The Handbook of Clinical Adult Psychology

The Handbook of Clinical Adult Psychology provides a comprehensive and thorough practical guide to modern clinical psychology. Clinical psychology is no longer devoted just to the traditional areas of neuropsychology and mental health but is now contributing to many other areas such as health promotion, behavioural medicine, issues of professional management and the presentation and management of forensic evidence. The Handbook covers all these areas which are of critical concern to clinical psychologists and related professions.

Clinical psychologists are called upon not only to treat mental illness and problems associated with medical afflictions but are also required to investigate, screen and advise on the treatment of clients referred to them by medical practitioners, social workers, nurses and others. In addition, one of the strengths of clinical psychology has been that careful investigation contributes to successful treatment. Therefore, investigation and treatment are clearly differentiated in separate chapters for most topics in this book, with each chapter written by a specialist in the area.

Many of the practices developed by clinical psychologists are now conducted by other professions in the course of their work. *The Handbook of Clinical Adult Psychology* will be immensely valuable for all professionals in training, such as clinical psychologists, nurses, psychiatrists, counsellors and social workers. It will also be a valuable reference work for members of those professions in practice.

Stan Lindsay is at the Institute of Psychiatry in London, and **Graham Powell** is in the Department of Psychology at the University of Surrey.

The Handbook of Clinical Adult Psychology

Second Edition

Edited by S.J.E. Lindsay and G.E. Powell

London and New York

First edition published 1987
by Gower Publishing Company Ltd

Second edition first published 1994
by Routledge
11 New Fetter Lane, London EC4P 4EE

Simultaneously published in the USA and Canada
by Routledge
25 West 35th Street, New York, NY 10001

Routledge is an imprint of the Taylor & Francis Group

Reprinted 1995, 1997, 1999

© 1994 Selection and editorial matter, S.J.E. Lindsay and G.E. Powell;
individual chapters, the contributors

Typeset in Times by LaserScript, Mitcham, Surrey
Printed and bound in Great Britain by
Mackays of Chatham PLC, Chatham, Kent

British Library Cataloguing in Publication Data
A catalogue record for this book is available from the British Library

Library of Congress Cataloguing in Publication Data
A catalogue record for this book is available from the Library of Congress

ISBN 0-415-07215-8 (hbk)
ISBN 0-415-07216-6 (pbk)

Contents

Illustrations

TABLES

Contributors

Ian Bennun, University of Exeter

Brendan P. Bradley, University of Cambridge

C. Bundy, University College North Wales, Bangor

A.G.M. Canavan, Institut an der Heinrich-Heine-Universität, Düsseldorf

A.J. Chalkley, Bath Mental Health Care Trust, Bath

P. de Silva, Institute of Psychiatry, University of London

Catherine Dooley, Psychological Department, Long Grove Hospital, Epsom, Surrey

Robert J. Edelmann, University of Surrey

B.S. Everitt, Institute of Psychiatry, University of London

Michael Gossop, Bethlem Royal and Maudsley Hospital, Kent

Gisli H. Gudjonsson, Institute of Psychiatry, University of London

David R. Hemsley, Institute of Psychiatry, University of London

M. Jahanshahi, Institute of Neurology, University of London

A. Lavender, Salomons Centre, Tunbridge Wells, Kent

S.J.E. Lindsay, Institute of Psychiatry, University of London

Joyce Mays, University College London, University of London

Stephen Morley, School of Medicine, University of Leeds

Shirley Pearce, University of East Anglia

G.E. Powell, University of Surrey

V. Rippere, formerly Institute of Psychiatry, University of London

Susan H. Spence, University of Brisbane

Jane Wardle, Institute of Psychiatry, University of London

F.N. Watts, Medical Research Council Applied Psychology Unit, Cambridge

Barbara A. Wilson, Medical Research Council Applied Psychology Unit, Cambridge

R.T. Woods, University College London, University of London

Foreword

The first edition of *The Handbook of Clinical Adult Psychology* was authoritative and concise, the essential qualities for a book of this type. As anticipated, it was well received and widely used.

The time has come for a revision, and happily, the Editors succeeded in retaining all but one of the original team of experts, plus two additional writers. The Editors and writers are to be congratulated for producing an excellent and comprehensive collection of work. The final product is as impressive and valuable as the original, and will no doubt be welcomed as a timely replacement and dependable guide.

Professor S. Rachman
February 1994

Editors' introduction

In our Introduction to the first edition of this book we drew attention to the importance of careful investigation in clinical practice. New tests and other assessment procedures are being published at a bewildering rate, often based on superficial research and on very small samples of subjects. It is also easy to devise rough-and-ready procedures for *ad hoc* assessment. This situation makes it all the more necessary that data gathered by such means are worth collecting. Therefore, the second edition of this book continues the strong emphasis on clinical investigation.

The book has had to reflect the rapid expansion in the application of cognitive approaches to clinical problems. This is evident not only in published research throughout clinical psychology but also in surveys of the activities of clinical psychologists. However, the book has had to acknowledge that pharmacotherapy and psychological treatment other than cognitive therapy can have beneficial effects on cognitions. This has suggested that certain effective attributes common to different psychological therapies should be identified especially in the treatment of emotional disorders. Unfortunately, we believe that the search for such attributes among psychotherapies has been disappointing and so the book has not drawn extensively on such work.

The continuing expansion of clinical psychology into areas hitherto the province only of medical practitioners has required that the book should increase its scope there. This has been met by an additional chapter.

Since the publication of the first edition there have been rapid changes in the health services in which clinical psychology and related disciplines operate. This has exposed clinical psychologists to competition with one another and with other professions, which has meant that those providing clinical psychology services should be able to justify the effectiveness and costs of what they do. This need is, therefore, met in this book not only by the emphasis on careful clinical investigation but also on the description of treatment which has been shown by research to be effective. However, we also believe that clinicians should be able to evaluate their own services and innovate where necessary. Therefore, we include several chapters on methods of clinical research.

Chapter 1

Practical issues of investigation in clinical psychology

S.J.E. Lindsay and G.E. Powell

Clinical psychology has developed out of a tradition of careful and painstaking investigation of the problems and characteristics which are presented by clients (see, for example, Mittler, 1970). Such investigation has been regarded as essential to the identification of effective remedies for the difficulties brought by those clients (Matarazzo, 1983). In the last twenty years there has been an enormous increase in the development of effective psychological treatment which has transformed clinical psychology. There have been similar developments in the psychiatric and neurological treatment of patients. This chapter therefore reviews practical issues in psychological investigation to promote the effective delivery of all such sources of help.

There are two notable stages in the gathering of clinical information and in making decisions about clients' difficulties. The first stage might be described as comprehensive information-gathering from which the clinician develops hypotheses (the formulation) about the causes and maintenance of those difficulties. The second consists in a more selective collection of data with greater precision and hypothesis-testing. This will continue throughout treatment.

There have been many schema for the first process as practised by clinical psychologists (Nay, 1979; Lazarus, 1976; Cone, 1978). There have, however, been very few attempts to determine the reliability and validity of these methods. Unfortunately the identification of the client's main difficulties and how they are maintained has been shown to be unreliable. There has been poor agreement among psychologists in their conclusions when they have been confronted with the same data about clients (Fewtrell, 1981; Hay *et al.*, 1979). Not surprisingly, agreement about corresponding treatments has also been poor (Fewtrell, 1981). These have been small-scale studies and perhaps insufficient data for reliable clinical judgements were available. However, the complexity of interactions among behaviours, cognitions, internal and external influences and different problems which can frequently occur in the same client (see, for example, Haynes and O'Brien, 1990, and Figure 1.1) would not favour agreement among clinicians about how to intervene.

However, it is suggested here that single-case experimental investigation (see Morley, Chapter 37) is probably a more reliable means of problem-analysis, testing hypotheses and the effects of treatment. The poor quality of clinical judgement as practised in case conferences and the neglect of statistical information in particular has long been recognised (Meehl, 1973).

If problem identification by these means is generally as poor as these observations suggest, it becomes difficult to understand why some psychological treatments may be recommended for some problems and not others. Thus for agoraphobia, exposure methods have been widely recommended (see Lindsay, Chapter 8) but other treatments, such as assertiveness training, have not been well supported. Unfortunately, it is notable that most published studies of behaviour therapy describe the target behaviour but rarely identify any other behavioural difficulties or independent and dependent variables which may be of note. Hence it is usually impossible to say how well-judged or arbitrary is the choice of treatment. Thus, for example, many studies of the treatment of depression describe the clients in terms of their scores on the Beck Depression Inventory but omit any evaluation of other problems, such as marital distress, which might be occurring and how those might be contributing to the central problem. Nevertheless, it has frequently been recognised (Yates, 1976) that the clinician for each case has to answer the questions: 'What treatment, by whom, is most effective for this individual with the specific problem, under which set of circumstances and how does it come about?' (Paul, 1969).

Although clinical psychologists now rarely contribute to psychiatric diagnosis, current developments in that discipline may yet have some lessons for the investigative procedures which psychologists themselves practise. For example, the *Diagnostic and Statistical Manual of Mental Disorders III – Revised (DSM III–R*; American Psychiatric Association, 1987) gives explicit rules for classification of patients into traditional and less traditional categories. The criteria which are necessary for inclusion in each category as well as symptoms which are not present for each diagnosis are both given: inclusion and exclusion criteria. In addition to psychiatric diagnostic categories, such as depression and anxiety, which are ascribed to the first diagnostic axis – 'mental categorisation' – other dimensions are provided. Axis 2 presents descriptions of personality disorders and developmental disorders; 3 is physical illness. Two other axes are identified to describe 4, 'the severity of psychosocial stressors' consisting of environmental influences and life crises, and 5, 'Global Assessment of Functioning', the 'highest level of adaptive functioning in the past year' recorded on a five-point scale. The latter takes into account the client's occupational functioning, the use of leisure time and social relationships. Some conditions, such as obsessions and compulsions, may require intervention only when they influence these variables critically.

The information necessary to implement this classification can be gathered according to recommendations published elsewhere. Structured interviews such as the Renard Diagnostic Interview (RDI) developed by Helzer *et al.* (1981) and the Diagnostic Interview Schedule (DIS) produced by Robins *et al.* (1981) have been used in reliability trials for the original *DSM III* (American Psychiatric Association, 1980). Robins *et al.* have described such a study in which lay persons' categorisation of over 400 clients was compared with that of experienced psychiatrists. Inter-observer agreement ranged from perfect for anorexia nervosa, through moderate for phobias to poor for panic disorder. Interview schedules have also been developed for *DSM III–R*, notably the Anxiety Disorders Interview Schedule (DiNardo *et al.*, 1985).

Hence the *DSM III* has been interesting in that it has drawn attention to the association of psychological disturbance with environmental influences and stresses and impairment in the client's functioning. The elaboration of rules for collecting data and classification has made this system more reliable than its predecessors (Matarazzo, 1983).

There are, however, other grounds for criticising it that are reviewed elsewhere (Eysenck *et al.*, 1983). These include the omission of some behavioural problems for which psychologists have developed interventions. The *DSM III* also ignores functional analysis which might more readily indicate treatment interventions. In addition, for many afflictions, a dimensional rather than a categorical approach would be more valid. The *DSM III* has also been criticised because it includes behavioural disturbances which are therefore assumed to be medical problems. Ironically also the *DSM III–R* gives little indication of the ways in which psychologists could be, and are, intervening in behavioural medicine (see Edelmann, Chapter 25).

Unfortunately, although psychologists have often drawn attention to the inadequacy of such psychiatric diagnostic systems (McGuire, 1973), they have adopted several of the traditional psychiatric classifications and so have found it difficult to ignore the *DSM III*. This is evident even in fears and anxiety, where psychologists have been most active in proposing their own models of causation. For example, panic attacks can occur in almost all fears but the nature of psychological treatment of panics depends largely upon the significance of the panic to the client (see Lindsay, Chapter 8). The organisation of chapters in this book reflects the mixture of such traditional psychiatric and more recent behavioural nomenclature.

INITIAL INFORMATION-GATHERING

The preceding discussion has indicted the value of clinical information and investigation for behaviour therapy and modification but clinical psychologists are still involved in more traditional diagnostic assessment, notably for neurological problems. In addition, although most referrals come to psychologists from medical colleagues, it would be advisable for psychologists to be aware of changes in the client's behaviour which might be treated more appropriately by a physician. Clinical psychologists must be able to refer the client back to the referring clinician or to a medical team colleague when changes attributable to the client's physical condition cause concern. It would also be advisable for the client to have a physical screening before behavioural investigation. This has been emphasised in several chapters throughout this book. Nevertheless, the clinical psychologist will at times gather information which will reflect the client's neurological state and other physical conditions.

Information-gathering guidelines which are thus sufficiently comprehensive have been described by Russell *et al.* (1987) and Nay (1979). The following is an outline of the information which they and others recommend should be available to the clinician. Some of this material may already have been collected by the referring clinician and may therefore be available in a letter or in the client's file. Some areas of enquiry may be of little or no relevance to some clients and so the clinician has to be selective in gathering information from the client directly. Exhaustive, over-inclusive interviewing may antagonise the client especially at a time when he or she is in considerable distress and may have already despaired of receiving effective help. To avoid repetitive and redundant questioning and for other reasons of efficiency, the clinician should record his or her observations as they are made. With some very distressed clients, however, the first interview might have to be spent in getting to know the client with very little recording.

For some clients it will be necessary to seek information from other parties who know the difficulties of the client well: parents, spouse, social workers, occupational therapists and care staff. This will be essential for mentally handi-capped clients and disturbed elderly or psychotic clients, who may be unable to communicate reliably. In addition, many problems influence and are affected by people in the client's environment. Also many interventions require the co-operation of the client's family or caretaker, who therefore have to be consulted during investigation. Wherever possible, nevertheless, the client's full approval should be obtained before the clinician consults other informants. Finally it should be emphasised that there will always be the possibility that some obser-vations made by the client will be unreliable or inaccurate and so will require corroboration from other parties. Sources of such bias and inaccuracy will be discussed below.

In most cases the *reason for the client's referral* will have been given in an introductory note from the referring agent or will have been communicated at a clinical team meeting. This issue should be clarified with the client or whoever is giving information on the client's behalf – the informant. It will be highly desirable in any case to hear the client describe the main difficulties in his or her own words if only to encourage cooperation in obtaining further information and in implementing treatment.

Most frequently it will be valuable first to enquire why help has been sought and how long the main complaint has persisted. It will often be important at this point, if possible, to reassure the client or whoever is most concerned that the complaint is not exceptional or outrageous in the clinician's experience and that it should be possible to offer some help. The clinician should explain that in order to understand the client's difficulties it will be necessary to obtain as much information about the problem as possible. The clinician should show some sympathy for and understanding of the client's concerns by, for example, saying that it is not at all surprising that he or she is so distressed by the problem.

A more detailed but *brief chronological history* of the complaint should follow. When did the informant first notice the problem and how did the client and others react to it? What was the client's situation at its outset and at times during its subsequent development – occupation, marital status, living with parents, at school? What attempts have been made to treat the problem or help the client in other ways?

An important but frequently neglected area of enquiry in behavioural investigation concerns the *impairments which have been produced by the client's difficulties.* How have the client's relationships with his or her family, work colleagues or other patients changed with the problem? How have performance and interest at work or in recreation changed? How has the client's biological functioning altered – in sleeping, sexual activity, eating and maintenance of body weight? Have there been any difficulties in coping with responsibilities, such as managing household budgets, and in taking decisions?

With many clients the concept of a change or onset of the problem may not be appropriate or may not be easy to pinpoint. Many problems, such as difficulties in meeting and speaking to other people, may have been present to some extent throughout the client's life and have only recently become of critical concern. This can arise when such a client applies for a job for the first time.

For such clients it may be necessary to compare functioning in such areas with certain standards: the performance of others of similar age, intellectual development, education and social and cultural background. The availability of such norms will be discussed later in this chapter.

How has the client coped with the problem? Drinking alcohol to excess, smoking heavily, taking tranquillisers, withdrawing to a bedroom for long periods, having friends and relatives take on the client's tasks, seeking reassurance? *How have others coped* with the client's difficulties?

The clinician should also investigate a number of variables which may not be the substance of the main referred complaint. What is the client's *prevailing mood* or what emotional state does the client experience at certain times and circumstances? Fear, anxiety, anger, frustration, sadness, irritation?

Sometimes the client will have difficulty in reporting any such mood. Some clients may not experience strong emotions even when these would be expected – flatness of affect. Sudden mood swings may also occur. The clinician will have to rely on the client or other informants' reporting these changes since, for example, even chronically anxious clients need not be continuously anxious and so may not be in such discomfort during the interview. Also it should be noted that spontaneous emotions may not be reliably evident in the client's facial expression (Ekman and Oster, 1979).

The *content of the client's reported thoughts* will also be of interest – troublesome intrusive thoughts or preoccupations especially as these relate to changes in emotion; plans and ambitions, realistic or otherwise. What does the client think will happen at times when he or she is in greatest distress?

The client's *reported beliefs* and interpretations of events will often be of significance. Are there abnormal beliefs about the environment including the behaviour and attitudes of other people towards the client? Does the client have unrealistic beliefs about his or her physical attributes or functioning? Facial appearance or body size may be of abnormal concern. Inappropriate persistent beliefs about the client's worth are frequently held to be unrealistic sources of distress. The client may believe that certain experiences, such as intrusive thoughts, mean that he or she is going mad or that such experiences are unique. Does the client believe that he or she has no control over events? What does the client think about the difficulties that have been presented?

Abnormal experiences in auditory, visual or other sensory modalities should be noted for the client's experience of: the environment (such as hallucinations or feelings of unreality or *déjà vu*); his or her body (such as feelings of numbness or tingling sensations in fingers, toes and scalp); or the self (such as depersonalisation or awareness of disturbances in thinking).

The client's *appearance and behaviour* during the interview should also be recorded – characteristic unusual movements and posture; abnormalities of speech, such as being inaudible or very loud, speaking fast or slowly, requiring prompting or being difficult to interrupt, answering questions directly or rambling away from the issues. Is the client attending to the interviewer or to something else in the environment which is evident or not apparent to the interviewer?

An assessment of the client's *cognitive-intellectual functioning* (memory, orientation in time and place, attention and concentration) will be of importance especially in clients in whom behavioural problems could be associated with difficulties in coping with work or self-care. This area of enquiry will also be especially important where neurological damage is suspected.

An assessment of the client's *attitudes to his or her difficulties* could be instructive: whether he or she considers them trivial or life-threatening; whether he or she is resigned to them as hopeless; what hypotheses the client has formulated for them.

Whatever the objective, it will be important to determine during the initial interview whether the client is working, thinking and concentrating as efficiently as would be expected from his or her level of education or employment. Does the client or informant believe that the client has difficulty in remembering information? Can the client report his or her name, age, other biographical information, present orientation in time and place, together with a brief account of current news events?

Having obtained a comprehensive picture of the client's current difficulties, the clinician should then seek to discover how these have developed. In therefore obtaining a corresponding history, the clinician will have to be selective in determining which aspects of the client's history will be worth investigating. For example, it will probably be of little interest to enquire about elderly people's sexual interests where some difficulties in coping with self-care have been pinpointed, although in young adults sexual behaviour may be of paramount concern.

In the case history, data can be obtained about *the client's family – parents and siblings*. Their occupations, illnesses and especially psychiatric history may be noted. In particular, are there precedents for the client's own difficulties in other family members or close peers? What family crises have occurred, such as deaths, sudden changes in income, marital difficulties in the parents? How did these affect the client?

The client's own early *developmental history* should be investigated especially if the client is still young. What sort of school did the client go to? Did the client go to school at the normal age and how did he or she cope with schooling?

Behavioural difficulties at school will be of interest in young adults. Were there any conduct problems, such as truancy or school refusal, stealing, fighting, difficulty in making friends? In order to understand the impairment produced by current complaints, it will often be essential to determine the client's academic attainments at school and after. Difficulties in attaining goals at school or matching achievements with other children may have contributed to the occurrence of behavioural and emotional problems; especially important: how well can he or she read?

For similar reasons the client's occupational history will frequently be of considerable interest. Have the client's jobs matched his or her educational history? Has the client had long periods out of work, frequent changes of occupation or been continually dissatisfied with work? Again occupational history, when compared with current occupational data, may indicate the client's current level of difficulty. Occupational difficulties may contribute to, or be the product of, behavioural and other problems of interest to the clinician.

The client's experience of *adolescence* may often indicate the onset of social and sexual difficulties. Hence that stage in development may be investigated for problems in relating to other adolescents: How did the client cope with the standards set by peers for sexual and social behaviour? Were there any notable periods of unhappiness, extreme and prolonged withdrawal?

The client's *sexual history* will be of interest certainly where marital, sexual or other relationship problems have been pinpointed.

How have the client's *marital history and experiences* related to the development of the main difficulties? For example, how has the client's husband or wife coped with the client? Have there been frequent quarrels, threats of, or actual, separation? How are the children? Do they have any notable difficulties at home or in school?

It would be important to determine what *previous psychiatric, psychological or medical help* has been given to the client for the current or other problems. What medication, if any, is the client taking? The success or failure of any such interventions, especially as the client sees them, should be ascertained because that information will probably influence the client's expectations about forthcoming treatment.

The client's *medical history* may be of direct or indirect significance. For example, frequent hospitalisation in childhood has been associated with conduct disorders even into adolescence (Rutter, 1977). The medical history will be of more direct concern where the client complains of physical symptoms, such as headaches or dizzy spells, for which the client has been referred. These should be the subject of a physical examination, if not already carried out. There may also be physical symptoms which may be related to the behaviour which is of direct concern to the clinician but which may not themselves be target variables in treatment. The symptoms of drug and alcohol withdrawal are in this category as are the signs of more permanent neurological damage with drug and alcohol addiction.

The clinician should be able to consult medical colleagues when physical symptoms change for the worse or do not respond to behavioural treatments as predicted. It should be made clear to the client at the outset that the responsibility for any medical condition or treatment remains with the psychologist's medical

Table 1.1 Summary of information-gathering

Reason for referral.
Client's own description of difficulties.
Why help sought (why now?)?
Chronological history of difficulties.
Client's situation: marital, occupation, living where and with whom.

Client's opinion of impairments produced by difficulties (in occupation, recreation, social relationships, his own happiness).

Client's biological functioning as affected by difficulties (eating, sleeping, sexual activity, maintenance of body weight).

How has the client coped with the difficulties; how have others coped with the clients difficulties; what professional treatment received?

Prevailing mood; mood at its worst.
Content of the client's thoughts.
Degree of intrusiveness of those thoughts.
Abnormal experiences in all sensory modalities.
Abnormal experiences in relation to the client's environment, his or her body, his or her self.
Client's appearance and behaviour during interview.
Cognitive-intellectual functioning (orientation in time and place, memory for recent information).

Client's attitudes to his or her difficulties.
Developmental, educational and occupational, sexual and marital history.
History of serious medical illnesses.
Current intake of drugs (alcohol etc.).
Remainder of family: their experience of psychological problems.

Provisional formulation: what is the most disturbing difficulty for the client; what are the influences on this difficulty; what effects does the difficulty have (or would have if it remained untreated); do those effects warrant intervention; what further data (e.g. by more interviewing, tests) are necessary to test these hypotheses; what intervention would be necessary?

colleagues or with the client's own doctor. The psychologist has responsibility only for psychological investigation and help.

PSYCHOMETRIC SCREENING

The foregoing discussion has outlined the areas of enquiry which the clinician should have in mind when conducting initial investigations. A number of attempts have been made to develop self-report inventories which would limit the workload of the clinician at this stage, avoid omissions of crucial subjects of enquiry and leave the clinician to concentrate on more selective investigation. Such inventories might be more easily subjected to tests of reliability and validity than open-ended investigations of the kind described above.

Cautela and Upper (1976), for example, described a four-part screening procedure for adults, the Behavioural Inventory Battery, using a Behavioural Analysis History Questionnaire (BAHQ; ibid.), a Behavioural Self-Rating Checklist (BSRC; ibid.), a Behavioural Self-Rating Checklist (BSRC; Cautela and Upper, 1975) together with a Reinforcement Survey Schedule (RSS; Cautela and Upper, 1976), and a Fear Survey Schedule (FSS; Geer, 1965).

Unfortunately, the authors reported no psychometric data for the BAHQ or the BSRC. In addition, there are areas of information such as sexual behaviour in which it might not always be prudent or necessary to enquire. Also, certain areas such as intellectual functioning are not well covered and so this approach is unsuitable, both in not covering sufficient information and in being too inclusive. It is therefore unlikely that this particular inventory can offer any advantages over the selective investigation described above.

The Wechsler Adult Intelligence Scale (WAIS; Wechsler, 1981) has been used as a screening test to try to detect almost every psychological affliction, but the lack of validity of much of this work is widely apparent (Frank, 1983).

The General Health Questionnaire (GHQ)

The GHQ (Goldberg and Williams, 1988) is a questionnaire which is widely used to screen samples of adults for the presence of psychiatric distress as would be identified by a standard psychiatric interview. The original version had 60 questions but, guided by cluster and factor analyses, shorter versions of 30, 28 and 12 items have been produced. These analyses have suggested that the GHQ is sensitive most notably to psychiatric distress as a non-specific variable, and to anxiety, depression and somatic complaints, such as headaches. Some analyses have suggested other components, such as social functioning and sleep disturbance (Goldberg and Williams, 1988).

The GHQ uses cut-off points for the numbers of complaints acknowledged by the respondents to determine whether the respondents are in psychiatric distress. Cut-off points are set to minimise the risk of incorrect decisions: wrongly identifying a respondent as well, or incorrectly identifying a client as in distress.

Analysis by Receiver Operating Characteristics can show the advantages and disadvantages of different cut-off points in surveys. These cut-off points have varied considerably from study to study especially with the 28- and 12-item versions. The most common cut-off scores are 11 complaints for the 60-item GHQ; 6 for the 30-item version (Goldberg and Williams, 1988).

The GHQ–60 and the GHQ–30 both have high internal consistency. They also have high test-retest reliability for the subjects who show an unchanging picture of psychiatric distress (Goldberg and Wiliams, 1988).

The GHQ is probably best designed to detect distress of recent onset, all the questions being prefaced by the phrase 'Have you recently . . .'. Patients with chronic serious difficulties, such as generalised anxiety, can fail to acknowledge symptoms with the answer 'No, I have always felt like this'. Other question-naires, such as the SCL–90–R (see below), are more suitable for detecting prolonged difficulties.

The Symptom Check-List–90–Revised (SCL–90–R)

The SCL–90–R (Derogatis, 1977), one of the most widely used screening questionnaires, consists of ninety questions designed to measure nine dimensions of psychopathology as determined by factor analyses: somatisation (such as 'trouble in getting your breath'), obsessive-compulsive difficulties, interpersonal sensitivity (such as 'feeling inferior to others'), depression, anxiety, anger–hostility, phobic anxiety, paranoid ideation and psychoticism (such as 'having thoughts that are not your own'). There are also seven questions about miscel-laneous problems such as 'trouble in falling asleep'. The subject responds to each question by selecting, for each item, one of five alternatives from 'not at all' to 'extremely' in answer to the question 'How much are you bothered by . . .'. There is a short form of the inventory (Derogatis and Melisaratos, 1983) with norms for a large sample of the adult population in the UK (Francis *et al.*, 1990). Unfortunately, the response rate in that survey was so poor that the sample could not be said to be representative of the population.

The SCL–90–R is intended to provide a profile of psychopathology for each respondent. The original reference provides normative data for clinical and normal samples. Unfortunately, only four of the nine dimensions identified in the original reference (Derogatis, 1977) have been reproduced in later independent research (Cyr *et al.*, 1988). A literature search for this chapter has revealed no satisfactory attempts to determine external validity, a comparison with other diagnostic procedures. Therefore, the SCL–90–R should only be used as a supplement to a clinical interview to identify different psychiatric problems.

The original version of the scale (SCL–90; Derogatis *et al.*, 1973) is probably still frequently used because of its easy availibility (ibid.). This should be used only with similar cautions.

PROBLEM FORMULATION

On the basis of information obtained in the initial interviews with the client or other informants, the clinician has to make a number of decisions. First, what is the client's outstanding problem and what should the target variables be during treatment? The answers to these questions may differ. For example, a man's problem may be his aggression and prickliness towards colleagues yet the target may be reading skills which have been poorly developed and which could be the subject of tuition. On the other hand, the target behaviour and the outstanding problem may coincide more directly. For example, the difficulties of an agoraphobic client might be characterised principally by her not venturing out of doors and in being unable to visit local shops. The target behaviour may be this avoidance which may be tackled directly in a programme of graded exposure.

The clinician will then have to decide on more detailed but selective investigation to determine whether treatment is necessary and what the target variables should be in that intervention whether it is conducted by the psychologist or by colleagues. Thus, recording of detail that can be reliably obtained, and which is described throughout the remainder of this book, will be the next stage of investigation.

The choice of investigation for this phase will depend at least in part on the hypothesis which the clinician has formulated about the maintenance of the client's difficulties. Unfortunately, this decision-process is probably the weakest link in psychological assessment, the most popular and influential textbooks of behavioural assessment paying very little attention to this topic (for example, Hersen and Bellack, 1981; Ciminero et al., 1977).

Two approaches have been favoured by psychologists, nevertheless. The first has consisted largely of an exercise in which clients are assigned to categories of difficulties according to the presence of certain symptoms or complaints. Cautela and Upper (1973) have described a Behavioural Coding System (BCS) which includes nearly 300 maladaptive behaviours divided into 21 major categories. Unfortunately O'Farrell and Upper (1977) report only modest inter-observer reliability for the categorisation of a sample of twenty patients.

The second approach has consisted in a functional analysis which seeks to identify mechanisms of the maintenance of clients' difficulties (Owens and Ashcroft, 1982; Cullen, 1983; Haynes and O'Brien, 1990) and which has relied frequently on operant explanations for this.

Little empirical work has yet been done to test reliability and validity and the processes of decision-making in functional analysis (Haynes and O'Brien, 1990)

It is suggested here that a combination of functional and descriptive analyses is necessary. Hence the following list of categories is a rough attempt to guide the clinician in making further investigations which are described by subsequent chapters in this book. Categorisation of this kind should be qualified by functional analyses which have been illustrated below. No claims are made for the comprehensiveness of this listing. It has been compiled from a consideration of psychiatric diagnostic classifications (for example, American Psychiatric Association, 1987) and categorisations favoured by the clinical psychology research literature.

Clinical psychologists are thus actively involved in the investigation and treatment of mood disorders (for example, anxiety, depression and fears); obsessive-compulsive disorders; impairment of intellectual functioning; widespread arrested development of intellectual and living skills; poor development or impairment of selected skills (self-help skills, such as organising daily routine or managing household budgets, social behaviour including appropriate assertiveness, educational attainment such as reading skills); conduct disorders, such as aggression or stealing; substance abuse of alcohol, drugs and so on; appetitive disorders (excessive, disruptive or inadequate intake); deviant in which abnormal objectives are the subject of sexual attraction; physical problems, such as chronic pain, sleep disturbance and cardiovascular and respiratory disorders; promoting physical health; the effects of neurological, especially cerebral, damage.

FUNCTIONAL ANALYSIS

By means of a functional analysis the clinician seeks to identify the discriminative stimuli and reinforcements which are associated with the occurrence of the behaviour of clinical interest. The setting conditions are also identified. For this, the occurrence of the chosen behaviour is recorded, together with the antecedent stimuli and the consequences of that behaviour (Haynes and O'Brien, 1990), over a period of, say, a week. The preceding stimuli may include what other people were doing or the arrival of certain people. The consequences may include a material object given to or acquired by the client or a social event, such as praise or laughter by others. For example, a client who suffers from a chronic pain disorder such as low back pain may, on seeing what she perceives as anger in her husband, complain that she is in discomfort. As a result, the husband looks less irritated, offers to make his wife a cup of tea or is solicitous in other ways. Behaviour analysis of this kind has also drawn attention to the influence of setting events, prolonged ongoing activity or situations. For example, the foregoing sequence might occur only when no other people were present.

It should be emphasised that analyses to identify reliably consistent discriminative stimuli, setting conditions and reinforcers depend on the adequate collection of data. It is unwise to assume that certain events, such as praise (Cullen, 1983), act as reinforcement for all clients. Praise may be encouraging for some clients but belittling and patronising for others. In addition, relationships can be perceived among variables which will turn out to be spurious on careful examination of data carefully collected.

Other concepts have been described by Owens and Ashcroft (1982) emphasising the effect of feedback loops. They describe a client who felt highly anxious about speaking in conversations. This client then avoided situations where she would be required to speak. As a result she became less practised in speaking aloud and this, together with impairment of fluent speech associated with that nervousness, made speaking even more difficult for her. The client, perceiving that she did not speak fluently when in company, became more nervous of company and this in turn contributed to her being more reclusive. This could have arisen because of beliefs that she was the focus of attention in social situations. In addition, as with so many socially phobic people, she could have applied double standards: expecting herself, but not others, to be fluent always while speaking in public. This illustrates the importance of cognitive influences which are now held to play a crucial part in most psychological problems, especially emotional disorders.

Haynes and O'Brien (1990) draw attention to the interrelationships among different problem behaviours, cognitions, feedback and environmental events in clients (see Figure 1.1). Some ('residual') causal influences, such as biological influences on depression and sleep, may no longer be operating. This complex picture is commonplace in clinical practice where clients are experiencing numerous difficulties by the time they seek professional help. Hence the foregoing discussion of initial information-gathering in emphasising the identification of single problems, has been simplistic. Emmelkamp (1982), for example, describes a hypothetical case where fear of being looked at leads to social withdrawal. The husband of the client finds more rewarding activity when he goes out alone in the evenings and friends also visit the house less and less. Quarrelling between the couple over this contributes to sexual problems, and the widespread loss of rewarding activities for the wife leads to depressed mood and sleeping difficulties.

The hypotheses which the clinician formulates in such a case will determine what treatment strategies are adopted: which problems will be treated directly and which difficulties will be treated first. For example, the clinician in this case may consider it necessary to reduce initially the client's levels of depression and insomnia as those problems might make cooperation in treatment especially difficult. These might be tackled, at any rate in the short term, with the help of medication.

Frequently the client's response to treatment will help to test hypotheses and so the clinician must be prepared to reformulate these as treatment progresses. The relationships among different variables and the nature of the corresponding clinical task may also change with treatment. Barlow and Mavissakalian (1981) describe how improvement in agoraphobia was accompanied by increased marital satisfaction in some clients but decreased satisfaction in others.

Single-case experimental investigation of such issues is therefore critically important (see Morley, Chapter 37)

In the collection of data and in developing hypotheses, certain sources of bias should be avoided. The accuracy of clinical judgement may even be impaired with experience as clinicians, perhaps with increasing confidence, seek to make intuitive judgements with insufficient information at their disposal (Watts, 1980). Fortunately, on the other hand, supervision and feedback can help clinicians to collect data with greater accuracy (Brown et al., 1982) in interview. Gentle

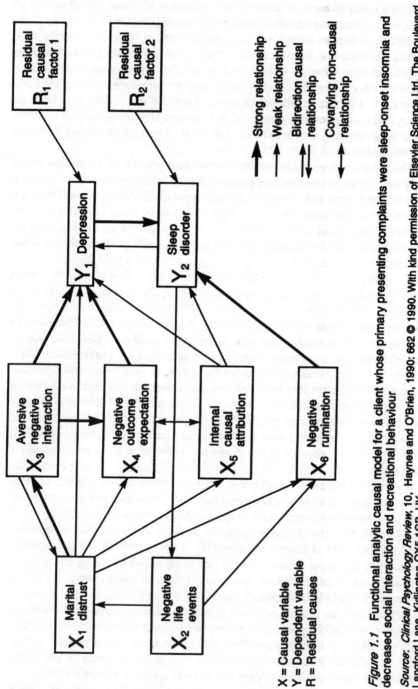

Figure 1.1 Functional analytic causal model for a client whose primary presenting complaints were sleep-onset insomnia and decreased social interaction and recreational behaviour

Source: Clinical Psychology Review, 10, Haynes and O'Brien, 1990: 662 © 1990. With kind permission of Elsevier Science Ltd, The Boulevard, Langford Lane, Kidlington OX5 1GB, UK.

probing questions may be used for this without prejudicing the gathering of information about feelings and emotions (Cox *et al.*, 1981a;b).

Additional sources of bias can lie in the tendency in observers to attribute the causes of behaviour to internal factors, such as personality, rather than to environmental variables (Watson, 1982). Also, observers tend to emphasise the effects of internal events in clients to the neglect of base-rate information and other estimates of statistical likelihood (Tversky and Kahneman, 1982; Meehl, 1973). Hence an investigator might concentrate on a cognitive investigation of a client without considering the likelihood of certain behaviour estimated from epidemiological data.

Therefore, there might be some advantage in remembering that, for example, between 12 and 20 per cent of men and between 20 and 30 per cent of women acknowledge depressive experiences at any given time (Boyd and Weissman, 1982). Also for example, as many as 8 per cent of adults in the UK have a serious alcohol consumption problem and the likelihood of this will be increased in young, single or divorced males and in those with depressive problems (Office of Health Economics, 1981).

THE APPRAISAL OF COGNITIVE ABILITY

The routine investigation of important cognitive abilities, notably of memory and intelligence, is now rarely undertaken except in neuropsychological investigation and in children. It is suggested here that such enquiry should be conducted only where clear predictions can be made from the data. Hence educational attainment, especially in reading and numerical skills, would be predicted with limited accuracy from estimates of IQ on the WAIS–R (Frank, 1983). Predicting vocational attainment – identifying the employment for which a client would be best suited – may also benefit from a knowledge of intelligence test data (Salmon, 1970). However, it has been recognised that the WAIS–R and tests favoured by neuropsychologists have had limited validity data to predict clients' functioning in everyday life (Heaton and Pendleton, 1981). Such tests often fail to provide the answer to the question: What score is necessary on this test to predict that the client will be able, for example, to resume his or her work successfully?

A frequently referred query, prediction of the client's ability to practise domestic self-help skills, is unlikely to be made accurately with such information. It is more appropriate to investigate these skills directly by, for example, Hall and Baker's Rehabilitation Assessment (Hall and Baker, 1983).

Certain diagnostic issues which have long been the subject of psychometric inquiry, such as the discrimination of the effects of brain damage from those of schizophrenia and the discrimination between depression and other sources of impairment, are either not plausible questions or could not be reliably investigated with WAIS–R and memory test data (Heaton *et al.*, 1979; Miller, 1975) and so these tests have been largely abandoned for such purposes also.

However, where crude predictions can be made from IQ information, a rapid screening test, such as the Raven's Progressive Matrices (Raven, 1992) and the Mill Hill Vocabulary Scale (Raven, 1994), will be adequate.

Under some circumstances the clinician may be interested in knowing whether medical or surgical intervention has impaired the client's level of functioning without the clinician's having to specify and observe the skills which the client uses in daily living. Thus a wide range of ability tests including the WAIS–R and memory tests may be used. Again, however, changes in results of such testing with treatment should be interpreted with caution. For example, memory testing may not reflect the client's memory skills in daily living (Erickson and Scott, 1977).

Medical colleagues are frequently concerned with screening the client for brain damage and they request psychological testing for this. However, the widespread and tenacious belief amongst clinicians that the discrepancy between Verbal and Performance IQs can detect brain damage irrespective of its nature and location is unwarranted (Todd *et al.*, 1977; Golden, 1979). For example, Todd *et al.* investigated the WAIS IQs of five groups of subjects, who, on neurological investigation, had demonstrated right or left localised cerebral damage, diffuse damage or non-specific brain damage. A group of psychiatric patients formed a control group. There was no significant difference in the size of Verbal-Performance discrepancy among the groups. Hence the authors conclude that the WAIS Discrepancy Index (superiority of Verbal over Performance IQs) is an insensitive indicator of brain damage or for the localisation of such damage.

Recent research has claimed to identify a factor structure of the WAIS–R which distinguishes right- from left-sided brain damage (Canavan and Beckman, 1993). This appears to be misleading.

Another means of detecting impairment in cognitive abilities which might be associated with brain damage has been described by Nelson (1991). This uses a test of reading ability, the National Adult Reading Test, to predict pre-morbid IQ. However, the prediction thus obtained has a large standard error so that the predicted full-scale IQ lies only within the range ± 15.2 points for the 95 per cent level of confidence.

IMPAIRMENT IN SOCIAL FUNCTIONING

A number of authors (e.g. Brown and Harris, 1978) have associated adverse living conditions with psychiatric disturbance. These authors found that depression in women was more likely if they had no employment outside the home, had four or more young children and no confidant. Other authors have noted poorer levels of attainment in income, living conditions, leisure activities, social contacts and occupation (Cooper, 1973). This may be the product or the consequence of psychiatric disturbance.

However, the extent to which it appears that a client's difficulties may have contributed to such impairment might be considered in deciding upon intervention.

For example, the client whose handicap consists, because of anxiety in travelling on public transport, in being unable to travel abroad on holiday might not be seen with the same urgency as a client who is unable to travel to work and whose marriage consequently may be in trouble.

The *DSM III–R* (American Psychiatric Association, 1987) describes a brief rating scale, Global Assessment of Functioning (GAF) which outlines areas of social functioning that may be assessed to provide a single score. There are guidelines for completion of this scale in the *DSM III–R*.

Much more extensive assessment of social functioning is provided by a standardised interview, the Adult Personality Functioning Assessment (APFA; Hill *et al.*, 1989). This has had extensive psychometric evaluation but is much too cumbersome for routine clinical use.

Clare and Cairns (1978) have described a standard 45-minute interview in which material conditions, competence and the client's satisfaction are each estimated for several areas. These are housing, occupation together with social roles, economic situation together with leisure and social activities, family and marital relationships.

The authors claim a high inter-observer reliability for most items for a sample of four observers. However, it is not clear how discriminating or sensitive to bias are some of the rating scales, notably those designed to measure the client's level of satisfaction with different activities and accomplishments. (Compare the discussions of the statistical properties of investigation and scaling later in this chapter.) Nevertheless, the scope of the interview gives useful guidelines for enquiry about the impairment associated with psychological disturbance.

Cooper *et al.* (1982) describe a self-report inventory which covers similar content. An earlier version had been published in the USA (Weissman and Bothwell, 1976). The scale covers levels of functioning at work (at home and outside), housework, social and leisure activities, and relationships with the rest of the family.

OCCUPATIONAL ASSESSMENT

The test battery, Assessment for Training and Employment (ATE; Psychological Corporation, 1992) contains a number of tests for assessing in adults, basic numeracy and literacy skills, work-related aptitudes, vocational interests and social behaviour appropriate for employment. There is a brief screening test which allows the clinician to select the appropriate tests for the substantive assessment.

Assessment of literacy and numeracy in the ATE   Self-administered paper and pencil tests allow the clinician to compare clients' performance on the Foundation Tests of vocabulary, reading comprehension, number operations and problem-solving. These tests might be considered to determine if a client needed help to boost his or her attainment in literacy or numeracy as the result, say, of interrupted schooling. Such deficits can contribute to social anxiety and other difficulties in adults.

Scores on the Foundation Tests can be compared with norms by conversion to percentiles based on the standardisation sample, nearly 800 participants in Employment Training and Youth Training throughout the UK. It is not clear how this sample was selected or what levels of ability, as determined by tests of general intelligence, were represented. Therefore, predictions on these tests of what levels of numeracy and literacy would be expected from a client, given his or her score on tests of intelligence such as the WAIS–R or the Raven's Progressive Matrices, should be made with caution. It is not clear, therefore, if a client with an average score on the WAIS–R (full-scale IQ of around 100) would be expected to produce an average performance on the ATE Foundation Tests.

Differential Aptitude Tests (DAT) in the ATE   The DAT are intended to measure eight basic aptitudes: verbal reasoning, numerical ability, abstract reasoning, clerical speed and accuracy, mechanical reasoning, ability for perceiving space relations, spelling ability and language usage. These tests have a long history and have been standardised on samples in the UK. They are probably the best tests for use with patients because they do not have time-limits for their completion.

Vocational guidance   The ATE gives guidelines for suggesting occupation, suited to clients based on assessment with the above tests and in consideration of the client's educational history and answers to the Vocational Interest Exploration test and the Personal Qualities Inventory.

SOCIAL SUPPORT

The Significant Others Scale (SOS)   Lack of social support is frequently believed to contribute to the seeking of professional help by people in distress. The presence of effective support from friends and relatives may help people to recover from, or cope with, serious distress without professional help. Clinicians may help patients to develop that sort of support. A formal measure of social support such as the SOS (Power *et al.* 1988; reproduced by Milne, 1992) might be useful for that.

The SOS is designed to measure emotional and practical support, both actual and ideal. The latter is the amount of which the client 'thinks things should be, if . . . things worked out exactly as you hoped . . . '.

There are short and long versions of the SOS. In both, the client is asked to provide the names of up to six people known to him or her and is asked to rate on a seven-point scale ('never' to 'always') how often he or she can (actual support) or should (ideal support) rely on the support of each of those people in a number of activities. For example, the client is asked to describe how often he or she gets support from X to 'lean on and turn to in times of difficulty'.

Test-retest reliability has been moderate (Power *et al.* 1988). Validity has been tested, amongst other methods, by the ability of the SOS to distinguish among different groups (undergraduates, elderly people and adults with Parkinson's disease and their carers), who the authors suggest should differ in perceived and ideal social support (Milne, 1992).

The SOS is in its early stages of development and data are needed to testify to its validity and reliability. It is difficult, moreover, to predict what level of social support would be desirable. The authors suggest that the discrepancy between ideal and actual support should be minimal. Indeed, experiencing much less support than their ideal would be a source of distress for some clients. However, some clients could argue that the less support they should have, the more satisfactory is their position. Indeed, elderly people appear to tend to this view (Lam and Power, 1991).

Many clients encountered in clinical practice will be very isolated from any sources of support. Others will have several friends and relatives on whom they rely. Often, however, it will be necessary to decide if that support is helpful or is likely to continue as long as the client's difficulties persist. Many patients with chronic difficulties lose or even antagonise the support upon which they rely initially.

CLINICAL DECISION-MAKING

The preceding discussions have indicated some of the influences on clinical decision-making, notably the functional relationships between the client's main difficulties and other variables as well as the degree of impairment which appears to have been produced by those difficulties. Other questions must also be considered.

The first decision will be whether or not treatment is warranted. Hence it will be necessary to ask: What will be the cost to the client and others of leaving the client's difficulties untreated? Will the client become more or less distressed; or will the client cause more distress to others if the problems remain untreated? Conversely, what would be the costs of the contemplated intervention, say, in the excision of a benign tumour?

The severity of the problem might also be considered although rarely in isolation from the variables noted above. The severity might be assessed by comparing measures of the variable of interest with data obtained from other subjects of similar age and other characteristics – a normative comparison. It would be comforting, therefore, if the clinician could consult a table of norms for a given variable and decide upon implementing treatment if it appeared that the client was exceptionally troubled on the target variable (Hartmann et al., 1979). For example, if a client was substantially less skilled in reading than clients of a similar age, social background and ability, it would be appropriate to offer coaching in reading skills (Rutter and Yule, 1977). This would be particularly important where the client perceives that he or she is less accomplished than his or her peers.

As noted above, clients will often present several major difficulties which may be targets for intervention. Decisions about which of them should receive priority may be made on grounds of functional relationships but the comparative severity of different problems may also be considered. For such a comparison, the data from the different variables must be in comparable form, notably in standard scores obtained from a normal distribution of the standardisation sample (Guilford and Fruchter, 1981). If the different variables have been recorded in different normative groups, they should be similar in composition.

Comparisons of this kind have been commonplace in personality testing (Harris, 1982), and the Minnesota Multiphasic Personality Inventory (MMPI) was once recommended for this (Meehl, 1973), but it would appear that poor standardisation (sampling differences, the absence of standard scores and non-normal distribution of data) makes it difficult in clinical practice to compare clients' scores on commonly used scales, such as the Social Avoidance and Distress Scale and the Beck Depression Inventory (see Table 1.2). Such a comparison may be necessary in evaluating a case where agoraphobic difficulties had been referred. The cognitive therapy of depression (see Bradley, Chapter 6) can require some evaluation of the client's capacity for assertiveness but actuarial comparisons in measures of this and of anxiety and depression must be hazardous. Self-report measures of assertiveness have poor validity (Arkowitz, 1981) and the BDI has shown significant correlations with measures of anxiety (Beck *et al.*, 1988).

Unfortunately, as indicated above, clinical judgements about the relative severity of different difficulties are also likely to be subject to substantial error. For this reason also, such variables should be monitored continuously and subject to single-case experimental analysis (see Morley, Chapter 37).

THE STATISTICAL REQUIREMENTS OF PSYCHOLOGICAL INVESTIGATION

There have been numerous discussions of the requirements of psychological investigation in clinical work (Ghiselli *et al.*, 1981; Anastasi, 1988; Cronbach *et al.*, 1972; Cone, 1981). Hence this review has concentrated on a number of issues which appear to be of critical importance in clinical practice. Statistical procedures associated with single-case experimentation are described by Morley in Chapter 37.

The principal sources of data for variables of interest in the second stage of clinical investigation lie in self-report from the client and in data recorded in observation by the clinician or other parties such as care staff or the client's family. Sometimes ready-made procedures, such as checklists, inventories and rating scales and tests, will be available. On other occasions the clinician will have to devise procedures *ad hoc*. The following discussion will indicate what are the outstanding considerations in selecting and constructing these devices.

Validity

Does the procedure detect and measure the variable which it purports to identify?

First, does it measure all the different aspects which are held to describe the variable of interest, that is, does the measurement procedure have *content validity* (Linehan, 1980)? For example, in devising a checklist to describe aggressive behaviour in a client, the clinician might have to ensure that all behaviour which the client presents in that category is detailed. Hence, striking others, throwing objects, pushing and screaming might all be included for that client.

Does the measure have *convergent validity* (Campbell and Fiske, 1959)? That is, does it correlate highly with another variable which is closely related to the variable of interest? For example, a checklist which purports to identify and record all the rituals and compulsions which a client can produce to disrupt a particular activity should produce data which correlate highly with the time taken by the client to complete that activity.

Does the procedure have high *divergent validity*? That is, how consistently does the test measure the hypothetical variable of interest? For example, a checklist designed to measure pain might consist of items which did not correlate highly with one another. It might be found that the data from only certain items were highly intercorrelated and these might describe sensations such as 'tingling' or 'throbbing'. Other items, such as 'cruel' or 'punishing', might not correlate highly with those items and they might describe a variable which could be described as an affective component of the experience (Melzack and Wall, 1988).

Reliability

When a client produces a certain score on an inventory, test or rating scale, it should be remembered that the score has been subject to sampling error. The clinician should consider that the score (described as the 'true score' in classical test theory), on which his decision-making will depend, will lie somewhere within a certain range of the obtained score determined by the standard error of measurement for the scale (Ghiselli *et al.*, 1981).

Guilford and Fruchter (1981) describe procedures for predicting 'true scores' within certain degrees of confidence. The *standard error of an obtained score* is equal to $\sigma_t \sqrt{1-r_{tt}}$ where σ_t is the reliability coefficient for the scale. The clinician should know that if it were possible to sample the subject's score repeatedly, 95 per cent of those scores would lie within the range ± two standard errors of the obtained score. In other words, the clinician would know at the 95 per cent level of confidence that the client's 'true score' lies within that range.

Where it is possible to obtain more than one estimate of a client's score for a given variable, the standard error of measurement decreases as more estimates are obtained. This can be accomplished by administering several homogeneous test items (Ghiselli *et al.*, 1981). This is illustrated by the State-Trait Anxiety Inventory (Spielberger *et al.*, 1983) in which the client is asked to describe the experience of anxiety by completing several very similar rating scales in quick succession.

Hence one source of determining a scale's capacity for giving estimated true scores with minimum error is the scale's *internal consistency reliability* (Guilford and Fruchter, 1981). This can be estimated from the correlation of the scores on each item with the total scores for the remainder of the test – the item–remainder correlations.

Another method of making the same prediction is *alternate or parallel forms reliability*, estimated by the correlation between such versions of the scale.

A third method which can be applied to variables for which temporal stability is the relevant criterion of reliability, is *test–retest reliability*, estimated by the correlation between scores obtained on the same scale completed on different occasions.

It should be emphasised here that such correlation analyses are only estimates of reliability. Therefore, when considering published coefficients of reliability expressed in these terms for psychometric purposes, the clinician must bear in mind that these too have been subject to sampling error. Again, the true reliability will lie within a certain range determined by the standard error of the correlation coefficient. The standard error of, for example, a product–moment correlation coefficient decreases with the size of the obtained correlation (r) and the number of observations (N) on which that correlation is based according to the formula:

standard error $= \dfrac{1 - r^2}{\sqrt{N - 1}}$ (Guilford and Fruchter, 1981).

Table 1.2 illustrates these points for a number of tests and scales.

It has often been pointed out that the validity of a measure depends in part on its reliability. However, a test with high inter-observer reliability need not accurately predict a client's status on the variable thus represented. For some variables there may be systematic differences between observers so that, for example, on an observation schedule which has a high inter-observer correlation, certain observers may give consistently lower scores for clients than would others (for example, Rutter and Cox, 1981). Other instances of such discrepancies can lie in comparisons between clinician's and client's observations (for example, Cooper *et al.*, 1982).

These illustrations of measurement accuracy have been used to qualify reliability of measurement. However, validity may also be limited by accuracy. For example, two measures which demonstrate high convergent validity may also present systematic discrepancies. Consider different estimates of the time required by subjects to fall asleep after a given signal. The time to stage 1 of an EEG sleep record may be positively correlated with the time to fall asleep which is reported by the subjects themselves (see Lindsay and Jahanshahi, Chapter 30). However, frequently subjects overestimate, compared with EEG criteria, the time which they take to fall asleep and so, although these measures of insomnia are positively correlated, they differ systematically. One variable may be a more accurate measure of insomnia than the other but in such cases it may be difficult to determine which is the more accurate estimate.

Hence high and reliable correlation coefficients and other measures of agree-

Table 1.2 Psychometric data for some commonly used tests and scales

Test	Principle sources	Reliability* ±standard error	Standard error of obtained score	Nature of scores	Distribution of scores	Nature of sample	Validity
Beck Depression Inventory (BDI)	Beck et al. (1988) Beck (1988)	0.73 0.95	2.80	Raw totals (means for 'not depressed' =11; 'mildly depressed' =19; 'moderately depressed' =25; 'severely depressed' = 28)	skewed?	depressed patients	Severity scores according to ratings by psychiatrists (not clear what diagnostic criteria they were using)
Self-rating for phobic patients (main phobia rating)	Marks and Mathews (1979)	0.93 ±0.01	0.56	Single rating on 9-point scale	?	20 phobic in-patients	?
Social avoidance and distress (SAD)	Watson and Friend (1969)	0.77 ±0.33	3.84	Raw totals (mean = 9.11 + s.d. 8.01)	skewed (modal score = 0)	205 Canadian summer-school students	?
State-Trait Anxiety Inventory (State scale)	Spielberger et al. (1983)	0.86 ±0.008	3.08	Raw totals (mean = 39.70 + s.d. 8.24)	?		Mean scores are greater under stress than non-stress (e.g. before/after surgery)
Sickness Impact Profile	Pollard et al. (1976); Bergner et al. (1976a)	0.77 ±0.05	4.24	Weighted raw scores; Percentage of total possible dysfunction score etc.	?		Mean scores greater for subjects with chronic illness than for those without
Severity of Alcohol Dependence Questionnaire	Stockwell et al. (1979)	0.51 0.80	3.28	Raw totals	?	104 patients in alcohol unit	Scores compared with ratings (validity not determined) of dependence by experienced psychiatrist
Aptitude Test for Employment (ATE) (Foundation Skills – A e.g. reading comprehension)	Psychological Corporation (1992)	0.91	2.01	Raw scores converted to percentiles or standard scores	normal	500 employees on work experience courses throughout the UK	?

* For nature of reliability (test-retest etc.), see quoted sources.

ment are necessary but not sufficient to support the reliability and validity of measurement procedures in clinical investigation. Measures of discrepancy such as t-tests are also necessary. As a measure of agreement, kappa, which allows for the influences of chance is more appropriate than correlation coefficients (Siegel and Castellan, 1988).

Sometimes there can be conflict in ensuring the validity and reliability of a measure. For example, in order to increase the content validity of a scale it may be necessary also to increase the number of different attributes which are sampled, thus decreasing the internal consistency of the test (Ghiselli *et al.*, 1981). The result may have to be a compromise between the content validity and the measurement reliability, especially if attempts to ensure that both are high result in a long and clumsy investigative procedure. This conflict has been noted in scales which seek to measure depression (Boyle, 1985).

Discriminant capacity

It should also be possible to determine the sensitivity of a given measure for detecting change reliably with treatment (Agras and Jacob, 1981). Hence for a representative sample of subjects undergoing a standard treatment procedure, the capacity of a variable, such as a self-rating of anxiety, for measuring change with that treatment would be determined by the ratio of the difference between mean scores, before and after treatment, to the pooled within-group standard deviation (Cohen, 1977). However, even for scales designed to measure change this information is usually not readily available.

Sources of bias in investigation

Several sources of systematic bias have been noted in the recording of behavioural data. The recording of self-report information by clients can influence their behaviour – the reactivity of client's behaviour (Nelson, 1977). The recording of observations by clinicians can have similar influences on the client (Harris and Lahey, 1983a; Haynes and Horn, 1982) and certain variables may influence the accuracy of the clinician's observation (Harris and Lahey, 1983b).

Reactivity

Several sources of reactivity in clients have been discussed. These have been especially evident where the client knows that his behaviour is being monitored. For example, observers who have already acted in a punitive fashion to clients may have a different reactive effect than observers who have used reinforcement to encourage appropriate behaviour. Hence the clinician would have to consider what effect would result from choosing an observer who was already known to the client. The presence of a stranger who is known to the client to be monitoring behaviour has shown surprisingly variable results. Undesirable activities may be discouraged by such monitoring whereas desirable behaviour may be increased. However, it is not unknown to the present authors for clients to accelerate disruptive behaviour when being the sole target of observation.

A number of recommendations can therefore be made to minimise the effects of such biases. Observational recording should be as unobtrusive as possible. Video and audio recording may help to attain this objective and will also assist the accuracy of recording because they can be played and replayed to check observations. These methods could be used over long periods without the cost entailed by the continuous presence of an observer and would allow the clients to become accustomed to, and perhaps less anxious about, their being observed. Participant observers, such as the client's family or care staff, may be less intrusive and again minimally expensive but the previous effect of the observer on the client's behaviour should be taken into account. If that source of influence was suspected, it would be advisable to have an independent observer also record data at intervals if possible.

It would be advisable also to look for systematic changes with time in recording before and after implementing changes in the environment, such as treatment and different observation procedures. Intermittent checks on the observer or the client's own recording might encourage more accurate and reliable recording and intermittent observation of a standard video demonstration of another client exhibiting the same target behaviour might refresh the criteria which are being used for recording.

Finally, but probably most important of all, the client's full approval for the collection of data should be sought at the outset wherever possible.

Impressionistic observations compared with recorded data

The accuracy of observations may be influenced by different expectations in the observer, and certain methods of observational recording may be especially sensitive to this bias. For example, recordings on rating scales used by observers to estimate hostility, sociability and hyperactivity in children were shown by Shuller and McNamara (1976) to be significantly influenced by instructions to the observers to expect high levels of those activities. Recordings of specific instances of aggressive, sociable or hyperactive behaviour were not influenced by the instructions. This finding is particularly important in view of the high frequency with which rating scales appear to be used in research and clinical practice.

Panic attacks have been shown to be less frequent, according to daily records of their occurrence kept by clients, than the clients had estimated in interview (Rapee *et al.*, 1990).

Relationships perceived among variables can turn out to be non-significant when data are carefully recorded. This has been observed for the association between panic attacks and menstruation in women (Cook *et al.*, 1990).

Scaling procedures

In practice the clinician will rarely be called upon to construct a multiple-item scale to measure single attributes such as extraversion, depression or short-term recall of visual information. This will be particularly true for the measurement of hypothetical constructs such as these. Such tests are usually readily available and the clinician may find them documented in the publications edited by Buros (Conoley and Kramer, 1992) and Hersen and Bellack (1988). The principles and practice of test construction will therefore be found elsewhere (Nunally, 1978; Anastasi, 1988).

However, frequently the clinician will be called upon to identify and devise a scale to measure change in a variable which has been identified for a given client as of central importance, the target variable, and for which no suitable scale is available for recording. A single symptom, such as the experience of a certain pain, may be reported by the client. The occurrence of behaviour such as crying can be observed by the client's family, the clinician and others. Such behaviour can vary in frequency, intensity and duration.

The behaviour should be defined as specifically as possible – 'crying' rather than 'appearing unhappy', or 'striking another patient' rather than 'being aggressive'. Several target variables, such as 'waking before 5 a.m.' and 'not going to work' may be recorded separately for the same client.

The occurrence of these events can then be recorded against a timescale on a checklist to determine their frequency over a given period. Time-sampling and interval-sampling may be used to limit the time required for observation (Marholin and Bijou, 1978). The duration of activities may be recorded in a similar fashion.

The intensity of symptoms, however, may require the construction of a rating scale unique to the client (Guilford, 1954; MacKay, 1980). Figure 1.2 illustrates different formats for such scales. They can differ in the number of points which anchor the scale, and the number of descriptors for those anchor points can be two or more.

Some scales have hypothetical zero points; others, such as the Semantic Differential Rating Scales (Osgood et al., 1957), are bipolar (for example, b on Figure 1.2). Some have equally spaced anchor points, others have unequal intervals. Hence some scales purport to be *ratio scales* with a zero point and equal intervals between the anchoring points. Some are *interval scales* with no determined zero but with equal intervals between points. Others have the anchoring points arranged in sequence for the given variable but make no assumptions about the size of the intervals or the location of the zero points (Siegel and Castellan, 1988).

Ratio, interval and ordinal scales differ in the statistical operations which may be conducted on them. This will be important in determining the significance of change in a given activity or symptom.

In addition, determining the clinical significance of change will also be

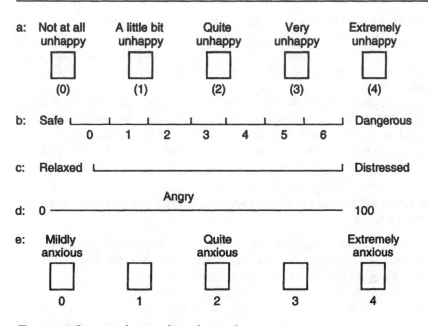

Figure 1.2 Common formats for rating scales

influenced by the intervals on the scale. Hence for a given client an improvement from point a to point b will probably be less notable than a change from b to c if the interval between a and b is less than that between b and c.

There are established procedures for determining anchoring points for ratio and interval scales (Ghiselli *et al.*, 1981). However, the amount of work required may make this impractical where a scale has to be constructed afresh for each client. Examples of such scale construction for personal questionnaires are described by Mulhall (1978) and Chalkley and Mulhall (1991). Such procedures generally require several samples of measurement for a given symptom on each occasion of estimate.

It is not clear if there is any advantage in defining rating scales with more than two descriptors where only one estimate of measurement is obtained as in a single use of scale c in Figure 1.2. Some clients, nevertheless, may find it difficult to translate their experience into numerical terms as in scale d of Figure 1.2. For them it would be more appropriate to use descriptors from an already constructed scale such as the Personal Questionnaire Rapid Scaling Technique (PQRST) (Mulhall, 1978). This has the additional advantages of being applicable to any attribute or symptom described by the client; it also gives an indication of inconsistency in the ratings produced by the client when it is used as a personal questionnaire. It comes already prepared.

In the construction of rating scales where the client gives only one estimate on an occasion of measurement, it is probably not necessary to use more than five or six anchoring points for reliable and discriminating measurement (McKelvie, 1980). In addition, although it will be necessary to ensure that descriptors for the scale are in correct sequence, there may be no significant advantage for reliability in ensuring that they are on an interval scale (Spector, 1980).

Finally, care must be taken to ensure that the descriptors for a scale do not confound poorly related variables. Hence, for example, the scale in Figure 1.3 would be difficult to complete if crying was not clearly associated with acute sadness for a given client. It would be better, therefore, to scale these variables separately.

ACCESS TO INFORMATION ABOUT COGNITIONS PROVIDED BY THE CLIENT

The development of cognitive therapy and the recognition of cognitive influences on behaviour and emotions has drawn renewed attention to difficulties which the client may have in disclosing information.

There can be many such impediments in the client: inability of the client to remember the information, difficulties in putting the information into words, being unaware of the significance of certain information, finding it difficult because of social desirability to disclose some matters (Watts, 1983). For example, a client with a panic disorder described his first panic as happening without warning and he was able to remember only a few of the events which led up to it. He vividly described in the clinic its onset having occurred as he drove in his car along a motorway. Having so little information about that panic contributed to his belief that some serious defect of his health was responsible for his panics. However, as treatment progressed, he remembered that he had started his journey on the day of the first panic without breakfast and having consumed only strong black coffee. As he had already discussed the importance of limiting his intake of caffeine, an anxiogenic substance, with the therapist, he now had crucial information to challenge his belief about his ill-health.

Nisbett and Wilson (1977), in a very influential paper, noted several instances where respondents were unable to describe influences on their behaviour. Nevertheless, the client must be the most dependable source of his or her own cognitions (White, 1988). The therapist may be able to prompt the client by, for

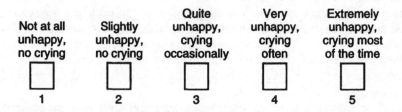

Figure 1.3 A rating scale with scale confounding

example, pointing out that certain cognitions which he or she has disclosed do not appear to be sufficient to account for the distress which the client is apparently experiencing. Under those circumstances, however, there is a risk that the client will produce spurious cognitions which he or she thinks are being sought by the therapist.

Nevertheless, the identification of cognitions which may be of unique importance to the client is of critical importance in cognitive therapy and will be stressed by several contributors throughout this book. It is rarely sufficient to ask the client to complete a standard check list of cognitions. Such lists will often fail to include crucial matters.

Hollon and Kendall (1981) have pointed to undesirable emotion-arousing effects which can occur with cognitive monitoring notably in thought-sampling, a technique which requires the client to record his or her thoughts when he or she hears a signal generator. Rippere (Chapter 5) has noted similar effects in a client who was completing a depression inventory. Hence the clinician should be prepared to help the client cope with these effects.

REFERENCES

Agras, W. S. and Jacob, R. G. (1981) 'Phobia: nature and measurement', in M. Mavissakaliam and D. H. Barlow (eds) *Phobia: Psychological and Pharmacological Treatment*, New York: Guildford Press.

American Psychiatric Association (1980) *Diagnostic and Statistical Manual of Mental Disorders, 3rd edn (DSM III)*, Washington, DC: American Psychiatric Association.

American Psychiatric Association (1987) *Diagnostic and Statistical Manual of Mental Disorders, 3rd edn Revised (DSM III–R)*, Washington, DC: American Psychiatric Association.

Anastasi, A. (1988) *Psychological Testing, 6th edn*, New York: Macmillan.

Arkowitz, H. (1981) 'Assessment of social skills', in M. Hersen and A. S. Bellack (eds) *Behavioural Assessment. A Practical Handbook*, New York: Pergamon.

Barlow, D. H. and Mavissakalian, M. (1981) 'Directions in the assessment and treatment of phobia: the next decade', in M. Mavissakalian and D. H. Barlow (eds) *Phobia: Psychological and Pharmacological Treatment*, New York: Guilford Press.

Beck, A. T. (1967) *Depression: Causes and Treatment*, Philadelphia: University of Philadelphia Press.

Beck, A. T. (1988) *Beck Depression Inventory*, Sidcup, Kent: Psychological Corporation.

Beck, A. T., Steer, R. A. and Garbin, M. G. (1988) 'Psychometric properties of the Beck Depression Inventory: twenty-five years of evaluation', *Clinical Psychology Review* 8: 77–100.

Bergner, M., Bobbitt, R. A., Pollard, W. E., Martin, D. P. and Gilson, B. S. (1976a) 'The Sickness Impact Profile: validation of a health status measure', *Medical Care* 14: 57–67.

Bergner, M., Bobbitt, R. A., Kressel, S., Pollard, W. E., Gilson, B. S. and Morris, J. R. (1976b) The Sickness Impact Profile: conceptual formulation and methodology for the development of a health status measure, *International Journal of Health Services* 6: 393–415.

Boyd, J. H. and Weissman, M. M. (1982) 'Epidemiology', in E. S. Paykel (ed.) *Handbook of Affective Disorders*, Edinburgh: Churchill Livingstone.

Boyle, G. J. (1985) 'Self-report measures of depression: some psychometric considerations', *British Journal of Clinical Psychology* 24: 45–59.

Brown, D. K. , Kratochwill, T. R. and Bergan, J. R. (1982) 'Teaching interview skills for problem identification: an analogue study', *Behavioural Assessment* 4: 63–73.

Brown, G. W. and Harris, T. (1978) *Social Origins of Depression: A Study of Psychiatric Disorders in Women*, London: Tavistock.

Campbell, D. T. and Fiske, D. W. (1959) 'Convergent and discriminant validation by the multitrait-multimethod matrix', *Psychological Bulletin*, 56: 81–105.

Canavan, A. G. M. and Beckman, J. (1993) 'Deriving principal component IQ scores from the WAIS-R, *British Journal of Clinical Psychology* 32: 81–6.

Cautela, J. R. and Upper, D. (1973) 'A behavioural coding system', Annual Meeting Association for the Advancement of Behaviour Therapy.

Cautela, J. R. and Upper, D. (1975) 'The process of individual behavior therapy', in M. Hersen et al. (eds.) *Progress in Behavior Modification, I*, New York: Academic Press.

Cautela, J. R. and Upper, D. (1976) 'The Behavioral Inventory Battery: the use of self-report measures in behavioral analysis and therapy', in M. Hersen and A. S. Bellack (eds.) *Behavioral Assessment. A Practical Handbook, 1st edn*, New York: Pergamon.

Chalkley, A. J. and Mulhall, D. J. (1991) 'The PQRSTUV: The Personal Questionnaire Rapid Scaling Technique – "Ultimate Version"', *British Journal of Clinical Psychology* 30: 181–4.

Ciminero, A. R., Calhoun, K. S. and Adam, H. E. (eds.) (1977) *Handbook of Behavioral Assessment* New York: Wiley.

Clare, A. W. and Cairns, V. E. (1978) 'Design, development and use of a standardised interview to assess social maladjustment and dysfunction in community studies', *Psychological Medicine* 8: 589–604.

Cohen, J. (1977) *Statistical Power Analysis for the Behavioral Sciences*, New York: Academic Press.

Cone, J. D. (1978) 'The Behavioral Assessment Grid (BAG): a conceptual framework and a taxonomy', *Behavior Therapy* 9: 882–8.

Cone, J. D. (1981) 'Psychometric considerations', in M. Hersen and A. S. Bellack (eds) *Behavioral Assessment, A Practical Handbook, 2nd edn*, New York: Pergamon Press.

Conoley, J.C. and Kramer, J.J. (eds) (1992) *The Eleventh Mental Measurements Year Book*, Lincoln Neb: Buros Institute.

Cook, B. L., Noyes, R., Garvey, M. J., Beach, V., Sobotka, J. and Chaudry, D. (1990) 'Anxiety and the menstrual cycle in panic disorders', *Journal of Affective Disorders* 19: 221–6.

Cooper, B. (1973) 'Clinical and social aspects of chronic neurosis', *Proceedings of the Royal Society of Medicine* 65: 509–12.

Cooper, P., Osborn, M., Gath, D. and Feggetter, G. (1982) 'Evaluation of a modified self-report measure of social adjustment', *British Journal of Psychiatry* 141: 68–75.

Cox, A., Holbrook, D. and Rutter, M. (1981a) 'Psychiatric interviewing techniques. VI. Experimental study: eliciting feels', *British Journal of Psychiatry* 139: 144–52.

Cox, A., Rutter, M. and Holbrook, D. (1981b) 'Psychiatric interviewing techniques. V. Experimental study: eliciting factual information', *British Journal of Psychiatry* 139: 29–37.

Cronbach, L. J., Gleser, G. C., Nanada, H. and Rajaratnam, N. (1972) *The Dependability of Behavioral Measurements: Theory of Generalisability for Scores and Profiles*, New York: Wiley.

Cullen, C. (1983) 'Implications of functional analysis', *British Journal of Clinical Psychology* 22; 137–8.

Cyr, J. J., Doxey, N. and Vigna, C. M. (1988) 'Factorial composition of the SCL–90–R, *Journal of Social Behaviour Personality* 3: 245–52.

Derogatis, L. R. (1977) *SCL–R–90: Administration, Scoring and Procedures Manual*, Baltimore: Clinical Psychometrics Research.

Derogatis, L. R. and Melisaratos, N. (1983) 'The Brief Symptom Inventory: an introductory report', *Psychological Medicine* 13: 595–605.

Derogatis, L. R. and Spencer, P. M. (1982) *The Brief Symptom Inventory. Administration, Scoring and Procedures Manual*, Baltimore: Clinical Psychometric Research.

Derogatis, L. R., Lipman, R. S. and Covi, L. (1973) 'SCL–90: an outpatient psychiatric rating scale – preliminary report', *Psychopharmacological Bulletin* 9: 13–25.

DiNardo, P. A., Barlow, D. H., Cerny, J. A., Vermilyea, B. B., Vermilyea, J. A., Himadi, W. G. and Waddell, M. T. (1985) *Anxiety Disorders Interview Schedule–Revised* (ADIS–R), New York: Phobia and Anxiety Disorders Clinic, State University of New York.

Ekman, P. and Oster, H. (1979) 'Facial expressions of emotion', *Annual Review of Psychology* 30: 527–54.

Emmelkamp, P. M. G. (1982) *Phobic and Obsessive–Compulsive Disorders: Theory, Research and Practice*, New York: Plenum.

Erickson, R. C. and Scott, M. L. (1977) 'Clinical memory testing: a review', *Psychological Bulletin* 84: 1130–49.

Eysenck, H. J., Wakefield, J. A. and Friedman, A. F. (1983) 'Diagnosis and clinical assessment: the *DSM III*', *Annual Review of Psychology* 34: 167–193.

Fewtrell, W. D. (1981) 'Variations in clinical opinion between psychologists treating a single case of sleep dysfunction', Annual Conference, British Psychological Society.

Fordyce, W. E. (1976) *Behavioural Methods for Chronic Pain and Illness*, St. Louis: Mosby.

Francis, V. M., Rajan, P. and Turner, N. (1990) 'British community norms for the Brief Symptom Inventory', *British Journal of Clinical Psychology* 29: 115–16.

Frank, G. (1983) *The Wechsler Enterprise*, New York: Pergamon.

Geer, J. H. (1965) 'The development of a scale to measure fear', *Behaviour Research and Therapy* 3: 45–53.

Ghiselli, E. E., Campbell, J. P. and Zedeck, S. (1981) *Measurement Theory for the Behavioral Sciences*, San Francisco: Freeman.

Goldberg, D. and Williams, P. (1988) *A User's Guide to the General Health Questionnaire*, Windsor: NFER-Nelson.

Golden, C. J. (1979) *Clinical Interpretation of Psychological Tests*, New York: Grune and Stratton.

Guilford, J. P. (1954) *Psychometric Methods, 2nd edn*, New York: McGraw-Hill.

Guilford, J. P. and Fruchter, R. (1981) *Fundamental Statistics in Psychology and Education, 6th edn*, New York: McGraw-Hill.

Hall, J. N. and Baker, R. (1983) *Rehabilitation Evaluation*, Aberdeen: Vine Publishing Ltd.

Harris, F. C. and Lahey, B. B. (1983a) 'Subject reactivity in direct observational assessment: a review and critical analysis', *Clinical Psychology Review*, 2: 523–38.

Harris, F. C. and Lahey, B. B. (1983b) 'Recording system bias in direct observational methodology', *Clinical Psychology Review* 2: 539–56.

Harris, J. G. (1982), 'The assessment of personality profiles', *Clinical Psychology Review* 2: 27–48.

Hartmann, D. P., Roper, B. L. and Bradford, D. C. (1979) Some relationships between behavioral and traditional assessment', *Journal of Behavioral Assessment* 1: 3–21.

Hay, W. M., Hay, L. R., Angle, H. V. and Nelson, R. O. (1979) 'The reliability of problem identification in the behavioral interview', *Behavioral Assessment* 1: 107–18.

Haynes, S. N. and Horn, W. F. (1982) 'Reactivity in behavioral observation: a review', *Behavioral Assessment* 4: 369–85.

Haynes, S. N. and O'Brien, W. H. (1990) 'Functional analysis in behaviour therapy', *Clinical Psychology Review* 10: 649–69.

Heaton, R. K. and Pendleton, M. G. (1981) 'Use of neuropsychological tests to predict adult patients' everyday functioning', *Journal of Consulting and Clinical Psychology* 49: 807–21.

Heaton, R. K., Beade, L. E. and Johnson, K. L. (1979) 'Neuropsychological test results associated with psychiatric disorders in adults', *Psychological Bulletin* 85: 141–62.

Helzer, J. E., Robins, L. N., Croughton, J. L. and Welner, A. (1981) 'Renard diagnostic interview', *Archives of General Psychiatry* 38: 393–98.

Hersen, M. and Bellack, A. S. (eds) (1981) *Behavioral Assessment. A Practical Handbook,* 2nd edn. New York: Pergamon.

Hersen, M. and Bellack, A. S. (eds) (1988) *A Dictionary of Behavioral Assessment Techniques,* New York: Pergamon Press.

Hill, J., Harrington, R., Fudge, H., Rutter, M. and Pickles, A. (1989) 'Adult Personality Functioning Assessment (APFA): an investigator-based standardised interview', *British Journal of Psychiatry* 155: 24–35.

Hollon, S. D. and Kendall, P. C. (1981) 'In vivo assessment techniques for cognitive-behavioral processes', in P. C. Kendall and S. D. Hollon (eds) *Assessment Strategies for Cognitive-Behavioral Interventions,* New York: Academic Press.

Lam, D. and Power, M. (1991) 'Social support in a general practice elderly sample', *International Journal of Geriatric Psychiatry* 6: 89–93.

Lazarus, A. A. (1976) *Multimodal Behavior Therapy,* New York: Springer.

Lewinsohn, P. M. (1975) 'The behavioral study and treatment of depression', in M. Hersen *et al.* (eds) *Progress in Behavior Modification I,* New York: Academic Press.

Linehan, M. M. (1980) 'Content validity: its relevance to behavioral assessment', *Behavioral Assessment* 2: 147–159.

McGuire, R. J. (1973) 'Classification and the problem of diagnosis', in H. J. Eysenck (ed.) *Handbook of Abnormal Psychology,* London: Pitman Medical.

MacKay, C. J. (1980) 'The measurement of mood and psychophysiological activity using self-report techniques', in I. Martin and P. H. Venables (eds) *Techniques in Psychophysiology,* New York: Wiley.

McKelvie, S. J. (1980) 'Graphic rating-scales: how many categories?' *British Journal of Psychology* 69: 185–202.

Marholin, D. H. and Bijou, S. W. (1978) 'Behavioral assessment. Listen when the data speak', in D. H. Marholin (ed.) *Child Behavior Therapy,* New York: Gardner Press.

Marks, I. and Mathews, A. M. (1979) 'Brief standard self-rating for phobic patients', *Behaviour Research and Therapy* 17: 263–67.

Matarazzo, J. D. (1983) 'The reliability of psychiatric and psychological diagnosis', *Clinical Psychology Review* 3: 103–45.

Meehl, P. E. (1973) 'Why I do not attend case conferences', in P. E. Meehl (ed.) *Psycho-diagnosis. Selected Papers,* Minneapolis: University of Minnesota Press.

Melzack, R. and Wall, P. (1988) *The Challenge of Pain,* Harmondsworth: Penguin Books.

Metcalfe, M. and Goldman, E. (1965) 'Validation of an inventory for measuring depression', *British Journal of Psychiatry* 111: 240–42.

Miller, W. R. (1975) 'Psychological deficit in depression', *Psychological Bulletin* 82: 238–60.

Milne, D. (1992) *A Mental Health Portfolio,* Windsor: NFER-Nelson.

Mittler, P. (ed.) (1970) *The Psychological Assessment of Mental and Physical Handicaps,* London: Metheun.

Mulhall, D. J. (1978) *Manual for the Personal Questionnaire Rapid Scaling Technique,* Windsor: NFER.

Nay, W. R. (1979) *Multimethod Clinical Assessment,* New York: Gardner.

Nelson, H. E. (1991) *National Adult Reading Test 2nd edn*, Windsor: NFER-Nelson.

Nelson, R. O. (1977) 'Assessment and therapeutic functions of self-monitoring', in M. Hersen *et al.* (eds) *Progress in Behavior Modification 5*, New York: Academic Press.

Nisbett, R. E. and Wilson, T. D. (1977) 'Telling more than we know: verbal reports on mental processes', *Psychological Review* 84: 231–59.

Nunally, J. C. (1978) *Psychometric Theory*, New York: McGraw-Hill.

O'Carroll, R. E., Baikie, E. M. and Whittick, J. E. (1987) 'Does the National Adult Reading Test hold in dementia?' *British Journal of Clinical Psychology* 26: 315–16.

O'Farrell, T. J. and Upper, D. (1977) 'The interjudge reliability of Cautela and Upper's Behavioral Coding System', *Journal of Behavior Therapy and Experimental Psychiatry* 8: 39–43.

Office of Health Economics (1981) *Reducing the Harm*, London: Office of Health Economics.

Osgood, C. E., Suci, G. J. and Tannenbaum, P. H. (1957) *The Measurement of Meaning*, Urbana, Ill.: University of Illinois Press.

Owens, R. G. and Ashcroft, J. B. (1982) 'Functional analysis in applied psychology'. *British Journal of Clinical Psychology* 21: 181–89.

Paul, G. L. (1969) 'Behavior modification research: design and tactics', in C. M. Franks (eds) *Behavior Therapy: Appraisal and Status*, New York: McGraw-Hill.

Pollard, W. E., Bobbitt, R. A., Bergner, M., Martin, D. P and Gilson, B. S. (1976) 'The Sickness Impact Profile: reliability of a health status measure', *Medical Care* 14: 146–55.

Power, M. J., Champion, L. A. and Aris, S. J. (1988) 'The development of a measure of social support: the Significant Others Scale (SOS)', *British Journal of Clinical Psychology* 27: 349–58.

Psychological Corporation (1992) *Assessment for Training and Employment (ATE)*, Sidcup, Kent: Psychological Corporation.

Rapee, R., Craske, M. G. and Barlow, D. H. (1990) 'Subject-described features of panic attacks using self-montioring', *Journal of Anxiety Disorders* 4: 171–81.

Raven, J. C. (1992) (Research supplements 1979, 1982) *Standard Progressive Matrices*, Oxford: Oxford Psychologists' Press.

Raven, J. C. (1994) *Mill Hill Vocabulary Scale*, Oxford: Oxford Psychologists' Press.

Robins, L. N., Helzer, J. E., Croughan, J. and Ratcliff, K. S. (1981) 'National Institute of Mental Health Diagnostic Interview Schedule', *Archives of General Psychiatry* 38: 381–89.

Russell, G. *et al.* (1987) *Notes on Eliciting and Recording Clinical Information in Psychiatric Patients, 2nd edn*, Oxford: Oxford University Press.

Rutter, M. (1977) 'Separation, loss and family relationships', in M. Rutter and L. Hersov (eds) *Child Psychiatry Modern Approaches*, Oxford: Blackwell.

Rutter, M. and Cox, A. (1981) 'Psychiatric interviewing techniques. I. Methods and measures', *British Journal of Psychiatry* 138: 273–82.

Rutter, M. and Yule, W. (1977) 'Reading difficulties', in M. Rutter and L. Hersov (eds) *Child Psychiatry, Modern Approaches*, Oxford: Blackwell.

Salmon, P. (1970) 'Vocational guidance', in P. Mittler (ed.) *The Psychological Assessment of Mental and Physical Handicaps*, London: Methuen.

Shuller, D. Y. and McNamara, J. R. (1976) 'Expectancy factors in behavioral observation', *Behavior Therapy* 7: 519–27.

Siegel, S. and Castellan, N. J. (1988) *Nonparametric Statistics for the Behavioral Sciences*, New York: McGraw-Hill.

Spector, P. E. (1980) 'Ratings of equal and unequal response choice intervals', *Journal of Social Psychology* 112: 115–19.

Spielberger, C. D., Gorsuch, R. L. and Lushene, R. E. (1983) *Manual for the State-Trait Anxiety Inventory*, Palo Alto, Calif.: Consulting Psychologist Press.

Stockwell, T., Hodgson, R., Edwards, G., Taylor, C. and Rankin, H. (1979) 'The development of a questionnaire to measure severity of alcohol dependence', *British Journal of Addiction* 74: 79–87.

Todd, J., Coolidge, F. and Satz, P. (1977) 'The Wechsler Adult Intelligence Scale Discrepancy Index: a neuropsychological evaluation', *Journal of Consulting and Clinical Psychology* 45: 450–54.

Tversky, A. and Kahneman, D. (1982) 'Evidential impact of base rates', in D. Kahneman, P. Slovic and A. Tversky (eds) *Judgement Under Uncertainty: Heuristics and Biases*, Cambridge: Cambridge University Press.

Watson, D. (1982) 'The actor and observer: how are their perceptions of causality divergent?' *Psychological Bulletin* 92: 682–700.

Watson, D. and Friend, R. (1969) 'Measurement of social evaluative anxiety', *Journal of Consulting and Clinical Psychology* 33: 448–51.

Watts, F. N. (1980) 'Clinical judgement and clinical training', *British Journal of Medical Psychology* 53: 95–108.

Watts, F. N. (1983) 'Strategies of clinical listening', *British Journal of Clinical Psychology* 56: 113–23.

Wechsler, D. (1981) *Manual for the Wechsler Intelligence Scale for Adults – Revised (UK Supplement, 1988)*, New York: Psychological Corporation.

Weissman, M. M. and Bothwell, S. (1976) 'Assessment of social adjustment by patient self-report', *Archives of General Psychiatry* 33: 1111–15.

White, P. A. (1988) 'Knowing more about what we can tell: "Introspective access" and causal report accuracy 10 years later', *British Journal of Psychology* 79: 13–45.

Yates, A. J. (1976) 'Research methods in behavior modification: a comparative evaluation', in M. Hersen *et al.* (eds) *Progress in Behavior Modification 2*, New York: Academic Press.

Chapter 2

An introduction to treatment

G.E. Powell and S.J.E. Lindsay

This book describes scientific approaches to the investigation, treatment and management of psychological problems. In tackling the main issues chapter by chapter, some of the broader or background issues can become lost or obscured to the reader, and so a few general comments are in order.

BEING A THERAPIST

To begin with, therapists from any discipline or adhering to any school should try to establish (1) what they are aiming to achieve, (2) how they intend to achieve it, (3) the rationale or theory behind their chosen course of action, (4) the effects of such an intervention, (5) the limitations of that intervention, and (6) when to consult professional colleagues. Often these aims are easier to state than to achieve.

Consider the problems in defining the technique which we are using. There are some techniques which can be easily defined at a practical level, such as systematic desensitisation where the procedures of relaxation training, hierarchy construction and item presentation can all be listed in detail (see Lindsay, Chapter 7). Other therapies can only be listed as a set of principles which guide the therapist, such as the use of 'contracting' strategies in marital therapy (Holtzworth-Munroe and Jacobson, 1991), the use of 'graded retraining' in the rehabilitation of chronic psychiatric cases (Watts and Bennett, 1983) or imagery-recoding strategies in helping those with memory problems (Wilson, 1987). Many therapies, then, are really a description of strategies which guide therapist behaviour but do not dictate all of the small tactical steps which must remain at the discretion of the therapist.

Treatment corresponding to the formulation

The previous chapter described how formulations can be made to describe a client's difficulties. Such formulations should enable the clinician to plan the intervention, usually one or two different approaches in each case. Unfortunately, some problems are so complex and corresponding formulations so uncertain that a large battery of treatments may be applied almost regardless of the formulation, in shot-gun fashion, to make sure that all possible difficulties are tackled. Thus, for example, patients with chronic occupational pain may receive assertiveness training, cognitive treatment for their beliefs about their pain, relaxation training to reduce the pain itself, and exposure to reduce the avoidance of activity by which the clients have learned to cope with pain (Spence, 1989).

Moreover, several different ways of helping a client with a given difficulty, such as agoraphobia, can be effective. Some clients will recover normal activity with no formal intervention from the therapist (Gelder, 1981; de Silva and Rachman, 1981). Outcomes such as this may come about because the different treatment or the therapist alone have led the client to believe that he can cope (Bandura, 1977), or because of other changes in the client's beliefs (Ellis and Grieger, 1977). It follows directly from this that the precise nature of any treatment and (perhaps therefore) its efficacy depends in part upon characteristics of the therapist, including degree of ingenuity, experience, skills and biases. For example, considerable persuasion and support may have to be offered before a patient will volunteer for a potentially threatening treatment, such as high-intensity exposure to feared objects or the response prevention of obsessional rituals (Foa and Goldstein, 1978).

Nevertheless, for the most effective intervention, the therapist should be able to explain the rationale for the chosen course of action. First, it must be understood that this represents a series of questions reflecting different levels of explanation. Consider an example.

Q   Why are you taking Mrs X across the road each day?
A   To desensitise her to traffic.
Q   Why?
A   To enable her to get to the shops.
Q   Why?
A   As part of a marital contract hoping to reduce marital friction:
    Mr X is fed up with doing all the shopping.
Q   Why is there a marital contract to reduce friction?
A   To save the marriage.
Q   Why are you trying to save the marriage? Will this help fulfil the aspirations of both partners?

Second, the word 'why' also demands an account of theory or knowledge.

Q   Why are you taking Mrs X across the road each day?
A   Repeated presentation of a noxious stimulus leads to reduction of anxiety under appropriate conditions (Lindsay, Chapter 8).
Q   Why are you doing this?
A   Mrs X's failure to shop is in part a learned avoidance response which will diminish once aversive experiences associated with the act of shopping

are diminished or eliminated and thus lead to disconfirmation of X's worst thoughts underpinning her fear (Lindsay, op. cit.).

Q   Why do you use marital contracting?

A   As a way of structuring and ensuring an exchange of positively reinforcing behaviours in view of the fact that the number of these emitted by spouses is positively correlated with ratings of marital satisfaction (Gottman, 1979).

Next is the problem of monitoring – knowing the effect that the treatment is having. Some target variables are easier to measure than others. In the above case, for example, anxiety responses can be measured by self-report, and the hypothesis that a reduction in such responses will allow Mrs X to shop more often is again directly testable by a frequency count of the latter. But what about measuring the emission of positive reinforcers in a domestic context not open to easy direct observation? What happens if partners disagree over whether a positive reinforcer has been emitted or not? How valid are self-report measures of marital satisfaction? How does one measure the satisfaction that is presumed to accrue from saving the marriage? Then there are the unexpected effects of treatment: Mrs X becomes more competent than even she expected and her whole self-confidence increases; she begins to resent being treated as ill by her husband and to demand a different and greater decision-making role in the marriage; Mr X sees this as a threat; he preferred taking decisions without having to consult his wife and he had felt proud of his ability to cope with a sick woman. In this set of circumstances, how might one measure such things as degree of threat or loss of self-esteem? Perhaps one should have predicted this possible outcome and taken baseline measures to do with marital roles? This might have given warning of arising complications but is it efficient or even possible to measure all aspects of a case just on the chance that they will later prove relevant?

Monitoring the effects of treatment is therefore almost always a compromise between what should and what can be measured at a theoretic level, and between what should and what can be measured at a practical level, taking into account pressures upon professional time. All therapists use measurement to monitor progress and assess efficacy, even if it is only the observation of the patient's behaviour or mood during the sessions or the simple request as to how things have been in the previous week. But emphasis upon measurement above and beyond this minimal level requires not only rigorous expertise and application (Chapter 1) but also flexibility. Often, however, changes will take place in variables which the clinician has not anticipated or recorded.

BEING A SCIENTIFIC THERAPIST

The ensuing chapters are all written by people taking a broadly scientific or experimental approach to problems and treatment, meaning that their work is open to public inspection in the scientific journals and that their theories and treatments are open to experimental validation or rejection. What does being 'broadly scientific' mean in a practical sense?

Aims defined

Aims or targets are agreed with the client at the outset of treatment following a sometimes lengthy process of measurement or investigation using wherever possible techniques or instruments of known adequacy, reliability and validity (Chapter 1).

Continuous assessment

Such assessment continues throughout treatment to monitor progress and provide evidence of efficacy. The original formulation remains no more than a provisional framework within which a hypothesis is constructed that strategy X will achieve Y. Treatment therefore is also used as hypothesis-testing. In addition, treatment is not pursued regardless of outcome and it is not assumed that the client will inevitably derive benefit from a given intervention.

Strategies and techniques defined

Treatment strategies and specific techniques are defined as accurately as possible and preferably in operational terms – in the same way that experimental methods in research papers should be extremely detailed, and for precisely the same reason, that is, to allow as exact a replication as possible. Tight definition of clinical psychology methods helps to keep sources of unknown variance to a minimum (say, from idiosyncratic interpretation and behaviour of the therapist); it allows a more or less uniform technique to be used across individuals in group research studies; it helps ensure comparability of studies across different research groups, perhaps in different countries; it aids the process whereby techniques are experimentally broken down into constituent elements to find the 'active ingredients'; and in clinical practice it facilitates the teaching of the technique to other psychologists, nurses and parents or relatives who all might be involved in treatment of the client. Such description also favours constructive discussion of the case with professional colleagues.

Ironically, it has been noted that the reliability with which experimental and treatment procedures have been implemented has received very little attention in research studies (Billingsley et al., 1980). Correspondingly there have been few recommendations in the treatment literature on methods for estimating the accuracy or consistency or even validity with which certain treatments have been carried out.

For example, reports of research in behaviour therapy for agoraphobia are discussed in by Lindsay (Chapter 8) but there is almost no information in those reports about how accurately or consistently the treatments were implemented. There is often little information about whether or not the intermediate and the presumed essential changes were observed (in cognitions, physiological arousal or other activity such as breathing patterns): the validity of the specified treatments was not determined. Was the cognitive therapy really cognitive?

Nevertheless, in clinical practice in order to achieve the foregoing objectives, treatment procedures should be described specifically. A general expression, such as 'anxiety management,' should be replaced with an account of a particular course of action; such as 'progressive muscular relaxation practised during imaginary rehearsal of waiting to board a plane was implemented whenever the client was seated while waiting on board the aircraft'.

The consistency of the client's behaviour should also be noted. How consistently does the client implement cue-controlled relaxation under conditions of stress? How often does he or she list negative thoughts and corresponding challenges when depressed?

Progress through controlled investigation

Progress and advances are generally made through controlled scientific investigation. Hence only interventions supported by scientific trials have been recommended in this book. However, such research has never been so precise that single-case experimentation by the clinician will not be necessary for each clinical case.

SOME COMMON PRINCIPLES OF TREATMENT

Acquiring realistic expectations

An important first step in treatment will consist in giving the client realistic but encouraging expectations about the conduct and the effects of treatment. At first it may be necessary to deal with some of the client's own assumptions and any disagreement or puzzlement that the client may have with the hypothesis the clinician has formulated about the difficulties.

Some clients expect to be given medication that will be quickly effective; others will expect that finding the historic 'causes' of their difficulty, without further intervention, will bring about their recovery. Many clients will anticipate that the burden of treatment will fall upon the therapist and that they will be the passive recipients of treatment; others expect that psychological treatment consists only of talking and indeed they may wish simply to unburden themselves in that way.

Hence, for many clients, it will be necessary to explain gently that a change for the better will come about slowly. Also it will be important to indicate that treatment will consist in practising new ways of behaving and that the client will be required to do this outside the clinic as 'homework'. In addition, a corresponding goal in treatment will consist of helping the client himself or herself to control, manage and overcome the main difficulties: to help the client become independent of the therapist and similar help. It may be necessary to explain that although it will probably be impossible to be sure about the original cause of the difficulties, certain factors will be contributing to its persistence and it is those that will be tackled in treatment. The experimental approach to treatment should be outlined. Finally it should be indicated that treatment will not last indefinitely. The therapist may anticipate that, say, about twenty weekly sessions will be required by which time the client should have experienced some benefits. There-after follow-up visits at, say, monthly intervals might be valuable for a period.

As a constructive introduction to treatment, a modelling demonstration on video or audiotapes of treatment sessions might be used. The therapist might describe the treatment and outcome of a similar case. Illustrating the different effects of encouraging and discouraging cognitions would be a useful entry to cognitive therapy (see Bradley, Chapter 6) and experiencing habituation by means of imaginal rehearsal might be an encouraging introduction to flooding *in vivo*. Bandura (1977) has suggested that giving clients expectations that they will be able to cope is an important contribution to successful treatment whatever the nature of the latter. There have been a few attempts to prepare patients by means of a leaflet and booklets before they attend psychology clinics. The result have not been encouraging (e.g. Schumann, 1987), some clients finding the material daunting. This approach cannot yet therefore be a substitute for the therapist's discussing the above matters and answering the client's corresponding concerns.

Reinforcement

During treatment it will often be important to reinforce progress made by the client. Hence an agoraphobic may visit interesting department stores. Clients with social fears may find new friends and join special interest clubs. Such reinforcement would be important where some other procedure such as social skills training was the main treatment.

Withdrawal of the reinforcement of undesired behaviour may be important in some cases. In others, reinforcement of desired behaviour may be implemented by means of tokens which can be accumulated and exchanged for back-up rewards by the client according to a pre-agreed economy (token economy pro-grammes, TEP; Kazdin, 1982).

Provision of feedback

Sometimes feedback is the prime treatment technique, as in relaxation training based on psychophysiological feedback or the feedback of rolandic cortex sensori-motor rhythm to control seizures. Often, like star charts in a TEP programme for a disruptive client, video feedback during social-skills training, or graphs of time spent on rituals by the obsessional, feedback is more of an adjunct. In fact, because this volume stresses the continuous measurement and monitoring of progress, suitable feedback can nearly always be made available to the patient and, in general, feedback should be maximised.

Feedback will be valuable where change in the target behaviour is slow and imperceptible from session to session. The therapist should think carefully, however, about giving feedback likely to undermine the confidence of the patient. For instance, once, in the treatment of a stutterer we were using video-tapes to measure degree of facial grimacing as one index of improvement, but the early tapes were so painful to watch, and so clearly worse than the patient's own perception of his facial appearance, that we did not show them to him. Later, when he was much improved, the better tapes were usefully shown to him to indicate which muscle groups he still needed to relax.

Some clients, especially those who are socially anxious, may find video replay very threatening in group treatment and it might be advisable to give them such experience in one-to-one sessions at first. Video feedback may then be reassuring to such clients when they see that their discomfort is not visible.

Graded approaches

Graded approaches all concern facing the patient with a goal that is manageable and there are at least three varieties. First, there is breakdown of a large task into constituent elements or subgoals. As each subgoal is achieved, steady progress is made towards the ultimate aim. For example, the aim 'to get married and have a normal life' in an extremely shy man might involve anxiety management, social skills training, family therapy to reduce the domination of overbearing parents, the establishment of low-level social activities such as joining clubs or societies, and so on. Second, there is the 'shaping' of behaviour (to borrow the term from operant theory) in which increasingly strict demands are placed upon the individual. For example, in reteaching language to a brain-damaged man, any utterance contingent upon the therapist's question might be reinforced initially. Later, any rough approximation to a word, then a properly pronounced word and lastly a few words will in turn be rewarded. Third, there is the grading of tasks according to their fear-arousing properties, whereby, as a general principle, patients tackle least disturbing tasks first, in the hope that fear will diminish and competence will increase by the time very difficult situations must be faced.

Modelling

This is the demonstration of a skill which the patient is to acquire. Sometimes it is a major form of treatment in its own right, as a major part of social skills training or in showing a couple how to discuss an issue constructively. Frequently, modelling is used to train others in behavioural skills, demonstrating to teachers how to obtain classroom control, for example, or showing mothers how to cope with a child having a temper tantrum: how to ignore and/or restrain the child in silence at such times and to praise and cuddle the child when well behaved. There are many times when a verbal explanation is inadequate and it is then that modelling is invaluable.

Rehearsal

Progressive relaxation for reducing headaches and anxiety, ignoring tantrums in a child in a supermarket rather than pacifying it with sweets, and making eye-to-eye contact with a stranger in spite of intense anxiety, are all skills which may be easy to rehearse in the secure environment of the clinic but impossible for the client to implement under those stresses. Hence, wherever possible, these skills should be rehearsed under conditions of simulated stress. New skills should also be exercised until they are overlearned, otherwise previous habits (possibly of greater 'habit strength' to borrow an old terminology) will come drifting back, or the new skills will disintegrate in times of pressure or stress. Hence most treatment programmes have 'homework'. The client must, in his or her own time between visits to the therapist, exercise and extend the skills learned in previous sessions. This is naturally especially relevant to out-patient treatment.

Changing dysfunctional beliefs

Cognitive therapy is now part of psychological treatment for almost all problems brought to psychologists, as most of the chapters in this book will show. The most widespread practice consists of the following (see, for example, Bradley, Chapter 6): By means of daily written records, list as they occur

1 Dysfunctional emotions (e.g. anger, sadness) and their degree of severity
2 The corresponding thoughts (e.g. a clinician might say, 'These patients are far too complex for these simplistic approaches', 'It's hopeless', 'I don't help anybody')
3 Corresponding challenges
4 Changes in the negative emotions as the result of such challenges

Transferring treatment and management to the patient and his or her environment

Most of the treatments to be described later require the patient to assume greater responsibility for his or her own behaviour; to learn the problem management and monitoring skills which will have been modelled by the therapist and to know how to tackle any resurgence of the problems. Therefore, most treatment requires the explicit education of the patient (and/or those involved with the patient) in the same principles that the therapist has been using.

For example, a phobic client should appreciate that anxiety habituates and that he or she should remain in a situation where he or she feels suddenly anxious until that feeling subsides. It would be wise also to warn the client about recurrences of such events even after the successful conclusion of treatment since their unexpected occurrence would probably be especially difficult to manage.

SOME COMMON PROBLEMS

There are many problems or issues surrounding treatment which have no clear-cut answer and for which the scientific literature often as yet provides little firm guidance. But it is as well to be aware of them from the outset because they will eventually be encountered and must be faced constructively.

Lack of compliance with therapist's advice

Research in general medical consultations has shown that much of treatment advice is not implemented by patients (Ley, 1983). In behaviour therapy, Hoelscher *et al.* (1984) have shown that the home practice of relaxation training was conducted much less frequently than the clients had reported. Compliance must of course be an important influence on the success or failure of treatment.

Nevertheless, the therapist has no unchallengeable right to expect compliance. Indeed a client who accepts and follows all advice may have trouble in managing difficulties independently following the conclusion of treatment. Moreover, it would be unethical to expect a client to comply with all advice except on the basis of informed consent to treatment.

Lack of compliance may result from failure to remember treatment advice, from failure to understand the nature of treatment and why it is required or from dissatisfaction with some aspect of the consultation (Pendleton, 1983). The client's beliefs about the treatment and his or her own difficulties, the Health Belief Model (Becker, 1974; King, 1983), will also be important.

Remembering treatment advice

Advice is probably best remembered if it is given last in the consultation and if attention is drawn to essential aspects with phrases such as, 'It will be important to remember . . .'. Advice is more likely to be remembered if it is broken into headings – 'what you do', 'what your husband does', 'how you record what happens', and so on. Fortunately in most psychologists' consultations there should be time for the client or therapist to write down instructions. Prepared written record sheets often act as *aides-mémoire* for treatment.

Understanding treatment advice

All advice should be given in simple language in the client's own terms wherever possible. A word such as 'rewards', should be used instead of 'reinforcement'. The clinician should check that the client has understood by asking the client to rephrase important points about treatment and to explain why they are necessary. In our experience it has been quite disturbing, although instructive, to find that a client has not understood essential information which we assumed was straightforward.

Being satisfied with the consultation

Evidence summarised by Pendleton (1983) indicates that the client will be satisfied with the consultation if he or she believes that the clinician has discovered, understood, sympathises with, and is interested in, his or her concerns and expectations. For example, a client who is looking simply for an opportunity to unburden themselves, perhaps by complaining about the attitude of relatives and friends, may not cooperate readily in treatment designed to change the ways in which he or she reacts to the reactions of others. Hence the clinician may seek a trade-off in which the client sees that if he or she seeks to change his or her own behaviour the clinician gives them a sympathetic hearing for their more realistic troubles. This arrangement should be discussed and made clear with the client.

The Health Belief Model and attitude-behaviour relationships

The Health Belief Model (Becker, 1974; King, 1983) and models of attitude-behaviour relationships (Ajzen and Fishbein, 1980; Bentler and Speckart, 1979) assume a number of influences – clients' desire to see an improvement in their difficulties, their perception of the short-term and long-term outcome if the problem remains untreated, their assessment of the degree of handicap produced by the difficulties, and the costs of treatment balanced against its benefits as they see them. A client who sees that treatment would require many sessions' attendance at the clinic and expensive time off work for uncertain benefit may be unwilling to devote more time to carrying out treatment homework. Beliefs about how others would regard his or her difficulties can be important. It can be humiliating for some people to be seen to attend a psychiatric clinic and to believe that they run the risk of being described as 'mentally ill'.

The client's evaluation may be realistic or the clinician may have to work harder at demonstrating the effectiveness of treatment. The client may be afraid of raising false hopes or that his or her 'illness behaviour' perhaps may be encouraged and reinforced by friends and relatives.

Other uncooperative behaviour

Besides not complying with treatment advice, clients can show lack of co-operation in many other ways, such as in failing to keep, or being late for, appointments; self-destructive behaviour such as drug overdoses and seeking conflicting help from other clinicians such as their general practitioner.

It would be helpful for clinicians in training to recognise that these problems are encountered even by experienced practitioners. It may not be possible to solve them but a consideration of the influences described in the preceding section may be helpful.

Curing or controlling?

With many clinical problems a total disappearance of all difficulties is probably out of the question. For example, chronic schizophrenia may persist inter- mittently over many years and so the clinician may simply be concerned with management during its more acute phases (see Hemsley, Chapter 16) and with the rehabilitation when it has largely remitted (Lavender and Watts, Chapter 24). Even the client with panic attacks who experiences a complete cessation of their occurrence with treatment may remain uneasy about possible recurrence for years afterwards.

It is important therefore to decide upon realistic goals as early as possible. Cognitive therapies and other adaptive skills treatments have been recommended for long-term and recurrent disabilities and these are discussed throughout this book. The reader should note that this situation is different from treatment failure (Foa and Emmelkamp, 1983).

Priorities in targets

A cognitive-behavioural analysis usually pinpoints a whole series of targets which would be impractical and confusing to tackle all at once. There will be certain targets that must be approached first because they have a pervasive negative influence upon all behaviour: depression, insomnia and excessive drinking are all targets that might fall into this category. After that, the designation of priorities will depend in part upon agreement between the patient and therapist, who will also have some responsibility towards society and those in the patient's environment.

The problem of not knowing enough

Most therapists feel inadequate at some stage in the course of any treatment. That is when other people's advice is important and should be sought. It is not a sign of weakness or ignorance to consult specialists in a particular field or to ask the advice of those more experienced. Indeed, so many programmes are technically complex that consultation with colleagues should perhaps be considered the norm. In addition, the therapist should not focus too narrowly on just the psychological aspects of immediate concern, but be prepared to note other problems (with health, perhaps, or with schooling or housing) and ensure that they have been picked up by the relevant professional colleague, such as physician, social worker or educational psychologist, otherwise these problems will often interfere with treatment. Regular multidisciplinary case conferences and case discussions with other psychologists are thus important.

Cost effectiveness and resources

Every therapist is frustrated by a lack of time and resources. Cost effectiveness or cost benefit should be taken into account when designing the type of service provision. For example, it may be impractical for a clinical psychologist to provide a service to each individual on a chronic ward. Rather, the psychologist could take on groups of patients with related problems or spend his or her sessions encouraging and teaching an overall style of care, or establish with care staff a general ward programme. In this way, the maximum number of patients benefit from the minimum of therapist time. More time could be spent on problem-analysis and in the construction of the treatment programme. This may delay things initially but will avoid wasted effort later.

Discharge

Where appropriate, the therapist should hand over treatment to the patient by stressing self-management skills from early on, and by describing the process of fading out of therapist support and the time-limited nature of treatment. This approach limits the patient's feelings of being rejected at the time of discharge because he or she comes to view it in a positive light. Planning ahead for discharge also assuages the guilt often felt by therapists that stems from the uneasy feeling at discharge that one 'could do more' or 'didn't do enough'. Unfortunately, lingering over discharge wastes a great deal of time and blocks the treatment of waiting clients.

Relapse

The likelihood of relapse after behavioural treatment has not been widely investigated, few studies having reported follow-up investigations six months or more after discharge (Jansson et al., 1984). Munby and Johnston (1980), in an exceptional study, reported data gathered up to four years after behavioural treatment in agoraphobics. Several had experienced a temporary 'severe relapse'.

The possibility of relapse should be discussed with the client before discharge. Identification of high-risk situations and sources of stress in the client's daily living that might contribute to relapse should all be discussed.

Follow-up visits at, say, monthly or six-weekly intervals should be made to rehearse treatment strategies and to encourage independent coping behaviour.

CLINICAL SKILLS IN PSYCHOLOGICAL THERAPIES

The search for both the skills possessed by effective clinicians and the essential ingredients possessed by psychological therapies has been pursued for many years (see, for example, Goldstein et al. 1966; Garfield and Bergin, 1986). This venture has been given recent impetus by similar outcomes for cognitive therapy, interpersonal therapy and pharmacotherapy for depression in the NIMH trial in the USA (see, for example, Imber *et al.*, 1990). Although it has been concluded that changes for the better in negative thinking precede recovery and contribute to the effectiveness of therapy (DeRubeis *et al.*, 1990), the NIMH study showed that cognitions were influenced equally well by the cognitive and pharmaco-logical therapies (Imber *et al.*, 1990). These findings have suggested that aspects of interpersonal therapy could improve cognitive therapy (Safran, 1990).

In the application of cognitive-behaviour therapies there has been conflicting evidence about the effect on outcome of the quality of the relationship between therapist and client. Hoogduin *et al.* (1989), for example, found a significant effect of the nature of the therapeutic relationship in behaviour therapy of obsessive-compulsive problems. On the other hand, Marks (1991) argues that it should not be necessary for the therapist to accompany the client in treatment. This could be accompanied in part by the use of self-help manuals. They would provide much less expensive help than treatment requiring the continual atten-tion of a therapist and so should always be considered. Several chapters in this book make such recommendations (for a review, see Gould and Clum, 1993).

However, for treatment which does require continual attention from a therapist, there has not been much agreement in surveys seeking to determine essential properties of psychological therapy and therapists (e.g. Orlinsky and Howard, 1986; Beutler *et al.* 1986). Some matters suggested by such surveys, neverthe-less, are probably worth consideration: the therapist should adhere to a contract established with the client; 'empathic resonance' – client and therapist should perceive and acknowledge each others' emotions during consultations; and 'mutual affirmation' should be established – a warm supportive relationship between therapist and client. Not surprisingly, the 'quality of the therapeutic bond', a global concept, and 'therapeutic realisation' (therapeutic effectiveness?) are both said to be particularly important (Orlinsky and Howard, 1986). Unfortunately, it appears that the more comprehensive are such reviews of widely differing psychological therapies, the more imprecise become the defini-tions of these skills and processes.

There are widespread, tenacious beliefs about what constitutes desirable skills in clinicians. For example, Fordham *et al.* (1990) described the attributes which a sample of supervisors, associated with two training courses, believed that 'good trainees' should possess. These attributes clustered on two dimensions, inter-personal skills and organisational ability. 'Good trainees' on the former would be 'warm', have a 'good physical appearance' and be 'careful about hygiene'. On the second dimension, 'good trainees' would 'meet deadlines', 'formulate plans', etc. It is not clear if these attributes were associated with the effectiveness of trainees in therapy.

While these attributes are unexceptionable, it is disappointing to the present authors that variables such as inventiveness and intelligence do not appear to have been considered. However, it has been clear to course tutors in the UK that the attributes on which clinical psychology trainees are assessed vary considerably (P. de Silva, personal communication).

While requisite clinical skills remain a matter for debate, it is disappointing that the training of clinical skills appears to be not very effective (Alberts and Edelstein, 1990). Such evidence favours the argument that good clinicians are born not made and should be selected for training accordingly.

The present authors and the contributors to this book take a somewhat more optimistic line. The present book describes skills and knowledge which can be used to good effect in promoting the health of troubled and not so troubled clients.

CONCLUDING REMARKS

There are two final points to make. First, it is not possible in a single chapter to cover all the general issues that may confront clinicians. For example, how does a clinician cope with a strong dislike for a client or with intense inter-disciplinary rivalry? Indeed, some problems arise in treatment that are unique. One of us was treating a client only to discover halfway through that the client was a relative, a fact bound in some way to distort the therapeutic relationship. Issues such as these should be frankly discussed with colleagues, hopefully in the context of a supportive department. To ignore them would be of no benefit either to the client, the therapist or the service.

Second, what should be done in the event of the failure which sometimes occurs with all interventions (Foa and Emmelkamp, 1983)? It may be possible to refer the client to a colleague who can offer a more promising intervention. It may be possible to discharge the client without causing him or her great distress, or the clinician may offer to give the client some supportive counselling for a limited period. For this help there may also be other organisations – local self-help groups or local authority counselling services. The client may be advised of these or of emergency services. In any case the clinician should be aware that he or she has responsibilities to other clients and that less specialist supportive help may be available for the present client elsewhere. It must be remembered that the referring agent such as the client's own doctor will probably still have a responsibility for the client and so should be fully informed about the outcome of the referral.

It is hoped here that such experiences will encourage clinicians to discover, through controlled research, more effective ways of helping their clients (see Morley, Chapter 37).

REFERENCES

Ajzen, I. and Fishbein, M. (1980) *Understanding Attitudes and Predicting Social Behavior*, Engelwood Cliffs, NJ: Prentice-Hall.
Alberts, G. and Edelstein, B. (1990) 'Therapist training: a critical review of skill training studies', *Clinical Psychology Review* 10: 497–512.

Bandura, A. (1977) 'Self-efficacy: toward a unifying theory of behavioral change', *Psychological Review* 84: 191–215.

Becker, M. H. (1974) 'The Health Belief Model and personal health behaviour', *Health Education Monograph* 2: 238–335.

Bentler, P. M. and Speckart, G. (1979) 'Models of attitude-behaviour relations', *Psychological Review* 86: 452–64.

Beutler, L. E., Crago, M. and Arizmendi, T. G. (1986) 'Therapist variables in psychotherapy process and outcome', in S. Garfield and A. Bergin (eds) *A Handbook of Psychotherapy and Behavior Change, 3rd edn,* New York: Wiley.

Billingsley, F., White, O. R. and Munson, R. (1980) 'Procedural reliability: a rationale and example', *Behavioural Assessment* 2: 229–41.

Brewin, C. R. (1988) *Cognitive Foundations of Clinical Psychology,* London: Erlbaum.

de Silva, P. and Rachman, J. (1981) 'Is exposure a necessary condition for fear-reduction?' *Behavioural Research and Therapy* 19: 227–32.

DeRubeis, R. J., Evans, M. D., Hollon, S. D., Garvey, M. J., Grove, W. M. and Tuason, V. B. (1990) 'How does cognitive therapy work? Cognitive change and symptom change in cognitive therapy and pharmacotherapy for depression', *Journal of Consulting and Clinical Psychology* 58: 862–69.

Ellis, A. and Grieger, G. (1977) *Handbook of Rational Emotive Therapy,* New York: Springer.

Foa, E. B. and Goldstein, A. (1978) 'Continuous exposure and strict response prevention in the treatment of obsessive-compulsive neurosis', *Behavior Therapy* 17: 169–76.

Foa, E. B. and Emmelkamp, P. M. G. (eds) (1983) *Failures in Behavior Therapy,* New York: Wiley.

Fordham, A. S., May, B., Boyle, M., Bentall, R. P. and Slade, P. D. (1990) 'Good and bad clinicians: supervisors' judgements of trainees' competence', *British Journal of Clinical Psychology* 29: 113–14.

Garfield, S. and Bergin, A. (eds) (1986) *A Handbook of Psychotherapy and Behavior Change, 3rd edn,* New York: Wiley.

Gelder, M. (1981) 'Is exposure a necessary and sufficient condition for the treatment of agoraphobia?' in J. C. Boulougouris (ed.) *Learnng Theory Approaches to Psychiatry,* Chichester: Wiley.

Goldstein, A. P., Heller, L. B. and Sechrest, K. (1966) *Psychotherapy and the Psychology of Behavior Change,* New York: Wiley.

Gottman, J. (1979) *Marital Interaction: Experimental Investigations,* London: Academic Press.

Gould, R. A. and Clum, G. A. (1993) 'A meta analysis of self-help treament approaches', *Clinical Psychology Review* 13: 169–86.

Hoelscher, T. J., Lichstein, K. L. and Rosenthal, T. L. (1984) 'Objective vs. subjective assessment of relaxation compliance among anxious individuals', *Behaviour Research Therapy* 22: 184–94.

Holtzworth-Munroe, A. and Jacobson, N. (1991) 'Behavioural Marital Therapy', in A. Gurman and D. Kniskern (eds) *Handbook and Family Therapy Vol. 2,* New York: Brunner-Mazel.

Hoogduin, C. A. L., de Haan, E. and Schaap, C. (1989) 'The significance of the therapist–patient relationship in the treatment of obsessive-compulsive neurosis', *British Journal of Clinical Psychology* 28: 185–6.

Imber, S. D., Pilkonis, P. A., Sotsky, S. M., Elkin, I., Watkins, J. T., Collins, J. F., Shea, M. T. and Leber, W. R. (1990) 'Mode-specific effects among three treatments for depression', *Journal of Consulting and Clinical Psychology* 58: 352–9.

Jacobson, N. and Margolis, G. (1979) *Marital Therapy: Strategies based on Social Learning and Behaviour Exchange Principles,* New York: Brunner-Mazel.

Jansson, L., Jerremalm, A. and Ost, L. G. (1984) 'Maintenance procedures in the behavioural treatment of agoraphobia: a program and some data', *Behavioural Psychotherapy* 12: 109–16.

Kazdin, A. E. (1982) 'The token economy: a decade later', *Journal of Applied Behaviour Analysis* 15: 431–45.

King, J. (1983) 'Health beliefs in the consultation', in D. Pendleton and J. Hasler (eds) *Doctor–Patient Communication*, London: Academic Press.

Ley, P. (1983) 'Patients' understanding and recall in clinical communication failure', in D. Pendleton and J. Hasler (eds) *Doctor–Patient Communication*, London: Academic Press.

Marks, I. (1991) 'Self-administered behavioural treatment', *Behavioural Psychotherapy* 19: 42–6.

Munby, M. and Johnston, D. W. (1980) 'Agoraphobia: the long-term follow-up of behavioural treatment', *British Journal of Psychiatry* 137: 418–27.

Orlinsky, D. E. and Howard, K. I. (1986) 'Process and outcome in psychotherapy', in S. Garfield and A. Bergin (eds) *A Handbook of Psychotherapy and Behavior Change, 3rd edn*, New York: Wiley.

Pendleton, D. (1983) 'Doctor–patient communication: a review', in D. Pendleton and J. Hasler (eds) *Doctor–Patient Communication*, London: Academic Press.

Powell, G. E. (1984) 'Psychological assessment and treatment strategies in the rehabilitation of brain-damaged patients', in S. Rachman (ed.) *Contributions of Medical Psychology Vol. III*, Oxford: Pergamon.

Safran, J. D. (1990) 'Towards a refinement of cognitive therapy in light of interpersonal theory: II practice', *Clinical Psychology Review* 10: 107–12.

Schumann, H. (1987) 'The use of leaflets to prepare patients for psychological treatment', unpublished M. Sc. thesis, Institute of Psychiatry, University of London.

Spence, S. H. (1989) 'Cognitive-behaviour therapy in the management of chronic, occupational pain of the upper limbs', *Behaviour Research and Therapy* 27: 435–46.

Watts, F. N. and Bennett, D. H. (eds) (1983) *Theory and Practice of Psychiatric Rehabilitation*, Chichester: Wiley.

Wilson, B. A. (1987) *Rehabilitation of Memory*, New York: Guilford Press.

Chapter 3

Obsessions and compulsions
Investigation

P. de Silva

INTRODUCTION

Obsessions and compulsions come under the term 'obsessive-compulsive neurosis' in traditional psychiatric classifications. Obsessive-compulsive neurosis, or obsessive-compulsive disorder, is one of several anxiety disorders. Recent epidemiological studies show that the disorder is much more common than previously thought. A lifetime prevalence of up to 3 per cent in the general population has been reported (Karno *et al.*, 1988; Robins *et al.*, 1984). The phenomena of obsessive-compulsive neurosis are so striking that they are very well described and recognised (see de Silva, 1992; de Silva and Rachman, 1992; Emmelkamp, 1982; Rachman and Hodgson, 1980).

Before examination of the definitions of obsessions and compulsions as they occur in patients described as obsessive-compulsive neurotics, a point should be made on obsessional personality. Traits such as excessive cleanliness, meticulousness, perfectionism, a strong need for order, rigidity, and indecisiveness, which are loosely called 'obsessional', do of course occur in normal persons, and when these features appear as a strong cluster in someone, the terms 'obsessional personality' and 'anankastic personality' are used. Those with an obsessional personality do not necessarily become obsessive-compulsive neurotics, nor do obsessive-compulsive patients necessarily have a pre-morbid personality of this type, although there is some overlap between the two categories (Pollack, 1979; Rachman and Hodgson, 1980).

DEFINING FEATURES OF OBSESSIVE-COMPULSIVE DISORDER

The American Psychiatric Association's *Diagnostic and Statistical Manual of Mental Disorders, 3rd Edition, Revised* (1987) (*DSM III–R*) describes the obsessive-compulsive disorder as having the following characteristics:

1 The essential features are recurrent obsessions or compulsions. For a diagnosis, the person must have either obsessions or compulsions, or both.
2 Obsessions are recurrent, persistent thoughts, images or impulses that intrude into consciousness. They are not experienced as voluntarily produced. They

are seen as senseless or repugnant, and attempts are made to ignore or suppress them.

3 Compulsions are repetitive and purposeful forms of behaviour that are performed according to certain rules or in a stereotyped fashion, and are carried out with a sense of subjective compulsion and with a desire to resist. The behaviour is not an end in itself, but is aimed at producing or preventing some event or situation. However, the activity is not connected in a realistic way with what it is aimed to produce or prevent, or it is clearly excessive. The person generally recognises the senselessness of the behaviour and does not derive pleasure from carrying out the activity, although it provides a release of tension.

4 The obsessions or compulsions cause impairment of the person's functioning and/or cause distress.

5 The obsessions or compulsions are not due to any other disorder, such as schizophrenia, organic syndrome or major affective disorder.

The features noted in the *DSM III–R* are generally agreed on by most practitioners (e.g. Emmelkamp *et al.* 1992).

Obsessions

Obsessions are unwanted and intrusive thoughts, impulses or images, or a combination of them, which are generally resisted. They are also recognised to be of internal origin (Rachman and Hodgson, 1980). Some clinical examples may be given.

1 A young woman had the recurrent intrusive thought that her husband would die in a car crash. She also had vivid imagery accompanying this thought.

2 A man had the recurrent intrusive doubt that he may have knocked down someone while they were crossing the road.

3 A young married woman had the recurrent intrusive impulse to strangle children and animals. This would be followed by the thought/doubt that she may actually have done this.

4 A man had the recurrent intrusive impulse to shout obscenities in public, or on solemn occasions.

5 A young man had recurrent intrusive images of himself violently attacking, with an axe, his elderly parents. He also had the thought that he might actually commit this act. This experience included images of the victims, of blood flowing and of injuries caused.

The content of obsessions is usually associated with contamination, violence and aggression, harm, disease, orderliness, sex and religion, and with pervasive doubting, although obsessions which relate to unusual and seemingly trivial matters can also occur (Akhtar *et al.* 1975; Khanna and Channabasavanna, 1988; Rachman and Hodgson, 1980; Rasmussen and Tsuang, 1986). It is also worth pointing out that most normal persons too have such unwanted, intrusive obsessions, but they are less intense and less frequent, and neither disabling nor unduly distressing (Rachman and de Silva, 1978; Salkovskis and Harrison, 1984).

Compulsions

Compulsions are repetitive and seemingly purposeful behaviours, preceded or accompanied by a subjective sense of compulsion, and generally resisted by the person. They are performed according to certain rules or in a stereotyped fashion. Despite the resistance, these behaviours are actively carried out by the person.

Common conpulsions are ritualistic behaviours involving checking and washing/cleaning. Other compulsive behaviours include doing things in a certain stereotyped way, ordering inanimate things and doing things in a strictly rigid sequence. Sometimes a certain special number is involved, in that the behaviour has to be carried out that number of times. A few clinical examples may be given.

1   A young woman felt contaminated every time she touched door handles, money, and so on, and washed her hands thoroughly and repeatedly in an elaborate ritual.
2   A young man had to check that he had correctly locked the doors and windows, drawers, cupboards, and so on every time he left his room/house. He would do this seven times.
3   A man opened letters he had written and sealed to make sure that he had written the correct things. Thus he would rip open the envelope, re-read the letter, and put it into a new envelope, several times before eventually posting it.
4   A young man had the compulsion to touch with the left hand anything he had touched with the right hand, and vice versa.
5   A woman in her forties complained that every time she entered a room, she had to touch the four corners of it, starting from the left.

Overt and covert compulsions

The preceding examples are all of compulsive behaviours which are overt and thus observable by others. They involve motor actions. It is in fact generally assumed that compulsive behaviours are overt and motor, while obsessions are covert and cognitive. The traditional classifications and descriptions foster and encourage this way of defining obsessions and compulsions. It is clear, however, that this scheme is incorrect (de Silva and Rachman, 1992; Foa and Tillmanns, 1980; Kozak et al., 1988a). Compulsions can take the form of covert behaviours as well. Consider this example.

A middle-aged woman was very distressed by the intrusive, repetitive appearance in her consciousness of obscene words. They came as visual images. She would then compulsively carry out the covert ritual of silently saying these same words but now changed into acceptable ones (for example, 'well' for 'hell') four times.

Many obsessive-compulsive patients have compulsions that are cognitive and covert, like the previous example, rather than motor and overt. For this reason, it is fruitful to move away from the modality-based distinction between obsessions and compulsions towards a loosely functional approach, in which a compulsion is an activity carried out as the result of a compulsive urge, and serving the same psychological function whether it is overt or covert – namely, reduction of tension or discomfort in the person. This discomfort is usually, but not always, the result of a preceding obsession. Thus, a person who experiences the thought 'Did I stab a cat?' (obsession) and looks ten times at his hands for bloodstains (compulsion) to relieve his discomfort is directly comparable to the person who gets the thought 'God is evil' (obsession) and silently recites a prayer (compulsion) to relieve his discomfort.

It must be noted, however, that this proposed classification does not extend the concept of obsession to include anything other than cognitive events. Foa and her colleagues have suggested that obsessions should be defined to include 'thoughts, images and actions that elicit anxiety or discomfort' (Foa and Tillmanns, 1980: 417). Although this yields a symmetrical relationship between obsessions and compulsions, the inclusion of actions among obsessions is unwarranted; by definition, obsessions are cognitive events.

Relationship of obsessions and compulsions

It must not be assumed that every obsession leads to a compulsion, or that every compulsive behaviour is preceded by a clear and distinct obsession. In order to examine the relationship between the two sets of phenomena, it will be useful to consider the events which may be present in an episode of obsessive-compulsive experience and their relationships. Table 3.1 attempts to present such a sequence.

Table 3.1 Possible sequence of events in an obsessive-compulsive experience

(a) Trigger	(b) Obsession	(c) Discomfort	(d) Compulsive urge	(e) Compulsive behaviour	(f) Discomfort reduction
external/ internal/ none	thought/ doubt/ image/ impulse/ none	+	+ –	overt/ covert/ none	+ ?

+ = yes
– = no

Thus, an obsession may arise with or without a trigger which in turn can be external (e.g. sight of knife: doubt, 'Did I stab someone?') or internal (e.g. remembering a meeting with someone: thought, 'I am taller than he, am I not?'). The obsession can take the form of a thought, image or impulse, or a combination of these. The obsession usually leads to discomfort/anxiety/distress. This could lead to an urge to engage in a certain compulsive behaviour or ritual, and this behaviour could be either overt (e.g. washing), or covert (such as counting backwards in silence). Carrying out this compulsive behaviour would, normally, lead to a reduction of discomfort, though there can be exceptions (see Beech, 1971).

A compulsive behaviour can sometimes arise without a preceding obsession. Consider a man who accidentally touches a part of the wall of a public toilet and immediately rushes into a washing ritual. It can be argued, of course, that the touching of the wall in this case led to a fleeting obsession ('I am contaminated', 'I am dirty') which was directly responsible for the compulsive behaviour, but it is doubtful whether the postulation of such a step is of any value. To all intents and purposes, the trigger would, without a well formed and distinct obsession, lead to discomfort and then to an urge to carry out the ritualistic behaviour. This is particularly so with long-standing compulsive behaviours which have, over the years, acquired a habit-like quality.

Thus, obsessions and compulsions can take place in the absence of each other, although in practice they are commonly found to occur together. In clinical practice one often comes across patients described as having obsessions only ('obsessional thoughts', 'obsessional ideas', and so on) and the relatively high frequency of such descriptions tempts one to assume that obsessions without compulsions are quite frequent. However, many of the patients described in this way in fact have covert compulsive behaviours, the details of which one has to elicit by careful enquiry.

Other major features

Avoidance

An important feature of obsessive-compulsive disorder that does not appear in the scheme proposed (Table 3.1) is avoidance, and this needs to be discussed here. Many obsessive-compulsive patients have avoidance, almost like phobic avoidance in some cases (e.g. Rachman and Hodgson, 1980: 94). The avoidance behaviour concerns stimuli, and sometimes behaviours, that can potentially trigger the obsession or compulsion. Those with contamination/washing/cleaning type problems, for example, strive to avoid what they believe to be dirty or contaminating. Those with checking rituals may avoid situations which lead to checking.

1 A young woman developed fear of contamination by faeces and other 'dirty' substances, and began to engage in excessive cleaning rituals. She also began

to avoid potentially contaminating things and places, such as public toilets, drains and drain covers. Since drain covers could not easily be avoided on the roads, she became unable even to go for a walk down the road.

2 A married woman had the obsessional thought that she had cancer. After several years of checking for cancer symptoms, she then began to avoid any situation where, she feared, she might discover evidence of cancer. Thus she could not make her bed in the morning, or look at her used underwear, for fear of discovering bloodstains which to her would be a sign of the illness. She completely stopped washing herself properly as she feared she would discover lumps and suchlike on her body.

Such extensive avoidance is not unusual in obsessionals, and can form an important part of the clinical picture.

Fears of disaster

These patients not infrequently report a fear of disastrous consequences if they neglect their compulsive behaviour: the reason given for carrying it out is often that the behaviour wards off some danger, usually to the patient him- or herself or to someone he or she loves. In some cases the feared disaster and the action intended to ward it off are closely related, such as infection by germs and handwashing, but this is not always the case.

A married woman compulsively washed her hands every time she heard or read about accidents. She felt that by doing this she was protecting her husband, who was a travelling salesman, from meeting with a fatal accident.

Resistance

Resistance to the obsession or compulsion has been considered traditionally as a central feature in obsession-compulsive neurosis. Lewis (1936), for example, considered it to be its cardinal feature. More recent empirical work, however, suggests that this is not entirely correct (e.g. Stern and Cobb, 1978). While obsessions and compulsions are mostly resisted by the person, in some patients there is no strong resistance. It is as if after resisting the unwanted phenomenon in the early stages of the disorder they have almost given up resisting (Rachman and Hodgson, 1980; Rasmussen and Tsuang, 1986).

Reassurance seeking

Many obsessive-compulsive patients resort to reassurance seeking, usually from family members. Often, obsessional thoughts, such as 'Will I go insane?' or 'Do I need to check the taps again?' lead to the patients asking for reassurance. When reassurance is elicited, the patient feels relief from discomfort, although it is often short-lived and the request for reassurance is repeated.

Disruption

When obsessive-compulsive patients engage in their compulsion, they feel a need to carry it out precisely as they feel it ought to be done. If the behaviour is disrupted by, say, an external event or another unwanted thought, the ritual is invalidated and may need to be re-started. For long and complicated compulsive rituals, this can be extremely time-consuming (de Silva and Rachman, 1992).

Ruminations

A rumination is a somewhat complex phenomenon sometimes found in obsessive-compulsive disorder. The patient attempts to think through a question or topic, such as 'Is there a life after death?' or 'Am I genetically abnormal?' and this thinking is inconclusive, prolonged and frustrating. The patient does this compulsively, and the compulsion is often triggered by the appearance of the relevant obsessional thought.

COMMON CLINICAL PRESENTATIONS

While the above analysis is useful, indeed essential, for a proper understanding of the disorder and its modification, it is also necessary to look at the common clinical presentation of these patients. Typically, an individual will come for help suffering from a disability arising from one major aspect of the disorder, which is the predominant problem for that individual. Thus, on initial clinical present-ation, patients fall into a few conveniently defined categories. It is important to bear in mind, however, that this is a superficial classification based only on the predominant feature of the presenting problem. A full assessment of the individual case is needed before a proper description of the patient, let alone therapy, can begin.

Main categories

Such a convenient classification based on predominant problems is given below:

1 Those with washing/cleaning type compulsions
2 Those with checking type compulsions
3 Those with other kinds of overt compulsions
4 Those whose obsessive-compulsive problems do not include overt compulsions
5 Those with primary obsessional slowness

Primary slowness

A word of explanation is necessary about the patients described as 'primarily obsessionally slow'. Rachman (1974; Rachman and Hodgson, 1980) has des-cribed a small number of obsessional patients whose main problem was excessive slowness. Most obsessionals would be slow anyway but that slowness is secondary to their compulsive behaviour or repeated obsessions which can be time-consuming. These patients, on the other hand, are *primarily* slow: their slowness is not a secondary consequence of other difficulties. Simple tasks of daily living take up a great deal of time in their lives. They do things correctly and meticulously. They are very concerned about the manner in which they do things, and the main area where this affects them is self-care. Rachman (1974) and Rachman and Hodgson (1980) believe they are profitably treated as a distinctive subgroup of obsessive-compulsive patients, and a number of case reports supporting their claims are available (e.g. Bilsbury and Morley, 1979).

Exclusions

A note on certain other behavioural problems which are given the descriptive term 'compulsive' but which do not come under the disorder in question is warranted. These are certain addictive behaviours (such as compulsive drinking, compulsive gambling) and habit disorders (such as compulsive nail-biting, compulsive hair-pulling). Despite the loosely used term 'compulsive', they are different problems from obsessions and compulsions as defined above, and will not be dealt with here.

ASSESSMENT

Introduction

The clinical assessment of obsessive-compulsive disorders is in principle no different from the assessment of other disorders. The aim is to obtain as full a picture of the problem as possible, using a variety of data-collection techniques. The nature of the difficulty, its extent and severity, the degree of disability it has caused and the factors that may be relevant to its possible modification have all to be examined. Where possible, quantifiable data should be obtained. The assessment approach should be comprehensive, and may profitably include a behavioural analysis as described, among others, by Kanfer and Saslow (1969).

Clinical interview

The clinical interview is the main data source in the assessment. Obsessive-compulsive patients are usually cooperative and will give a good account of the difficulties as they see them. One problem is that – unlike many other groups of patients – they may talk too much and give too many details, so that the main thrust of the interview can get affected and the whole process delayed. Some tend to take a very long time giving answers because of their own doubts about what to say; others check with the interviewer repeatedly about previous answers, to make sure they did not give wrong details. It is therefore important for the assessor to maintain control of the interview and follow a loose but clear structure. Additional details may be discouraged when clearly irrelevant, at least in the initial interview. Detailed discussions of interviews with obsessive-compulsive patients are found in, among others, Turner and Beidel (1988) and Steketee and Foa (1985).

Areas of enquiry during interview

The interview should aim to get information about what the main problems are, when and where they occur, how they affect the patient's life and work, how the patient's family are affected, and of course the history. The sequence of events suggested in Table 3.1 would be a useful basis to make specific enquiries about the phenomena themselves with regard to each problem area. For compulsive behaviour, the time taken for the rituals and the number of times they are repeated must be enquired about. The degree of disability has to be assessed in different areas of life, such as work, leisure, family and sex. The role of anxiety/discomfort is an important aspect that will have bearing on therapy. What brings on anxiety/discomfort? What compulsive activity, if there is any, brings it down? Does the patient believe that unless the compulsion is carried out some unpleasant consequences will befall? Foa's (1979) findings suggest the need to enquire about the strength of the patient's obsessional or obsession-related beliefs. Are there other ways in which the patient can reduce anxiety, such as asking for reassurance from a family member or getting someone else to do some of the checking? The nature and extent of avoidance needs to be gone into fully, as does the presence or absence of identifiable triggers. An assessment of mood, using a simple depression scale (see Chapter 5) should be undertaken. The effects of mood on the obsession/compulsion, and vice versa, should also be examined (see pp. 64–5).

The stimuli/situations that cause problems or are avoided have to be explored in detail. A list of such situations should be constructed, graded in terms of how much discomfort they arouse as estimated by the patient (see pp. 63–4). This is broadly similar to a fear hierarchy used with phobic patients in desensitisation (Wolpe, 1958; 1991) – that is, it will include diverse situations which have a basic discomfort-arousing quality (for example, contamination) in common, rather than a series of finely graded events different in the degree of closeness to the main problem stimulus in space or time.

It will often be found in clinical assessment interviews that the patient has not looked at the problem closely, or in terms of what would be valuable clinical data, and may not thus volunteer details unless asked. So careful questioning and prompting will be needed. Sometimes the patient may have to be asked keep a daily record (see pp. 60–1) in order to be able to provide some of the required details.

Differentiation from other disorders

Patients who are referred to clinical psychologists for assessment of their disorder are generally assumed to have been screened previously. It is not, however, entirely unusual to have as referrals patients whose obsession-like and compulsive-like features may in fact reflect a different illness. It is worth remembering, therefore, some distinguishing features of apparently similar phenomena as they occur in other conditions. Following Rachman and Hodgson (1980), these may be summarised as follows:

1 In schizophrenia, intrusive ideas and so on are attributed to external sources, are not necessarily ego-dystonic, are not regarded as senseless, and are not generally resisted.
2 In organic impairments, repetitive ideas or acts lack intellectual content, lack intentionality, and have a mechanical and/or primitive quality.

The stereotyped behaviours in severe mental retardation and the repetitive responses in Gilles de la Tourette Syndrome should hardly ever present a problem of differential diagnosis. A good discussion of the problems of differential diagnosis is available in Rasmussen and Eisen (1992).

Key informants

An interview with a key person in the patient's life, usually parent or spouse, will help in getting a valuable complementary account of the problems in question. The time taken by rituals, the number of times a ritual is performed per day, the specific situations and stimuli that provoke problem behaviours, the extent of avoidance and reassurance-seeking, and the degree to which the immediate family has been drawn into, and affected by, the patient's obsessive-compulsive problems can usually be elucidated by such an informant. Equally important, perhaps, is the role of the family in maintaining and fostering the patient's problems. A somewhat extreme, but instructive, clinical example will illustrate this point.

A 17-year-old female patient was referred with severe contamination fears and related washing and cleaning rituals. Her main focus as a contamination source was the boyfriend of her older sister. She became upset if she came in contact with anything he had touched, and had to engage in extensive washing. The parents did not approve of the boyfriend for various reasons but would not express their disapproval to the daughter as they felt – and said – the girls were old enough to make their own decisions, and were free to bring home anyone they wished. The patient's inability to tolerate her sister's boyfriend coming to stay for weekends was, however, a great relief to the parents, who used it as a reason to keep the young man away.

Daily records/diaries

A fairly simple assessment technique is to ask the patient to keep a daily diary of relevant cognitions and behaviours, with details of time, circumstances, and so on. This is particularly valuable as a source of baseline data. Many obsessive-compulsive patients keep meticulous and detailed diaries when asked to. To avoid being flooded with hundreds of pages, the investigator may supply a structured format, concentrating on a few relevant headings. An example of a daily record sheet used for this purpose is given in Table 3.2. A simple counter to keep frequency counts can be a useful addition.

Questionnaires and inventories and rating scales

Several questionnaires/inventories are available for the assessment of these patients. These are not intended to be substitutes for clinical assessment. They supplement interview assessment and also provide quantified scores.

Leyton Obsessional Inventory The Leyton Obsessional Inventory (Cooper, 1970) is one of the oldest and best known. It is standardised on normal subjects and obsessive-compulsive patients, and differentiates well between the two groups (Cooper and Kelleher, 1973; Murray *et al.*, 1979). It has sixty-nine items,

Table 3.2 An example of a daily record sheet

Date   Target[a]

Time	Frequency[b]	Highest discomfort [c]	Highest compulsive urge[d]	Details and comments[e]
Before 7 a.m.				
7 – 10 a.m.				
10 a.m. – 1 p.m.				
1 – 4 p.m.				
4 – 7 p.m.				
7 – 10 p.m.				
After 10 p.m.				

a   The particular obsession or compulsion monitored.
b   How many times it happened in each time period.
c,d Rated on a 0–100 scale. Give the highest felt during the time period.
e   Details of what happened: when, where, what was the trigger, how long taken, number of repetitions, etc. of the *worst* episode.

forty-six of them relating to obsessive-compulsive symptoms, and the others to obsessional personality traits. The questions are printed on separate cards which the patient puts into either the 'yes' or the 'no' slot of an answer box. Questioning regarding some of the cards is required in order to derive the resistance and interference scores. It yields a total symptom score, a trait score and resistance and interference scores. The resistance score measures the severity rather than the extent of the symptoms and the interference score measures the disability caused by the symptoms. These scores, however, are not independent of the symptom score.

The Leyton Obsessional Inventory is not very convenient for routine clinical use as it is time-consuming. Also, the assignment of some of the items to trait or symptom scores seems somewhat arbitrary.

Pencil-and-paper and shorter versions of this instrument are also available (Allen and Tune, 1975; Snowdon, 1980).

Compulsive Activity Checklist   This instrument is used both for self-rating by the patient and for rating by the therapist (Marks *et al.* 1977). This consists of thirty-eight specific activities (for example, having a bath or shower, touching door handles). Each activity is rated on a four-point scale of severity, from 0 (no problem) to 3 (unable to complete or attempt the activity). A total score is obtained by adding the individual score items. What is more important, however, is the identification of the activities that cause real difficulty for the patient. A shorter version has recently been reported (Steketee and Freund, 1993).

Maudsley Obsessional-Compulsive Inventory   The Maudsley Obsessional-Compulsive Inventory is easy and quick to administer, being made up of 30 items with 'true'/'false' answers (Hodgson and Rachman, 1977; Rachman and Hodgson, 1980). In addition to a global obsessionality score, it gives four sub-scores: checking, washing/cleaning, slowness/repetitiveness and doubting/conscientiousness. Unfortunately, the inventory has only two items covering thoughts (obsessions). Nor does it assess degree of disability and severity as opposed to extent of the problem. However, it does differentiate between obsessional-compulsive patients and other neurotics. On the whole, the Maudsley Obsessional-Compulsive Inventory is a useful and easy-to-use instrument, and can be easily included in the routine assessment procedure. It is particularly useful for monitoring change with therapy. It is reproduced as an appendix to this chapter.

Padua Inventory   This is an instrument developed recently in Italy (Sanavio, 1988). It consists of sixty items, using five-point ratings, and is designed to evaluate the range of clinical obsessions and compulsions.

Yale–Brown Obsessive-Compulsive Scale   This is an observer-rated scale which consists of ten items, each rated on a 0–4 scale. Five of the items focus on obsessions, and the other five on compulsions. The total maximum score is 40. This instrument is rapidly gaining popularity among clinicians in the USA (Goodman *et al.* 1989).

Psychophysiological assessment

Psychophysiological measures – heart-rate, pulse-rate and skin-conductance – have been used in a few studies of obsessive-compulsive phenomena (e.g. Boulougouris et al., 1977; Grayson et al., 1980; Kozak et al., 1988b), but there is insufficient evidence to recommend the use of these measures in routine clinical assessment. It has also been argued that caution is needed in the use and interpretation of these measures (Salkovskis, 1990).

Behavioural tests

Behavioural performance tests are perhaps the most useful and most direct assessment method available. Simple behavioural tests can be carried out in a clinical interview setting – for example, asking patients to touch a 'contaminating' object, and observing the reaction and degree of avoidance, and getting a self-rated measure of discomfort and of urge to wash (see below) This should be done for selected target problems – usually the ones that cause greatest difficulty to the patient. More structured and better planned behavioural tests will attempt to sample the relevant problems more fully (e.g. Steketee and Foa, 1985). Such a planned assessment will ideally include systematic manipulation of several variables, including presence or absence of trigger, different triggers, permission to engage in compulsive behaviour, presence or absence of family, and so on. It must be remembered, however, that the degree of obsessive-compulsive problems is likely to be temporarily lessened in a new environment. Thus, in the first few days of hospitalisation, even a usually severely affected patient may not demonstrate the phenomena they have reported.

Behavioural tests carried out in the home environment by the patient can also be used and provide valuable information.

Naturalistic observation

Observation of the patient in the natural environment can throw valuable light on the nature of the problems but this is usually difficult in practice. However, if there are problems in specific situations (such as excessive checking at work, avoidance of any contact with people in public transport), direct observation by the assessor in the target situations should be seriously considered. More usually, the patient and the key informants are relied on to supply details of what happens in such situations.

Self-ratings

In behavioural tests, as indeed in interview assessment and diary-keeping, the patient should be asked to rate his or her subjective reactions (Rachman and Hodgson, 1980; Salkovskis, 1990). A 0–100 scale, similar to a 'fear thermometer', is a relatively easy scale to use for these purposes. Some clinicians use 0–8 scales (e.g. Marks *et al.* 1977). The patient will rate his or her 'discomfort' (a more neutral term than 'anxiety'), and – where relevant – the strength of the urge to engage in compulsive behaviour. Despite problems of reliability and validity, these simple self-rating measures are easy for patients to learn to use, and add a useful dimension to purely verbal self-reports. The discomfort ratings are particularly useful in preparing hierarchies of difficult situations (see p. 76).

Special problems

Absence of overt phenomena

In cases where the predominant problem presents as cognitive phenomena – that is, with no external manifestations – special care has to be taken in assessing the problem. While the basic techniques and tools described above are all generally relevant, particular enquiry must be made about covert rituals. The performance tasks for the patient in such cases would include producing the obsession upon instruction, and then recording the reactions in terms of discomfort, urge to ritualise, and so on. A verbatim report of the obsession and covert compulsions should be recorded. The actual form the obsession takes – that is, whether it is a thought, image or an impulse – is also important to record (de Silva, 1986). A number of additional dimensions that may be useful in the assessment of these phenomena may be found in Salkovskis (1990).

Primary slowness

Where the problem is primary slowness, particular attention has to be paid to the time taken for various day-to-day activities, mainly the patient's self-care. The order of behaviour sequences also needs to be elicited and observed. Behavioural tests will involve the patient carrying out specific self-care or other relevant activities.

Depression

It was noted in the section on interview assessment that the patient's mood needs to be assessed. This is because there is a relationship between depression and obsessive-compulsive disorder. It is well known that when the patient is significantly depressed, obsessions and compulsions can get worse (Rachman and Hodgson, 1980). In addition, obsessions are common in depressive illness as a secondary feature (de Silva and Rachman, 1992; Zohar and Insel, 1987). A further relevant consideration is that obsessive-compulsive patients are less likely to respond to behavioural treatment when they are significantly depressed (Foa, 1979). Given this interrelationship between obsessive-compulsive disorder and depression, careful enquiry into mood is an essential aspect in the investigation of patients presenting with obsessive-compulsive symptoms.

Cognitive factors

Some authors have argued that cognitive factors are of crucial importance in obsessive-compulsive disorder. Reed (1985), for example, takes the view that obsessive-compulsive disorder is essentially a manifestation of particular cognitive style (see also Reed, 1991). Salkovskis (1985) has offered an analysis of obsessive-compulsive problems within the framework of Beck's concept of negative automatic thoughts (e.g. Beck, 1976). There is, however, no convincing evidence at present for these or other cognitive models of obsessive-compulsive problems. A fuller discussion is available in de Silva (1992).

Biological and neuropsychological aspects

Several investigators have looked for a biological basis for obsessive-compulsive disorder, and many claims have been made. Some have suggested, citing evidence from brain-imaging techniques, that abnormalities in the frontal lobe and the basal ganglia may be involved (e.g. Malloy, 1987; Wise and Rapoport, 1989). The current evidence on the role of these in the genesis of obsessive-compulsive disorder is, at best, unclear. There is little relevance of these considerations for the clinical assessment of this disorder at the present time. In recent years, strong claims have been made that a neurotransmitter, serotonin, may be involved in the disorder. Certain drugs that act on serotonin have been shown to have some, limited, effect in patients with this disorder (e.g. Cobb, 1992). However, the current evidence for a direct causal role for serotonin, or any other substance, in obsessive-compulsive disorder is not persuasive. More light will no doubt be thrown on these issues by further research.

CONCLUDING COMMENTS

Needless to say, the assessment package a psychologist uses for any individual patient will depend on the nature of the presenting problems and circumstances. The preceding sections have attempted to indicate what main types of measure are available in the assessment of obsessions and compulsions. A comprehensive assessment will include self-report, key informant interviews and behavioural assessments, and data from the patient's natural environment for a sufficiently lengthy period of time. More emphasis will be placed on types of data particularly relevant to the specific problems (for example, duration of obsession, where the obsessional cognition is the main problem; number of times ritual is performed, where the major problem is overt compulsive behaviour) and on data that have a direct bearing on the therapeutic strategy to be used. Assessment will also aim at eliciting data that will allow for measuring change.

APPENDIX: THE MAUDSLEY OBSESSIONAL-COMPULSIVE INVENTORY*

(a) The inventory

Instructions: Please answer each question by putting a circle around the 'True' or 'False' following the question. There are no right or wrong answers, and no trick questions. Work quickly and do not think too long about the exact meaning of the question.

1	I avoid using public telephones because of possible contamination	TRUE FALSE
2	I frequently get nasty thoughts and have difficulty in getting rid of them	TRUE FALSE
3	I am more concerned than most people about honesty	TRUE FALSE
4	I am often late because I can't seem to get through everything on time	TRUE FALSE
5	I don't worry unduly about contamination if I touch an animal	TRUE FALSE
6	I frequently have to check things (e.g. gas or water taps, doors, etc.) several times	TRUE FALSE
7	I have a very strict conscience	TRUE FALSE
8	I find that almost every day I am upset by unpleasant thoughts that come into my mind against my will	TRUE FALSE
9	I do not unduly worry if I accidentally bump into somebody	TRUE FALSE
10	I usually have serious doubts about the simple everyday things I do	TRUE FALSE
11	Neither of my parents was very strict during my childhood	TRUE FALSE
12	I tend to get behind in my work because I repeat things over and over again	TRUE FALSE
13	I use only an average amount of soap	TRUE FALSE
14	Some numbers are extremely unlucky	TRUE FALSE
15	I do not check letters over and over again before posting them	TRUE FALSE
16	I do not take a long time to dress in the morning	TRUE FALSE
17	I am not excessively concerned about cleanliness	TRUE FALSE
18	One of my major problems is that I pay too much attention to detail	TRUE FALSE
19	I can use well-kept toilets without any hesitation	TRUE FALSE
20	My major problem is repeated checking	TRUE FALSE
21	I am not unduly concerned about germs and diseases	TRUE FALSE
22	I do not tend to check things more than once	TRUE FALSE
23	I do not stick to a very strict routine when doing ordinary things	TRUE FALSE
24	My hands do not feel dirty after touching money	TRUE FALSE
25	I do not usually count when doing a routine task	TRUE FALSE
26	I take rather a long time to complete my washing in the morning	TRUE FALSE
27	I do not use a great deal of antiseptics	TRUE FALSE
28	I spend a lot of time every day checking things over and over again	TRUE FALSE
29	Hanging and folding my clothes at night does not take up a lot of time	TRUE FALSE
30	Even when I do something very carefully I often feel that it is not quite right	TRUE FALSE

(b) Scoring key

Score 1 when a response matches that of this key, and 0 when it does not. The maximum scores are given at the foot of the key. Only two items (2 and 5) are loaded on ruminations, so they are not scored separately.

	Total obsessional score	Checking	Washing	Slowness/ repetition	Doubting/ Conscientious
1	True	–	True	–	–
2	True	True	–	False	–
3	True	–	–	–	True
4	True	–	True	True	–
5	False	–	False	–	–
6	True	True	–	–	–
7	True	–	–	–	True
8	True	True	–	False	–
9	False	–	False	–	–
10	True	–	–	–	True
11	False	–	–	–	False
12	True	–	–	–	True
13	False	–	False	–	–
14	True	True	–	–	–
15	False	False	–	–	–
16	False	–	–	False	–
17	False	–	False	–	–
18	True	–	–	–	True
19	False	–	False	–	–
20	True	True	–	–	–
21	False	–	False	–	–
22	False	False	–	–	–
23	False	–	–	False	–
24	False	–	False	–	–
25	False	–	–	False	–
26	True	True	True	–	–
27	False	–	False	–	–
28	True	True	–	–	–
29	False	–	–	False	–
30	True	–	–	–	True
	30	9	11	7	7

* Reproduced with permission.

REFERENCES

Akhtar, S., Wig, N. H., Varma, V. K., Pershad, D. and Verma, S. K. (1975) 'A phenomenological analysis of symptoms in obsessive-compulsive neurosis', *British Journal of Psychiatry* 127: 342–48.

Allen, J. J. and Tune, G. S. (1975) 'The Lynfield Obsessional-Compulsive Questionnaire', *Scottish Medical Journal* 20: 21–4.

American Psychiatric Association (1987) *Diagnostic and Statistical Manual of Mental Disorders 3rd Edn Revised*, Washington DC: American Psychiatric Association.

Beck, A. T. (1976) *Cognitive Therapy and the Emotional Disorders*, New York: International Universities Press.

Beech, H. R. (1971) 'Ritualistic activity in obsessional patients', *Journal of Psychosomatic Research* 15: 417–22.

Bilsbury, C. and Morley, S. (1979) 'Obsessional slowness: a meticulous replication', *Behaviour Research and Therapy* 17: 405–8.

Boulougouris, J. C., Rabavilas, A. D. and Stefanis, C. (1977) 'Psychophysiological responses in obsessive-compulsive patients', *Behaviour Research and Therapy* 15: 221–30.

Cobb, J. J. (1992) 'Serotonin re-uptake inhibitors in obsessive-compulsive disorder: What is their therapeutic role?' in K. Hawton and P. Cowen (eds) *Practical Problems in Psychiatry*, Oxford: Oxford University Press.

Cooper, J. (1970) 'The Leyton Obsessional Inventory', *Psychological Medicine* 1: 48–64.

Cooper, J. and Kelleher, M. (1973) 'The Leyton Obsessional Inventory: a principal component analysis on normal subjects', *Psychological Medicine* 3: 204–8.

de Silva, P. (1986) 'Obsessional-compulsive imagery', *Behaviour Research and Therapy* 24: 333–50.

de Silva, P. (1988) 'Obsessive-compulsive disorder', in E. Miller and P. J. Cooper (eds) *Adult Abnormal Psychology*, Edinburgh: Churchill Livingstone.

de Silva, P. (1992) 'Obsessive-compulsive disorder', in L. A. Champion and M. Power (eds) *Adult Psychological Problems: An Introduction*, London: Falmer Press.

de Silva, P. and Rachman, S. (1992) *Obsessive-Compulsive Disorder: The Facts*, Oxford: Oxford University Press.

Emmelkamp, P. M. G. (1982) *Phobic and Obsessive-Compulsive Disorders: Theory, Research and Practice*, New York: Plenum.

Emmelkamp, P. M. G., Bouman, T. K. and Scholing, A. (1992) *Anxiety Disorders: A Practitioner's Guide*, Chichester: Wiley.

Foa, E. B. (1979) 'Failure in treating obsessive-compulsives', *Behaviour Research and Therapy* 17: 169–76.

Foa, E. B. and Tillmanns, A. (1980) 'The treatment of obsessive-compulsive neurosis', in A. Goldstein and E. B. Foa (eds) *Handbook of Behavioral Interventions: A Clinical Guide*, New York: Wiley.

Goodman, W. K., Price, L. H., Rasmussen, S. A., Mazure, C., Fleischmann, R. L., Hill, C. L., Heninger, G. R. and Charney, D. S. (1989) 'Yale–Brown Obsessive-Compulsive Scale (Y-BOCS), Part I: Development, use and reliability', *Archives of General Psychiatry* 46: 1006–11.

Grayson, J. B., Nutter, G. and Mavissakalian, M. (1980) 'Psychophysiological assessment of imagery in obsessive-compulsives: A pilot study', *Behaviour Research and Therapy* 18: 580–93.

Hodgson, R. J. and Rachman, S. (1977) 'Obsessional-compulsive complaints', *Behaviour Research and Therapy* 15: 389–95.

Kanfer, R. H. and Saslow, G. (1969) 'Behavioral diagnosis', in C. M. Franks (ed.) *Behavior Therapy – Appraisal and Status*, New York: McGraw-Hill.

Karno, M., Golding, J. M., Sorenson, S. B. and Burnham, A. (1988) 'The epidemiology of obsessive-compulsive disorder in five US communities', *Archives of General Psychiatry* 45: 1094–99.

Khanna, S. and Channabasavanna, S. M. (1988) 'Phenomenology of obsessions in obsessive-compulsive disorder', *Psychopathology* 21: 12–18.

Kozak, M. J., Foa, E. B. and McCarthy, P. R. (1988a) 'Obsessive-compulsive disorder', in C. G. Last and M. Hersen (eds) *Handbook of Anxiety Disorders*, New York: Pergamon.

Kozak, M. J., Foa, E. B. and Steketee, G. S. (1988b) 'Process and outcome of exposure treatment with obsessive-compulsives: Psychophysiological indicators of emotional processing', *Behavior Therapy* 19: 157–69.

Lewis, A. J. (1936) 'Problems of obsessional illness', *Proceedings of the Royal Society of Medicine* 29: 325–36.

Malloy, P. (1987) 'Frontal lobe dysfunction in obsessive-compulsive disorder', in E. Perecman (ed.) *The Frontal Lobe Revisited*, New York: IRBN Press.

Marks, I. M., Hallam, R. S., Connolly, J. and Philpott, R. (1977) *Nursing in Behavioural Psychotherapy*, London: Royal College of Nursing.

Murray, R. M., Cooper, J. E. and Smith, A. (1979) 'The Leyton Obsessional Inventory: an analysis of the responses of 73 obsessional patients', *Psychological Medicine* 9: 305–11.

Pollack, J. M. (1979) 'Obsessive-compulsive personality: a review', *Psychological Bulletin* 86: 225–41.

Rachman, S. (1974) 'Primary obsessional slowness', *Behaviour Research and Therapy* 11: 463–71.

Rachman, S. and de Silva, P. (1978) 'Abnormal and normal obsessions', *Behaviour Research and Therapy* 16: 233–48.

Rachman, S. and Hodgson, R. J. (1980) *Obsessions and Compulsions*, Englewood Cliffs, NJ: Prentice-Hall.

Rasmussen, S. A. and Eisen, J. L. (1992) 'The epidemiology and differential diagnosis of obsessive-compulsive disorder', *Journal of Clinical Psychiatry* 53(4) Supplement: 4–10.

Rasmussen, S. A. and Tsuang, M. T. (1986) 'Clinical characteristics and family history in DSM-III obsessive-compulsive disorders', *American Journal of Psychiatry* 143: 317–22.

Reed, G. (1985) *Obsessional Experience and Compulsive Behaviour*, London: Academic Press.

Reed, G. (1991) 'The cognitive characteristics of obsessional disorder', in P. A. Magaro (ed.) *Cognitive Bases of Mental Disorders*, Newbury Park: Sage.

Robins, L. N., Helzer, J. E., Weissman, M. M., Orvaschel, H., Greenberg, E., Burke, J. D. Jr and Regier, D. A. (1984) 'Lifetime prevalence of specific psychiatric disorders at three sites', *Archives of General Psychiatry* 41: 949–58.

Salkovskis, P. M. (1985) 'Obsessional-compulsive problems: A cognitive-behavioural analysis', *Behaviour Research and Therapy* 23: 571–83.

Salkovskis, P. M. (1990) 'Obsessions, compulsions and intrusive cognitions', in D. F. Peck and C. M. Shapiro (eds) *Measuring Human Problems: A Practical Guide*, Chichester: Wiley.

Salkovskis, P. M. and Harrison, J. (1984) 'Abnormal and normal obsessions: A replication', *Behaviour Research and Therapy* 22: 549–52.

Sanavio, E. (1988) 'Obsessions and compulsions: The Padua Inventory', *Behaviour Research and Therapy* 26: 169–77.

Snowdon, J. A. (1980) 'A comparison of written and postbox forms of the Leyton Obsessional Inventory', *Psychological Medicine* 10: 165–70.

Steketee, G. S. and Foa, E. B. (1985) 'Obsessive-compulsive disorder', in D. H. Barlow (ed.) *Handbook of Psychological Disorders*, New York: Guilford Press.

Steketee, G. S. and Freund, B. (1993) 'Cognitive Activity Checklist (CAC): Further psychometric analysis and revision', *Behavioural Psychotherapy* 21: 13–25.

Stern, R. S. and Cobb, J. (1978) 'Phenomenology of obsessive-compulsive neurosis', *British Journal of Psychiatry* 132: 233–9.

Turner, S. M. and Beidel, D. C. (1988) *Treating Obsessive-Compulsive Disorder*, New York: Pergamon.

Wise, S. P. and Rapoport, J. L. (1989) 'Obsessive-compulsive disorder: Is it a basal ganglia dysfunction?', in J. L. Rapoport (ed.) *Obsessive-Compulsive Disorder in Children and Adolescents*, Washington, DC: American Psychiatric Press.

Wolpe, J. R. (1958) *Psychotherapy by Reciprocal Inhibition*, Stanford: Stanford University Press.

Wolpe, J. R. (1991) *The Practice of Behavior Therapy, 4th edn*, New York: Pergamon Press.

Zohar, J. and Insel, T. R. (1987) 'Obsessive-compulsive disorder: Psychobiological approaches to diagnosis, treatment and pathophysiology', *Biological Psychiatry* 22: 667–87.

Chapter 4

Obsessions and compulsions
Treatment

P. de Silva

INTRODUCTION

The treatment of obsessions and compulsions has witnessed considerable progress in recent decades. The almost resigned acceptance seen very commonly even in the 1960s (for example, Slater and Roth, 1969: 135) of the poor outcome of therapy in these disorders has given way to an attitude of optimism (e.g. Emmelkamp *et al.*, 1992; Greist, 1992; Rachman and Hodgson, 1980; Turner and Beidel, 1988). Psychologists have been developing and using increasingly effective and refined behavioural intervention techniques for these disorders, and it is common practice today for obsessive-compulsive patients to be referred to clinical psychologists for therapy of their difficulties.

Before we look in some detail at these behavioural techniques, reference must be made to other forms of therapy that have a longer history and are still used by some clinicians.

PSYCHOTHERAPY

In psychodynamic theory, obsessions and compulsions are symptoms of underlying psychic conflicts and other repressed material in the way that all neurotic symptoms are. The individual finds a relatively safe way of giving expression to repressed thoughts, feelings and so on, through his or her obsessions and/or compulsions. The individual's experiences during the so-called anal stage of development are considered to be particularly important in causing these symptoms in later life (see, for example, Fenichel, 1946). Psychotherapy would aim at exploring the patient's unconscious phenomena in order to unravel the hidden conflicts and anxieties. The results of such therapy, which is time-consuming, have not been established to be satisfactory for any neurotic disorder (Eysenck, 1952). The problems in evaluating the outcome of psychotherapy are many, and these have been discussed fully in the literature (Rachman and Wilson, 1981). One of the problems is whether a treatment produces better results than the improvement rate that spontaneously occurs. This makes it particularly difficult to evaluate therapies that are carried out over a long period of time. The results of psychotherapy for obsessive-compulsive problems are not successful or impressive (Cawley, 1974). To quote one recent reviewer: 'Traditional psycho-dynamic psychotherapy is not an effective treatment for obsessions or rituals in patients meeting the criteria for obsessive-compulsive disorder . . . . There are no reports in the modern psychiatric literature of patients who stopped ritualising when treated with these methods alone' (Jenike, 1990: 295).

PSYCHOSURGERY

Another form of treatment that has been popular for these disorders is psycho-surgery. It is worth noting that what goes on as psychosurgery is not one uniform procedure, but several different ones, including standard leucotomy, modified leucotomy and stereotactic limbic surgery.

It has been pointed out (Rachman, 1980; Rachman and Hodgson, 1980) that no logical explanation has been given as to why brain surgery should be expected to help these patients. As for empirical data, reviews of psychosurgical treatment for obsessive-compulsive patients indicate that the results are at best unclear (Rachman, 1980; O'Callaghan and Carroll, 1982). There is clearly no evidence to show that this drastic and invasive form of therapy is a more effective treatment for obsessionals than less intrusive psychological methods. The claim that this treatment has a place in the management of chronic intractable cases has been made by some practitioners (e.g. Chiocca and Martuza, 1990; Cobb and Kelly, 1990). Even as a last resort treatment, psychosurgery must be viewed with much caution.

PHARMACOLOGICAL TREATMENT

Many psychiatrists believe that pharmacological treatment is of considerable value in obsessive-compulsive disorder. Although anxiolytic drugs and major tranquillisers are sometimes prescribed, there is no real benefit from them. On the other hand, anti-depressant drugs are often prescribed, and varying degrees of success have been reported (Cobb, 1992; Goodman et al., 1992). It is clear that when concurrent depression is present, these drugs have a role to play in lifting the patient's mood. (See discussion of depression in the preceding chapter.) More recently, specific anti-obsessive-compulsive effects have been claimed for some anti-depressants. These are preparations which act to inhibit serotonin re-uptake in the brain (e.g. Insel, 1990). An examination of the rapidly growing literature addressing this issue shows that some obsessive-compulsive patients do indeed benefit from such medication. However, once the drug is stopped, symptoms tend to return (e.g. Pato et al. 1988). They also have unpleasant side effects. Many psychiatrists have considered the use of such anti-depressants along with behaviour therapy as an effective way of treating these patients (e.g. Greist, 1992). Used on their own, they are not as effective as behavioural treatment. It is worth noting that there is much ongoing research in this area, and the subject needs to be kept under review.

BEHAVIOURAL TREATMENT

The treatment of choice with obsessive-compulsive patients is behaviour therapy. The early work of Wolpe (1958) and of Meyer (1966) have led to the development of a group of techniques which have been used with considerable success and shown to be more effective than the treatments used until their advent (Foa and Tillmanns, 1980; Foa et al., 1985; Meyer et al., 1974; Minichiello, 1990; Rachman and Hodgson, 1980; Turner and Beidel, 1988).

In clinical practice, the specific treatment strategy to be used for a given patient will be determined by the nature of the main or predominant problem. As Chapter 3 shows, the events comprising an obsessive-compulsive experience are many and they may occur in different combinations. The decision as to what specific treatment strategy is to be used depends largely on which of these events predominates, and how they interfere with the individual's functioning.

Therapy for overt compulsions

The example of washers/cleaners

Those whose main problems are overt compulsions, like washing and/or cleaning rituals, are best treated with a therapy package of which the ingredients are exposure, modelling, and response prevention (Foa and Tillmanns, 1980; Foa et al., 1985; Meyer et al., 1974; Rachman and Hodgson, 1980; Turner and Beidel, 1988).

Elements of therapy

Exposure refers to exposing the patient to stimuli or situations that provoke the compulsive urge. Thus, someone whose rituals are based on the belief that he will be contaminated by coming into contact with dustbins and kitchen floors will be asked to touch these objects repeatedly and quite thoroughly. This may seem to be an exaggerated act, but it is useful in that it provokes the compulsion, usually via a strong feeling of discomfort.

Modelling refers to the therapist demonstrating to the patient the behaviour that he instructs the latter to engage in – touching the dustbin, for instance. He does this in a calm and controlled way, with no sign of anxiety; he also models coping with this exposure without rushing out to wash and clean. It should be noted that passive modelling, where the patient simply observes, is not an effective element of therapy for these patients. What is needed is participant modelling, where the patient copies the therapist. It must be noted that modelling, while it clearly facilitates therapy, is not always considered essential.

Response prevention requires the patient to refrain from engaging in his usual compulsive behaviour. After touching the dustbin, for example, the patient may wish immediately to decontaminate himself by a great deal of washing, but this is strictly prevented – perhaps for several hours or even days where this is feasible.

Of these three, exposure and response prevention are the crucial elements of therapy. Modelling has clear uses as an additional strategy, and certainly helps in persuading many patients to engage in behaviour they would hesitate to undertake otherwise.

Rationale

The rationale for this standard treatment package comes from both animal studies and clinical/experimental investigations. The blocking of avoidance responses has been shown to lead to the reduction of these responses in animal studies (e.g. Baum, 1969; 1970). Similarly, Maier and Klee (1945) and Maier (1949) have shown how manually guiding rats towards a previously avoided situation was successful in eliminating established stereotyped responses. Meyer's use of this form of therapy was based on the assumption that prolonged prevention of ritual would lead to changes in the patient's expectancies and thus in the strength of the urge to ritualise (Meyer, 1966). A series of studies carried out at the Maudsley Hospital has shown that:

1 Typically, an obsessive-compulsive patient with rituals experiences discomfort and a strong urge to ritualise when provoked by exposure to the trigger stimulus or situation.
2 When the patient engages in the compulsive behaviour, say, hand-washing, the discomfort goes down.
3 When, however, the discomfort and the urge to engage in the compulsive behaviour are provoked but the patient is prevented from carrying out the response, the urge and the discomfort still dissipate, but much more slowly.

This spontaneous decay of the compulsive urges and associated discomfort may be regarded as the main cornerstone of response prevention therapy (Rachman *et al.*, 1976). With repeated sessions, there is a cumulative effect leading to progressively less discomfort and urge to engage in compulsive behaviour, and – more markedly – progressively quicker dissipation of these (Likierman and Rachman, 1980).

Implementation of therapy

In order to carry out this treatment package, the therapist has to get a clear idea as to what stimuli, or cues, trigger the compulsions. A comprehensive assessment will elicit this information (see Chapter 3). A hierarchy of these stimuli/situations will need to be prepared (see Table 4.1). Therapy begins with a clear explanation of the rationale of therapy and a statement of the requirements to be fulfilled by the patient. The difficulty the patient may experience in complying should not be denied, but he or she should be supportively persuaded to go through with the therapy. The treatment is never imposed on an unwilling patient.

Explaining the rationale   How should the rationale of therapy be explained? It is useful to stress that the patient's problems are a learned behaviour pattern. The relationship between discomfort arising from the stimuli in question and the compulsion should be explained, using examples from the patient's own account, such as:

> 'As you have noticed yourself, when you touch money you feel you have become contaminated. So you feel quite anxious and – naturally – you feel a strong need to wash your hands, which you then do. This clearly helps you at the time, but it also strengthens the link between touching money and washing, doesn't it? Washing makes you feel relieved and so you want to wash every time you touch money.'

How the therapy aims to break this relationship should then be explained.

> 'The treatment programme is intended to break this relationship, and for this we would want you to touch money and other worrying things but *not* wash, perhaps for several hours. You will, of course, feel quite dirty and quite anxious, but after some time you will begin to feel better. It is important that we do it this way, for within a few days you will be able to break the link between money and washing. We'll help you with this as much as we can. I shall touch the money with you, and I shall stay without washing my hands, just as you will.'

Graded or rapid exposure?   There is no need, as there is in systematic desensitisation, to work gradually from the least to the most anxiety-arousing situation in a series of graded steps, although some experts recommend this (e.g. Foa and Tillmanns, 1980). It is expedient to concentrate on situations/items which are high on the list, and go for lower items only as part of generalisation training.

An example of a hierarchy of situations, treated with concentration on the top items first, is given in Table 4.1. The patient was a young man who had extensive washing rituals arising from a feeling of being contaminated by dogs.

In this case the patient was exposed to the first four situations in the initial part of therapy, and the gains were generalised to the items lower in the hierarchy without much additional effort.

On the other hand, it may be necessary to begin working at a somewhat lower level in the hierarchy if the patient is unable to cooperate with a programme which commences with a very high anxiety situation. In practice, the best strategy is to start at the highest level the patient is willing to try.

Table 4.1 A hierarchy of stimuli triggering the compulsion to wash in one patient

No. Items	Rated discomfort 0–100
1 Touching a dog with both hands	100
2 Touching a bowl from which a dog had eaten	90
3 Touching a piece of cloth which had come in contact with a dog	80
4 Walking barefoot on the ground where dogs had been previously	75
5 Wearing a shirt which he had been wearing at the time of passing near a dog	65
6 Holding hand of someone who had been feeding a dog	50
7 Touching the clothes of an unknown person in hospital	50
8 Walking past dustbins in the hospital premises	40
9 Walking on the road during rush hours	30

Source: de Silva, 1978

Issues in response prevention

The most important aspect of this package, in terms of practical issues, is the response prevention. This may require direct and close supervision of the patient for two to three hours – even twenty-four hours in some programmes (e.g. Sturgis and Meyer, 1981). On the other hand, a well-motivated patient with a clear commitment to therapy can be expected to cooperate fully so that such supervisory measures may not always be necessary (Emmelkamp, 1982). It is important to discuss with the patient the difficulties that this phase of therapy brings. For example, the patient may carry out an unnoticeable abbreviated ritual to bring down discomfort, or the patient may happily survive even a relatively long response prevention period with the internal resolve that he or she will, at the end of it, carry out the necessary ritual. These expedients are not unusual and the therapist needs to discuss them, and how they can be controlled, with the patient (de Silva and Rachman, 1992).

It is necessary to make clear that while in some programmes the response prevention is specific and time-limited, for example the patient is exposed to a contaminating object and then not allowed to clean or wash for a limited period of two hours or so, in others it is general and relatively unlimited, for example, the patient is prevented from engaging in any of his target behaviours for the whole duration of the intensive treatment period. Foa and Tillmanns (1980), for example, describe a programme where washing of any sort is banned, except for a quick supervised shower followed by recontamination, in the initial phase of therapy (see also Foa and Goldstein, 1978). The latter seems to be the more desirable in general, but would require a great deal of motivation from the patient and/or facilities for full supervision. In practice, the important factor is to prevent the target response for a period long enough to bring down the urge to engage in the behaviour and the associated discomfort (Rachman *et al.* 1976; Sturgis and Meyer, 1981). Hence it is important to monitor the strength of the urge carefully.

Issues in exposure

The exposure itself can lead to practical difficulties. The patient may touch only a 'safe corner' of the contaminating stimulus, or touch it with only the back of his or her hand. If the patient is required to carry a contaminating item, he or she may carry it wrapped in several handkerchiefs, which makes the item, to the patient, not so bad. Efforts must be made to ensure that there is full and clear exposure; the use of exaggerated exposure, such as thoroughly touching inside and outside a dustbin, rubbing the hands hard on the floor several times, rubbing the now contaminated hands on one's face, hair or clothes, usually guarantees effective exposure. The use of modelling is invaluable here. The point is that the exposure exercise should lead to a substantial degree of discomfort and a subtantially high urge to engage in the compulsion. Clearly it has to be more than nominal.

Like response prevention, the practice of exposure too can be diverse. It can be a time-limited exposure to a stimulus (for example, getting a patient to touch an animal which he considers contaminating); or it can be continuous (getting the patient to carry a small packet of dog hair in his pocket all the time). It is possible to expose the patient to several stimuli at the same time, together or in close succession (for example, getting the patient to touch a dog, handle the feeding bowl, thoroughly rub the dog collar on his clothes, use a public telephone and handle money given by outsiders). In an intensive programme for a patient with a disabling range of difficult stimuli, such a multiple-exposure programme may be desirable.

Desensitisation   Is there a role for desensitisation (that is, graded exposure with or without relaxation)? The patient who avoids certain stimuli for fear that they will generate discomfort/anxiety and compulsions can in theory be treated with a desensitisation paradigm, in the same way as a phobic patient is treated. In fact some obsessional patients, especially those with washing compulsions, do have a strong phobic component in their problems and this may seem particularly appropriate for them. However, desensitisation alone in obsessional-compulsives is, in general, not found to be very successful. The results of available reports are mixed (e.g. Furst and Cooper, 1970). The addition of response prevention gives clearly superior results.

Imaginal exposure   Some therapists use imaginal exposure as an additional ingredient in an exposure/response prevention package (e.g. Foa and Tillmanns,

1980; Steketee *et al.*, 1982). This may be done for situations to which, for practical reasons, it is difficult to arrange *in vivo* exposure, and also as an initial step in a therapy package. Work at the Temple University (e.g. Foa *et al.* 1980; Steketee *et al.*, 1982) suggests that the addition of imaginal exposure involving the disasters that the patient believes will occur if he or she does not ward them off with his or her compulsive behaviours, may lead to better long-term results than a package that does not include this step.

Therapy for other overt compulsions

We have concentrated so far on the therapy of patients who have washing compulsions. Patients whose main problems consist of other overt compulsions, such as those with checking compulsions and those with other rituals (for example, those who compulsively straighten anything that is not straight, or compulsively touch corners of a room whenever entering it, or carry out a sequence of responses in a given order before having a meal) can also be treated on the basis described above. The exposure might include, for instance, sitting at or working at a desk where the items on it are disordered, the patient, preferably, having disturbed the order; the patient will not then be allowed to put them in the right order or straighten them. A patient might be required to have supervised meals with none of the unnecessary rituals, any fixed order of responses being deliberately disarranged.

For checkers, engaging in the checking-generating activity (for example, closing doors, switching off gas heaters, closing drawers), without being allowed to check or repeat, will be the main thrust of therapy. Steps should be taken to expose checkers to most, if not all, of the risk situations. Since checking urges tend to be associated with the patient's feeling of responsibility, it may be necessary to set up situations where the patient is made to feel responsible for certain actions and where the responsibility is not taken over by the care staff or others. Checkers also seem particularly to benefit from added imaginal exposure to the disasters which they think their checking rituals prevent (Foa *et al.*, 1980; Steketee *et al.*, 1982).

Avoidance-reduction

Avoidance-reduction should be built into the therapy programme as a general rule. Even after successful exposure therapy to items high on a hierarchy, patients may still avoid many situations, partly out of habit. Rather than expecting automatic generalisation, it is useful to help the patient with these situations; often self-administered homework tasks will suffice, but this should not be taken for granted. Ideally, as many relevant target situations should be incorporated into the treatment programme as possible.

In cases where the main problem is compulsive avoidance, the main therapeutic strategy will be extensive exposure to the avoided stimuli or situations.

A young married woman avoided the number four, in all its forms, in her obsessional belief that if she did not, her husband would be harmed. She would not read or write on the fourth (or the fourteenth, twenty-fourth, and so on) page of a book, would not say or look at the number four, would not do anything four times. This extended to all areas of her life and restricted her functioning dramatically. Therapy involved exposing her to the number four in numerous ways, many of them continuous. She was made to do many activities four times, she had the number four painted all over the wall in her hospital room, she carried pieces of paper with it written on them in her pockets and handbag, and so on. No escape was permitted. She improved considerably very quickly.

Some practical considerations

Intensity of therapy

How intensive should behavioural therapy for these patients be? Some of the more successful programmes have included very intensive therapy. Foa and Tillmanns (1980), for example, describe an impressive programme in which almost daily therapy sessions are conducted for about two weeks, in the initial stages. It is clear from both the literture and clinical experience that once-a-week or once-a-fortnight out-patient sessions are an unsatisfactory arrangement for these patients. (See, however, Emmelkamp, 1982; Kirk, 1983.) The intensive therapy may in fact require hospitalisation. If intensive therapy is to be undertaken on an out-patient basis, arrangements should be made for frequent sessions, and also for the help and support of a key person in the patient's life, such as spouse, parent or friend.

Therapist's attitude

Equally importantly, a consistent and firm attitude needs to be shown by the therapist and others involved. It is not unusual for the patient to want to dilute the programme or circumvent the requirements of it. An understanding and sympathetic, yet firm, stand has to be taken by the therapy team. Making *ad hoc* concessions to an obsessive-compulsive patient once the programme is agreed on and under way is one of the commonest causes of failure of therapy. Sometimes a therapist and/or family will make concessions as an easy compromise, or indeed as the only way in which the patient will continue with any therapy, only to find that this leads to the patient making no progress, or making such limited and/or slow progress that the patient and family lose both motivation and their faith in therapy.

A 17-year-old female student had contamination obsessions about her sister's new boyfriend. She would avoid anything that she felt he had touched or come in contact with, and engage in excessive washing and cleaning to cancel out any feared contamination. Although she agreed to cooperate with a treatment programme, she constantly protested to the hospital staff about the harshness of the regime and demanded to be allowed concessions. One concession thus made by the staff, largely because they felt she would not continue to co- operate otherwise, was to let her use 'wet wipe' tissues to clean her hands, as washing had been prohibited. This won her continued cooperation all right, but diluted the programme so dramatically that her progress became stagnant.

Family involvement

The involvement of family or key person will normally be required even in in-patient therapy, as far as possible, to help in the adjustment of the patient after discharge. Patients who have been severely disabled by their problems and have evolved a limited and distorted lifestyle need help to establish or re-establish normal functioning. It is not unusual for severely disabled obsessive-compulsive patients to have had almost no time for social or leisure activities, and the improvement after therapy will leave them with a good deal of unfilled time. New activities, even a new lifestyle, may have to be developed. This requires the cooperation and help of those in the home environment.

Need for a consistent approach

In any therapy programme, whether in hospital or on an out-patient basis, there needs to be consistency in the approach to the patient and the patient's problems from all concerned. In hospital, for example, all staff who come into contact with the patient need to be familiar with the patient's programme and what is and is not allowed. The same applies to family members. For instance, a common feature with some obsessive-compulsive patients is their asking for reassurance (for example, 'Do you think that I closed the window properly?' 'Are you sure it's all right if I didn't wash my hands?'). In so far as reassurance-giving counters the aim of the therapy programme, by reducing anxiety/discomfort by external means and thus not allowing it to dissipate, it should be withheld from the patient by all in his environment. A good response to such requests for reassurance would be to say something like: 'We agreed not to talk about that, didn't we?'

Help for the family

For the family, the problems can be even more serious and complex. Not infrequently, the obsessive-compulsive patient gradually succeeds in establishing great control over the lives of all members of the household. Cleaning, eating, closing doors, dressing, and so on have to be done according to the wishes of the patient; the patient's avoidance of certain behaviours and situations is tolerated and accepted; no one dares to challenge him or her. This happens usually as an adaptive response after early resistance and clashes have led only to quarrels and scenes, and also as an act of kindness. The way in which the life pattern of an entire household can be allowed to be controlled by an obsessive-compulsive patient is indeed amazing.

In therapy, therefore, and in post-therapeutic adjustment, the family faces an enormous task in readjusting to a more normal life. The breaking-up of established patterns, however absurd they are, may prove as difficult for the family as they are for the patient. Joint discussions with the family and patient, and where necessary rehearsal sessions with the therapist involved, will be an additional step that will prove profitable.

Therapy for covert obsessional phenomena

The therapy for covert obsessional phenomena needs to be discussed as a separate problem. It is unfortunately the case that the success of therapy with these is not as impressive as with overt compulsions discussed above. There are, however, some indications as to how they might be dealt with (de Silva and Rachman, 1992; Rachman, 1978; Salkovskis and Westbrook, 1989).

Main strategies

The main therapeutic strategies used for covert obsessional phenomena have been thought-stopping and related thought-control procedures, and habituation/satiation procedures.

Thought-stopping

Thought-stopping is a simple technique in which the patient is trained to bring the unwanted cognition to an end by a simple command (e.g. Kirk, 1983; Stern, 1970; Wolpe, 1958; 1991). In the initial stage, the therapist gets the patient to sit or lie down, relaxed, and instructs him or her to get the thought in question. The patient is asked to indicate the appearance of the thought by a sign – for example, raising the index finger. When the patient gets the thought, the therapist shouts 'Stop!' quite loudly; this can be accompanied by another auditory stimulus, such as banging a ruler on the table. The procedure is repeated several times. In the next stage, the patient him- or herself delivers the command to stop; and, in the final stage, which typically will take place three or four sessions into therapy, the self-command is made only sub-vocally. Some therapists recommend the addition of aversive stimulus for the patient to use with the self-command to stop; an elastic band, pulled and released against the wrist, is commonly used clinically (e.g. Bass, 1973; Mahoney, 1971).

Variants of thought-stopping include thought-switching procedures, whereby the patient is trained to dismiss the unwanted thought and substitute another in its place, and thought-control, where dismissing and re-obtaining the thought in question is encouraged as a means of developing voluntary control over an otherwise intrusive thought (Daniels, 1976; Sturgis and Meyer, 1981).

The results of thought-stopping as reported in the literature are mixed (e.g. Stern, 1978, Tryon, 1979). Clearly, some patients benefit from this and others do not. The reports by Kirk (1983) and Turner *et al.* (1983) of its usefulness are encouraging. Further research is needed before firm conclusions can be drawn.

Habituation training

The satiation/habituation procedure is almost the opposite of thought-stopping in that the patient is asked to get the thought, keep it without losing it, and dwell on it (Rachman, 1976; Rachman and Hodgson, 1980). Prolonged exposure to the thought is carried out in this way – for up to several minutes per trial (Likierman and Rachman, 1982); longer exposures, of up to one hour or more, have also been used (e.g. Emmelkamp, 1982; Emmelkamp and Kwee, 1977; Gurnani and Vaughan, 1981). This may be done under relaxation (e.g. Rachman, 1976). The patient may need help to get and keep the thought from slipping away, para-doxical as it may seem. Verbal prompts, physical exposure to the trigger stimulus if there is any such trigger, playing back a recorded version of the thought in the patient's own voice, or getting the patient to write out the thought repeatedly for up to one hour per session are all aids (Farkas and Beck, 1981; Salkovskis and Westbrook, 1989).

A note must be added on the distinction between satiation, where exposure to the thought is continued until it arouses no reaction, and habituation, where exposure is carried out repeatedly. In habituation training, not only the thought itself but the imagined disastrous consequences, if there are any, may be made the content of exposure (e.g. Crook and Charney, 1982).

The results of satiation/habituation training and similar exposure techniques are on the whole promising (e.g. Parkinson and Rachman, 1980, Emmelkamp and Kwee, 1977; Rachman, 1976; Rachman and Hodgson, 1980; Salkovskis and Westbrook, 1989) but not yet conclusive (e.g. Likierman and Rachman, 1982). As in the case of thought-stopping, more and better controlled studies are needed before definite conclusions can be drawn.

Exposure to triggers

Exposure to the trigger stimuli may be used both as an aid to the patient to get the thought to mind as mentioned above, or as the main therapeutic strategy in a desensitisation paradigm, when appropriate. This latter strategy is to be con-sidered in cases where there are clear and significant triggers, which the patient has been avoiding.

Matching phenomena to therapeutic strategy

It is important to recognise that some cases described as ones with 'pure obsessions', that is, without compulsions, may in fact have compulsive behaviour (see Chapter 3). When this is present, it is necessary to prevent its being carried out after exposure to the thought. When the compulsive behaviour is entirely covert, which is more likely, again prevention of its occurrence is necessary (e.g. de Silva and Rachman, 1992; Emmelkamp and Kwee, 1977; Rachman, 1976; Rachman and Hodgson, 1980). This is much harder to achieve than prevention of overt rituals, for the therapist has no direct control over, or even direct access to, the phenomenon in question. The individual's own ability to control covert behaviour is also limited, when compared to overt behaviours. The same applies to cases where there is simply an overt compulsion. In addition to issuing clear instructions to the patient not to engage in the covert compulsive behaviour once the urge is provoked, it may be necessary to give further help by, for example, giving the patient distracting, demanding mental tasks. Thought-stopping can have a particularly useful role here, as a means of stopping the unwanted internal act. Thus, in a typical situation of this sort, the patient will be exposed to the trigger and/or obsession, so that the urge to engage in the covert ritual is provoked, but the patient will be clearly instructed, and helped, not to carry it out.

> A middle-aged woman had the covert compulsion of mentally correcting any asymmetrical figure that she saw by imagining it in symmetrical form. She did this both immediately and every time she remembered it. This compulsive covert act was done repetitively until she had felt she got it right. Therapy consisted of exposing her to asymmetrical patterns, which she was instructed to look at carefully, and then blocking her compulsive thoughts/images with self-administered thought-stopping. Distraction by mental arithmetic was also used.

It can be argued that, by carefully matching the therapeutic strategy to the type of covert obsessional problem the patient has, one could expect better results than those so far clinically available (see Rachman, 1982). The clinical and clinical/experimental literature describes mostly therapy for obsessional thoughts and so on with either thought-stopping or habituation training. If an effort is made to make sure that the thought-stopping, which is a blocking or response-prevention procedure, is used for cases where there is a clear covert ritual, and habituation training is used for the discomfort-generating obsession, more satisfactory results may be obtained (Foa and Steketee, 1979; Rachman, 1982). This is, of course, not to claim that such differentiation and matching are always easy to achieve, only to point out the theoretical advantages of such an approach. It also runs parallel to the generally successful therapy of patients with overt compulsions.

The problem of images

In some cases, the obsession takes the form of mental imagery (see Table 3.1,

p. 54). When the main presenting problem of the patient is an intrusive image, special techniques can be used. With some practice, one can learn to manipulate and play about with one's mental images. In experiments, normal subjects have been shown to be able to rotate, expand, shrink and otherwise manipulate their visual images (e.g. Kosslyn, 1980). This facility can be improved with practice. When an obsessive-compulsive patient complains of distressing visual images, he may be instructed to deal with the image by modifying it in various ways (de Silva, 1986). A patient whose unwanted, intrusive image was of dog faeces, was trained to shrink this image. With practice, he acquired the ability to make the image smaller and smaller, until it became just an innocuous dot. Another patient who complained of distressing images of a violent scene was trained to focus on a marginal detail of the image and 'zoom in' on this part. In this way it was possible to make this part of the image, which did not arouse discomfort, larger and larger, so that the discomfort-arousing parts of the image 'overflowed' from the image space. Such techniques as these are effective probably because of the sense of control the patient gets in successfully using them (de Silva and Rachman, 1992).

Practical aspects of therapy

In terms of the practical aspects of therapy, covert obsessional phenomena can be usually dealt with on an out-patient basis, except when the problem is all-pervasive in the patient's life and/or has led to extensive avoidance. Of particular importance is the reassurance-seeking in these patients. When the thought is in the nature of a doubt, the patient may constantly ask for reassurance from family members or therapists, for temporary relief. In a properly planned treatment programme, steps will be taken to withhold reassurance-giving, either by family or by other key persons.

Therapy for obsessional slowness

Finally, the small subgroup of patients described as primarily obessionally slow (see p. 57) should be treated with a package involving pacing, prompting and shaping, with modelling, feedback, target-setting and verbal reward as additional elements (Rachman, 1974; Rachman and Hodgson, 1980; Bilsbury and Morley, 1979). These patients require a good deal of therapeutic input, usually hospital-based, and also additional home-based therapy. Further, many regular booster sessions are needed in order to maintain their gains. Their improvement can be slow, with plateau periods where no further improvement takes place for a time.

Group approaches

While group therapy is commonly used in many psychiatric disorders, it has been of limited popularity among clinicians treating obsessive-compulsive patients.

There is some recent evidence that a group approach may be beneficial, both for obsessive-compulsive patients and their families, as an adjunct to individual treatment (Tynes *et al.*, 1992; Van Noppen *et al.*, 1991). Group therapy as a substitute for individual therapy is not justified.

Self-therapy and education

It has recently been argued that much of the behavioural treatment of obsessive-compulsive disorder can be undertaken by the patient him- or herself, with little involvement of the therapist (e.g. Hoogduin and Hoogduin, 1984). In many therapy programmes, clinic-based treatment is augmented by self-administered therapy sessions, sometimes involving a family member. However, the problems need to be carefully assessed by an experienced therapist, and the treatment well supervised. Except in very mild cases, unsupervised self-treatment is not advisable.

An important aspect of an overall treatment programme, however, should be the education of the patient and family members, and other key persons, about the disorder, its nature and treatment. Prescribing suitable reading is an obvious way of doing this. Publications intended for this purpose include de Silva and Rachman (1992), Foa and Wilson (1991), Greist (1989) and Marks (1978).

Some other behavioural therapies

For the sake of completeness, other forms of behavioural therapy that have been used with obsessive-compulsive patients will be mentioned briefly.

Aversion

Aversion therapy using mild shock has been used for obsessions (e.g. Kenny *et al.*, 1973). The elastic-band addition to thought-stopping already mentioned (see p. 81) may also be considered a form of aversion therapy.

Aversion relief

Aversion relief therapy, in which the cessation of an aversive stimulus such as shock is used as the key variable in order to effect the relationship of the target behaviour and the emotional responses that are normally associated with it, has been reported (e.g. Solyom, 1969).

Self-monitoring

Self-monitoring, an important aspect of assessment, can often have therapeutic effects (Nay, 1979), and it has been shown to be of some use with these problems (Paquin, 1979).

Contingency management

Finally, the use of comprehensive contingency management must be considered. Like any other behavioural disorder, the problems in question are amenable to functional analysis (see Chapter 1), and on this basis a therapy programme can be designed and carried out within an operant framework. The thrust of the programme will be to identify and remove the factors that maintain or encourage the unwanted behaviours, and to develop and strengthen alternative behaviours by reinforcement (e.g. Queiroz *et al.*, 1981; Vingoe, 1980; Vogel *et al.*, 1982).

Often in clinical practice this kind of approach is used as part of the main therapy programme – for example, ensuring that the patient's obsession-based demands are not positively responded to by family members. On the other hand, an approach based entirely on the management of contingencies between the problem behaviours and external factors is not likely to be adequate.

Factors contributing to poor outcome

It has been shown that severe depression can lead to failure of behavioural treatment in obsessive-compulsive patients (Foa *et al.*, 1983). This points to the need to treat their depression as part of a comprehensive therapy package. The finding that initial low anxiety correlates with good outcome (ibid.) suggests that reduction of anxiety, by such means as relaxation, could be useful.

Foa (1979) also found that those patients who held that their obsessions or obsession-related beliefs were realistic (that is, they had overvalued ideas) tended to have poor treatment outcome. The implications of her finding are, at the moment, not clear. For one thing, the assessment of a belief as strongly held or otherwise is itself beset with problems, and there are obvious difficulties arising from identifying a belief in an obsessional patient as an overvalued idea. What, for example, would distinguish such a belief from a delusion? If this notion is confirmed by more research and sufficiently clarified to be useful, a cognitive-therapy approach for such cases might perhaps be considered as an additional part of therapy. A tentative outline for cognitive therapy for obsessive-compulsive disorder is given by McFall and Wollersheim (1979) and - from a different point of view – by Salkovskis and Warwick (1988). The latter authors provide a discussion of how delusion-like cognitions in some of these patients may be dealt with.

Treatment acceptance and compliance

Sometimes patients find the treatment too difficult to accept. The Temple University team (Steketee *et al.*, 1982) have reported that 25 per cent of the patients requesting help at their centre refuse to accept the package offered. It is tempting to offer a diluted programme to make the therapy acceptable to such patients, but this is not to be recommended, as such a programme often leads to only minimal gains. Clinical judgement may allow a certain amount of flexibility without admitting self-defeating compromises; but, in the end, the therapist has to use his or her ingenuity in persuading patients to accept therapy. One useful strategy is to provide such patients with the opportunity to discuss the treatment with people who have already been treated successfully. Even then, there will still be some patients who are unable to accept what is offered.

References

Bass, B. A. (1973) 'An unusual behavioral technique for healing obsessional ruminations', *Psychotherapy: Theory, Research and Practice* 10: 191–2.

Baum, M. (1969) 'Extinction of an avoidance response following response prevention: some parametric investigations', *Canadian Journal of Psychiatry* 23: 1–10.

Baum, M. (1970) 'Extinction of avoidance responding through response prevention (flooding)', *Psychological Bulletin* 74: 276–84.

Bilsbury, C. and Morley, S. (1979) 'Obsessional slowness: A meticulous replication', *Behaviour Research and Therapy* 17: 405–8.

Cawley, R. H. (1974) 'Psychotherapy and obsessional disorders', in H. R. Beech (ed.) *Obsessional States*, London: Methuen.

Chiocca, E. A. and Martuza, R. L. (1990) 'Neurosurgical therapy of obsessive-compulsive disorder', in M. A. Jenike, L. Baer and W. E. Minichiello (eds) *Obsessive-Compulsive Disorders: Theory and Management, 2nd edn*, Chicago: Year Book Medical Publications.

Cobb, J. (1992) 'Serotonin re-uptake inhibitors in obsessive-compulsive disorder: What is their therapeutic role?', in K. Hawton and P. Cowen (eds) *Practical Problems in Psychiatry*, Oxford: Oxford University Press.

Cobb, J. and Kelly, D. (1990) 'Psychosurgery: Is it ever justified?', in K. Hawton and P. Cowen (eds) *Dilemmas and Difficulties in the Management of Psychiatric Patients*, Oxford: Oxford University Press.

Crook, J. O. and Charney, D. L. (1982) 'A new technique for treating obsessions: paradoxical practice with cassette recorder', in R. L. Du Ponty (ed.) *Phobia*, New York: Brunner/Mazel.

Daniels, L. K. (1976) 'An extension of thought-stopping in the treatment of obsessional thinking', *Behavior Therapy* 7: 131.

de Silva, D. (1978) 'Behaviour therapy for obsessional neurosis', *Nursing Mirror* 146: 15–17.

de Silva, P. (1986) 'Obsessional-compulsive imagery', *Behaviour Research and Therapy* 24: 333–50.

de Silva, P. and Rachman, S. (1992) *Obsessive-Compulsive Disorder: The Facts*, Oxford: Oxford University Press.

Emmelkamp, P. M. G. (1982) *Phobic and Obsessive-Compulsive Disorders: Theory, Research and Practice*, New York: Plenum.

Emmelkamp, P. M. G. and Kwee, K. (1977) 'Obsessional ruminations: a comparison between thought-stopping and prolonged exposure in imagination', *Behaviour Research and Therapy* 15: 441–4.

Emmelkamp, P. M. G., Bouman, T. K. and Scholing, A. (1992) *Anxiety Disorders: A Practitioner's Guide*, Chichester: Wiley.

Eysenck, H. J. (1952) 'The effects of psychotherapy: An evaluation', *Journal of Consulting Psychology* 16: 319–24.

Farkas, G. M. and Beck, S. (1981) 'Exposure and response prevention of morbid ruminations and compulsive avoidance', *Behaviour Research and Therapy* 19: 257–61.

Fenichel, O. (1946) *The Psychoanalytic Theory of Neurosis*, London: Kegan Paul.

Foa, E. B. (1979) 'Failure in treating obsessive-compulsives', *Behaviour Research and Therapy* 17: 169–76.

Foa, E. B. and Goldstein, A. (1978) 'Continuous exposure and strict response prevention in the treatment of obsessive-compulsive neurosis', *Behavior Therapy* 9: 821–9.

Foa, E. B. and Steketee, G. (1979) 'Obsessive-compulsives: Conceptual issues and treatment interventions', in M. Hersen, R. M. Eisler and P. M. Miller (eds) *Progress in Behavior Modification, Vol. 8*, New York: Academic Press.

Foa, E. B. and Tillmanns, A. (1980) 'The treatment of obsessive-compulsive neurosis', in A. Goldstein and E. B. Foa (eds) *Handbook of Behavioral Interventions: A Clinical Guide*, New York: Wiley.

Foa, E. B. and Wilson, R. (1991) *S.T.O.P. Obsessing: How to Overcome Your Obsessions and Compulsions*, New York: Bantam Books.

Foa, E. B., Steketee, G., Turner, R. M. and Fischer, S. C. (1980) 'Effects of imaginal exposure in feared disasters in obsessive-compulsive disorders', *Behaviour Research and Therapy* 18: 449–55.

Foa, E. B., Grayson, J. B. and Steketee, G. (1982) 'Depression, habituation and treatment outcome in obsessive-compulsives', in J. Boulougouris (ed.) *Learning Theory Approaches to Psychiatry*, New York: Wiley.

Foa, E. B., Grayson, J. B., Steketee, G. S., Doppelt, H. G., Turner, R. M. and Latimer, P. R. (1983) 'Success and failure in the behavioral treatment of obsessive-compulsives', *Journal of Consulting and Clinical Psychology* 51: 287–97.

Foa, E. B., Steketee, G., Grayson, J. B. and Doppelt, H. G. (1982) 'Treatment of obsessive-compulsives: Where do we fail?' in E. B. Foa and P. M. G. Emmelkamp (eds) *Failures in Behavior Therapy*, New York: Wiley.

Foa, E. B., Steketee, G. S. and Ozarow, B. J. (1985) 'Behavior therapy with obsessive-compulsives: From theory to treatment', in M. Mavissakalian, S. M. Turner and L. Michelson (eds) *Obsessive-Compulsive Disorder: Psychological and Pharmacological Treatment*, New York: Plenum Press.

Furst, J. B. and Cooper, A. (1970) 'Failure of systematic desensitization in two cases of obsessional-compulsive neurosis marked by fear of insecticide', *Behaviour Research and Therapy* 8: 203–6.

Goodman, W. K., McDougle, C. J. and Price, L. H. (1992) 'Pharmacotherapy of obsessive-compulsive disorder', *Journal of Clinical Psychiatry* 53 (4 supplement): 29–37.

Greist, J. H. (1989) *Obsessive-Compulsive Disorder: A Guide*, Madison, Wis.: Anxiety Disorders Centre.

Greist, J. H. (1992) 'An integrated approach to treatment of obsessive-compulsive disorder', *Journal of Clinical Psychiatry* 53 (4 supplement): 38–41.

Gurnani, P. D. and Vaughan, M. (1981) 'Changes in frequency and distress during prolonged repetition of obsessional thoughts', *British Journal of Clinical Psychology* 20: 79–81.

Hackman, A. and McClean, C. (1975) 'A comparison of flooding and thought-stopping treatment', *Behaviour Research and Therapy* 13: 263–9.

Hoogduin, G. A. C. and Hoogduin, W. A. (1984) 'The out-patient treatment of patients with obsessive-compulsive disorder', *Behaviour Research and Therapy* 22: 455–9.

Insel, T. R. (1990) 'New pharmacologic approaches to obsessive-compulsive disorder', *Journal of Clinical Psychiatry* 51 (10 supplement): 47–51.

Jenike, M. A. (1990) 'Psychotherapy of obsessive-compulsive personality disorder', in M. A. Jenike, L. Baer and W. E. Minichiello (eds) *Obsessive-Compulsive Disorders: Theory and Management, 2nd Edition*, Chicago: Year Book Medical Publications.

Kenny, F. T., Solyom, L. and Solyom, C. (1973) 'Faradic disruption of obsessive ideation in the treatment of obsessive neurosis', *Behavior Therapy* 4: 448–57.

Kirk, J. W. (1983) 'Behavioural treatment of obsessional-compulsive patients in routine clinical practice', *Behaviour Research and Therapy* 21: 57–62.

Kosslyn, S. (1980) *Image and Mind*, Cambridge, Mass.: Harvard University Press.

Likierman, H. and Rachman, S. (1980) 'Spontaneous decay of compulsive urges: cumulative effects', *Behaviour Research and Therapy* 18: 387–94.

Likierman, H. and Rachman, S. (1982) 'Obsessional ruminations: An experimental investigation of thought-stopping and habituation training', *Behavioural Psychotherapy* 10: 324–38.

McFall, M. E. and Wollersheim, J. P. (1979) 'Obsessive-compulsive neurosis: A cognitive-behavioral formulation and approach to treatment', *Cognitive Therapy and Research* 3: 333–48.

Mahoney, M. J. (1971) 'The self-management of covert behavior: a case study', *Behavior Therapy* 2: 575–8.

Maier, N. R. F. (1949) *Frustration*, New York: McGraw-Hill.

Maier, N. R. F. and Klee, J. B. (1945) 'Studies of abnormal behavior in the rat XVII: Guidance versus trial and error in the alteration of habits and fixations', *Journal of Psychology* 19: 133–63.

Marks, I. M. (1978) *Living With Fear*, New York: McGraw-Hill.

Marks, I. M., Hodgson, R. and Rachman, S. (1975) 'Treatment of chronic obsessive-compulsive neurosis by *in vivo* exposure', *British Journal of Psychiatry* 127: 349–64.

Meyer, V. (1966) 'Modification of expectations in cases with obsessional rituals', *Behaviour Research and Therapy* 4: 273–80.

Meyer, V., Levy, R. and Schnurer, A. (1974) 'The behavioural treatment of obsessional-compulsive disorders', in H. R. Beech (ed.) *Obsessional States*, London: Methuen.

Minichiello, W. E. (1990) 'Clinical case examples of behavioral therapy of obsessive-compulsive disorder', in M. A. Jenike, L. Baer and W. E. Minichiello (eds) *Obsessive-Compulsive Disorders: Theory and Management, 2nd Edn*, Chicago: Year Book Medical Publications.

Nay, W. R. (1979) *Multimethod Clinical Assessment*, New York: Gardner Press.

O'Callaghan, M. A. J. and Carroll, D. (1982) *Psychosurgery: A Scientific Analysis*, Lancaster: MTP Press.

Paquin, M. J. (1979) 'The treatment of obsessive compulsions by information feedback: A new application of a standard behavioral procedure', *Psychotherapy: Theory, Research and Practice* 16: 292–6.

Parkinson, L. and Rachman, S. (1980) 'Are intrusive thoughts subject to habituation?' *Behaviour Research and Therapy* 18: 409–18.

Pato, M. T., Zohar-Kadouch, R., Zohar, J. and Murphy, D. L. (1988) 'Return of symptoms after discontinuation of domipramine in patients with obsessive-compulsive disorder', *American Journal of Psychiatry* 145: 1521–5.

Queiroz, I. O., Motta, M. A., Madi, M. B., Sissai, D. L. and Boren, J. J. (1981) 'A functional analysis of obsessive-compulsive problems with related therapeutic procedures', *Behaviour Research and Therapy* 19: 377–88.

Rachman, S. (1971) 'Obsessional ruminations', *Behaviour Research and Therapy* 9: 229–35.

Rachman, S. (1974) 'Primary obsessional slowness', *Behaviour Research and Therapy* 12: 9–18.

Rachman, S. (1976) 'The modification of obsessions: A new formulation', *Behaviour Research and Therapy* 14: 437–43.

Rachman, S. (1978) 'An anatomy of obsessions', *Behaviour Analysis and Modification* 2: 253–78.

Rachman, S. (1980) 'Psycho-surgical treatment of obsessional-compulsive disorders', in E. S. Valenstein (ed.) *The Psychosurgery Debate*, San Francisco: W. H. Freeman.

Rachman, S. (1982) 'Obsessional-compulsive disorders', in A. S. Bellack, M. Hersen and A. G. Kazdin (eds) *International Handbook of Behavior Modification and Therapy*, New York: Plenum Press.

Rachman, S. and Hodgson, R. (1980) *Obsessions and Compulsions*, Englewood Cliffs, NJ: Prentice-Hall.

Rachman, S. and Wilson, G. T. (1981) *The Effects of Psychological Therapy*, New York: Pergamon.

Rachman, S., de Silva, P. and Roper, G. (1976) 'The spontaneous decay of compulsive urges', *Behaviour Research and Therapy* 14: 445–53.

Rachman, S., Hodgson, R. and Marks, I. (1971) 'The treatment of chronic obsessional neurosis', *Behaviour Research and Therapy* 9: 237–47.

Rachman, S., Cobb, J., Grey, S., McDonald, B., Mawson, D., Sartory, G. and Stern, R. (1979) 'The behavioural treatment of obsessive-compulsive disorders, with and without clomipromine', *Behaviour Research and Therapy* 17: 467–78.

Salkovskis, P. M. and Warwick, H. M. C. (1988) 'Cognitive therapy of obsessive-compulsive disorder', in C. Perris, L. M. Blackburn and H. Perris (eds) *The Theory and Practice of Cognitive Therapy*, Heidelberg: Springer.

Salkovskis, P. M. and Westbrook, D. (1989) 'Behaviour therapy and obsessional ruminations: Can failure be turned into success?' *Behaviour Research and Therapy* 27: 149–60.

Slater, E. and Roth, M. (1969) *Clinical Psychiatry* (3rd edn of W. Meyer-Gross, E. Slater and M. Roth's *Clinical Psychiatry*), London: Balliere, Tindall & Cassell.

Solyom, L. (1969) 'A case of obsessive neurosis treated by aversion relief', *Canadian Psychiatric Association Journal* 14: 523–626.

Steketee, G., Foa, E. B. and Grayson, J. B. (1982) 'Recent advances in the behavioural treatment of obsessive-compulsives', *Archives of General Psychiatry* 39: 1365–71.

Stern, R. (1970) 'Treatment of a case of obsessional neurosis using thought-stopping technique', *British Journal of Psychiatry* 117: 441–2.

Stern, R. S. (1978) 'Obsessive thoughts: The problem of therapy', *British Journal of Psychiatry* 133: 200–5.

Sturgis, E. T. and Meyer, V. (1981) 'Obsessive-compulsive disorders', in S. M. Turner, R. S. Calhoun and H. E. Adams, (eds) *Handbook of Clinical Behavior Therapy*, New York: Wiley.

Tryon, G. S. (1979) 'A review and critique of thought-stopping research', *Journal of Behavior Therapy and Experimental Psychiatry* 10: 189–92.

Turner, S. M. and Beidel, D. C. (1988) *Treating Obsessive-Compulsive Disorder*, New York: Pergamon.

Turner, S. M., Hersen, M., Bellack, A. S. and Wells, K. C. (1973) 'Behavioral treatment of obsessive-compulsive neurosis', *Behaviour Research and Therapy* 17: 95–106.

Turner, S. M., Holzman, A. and Jacob, R. B. (1983) 'Treatment of compulsive looking by imaginal thought-stopping', *Behavior Modification* 7: 576–89.

Tynes, L. L., Salins, C., Skiba, W. and Winstead, D. K. (1992) 'A psycho- educational and support group for obsessive-compulsive disorder patients and their significant others', *Comprehensive Psychiatry* 33: 197–201.

Van Noppen, B. L., Rasmussen, S. A., Eisen, J. and McCartney, L. A. (1991) 'A multifamily group approach as an adjunct to treatment of obsessive-compulsive disorder', in M. T. Pabo and J. Zohar (eds) *Current Treatment of Obsessive-Compulsive Disorder*, Washington DC: American Psychiatric Press.

Vingoe, F. J. (1980) 'The treatment of a chronic obsessive condition via reinforcement contingent upon success in response prevention', *Behaviour Research and Therapy* 18: 212–17.

Vogel, W., Peterson, L. E. and Broverman, I. K. (1982) 'A modification of Rachman's habituation technique for treatment of obsessive-compulsive disorder', *Behaviour Research and Therapy* 20: 101–4.

Wolpe, J. (1958) *Psychotherapy by Reciprocal Inhibition*, Stanford: Stanford University Press.

Wolpe, J. (1991) *The Practice of Behavior Therapy, 4th edn*, New York: Pergamon.

Chapter 5

Depression
Investigation

V. Rippere

WHAT IS MEANT BY 'DEPRESSION'?

The term 'depression' is used in several ways, in describing mood, in identifying a syndrome and as a psychiatric nosological concept. 'Depressed mood' is familiar to most of us in the sense of 'experience of unhappiness' or 'distress': it may involve feelings of being fed up, of guilt, worthlessness, self-deprecation, listlessness and apathy. There is little disagreement over what constitutes 'depressed mood' and there is a variety of checklists available for assessment of the degree of its severity.

'Depressive syndrome' describes a cluster of symptoms which are commonly seen in psychiatric practice. These generally comprise depressed mood, loss of interest, anxiety, sleep disturbance, loss of appetite, lack of energy and suicidal thoughts. Weeping and slowness of speech and action may be apparent; sometimes extreme withdrawal is manifest. Some patients experience hallucinations, often of voices ridiculing them, and may have delusions that they have been responsible for a horrific catastrophe.

Depression is also a nosological concept. It has been subdivided into bipolar (manic-depressive), endogenous, reactive, neurotic and psychotic varieties on the basis of history and symptoms. Currently, much energy is being expended on investigating biological markers to help support these clinical classifications. Different diagnoses may favour different treatments, for example, ECT for severe endogenous patients or lithium for manic-depressives.

In the following discussion issues of classification will not be dealt with. In the first place, formulations of depression in terms of behavioural and cognitive concepts are not related to differences in psychiatric classifications of depression; secondly there is limited agreement between observers about the value of identifying different subtypes of depression; and thirdly, the agreement between different raters is not always good (Kendell, 1976). The term 'depression' therefore is used here simply to refer to a clinical syndrome or cluster of symptoms covering changes in affect, cognition and behaviour.

The psychometric investigation of depression

There are three main types of investigation in cases of depression.

The first is for diagnostic purposes: a number of variables – mood, activity, and so on – are investigated to determine whether a client could be characterised as depressed. This is rarely done now by clinical psychologists as there are probably no instruments (by reason of poor standardisation) for doing this satisfactorily. Most psychometric procedures are designed rather to measure the severity of depression.

The second is to provide measures with which to monitor, from baseline, changes with treatment such as medication or behaviour therapy.

The third is to determine the patient's suitability for cognitive behavioural treatment. This objective is probably least satisfactorily dealt with by psychometric means.

There are many other psychometric procedures for assessing depression but few are adequately standardised. Of perhaps greatest interest are techniques for recording data of value to cognitive therapy. These are the Automatic Thoughts Questionnaire (Hollon and Kendall, 1980; Harrell and Ryon, 1983), the Dysfunctional Attitude Scale (Weissman and Beck, 1978; Beck, 1976) and the Cognitive Style Test (Wilkinson and Blackburn, 1981). There have been few data to support the use of the two former techniques (Dobson and Breiter, 1983). Beck *et al.* (1979) recommend the use of a recording procedure for negative thoughts unique to the patient (see Chapter 6). Unfortunately, because of the highly varied and rapidly changing nature of negative thoughts, the conventional methods of assessing reliability (Chapter 1) would not be appropriate for that procedure.

Finally, the clinician should be alert to record certain depressive behaviours which may be of interest, for example, the number of times the client is observed crying; how much time is spent alone in his or her room.

Depression measures as psychometric instruments

Because depression measures are psychometric instruments, the numerical scores representing a patient's performance have no prior significance. In order to be meaningful, they must be compared to existing normative data, which are derived in most cases from other patients. The meaning of a depression score depends upon the purpose for which the measure was constructed and the adequacy of the norms. Scores on different measures may accordingly have different meanings. Thus, some measures, like the Beck Depression Inventory, indicate the severity of a depressive condition that has been identified by other means (Beck *et al.*, 1979); others, such as the Wakefield Self-Assessment Depression Inventory (Snaith *et al.*, 1971), give a cut-off score above which a patient may be considered to be clinically depressed; while still others refer to mood only rather than to clinical depressive illness. In the Wessman–Ricks Scale (Wessman and Ricks, 1966), for example, the norms take the form of the means

and standard deviations attained by an undergraduate sample and the respondent's score is simply compared with the average. There are measures, such as the
widely used visual analogue scale (see Chapter 1) for which no norms are
available. The patient's current score is compared to his or her previous score on
the same instrument.

Since many depression measures yield a global score, usually indicating
degree of severity, they provide in many cases only an oblique view of a given
patient's individual state. In the case of sub-maximal scores, the final total may
be derived from endorsement of many differently weighted response options and
two patients with the same sub-maximal score may gain by very different
performances. Thus on a fifteen-item questionnaire, each item having four
response options weighted 0, 1, 2, 3, one patient with a score of 15 may have
endorsed all fifteen symptoms at severity level 1 (global mild impairment),
whereas another, also scoring 15, may have endorsed five symptoms at severity
level 3 (patchy severe impairment) and scored noughts on the rest. The user of
depression measures needs to remain constantly aware that the same numerical
score may have very different clinical meanings, both between and within
individuals.

The prospective user of any depression measure needs to ascertain what kind
of information the scores obtained will yield and how reliable and valid the
measure has been found to be for different purposes. The choice of measure will
depend, among other things, on the nature of the problem presented by the
patient, on the user's purpose in doing the assessment, and on the kind of
information the measure provides. It is recommended that intending users of
formal depression measures go beyond this practically oriented chapter and read
some of the helpful review papers which may clarify theoretical issues, such as
the types of reliabilities and validities relevant to depression measures, more
than it has been possible to do here in the limited space available (e.g. Boyle,
1985; Lader, 1981).

It should be noted that self-administered depression scales correlate as highly
with measures of social desirability as they do with each other (Langevin and
Stancer, 1979).

Some measures of depression

The coverage here omits experimental tests (such as Lehmann, 1974; Cohen and
Hunter, 1978); measures of mood (such as the Depression Adjective Checklists:
Lubin, 1966; 1967); measures designed for use with normals (for example,
Berndt et al., 1980); physiological and biochemical tests (for examples see Noble
and Lader, 1972, and American Psychiatric Association, 1987); and tests designed for use with children (for example, Birleson, 1981). It includes measures
that cover depressed patients of all degrees of severity, chronicity, articulateness
and cooperativeness. Measures of other variables, such as anxiety, suicidal
intent, anhedonia, reinforcers, or whatever, are not included, but their exclusion

should not be taken to have any implications for the relevance to assessing individual depressed patients.

Observer rating scales

Observer rating scales should include *ad hoc* measures for, for example, time spent alone in bedroom. However, the following have established psychometric data.

Hamilton Rating Scale

The Hamilton Rating Scale (HRS) (Hamilton, 1960; 1967) is the most widely used observer scale for rating depressed patients. It is not a diagnostic instrument but a measure of severity.

The twenty-one items in the initial version include mood, guilt, suicidal tendencies, insomnia, work and interests, activity level, anxiety, somatic symptoms, hypochondriasis, weight, insight, diurnal variation, depersonalisation, paranoid and obsessional symptoms. Each is rated on either a 0 to 2 or a 0 to 4 scale.

It is recommended that two raters independently score a patient at the same interview, as a check on inter-rater reliability. The patient's score is the sum of scores given by the two raters. If resources do not run to having two observers rate the patient, the one rater's scores are doubled to render them comparable to norms.

The HRS has been found to have high inter-rater reliability. Hamilton (1960) reported a correlation of +0.90 for two raters observing seventy patients. Bech *et al.* (1975a) reported inter-rater reliabilities amongst four psychiatrists ranging from +0.88 to 0.98 for individual items and +0.94 for total score.

Validation studies have shown variable correlations with other depression measures, as shown in Table 5.1.

Table 5.1 Validation studies of the Hamilton Rating Scale for Depression, showing correlations with other measures of depression

Depression measure	Correlations	Source
MMPI–D	+0.34	Schnurr *et al.*, 1976
Zung SDS	from +0.22 to +0.95	Schnurr *et al.*, 1976 Davies *et al.*, 1975
Beck Depression Inventory	from +0.16 to +0.82	Schnurr *et al.*, 1976 Williams *et al.*, 1972
Behavioural ratings	+0.71	Williams *et al.*, 1972
Clinical assessment	+0.84	Bech *et al.*, 1975a,
Psychiatrist's global rating	+0.89	Knesevich *et al.*, 1977
Wechsler Depression Scale	+0.23	Schnurr *et al.*, 1976

Despite this generally impressive performance, the HRS has been criticised for failing to differentiate adequately between moderate and severe depression, as measured by a psychiatrist's global clinical assessment (Bech *et al.*, 1975a) and for lack of homogeneity (Bech *et al.*, 1981).

The scale's chief advantages are high reliability, validity and international acceptance; the chief disadvantage is the time required to interview the patient and complete the complex ratings.

The Inventory for Depressive Symptomatology

The Inventory for Depressive Symptomatology (IDS; reproduced in D. Milne, 1992 and in Rush *et al.*, 1986a) can be administered either by the clinician as a result of an interview and observations of the patient or as a self-report question-naire by the patient.

The IDS consists of twenty-eight items and is thus slightly more compre-hensive than the HRS and the Beck Depression Inventory (BDI; see following sections) although it has been reported (Rush *et al.*, 1987) to have high internal consistency (Cronbach's alpha = +0.85). The IDS has been moderately correlated (+0.61 for the clinician-administered version, +0.78 for the self-completed version) with the BDI (Rush *et al.*, 1986b).

Self-rating scales

Visual analogue scales

A visual analogue scale (VAS) consists of a straight line, usually 100 mm long, with labelled, usually bipolar, endpoints, such as 'extremely depressed' and 'not at all depressed', or whatever other constructs suit the clinician's purpose (Chapter 1).

The results of VAS ratings have been found to correlate highly with scores on several standardised depression scales, as shown in Table 5.2.

These results have led to the general consensus that simple, quick and easy-to- administer visual analogue scales perform efficiently when compared to the more complex and time-consuming standardised rating procedures.

Table 5.2 Validation of visual analogue scales as measures of depression, showing correlations with other measures of depression

Depression measure	Correlation variability	Source
HRS	from +0.79 to +0.88	Zealley and Aitken, 1969 Davies *et al.*, 1975
Beck Depression Inventory	from +0.65 to +0.76	Davies *et al.*, 1975 Little and McPhail, 1973
Self- and Observer VAS	+0.44	Pilowsky and Spalding, 1972

Variants of VAS have been proposed. Gringras (1977), for example, suggested a version for use in assessing change on anti-depressant treatment in general practice. His scale consists of a 100 mm line with labelled endpoints and midpoint labelled 'My feelings at last visit'. The endpoints are 'As bad as you can imagine' and 'Completely symptom-free'. The spaces between the 'bad' end and the middle, and the 'symptom-free' end and the middle are designated 'worse' and 'better', respectively.

The scale is reported to be useful for its intended purpose and extremely sensitive, especially where very short-term fluctuations of mood are of interest (Rippere and Gledhill, unpublished data, 1976).

Bond and Lader (1974) mention several studies in which visual analogue scales have been found to be sensitive to drug effects; their own study demonstrated sensitivity to drug after-effects. They also found that data from sixteen such scales administered to 500 normals yielded a three-factor structure.

Beck depression inventory

There are two forms of the Beck Depression Inventory (BDI) (Beck *et al.*, 1961: Beck and Beck, 1972; Beck *et al.*, 1979; Beck, 1988): the original 21-item form published in 1961 and subsequently revised, and a shortened, 13-item version which was introduced in 1972. We shall consider them separately. They have been used especially for monitoring changes with cognitive therapy (see Chapter 6).

Long form

The purpose of the long form of the BDI is to provide a quantitative assessment of the severity of depression. It is not a diagnostic instrument. This point must be emphasised because the BDI has often been used in psychological research as if it were such and a score above a certain point meant that the subject was suffering from a clinical depression. Hammen (1980) has shown that this assumption is rarely warranted.

In that light, the cut-off scores recommended by the authors (Beck *et al.*, 1988) should be considered with caution: < 10 representing minimum or no depression; 10–18 indicating mild to moderate depression; 19–29 showing moderate to severe depression; 30–63 is severe depression.

The items in the BDI cover mood, pessimism, sense of failure, lack of satisfaction, guilt, sense of punishment, self-hate, self-accusation, self-punitive wishes, crying spells, irritability, social withdrawal, indecisiveness, body image, work inhibition, sleep disturbance, fatigue, appetite, weight, somatic preoccupation and libido. Each item has four or five verbally anchored response options with scores ranging from 0 to 3 for each option. The scale was originally intended to be read out to the patient and marked by the interviewer, but it is often given to patients to fill in themselves. The score is the sum of all individual item scores.

Reliability studies (Beck *et al.*, 1988) have shown a high degree of internal consistency, in that all item scores correlate highly with total score and high split-half reliability has invariably been found. Test–retest reliability has been studied indirectly (Beck *et al.*, 1961) and directly, test–retest correlations having ranged from 0.48 to 0.90 with intervals varying from a few hours to four months (Beck *et al.* 1988).

Validation studies by Beck and his collaborators include a demonstration that mean BDI scores increased with increases in psychiatrist's global severity ratings and that clinician's ratings and BDI scores were significantly correlated (+0.65 and +0.67 in two separate studies). The authors also found that patients whose global clinical ratings changed two to five weeks after admission also showed changes in BDI scores consistent with the direction of clinical change (Beck *et al.*, 1961).

Independent validation studies have shown a range of usually high correlations of BDI scores with other depression measures (Beck *et al.*, 1988).

Analyses of the readability of the BDI indicate that it can be read, and probably understood, by average children as young as 12 years (Beck *et al.*, 1988).

The BDI has been criticised for failing to differentiate adequately between moderate and severe depression as measured by a global clinical assessment (Bech *et al.*, 1975a) and for being open to observer bias when the interviewer rates the patient (Carroll *et al.*, 1973). Both patients and students have complained to the writer that they found the scale depressing to complete. An indecisive patient reported finding it impossible to choose between the different response options. One medical student, who completed it as part of a class exercise, noted that he had lost weight not because he was depressed but because he was deliberately slimming. This objection has been met in a 1978 revision by the inclusion of the statement 'I am purposely trying to lose weight by eating less: Yes/No' alongside the weight loss item (Beck *et al.*, 1979).

Significant correlations (Beck *et al.*, 1988) have also been reported with measures of suicidal behaviour and alcohol abuse. This is not surprising because these are ways in which many people react to depression. Significant correlations have also been noted with measures of anxiety, in part probably because depres- sion and anxiety can have some symptoms in common.

Short form

Beck and Beck (1972) presented a thirteen-item shortened version of the BDI for use by general practitioners in screening patients for depression. The item content includes sadness, pessimism, sense of failure, dissatisfaction, guilt, self-dislike, self-harm, social withdrawal, indecisiveness, self-image, work difficulty, fatigue and appetite. The questionnaire is self-administering and is said to take five minutes for the patient to complete. Each item has four response options, scored, 0, 1, 2 or 3. The patient's score is the sum of item total. Data are presented showing the means and standard deviations for patients rated clinically as not depressed, mildly, moderately or severely depressed.

In a subsequent study (Beck *et al.*, 1974b) correlations were reported between short BDI scores and clinicians' ratings of the order of +0.55 for a hospitalised depressed sample and +0.67 for general practice medical patients. Correlations between long and short BDI scores were reported as +0.89 (suicide attempters) and +0.96 (schizophrenics). Correlations between short BDI scores and age, sex and race were non-significant. The authors suggested that in clinical practice short BDI scores must be regarded as suggestive and followed up with more intensive interviews. The short form probably samples non-cognitive aspects of depression less thoroughly (Beck *et al.*, 1988). In research, however, the short form could be used as equivalent to the long form and would be especially useful where repeated measurements were made.

Reynolds and Gould (1981) compared the long and short forms in a sample of participants in a methadone maintenance programme. They reported internal consistency reliabilities of 0.85 (standard) and 0.83 (short form) and a correlation of +0.93 between the two scales. They concluded that the short BDI was a reliable and valid brief measure of depression.

Zung Self-rating Depression Scale

The Zung Self-rating Depression Scale (SDS) (Zung, 1965) is a twenty-item scale involving ratings on a four-point qualitative temporal scale ('a little of the time', 'some of the time', 'good part of the time' and 'most of the time'). The items are discursive propositions, ten worded positively (for instance, 'I feel hopeful about the future') and ten worded as statements of depressive symptomatology ('I have crying spells or feel like it'). Items are scored 1, 2, 3 and 4 respectively, with higher scores indicating more depression.

Zung presents evidence that the scale differentiates between depressed patients, other psychiatric patients and normals. Scores of depressed patients were also shown to be significantly lower after treatment than before.

Zung has used the scale to examine the frequency and severity of depression in the normal adult population (Zung, 1971) and in the normal aged (Zung, 1967b). Scores have been found to be higher in adolescents and in the aged generally, but in a study of patients they were found to be unaffected by the patient's age, sex, marital status, educational level, financial status or intelligence (Zung, 1967a).

In validation studies, the SDS has been found to correlate variously with other depression measures, as shown in Table 5.3.

However, the scale has also come in for criticism for insensitivity to clinical differences at the lower end of the severity range, awkward wording of items, and lack of a rating category to indicate absence of a symptom (Carroll, 1978; Carroll *et al.*, 1973; Gringras, 1980). The last of these criticisms, at least, has been met in a revision where the rating category is reworded 'None or a little of the time' (Zung, 1973).

Table 5.3 Validation of the Zung Self-Rating Depression Scale, showing correlations with other measures of depression

Depression measure	Correlations	Source
HRS	+0.22	Schnurr *et al.*, 1976
BDI	+0.57	Reynolds and Gould, 1981
	+0.52 to +0.80	Davies *et al.*, 1975

Change scales

Montgomery–Asberg Scale

This ten-item scale (Montgomery and Asberg, 1979) was designed specifically to be sensitive to the effects of treatment for depression, in contrast to being used for screening or diagnostic purposes. The items include apparent and reported sadness, inner tension, reduced sleep and appetite, concentration difficulties, lassitude, inability to feel, pessimistic and suicidal thoughts. The ratings, based on a semi-structured interview, are made on a scale running from 0 to 6, points 0, 2, 4 and 6 of which are precisely defined for each item, the rest being intermediate.

High inter-rater reliabilities (0.89 to 0.97) are reported for various pairs of raters and patients at different stages of treatment. The scale was also found to differentiate better than the HRS between responders and non-responders to treatment.

Mania scales

Manic State Scale

This 26-item observer rating scale (Beigel *et al.*, 1971) was developed in order to measure manic symptomatology in hospitalised patients. Items cover apparent mood, cognitions, speech, attitude and behaviour. Items are to be rated on both frequency (F) and intensity (I) scales, each with five verbally anchored points. The score is the total of the products of F × I scores for all items.

High intra-class correlations for individual items showing high inter-rater reliability and adequate correlations between the scale and independent psy-chiatrist and nurse global ratings have been reported for twenty-two items. The authors found that six items best characterised changes in severity of mania. In a later study they reported that eleven items characterised common elements of mania (Beigel and Murphy, 1971).

Bech *et al.* (1975b) have independently validated the instrument. They reported finding a different six items to be valid for their criteria.

A modified twenty-eight-item version incorporating a glossary has been developed by British investigators Blackburn *et al.* (1977).

Miscellaneous

Research Diagnostic Criteria

Among the few instruments which have been designed to detect the presence of depression according to a medical model are the Research Diagnostic Criteria (RDC) (Feighner *et al.*, 1972).

Feighner and his co-workers recommended the adoption of standardised criteria for selection of patients for research in different centres. The RDC for depression have been widely used in research and are as follows:

A Dysphoric mood and

B at least five of the following for 'definite' depression and four for 'probably' depression:

1 Poor appetite or weight loss
2 Sleep difficulty
3 Loss of energy
4 Agitation or retardation
5 Loss of interest in usual activities or decrease in sexual drive
6 Feelings of self-reproach or guilt
7 Worsened ability to think or concentrate
8 Recurrent thoughts of suicide or death

C A psychiatric illness lasting at least one month with no pre-existing psychiatric conditions or serious medical illness.

Comparable criteria are given for mania.

The RDC may be of interest to clinical psychologists for research purposes, but Zwick (1983) has noted that further investigation of their psychometric properties is needed.

The Cognitive Style Test

The Cognitive Style Test (CST; Blackburn *et al.*, 1986) contains descriptions of thirty everyday events about which respondents describe, each with four alternatives, how they would think. For example, 'You meet friends whom you haven't seen for a long time.' The possible responses are, 'I wonder if they still like me' or 'It's good to see old friends' or 'They won't like me any more' or 'They like me a lot.' Subjects producing high scores on this test are thus producing evidence characteristic of thinking in depression.

Blackburn *et al.* (1986) found that the test significantly discriminated clinically anxious from clinically depressed patients but no data are given to test aspects of reliability directly. There have been very few published studies to confirm these findings for the validity of the test.

The Dysfunctional Attitude Scale

The Dysfunctional Attitude Scale (DAS; Weissman and Beck, 1978) was the principal measure of cognitive style in the multi-centre trials of cognitive therapy in the USA (see Chapter 6).

The DAS consists of forty items in each of which the respondent is asked to give a rating of agreement, having been given seven alternatives from 'disagree totally' to 'agree totally'. For example, consider 'People will probably think less of me if I make a mistake.'

There are two parallel forms of the DAS, each having internal consistency of 0.89 or higher. Responses to the two forms have also been highly correlated with one another when given to undergraduates on two occasions at an interval of eight weeks (Weissman and Beck, 1978).

The Hopelessness Scale

This scale (Beck et al., 1974a) consists of twenty self-report items designed to predict suicidal behaviour. Consistent with this, Beck et al. (1990) found that a score of 9 or higher identified all but one of seventeen out-patients who later committed suicide, even several months after completing the questionnaire, in a sample of nearly 2,000. This had confirmed results of an earlier study of in-patients.

ASSESSMENT OF DEPRESSED PATIENTS FOR PSYCHOLOGICAL TREATMENT

Assessing a depressed patient for treatment (especially to determine if psychological treatment is appropriate) is rather a different matter from assessing the patient's level of depression per se. This section of the chapter concerns some basic principles and problems, considered from the standpoint of most clinical psychology practice (as opposed to private, fee-paying practice).

Although psychological treatment of depressed patients has generated a number of ambitious, elaborate and comprehensive schemes (e.g. McLean, 1976; Lewinsohn et al., 1976), it is probably fair to say that, in principle, the assessment of a depressed patient for treatment does not differ in any radical way from the assessment of any other type of patient. Indeed, most patients who are referred to the psychologist for treatment will be depressed to some degree, even if they do not necessarily suffer from a formal clinical depressive illness, and the vast majority of psychologist referrals with an unequivocal diagnosis of depression will have at least one, and typically more than one, other problem, commonly including anxiety, panic attacks, agoraphobia, bereavement, specific phobias, eating disorders, headaches or migraine, obsessions, difficulties in social adjustment, social skills, work, marriage, family, finance, education, behaviour, nutrition, or health, among many others. The line which can be drawn between the 'depressed' patient and the 'non-depressed' patient is almost purely hypothetical.

Since most clinically depressed patients who are referred to the psychologist will be on some form of anti-depressant medication, the referral may well concern one or more of the patient's other problems rather than the patient's depression *per se*. The psychologist's first task, therefore, is to ascertain which aspect of the patient's difficulties the psychologist is being asked to deal with, or to which the psychologist might most promisingly contribute some amelioration.

The second task is to find out, if at all possible, which problem(s) the patient wants help with. The problem(s) which the patient presents for treatment and the problem(s) mentioned in the referral may or may not be the same. Considerable trouble may be avoided if any differences can be reconciled early on. Efforts to treat the patient for a problem that the patient would prefer not to have treated are likely to be unsuccessful.

The task of discovering which problem(s) the patient wants help with may be complicated by the patient's unwillingness or inability to say what the problem is. For example, the grossly institutionalised chronically depressed in-patient who has been sent to the hospital for a second opinion after mouldering for years in a large custodial establishment and is thence referred to the team psychologist for a 'ward behavioural programme' may have forgotten how to talk, much less how to conceptualise and differentiate his or her needs and problems. Passive-aggressive personality-disordered out-patients may get their kicks in life by programmatically frustrating intending therapists through screaming if help is wanted and by systematically rejecting all suggestions. As for weepy patients (whose complaints concern the miserable way other people treat them and whose view of what needs to be done is that these others will have to be changed), they will probably collapse into a flood of tears or explode with indignation at the suggestion that perhaps they might need to change in some way. And finally, the therapist may encounter the inarticulate post-adolescent who is still too ashamed of his or her problems to bring himself to talk about them.

In cases where the patient cannot or will not present a problem, several options are available. The psychologist may seek relevant information from sources other than the patient, such as ward staff or the patient's significant others. He or she may send the games-playing patient away until that patient can formulate a reasonable problem, carry on talking to the patient in the hope that a suitable problem will emerge, send the patient back to the referring source saying that the psychologist regrets being unable to find a way to help, or, on the basis of what the patient has said, formulate a potentially treatable problem and try to persuade the patient to accept the formulation. Other options include suggesting to the patient the kinds of problems that one can help, in the hope that the patient will recognise one as his or her own; confronting the patient with his or her passive-aggressive stance; and even, on occasion, judiciously interpreting the patient's reluctance ('Could it be that you're hesitant to tell me what's really bothering you because you're afraid I'll think it's stupid?').

The psychologist should not be too surprised if it transpires that the patient's problem is not really a psychological one. The psychologist should be bold enough to say to the referring agent that he cannot offer the patient much help.

There are also others whose despondency, on close examination, turns out to seem entirely appropriate and proportionate to their depressing circumstances; these folk are not suffering from a pathology of affect but rather from a pathology of circumstances – squalid housing, dire poverty, chronic ill health, under-employment, unemployment, linguistic handicap, racial prejudice, or a host of other real oppressions. Such patients, on inspection, may appear to be coping admirably well with circumstances so dreadful that no one could reasonably be expected to withstand them for long. Some may be depressed needlessly: the majority of people are not clinically depressed by such circumstances, and it is of course possible that the patient's depiction may distort the degree of hardship involved, but the writer has been impressed with how often, on further enquiry, the patient's version of events has proved to be veridical.

In such cases, it is essential that the psychologist does not augment the patient's problems by confounding normal unhappiness in the face of heroic difficulties with an abnormal affective state and so demoralise the patient further by treating him or her as if he or she were 'mental'. In many cases, the patient will be found to have fallen through the net of available services and in these circumstances the kindest thing the psychologist can do may be to refer the patient on to the appropriate agency and follow up the referral with the nagging which may be necessary to ensure that the required help is forthcoming.

If appropriate service provision has already been set in motion, explaining to the patient that his or her reaction to events seems to be entirely normal and that it is the events that are abnormal may be therapeutic in its own right. Here I am not suggesting collusion with an evidently distorted view of how awful everything is but suggesting an avoidance of the unwarranted assumption that all unhappy people seen in mental health settings are *ipso facto* abnormally disordered in affect.

Now, assuming that the patient does produce a problem potentially treatable by psychological means, what other questions does the clinical psychologist need to ask before deciding what to do about it? Although most clinicians will want to evolve their own individual approaches, the following questions may be suggested as a rough guide:

1 Is the patient in a potentially treatable condition? Some depressed patients may be simply too ill for meaningful participation in psychological or behaviour treatment and will need to have physical treatment before they are fit for psychological intervention. Cognitive therapy, for example, is recommended only for unipolar depressed out-patients (Beck *et al.*, 1979).

2 Besides the main problem(s), which other difficulties, psychological and otherwise, lurk in the background? Which are potentially treatable and which might constitute potential obstacles to treatment?

Efforts to see the patient as an individual in his or her own social matrix may also help one to avoid the generally unproductive but increasingly widespread assumption – which is fostered by the progressively more schematic and theoretical manner in which psychology undergraduates and clinical trainees are taught abnormal psychology – that just because a particular individual labels himself or herself 'depressed' or is thus diagnosed, that individual therefore necessarily corresponds to a theoretical psychology-of-depression paradigm. While some people's depression appears to fit, say, a 'learned helplessness', a 'negative cognitive triad' or a 'low response-contingent positive reinforcement' model (see Chapter 6), the 'depression' of many patients encountered in clinical practice does not fit readily into these models. We are not likely to benefit those patients by Procrustean attempts to cram them into a particular theoretical box.

The question of how the therapist decides what treatment, if any, to offer cannot be dealt with here in any detail. The decision rests on what problems the patient presents, the patient's personal attributes and resources, his or her circumstances and preferences, the therapist's skills and knowledge of the literature, and the amount of time participants have available to devote to the treatment. Unless a therapist indiscriminately offers the same treatment to all depressed patients, it is nearly impossible to predict exactly what treatment a given patient will end up having simply on the basis of knowing that the patient is 'depressed'.

The range of treatments that may be offered extends far beyond the usual gamut of cognitive restructuring, supportive chat, social skills and assertiveness training, contingency management, ward-based token programmes, deconditioning therapies, relaxation training, self-monitoring, modelling, increasing participation in rewarding activities, marital counselling and the like. In the name of therapy for patients suffering from the spectrum of depressive disorders, the writer has at times used not only all of the above but also factual advice, instigation therapy, running, bibliotherapy, psychometric testing, vocational guidance, telephone and correspondence therapy, abreaction, clinical ecology and orthomolecular treatment; referrals have been arranged for physical investigations and treatment, group therapy, the strenuous encouragement of self-help, and even, upon rare occasions, psychodynamic interpretations, among others. In the case of an electively mute depressed adolescent in-patient, treatment for the first few months took the form of going to the ward and sitting with her for half an hour several times a week, to convey to her that when she was ready to talk, someone would be ready to listen. Because patients who are depressed comprise such an enormously heterogeneous group, there is a very real danger of allowing theoretical preconceptions to dictate stereotyped approaches to our assessment of, and intervention in, their difficulties.

One final point concerning the assessment of depressed patients is that assessment does not end with the conclusion of the initial assessment interview. The decision to offer a particular form of treatment may entail further, more focal assessment of specific aspects of the patient's problems (for example, specific questionnaires, behavioural assessment, self-monitoring, baseline ward observations, and so on). Many forms of treatment themselves entail a formal assessment component in order to enable outcome to be evaluated. And if several treatments for different problems have been offered as a sequence, re-evaluation of future plans will be required on the basis of past outcome, changes in circumstances and changes, for better or worse, in the patient's clinical state.

REFERENCES

American Psychiatric Association (1987) *Diagnostic and Statistical Manual of Mental Disorders, 3rd edn, Revised,* Washington, DC: American Psychiatric Association.

Bech, P., Gram, L. F., Dein, E., Jacobsen, O., Vitger, J. and Bolwig, T. G. (1975a) 'Quantitative rating of depressive states. Correlation between clinical assessment, Beck's self-rating scale and Hamilton's objective rating scale', *Acta Psychiatica Scandinavia* 51: 161–70.

Bech, P., Bolwig, T. G., Dein, E., Jacobsen, O. and Gram, L. F. (1975b) 'Quantitative rating of manic states', *Acta Psychiatica Scandinavia* 52: 1–6.

Bech, P., Allerup, P., Gram, L. F., Reisby, N., Rosenberg, R., Jacobsen, O. and Nagy, A. (1981) 'The Hamilton Depression Scale. Evaluation of objectivity using logistic models', *Acta Psychiatica Scandinavia* 63: 290–9.

Beck, A. T. (1967) *Depression. Clinical, Experimental and Theoretical Aspects,* London: Hoeber Medical Division, Harper and Row.

Beck, A. T. (1976) *Cognitive Therapy and the Emotional Disorders,* New York: International Universities Press.

Beck, A. T. (1988) *Beck Depression Inventory (BDI),* Sidcup: The Psychological Corporation.

Beck, A. T. and Beck, R. W. (1972) 'Screening depressed patients in family practice. A rapid technique', *Postgraduate Medicine* 52: 81–5.

Beck, A. T., Ward, C. H., Mendelson, M., Mock, J. and Erbaugh, J. (1961) 'An inventory for measuring depression', *Archives of General Psychiatry* 4: 561–74.

Beck, A. T., Weissman, A. W., Lester, D. and Trexler, L. (1974a) 'The assessment of pessimism: the Hopelessness Scale', *Journal of Consulting and Clinical Psychology* 42: 861–5.

Beck, A. T., Rial, W. Y. and Rickels, K. (1974b) 'Short form of depression inventory: cross-validation', *Psychological Reports* 34: 1181–6.

Beck, A. T., Rush, A. J., Shaw, B. F. and Emery, G. (1979) *Cognitive Therapy of Depression,* Chichester: Wiley.

Beck, A. T., Steer, R. A. and Garbin, M. G. (1988) 'Psychometric properties of the Beck Depression Inventory: twenty-five years of evaluation', *Clinical Psychology Review* 8: 77–100.

Beck, A. T., Brown, G., Berchick, R. J. and Stewart, B. L. (1990) 'Relationship between hopelessness and ultimate suicide: a replication with psychiatric out-patients', *American Journal of Psychiatry* 147: 190–5.

Beigel, A. and Murphy, D. L. (1971) 'Assessing clinical characteristics of the manic state', *American Journal of Psychiatry* 128: 688–94.

Beigel, A., Murphy, D. L. and Bunney, W. E. Jr (1971) 'The Manic State Rating Scale', *Archives of General Psychiatry* 25: 256–62.

Berndt, D. J., Petzel, T. P. and Berndt, S. M. (1980) 'Development and initial evaluation of a multiscore depression inventory', *Journal of Personal Assessment* 44: 396–403.

Birleson, P. (1981) 'The validity of depressive disorder in childhood and the development of a self-rating scale', *Journal of Child Psychology and Psychiatry* 22: 73–88.

Blackburn, I. M., Loudon, J. B. and Ashworth, C. M. (1977) 'A new scale for measuring mania', *Psychological Medicine*, 7: 453–8.

Blackburn, I., Jones, S. and Lewin, R. J. P. (1986) 'Cognitive style in depression', *British Journal of Clinical Psychology* 25: 241–51.

Bond, A. and Lader, M. (1974) 'The use of analogue scales in rating subjective feelings', *British Journal of Medical Psychology* 47: 211–18.

Boyle, G. J. (1985) 'Self-report measures of depression: some psychometric considerations', *British Journal of Clinical Psychology* 24: 45–59.

Carroll, B. J. (1978) 'Validity of the Zung Self-rating Depression Scale', *British Journal of Psychiatry* 133: 379–84.

Carroll, B. J., Fielding, J. M. and Blashki, T. G. (1973) 'Depression rating scales. A critical review', *Archives of General Psychiatry* 28: 361–6.

Cohen, E. and Hunter, I. (1978) 'Severity of depression differentiated by a colour selection test', *American Journal of Psychiatry* 135: 611–12.

Davies, B., Burrows, G. and Poynton, C. (1975) 'A comparative study of four depression rating scales', *Australian and New Zealand Journal of Psychiatry* 9: 21–4.

Dobson, K. S. and Breiter, H. J. (1983) 'Cognitive assessment of depression: reliability and validity of three measures', *Journal of Abnormal Psychology* 92: 107.

Feighner, H. P., Robins, E., Guze, S. B., Woodruff, R. A. Jr, Winokur, G. and Munoz, R. (1972) 'Diagnostic criteria for use in psychiatric research', *Archives of General Psychiatry* 26: 57–63.

Gringras, M. (1977) 'Experiences with some new scales for use in general practice', *Journal of International Medical Research* 5 (supplement): 61–5.

Gringras, M. (1980) 'Validation of the general practitioner clinical research group, 11-item depression scale', *Journal of International Medical Research* 8: (supplement 3): 45–8.

Hamilton, M. (1960) 'A rating scale for depression', *Journal of Neurosurgery and Psychiatry* 23: 56–62.

Hamilton, M. (1967) 'Development of a rating scale for primary depressive illness', *British Journal of Social Clinical Psychology* 6: 278–96.

Hammen, C. L. (1980) 'Depression in college students: beyond the Beck Depression Inventory', *Journal of Consulting and Clinical Psychology* 48: 126–8.

Harrell, T. H. and Ryon, N. B. (1983) 'Cognitive-behavioural assessment of depression: clinical validation of the Automatic Thoughts Questionnaire', *Journal of Consulting and Clinical Psychology* 51: 721–5.

Hollon, S. D. and Kendall, P. C. (1980) 'Cognitive self-statements in depression: development of an automatic thoughts questionnaire', *Cognitive Therapy and Research* 4: 383–95.

Hollon, S. D. and Kendall, P. C. (1981) 'In vivo assessment techniques for cognitive-behavioural processes', in P. C. Kendall and S. D. Hollon (eds) *Assessment Strategies for Cognitive-Behavioral Interventions*, New York: Academic Press.

Kendell, R. E. (1976) 'The classification of depressions: a review of contemporary confusion', *British Journal of Psychiatry* 129: 15–28.

Knesevich, J. W., Biggs, J. T., Clayton, P. J. and Ziegler, V. E. (1977) 'Validity of the Hamilton Rating Scale for Depression', *British Journal of Psychiatry* 131: 49–52.

Lader, M. H. (1981) 'The clinical assessment of depression', *British Journal of Clinical Pharmacology* 1: 5–14.

Langevin, R. and Stancer, H. (1979) 'Evidence that depression rating scales primarily measure a social undesirability response set', *Acta Psychiatica, Scandinavia* 59: 70–9.

Lehmann, H. E. (1974) 'Experimental criteria of depression', in N. S. Kline (ed.) *Factors in Depression*, New York: Raven Press.

Lewinsohn, P. M., Biglan, A. and Zeiss, A. M. (1976) 'Behavioural treatment of depression', in P. O. Davidson (ed.) *The Behavioural Management of Anxiety, Depression and Pain*, New York: Brunner/Mazel.

Little, J. C. and McPhail, N. I. (1973) 'Measures of depressive mood at monthly intervals', *British Journal of Psychiatry* 122: 447–52.

Lubin, B. (1966) 'Fourteen brief depression adjective check lists', *Archives of General Psychiatry* 15: 205–8.

Lubin, B. (1967) *Depression Adjective Check Lists: Manual*, San Deigo, Calif.: Education and Industrial Testing Service.

McLean, P. (1976) 'Therapeutic decision-making in the behavioural treatment of depression', in P. O. Davidson (ed.) *The Behavioural Management of Anxiety, Depression and Pain*, New York: Brunner/Mazel.

Milne, D. (1992) *A Mental Health Portfolio*, Windsor: NFER-Nelson.

Montgomery, S. and Asberg, M. (1979) 'A new depression scale designed to be sensitive to change', *British Journal of Psychiatry* 134: 382–9.

Noble, P. and Lader, M. (1972) 'A physiological comparison of "endogenous" and "reactive" depression', *British Journal of Psychiatry* 120: 541–2.

Pilkowsky, L. and Spalding, D. (1972) 'A method for measuring depression: validity studies on a depression questionnaire', *British Journal of Psychiatry* 121: 411–16.

Reynolds, W. M. and Gould, J. W. (1981) 'A psychometric investigation of the standard and short form of the Beck Depression Inventory', *Journal of Consulting and Clinical Psychology* 49: 306–7.

Rippere, V. and Gledhill, C. (1976) Unpublished data.

Rush, A. J., Hiser, W. and Giles, D. E. (1987) 'A comparison of self-reported versus clinical-rated symptoms of depression', *Journal of Clinical Psychiatry* 48: 246–8.

Rush, A. J., Giles, D. E., Schlesser, M. A., Fulton, C. L., Weissenburger, J. and Burns, C. (1986a) 'The Inventory for Depressive Symptomatology (IDS): preliminary findings', *Psychiatry Research* 18: 65–87.

Rush, A. J., Giles, D. E., Schlesser, M. A., Fulton, C. L., Weissenburger, J. and Burns, C. (1986b) 'The Inventory for Depressive Symptomatology (IDS): preliminary findings', *Psychopharmacology Bulletin* 22: 985–90.

Schnurr, R., Hoaken, P. C. S. and Jarrett, F. J. (1976) 'Comparison of depression inventories in a clinical population', *Canadian Psychiatric Associate Journal* 21: 473–76.

Snaith, R. P., Ahmed, S. N., Mehta, S. and Hamilton, M. (1971) 'Assessment of the severity of primary depressive illness. Wakefield Self-assessment Depression Inventory', *Psychological Medicine* 1: 143–49.

Weissman, A. and Beck, A. T. (1978) 'Development and validation of the Dysfunctional Attitude Scale: a preliminary investigation', unpublished paper, read to American Educational Research Association.

Wessman, A. E. and Ricks, D. F. (1966) *Mood and Personality*, London: Holt, Rinehart and Winston.

Wilkinson, I. M. and Blackburn, I. M. (1981) 'Cognitive style in depressed and recovered patients', *British Journal of Clinical Psychology* 20: 283–92.

Williams, J. G., Barlow, D. H. and Agras, W. S. (1972) 'Behavioural measurement of severe depression', *Archives of General Psychiatry* 27: 330–3.

Zealley, A. K. and Aitken, R. C. B. (1969) 'Measurement of mood', *Proceedings of the Royal Society of Medicine* 62: 993–6.

Zubin, J., Salzinger, K., Fleiss, J. L., Gurland, B., Spitzer, R. L., Endicott, J. and Sutton, S. (1975) 'Biometric approach to psychopathology: abnormal and clinical psychology – statistical, epidemiological and diagnostic approaches', *Annual Review of Psychology* 26: 621–71.

Zung, W. W. K. (1965) 'A Self-Rating Depression Scale ', *Archives of General Psychiatry* 12: 63–70.

Zung, W. W. K. (1967a) 'Factors influencing the Self-Rating Depression Scale', *Archives of General Psychiatry* 16: 543–7.

Zung, W. W. K. (1967b) 'Depression in the normal aged', *Psychosomatics* 8: 287–292.

Zung, W. W. K. (1971) 'Depression in the normal adult population', *Psychosomatics* 12: 164–7.

Zung, W. W. K. (1972a) 'How normal is depression?', *Psychosomatics* 13: 174–8.

Zung, W. W. K. (1972b) 'The Depression Status Inventory: an adjunct to the Self-Rating Depression Scale', *Journal of Clinical Psychology* 28: 539–43.

Zung, W. W. K. (1973) 'From art to science: the diagnosis and treatment of depression', *Archives of General Psychiatry* 29: 328–37.

Zwick, R. (1983) 'Assessing the psychometric properties of psychodiagnostic systems: how do the research diagnostic criteria measure up? *Journal of Consulting and Clinical Psychology* 51: 117–31.

Chapter 6

Depression
Treatment

Brendan P. Bradley

INTRODUCTION

Depression is one of the most common psychological conditions. Some studies suggest rates of major depressive disorder ranging from 2.2 to 3.5 per cent, and rates of dysthymia varying from 2.1 to 3.8 per cent (Myers *et al.*, 1984). Depression which does not meet full *DSM III–R* criteria is more common. It has been estimated that, at any one time, between 9 per cent and 20 per cent of the population has significant symptoms of depression (Boyd and Weissman, 1981). The latter study estimated that women are about twice as likely to experience clinical depression as men.

A number of psychological approaches to the treatment of depression have been used but it is only in the last two decades that controlled evaluations comparing these different approaches have been carried out. Current treatments for depression include both physical and psychological means. The former include the use of anti-depressant medication (such as tricyclics, monoamine oxidase inhibitors [MAOIs], lithium carbonate); electroconvulsive therapy (ECT); and, for patients whose depression is severe enough and resistant to other approaches, modified narcosis with ECT, or even psychosurgery (Kelly, 1982). Non-physical approaches have also been diverse, including behavioural methods (for example, progressive muscular relaxation, flooding, contingency contracting, increasing participation in pleasant activities, social-skills training, behavioural marital therapy); cognitive methods (Beck's Cognitive Therapy, Ellis's Rational Emotive Therapy, problem-solving, covert conditioning); and approaches such as exercise, Interpersonal Therapy and helplessness reduction. In some studies, cognitive, behavioural and pharmacological approaches have all been used, and such treatments have been administered individually or in groups. Recipients of these treatments for depression have ranged from volunteer college students to in-patient, severe, retarded depressives.

In this chapter, extreme selectivity is necessary given the variety of psychological therapies for depression. Many of the approaches mentioned above have produced favourable outcomes in single-case reports. However, one should be wary of this method, especially in the treatment of depression, because by its very nature depression is an intermittent condition (Clayton, 1984), and an episode often lasts for a few months, being followed by a period of normal mood. Therefore controlled studies, where treatments are compared with each other and with a waiting list condition, are especially valuable in allowing a proper evaluation of relative effectiveness.

THE PLACE OF PSYCHOLOGICAL METHODS IN THE TREATMENT OF DEPRESSION

Psychological treatments of depression are time-consuming and expensive compared to pharmacological treatments and electroconvulsive therapy (ECT). Why, then, should psychological treatments be used? One reason for examining psychological approaches is that pharmacological treatments, while commonly producing marked reductions in symptomatology, often leave patients well above normative levels for non-depressed subjects on measures of depression (McLean and Hakstian, 1979). Furthermore, the generality of improvement across the various components of depression (self-reported mood, somatic symptoms and behaviour) is unclear (Hollon, 1981). Some patients respond over more variables than others but these differences are difficult to predict (Rogers and Clay, 1975). Moreover, not all patients can be treated by drugs. Pregnant women, patients with severe physical disorders and many older patients often cannot be treated with the appropriate anti-depressants at adequate dosages.

Side effects of pharmacological treatments can be distressing enough for patients to discontinue treatment, and Hollon (1981) reports drop-out rates ranging from 20 to 50 per cent, adding that estimates of drug-response may be inflated by proportionately more non-responders dropping out of the trials. Maintenance of treatment gains can be problematic; depression commonly recurs and therefore pharmacological approaches have been used for long periods for maintenance (Davis, 1976; Schon, 1976). The hazards of such chronic use are not well documented. Tricyclic anti-depressants are a major problem in overdose and even a week's full dose can be lethal (Lader and Herrington, 1990).

ECT is typically given to severely depressed in-patients and very high rates of improvement are reported (Lehmann, 1977). But these high rates refer to the proportions of patients showing some degree of improvement: the magnitude of such improvement may differ widely. There is no indication that ECT has a prophylactic effect and fears about its safety are common, limiting its acceptability to patients and, occasionally, care staff.

Traditional psychodynamic treatments are generally time-consuming and expensive compared to cognitive-behavioural approaches and have not been shown to be effective when compared with non-specific controls or with pharmacological or somatic treatments (Hollon and Beck, 1978; 1979). An exception is Weissman's Interpersonal Psychotherapy which appears to have a therapeutic effect specific to depression and social functioning (Weissman *et al.*, 1979; Elkin *et al.*, 1989). Moreover, Shapiro *et al.* (1990) report preliminary positive results for a form of exploratory relationship-orientated therapy. As Williams (1984) has pointed out, these approaches may share a number of techniques with cognitive- behavioural approaches.

It is clear that while considerable progress has been made in the treatment of depression by pharmacological means and ECT, there are drawbacks and thus the application of psychological approaches is welcome. Behavioural and cognitive treatments have received most research attention in recent years, and a general conclusion is that those treatments which combine both approaches perform better than those which confine themselves purely to behavioural or to cognitive techniques alone (Taylor and Marshall, 1977). The most comprehensively re-searched cognitive-behavioural treatment is Cognitive Therapy (CT; Beck *et al.*, 1979b) and, with rare exceptions, its effectiveness in the treatment of, and prevention of relapse in, unipolar non-psychotic depression is substantial. There are more consistent positive results reported for this treatment, from more centres and from more countries, than for other psychological treatments and hence this is the treatment on which I concentrate here.

EFFECTIVENESS OF COGNITIVE-BEHAVIOURAL THERAPY

In one of the most comprehensive reviews in this field, Dobson (1989) examined twenty-eight outcome studies and concluded that Beck's Cognitive Therapy seems to be more effective than behaviour therapy or pharmacotherapy (and more effective than a no-treatment condition) in the treatment of clinical de-pression. He also concluded that it is superior to other forms of psychotherapy in the treatment of depression, although admitting that further comparisons are required before drawing closure on this issue. In the studies examined, the average cognitive therapy patient did better than 98 per cent of the no-treatment controls, 67 per cent of the behaviour therapy clients, 70 per cent of anti-depressant drug clients, and 70 per cent of the other psychotherapy clients. CT was equally effective for men and women.

Hollon *et al.* (1991) in their review agree that CT is a promising alternative to pharmacotherapy and indicate (a) that there is evidence that CT is comparable to tricyclic pharmacotherapy in the treatment of the acute episode, (b) with some exceptions combined CT and pharmacotherapy does not appear superior to either modality alone, and (c) CT during the acute episode may protect against relapse. They are justifiably more guarded in their conclusions than Dobson and point out that these conclusions can only be considered as suggestive because of limita-tions in study design and execution.

Results from a large scale NIMH study (Elkin *et al.*, 1989) are somewhat less positive concerning initial treatment efficacy than Dobson's conclusions would suggest, although fewer CT patients required treatment over the one-year follow-up (Shea *et al.*, 1992). Elkin *et al.* (1989) randomly assigned 250 out-patients with Major Depressive Disorder to four treatments, namely, Cognitive-Behavioural Therapy (CBT); Interpersonal Therapy (IPT, a short-term psychoanalytically orientated approach; Klerman *et al.*, 1979); imipramine + clinical management; and placebo + clinical management. In the overall analysis, at termination of treatment there were few significant differences in effectiveness among the four treatments, but what differences there were suggested that imipramine together with clinical management did best, the two psychotherapies came next and were very close in effectiveness, while placebo together with clinical management came last. For the more severely depressed and impaired, Interpersonal Therapy and imipramine with clinical management seemed more effective. It should be noted that there has been some discussion concerning how effective the supervision was for the cognitive therapists in the latter trial (Hollon and Najavits, 1988).

Another recent study supports the view that some short-term psychotherapies not derived from a behavioural or cognitive tradition may be helpful for depression. Shapiro *et al.* (1990) found that exploratory (relationship-orientated) therapy was equivalent in effectiveness to CT in terms of depression symptoms but that the exploratory therapy seemed to give a better outcome with interpersonal difficulties. These findings are intriguing but should not divert us from recognising that on balance there is much more support from controlled, carefully conducted studies for the efficacy of CT for depression than for any other psychotherapeutic approach.

The combination of CT and pharmacotherapy has been used in a number of studies. Hollon *et al.* (1991) review these and conclude that CT alone provides as much protection against relapse as the combination. The relapse-prevention aspect of CT is supported by a number of studies (Kovacs *et al.*, 1981; Blackburn *et al.*, 1986; Simons *et al.*, 1986; Hollon *et al.*, 1991; Shea *et al.*, 1992). There is some suggestion that the combination may be better than pharmacotherapy alone for severe in-patient depression in a study by Bowers (1990). Furthermore, Miller *et al.* (1989) found that cognitive therapy and cognitive-behaviourally orientated social skills training each improved the outcome of depressed in-patients who received standard treatment consisting of pharmacotherapy, clinical management sessions and hospital milieu therapy. Moreover there was a lower rate of relapse over the one-year follow-up period in the CBT groups.

Both CT and pharmacotherapy appear to produce similar cognitive changes in that negative thoughts and attitudes become less negative as mood improves, irrespective of the type of treatment (Simons *et al.*, 1984b; Zeiss *et al.*, 1979; Imber *et al.*, 1990). However, while such cognitive change predicts improvement in the later sessions of CT, it does not seem to predict improvement when drug treatment is used (DeRubeis *et al.*, 1990), suggesting that cognitions may play a mediating role during the course of CT, but that they may not have such a role during drug treatment. While the processes of change differ between these two treatments, both may be employed together without apparent detriment (Hollon *et al.*, 1991). Moreover, the results of De Rubeis *et al.* (1990) suggest that, since tricyclic anti-depressant drugs and CT both alter cognitions, the use of drugs may be considered not only as a treatment in itself, but also in conjunction with CT, in cases where difficulties are encountered in challenging negative cognitions. Hollon *et al.* (1991) found some suggestion of potential enhancement of treatment effects when the two treatments were combined, although more systematic study of this possibility is warranted.

Barber and DeRubeis (1989) consider three possible mechanisms underlying CT's effectiveness. First, CT may alter basic negative schemata, but there is little evidence of this, since changes in cognition are not unique to CT. A second possibility is that negative schemata are de-activated while adaptive schemata are activated. This may indeed underlie the effectiveness of pharmacotherapy but it would not readily explain why CT is effective in preventing relapse. Barber and DeRubeis favour the third mechanism which holds that CT provides a set of 'compensatory skills' which can be used to deal with depressive cognitions when they occur. They allow the possibility that, with repeated practice, schema change may occur but regard this as unlikely within the typical course of short-term cognitive therapy.

Returning to the issue of cost-effectiveness of psychological treatment, it has been acknowledged that such treatment generally requires more therapist contact time than is required by drug therapy. However, the evidence that CT reduces the risk of relapse, compared to drug treatment given in the acute phase, suggests that CT is more effective and may lead to less therapist time in the long run. Moreover, there is evidence that the saving for drug treatment in therapist contact time necessary for symptom remission may be much more modest than one might expect. Freeman's work (cited by Williams, 1992) suggests that while drug therapy took on average 11 hours before remission occurred, CT took 14.6 hours and dynamic counselling took 20.9 hours. Therefore the advantage for drug treatment was only 3.6 hours, a benefit which could be eliminated in one relapse episode. Readers interested in a more detailed discussion of differential effectiveness and relapse should consult Williams (1992).

Beck's Cognitive Therapy – overview

Beck's theory of depression claims that depressed affect results from negative thoughts and negatively biased perception. He claims that depressed individuals are typically pessimistic in outlook, and show negative distortions in their interpretations of experience, whether past or present. Beck (1976) has outlined various types of distorted processes, such as overgeneralisation (for example, on making a mistake the depressed individual thinks, 'I always get it wrong'); selective abstraction (for example, attending to negative aspects of experiences); magnification and minimisation (for example, exaggerating negative and underplaying positive qualities); dichotomous reasoning or thinking in all-or-nothing terms (for example, 'If I lose him I might as well be dead').

Beck has used a schema or cognitive structure concept to explain this wide array of negative distortions. When a person is depressed, negative schemata are activated and they govern the processing of information. Beck regards depressed individuals' negative outlook as encompassing the self, their world and their future. These constitute the negative cognitive triad. The self is regarded as defective or inadequate in a psychological, moral or physical sense, and unpleasant experiences tend to be attributed to this defect. Experiences are interpreted in a negative way. Life is seen as making extreme demands and interactions with the environment are interpreted as representing defeat or deprivation. The depressed person's view of the future leads to negative expectations and failure is anticipated. Beck sees this as an explanation of the reduced motivation that commonly accompanies depression. Given that depressed people expect unpleasant outcomes from their actions, the characteristic inactivity and inertia seem understandable. The empirical support for Beck's theory of depression has been reviewed by Haaga *et al.* (1991) who conclude that, during a depressed episode, people show evidence of cognitive distortion, although there is little evidence in favour of cognitive vulnerability when they are free of depression.

Beck's Cognitive Therapy (Beck *et al.*, 1979b) is a treatment package derived from this theory, the aims of which are to identify and challenge negative thoughts, to develop alternative more accurate and adaptive thoughts, and to promote cognitive and behavioural responses based on these adaptive thoughts. The relationship between therapist and patient is stressed. Empathy, that is, where the therapist understands how the patient feels and communicates this to the patient, is seen as important in applying the therapy, as are genuineness and an attitude of concern for the patient's well-being. The approach embodies a significant educational component in which patients are introduced to the idea that negative thoughts are of critical importance in depression, and ways of changing these thoughts are illustrated. Patients are encouraged to see therapy as a joint venture where both therapist and patient define target problems which are to be dealt with during the course of therapy. These might include depressive symptoms themselves, such as difficulty in concentration, or external problems such as relationship difficulties. When agreement is reached on the main problems, a priority for tackling these is set, taking into account both how important they are to the patient and how amenable to change they seem to be. An agenda of items is set at the beginning of each session, covering the points to be discussed within that session. Patients' reactions to the therapist's intervention are carefully monitored so that potentially negative views may be discussed and answered. A look-out is kept for indications of misunderstanding or of negative reactions such as failure to record negative thoughts, since some patients appear to be compliant while silently disagreeing with what they are being asked to do. Cognitive therapy is a short-term treatment and the average length of therapy is generally less than fifteen weeks. In fact, as discussed later, Fennell and Teasdale (1987) found that most treatment response in straightforward cases occurred in the first few sessions. This information may be used in order to decide whether a patient is suitable for CT. A trial of up to five sessions may be used in order to establish whether improvement is shown. Of course it is necessary for the patient to be told in advance of the trial period.

The course of Beck's Cognitive Therapy – early sessions

The therapist's goals at the beginning are: (1) assessment; (2) socialising the patient into the cognitive model; and (3) dealing with the patient's pessimism about treatment and in general (DeRubeis and Beck, 1988). Specific problems are identified, depression is measured by the BDI or other instruments (see Rippere, Chapter 5), and background information concerning the patient's life is obtained. The presence of suicidal wishes is ascertained. Priorities are then set as to which problems are to be dealt with first. This is normally done on the basis of how important and how easily altered the difficulty seems to be, how active the patient is and how much pleasure is obtained from such activity. Patients are introduced to the idea of the influence of thoughts on feelings. They are asked to try to remember what thoughts occurred during a recent episode of low mood. Did these thoughts produce unhappiness or do they now have that effect on recalling them? These negative thoughts may be contrasted with thoughts associated with a time when the patient has felt happier.

The relationship and distinction between thoughts and feelings can be illustrated by the therapist. A common example consists in asking what thoughts and feelings would result if in the middle of the night whilst sleeping in an unfamiliar house, the patient heard the crash of breaking glass. Feelings of alarm and fear, and the thought of a burglary might be elicited. The therapist could then ask the patient to question that thought and think of alternative explanations, such as, 'Maybe the cat has knocked something over'. What would the patient then feel – relief? The booklet *Coping with Depression* by Beck and Greenberg (1974) can be very helpful in providing background information and helpful hints about the treatment, as can the book *Feeling Good* by Burns (1980).

Patients would be assisted in challenging one of their own negative thoughts by obtaining a disconfirming piece of evidence or by revealing the distorted quality of the negative thoughts. Thus, the therapist would demonstrate that such automatic, negative and distressing thoughts need not be accepted as true and that they can be controlled.

Patients are next shown how to list their thoughts on a record sheet as they happen, noting the situations where they occur and the emotions which accompany them (anger, frustration, despair, and so on). Patients are usually asked as a homework exercise to complete such a list daily on a prepared form. It is important at this stage to ensure that the patient can distinquish clearly between thoughts and feelings. Once this has been accomplished successfully the intensity of such symptoms and the strength of belief in the validity of the thoughts are recorded. Challenges to those thoughts and the corresponding changes in feelings and beliefs are also noted on the record (Table 6.1).

If the initial investigation has shown that the patient is inactive, perhaps spending many hours lying in bed passively or watching TV, it would be more appropriate to introduce an activity schedule first. Simple activities which the patient should find rewarding but not very demanding would be identified.

Clients may claim that they do nothing or derive no enjoyment from daily activities and so recording of those activities and ratings of accomplishment and pleasure (an activity schedule) can provide an important test of this hypothesis which often turns out to be false. The patient is seen twice weekly or even more frequently at first if very distressed.

Structure within sessions

At the beginning of each session, patients complete the BDI or a similar scale and both therapist and patient jointly set the agenda. Homework exercises, any serious difficulties which have emerged since the previous session and thoughts about that session (feedback) are discussed. When a list of items has been compiled, patient and therapist agree on the order of dealing with the items and on whether all the items can be dealt with adequately during the session. If, however, patients desire to talk about other matters which they see as important, the therapist should be flexible in imposing the structure outlined above. This flexibility is necessary to preserve a constructive relationship.

Data which the patient provides in the activity schedule and recording of negative thoughts will help to identify other interventions that may be needed, such as assertiveness training, social skills training, marital therapy, graduated exposure for a phobia, and so on.

Challenging negative automatic thoughts

Central to cognitive therapy is the identification and challenging of negative thoughts. Such thoughts occur automatically and embody a number of distortions. They can be challenged by identifying and avoiding these distortions, by trying to determine whether there really is any evidence to support the negative thoughts, by gathering evidence to contradict them, and by trying to see what action could be taken to test the validity of the thoughts or to change the situation. For example, if the negative thought were 'I am useless at everything', the patient could be encouraged to recall specific success experiences, and a homework task could be devised where the depressed individual predicts failure but where past performance suggests that success is likely.

A further tactic involves the alteration of attributions for unpleasant events. For example, a depressed patient did not get the job she wanted. She interpreted this to mean that she was not good enough. The therapist encouraged her to formulate other possibilities, such as, 'There were fifteen applicants for this job', or 'I was over-qualified for it', or 'I had not got the right experience'. It may be helpful to give the patient a list of guidelines on challenging negative thoughts (such as that shown in Table 6.2). Examples of such ways of challenging negative thoughts follow.

Table 6.1 Example of recording alternative thoughts

Date	Emotion (0–100)	Situation	Negative thought (belief 0–100)	Alternative thought	Belief in negative thought Emotion What can you do now?
7 Dec	Depressed (70)	Arrived home from work	I didn't do a thing right today (90)	That's not true I made five phone calls and cleared my desk	(1) 50 (2) 40 (3) Plan to do one satisfying activity at work tomorrow
7 Dec	Fed up (80)	Argument with husband	I'm always in the wrong (90)	We're both contributing to this/I don't usually argue	(1) 20 (2) 40 (3) We can sit down and discuss this issue when we're not tired

What is the evidence?

John, a 39-year-old actor, indicated that he was a 'has-been' who had no future on the stage. On being asked what evidence backed this up, he said that he had not received an offer of a job for the previous few weeks. Further discussion revealed that this was not uncommon among actors and, in any case, he had tended to avoid chasing up offers which had been made to him in the past, disliking the idea of 'selling himself'. Following the discussion, he realised that the evidence which he had used did not in fact support his original conclusion. When asked to provide evidence against his negative thoughts, John revealed that he had recently acted in a well-received play, he had broadened his acting style and had, a few months previously, been approached by two leading agents.

What are the alternatives?

John attributed his failure to receive any offer of work in the previous few weeks to an internal and stable factor, namely that he was a 'has-been'. But he was able to produce two alternatives which he regarded as plausible:

1 'Not receiving an offer of a job for a few weeks is relatively common in my business and this has happened to me and to others many times before and was always followed by work.'
2 'I fail to get work because I do not let people know that I want work.'

Jill, a 30-year-old secretary, believed that her work colleagues did not want to talk to her. She was unable to provide evidence of this and she generated the alternative thought that if she made more effort to talk to them, then they would be more friendly and would talk to her more. Her rating of strength of belief in this thought was 50 per cent and she agreed to subject her thoughts to a test. Initially in homework she noted what the other secretaries talked about. She found out that one of them, a woman she particularly wanted to get to know, was interested in tennis. In a therapy session she role-played what to say. At work she managed to choose an appropriate moment to say a few words. Her colleague smiled and followed up on Jill's remarks. The conversation lasted between five and ten minutes. Jill reported back that her belief in the alternative thought was now 90 per cent and her belief in the negative thought had reduced from 100 per cent to 30 per cent.

What is the effect of thinking the way I do?

John had already identified that one of his main difficulties was his tendency to procrastinate. He revealed that by dwelling on possible complications or draw-backs he tended to hold himself back from embarking on a course of action. His record of negative automatic thoughts illustrated how he did this. On being reminded by his wife that he should make an appointment with a dentist he thought, 'I'll do it later', 'I can't afford the dental fees anyway', and 'If I put it off I may be able to afford it later'.

What thinking error am I making?

Mary, a moderately depressed patient, learned to challenge her negative thoughts by noting the types of distortions which they exemplified. On being rejected for a job, her negative automatic thought was 'I'm just no good – I'll never get a job again'. She decided that her distortions were over-generalisation, arbitrary inference and catastrophising. She found this helpful in reminding herself that the thoughts did not describe the reality of the situation but tended to paint it blacker than it really was.

What action can I take?

John managed to answer his negative thoughts and proceeded to carry out the tasks he had put off for months. When he postponed his dental appointment, thinking, 'I'll do it later', he replied by writing down, 'I've been saying this for months now – I'm just fooling myself'. On thinking 'I can't afford dental treatment. If I wait a bit longer I might have enough money', he answered by writing, 'If I wait longer the dental problem may get worse. It's best to have it done now'. After writing down his alternative thoughts he picked up the telephone to ring the dentist and felt a considerable sense of achievement.

The downward arrow technique

Sometimes it is helpful not to assess the validity of a negative thought but instead to ask, 'Supposing that were true, what would that mean to me?' (Burns, 1980). Such a technique can help draw out an underlying more 'core' meaning of the negative interpretation, and expose a more fundamental underlying assumption which can then be challenged. For example, Tony felt defeated when a woman he spoke to at a garden party made her excuse and left. His thought was, 'she didn't want to talk to me, she doesn't find me interesting enough'. Instead of asking questions such as 'What is the evidence?' or 'What are the alternatives?', the therapist asked, 'If that were true, what would it mean to you?'. Tony indicated that it would mean that he was basically a boring person and that he would never form a satisfying relationship. This underlying assumption was then challenged by means of the methods outlined above.

Homework

It is important that homework is set to give the patient practice in challenging negative thoughts and in solving problems. Recording homework exercises, negative thoughts, alternative thoughts and mood states are key features of CT.

Table 6.2 Guidelines on challenging negative thoughts

Looking for rational answers

1 *What is the evidence?*
   What evidence do I have to support my thoughts?
   What evidence do I have against them?
2 *What alternative views are there?*
   How would someone else view this situation?
   How would I have viewed it before I got depressed?
   What evidence do I have to back these alternatives?
3 *What is the effect of thinking the way I do?*
   Does it help me, or hinder me from getting what I want? How?
   What would be the effect of looking at things less negatively?
4 *What thinking error am I making?*
   Am I thinking in all-or-nothing terms?
   Am I condemning myself as a total person on the basis of a single event?
   Am I concentrating on my weaknesses and forgetting my strengths?
   Am I blaming myself for something which is not my fault?
   Am I taking something personally which was little or nothing to do with me?
   Am I expecting myself to be perfect?
   Am I using a double standard – how would I view someone else in my
      situation?
   Am I paying attention only to the black side of things?
   Am I overestimating the chances of disaster?
   Am I exaggerating the importance of events?
   Am I fretting about the way things ought to be instead of accepting and
      dealing with them as they come?
   Am I assuming I can do nothing to change my situation?
   Am I predicting the future instead of experimenting with it?
5 *What action can I take?*
   What can I do to change my situation?
   Am I overlooking solutions to problems on the assumption they won't work?
   What can I do to test the validity of my rational answers?

Source: Adapted by M. Fennell (unpublished) from Emery (1981) and reproduced here
with permission from M. Fennell gratefully acknowledged

Treatment in later sessions

As treatment progresses, the same structure is used. However, as the patient
becomes less depressed, certain techniques become less likely to be used, for
example, scheduling activities in order to counteract inactivity and listlessness.
In addition, more general issues or maladaptive assumptions may emerge. These

are similar to Ellis's 'irrational beliefs' and consist of general attitudes or beliefs which often incorporate perfectionistic or dependent ways of interacting or reacting to circumstances. One such assumption might be: 'I should be liked by everyone I meet'. Another is: 'I must always do things perfectly'. The therapist may question the patient in an attempt to show contradictions or problems resulting from such assumptions. Advantages and disadvantages of changing an assumption may be elicited, and discussion of these may help the patient to change his or her viewpoint.

Behavioural techniques within cognitive therapy

The use of homework exercises has already been referred to in connection with testing the accuracy or usefulness of negative thoughts or assumptions. This is a key use of behavioural prescriptions – to help modify maladaptive cognitions. However, in the early stages of therapy they may be used in order to counteract the inactivity and social withdrawal of severely depressed patients. Indeed a behavioural, activity-orientated intervention at the beginning of therapy was particularly helpful with severe and chronic depressives (de Jong *et al.*, 1986). Some particularly useful techniques are briefly described below.

Graded task assignments

Where patients experience difficulty in carrying out tasks, these may have to be broken up into component parts and only the simplest parts undertaken first. For example, a patient who avoided cleaning her flat but instead got her sister to do it was asked to outline the various tasks and rooms involved. She revealed that, when she thought of the cleaning, she thought of all the tasks that needed to be done, such as dusting the furniture in four rooms, vacuum-cleaning all the floor area, washing the paintwork on the stairs, and so on. Probing revealed that the living area was seen as in most urgent need of cleaning and that, at the most, ten minutes of vacuum-cleaning would be adequate, and so this was then set as the task to be done first. By this sort of simplification, depressed patients can be helped to take on tasks which had seemed overwhelming and impossible for them. Participating in activities may also help in distracting patients from depressive ruminations.

Activity scheduling

Some patients complain of doing very little and experiencing no sense of accomplishment or pleasure in everyday life. An activity schedule, where activities are recorded each hour of the day can help give a clear idea of exactly how time is spent. Patients may be asked to rate their sense of accomplishment and pleasure after each activity. This may reveal that the picture is not as bleak as the patient recalls in retrospect; alternatively it can help in indicating which activities may be increased in frequency – in particular those associated with mastery or pleasure; or it may indicate problems which can be tackled in therapy. Scheduling activities can increase the chance of patients engaging in an activity that they have been avoiding and it removes decision-making as an obstacle in initiating action (DeRubeis and Beck, 1988). An increase in activity level often produces an improvement in mood. Useful activities are often ones which occupy the mind, involve exertion or exercise, are potentially enjoyable, or are seen as 'worthwhile' (Freeman *et al.*, 1990). Activities to be scheduled can be: (1) those associated with good mood, mastery or pleasure as shown by the activity schedule, (2) those which have been rewarding in the past but which are now being avoided, and (3) new activities which both therapist and patient agree may be rewarding or informative (DeRubeis and Beck, 1988).

Behavioural experiments

An effective way of getting cognitive change consists in obtaining evidence from personal experience which is incompatible with the target thought. Patients are encouraged to formulate and carry out behavioural tests of their thoughts. Some examples of this are given above.

In-vivo exposure

Anxiety states often co-exist with depression and graduated exposure to the feared situation is particularly advisable to deal with phobic anxiety states, such as specific phobias, agoraphobia or social phobia (see Chapter 8).

Role-playing

Role-playing may be used to practise new behaviours as in social skills training. In addition, it may aid assessment of cognitions occurring in patients' social situations. It may also be used to practise cognitive coping-strategies for dealing with social interactions. The patient may be asked to imagine the sequence of steps involved in carrying out a task in order to reveal problems which may impede success in completing the task. Furthermore, it may help in preparing the patient to achieve the task, to take him or her through the planning stage. This would mean that the patient could then simply execute the plan rather than having to generate and execute it at the same time.

Distraction

Distraction can be used at times when unpleasant thoughts become prominent. It may be particularly appropriate early on in therapy before patients have learned to challenge effectively their negative thoughts. Distraction involves carrying out some activity which directs attention away from the unpleasant feelings; for example, work, exercise, or some cognitive strategy such as imagining or recalling a success experience.

Social skills training and assertiveness training

Many depressed individuals have real difficulties in these areas, and they complain of loneliness and social isolation. It is helpful to assess whether the difficulties pre-date the depressed episode or whether they covary with depression. Learning how to make social contact, starting and maintaining conversations, not dwelling on one's own problems, and being a good listener are important in developing and maintaining friendships. See Spence (Chapters 11 and 12) for further accounts of this approach.

Marital interventions

There is evidence (O'Leary and Beach, 1990) that, where there are marital problems and one partner is depressed, behavioural marital therapy may be worth implementing first since it can improve both marital satisfaction and depression, whereas the cognitive-behavioural therapy used in the quoted study helped only the depression.

Therapist's competence

The Cognitive Therapy Scale (CTS; Young and Beck, 1980) is a measure of therapist's competence and may be used to summarise requirements for good cognitive therapy. Freeman *et al.* (1990) include a revised CTS in the appendix to their book. The scale was developed for use in the training and evaluation of cognitive therapists. It gives guidelines for rating the following items: agenda-setting (appropriate target problems suitable for discussion in the time available); feedback to determine how well the patient understood and was satisfied with the session; understanding of what the patient says and feels, and communication of this understanding to the patient; interpersonal skills; collaboration in which the therapist encourages the patient to take an active part in the session; and efficient use of time in the session.

The CTS also contains items referring to 'guided discovery' where the therapist, rather than lecturing the patient, encourages him or her to challenge negative thoughts and provide solutions, focusing on crucial cognitions so that the therapist and patient identify thoughts or 'key cognitions' which are principally responsible for the level of reported distress. For example, if a patient describes being intensely unhappy after a quarrel with his wife and attributes this to the thought that he doesn't like losing an argument, the therapist might ask how that should make him so unhappy. This may lead to a realisation that the underlying thought is that their marriage is really over. Other considerations for effective therapy include the therapist's demonstration of a coherent strategy within and between sessions for changing the patient's behaviour.

The psychometric properties of the CTS have been evaluated by Dobson *et al.*, (1985) who found it to be homogeneous, with high item-total correlations and good inter-rater reliability for total scores. The latter finding was corroborated by Williams *et al.*, (1991). Only total scores are recommended for use in prediction of therapeutic outcome.

Two other related scales should be mentioned. The Collaborative Study Psychotherapy Rating Scale (CSPRS; Hollon *et al.*, 1985) was devised to distinguish objectively sessions of CT from those of other forms of therapy. Another scale was devised by Luborsky *et al.*, (1982) to measure therapists' adherence to the 'core characteristics' of cognitive therapy (as well as measuring characteristics of other therapies). This scale has predicted good outcome (Luborsky *et al.*, 1985).

Problems in carrying out cognitive therapy

The principles of CT are simple and clear but carrying out CT can be complex and difficulties commonly arise. The therapist and the patient should identify specific points where problems arise, such as not doing homework assignments, or interventions which do not work or which backfire. Freeman *et al.* (1990) discuss a number of commonly experienced stumbling blocks:

Lack of collaboration   Difficulties are unlikely here if there is a good working relationship, if the homework relates clearly to mutually agreed goals, and if both therapist and patient have jointly developed the assignment. With unassertive patients in particular, the therapist should actively seek their views in setting the agenda, determining the therapeutic focus, and developing homework assignments. It is clearly important to ensure that the patient understands what is expected and to this end therapists should encourage patients to question, give feedback, and to raise concerns.

Anticipation of failure   A patient's prediction of failure can prevent the completion of homework assignments. Tasks must be chosen which are within the patient's current capability, making sure that the instructions are understood, and encouraging an objective view of the likelihood and probable consequences of failure. It will generally be necessary to alter the assignment if failure seems likely or if its consequences are serious. Therapists should respond to noncompliance without being punitive but instead work with the patient to understand the causes. Perfectionistic patients often anticipate extreme reactions if the assignments are not carried out perfectly. It can be very useful to present homework as a 'no-lose' situation, where if the assignment is successful then all well and good, but if it is not then it is possible to discover a previously unrecognised aspect of the depression which should help future progress.

Patient's lack of skill   Some assignments, such as establishing social contact, tackling a financial problem, or dealing with a difficult work colleague, may require a series of skilled performances where the patient may be deficient. Role-playing, instruction and rehearsal may all be necessary in order that the patient develops the necessary skill to perform the task.

Lack of motivation   Severely depressed patients often require scheduling of activities together with self-motivational training and graded task assignment. Self-motivational training involves establishing clear goals and identifying a course of action which results in attaining them. Sometimes fears about the consequences of their actions or indirectly expressed resentment can result in reduced motivation.

Anti-depressant medication can help in mobilising patients to overcome torpor and lethargy and may even help to bring about cognitive changes.

Trying to make progress too quickly   Therapists who push too much may find that the patient fails to attend, is reluctant to comply with assignments, or the collaborative relationship is impaired. Patients themselves may be in too much of a rush to get better. One guideline suggested by Freeman *et al.* (1990) is the patient's level of anxiety while discussing or doing the homework task. If patients feel entirely comfortable, the task is probably too easy; if they feel very anxious, it could be too difficult.

Concerns about the consequences of change   For example, some patients may fear that if they reduce their perfectionistic standards, they will become mediocre or will fail.

External barriers to change   Sometimes barriers to change reflect problems which had been overlooked in the initial assessment session, such as drug or alcohol abuse, or chronic personality problems.

Therapist's blind spots   Where the patient's problem reveals dysfunctional attitudes which are shared by the therapist there are often difficulties in making progress. Sometimes the therapist's own emotional reactions of frustration with slow progress, irritation at the patient, or guilt about not helping the patient more can be problematic. Some acknowledgement of one's own limitations is helpful as is a recognition that lack of progress is often neither the therapist's nor the patient's fault. Consultation with an experienced and trusted colleague may be warranted.

Training in cognitive therapy

As indicated above, the practice of cognitive therapy is not always straightforward and the availability of systematic training is quite limited. Those who wish to practice this method should select from the introductory readings noted here, review the many videotapes or audiotapes now available, and attend workshops or seminars run by established and experienced practitioners. Personal or group supervision by an experienced cognitive therapist is recommended. Peer supervision groups of qualified professionals who are interested in cognitive therapy may be very valuable. In the UK there are at least four centres, in London at the Institute of Psychiatry and at Goldsmiths' College, in Oxford at the Warneford Hospital and in Newcastle, where training courses are run. Throughout the USA there are a number of cognitive therapy centres affiliated with Beck's Center for Cognitive Therapy at the University of Philadelphia.

Predictors of response to cognitive therapy

Patient factors

Fennell and Teasdale (1987) found marked differences among patients in responsiveness to CBT within two weeks of entering treatment, and this strongly predicted post-treatment outcome. More complete and fast improvement appeared to occur in those who showed 'depression about depression', that is, where the negative ruminations concerned symptoms of depression. For example, some depressed patients interpret their lack of energy and initiative, and poor work performance as evidence that they are lazy, stupid or incompetent. Reading the booklet *Coping with Depression* (Beck and Greenberg, 1974) can help patients realise that their disturbing feelings are common symptoms of depression, rather than signs of personal inadequacy, that depression can be understood in terms of negative thinking, and that it can be controlled by using logical and clearly specified strategies. Indeed those who responded rapidly felt that the description of the cognitive model, as outlined in *Coping with Depression*, was especially relevant to their problems. Moreover, those who improved rapidly also responded positively to initial homework assignments. The latter finding was supported by Persons et al. (1988), who found that those who carried out homework improved by 16.6 BDI points while those who did not improved by only 2.4 points. The importance of homework was particularly marked for those whose initial BDI scores were greater than 20. The beneficial role of homework is further supported by Neimeyer and Feixas (1990), who found that those depressives who were assigned to a homework condition showed a better response than those who were not required to do homework, at the end of the treatment phase. Interestingly, at six-month follow-up the homework condition made no difference, but those who had mastered the cognitive restructuring technique did best. Dysfunctional cognitions, as assessed by the Attributional Style Questionnaire, the Dysfunctional Attitude Scale and the Hopelessness Scale, appear to play a mediational role in CT in that changes in these scales predict later improvement in CT. They do not appear simply to reflect symptomatic improvement because such cognitive changes do not predict improvement in a group treated with pharmacotherapy (DeRubeis et al., 1990).

Drop-out from treatment was studied by Persons et al. (1988) who found that

50 per cent of their patients dropped out of treatment, a higher rate than generally found in controlled outcome studies, although this was a private patient sample in the USA who had not been screened to exclude alcoholism, drug abuse or borderline conditions. The drop-outs were more likely to have personality disorders, less education, no endogenous symptoms, and high initial BDI scores. Simons *et al.* (1984a) found that drop-outs had been slower responders to therapy in comparison with those who remained in treatment.

Hollon has formulated a Global Chronicity/Severity Index (cited in Fennell and Teasdale, 1982) which identifies seven critical depression characteristics:

1 Severity on the Beck Depression Inventory (BDI) > 30
2 Duration of current episode > 6 months
3 Poor prior treatment response
4 More than one previous episode
5 The presence of psychopathology other than depression
6 Overall impairment estimated as moderate or severe
7 Poor estimated tolerance for life stress

Scores on four or more items predict a poor response to treatment. Fennell and Teasdale (1982) provide results consistent with Hollon's claims. Zeiss and Jones (1983) discuss some similar predictors and add that 'entrenchment in potent and dysfunctional environmental systems' seems to be a cause of failure. Rush and Shaw (1983) extend the discussion and consider patient motivation, ability level, underlying medical disorders, unresponsive depressive disorders, social system forces, and technical problems in applying cognitive-behavioural therapy as causes of failure. See also Scott (1992) who developed CT to deal with difficult and chronic cases. This approach is outlined later.

Therapist factors

Therapists who encourage their patients to be problem-focused, to examine their beliefs, and to undertake straightforward focused homework tasks between sessions, who attempt to promote symptom relief and to teach patients ways of controlling their own symptoms had better results than therapists who were less specific in their intervention approach (DeRubeis and Feeley, 1990). Facilitative conditions (empathy, warmth, genuineness) were not significantly related to outcome nor did the quality of the therapist–patient relationship predict change, suggesting that technical factors are very important in cognitive therapy. Therapists' empathy, warmth and congruence did not predict response over six treatment sessions in a study by Beckham (1989). However, it would seem unwise to conclude that therapists' setting conditions are unimportant. Rather, most therapists in these studies may have provided adequate levels of these factors. Certain minimum levels of facilitative conditions and of the quality of the relationship seem necessary for patients to reveal their problems and to persist with therapy. While this latter conclusion would probably be accepted by many contemporary cognitive-behavioural therapists, there is some further intriguing evidence that a relationship with a therapist may be unnecessary, at least for volunteer patients. Selmi *et al.* (1990) found a six-session interactive computer-administered CBT was as effective for volunteer patients as therapist-administered CBT at the end of treatment and at two months follow-up, and both conditions were superior to waiting list control.

The delivery of effective treatment

Given the widespread extent of depression and the limited number of therapists trained to deal with the problem, how can effective therapy be made more widely available? CT training is now more widespread than only a few years ago, particularly in the USA, and this trend is to be encouraged. In addition to greater numbers of therapists it is clearly desirable to have more efficient delivery of treatment. This would involve therapists being more selective, and taking on only those who are likely to respond, or terminating treatment when it is clear that a favourable response is unlikely.

Psychiatrists and general practitioners tend to favour medication for patients with biological signs of depression (such as sleep and appetite disturbance, etc.) and many refer depressed patients with personal problems without biological signs to psychologists. However, there seems to be little objective support for both these practices. Joyce and Paykel (1989) found no evidence that the presence of endogenous symptoms predicted response to drug treatment. Moreover, such symptoms do not seem to predict response to CT (Blackburn *et al.*, 1981; Kovacs *et al.*, 1981; and Beck *et al.*, 1985). It should be noted that the latter studies, like most studies using CT, used out-patients and excluded those suffering from delusions or hallucinations. Moreover, a specific biological marker of depression, namely, sleep disturbance measured by EEG, also failed to predict response to CT (Simons and Thase, 1992). Despite clinical lore about which types of depressed patients respond to which treatments, there is little reliable data on which to base recommendations. While interactions have been found between pre-treatment patient factors and treatment type, there are few replicated findings.

The use of group treatment obviously allows a therapist to reach more patients but further research into effectiveness appears necessary, with existing studies being inconsistent as to how effective group approaches are, compared to individual therapy (e.g. Nietzel *et al.*, 1987; Robinson *et al.*, 1990). See the section below on group treatment for a further brief discussion. Written material is often used within individual CT, and bibliotherapy with minimal support from therapists has been used sucessfully by Scogin and colleagues for elderly individuals suffering from mild to moderate depression (Scogin *et al.*, 1987; Scogin *et al.*, 1989). In the latter study both a cognitive- and a behaviourally-orientated approach were equally effective. Some caveats should be mentioned. Bibliotherapy relies on a certain level of concentration, reading ability and motivation towards a self-help approach. The more educated clients seemed to find it more useful.

Scogin and colleagues recommend at least minimal contact between therapist and client. Programmes which are completely self-administered are not recommended for ethical and practical reasons.

Research may help in identifying effective ingredients of successful therapy so that simplified versions of psychological treatments may be devised. This holds out the promise of shorter treatments and of methods which may be taught more widely to other health professionals, given the scarcity of clinical psychologists.

New developments in cognitive therapy

A number of developments of CT are indicated which generally require further evaluative work before acceptance but they are included here because they suggest promising avenues for development.

Depression about depression

Individual case studies by Fennell, Teasdale and colleagues (cited by Fennell and Teasdale, 1987) suggest that some patients who are highly motivated to work independently and able to form a collaborative therapeutic relationship may benefit from a much shorter CT package than the maximum of twenty sessions commonly offered. Their work would suggest that those who show 'depression about depression', that is, those whose focus of concern surrounds the symptoms of depression themselves (apathy, problems in concentration, sleep disruption, temporarily impaired problem-solving ability, crying spells, etc.) would be most likely to benefit from such a short treatment. Fennell and Teasdale (1987) stress that it is important not to ignore underlying factors such as chronic environmental stressors or dysfunctional underlying assumptions in providing such a brief treatment. Nevertheless they suggest that it may be advisable to offer initially, say, five sessions, given that the therapy is not appropriate for all patients. Where rapid response was noted, say, on the BDI, five sessions might be enough. Where a limited degree of improvement was noted, the full twenty sessions might be warranted, or the techniques suggested by Young (1989) might be employed (see p. 132). Young's approach might also suit those who do not respond within five sessions.

Group cognitive therapy

There is some recent evidence that cognitive therapy (in addition to treatment as usual) conducted in groups with a community sample can be as effective as individual work (Scott and Stradling, 1990), although this conclusion requires corroboration (see Scott and Stradling ibid. for a discussion). In particular it should be noted that patients received three sessions of individual therapy prior to the group work and in the light of the findings of Fennell and Teasdale (1987) it is possible that by this stage much improvement had already occurred.

Cognitive therapy for dysthymic disorder

Stravynski *et al.* (1991) found that fifteen sessions of CT produced significant improvements in depression at post-treatment and six-month follow-up in five out of six patients who met *DSM III–R* criteria for dysthymic disorder, a mild but chronic form of depression. At follow-up, four patients had improved sufficiently that they no longer met the diagnostic criteria.

Chronically depressed in-patients who have not responded to other treatments

A substantial minority of depressed patients (15 to 20 per cent) experience persistent depression which is resistant to standard treatments (Scott, 1988). Scott (1992) reported very encouraging results from a modified cognitive therapy approach together with pharmacotherapy (lithium carbonate, phenelzine and L-tryptophan). Patients were admitted to a special unit for about twenty-six in-patient sessions plus at least six months of out-patient treatment. Initially the emphasis was on behavioural techniques, together with considerable discussion about CT. Due to the severity of the depression many patients could not cope with a 45-minute session, and so the initial CT sessions lasted 20 minutes, three times a week. Nursing staff incorporated CT techniques into the in-patient treatment programme. Given the prevalence of interpersonal problems it was seen as important to involve the family in treatment. There were a number of CT sessions with the patient and family which focused on the nature of CT and also used specific cognitive techniques to deal with negative automatic thoughts of family members. Coping strategies of family members were reviewed. Results suggested that up to 70 per cent of these patients who had been chronically depressed and had failed previous treatment attempts made significant improvements. Mean BDI scores had improved from 38.7 to 14.7 over twelve weeks, and 11 out of 16 patients regarded themselves as 'much improved' or 'back to my normal self'.

Those interested in CT with this population of patients should consult Scott (1988; 1992). She stresses that experienced therapists should be used because novices become de-skilled and demoralised in response to repeated failures of their interventions. Such demoralisation influences the patient and can precipitate crises.

Cognitive therapy for patients with personality disorders

There is evidence from the NIMH Treatment of Depression Collaborative Research Program that patients with personality disorders (PD) tended to improve more with cognitive-behavioural therapy, while subjects without PD tended to do better in other treatments (Shea *et al.*, 1990). Moreover, Miller *et al.*, (1985) produced substantial improvement in six chronic drug-resistant depressed women who were admitted as in-patients and given CBT together with pharmacotherapy. Treatment continued for four months in an out-patient setting.

Young (1989) has developed cognitive therapy to deal specifically with personality disordered and difficult patients. He points out that normal short-term CT makes seven assumptions about patients:

1 They can report on their feelings. But many long-term patients find this difficult.
2 They can report on their thoughts and images with little training. Again this is not so with many patients.
3 There are identifiable problems to focus on. However, some difficult patients have vague problems or a general malaise with no apparent triggers.
4 They are motivated to do homework assignments and to learn self-control strategies. But some patients show considerable dependence on the therapist and are reluctant to help themselves.
5 There is a collaborative relationship. On the other hand, some patients try desperately to get the therapist to meet their needs, or alternatively are so disengaged or hostile that they cannot collaborate.
6 Difficulties in the therapeutic relationship are not a major issue. However, the essence of the problem is sometimes interpersonal, and dealing with the therapeutic relationship as a primary focus may be beneficial.
7 All cognitions and behaviours can be modified by empirical analysis, logic, experiment and graduated practice. But many chronic patients do not change in spite of these techniques.

In personality disorders there is often extreme rigidity and inflexibility in thought and behaviour. Some emotive thoughts and feelings are avoided, probably through aversive conditioning, and there are often long-term interpersonal problems.

The assessment of Early Maladaptive Schemas

Young indicates that Early Maladaptive Schemas (EMSs) underlie these patterns and a first step is to identify those of the patient. Such schemas are regarded as being extremely stable and enduring patterns of thinking which develop during childhood and which serve as templates for the processing of later experience. While Beck also regards negative schemas as underlying depression, in practice normal short-term cognitive therapy does not put so much stress on dealing with schemas. As noted elsewhere in this chapter, improvement in treating fairly straightforward cases of depression often occurs in only a few sessions. Young regards EMSs as being more unconditional and more rigid than the underlying assumptions described by Beck. Underlying assumptions take the form 'If I can be perfect, then I am worthwhile'. However, an EMS may have the form 'No matter what I do, I'm incompetent, unlovable, ugly; I'll be abandoned; I'll be punished'. Young also regards EMSs as being much more resistant to change than underlying assumptions, since they often form the core of the individual's self-concept. Young groups EMSs into four categories: autonomy, connected-ness (relating to other people), limits and standards, and worthiness.

Young uses the Lazarus Multimodal Life History Questionnaire (Lazarus, 1980) and the Schema Questionnaire (Young, 1989) to help identify the EMSs. In the course of enquiry about life events and symptoms, the therapist tries to identify themes concerning autonomy, connectedness, worthiness, reasonable expectations, and realistic limits. Patients are educated about their schemas. In the session the therapist then tries to trigger those schemas which are assumed to be problematic. Patients may be asked to close their eyes and report what images come to mind spontaneously, they may be asked to report on current distressing events, or to discuss distressing experiences from the past. The therapist pays close attention to the therapeutic relationship to find out what triggers schemas during the session. Use is made of books and films which deal with themes of abandonment, autonomy, etc. Group therapy can be used to trigger schemas which are interpersonal in nature. Young also makes use of dreams where the basic themes may be represented. Finally, homework assignments, such as keeping a daily record of dysfunctional thoughts or writing about a specific schema-related topic, are prescribed.

Young recommends confronting patients who show 'schema avoidance', that is, when they feel distress but cannot identify the content. Schema-driven be-haviours are identified. A final step in the assessment means formulating the patient's problems in schema terms, and identifying the primary or core schemas which are responsible for the most intense emotions.

Young's intervention

In order to change schemas, Young advocates four types of intervention: emotive, interpersonal, cognitive, and behavioural. Many of the emotive techniques are drawn from gestalt therapy and involve triggering the schemas in the session. One such technique is to encourage patients to carry on an imaginary conver-sation with their parents, telling the parents how they feel and what they want. By role-playing themselves as they would have liked to respond to their parents they may be able to change their beliefs about themselves and begin to see the role of their parents in helping to form their schemas.

Emotional catharsis is also advocated to help patients let go of unexpressed anger based on early life experiences. Interpersonal techniques may involve encouraging the patient to test the schemas directly by obtaining feedback about the therapist's perceptions of the patient. Another strategy is for the therapist to recreate a relationship which counteracts early maladaptive schemas by, for example, being nurturing and caring if the patient has suffered a great deal of emotional deprivation. Cognitive techniques have already been described above. These involve reviewing evidence in support of the schemas. Young counsels that the therapist must be careful of being too confrontational, since this can result in the patient's ignoring the therapist's counter-arguments. One key way of invalidating evidence is to point out how the schemas were formed through distorted parental and family standards and expectations. Patients are shown how schema-driven behaviours result in validation of the schema. Next therapist and patient look for positive information which contradicts the schema, for example, evidence of the patient's effectiveness, ability to take responsibility, areas of competence and success, and examples of good interpersonal relationships. The therapist illustrates how the patient discounts contradictory evidence, often getting the patient to role-play the schema while the therapist takes the role of Reason. Then they exchange roles. Patients are encouraged to get angry at the schema in order to distance themselves further from it. Rational responses are constantly rehearsed by writing the most powerful counter-arguments against the schema on a card which is then read repeatedly as necessary. Thus, the schema is challenged whenever it is activated.

Patients are encouraged to change long-term behavioural patterns which have reinforced the schemas. To this end, changes in the patient's environment may be made, for example, by working with the patient's spouse in conjoint therapy, encouraging new friendships or new hobbies. Finally, Young finds that the adjunctive use of medication may be helpful in reducing depression or anxiety sufficiently to allow patients to be receptive to schema-focused therapy.

In summary, Young's (1989) schema-focused cognitive therapy extends cognitive therapy to deal with difficult patients with long-term personality disorders and those with chronic anxiety or depression. It differs from short-term cognitive therapy in the following ways.

There is more confrontation and less guided discovery, the therapeutic relationship is used much more to encourage change, the therapy lasts longer, the level of emotion is greater, dealing with cognitive and behavioural avoidance is more important, and childhood origins of schemas and emotive gestalt-inspired techniques are used. The efficacy of this approach awaits controlled evaluation.

Depression in adult victims of child sexual abuse

Very high prevalence rates for mood disturbances, interpersonal problems and sexual dysfunction are reported for previously abused women who enter therapy. Jehu (1988) reports in detail on a range of cognitive-behavioural approaches to treatment, while Cahill et al., (1991) review treatments for this population. The section below will, largely, summarise Jehu's guidelines for dealing with the mood disturbances which commonly accompany such abuse. These approaches are based on clinical experience and reports rather than on controlled evaluations, and this should be borne in mind.

It is common for such patients to experience self-blame for the abuse, self-injurious impulses, anger and revenge towards the offender, and feelings of hostility and betrayal towards parents who did not protect them from abuse or who themselves were the abusers. Disclosure of the abuse is often associated with intense shame, and associated fear of being rejected by the therapist. Female therapists are especially important for sex-abused girls or women.

Acceptance and support from the therapist is especially important. It is necessary to be empathic concerning the victim's feelings of being responsible for and therefore guilty about the abuse. It is also important to acknowledge the common experience of the victim's positive feelings of loyalty and love, as well as anger towards the abuser where this was a family member. Commonly, victims experience flashbacks, dissociative reactions and sexual aversion. It is important that these problems, which may appear bizarre and be interpreted by the victim as indications that they are mad, are acknowledged by the therapist as common sequelae of abuse and that the victim is helped to see these experiences as such.

The principles of such treatment are essentially as described earlier under Beck's Cognitive Therapy, although the particular maladaptive thoughts have certain specific themes illustrated below.

Examples of distortions or maladaptive thoughts characteristic of sexual abuse victims

Overgeneralisation: 'I can't trust my [male] therapist not to be sexual with me.' 'All that men are interested in, in a relationship, is sex.' 'I'm a weak and inadequate person because I haven't got over the abuse' (ignoring all the other areas of life where she performed well).
Disqualifying the positive: 'When a man pays me a compliment, all he wants is sex.'
Jumping to conclusions (arbitrary inference): 'My friends will shun me if they know I've been abused.'
Magnification: 'I will never be able to lead a normal life, the damage is permanent.'
Misattribution or personalisation: 'I must have been responsible for sex when I was a child because I wasn't forced into it and it went on so long.'
'Should' statements: 'I should have known better than to have gone into his room.'

Another way of classifying these thoughts is in terms of their themes. Jehu divides them into self-blaming and self-denigratory beliefs. The former includes beliefs in one's own responsibility for what happened. Passive compliance and not telling others were interpreted by over 80 per cent of Jehu's sample as evidence of personal responsibility. Most also thought that they had been sexually provocative as a child. Their memories of sexual pleasure during the abuse was often a source of profound guilt. Often the victim holds certain beliefs which exonerate or excuse the offender's responsibility, for example, belief that the offender was 'sick', that the acts were in order to enhance the emotional relationship between offender and victim, or that it was part of an attempt at making her a better sexual partner when she grew up. Self-denigratory beliefs include victims' beliefs that they are 'worthless and bad' (endorsed by almost 80 per cent of Jehu's sample), being inherently different from others, being shunned by others as a result of the abuse, being inadequate or useless, or having to subordinate their rights to men.

Jehu advocates a cognitive restructuring approach. First the relation between beliefs and feelings is demonstrated in the manner described earlier. Next the specific beliefs which contribute to the mood disturbance are identified by means of questions, 'remote recall', role-play, imagery, diary recording, or the Belief Inventory (Jehu et al., 1986) as a measure of some common distorted beliefs associated with child sexual abuse. The therapist explores with the victim some more accurate and realistic beliefs as alternatives to the distorted or maladaptive ones.

Summary of Jehu's cognitive-behavioural treatment of mood disturbance associated with sexual abuse victims

Provision of information. Information about the prevalence of sexual abuse may help to reduce the patient's ideas that she is different from everyone else. Gil (1984) describes the emotional problems of previously sexually abused women which can be very helpful for victims to read.

Logical analysis. Does the evidence necessarily support the victim's conclusion? For example, 'I must have been to blame because I was removed from home' (after the abuse was discovered). Another conclusion is that she was removed for her own safety.

Decatastrophising. A victim who believes that she has been permanently damaged and will always be unable to lead a normal life may find it helpful to learn that many victims can and do lead normal lives.

Distancing. This means making a distinction between 'I believe', an opinion which is open to dispute, and 'I know', an undisputable fact. For example, a woman who 'knows' that she was to blame for her abuse may be enabled to distance herself from this by hearing the testimonies of other abused victims who equally believed themselves to be to blame.

Re-attribution. Therapist and victim review the evidence of the abuse to arrive at a more appropriate assignment of responsibility for the abuse. For example: 'I must have been responsible for sex when I was a child because I wasn't forced into it and it went on so long'. Alternative formulation: 'In a sense I was forced into it and could not stop it because: (a) the offender kept persuading me by saying, "what's the matter, don't you want to help an old man?". I had been indoctrinated with the belief that nice little girls were supposed to help and please people, especially older people, and did not want to hurt him by not continuing to participate'; (b) I desperately wanted attention from someone outside my family and he gave me this; (c) I could not refuse to take his lunch out to the field where the abuse often happened because I would have to explain to his wife why I was refusing, and I did not want to upset her; (d) I feared that if I told my mother she would do nothing to protect me; (e) I could not consider telling my father because I hated him, I feared that he would blame or punish me, or not do anything.'

Jehu (1988) presents very promising results from this treatment, with clinically significant improvements in depression being noted in 95 per cent of his cases, together with reductions in distorted beliefs, and beneficial effects on marital and sexual relationships of substantial proportions of victims.

Assessment of suicidal behaviour

The single best predictor of suicide is a previous episode of parasuicide but only around 1 per cent will proceed to kill themselves in the following year (MacLeod et al., 1992). Kreitman and Foster (1991) found the following predictors of parasuicide: previous parasuicide; personality disorder; alcohol consumption > 21 units per week in males and > 14 in females; previous psychiatric treatment; unemployment; low social class; drug abuse; criminal record; violence given or received in the past five years; aged between 25 and 54; and single, widowed or divorced. Those with three or less of these factors had a repetition rate of 4.9 per cent, those with a score between 4 and 7, 20.5 per cent, and those scoring above 8, 41.5 per cent. Some important factors in assessing suicidal intent after a parasuicide attempt are discussed by MacLeod et al. (1992) and by Beck et al., (1974). They include:

External circumstances. How isolated was the person at the time of the attempt? Was intervention likely or unlikely? Any precautions taken against discovery? Did the person seek help during the attempt or afterwards? Did the person carry out a final act anticipating that he or she would die? Did the person write a suicide note?

Self-report. Did the person believe that what he or she did would kill him or her? Did the person say he or she wanted to die? How premeditated was the act? Is the person sorry or glad to have recovered?

MacLeod et al. (1992) discuss some psychological factors associated with increased likelihood of parasuicide, namely, poor interpersonal problem-solving, hopelessness about the future, and failure to regulate one's own affective responses. Freeman et al. (1990) include a Scale for Suicidal Ideation (SSI; Beck et al., 1979a) and the Hopelessness Scale (Beck et al., 1975) in the Appendix to their book. See also Appleby's (1992) review.

Linehan's Dialectical Behaviour Therapy is a multi-component treatment which has shown encouraging results in reducing suicidal behaviour in Borderline Personality Disorder patients. A description of this treatment is outside the scope of this chapter but interested readers are referred to Linehan et al. (1991).

Risk and therapist's responsibility

The therapist should carefully assess suicide risk (e.g. Kreitman and Foster, 1991; Freeman et al., 1990; MacLeod et al., 1992). Therapists are advised to discuss progress in the management of seriously depressed patients with other professional colleagues since medication and in-patient care may be necessary.

GUIDELINES FOR CONDUCTING THERAPY WITH DEPRESSED PATIENTS

1 Investigation should concentrate on functional analyses (Chapter 1) to establish factors influencing daily occurrences of depressed mood and depressed behaviour.
2 Recording of daily activity schedules may contribute to this but will also establish whether patients have correctly described their daily activities and pleasure and sense of accomplishment in them.
3 The therapist should assess whether training in assertiveness skills or other social skills is desirable.
4 Other psychological problems such as general anxiety or agoraphobia may be reducing sources of reinforcement for non-depressive behaviour and may be priority targets.
5 The severity of the patient's distress may indicate whether or not procedures such as distraction, programming daily activities or daily therapy sessions will be necessary at first.
6 Certain depressed patients may prove difficult to treat. See Predictors of Response (p. 127).
7 Some measure of the patient's level of depression should be recorded in each therapy session. The reduction of this to a minimum level should be the main goal of treatment.
8 An approach which uses components of both cognitive and behavioural interventions is probably optimal.
9 It may be helpful to agree initially on a small number of sessions, such as five.
10 The distinction between emotions and thoughts must be established and understood by the patient. An introductory booklet (Beck and Greenberg, 1974) may be given to illustrate negative thoughts, their role in depression, and the process of cognitive therapy.
11 The influence of thoughts on emotions should be illustrated and the recording of these (Table 6.1) should be discussed.
12 Therapy should be discussed as a collaborative venture. Patients should be encouraged to present problems which have been distressing them recently, to set goals for therapy and to query the therapist's remarks.
13 For each session an agenda should be established collaboratively at the start of the session.
14 Items on the agenda should include reflections (feedback) on matters discussed in the previous session (has the patient understood and accepted what was discussed?), discussion of homework such as activity schedules and recording of negative thoughts.

15 The identification of errors in thinking and methods of challenging negative thoughts (Table 6.2) should be discussed and illustrated. The patient and therapist should look for challenges which reduce the distress associated with negative thoughts.

16 Negative thoughts and alternative thoughts should be recorded as homework (Table 6.1).

17 Behavioural methods, especially role-playing, may be used within sessions, for example, to pinpoint discouraging thoughts which the patient experiences in social interactions at work.

18 Role-playing, social skills training, problem-solving training, or marital therapy may be used especially to establish and practise behaviour which may resolve problems including the behaviour of others towards the patient.

19 Homework exercises should then be agreed in order to implement behaviour rehearsed in role-plays.

20 In relatively straightforward cases some reduction of depression should be observed within four to five sessions if a complete course of therapy is to be pursued. Where clients are in-patients, have failed other treatments, or have associated personality disorders, then treatment will generally require modification. (See Scott, 1988 and Young, 1989.)

REFERENCES

Appleby, L. (1992) 'Suicide in psychiatric patients: risk and prevention', *British Journal of Psychiatry* 161: 749–58.

Barber, J. P. and DeRubeis, R. J. (1989) 'On second thoughts: Where the action is in cognitive therapy for depression', *Cognitive Therapy and Research* 13: 441–57.

Beck, A. T. (1976) *Cognitive Therapy and the Emotional Disorders*, New York: International Universities Press.

Beck, A. T. (1990) *Cognitive Therapy of Personality Disorders*, New York: Guilford.

Beck, A. T. and Greenberg, R. L. (1974) *Coping with depression*, New York: Institute for Rational Living.

Beck, A. T., Kovacs, M. and Weissman, M. (1975) 'Hopelessness and suicidal behavior: an overview', *Journal of the American Medical Association* 234: 1146–9.

Beck, A. T., Kovacs, J. and Weissman, M. (1979a) 'Assessment of suicidal ideation: The Scale of Suicidal Ideation', *Journal of Consulting and Clinical Psychology*, 47: 343–52.

Beck, A. T., Rush, A. J., Shaw, B. F. and Emery, G. (1979b) *Cognitive Therapy of Depression*, New York: Guilford Press.

Beck, A. T., Schuyler, D. and Herman, J. (1974) 'Development of suicidal intent scales', in A. T. Beck, H. L. P. Resnick and D. J. Lettieri (eds) *The Prediction Suicide*, Maryland: Charles Press.

Beck, A. T., Steer, R. A., Kovacs, M. and Garrison, B. E. (1985) 'Hopelessness and eventual suicide: A ten-year prospective study of patients hospitalized for suicidal ideation', *American Journal of Psychiatry* 142: 559–63.

Beckham, E. E. (1989) 'Improvement after evaluation in psychotherapy of depression: Evidence of a placebo effect?', *Journal of Clinical Psychology* 45(6): 945–50.

Blackburn, I. M., Bishop, S., Glen, I. M., Whalley, L. J. and Christie, J. E. (1981) 'The efficacy of cognitive therapy in depression: a treatment trial using cognitive therapy and pharmacotherapy, each alone and in combination', *British Journal of Psychiatry* 139.

Blackburn, I. M., Eunson, K. M. and Bishop, S. (1986) 'A two-year naturalistic follow-up of depressed patients treated with cognitive therapy, pharmacotherapy and a combination of both', *Journal of Affective Disorders* 10: 67–75.

Bowers, W. A. (1990) 'Treatment of depressed in-patients: Cognitive therapy plus medication, relaxation plus medication, and medication alone', *British Journal of Psychiatry* 156: 73–8.

Boyd, J. H. and Weissman, M. M. (1981) 'Epidemiology of affective disorders', *Archives of General Psychiatry* 38: 1039–46.

Burns, D. D. (1980) *Feeling Good: the new mood therapy*, New York: William Morrow.

Cahill, C., Llewelyn, S. P. and Pearson, C. (1991) 'Treatment of sexual abuse which occurred in childhood: a review', *British Journal of Clinical Psychology* 30: 1–12.

Clayton, P. J. (1984) 'Overview of recurrent mood disorders: Definitions and natural course', paper presented at the National Institute of Mental Health Consensus Develop- ment Conference, Washington, DC.

Davis, J. M. (1976) 'Overview: maintenance therapy in psychiatry: II. Affective disorders', *American Journal of Psychiatry* 133: 1–14.

de Jong, Treiber and Henrich (1986) 'Effectiveness of two psychological treatments for inpatients with severe and chronic depressions', *Cognitive Therapy and Research* 10(6): 645–63.

DeRubeis, R. J. and Beck, A. T. (1988) 'Cognitive Therapy', in K. S. Dobson (ed.) *Handbook of Cognitive-Behavioral Therapies*, New York: Guilford.

DeRubeis, R. J. and Feeley, M. (1990) 'Determinants of change in cognitive therapy for depression', *Cognitive Therapy and Research* 14(5): 469–82.

DeRubeis, R. J., Evans, M. D., Hollon, S. D., Garvey, M. J., Grove, W. M. and Tuason, V. B. (1990) 'How does cognitive therapy work? Cognitive change and symptom change in cognitive therapy and pharmacotherapy for depression', *Journal of Consulting and Clinical Psychology* 58(6): 862–9.

Dobson, K. S. (1989) 'A Meta-analysis of the efficacy of cognitive therapy for depression', *Journal of Consulting and Clinical Psychology* 57(3): 414–19.

Dobson, K. S., Shaw, B. F. and Vallis, T. M. (1985) 'Reliability of a measure of the quality of cognitive therapy', *British Journal of Clinical Psychology* 24: 295–300.

Elkin, I., Shea, M. T., Watkins, J. T., Imber, S. D., Sotsky, S. M., Collins, J. F., Glass, D. R., Pilkonis, P. A., Leber, W. R., Docherty, J. P., Fiester, S. J. and Parlott, M. B. (1989) 'NIMH Treatment of Depression Collaborative Research Program: 1 General effectiveness of treatments', Archives of General Psychiatry 46: 971–82.

Emery, G. (1981) *A New Beginning: How You Can Change Your Life Through Cognitive Therapy*, New York: Simon & Schuster.

Fennell, M. J. V. (1989) 'Depression', in K. Hawton, P. M. Salkowskis, J. M. Kirk and D. M. Clark (eds) *Cognitive Behaviour Therapy for Psychiatric Problems: A practical guide*, Oxford: Oxford Medical (Ch .6)

Fennell, M. J. V. and Teasdale, J. D. (1982) 'Cognitive therapy with chronic, drug- refractory depressed out-patients: a note of caution', *Cognitive Therapy and Research* 6 (4): 455–60.

Fennell, M. J. V. and Teasdale, J. D. (1987) 'Cognitive therapy for depression: individual differences and the process of change', *Cognitive Therapy and Research* 11(2): 253–71.

Freeman, A., Pretzer, J., Fleming, B. and Simon, K. M. (1990) *Clinical applications of cognitive therapy*, New York: Plenum.

Gil, E. M. (1984) *Outgrowing the Pain: a book for and about adults abused as children*, 2nd edn, San Francisco: Launch.

Gotlib, I. H. and Hammen, C. L. (1992) *Psychological Aspects of Depression: towards a cognitive-interpersonal integration*, Chichester, Wiley.

Haaga, D. A. F., Dyck, M. J. and Ernst, D. (1991) 'Empirical status of Cognitive Theory of Depression', *Psychological Bulletin* 110(2): 215–36.

Hollon, S. D. (1981) 'Comparisons and combinations with alternative approaches', in L. P. Rehm (ed.) *Behavior Therapy for Depression: Present status and Future Directions*, New York: Academic Press.

Hollon, S. D. and Beck, A. T. (1978) 'Psychotherapy and drug therapy: comparison and combinations', in S. L. Garfield and A. E. Bergin (eds) *The Handbook of Psychotherapy and Behavior Change, 2nd edn* New York: Wiley.

Hollon, S. D. and Beck, A. T. (1979) 'Cognitive therapy for depression', in P. C. Kendall and S. D. Hollon (eds) *Cognitive Behavioral Interventions: Theory, Research and Procedures*, New York: Academic Press.

Hollon, S. D., Evans, M. D., Auerbach, A., DeRubeis, R. J., Elkin, I., Lowery, A., Tuason, V. B., Kriss, M. and Piasecki, J. (1985) 'Development of a system of rating therapies for depression', unpublished manuscript, University of Minnesota and St. Paul–Ramsay Medical Center, Minneapolis-St. Paul, Minn.

Hollon, S. D. and Najavits, L. (1988) 'Review of empirical studies on cognitive therapy', in A. Tasman, R. Hales, and A. Frances (eds) *Review of Psychiatry* 7: 643–666.

Hollon, S. D., Shelton, R. C. and Loosen, P. T. (1991) 'Cognitive therapy and pharmacotherapy for depression', *Journal of Consulting and Clinical Psychology* 59(1): 88–99.

Imber, S. D., Pilkonis, P. A., Sotsky, S. M., Elkin, I., Watkins, J. T., Collins, J. F., Shea, M. T., Leber, W. R. and Glass, D. R. (1990) 'Mode-specific effects among three treatments for depression', *Journal of Consulting and Clinical Psychology* 58: 352–59.

Jehu, D. (1988) *Beyond Sexual Abuse: Therapy with women who were childhood victims*, Chichester: Wiley.

Jehu, Klassan and Gazan (1986) 'Cognitive restructuring of distorted beliefs associated with childhood sexual abuse', in J. Gripton and M. Valentich (eds), *Social Work Practice in Sexual Problems*, New York: Haworth.

Joyce, P. R. and Paykel, E. S. (1989) 'Predictors of drug response in depression', *Archives of General Psychiatry* 46: 89–99.

Kelly, D. (1982) 'Leucotomy', in E. Paykel, (ed.) *Handbook of Affective Disorders*, London: Churchill Livingstone.

Klerman, G. L., Rounsaville, B., Chevron, E., Neu, G. and Weissman, M. M. (1979) *Manual for Short-term Interpersonal Psychotherapy (IPT) of Depression, 4th rev.*, mimeographed publication distributed by Yale University School of Medicine, New Haven, Conn.

Kovacs, M., Rush, A. J., Beck, A. T. and Hollon, S. D. (1981) 'Depressed out-patients treated with cognitive therapy or pharmacotherapy: a one-year follow-up', *Archives of General Psychiatry* 38; 33–9.

Kreitman, N. and Foster, J. (1991) 'The construction and selection of predictive scales with particular reference to parasuicide', *British Journal of Psychiatry* 159: 185–92.

Lader, M. and Herrington, R. (1990) *Biological Treatments in Psychiatry*, Oxford: Oxford Medical.

Lazarus, A. (1980) *Multimodal Life History Questionnaire*, Kingston, NJ: Multimodal Publications.

Lehmann, H. E. (1977) 'Depression: somatic treatment methods, complications, failures', in G. Usdin (ed.) *Depression: Clinical, Biological and Physiological Perspectives*, New York: Brunner/Mazel.

Linehan, M. M., Armstrong, H. E., Suarez, A., Allmon, D. and Heard, H. L. (1991) 'Behavioral treatment of chronically parasuicidal borderline patients', *Archives of General Psychiatry*.

Luborsky, L., McClelland, G. E., Woody, G. E., O'Brien, C. P. and Auerbach, A. (1985) 'Therapist success and its determinants', *Archives of General Psychiatry* 42: 602–11.

Luborsky, L., Woody, G. E., McClelland, G. E., O'Brien, C. P. and Rosenzweig, J. (1982)

'Can independent judges recognize different psychotherapies? An experience with manual-guided therapies', *Journal of Consulting and Clinical Psychology* 50: 49–62.

McLean, P. and Hakstian, A. R. (1979) 'Clinical depression: comparative efficacy of out-patient treatments', *Journal of Consulting and Clinical Psychology* 47: 813–36.

MacLeod, A. K., Williams, J. M. G. and Linehan, M. M. (1992) 'New developments in the understanding and treatment of suicidal behaviour', *Behavioural Psychotherapy* 20(3): 193–218.

Miller, I. W., Norman, W. H. and Keitner, G. I. (1989) 'Cognitive-behavioural treatment of depressed in-patients: six- and twelve-month follow-up', *American Journal of Psychiatry* 146(10): 1274–79.

Miller, I. W., Bishop, S. B., Norman, W. H. and Keitner, G. I. (1985) 'Cognitive/ behavioural therapy and pharmacotherapy with chronic, drug-refractory depressed in-patients: a note of optimism', *Behavioural Psychotherapy* 13: 320–7.

Myers, J. K., Weissman, M. M., Tischler, G. L., Holzer III, C. E., Leaf, P. J., Orvaschel, H., Anthony, J. C., Boyd, J. H., Burke, J. D., Kramer, M. and Stoltzman, R. (1984) 'Six-month prevalence of psychiatric disorders in three communities: 1980–1982', *Archives of General Psychiatry* 41: 959–67.

Neimeyer, R. A. and Feixas, G. (1990) 'The role of homework and skill acquisition in the outcome of group cognitive therapy for depression', *Behavior Therapy* 21(3): 281–92.

Nietzel, M., Russell, R., Hemmings, K. and Gretter, M. (1987) 'Clinical significance of psychotherapy for unipolar depression: a meta-analytic approach to social comparison', *Journal of Consulting and Clinical Psychology* 55: 156–61.

O'Leary, K. D. and Beach, S. R. (1990) 'Marital therapy: a viable treatment for depression and marital discord', *American Journal of Psychiatry* 147(2): 183–6.

Persons, J. B., Burns, D. D. and Perloff, J. M. (1988) 'Predictors of dropout and outcome in cognitive therapy for depression in a private practice setting', *Cognitive Therapy and Research* 12(6): 557–75.

Robinson, L. A., Berman, J. S. and Neimeyer, R. A. (1990) 'Psychotherapy for the treatment of depression: a comprehensive review of controlled outcome research', *Psychological Bulletin* 108: 30–49.

Rogers, S. C. and Clay, P. M. (1975) 'A statistical review of controlled trials of imipramine and placebo in the treatment of depressive illness', *British Journal of Psychiatry* 127: 599–603.

Rush, A. J. and Shaw, B. F. (1983) 'Failures in treating depression by cognitive behavior therapy', in E. B. Foa and P. M. G. Emmelkamp (eds) *Failures in Behavior Therapy*, New York: Wiley.

Schon, M. (1976) 'Prophylactic and maintenance therapy in permanent affective disorders', in D. M. Galland and G. M. Simpson (eds) *Depression: Behavioral, Biochemical, Diagnostic and Treatment Concepts*, New York: Spectrum Publications.

Scogin, F., Hamblin, D. and Beutler, L. E. (1987) 'Bibliotherapy for depressed older adults: a self-help alternative', *The Gerontologist* 27: 383–7.

Scogin, F., Jamison, C. and Gochneaur, K. (1989) 'Comparative efficacy of cognitive and behavioral bibliotherapy for mildly and moderately depressed older adults', *Journal of Consulting and Clinical Psychology* 3: 403–7.

Scott, J. (1988) 'Cognitive therapy with depressed in-patients', in W. Dryden and P. Trower (eds) *Developments in Cognitive Psychotherapy*, London: Sage.

Scott, J. (1992) 'Chronic depression: can cognitive therapy succeed when other treatments fail?' *Behavioural Psychotherapy* 20: 25–36.

Scott, M. J. and Stradling, S. G. (1990) 'Group cognitive therapy for depression produces clinical significant reliable change in community-based settings', *Behavioural Psychotherapy* 18(1): 1–19.

Selmi, P. M., Klein, M. H., Greist, J. H., Sorrell, S. P. and Erdman, H. P. (1990)

'Computer-administered cognitive-behavioral therapy for depression', *American Journal of Psychiatry* 147(1): 51–6.

Shapiro, D. A., Barkham, M., Hardy, G. E., Morrison, L. A. (1990) 'The second Sheffield psychotherapy project: rationale, design and prelimary outcome data', *British Journal of Medical Psychology* 63(2): 97–108.

Shea, M. T., Elkin, I., Imber, S. D., Sotsky, S. M., Watkins, J. T., Collins, J. F., Pilkonis, P. A., Beckham, E., Glass, D. R., Dolan, R. T. and Parloff, M. B. (1992) 'Course of depressive symptoms over follow-up: findings from the National Institute of Mental Health Treatment of Depression Collaborative Research Program', *Archives of General Psychiatry* 49: 782–7.

Shea, M. T., Pilkonis, P. A., Beckham, E., Collins, J. F., Elkin, I., Scotsky, S. M. and Docherty, J. P. (1990) 'Personality disorders and treatment outcome in the NIMH Treatment of Depression Collaborative Research Program', *American Journal of Psychiatry* 147(6): 711–18.

Simons, A. D., Levine, J. L., Lustman, P. J. and Murphy, G. E. (1984a) 'Patient attrition in a comparative outcome study of depression: a follow-up report', *Journal of Affective Disorders* 6(2): 163–73.

Simons, A. D., Garfield, S. L. and Murphy, G. E. (1984b) 'The process of change in cognitive therapy and pharmacotherapy: changes in mood and cognitions', *Archives of General Psychiatry* 41: 45–51.

Simons, A. D., Murphy, G. E., Levine, J. L. and Wetzel, R. D. (1986) 'Cognitive therapy and pharmacotherapy for depression: sustained improvement over one year', *Archives of General Psychiatry* 43: 43–9.

Simons, A. D. and Thase, M. (1992) 'Biological markers, treatment outcome, and 1-year follow-up in endogenous depression: electroencephalographic Sleep Studies and Response to cognitive therapy', *Journal of Consulting and Clinical Psychology* 60(3): 392–401.

Stravynski, A., Shahar, A. and Verreault, R. (1991) 'A pilot study of the cognitive treatment of dysthymic disorder', *Behavioural Psychotherapy* 19(4): 369–72.

Taylor, F. G. and Marshall, W. L. (1977) 'Experimental analysis of a cognitive-behavioral therapy for depression', *Cognitive Therapy and Research* 1: 59–72.

Weissman, M. M., Prusoff, B. A., Di Mascio, A., Neu, C., Goklaney, M. and Klerman, G. L. (1979) 'The efficacy of drugs and psychotherapy in the treatment of acute depressive episodes', *American Journal of Psychiatry* 136: 555–8.

Williams, J. M. G. (1984) *The Psychological Treatment of Depression* London: Croom Helm.

Williams, J. M. G. (1992) *The Psychological Treatment of Depression, 2nd edn*, London: Routledge.

Williams, R., Moorey, S. and Cobb, J. (1991) 'Training in cognitive-behaviour therapy: pilot evaluation of a training course using the cognitive therapy scale', *Behavioural Psychotherapy* 19(4): 373–6.

Young, J. E. (1989) *Schema-focused Cognitive Therapy for Personality Disorders and Difficult Patients'*, Sarasota, Fla.: Professional Resource Exchange.

Young, J. and Beck, A. J. (1980) 'Cognitive therapy scale and rating manual', unpublished manuscript.

Zeiss, A. M. and Jones, S. L. (1983) 'Behavioral treatment of depression: examining treatment failures', in E. B. Foa and P. M. G. Emmelkamp (eds) *Failures in Behavior Therapy*, New York: Wiley.

Zeiss, A. M., Lewinsohn, P. M. and Munoz, R. F. (1979) 'Nonspecific improvement effects in depression using interpersonal, cognitive, and pleasant events focused treatments', *Journal of Consulting and Clinical Psychology* 47: 427–39.

Chapter 7

Fears and anxiety
Investigation

S.J.E. Lindsay

INTRODUCTION: THE IMPACT OF FEARS

It is evident even to a cursory review of daily newspapers, television and radio that we are continually exposed to a deluge of evidence which should make us dread threats to our health, environmental disasters and other risks. Even information designed to encourage us to take better care of our health, about incurable illness and risks from consumption of commonplace foods, appears designed to encourage helplessness and fear, so numerous are the sources of danger (Berger *et al.*, 1991). It is surprising, therefore, that many people remain optimistic about these risks, even to their disadvantage (Taylor and Brown, 1988). Nevertheless, for some fears, especially those associated with expectations of pain, notably in routine dental treatment, pessimism is probably common and even prudent. It may protect patients from pain (Lindsay and Jackson, 1993).

How does intense fear affect those of us who succumb to it? Agoraphobics may expect to collapse, to have heart attacks or die in the street while out shopping (Thorpe and Burns, 1983). Dental phobics believe that they will continually think during treatment that they will experience sudden pain and that they will have dificulty controlling those thoughts (Kent and Gibbons, 1987). People who become very anxious in company may report that they believe it to be very obvious that they are uncomfortable and that, if they are spoken to, they will appear hesitant and foolish (see Glass *et al.*, 1982; Halford and Foddy, 1982).

Often, however, people who are afraid in such situations have difficulty in saying what is distressing them or how they feel (Meyer and Reich, 1978). For example, during panics, their minds go blank. In addition, even where phobic clients clearly anticipate a particular, threatening outcome, their distress can be aggravated by uncertainty about whether it will occur or when or where it will happen. Thus agoraphobics may be uncertain about whether they will feel faint or dizzy even in situations where they expect it to be most likely. Dental phobics are often especially afraid just because they are not sure when they will experience pain (Lindsay, 1984). Socially anxious people may be especially nervous because they do not know when they may be required to speak or answer a question in company. Some people plagued by continual anxiety, can be unpredictably nervous of many events and situations.

Fears and anxiety can be distressing simply because of their intensity. Continuous preoccupation with certain fears, such as of risks to one's health in panic disorders, can also make the fear less easy to tolerate. In addition, fears and panic may be associated with a higher risk of suicide (Marks, 1987) or of serious cardiovascular disease (Haines *et al.*, 1987). However, the causal mechanisms of these relationships are far from clear. More clearly, chronic fears and anxiety can impair social relationships, work and recreation.

For example, in Kent, south-east England, a woman with a phobia of snakes experienced severe panic attacks whenever she saw a snake on television. Members of her family had to screen magazines for pictures of snakes in order to prevent panics. A young man who experienced extreme tension and occasional panic attacks in crowded rooms could tolerate only with great difficulty friends visiting himself and his wife. As a result they rarely entertained visitors. Because she had young children and did not work outside the home, this placed a strain on the wife and on the marriage.

Avoidance is most often coupled with the expression of fear. Thus agoraphobics avoid going out of doors or doing the shopping. Social phobics avoid gatherings of strangers, or even friends, and may be unable to speak in company. Dental phobics avoid dental treatment. However, many factors can limit the correlation between avoidance and the expression of fear and anxiety. For example, clients will tolerate intense distress during flooding treatment, when they are introduced to the situation which they dread most, because they understand that by doing so they will overcome their fear. Clients may also agree to medical and dental treatment even though very nervous at the prospect, because they wish to avoid an even more distressing outcome from ill-health. Socially anxious people attend meetings at work because of a greater fear of being reprimanded or of losing their jobs.

Other behaviours are associated with fear, for example, seeking reassurance from family, friends and doctors about risks to health. This is notable in fears in which panic attacks are prominent. Other ways of reacting to fears include drinking alcohol and abusing other drugs.

AETIOLOGY

An exhaustive review of aetiology is beyond the scope of this discussion but is available elsewhere (Marks, 1987; Edelmann, 1992).

Conditioning influences

The most influential theories of fear and anxiety in clinical psychology have been those which have emphasised the effects of an unpleasant experience occurring in association with an otherwise unthreatening situation: classical conditioning models (Rachman, 1991; Wilson, 1982). Such theories are in part consistent with the following example:

> An elderly woman at home is telephoned urgently by her husband from a public call-box because he has become ill while out exercising the dog. Unfortunately he collapses and dies before reaching home. The acute distress of this sudden bereavement is followed in his widow by an increasing reluctance to venture out of doors. She then has a panic attack when she is in a shopping centre some weeks later and the symptoms of breathlessness, palpitations and dizziness suggest to her that she too is likely to die suddenly while away from home and thus not close to help. Because she believes that she is safe only when at home and near a telephone, she becomes dependent on friends and neighbours to do her shopping. This client can remember a similar experience when she was much younger – dizziness and palpitations in such situations. This encourages her belief that she has a weak heart.

The neutral conditional stimulus is the shopping centre; the panic attack appears to be the unconditioned response. However, as in so many cases of agoraphobia, the unconditioned stimulus for that response is not clear.

Similar precipitating events have been reported in over 70 per cent of one sample of agoraphobics according to Thorpe and Burns (1983), but other surveys and analyses of this and other fears identify fewer instances where such a precipitant is evident (Murray and Foote, 1979; Lindsay and Jackson, 1993).

Although conditioning models have received increasingly less attention, they have been of considerable importance in supporting the initial developments of behavioural treatments for those problems. In addition, some of the behaviour, such as increases in heart rate and blood pressure, trembling and agitation, which is held to characterise fear and anxiety, has been highlighted by demonstrations of classical avoidance and non-avoidance conditioning (See Dykeman *et al.*, 1965).

These demonstrations appear to be most pertinent to explanations for those human fears such as post-traumatic stress disorder (Litz, 1992) and fears of pain in medical and dental treatment where there is a clear traumatic precipitant. However, even for the latter, cognitive influences such as changing memories and expectations of pain probably influence the development and persistence of fear (Lindsay, 1984; Lindsay and Jackson, 1993).

Other aetiological hypotheses

The observation of fear and avoidance in other people can serve as a model for that reaction in the client – a social learning hypothesis. Consistent with this, Windheuser (1978) has shown that children have similar fears to their mothers. Some authors have emphasised that certain stimuli such as snakes become more readily associated with fear because of some biological survival value (Seligman, 1971) – the preparedness hypothesis. Attention has also been drawn to the possible influence of ongoing stress on the development of acute fear and anxiety (Emmelkamp, 1982). Some authors have noted the high likelihood that children will develop additional fears when they already have many fears (e.g. Liddell, 1990). Adults with intense fears can present higher levels of neuroticism (Lautch, 1971). These observations have favoured arguments for biological and genetic influences on fears.

Rachman (1980) has reviewed those influences which have been implicated with varying degrees of certainty in laboratory and clinical research in the inability to overcome fear and stress. These include, in the subject, high arousal and fatigue at the time of stress, neuroticism and introverted personality. The stress is less easily overcome if it is sudden, intense, unpredictable, uncontrollable, and if other stresses, such as heat and noise, are present.

Foa and Kozak (1986), in an important theoretical paper, frequently illustrate, with psychophysiological data, the activation of fear. However, for many clinical purposes a theory which emphasises the association between physiological arousal, avoidance and cognitions (e.g. Zander and McNally, 1988) is not very constructive because in clinical practice it is the client's expression and experience of distress and behaviour, such as avoidance, reassurance-seeking and consumption of alcohol, which is of immediate concern. For example, consider the client who has been unable to drive to work in the centre of London because he is afraid of being caught in stationary traffic. He anticipates that, if that happened, he would find the entrapment so distressing that he would have to leave his car where it had stopped and run off. He expects that this would be highly embarrassing to him as he imagines being laughed and jeered at by the other motorists.

The priorities in treatment would appear to be a reduction in the distress (fear, anxiety, tension?) which the client experiences while he is in his car in a traffic jam for prolonged periods. It would be equally important to make it possible for him to drive in busy city streets with the considerable risk of being stopped on the way. Changing the client's expectancies about his experiences would probably be necessary for this. Hence it does not appear at first glance necessary to monitor and change physiological activity such as heart rate or skin conductance which appear to have no immediate part in the client's experience. Expression of fears and avoidance, unlike physiological activity, also have effects on observers, including clinicians and the patient's family. However, the monitoring of physiological activity will be discussed below. In some conditions physiological arousal will be of more direct concern than in this case.

Cognitive influences

Theories emphasising cognitive influences have recently had a major influence on the treatment of social fears (Butler, 1989), generalised anxiety and panic disorders (Clark *et al.*, 1988). These emphasise the sensitivity of fearful and panic-prone people to cues predictive of danger (see, for example, Mathews and

MacLeod, 1986). The interpretation of such experiences in a threatening manner then exacerbates the anxiety, which produces symptoms to which the client reacts with more anxiety. Such influences would thus be said to have contributed to the distress in the elderly woman described above. Much attention in experimental research has been devoted in recent years to the recall of material presumed to be alarming to subjects with anxiety disorders. Clinical experience suggests that such people often remember episodes in their lives which add to their present anxieties. For example, one socially anxious patient known to the author frequently remembered having been humiliated in school by teachers when he was much younger. Also, Post-Traumatic Stress Disorder is notable for the frequency with which sufferers describe vivid, intrusive flashbacks of the traumatic event, such as a mugging or a traffic accident, which has caused their distress.

Foa and Kozak (1986) frequently describe the activation of fear, in situations threatening to phobic subjects, as requiring an activation of memories. However, most experimental studies have failed to confirm that subjects with anxiety disorders have enhanced or impaired recall of material which has been presumed to be especially alarming for them: in agoraphobics (Pickles and van den Broek, 1988); in patients with panic disorder (Beck *et al.*, 1992) or generalised anxiety disorder (Mogg *et al.*, 1987). However, in veterans of the Vietnam War, Post-Traumatic Stress Disorder promotes efficient recognition of words evoking combat such as 'bodybags' (Zeitlin and McNally, 1991). This was in contrast to their poor recall of information in general.

In patients highly anxious about dentistry, Kent (1985) concluded that memories changed, so that three months after treatment, the patients described the experience as more painful than they had at the time of treatment. This raises the possibility that patients with anxiety disorders need not be especially efficient at remembering information which alarms them. Instead they may construct memories even inaccurately, to threaten them, consistent with other information.

More consistently, patients with anxiety disorders appear to be more efficient than normal subjects in detecting alarming information in tasks such as the Stroop test and dichotic listening (Mathews and MacLeod, 1986). In the reporting of the characteristics of frightening stimuli, snake phobic subjects reported that snakes showed more movement than was reported by control subjects (Rachman and Cuk, 1992).

Most of the studies of cognitive influences have not studied the impact of information of unique importance to each subject, such as the recall of childhood memories in the client described above. In addition, although these studies suggest that subjects with anxiety disorders can demonstrate biases of attention and recall for alarming material, it is not clear if this influences the generation of fear and anxiety day-to-day. These studies do, however, suggest that cognitive investigation of fears should be considered in clinical practice, especially because decline in sensitivity to such biases does appear to occur with successsful treatment (Rachman and Cuk, 1992; Horowitz *et al.*, 1979). Discussion of the different anxiety disorders below will show what is practicable. The next chapter will show that identifying with each patient his or her own concerns is the crux of successful cognitive therapy.

THE PRELIMINARY INVESTIGATION OF PHOBIAS

Psychophysiological recording

Psychophysiological recording, particularly of skin conductance and heart rate (Martin and Venables, 1980) was once favoured because such variables can be recorded continuously from the subject in situations where it may be difficult to obtain frequent verbal reports of anxiety. The continuous recording of physiological activity, especially of skin conductance, under repeated stimulation, has shown that anxious and some phobic clients demonstrate little of the decline in arousal (habituation) that is evident in control subjects (Lader and Wing, 1967; Lader, 1967). The decline in activity such as heart rate has been used to demonstrate the successful effects of the treatment of phobias and was very influential in the initial development of behaviour therapy (see for examples, Lader and Mathews, 1968; Watson et al., 1972).

There are other clinical indications for the use of psychophysiological investigation. It is possible that clients whose physiological reactions to phobic situations have not shown significant change with treatment are likely to relapse even though their reports of distress and avoidance have improved (e.g. Barlow et al., 1980). Craske and Rachman (1987) have shown that fast heart rate immediately before a behavioural test preceding a course of therapy can predict the return of fear after successful treatment. High heart rates during behavioural testing after treatment may also predict relapse. However, in clinical practice where a single subject is being assessed, it would be difficult to know what level of heart rate before or after treatment could reliably predict this. Caution would advise that failure to show any decline in heart rate with treatment should be regarded as a possible predictor of relapse even if the subject reported little fear or avoidance on completion of treatment.

Physiological recording may be advisable where the subject is unable to say how afraid he or she is, and so heart rate and other physiological variables, such as skin conductance, may provide a more accurate representation of how the subject is really feeling under stress.

Unfortunately, however, the correlation among the many physiological variables used for such purposes has long been recognised as low, variable and certainly not simple (Duffy, 1962). Moreover, the relationship between the client's expression of fear, approach-avoidance behaviour and physiological activity can also be low (Andrasik et al., 1980; Hodgson and Rachman, 1974), and so it has been suggested that these three domains of measurement should all be sampled in the clinical investigation of phobic subjects (Lang, 1979). However, this approach has made it difficult to interpret the different sources of data (Kozak and Miller, 1982) especially when they present conflicting information.

Although many attempts have been made to identify how physiological activity relates to the other variables of interest in fear, the value of collecting physiological data routinely in clinical work has not been established. In addition, the recording of physiological data free from artefact is difficult and expensive in clinical practice (Martin and Venables, 1980; Ray and Kimmel, 1979). Heart rate should be recorded only when the subject has been at rest for at least fifteen minutes and even then the recording should be done with as little movement by the subject as possible, say, immediately before undergoing a behavioural task which has been described to the client (see, for example, Craske and Rachman, 1987).

Under some circumstances, heart rate may show mainly deceleration rather than an acceleration to stimulation. The direction of the subject's attention has been postulated to account for this (Lacey and Lacey, 1980). Heart rate is therefore difficult for assessing brief reactions to discrete stimuli. It is probably best monitored over a period such as ten minutes and the average level recorded.

Lang (1979) has suggested that in the recording of heart rate, for example, there may be an increase for some phobic subjects as they imagine their encountering the situation, say dental treatment, which they dread, but only if they imagine also running off. However, not all fears are evident in this way. Agoraphobics would present little increase in heart rate when imagining standing in a supermarket queue, dropping the basket and running out of the store, even after training to promote imaginal attention to such events (cf. Zander and McNally, 1988). Foa and Kozak (1986) believe that subjects need to be aware during fear-provoking situations of all the following in order to show physiological arousal: the meaning of the experience (e.g. 'I could die, I'm ill'); the critical responses (e.g. 'I feel faint, I'm finding it impossible to get enough air'); the critical stimuli (e.g. 'everybody's looking at me'). Such engagement, evident in, say, increased heart rate, is probably necessary for a successful outcome to treatment (Foa and Kozak, 1986) although the evidence for this is weak (Marks, 1987).

There have been attempts, notably by Ost and his colleagues (e.g. Ost *et al.*, 1984), to characterise phobic subjects as physiological or behavioural responders to fear-provoking situations. The former are characterised as responding with increases in heart rate but are able to accomplish behavioural tests, such as a walk down a busy city street; the latter are unable to make the trip so far along the street but do not react with a similar increase in heart rate for the distance which they do travel. However, it is not clear if this has acceptable test-retest reliability; and some subjects can fall into both categories.

Perhaps it is not surprising that psychophysiological recording is no longer fashionable in clinical practice and most emphasis is now placed on clients' behaviour and reports of fear and avoidance. Even for the continuous monitoring of levels of distress in clients, subjective reports may be adequate. Lande (1982; Figure 8.1, p. 176) has demonstrated such minute-to-minute changes in clients' reports during flooding sessions.

Patients' reports of fear and other information

The following should be considered when investigating most fears. All this information may be obtained in an interview with the client, or when the client is asked to imagine being in a given situation, or during a rehearsal or role-play of such a situation or during an *in vivo* test of his or her fear. It will be more appropriate to describe how such data can be collected when behavioural testing is described (see p. 155). Throughout the following discussion, the clinician should distinguish carefully between what the client expects will happen and the client's experience of what has happened or what is happening to him or her in the situations of which he or she is most apprehensive. For example, an agoraphobic client may expect to fall down or faint in public as the result of a dizzy episode but may never have experienced that outcome in a panic attack. Treatment goals and procedures may differ considerably according to whether the client only expects to, or has in fact, collapsed in public.

It will probably be important to identify the *situations and stimuli* which the client expects to cause, or has experienced as causing, the most severe distress. Hence for an agoraphobic client it would be essential to identify stores, streets and other places which he associates with fear, acute tension, panic or some other strong negative emotion. For a client who is terrified of thunder, being in a caravan in a field during a thunderstorm might be the most distressing experience. It will be particularly constructive to identify situations the client has a strong likelihood of encountering in normal day-to-day activities.

Certain *attributes of these situations* may be important, such as distances from home, the presence/absence of a trusted friend, the noise of traffic, bright light, and the reactions of other people, especially strangers, to the client's distress. For example, has a client who is terrified of moths, and is thus prevented from going on holiday with the family, been teased when alarmed at the presence of a moth and has that been especially upsetting? In agoraphobic clients the absence of exits close to hand in supermarkets, or being confined in a hairdresser's chair or checkout queue, may aggravate their distress. Thus the clinician has to identify which features of the situation are most upsetting.

It will be essential to identify in more accurate terms than may have been possible during a first interview, *what the client has experienced or expects to experience* in the situations which the client has come to dread. How has the client felt or does he or she expect to feel – terrified, shaky, uneasy, tense, puzzled? Are physical sensations predominant – dizziness, trembling, feeling hot and cold, difficulty in breathing, strange sensations in the stomach?

Experienced to intense degrees, these can be the symptoms of a panic attack (Table 7.1), which can occur in association with most phobias (Barlow *et al.*, 1985).

What avoidance does the client report? Does the client take a taxi home rather than completing the shopping or does he or she have to sit down in a cafe? Other less obvious avoidance may occur, such as not looking at the most distressing aspects of the situation – the agoraphobic keeps looking at the pavement rather than at the crowds or the traffic. Others may devise distracting tasks to similar effect. Clients who are afraid of thunderstorms may prevent the family from going on holiday or may not venture out of doors without listening to the weather forecast. Clients with medical or dental fears may delay seeking medical or dental help. Clients with social fears may conceal themselves behind newspapers when in public or avoid commonplace topics of conversation.

What else does the subject do as a result of anticipating the worst: seek frequent reassurance from family, friends and doctors? Search for books and newspaper articles about illness such as heart disease and HIV infection? One woman known to the author, afraid that she had contracted an HIV infection and had passed it to her husband, telephoned him at work several times a day to ask him if his frequent cough (which she believed was evidence of his succumbing to AIDS) was becoming better. Other patients will, for example, drink alcohol before doing a feared task such as shopping.

Is there any *impairment of the performance of skills?* Does the client dry up in the middle of speaking or does he hesitate or stammer? Does an agoraphobic woman have difficulty in counting her money or remembering her shopping-list while in a crowded store? Clients with social anxieties may forget what they wanted to say, or even how to say it, when in company. Many clients who have practised relaxation at home or in the clinic may be overwhelmed by stress and thus be unable to implement that skill when it is most needed.

What *beliefs and expectations does the client report about his or her fears?* Does the agoraphobic woman think that the physical sensations mean that she will have a heart-attack? Do people with social anxieties believe that others will think them stupid if they say something trivial? Does a dental phobic believe that dentists almost always extract teeth when confronted with a patient? A critical question will probably be: what does the client think will happen or what is the worst that he or she believes could happen? Some women with panic disorders believe that panics are more frequent immediately before menstruation (Cook *et al.*, 1990). A daily diary recording panics and the onset and termination of menstruation did not confirm the clients' beliefs (ibid.)

With many subjects, distress will be experienced with varying degrees of *uncertainty* about the outcome. With some fears it may be the uncertainty or lack of control over events which is most upsetting (Miller, 1979; Thompson, 1980).

It may also be valuable to discover *how well the client thinks he or she will cope* when under stress, that is, how well the client thinks he or she will be able to implement the behaviour which has been avoided (see Cone, 1979). Some authors have demonstrated that such estimates of self-efficacy are good predictors of the client's avoidance behaviour, but one report suggests that such a prediction is equally well made from the client's expectations of how anxious he or she will feel when in the situation which has been avoided (Kirsch *et al.*, 1983).

What *notable substances does the client consume?* Many can exacerbate anxiety and contribute to the onset of panic attacks: these include alcohol (Cox *et al.*, 1990); caffeine in soft drinks such as Coke, Pepsi and Irn-Bru, and in coffee and tea (Charney *et al.*, 1985); cannabis, cocaine and other illicit drugs (Cox *et al.*, op. cit.); benzodiazepines such as diazepam and lorazepam (Petursson and Lader, 1984); some anti-depressants such as Seroxat; other medication such as salbutamol for asthma (British Medical Association, 1993). Ironically many of these substances are consumed in the client's belief that they will help anxiety. One estimate suggests that 20 per cent of people with anxiety disorders drink alcohol to excess (Cox *et al.*, op. cit.).

Is the client's *intake of food* normal? In the author's clinical experience, a low intake of food can be associated with panic attacks and sudden increases in anxiety especially if anxiogenic substances such as black coffee are consumed. This can occur in people who are concerned about being overweight and so have only black coffee for breakfast.

Medical screening

There are several illnesses in which anxiety can be prominent: hypoglycaemia from diabetes, low food intake and other causes; chronic hypertension; caffeine intoxication; Ménière's syndrome; hyperthyroidism; hypoparathyroidism; Cushing's syndrome (due to increased level of circulating cortisol); pheochromocytoma due to a tumour in the adrenal glands, which provokes the secretion of epinephrine and norepinephrine; mitral valve prolapse; and infectious illness in the elderly (Marks, 1987). These observations confirm the necessity of a physical examination for all cases where anxiety and its physical correlates are evident.

Self-report rating scales

Single-item scales

In recording clients' experiences of fear and anxiety, single rating scales have been ubiquitous. They have consisted of four or more points up to 100 with descriptors to anchor the end and intermediate points (see Chapter 1). These descriptors have differed considerably, with some scales confounding the experience of fear and physiological reactions, or fear and some other variable, such as avoidance or the difficulties caused by the fear.

Gelder and Marks (1966) devised a scale in which 0 was described as 'no uneasiness when meeting feared object'; 2 was given the description 'uneasiness but no avoidance', while 5 was 'terrifying, panic attack when avoidance impossible'. Other scales were used to describe the symptoms of sweating, palpitations or breathlessness, again on a six-point dimension of severity-frequency. Similar ratings were made in that study by the therapist, the patients and an independent assessor. The inter-rater correlations ranged from 0.69 to 0.82. Other authors unfortunately have found non-significant correlations (e.g. Solyom *et al.*, 1973) among different sources of measurement with these scales.

Marks and Mathews (1979) have produced an inventory which is widely used and which asks the client to rate the likelihood of avoiding seventeen situations, including the client's own main fear, on a nine-point scale. The 'troublesome' nature of six symptoms, such as 'feeling tense or panicky' and 'upsetting thoughts coming into your mind', is also quantified on nine-point scales. Finally, the client's main phobic symptoms are described on a scale of 'disturbance-disablement', again on a nine-point scale. While for some clients it may be appropriate in clinical practice to use scales such as these, it may be more appropriate to devise scales to correspond to each of the client's fears as he or she reports them (see Chapter 1).

Unfortunately, where only a single symptom is being rated and is not highly correlated with some clearly detectable evidence such as avoidance or increased heart rate, the anchoring of the scale becomes very difficult. The low correlations among the different variables of fear and anxiety noted above make this inevitable. For example, the anchoring point, 'so nervous in front of people that I could not present my research proposal at a meeting' would not be valid for clients who did make such presentations, in spite of their anxiety, because their jobs would be at risk.

Although single bipolar rating scales of the kind 0 = 'no anxiety' to 10 = 'extremely anxious' may be quick and easy to administer, they may be sensitive to sources of bias recognised in Chapter 1 for such poorly anchored scales. The variable test-retest reliability of ratings of symptoms which are thought to be stable in agoraphobia (Michelson and Mavissakalian, 1983) has led these authors to query the psychometric properties of such assessment.

Unfortunately, it is often necessary to determine the client's change in distress within a short period, such as a thirty-minute session of treatment, and single-rating scales administered repeatedly may be the only way of doing so (Figure 8.1, p. 176). One or two items from the Spielberger State-Trait Anxiety Inventory (State version) (Spielberger et al., 1983; see following section) can be used for this.

Multiple-item self-report scales

Questionnaires have been designed to reduce the standard error of measurement by sampling the client's estimates of fear or anxiety several times on a single occasion (e.g. Spielberger et al., 1983). Some scales have attempted to increase content validity by sampling the client's physical experiences as well as his or her semantic structure of anxiety (e.g. Husek and Alexander, 1963). Both these scales can be applied to any fear and free-floating anxiety. Some scales have been designed to sample the client's experience only of physical symptoms (Lay et al., 1974).

Many scales have been designed to measure the severity of specified fears – test-anxiety, fears of heights, snakes, spiders, dentistry (Haynes and Wilson, 1979; Corah, 1969). However, most have been investigated only in small samples mainly of undergraduates in the USA. Hence, estimates of their reliability and validity should be interpreted with considerable caution.

A number of scales, in particular, may be considered in greater detail for the measurement of transient anxiety, regardless of what has provoked the anxiety. That is, the subject is asked to complete the scale to describe how he or she is now. This may be during a behavioural test, or sitting in the clinic, or immediately before undergoing an alarming experience such as minor surgery.

The scale most often used for this, the State-Trait Anxiety Inventory (State version) (STAI; Spielberger *et al.*, 1983) consists of twenty adjectives, all synonyms or antonyms of 'anxious', each of which is rated on a four-point scale, 'not at all/somewhat/moderately so/very much so'. This scale has been widely documented (Smith and Lay, 1974; Buros, 1978) and has shown high criterion-validity in subjects under a wide range of stresses and both before and after behavioural treatment. High internal consistency has also been shown (Spielberger *et al.*, 1983) and so theoretically the STAI should have a low standard error of measurement. However, some subjects can be irritated by the presentation of similar adjectives as in the items 'I feel jittery' and 'I feel highly strung' or 'I feel calm' and 'I am relaxed'. Not surprisingly subjects give similar answers to the synonyms for anxiety and consistent answers for the antonyms but there is less correspondence between the two categories (Kendall *et al.*, 1976). The authors of the STAI and others (Knight *et al.*, 1983) have produced norms for psychiatric patients and normal subjects. Again the anchoring of the rating scale 'not at all' to 'very much so' makes comparison between subjects hazardous and so the STAI may be recommended for investigating changes within subjects only.

Behavioural testing

Wherever possible, some measure of the subject's ability to tolerate hitherto avoided situations should be recorded before, during and after treatment. This should be possible for most fears but may not be readily applied to generalised anxiety or in some situations, such as flying or medical treatment.

Perhaps the most simple avoidance measures have been recorded in phobias of animals and insects where the client is asked to proceed as near to the creature as possible without feeling anxious. The distance which remains between the client and the target when the client stops moving is the measure of the client's avoidance (Lang and Lazovik, 1963).

Such univariate scales of avoidance are often not practical or realistic in clinical work, however. It is much more common to consider a series of situations which can be graded by the client in a composite scale which is directly related to the distress they provoke. Hence the client describes the situation in which he or she anticipates experiencing most anxiety. This might be standing in the middle of a long checkout queue in a noisy crowded supermarket in bright artificial light. Tolerating this would probably be the final goal of treatment. A similarly demanding situation for that client might be standing in a bus queue. Slightly less distressing might be going through the supermarket checkout without having to wait. A situation in which no anxiety would be experienced should also be described and so a series of about a dozen such situations – *a hierarchy* – can be presented by the client down to the least stressful, which might be in this case sitting at home with the family.

An important exercise in behavioural testing sometimes lies in determining which of these situations the client can tackle without experiencing anything more than, say, mild unease. The clinician or someone else, who may be a co-therapist or the client's husband or wife, should observe the client in this situation. *In vivo testing* of this kind is highly desirable because several aspects of avoidance and other behaviour may be evident which were not described by the client in interview. These might include not looking up, or holding on to a companion. In addition, the client may anticipate being able to tolerate a situation but in reality find it too threatening. Also the client will probably be able to give a more accurate account of how he or she is feeling (on a rating scale) than could have been anticipated in the clinic.

Other criteria for the client's tolerance of each item of the hierarchy can be suggested by the clinician, such as the highest item which the client could tackle. *Time that the client can spend in a given situation* may be another measure of approach-avoidance. Distance which the client can proceed down a busy street before having to turn back could be another.

The situations which are described above might be appropriate for some agoraphobic clients. Other items which might be of value for agoraphobics have been described by Mathews *et al.* (1981: 202–5). Clients whose fears are associated mainly with encountering and relating to other people might describe such items as, 'walking along a busy street, not stepping aside for anyone and looking at passers-by straight in the eyes' or 'buying a piece of cheese and asking if you can taste it first' (Emmelkamp, 1982). Some such clients would find it difficult to look up from a newspaper or book when in a public situation such as sitting in a bus or hospital waiting-room. A series of items for dental and needle phobias have been described by Lindsay (1985).

It should be emphasised that a client's tolerance of a given item in reality may be influenced by instructions from the therapist or by similar demands from other sources (Trudel, 1978). According to how persuasive the therapist appears to the clients, they may remain in a highly distressing situation almost indefinitely (as they would in flooding treatment, see Chapter 8). Behavioural tolerance is therefore not an unbiased measure of fear (Trudel, op. cit.).

Sampling self-reports of fear and anxiety

It is suggested here that the clinician, in assessing fear, should record both the client's experience and his or her expectations of fear. When the client is about to encounter a given situation either in imagination or in reality, two questions should be asked:

1 How anxious is the subject *now?* (Subject completes rating)
2 How anxious does the subject *expect* to be or how well does the subject think he or she *will* cope? (Subject completes rating.)

In addition, for certain fears (see following sections), the client should record his or her negative thoughts in a daily record at the times of greatest fears.

DESCRIPTIONS OF COMMON ANXIETY DISORDERS

Structured diagnostic interviews corresponding to the criteria of *DSM III–R* are available (DiNardo *et al.*, 1985). The following outlines the characteristics of the major disorders of anxiety.

Panic disorder

The symptoms commonly associated with panic (*DSM III–R*; American Psychiatric Association, 1987) are shown in Table 7.1. The assessment of panic disorder is summarised in Table 7.2. Panic disorder, as characterised by *DSM III–R* requires that at least four symptoms (Table 7.1) are experienced during at least one panic; panics are unexpected and not triggered by some organic cause or identifiable circumstance; at least four panics occur in a period of four weeks; alternatively, one or more of the panics are followed by at least a month in which the subject dreads their reoccurrence; at least some of the panics reach maximum intensity in ten minutes. These characteristics can be identified in the Panic Attack Questionnaire[1] (PAQ; Norton *et al.*, 1985) updated for *DSM III–R*, completed by subjects themselves. Clum *et al.* (1990) have produced a questionnaire listing many additional symptoms which can be experienced in panics.

One of the most influential hypotheses has claimed that panics are caused by

Table 7.1 Symptoms of panic

1 Difficulty in breathing
2 Choking
3 Palpitations or feeling of racing heartbeat
4 Sweating
5 Feeling faint
6 Feeling dizzy, light-headed or unsteady
7 Nausea or uncomfortable stomach
8 Feeling unreal
9 Pains or other discomfort in chest
10 Numbness or tingling sensations
11 Hot/cold sensations
12 Trembling or shaking
13 Being afraid of dying
14 Being afraid of losing control, becoming insane

hyperventilation, breathing in excess of metabolic requirements. This blows off carbon dioxide (CO_2) from the lungs, and reduces CO_2 levels in the blood. Because CO_2 via chemoreceptors is a stimulus to breathing, when CO_2 reaches critical levels (hypocapnia), breathing stops (apnoea) to allow CO_2 to be replenished from the metabolism of oxygen. The depletion of CO_2 produces changes in musculature and vasoconstriction notably in the brain and in coronary arteries. These changes can be produced in human subjects by voluntary deep overbreathing at 30 or more breaths per minute for three minutes or longer (Keele *et al.*, 1982). Effects of this include dizziness, tingling in fingers and toes, faintness, sweating (Lindsay *et al.*, 1991) and cognitive impairment (Ley, 1989).

The correspondence between many of the symptoms of panic (Table 7.1) and overbreathing is clear. At one time voluntary overbreathing, the hyperventilation provocation test (HVPT), was used to determine with patients whether hyperventilation contributed to their panic attacks. If they recognised the symptoms of voluntary hyperventilation in the clinic as similar to those of a typical panic attack, hypocapnia was said to have contributed to that panic. However, recent studies (e.g. Hibbert and Pilsbury, 1989) have shown that hypocapnia takes place infrequently during panic in subjects diagnosed as being afflicted with panic disorder. In addition, performing laboratory tasks such as the Stroop test (Hornsveld *et al.*, 1990) can produce symptoms similar to those of hypocapnia, even in the absence of hypocapnia in patients with panic disorder. Also the HVPT has only moderate test-retest reliability (Lindsay *et al.*, 1991). Therefore the HVPT cannot now be used to determine that hyperventilation has contributed to a patient's panics. It can, however, sometimes be used to reproduce experiences similar to those of panics. Even without such close resemblance, this can be very alarming to some patients and so it can be used as an exposure exercise for treatment (see Chapter 8).

It is important to note that, because of the vasoconstrictive effects of hyperventilation, patients with cardiovascular disease should not be subjected to the HVPT. That could provoke angina, for example, in such subjects.

A number of other tests ('provocation tests') have been used to simulate or trigger panic attacks. They include inhalation of very high concentrations of CO_2 (35 per cent of inhaled atmospheres), ingestion of caffeine, and imagining and rehearsing panic attacks.

Panic cognitions

A number of psychological tests, notably the Anxiety Sensitivity Index (ASI; Reiss *et al.*, 1986), the Agoraphobia Cognitions Questionnaire (ACQ; Chambless *et al.*, 1984) and the Panic Attack Cognitions Questionnaire (PACQ; Clum *et al.*, 1990), can sample the worries which are believed to favour the development of distress and panics. For example, a panic-prone subject is likely to acknowledge on the ASI that 'it scares me when I feel shaky' (Reiss *et al.*, 1986). Patients with panic disorder and phobias who score high on the ASI are likely to report frequent panic attacks (Marks, 1988) and high levels of distress during an HVPT in the clinic. On the PACQ, a patient prone to panic attacks is likely to say that he was 'dominated' by the thought that his last panic would never end and that he would not be able to breathe.

It is advisable to supplement such questionnaires with a record *ad hoc* of preoccupations taken at the time of a panic. This can identify idiosyncratic worries such as, 'I am nowhere near a hospital.'

Physiological sensitivity

It is notable that patients subject to panic attacks are likely to describe more, and more intense, symptoms during HVPTs and during panics than do subjects who are not afflicted by panics or who do not seek help for them (e.g. Lindsay *et al.*, 1991). This and other evidence (Clark *et al.*, 1988) has suggested that patients with panic disorder are more sensitive to their physiological changes. However, recent evidence has been unable to confirm this. Patients with panic disorder are not especially adept at detecting false feedback of heart rate (Asmundson *et al.*, 1993).

Nevertheless, standard excercises such as stair-climbing which can increase physiological activity can be a useful basis for treatment. Ratings of anxiety under such tests could be used to demonstrate patients' response (reduction in ASI scores) to treatment.

Agoraphobia

People who suffer from agoraphobia, a fear or avoidance of being alone in public places (*DSM III–R*; American Psychiatric Association, 1987), often experience physical sensations continuously like patients with panic disorder: for example,

Table 7.2 Summary of assessment of panic disorder

---

1 Diary: daily recording of the occurrence/non-occurrence of panics, rating of severity (1–10) and duration; record also time of day, circumstances and consequences.
2 Before treatment to describe panic disorder and to diagnose (cf. *DSM III–R*) if necessary: Panic Attack Questionnaire (PAQ; Norton *et al.*, 1985).
3 To assess influences on panics before and after treatment: Anxiety Sensitivity Index (ASI; Reiss *et al.*, 1986); Panic Cognitions Questionnaire (PSQ; Clum *et al.*, 1990).
4 Before and after treatment: Panic Symptoms Questionnaire (PSQ; Clum *et al.*, 1990).
5 Provocation test before and after treatment to reproduce symptoms similar to those of panic: e.g. overbreathing (30+ deep breaths per minute for 3 minutes) or exercise test.
6 *Ad hoc* daily record of cognitions and their circumstances and challenges for sample of panics.

tension, feeling vague or unreal, trembling, a dry mouth (Arrindell, 1980). These symptoms can increase in intensity and, with the addition of other symptoms such as pains in the chest, can suddenly become panic attacks (see above). Many authors (e.g. Emmelkamp, 1982) have attributed these to hyperventilation. The association of hyperventilation with agoraphobia has been disputed, however, on the basis of clinical observations: agoraphobics are rarely seen to overbreathe (Mathews *et al.*, 1981). Nevertheless, panic attacks are common though not universal in agoraphobic clients (Barlow *et al.*, 1985; Wittchen, 1986). Moreover, many agoraphobic patients describe the onset of their difficulties as the occurrence of panic attacks (Franklin, 1987) which they then seek to curtail by avoiding places which they see as unsafe, such as supermarkets or anywhere outside home.

Factor analytic studies of fear surveys have shown that other fears, notably of enclosed places and of crowds of people, are also commonly associated with agoraphobia (e.g. Hamann and Mavissakalian, 1988). For many agoraphobics living in large cities, being in a stationary train between stations in the Underground would be the most terrifying experience. For many agoraphobics also, the embarrassment of being observed in a panic is very troubling.

Hallam (1978) has criticised the concept of agoraphobia, proposing that it should be seen as an aspect of diffuse, generalised anxiety. This is perhaps inappropriate because follow-ups of treatment in agoraphobics (Munby and Johnston, 1980) do not report any change in categorisation of such patients to generalised anxiety. However, these studies do not highlight those clients who had persistent difficulties and who might therefore have given reason for a redefinition of their problems. Hallam's more recent criticisms (Hallam, 1983) draw attention to the more frequent diagnosis of agoraphobia in women. This may be due to a greater readiness to allow women to be confined at home in response to psychological distress while men are encouraged to cope in other ways, such as by abusing alcohol.

Other authors, notably Goldstein and Chambless (1978) have maintained that agoraphobia, being evident mostly in women, arises in response to interpersonal stress and in dependent people with limited assertiveness. There is probably little evidence to support this as a generalisation except in the observation that female agoraphobics respond less well to treatment where the marriage is in difficulties (Bland and Hallam, 1981). It is not surprising, therefore, that assertiveness training alone is not as effective as exposure treatments (Emmelkamp *et al.*, 1983) in treating avoidance in agoraphobia.

Other problems occur with agoraphobia, notably depression, general anxiety, depersonalisation and loss of libido (Buglass *et al.*, 1977). Therefore, clinicians should be aware that almost all varieties of non-psychotic disturbance and interpersonal difficulties may be found.

Marks (1981) proposed that a phobia which occurs in clients aged 55 on average, older than the average age of agoraphobics, and which is characterised principally by a fear of falling, especially while out of doors, should be distinguished from agoraphobia. Marks believed that the high incidence of numerous physical symptoms, such as tinnitus and hypertension, in such cases indicated that a disorder of oculo-vestibular mechanisms was involved, and the condition has been called 'space phobia'. However, the separation of this from agoraphobia is questionable (Gelder, 1982). Other authors (Kantor *et al.*, 1980) have drawn attention to the presence of mitral valve prolapse in female agoraphobics who have reported experiencing palpitations. This condition was observed by these authors in only eleven out of twenty-five such cases but it is probably quite common amongst women. There is as yet no evidence to suggest that these cases should receive a different approach from that recommended for agoraphobics generally and all such referrals should receive medical screening in any case.

Cognitive theories of panic have led to studies of cognitions in agoraphobics. Compared with subjects with specific phobias, such as of spiders (Marks, 1988), agoraphobics show much higher fear of common agoraphobic symptoms, such as shortness of breath and feeling faint, as shown by the Anxiety Sensitivity Index (ASI; Reiss *et al.*, 1986). However, agoraphobics do not believe that these symptoms are more threatening to health than do normal subjects (Ahmad *et al.*, 1992). The ASI does predict the occurrence of panic in agoraphobics (Marks, 1988), high ASI scores being associated with high frequency of panic. ASI scores decline with successful treatment (Marks, ibid.). However, neither the ASI nor the Agoraphobia Cognitions Questionnaire (ACQ; Chambless *et al.*, 1984) can identify idiosyncratic fears or cognitions associated with agoraphobia.

For example, one agoraphobic known to the author was afraid of standing on loose floorboards because they made his knees unsteady, reminding him of his symptoms in panic attacks. For him, standing astride the junction of the two spans of Tower Bridge in London was particularly trying because they shook independently as traffic passed by. Hot air fans in stores can be similar triggers for other patients.

Physiological fears

In many fears (see above) the client may report the physiological arousal that can be associated with the experience of fear. In some cases the physiological reaction will be so prominent that it will be the clinician's main target in treatment as in fainting at the sight of blood, medical syringes or injury (Connolly *et al.*, 1976). There, a temporary increase in heart rate, a response associated with fear in other situations, is followed by a sharp decrease, a drop in peripheral blood pressure and fainting (Speirs, 1983). The nature of the association between the experience of fear and these physiological reactions is, however, even more puzzling in blood and injury phobia than it is for other fears. In exceptional cases, clients will describe how they always faint when they receive an injection but are not correspondingly afraid. Fainting is, nevertheless, not a common reaction associated with fears of injections and surgical inter-

Table 7.3 Summary of assessment for agoraphobia

1　Diary: daily recording of the occurrence/non-occurrence of panics (definition as agreed with the patient); rating of severity (1–10) and duration of each panic; record also time of day, circumstances and consequences.
2　Diary: daily record of activities done, places visited and with whom.
3　Compile in interview a detailed hierarchy of fear-provoking situations (e.g. the worst: being alone in supermarket when crowded; the easiest: sitting in the car outside the supermarket).
4　As measure of agoraphobic fear and avoidance before and after treatment: the Agoraphobia Scale (AS; Ost, 1990).
5　As indices of influences on agoraphobia before and after treatment: Anxiety Sensitivity Index (ASI; Reiss *et al.*, 1986); Agoraphobia Cognitions Questionnaire (ACQ; Chambless *et al.*, 1984).
6　Behavioural testing before and after treatment: e.g., how far patient can proceed down a certain street at, say, noon; or how long he or she can stay in a certain supermarket at a certain time. Observe avoidance behaviour, such as looking downwards.
7　Record state anxiety before and during each behavioural test (use *ad hoc* rating scale or choose items from State-Trait Anxiety Inventory (State version) (Spielberger, 1983).

vention. Most often, especially in dentistry, the client's main difficulty is an acute fear of experiencing pain (Lindsay and Jackson, 1993).

For them, behavioural tests such as the presentation of a syringe together with ratings of fear would be the main elements of the assesment. Recording blood pressure at the start of, and during, presentation could be instructive for patients who faint. There are now many user-friendly devices readily available for recording blood pressure. The most reliable and long-establised but cumbersome method is described in this book by Bundy (Chapter 28). A hierarchy of fear-provoking stimuli would be appropriate for determining treatment progress.

There are are other fears in which a physiological reaction is prominent. Patients may be unable to swallow and are afraid of choking to death. Being unable to pass urine in public toilets, especially with somebody close by, is common in men. In elderly patients, similar difficulties in urinating can be produced by a fear of severe urinary retention which can be very painful. Retching (a hypersensitive gag reflex) in response to the soft tissue of the mouth being touched by implements such as toothbrushes and dental mirrors can produce intense fears of any such object entering the mouth, so much so that clients may start to gag and initiate a panic as the implement approaches.

Social fears

Many people are afraid of social situations because they are apprehensive about the reactions of other people to their behaviour or appearance. For example, such people can believe that they will appear stupid if they make trivial comments about the weather. Similar beliefs are described elsewhere (Halford and Foddy, 1982; Glass *et al.*, 1982).

Social phobics can show a wide variety of avoidance behaviour. They may be unable to sit with colleagues at meal times and coffee breaks. They may conceal themselves behind newspapers in buses and in other public places. By such behaviour they can avoid seeing others looking at them, because being watched may be especially distressing.

In addition, people with social fears may behave awkwardly. For example, very frequently such people are unable to look at someone they are speaking to and so they look at the floor instead. Their speech may be inaudible or especially hesitant. The client, inhibited by anxiety from practising these everyday social skills, may or may not be aware of his or her deficiency, but it may provoke intolerant or unfriendly behaviour by others which then reinforces further anxiety and avoidance in the client. A more extensive discussion of social behaviour is presented by Spence in Chapter 11.

Panics can afflict subjects with social fears (Barlow *et al.*, 1985). Instead of being intensely afraid that they are experiencing some serious threat to life during a panic, socially phobic subjects can be afraid that their panics are evident to others and will become an object of ridicule, or will require some explanation from them under circumstances where they already find conversation difficult. In addition, socially phobic clients can be afraid that panics will impair further their performing in public.

Two commonly used questionnaires for measuring social anxiety are the Fear of Negative Evaluation (FNE) and the Social Avoidance and Distress (SAD) scales (Watson and Friend, 1969). However, the original report quotes data only from Canadian University students. The data were not normally distributed for either questionnaire, thus making normative analysis difficult. A short version of the FNE, again standardised on college students, has been reported by Leary (1983).

Turner *et al.* (1989) have produced a questionnaire[2] which discriminates social phobia from general anxiety disorder more clearly than the FNE and the SAD. However, this was shown in a sample of only twenty-one socially phobic subjects. There are several further studies of the questionnaire's other properties.

The worries which can preoccupy socially anxious subjects are sampled by the Social Interaction Self-Statement Test (SISST; Glass *et al.*, 1982). This is administered immediately before a rehearsal of a social encounter or a behavioural test consisting of a meeting and discussion with a member of the opposite sex. The SISST is probably best used for young subjects, being developed initially on samples of students.

Unfortunately, the SISST is also not adaptable to assessing cognitions in subjects as they encounter people in their daily lives. In addition, it may not sample idiosyncratic cognitions and so it is usually necessary to ask clients to keep a daily diary to record their worries as they occur from day to day.

Table 7.4 Summary of investigation in social phobia

1   Before and after treatment: Fear of Negative Evaluation (FNE); Social
    Avoidance and Distress (SAD; Watson and Friend, 1969) [short form of
    FNE; Leary, 1983]; Social Interaction Self-Statement Test (SISST; Glass *et
    al.*, 1982) before social interaction (real or simulated).
2   Daily diary: *ad hoc* recording of anxiety and other emotions, circumstances,
    negative thinking, constructive challenges.

Generalised anxiety disorder

Unfortunately there is a 'dearth of research aimed specifically at investigation of generalised anxiety disorder' (Rapee, 1991). Multiple-item scales which are completed by the client for measuring transient anxiety and fear have been produced, including the Multiple Affect Adjective Check-List (MAACL; Zuckerman and Lubin, 1965) and the Beck Anxiety Inventory (BAI; Beck, 1990). For the BAI, normative data for a wide range of different anxiety disorders are available (ibid.). The Penn Worry Questionnaire (Meyer *et al.*, 1990) allows subjects to describe their beliefs about their propensity to worry.

Structured interviews and corresponding ratings have been described, most notably the Hamilton Anxiety Scale (Hamilton, 1959) for the measurement of anxiety regardless of its source. A shorter version of the scale, the Clinical Anxiety Scale, with clearer instructions for scoring, has been developed (Snaith *et al.*, 1982). Normative data indicating need for treatment are available (Snaith *et al.*, 1986) but there is little information about the scale's internal consistency or inter-observer reliability.

The process by which anxious patients can produce a torrent of concerns during an interview, and thus rapidly escalate their anxiety, has been difficult to characterise and assess. Perhaps only psychophysiological variables could do that (cf. Lader and Mathews, 1970) but this remains to be exploited.

Post-Traumatic Stress Disorder (PTSD)

PTSD arises from catastrophic experiences, such as war-time combat, and civil disasters, such as train crashes, ferry sinkings, and being raped. There have been many theoretical reviews (e.g. Litz, 1992; Jones and Barlow, 1990) but there have been few corresponding developments in treatment for victims of civilian tragedies.

PTSD has now been established as grounds for successful litigation against those responsible for such disasters. This depends on the reliable diagnosis of PTSD for which DSM III-R (American Psychiatric Association, 1987) provides the criteria. These are summarised in Table 7.5.

A questionnaire, the Impact of Events Scale (revised), has been developed to allow clients to report their experience of (1) avoidance of reminders about the traumatic event; and (2) the extent to which cognitions about the event intrude into daily thinking (Horowitz *et al.*, 1979). Comparison data are available in the original reference from adult clients who had received treatment for distress associated with bereavement and other stresses. Clients can sometimes be so highly distressed by the questionnaire and other reminders of the trauma that a version completed by the interviewer can be useful (Weiss *et al.*, 1984).

Table 7.5 Summary of diagnostic criteria for Post-Traumatic Stress Disorder (PTSD)

1 The client has experienced an event which is beyond the range of normal human experience and would be very distressing to almost anybody.

2 That event is persistently re-experienced in at least one of the following ways:
   (a) Recurrent and intrusive distressing recollections of the event
   (b) Recurrent dreams of the event
   (c) Sudden acting or feeling as if the event were recurring, including vivid flashback memories
   (d) Intense psychological distress at exposure to events and stimuli that symbolise or resemble the event.

3 Persistent avoidance of stimuli associated with the event or numbing (not present before the event) of general responsiveness, as shown by at least three of the following:
   (a) Deliberate efforts to avoid thoughts or feelings associated with the event
   (b) Deliberate efforts to avoid avoid activities or situations that arouse memories of the event
   (c) Inability to recall an important aspect of the event
   (d) Greatly diminished interest in significant activities
   (e) Feeling of detachment or estrangement from others
   (f) Restricted range of affect (e.g. unable to have loving feelings)
   (g) A sense of a foreshortened future.

4 Persistent symptoms of increased arousal as shown by at least two of the following:
   (a) Difficulty in falling asleep or maintaining sleep
   (b) Irritability or outbursts of anger
   (c) Difficulties in concentrating
   (d) Hypervigilance
   (e) Exaggerated startle response
   (f) Physiological reactivity at exposure to events that symbolise or resemble an aspect of the event (e.g. shaking or feeling cold or perspiring at the scene of the event).

5 Duration of the psychological disturbance has been at least one month even though the onset was delayed. The length of the delay should be specified.

Source: Reprinted with permission from the *Diagnostic and Statistical Manual of Mental Disorders, 3rd edn, Revised.* © 1987 American Psychiatric Association.

Aspects of PTSD, notably emotional numbing experienced by some patients, have been difficult to assess. Measures of depression have been used but may not adequately represent this problem (Litz, 1992).

NOTES

Acknowledgement   The author wishes to express his gratitude to Dr. P. Hayward for his comments on a draft of this and the next chapter.
1   Available from Dr. R. Norton, Psychology Dept., University of Winnipeg, Manitoba, Canada, R3B 2E9.
2   Revised for *DSM III–R* and available from Multi-Health Systems Inc., 65 Overlea Boulevard, Suite 210, Toronto, Ontario, Canada M4H 1P1.

REFERENCES

Ahmad, T., Wardle, J. and Hayward, P. (1992) 'Physical symptoms and illness attributions in agoraphobia', *Behaviour Research and Therapy* 30: 493–500.

American Psychiatric Association (1987) *Diagnostic and Statistical Manual of Mental Disorders, 3rd edn Revised*, Washington, DC: American Psychiatric Association.

Andrasik, F., Turner, S. M. and Ollendick, T. H. (1980) 'Self-report and physiologic responding during in vivo flooding', *Behaviour Research and Therapy* 18: 593–5.

Arrindell, W. A. (1980) 'Dimensional structure and psychopathology correlates of the Fear Survey Schedule (FSS III) in a phobic population: a factorial definition of agoraphobia', *Behaviour Research and Therapy* 18: 229–42.

Asmundson, G. J. G., Sandleer, L. S., Wilson, K. G. and Norton, G. R. (1993) 'Panic attacks and interoceptive acuity for cardiac sensations', *Behaviour Research and Therapy* 31: 193–8.

Barlow, D. H., Mavissakalian, M. R. and Schofield, L. D. (1980) 'Patterns of desynchrony in agoraphobia: a preliminary report', *Behaviour Research and Therapy* 18: 441–8.

Barlow, D. H., Vermilyea, J., Blanchard, E. B., Vermilyea, B. B., DiNardo, P. A. and Cerny, J. A. (1985) 'The phenomenon of panic', *Journal of Abnormal Psychology* 94: 320–8.

Beck, A. (1990) *Beck Anxiety Inventory*, New York: Psychological Corporation.

Beck, J. G. and Scott, S. K. (1987) 'Frequent and infrequent panic: a comparison of cognitive and autonomic reactivity', *Journal of Anxiety Disorders* 1: 47–58.

Beck, J. G., Stanley, M. A., Averill, P. M., Baldwin, L. E. and Deagle, E. A. (1992) 'Attention and memory for threat in panic disorder', *Behaviour Research and Therapy* 30: 619–30.

Beidel, D. C., Turner, S. M. and Cooley, M. R. (1993) 'Assessing reliable and clinically significant change in social phobia: validity of the social phobia and anxiety inventory', *Behaviour Research and Therapy* 31: 331–7.

Berger, P., Browning, R., Anderson, D., Skrabanek, P., Johnson, J. R., Finch, P. D., Le Fanu, J., Mills, M., Wildavsky, A. and Kristol, I. (1991) *Health, Lifestyle and Environment: Countering the Panic*, London: The Social Affairs Unit/The Manhattan Institute.

Bland, K. S. and Hallam, R. S. (1981) 'Relationship between response to graded exposure and marital satisfaction in agoraphobics', *Behaviour Research and Therapy* 19: 335–8.

British Medical Association and The Pharmaceutical Society of Great Britain (1993) *British National Formulary*, London: BMA & PSGB.

Buglass, D., Clarke, J., Henderson, A. S., Kreitman, N. and Presley, A. S. (1977) 'A study of agoraphobic housewives', *Psychological Medicine* 7: 73–86.

Buros, O. (1978) *The Eighth Mental Measurements Year Book*, New York: Griffin Press.

Butler, G. (1989) 'Issues in the application of cognitive and behavioural strategies to the treatment of social phobia', *Clinical Psychology Review* 9: 91–106

Chambless, D. L., Caputo, C., Bright, P. and Gallagher, R. (1984) 'Assessment of fear of fear in agorpahobics: the Body Sensations Questionnaire and the Agorpahobia Cognitions Questionnaire', *Journal of Consulting and Clinical Psychology* 62: 1090–7.

Charney, D. S., Heninger, G. R. and Jatlow, P. I. (1985) 'Increased anxiogenic effects of caffeine in panic disorders', *Archives of General Psychiatry* 42: 233–43.

Chemtob, C., Roitblat, H. C., Hamada, R. S., Carlson, J. G. and Twentyman, C. T. (1988) 'A cognitive action theory of post-traumatic stress disorder', *Joural of Anxiety Disorders* 2: 253–75.

Clark, D. M., Salkovskis, P., Gelder, M., Koehler, J., Martin, M., Anastasiades, P., Hackman, A.; Middleton, H. and Jeavons, A. (1988) 'Tests of a cognitive theory of panic', in I. Hand and H. Wittchen (eds) *Panic and Phobias II*, Heidelberg: Springer.

Clum, G. A., Broyles, S., Borden, J. and Watkins, P. L. (1990) 'Validity and reliability of the Panic Attack Symptoms and Cognitions Questionnaire', *Journal of Psychopathology and Behavioral Assessment* 12: 233–45.

Cone, J. D. (1979) 'Confounded comparisons in triple response mode assessment research', *Behavioral Assessment* 1: 85–9.

Connolly, J., Hallam, R. S. and Marks, I. M. (1976) 'Selective association of fainting with blood-injury phobias', *Behavior Therapy* 7: 8–13.

Connolly, J. F. (1979) 'Tonic physiological responses to repeated presentations of phobic stimuli', *Behaviour Research and Therapy* 17: 189–96.

Cook, B. L., Noyes, R., Garvey, M. J., Beach, V., Sobotka, J. and Chaudry, D. (1990) 'Anxiety and the menstrual cycle in panic disorder', *Journal of Affective Disorders* 19: 221–6.

Corah, N. L. (1969) 'Development of a dental anxiety scale', *Journal of Dental Research* 48: 596.

Cox, B. J., Norton, G. R., Swinson, R. P. and Endler, N. S. (1990) 'Substance abuse and panic-related anxiety: a critical review', *Behaviour Research and Therapy* 28: 385–94.

Craske, M. G. and Rachman, S. J. (1987) 'Return of fear: perceived skill and heart-rate responsivity', *British Journal of Clinical Psychology* 26: 187–99.

DiNardo, P. A., Barlow, D. H., Cerny, J. A., Vermilyea, B. B., Vermilyea, J. A., Himadi, W. G. and Waddell, M. T. (1985) *Anxiety Disorders Interview Schedule – Revised (ADIS–R)*, New York: Phobia and Anxiety Disorders Clinic, State University of New York at Albany.

Donnell, C. and McNally, R. J. (1989) 'Anxiety sensitivity and history of panic as predictors of response to hyperventilation', *Behaviour Research and Therapy* 27: 325–32.

Duffy, E. (1962) *Activation and Behavior*, New York: Wiley.

Dykeman, R. A., Mack, R. L. and Ackerman, P. T. (1965) 'The evaluation of autonomic and motor components of nonavoidance conditioned response in the dog', *Psychophysiology* 1: 209–30.

Edelmann, R. J. (1992) 'Anxiety: Theory, Research and Intervention', in *Clinical and Health Psychology*, Wiley: Chichester.

Emmelkamp, P. M. G. (1982) *Phobic and Obsessive-Compulsive Disorders. Theory, Research and Practice*, New York: Plenum.

Emmelkamp, P. M. G., Van der Hout, A. and de Vries, K. (1983) 'Assertive training for agoraphobics', *Behavioural Research and Therapy* 21: 63–8.

Foa, E. B. and Kozak, M. J. (1986) 'Emotional processing of fear: exposure to corrective information', *Psychological Bulletin* 99: 20–35.

Franklin, J. A. (1987) 'The changing nature of agoraphobic fears', *British Journal of Clinical Psychology* 26: 127–33.

Gelder, M. (1982) 'Agoraphobia and space phobia', *British Medical Journal* 284: 72.
Gelder, M. G. and Marks, I. M. (1966) 'Severe agoraphobia: a controlled prospective therapeutic trial', *British Journal of Psychiatry* 112: 309–19.
Glass, C. R., Merluzzi, T. V., Biever, J. L. and Larsen, K. H. (1982) 'Cognitive assessment of social anxiety: development and validation of a self-statement questionnaire', *Cognitive Therapy and Research* 6: 37–9.
Goldstein, A. J. and Chambless, D. L. (1978) 'A reanalysis of agoraphobia', *Behavior Therapy* 9: 47–59.
Haines, A. P., Imeson, J. D. and Meade, T. W. (1987) 'Phobic anxiety and ischaemic heart disease', *British Medical Journal* 295: 297–9.
Halford, K. and Foddy, M. (1982) 'Cognitive and social skills correlates of social anxiety', *British Journal of Clinical Psychology* 21: 17–28.
Hallam, R. S. (1978) 'Agoraphobia: a critical review of the concept', *British Journal of Psychiatry* 133: 314–19.
Hallam. R. S. (1983) 'Agoraphobia: deconstructing a clinical syndrome', *Bulletin of the British Psychological Society* 36: 337–40.
Hamann, M. S. and Mavissakalian, M. (1988) 'Discrete dimensions in agoraphobia: a factor analytic study', *British Journal of Clinical Psychology* 27: 137–44.
Hamilton, M. (1959) 'The assessment of anxiety states by rating', *British Journal of Medical Psychology* 32: 50–5.
Haynes, S. N. and Wilson, C. C. (1979) *Behavioral Assessment. Recent Advances in Methods, Concepts and Applications*, San Francisco: Jossey-Bass.
Heimberg, R. G., Hope, D. A., Rapee, R. M. and Bruch, M. A. (1988) 'The validity of the Social Avoidance and Distress Scale and the Fear of Negative Evaluation Scale with social phobic Patients', *Behaviour Research and Therapy* 26: 407–11.
Hibbert, G. and Pilsbury, D. (1989) 'Hyperventilation: is it a cause of panic attacks?' *British Journal of Psychiatry* 155: 805–9.
Hodgson, R. and Rachman, S. (1974) 'Desynchrony in measures of fear', *Behaviour Research and Therapy* 319–26.
Hope, D. A., Gansler, D. A. and Heimberg, R. G. (1989) 'Attentional focus and causal attributions in social phobia: implications from social psychology', *Clinical Psychology Review* 9: 49–60.
Hornsveld, H., Garssen, B., Fiedeldij, D. and Van Spiegel, P. (1990) 'Symptom reporting during voluntary hyperventilation and mental load: implications for diagnosing hyperventilation syndrome', *Journal of Psychosomatic Research* 34: 687–97.
Horowitz, M., Wilner, N. and Alvarez, W. (1979) 'Impact of Event Scale: a measure of subjective stress', *Psychosomatic Medicine* 41: 209–18.
Husek, T. R. and Alexander, S. (1963) 'The effectiveness of the anxiety differential in examination stress situations', *Educational and Psychological Measurements* 23: 309–18.
Jones, J. C. and Barlow, D. H. (1990) 'The etiology of post-traumatic stress disorder', *Clinical Psychology Review* 10: 299–328.
Kantor, J. S., Zitrin, C. M. and Zeldis, S. M. (1980) 'Mitral valve prolapse syndrome in agoraphobic patients', *American Journal of Psychiatry* 137: 467–9.
Keele, C. A., Neil, E. and Joels, N. (1982) *Samson Wright's Applied Physiology, 13th edn* Oxford: Oxford University Press.
Kendall, P. C., Finch, A. J., Auerbach, S. M., Hooke, J. F. and Mikulka, P. J. (1976) 'The State-Trait Anxiety Inventory: a systematic evaluation', *Journal of Consulting and Clinical Psychology* 44: 406–12.
Kent, J. (1985) 'Memory of dental pain', *Pain* 21: 187–94.
Kent, J. and Gibbons, R. (1987) 'Self-efficacy and the control of anxious cognitions', *Journal of Behavior Therapy and Experimental Psychiatry* 18: 33–40.
Kirsch, I., Tennen, H., Wickless, C., Saccone, A. J. and Cody, S. (1983) 'The role of expectancy in fear reduction', *Behavior Therapy* 14: 520–33.

Knight, R., Waal-Manning, H. J. and Spears, G. F. (1983) 'Some norms and reliability data for the State-Trait Anxiety Inventory and the Zung Self-Rating Depression Scale', *British Journal of Clinical Psychology* 22: 245–9.

Kozak, M. J. and Miller, G. A. (1982) 'Hypothetical constructs v. intervening variables: an appraisal of the three systems model anxiety assessment', *Behavioural Assessment* 4: 347–58.

Lacey, B. C. and Lacey, J. I. (1980) 'Sensorimotor behaviour and cardiac activity', in I. Martin and P. H. Venables (eds) *Techniques in Psychophysiology*, Chichester: Wiley.

Lader, M. H. (1967) 'Palmar skin conductance measures in anxiety and phobic states', *Journal of Psychosomatic Research* 11: 271–81.

Lader, M. H. and Marks, I. (1971) *Clinical Anxiety*, London: Heinemann.

Lader, M. H. and Mathews, A. M. (1968) 'A physiological model of phobic anxiety and desensitisation', *Behaviour Research and Therapy* 6: 411–21.

Lader, M. H. and Mathews, A. M. (1970) 'Physiological changes during spontaneous panic attacks', *Journal of Psychosomatic Research* 14: 377–82.

Lader, M. H. and Wing, L. (1967) *Physiological Measures, Sedative Drugs and Morbid Anxiety*, Oxford: Oxford University Press.

Lande, S. D. (1982) 'Physiological and subjective measures of anxiety during flooding', *Behaviour Research and Therapy* 20: 81–8.

Lang, P. J. (1977) 'Imagery in therapy: an information processing analysis of fear', *Behaviour Therapy* 8: 862–86.

Lang, P. J. (1978) 'Anxiety: toward a psychophysiological definition', in H. S. Akiskal and W. L. Webb (eds) *Psychiatric Diagnosis: Exploration of Biological Predictors*, New York: Spectrum.

Lang, P. J. (1979) 'A bio-informational theory of emotional imagery', *Psycho-physiology* 16: 495–512.

Lang, P. J. and Lazovik, A. D. (1963) 'Experimental desensitisation of a phobia', *Journal of Abnormal and Social Psychology* 66: 519–25.

Lautch, H. (1971) 'Dental phobia', *British Journal of Psychiatry* 119: 151–8.

Lay, C., Ziegler, M., Herschfield, L. and Miller, D. (1974) 'The perception of situational consistency in behaviour; assessing the actor-observer bias', *Canadian Journal of Behavior Science* 6: 376–84.

Leary, M. R. (1983) 'A brief version of the Fear of Negative Evaluation Scale', *Personality and Social Psychology Bulletin* 9: 371–5.

Ley, R. (1989) 'Dyspneic-fear and catastrophic cognitions in hyperventilatory panic attacks', *Behaviour Research and Therapy* 27: 549–54.

Liddell, A. (1990) 'Personality characteristics versus medical and dental experiences of dentally anxious children', *Journal of Behavioral Medicine* 13: 183–94.

Lindsay, S. J. E. (1984) 'The fear of dental treatment: a critical and theoretical analysis', in S. Rachman (ed.) *Contributions to Medical Psychology III*, Oxford: Pergamon.

Lindsay, S. J. E. (1985) 'The anxious patient 2: The casual attender', *Dental Update* 12: 177–80.

Lindsay, S. J. E. and Jackson, C. (1993) 'The fear of dental treatment in adults: its nature and management', *Psychology and Health* 8: 135–54.

Lindsay, S. J. E., Saqi, S. and Bass, C. (1991) 'The test-retest reliability of the hyperventilation provocation test', *Journal of Psychosomatic Research* 35: 155–62.

Litz, B. T. (1992) 'Emotional numbing in combat-related post-traumatic stress disorder: a critical review and reformulation', *Clinical Psychology Review* 12: 417–32.

Marks, I. (1981) 'Space phobia: a pseudoagoraphobic syndrome', *Journal of Neurology, Neurosurgery and Psychiatry* 44: 387–91.

Marks, I. (1987) *Fears, Phobias and Rituals*, Oxford: Oxford University Press.

Marks, I. and Mathews, A. M. (1979) 'Brief standard self-rating for phobic patients', *Behaviour Research and Therapy* 17: 263–7.

Marks, M. (1988) 'Fear of fear in different phobic groups', Unpublished M. Sc. thesis, Institute of Psychiatry, University of London.

Martin, I. and Venables, P. H. (eds) (1980) *Techniques in Psychophysiology*, Wiley: Chichester.

Mathews, A. M. and MacLeod, C. (1986) 'Discrimination without awareness in anxiety states', *Journal of Abnormal Psychology* 95: 131–8.

Mathews, A. M., Gelder, M. G. and Johnson, D. W. (1981) *Agoraphobia: Nature and Treatment*, London: Tavistock.

Meyer, T. J., Miller, M. L., Metzger, R. L. and Borkovec, T. D. (1990) 'Development and validation of the Penn State Worry Questionnaire', *Behaviour Research and Therapy* 28: 486–96.

Meyer, V. and Reich, B. (1978) 'Anxiety management: the marriage of physiological and cognitive variables', *Behaviour Research and Therapy* 16: 177–82.

Michelson, L. and Mavissakalian, M. (1983) 'Temporal stability of self-report measures in agoraphobia-research', *Behaviour Research and Therapy* 21: 695–98.

Miller, S. M. (1979) 'Controllability and human stress: method, evidence and theory', *Behaviour Research and Therapy* 17: 287–304.

Mogg, K., Mathews, A. and Weinman, J. (1987) 'Memory bias in clinical anxiety', *Journal of Abnormal Psychology* 96: 94–8.

Munby, M. and Johnston, D. W. (1980) 'Agoraphobia: the long-term follow-up of behavioral treatment', *British Journal of Psychiatry* 137: 418–27.

Murray, E. J. and Foote, F. (1979) 'The origins of fear of snakes', *Behaviour Research and Therapy* 17: 489–93.

Norton, G. R., Harrison, B., Hauch, J. and Rhodes, L. (1985) 'Characteristics of people with infrequent panic attacks', *Journal of Abnormal Psychology* 94: 216–21.

Ost, L. G. (1990) 'The Agoraphobia Scale: an evaluation of its reliability and validity', *Behaviour Research and Therapy* 28: 323–30.

Ost, L. G., Jerremalm, A. and Jansson, L. (1984) 'Individual response patterns and the effects of different behavioral methods in the treatment of agoraphobia', *Behaviour Research and Therapy* 22: 697–708.

Peterson, R. A. and Heilbronner, D. (1987) 'The Anxiety Sensitivity Index: construct validity and factor analytic structure', *Journal of Anxiety Disorders* 1: 117–22.

Petursson, H. and Lader, M. H. (1984) *Dependence on Tranquillizers*, Oxford: Oxford University Press.

Pickles, A. J. and van den Broek, M. D. (1988) 'Failure to replicate evidence for phobic schemata in agoraphobic patients', *British Journal of Clinical Psychology* 27: 271–3.

Rachman, S. J. (1980) 'Emotional processing', *Behaviour Research and Therapy* 18: 51–60.

Rachman, S. J. (1991) 'Neo-conditioning and the classical theory of fear acquisition', *Clinical Psychology Review* 11: 155–74.

Rachman, S. J. and Cuk, M. (1992) 'Fearful distortions', *Behaviour Research and Therapy* 30: 583–9.

Rapee, R. M. (1991) 'Generalised Anxiety Disorder: a review of clinical features and theoretical concepts', *Clinical Psychology Review* 11: 419–40.

Ray, R. L. and Kimmel, H. D. (1979) 'Utilisation of psychophysiological indices in behavioral assessment: some methodological issues', *Journal of Behavioral Assessment* 2: 107–22.

Reiss, S., Peterson, R. A., Gursky, D. M. and McNally, R. J. (1986) 'Anxiety sensitivity, anxiety frequency and the prediction of fearfulness', *Behaviour Research and Therapy* 24: 1–8.

Seligman, M. E. P. (1971) 'Phobias and preparedness', *Behavior Therapy* 2: 307–20.

Smith, R. C. and Lay, C. D. (1974) State and trait anxiety: an annotated bibliography', *Psychological Reports* 34: 519–94.

Snaith, R. P., Baugh, S. J., Clayden, A. D., Husain, A. and Sipple, M. A. (1982) 'The Clinical Anxiety Scale: an instrument derived from the Hamilton Anxiety Scale', *British Journal of Psychiatry* 141: 518–23.

Snaith, R. P., Harrop, F. M., Newby, D. A. and Teale, C. (1986) 'Grade scores of the Montgomery–Asberg Depression and the Clinical Anxiety Scales', *British Journal of Psychiatry* 148: 599–601.

Solyom, L., Heseltine, G. F. D., McClure, D. J., Solyom, C., Ledwidge, B. and Steinberg, S. (1973) 'Behavior therapy v. drug therapy in the treatment of phobic neurosis', *Canadian Psychiatric Association Journal* 18: 25–31.

Speirs, R. L. (1983) 'Some reflections on the mechanism of the common faint', *Dental Update* 644–50.

Spielberger, C. D., Gorsuch, R. L., Lushene, R. E., Vagg, P. R. and Jacobs, G. A. (1983) *Manual for the State-Trait Anxiety Inventory*, Palo Alto, Calif.: Consulting Psychologists Press.

Taylor, S. E. and Brown, J. D. (1988) 'Illusion and well-being: a social psychological perspective on mental health', *Psychological Bulletin* 103: 193–210.

Thompson, S. (1980) 'Will it hurt if I can control it? A complex answer to a simple question', *Psychological Bulletin* 90: 89–101.

Thorpe, G. L. and Burns, L. E. (1983) *The Agoraphobic Syndrome. Behavioral Approaches to Evaluation and Treatment*, Chichester: Wiley.

Trudel, G. (1978) 'The effects of instructions, level of fear, duration of exposure and repeated measures on the behavioural avoidance test', *Behaviour Research and Therapy* 17: 113–18.

Turner, S. M., Beidel, D. C., Dancu, C. V. and Stanley, M. A. (1989) 'An empirically derived inventory to measure social fears and anxiety: the Social Phobia and Anxiety Inventory', *Psychological Assessment: a Journal of Consulting and Clinical Psychology* 1: 35–40.

Watson, D. and Friend, R. (1969) 'Measurement of social evaluative anxiety', *Journal of Consulting and Clinical Psychology* 33: 448–57.

Watson, J. P., Gaind, R. and Marks, I. M. (1972) 'Physiological habituation to continuous phobic stimulation', *Behaviour Research and Therapy* 10: 269–78.

Weiss, D. S., Horowitz, M. J. and Wilner, N. (1984) 'The Stress Response Rating Scale: a clinician's measure for rating the response to serious life events', *British Journal of Clinical Psychology* 23: 202–15.

Wilson, G. T. (1982) 'The relationship of learning theories to behavioural therapies: problems, prospects and preferences', in J. C. Boulougouris (ed.) *Learning Theory Approaches to Psychiatry*, Chichester: Wiley.

Windheuser, H. J. (1978) 'Anxious mothers as models for coping with anxiety', *Behavioural Analysis and Modification* 2: 38–58.

Wittchen, H. U. (1986) 'Epidemiology of panic attacks and panic disorders', in I. Hand and H. U. Wittchen (eds) *Panic and Phobias. Empirical Evidence of Theoretical Models and Long-Term Effects of Behavioral Treatments*, Berlin: Springer-Verlag.

Zander, J. R. and McNally, R. T. (1988) 'Bi-informational processing in agoraphobia', *Behaviour Research and Therapy* 26: 421–30.

Zeitlin, S. B. and McNally, R. J. (1991) 'Implicit and explicit memory bias for threat in post-traumatic stress disorder', *Behaviour Research and Therapy* 29: 451–8.

Zuckerman, M. and Lubin, B. (1965) *Manual for the Multiple Affect Adjective Check-List*, San Diego: Education and Industrial Testing Service.

Chapter 8

Fears and anxiety
Treatment

S.J.E. Lindsay

INTRODUCTION

The treatments which made the first major successful impact on fears were the behaviour therapies developed in the 1960s and 1970s. These were first tested on simple fears and then extended to agoraphobia. The 1980s have seen the development of treatment especially by cognitive therapies of more complex fears, notably social phobia, generalised anxiety, panic disorders and simple fears resistant to behaviour therapies.

Among the behaviour therapies there is a wide variety of techniques, and Marks (1981) has listed over forty which he has said, then and since (Marks, 1987), have the one outstanding principle of successful treatment, namely, the exposure of the client to the threat which is feared. Some authors have emphasised the necessity of exposure without distress (Gelder, 1975); others have claimed that treatment should have the aim of encouraging the subject to believe that he or she can cope with the threat and implement approach behaviour – self-efficacy (Bandura, 1977); others have emphasised that treatments are effective according to the extent to which they reduce discouraging cognitions (Goldfried, 1979) or disprove to the client that the worst outcome which the client expects in his or her most intense fears will not happen.

Behaviour therapy for fears may be conducted in the imagination of the client or in reality (*in vivo*); it may consist of a gradual introduction to the most threatening experience (graded exposure) or an introduction at the outset to that situation with very little preparation (flooding). Exposure may be indirect when the client sees a demonstration of another subject undergoing exposure (modelling).

Treatment of this kind may be preceded by the practice and encouragement of a number of skills, such as applied or progressive relaxation (Ost, 1987; Bernstein and Borkovec, 1973). Exposure to threatening situations may take place after activities to reduce anxiety (Johnson *et al.*, 1982; Wolpe, 1981), such as laughter, exhaustion, eating, and tranquilliser-induced equanimity (Zitrin, 1981). Reinforcement of coping behaviour and exposure together with feedback of success have also been used (O'Brien, 1981; Leitenberg *et al.*, 1969).

Whatever method is used successfully to treat and manage fear, there is much dispute about what contributes to that success (Foa and Kozak, 1986; Marks, 1987; Brewin, 1988). However, so vast is the literature that an assessment of these issues is beyond the scope of this review and is available elsewhere (op. cit.).

BEHAVIOUR THERAPY FOR PHOBIAS: GENERAL ISSUES

The components of the successful treatment of fear are summarised in Table 8.2. The first steps in treatment are as follows.

After discussing with clients a formulation of their difficulties, an explanation of the nature of fear and anxiety is probably essential: the symptoms of anxiety and the effects of cues and cognitions in triggering fear and symptoms.

The withdrawal of anxiogenic substances is probably the next step: substances such as caffeine, benzodiazepines and alcohol (see Chapter 7).

However, there has been no clear evidence that continued consumption of benzodiazepines impedes or facilitates psychological treatment especially in the dosages recommended for anxiolytic use (Wardle et al., 1993). Even sedation with Brevital (metho-hexitone sodium) during behaviour therapy has no clear advantage (Chambless et al., 1980). Nevertheless, it is possible that the reduction of the consumption of benzodiazepines alone can reduce anxiety (Petursson and Lader, 1984). This can be helped by information about the symptoms of withdrawal given by the patient's doctor or in books (e.g. Lacey and Woodward, 1985) and by mutually supportive groups of patients undergoing withdrawal (Cormack et al., 1989), or by anxiety management from psychologists (Fraser et al., 1990). However, there is no clear evidence in favour of any one of these procedures.

There appear to be few studies which test the effect of the continued consumption of benzodiazepines after successful behaviour therapy. It is not clear, therefore, if persistent dependence could favour relapse. However, consistent with arguments elsewhere in this chapter, fear would appear to have been inadequately processed in cases where benzodiazepines are still used by the patient. In addition, there is the risk that successful psychological treatment could be attributed by the patient to the benzodiazepines, thus reinforcing their continued use and discouraging the practice of the psychological skills acquired in treatment. There are also a number of side effects associated with addiction to benzodiazepines, including depression and symptoms resembling those of influenza (Petursson and Lader, 1984). Therefore, it would be advisable to eliminate dependence at the outset as part of treatment. Unfortunately, this is sometimes unacceptable to patients, the distress of withdrawal and belief in the efficacy of tranquillisers being too great. This belief can be reinforced in the patients by the increase in anxiety experienced when consumption is discontinued. Being unwilling to wait until these symptoms subside, they are thus convinced that they need tranquillisers indefinitely. Psychological treatment may therefore have to proceed in spite of this.

Similar arguments can be applied to the continuing consumption of alcohol, caffeine and other drugs in view of their anxiogenic properties, their reinforcement of dependence and other destructive effects.

EARLY BEHAVIOURAL TREATMENT: SYSTEMATIC DESENSITISATION

Procedure. Systematic desensitisation, graded exposure in imagination, was the earliest treatment to receive thorough scientific investigation (Wolpe, 1958; Paul, 1966) and required that the therapist and client first construct a hierarchy of threatening stimuli (see Chapter 7). Following training in progressive relaxation, the client imagined experiencing the first, most innocuous, of these. If the client experienced any anxiety, this was signalled to the therapist, who then prompted the client to dismiss that imagery, think of a neutral scene and resume intensive relaxation for about one minute. Once that had been accomplished, the client then imagined the same stimulus and if that was experienced with minimal anxiety, the client imagined the next most threatening situation. If the client experienced distress with that, he or she discontinued that item, practised further relaxation and either imagined again the previously experienced item or a neutral situation.

This procedure would continue until the most threatening situation had been experienced in imagination with minimal discomfort. Paul (1966) suggested that this procedure should be completed in five sessions with the therapist being careful to terminate each session successfully, that is, with an item that provoked no distress.

Sometimes it would be necessary to introduce additional items to deal with aspects which the subject had forgotten. For example, the client might remember being acutely nervous in a shopping crowd when her friend was no longer nearby. Hence, items in which the contact with a trusted companion varied, would have to be introduced. The imaginal rehearsal might also be enhanced by audiotapes and videotapes of situations of particular interest to the client (e.g. Solyom *et al.*, 1972). The therapist, to confirm engagement in the exposure, could also prompt the client to describe aspects of the situations as they are encountered (Tower and Singer, 1981).

Influences on the outcome of systematic desensitisation

Marks (1975) reviewed the early work on exposure much of which was on systematic desensitisation in fantasy. He concluded that the outcome was more favourable if exposure to individual items consisted of hours rather than minutes or half-a-minute rather than a few seconds. Frequent sessions (say twice a day) were no more effective than twice in two weeks. It was debatable whether it made any difference whether the therapist or the client controlled the presentation of the stimulus items.

Relaxation was concluded from several studies to be unimportant and a number of investigations suggested that shifting the subject's attention by means of instruction from the therapist or by playing music (Yulis *et al.*, 1975) had an effect as great as relaxation. One report (Sue, 1972) found that even increasing muscle tension was as effective as relaxation. Marks (1975) also noted some evidence that experiencing the hierarchy items in the reverse order was as effective as the orthodox procedure.

Desensitisation *in vivo* or in imagination?

Although Wolpe (1958) has concluded that the generalisation of desensitisation to the corresponding reality occurs rapidly, other authors have reported unsatisfactory generalisation (Leitenberg *et al.*, 1969; and see Emmelkamp, 1982: 45), and so it would be unwise to assume that generalisation is invariable. It would be advisable to arrange for corresponding *in vivo* exposure wherever possible, either as homework accompanying a clinic-based programme or as an *in vivo* programme within the environment to which generalisation is desired to take place.

For some fears, however, such as those of flying or of thunderstorms or of medical procedures, it may be difficult, if not impossible, to arrange more than a single exposure to target situations and so imaginal desensitisation or similar procedures may have to suffice (Ost, 1978; Howard *et al.*, 1983).

EXPOSURE WITHOUT FEAR

Where experience of a series of situations can be arranged, graded exposure in reality may follow a similar pattern to that of imaginal desensitisation except that it may be more difficult to arrange exposure to items without producing anxiety. It may be possible to present some material for specific fears, such as those of insects and of surgical procedures, in a manner similar to the desensitisation programme outlined above. In the simplest situation, for example, a spider can be brought nearer to the client in stages, the subject practising relaxation or retracing previously experienced exposure where necessary. A similar *in vivo* procedure has been described by Emmelkamp (1982: 282) even for the treatment of agoraphobia. In the self-controlled exposure programme which he describes, the client is asked to proceed into the situation which she fears until she begins to experience 'undue anxiety'. The client then retreats until that anxiety has diminished and then repeats that procedure throughout a ninety-minute period.

EXPOSURE WITH FEAR?

One treatment in particular which has been described as a quicker alternative to desensitisation or graded *in vivo* exposure is flooding. Marshall *et al.* (1979) have described this as a treatment which exposes the client to 'aversive stimuli for prolonged periods in the absence of actual physically injurious consequences' with the result that the client undergoes 'overwhelmingly provocative stimulation'.

In spite of the highly intense distress which frequently occurs in flooding, it has proved to be safe (Shipley and Bedouwyns, 1980). Most authors consider flooding to require, and to result in, the diminution of fear and physiological arousal within the duration of the sessions (Stern and Marks, 1973; Marshall *et al.*, 1979; Foa and Chambless, 1978; Lande, 1982). However, one study uses the term 'flooding' to describe exposure to stimuli provoking moderate levels of anxiety and where the client's distress increased towards the end of the sessions (Mathews and Shaw, 1973). Flooding is now widely applied to exposure where some fear is experienced.

Flooding may be conducted in imagination or *in vivo* (e.g. Emmelkamp and Wessels, 1975; Mathews *et al.*, 1976), and it has been concluded from these studies that the latter is more effective (Mathews *et al.*, 1981; Emmelkamp, 1982; Marshall *et al.*, 1979).

The changes in distress which are usually sought and experienced within sessions of flooding are illustrated in Figure 8.1 taken from Lande (1982). He obtained ratings of fear and recordings of respiration rate and heart rate. These all increased as the client imagined being criticised by a supervisor and declined as that experience was continued over twenty-four minutes. Foa *et al.* (1980) observed that reduction in distress to baseline took ninety minutes for another case of flooding in imagination.

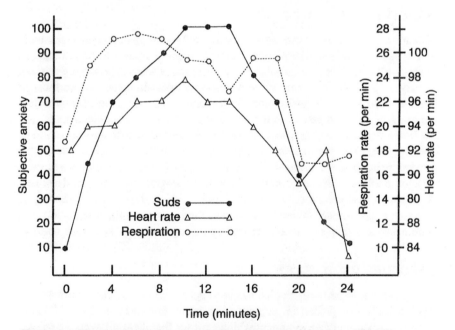

Figure 8.1 Changes in distress in a subject during one session of flooding

Source: Lande, *Behaviour Research and Therapy* 1982, 20, 81–8, with permission from Elsevier Science Ltd, Kidlington OX5 1GB, UK.

An alternative procedure for *in vivo* exposure has been described by Mathews *et al.* (1981). For this, the client is instructed to remain in a given situation until anxiety diminishes. (See also Marks, 1981; Marshall *et al.*, 1979.) A range of situations may be tackled in this way. Thus the client may enter a supermarket at a quiet time with a friend and stay there until she becomes less ill at ease; a subsequent stage might consist in going to a supermarket at a busier time. It may not be necessary for fear to be reduced to minimal levels thus within sessions (see the section on engagement and response prevention, on p. 178).

If *in vivo* exposure is practicable or is not too expensive in terms of therapist's time, why should not all treatment consist of *in vivo* exposure? Unfortunately, it may not be possible initially to find a situation which the client is prepared to face in reality. Under those circumstances, it may be less threatening for the client to undergo desensitisation to a hierarchy in which items range from some in imagination to others in reality. Hence for an agoraphobic client, these might include imagining stepping outside the front door and walking to the end of the street. Other items might consist in practising walking to the local shops.

It may also be helpful to demonstrate the procedure of exposure by a session in the clinic where only exposure in fantasy is experienced. Thus the client would learn how anxiety is to be controlled, by the self-control procedure or by allowing the anxiety to diminish as described above.

Clearly, also, there would be some cost benefits if imaginal desensitisation in the clinic were as effective as a similar procedure conducted *in vivo*. Unfortunately, Linden (1981) and James *et al.* (1983) have claimed that although studies have supported the superiority of *in vivo* graded exposure to imaginal desensitisation for non-clinical fears, this has not been satisfactorily tested for more serious problems. James *et al.* (ibid.), however, did find that for six cases of agoraphobia who had been seriously disabled for on average eight years, imaginal desensitisation was as effective as a corresponding *in vivo* treatment.

Procedures which limit the cost of treatment include the treatment of clients in groups (e.g. Hand *et al.*, 1974), the administration by the client of the programme in the client's own environment (Mathews *et al.*, 1981), the participation of nurse therapists (Ginsberg and Marks, 1977) or the client's relatives acting as co-therapists (Mathews *et al.*, 1981) and contact between the client and therapist by telephone (Taylor, 1984).

Manuals are useful to supplement treatment supervised by a therapist (for example, for agoraphobia, Mathews *et al.*, 1981). However, the evidence that self-help manuals are effective as the sole source of help is conflicting (Ghosh *et al.*, 1988; Holden *et al.*, 1983).

The duration of sessions

Many investigations have sought to determine how long flooding sessions should be (Marshall *et al.*, 1979). Sessions between thirty and sixty minutes are probably best (Marks, 1987), and it is often suggested that flooding should continue for each session until the client is experiencing minimal anxiety (Marshall *et al.*, op. cit.), confirmed by the client's verbal report (Gauthier and Marshall, 1977). Such complete reduction in anxiety may not be necessary (see below, this section).

It would appear appropriate, therefore, that the therapist should choose, from a range of situations for each client, an item which is likely to produce something less than maximum distress. It would be expected that such a procedure would result in the diminution of anxiety for that situation within an acceptable period, say, an hour. Unfortunately, the changes in distress for moderately threatening items may follow a different pattern from that observed for more provoking stimuli. As it was noted above in the Mathews and Shaw (1973) study, less threatening situations may result in increases in anxiety within the same period as reductions in fear are recorded for more intense reactions. Fortunately, in that investigation the presentation of moderately distressing stimuli nevertheless resulted in a more favourable outcome for treatment than high-intensity exposure.

The frequency of exposure sessions

The optimum frequency of flooding sessions may also be of critical importance, although this problem has received much less attention than the duration of sessions (Foa *et al.*, 1980). These authors have suggested that frequent sessions (daily in their study) are more productive than less frequent treatments (once a week). However, it is probably equally important to encourage the client to practise exposure at home between sessions. The observations of Foa *et al.* (ibid.) have also suggested that more frequent sessions should occur at the start of treatment, especially in highly distressed clients who are pessimistic about the outcome. This will be especially true with those clients who say, as do many agoraphobics, that the encouragement by the therapist is the most helpful aspect of treatment (Mathews, 1977).

Engagement and response prevention in exposure

It can be difficult sometimes, especially when the client expects to be seriously distressed as in a flooding session, to ensure that the client is fully attentive to the situation (Emmelkamp and Van den Hout, 1983). Hence, an agoraphobic may go through an entire programme of exposure without looking up or further than two or three feet ahead. He or she may spend all of the treatment time clutching on to railings or keeping close to walls or doorways and he or she may choose certain stores as targets because they have frequent and readily accessible exits. It is possible that such behaviour may be maintained after treatment has been discontinued and may be a considerable improvement on what has gone before. However, treatment can hardly be said to be complete until the client is encouraged to cope without these activities.

Evidence suggests that effective exposure requires that the client pays attention to the cues which provoke the fear. It may be helpful also to experience the images and memories and evaluations which have contributed to that fear (Marks, 1987; Foa and Kozak, 1986). Therefore, for example, the agoraphobic described in the preceding chapter should remember, while confined in a stationary car in a traffic jam, that he has had to abandon his car in those circumstances and that he fears being seen running off and causing a commotion.

It is thus also recommended that behaviour which has been used to curtail fear in the past, such as the seeking of reassurance from family, friends and doctors, should be discontinued. With the consent of the patient, it can be helpful to discuss this with those from whom the patient has sought reassurance. It can often be very difficult for others not to give in occasionally to frequent demands of that kind. The patient thus understands that persistence is the way to receive reassurance.

It is not clear if escape from demanding situations in a treatment programme should be prevented. For example, an agoraphobic leaves a supermarket when anxiety becomes intolerable. There are several accounts in which such escape does not appear to impede the success of treatment. It is probably necessary for the client to return to repeat the exercise (Marks, 1987; Emmelkamp, 1982).

THE PROBLEM OF RESISTANT FEAR AND GENERALISED ANXIETY

Although there is much evidence that exposure is very successful in effecting a sustained improvement in fear (e.g. Munby and Johnston, 1980), many patients do not recover completely (Emmelkamp and Van den Hout, 1983; Jacobson et al., 1988; Michelson and Marchione, 1991). For this problem and for more widespread anxiety, a number of authors have also recommended teaching more adaptive coping skills, cue-controlled relaxation, self-control desensitisation, anxiety-management training, stress inoculation, self-statement modification (Barrios and Shigetomi, 1979) and applied relaxation (Ost, 1987). These may be appropriate where exposure training is difficult to arrange, as in fear of flying, medical treatment and thunderstorms, or in widespread anxiety.

Table 8.1 Procedures to promote the efficacy of exposure conducted over several sessions

Long sessions (30+ minutes)
Frequent sessions (2+ per week)
Thorough engagement
Ensure some arousal but avoid high arousal during exposure
Homework between sessions
Exposure completed in a single session? (Ost, 1989)
Prevention of avoidance, reassurance, etc.
Booster sessions after completion of treatment
Reduction of fear in subjective report *and* physiological arousal *and* behavioural avoidance

Relaxation training

Relaxation might be more effective than hitherto demonstrated with systematic desensitisation if more rigorous criteria were adopted for identifying the state of relaxation itself, but the success of relaxation training in bringing about a reduction in appropriate physiological activity has been variable. Hence, only in cases where relaxation training has been shown to produce a significant reduction in physiological and subjective criteria of tension during training is it likely to be effective as a coping strategy in fear (Greenwood and Benson, 1977).

Unfortunately, there have been few studies which have investigated the effects of most of the coping skills noted above in clinical populations (Grimm, 1980; Barrios and Shigetomi, 1979; Ramm et al., 1981), relaxation being a notable exception, with several studies of its effects in clinical cases (Glaister, 1982; Ost, 1987).

The relaxation training which has been most widely recommended consists in the client's practising tensing and releasing different muscle groups in turn until he or she is able to relax and concentrate on the corresponding sensations with the minimum of prompting from the therapist (Bernstein and Borkovec, 1973). A notable review has emphasised the importance of feedback from the therapist about the quality of the client's relaxation; taped instructions alone may be of no value (Lehrer, 1982).

Bio-feedback of, for example, EMG electrical muscle potentials (electromyography), and other physiological activity probably has no greater benefit than progressive relaxation. Only for EMG bio-feedback have there, in any case, been significant reductions in reports of anxiety (Rice and Blanchard, 1982), and LeBoeuf and Lodge (1980) claim that these are of little clinical significance. In their study, clinically anxious clients showed significant reductions, following sixteen sessions of EMG bio-feedback training or relaxation training, in scores for trait-anxiety questionnaires but not in psychiatrists' ratings. The validity and reliability of the latter are unclear, however.

Distressing effects of progressive relaxation

Unfortunately, some subjects can become anxious and develop panic attacks during progressive relaxation, perhaps because: their attention is drawn to bodily activity about which they have already become anxious; or they feel that relaxation is making them lose control over these activities; or they are using too much effort, thus increasing their arousal; or relaxation reduces barriers which they normally have to worrisome thinking (Heide and Borkovec, 1984). Ley (1988a) has noted the possibility of hyperventilation contributing to panics in relaxation. This, he has said, also may provoke nocturnal panic attacks occurring with the relaxation at the onset of sleep (Ley, 1988b).

As a remedy, it has been suggested that another relaxing procedure, notably focusing more on imagery, should be tried. Alternatively, subjects should practise progressive relaxation so that they become less apprehensive as a result of exposure to fear-provoking cues of relaxation (Heide and Borkovec, 1984).

It would also be advisable to ensure that subjects breathe normally during relaxation: that they do not hold their breath during some exercises and then take deep gasps to recover. This may amount to hyperventilation. Average normal breathing consists in 14 to 18 breaths per minute with movement of the diaphragm.

Breathing retraining

Breathing retraining has been widely recommended to supplement behaviour therapy for anxiety disorders, especially those associated with panic attacks (Franklin, 1989; Bonn and Redhead, 1984). Unfortunately there are several different recommendations for breathing retraining: make inhalation longer than exhalation with each breath (e.g. Barlow and Cerny, 1988); make exhalation longer than inhalation (Grossman et al., 1985; Cappo and Holmes, 1984; British Medical Journal, 1978); reduce the number of breaths per minute (Grossman et al., 1985; Hibbert and Chan, 1989); increase the movement of the diaphragm especially during inhalation (Barlow and Cerny, 1988). Difficulties in respiration may not contribute to panics in the way which was once widely believed (see Chapter 7), and so it is not surprising that the effects of respiratory training have been weak and may amount to no more than treatment by placebo (Garssen et al., 1992).

Breathing retraining can produce symptoms of hyperventilation in some patients (Fried, 1987). This would be ironic if hyperventilation had not contributed to their panic attacks hitherto.

Different breathing exercises may be tried for different problems, as follow. Research has yet to confirm these recommendations, however, and so single-case experimentation testing the effects of different procedures on symptoms such as those listed in the Panic Symptoms Questionnaire (see Chapter 7) would be apropriate.

For racing pulse, say in excess of 95 beats per minute at rest: prolonged exhalation (inhaling for 3 seconds, exhaling for 6 seconds with each breath [Cappo and Holmes, 1984]); this allows the reflex for slowing heart rate which operates only during exhalation (British Medical Journal, 1978).

Difficulties in drawing sufficient breath: prolonged inhalation compared with exhalation could be helpful, especially if inhalation is accompanied by inflation of the diaphragm. This can be observed if the subject is reclining and has a hand on the upper half of the abdomen. Expansion of the diaphragm can account for more than 50 per cent of the volume of air inhaled into the lungs (Keele et al., 1982).

For fast shallow breathing, say in excess of 22 breaths per minute: breathing with the diaphragm and slowed to about 18 breaths per minute would be appropriate.

Anxiety management

Anxiety-management training (Suinn and Richardson, 1971) depends mainly on training in relaxation and consists in the subject's imagining, for an hour each session, alarming and relaxing situations. The final session requires the subject to imagine tension-provoking situations which are terminated as the subject again relaxes. The main benefit of treatment consists in the client's learning to identify anxiety-feelings and to control the production of tension-provoking imagery, being able to invoke such imagery, to dismiss it and to practise the relaxation, an activity assumed to be incompatible with tension and anxiety.

Applied relaxation

Applied relaxation (Ost, 1987) combines several different relaxation procedures. It consists of training in the following: (1) in order to make the client more aware of the feelings (especially physical sensations) of anxiety the client is asked to keep a daily record of his or her experiences; (2) tension-release progressive relaxation; (3) release-only relaxation; (4) cue-controlled relaxation to focus attention on the client's breathing, the words 'inhale' and 'relax' being used by the therapist in training (there appears to be no attempt to change the character-istics of respiration); (5) differential relaxation in which the client practises while in different situations, from sitting in an armchair to walking (the time to acccomplish this is reduced from exercise to exercise); (6) rapid relaxation to practise in non-stressful natural situations and to accomplish this more and more quickly; (7) relaxation is then practised under stresses in the clinic such as voluntary hyperventilation.

Applied relaxation has been used as an alternative to exposure (ibid.) although it is not clear if it has been practicable to exclude exposure during applied relaxation.

Early developments in cognitive treatments

Ramm *et al.* (1981) reported the effects of self-statement recital in twelve patients who suffered from acute anxiety and panic attacks which could not be predicted.

In the clinic, the clients imagined undergoing alarming experiences and read cue-cards listing a number of self-statements, such as 'I can cope with these feelings', 'these awful feelings don't mean anything dreadful will happen to me', 'these terrible feelings will pass eventually'. This was then practised *in vivo*, with the clients being encouraged to seek as many alarming situations as possible. General anxiety did not decline significantly but the number of panic attacks was reduced.

The self-statements may not have corresponded to the beliefs or negative cognitions which the clients themselves had entertained. Other early developments in cognitive therapy, such as paradoxical intention (Michelson *et al.*, 1985; Michelson and Marchione, 1991), would probably have shared that characteristic. Cognitive therapy now emphasises that the subject's own worries should be elicited in order to reduce their contribution to anxiety as illustrated below in the discussion of specific anxiety disorders.

Matching treatments to client's needs

A number of authors have remarked on the possible advantage of more closely matching clients' requirements to the treatments available (Emmelkamp and Foa, 1983; Barlow and Mavissakalian, 1981; Ley, 1992). There has been a notable lack of consideration of this possibility in published studies of the treatment of fear and anxiety, certain treatments being given to all subjects who present a given fear such as agoraphobia, irrespective of other characteristics and difficulties which may be present.

Ost *et al.* (e.g. 1981; 1982) have reported two studies where they sought to identify whether individual clients showed predominant physiological disturbance (in heart rate) or behavioural distress (assessed by an independent observer) during behavioural testing. In both quoted studies, one of claustrophobic patients (Ost el al., 1981), the other of clients with social difficulties (Ost *et al.* 1982), the behavioural reactors improved to a greater extent on measures of anxiety if clients were given a behavioural treatment (exposure or social skills training) than if they were given relaxation training. Among the physiological reactors, relaxation training, which was assumed to be a physiological therapy, produced greater benefits than the other treatments in the experience of anxiety. These data were obtained during the behavioural testing. Both treatments produced significant benefits in performance testing for the behavioural reactors. For the physiological reactions, no such improvements were possible. The difficulties of making such assessments reliably for specifying treatment were noted in Chapter 7.

The management of anxiety: control and predictability

For certain situations, especially those where *in vivo* practice is difficult to arrange, accurate information about the nature and likelihood of unpleasant threatening events may be helpful. Several sources of evidence (Miller, 1979; Thompson, 1981) indicate that if patients about to undergo surgical or medical treatment are given accurate information by the physician or nursing staff about procedures, they may experience less distress before and even during that treatment. Such information, if it contains material about pain management and how the patient could control the progress of treatment with signals, can reduce apprehension in dentistry before treatment (Lindsay and Jackson, 1993).

Accurate information about procedures has been recommended for fear of flying by Duckworth and Miller (1983). However, Girodo and Roehl (1978) have found that self-statement training has a similar effect.

Information about panic attacks and the symptoms of anxiety is probably an important aspect of the treatment of anxiety. Many patients with panic attacks have fallacious beliefs about physiology. For example, many believe that pains on the left side of the body are especially significant for heart disease. The pains of true cardiovascular disease are distributed more often toward the centre of the chest and frequently in the right arm as well (Beunderman and Duyvis, 1990).

Modelling and skills training

Modelling, the demonstration of another subject coping with a distressing situation, has been used as an exposure procedure and might be considered as an alternative to flooding. A particularly successful variant of this, participant modelling (Bandura 1977), requires the client to perform the behaviour simultaneously with its being demonstrated by the therapist. This has been used especially to treat compulsive behaviour (Rachman and Hodgson, 1980) where, for example, the therapist models handling some contaminated material.

In the treatment of other clinical fears and avoidance, modelling may be added to a programme of *in vivo* exposure. For example, a client who had a fear of choking while eating was unable to eat certain foods which she thought were most likely to go down her windpipe. This fear was probably aggravated by the inhibition of contractions in her oesophagus as she attempted to swallow. Treatment consisted first in her eating with the therapist the least frightening foods, mouthful by mouthful, as the therapist ate the same food. This was supplemented by similar exercises at home.

The preparation for unfamiliar surgical treatment is an appropriate target for modelling and this has been widely used for children (Melamed, 1977). Hence the procedures of giving blood samples before surgery could be demonstrated to advantage by film.

Modelling is also well suited to the teaching of complex skills which might be necessary for clients with anxieties about presenting themselves in social situations. For example, appropriate eye contact and variables of speech may be demonstrated by the therapist or another client in a rehearsal in the clinic. Again this should be followed by some *in vivo* exposure to situations such as those described in the preceding chapter and by Emmelkamp (1982).

Finally, for test-anxiety, skills-training may have to be considered together with anxiety management. Allen (1980) has discussed the role which study and examination-taking skills may have in treating this problem.

Pharmacological treatment

Sometimes clients can be so distressed by their experiences of anxiety, especially panic attacks, that they find it diffcult to collaborate in psychological treatment. For them there may be some avantage in attempting control by medication. Alprazolam, a benzodiazepine, and certain anti-depressants, notably imipramine and clomipramine, can control panics (Klosko *et al.*, 1990; Marks, 1987; Michelson and Marchione, 1991) but the danger is that the panics will return when the medication is discontinued (Michelson and Marchione, 1991). Some clients can develop panic attacks if they find that they have, for example, left home without taking the medication. Alprazolam, in any case, should be given only for a short period because of risks of tolerance and addiction (British Medical Association, 1993).

TREATMENT OF ANXIETY: SPECIFIC DISORDERS

Post-Traumatic Stress Disorder (PTSD)

Only in the last five years have there been thorough attempts to determine the efficacy of different treatments for PTSD associated with experiences other than war (Brom *et al.*, 1989; Foa *et al.*, 1991). Discussions of the aetiology and phenomenolgy of PTSD have thus had little opportunity to influence the evaluation of treatment. Problems of particular concern, such as numbness and alienation, have therefore been neglected.

In the study by Brom *et al.*, (1989) patients received by random allocation either hypnotherapy or 'trauma desensitisation', or psychodyamic therapy, or they remained untreated on a waiting-list. There were 21 outcome variables (10 representing symptoms, 11 describing traits of patients with PTSD) including measures of avoidance and intrusion of images and memories. Multivariate analysis of variance with statistical correction for differences between patients at the outset showed that the treatments were 'equally effective' in terms of improvement since baseline over all the variables. Only anger was not affected by any of the treatments. It is difficult, however, to see which variables, if any, were affected more by one treatment than another. Also it is not clear whch aspects of the different treatments were effective or how far the treatments were distinct from one another. For example, it is not clear how far were exposure or anxiety management common to all treatments.

A study by Foa *et al.* (1991) of victims of rape compared exposure with 'stress-inoculation' with 'supportive counselling' and remaining untreated on a

Table 8.2 Components of effective treatment for fear and anxiety in descending order of importance

Exposure to feared stimuli (external and internal to client)
Information about the nature and effects of fear
   and?
Withdrawal of anxiogenic substances
Training of skills (relaxation, cognitive challenging, breathing, social behaviour)
Pharmacological treatment

waiting-list. The 'stress inoculation' was a comprehensive package of anxiety management similar to that described above in this chapter. The exposure consisted of 'reliving the rape scene in imagination' over seven sessions. Each session of an hour required the patient to repeat this several times. Each patient then was asked to listen at home to tape-recordings of sessions.

Only small numbers of patients, between ten and fourteen per group, participated, and so generalisations from the conclusions should be made only with caution. The results showed that on measures of symptoms of PTSD and avoidance, 'stress inoculation' produced clearest immediate improvement, whereas both that treatment and exposure showed clear benefits on follow-up compared with the other interventions.

The authors suggest that exposure was less effective because of the very distressing experience of reliving the traumatic event. The authors thus proposed combining 'stress inoculation' and exposure.

In view of this and other studies (e.g. McFarlane, 1989), the following could be recommended for the treatment of PTSD:

1 Imaginal exposure to images and memories of the traumatic event particularly for reducing symptoms of intrusion; exposure *in vivo* where practicable to stimuli associated with distress
2 Anxiety management as discussed in the preceding sections of this chapter
3 Cognitive therapy (cf. Bradley, Chapter 6) to reduce guilt, depression, alienation and numbness.

The value of other possible interventions, such as support groups of other patients, is not clear. In the experience of the present author these can provoke distress without resolving difficulties. A report by Muss (1991) claims rapid success for a 'rewind-technique' but the details of this are not clear.

Finally, a number of cautions should be noted. First, victims of PTSD often find it difficult to accept help because they are reluctant to acknowledge that they are in psychological difficulties, believing that some other agency is to blame (the party who might be found liable in a legal action) or because of the alienation and demoralisation which they feel towards all aspects of their lives.

Second, victims of sexual assault would probably be helped by a therapist of the same sex (cf. treatment of victims of sexual abuse, Bradley, Chapter 6).

Third, in view of the suggestions above about factors which could influence relapse, it might be advisable to avoid exposure to intensely distressing experiences. However, much more evidence from follow-up studies of PTSD is necessary to test this.

Panic disorders

Effective treatment for patients who are troubled by panic attacks (in panic disorder, agoraphobia and other phobias) probably requires some form of cognitive treatment of the kind which identifies and challenges each patient's own concerns about his or her experiences of panic (e.g. Salkovskis *et al.*, 1991; Barlow *et al.*, 1989). Training in relaxation and breathing without cognitive therapy can help but is probably not very effective (e.g. Hibbert and Chan, 1989). However, that is the subject of debate and may yet be influenced by an improvement in discriminating between patients whose panics are influenced by respiratory difficulties and those affected by cognitive influences (Ley, 1992). Barlow and Cerny (1988) have written probably the most comprehensive description of treatment although recent evaluations of respiratory influences on panic must modify their recommendations for breathing retraining (see the section on breathing retraining on p. 181).

In light of the outcome studies quoted, recommendations for treatment are as follows:

1 It is probably important to acknowledge with the patient that he or she has a serious problem, and suffers from 'panic attacks'; many patients have sought medical advice only to understand that there is 'nothing wrong' with them.
2 From the patient's daily records of panic attacks, the thoughts associated with each panic should be examined to identify those which appear to cause most distress (these might be, 'I have no control over the panics, they come out of the blue and I cannot be ready for them; it feels like what I have read about heart-attacks, I have never collapsed but I thought that I was about to have a heart-attack; I am alone and noboby here knows what is wrong or how to help me').
3 Means of challenging the most distressing of these thoughts should be discussed with the patient.
4 For nocturnal panics, stimulus control (see Lindsay, Chapter 31).

All these steps can be difficult at first in patients who have been accustomed to visiting doctors in response to panic attacks in attempts to seek advice and information passively.

A number of possible challenges may be identified. *Evidence against illhealth* may be evident in the patient's lifestyle, signs of physical fitness and family history. *Evidence that the panic attacks are unpredictable* may be challenged by recording the panics and their association with variables such as time of day and intake of food and other substances (see Chapter 7). For example, it might be thus noted that most panics occur in the few hours after wakening when little but black coffee had been taken and the patient was very active preparing and taking the children to school. Evidence that the cause of panics is unpredictable could be challenged by a hyperventilation provocation test (see Chapter 7) which, if it produces symptoms similar to those of a panic, could be used to show that the patient does not collapse and that the symptoms pass quickly.

In normal subjects, the symptoms provoked by voluntary hyperventilation can diminish in severity as hyperventilation is continued for many more minutes than the two or three which are necessary to produce symptoms (Hout *et al.*, 1990). This is an exhausting procedure. It is notable that, consistent with the state of knowledge of hyperventilation, none of the subjects fainted in that study. It may be possible, therefore, thus to show patients that the symptoms of hyperventilation disappear no matter how long they overbreathe. However, this remains to be confirmed in patients with panic disorders.

Evidence that the symptoms are controllable could be provided again by a hyperventilation test following which the patient rebreathes from a paper bag covering the mouth and nose. This allows the patient to rebreathe the CO_2, depletion of which has produced the symptoms. This has been favoured by the hyperventilation hypothesis for panic attacks. Ironically, it has been shown that symptoms produced in this way can diminish if subjects are allowed to breathe normal room air in the belief that they are breathing his or her expired air. This can be achieved by having a bag-rebreathing system open to room air (Hout *et al.*, 1988). This, a placebo effect, could thus be effective to control the symptoms of a panic attack as it occurred, even if hyperventilation had not contributed to the panic. Other means of controlling panics, vagal innervation techniques to reduce increases in heart rate, are described by Sartory and Olajide (1988). These include massaging the carotid arteries to stimulate receptors sensitive to blood pressure.

The discussion may also identify that the patient should *take some action* to control, predict and test evidence about the panics. This might consist in taking exercise in a controlled way or under supervision, to increase physical fitness, to increase resistance to ill-health, and to prove that the patient is in good health.

Concerns about others not understanding what is happening to the patient in a panic might be tackled by the patient's agreeing and rehearsing to tell others about the panics. One patient was able to tell his girl-friend and then strangers. The latter occurred, for example, when, during a panic on his bicycle, he asked a policeman to hold the bicycle while he rebreathed from a paper bag. The patient was reassured by the policeman's helpful phlegmatic response.

With the cautions noted earlier, control over symptoms might be sought by practising relaxation and breathing. Many patients seek advice from the therapist about their breathing, especially if they have had difficulty breathing during panics.

Finally, exposure exercises can be arranged by, for example, repeated practice in overbreathing. Many patients find overbreathing so alarming at first that they can tolerate this for less than a minute. Other exposure exercises can be arranged by strenuous physical exercises which expose patients to being breathless and feeling their pulses racing.

Finally, a recent study supports the value of self-help by means of a published book giving guidance similar to the above (Gould *et al.*, 1993).

Social phobia

While exposure to anxiety-provoking situations is widely regarded as an important factor in the psychological treatment of social phobia, there are difficulties in putting this into effect (Butler, 1985). Social situations, such as parties, meetings at work and casual encounters with people in public, are highly variable and much less predictable than situations which are typically used to treat agoraphobics, for example. Critical aspects of situations suggested, such as challenging or complaining to a sales assistant, may be insufficiently prolonged or repeatable to permit much change in anxiety (cf. Figure 8.1) within and over sessions.

The development of cognitive treatment of social phobia (Butler, 1989; Mattick and Peters, 1988) suggests additional procedures:

1 Rehearsal of social meetings and conversations
2 Controlling the symptoms of anxiety by anxiety management
3 Changing and practising social behaviour (see Spence, Chapter 12)
4 Recording and challenging negative thinking

Treatment frequently needs to have the goals of drawing patients' attention away from their inner state and of challenging the belief that they are under close scrutiny and adverse, unspoken criticism from other people. Socially phobic patients often apply standards to their behaviour which they would not apply to others (Hope *et al.*, 1989).

However, comparison of social phobics with patients suffering generalised anxiety disorders has challenged the notion that the former continuously harbour thoughts about evaluation by others (Stopa and Clark, 1993; Turner *et al.*, 1987).

Some of the approaches which have been favoured by recent research in the treatment of social phobia are evident in the following illustrations. P., a 25-year-old man, frequently experienced panic attacks during meetings, especially during conversations with young women to whom he was attracted. During panics he complained particularly of shaking, perspiring and difficulties in breathing. He believed that the shaking was conspicuous to others and attempts to cope by remaining silent made him feel that he would be regarded as dull and unintelligent, which he felt was untrue given that he had been a university student. He had abused alcohol in the past to boost his confidence under such circumstances. Unfortunately, his abuse of alcohol had contributed to the destruction of his career as a student.

It was agreed that frequent practice of social encounters would help P. to build up his tolerance of conversations and would help him to develop the skills for appearing competent in the presence of young women. Because he was interested in painting and in martial arts, he decided to join art classes, five per week, and judo classes. This exposure had to be enhanced in the art classes by his sitting during meal breaks first of all next to other men, then next to women to whom he was not especially attracted, and then next to more attractive women of his own age.

'What action can I take?' tackled the risk of shaking at meal-times. This, daily recording suggested, was a realistic possibility. It was concluded that P. should choose certain items of food, the consumption of which would not be seriously impaired if he did shake. Unfortunately, he could afford only soup which, if drunk with a spoon, would be spilled when he shook. In addition, the spoon would rattle against his teeth. P. would then either use two hands to bring the spoon to his mouth or he would use his non-preferred hand, both of which measures he believed looked awkward thus drawing attention to his difficulties.

It was therefore decided that he should ask for soup in a cup which he could hold with both hands and from which there was little risk of spilling. However, it was decided that he could choose for the first meal an easier food, an apple, before trying the soup. P. was able to persevere in this way through two panics in company before they ceased altogether at the art classes.

Possible topics of conversation were rehearsed according to how appropriate they would be in the group. This was supplemented with challenging his beliefs that his shaking would result in his being regarded as stupid. The challenge that he was over-emphasising the impact of his shaking was not very reassuring. It was agreed that his shaking might be puzzling and unsettling to people who did not understand. However, he agreed that it would help to disclose this difficulty to one of the older women in the class who, he believed, would understand and sympathise.

The impact of this problem was also challenged by looking for attributes in himself which would be attractive and which could balance his shakiness in public. He concluded realistically that he had a sense of humour and was able to make people laugh when he became relaxed.

It was agreed also that anxiety management would be helpful in minimising the symptoms which he feared. This was practised as described earlier in this chapter.

Having had some success in thus tackling his anxiety in the art classes, P. decided to attend meetings of Alcoholics Anonymous in order to expand his practice in tackling his social phobia and to help him curtail his drinking. His first meeting illustrated the difficulty of controlling exposure in social situations. Each member of the group of thirty men had to introduce himself in turn and declare his drinking. P. was at the end of the sequence and became more and more anxious as his turn approached. At subsequent meetings, he arranged to be nearer the start.

Generalised anxiety

There are not many studies of the psychological treatment of generalised anxiety. Moreover, the effects of psychological treatment have not been impressive (Butler et al., 1991).

Possibly the most successful psychological treatment has been cognitive therapy (Borkovec et al., 1987; Butler et al., op. cit.) especially in which daily records of patients' worries and associated emotions, such as anxiety, are used to encourage patients to adopt a less passive role and challenge their worries as they arise (cf. Bradley, Chapter 6). Cognitive-behaviour therapy is probably more successful than treatment with benzodiazepines (Power et al., 1990).

Consider, for example, the following case. S., a 32-year-old man, a graduate in chemistry, had become disillusioned with work as an industrial chemist for a multi-national company. He undertook, at his own expense, a two-year course in furniture restoration. Unfortunately, following what was probably in part a depressive illness in which he had panic attacks and frequent difficulties in sleeping (sleep-maintenance insomnia), he was unable to seek work in furniture restoration on completion of the course because of a crisis in confidence. In addition, his wife had left him and he was afraid that he would be unable to establish any permanent relationship.

When first interviewed, he would express a torrent of worries: about being unable to work as a restorer and about remaining unmarried, jobs which were attempted were seen as full of flaws, difficulties in sleeping were reminders of his early depressive illness. This flow of worries, if unchecked, would result in his becoming tearful and incoherent. Being interviwed for the Present State Examination, a psychiatric interview for research, provoked distress in a similar way.

The first steps in treatment were therefore to agree to set an agenda at the start of each session of items to be discussed. In addition, practice in cue-controlled relaxation helped to curtail the spiralling of anxiety in sessions and, practised before sleep, helped sleep-onset also. Distraction tasks, such as naming all the items in the room beginning with the letter 'E', were used also to curtail the build-up of anxiety in early treatment sessions.

Sweeping generalisations in daily records of negative thinking, such as 'I lack confidence in everything', were resolved by itemising areas of concern. The daily records showed that being unable to take on restoration tasks was causing most anxiety. This was confirming to S. that he had wasted time and money and had made a mistake in leaving secure employment. This was taken by him as evidence also that he had failed to meet most of the challenges in his life. Further records showed that he believed that all his colleagues on the restoration course had work: further evidence of his life-long ineptness. These records also showed that he expected to be able to be instantly competent in all the tasks which could come his way.

These beliefs were challenged by asking how another inexperienced graduate would feel about unfamiliar restoration tasks. What steps could such a person take, being faced with unfamiliar tasks? S. suggested that he could seek information from books, other restorers and colleagues from the course with whom he was on close terms.

What further steps could he take in gaining confidence in restoration? It was suggested to S. that he could take on jobs which would make least demands on his skills at first and where the result would not be very important to the owner of the furniture. He was asked how he could find ways of obtaining experience along those lines. Easy restoration jobs for friends at minimal cost to them was his first step.

Peaks of anxiety recorded in doing jobs were associated with beliefs that he would make an error resulting in permanent damage to the furniture. This was challenged by asking whether he was overestimating the chances of disaster. S. agreed that this was possible but that such an error could have serious consequences. What steps could he therefore take to minimise that risk? Tests on inconspicuous parts of the furniture were suggested by him. Further challenges for this were set by asking what standards clients would expect. Was he setting standards higher than those expected by clients. How could he find this out?

Worries associated with social encounters – meetings with clients, especially in estimating costs, charges and deadlines; being interviewed for jobs – were tackled by rehearsal and discussion of what action he could take for possible contingencies.

Days when anxiety was intense were often followed by difficulties in sleeping. This increased his concerns that he would experience the sleeplessness which was particularly distressing at the start of his illness. However, as his daily anxieties were tackled successfully, his services as a restorer were being sought and he became more adventurous in seeking work. This was accompanied by a reduction in anxiety, as recorded on the Beck Anxiety Inventory, and his sleep became less frequently impaired, as shown by his records. Towards the end of treatment, he was advertising his services in galleries and in antique shops. This improvement was further evident in a more relaxed relationship with his girl-friend.

Physiological fears

For fears of blood and injury where fainting is a complication, graded exposure to stimuli, such as reading the word 'blood' and watching a video of an operation, have been successful (e.g. Yule and Fernando, 1980). Muscle-tensing has been used to increase blood flow to retard fainting in clients undergoing such exposure (Foulds *et al.*, 1990).

Fears which impede urination have also been treated by exposure (Marks, 1981) as can be fears of choking while eating (see the section on modelling and skills training on p. 184).

REFERENCES

Allen, G. J. (1980) 'The behavioral treatment of test anxiety: therapeutic innovations and emerging conceptual challenges', in M. Hersen, R. H. Eisler and P. M. Miller (eds) *Progress in Behavior Modification 9*, New York: Academic Press.

Bandura, A. (1977) 'Self-efficacy: toward a unifying theory of behavioral change', *Psychological Review* 84: 191–215.

Bandura, A., Blanchard, E. B. and Ritter, B. (1969) 'Relative efficacy of desensitisation and modelling approaches for inducing behavioral, affective and attitudinal changes', *Journal of Personality and Social Psychology* 13: 173–99.

Barlow, D. and Cerny, J. A. (1988) *The Psychological Treatment of Panic*, New York: Guilford Press.

Barlow, D. H. and Mavissakalian, M. (1981) 'Directions in the assessment and treatment of phobia: the next decade', in M. Mavissakalian and D. H. Barlow (eds) *Phobia, Psychological and Pharmacological Treatment*, New York: Guilford Press.

Barlow, D. H., Craske, M. G., Cerny, J. A. and Klosko, J. S. (1989) 'Behavioral treatment of panic disorder', *Behavior Therapy* 20: 261–82.

Barrios, B. A. and Shigetomi, C. C. (1979) 'Coping-skills training for the management of anxiety: a critical review', *Behavior Therapy* 10: 491–522.

Bernstein, D. A. and Borkovec, T. D. (1973) *Progressive Relaxation Training*, Champaign, Ill.: Research Press.

Beunderman, R. and Duyvis, D. J. (1990) 'Cardiac phobia', in A. A. Kaptein, H. M. van der Ploeg, B. Garssen, P. J. G. Schreurs and R. Beunderman (eds) *Behavioural Medicine. Psychological Treatment of Somatic Disorders*, Chichester: Wiley.

Bonn, J. A. and Redhead, C. P. A. (1984) 'Enhanced adaptive behavioural response in agoraphobic patients pretreated with breathing retraining', *Lancet* (September): 665–9.

Borkovec, T. D., Mathews, A. M., Chambers, A., Ebrahimi, S., Lytle, R. and Nelson, R. (1987) 'The effects of relaxation training with cognitive or non-directive therapy and the role of relaxation-induced anxiety in the treatment of generalised anxiety', *Journal of Consulting and Clinical Psychology* 55: 883–8.

Brewin, C. R. (1988) *Cognitive Foundations of Clinical Psychology*, London: Erlbaum.

British Medical Association and the Pharmaceutical Society of Great Britain (1993) *British National Formulary*, London: BMA & PSGB.

British Medical Journal (1978) 'Breathing and control of heart rate', *British Medical Journal* 2: 1663–4.

Brom, D., Kleber, R. J. and Defares, P. B. (1989) 'Brief psychotherapy for Posttraumatic Stress Disorders', *Journal of Consulting and Clinical Psychology* 57: 607–12.

Butler, G. (1985) 'Exposure as a treatment for social phobia: some instructive difficulties', *Behaviour Research and Therapy* 23: 651–7.

Butler, G. (1989) 'Issues in the application of cognitive and behavioral strategies to the treatment of social phobia', *Clinical Psychology Review* 9: 91–107.

Butler, G., Fennell, M., Robson, P. and Gelder, M. (1991) 'Comparison of behavior therapy and cognitive behavior therapy in the treatment of generalised anxiety disorder', *Journal of Consulting and Clinical Psychology* 59: 167–75.

Cappo, B. M. and Holmes, D. S. (1984) 'The utility of prolonged respiratory exhalation for reducing physiological and psychological arousal in non-threatening and threatening situations', *Journal of Psychosomatic Research* 28: 265–73.

Chambless, D. L., Foa, E. B., Groves, G. A. and Goldstein, A. J. (1980) 'Flooding with Brevital in the treatment of agoraphobia: countereffective?' *Behaviour Research and Therapy* 17: 243–51.

Clark, D. M., Salkovskis, P. M. and Chalkley, A. J. (1985) 'Respiratory control as a treatment for panic attacks', *Journal of Behavior Therapy and Experimental Psychiatry* 16: 23–30.

Cormack, M. A., Owens, R. G. and Dewey, M. E. (1989) *Reducing Benzodiazepine Consumption. Psychological Contributions to General Practice*, New York: Springer-Verlag.

Duckworth, T. and Miller, D. (1983) *Flying without Fear*, London: Sheldon Press.

Ellis, A. (1979) 'A note on the treatment of agoraphobics with cognitive modification versus prolonged exposure in vivo', *Behaviour Research and Therapy* 17: 162–4.

Emmelkamp, P. M. G. (1982) *Phobic and Obsessive-Compulsive Disorders. Theory, Research and Practice*, New York: Plenum Press.

Emmelkamp, P. M. G. and Foa, E. B. (1983) 'Failures are a challenge', in P. M. G. Emmelkamp and E. B. Foa (eds) *Failures in Behaviour Therapy*, New York: Wiley.

Emmelkamp, P. M. G. and Wessels, H. (1975) 'Flooding in imagination v. flooding in vivo: a comparison with agoraphobics', *Behaviour Research and Therapy* 13: 7–15.

Emmelkamp, P. M. G. and Van den Hout, A. (1983) 'Failures in treating agoraphobia', in E. B. Foa and P. M. G. Emmelkamp (eds) *Failures in Behavior Therapy*, New York: Wiley.

Emmelkamp, P. M. G., Mersch, P. P., Vissia, E. and Van Der Helm, M. (1985) 'Social phobia: a comparative evaluation of cognitive and behavioural interventions', *Behaviour Research and Therapy* 23: 365–70.

Foa, E. B. and Chambless, D. L. (1978) 'Habituation of subjective anxiety during flooding in imagery', *Behaviour Research and Therapy* 16: 391–9.

Foa, E. B. and Kozak, M. (1986) 'Emotional processing of fear', *Psychological Bulletin* 99: 20–35.

Foa, E. B., Jameson, J. S., Turner, R. M. and Payne, L. L. (1980) 'Massed v spaced exposure sessions in the treatment of agoraphobia', *Behaviour Research and Therapy* 18: 333–8.

Foa E. B., Rothbaum, B. O., Riggs, D. S. and Murdock, T. B. (1991) 'Treatment of Posttraumatic Stress Disorder in rape victims: a comparison between cognitive-behavioral procedures and counseling', *Journal of Consulting and Clinical Psychology* 59: 715–23.

Foulds, J., Wiedman, K., Patterson, J. and Brooks, N. (1990) 'The effects of muscle tension on cerebral circulation in blood-phobic and non-phobic subjects', *Behaviour Research and Therapy* 28: 481–6.

Franklin, J. A. (1989) 'A 6-year follow-up of the effectiveness of respiratory retraining, in-situ isometric relaxation and cognitive modification in the treatment of agoraphobia', *Behavior Modification* 13: 139–67.

Fraser, D., Peterkin, G. S. D., Gamsu, C. V. and Baldwin, P. J. (1990) 'Benzodiazepine withdrawal: a pilot comparison of three methods', *British Journal of Clinical Psychology* 29: 230–3.

Fried, R. (1987) *The Hyperventilation Syndrome. Research and Clinical Treatment*, Baltimore: John Hopkins Press.

Garssen, B., Ruiter, C. d. and Dyck, R. v. (1992) 'Breathing retraining: a rational placebo?', *Clinical Psychology Review* 12: 141–54.

Gauthier, J. and Marshall, W. L. (1977) 'The determination of optimal exposure to phobic stimuli flooding therapy', *Behaviour Research and Therapy* 15: 403–10.

Gelder, M. (1975) 'Flooding: results and problems from a new treatment for anxiety', in T. Thompson and W. S. Dockens (eds) *Applications of Behaviour Modification*, New York: Academic Press.

Ghosh, A., Marks, I. and Carr, A. C. (1988) 'Therapist contact and outcome of self-exposure treatment for phobias', *British Journal of Psychiatry* 152: 234–38.

Ginsberg, G. and Marks, I. (1977) 'Cost and benefits of behavioural psychotherapy: a pilot study of neurotics treated by nurse-therapists', *Psychological Medicine* 7: 685–700.

Girodo, M. and Roehl, J. (1978) 'Cognitive preparation and coping self-talk: anxiety management during the stress of flying', *Journal of Consulting and Clinical Psychology* 46: 978–89.

Glaister, B. (1982) 'Muscle relaxation training for fear reduction of patients with psychological problems: a review of controlled studies', *Behaviour Research and Therapy* 20: 493–504.

Goldfried, M. R. (1979) 'Anxiety reduction through cognitive-behavioral intervention', in P. C. Kendall and S. D. Hollon (eds) *Cognitive-Behavioral Interventions*, New York: Academic Press.

Gould, R. A., Clum, G. A. and Shapiro, D. (1993) 'The use of bibliotherapy in the treatment of panic: a preliminary investigation', *Behavior Therapy* 24: 241–52.

Greenwood, M. M. and Benson, H. (1977) 'The efficacy of progressive relaxation in systematic desensitisation and a proposal for an alternative competitive response: the relaxation response', *Behaviour Research and Therapy* 15: 337–43.

Grimm, L. G. (1980) 'The evidence for cue-controlled relaxation', *Behavior Therapy* 11: 283–93.

Grossman, P., De Swart, J. C. G. and Defares, P. B. (1985) 'A controlled study of a breathing therapy for treatment of hyperventilation syndrome', *Journal of Psychosomatic Research* 29: 49–58.

Hafner, J. and Marks, I. M. (1976) 'Exposure in vivo of agoraphobics: the contributions of diazepam, group exposure and anxiety evocation', *Psychological Medicine* 6: 71–88.

Hand, I., Lamontagne, Y. and Marks, I. (1974) 'Group exposure (flooding) in vivo for agoraphobics', *British Journal of Psychiatry* 124: 588–602.

Heide, F. J. and Borkovec, T. D. (1984) 'Relaxation-induced anxiety: mechanisms and theoretical implications', *Behaviour Research and Therapy* 22: 1–12.

Hibbert, G. A. and Chan, M. (1989) 'Respiratory control: its contribution to treatment of panic attacks. A controlled study', *British Journal of Psychiatry* 154: 232–6.

Holden, A. E., O'Brien, G. T., Barlow, D. H., Stetson, D. and Infantino, D. (1983) 'Self-help manual for agoraphobia: a preliminary report of effectiveness', *Behavior Therapy* 14: 545–56.

Hope, D. A., Gansler, D. A. and Heimberg, R. G. (1989) 'Attentional focus and causal attributions in social phobia: implications from social psychology', *Clinical Psychology Review* 9: 49–60.

Hout, M. van den; Jong, P., Zandbergen, J. and Mercklebach, H. (1990) 'Waning of panic sensations during prolonged hyperventilation', *Behaviour Research and Therapy* 28: 445–48.

Hout, M. A. van d., Boek, C., Molen, G. M. van d., Jansen, A. and Griez, E. (1988) 'Rebreathing to cope with hyperventilation: experimental tests of the paper bag method', *Journal of Behavioral Medicine* 303–10.

Howard, W. A., Murphy, S. M. and Clarke, J. C. (1983) 'The nature and treatment of fear of flying: a controlled investigation', *Behavior Therapy* 14: 557–67.

Jacobson, N. S., Wilson, L. and Tupper, C. (1988) 'The clinical significance of treatment gains resulting from exposure-based interventions for agoraphobia: a reanalysis of outcome data', *Behavior Therapy* 19: 539–54.

James, J. E., Hampton, B. A. M. and Larsen, S. A. (1983) 'The relative efficacy of imaginal and in vivo desensitisation in the treatment of agoraphobia', *Journal of Behavior Therapy and Experimental Psychiatry* 14: 203–7.

Johnson, C. H., Gilmore, J. D. and Shenoy, R. S. (1982) 'Use of feeding procedure in the treatment of a stress-related anxiety disorder', *Journal of Behaviour Therapy and Experimental Psychiatry* 13: 235–7.

Keele, C. A., Neil, E. and Joels, N. (1982) *Samson Wright's Applied Physiology, 13th edn*, Oxford: Oxford University Press.

Klosko, J. S., Barlow, D. H., Tassinari, R. and Cerny, J. A. (1990) 'A comparison of alprazolam and behavior therapy in treatment of panic disorder', *Journal of Consulting and Clinical Psychology* 58: 77–84.

Lacey, R. and Woodward, S. (1985) *That's Life Survey on Tranquilisers*, London,:British Broadcasting Corporation/Mind.

Lande, S. D. (1982) 'Physiological and subjective measures of anxiety during flooding', *Behaviour Research and Therapy* 20: 81–8.

LeBoeuf, A. and Lodge, J. (1980) 'A comparison of frontalis EMG feedback training and progressive relaxation in the treatment of chronic anxiety', *British Journal of Psychiatry* 137: 279–84.

Lehrer, P. M. (1982) 'How to relax and how not to relax: a re-evaluation of the work of Edmund Jacobson – I', *Behaviour Research and Therapy* 20: 417–28.

Leitenberg, H., Agras, W. S., Barlow, D. H. and Oliveau, D. C. (1969) 'The contribution of selective positive reinforcement and therapeutic instructions to systematic desensitisation therapy', *Journal of Abnormal Psychology* 74: 113–18.

Ley, R. (1988a) 'Panic-attack during relaxation and relaxation-induced anxiety: a hyperventilation interpretation', *Journal of Behavior Therapy and Experimental Psychiatry* 19: 253–59.

Ley, R. (1988b) 'Panic attacks during sleep: a hyperventilation-probability model', *Journal of Behavior Therapy and Experimental Psychiatry* 19: 181–92.

Ley, R. (1992) 'The many faces of Pan: psychological and physiological differences among three types of panic attacks', *Behaviour Research and Therapy* 30: 347–57 (see errata, *Behaviour Research and Therapy* 30: 657).

Linden, W. (1981) 'Exposure treatments for focal phobias: a review', *Archives of General Psychiatry* 38: 769–75.

Lindsay, S. J. E. (1985) 'The anxious patient 2. The casual attender', *Dental Update* 12: 177–80.

Lindsay, S. J. E. and Jackson, C. (1993) 'The fear of dental treatment in adults: its nature and management', *Psychology and Health* 8: 135–54.

McFarlane, A. C. (1989) 'The treatment of post-traumatic stress disorder', *British Journal of Medical Psychology* 62: 81–90.

McPherson, F. M., Broughan, L. and McLaren, L. (1980) 'Maintenance of improvement in agoraphobic patients treated by behavioral methods: a four year follow-up', *Behaviour Research and Therapy* 18: 150–2.

Marchione, K. E., Michelson, L., Greenwald, M. and Dancu, C. (1987) 'Cognitive behavioral treatments of agoraphobia', *Behaviour Research and Therapy* 25: 319–28.

Marks, I. (1975) 'Behavioral treatments of phobic and obsessive-compulsive disorders: a critical appraisal', in M. Hersen, R. M. Eisler and P. M. Miller (eds) *Progress in Behavior Modification I*, New York: Academic press.

Marks, I. (1981) *The Cure and Care of Neurosis*, New York: Wiley.

Marks, I. (1987) *Fears, Phobias and Rituals*, Oxford: Oxford University Press.

Marshall, W. L., Gauthier, J. and Gordon, A. (1979) 'The current status of flooding therapy', in M. Hersen, R. H. Eisler and P. M. Miller (eds) *Progress in Behavior Modification 7*, New York: Academic Press.

Mathews, A. M. (1977) 'Recent developments in the treatment of agoraphobia', *Behavioural Analysis and Modification* 2: 64–75.

Mathews, A. M. and Shaw, P. (1973) 'Emotional arousal and persuasion effects in flooding', *Behaviour Research and Therapy* 11: 587–98.

Mathews, A. M., Johnston, D. W., Lancashire, M., Munby, M., Shaw, P. M. and Gelder, M. G. (1976) 'Imaginal flooding and exposure to real phobic situations: treatment outcome with agoraphobic patients', *British Journal of Psychiatry* 129: 362–71.

Mathews, A. M., Gelder, M. G. and Johnson, D. W. (1981) *Agoraphobia: Nature and Treatment*, London: Tavistock.

Mattick, R. P. and Peters, L. (1988) 'Treatment of severe social phobia: effects of guided exposure with and without cognitive restructuring', *Journal of Consulting and Clinical Psychology* 56: 251–60.

Melamed, B. G. (1977) 'Psychological preparation for hospitalisation', in S. Rachman (ed.) *Contributions to Medical Psychology I*, Oxford: Pergamon.

Michelson, L. K. and Marchione, K. (1991) 'Behavioral, cognitive and pharmacological treatments of panic disorder with agoraphobia: a critique and synthesis', *Journal of Consulting and Clinical Psychology* 59: 100–14.

Michelson, L., Mavissakalian, M. and Marchione, K. (1985) 'Cognitive and behavioral treatments of agoraphobia: clinical, behavioral and psychophysiological outcomes', *Journal of Consulting and Clinical Psychology* 53: 913–25.

Miller, S. M. (1979) 'Controllability and human stress: method, evidence and theory', *Behaviour Research and Therapy* 17: 287–304.

Munby, M. and Johnston, D. W. (1980) 'Agoraphobia: the long-term follow-up of behavioural treatment', *British Journal of Psychiatry* 137: 418–27.

Muss, D. C. (1991) 'A new technique for treating post-traumatic stress disorder', *British Journal of Clinical Psychology* 30: 91–92.

O'Brien, G. T. (1981) 'Clinical treatment of specific phobias', in M. Mavissakalian and D. H. Barlow (eds) *Phobia, Psychological and Pharmacological Treatment*, New York: Guilford Press.

Ost, L. G. (1978) 'Behavioural treatment of thunder and lightning phobias', *Behaviour Research and Therapy* 16: 197–207.

Ost, L. G. (1987) 'Applied relaxation: description of a coping technique and a review of controlled studies', *Behaviour Research and Therapy* 25: 397–410.

Ost, L. G. (1989) 'One-session treatment for specific phobias', *Behaviour Research and Therapy* 27: 1–8.

Ost, L. G., Jerremalm, A. and Johansson, J. (1981) 'Individual response patterns and the effects of different behavioural methods in the treatment of social phobia', *Behaviour Research and Therapy* 19: 1–16.

Ost, L. G., Johansson, J. and Jerremalm, A. (1982) 'Individual response patterns and the effects of different behavioral methods in the treatment of claustrophobia', *Behaviour Research and Therapy* 20: 445–60.

Paul, G. L. (1966) *Insight v Desensitisation in Psychotherapy*, Stanford: Stanford University Press.

Petursson, H. and Lader, M. (1984) *Dependence on Tranquilisers*, Oxford: Oxford University Press.

Power, K. G., Simpson, R. J., Swanson, V. and Wallace, L. A. (1990) 'A controlled comparison of cognitive-behaviour therapy, diazepam and placebo alone and in combination for the treatment of generalised anxiety disorder', *Journal of Anxiety Disorders* 4: 267–92.

Rachman, S. (1989) 'The return of fear: review and prospects', *Clinical Psychology Review* 9: 147–68.

Rachman, S. and Hodgson, R. J. (1980) *Obsessions and Compulsions*, Englewood Cliffs, NJ: Prentice-Hall.

Ramm, E., Marks, I., Yuksel, S. and Stern, R. S. (1981) 'Anxiety management training for anxiety states: positive compared with negative self-statements', *British Journal of Psychiatry* 140: 367–73.

Rice, K. M. and Blanchard, E. B. (1982) 'Biofeedback in the treatment of anxiety disorders', *Clinical Psychology Review* 2: 557–77.

Salkovskis, P. M. and Warwick, H. M. C. (1986) 'Morbid preoccupations, health anxiety and reassurance: a cognitive-behavioral approach to hypochondriasis', *Behaviour Research and Therapy* 24: 597–602.

Salkovskis, P. M., Clark, D. and Hackmann, A. (1991) 'Treatment of panic attacks using cognitive therapy without exposure or breathing retraining', *Behaviour Research and Therapy* 29: 161–6.

Sartory, G. and Olajide, D. (1988) 'Vagal innervation techniques in the treatment of panic disorder', *Behaviour Research and Therapy* 26: 431–4.

Shipley, R. H. and Bedouwyns, P. A. (1980) 'Flooding and implosive therapy: are they harmful?' *Behavior Therapy* 11: 503–8.

Solyom, L., McClure, D. J., Heseltine, G. F. D., Ledwidge, B. and Solyom, C. (1972) 'Variables in the aversion relief of phobics', *Behavior Therapy* 3: 21–8.

Stern, R. and Marks, I. (1973) 'Brief and prolonged flooding. A comparison in agora-phobic patients', *Archives of General Psychiatry* 28: 270–6.

Stopa, L. and Clark, D. M. (1993) 'Cognitive processes in social phobia', *Behaviour Research and Therapy* 31: 255–68.

Sue, D. (1972) 'The role of relaxation in systematic desensitisation', *Behaviour Research and Therapy* 10: 153–8.

Suinn, R. M. and Richardson, F. (1971) 'Anxiety management training: a non-specific behavior therapy program for anxiety control', *Behavior Therapy* 2: 498–511.

Taylor, I. (1984) 'Self exposure instructions by telephone with a severe agoraphobic: A case study', *Behavioural Psychotherapy* 12: 68–72.

Thompson, S. (1981) 'Will it hurt if I can control it A complex answer to a simple question', *Psychological Bulletin* 90: 89–101.

Tower, R. B. and Singer, J. L. (1981) 'The measurement of imagery: how can it be clinically useful?' in P. C. Kendall and S. D. Hollon (eds) *Assessment Strategies for Cognitive-Behavioral Interventions*, New York: Academic Press.

Turner, S. M., McCanna, M. and Beidel, D. C. (1987) 'Validity of the social avoidance and distress and fear of negative evaluation scales', *Behaviour Research and Therapy* 25: 113–15.

Tyrer, P. J. (1984) 'Benzodiazepines on trial', *British Medical Journal* 288: 1101–2.

Wardle, J., Hayward, P., Higgitt, A., Stabl, M ., Blizard, R. and Gray, J. (1993) 'Effects of concurrent diazepam treatment on the outcome of exposure therapy in agoraphobia', *Behaviour Research and Therapy* (forthcoming).

Wolpe, J. (1958) *Psychotherapy by Reciprocal Inhibition*, Stanford: Stanford University Press.

Wolpe, J. (1981) 'Reciprocal inhibition and therapeutic change', *Journal of Behaviour Therapy and Experimental Psychiatry* 12: 185–8.

Woodward, R. and Jones, R. B. (1980) 'Cognitive restructuring treatment: a controlled trial with anxious patients', *Behaviour Research and Therapy* 18: 401–7.

Yule, W. and Fernando, P. (1980) 'Blood phobia – beware', *Behaviour Research and Therapy* 18: 587–90.

Yulis, S., Brahm, G., Charnes, G ., Jacard, L. M. Picota, E. and Rutman, F. (1975) 'The extinction of phobic behaviour as function of attention shifts', *Behaviour Research and Therapy* 13: 173–6.

Zitrin, C. M. (1981) 'Combined pharmacological and psychological treatment of phobias', in M. Mavissakalian and D. H. Barlow (eds) *Phobia, Psychological and Pharmacological Treatment*, New York: Guilford Press.

Chapter 9

Sexual dysfunction

Investigation

P. de Silva

DYSFUNCTION AND DEVIATION

Sexual dysfunctions are impairments or disturbances in sexual desire, arousal or orgasm. They are usually considered as a group of problems within 'normal' sexuality, different from sexual deviation, or paraphilias, and the two are treated as separate clinical categories. This is a convenient distinction, but it must be noted that there can be overlap between the two. For example, a male presenting with erectile difficulties with his wife may, upon close enquiry, show a history of paraphiliac sexual activity involving, say, leather and rubber garments, and the content of his sexual fantasies may be exclusively geared to these activities. Clearly this would be a case of sexual dysfunction and sexual deviation co-existing and interrelated. Similarly, it is not uncommon to find patients whose presenting problems take the form of sexual deviation and who also have difficulties in normal sexual activity. Thus one must consider the distinction between sexual dysfunction and sexual deviation not as a mutually exclusive and rigid one, but only as a convenient general grouping based on the nature of the presenting problem. In the assessment of patients with sexual dysfunction, enquiry has to be made about paraphiliac activities, desires and fantasies, and the relationship of these factors with the dysfunction needs to be examined.

Degrees of dysfunction

Another point to be borne in mind is that sexual dysfunction cannot be considered as a discrete phenomenon qualitatively different from non-dysfunction. It is not the case that there are persons who have developed sexual dysfunction and those who have not, in an absolute sense. More often, functional and dysfunctional presentations are on the same continuum; there are, in other words, degrees of dysfunction, and – in one person or couple – areas of very satisfactory sexual activity alongside areas of difficulty. Also, what is seen as dysfunctional may vary from person to person, couple to couple and society to society. It is worth noting that non-clinical populations – that is, couples who do not consider themselves to be sexually dysfunctional and who therefore do not attend clinics or go for other help – include among them a proportion whose sexual functioning is in some respects less than satisfactory. Frank *et al.* (1978) reported a study of 100 well-educated, happily married couples. Over 80 per cent of the couples reported that their sexual and marital relations were happy and satisfactory. However, 40 per cent of the men reported erectile or ejaculatory problems, and over 60 per cent of the women reported problems of arousal or orgasm.

CLASSIFICATION

With these constraints in mind, let us now look at the common categories of sexual dysfunction that present at clinics and other services for help. There are many useful classifications proposed (e.g. American Psychiatric Association, 1987; Hawton, 1985; Kaplan, 1974; 1979; Masters and Johnson, 1970); the following are offered as fairly simple classifications of male and female dysfunctions.

Male disorders

Male main sexual dysfunctions may be classified as follows. As can be seen, the categories are not necessarily mutually exclusive.

1 Low sexual interest/desire
2 Impotence
3 Premature ejaculation
4 Retarded ejaculation
5 Dyspareunia
6 Sexual aversion

Low sexual interest/desire is not uncommon (Kaplan; 1977, 1979). The individual will not normally complain of this except in the context of a relationship when it becomes a problem for the couple, or when there has been a marked reduction from a previous level.

Impotence refers to erectile failure or difficulty. There may be inability to get or to sustain an erection; often the problem may be lack of strong enough erections for successful sexual activity (Masters and Johnson, 1970). Erectile problems are quite common, and are probably the most common complaint of males who seek help in sex therapy clinics (Spector and Carey, 1990). Impotence may be primary (the person has always had the problem) or secondary (there was a time in the past when the problem did not exist). It can be total (the person is unable to get or sustain an erection in any situation) or situational (erections take place in certain situations – for example, in masturbation – but not in others). This latter distinction refers to the current situation, while the primary versus secondary distinction refers to the person's history.

Premature ejaculation refers to the reaching of sexual climax far too soon for satisfactory sexual activity for the couple. It is often cited as one of the most common sexual dysfunctions (e.g. Kaplan, 1974). The typical complaint of the male who seeks help with this problem is that he arrives at orgasm 'too quickly'. What is 'too quick'? This obviously can not be defined in terms of time, nor can it be defined in terms of the questionable concept of voluntary control (Kaplan, 1979). The problem has to be assessed in terms of how much it interferes with the sexual activity and enjoyment of the couple. For example, consistent ejaculation before the penis is inserted into the vagina or immediately after entry will clearly be a problem, while occasional climaxing within a short time will not. It is perhaps worth noting the Kinsey Report finding that 75 per cent of their sample of 6,000 American males reported that they reached a climax within two minutes of penetration (Kinsey *et al.*, 1948). Like impotence, premature ejaculation can be total or situational, and primary or secondary.

Retarded ejaculation, far more rare than either impotence or premature ejaculation, refers to the failure of ejaculation/climaxing despite a good deal of stimulation (Dow, 1981; Masters and Johnson, 1970). This can be total or situational: not infrequently, a man may complain of an inability to reach a climax inside a vagina, but is able to do so with self-stimulation or even manual stimulation by his partner. It is important to note that in some cases the male does reach an orgasm, but does not ejaculate. This is called 'retrograde ejaculation' as what happens is that the seminal fluid travels backwards into the bladder. This may occur as the result of certain drugs, or due to certain physical causes.

Dyspareunia, or pain in intercourse, is extremely rare in males (Bancroft, 1989), and usually has a physical cause.

Sexual aversion refers to a dislike of certain aspects of sex. For example, a man may dislike his penis being touched at all, whereas his sexual desire in general and ability to engage in satisfactory intercourse is not impaired. It is also possible for someone to have a more general sexual aversion, although there is no lack of sexual desire; thus he may have frequent and enjoyable masturbatory experiences, but would avoid, or not enjoy, interpersonal sex (American Psychiatric Association, 1987).

Female disorders

Female sexual dysfunction may similarly be classified into the following, not necessarily mutually exclusive, categories:

1 Low sexual interest/desire
2 Absence of responsiveness
3 Anorgasmia
4 Vaginismus
5 Dyspareunia
6 Sexual aversion

Low sexual interest/desire is similar to that in males (Lief, 1977). This becomes a presenting problem usually only within the context of a relationship. It is the commonest presented by females attending sex clinics (e.g. Bancroft, 1989).

Absence of responsiveness is a problem of sexual arousal (Kaplan, 1979). The usual physiological arousal, indicated by vaginal lubrication and expansion of the vaginal canal, is affected. This may be primary or secondary.

Anorgasmia is the inability to reach orgasm, and is a common clinical presentation (Bancroft, 1989; Masters and Johnson, 1970). This can be either primary (where the person has never had orgasm) or secondary. In terms of current functioning it can be either total (where the person does not reach orgasm at all) or situational (where orgasm is possible in certain situations but not in others). A common complaint is lack of orgasm with a partner despite achieving orgasm via masturbation.

Vaginismus refers to the involuntary spasm of vaginal muscles so that penetration is almost impossible (Masters and Johnson, 1970). Typically, the muscle spasms occur in anticipation of intercourse or when penetration is attempted (Lamont, 1978). Its presentation in cases of non-consummated marriage is well known (Duddle, 1977). Bancroft (1989) reported that 13 per cent of females presenting at his clinic (n = 577) complained of vaginismus.

Dyspareunia is painful intercourse, and is usually associated with other problems including physical ones (Masters and Johnson, 1970).

Sexual aversion refers to dislike either of all aspects of sex or of some specific aspects. For example, a woman may complain of an intense dislike of being touched on the breasts, or of being kissed on the mouth. Sometimes there will be aversion to sex with a partner, while self-stimulation is enjoyable (Kolodny *et al.*, 1979).

Some related factors

The above account of the main categories of sexual dysfunction did not refer to certain crucial variables which may contribute to the problem concerned. These are briefly mentioned below.

Ignorance   Lack of proper information about sexual functioning can be a major problem in sexual dysfunction (Bancroft, 1989). Not infrequently, the presenting problem is the result of either ignorance of basic facts about the sexual response system, or certain misconceptions about sex (Masters and Johnson, 1970; Zilbergeld, 1978). Young men sometimes worry a great deal about what they see as the rapidity with which they reach a climax in sex and, believing that the norm is much longer than it actually is, get into a state of stress and worry, which in turn can contribute to the development and maintenance of erectile or ejaculatory problems. In females, lack of knowledge or misconceived ideas can lead to fears about sex – such as that sexual intercourse is necessarily painful – which can cause real difficulties. In certain cultural groups some beliefs are fostered which can lead to difficulties in sexual adjustment: among some Asian communities, for example, loss of seminal fluid excessively, or in adolescence, is considered as a cause of major sexual and other pathology. This can lead to problems in men who believe that they have made themselves vulnerable to these illnesses (de Silva and Dissanayake, 1989; Malhotra and Wig, 1975).

The quality of a patient's knowledge about sex, and associated beliefs, are therefore as important to explore as the nature of the presenting problem itself.

Attitudes   Related to knowledge and beliefs are the attitudes of the person to sex and sexual activity. A person who has been brought up with an attitude to sex which is a strictly moralistic one, that is, that sex is for procreation only and not to be enjoyed, may find him- or herself sexually inhibited (Masters and Johnson, 1970). Such a person may also find a more libertarian attitude in his or her partner to be a source of conflict. One partner's desire for experimenting with different types of foreplay, with different positions for intercourse, and so on, may be unacceptable to the other partner whose attitudes reflect a stricter background. Attitudinal problems can thus play a crucial part in generating and perpetuating sexual dysfunction. Long-standing attitudes do not change easily, and need to be examined in assessing a person's or couple's sexual life. It is interesting to note that the prevalence of vaginismus is much higher among Irish women than in many other groups studied (Barnes, 1986a, 1986b; O'Sullivan, 1979).

Anxiety   Anxiety is a major factor associated with sexual dysfunction (Bancroft, 1989; Lief, 1979; Masters and Johnson, 1970). Some difficulties are caused, at least partially, by anxiety and many are maintained and perpetuated by it. Consider the example of a young man who fails to get an erection in an attempt to have intercourse in circumstances far from favourable for relaxed, comfortable sex (for example, in the back of a car, or in a place where there is the possibility of being observed or disturbed). This failure may lead to anxiety about possible failure on subsequent occasions where sexual intercourse is attempted or contemplated, and this anxiety can now lead to repeated failure which – in turn – increases the person's anxiety. With females, traumatic or unpleasant sexual experiences, such as being sexually assaulted or abused, may lead to generalised sexual anxiety that contributes to a sexual aversion. Sometimes the problem takes the form of a full-blown phobia of sex or of men or male genital organs. Current anxieties, such as fear of getting pregnant, can also cause sexual difficulties.

'Spectatoring'   Associated with anxiety is what has come to be called 'spectatoring' (Masters and Johnson, 1970). This refers to the tendency in a person to watch him- or herself during sexual activity. Sexually anxious persons may get into this role out of fear of failure. Rather than enjoying the sexual activity fully, the person is partly playing the role of spectator of his or her own activity and success or failure. This may then lead to inhibited sexual action and enjoyment

or even true failure. It must be noted, however, that spectatoring is not necessarily an inhibiting factor. Many men and women find watching themselves and their sexual reactions quite stimulating. The problem is that when spectatoring becomes a feature in the sexual activity of someone already anxious about sex, it can perpetuate and sometimes worsen the difficulty (cf. Beck *et al.*, 1983).

Relationship problems   The relevance of the quality of the relationship between a couple to their sexual problems is self-evident (Crowe and Ridley, 1990; Woody, 1992). Sexual difficulties can develop easily in the context of a poor marital relationship. Jealousy, fears and worries about infidelity, constant conflicts in areas of life other than sex, all may contribute to, or be reflected by, a sexual problem. When one considers the continuous nature of satisfactory sexual functioning and dysfunction, it is easy to see how non-sexual relationship problems can emphasise and exacerbate whatever minor difficulties there may be in a couple's sex life. Sex sometimes becomes the main battleground for marital conflicts such as those associated with dominance, jealousy and punitiveness (Harbin and Gamble, 1977). Equally, a frankly sexual problem can cause wider relationship difficulties, and when couples present with marital problems it is not unusual for enquiry to reveal that they are suffering from focal sexual dysfunctions (Zimmer, 1987). The overlap and interrelationship between the two types of problem can be significant.

Physical problems   Clearly some sexual problems are caused by, or associated with, physical factors. The relevance of such factors as prolonged alcoholism, diabetes, ageing, neurological damage, drugs, and so on to sexual activity is well established (Bancroft, 1989; Kolodny *et al.*, 1979). Sometimes a physical cause is directly responsible for the presenting problem but often the psychological effect of the condition, such as the feeling of being ill or invalidism, is the crucial intermediate variable.

The presenting sexual problem may simply be a manifestation of a physical condition. Pain in intercourse, for example, can be due to a very rigid hymen in the female, or a tight foreskin in the male. Similarly, vaginal irritation caused by an infection could lead to sexual aversion or loss of interest.

The need for ruling out physical causes before concluding that a problem is psychogenic may be quite strong in some cases. This will be discussed later.

ASSESSMENT

General issues

Assessment of sexual dysfunctions should be comprehensive, and cover the details of the presenting problem(s) and the relevant areas discussed in the previous section. Clinical assessment with sexual dysfunction patients is in theory no different from such assessment of other problems, but in practice it is a harder and more challenging task. Since sex is a very private aspect of one's life, detailed communication about it, however relevant clinically, can be difficult for the patient – and indeed for the inexperienced therapist. Also, some of the usual methods of assessment, such as direct observation and reports from independent observers, are not available for obvious reasons. Some of these matters and other general issues in sexual dysfunction assessment are discussed in detail in the literature (e.g. Bancroft, 1989; Hawton, 1985; Spence, 1991; Wincze and Carey, 1991).

The aim of the assessment should be to obtain as clear a picture as possible of the problem(s) and related factors. A full behavioural analysis (e.g. Kanfer and Saslow, 1969) will be particularly useful. Since one of the goals of clinical assessment is to obtain sufficient information to make possible a therapeutic programme, if indicated, areas that are relevant to possible treatment strategies need to be investigated. Different professionals emphasise different areas in assessment, reflecting their theoretical standpoints and therapeutic approaches. Thus a psychodynamically oriented therapist will enquire a great deal into the patient's childhood and childhood relationships. A behavioural psychologist, on the other hand, will want to enquire closely about relevant past experiences, such as sexual failures, disappointments and traumatic events; current factors, such as anxiety, expectations and skills; and factors that are related directly to the sexual behaviours as antecedents and consequences. Whatever the orientation, the assessment needs to cover details of the presenting problem, its correlates, and factors that are possibly linked to it, so that the therapist can arrive at a tentative formulation which will form the basis of therapy.

The interview

Special problems

The main source of information in assessment is the clinical interview, which in the case of sexual dysfunction has certain special problems associated with it (Bancroft, 1989; Hawton, 1985; Spence, 1991; Wincze and Carey, 1991). Some of the main ones are listed below.

1 The patient may be embarrassed about having to discuss intimate matters with a relative stranger. The fact that the person has come for therapy does not necessarily imply that he or she will be able to talk freely about sex. The therapist must therefore be sensitive to this problem and help the patient by building rapport, asking about more general matters first, and if necessary acknowledging that talking about sexual matters could be difficult.
2 The language used must be simple and easy to understand. The jargon one learns to take for granted as a professional is often quite unfamiliar to the patient. Even words like 'penetration' and 'arousal' often confuse patients.
3 Precise details must be obtained about the problems and behaviours in question. A general description that a patient may give, such as 'I don't seem

to want it any more', is meaningless without detailed enquiry and elaboration. The therapist must, however, handle this enquiry with patience, and pace it according to the ease or otherwise with which the patient responds in the interview (see below). Some details may have to be elicited at a second or even third interview when the patient is more comfortable with the therapist.

4 There should be an attitude of non-judgemental acceptance, on the part of the therapist, of all behaviours and likes and dislikes of the patient. Any display of disapproval – or even surprise – however unintended, may discourage the patient from giving full details of what one wishes to know.

5 It is possible that a patient may withhold some information in the initial interview, partly out of embarrassment and partly because the therapist is still an unfamiliar person to the patient. This can, of course, create difficulties as, in practice, a decision may have to be made on the basis of one or two assessment sessions. So it may perhaps be necessary gently to encourage the patient to divulge all relevant facts. On the other hand, it is equally important to allow the patient to give more information, when he or she seems ready to do so, in later sessions.

Areas of enquiry

The areas to enquire about in the interview include the following:

1 The nature of the problem in as much detail as required to obtain a full picture of the difficulty and all its associated factors, including anxiety and situational variations – in men with impotence, particular enquiry should be made about whether early morning erections are present or not, as their presence usually helps to rule out the possibility that the problem is organic
2 The history of the problem, its beginnings and course, and present sexual activity including masturbation
3 The partner's reactions to the problem, both in the sexual situation and in general
4 The person's sexual knowledge, beliefs and attitudes, including those determined by his or her religion and culture
5 The person's sexual likes, dislikes and preferences – and fantasies
6 Past sexual history including relevant early experiences
7 Psychiatric and medical factors, including drugs, alcohol, etc. – current depression is particularly important to assess
8 Menstrual history and relation of problem to menstrual cycle
9 Contraception and past pregnancies, and attitude to possibility of conception
10 General relationship factors
11 Background factors, such as job, income, accommodation, and so on, which can be sources of stress
12 Previous treatment, if any.

More details may be needed on some of the areas than on others in a given case, and this is a matter of clinical judgement as the interview proceeds. Needless to say, the assessor must be prepared to vary his or her enquiry to suit each patient, as needed. Most clinicians rely on a general checklist of topics to enquire about as a matter of routine. Examples of such checklists are available in, among others, Group for the Advancement of Psychiatry (1973); Hawton (1985); Lo Piccolo and Heiman (1978); and Spence (1991). In practice, while such detailed checklists are indeed useful, flexibility is needed in their use: such a list should serve as a general guide rather than as something to be rigidly followed.

Individual and couple interviews

One major issue in interviewing patients with sexual dysfunction is whether the partners – when a couple present themselves for help – should be interviewed together or not. Different viewpoints have been expressed about this (e.g. Bancroft, 1989; Masters and Johnson, 1970; Wincze and Carey, 1991). In general, a good arrangement is to see the couple jointly to start with, and then to conduct assessment interviews separately. If two therapists are available, this may be done in parallel sessions; if not, more time should be spent on the partner with the presenting problem, followed by a briefer interview with the other partner.

It is important that individual interview sessions are undertaken in all cases. This provides an opportunity for each partner to give his or her version of the problem, and to discuss with the therapist various matters, including feelings about the partner, without inhibition. It also gives an opportunity for him or her to divulge information which might have been kept away from the partner, such as an extra-marital relationship, or a particular aspect of the individual's past history.

Motivation and selection

Assessment of the motivation of the patient/couple for therapy is an important aspect of the interview, although this may not prove easy in one interview expect perhaps to identify those who are clearly unwilling to accept the therapy offered. As for suitability for therapy, an assessment comprising two interviews at most is usually sufficient to identify those who are clearly not likely to benefit from the therapy that can be offered. For example, presence of clear psychiatric illness will often require treatment of that condition first; serious marital difficulties may require referral to a specialist clinic – unless the therapist feels competent to deal with these him- or herself; and, when physical factors are probably involved, investigations of these, and a physical examination, will have to be arranged prior to acceptance for therapy.

Physical examination and investigations

Some clinicians believe that all patients presenting with sexual dysfunction should routinely be examined physically (e.g. Kolodny *et al.*, 1979; Spence,

1991). This is unnecessary, but it is essential to have the facilities to get this and relevant investigations done if required in a given case. Bancroft has given an extremely useful set of indications for physical examination (Bancroft, 1989: 417; 424). These are: complaints of pain or discomfort during sex; recent history of ill-health or physical symptoms other than the sexual problem; recent onset of loss of sex drive with no apparent cause; when the patient believes that a physical cause is most likely, or is concerned about the genitalia (for example, a man complaining that his penis is too small or bent; or a woman suspecting that there is something abnormal about her sexual organs); history of abnormal puberty or other endocrine disorder; in men, age over 50; in women, being in pre- or post-menopausal age group; and in women, history of marked menstrual irregularities or infertility.

Where appropriate, the medical practitioner carrying out the physical examination will also carry out, or arrange for, relevant laboratory investigations. Details of the common investigations may be found in Bancroft (1989), Hawton (1985), Kolodny *et al.*, (1979) and Wincze and Carey (1991).

Questionnaires and inventories

Data obtained from the interview can profitably be supplemented by the use of questionnaires and inventories. These help to cover some important areas quickly, but more importantly they provide quantitative data which are particularly useful in assessing differences between before and after treatment.

Several useful instruments are available for the measurement of sexual experiences, attitudes, dysfunctions, and other related matters. Hoon *et al.*, (1976a) provide an inventory for the assessment of female sexual arousal. Lo Piccolo and Steger (1974) have developed an inventory to assess sexual interaction and satisfaction of a couple. Lief and Reed (1972) provide a questionnaire to assess both sexual knowledge and sexual attitudes, while Wilson (1978) describes a useful fantasy questionnaire, which measures fantasies, desires and actual behaviours. The Derogatis Sexual Functioning Index (Derogatis and Melisaratos, 1979) is a wide-ranging scale of sexual functioning covering ten domains (e.g. information, desire, attitudes). While its comprehensiveness is no doubt an asset, its prohibitive length (245 items) makes it somewhat unwieldy for routine clinical use.

An interesting and valuable recent development is the Golombok–Rust Inventory of Sexual Satisfaction (GRISS; Rust and Golombok, 1986). This 28-item questionnaire, which is readily available, is intended for use with heterosexual couples or individuals with a current heterosexual relationship, and yields an overall score, for men and women separately, of the quality of sexual functioning. In addition, the following sub-scores can also be obtained: impotence, premature ejaculation, anorgasmia, vaginismus, infrequency, poor communication, dissatisfaction, non-sensuality and avoidance. This instrument has good reliability, and is easy to use. In view of the wide range of measures it yields, the GRISS is an economical instrument to use routinely.

A parallel, and equally economical, instrument for the assessment of the overall relationship is the Golombok–Rust Inventory of Marital State (GRIMS; Rust *et al.*, 1988). Other established marital questionnaires include the Locke–Wallace Marital Adjustment Scale (Locke and Wallace, 1959) and the Dyadic Adjustment Scale (Spanier, 1976).

When depression is a relevant factor needing to be assessed, a depression inventory such as the Beck Depression Inventory (Beck *et al.*, 1961), or the Wakefield Depression Inventory (Snaith *et al.*, 1971) may be used for this purpose (see Chapter 5).

Subjective ratings

Self-rating scales may be used as part of assessment of the major variables in question for a given patient. For example, anxiety in sex, desire and sexual arousal may be rated by the patient on a 0 to 100 scale indicating subjective estimates. Patients usually find these simple scales easy to use. Equally simple are frequency charts, recording the frequency of target behaviours on a daily basis. A pre-designed diary provided by the assessor/therapist, specifying the targets to be recorded, is an effective way of obtaining baseline data as well as of monitoring change. Conte (1986) and Spence (1991), among others, provide discussions of these.

Physiological measures

Physiological techniques have been used increasingly in the assessment of sexual function in recent years, receiving impetus from the work of Masters and Johnson (1966; 1970). Measuring techniques are available for both male and female arousal. Penile plethysmography for the assessment of erection is widely used in research and can be used in clinical practice where needed and practicable (e.g. Wagner and Green, 1981; Wincze *et al.*, 1988). The measure may be of either penile volume or penile circumference changes. Penile plethysmography has also been used to assess nocturnal erections in an attempt to distinguish psychogenic from organically caused impotence (Karacan, 1978). Detailed discussions of these, and other laboratory techniques for the assessment of erectile problems, are provided by Bancroft (1989) and Schiavi (1992). As for female arousal, the best established method is the photoplethysmography technique (Hoon *et al.*, 1976b), in which vasocongestion in the vaginal walls is measured with the help of a probe.

In a clinical setting, however, the use of physiological methods for routine assessment is not feasible. Also, the interpretation of their results in the clinical context is not always clear-cut (see Bancroft, 1989; Conte, 1986).

Formulation

The data obtained in the assessment will enable the assessor to arrive at a formulation of the problem. In the formulation, information from all sources is brought together, providing a brief descriptive account and a tentative explanation of the presenting problem. The formulation should include:

1 Description of the problem
2 Predisposing factors
3 Precipitating factors
4 Maintaining factors

The formulation will provide the basis for therapy.

CONCLUDING COMMENTS

In clinical practice, assessment is necessarily multifaceted. In the assessment of sexual dysfunction, the clinician has more constraints placed on him or her than in the assessment of most other disorders. Despite these constraints, the clinician still has a variety of techniques at his or her disposal. The interview will be the main source of information. Other techniques will be used, both within the interview and without, for obtaining additional data and for improving the quality of information. Which of these additional methods are to be used will depend on the nature of the presenting problem, its circumstances and the context of service.

REFERENCES

American Psychiatric Association (1987) *Diagnostic and Statistical Manual of Mental Disorders, 3rd edn Revised*, Washington, DC: American Psychiatric Association.
Bancroft, J. (1989) *Human Sexuality and Its Problems, 2nd edn*, Edinburgh: Churchill Livingstone.
Barnes, J. (1986a) 'Primary vaginismus I. Social and clinical features', *Irish Medical Journal* 79: 59–62.
Barnes, J. (1986b) 'Primary vaginismus II. Aetiological factors', *Irish Medical Journal* 79: 62–5.
Beck, A. T., Ward, C. H., Mendelsohn, M., Mock, J. and Erbaugh, J. (1961) 'An inventory for measuring depression', *Archives of General Psychiatry* 4: 561–71.
Beck, J. G., Barlow, D. H. and Sakheim, D. (1983) 'The effects of attentional focus and partner arousal on sexual responding in functional and dysfunctional men', *Behaviour Research and Therapy* 21: 1–8.
Conte, H. R. (1986) 'Multivariate assessment of sexual dysfunction', *Journal of Consulting and Clinical Psychology* 54: 149–57.
Crowe, M. J. and Ridley, J. (1990) *Therapy with Couples*, Oxford: Blackwell.
Derogatis, L. R. and Melisaratos, N. (1979) 'The DFSI: A multidimensional measure of sexual functioning', *Journal of Sex and Marital Therapy* 5: 244–81.
de Silva, P. and Dissanayake, S. A. W. (1989) 'The Loss of Semen Syndrome in Sri Lanka: A clinical study', *Sexual and Marital Therapy* 4: 195–204.
Dow, S. (1981) 'Retarded ejaculation', *Journal of Sex and Marital Therapy* 7: 49–53.

Duddle, M. (1977) 'Etiological factors in the unconsummated marriage', *Journal of Consulting and Clinical Psychology* 54: 157–60.

Frank, E., Anderson, C. and Rubinstein, D. (1978) 'Frequency of sexual dysfunction in normal couples', *New England Journal of Medicine* 299: 111–15.

Group for the Advancement of Psychiatry (1973) *Assessment of Sexual Function: A Guide to Interviewing*, Report No. 88, Vol. VIII.

Harbin, H. T. and Gamble, B. (1977) 'Sexual conflicts related to dominance and submission', *Medical Aspects of Human Sexuality* 11(1): 84–9.

Hawton, K. (1985) *Sex Therapy: A Practical Guide*, Oxford: Oxford University Press.

Hoon, E., Wincze, J. and Hoon, P. (1976a) 'The SAI: An inventory for the measurement of female sexual arousal', *Archives of Sexual Behavior* 5: 291–300.

Hoon, E., Wincze, J. and Hoon, P. (1976b) 'Physiological assessment of sexual arousal in women', *Psychophysiology* 13: 196–208.

Kanfer, F. H. and Saslow, G. (1969) 'Behavioral diagnosis', in C. M. Franks (ed.) *Behavior Therapy – Appraisal and Status*, New York: McGraw-Hill.

Kaplan, H. S. (1974) *The New Sex Therapy: Brief Treatment of Sexual Dysfunction*, New York: Brunner/Mazel.

Kaplan, H. S. (1977) 'Hypoactive sexual desire', *Journal of Sex and Marital Therapy* 3: 3–9.

Kaplan, H. S. (1979) *Disorders of Sexual Desire*, New York: Brunner/Mazel.

Kaplan, H. S. (1989) *How to Overcome Premature Ejaculation*, New York: Brunner/Mazel.

Karacan, I. (1978) 'Advances in the psychophysiological evaluation of male erectile impotence', in L. Lo Piccolo and J. Lo Piccolo (eds) *Handbook of Sex Therapy*, New York: Plenum Press.

Kinsey, A. C., Pomeroy, W. B. and Martin, C. G. (1948) *Sexual Behavior in the Human Male*, Philadelphia: Saunders.

Kolodny, R. C., Masters, W. H. and Johnson, V. (1979) *Textbook of Sexual Medicine*, Boston: Little Brown.

Lamont, J. A. (1978) 'Vaginismus', *American Journal of Obstetrics and Gynaecology* 131: 632–6.

Lief, H. I. (1977) 'Inhibited sexual desire', *Medical Aspects of Human Sexuality* 11(12): 51–7.

Lief, H. I. (1979) 'Anxiety, sexual dysfunctions and therapy', in W. E. Fann, I. Karacan, A. D. Pokorny and R. D. Williams (eds) *Phenomenology and Treatment of Anxiety*, New York: Spectrum.

Lief, H. I. and Reed, D. M. (1972) *Sexual Knowledge and Attitude Test (SKAT) 2nd edn*, Centre for the Study of Sex Education in Medicine, University of Pennsylvania.

Locke, H. J. and Wallace, K. M. (1959) 'Short marital adjustment and prediction tests: their reliability and validity', *Marriage and Family Living* 21: 251–5.

Lo Piccolo, J. and Steger, J. C. (1974) 'The Sexual Interaction Inventory: a new instrument for assessment of sexual dysfunction', *Archives of Sexual Behavior* 3: 585–95.

Lo Piccolo, L. and Heiman, J. (1978) 'Sexual Assessment and history interview', in J. Lo Piccolo and L. Lo Piccolo (eds) *Handbook of Sex Therapy*, New York: Plenum Press.

Malhotra, H. K. and Wig, N. (1975) 'Dhat Syndrome: a culture-bound sex neurosis of the Orient', *Archives of Sexual Behavior* 4: 519–28.

Masters, W. H. and Johnson, V. E. (1966) *Human Sexual Response*, Boston: Little Brown.

Masters, W. H. and Johnson, V. E. (1970) *Human Sexual Inadequacy*, Boston: Little Brown.

O'Sullivan, K. (1979) 'Observations on vaginismus in Irish women', *Archives of General Psychiatry* 36: 824–6.

Rust, J. and Golombok, S. (1986) *The Golombok–Rust Inventory of Sexual Satisfaction*, Windsor: NFER-Nelson.

Rust, J., Bennun, I., Crowe, M. J. and Golombok, S. (1988) *The Golombok–Rust Inventory of Marital State*, Windsor: NFER-Nelson.

Schiavi, R. C. (1992) 'Laboratory methods for evaluating erectile dysfunction', in R. C. Rosen and S. R. Leiblum (eds) *Erectile Disorders: Assessment and Treatment*, New York: Guilford Press.

Snaith, R. P., Ahmed, S. N., Mehta, S. and Hamilton, M. (1971) 'Assessment of the severity of primary depressive illness: Wakefield Self-Assessment Depression Inventory', *Psychological Medicine* 1: 143–9.

Spanier, G. B. (1976) 'Measuring dyadic adjustment: New scales for assessing the quality of marriage and similar dyads', *Journal of Marriage and the Family* 38: 15–23.

Spector, L. P. and Carey, M. P. (1990) 'Incidence and prevalence of the sexual dysfunctions: A critical review of the literature', *Archives of Sexual Behavior* 19: 389–408.

Spence, S. H. (1991) *Psychosexual Therapy: A Cognitive-Behavioural Approach*, London: Chapman and Hall.

Wagner, G. and Green, R. (1981) *Impotence: Physiological, Psychological, Surgical Diagnosis and Treatment*, New York: Plenum Press.

Wilson, G. D. (1978) *The Secrets of Sexual Fantasy*, London: Dent.

Wincze, J. P. and Carey, M. P. (1991) *Sexual Dysfunction: A Guide for Assessment and Treatment*, New York: Guilford Press.

Wincze, J. P., Bansal, S., Malhotra, C., Balko, A ., Susset, J. G. and Malamud, M. (1988) 'A comparison of nocturnal penile tumescence and penile response to erotic stimulation during working states in comprehensively diagnosed groups of males experiencing erectile difficulties', *Archives of Sexual Behaviour* 17: 333–47.

Woody, J. D. (1992) *Treating Sexual Distresss: Integrative Systems Therapy*, Newbury Park: Sage.

Zilbergeld, B. (1978) *Men and Sex*, Boston: Little Brown.

Zimmer, D. (1987) 'Does marital therapy enhance the effectiveness of treatment for sexual dysfunction?' *Journal of Sex and Marital Therapy* 13: 193–209.

Chapter 10

Sexual dysfunction

Treatment

P. de Silva

INTRODUCTION

Interest in sexual dysfunction and its therapy has witnessed a phenomenal increase in the last two decades. The impetus provided by the work of Masters and Johnson (1970), and the public awareness of availability of treatment for sexual problems, have contributed to the vast increase in those seeking and receiving help for these difficulties. In addition to the psychiatric and psychological services, marriage guidance organisations, counselling centres, family planning centres and general practitioner clinics have begun to include sexual dysfunction therapy among their services. In clinical psychology, this group of problems is now an integral part of the range of disorders with which a practitioner is expected to deal.

The therapies for sexual dysfunction used by clinical psychologists are, in the main, behavioural – the term 'behavioural' being used here in a wide sense. The original behaviour-therapeutic approach to problems, as described by Wolpe (1958) and other pioneer behaviour therapists, has been applied to sexual dysfunction for over three decades (e.g. Lazarus, 1963; Wolpe, op. cit.). In clinical practice today, however, the approach used most frequently is one based on that of Masters and Johnson (1970), which is itself largely behavioural but which includes elements that do not fall strictly within the spectrum of conventional behaviour therapy (cf. Murphy and Mikulas, 1974).

Before discussing these approaches, however, the alternative approaches need to be briefly mentioned.

NON-BEHAVIOURAL APPROACHES TO THERAPY

Psychotherapy

Psychotherapy based on psychodynamic principles has been used traditionally with sexual dysfunction cases (e.g. Rosen, 1977). The assumption is that the presenting problem is the result of an unconscious conflict or a repressed memory of a past experience, usually related to the Oedipal stage of development. The rationale, therefore, is to bring to surface the unconscious material by analysis. While orthodox analysts still use this form of psychotherapy for patients with sexual dysfunction, there is no good evidence for the efficacy of this time-consuming and usually expensive approach (Killman and Auerbach, 1979).

Kaplan (1974; 1979) has advocated an approach combining focal problem-oriented therapy with a psychodynamic orientation. The interest here is in exploring and resolving psychological conflicts and other relationship factors as they arise in therapy. This is, thus, not an entirely psychotherapeutic approach, as the main emphasis is on dealing with specific problems and is best described as eclectic. Kaplan (1987) has also made clear that psychodynamic exploration is undertaken only in a proportion of cases, where the behavioural approach fails to progress beyond a certain point.

Hypnosis

The use of hypnosis in sexual dysfunction has been described by several writers (e.g. Beigel, 1971; Cheek, 1976). It has been employed to explore 'hidden' sexual fears and memories, to reduce tension and induce relaxation, to attempt to change responses by post-hypnotic suggestion, and as an adjunct to other forms of therapy (e.g. Fuchs *et al.*, 1973). There is no convincing evidence of the efficacy of hypnosis as a therapeutical intervention in its own right in these problems.

Bio-feedback

Bio-feedback has been used to enhance erections in males with erectile problems. The patient is usually shown erotic material to encourage arousal, and changes in penile circumference are amplified and immediately fed back to him, by visual and/or auditory means. While this has some potential as a therapeutic strategy, bio-feedback training with these patients is not yet established. While the value of bio-feedback in research is beyond doubt, its role in clinical practice is still very limited. A useful review of this area is found in Rosen and Beck (1988).

Hormone therapy

A common treatment used in medical settings for sexual problems is hormonal therapy. While it is frequently used inappropriately, this form of therapy does have a role in the treatment of cases where there is a clear hormonal abnormality and, when used in this way, can be quite effective. Low sexual drive in males in whom the testosterone level is low may be corrected with testosterone supple-mentation. In post-menopausal women, in whom fall in oestrogens can lead to lack of responsiveness and/or loss of interest, oestrogen therapy is quite bene-ficial (Bancroft, 1989; Davidson and Rosen, 1992; Walling *et al.*, 1990).

As was pointed out in the preceding chapter, it is important to carry out the necessary physical examinations and investigations to identify those patients whose problems may be amenable to hormonal and other physical treatments. When the problem is psychogenic, these treatments are not only ineffective but can also be counter-productive. It is also worth noting that, even in those cases where these interventions are suitable, additional psychological therapy is often needed.

Surgical methods

Physical methods of treatment include surgery. An overtight foreskin or a tough hymen, causing pain in intercourse and/or difficulty in penetration, can be corrected by minor surgery. For men with erectile problems that are considered organic, penile prostheses can be used. Solid or inflatable implants have been used with these patients with some success (Wagner and Green, 1981). Relatively new developments in this field include corrective surgery on arterial supply and on abnormal drainage problems where necessary (Melman and Tiefer, 1992; Wagner and Green, op. cit.).

Mechanical aids

Mechanical devices or aids are also used in the treatment of sexual dysfunction. The best known perhaps are the penile ring, an ebonite ring claimed to help in maintaining erections (Cooper, 1974), and the vibrator (Gillan, 1987). The use of the vibrator as an aid in the treatment of both male and female dysfunction is now recognised. The proper use of the vibrator, however, is not as a sole therapeutic means but as part of a wider package. The use of vacuum devices as an aid for men to obtain erections has also become popular in recent years (Cooper, 1987). Several devices are currently on the market. Reviews of this field are available in Althof and Turner (1992) and Nadig et al. (1986).

Injections for inducing erections

In the past decade or so, many reports have appeared on the use of injections of papaverine (a smooth muscle relaxant) and similar substances into the corpus cavernosum of the penis, to induce erections (Brindley, 1983; 1986). The erections induced in this way may last from one to four hours and are in many cases adequate for satisfactory intercourse. The patient is taught to give these injections himself. The use of this method to help men with organically caused erectile problems, or those who have failed to respond to psychological or behavioural methods, is advocated by several authorities. There is, however, a need for further research, and the use of this approach needs caution (Althof and Turner, 1992; Crowe and Qureshi, 1991). Additional psychological counselling is also often needed.

BEHAVIOUR THERAPY – DESENSITISATION

The main standard behavioural treatment technique that has been used in this field is desensitisation. Where the problem is seen as primarily an anxiety-based one, reduction of anxiety by imaginal and *in vivo* desensitisation can be useful (see Wolpe, 1958). The anxiety-arousing situations are elicited from the patient and arranged in a hierarchy of lowest anxiety to highest (see Lindsay, Chapter 7), and these are then presented to the patient to imagine, in graded fashion, under relaxation. The hierarchy typically involves non-sexual items at the lower end (for instance, looking at partner in a crowded room), and moves upwards towards explicitly sexual situations (such as being in bed with partner, both nude). The desensitisation steps may of course be carried out *in vivo*, in a carefully graded way, or in a combination of imaginal and *in vivo* exposures (Obler, 1973; Wolpe, 1958; 1991). Successful desensitisation in group settings has also been reported (O'Gorman, 1978).

THE CONJOINT THERAPY APPROACH

While desensitisation represents the use of standard behaviour therapy for sexual dysfunction where suitable, it is profitable to consider this and other behavioural techniques as elements that may be incorporated into a wider treatment package. This is the approach taken in much of sex therapy today. The reason for this is that sexual problems are often multi-faceted (see Chapter 9), so that to deal with them effectively needs several methods, of which specific behavioural techniques for those aspects of the difficulty amenable to them are an important part. The general package most widely used in this way is the conjoint therapy of Masters and Johnson (1970), modified in its detail by subsequent writers (e.g. Bancroft, 1989; Gillan 1987; Hawton, 1985; Spence, 1991; Wincze and Carey, 1991).

In the Masters and Johnson conjoint therapy approach, the presenting partner and his or her spouse are seen as a couple for therapy. In the original programme, each couple was seen by a male and female co-therapist team. Therapy was carried out on an intensive basis – daily sessions over a two-week period (Masters and Johnson, 1970). Other researchers have found that the addition of a second therapist added little to the programme, and that sessions did not need to be so closely massed together (Arentewicz and Schmidt, 1983; Bancroft, 1989; Crowe *et al.*, 1982).

Features of the conjoint therapy approach

The main elements of the Masters and Johnson type conjoint therapy approach may be summarised as follows:

1 Treat the problem as a joint problem. This helps to reduce worry and guilt in the presenting partner and also emphasises that the need is to learn, or re-learn, how to have satisfactory sex jointly.

2 Reduce anxiety. This is usually achieved by banning any attempt at intercourse. This removes the pressure to perform. Relaxation training may also be used as an extra help.

3 Set sexual tasks or assignments to be carried out at home. These are specific behavioural tasks and involve touching, caressing and so on. The two main stages of this are 'non-genital sensate focus', where the touching excludes genitals and breasts, and 'genital sensate focus' where these are included. These basic tasks aim to help the couple to learn giving and receiving pleasure by touch, with no anxiety or performance demands, moving from less sexual to more intimate interactions.

4 Educate the couple in sexual knowledge – for example, anatomy, physiology, coital positions.

5 Help the couple to develop sexual communication skills.

6 Use specific techniques for specific dysfunctions. While 1 to 5 are common to all, there are specific interventions designed to deal with specific presenting problems. They are usually introduced after the common stages.

This programme may be considered a behavioural package in that there is no attempt to interpret the presenting symptoms in terms of psychodynamic constructs, and that behavioural tasks are a major part of the package. The degree to which an approach geared towards unravelling conflicts and relationship problems is incorporated into this varies from therapist to therapist and case to case (e.g. Beck, 1992; Woody, 1992). Bancroft (1989), for example, uses a programme which, while basically close to the Masters and Johnson format, emphasises these factors a great deal. It must be recognised that severe relationship problems could make the programme impossible for the couple to carry out successfully; and sometimes the relationship problems come to the forefront only when the couple have attempted some of the tasks. These problems need to be looked into where relevant (e.g Crowe and Ridley, 1990). Even in such cases, however, the thrust of the programme can remain behavioural. We shall return to this issue later in this chapter.

Anxiety reduction is a key part of this package. The prohibition of attempts at intercourse helps to achieve this, as immediately the performance anxiety in the male and fears of pain and so on in the female are removed. Other techniques of anxiety reduction may be added as required. McCarthy (1977; 1992), for example, has listed a number of ways, both general and specific, in which anxiety can be reduced in sexual problems.

The sensate focus assignments help a couple to learn to relax in each other's company and enjoy physical contact and interaction without worries of failure. In this relaxed, mutually pleasuring stage, they can acquire the confidence to move towards more intimate interactions. It is perhaps worth noting here that the progression from non-genital to genital sensate focus, and from there to more specific and more explicitly sexual acts, is similar in many ways to an *in vivo* desensitisation programme.

Self-exploration and self-stimulation may be incorporated into the programme where required. Communication, both verbal and non-verbal, on matters of pleasure, sensations and sexual responses is encouraged and taught (for example, how to indicate to the partner where and how to touch, and how to express pleasure at what the partner is doing). The verbal aspects of this kind of simple, but to many couples new, interaction may be role-played and rehearsed during sessions in the presence of the therapist.

The meetings with the therapist are crucial in discussing progress or otherwise of the assignments, and difficulties and problems are discussed fully. Not infrequently in these feedback discussions, relevant new materials about the relationship emerge for the first time (see Bancroft, 1989; Hawton, 1985).

Specific techniques used in conjoint therapy

The specific techniques that are incorporated into this general programme, usually after the initial stages are successfully completed, are summarised in the following sections.

Premature ejaculation

There are two, closely similar, techniques used for premature ejaculation. Masters and Johnson (1970) recommend what is called the 'squeeze' technique. The couple are asked to practise this in the genital touching stage. The female stimulates the penis of her partner with her hand, and when the man feels he is about to reach a climax he indicates this to her with a pre-arranged signal. She then squeezes the penis hard for two to three seconds. For squeezing, the penis is held with the thumb on the frenulum and the first and second fingers on the opposite surface, one on each side of the coronal ridge. The squeeze makes the man lose his urge to ejaculate, and also perhaps some of the erection. This process of stimulation and squeeze is repeated several times in a session. Several sessions of this leads to gradual increase in ejaculatory control, and the couple is then asked to effect vaginal entry, in the woman-above position. At first, entry is not followed by movement. If the man feels he is about to ejaculate, he communicates this to his partner who then lifts herself off him lightly and applies the squeeze. Kolodny et al. (1979) recommend a basilar squeeze technique at this stage so that the penis does not have to be completely disengaged. The penis is held at the base, anterior to posterior, and the pressure applied. Eventually the couple may revert to preferred positions.

The squeeze technique is, in fact, a variant of the start-stop method described in 1956 by Semans, which is used by many therapists (e.g. Kaplan, 1974; 1979). This consists of stimulating the penis and stopping at the point of near-climax, and repeating the process several times. Initially, the stimulation is with a dry hand; later a lubricant is used to increase sensitivity and make the sensations more like the experience of vaginal entry (Gillan, 1987). The rest of the programme consists of vaginal entry without movement, followed by movement in the woman-above position.

Impotence

In the genital sensate focus stage, 'teasing' is introduced, that is, periods of penile stimulation alternating with absence of stimulation. While erections may spon- taneously occur, these are not considered the aim of therapy, and the couple are encouraged to let the erection subside before re-stimulating. This helps in training them not to rush to intercourse once an erection is there, and also demonstrates that erections, when lost, can re-appear.

The next stage is vaginal entry, in the female superior position but with no movement. In the following stage the female makes slow movements, eventually leading to the male participating in and/or initiating movement, and using different positions.

Retarded ejaculation

The aim is to work towards intra-vaginal ejaculation, in a series of steps gradually approaching this goal. Again the instructions are introduced at the genital touching stage. For those males who do not ejaculate easily in any situation, vigorous stimulation with the aid of a lubricant is recommended. The use of a vibrator may also be considered. Once orgasm can be achieved in this way, vaginal entry, after some initial manual stimulation, may be attempted. In those men whose problem is that they cannot reach orgasm in the vagina but can do so with manual stimulation, a graded programme in which orgasm is achieved by manual stimulation, with the penis increasingly close to the vagina, is recommended. In the next stage vaginal entry is achieved, after stimulation by hand close to orgasm. Even then, some manual stimulation may be needed to achieve orgasm once the penis is in the vagina. Subsequently, vaginal stimulation alone will be sufficient for orgasm (Kaplan, 1987).

Vaginismus

This is treated by helping the patient to learn to relax and to explore her own genitals. Following this, a graded series of steps achieving penetration using own fingers, partner's fingers or dilators (or trainers) of increasing sizes, is undertaken (Gillan, 1987; Scholl, 1988). This is done with the patient retaining control. The use of imaginal desensitisation using scenes of varying degrees of sexual closeness and penetration may also be used (Fuchs *et al.*, 1973).

Anorgasmia

For females with orgasmic dysfunction, the main additional element in the therapy package is a good deal of self-focusing and self-stimulation (Barbach, 1975; 1980; Gillan, 1987; Heiman and Lo Piccolo, 1988; Lo Piccolo and Lobitz, 1972; Lo Piccolo and Stock, 1986; see also Nairne and Hemsley, 1983). This helps the patient to learn to enjoy the sexual sensations in a relaxed manner. These self-sessions, including stimulation until orgasm is achieved, can be built into the basic programme as parallel assignments. It has been shown that the use of vibrators can help these women to achieve orgasm; this may be done by the patient herself at first, and the partner may help her to achieve orgasm with the vibrator in later stages. The use of fantasy and erotic materials may also be used as an adjunct (Gillan, 1987; Spence, 1991).

Exercises to achieve control over the pubococcygeus muscle and to strengthen its tone, usually referred to as 'Kegel exercises', have also been recommended as an aid to achieving orgasm (Gillan, 1987; Kegel, 1952).

For females who are unable to achieve orgasm with the partner but have no problem in masturbation, other elements may need to be added to the programme. For example, orgasmic reconditioning may be attempted, in which the patient is taught to pair the positive pleasurable aspects of self-stimulation or other sexual situations with images of the partner in a fantasy-based graded programme (Asirdas and Beech, 1975; Gillan, 1987).

Lack of interest

Lack of interest usually begins to respond to the general treatment package if nothing more serious is underlying. Additional techniques are self-focusing, self-stimulation, use of vibrators, and stimulation with erotic material – pictures, videos, audiotapes, and so on (Gillan, 1987). It is important, however, that the kind of erotic material recommended or provided is not distasteful to the patients and so the choice is best left to them. Fantasy training is a related technique sometimes useful for those whose fantasies are minimal (Spence, 1991). To encourage fantasies, published fantasy materials may be used, such as the volumes of fantasies published by Nancy Friday (e.g. Friday, 1976; 1991). The use of agreed timetables for sex is also found to be helpful (e.g. Crowe and Ridley, 1990). The therapist would negotiate with the couple a timetable for sex; for example, intercourse will take place only on certain days of the week, or sex will be initiated by each partner on certain days only. This approach is often quite effective in cases where the partner with the low level of desire finds the demands made by the spouse too much, thus making the problem worse. The timetable helps to establish an acceptable pattern or schedule, within which further progress can be made.

Some additional considerations on conjoint therapy

Needless to say, the above is only a brief, and perhaps over-simplified, account of conjoint therapy. Some general points about this treatment approach need to be made.

1 The package in its basic form is for use with all sexual dysfunctions, with the specific elements added to suit specific difficulties. There are, however, instances where there is no need to apply the whole package, where perhaps sexual counselling and basic education are all that is needed (Hawton, 1985; Kaplan, 1987). Needless to say, the therapist must have a flexible approach in applying the therapy package or parts of it.

2 The programme is intended for psychogenic problems, as patients with organic problems need different forms of therapy (see pp. 214–15). On the other hand, there is no reason why the early stages of the programme should not be used even with those whose problems are not psychogenic, as a way of helping them to relax in their sexual activity and enhance their sexual experience. For example, in elderly men with impotence, who due to ageing and other physical causes may not be able to have erectile function restored, much can still be achieved by a programme aimed at enhancing their enjoyment of sexual activity, enabling them to accept that sex need not always mean vaginal intercourse (cf. Gibson, 1992). (Note also that couples can be encouraged to have and enjoy intercourse with a limp or semi-flaccid penis. Couples can achieve this with the aid of a good lubricant and using a position which permits easy access to the female genitals.) It is also important to remember that the psychogenic-organic distinction is not always clear cut, and often there is overlap. A problem caused, or triggered, by a physical condition may often be aggravated or maintained by psychological factors, such as anxiety, invalidism and diminished self-esteem. In many cases, psychological help is needed in addition to a physical intervention.

3 The programme is meant to be applied flexibly. The needs of each couple determine what changes to aim for, and the therapist must be prepared to alter the direction of a programme as and when required; for example, a couple presenting with a premature ejaculation problem may turn out to be one where the basic problem is lack of responsiveness in the female. Some couples require a good deal of direct education; a shy patient may not be able to participate fully in therapy sessions until his or her embarrassment is overcome, and will need considerable time and effort to reach the point where therapy can proceed. The need for flexibility is very well illustrated by Lobitz *et al.* (1976) and Winzce and Carey (1991).

4 The programme can sometimes meet with resistance. A couple may not carry out therapy assignments, or do them only infrequently or cursorily. Their difficulties will need to be fully explored. Marital problems may come to the surface at this stage, in which case the lack of progress with the assignments is entirely understandable and efforts should be directed towards resolving these (Bancroft, 1989; Crowe and Ridley, 1990).

5 Additions to the basic programme need not be confined to the specific techniques mentioned above. Any suitable behavioural technique for aspects of the problem may be incorporated as required. For example, when a strong phobic element is present, an intervention to deal with the phobia may be

attempted; for a man whose dysfunction is bound up with deviant desires, additional treatments may be required (see Chalkley, Chapter 18).

The idea of functional analysis (e.g. Kanfer and Saslow, 1969) is extremely useful in devising individualised treatment programmes. When the assessment shows clearly identifiable factors related to the problem behaviour, the systematic manipulation of these can achieve considerable results – usually as a part of the main programme, but also sometimes as the main intervention itself (Lobitz *et al.*, 1976).

Cognitive changes

An aspect of therapy which has increasingly been recognised as important is the modification of cognitions that are related to the dysfunction. Where maladaptive cognitions have a role in the maintenance of a problem, these need to be challenged and changed. Common myths, attitudes, and idiosyncratic beliefs, etc. often contribute to sexual difficulties (e.g. Baker and de Silva, 1988; Bishay, 1988; de Silva and Dissanayake, 1989). The use of cognitive techniques as part of the therapy package therefore often needs to be considered. Spence (1991) has provided a particulary helpful discussion of the use of cognitive strategies in the treatment of sexual difficulties. She includes fantasy training and attention-focusing skills as possible aspects of therapy. The major cognitive interventions, however, consist of identifying and restructuring the relevant cognitions. Maladaptive or negative thoughts need to be identified and changed as needed (e.g. Zilbergeld, 1978; 1992). For a full discussion see Spence (1991: 148–64).

The relationship context

The importance of relationship factors was referred to in several previous paragraphs. In conjoint therapy, relationship factors are taken into account in varying degrees. Some practitioners, such as Woody (1992), take the view that dealing with these is an essential aspect of sex therapy, and she proposes an integrative systems approach. Relationship factors are sometimes a key element in the aetiology of sexual problems; more often, they have a role in their maintenance. Issues in the relationship such as status, power and dominance, trust, jealousy and intimacy sometimes have a crucial role in the clinical picture. When this is the case, conjoint therapy needs to pay due attention to these and deal with them as required. Excellent discussions of these are available in Crowe and Ridley (1990), Leiblum and Rosen (1992) and Woody (op. cit.).

Some practical issues

As was noted in an earlier paragraph, Masters and Johnson (1970) used a male and female team of co-therapists in their programme, but others have shown that a second therapist adds little to the programme effectiveness. On the other hand, in certain cases an additional therapist of the opposite sex to the main therapist can be an advantage, for example, by making it easier for each of the partners to communicate about the problem and his or her feelings about it.

The individuals should be given an opportunity to report to the therapist individually, that is, in the absence of the partner, at least briefly in every session. This enables the therapist to gain a balanced account of the progress and related matters.

Giving written instructions, with illustrations, is a valuable addition to the therapy programme. While written instructions have been used with some success as the main mode of therapy (e.g. Lowe and Mikulas, 1975), they should be used as a supplement to verbal instructions. Equally useful is to recommend a well-written basic book on sex. There are many good books that may be recommended – for example, Barnes and Rodwell (1992) and Delvin (1974). Films, videos and slides may also be used (Gillan, 1987).

PATIENTS WITHOUT PARTNERS

When a patient comes for therapy without a partner, what help can be offered? If the patient has a steady partner who, though unwilling to come to the clinic, will cooperate with a therapy programme, a 'remote control' approach may be used, with the presenting partner also acting as communicator of instructions. The use of written material will be particularly useful in such cases. Clinical experience suggests that this is a less than ideal substitute for conjoint therapy, but should be considered in the right circumstances. If the refusal of the partner to attend clinic reflects a poor relationship, and an attitude that it is all the other's problem, then clearly the chances of joint work being successfully carried out are slim. On the other hand, if the reluctance of the spouse to come is more the result of shyness or embarrassment and cooperation at home is assured, the therapy has better prospects of succeeding.

A somewhat different problem arises when the patient has no partner available. Many young men with erectile or ejaculatory problems not only do not have a steady partner, but also avoid, through fear of failure and rejection, developing relationships. Individual therapy is the only option available in such cases, unless group therapy is considered and facilities are available for it (see p. 224).

The basic principles of individual sex therapy are the same as for couples: education, counselling, anxiety reduction in various ways including relaxation, self-focusing, self-stimulation and fantasy training, are all possible and useful elements in such a programme. As for specific techniques, premature ejaculators will find the start-stop technique more feasible than the squeeze. Imaginal desensitisation may be used for fear or anxiety, while role-play and social skills training can be useful in some cases (McCarthy, 1992). The sexual re-education programme of Zilbergeld (1978) is particularly appropriate for males with sexual worries and associated dysfunctions. Zilbergeld considers it important to dispel some widespread 'myths' about sex (such as that sex always means intercourse, that the male must always take the active role, and so on) in helping these persons, and exploration – and correction – of the individual's misconceptions about sex will be a useful element in an individual sex-therapy programme (Zilbergeld, 1992). For females, masturbatory exercises, Kegel exercises, vibrator use and other such techniques referred to in earlier paragraphs, which are possible for the individual to use without a partner, may profitably be used.

SURROGATES

The use of surrogate partners in the treatment of patients who come without partners has been used and recommended by some therapists. Masters and Johnson used surrogates for some of their male patients but later gave up this practice. Several sex therapists in the USA still use surrogate therapy (Dauw, 1988; Sommers, 1980), while in the UK Cole has been using this form of therapy for some time. Cole (1988) has described surrogate therapy with 425 patients, 390 men and 35 women. Of these, 316 (74.4 per cent) completed therapy; unfortunately, follow-up was possible in only 13.3 per cent of these.

There are serious problems with the use of surrogate therapy, including obvious legal and ethical issues. For example, in the Cole sample, nearly a quarter were married and in many of them the spouse was not even aware that the patient had come for therapy. A serious clinical question is whether someone who has been treated with a surrogate partner will be able to generalise his or her gains to other situations. In view of these reservations it is difficult to recommend surrogate therapy as an option in the management of sexual dysfunction.

GROUP THERAPY

In recent years, an increasing number of therapists have treated sex-dysfunction patients in groups. There have been male groups, female groups, couple groups and mixed-single groups; and there have been groups for patients with similar problems and groups for heterogeneous problems (Auerbach and Killman, 1977; Barbach and Flaherty, 1980; Kayata and Szydlo, 1988; Spence, 1985; Zilbergeld, 1975). The groups have used a variety of techniques – including education, task-setting, relaxation, desensitisation, instructions to use masturbation and vibrators, and open discussion of problems. Particularly for young and sexually diffident persons, the experience of group therapy can have benefits (Bancroft, 1989) over and above the specific gains they make.

HELPING GAY COUPLES AND INDIVIDUALS

Gay couples, and single gay persons, increasingly present at clinics seeking help for sexual dysfunctions. Their difficulties are largely similar to those of heterosexuals seeking help, and the principles outlined above should be used in treating them. However, they may also have different concerns, for example with regard to attitudes towards certain acts such as oral or anal sex (Reece, 1988; Spence, 1991). Worries about the sexual orientation itself may sometimes contribute to the problem, as may particular fears and concerns about 'safe' sex. The therapist needs to elicit the patient's worries and concerns carefully and patiently, and deal with them as appropriate. Some of the special issues in the treatment of gay men are well discussed by Gordon (1988).

EFFICACY OF THERAPY

What about the efficacy of the various therapeutic approaches and techniques that have been discussed above? The very high success rates reported by Masters and Johnson (1970; also Kolodny, Masters and Johnson, 1979) have not been matched by other investigators, but there is, generally, evidence that the conjoint approach and other behavioural techniques referred to in this chapter are beneficial to many patients (Arentewicz and Schmidt, 1983; Bancroft, 1989, Spence, 1991). A thorough critical evaluation of these is not easy to undertake because of various factors: heterogeneity of samples, lack of uniformity in outcome meas- ures, ambiguity of criteria of improvement, preponderance of single-case reports, poor description of patient characteristics, absence of data on drop-outs and failures, and so on (Beck, 1992). Within these limitations, the available data are encouraging. While the conjoint therapy approach is the best option when it is feasible, it is up to the individual clinician to use his or her ingenuity and judgement in choosing, for each case, those elements of therapy that are particularly suitable for the problems he or she is called upon to deal with.

REFERENCES

Althof, S. E. and Turner, L. A. (1992) 'Self-injection therapy and external vacuum devices in the treatment of erectile dysfunctions: Methods and outcome', in R. C. Rosen and S. R. Leiblum (eds) *Erectile Disorders: Assessment and Treatment*, New York: Guilford Press.

Arentewicz, G. and Schmidt, G. (1983) *The Treatment of Sexual Disorder: Concepts and Techniques of Couple Therapy*, New York: Basic Books.

Asirdas, S. and Beech, H. R. (1975) 'The behavioural treatment of sexual inadequacy', *Journal of Psychosomatic Research* 19: 345–53.

Auerbach, R. and Killman, P. R. (1977) 'The effects of group systematic desensitisation on secondary erectile failure', *Behaviour Therapy*, 8: 330–9.

Baker, C. D. and de Silva, P. (1988) 'The relationship between male sexual dysfunction and belief in Zilbergeld's myths: An empirical investigation', *Sexual and Marital Therapy* 3: 229–38.

Bancroft, J. (1989) *Human Sexuality and Its Problems, 2nd edn*, Edinburgh: Churchill Livingstone.

Barbach, L. (1975) *For Yourself: The Fulfillment of Female Sexuality*, New York: Signet.

Barbach, L. (1980) *Women Discover Orgasm*, New York: Free Press.

Barbach, L. G. and Flaherty, M. (1980) 'Group treatment of situationally anorgasmic women', *Journal of Sex and Marital Therapy* 6: 19–29.

Barnes, T. and Rodwell, L. (1992) *A Woman's Guide to Loving Sex*, London: Boxtree.

Beck, J. G. (1992) 'Behavioral approaches to sexual dysfunction', in S. M. Turner, K. S. Calhoun and H. E. Adams (eds) *Handbook of Clinical Behavior Therapy, 2nd edn*, New York: Wiley.

Beigel, H. (1971) 'The hypnotherapeutic approach to male impotence', *Journal of Sex Research* 7: 168–76.

Bishay, N. R. (1988) 'Cognitive therapy for sexual dysfunction: A preliminary report', *Sexual and Marital Therapy* 3: 83–90.

Brindley, G. S. (1983) 'Cavernosal alpha-blockade: A new technique for investigating and treating erectile impotence', *British Journal of Psychiatry* 143: 332–7.

Brindley, G. S. (1986) 'Maintenance treatment of erectile impotence by cavernosal unstriated muscle relaxant injection', *British Journal of Psychiatry* 149: 210–15.

Cheek, J. B. (1976) 'Short-term hypnotherapy for frigidity using exploration of early life attitudes', *American Journal of Clinical Hypnosis* 19: 20–7.

Cole, M. (1988) 'Sex therapy for individuals', in M. Cole and W. Dryden (eds) *Sex Therapy in Britain*, Milton Keynes: Open University Press.

Cooper, S. J. (1974) 'A blind evaluation of a penile ring – a sex aid for impotent males', *British Journal of Psychiatry* 124: 402–6.

Cooper, S. (1987) 'Preliminary experience with a vacuum tumescence device (VTD) as a treatment for impotence', *Journal of Psychosomatic Research* 31: 413–18.

Crowe, M. J. and Qureshi, M. J. H. (1991) 'Pharmacologically induced penile erections (PIPE) as a maintenance treatment of erectile impotence: A report of 41 cases', *Sexual and Marital Therapy* 6: 273–85.

Crowe, M. J. and Ridley, J. (1990) *Therapy with Couples*, Oxford: Blackwell.

Crowe, M. J., Gillan, P. and Golombok, S. (1982) 'Form and content in the conjoint treatment of sexual dysfunction: a controlled study', *Behaviour Research and Therapy* 19: 47–54.

Dauw, D. C. (1988) 'Evaluating the effectiveness of the SECS surrogate-assisted sex therapy model', *Journal of Sex Research* 24: 269–75.

Davidson, J. M. and Rosen, R. C. (1992) 'Hormonel determinants of erectile function', in R. C. Rosen and S. R. Leiblum (eds) *Erectile Disorders: Assessment and Treatment*, New York: Guilford Press.

Delvin, D. (1974) *The Book of Love*, London: New English Library.

de Silva, P. and Dissanayake, S. A. W. (1989) 'The Loss of Semen Syndrome in Sri Lanka: A clinical study', *Sexual and Marital Therapy* 4: 195–204.

Friday, N. (1976) *My Secret Garden: Women's Sexual Fantasies*, London: Quartet.

Friday, N. (1991) *Women on Top*, London: Hutchinson.

Fuchs, K., Hoch, L., Paldi, E., Abramovici, H., Brandes, J., Timor-Tritisch, I. and Kleinhaus, M. (1973) 'Hypnodesensitization therapy of vaginismus, I. In vitro method; II. In vivo method', *International Journal of Clinical and Experimental Hypnosis* 21: 144–56.

Gibson, N. B. (1992) *Love, Sex and Power in Later Life*, London: Freedom Press.

Gillan, P. (1979) 'Stimulation therapy for sexual dysfunction', *British Journal of Sexual Medicine* 6: (June): 13–14.

Gillan, P. (1987) *Sex Therapy Manual*, Oxford: Blackwell.

Gordon, P. (1988) 'Sex therapy with gay men', in M. Cole and W. Dryden (eds) *Sex Therapy in Britian*, Milton Keynes: Open University Press.

Hawton, K. (1985) *Sex Therapy: A Practical Guide*, Oxford: Oxford University Press.

Heiman, J. R. and Lo Piccolo, J. (1988) *Becoming Orgasmic*, Englewood Cliff, NJ: Prentice-Hall.

Kanfer, F. H. and Saslow, G. (1969) 'Behavioral diagnosis', in C. M. Franks (ed.) *Behavior Therapy: Status and Appraisal*, New York: McGraw-Hill.

Kaplan, H. S. (1974) *The New Sex Therapy: Active Treatment of Sexual Dysfunction*, London: Bailliere Tindall, New York: Brunner/Mazel.

Kaplan, H. S. (1979) *Disorders of Sexual Desire*, New York: Brunner/Mazel.

Kaplan, H. S. (1987) *The Illustrated Manual of Sex Therapy*, 2nd edn, New York: Brunner/Mazel.

Kaplan, H. S., Kohl, R. M., Pomeroy, W. B., Offit, A. K. and Hogan, B. (1978) 'Group treatment of premature ejaculation', *Archives of Sexual Behavior* 3: 443–52.

Kayata, L. and Szydlo, D. (1988) 'Sex therapy in groups', in M. Cole and W. Dryden (eds) *Sex Therapy in Britain*, Milton Keynes: Open University Press.

Kegel, A. (1952) 'Sexual functions of the pubococcygeus muscle', *Western Journal of Surgery, Obstetrics and Gynaecology* 60: 521–4.

Killman, P. R. and Auerbach, R. (1979) 'Treatment of premature ejaculation and psychogenic impotence: a critical review of the literature', *Archives of Sexual Behavior* 8: 81–100.

Kolodny, R. C., Masters, W. H. and Johnson, V. E. (1979) *A Textbook of Sexual Medicine* Boston: Little Brown.

Lazarus, A. A. (1963) 'The treatment of chronic frigidity by systematic desensitization', *Journal of Nervous and Mental Disease* 136: 272–8.

Leiblum, S. R. and Rosen, R. C. (1992) 'Couples therapy for erectile disorders: Observations, obstacles and outcomes', in R. C. Rosen and S. R. Leiblum (eds) *Erectile Disorders: Assessment and Treatment*, New York: Guilford Press.

Lobitz, W. C., Lo Piccolo, J., Lobitz, G. K. and Brockway, J. (1976) 'A closer look at simplistic behaviour therapy for sexual dysfunction: two case studies', in H. G. Eysenck (ed.) *Case Studies in Behaviour Therapy*, London: Routledge & Kegan Paul.

Lo Piccolo, J. and Lobitz, W. C. (1972) 'The role of masurbation in the treatment of orgasmic dysfunction', *Archives of Sexual Behavior* 2: 163–71.

Lo Piccolo, J. and Stock, W. (1986) 'Treatment of sexual dysfunction', *Journal of Consulting Clinical Psychology* 54: 158–67.

Lowe, J. C. and Mikulas, W. L. (1975) 'Use of written material in learning self-control of premature ejaculation', *Psychological Reports* 37: 295–8.

McCarthy, B. W. (1977) 'Strategies and technique for the reduction of sexual anxiety', *Journal of Sex and Marital Therapy* 3: 243–8.

McCarthy, B. W. (1992) 'Treatment of erectile dysfunction with single men', in R. C. Rosen and S. R. Leiblum (eds) *Erectile Disorders: Assessment and Treatment*, New York: Guilford Press.

Masters, W. H. and Johnson, V. E. (1970) *Human Sexual Inadequacy*, Boston: Little Brown.

Melman, A. and Tiefer, L. (1992) 'Surgery for erectile disorders: Operative procedures and psychological issues', in R. C. Rosen and S. R. Leiblum (eds) *Erectile Disorders: Assessment and Treatment*, New York: Guilford Press.

Murphy, C. V. and Mikulas, W. L. (1974) 'Behavioural features and deficiencies of the Masters and Johnson programme', *Psychological Record* 24: 221–7.

Nadig, P., Ware, J. and Blumoff, R. (1986) 'Non-invasive device to produce and maintain an erection-like state', *Urology* 27(2): 126–31.

Nairne, K. D. and Hemsley, D. R. (1983) 'The use of directed masturbation training in the treatment of primary anorgasmia', *British Journal of Clinical Psychology* 22: 183–94.

Obler, M. (1973) 'Systematic desensitization in sexual disorders', *Journal of Behaviour Therapy and Experimental Psychiatry* 4: 93–101.

O'Gorman, E. (1978) 'Treatment of frigidity: a comparative study of group and individual desensitization', *British Journal of Psychiatry* 132: 580–4.

Reece, R. (1988) 'Special issues in the etiologies and treatments of sexual problems among gay men', *Journal of Homosexuality* 15: 43–57.

Rosen, J. (1977) 'The psychoanalytic approach to individual therapy', in J. Money and H. Musaph (eds) *Handbook of Sexology*, Amsterdam: Elsevier.

Rosen, R. C. and Beck, G. J. (1988) *Patterns of Sexual Arousal: Psychophysiological Processes and Clinical Applications*, New York: Guilford Press.

Scholl, G. M. (1988) 'Prognostic variables in treating vaginismus', *Obstetrics and Gynaecology* 72: 231–5.

Semans, J. H. (1956) 'Premature ejaculation: A new approach', *Southern Medical Journal* 49: 353–8.

Sommers, F. G. (1980) 'Treatment of male sexual dysfunction in a psychiatric practice integrating the sexual therapy practitioner (surrogates)', in R. Farleo and W. Pasini (eds) *Medical Sexology*, Amsterdam: Elsevier.

Spence, S. H. (1985) 'Group versus individual treatment of primary and secondary orgasmic dysfunction', *Behaviour Research and Therapy* 23: 539–48.

Spence, S. H. (1991) *Psychosexual Therapy: A Cognitive-Behavioural Approach*, London: Chapman and Hall.

Wagner, G. and Green, R. (1981) *Impotence: Physiological, Psychological, Surgical Diagnosis and Treatment*, New York: Plenum Press.

Walling, M ., Andersen, B. L. and Johnson, S. R. (1990) 'Hormonal replacement therapy for post-menopausal women: A review of sexual outcomes and gynaecologic effects', *Archives of Sexual Behavior* 19: 119–37.

Wincze, J. P. and Carey, M. P. (1991) *Sexual Dysfunction: A Guide for Assessment and Treatment*, New York: Guilford Press.

Wolpe, J. (1958) *Psychotherapy by Reciprocal Inhibition*, Stanford: Stanford University Press.

Wolpe, J. (1991) *The Practice of Behavior Therapy, 4th edn*, New York: Pergamon.

Woody, J. D. (1992) *Treating Sexual Distress: Integrative Systems Therapy*, Newbury Park: Sage.

Zilbergeld, B. (1975) 'Group treatment of sexual dysfunction in men without partners', *Journal of Sex and Marital Therapy* 1: 204–14.

Zilbergeld, B. (1978) *Men and Sex*, Boston: Little Brown.

Zilbergeld, B. (1992) 'The man behind the broken penis: Social and psychological determinants of erectile failure', in R. C. Rosen and S. R. Leiblum (eds) *Erectile Disorders: Assessment and Treatment*, New York: Guilford Press.

Chapter 11

Interpersonal problems
Investigation

Susan H. Spence

INTRODUCTION

The ability to interact with others in a competent and successful way is of great importance at all stages of our lives. Failure to do so may have far-reaching consequences. For example, children who exhibit poor peer relations have been shown to be more likely to experience a range of adult problems, such as psychiatric disturbance and unfavourable army discharges (Cowen *et al.*, 1973; Roff, 1970; Roff *et al.*, 1972). The greatest predictor of post-hospital adjustment amongst psychiatric patients has been suggested to be the level of pre-morbid social competence (Zigler and Phillips, 1961). Similarly, the frequency of psychiatric hospitalisation has been shown to be related to the person's level of social competence (Lowe, 1985). Given the importance of this attribute, it is distressing to find that a large number of people experience considerable difficulty or lack of success in social interactions. Research amongst children suggests that many have few or no friends. For example, Hymel and Asher (1977) found that 11 per cent of children surveyed had no friends. However, within the general adult population evidence on the extent of social inadequacy is lacking, with most research having focused on psychiatric patients. The evidence suggests that between 7 and 16 per cent of psychiatric patients are judged to be socially inadequate (Bryant *et al.*, 1976; Curran *et al.*, 1980).

THE NATURE AND DETERMINANTS OF INTERPERSONAL PROBLEMS

At this point it is important to clarify what is meant by social competence or social adequacy and their corollaries, social incompetence and social inadequacy. Trower *et al.* (1978a) stated that a person can be regarded as socially adequate if he is able to affect the behaviour of others in the way that he intends and society accepts. McFall (1982), however, took a different approach, defining social competence as a general evaluative term reflecting somebody's judgement, on the basis of certain criteria, that a person's performance is adequate on a given social task. Thus, social competence is seen as dependent upon the consequences or outcome of a person's social interactions as determined by the reaction of other people. Social competence is not so much what a person does, as how the performance is evaluated by others. It follows, therefore, that social incompetence reflects a failure to achieve successful outcomes or favourable judgements from social interactions.

Cavell (1990) emphasised the many factors that influence whether a person is judged by others to be socially competent, over and above the performance of specific behaviours. These factors relate to the context in which the behaviour occurs, characteristics of the person who is evaluating the behaviour, and a range of non-social characteristics of the performer. Cavell outlined a tri-component, hierarchical model of social competence. At the top of the hierarchy is social adjustment, defined as the extent to which individuals are currently achieving societally determined, developmentally appropriate goals. Such goals relate to various aspects of functioning, including social, emotional, familial and relational aspects of life. Cavell makes the point that social adjustment, as defined in this way, is determined by multiple factors (for example, sex, race, physical appearance, athletic ability, academic and work skills) of which actual social performance is just one aspect. The second level of the hierarchical model of social competence is labelled 'social performance' and is defined as the degree to which an individual's responses to relevant, primarily social situations meet socially valid criteria. In line with the position of McFall (1982), Cavell makes a distinction here between performance and skills. Performance is what the person does, but implies an evaluation regarding whether the response is judged to be socially appropriate for a specific social task. This position agrees with Dodge and Murphy (1984) who stated that we need to look at social responding to different social tasks (for example, dealing with conflict, initiating a conversation with a stranger, or saying 'no' to an unreasonable request), rather than looking at rate of interaction or discrete behaviours which are assumed to be important globally across all social situations.

Finally, Cavell (1990) outlines the third level, namely that of social skills. In line with the social information processing models of McFall (1982) and Dodge and Murphy (1984), Cavell describes a sequence of overt and cognitive skills and processes that are involved in determining how a person behaves in a particular social situation.

Although the models of Cavell (1990), Dodge and Murphy (1984) and McFall (1982) are all valuable in facilitating our understanding of the nature and determinants of social competence, the utility of these models is limited in clinical practice. It is frequently difficult to separate out the different levels when it comes to assessment and it is also difficult to imagine most clinicians having the time to assess separately the many social tasks that most adults are required to deal with. What follows, therefore, is a practically based system for the assessment of social competence which tries to retain some of the important features of the academic models proposed by the above authors.

A PRACTICAL MODEL FOR THE ASSESSMENT OF SOCIAL FUNCTIONING

The practical model outlined here focuses on four levels of assessment, namely (1) long-term social outcomes, (2) short-term social outcomes, (3) social behaviour (i.e. what the person actually says and does), and (4) social-cognitive skills and processes. Table 11.1 outlines the way in which these four levels of assessment relate to one another. This model is not intended to represent a theoretical account of social functioning and is designed for practical utility. Each level reflects the type of information that may be considered during the assessment process. It is recognised that the relationship between each level is only hierarchical in a very loose sense and each level is determined by many factors, both social and non-social, in addition to the previous level.

Level 1: long-term social outcomes

Various long-term social outcomes are proposed to result from the way in which a person behaves in a social situation. Long-term outcomes relate to adequacy of functioning within the various domains of life, such as the family, marriage, the workplace, friendships and recreation pursuits. Functioning at this level may be assessed in terms of the quantity and quality of various outcomes (for example, occurrence of and satisfaction with marriage or employment). Satisfaction may be determined by the self or by others. In addition to the long-term impact upon

Table 11.1 A practical model for the assessment of interpersonal problems

Level	Content	What is assessed
Level 1	Long-term social outcomes	Qualitative and quantitative aspects of relationships in marital, family, occupational and friendship domains as judged by self or others

Level 2	Short-term social outcomes	Immediate impact from social interactions as judged by self and others or objective outcomes
		  e.g. ratings of assertiveness, social skilfulness
		or/ objective measures of succcess
		  e.g. obtaining a job
		or/ subjective feelings
		  e.g. distress

Level 3	Overt social behaviour	Use of micro- and macro-performance skills Frequency, intensity, duration of specific responses Sequencing and blending of responses Micro-skills e.g. eye-contact, facial expression Macro-skills e.g. refusing an unreasonable request
Level 4	Social-cognitive skills and processes	Social perception, social knowledge Social problem-solving, self-monitoring Maladaptive/negative or irrational thoughts, attitudes and beliefs

interpersonal relationships, social adjustment at this level may also be assessed in terms of psychological consequences for the individual. Thus, psychological difficulties such as anxiety or depression may also be considered as possible long-term consequences of an individual's social behaviour. Again, it must be emphasised that many factors other than the previous levels outlined here are important in determining long-term social outcomes. A wide range of environmental and non-social factors are obviously involved, but are not the focus of the present chapter. For example, a person's success in the area of employment may be determined by numerous variables, such as the state of the economy, intellectual and motivational factors, physical attractiveness, characteristics of colleagues and superiors, and so on, rather than purely by the way in which the person interacts with others in the workplace.

Assessment at this level asks the question 'Is there a problem in social adjustment?' and, if so, 'in which domain?' If a problem is identified, then it is important to proceed to the next level of assessment, in order to determine whether the problem relates to difficulties in social interactions, or whether other, non-social factors are involved.

Level 2: short-term social outcomes

Short-term outcomes relate to the immediate impact of a person's behaviour in a social interaction upon the performer and other people who are witness to, or influenced by, the interaction. The outcome may be viewed in terms of subjective judgements, or in terms of objective consequences such as the presence/absence of particular events. Examples of subjective judgements include ratings of assertiveness and assessment of the success or appropriateness of the person's behaviour during the interaction. Objective consequences include the degree to which specific outcomes occur, such as the resolution of a conflict or success in obtaining a job from an interview situation. This level of assessment also permits the assessor to identify the specific tasks in which the client has difficulty. There is an enormous range of social tasks that we all have to be able to deal with. Some common examples of social tasks include resolution of conflicts, beginning conversations with strangers, making assertive responses to unreasonable demands from others, giving compliments and asking for help.

As with long-term outcomes, there are many factors which influence the impact of social behaviour over and above what a person actually says and does. These factors will be discussed in more detail below, but to summarise briefly they may concern characteristics of the individual (for example, physical attractiveness or sex), characteristics of the person making the evaluation, and a wide range of non-social and contextual variables.

Level 3: overt social behaviour

At this level of assessment, one is concerned with what the person actually says and does in specific social situations. Having identified the type of situations in which short-term negative outcomes occur, it is important that the assessor identifies the exact behaviours engaged in by the client during such interactions. The assessment of overt social behaviour should consider the occurrence/non-occurrence, frequency, duration and intensity of specific behaviours. It is this overt, behavioural aspect of social functioning that has been the focus of much of the social-skills literature. It is accepted here that social skills refer to those behaviours which are required in order to lead to successful outcomes from specific social situations. Implicit in this position is the assumption that we are able to identify which behaviours are social skills in particular social situations and which are not. This assumption is questionable but does not prevent practitioners from proceeding upon this assumption in clinical practice. We are frequently guilty of assuming that we can determine whether a person's behaviour is appropriate for a given situation, such as whether his or her level of eye contact, posture or social distance is adequate or not. In reality we do not have the empirical evidence to justify such judgements, and much of what goes on in the area of assessment and training of social skills is based on personal intuition and folklore.

Programmes have varied in the degree to which they have focused on micro- versus macro-skills during assessment and training. Micro-skills refer to the basic responses of social interaction, such as eye contact, posture and facial expression. Macro-skills, on the other hand, represent a more complex level of behaviour in which micro-skills are integrated into strategies for dealing with specific social tasks. Starting a conversation, giving a compliment or dealing with an accusation would all be examples of macro-, complex behaviours which integrate a wide range of micro-skills.

Level 4: social-cognitive skills and processes

Overt social behaviour is strongly influenced by thought processes and these need to be considered in the assessment of social functioning. There are two separate aspects to this level of assessment. One aspect concerns the person's ability to perform a range of social-cognitive skills that are important in deter- mining what is said and done. The other aspect relates to the influence of thoughts, attitudes and beliefs in deciding how we behave. Ultimately, these two aspects interact but for practical purposes we consider them separately below.

The way in which a person behaves overtly is determined to a large degree by a series of cognitive processes. Argyle and Kendon (1967) stressed a variety of cognitive processes considered necessary to enable a person to perform in a socially skilled manner. Their model highlighted the importance of the person's motivations and goals, the ability to perceive information correctly from the outside world and to monitor changes. The individual must then process this information, and bring into play appropriate motor responses which must be correctly performed. McFall (1982), Morrison and Bellack (1981), Spivack and Shure (1976) and Trower (1979) have all expanded on this model and have suggested a series of cognitive processes which are viewed as necessary but not sufficient conditions for competent responding. Deficits at any one stage can have devastating effects on what a person finally does in a social situation.

Table 11.2 summarises a wide range of cognitive skills which have been suggested to influence the way in which a person behaves in a given social interaction.

Social perception

It is important that we are able to attend to, and correctly interpret, the behaviour and feelings of others. Failure to do so may result in inappropriate social responding. As an illustration, take the hypothetical example of the male client

Table 11.2 Social-cognitive skills

1 *Social perception*
   Receiving information from others and environment relevant to the
      interaction
   Attention to relevant aspects of information received
   Knowledge of social rules
   Knowledge of the significance or meaning of various responses
   Correct interpretation of information receive
   Perspective-taking ability

2 *Social problem-solving skills*
   Identification of the nature and existence of a problem situation
   Determination of goals for the situation
   Generating ideas regarding possible alternative responses
   Predicting likely consequences of each course of action
      (requires knowledge of social rules for different situations)
   Selecting the response most likely to lead to desired consequence
   Searching own repertoire for a similar response
   Generating new repertoires of responding
   Plan and sequence a wide range of responses to execute selected course
      of action

3 *Self-monitoring*
   Observe, and correctly perceive, outcome of own actions, and response of
      others
   Adjust responses where appropriate
   Accurate labelling of own behaviour

who was found to talk excessively and to ask inappropriate, personal questions of the female staff while others were trying to work. There are several possible explanations here. For example, this client may have failed to notice the annoyed interpersonal cues in the facial expression, tone of voice and averted stance of his colleagues and may not have realised that they did not wish to continue the interaction with him. Alternatively, he may have been unaware of the social rule that it is inappropriate to ask very personal questions of females whom one hardly knows. Another hypothesis could be that he may have misinterpreted the aversive cues of others as being friendly or encouraging, causing him to persist with his inappropriate behaviour. These examples illustrate deficits in social perception as outlined in Table 11.2. Sensory handicaps, such as blindness or deafness, may also seriously interfere with social perception, as may limitations in intellectual ability and attentional skills (Rathjen, 1980).

Social problem-solving skills

In some instances, social perception skills may be adequate but deficits occur in a second area, that of social problem-solving skills. If a person has difficulty in any of the problem-solving stages outlined in Table 11.2 he or she will be less likely to choose an adequate course of action in a given situation.

Take the case of a female client who rarely interacts with her workmates. It is found that she feels very lonely and wishes very much to make friends. During assessment, however, it is revealed that she has few ideas regarding ways in which to initiate or join in coffee- and meal-breaks with colleagues. Her only suggestion is to wait until she is asked. As a result she is seen as unfriendly and aloof by others who consequently ignore her.

Individuals who are unable to identify the nature of occurrence of a problem situation, to generate alternative responses, to predict likely consequences and to select appropriate responses are unlikely to behave in the most suitable manner in social interactions. Even if these skills do exist, it is still necessary for the person to be able to plan out a response incorporating a wide range of behaviours and sequence them appropriately.

For example, even the simple act of approaching a stranger to request the time requires an enormously complex sequence of responses. A wide range of micro-response such as use of eye-contact, tone of voice, facial expression, body position and wording of question must be brought into play, requiring careful timing and integration. With the majority of people the integration of these micro-skills appears to have reached an 'automatic' level of cognitive processing where one is no longer aware of controlling and regulating their occurrence (Argyle and Kendon, 1967). A prerequisite for adequacy at this stage, however, is knowledge that various responses are important in determining the outcome of social interactions. Hence, if a person is unaware that failure to use eye-contact, or the use of an aggressive tone of voice, results in an unfavourable impression upon others, then he or she is unlikely to bring about desirable changes in behaviour. Similarly, it is essential that a person has the knowledge that different combinations and sequences of behaviours are necessary in different locations, with different people. For example, different behaviours are judged as appropriate with intimate friends at home compared to relative strangers in elevators. The assessment process therefore needs to confirm that the client is aware of these complex social rules in addition to possessing the necessary problem-solving skills.

Self-monitoring

A third area of cognitive skills which may influence social responding is the ability to monitor accurately one's own behaviour and then make necessary adjustments in responding (Argyle and Kendon, 1967; McFall, 1982). This requires that attention is paid to one's own behaviour and that the outcome of the interaction is correctly perceived (which brings us back to social perception skills!). This process necessitates that a person is able to label his or her own behaviour correctly. If the person cannot do so, for example if he or she is unaware of having a facial expression that is likely to be perceived by others as aggressive, this aspect of responding is unlikely to be changed despite an awareness of aversive responses from others.

It must be remembered that the cognitive aspect of responding is closely linked to the performance aspect and having developed the necessary plan of action in terms of cognitive schema, the person must then be able to execute this response correctly at a overt-behavioural level. As with any motor skill, repeated practice improves performance as the overt response becomes closer to that which the person is attempting to achieve.

Thoughts, attitudes and beliefs

Our thoughts, attitudes and beliefs have considerable influence over the way in which we interpret social situations and the solutions which we select for social problems. There are many occasions in which a person is capable of selecting and performing an appropriate solution to a particular social problem but is influenced by thoughts, attitudes and beliefs to behave in an inappropriate or unsuccessful manner. For example, maladaptive thoughts and negative attitudes or beliefs may inhibit the selection of appropriate responses during conflict situations or during tasks which involve evaluation by others (Halford and Foddy, 1982).

Here are two case descriptions. In the first case, a young male presented to the clinic with problems in controlling his temper with his superiors at work. During assessment, he revealed many negative attitudes towards authority, such as, 'No one has the right to criticise me; if they do, that is terrible and I will not tolerate such behaviour'. Perhaps not surprisingly, he tended to deal with instructions and criticism from superiors at work in an aggressive manner. Technically, he was able to generate appropriate solutions to such situations, but in practice his selection of a response was strongly influenced by his maladaptive thoughts and attitudes.

A similar process of inhibition of social-cognitive skills has been found amongst many cases of social anxiety in which people experience fears of situations in which they are subject to evaluation by others. The following case illustrates this point: a 46-year-old woman was referred to the clinic following a long history of avoidance of many social situations, such as meeting new people, eating in public and going to parties. During assessment, we identified many maladaptive thoughts and attitudes. For example, if she was invited out to a party, she would report thoughts such as, 'I can't possibly go. Who would I talk to? I wouldn't know what to say to anyone. They would all think I am stupid. Everyone will laugh at me'. On social problem-solving tests, it was clear that this woman was able to problem-solve effectively but, in real-life situations, her solutions tended to be inhibited by her negative thoughts and beliefs.

Rathjen (1980) stressed the importance of irrational beliefs and distorted thinking processes, such as arbitrary inference, magnification, over-generalisation, dichotomous reasoning and catastrophising, in determining how we respond socially. Maladaptive or incorrect attributions, self-appraisal, values, attitudes and expectancies are also suggested to influence social responding. It is therefore proposed here that the assessment of social functioning should fully explore the possible involvement of maladaptive cognitions in social inadequacy. There seems little point in spending considerable time developing sophisticated social skills if the person is not going to use them as a result of competing maladaptive thoughts.

OTHER FACTORS INFLUENCING SOCIAL RESPONDING

The previous section outlined various cognitive processes which determine the way in which a person responds in a social situation, but unfortunately there is a whole range of other variables which influence what a person actually does. These are outlined in Table 11.3 below.

For example, a client may be aware of what he or she should do in a particular interaction and may be capable of performing the response successfully, but for some reason may choose an alternative and less appropriate course of action. Various explanations for this are possible and need to be considered during assessment. Part of the assessment process will require consideration of environmental contingencies, either antecedents or consequences of both competent and incompetent responding. It may be found in some instances that a person's inadequate social behaviour may be accounted for by factors such as the modelling, prompting and reinforcement of undesirable actions rather than a social-skills deficit. Take the example of John, a 27-year-old schizophrenic, who frequently shouts aggressively at care staff in the hostel where he lives. Behavioural analysis revealed that this behaviour was being maintained by the peer

Table 11.3 Factors involved in the determination of interpersonal problems

RELATING TO THE INDIVIDUAL	RELATING TO ENVIRONMENT/OTHERS

1 *Personal characteristics*
  – physical attractiveness
  – grooming, dress
  – physical handicap
  – age, sex, status, culture
  – prior learning history
	1 *Environmental contingencies*
	  – antecedents and consequences
	   of competence/incompetent
	   behaviour, including modelling
	   and prompting

2 *Maladaptive affect and cognitions*
  – control over physiological, motor
   and cognitive components of
   emotional states e.g. anxiety,
   fear, anger
  – control over avoidance
   responses
  – attitude, beliefs, attributions
  – expectations
  – aims, intentions motivation
  – values
  – self-concept, self-appraisal
	2 *Characteristics of others in interaction*
	  – age, sex, status, culture, physical
	   attraction, etc.
	  – aims, goals, expectations
	  – response to individual

	3 *Characteristics of judge*
	  – personal characteristics e.g. age,
	   sex, status
	  – knowledge of situation and
	   performer
	  – expectations, values, norms
	  – personal and cultural beliefs
	  – criteria used in making judgement

3 *Social-cognitive skills*
  (see Table 11.2)
	4 *Characteristics of social situation*
	  – location
	  – task analysis (McFall, 1982):
	   difficulty and nature of
	   components of task
	  – combined aims of all persons
	   involved in interaction

4 *Overt-behavioural social skills*
  – verbal skills
  – non-verbal skills
	5 *Social-cultural determinants*
	  – norms and values, expectations
	   of society/culture to which all
	   involved belong

	6 *Social contacts/networks*
	  – availability of others with whom
	   individual has opportunity to
	   interact

group, who laugh and cheer whenever John behaves aggressively towards the care staff. In role-play tasks John was found to be capable of approaching the staff appropriately and of making polite requests, but he failed to do so in the real-life situation. The intervention used here was the removal of the reinforcing contingencies of the peer group and the reinforcement of appropriate approaches to staff.

A further area that may influence social functioning concerns the range of a person's social contacts and the social network. Different people vary in their opportunity for social interactions. We all have varying family sizes, live at various degrees of proximity to friends and relatives, work with varying numbers and types of people and live in different locations with different social facilities. The opportunity that a client has to engage in particular social interactions must be considered, as social competence is likely to be influenced by the frequency of practice of target responses. Where necessary, intervention may be more usefully focused on extending social contacts, identifying local facilities and arranging the opportunity for interactions, such as dates or interviews, than on enhancing other aspects of social behaviour.

FACTORS INFLUENCING OUTCOMES AND CONSEQUENCES OF SOCIAL RESPONDING

As mentioned above, the short-term and long-term outcomes of social functioning are not merely dependent upon what a person does, but also upon a wide range of non-social factors and also factors relating to the characteristics of the person making the judgement about social competency (see Table 11.3). These factors must also be considered in deciding whether intervention is warranted, and the type of intervention to be used.

Personal characteristics of the performer

There is now abundant evidence that a range of personal characteristics may influence the outcome of social interactions. For example, physical attractiveness, mode of dress, personal grooming and presence of physical handicaps have all been suggested to be important (Glasgow and Arkowitz, 1975; Rathjen, 1980; Trower, 1979). For example, a person's failure in specific social situations, such as dating or job interviews, may be related to problems in any of these areas rather than to inappropriate social behaviour. Where this is the case, intervention should aim to deal with these factors, rather than attempting to change what the person says or does. The individual's age, sex, status, socio-economic level, social class and culture have also been suggested to influence judgements of social competence (Rathjen, op. cit.).

Characteristics of others and the situation

Different behaviours are required in different physical locations (for instance, work and home) and with different people (for example, males and females). The combination of the aims of all persons involved, and the circumstances, define the nature of the interaction (say, job interview or making friends) and the type of behaviour required for social success. McFall (1982) discusses the need for a task-analysis in which each social interaction that a client is required to handle is broken down into a large number of steps, which take into account the characteristics of the situation and all persons involved. The type of behaviour required for a successful outcome in a social interaction will be influenced by the characteristics of other persons involved in the interaction. For example, different behaviours may be required for successful handling of a social task depending upon factors such as the age, sex, status, social class, culture, expectations, values, personal cultural beliefs and information of the other person.

In some instances it may be found that a client referred as being socially incompetent is assessed as sufficiently competent by the therapist but fails to reach the criteria of certain others such as spouse, colleague or employer. The problem is therefore seen as excessively high expectations on the part of others rather than as inadequate performance on the part of the client. As McFall (1982) points out, social incompetence can be seen as the product of a mismatch between a person's performance abilities and the task demands imposed on the person. Intervention may therefore need to focus on reducing the task demands or the criteria set by others.

Social-cultural determinants

During assessment it is important to consider the social-cultural background of the client as this may have important implications in explaining a judgement of social incompetence and in designing treatment programmes. Little information regarding cultural and social background determinants of social behaviour is available and many assessment instruments have been standardised only in the USA. Hence the therapist will need to do some researching of his or her own. Undoubtedly different cultures and social groups have different social rules and norms for behaviour. Problems may arise when a person from one cultural group engages in social responses considered appropriate in the person's own culture but not in others. This is important to remember when working with minority groups where assessment must investigate which groups the client finds problematic and in which groups the client is found to be competent. Assessment must also identify the social tasks the client must be able to perform in the various cultures. Part of intervention will then need to focus on teaching appropriate ways of responding according to the different cultures and situations involved.

THE ASSESSMENT PROCESS

In the past, therapists have tended to take a very narrow view of social behaviour, with the majority of developments in research and practice focusing on the overt, motor, social-skill aspects of social competence. Inspection of the research data, however, reveals that there is minimal evidence to suggest that merely improving the performance of basic social skills, such as eye-contact, tone of voice or posture, leads to dramatic, long-lasting benefits in terms of social behaviour in the client's day-to-day interactions (Benton and Schroeder, 1990).

Generally, clients are referred to clinical psychologists for intervention in the area of social competence as the result of long-term, negative social consequences, such as lack of friends, difficulty in getting on with others, difficulty in self-assertion in conflict situations or controlling temper outbursts when provoked. Successful intervention requires significant and long-lasting improvements in these major problem areas. It is proposed here that therapists must take an expanded view of social functioning in both assessment and intervention and that this requires consideration of the multiple factors determining social competence as outlined above.

A variety of assessment methods may be used to follow the four levels of assessment already described. The four levels of assessment outlined previously allow identification of persons who experience interpersonal problems at levels 1 and 2, and then to examine the degree to which these are the result of overt behavioural or social cognitive skills deficits at levels 3 and 4. The following sections discuss the sources of information that may be used at each level of assessment. Several factors should be taken into account in the selection of assessment measures. For example, the assessment methods used must be appropriate to the characteristics of the client. Hence different instruments are available for psychiatric patients as opposed to college students. The assessor should also consider the psychometric properties of the instrument being used, in terms of its reliability and validity. Unfortunately, many methods used in the assessment of interpersonal problems are of dubious reliability and validity, and should be used with caution.

METHODS OF ASSESSMENT

There are many sources of information which may be used in the assessment of interpersonal problems. Data may be obtained from the client him- or herself, from significant others such as a spouse, friend or parent, by observing the client in a simulated situation in the clinic, or by observing him or her in a real-life situation. The methods used may include interviews, questionnaires, checklists, diaries and direct or videotaped observation. Each information source and method of data collection has its own set of advantages and disadvantages. In practice, the assessor tends to use a combination of approaches in order to obtain a full picture of the problems presented by the client.

The following section attempts to review the methods frequently used in the assessment of interpersonal problems within the context of the four levels of assessment outlined at the beginning of this chapter.

Self-report methods

Self-report methods have been the most widely used sources of information in the assessment of social competence, particularly at the initial screening stage and in the assessment of social anxiety and maladaptive cognitions. Obviously, the client is the only available source of data regarding cognitive events, such as feelings of anxiety or irrational thoughts. Similarly the individual is the only person who is always present during his or her social interactions. The information obtained, however, merely provides data on how and what the person attends to, perceives and remembers regarding social interactions. This may be at considerable variance with what actually occurs. Hence the use of self-report data, while being extremely valuable, should be treated with caution and checked against other sources of information to identify areas of discrepancy.

The cognitive-behavioural interview and personal history

The cognitive-behavioural interview and personal history (see Chapter 1) provide useful screening information to determine whether the client judges his or her behaviour to be problematic in any social interactions and wishes to bring about changes. This represents level 1 of the assessment process at which the aim is to assess whether the client does experience negative long-term outcomes from social relationships in relevant domains, such as the marriage, family, employment and social friendships. Questions need to be asked about the quality of relationships in these domains, whether the client is satisfied with these and whether other people view these relationships as problematic. For example, the assessor may ask whether the client has close friendships, whether he or she attends social functions, or whether he or she is popular with colleagues at work. Subjective feelings which reflect long-term satisfaction with relationships, such as feelings of loneliness, should also be examined.

If problems are identified in any of these or other areas, then it is appropriate to proceed to level 2 of assessment to consider whether these difficulties are the result of negative outcomes from social interactions, or reflect other, non-social determinants of social competence. Questions should examine the occurrence of specific short-term, negative outcomes from social interactions in domains in which problems occur. For example, if problems are noted in the work environment, then assessment should now try to specify the exact social situations in which problems occur, exactly what these negative outcomes are, how often and who with. The following case example may illustrate this point.

Brian, aged 45, referred himself to the clinic initially as the result of feelings of depression. During assessment, Brian reported considerable difficulties at work and that he was taking a large number of sick days off. Further assessment revealed that he was a manager of a small department of women and he experienced great difficulty in acting in an assertive manner in his managerial capacity. He reported that he frequently gave the women instructions which they appeared to ignore and, as a result, he was often required to work late in order to complete the tasks himself.

In some instances, the client is not the best person to provide information about the way in which he or she is judged by other people or the impact of his or her behaviour upon others. Thus, it is important to obtain additional information about short-term consequences of social interactions from other assessment sources. For example, role-played interactions may be observed and rated by independent judges in order to assess level of social skilfulness or assertiveness in specific types of social interactions (see p. 248). In Brian's case, we asked him to role-play a situation in which he was required to instruct one of his employees to stop the task that she was working on and to complete a more urgent assignment. We videotaped the roleplay and asked an independent assessor to rate the level of assertiveness and probability of the employee's completing the assignment on time. Brian was rated as not at all assertive in making his request and it was considered highly unlikely that the employee would comply with his instruction. Thus, the assessment moved on levels 3 and 4 of the assessment in order to identify exactly what Brian was saying and doing that produced a negative impression upon others and why this was the case. A detailed behavioural analysis of his behaviour during roleplay was useful here, in addition to other sources of information as outlined below.

When it comes to assessment of social anxiety and attitudes, beliefs or maladaptive cognitions, the interview can also provide valuable information. This area is discussed in depth by Arnkoff and Glass (1989). In the case of Brian, he reported feeling highly anxious before giving instructions to the women in his department and anticipated a negative outcome, typically the case. He reported thoughts such as, 'I know that Janine doesn't like me and these women laugh behind my back. How on earth am I going to get this work done by Monday? She'll be furious if I ask her to do this. I can't ask her. I'm no good at this job. This is terrible'.

Finally, the interview is a useful way of exploring some of the non-social determinants of social inadequacy, such as the range of social contacts and personal characteristics.

Self-report questionnaires

A variety of self-report questionnaires are available, designed for different purposes. Some are more useful at levels 1 and 2 of the assessment process, whereas others can be used to assess overt behaviour or social-cognitive skills, at levels 3 and 4. Unfortunately, many questionnaire methods confuse the different levels of assessment and confound outcomes with behaviours and skills. This produces problems at a theoretical level, because many questionnaires that purport to assess social competence are actually assessing the occurrence of specific behaviours which are merely assumed to lead to negative outcomes and which may not necessarily be the case. Similarly, some measures claim to assess social skills and yet actually ask questions about outcomes. For example, the question 'Does he or she makes friends easily?' reflects a social outcome and not a social skill. This distinction should be considered in the selection of assessment devices.

Some self-report questionnaires try to get round this problem by assessing outcomes and behaviours. For example, the Social-Situation Questionnaire (SSQ) devised by Bryant and Trower (1974) requests self-rating of both the frequency and the difficulty of performing certain social behaviours. This method was initially developed from social situations identified by university students, but has since been used with adult psychiatric patients. Trower *et al.* (1978b) report the measure to have good internal consistency and to be sensitive to change following intervention. Another questionnaire measure which considers the subjective aspects and behaviour separately is the Assertion Inventory of Gambrill and Richey (1975). This measure is limited to situations which require an assertive response, but asks clients to rate the degree of discomfort that they would experience if they were to perform a particular behaviour and the probability that they would engage in such a response. Again, this measure was initially developed for use with college students but its psychometric properties are good and it has been widely used with clinic populations (Baggs and Spence, 1990).

The area of assertiveness has attracted the development of numerous self-report questionnaire measures. The Rathus Assertiveness Scale (Rathus 1973) is probably the most widely used and well established. It also was designed, however, for use with college students with whom most of the psychometric evaluations have been performed. The test-retest reliability is reported to be adequate, with good split-half reliability and correlation with judgements made by peers. A simplified version of the Rathus was developed by McCormick (1984) and this has been used successfully with a variety of clinic groups including schizophrenics (Payne and Halford, 1990). The Wolpe–Lazarus Assertiveness Questionnaire (Wolpe and Lazarus, 1966) also contains thirty items which sample a number of assertive behaviours in various situations. Little information is available regarding reliability and validity, although Eisler *et al.* (1973; 1975) have shown it to discriminate between hospitalised psychiatric patients who were judged as high/low on behavioural tests of assertion. Other frequently used self-report methods for assessing assertive responding are the Conflict Resolution Inventory (McFall and Lillesand, 1971) and the College Self-Expression Scale (Galassi *et al.*, 1974). Some evidence is available to confirm the reliability or validity of these scales and the reader is referred back to the original sources.

Self-report questionnaires have also proliferated in the assessment of social anxiety. Although various authors have stressed the need for separate evaluation of the physiological, cognitive and motor components of social anxiety, most attention has been paid to self-report methods, focusing on the cognitive and behavioural aspects. Questions have typically related to avoidance behaviour and subjective feelings of fear or anxiety. The pioneers in this area were Watson and Friend (1969), who explored two components of social anxiety in summer school students in Canada, first the tendency to avoid and experience discomfort in social situations as assessed by the Social Avoidance and Distress (SAD) scale, and second, the fear of negative evaluation by others assessed by the Fear of Negative Evaluation (FNE) scale. Both measures were found to have good test-retest reliability, good questionnaire homogeneity, and to discriminate between high- and low- frequency daters (Arkowitz, 1977). These scales continue to be used extensively in research and clinical practice.

Richardson and Tasto (1976) developed the Social Anxiety Inventory which incorporates 100 items derived from hierarchies of socially anxious clients. Seven distinct fear factors were identified: fear of disapproval or negative evaluation; social assertiveness and visibility; confrontation and anger expression; heterosexual contact; intimacy and interpersonal warmth; conflict with, or rejection by, parents; and interpersonal loss. This method has been further developed by Curran *et al.* (1980) to incorporate ratings of both skill and anxiety. A final social anxiety measure worth mentioning is the Survey of Heterosexual Interactions (Twentyman and McFall, 1975) which involves a twenty-item, seven-point rating scale designed to explore the specific area of interaction with the opposite sex by college males. The scale is reported to have good test-retest reliability and construct-validity (Twentyman and Zimering, 1979) but is claimed to be poor in terms of its ability to discriminate between social-skills and social-anxiety problems (Mariotto *et al.*, 1979).

Much less attention has been paid to the development of questionnaires which assess behaviour across other types of social interactions. However, the Social Performance Survey Schedule of Lowe and Cautela (1978) represents an attempt to examine a wide range of social-skills across several domains of social functioning. The schedule comprises 100 items, divided into positive and negative aspects of social behaviour, each to be rated on a five-point scale of frequency of occurrence. The scale is reported to have good test-retest reliability, and significant correlations of total score with depression level, social activity level, general ratings of social-skills made by staff and number of previous hospitalisations (Lowe and Cautela, op. cit.; Lowe, 1985).

The final area of the use of self-report questionnaires to be mentioned here is in the assessment of attitudes and maladaptive cognitions (see also Rippere, Chapter 5, and Bradley, Chapter 6). A useful summary of this area is provided by Arnkoff and Glass (1989). Questionnaires such as the Social Interaction Self-Statement Test (Glass *et al.*, 1982), the Social Anxiety Thoughts Questionnaire (Hartman, 1984) and the Irrational Beliefs Test (Jones, 1969) are all useful in the assessment of this area.

Self-monitoring, self-recording and diaries

Self-monitoring, self-recording and the keeping of diaries can provide valuable information to aid in the assessment process. This is particularly important in clarifying the nature of the problem and exploring causal factors. Information can be obtained regarding success in different situations, subjective distress, cognitions and the frequency of occurrence of various behaviours.

Social-cognitive tasks

Few methods are as yet available to assess social-cognitive skills at level 4 of the assessment process and those that do exist rarely provide satisfactory information regarding psychometric properties. In the area of social perception, Archer and Akert (1977), have developed the Social Interpretation Task which assesses the ability to decode verbal and non-verbal cues. Clients are shown a series of videotaped interactions and then required to provide information regarding the motives and relationships of the characters observed. A similar procedure is reported by Morrison and Bellack (1981). Other methods to assess social sensitivity and perception have been developed by Ekman (1971), Rosenthal *et al.* (1979), and Buck (1984) but these methods tend to be more suitable for research studies than for routine clinical practice.

A useful clinical assessment method which explores accuracy in labelling emotions from posture, facial expression, tone of voice and gestures is reported by Spence (1980). Although this measure was developed for use with children, it has been used successfully with adults who have experienced head injury (Jackson and Moffat, 1987).

Finally, it is important to consider the assessment of social problem-solving skills. Developments in this area are still very experimental and the majority have been developed for use with children. Butler and Meichenbaum (1981) review the research evidence regarding the reliability and validity of the limited measures available. Typically, the results have been mediocre but pave the way for further developments. The most commonly used measure is the Means–End Problem-Solving (MEPS) test developed by Platt and Spivack (1975). The measure evaluates ability to generate alternative solutions to problem situations. Individuals are presented with the beginning and ending of ten problem situations and are asked to make up the middle of the story. Bellack *et al.*, (1989) were highly critical of the MEPS and commented upon its low test–retest reliability and lack of established criterion validity. These authors also suggested that the contents of some stories in the MEPS are not relevant to the lives of most people. Scoring of the MEPS in terms of total number of solutions generated, rather than quality or social acceptability of the solutions suggested, was also criticised. The Problem-Solving Inventory produced by Heppner and Peterson (1982) is a possible alternative, but this is a more general measure of problem-solving ability, rather than of interpersonal problem-solving skill *per se*. It is clear that there is an urgent need for a reliable and valid measure of interpersonal problem-solving ability.

Information from significant others

Valuable information may be obtained from other people with whom the client interacts on a regular basis. For example, the spouse, employers, friends or care staff may be used to provide information through interviews and questionnaire, where appropriate. One example here is the 'significant other' version of Lowe and Cautela's Social Performance Survey Schedule outlined on p. 245. This may be used to provide validation of self-report information or may be useful if the client is unable to complete a self-report version, for example with certain intellectually handicapped individuals.

Other people may be asked to provide information in the initial stages of assessment (i.e. at levels 1 and 2) in order to determine the nature and extent of interpersonal difficulties but also make an important contribution to the assessment process at level 3. At this stage, significant others may be valuable in describing exactly what a person says and does and in clarifying the presence and absence of specific overt behavioural social skills.

Direct behavioural observation in the natural environment

Obviously it would be preferable if all clients could be carefully observed during their day-to-day interactions This would provide important information regarding what social activities a person engages in, what social skills are used and with what consequences at level 3 of the assessment process, to clarify the problem behaviour and environmental determinants of social incompetence, and to assess the occurrence and level of specific social skills. Unfortunately, however, direct behavioural observation in the natural setting is a time-consuming process beyond the scope of many clinicians. Furthermore, it is difficult to obtain reliable data in terms of accuracy as to what actually occurred, and substantial training of observers is necessary. There is typically a trade-off between reliability and validity in the assessment of social competence. Real-life observation may be more valid in that it should reflect the client's natural responding, but it is difficult to achieve observation methods that are highly reliable. Reliability can be increased by introducing more controlled and contrived situations but this tends to be at the expense of validity.

It is relatively easy to observe and record one simple unit of behaviour, but this obviously results in much lost information regarding other behaviours and the response of others. To overcome this problem, complex coding systems have been developed to assess social interaction between individuals (e.g. Patterson *et al.*, 1975a). Such methods are useful but the influence of observer presence and reliability between raters must be carefully considered. Furthermore, considerable training of observers is required before adequate reliability of observation can be attained. Observations are also costly in terms of therapist time. Most practitioners do not, therefore, have the resources required for satisfactory use of most complex observation systems. It may be possible, however, to use less complex forms of direct behavioural observation, such as the use of telephone calls in which a standard request is made and the response recorded and rated (e.g. McFall and Marston, 1970). Other authors have suggested using rating scales to assess the quality of a behavioural response, rather than using a quantitative measure of frequency or duration. These may be used to facilitate the assessment of specific motor social skills in both simulated and natural situations. For example, Spence (1980) outlined a detailed rating scale with descriptive statements, for use with adolescents. Trower *et al.* (1978b) report a similar method designed for use with adults. Both methods are restricted by lack of data regarding reliability and validity and absence of normative information to help in deciding when a response is considered to be problematic. Indeed, this latter point can be made of the majority of assessment devices available to date.

It is also important to stress that it is not necessarily the absolute quantity, intensity or rate of a response that is important in the assessment of overt, behavioural social skills. The crucial factor in determining judgements of social competence may be when and how the response is made. Attention needs to be paid to the interactive sequencing of behaviour during assessment (Becker *et al.*, 1987). Similarly, problem behaviour is not necessarily uni-directional, in that responding may occur to excess or deficit. For example, excessive speech may be as much of a problem as minimal verbal output.

Behavioural observation in analogue situations

As the result of difficulties in carrying out observations in natural settings, simulated interactions and methods such as role-play and contrived situations using stooges have been regularly employed. One of the earliest reports on the use of role-play in the assessment of social adequacy was by Rehm and Marston (1968) who developed what was to become the prototype for many later role-play batteries – the Role-Play Situation Test. In this, ten situations related to heterosexual activities are described to the subjects over an intercom, and the responses made are rated by trained judges on various global measures. Since then, a similar method has been reported by Goldsmith and McFall (1975) for use with psychiatric patients and by Eisler *et al.* (1973) with the Behavioural Assertiveness Test (BAT). The BAT and revised version BAT–R (Eisler *et al.*, 1975) have been most widely researched, Bellack *et al.* (1978) reporting a good correlation between judges' ratings and the patients' therapists' ratings and good inter-rater reliability, and Eisler *et al.* (1975) giving evidence of good internal consistency between items.

Another widely used role-play test is the Simulated Social Interaction Test (SSIT; Curran, 1982). This involves eight standardised role-play scenes, and clients are rated on two 11-point scales of social skill and anxiety. Inter-observer reliability of this measure is reported to be good (Payne and Halford, 1990). Despite the good reliability of role-play assessments, Bellack *et al.* (1978) question the validity of the claim that role-play is representative of 'real-life' behaviour. Little correlation was found between BAT–R ratings of specific behaviours, such as latency of response, and behavioural measures taken in ward-group situations. Given the questions raised by Bellack *et al.* (ibid.) regarding the validity of role-play, caution should be exerted with its use. Wherever possible, the information obtained should be cross-checked against other data sources. Other authors support its use, in that useful data can be obtained regarding global judgements of social competence and the use of specific social skills, and the client can be questioned regarding feelings of anxiety and occurrence of maladaptive thoughts in specific role-play situations. Wessburg *et al.* (1979) provide data that suggest that role-play assessments may be valid in some situations: the response of college students was compared in two simulated, opposite-sex interactions and in two waiting-room situations. A good correlation was found for global judgements of social competence between the waiting-room and simulated interactions and between the two simulated interactions. Whether a waiting-room setting is equivalent to a natural, day-to-day situation is highly questionable, and the reservations of Bellack *et al.* (1978) should still hold.

Physiological assessment

One final area that should be mentioned is that of physiological assessment. As previously discussed, there is a need to investigate the ability to regulate and control various physiological response systems, such as those involved in anxiety, fear and anger. Excessive responding in these areas is likely to interfere with competent social responding (McFall, 1982) and intervention may be necessary. Eisler (1976) questions the relationship between social competence and high physiological arousal, suggesting that some people may be highly socially skilled during states of high physiological arousal (for example, public speaking). Others may be adversely affected under states of high physiological arousal. Hence the relationship between physiological and motor responding is not consistent, but should at least be considered in the assessment of social competence.

SUMMARY AND CONCLUSIONS

This chapter has outlined a multi-level, practical approach to the assessment of interpersonal problems. It is clear that social competence is determined by a wide range of factors relating to the individual, the environment and other people. The assessment process aims to identify the nature and causes of a client's interpersonal difficulties in order that these factors can be tackled during therapy. Information needs to be obtained from a variety of assessment sources, including the individual, significant others, and through behavioural observation. Unfortunately, many of the assessment methods available still lack confirmation regarding reliability and validity. In other areas of assessment, such as cognitive tasks for evaluating problem-solving skills, there is a noticeable lack of clinically useful assessment methods. Overall, an assessment plan is proposed which explores a wide range of potential explanations for social inadequacy, using a variety of methods designed to reveal reliable and valid data.

REFERENCES

Archer, D. and Akert, R. M. (1977) 'Words and everything else: verbal and non-verbal areas in social interpretation', *Journal of Personality and Social Psychology* 35: 443–9.

Argyle, M. and Kendon, A. (1967) 'The experimental analysis of social performance', in L. Berkowitz (ed.) *Advances in Experimental Social Psychology. Vol. 3*, New York: Academic Press.

Arkowitz, H. (1977) 'Measurement and modification of minimal dating behaviour', in M. Herson, R. Eisler and P. Miller (eds) *Progress in Behaviour Modification. Vol. 5*, New York: Academic Press.

Arnkoff, D. B. and Glass, C. R. (1989) 'Cognitive assessment in social anxiety and social phobia', *Clinical Psychology Review*, 9: 61–74.

Baggs, K. and Spence, S. H. (1990) 'Effectiveness of booster sessions in the maintenance and enhancement of treatment gains following assertion training', *Journal of Consulting and Clinical Psychology* 58: 845–54.

Becker, R. E., Heimberg, R. G. and Bellack, A. S. (1987) *Social-skills Training for Depression*, New York: Pergamon Press.

Bellack, A. S., Hersen, M. and Turner, S. M. (1978) 'Role-play tests for assessing social-skills. Are they valid?' *Behaviour Therapy* 9: 448–61.

Bellack, A. S., Morrison, R. L., and Mueser, K. T. (1989) 'Social-problem-solving in schizophrenia', *Schizophrenia Bulletin* 15: 101–16.

Benton, M. K., and Schroeder, H. E. (1990) 'Social skills training with schizophrenics: A meta-analytic evaluation', *Journal of Consulting and Clinical Psychology* 58: 741–7.

Bryant, B. M., and Trower, P. E. (1974) 'Social difficulty in a student sample', *British Journal of Educational Psychology* 44: 13–21.

Bryant, B. M., Trower, P., Yardley, K., Urbieta, H. and Letemendia, F. (1976) 'A survey of social inadequacy among psychiatric out-patients', *Psychological Medicine* 6: 101–12.

Buck, R. (1984) *The Communication of Emotion*, New York: Guilford.

Butler, L. and Meichenbaum, D. (1981) 'The assessment of interpersonal problem-solving skills', in P. C. Kendall and S. D. Hollon (eds) *Assessment Strategies for Cognitive Behavioural Interventions*, New York: Academic Press.

Cavell, T. A. (1990) 'Social adjustment, social performance and social skills: A tri-component model of social competence', *Journal of Clinical Child Psychology* 19: 111–22.

Cowen, E. L., Pederson, A., Babigon, H., Izzo, L. D. and Trost, M. A. (1973) 'Long-term follow-up of early detected vulnerable children', *Journal of Consulting and Clinical Psychology* 41: 438–46.

Curran, J. P. (1982) 'A procedure for the assessment of social-skills: The Simulated Social Interaction Test', in J. P. Curran and P. M. Monti (eds) *Social-skills Training: A Practical Handbook for Assessment and Treatment* (348–73), New York: Guilford.

Curran, J. P., Corriveau, D. P., Monti, P. M. and Hagerman, S. (1980) 'Social-skill and social anxiety: self-report measurement in a psychiatric population', *Behaviour Modification* 4: 493–512.

Dodge, K. A., and Murphy, R. R. (1984) 'The assessment of social competence of adolescents', in P. Karoly and J. J. Steffen (eds) *Adolescent behaviour disorders: Foundations and contemporary concerns* (61–173), Lexington, Mass.: Lexington.

Eisler, R. M. (1976) 'Behavioural assessment of social-skills', in M. Hersen and A. S. Bellack (eds) *Behavioural Assessment: A Practical Handbook*, New York: Pergamon Press.

Eisler, R. M., Miller, P. M. and Hersen, M. (1973) 'Components of assertive behaviour', *Journal of Clinical Psychology* 29: 295–99.

Eisler, R. M., Hersen, M., Miller, P. M. and Blanchard, E. B. (1975) 'Situational determinants of assertive behaviour', *Journal of Consulting and Clinical Psychology* 43: 330–40.

Ekman, P. (1971) 'Universal and cultural differences in facial expressions of emotions', in J. K. Cole (ed.) *Nebraska Symposium on Motivation*, Nebraska: University of Nebraska Press.

Ellis, A. (1958) 'Rational psychotherapy', *Journal of General Psychology* 59: 35–49.

Feffer, M. H. (1959) 'The cognitive implications of role-taking behaviour', *Journal of Personality* 27: 152–68.

Gambrill, E. E., and Richey, C. A. (1975) 'An assertion inventory for use in assessment and research', *Behaviour Therapy* 6: 550–61.

Galassi, J. P., DeLo, J. S., Galassi, M. D. and Bastein, S. (1974) 'The College Self-expression Scale: a measure of assertiveness', *Behaviour Therapy* 5: 165–71.

Glasgow, R. E. and Arkowitz, H. (1975) 'The behavioural assessment of male and female social competence in hyadic heterosexual interactions', *Behaviour Therapy* 6: 488–98.

Glass, C. R., Merluzzi, T. V., Biever, J. L., and Larsen, K. H. (1982) 'Cognitive assessment of social anxiety: Development and validation of a self-statement questionnaire', *Cognitive Therapy and Research* 6: 37–55.

Goldsmith, J. D. and McFall, R. M. (1975) 'Development and evaluation of an interpersonal skill-training program for psychiatric in-patients', *Journal of Abnormal Psychology* 84: 51–8.

Halford, W. K. and Foddy, M. (1982) 'Cognitive and social-skill correlates of social anxiety', *British Journal of Clinical Psychology* 21: 17–28.

Hartman, L. (1984) 'Cognitive components of social anxiety', *Journal of Clinical Psychology* 40: 137–9.

Heppner, P. P., and Peterson, C. H. (1982) 'The development and implementation of a personal problem-solving inventory', *Journal of Counselling Psychology* 29: 66–75.

Hymel, S. and Asher, S. R. (1977) 'Assessment and training of isolated children's social-skills', paper presented at the biennial meeting of the Society for Research in Child Development, (March) New Orleans, Louisiana.

Jackson, H., and Moffat, N. J. (1987) 'Impaired emotional recognition following severe head injury', *Cortex* 23: 293–300.

Jones, R. G. (1969) 'A factored measure of Ellis' irrational belief system, with personality and adjustment correlates', doctoral dissertation, Texas Technological College, 1968, Dissertation Abstracts International 29: 4379B–4380B (University Microfilms No. 69–6443).

Lowe, M. R. (1985) 'Psychometric evaluation of the Social Performance Survey Schedule: Reliability and validity of the positive subscale', *Behaviour Modification* 9: 193–210.

Lowe, M. R. and Cautela, J. R. (1978) 'A self-report measure of social-skill', *Behaviour Therapy* 9: 535–44.

McCormick I. A. (1984) 'A simplified version of the Rathus Assertiveness Schedule', *Behavioural Assessment* 7: 95–9.

McFall, R. M. (1982) 'A review and reformulation of the concept of social skills', *Behavioural Assessment* 4: 1–33.

McFall, R. M. and Lillesand, D. B. (1971) 'Behaviour rehearsal with modelling and coaching in assertion training', *Journal of Abnormal Psychology* 77: 313–23.

McFall, R. M. and Marston, A. B. (1970) 'An experimental investigation of behaviour rehearsal in assertive training', *Journal of Abnormal Psychology* 76: 295–303.

Mariotto, M. J., Farrell, A. D. and Wallender, J. L. (1979) 'A multimethod validation of the survey of heterosexual interactions as a screening instrument for heterosocial-skill and anxiety research', unpublished manuscript, University of Houston.

Morrison, R. L. and Bellack, A. (1981) 'The role of social perception in social skills', *Behaviour Therapy* 12: 69–79.

Patterson, G. R., Hops, H. and Weiss, R. L. (1975a) 'Interpersonal skills training for couples in early stages of conflict', *Journal of Marriage and the Family* 37: 295–303.
Patterson, G. R., Reid, J. D., Jones, R. R. and Conger, R. E. (1975b) *A Social Learning Approach to Family Intervention. Vol. 1*, Eugene, Oregon: Castalia.
Payne, P. V. and Halford, W. K. (1990) 'Social skills training with chronic schizophrenic patients living in community settings', *Behavioural Psychotherapy* 18: 49–64.
Platt, J. J. and Spivack, G. (1975) *Manual for the Means–Ends Problem-Solving Procedures (MEPS)*, Philadelphia: DMHS.
Rathjen, D. P. (1980) 'An overview of social competence', in D. P. Rathjen and J. P. Foreyt (eds) *Social Competence. Interventions for Children and Adults*, New York: Pergamon.
Rathus, S. (1973) 'A 30-item schedule for assessing assertive behaviour', *Behaviour Therapy* 4: 398–406.
Rehm, L. P. and Marston, A. R. (1968) 'Reduction of social anxiety through modification of self-reinforcement: an instigation therapy technique', *Journal of Consulting and Clinical Psychology* 32: 565–74.
Richardson, F. C. and Tasto, D. L. (1976) 'Development and factor analysis of a social anxiety inventory', *Behaviour Therapy* 7: 453–62.
Roff, M. (1970) 'Some life history factors in relation to various types of adult maladjustment', in M. Roff and D. Ricks (eds) *Life History Research in Psychopathology*, Minneapolis: University of Minnesota Press.
Roff, M., Sells, B. and Golden, M. (1972) *Social Adjustment and Personality Development in Children*, Minneapolis: University of Minnesota Press.
Rosenthal, R., Hall, J. A., DiMatteo, M., Rogers, P. and Archer, D. (1979) *Sensitivity to Nonverbal Communications: The PONS Test*, Baltimore: Johns Hopkins University Press.
Spence, S. H. (1980) *Social-skills Training with Children and Adolescents: A Counsellor's Manual*, Windsor: NFER.
Spivack, G. and Shure, M. B. (1976) *Social Adjustment of Young Children. A Cognitive Approach to Solving Real Life Problems*, London: Jossey Bass.
Trower, P. (1979) 'Fundamentals of interpersonal behaviour: a social-psychological perspective', in A. S. Bellack and M. Hersen (eds) *Reseach and Practice in Social-skills Training*, New York: Plenum Press.
Trower, P., Bryant, B. and Argyle, M. (1978a) *Social-skills and Mental Health*, London: Methuen.
Trower, P., Yardley, K., Bryant, B., and Shaw, P. (1978b) 'The treatment of social failure: A comparison of anxiety-reduction and skills-acquisition procedures on two social problems', *Behaviour Modification* 2: 41–60.
Twentyman, C. T. and McFall, R. M. (1975) 'Behavioural training of social skills in shy males', *Journal of Consulting and Clinical Psychology* 43: 384–95.
Twentyman, C. T. and Zimering, R. T. (1979) 'Behavioural training of social skills: a critical review', in M. Hersen, R. M. Eisler and P. M. Miller (eds) *Progress in Behaviour Modification. Vol. 7*, New York: Academic Press.
Van Hasselt, U. B., Hersen, M. M., Whitehall, N. B. and Bellack, A. S. (1979) 'Social-skill assessment and training for children: an evaluative review', *Behaviour Research and Therapy* 17: 413–439.
Watson, D. and Friend, R. (1969) 'Measurement of social evaluative anxiety', *Journal of Consulting and Clinical Psychology* 33: 448–57.
Wessburg, H. W., Mariotto, M. J., Congor, A. J ., Farrell, A. D. and Congor, J. C. (1979) 'Ecological validity of roleplays for assessing heterosexual anxiety and skill of male college students', *Journal of Consulting and Clinical Psychology* 47: 525–35.
Wolpe, J. and Lazarus, A. A. (1966) *Behaviour Therapy Techniques*, New York: Pergamon.
Zigler, E. and Phillips, L. (1961) 'Social competence and outcome in mental disorder', *Journal of Abnormal Psychology* 63: 264–71.

Chapter 12

Interpersonal problems
Treatment

Susan H. Spence

INTRODUCTION

There are many reasons to explain why a person experiences difficulty during interactions with other people, as outlined in the preceding chapter. Not surprisingly, then, a wide range of methods have been developed to enhance social competence, each of which has been designed to tackle a different causal factor. For example, techniques to improve social competence have included social-skills training (SST), anxiety-reduction methods, cognitive restructuring and modification, social-perception training and social-problem-solving skills training. Social-skills training methods are designed to teach behavioural responses necessary for successful outcomes in social situations, with individuals who show lack of skills in certain areas. Anxiety management methods are relevant to those individuals who may have the necessary skills but who are either inhibited from using their skills or who avoid certain social situations as the result of anxiety. Cognitive restructuring methods, on the other hand, are designed to reduce negative or maladaptive thoughts and attitudes which may lead a person to behave in a way that causes interpersonal difficulties. Social-perception training represents another form of intervention that may be important for people whose inappropriate social behaviour stems from errors in the perception or interpretation of other people's social cues. This chapter reviews the use of these methods to enhance social functioning and examines their effectiveness in clinical practice. It should be read as an extension of the preceding chapter, in which a working model of social competence and its assessment was outlined.

The model outlined in the preceding chapter stressed the need for individual tailoring of intervention programmes for each person according to the outcome of assessment. The methods used in therapy are therefore designed to bring about change in the area suggested to account for the client's social problems which are identified during assessment. This is an important point, as clients with interpersonal problems can prove to be markedly different in the nature of their difficulties. Unfortunately, many studies investigating the treatment of social inadequacy have failed to assess each client to ensure that the assumed problem, such as social-skills deficit or maladaptive cognitions, actually exists. Examination of recent studies confirms that this practice continues and that individuals continue to be referred into SST or other programmes on the basis of some diagnostic category such as schizophrenia or depression, rather than on the basis of demonstrated problems in social skills (e.g. Hogarty *et al.*, 1991; Miller *et al.*, 1989). This problem, therefore, makes it hard to evaluate the outcome of many group-design research studies. Group data tend to mask individual differences in response to treatment, hiding the fact that many clients fail to improve. It could be suggested that, in most group-research studies in the area of social inadequacy, the treatment given may be of relevance only to certain individuals. This may well explain the mediocre results of many studies which attempt to enhance social competence of groups of clients (Benton and Schroeder, 1991; Heimberg, 1989). Many studies fail to consider the relevance of particular therapy approaches for individual clients.

Some programmes attempt to overcome the lack of individual assessment and personally tailored interventions by incorporating a wide range of therapy techniques within a package approach. Such packages frequently involve numerous components, such as the training of basic and complex motor social skills, relaxation training, systematic desensitisation, social-problem-solving and social-perception skills. These 'package' attempts may still be criticised, however, on the grounds of inefficient use of therapist and client time. Package approaches are based on the assumption that some of the content will be applicable to some of the clients some of the time.

METHODS OF ENHANCING INTERPERSONAL COMPETENCE

The following section outlines the most widely used approaches to the enhancement of social competence. Each approach will be discussed separately, prior to a review of more complex programmes which incorporate a variety of social enhancement methods.

Overt-behavioural social-skills training

Social-skills training (SST) was developed as a technique for teaching specific, overt-behavioural social skills to persons deficient in such responses. Similar teaching methods to those involved in training other motor skills, such as playing tennis, are therefore used, including instructions and discussion, modelling, behaviour rehearsal, feedback, reinforcement and homework tasks. Most current approaches to the training of social skills combine the training of micro-skills, such as eye-contact, appropriate voice volume or posture, along with more complicated macro-skills, such as giving a compliment, making a complaint, or refusing an unreasonable request (Hogarty *et al.*, 1991; Miller *et al.*,1989; Bellack *et al.*, 1984). There are numerous practical texts available which outline the potential content of SST programmes. Although some of these are now rather dated, the texts by Becker *et al.*, (1987); Trower *et al.* (1978); Spence and Shepherd (1983), Kelly (1982), Wilkinson and Canter (1982), Curran and Monti (1982), Goldstein (1973) and Liberman *et al.* (1975) all retain their value for therapists who are developing SST programmes.

Training components

The characteristic methods used in SST programmes include instructions, coaching, discussion, modelling (live or taped), rehearsal, role-play, feedback (verbal or videotaped), social reinforcement and home-based tasks.

Instructions, coaching and discussion

Most programmes involve a certain degree of verbal tuition in the form of giving instructions, verbal coaching of clients and encouraging client awareness of target skills through discussion. Indeed, it seems that for some clients, merely discussing problem situations and ways of dealing with them may be sufficient to result in a marked improvement in social competence (Stravynski *et al.*, 1989; Twentyman and Zimering, 1979).

Modelling

Modelling refers to the demonstration of the use of a particular skill or behaviour by another individual, while being observed by the trainee. Various types of modelling have been used, including therapist demonstration, videotaped or audiotaped modelling, or live modelling by other persons within the group. Modelling when used on its own may produce some improvement in the target behaviour. The durability and transfer of benefits beyond the training situation, however, are questionable, and modelling is generally used as part of the overall SST package. Most authors, following the work of Bandura (1977), have stressed the need to use models of similar age, sex and status to the clients in order to produce maximal learning. It has also been suggested that showing that the model's performance leads to positive rather than negative consequences increases the likelihood of imitation (Bandura, op. cit.).

Behaviour rehearsal/role-playing

After the trainees have observed the model's performance, SST typically encourages practice of the target skill. This may take the form of a simple rehearsal of the target behaviour or may be incorporated into a role-play. The practice of the skill may be carried out overtly or in imagination. Both techniques have been shown to lead to short-term improvements in social skills and there appears to be little difference in effectiveness (Kazdin, 1982). The addition of modelling, however, seems to increase the efficacy of both overt and covert practice (Friedman, 1971; Prince, 1975).

Feedback and reinforcement

Feedback to clients about the adequacy of their performance is another major feature of SST. It may take the form of comments by the therapist and/or group members about which behaviours were performed correctly and which required change, or it may involve audio- or videotaped playback. The effectiveness of feedback as a teaching method, as shown by outcome research, has been mixed but it generally appears that feedback adds to the effectiveness of other training components (Twentyman and Zimering, 1979). These authors also suggest that subject factors, such as high anxiety levels or severe skills deficits, may interact with the use of feedback procedures, indicating a need for caution on the part of therapists.

Reinforcement methods are also important in the shaping-up of target behaviours towards successive approximations to the final goal. Most authors have stressed the value of appropriate social reinforcement, such as praise and approval from the therapist and group members. Other forms of reinforcement which may be used within SST programmes include financial contingencies, tokens and self-reinforcement. Research, however, suggests that although reinforcement may be an important adjunct to training, it is insufficient to produce marked improvements in new behavioural repertoires (Spence, 1983). Merely reinforcing increased frequency of interaction may lead to improved quantity, but not necessarily improved quality, of interaction.

Homework assignments

Most SST programmes have involved the setting of homework assignments in which the trainee is requested to practise the skills learned in the session. The rehearsal of new skills in real-life situations in addition to the training setting is suggested to facilitate the carry-over of improvements in performance to the natural setting (Goldstein *et al.*, 1978; Lalli *et al.*, 1991).

Practical concerns

There are many questions which may be asked about the best way to conduct SST programmes. These issues include whether it is preferable to use group versus individual therapy sessions, the number, duration and frequency of sessions, the number of therapists, and open versus closed groups. The practical texts mentioned earlier discuss these topics in detail, although there appears to be little evidence to allow conclusions to be drawn about the most suitable form of SST for different client groups. There has been marked variation in the amount of training given to clients, ranging from one to one hundred sessions, with various spacings and session durations (Shepherd, 1983; Benton and Schroeder, 1990). The location of intervention has also varied, ranging from clinic or hospital settings to colleges or workplace programmes.

The need to programme for the maintenance and generalisation of skill improvement from the training setting to the natural environment and to new interpersonal situations, is repeatedly stressed (Benton and Schroeder, 1990; Kelly, 1982). Methods such as increasing the number of trainers, introducing visitors to the group, selection of valid target behaviours, and arranging for modelling, prompting and reinforcement of target skills outside sessions have all been suggested as ways of encouraging the transfer of skill acquisition from the clinic to real-life interactions (Goldstein *et al.*, 1978). Booster sessions have also been found to be a valuable means of improving the durability of SST gains after the end of treatment (Baggs and Spence, 1990).

Outcome studies

In order to draw conclusions about the effectiveness of training overt-behavioural social skills, it is important to ensure that the research studies considered do not include other methods of enhancing social competence. Many intervention programmes quite appropriately include a variety of methods, such as relaxation training, teaching of social-perception skills, interpersonal problem-solving skills training and cognitive restructuring, where appropriate to the clients' needs. The studies reviewed in this section, however, have been selected as being restricted to the use of overt-behavioural SST.

Unfortunately, there are many methodological shortcomings in most outcome studies. For example, the reliability and validity of many of the outcome measures used is questionable and studies frequently rely on self-report measures of change rather than objective criteria, thereby increasing the chance of bias. If observation methods are used, such as the coding or rating of specific behaviours during role-played interactions or naturalistic settings, the accuracy of the recordings is often limited. Furthermore, the use of role-play in assessment is of questionable validity, given that the behaviour obtained may not be representative of responses in the natural environment (Bellack, 1983). Yet another methodological limitation relates to the failure of many studies to ensure that the skills being trained were initially lacking in the people being trained. Long-term follow-up measures are frequently lacking, or the follow-up period is of insufficient duration. Similarly, the assessment of generalisation of behaviour change from the training situation to real-life settings is often not considered. All these limitations combine to make it difficult to determine the degree to which behavioural SST really is effective in producing improvements in specific behaviours, and whether the changes are long-lasting and occur in real-life situations. Of even greater importance is whether the changes in behaviours lead to improvements in social competence, such as development of friendships and improved interpersonal relationships (Benton and Schroeder, 1990; Shepherd, 1983).

There is now much literature to confirm that individuals can be taught to increase their use of a wide range of specific behaviours such as eye-contact, posture or facial expression. The use of these skills is generally assessed from role-play situations in the clinical setting, but the improvements have been found to generalise to natural situations and to be maintained over time (Benton and Schroeder, 1990; Shepherd, 1983). Social-skills training has also been found to produce beneficial changes in the quality of performance of more complicated skills, such as giving compliments, expressing criticism or commencing conversations with another person. These improvements do not occur in untrained groups or attention-placebo control groups and are found to transfer outside the training situation, albeit not as well as in the therapy setting (Payne and Halford, 1990; Lalli et al., 1991; Foxx et al., 1985). If self-assessment of quality of social functioning is examined, such as ratings of assertiveness, then the results are also encouraging (Benton and Schroeder, 1990). Unfortunately, the effects of SST on more global indices of social functioning, completed by other people, are typically not so positive and suggest that overt-behavioural changes are not always associated with concurrent improvements in more general measures of social competence (Benton and Schroeder, op. cit.; Bramston and Spence, 1985).

In summary, it seems that SST methods can be effective in producing improvements in the performance of specific overt behaviours at both a basic and complex skill level. Methodological limitations in the design of many studies limits the conclusions that may be drawn, but there does appear to be some evidence to suggest that the maintenance and generalisation of improved skills to natural situations does occur. Self-reported improvements in social responding are also found. Whether improvements in behavioural performance would be maintained if adequate durations of follow-up (e.g. of 1 to 2 years) were used, with rigorous assessment of naturalistic settings, remains to be determined. The degree to which improvement in specific skill performance affects the degree to which individuals are judged to be socially competent by others is also unclear, and the available evidence in this area is not so encouraging.

Training social-perception skills

Social perception is the ability to receive and translate social cues accurately in order to interpret the feelings and intentions of others and the ability to discern the particular norms and conventions operating in a given social interaction. Most research in the area of social perception, however, has been focused on information conveyed from facial expression, posture, gestures and tone of voice. Many authors have emphasised the importance of social-perception skills (e.g. Morrison and Bellack, 1981; Hollin and Trower, 1986; Shepherd, 1984), and the training of such skills is frequently included within interpersonal skills training programmes (e.g. Becker et al., 1987; Hogarty et al., 1991; Trower et *al.*, 1978). Becker *et al.* (op. cit.) include a therapy component which teaches clients: (1) to recognise the various dynamic cues as they are presented, (2) to understand social norms, (3) to imagine and carry out several responses to these dynamic cues, and (4) to monitor their own dynamic cues and modify them to improve communication. This programme gives an excellent outline of the way in which people can be taught to pay attention to, and interpret the meaning of, other people's social cues. Specific situations are taken in order to teach these skills. For example, one target area relates to monitoring the conversation and cues of others during conversations in order to identify when a person is about to finish a message and hand over to the listener who is now expected to speak. The methods used to teach this skill include direct instructions and explanations concerning the type of cues which signal what the authors call a 'floor shift', demonstration of how these cues are used to signal a floor shift, discussion and demonstration of appropriate responses to these cues, practice in cue observation and use of appropriate responses, feedback and homework tasks. Thus, the methods used in overt-behavioural SST may be used equally appropriately to teach the cognitive-social skills of social perception.

Although the training of social-perception skills obviously makes much sense, there is actually very little evidence to determine whether such training is actually effective and whether the inclusion of this therapy component adds to the efficacy of overt-behavioural SST. One of the few studies to examine this area was reported by Bullmer (1972). Techniques of instructions modelling and feedback were reported to be effective in improving social-perception skills with undergraduate education-counsellor students. Obviously the training of social-perception skills is an area wide open to research and the existence of several techniques for assessing social perception (Archer and Akert, 1977; Ekman, 1971; Rosenthal *et al.*, 1979; Spence, 1980) should make evaluative studies relatively easier to perform.

The areas of role-taking, social-perspective-taking skills and empathy skills have frequently been included under the topic of interpersonal perception. Again, the main emphasis of research has been on the existence, importance and use of such skills rather than on their enhancement (Hughes, 1978).

Given the lack of evaluative research in the area of training in social-perception skills, few conclusions can be drawn. It would seem that further developments are urgently needed, given the enormous impact that deficits in social-perception skills may have on social competence (Morrison and Bellack, 1981).

Social-problem-solving skills training (SPSST)

Social-problem-solving skills enable an individual to identify the presence of a problem situation, to identify a range of alternative responses, to predict the likely outcomes of each alternative, and then select the response most likely to lead to a successful outcome. The importance of social-problem-solving skills has been discussed by various authors (e.g. McFall, 1982) and was outlined in detail in Chapter 11. Deficits in social-problem-solving have been implicated in the maintenance of a variey of psychological disorders including depression (Nezu, 1986) and schizophrenia (Platt and Spivack, 1972).

The limited number of studies which have investigated the effectiveness of social-problem-solving skills training (SPSST) have produced encouraging results. Twentyman *et al.* (1978) reported some improvement in assertive responding following problem-solving training. This study compared a procedure involving modelling, coaching and rehearsal of positive self-statements with SPSST and a standard SST approach. All groups were superior to the no-treatment control group on behavioural measures of assertion but no differences emerged between the procedures. Nezu (1986) compared SPSST with problem-focused therapy and a wait-list control in the treatment of depression. SPSST produced a significant decrease in depression levels which was associated with improvements in problem-solving skills. The benefits were maintained at six-month follow-up and were not evident in the two comparison conditions, suggesting that SPSST is valuable in the treatment of depression.

Bellack at al. (1989) reviewed the outcome studies relating to SPSST with schizophrenics. These authors noted the many methodological problems, such as small sample sizes, lack of adequate outcome measures and inclusion of additional therapy components which made it difficult to draw any firm conclusions about the value of SPSST with schizophrenic patients. SPSST has also been used with intellectually handicapped adults. A study reported by Bramston and Spence (1985) found that SPSST produced significant improvements in the generation of alternative solutions with moderately intellectually handicapped adults, but this effect was short-lived and did not lead to improvements in global ratings of social competence made by staff. Interestingly, an overt-behavioural SST procedure did not produce the same increase in the generation of alternative solutions but did produce improvements in the use of specific social skills, an effect which was not produced by SPSST. Thus, with moderately intellectually handicapped adults, cognitive SPSST produced benefits which were limited to cognitive changes, whereas overt-behavioural SST produced benefits which were limited to overt behaviours.

Again it must be pointed out that, as with the majority of SST studies, subjects selected for SPSST have not generally been selected on the basis of deficits in the skill to be taught, namely social-problem-solving skills deficits. The benefits of SPSST may be much more marked if applied to clients with poor problem-solving abilities, rather than to clients for whom such deficits are merely assumed to exist.

Affect control: anxiety and anger reduction

Anxiety reduction

The importance of social anxiety in the development and maintenance of social inadequacy was strongly emphasised in the preceding chapter. For some clients, the use of their social skills may be inhibited by high levels of anxiety or they may avoid certain social situations, thereby producing interpersonal difficulties (Curran, 1977). In such cases, it is important that therapy focuses on teaching anxiety reduction methods. The most widely used methods of anxiety reduction include relaxation training and systematic desensitisation. In this latter procedure, the therapist identifies a hierarchy of feared situations and encourages the client to expose him- or herself to these feared situations while engaging in responses which are incompatible with anxiety (i.e. being in a relaxed state). The exposure programme is gradual, with the client learning to cope with the least fearful situations first and systematically working up the hierarchy. There is now considerable evidence that systematic desensitisation and exposure methods of this type can be effective with clients who experience problems of social phobia, social anxiety and extreme shyness (Heimberg, 1989). Exposure also seems to be effective with social phobic clients who initially show social-skills deficits in addition to social phobia. However, because of difficulties in arranging prolonged exposure and because of cognitive influences on social fears, cognitive therapy is often necessary to supplement these treatments (see below; and Lindsay, Chapter 8).

It is unclear, therefore, whether SST or systematic desensitisation is the most suitable treatment for social phobic clients who experience deficits in social skills. Wlazlo *et al.* (1990) reported both approaches to be equally effective after treatment, at three-months follow-up and at two-years follow-up, even for social phobics with social-skills deficits. Trower *et al.* (1978), however, reported that social anxious patients with social-skills deficits responded best to SST rather than systematic desensitisation. The socially anxious patients who did not have social-skills deficits did equally well with SST and systematic desensitisation. It is interesting to find that SST produces reductions in social anxiety in persons who do not have social-skills deficits. This effect can probably be explained by the 'safe' environment which is produced during SST groups, in which fearful social tasks can be tried and practised without fear of ridicule or negative outcomes. The homework tasks also provide an opportunity for exposure to previously avoided situations and the SST approach may therefore produce a desensitising experience, thereby producing fear reduction.

Interestingly, the characteristic feature of social phobia and social anxiety appears to be not just a fear of social situations but a fear of being scrutinised and negatively evaluated by other people. This has led to the development of cognitive restructuring methods designed to tackle the thoughts and attitudes that are proposed to lead to the emotional responses of fear and anxiety in trigger situations (Butler, 1989). This area is dealt with in more detail below.

Anger control

The inability to self-regulate the emotion of anger has been suggested to account for some instances of inappropriate social responding in stressful or provocative interactions (Novaco, 1975; 1977). In order to enhance control over anger, Novaco stresses the need to focus on cognitive, somatic-affective and behavioural response. This has led to the development of an extensive programme for anger control, incorporating various cognitive-modification procedures, relaxation and overt-behavioural SST methods. Typically, clients are taught to identify the situations which tend to trigger off anger responses and to notice the physiological reactions that indicate the early stages of anger. Once this step has been achieved, clients are trained to 'stop' rather than react when they observe the trigger situations and physiological responses. They are then trained to relax and to use interpersonal problem-solving strategies as outlined above in order to select socially appropriate responses. Self-talk strategies may be used to teach people to carry out the necessary problem-solving steps. Social-skills training methods are then used to teach the client how to perform appropriate responses in a competent manner. At a cognitive level, therapy aims to correct faulty appraisals, attributions and expectations, and to challenge negative self-statements, as described in the next section. Novaco has reported several studies in which clients are taught cognitive, somatic and behavioural-coping skills which they then practise in provocative situations. Evidence to support the benefits of this type of approach to anger management has been produced by other researchers (e.g. Moon and Eisler, 1983), indicating the value of cognitive-behavioural approaches with clients whose interpersonal difficulties are associated with problems of temper or anger control.

Reducing maladaptive cognitions

Three types of cognitive intervention methods have already been mentioned, the training of social-perception, social-problem-solving skills, and use of self-talk strategies. Other authors (Rehm and Marston, 1968; Becker et al., 1987) have outlined the use of self-monitoring, self-evaluation and self-reinforcement techniques to improve social competence with some clients. The need to modify negative and maladaptive cognitions, however, has also received attention in relation to social enhancement programmes (Glass et al., 1976; Halford and Foddy, 1982; Butler, 1989).

The little research available to date has focused primarily on social phobia and heterosexual-social anxiety. Several studies have demonstrated the benefits of cognitive restructuring methods in the treatment of social phobia (Heimberg, 1989). For example, Mattick et al., (1989) reported cognitive restructuring to be more effective than exposure on measures of phobic avoidance, negative self-evaluation and irrational beliefs. Kanter and Goldfried (1979) and Malkiewich and Merluzzi (1980) both report effectiveness of cognitive rational-restructuring procedures in reducing anxiety and increasing the ability to approach and deal effectively with a variety of heterosexual-social situations. Glass et al. (1976) also reported a positive outcome using a cognitive self-statement procedure with socially anxious males. This procedure involved a semi-automated, audiotaped programme in which heterosexual situations were described and a model was demonstrated in which negative thoughts were replaced with positive ones. Clients were then required to rehearse positive self-statements aloud, during which they received feedback and coaching. Significant improvements in behavioural measures were found after intervention in frequency of phone calls for dates and in the impression made upon females during the phone calls. Similar results were found, however, with a more traditional motor SST procedure, although there was some evidence of greater generalisation of behaviour change with the cognitive procedure. No superiority was found with a combined cognitive-behavioural procedure and all treatments were superior to the no-treatment control group.

The use of cognitive-restructuring methods such as those of Beck (1976) or Ellis (1958), when applied to problems of social competence, would therefore seem encouraging from the few studies available to date (see Lindsay, Chapter 8 and Bradley, Chapter 6). Such methods already form an integral part of many assertiveness training programmes (e.g. Lange and Jakubowski, 1976) and integrated treatments for social phobia (e.g. Heimberg *et al.*, 1985).

SOCIAL ENHANCEMENT APPROACHES WITH SPECIFIC DISORDERS

We will now look at the application of the methods outlined above with specific client groups. A review of studies in this area reveals that authors typically use the term social-skills training (SST) to cover a wide range of approaches generally involving some or all of the methods outlined above. The term social-skills training will therefore be used in the 'umbrella' way in the following review, clarifying where possible the components used in different studies. Social-skills training approaches of various types have been applied to almost every conceivable client group and to a wide range of target skills. It is not possible to discuss all these areas here, thus only certain client groups will be mentioned.

Intellectual handicap

There have been many studies evaluating the benefits of SST with intellectually handicapped adults. The type of training used and targets for intervention vary according to the severity of the cognitive deficits. The training of interpersonal skills has an important place in the education of many intellectually handicapped persons. It has been conclusively demonstrated that intellectually handicapped adults can be trained to improve their use of specific, basic and complex social skills in the short term, but the durability of the benefits and degree of generalisation to naturalistic interactions is less dramatic (Foxx *et al.* 1983; Bates, 1980; Lalli *et al.*, 1991). Furthermore, the impact of training specific social skills upon more global measures of social competence is often weak (Bramston and Spence, 1985; Matson and Senatore, 1981). Future effort should therefore focus on the development of methods to maintain training improvements and to enhance generalisation to everyday situations.

Given the cognitive deficits involved in intellectually handicapped persons, it makes sense to suggest that cognitive deficits in interpersonal problem-solving skills will play an important part in producing inappropriate interpersonal responding. Training in interpersonal problem-solving skills would thus seem to be an important component of intervention for those intellectually handicapped adults who experience social difficulties. As mentioned above, intellectually handicapped adults can be trained to increase their ability to generate alternative solutions to social problems but this effect does not appear to be maintained without further intervention and does not result in significant improvements in overall social competence (Bramston and Spence, 1985). It is possible that a combined cognitive-overt-behavioural approach to intervention would be more beneficial than either method used in isolation.

Obviously, the manner in which SST is presented must be adapted to the cognitive skills and attention span of the clients. Foxx et al., (1983) describe the use of a board game and role-play approach to the teaching of skills, such as giving and receiving compliments or criticism. This method has been reported to produce short-term improvements in target social skills and represents a novel method of applying SST with intellectually handicapped adults.

Schizophrenia

Difficulties in social functioning are a common feature of schizophrenia, resulting from a range of factors which may vary for different individuals. These variables include limited social networks, cognitive deficits in social-perception skills and deficits in behavioural-social skills (Shepherd, 1986). Shepherd argues that intervention programmes need to consider the range of variables that may contribute to difficulties in social functioning, over and above behavioural SST approaches. For example, methods are needed to enhance social networks, to reduce social anxiety or to control anger outbursts, according to the characteristics of each client. Furthermore, the type of specific, behavioural social skills deficits may also differ markedly for different clients, which needs to be considered in designing intervention programmes.

Many studies have demonstrated the feasibility of training specific behavioural-social skills with schizophrenic patients, although the benefits appear to generalise only partially to naturalistic interactions and show some deterioration over time (Benton and Schroeder, 1990; Payne and Halford, 1990). The long-term impact upon social adjustment, however, is disappointing, even with prolonged, intensive SST programmes. For example, Hogarty et al. (1991) reported that the effects of SST were found to deteriorate after two years of ongoing intervention, whereas family interventions continued to prevent relapse and enhance social adjustment. It seems likely that the biological mechanisms involved in schizophrenia ultimately override the benefits of SST, whereas family-based interventions, which directly aim to reduce the trigger events within the family environment that are believed to be capable of provoking new episodes of the disorder, are more successful in preventing relapse.

Depression

The application of SST methods with depressed persons is based on the assumption that deficits in social skills play a role in the aetiology of depression. Studies investigating social-skill deficits in depression, however, have produced conflicting results. Williams (1992) reviews this evidence and concludes that depressed persons certainly seem to produce a negative impact upon others in terms of judgements of social competence. Interestingly, this effect cannot be attributed to deficits in specific, molecular social skills. These do not appear to be significantly different in depressed persons compared to non-depressed samples. Williams suggests that it may be the content of the conversation of depressed persons that produces the alienation effect, rather than the manner in which the information is presented. It should be pointed out that, although depressed individuals as a group may not demonstrate behavioural-social skills deficits at a molecular level, SST approaches may still be beneficial in changing the content of conversations and in producing a more positive impact upon other people.

As with other populations, there is considerable evidence for the effectiveness of SST in enhancing behavioural-social skills, but the impact upon more global measures of social competence and upon measures of depression is less convincing. Hersen et al., (1984) assigned 120 depressed women to one of four treatments, namely, amitriptyline, amitriptyline plus SST, placebo plus SST, or placebo plus psychotherapy. All treatments lasted for twelve weeks, with a further 6 to 8 booster sessions during the six-month follow-up. No difference was found between groups on measures of depression, but SST produced significantly greater improvements on measures of basic social skills and overall ratings of assertiveness during role-play. This difference was maintained at six-month follow-up. It is possible that a longer period of SST is required in order to produce a positive impact upon depression. Miller et al., (1989) reported SST to produce significant reductions in depression which were maintained after six months. This programme involved around thirty sessions, occurring daily during in-patient hospitalisation and weekly over a twenty-week out-patient phase. Unfortunately, this study did not assess changes in social skills, thus it is not possible to determine whether the reductions in depression were associated with improvements in social skills and social competence.

Social phobia

Social anxiety, shyness and social phobia have much in common and the terms are frequently used interchangeably. The characteristics include subjective feelings of anxiety concerning social situations, particularly those involving evaluation by others, which may lead to avoidance of the feared situations. The role of social-skills deficits in social anxiety is unclear. Studies have failed to find convincing evidence of social-skills deficits at a molecular level, although global ratings of social competence by independent judges tend to be lower for social phobics compared to non-socially anxious controls (Beidel *et al.*, 1985, Turner *et al.*, 1986). Despite the lack of obvious deficits in molecular social skills, many programmes have applied overt-behavioural SST approaches to the treatment of social anxiety and social phobia.

Interestingly, there are several reports that indicate SST to be effective in the treatment of social phobia, and SST appears to be equally beneficial for clients with or without social-skills deficits (Falloon *et al.*, 1981; Wlazlo *et al.*, 1990; Mersch *et al.*, 1989). Similarly, socially phobic clients with social-skills deficits are found to respond equally well to exposure treatments, cognitive therapy methods and SST, as discussed above. These results lead to the suggestion that SST may be successful with social phobics because of the opportunity it provides for practice of previously avoided social responses in a non-threatening environment. This exposure may then result in an alteration of negative beliefs relating to likely aversive outcomes from evaluation by other people.

CONCLUSIONS

This chapter has outlined a variety of methods which have been commonly applied to the modification of social inadequacy. With each method discussed, whether it be SST, anxiety reduction, social-problem-solving or anything else, two common themes have emerged. First, methods have generally been applied as part of a package, which makes it hard to recommend one technique rather than another. Second, most studies have selected clients for the intervention on the basis of some form of psychopathology (e.g. schizophrenia or depression) or inadequacy in particular social situations (e.g. difficulty in dating). Rarely have attempts been made to check that all clients actually experience the assumed problem, such as lack of social skills, high social anxiety or poor problem-solving skills. These problems make it difficult to draw firm conclusions about the impact of specific social competence interventions.

Future studies should therefore focus on the matching of treatments to the needs of each client, with therapy being designed to tackle the factors that cause the person to experience interpersonal difficulties. Greater attention should also be paid to ways of enhancing the generalisation of therapy improvements from the clinical situation to everyday interactions. Similarly, we need to investigate ways of producing long-lasting benefits which are sufficiently strong to impact upon the quality of interpersonal relationships and global social functioning. Improvements in specific behaviours such as molecular social skills or cognitive social-problem-solving skills are only beneficial if they are of sufficient magnitude and relevance to the client that they result in positive improvements in overall social competence.

REFERENCES

Archer, D. and Akert, R. M. (1977) 'Words and everything else: verbal and non-verbal areas in social interpretation', *Journal of Personality and Social Psychology* 35: 443–49.

Baggs, K. and Spence, S. H. (1990) 'Effectiveness of booster sessions in the maintenance and enhancement of treatment gains following assertion training', *Journal of Consulting and Clinical Psychology* 58: 845–54.

Bandura, A. (1977) *Social Learning Theory*, Englewood Cliffs, NJ.: Prentice-Hall.

Bates, P. (1980) 'The effectiveness of interpersonal skills training on the social skill acquisition of moderately and mildly retarded adults', *Journal of Applied Behaviour Analysis* 13: 237–48.

Beck, A. T. (1976) *Cognitive Therapy and the Emotional Disorders*, New York: International Universities Press.

Becker, R. E., Heimberg, R. G., and Bellack, A. S. (1987) *Social-Skills Training for Depression*, New York: Pergamon.

Beidel, D. C., Turner, S. M. and Dancu, C. V. (1985) 'Physiological, cognitive and behavioural aspects of social anxiety', *Behaviour Research and Therapy* 23: 109–17.

Bellack, A. S. (1983) 'Recurrent problems in the behavioural assessment of social skill', *Behaviour Research and Therapy* 21: 29–41.

Bellack, A. S. Turner, S. M. Hersen, M and Luber, R. F. (1984) 'An examination of the efficacy of social skills training for chronic schizophrenic patients', *Hospital and Community Psychiatry* 35: 1023–8.

Bellack, A. S., Morrison, R. L. and Mueser, K. T. (1989) 'Social-problem-solving in schizophrenia', *Schizophrenia Bulletin* 15: 101–16.

Benton, M. K. and Schroeder, H. E. (1990) 'Social skills training with schizophrenics: A meta-analytic evaluation', *Journal of Consulting and Clinical Psychology* 58: 741–7.

Bramston, P. and Spence, S. H. (1985) 'Behavioural versus cognitive social skills training with intellectually handicapped adults', *Behaviour Research and Therapy* 23: 239–46.

Bullmer, K. (1972) 'Improving accuracy of interpersonal perception through a direct teaching method', *Journal of Counselling Psychology* 19: 37–41.

Butler, G. (1989) 'Issues in the application of cognitive and behavioural strategies to the treatment of social phobia', *Clinical Psychology Review* 9: 91–106.

Curran, J. P. (1977) 'Skills training as an approach to the treatment of heterosexual-social anxiety: a review', *Psychological Bulletin* 84: 140–57.

Curran, J. P. and Monti, P. M. (eds) (1982) *Social Skills Training*, New York: Guilford.

Ekman, P. (1971) 'Universal and cultural differences in facial expressions of emotions', in J. K. Cole (ed.) *Nebraska Symposium on Motivation*, Nebraska: University of Nebraska Press.

Ellis, A. (1958) 'Rational psychotherapy', *Journal of General Psychology* 59: 35–49.

Falloon, I. R. H., Lloyd, G. G. and Harpin, R. E. (1981) 'The treatment of social phobia: Real-life rehearsal with nonprofessional therapists', *Journal of Nervous and Mental Disease* 169: 180–3.

Foxx, R. M., McMorrow, R. J. and Schloss, C. N. (1983) 'Stacking the Deck: Teaching social skills to retarded adults with a modified table game', *Journal of Applied Behaviour Analysis* 16: 157–70.

Foxx, R. M., McMorrow, R. J. Bittle, R. G. and Fenlon, J. (1985) 'Teaching social skills to psychiatric in-patients', *Behaviour Research and Therapy* 23: 531–7.

Friedman, P. H. (1971) 'The effects of modelling and role playing on assertive behaviour', in R. D. Rubin, H. Fensterheim, A. A. Lazarus and C. M. Franks (eds) *Advances in Behavior Therapy*, New York: Academic Press.

Glass, C. R., Gottman, J. M. and Schmirak, S. H. (1976) 'Response-acquisition and cognitive self-statement modification approaches to dating skills training', *Journal of Counselling Psychology* 23: 520–6.

Goldstein, A. P. (1973) *Structured Learning Therapy: Towards a Psychotherapy for the Poor*, New York: Academic Press.

Goldstein, A. P., Sherman, M., Gershaw, N. J., Sprafkin, R. P. and Glock, B. (1978) 'Training aggressive adolescents in prosocial behaviour', *Journal of Youth and Adolescence* 7: 73–93.

Halford, W. K. and Foddy, M. (1982) 'Cognitive and social-skill correlates of social anxiety', *British Journal of Clinical Psychology* 21: 17–28.

Heimberg, R. G. (1989) 'Cognitive and behavioural treatments for social phoboa: a critical analysis', *Clinical Psychology Review* 9: 107–28.

Heimberg, R. G., Becker, R. E., Goldfinger, K., and Vermilyea, J. A. (1985) 'Treatment of social phobia by exposure, cognitive restructuring and homework assignments', *Journal of Nervous and Mental Disease* 173: 236–45.

Hersen, M., Bellack, A. S., Himmelhoch, J. M. and Thase, M. E. (1984) 'Effects of social skills training, amitriptyline and psychotherapy in unipolar depressed women', *Behaviour Therapy* 15: 21–40.

Hogarty, G. E., Anderson, C. M., Reiss, D. J., Kornblith, S. J., Greenwald, D. P., Ulrich, R. F., and Carter, M. (1991) 'Family psychoeducation, social skills training, and maintenance chemotherapy in the aftercare treatment of schizophrenia', *Archives of General Psychiatry* 48: 340–6.

Hollin, C. R. and Trower, P. (1986) 'Social skills training: critique and future development', in C. R. Hollin and P. Trower (eds) *Handbook of Social Skills Training: Clinical Applications and New Directions* 10: 237–58, Oxford: Pergamon.

Hughes, M. (1978) 'Selecting pictures of another person's view', *British Journal of Educational Psychology* 48: 210–19.

Kanter, N. J. and Goldfried, M. R. (1979) 'Relative effectiveness of rational restructuring and self control desensitization in the reduction of inter-personal anxiety', *Behaviour Therapy* 10: 472–90.

Kazdin, E. A. (1982) 'The separate and combined effects of covert and overt rehearsal in developing assertive behaviour', *Behaviour Research and Therapy* 20: 17–25.

Kelly, J. A. (1982) *Social Skills Training: a Practical Guide for Interventions*, New York: Springer.

Lalli, J. S., Pinter-Lalli, E., Mace, F. C. and Murphy, D. M. (1991) 'Training interactional behaviours of adults with developmental disabilities: A systematic replication and extension', *Journal of Applied Behaviour Analysis* 24: 167–74.

Lange, A. J. and Jakubowski, P. (1976) *Responsible assertive behaviour: Cognitive-behavioural procedures for trainers*, Champaign, Ill.: Research Press.

Liberman, R. P., King, L. W., De Risi, W. J. and McCann, M. (1975) *Personal Effectiveness: Guiding People to Assert Themselves and Improve their Social Skills*, Champaign, Ill.: Research Press.

McFall, R. M. (1982) 'A review and reformulation of the concept of social skills', *Behavioural Assessment* 4: 1–33.

Malkiewich, L. E. and Merluzzi, T. V. (1980) 'Rational restructuring versus desensitization with clients of diverse conceptual levels: a test of client-treatment match model', *Journal of Counselling Psychology* 27: 453–61.

Matson, J. L. and Senatore, V. (1981) 'A comparison of traditional psychotherapy and social skills training for improving interpersonal functioning of mentally retarded adults', *Behavior Therapy* 12: 369–82.

Mattick, R. P., Peters, L. and Clarke, J. C. (1989) 'Exposure and cognitive restructuring for social phobia: A controlled study', *Behaviour Therapy* 20: 3–24.

Mersch, P. P. A., Emmelkamp, P. M. G., Bogels, S. M. and Van der Sleen, J. (1989)

'Social phobia: individual response patterns and the effects of behavioral and cognitive interventions', *Behaviour Research and Therapy* 27: 421–34.

Miller, I. W., Norman, W. H., Keitner, G. I., Bishop, S. B. and Dow, M. G. (1989) 'Cognitive-behavioral treatment of depressed inpatients', *Behavior Therapy* 20: 25–47.

Moon, J. R. and Eisler, R. M. (1983) 'Anger control: an experimental comparison of three behavioral treatments, *Behavior Therapy* 14: 493–505.

Morrison, R. L. and Bellack, A. (1981) 'The role of social perception in social skills', *Behavior Therapy* 12: 69–79.

Nezu, A. M. (1986) 'Efficacy of social-problem-solving therapy approach for unipolar depression', *Journal of Consulting and Clinical Psychology* 54: 196–202.

Novaco, R. W. (1975) *Anger Control: the Development and Evaluation of an Experimental Treatment*, Lexington Mass.: Lexington Books.

Novaco, R. W. (1976) 'The treatment of anger through cognitive and relaxation controls', *Journal of Consulting and Clinical Psychology* 44: 681.

Novaco, R. (1977) 'Stress inoculation: a cognitive therapy for anger and its application to a case of depression', *Journal of Consulting and Clinical Psychology* 45: 600–8.

Payne, P. V. and Halford, W. K. (1990) 'Social skills training with chronic schizophrenic patients living in community settings', *Behavioural Psychotherapy* 18: 49–64.

Platt, J. J. and Spivack, G. (1972) 'Problem-solving thinking of psychiatric patients', *Journal of Consulting and Clinical Psychology* 43: 148–51.

Prince, H. F. (1975) 'The effects of covert behavioural rehearsal, modelling and vicarious consequences in assertive training', unpublished doctoral dissertation, University of Texas at Austin.

Rehm, L. P. and Marston, A. R. (1968) 'Reduction of social anxiety through modification of self-reinforcement: an instigation therapy technique', *Journal of Consulting and Clinical Psychology* 32: 565–74.

Rosenthal, R., Hall, J. A., DiMatteo, M., Rogers, P. and Archer, D. (1979) *Sensitivity to Nonverbal Communications: The PONS Test*, Baltimore: John Hopkins University Press.

Shepherd, G. (1983) 'Introduction. Chapter 1', in S. H. Spence and G. Shepherd (eds) *Developments in Social Skills Training*, London: Academic Press.

Shepherd, G. (1984) 'Assessment of cognitions in social skills training', in P. Trower (ed.) *Radical Approaches to Social Skills Training*, London: Croom Helm.

Shepherd, G. (1986) 'Social skills training and schizophrenia', in C. R. Hollin and P. Trower (eds) *Handbook of Social Skills Training: Clinical Applications and New Directions*, 1: 9–38, Oxford: Pergamon.

Spence, S. H. (1980) *Social-Skills Training with Children and Adolescents: A Counsellor's Manual*, Windsor: NFER.

Spence, S. H. (1983) 'Teaching social skills to children: an annotation', *Journal of Child Psychology and Psychiatry* 24: 621–7.

Spence, S. H. and Shepherd, H. (eds) (1983) *Developments in Social Skills Training*, London: Academic Press.

Stravynski, A., Lesage, A., Marcouiller, M. and Elie, R. (1989) 'A test of the therapeutic mechanism in social skills training with avoidant personality disorder', *Journal of Nervous and Mental Disease* 177: 739–44.

Trower, P., Bryant, B. and Argyle, M. (1978) *Social Skills and Mental Health*, London: Methuen.

Turner, S. M., Beidel, D. C. and Larkin, K. T. (1986) 'Situational determinants of social anxiety in clinic and nonclinic samples: Physiological and cognitive correlates', *Journal of Consulting and Clinical Psychology* 54: 523–7.

Twentyman, C. T. and Zimering, R. T. (1979) 'Behavioural training of social skills: a critical review', in M. Hersen, R. M. Eisler and P. M. Miller (eds) *Progress in Behavior Modification. Vol. 7*, New York: Academic Press.

Twentyman, C. T ., Pharr, D. and Connor, J. M. (1978) 'A comparison of three cognitive modification programmes in assertion training', unpublished manuscript, State University of New York.

Wilkinson, J. and Canter, S. (1982) *Social Skills Training Manual*, Chichester: Wiley.

Williams, J. M. G. (1992) *The Psychological Treatment of Depression. 2nd edn*, London: Routledge.

Wlazlo, Z., Schroeder-Harwig, K., Hand, I., Kaiser, G. and Munchau, N. (1990) 'Exposure in vivo vs social skills training for social phobia: Long-term outcome and differential effects', *Behaviour Research and Therapy* 28: 181–93.

Chapter 13

Marital conflict
Investigation

Ian Bennun

INTRODUCTION

The assessment of marital conflict and indeed any relationship problem is based on the assumption that the information gathered during this phase of treatment will determine, among other things, an intervention plan. The assessment could indicate the pros and cons of particular intervention strategies, indicate the participants' commitment to the relationship, and then help the practitioner aim towards realistic goals. However, implicit in this is the position that there is a distinction between assessment and therapy/intervention. This assumption is not universally accepted because some therapeutic models deliberately attempt to blur this distinction (Pallazzoli *et al.*, 1980). For example, the question to the couple enquiring whose idea it was to seek treatment would be considered an intervention within this therapeutic approach. Other approaches clearly differentiate assessment from therapy (Jacobson and Margolin, 1979). A second issue which needs to be considered within the context of a recognised assessment of marital conflict is the parameters to be examined. Previously behaviour was seen as the primary target of assessment and marital behaviours were defined as those overt interactions occurring between partners. However, as our understanding of marriage has become increasingly sophisticated, so has the need to expand traditional areas of assessment. Research into affect and the social cognitions in marriage has illustrated the weakness in assessing just 'marital behaviour', and comprehensive assessments should now include these factors. Vincent and Carter (1987) define assessment as the process of measuring behavioural, cognitive and affective components of all relationships.

In this chapter, the focus will go beyond the assessment of dysfunctional marital behaviours as described in the first edition of this *Handbook* (Bennun, 1987). It will therefore include discussions of the cognitive and affective factors contributing to marital distress. Although it can be argued that cognition, affect and behaviour are not easily separated, for the purposes of assessment, the generally accepted emphasis on 'what is observed' has to be extended to cover other aspects that influence behaviour.

MARRIAGE LIFE CYCLE

Before examining some specific issues and methods in marital assessment, it is worth noting some of the general aspects that are involved, specifically the range of information required by a therapist as part of the overall process of assessment. Having invited the couple to offer their view of the presenting problem, it will be necessary to place their marriage in a developmental context. One way of achieving this is to locate the couple within the family life cycle (Carter and McGoldrick, 1989; Falicov, 1988). This model identifies specific stages which marriages move through and identifies some of the tasks that accompany each stage.

The life cycle paradigm has had a major impact on the way marital therapists view and assess both marital and family functioning. Some authors have suggested that marital and family problems are the result of a disruption in the natural progression of the marital and family life cycle. Intimate relationships pass through critical phases in their development and each of these has a number of associated tasks. It is possible to identify seven stages and consider some of the tasks and functions associated with each. As a tool in the assessment of marital conflict, clinicians could consider whether the couple are struggling with a particular task, once they have located the couple within the following framework (Bennun, 1988):

1 Beginning families include courtship and marriage prior to the couple starting a family.
2 Child-bearing families begin with the birth of the couple's first child and continue until this child begins school.
3 Child-rearing families are a continuation of the previous stage until the oldest child becomes a teenager.
4 Families with teenagers begin with the first teenage child and continue until the oldest child leaves home.
5 Families as launching centres comprise the duration of time during which the first and last child leave home and commence their more independent living.
6 Families in the middle years span the time when the parental couple are together without their children until one or both retire.
7 Ageing families incorporate the remaining portion of the couple's lives.

Falicov (1988) suggests that the restructuring of marital relationships during periods of transition is extremely stressful as new processes generate anxiety and confusion which compounds manifest difficulties. The pace of change during transitions is also essential to assessing marital conflict. If a transition occurs too slowly or rapidly, the couple could face difficulties which escalate as they repeatedly fail in their attempts at solving their difficulties. While it is easier to place a couple within this developmental model, identifying the tasks to be negotiated is more difficult. It is useful to recall with the couple the stages they have already negotiated and to identify the tasks they faced at each time. The hypotheses that are generated relating to each stage will be a helpful adjunct to the assessment and can be used productively to engage the couple in treatment. Thus, a more comprehensive assessment will go beyond the presenting problem and place it within this paradigm as a way of presenting problems as developmental issues.

PRESENTING PROBLEMS: CONCRETE OR FUNCTIONAL?

Problems can be seen to have both concrete and functional aspects. A concrete approach examines the problems and assumes that they arise from behavioural or cognitive dysfunctions. Behavioural dysfunctions include those aspects identified as characterising distressed marriages and include poor or inappropriate patterns of communication, inability to overcome behavioural change deficits and inadequate problem-solving skills (Jacobson and Margolin, 1979). Other presenting problems within a concrete model could include difficulties in overcoming the effects of particular events (extra-marital affairs) or difficulties related to child rearing. Broadly this approach considers presenting problems as manifestations of a deficit in skills.

Alternatively, a functional approach (as distinct from functional analysis) assumes that the presenting problem is a 'metaphor' for the relationship and, as such, is functional and purposeful. Within this analysis, the presenting problem is explored for its role in a distressed relationship. A communication problem, for example, will not be seen as a sign of a skills deficit, but rather as a way in which the couple regulate the intimacy within their relationship: an avoidance of intimate discussion keeps the partners at a safe distance. Similarly, the presenting problem may indicate difficulties in negotiating a developmental task within the marriage. While the 'problem' is evident, the developmental difficulties have yet to be appropriately acknowledged.

Having considered the concrete and/or functional nature of the problem, a range of related issues need to be addressed:

1 Why are the couple seeking treatment at this particular point in time?
2 The duration of the problem and previous attempts to resolve it.
3 Are there any other people affected by the difficulties (e.g. children)?
4 Are there any impinging factors, external to the marriage, that require consideration (socio-economic factors, life events)?
5 Are both partners equally committed to therapy?
6 A consideration of clinical outcome.
7 Monitoring the therapeutic relationship specifically relating to trust, positive expectancy, gender roles, etc.

Sometimes practitioners prefer to assess partners separately in an attempt to determine whether there are individual problems that could interfere with marital functioning. Alcohol abuse clearly undermines marital satisfaction and the role of abuse in the context of marriage requires consideration. Many couples requesting help do so following an extra-marital affair. Practitioners have to decide whether the affair should stop while the couple are in treatment and to discuss the impact on the outcome of treatment of the affair being a secret. The existence of individual psychopathology, undeclared sexual problems and physical abuse should be part of all assessments with varying emphasis on how explicit these enquiries should be. The possibility of these problems coming to the surface exists throughout the course of treatment. Practitioners should be vigilant in recognising any hints that the couple make within these sensitive areas.

SOCIAL COGNITION AND ATTRIBUTIONS

Social cognition as linked to attributional processes has been ignored within the mainstream of assessing marital conflict. The definitions of social cognition vary, but all consider it to refer to how individuals acquire, represent and retrieve information within interpersonal contexts. The judgements that partners make of one another can, in part, be the result of processes linked to assumptions made about other relationships, repeated patterns within their own relationships or from the early dyadic relationships that they may have witnessed (for example, their parents' marriage). The link between social cognition and attributional processes is important as attributions can develop following inferences made from the way perceivers understand their social world and the explanations (correct or otherwise) used in making sense of their reality (Zajonc, 1980). Because attributional processes involve the observation of events and the subsequent inferences about their causes, there is the obvious potential for cognitive distortion within these processes. As the observations will in the context of marriage be interpersonal, social and cognitive distortions will then undoubtedly influence the functioning of intimate relationships.

ASSESSING ATTRIBUTIONS AND COGNITIVE DISTORTION

Despite the finding that questionnaires can discriminate between distressed and non-distressed couples, doubts have always existed about correlations between behavioural and self-report assessment procedures. Furthermore, it is assumed, perhaps incorrectly, that self-report measures provide accurate information about actual communication behaviour. It could be argued, however, that self-reports by spouses of marital communication provide only perceptions of the communication rather than the actual behaviour. This distinction is important given that research evidence suggests that dysfunctional cognitions and distortions in the recall and evaluation of spouse behaviour are contributors to marital distress (Berley and Jacobson, 1984). The types of cognitive variables that have received attention are beliefs about the standards for relationships, marital attributions for the causes of conflict, responsibility, intent and motivation behind behaviours. If these theoretical models are indeed correct, it could be reasonably expected that evidence for unrealistic beliefs and standards will result in marital distress and that negative attributions will exacerbate feelings of hopelessness, anger and distrust within intimate relationships.

CLINICAL IMPLICATIONS FOR ASSESSMENT

The research undertaken examining the various differences between distressed and non-distressed couples has shown that distressed partners are more likely to attribute their partner's unpleasant behaviours to negative intent and their positive behaviours to specific unstable and unintentional causes. These biased attributions elicit a sense of hopelessness and helplessness regarding the improvement of the relationship and are obstacles towards developing the atmosphere for exploring possibilities for change.

The primary mechanisms for examining the attributions which partners make about their relationship and events within it are the clinical interview, questionnaires, behavioural observations, and the content analysis of communication samples. During clinical assessment interviews, the clinician will attempt to elicit perceptions and meanings which act as mediators to the emotional and behavioural responses and attitudes within the relationship. The way partners interpret events, overgeneralise, and make arbitrary inferences are the cognitive and attributional distortions which will help the clinician focus interventions. Within an interview, the marital therapist will have the opportunity to witness each spouse's cognitive and emotional responses to the other's in-session behaviour. When attributions or 'explanations' are forthcoming, the therapist then has a chance to explore how these have developed and the evidence that exists for their continued impact on interaction, as well as to explore opportunities to challenge and alter them. Comparing how two partners perceive and explain a shared interaction or event can be helpful in gaining information on how partners' attributions and automatic thoughts contribute to cognitive distortions and misinterpretations.

In addition to the clinical interview, there are a number of questionnaires that have been developed to assess dysfunctional marital relationships (see Epstein, 1986). For example, the Relationship Belief Inventory (Eidelson and Epstein, 1982) assesses dysfunctional beliefs that spouses may hold about the nature of their intimate relationships. This scale has five subscales which include beliefs such as 'disagreement is destructive', 'mind reading is expected', 'partners cannot change', 'sexual perfectionism' and 'the sexes are different'.

ASSESSING AFFECT IN MARRIAGE

Positive affect, that is, the expression of emotion and love, is difficult to define, but research has shown that affect is judged by women to be the primary characteristic of positive marriages, whereas men rate important both love and understanding (Broderick, 1981).

Gottman and colleagues have suggested that autonomic arousal measured during couple interaction offers a reliable measure of dyadic affect (Gottman, 1979; Levenson and Gottman, 1985). Those behaviours that decrease arousal will be reinforced and those which increase arousal should be targeted for change. Interventions could be tailored to alter these interactions particularly within the three dimensions described above. A fourth dimension, reactivity, has also been considered as contributing to marital affect. Within dyadic relationships, reactivity is the extent to which specific behaviours in one partner produce reciprocal behaviours in the other (the more one partner nags, the more the other will withdraw, for example). Thus an indication of affect within marriages would include positiveness, reciprocity, dominance and reactivity.

The assessment of affect takes three factors into account: physiological, cognitive and motivational. Gottman's (1979) important research attempted to identify the ways of exploring affect within marriages. He suggested a structural model within marital interactions comprising positiveness, reciprocity and dominance as three affective dimensions. The hypotheses that have been generated and studied empirically have shown that there are distinct differences between distressed and non-distressed couples within these domains. Distressed couples are distinguished by less positive and more negative affect, a greater degree of negative affect reciprocity (exchanges of negative affect) and greater symmetry in predictability of affect. Although the research that has looked at marital affect has become increasingly sophisticated, moving theory and research to practice has lagged behind.

Two related questions arise when considering the relationship between affect and marital satisfaction. The first is quantitative and relates to the degree to which affect is a component of marital satisfaction. If emotion does colour marriage, how does affect influence marital satisfaction?

Levenson and Gottman (1985) conducted a three-year follow-up study of the extent to which physiological and affective factors predict change in marital satisfaction. Physiological measures were used because they were considered to be independent of the more sociologically based marital satisfaction outcome criteria. Physiological and affective measures were predictive of current satisfaction and were found to predict relationship satisfaction at three years post-test. The results indicated that the amount of positive and negative affect and certain patterns of negative affect reciprocity were predictive of changing levels of relationship satisfaction; increased marital satisfaction was associated with less negative reciprocity. There were also gender differences; satisfaction declined most when male partners did not and female partners did reciprocate negative affect.

Emotion is not always directly assessed in studies of marital satisfaction. In order to do so, specific items or components of assessment procedures measuring affect would need to be looked at separately in order to see how affective reactions/factors relate to marital satisfaction. In this way, it would be possible to see whether affective reactions are involved in the reciprocity of positive and negative behaviours. There are a number of ways to assess dyadic affect. Self-report measures can be either paper-and-pencil measures (of intimacy, trust and feelings) or observation systems where spouses observe and then record events and their affective consequences. The Positive Feelings Questionnaire (O'Leary *et al.*, 1983) is a seventeen-item instrument designed to measure positive feelings towards a partner. Each item is scored on a seven-point scale. Another method requires partners to review a videotape of their interaction while manipulating a dial denoting negative, neutral or positive affect (Levenson and Gottman, 1985). Physiological measures are taken simultaneously to identify specific interactional sequences and the relationship between behaviour, affect and arousal. These are then correlated with marital satisfaction scores. As the dimensions under investigation increase, so the complexity characterising affect in marriage increases, limiting the conclusions one can draw from a single measurement system.

ASSESSING MARITAL SATISFACTION

Marital satisfaction is a multi-dimensional concept and encompasses a variety of factors all of which contribute to a general satisfaction (or dissatisfaction) within relationships. Yet different partners want different things of their relationships, although it could be argued that there is basic agreement on what constitutes a happy marriage/relationship. However, partners require a range of changes within relationships when there are problems, and obviously different individuals are able to tolerate different levels of conflict or dissatisfaction.

Assessment questionnaires essentially reflect aspects which distinguish distressed and non-distressed relationships. Further, they include specific target behaviours which can be observed (and counted) or they assess attitudes, beliefs and experiences of the relationship. To varying degrees, sexual satisfaction is included, although there are specific questionnaires designed to assess sexual relationships (e.g. Golombok and Rust, 1986). One way to consider the variety of satisfaction measures is to differentiate quantitative measures, which include activities and observable behaviours (decision-making, reliability, arguments, praise, affection, communication, etc.), from qualitative measures, which include attitudes, beliefs and expectations (damage is irreversible, emotional needs do not vary, disagreements are bad, etc.). Emphases within questionnaires vary: it is important to select the one which addresses the dimension of marital satisfaction under review. The more general the questionnaire, the less specific are the items and the more global is the overall description.

BEHAVIOURAL ASSESSMENT AND OBSERVATION

Behavioural observation was included in most outcome studies during the 1980s. Numerous coding schemes were developed to assess behavioural samples and interaction sequences. These provided valuable information for therapists about how couples interacted and enabled them to modify dysfunctional behaviour and investigate the efficacy of their methods.

The Marital Interaction Coding System (Hops *et al.*, 1972) is the most widely used scheme and is used by an observer to code behaviour as couples attempt to resolve a pre-set task or discuss an issue suggested by the therapist/investigator. The interaction is usually recorded on videotape and the trained raters then code the interactions into verbal and non-verbal codes. The verbal codes include problem-solving, problem description, negative and positive behaviours. The non-verbal codes include positive and negative behaviours, such as criticism, complaining and turning off. Couples are videotaped before and after treatment and usually the behaviour is coded in ten-minute segments.

The Category System for Coding Interpersonal Communications (Hahlweg *et al.*, 1984) was developed from a behavioural marital therapy treatment package and examines both speaker and listener skills. The basic coding units are verbal responses, disregarding their duration or syntactical structure. Each content code is assigned a non-verbal rating (positive, negative, neutral). The content codes include self-disclosure, positive solution, acceptance of the other, agreement, problem description, meta communication, rest, listening, criticism, negative solution, justification and disagreement. The non-verbal codes include facial cues, voice tone and body cues.

These methods, while reliable, are not easily applied in clinical settings. They require the agreement of couples to interact in a laboratory setting, and the interaction is assumed to provide a valid and reliable sample of their everyday behaviour. The extent to which laboratory behaviour generalises to the natural setting is, of course, questionable. The coding of behaviours will necessarily involve both the equipment and training of raters, which is expensive. It is not surprising that these methods are not used regularly, and more recently there has been a greater reliance on other forms of assessment.

QUESTIONNAIRES ASSESSING MARITAL SATISFACTION

Questionnaires are extensively used in the assessment of marital satisfaction. They have all the limitations of self-report methods, but they are generally easy to administer and score, are a cost-effective method of assessment, and have usually been developed in clinical settings using valid and reliable method-ologies. The range of target behaviours is wide, and a few are discussed below. All have been published, and some are marketed by publishing companies (e.g. Golombok–Rust Inventory of Marital Satisfaction; Golombok and Rust, 1986). Nevertheless, like most questionnaires measuring interactional processes, the domains assessed are quite restricted and the items are often confounded both by theory and the assumption that non-distressed marriages are homogeneous and are the 'accepted norm'. When the questionnaires are developed within a partic-ular theoretical approach (for example, behavioural marital theory), then the items are restricted to assessing outcome or change only within that approach. Similarly, the laboratory research on distinguishing distressed and non-distressed couples also is biased within just that one approach.

The Marital Pre-Counselling Inventory (Stuart and Stuart, 1973) is a compre-hensive self-report inventory comprising nine components: assess goals for behaviour change, resources for change, degree of marital understanding, power distribution, congruence of priorities, communication effectiveness, sexual satisfaction, congruence in child management and general marital satisfaction. This inventory has not been revised recently and is therefore somewhat dated in considering contemporary relationships.

The Daily Checklist of Marital Activities (Broderick, 1980) is a 109-item spouse observation checklist. Half the items are judged positive and half are judged negative. There is also a Daily Satisfaction Rating which is completed each day by the individual partners. The items included have been derived from the 400-item Spouse Observation Checklist (Weiss and Margolin, 1977) which comprises the following categories: companionship, affection, consideration, sex, communication process, child care, household management, financial decision-making, employment–education, personal habits and appearance, and spouse independence. As an observational checklist, this measure tends to focus more on the concrete observable aspects of relationships.

The Golombok–Rust Inventory of Marital State (Rust *et al.*, 1990) is a 28-item inventory. In developing this scale two axes were identified. The first included shared interests, communication, sex, warmth/love/hostility, trust, roles, decision-making and coping; the other identified areas which could be assessed against the first axis as they became manifest: beliefs/insight/understanding, behaviour, attitudes/feelings, motivation for change and agreement.

The Personal Assessment of Intimacy in Relationships Inventory (Schaefer and Olson, 1981) is a 36-item scale, which includes 7 subscales: emotional, social, sexual, intellectual, recreational, intimacy and conventionality. The construction of this test enables researchers and clinicians to obtain a difference score between perceived and expected levels of intimacy. Couples are required to score each item on a five-point Likert-type scale.

Other questionnaires which have been used include the Marital Adjustment Scale (Kimmel and van der Veen, 1974; Locke and Wallace, 1959), the Marital Conflict Form (Weiss and Margolin, 1977), the Marital Status Inventory (Weiss and Cerreto, 1980), the Dyadic Adjustment Scale (Spanier, 1976), the Primary Communication Inventory (Navran, 1967), the Marriage Inventory (Knox, 1971), and the Areas of Change Questionnaire (Weiss *et al.*, 1973).

INDIVIDUALISED MEASURES

In addition to questionnaire and behavioural observation measures, the use of couples own identified target problems (e.g. Woodward *et al.*, 1978) has obvious advantages. Apart from its face validity, assessing change on specific target problems as identified by the couple themselves ensures that targets/goals are relevant and specific. Bennun *et al.*, (1987) adapted Shapiro's Personal Questionnaire (PQ; Shapiro, 1961) for use in assessing treatment outcome. In developing the original PQ, it was considered advantageous that partners/couples be rated on their own set of problems rather than on the basis of a pre-determined set, as happens when standardised questionnaires and inventories are used. Although the questionnaires have obvious advantages in the area of couple therapy, their clinical relevance is frequently open to question. The gender bias (men and women score differently for identical responses) in the Marital Adjustment Scale, the length and tedium of the Spouse Observation Checklist and the theoretical bias in the Areas of Change Questionnaire illustrate this point.

Attention has been drawn to the contrast between individualised measures (for example, PQ) and those procedures more closely associated with the psychometric tradition. The major difficulty of the psychometric approach is the need to assess all cases on the same items of the chosen test, regardless of the relevance of particular items. In the field of marital therapy, this results in couples being rated on 'irrelevant' variables as well as 'relevant' ones. There are inherent difficulties in defining and assessing 'marital satisfaction' and in the assumption that it is a unidimensional construct. One way of addressing this and the other limitations is by applying assessment procedures that can account for the specifics of the individual case. Using individualised measures gives priority to the couple's report of their difficulties and, if necessary, separate spouse assessments can be made of the severity of the presenting problems. The couple need to agree on the list of target complaints but the clinician, as assessor, can then be flexible in how the identified problems are used. While changes are usually specific to individuals, the changes as described by one or both partners will help the clinician in deciding on realistic goals, outcomes and longer term prognoses.

REFERENCES

Bennun, I. (1987) 'Marital dysfunction: Investigation', in S. Lindsay and G. Powells (eds) *A Handbook of Clinical Adult Psychology*, Aldershot: Gower.

Bennun, I. (1988) 'Systems theory and family therapy', in E. Street and W. Dryden (eds) *Family Therapy in Britain*, Milton Keynes: Open University Press.

Bennun, I., Chalkley, A. and Donnely, M. (1987) 'Research applications of Shapiro's personal questionnaire in marital therapy', *Journal of Family Therapy* 9: 131–44.

Berley, R. and Jacobson, N. (1984) 'Causal attribution in intimate relationships: toward a model of cognitive behavioural marital therapy', in P. Kendall (ed.) *Advances in Cognitive Behavioural Research and Therapy. Vol. 3*, New York: Academic Press.

Broderick, J. (1980) 'Attitudinal and behavioural components of marital satisfaction', unpublished doctoral dissertation, State University of New York at Stony Brook.

Broderick, J. (1981) 'A method for derivation of areas for assessment in marital relationships', *American Journal of Family Therapy* 9: 25–34.

Carter, B. and McGoldrick, M. (1989) *The Changing Family Life Cycle: Framework for Family Therapy*, London: Allyn and Bacon.

Eidelson, R. and Epstein, N. (1982) 'Cognition and relationship maladjustment: development of a questionnaire of dysfunctional relationship beliefs', *Journal of Consulting and Clinical Psychology* 50: 715–20.

Epstein, N. (1986) 'Cognitive marital therapy: multi-level assessment and intervention', *Journal of Rational Emotive Therapy* 4: 68–81.

Falicov, C. (1988) *Family Transitions: Continuity and Change Over the Lifecycle*, New York: Guilford Press.

Golombok, S. and Rust, J. (1986) *GRISS: Golombok–Rust Inventory of Sexual Satisfaction*, Windsor: NFER-Nelson.

Gottman, J. (1979) *Marital Interaction: Experimental Investigations*, New York: Academic Press.

Hahlweg, K., Reisner, L., Kohli, J., Volmmer, M., Schindler, L. and Revenstort, D. (1984) 'K.P.I. Category System for Partnership Interaction', in K. Hahlweg and N. Jacobson (eds) *Marital Interaction: Analysis and Modification*, New York: Guilford Press.

Hops, H., Wills, T., Paterson, G. and Weiss, R. (1972) 'Marital Interaction Coding System', unpublished manuscript, University of Oregon and Oregon Research Institute.

Jacobson, N. and Holtzworth-Munroe, A. (1986) 'Martial therapy: a social-learning cognitive perspective', in N. Jacobson and A. Gurman (eds) *Clinical Handbook of Marital Therapy*, New York: Guilford Press.

Jacobson, N. and Margolin, G. (1979) *Marital Therapy: Strategies Based on Social Learning and Behaviour Exchange Principles*, New York: Brunner/Mazel.

Kimmel, D. and van der Veen, F. (1974) 'Factors of marital adjustment in Locke's marital adjustment test', *Journal of Marriage and the Family* 36: 57–63.

Knox, D. (1971) *Marriage Happiness*, Champaign, Ill.: Research Press.

Levenson, R. and Gottman, J. (1985) 'Physiological and affective predictors of change in relationship satisfaction', *Journal of Personality and Social Psychology* 49: 85–94.

Locke, H. and Wallace, K. (1959) 'Short marital adjustment and prediction tests: their reliability and validity', *Marriage and Family Living* 21: 251–5.

Navran, L. (1967) 'Communication and adjustment in marriage', *Family Process* 6: 173–84.

O'Leary, K. and Arias, I. (1987) 'Marital assessment in clinical practice', in K. A. O'Leary (ed.) *Assessment of Marital Discord*, NJ: Lawrence Erlbaum.

O'Leary, K., Fincham, F. and Turkewitz, H. (1983) 'Assessment of positive feelings towards spouse', *Journal of Consulting and Clinical Psychology* 51: 949–51.

Pallazzoli, M., Bascolo, L., Cecchin, G. and Prata, G. (1980) 'Hypothesising circularity and neutrality', *Family Process* 19: 3–12.

Rust, J., Bennun, I., Crowe, M. and Golombok, S. (1990) 'The GRIMS: psychometric instrument for the assessment of marital discord', *Journal of Family Therapy* 12: 45–57.

Schaefer, M. and Olson, D. (1981) 'Assessing intimacy. the P.A.I.R. inventory', *Journal of Marital and Family Therapy* 1: 47–60.

Shapiro, M. (1961) 'A method of measuring psychological change specific to the individual psychiatric patient', *British Journal of Medical Psychology* 34: 151–55.

Spanier, G. (1976) 'Measuring dyadic adjustment: new scales for assessing the quality of marriage and similar dyads', *Journal of Marriage and the Family* 38: 15–28.

Stuart, R. and Stuart, F. (1973) *Marital Pre-Counselling Inventory*, Champaign, Ill.: Research Press.

Vincent, J. and Carter, A. (1987) 'Family assessment: practical and methodological considerations', in K. A. O'Leary (ed.) *Assessment of Marital Discord*, NJ: Lawrence Erlbaum.

Weiss, R. and Cerreto, M. (1980) 'The marital status inventory: development of a measure of dissolution potential', *The American Journal of Family Therapy* 8: 80–5.

Weiss, R. and Margolin, G. (1977) 'Assessment of marital conflict and accord', in A. Ciminero, K. Calhoun and H. Adams (eds) *Handbook of Behavioural Assessment*, Chichester: Wiley.

Weiss, R., Hops, H. and Paterson, G. (1973) 'A framework for conceptualising marital conflict, technology for altering it, some data for evaluating it', in L. Hammerlynch,

L. Handy and E. Mash (eds) *Behaviour Change: Methodology Concepts and Practice*, Champaign, Ill.: Research Press.

Woodward, C., Santa-Barbara, J., Leven, S. and Epstein, N. (1978) 'The role of goal attainment scaling in evaluating family therapy outcome', *American Journal of Orthopsychiatry* 48: 464–76.

Zajonc, R. (1980) 'Cognition and social cognition: A historical perspective', in L. Festinger (ed.) *Retrospections on Social Psychology*, Oxford: Oxford University Press.

Chapter 14

Marital conflict

Treatment

Ian Bennun

INTRODUCTION

A provocative critique of marital therapy some two decades ago suggested that
therapists were treating marital problems without the required conceptual clarity
(Manus, 1966). There was at the time a psychoanalytic perspective on marriage
and marital conflict which was unchallenged by other clinicians (Dicks, 1967;
Mittlemann, 1944). As psychoanalytic thinking was already at an advanced stage
in both practice and theory, it is not altogether surprising that early marital
intervention strategies had developed from psychoanalytic and object-relations
theory. A further obstacle to the development of a theory of marital relationships
was the idea that marital therapy was an element (or sub-system) within family
therapy. It was argued that the marital relationship within a family system was
not a conceptual unit and that the focus only on dyads ignored the structure in
which they were embedded. As such, the conceptual and technical emphasis on
marital dyads was considered a hindrance to useful theory building (Haley,
1984).

In some respects, this debate continues at present, yet there now seems to be
an acceptance that a key stage in the developmental cycle of families is the
emergence of the adult twosome. The development of an intimate relationship
which then, other things being equal, evolves into a two-generation system, is a
necessary element in understanding family theory. Over the last two decades,
alternative models of marital therapy have been generated. Theory and research
in some of these is as sophisticated as the early psychoanalytic writings.
Empirically they have also shown to be clinically effective.

Recent advances in marital intervention have identified that differentiating
between models of therapy, while necessary, has led to considering whether
couples and families can be effectively utilised in the treatment of specific
disorders (see Bennun, 1988a). Further, there is the evidence to suggest that
marital therapy can be effective even if one partner is reluctant to attend. This
chapter will examine these issues by considering some models of marital therapy.
It will also consider some new developments, particularly unilateral marital
therapy, and note the use of dyads in the treatment of specific disorders.

There are a variety of agencies providing treatment for distressed couples. In addition to Health Service provision, others include RELATE (formerly the National Marriage Guidance Council), the Catholic Marriage Advisory Council and the Jewish Marriage Council. Health Service provision may be offered by a number of departments (Psychotherapy, Family Therapy, Mental Health) some of which will include clinical psychologists. However, as most of the referrals originate from general practitioners, these rates of referral may alter as a result of the NHS reforms and the development of general practitioner fundholding. The prevalence of marital problems is high, and access to services may become more difficult even though there is recognition at government level for the provision of these services for couples and families. One obvious risk will be greater reliance on private practitioners and charitable organisations who will levy charges.

RECENT DEVELOPMENTS IN BEHAVIOURAL MARITAL THERAPY

Behavioural marital therapy has generally been the clinical application of social learning and behaviour exchange principles to the treatment of marital discord. This approach has comprised three basic components, each of which has been empirically validated both separately and in combination. The behavioural formulation of marriage and marital distress views marital disharmony as being characterised by lower rates of behavioural exchange and problem-solving skills and higher rates of conflict and negative reciprocity. It is also characterised by poor communication skills and lower rates of shared recreational activities.

The early behavioural interventions included communication training to improve deficits in verbal and non-verbal interactions, teaching problem-solving skills as a systematic form of negotiating conflictual issues and contingency contracting to achieve a balance in the reciprocation of constructive dyadic behaviours. This approach incorporated the functional analytic method, which focused on the topography of conflict in terms of causal factors, behavioural conflict and maintenance mechanisms (i.e. antecedents and consequences). The most expansive theoretical development within behavioural marital therapy has been the recognition and inclusion of cognitive and perceptual processes as determinants of marital interaction. These cognitive and perceptual processes are seen as mediators within marital satisfaction–distress. The mediational model considers the role of affect and cognition in the development of dysfunctional marital processes (Levenson and Gottman, 1985), acknowledging the existing research on the role of causal attributions in producing, maintaining and exacerbating marital distress.

The cognitive model of marital distress includes *perceptions* about what events occur: *attributions* about why they occur: *expectancies* of what will occur: *assumptions* about the nature of events; and *beliefs/standards* about how things should be. These are all cognitive phenomena about the way information-processing occurs and, in the context of dyadic relationships, are active in the cognitive assessment and treatment of marital distress (Baucom and Epstein, 1989).

Including cognitive interventions within behavioural treatments enables the clinician to modify those cognitive phenomena that distort spouses' experiences of their interactions, that exacerbate their distress about their marriage, and induce them to interact in ways detrimental to their general well-being. In order to achieve this, each element listed above should be addressed in turn within the overall context of the couple's relationship.

Partners develop particular *perceptions* about events which may or may not reflect reality. The way these perceptions develop should be explored in order to assess whether all the relevant information underlying the perceptions is available, valid and complete. If a partner experiences criticism as rejection, it would be necessary to enquire whether the criticism is intended to convey rejection or whether it is just experienced as such. Often, partners are selective in their perceptions and tend to ignore factors or evidence which is contrary to their assumptions about the events they observe.

Attributions can be introduced into treatment by seeking the couple's explanation/ understanding of the events and factors that account for their difficulties. The causal attributions can be global–specific, stable–unstable, originate from self–partner, and include blame–intent. Attributing a partner's behaviour as global and stable would involve over-generalising with a view to being selective in ignoring or discounting behaviours or gestures that disconfirm the attribution. Within the therapeutic dialogue, it would be necessary to explore attributions and modify the mechanisms that are active in maintaining the chosen explanation; for example, arbitrary inference, over-generalisation, automatic thoughts about the partner and relationship.

Within the context of treatment, it is important to distinguish between broad beliefs that individuals hold about what will occur within their marriage and specific *expectancies* which they have about their relationship. Expectancies involve probabilities that certain events will occur. These are usually adaptive in that they produce the expected or desired outcome based on past experiences. Clinically, it is equally important to explore the content of the expectancy as well as its formation. It is likely that negative expectancies are the subject of cognitive distortions. A partner will predict a particular behavioural sequence (nagging, hostility) based on dysfunctional assumptions of the rules governing previous interactions. For example, one partner may hold the following expectation, which will determine her behaviour: 'He always behaves like that, and if I raise the issue, then I know he will be hostile'.

Assumptions determine how individuals develop ideas about how particular characteristics of people and relationships are associated. These assumptions can include automatic thoughts and the loose connections that couples make about the 'data' available to them. When exploring sexual relationships within marital therapy, couples often consider their difficulties as unique to them, assuming that they are atypical and alone in their difficulty. It would be necessary to correct this distortion and enquire about the basis on which their assumption is made.

Finally, *beliefs and standards* about relationships need to be examined, as they often produce information based on the experiences of others (friends, relatives) or on custom (religious beliefs). Couples often enter therapy recognising (or complaining about) the discrepancy between their relationship and their basic philosophies about the nature of satisfactory marriages. In discussion, spouses are less likely to see their own standards as unrealistic than to see those of their partner as extreme and problematic.

These cognitive components have augmented behavioural marital therapy and have enabled the approach to consider areas previously ignored. Behavioural marital therapy has been replaced by a social–learning–cognitive perspective (Jacobson and Holtzworth-Munroe, 1986; Holtzworth-Munroe and Jacobson, 1991), which has been a clinical development within the treatment of distressed marriages.

SYSTEMS THEORY APPROACHES

Most marital and family therapy approaches draw on systems theory in both formulating hypotheses about distress and planning interventions (Bennun, 1988b). Systemic therapists invariably construct a map defining the organisation, roles and rules of the family and couples they treat. It is possible to list some of the systemic characteristics of couple and family relationships as follows:

1 Families and couples, like other social groups, are systems having properties which are more than the sum of their attributes or their parts.
2 The family system comprises sub-systems which together constitute the relationships within the family. The marital couple is one such sub-system.
3 Each system and sub-system has a set of boundaries differentiating them from other systems and sub-systems. The boundaries define the flow of communication and feedback within the organisation and the individuation of each member.
4 Communication within the system and between the constituent parts is important in contributing to the system's overall functioning.
5 The family and couple stand in relation to a supra-system which represents the external environment within which it operates.
6 Circular rather than linear models of causality apply in understanding the genesis and maintenance of family and couple problems.
7 Any tendency of the system to move away from a steady state of functioning (equilibrium) is corrected through negative feedback; changes in the system's functioning (as opposed to stability) are achieved through positive feedback.

Clinical approaches derived from a systems perspective incorporate these systemic principles but emphasise some aspects more than others. For example, some approaches focus more on the structure of the system and intervene by attempting to reorganise boundaries, hierarchies or power relationships. Others may deliberately attempt to challenge the equilibrium/homeostasis through the introduction of rituals or strategies to change ongoing patterns of interaction. To examine all the approaches is beyond the scope of this chapter, so just two will be introduced by way of illustration.

STRUCTURAL AND STRATEGIC THERAPIES

Both structural and strategic therapists view marriage as a relatively stable interactional system. Considering marital relationships as systems implies that the behaviour of the marital dyad is governed by the state of each partner individually, the feedback between them, and the impact of the external environment (for example, children). The dyad is essentially goal-oriented, attempting to satisfy the needs of each partner. These needs are based on the evolving life cycle (Carter and McGoldrick, 1989) and the developmental cycles of each partner (Bennun, 1991).

Structural and strategic therapies place greater importance on the current marital context than on a historical perspective (c.f. psychoanalytic models). Symptoms are considered within a developmental context as conflicts or manifestations of the evolving life cycle (see Chapter 13). When seen in this way, marital distress is maintained by the marital system and in order to relieve the distress, the system requires reorganisation. Structural approaches in particular study the transactions between participants, paying specific attention to what couples do to, and for, each other as well as their emotional needs. Treatment is usually active and directive with the distinction between assessment/diagnosis and intervention being deliberately unclear. The approach is a pragmatic one, considering strategies or organisational patterns/changes as the medium for intervention.

Specific notions of power, boundaries, rules and interactional styles have been incorporated from systems theory. Rigid boundaries, either between partners or between the couple and the external environment, block the flow of information and feedback and can prevent contact with outside influences. Boundaries can also define rules governing who participates in the system functioning and determine how their influence can be integrated within the whole. Closely related are concepts of enmeshment and disengagement which refer to interactional styles. Enmeshment suggests little separateness or autonomy, with each spouse talking, thinking and reacting for the other. At the other end of the continuum, disengaged couples are characterised by minimal connectedness, reduced interaction and little support to one another in times of crisis. Alliances and coalitions within the dyad are important in understanding its functioning. Clinically, each partner is involved in external alliances and coalitions (work colleagues, extended family) or may implicitly appeal to the therapist to join in a marital system triangle (therapist–partner coalition).

The goal of structural therapy is to restructure the system so as to permit it to deal competently with those life tasks that are most salient at the particular time. Means towards achieving this goal include examining the power relationships within the dyad, and enabling the participants separately and the couple together to interact with each other through improved styles of communication, as well as examining the rules which have developed that determine their behaviour and responses. The model of therapy that has developed from this approach emphasises carefully planned action on the therapist's part towards achieving these specific goals. Having established a working therapeutic alliance, the therapist will initially join with the couple, accepting their organisational style in order to begin altering it. Failing to join effectively can prevent the therapist from establishing the necessary influence to become a trusted change agent.

A clinical illustration of this approach is described by Palazzoli *et al.* (1978) in their application of the 'odd and even day ritual'. A couple requesting therapy reported that virtually every day they had disagreements, some of which were trivial, some others more serious. The information gathered in the assessments led the therapist to a formulation that the rows and disagreements represented the couple's attempt to negotiate the power relationship between them. A 'rule' that appeared to exist within their relationship is that trying to exert power and dominance over each other was more important than taking care of one another. The information was then used to develop an intervention which addressed the dyadic structure as well as the processes that maintained the conflict. By joining with the couple and establishing a therapeutic alliance, the therapist gained a perspective of the nature and function of the conflictual interactions. The intervention was then used as a way of addressing both the power struggle and those factors maintaining it once the row had commenced. Using this ritual, it was suggested to the couple that on Mondays, Wednesdays and Fridays, the husband had responsibility for ensuring that his wife 'is well cared for' and on the other days of the week, the wife assumed that responsibility. 'Care' was defined as safeguarding against emotional upsets as well as doing something concrete for the partner. The intervention tested the couple's motivation and compliance and gave them the opportunity to interact differently when the setting required it.

If the formulation is valid, the therapist has the opportunity of addressing explicitly how the couple struggle with power and dominance within their relationship. The theoretical premises behind this particular intervention aims to detect quickly the rule or rules which generate and maintain the problematic behaviour and to devise interventions or prescriptions (rather than interpretations) aimed at altering the rules which perpetuate the dysfunction.

Todd (1986) has listed a number of assumptions of the approach as a useful therapeutic guide. At the outset, the primary therapeutic role is to help the couple find new ways of behaving towards each other. Insight is not necessary in producing behavioural change; rather, relabelling or redefining the problem with a new focus is deemed a more potent mechanism of change. Behavioural change can only be achieved with the active participation of the therapist. It does not need to address behavioural deficits but rather strategies for change. The therapist should work towards creating a new context for using constructive new skills and encourage the partners to implement these. Symptoms are seen as serving an adaptive function, yet these are at the expense of enabling the couple to adapt to change in circumstances. Finally, the therapist needs to help the couple find new adaptive solutions without the need to resort to symptomatic behaviour. (For a more comprehensive discussion of the approaches, see Calapinto, 1991; Madanes, 1991; Minuchin, 1974; Stanton, 1981.)

UNILATERAL MARITAL THERAPY

The conjoint interview is a distinctive feature of contemporary marital therapy. Both partners attend together and are seen by either one or two therapists. Despite the controversies surrounding individual treatment for relationship problems, treating just one partner has always been recognised as one form of marital therapy and indeed, couples have sometimes requested this as a treatment of choice (Fibush, 1957). Nadelson (1978) has suggested that partners who find conjoint sessions competitive, or are too immature to tolerate the stress of conjoint sessions, should be seen individually. In some instances the presenting problem may indicate individual rather than conjoint work, such as difficulties with dependence–independence, problems sustaining two-person relationships, violence or jealousy (Bennun, 1991).

One of the consequences of the application of systems theory is the apparent loss of the individual within systemic thinking. Walter (1989) has argued that systemic therapies need to consider how to integrate individual models of psychological functioning into systemic work and recognise the indications for individual treatment when appropriate.

Before briefly examining some of the models of unilateral therapy that have developed in response to clinical need it is worth considering how this approach can be used more generally in clinical practice. Within the couple context, treating just one partner should always remain an option. However, the therapist must be clear in distinguishing intrapsychic from interpersonal processes (Walter, 1989). These two processes should be thought of as coexisting rather than reflecting conflicting realities. Systemic enthusiasm should be tempered by remaining cognisant of individual dynamics and how these interact with interpersonal processes.

Apart from some clinical problems responding more favourably to unilateral therapy, seeing one partner alone can be used in preparation for later conjoint sessions. Therapists should respond favourably to a partner's request to be seen alone, although the nature and meaning of the request should be explored. A case can be made for this approach when particular family systems have undermined a person's individual resources. The role of mother, father, husband or wife implies a dualism, and after years of performing these dual roles the person may be left with an impaired sense of self which could be repeated or re-enacted within a conjoint setting. Another consideration for using these approaches is when an identifiable problem is both systemic and intrapsychic in nature. Individual therapy would then have two foci: one to explore individual psychological processes and one exploring how the system maintains them.

Szapocznik *et al.* (1983; 1984) have developed and evaluated their one-person method of family therapy. Both structural and strategic theory has informed their approach, with the intervention itself being brief, usually around ten sessions. The goal of one-person family therapy is to bring about changes in repetitive dysfunctional sequences by using the most important family member as the agent of change. In a marital context, the therapist could decide which partner was the most appropriate to engage in treatment. During sessions with the one person, the therapist monitors, through feedback, the marital interactional structure, and then initiates change through the one attending partner.

As the approach relies on the basic systemic premise that a change in one element of the system will necessitate change in others, the therapist can influence the dyadic structure through the interventions with the attending partner. The therapist may instruct the partner to behave in new ways or explore their particular perceptual processes as a means of reorganising the rules and structure that determine the couple's functioning.

With just one partner attending, the therapist would need to explore how this individual has internalised or incorporated his or her complementary role within the dyadic interactions. Although there is no one present in the session to confirm or disconfirm his or her perceived reality, it is a therapeutic task to maintain a reality-oriented position within treatment, possibly using some of the methods outlined previously describing the cognitive approach.

Having identified the interactions and processes operating within the dyad from the attender's point of view, the therapist then attempts to construct the non-attender's view, so developing the complementary map describing the total dyadic process. Having done so, the intervention is directed through altering the one person's reported behaviour or perceptions.

The empirical outcome data from this clinical research group are encouraging, although it is difficult to ascertain the mechanisms through which change is achieved. As in many intervention packages, the relative efficacy of component parts remains unclear.

INDIVIDUAL COUPLE THERAPY

A different model using one partner for the treatment of marital distress has been developed by Bennun (1984; 1991) in response to the increasing number of partners requesting marital therapy yet having to attend without their spouse. Some reluctance to developing this approach has been expressed on the basis that the therapist should always attempt to convene a conjoint session. However, as described above, there may be circumstances where seeing one partner is appropriate. Other reservations about this approach include gaining a biased account of the existing problem, becoming involved in marital secrets and the therapeutic relationship being used as a competing relationship. In developing this unilateral model, these concerns have been taken into account, although the possibility of at least a conjoint assessment/initial interview is to be recommended.

Three elements best describe the approach: these include a dyadic focus, giving attention to the non-attending partner and exploring contributions to conflict. These are considered simultaneously in each session and are made explicit during treatment.

The *dyadic focus* stresses the balance to be maintained between individual and dyadic processes. Relationships fulfil a range of psychological and physical needs for both the individual and couple. When these are unfulfilled, the ensuing distress affects the individual, their partner and the relationship. The dyadic focus guides the therapist and the attending partner in looking at relationship issues primarily, rather than individual psychological problems. Should these arise from within the relationship, then they are obviously explored in the appropriate way.

An essential principle of the dyadic focus is the way in which problems are defined and formulated. If the therapist is working towards the resolution of a specific problem, the treatment needs to be formulated in terms that include both partners. For example, in the case of an agoraphobic woman, the dyadic focus would necessitate the problem being understood as both fear and her partner's inability to provide her with the appropriate reassurance to leave the house. The exact formulation will obviously develop from a full clinical assessment.

The second element, *the non-attending partner*, aims to direct the therapist in gaining the cooperation and involvement of this partner. The attending partner must be encouraged to give his or her spouse an account of the session, preferably on the same day that it takes place. It is useful to negotiate this at the outset of treatment. If home assignments are set, then it is important to ensure that the non-attending partner participates where appropriate. The therapist must also encourage feedback from the non-treated partner about the tasks or topics that he or she may wish to share. This highlights the value and importance of the conjoint assessment session which can be used flexibly and creatively without insisting that a reluctant partner necessarily attends each subsequent session. By giving 'permission' not to attend, this may decrease resistance and improve compliance with the treatment regime.

Thirdly, both partners' *contribution to conflict* must be acknowledged. Therapists can easily step out of their neutral role and join with one partner in a treatment coalition. A pivotal factor in working with one partner is adherence to the systemic assumption that conflict is the result of interaction and feedback and that one partner is not solely to blame. The paradigm acknowledges that both partners contribute to conflict and both are responsible for its resolution. Yet this must be viewed pragmatically; episodes of marital violence, physical abuse, and the like need not be viewed as both partners having equal responsibility for these occurrences. However, maintaining this view of conflict brings together all three elements and allows the therapist to maintain the balance between individual and interpersonal processes.

These three elements of the approach are illustrated in the treatment of a woman who presented with low self-esteem and a sense of personal inadequacy which undermined the stability of her marriage. The problem as described was reformulated with a dyadic focus, acknowledging the source of these feelings (her previous relationship with her father) and her husband's apparent inability to help her alter her self-perception. The reformulation of the presenting problem thus included her husband as not being able to help her in overcoming these distressing feelings. The second element involved the couple having detailed conversations, sharing their respective reasons as to why and how they thought the problem had developed. The therapist role-played the partner's role with the woman and showed her how to challenge some of the assumptions she had about herself, particularly in relation to her father, and how these had generalised to her husband. Thirdly, both partners owned the difficulty without it being seen as 'her problem'. From the role-play, the wife was able to teach her husband to challenge her own beliefs as well as demonstrate to her that she was not as inadequate as she believed and that he did not necessarily see her in this way.

This particular model has been evaluated and has been shown to be as effective as both conjoint marital therapy and couples groups. While there are theoretical arguments against these unilateral methods, the outcome data does not support these doubts.

OTHER APPLICATIONS OF COUPLES THERAPY

The family or couple unit essentially carries the initial burden of a developing psychological problem in one of its members. As already noted in other sections of this chapter, the reciprocal effects between individuals with the identified problem and their family/spouse can lead to either an exacerbation or a containing of the problem. Although there is a wealth of theoretical coverage on the issue, this has not necessarily informed clinical practice (Kuipers and Bebbington, 1985).

There are three lines of thinking on the use of partner in treating adult psychological problems (see Bennun, 1988a). Firstly, partners can be included in treatment in order to enhance treatment compliance, given that poor treatment outcomes from non-compliance do account for a significant proportion of clinical cases. Secondly, Hafner et al. (1983) have developed spouse-aided therapy where the spouse plays a direct and active role in the treatment process as a co-therapeutic agent. These authors have also viewed this approach as 'marriage resource therapy'. Finally, marital therapy has been used when it is considered that marital problems are being manifest through psychiatric or psychological problems, such as agoraphobia (Hafner, 1986), depression (Jacobson and Holtzworth-Munroe, 1986), drinking problems (O'Farrell, 1986), jealousy (Im et al., 1983) and eating disorders (Foster, 1986).

Couples therapy has also been used with specific populations and social groupings, such as unmarried couples, remarried couples, cross-cultural marriages, gay and lesbian couples (see Dryden, 1985; Hooper and Dryden, 1991; Jacobson and Gurman, 1986). A review of ethical issues in marital therapy has been usefully discussed by Margolin, (1982, 1986).

Marital therapy developed as an intervention to help couples in distressed marriages. This chapter has attempted to illustrate that relationship issues can extend beyond 'marriage counselling' and may be useful in planning treatment where using the partner may improve outcome. There needs to be some clarity when seeing couples together: inviting the partner to attend should not necessarily convey marital distress, but clinical experience suggests the presence of dysfunctional dyadic issues when they are not always expected.

REFERENCES

Baucom, D. and Epstein, N. (1989) *Cognitive-Behavioral Marital Therapy*, New York: Brunner/Mazel.

Bennun, I. (1984) 'Marital therapy with one spouse', in: K. Hahlweg and N. Jacobson (eds) *Marital Interaction: Analysis and Modification*, New York: Guilford Press.

Bennun, I. (1988a) 'Involving spouses and families in the treatment of adult psychological problems', in F. N. Watts (ed.) *New Developments in Clinical Psychology. Vol. 2*, Chichester: Wiley.

Bennun, I. (1988b) 'Systems theory and family therapy', in E. Street and W. Dryden (eds) *Family Therapy in Britain*, Milton Keynes: Open University Press.

Bennun, I. (1991) 'Working with the individual from the couple', in D. Hooper and W. Dryden (eds) *Couple Therapy: A Handbook*, Milton Keynes: Open University Press.

Calapinto, J. (1991) 'Structural family therapy', in A. Gurman and D. Kniskern (eds) *Handbook of Family Therapy. Vol. 2*, New York: Brunner/Muzel.

Carter, B. and McGoldrick, M. (1989) *The Changing Family Life Cycle: Framework for Family Therapy*, London: Aylen and Bacon.

Dicks, H. (1967) *Marital Tensions*, London: Tavistock.

Dryden, W. (1985) *Marital Therapy in Britain. Vol. 2*, Milton Keynes: Open University Press.

Fibush, E. (1957) 'The evaluation of marital interaction in the treatment of one partner', *Social Casework* 38: 303–7.

Foster, S. (1986) 'Marital treatment of eating disorders', in N. Jacobson and A. Gurman (eds) *Clinical Handbook of Marital Therapy*, New York: Guilford Press.

Hafner, R. (1986) 'Marital therapy for agoraphobia', in N. Jacobson and A. Gurman (eds) *Clinical Handbook of Marital Therapy*, New York: Guilford Press.

Hafner, R., Badenoch, A., Fisher, J. and Swift, H. (1983) 'Spouse aided versus individual therapy in persisting psychiatric disorders: a systematic comparison', *Family Process* 22: 385–99.

Haley, J. (1984) 'Marriage or family therapy?' *American Journal of Family Therapy* 12: 3–14.

Holtzworth-Munroe, A. and Jacobson, N. (1991) 'Behavioural marital therapy', in A. Gurman and D. Kniskern (eds) *Handbook of Family Therapy. Vol. 2*, New York: Brunner/Muzel.

Hooper, D. and Dryden, W. (1991) *Couple Therapy: A Handbook*, Milton Keynes: Open University Press.

Im, W., Wilner, R. and Breit, M. (1983) 'Jealousy: interventions in couples therapy', *Family Process* 22: 211–19.

Jacobson, N. and Gurman, A. (1986) *Clinical Handbook of Marital Therapy*, New York: Guilford Press.

Jacobson, N. and Holtzworth-Munroe, A. (1986) 'Marital therapy: a social learning-cognitive perspective', in N. Jacobson and A. Gurman (eds) *Clinical Handbook of Marital Therapy*, New York: Guilford Press.

Jacobson, N., Dobson, K., Fruzzetti, A., Schmaling, K. and Salinsky, S. (1991) 'Marital therapy as a treatment for depression', *Journal of Consulting and Clinical Psychology* 59: 547–57.

Kuipers, L. and Bebbington, P. (1985) 'Relatives as a resource in the management of functional illness', *British Journal of Psychiatry* 147: 465–70.

Levenson, R. and Gottman, J. (1985) 'Physiological and affective predictors of change in relationship satisfaction', *Journal of Personality and Social Psychology* 49: 85–94.

Madanes, C. (1981) *Strategic Family Therapy*, San Francisco: Jossey Bass.

Madanes, C. (1991) 'Strategic Family Therapy', in A. Gurman and D. Kniskern (eds) *Handbook of Family Therapy. Vol. 2*, New York: Brunner/Muzel.

Manus, G. (1966) 'Marriage counselling: a technique in search of a theory', *Journal of Marriage and the Family* 28: 449–53.

Margolin, G. (1982) 'Ethical and legal considerations in marital and family therapy', *American Psychologist* 37: 788–801.

Margolin, S. (1986) 'Ethical issues in marital therapy', in N. Jacobson and A. Gurman (eds) *Clinical Handbook of Marital Therapy*, New York: Guilford Press.

Minuchin, S. (1974) *Families and Family Therapy*, Cambridge Mass.: Harvard University Press.

Mittlemann, B. (1944) 'Complementary neurotic reactions in intimate relationships', *Psychoanalytic Quarterly* 13: 479–91.

Nadelson, C. (1978) 'Marital therapy from a psychoanalytic perspective', in T. Paolino and B. McCrady (eds) *Marriage and Marital Therapy*, New York: Brunner/Muzel.

O'Farrell, T. (1986) 'Marital therapy in the treatment of alcoholism', in N. Jacobson and A. Gurman (eds) *Clinical Handbook of Marital Therapy*, New York: Guilford Press.

Palazzoli, M., Boscolo, L., Cecchin, G. and Prata, G. (1978) 'A ritualized prescription in family therapy: odd days and even days', *Journal of Marriage and Family Counselling* 4: 3–9.

Stanton, M. (1981) 'Marital therapy from a structural-strategic viewpoint', in G. Sholevar (ed.) *The Handbook of Marriage and Marital Therapy*, Philadelphia: MTP Press.

Szapocznik, J., Kurtines, W., Foote, F., Peres-Vidal, A. and Hervis, O. (1983) 'Conjoint versus one person family therapy: Some evidence for the effectiveness of conducting family therapy through one person', *Journal of Consulting and Clinical Psychology* 51: 889–99.

Szapocznik, J., Kurtines, W. and Spencer, F. (1984) 'One-person family therapy', in W. O'Conner and B. Lubin (eds) *Ecological Approaches to Clinical and Community Psychology*, New York: Wiley.

Todd, T. (1986) 'Structural-strategic marital therapy', in N. Jacobson and A. Gurman (eds) *Clinical Handbook of Marital Therapy*, New York: Guilford Press.

Walter, J. (1989) 'Not individual, not family', *Journal of Strategic and Systemic Therapies* 8: 70–7.

Chapter 15

Schizophrenia
Investigation

David R. Hemsley

HISTORICAL INTRODUCTION TO THE CONCEPT OF SCHIZOPHRENIA

The major step towards distinguishing from the other psychotic conditions that which is today referred to as schizophrenia, was taken by Kraepelin (1896). He brought together the previously employed terms of paranoia, catatonia and hebephrenia under the general term 'dementia praecox'. The fundamental features of this group, as implied by the name, were an early onset (praecox) and a progressive intellectual deterioration. Symptoms noted by Kraepelin included hallucinations (especially in the auditory modality), delusions, thought-broadcasting and influencing, poor judgement, disturbances of emotional expression, bizarre and stereotyped behaviour, and negativism. Thus, in defining the disorder, both course and symptoms were employed, although the former was often emphasised.

In contrast, Bleuler (1911/1950) rejected Kraepelin's view of a necessary progressive deterioration and preferred to call dementia praecox 'schizophrenia', a name that reflected his view that there is a loss of harmony between various groups of mental functions. Noting the wide variety of disturbances displayed, he sought to understand the symptoms of schizophrenia in terms of their basic components. Thus he wrote, 'The fundamental symptoms consist of disturbances of association and affectivity, and the inclination to divorce oneself from reality' (Bleuler 1950: 14). These are often referred to as the four As: association, affect, autism and ambivalence. In contrast, such symptoms as hallucinations and delusions were seen as accessory symptoms: their presence varied from individual to individual. Bleuler made a further distinction – between primary and secondary symptoms. The former are those resulting directly from the organic disease that he presumed to underlie schizophrenia – the disruption of the associative threads linking not only words but thoughts was considered a primary symptom. In contrast, secondary symptoms reflect the normal psychic processes and are attempts at adaptation to the primary disturbance. Much psychological research (e.g. Hemsley, 1977) has also viewed aspects of schizophrenic symptomatology as resulting from the interaction of the cognitively impaired individual with his environment. This will be considered in a subsequent section.

THE DIAGNOSTIC PROCESS

It is apparent that various kinds of information may be employed in reaching a diagnosis, the major categories being current behaviour, history and course, and aetiology. As yet there is minimal use of the last of these in the field of psychopathology. Although it is not the concern of the present chapter, it is perhaps appropriate that the author makes explicit his own views as to the aetiology of schizophrenia. Broadly, he supports Zubin and Spring's (1977) vulnerability-stressor model for the disorder, vulnerability resulting from genetic inheritance and acquired propensities.

A wide range of diagnostic systems have been employed, some developed purely as research tools, others for clinical use. These have been summarised by Landmark (1982). Following Bleuler, many have given prominence to presenting symptoms, rather than the course of the disorder, for example the Research Diagnostic Criteria (RDC) of Spitzer and Endicott (1978). Here, the diagnostic terms are well defined, and precise information is presented indicating what is required for a diagnosis of schizophrenia. The reliability of diagnosis of schizophrenia has been subject to considerable criticism, a review of studies (Spitzer and Fleiss, 1974) concluding that, although schizophrenia could be diagnosed with some degree of reliability, there remained considerable room for improvement. This has been achieved by the use of systematic and structured interviews to cover all aspects of a patient's current mental status, among the best known being the Present State Examination (PSE) (Wing *et al.*, 1974).

The above endeavours presuppose that the resultant groupings possess utility at either a theoretical or practical level. The present author would follow Neale and Oltmanns (1980) in viewing schizophrenia as an open scientific construct capable of being partially defined via a series of measurement operations. The definition of the construct involves the specification of the lawful relationships into which it enters. The importance of specific symptoms is thus dependent on their relationship to other factors, and they can be seen as mediated by a range of biological and psychological processes.

However, many would now argue that it is preferable to assess the correlates and properties of discrete aspects of psychotic behaviour and experience (see Bentall, 1992), rather than be concerned with the schizophrenia syndrome. Although this approach has many advantages, it cannot be assumed that a given abnormality has equivalent implications regardless of the presence or absence of accompanying disturbances. That is, we must allow for the possible importance of patterns of psychological dysfunction. At present these two approaches to research appear complementary.

Linked to the above is the question of whether the abnormal phenomena characteristic of schizophrenia are continuous or discontinuous with normality. This clearly has important implications for the assessment process.

Scales have been developed purporting to measure the predisposition to psychotic symptoms. Thus questionnaires have been constructed to assess non-clinical levels of abnormal experiences (Perceptual Aberration Scale; Chapman et al., 1978) and beliefs (Magical Ideation Scale; Eckblad and Chapman, 1983). Chapman and Chapman (1980) have also developed scales for rating, at interview, psychotic and psychotic-like experiences as continua. The type of experience at the high end of each continuum is a Schedule of Affective Disorders and Schizophrenia (SADS) psychotic symptom (Spitzer and Endicott, 1978). The other types of experience on each scale have a similar theme but are to varying degrees less deviant. Areas covered by the scales are transmission of own thoughts, passivity experiences, auditory hallucinations, thought withdrawal, other personally relevant aberrant beliefs and abnormal visual experiences. A longitudinal study employing these scales (Chapman and Chapman, 1988) indicated that in the three subjects developing clinical levels of psychosis, their earlier abnormal beliefs appeared continuous with the later delusions both in content and degree of deviancy.

The acceptance of a vulnerability-stressor model not only suggests the potential importance of identifying those with a long term predisposition to psychotic phenomena, but also those whose present temporary condition may alert the clinician to potential relapse. This will be considered below. It further highlights the need to assess those aspects of the environment which may increase the likelihood of disturbance, i.e. the potential stressors.

The reasons for psychological assessment in schizophrenia

Diagnosis or description?

Even if one accepts the utility of the diagnostic approach, the limitations of many early cognitive assessment procedures for diagnostic purposes have long been apparent (see Hemsley, 1976). Instead it is preferable to develop direct and reliable measures of those abnormalities considered important. Such assessments may clarify the psychological structure of a particular symptom. Thus Garety and Hemsley (1987) have emphasised the multi-dimensional nature of delusional beliefs, and it cannot be assumed that change on one dimension will be accompanied by equivalent alteration in others (Brett-Jones et al., 1987).

To monitor changes in functioning

A second rationale for psychological assessment of the schizophrenic patient is to monitor changes in functioning, whether they occur spontaneously or as a result of psychological or pharmacological intervention procedures. Ratings of gross clinical behaviour indicate the end product of complex determinants. More specific measures may permit an analysis of underlying change processes. For example, Depue et al. (1975) employed intellectual, associational and psychophysiological measures to monitor the differential rates of recovery in withdrawn and active schizophrenics, and Rosen et al. (1980) used time-sampled observations of objectively defined ward behaviour to explore changes occurring subsequent to medication. In considering the overall effects of intervention it is clearly important to distinguish a number of separate outcome systems. Thus symptoms, social functioning, employment and hospitalisation may show quite different patterns of change over time. Strauss and Carpenter (1972) provide a simple scale for the assessment of these four major aspects of outcome, and have demonstrated high inter-rater reliability.

Functional analysis

Assessment may also be carried out in an attempt to establish the determinants and maintaining factors of aspects of the schizophrenic disturbance, that is, to carry out a functional analysis. Thus Slade (1972) required a patient to complete a record of auditory hallucinations three times a day; he also rated his mood and noted environmental variables. Hallucinations were associated with states of high arousal, noisy crowded situations, and the patient not being engaged in conversation. This led to a subsequent treatment programme (see Chapter 16). Margo et al. (1981) were also able to demonstrate variations in reported hallucination as a result of manipulation of auditory input. More recently, Brett-Jones et al. assessed deluded subjects' responses to hypothetical contradictions and concluded that 'those subjects who ultimately entirely rejected their delusional beliefs dealt with hypothetical contradiction in a more rational way than those that did not' (Brett-Jones et al., 1987: 261).

Assessment of prodromal symptomatology

It is increasingly recognised that psychotic relapse is frequently preceded by a period during which a variety of psychological abnormalities may become apparent. Thus Subotnik and Nuechterlein concluded that, 'Even small elevations in odd thought content, unusual perceptual experiences, depression, somatic concern and guilt above the levels usually present for a given patient may presage psychotic relapse during the 6 to 8 weeks prior to its occurrence' (Subotnik and Nuechterlein, 1988: 405). The regular assessment of such disturbances, particularly during periods of stress or while medication is being reduced, may permit pharmacological and psychological intervention to avert psychotic relapse. For example, Herz et al. (1982) carried out assessments during drug withdrawal in a group of schizophrenic patients. Ten out of nineteen showed increases in symptomatology of a non-psychotic type, typical being sleep disturbances, agitation, anger, social withdrawal and impaired social relations.

The assessment of schizophrenic symptomatology

The detailed assessment of symptomatology may be achieved by trained interviewers using the Present State Examination (PSE; Wing *et al.*, 1974). The manual lists more than 500 questions designed to elicit information allowing the interviewer to rate 107 symptoms based on the patient's self-report. Delusions and hallucinations are covered in great detail. The recommended questions, such as, 'Do you ever seem to hear your own thoughts repeated or echoed?' may be followed up in order to specify the nature and degree of each symptom. These are rated on a scale from 0 (absent) to 2 (present in severe form). The PSE also allows the rating of patients' behaviour, affect and speech, and extensive definitions are provided for the symptoms. Problems with the PSE are the need for specific training and the fact that it is concerned solely with the current state of the patient. This is in contrast to the SADS (Spitzer and Endicott, 1978), another extensive structured interview, which, with trained raters, provides reliable information about both present and past mental status.

Such interviews are designed primarily to establish the presence or absence of categories of symptoms, to determine diagnosis. They provide relatively limited information concerning the severity or frequency of particular abnormalities. In contrast, general symptom rating scales, such as the Brief Psychiatric Rating Scale (BPRS) (Overall and Gorham, 1962) and the Manchester Scale (Krawiecka *et al.*, 1977), are better designed to assess change.

A frequently encountered distinction is between the 'positive' symptoms of schizophrenia, such as delusions, hallucinations and thought disorder, and 'negative' symptoms, such as flatness of affect, retardation, apathy, social withdrawal and poverty of speech. Schizophrenic patients most frequently show both positive and negative symptomatology (e.g. Guelfi *et al.*, 1989), and it is unclear whether the distinction represents: (a) two underlying and distinct disorders; (b) differing severity of the same disorder; (c) individual differences in reaction to the same disorder; (d) different stages of the same disorder; or a combination of (b), (c) and (d). A further complication is the suggestion (e.g. Liddle, 1987) that a third dimension of 'cognitive disorganisation' is required to explain the structure of schizophrenic symptomatology.

Despite these difficulties, scales for the separate assessment of positive and negative symptoms can be useful. The best known are those developed by Andreasen (1982; 1984), the Scale for the Assessment of Positive Symptoms (SAPS), and the Scale for the Assessment of Negative Symptoms (SANS). The latter, for example, provides detailed clinical descriptions of five global symptom groups: alogia, anhedonia–asociality, avolition–apathy, affective flattening, and attentional impairment, although the status of the last of these as a 'negative symptom' has been disputed. These are broken down into twenty-five observable behavioural components, which are rated on a six-point severity scale. Satisfactory reliability has been demonstrated.

All of the above make certain assumptions about the structure of an individual psychotic symptom. Thus it cannot be assumed that reported frequency, clarity and loudness of hallucinatory experiences will be closely related (see Margo *et al.*, 1981). Hustig and Hafner (1990) take this into account in their description of a self-report method for assessing auditory hallucinations. Subjects complete three times a day visual analogue scales dealing with the loudness, clarity, distress, and distractibility of the experiences. Adequate test-retest reliability is reported. Similarly it has become apparent that delusions are best conceptualised as multi-dimensional. The Personal Ideation Inventory (Rattenburg *et al.*, 1984) is a semi-structured interview yielding scores on the three hypothesised major dimensions of content, commitment and conviction. In contrast, Garety and Hemsley (1987) assessed eleven subjective belief characteristics employing a visual analogue technique. The Characteristics of Delusions Rating Scale measures the following dimensions: conviction, preoccupation, worry, unhappiness, reassurance seeking, interference, resistance, dismissibility, absurdity, self evidentness, and pervasiveness. A principal components analysis indicated four components: distress, belief strength, obtrusiveness, and concern. However, the potentially important dimension of 'bizarreness' is, inevitably, not covered by this self-report procedure.

Garety (1985) and Brett-Jones *et al.* (1987) have modified Shapiro's (1961) Personal Questionnaire technique to make assessments of delusional preoccupation and conviction sensitive to small changes of symptom intensity over time. Chadwick and Lowe (1990) have recently employed this in a cognitive-behavioural intervention study with delusional beliefs. The dimensions of preoccupation, conviction, and anxiety while thinking of the delusional beliefs, covaried in some subjects but not in others. Brett-Jones *et al.* (op. cit.) also argue for the potential utility of assessing patients' reactions to hypothetical contradiction, and the extent to which they are aware of actual occurrences contradictory to their belief. Both may have implications for cognitive-behavioural intervention (see Chapter 16).

It has long been apparent that symptoms of anxiety and depression are frequently observed preceding, during, and subsequent to a psychotic episode (see Giris, 1991). Their assessment and management may be crucial to successful social and occupational outcome. In assessing depression it is convenient to distinguish cognitive disturbances, such as the negative view of self, future and the world, from behavioural indices, such as apathy, withdrawal, retardation, and loss of interest. There are particular problems in assessing depression in schizophrenic patients: (1) it may be masked by more dramatic positive symptomatology; (2) it can be difficult to distinguish flat affect from depressed mood; (3) other negative symptoms, such as poverty of speech, may be mistaken for depression; (4) anti-psychotic medication may produce both motor and behavioural side effects which may be mistaken for depression. However, anti-psychotic medication frequently has a genuinely 'depressing' effect. Animal research suggests that reward and reinforcement mechanisms are mediated by dopamine. For example, self-stimulation is reduced by major tranquillizers even when levels of motor activity are controlled for. The issue of the depressogenic role of the major tranquillisers is receiving increasing attention (see Emerich and Sanberg, 1991).

A review of studies of suicide among schizophrenic patients concluded that the incidence was approximately 10 per cent (Miles, 1977) and a more recent report (Westermeyer *et al.*, 1991) produced a similar figure. The assessment of suicide risk is therefore of considerable importance. Roy (1982) suggests that the appearance of depressive symptoms is one of the most frequently identified risk factors, and Addington *et al.* (1990) have developed a depression rating scale for schizophrenics which attempts to deal with some of the problems described in the previous paragraph. It has also been claimed by Drake and Cotton that schizophrenics who committed suicide 'typically exhibited the psychological but not somatic symptoms' of depression (Drake and Cotton, 1986: 554). The frequent consequences of a schizophrenic illness, in terms of broken relationships and disruption of career plans make negative views of the future all too understandable. The assessment and modification of such cognitions is likely to become increasingly important.

The assessment of functioning of long-term psychiatric patients

Ward-behaviour rating scales have long been employed in the assessment of schizophrenic patients. Criteria for the selection of items vary widely, as Hall has noted. He argues that inclusion should be influenced by '(a) demonstrated association with response to medication or other types of treatment; (b) demonstrated association with long term status or follow up; (c) actual frequency of behaviour; (d) opinions of primary care personnel regarding effects of behaviour on ward, home, or community.' (Hall, 1977: 288). It is also pointed out that factors relevant to the general behaviour of chronic patients may not be so for more acute schizophrenics. In a subsequent publication Hall (1980) reviewed twenty-nine published ward rating scales, paying attention to details of the rating setting, the rating procedure and scale construction and evaluation. Unfortunately those shown to be useful for their stated purpose are often employed subsequently with different aims – a practice which amounts to vandalisation when there is no re-evaluation of their reliability, validity, and so on. Hall reviews the adequacy of scales according to the following minimal criteria:

1 Has the content of the scale been pre-selected on any rational basis?
2 Is the observation period specified on which ratings are to be based?
3 Are there any norms?
4 Has reliability been assessed?
5 Has validity been assessed?

He concluded that only four scales meet all five criteria, and that none of the scales reviewed provided anything approaching a manual for rater use. In addition, the use of such scales requires repeated monitoring if assessments are to be made over an extended period because of the decreases in inter-rater reliability that may occur when raters no longer believe that checks on accuracy are being made.

Baker and Hall (1983) subsequently developed the REHAB scale based on care staff observations during the preceding week. This results in a general behaviour score, based on sixteen items, and a deviant behaviour score, based on seven items. The former includes areas such as the quality of speech and level of interpersonal relationships, and the latter anti-social behaviours such as violence or verbal abusiveness. There are extensive long-stay patient norms, and the scales possess satisfactory reliability. The Social Behaviour Schedule (Wykes and Sturt 1986) also includes challenging and bizarre behaviours. However, it is completed on the basis of an interview with an informant concerning the patient's behaviour over the previous month, and ratings are made on the basis of severity or frequency.

Farrell and Mariotto (1982) have provided data on the concurrent validity of two rating scales with a pre-chronic in-patient population, predominantly schizophrenic. The scales employed were the Nurses' Observation Scale for In-patient Evaluation (NOSIE; Honigfeld and Klett, 1965) and the Psychotic In-patient Profile (PIP; Lorr and Vestre, 1969). Ratings were obtained from aides and professional observers, the latter also providing measures of behaviour on the Time Sample Behavioural Checklist (Power, 1974). Scores on the PIP and NOSIE showed fairly good convergent and discriminant validity across instruments and across different raters. Rating-scale measures of social interaction and withdrawal related strongly to observational measures of similar content; for psychotic behaviour, there was a moderately strong relationship to behavioural indices. For irritability and self-care, the relationship was less clear cut. The authors concluded that rating scales, while an important approach to assessment, may not provide completely comparable data to those resulting from the direct assessment of patients' behaviour on the ward.

Measures of frequency and duration of specified behaviours were among the most important assessment procedures in the major research project on the psychosocial treatment of chronic patients carried out by Paul and Lentz (1977). However, rating scales were also employed, including the NOSIE, and the in-patient scale of minimal functioning, a ward rating developed for assessing low-level functioning and troublesome behaviour in chronic populations (Paul *et al.*, 1976).

Cognitive assessment

Both Bleuler and Kraepelin indicated that cognitive disturbances are important mediators between overt schizophrenic symptoms and what they believed to be an underlying neurological defect, and there has been considerable psychological research on the topic of schizophrenic cognition; for a review, see Hemsley, 1988. Recent integrative models of the disorder (e.g. Gray *et al.*,

1991a,b; Hemsley, 1990; Hemsley *et al.*, 1993) emphasise the crucial role of perceptual/cognitive abnormalities in the emergence of psychotic symptoms. However, the measures employed have limited clinical utility at present. Instead, there is increasing awareness of the importance of residual cognitive deficits once optimal levels of medication have been achieved. For example, Saccuzzo and Braff (1981) have shown that slow information-processing is a relatively stable deficit in schizophrenic patients with a poor prognosis but that those with a good prognosis had a similar but reversible deficit. It is also of interest that both Cancro *et al.* (1971) and Zahn and Carpenter (1978) report significant relationships between simple reaction time and prognosis. This is reminiscent of earlier work indicating that psychomotor assessments may have value in predicting the subsequent work behaviour of schizophrenics.

More recently, Mueser *et al.* (1991) examined memory and symptomatology as predictors of social skill acquisition in patients participating in a social-skills training programme. Poor memory was related to pre-treatment social-skills impairments and slower rates of skill improvement in those with a diagnosis of schizophrenia, but not affective disorder. In contrast, levels of symptomatology were not consistently related to either measure. They conclude that cognitive deficits in schizophrenia are associated with impairments in social skill and may limit the rate of skill acquisition and clinical response.

The relevance of residual cognitive impairment to rehabilitation outcome has also been emphasised by Wykes and her colleagues. Indices of performance derived from a choice reaction time task were predictive of service use within a chronic psychiatric group, the majority of whom had a diagnosis of schizophrenia; patients with continuing cognitive difficulties were likely to remain in more supportive settings. In a series of regression analyses, cognitive indices added significantly to the variance accounted for by traditional prognostic measures (Wykes *et al.*, 1992). The relationship between cognitive impairment and service use was most marked for those with a diagnosis of schizophrenia, an instance of diagnosis acting as a 'moderator variable'. For those patients in the long-stay group, the distribution of reaction time scores was bi-modal and this measure was not related to levels of symptomatology. However, in a longitudinal study (Wykes *et al.*, 1990), reaction time measures predicted service use after three years. Those showing slower responses were less likely to move to more independent care during this period. The authors suggest the need for alternative rehabilitation strategies within this group.

Assessment of family atmosphere

As indicated previously, the acceptance of a vulnerability-stressor model for schizophrenic symptoms implies an important role for the assessment of environmental factors related to relapse. Among the best established is that linking relapse to the attitudes of key relatives.

Brown *et al.* (1962) rated the emotion, hostility and dominance expressed by the key relative towards the patient. Patients from high expressed emotion (EE) homes showed a greatly increased relapse rate. High contact, arbitrarily defined here as more that thirty-five hours a week together, also had an adverse effect, particularly when combined with high expressed emotion. Techniques for assessing expressed emotion have been refined, and replications have followed (e.g. Brown *et al.*, 1972; Vaughn and Leff, 1976). The latter study found that an additional protective factor was regular medication.

The ratings were initially developed from a semi-structured interview, the Camberwell Family Interview (Rutter and Brown, 1966). The Brown *et al.* (1972) study describes and defines the affect ratings, these being made from audiotapes of the interview by raters who were trained for at least three months using well-established criteria. Both critical and positive remarks were counted, and ratings of criticism, hostility, warmth, emotional over-involvement and dissatisfaction were made. High EE was indicated by a rating of marked emotional over-involvement or by seven or more critical remarks or by hostility, or by any combination of these. Critical remarks accounted for 77 per cent of high EE families. Vaughn and Leff (1976) employed a shortened version of the CFI, as it was found that the number of critical remarks was independent of interview length. Although it remains time-consuming to administer and rate the interview – an average of four hours – it appears to be a reliable method of assessing attitudes and coping response in relatives faced with the disturbing behaviour of the schizophrenic patient.

The present status of the expressed emotion concept has been reviewed by Falloon (1988). Although the association between EE and the course of schizophrenia is relatively well established, Falloon cautions that 'current understanding of the exact nature of its predictive function is limited' (Falloon, op. cit.: 272). He also notes the need for further research on the relationship between EE and the need for continuous neuroleptic medication, given the known harmful side effects of the latter.

Assessment of coping strategies

It has often been argued that certain of the behaviours shown by the schizophrenic patient represent attempts at adaptation to the disorder, either to alleviate distress or to reduce disorganisation; this is often ignored in clinical assessment. Those studying cognitive disturbance have suggested that behaviours such as slowed responding, narrowed attention, social withdrawal, and verbal underresponsiveness ('poverty of speech') may sometimes represent attempts to minimise the effects of the cognitive abnormality (Hemsley, 1977). The implications of this view for intervention procedures based on operant principles are presented in Chapter 16. There is now considerable evidence for the existence of such coping strategies. For example, Falloon and Talbot (1981) interviewed forty chronic schizophrenic out-patients with persistent auditory hallucinations and enquired as to the techniques employed to cope with the intrusive phenomena.

Frequent coping mechanisms included changes in activity, interpersonal contact, manipulations of physiological arousal, and attentional control. Patients who appeared to be least handicapped by the persistent hallucinations often used fewer methods but had found strategies that proved highly effective. Later studies (e.g. Breier and Strauss, 1983; Tarrier, 1987), also indicate the existence of spontaneous coping strategies in the majority of patients. It therefore appears important to assess the strategies currently employed, and their efficacy, with a view to providing systematic guidance as to when certain coping behaviours might best be used. Such interventions will be considered in the next chapter.

REFERENCES

Addington, D., Addington, J. and Schissel, B. (1990) 'A depression rating scale for schizophrenics', *Schizophrenia Research* 3: 247–51.

Andreasen, N. C. (1982) 'Negative symptoms in schizophrenia: definition and reliability', *Archives of General Psychiatry* 36: 1325–30.

Andreasen, N. C. (1984) *Scale for the Assessment of Positive Symptoms (SAPS)*, Iowa: Dept. of Psychiatry, University of Iowa.

Andreasen, N. C. and Olsen, S. (1982) 'Negative v. positive schizophrenia', *Archives of General Psychiatry* 39: 789–94.

Baker, R. D. and Hall, J. N. (1983) *Rehab: a multipurpose assessment instrument for long stay psychiatric patients*, Aberdeen: Vine Publishing.

Bentall, R. P. (1992) 'Reconstructing psychopathology', *Psychologist* 5: 61–5.

Bleuler, E. (1950) *Dementia Praecox or the Group of Schizophrenias*, New York: International Universities Press, (Originally published 1911.)

Breier, A. and Strauss, J. S. (1983) 'Self control in psychotic disorders', *Archives of General Psychiatry* 40: 1141–5.

Brett-Jones, J., Garety, P. A. and Hemsley, D. R. (1987) 'Measuring delusional experiences: a method and its application', *British Journal of Clinical Psychology* 26: 257–65.

Brown, G. W., Monck, E. M. and Carstairs, G. M. (1962) 'Influence of family life on the course of schizophrenic illness', *British Journal of Preventive and Social Medicine* 16: 55–68.

Brown, G. W., Birley, J. L. T. and Wing, J. K. (1972) 'Influence of family life on the course of schizophrenic disorders: a replication', *British Journal of Psychiatry* 121: 241–58.

Cancro, R., Sutton, S., Kerr, J. and Sugerman, A. A. (1971) 'Reaction time and prognosis in acute schizophrenia', *Journal of Nervous and Mental Disease* 153: 351–9.

Chadwick, P. D. J. and Lowe, C. F. (1990) 'The measurement and modification of delusional beliefs', *Journal of Consulting and Clinical Psychology* 58: 225–32.

Chapman, L. J. and Chapman, J. P. (1980) 'Scales for rating psychotic and psychotic-like experiences as continua', *Schizophrenia Bulletin* 6: 476–89.

Chapman, L. J. and Chapman, J. P. (1988) 'The genesis of delusions', in T. F. Oltmanns and B. A. Maher (eds) *Delusional Beliefs*, New York: Wiley, (167–83).

Chapman, L. J., Chapman, J. P. and Raulin, M. L. (1978) 'Body image aberration in schizophrenia', *Journal of Abnormal Psychology* 87: 399–407.

Depue, R. A., Dubicki, M. D. and McCarthy, T. (1975) 'Differential recovery of intellectual, associational and psychophysiological functioning in withdrawn and active schizophrenics', *Journal of Abnormal Psychology* 84: 325–30.

Drake, R. E. and Cotton, P. G. (1986) 'Depression, hopelessness and suicide in chronic schizophrenia', *British Journal of Psychiatry* 148: 554–9.

Eckblad, M. and Chapman, L. J. (1983) 'Magical ideation as an indicator of schizotypy', *Journal of Consulting and Clinical Psychology* 51: 215–25.

Emerich, D. F. and Sanberg, P. R. (1991) 'Neuroleptic dysphoria', *Biological Psychiatry* 29: 201–3.

Falloon, I. R. H. (1988) 'Expressed Emotion: current status', *Psychological Medicine* 18: 269–74.

Falloon, I. R. H. and Talbot, R. E. (1981) 'Persistent auditory hallucinations: coping mechanisms and implications for management', *Psychological Medicine* 11: 329–34.

Farrell, A. D. and Mariotto, M. J. (1982) 'A multimethod validation of two psychiatric rating scales', *Journal of Consulting and Clinical Psychology* 50: 273–80.

Garety, P. A. (1985) 'Delusions: problems in definition and measurement', *British Journal of Medical Psychology* 58: 25–34.

Garety, P. A. and Hemsley, D. R. (1987) 'Characteristics of delusional experience', *European Archives of Psychiatry and Neurological Science* 236: 294–8.

Giris, S. G. (1991) 'Diagnosis of secondary depression in schizophrenia: Implications for DSM IV', *Schizophrenia Bulletin* 17: 75–98.

Gray, J. A., Feldon, J., Rawlins, J. N. P., Hemsley, D. R. and Smith, A. D. (1991a) 'The neuropsychology of schizophrenia', *Behavioural and Brain Sciences* 14: 1–20.

Gray, J. A., Hemsley, D. R., Gray, N., Feldon, J. and Rawlins, J. N. P. (1991b) 'Schiz Bits: Misses, mysteries and hits', *Behavioural and Brain Sciences* 14: 56–84.

Guelfi, G. P., Faustman, W. O. and Csernansky, J. G. (1989) 'Independence of positive and negative symptoms in a population of schizophrenic patients', *Journal of Nervous and Mental Disease* 177: 285–90.

Hall, J. N. (1977) 'The content of ward rating scales for long stay patients', *British Journal of Psychiatry* 130: 287–93.

Hall, J. N. (1980) 'Ward rating scales for long stay patients: a review', *Psychological Medicine* 10: 277–88.

Hall, J. (1989) 'Chronic psychiatric handicaps', in K. Hawton, P. M. Salkovskis, J. Kirk and D. M. Clark (eds) *Cognitive Behaviour Therapy for Psychiatric Problems*, Oxford: Oxford University Press (315–38).

Hemsley, D. R. (1976) 'Problems in the interpretation of cognitive abnormalities in schizophrenia', *British Journal of Psychiatry* 129: 332–5.

Hemsley, D. R. (1977) 'What have cognitive deficits to do with schizophrenic symptoms?', *British Journal of Psychiatry* 130: 167–73.

Hemsley, D. R. (1988) 'Psychological models of schizophrenia', in E. Miller and P. Cooper (eds) *Adult Abnormal Psychology*, London: Churchill Livingstone (101–27).

Hemsley, D. R. (1990) 'What have cognitive deficits to do with schizophrenia?' in G. Huber (ed.) *Idiopathische Psychosen*, Stuttgart: Schattauer (111–25).

Hemsley, D. R., Rawlins, J. N. P., Feldon, J., Jones, S. H. and Gray, J. A. (1993) 'The Neuropsychology of schizophrenia: Act 3', *Behavioural and Brain Sciences* 16(1): 209–15.

Herz, M., Szymanski, H. and Simon, J. (1982) 'Intermittent medication for stable schizophrenic out-patients: an alternative to maintenance medication', *American Journal of Psychiatry* 139: 918–22.

Honigfeld, G. and Klett, C. J. (1965) 'The nurse's observation scale for in-patient evaluation', *Journal of Clinical Psychology* 21: 65–71.

Hustig, H. H. and Hafner, R. J. (1990) 'Persistent auditory hallucinations and their relationship to delusions and mood', *Journal of Nervous and Mental Disease* 178: 264–7.

Kraepelin, E. (1896) *Psychiatrie: Ein Lehrbuch fur Studierende und Aertze (5th edn)*, Leipzig: Barth.

Krawiecka, M., Goldberg, D. and Vaughan, M. (1977) 'A standardized psychiatric assessment scale for rating chronic psychometric patients', *Acta Psychiatrica Scandinavica* 55: 299–308.

Landmark, J. (1982) 'A manual for the assessment of schizophrenia', *Acta Psychiatrica Scandinavica*, supplement 298, vol. 65.

Liddle, P. F. (1987) 'The symptoms of chronic schizophrenia: a re-examination of the positive-negative dichotomy', *British Journal of Psychiatry* 151: 145–51.

Lorr, M. and Vestre, N. D. (1969) 'The psychotic in-patient profile: a nurse' observation scale', *Journal of Clinical Psychology 25: 137–40.*

Margo, A., Hemsley, D. R. and Slade, P. D. (1981) 'The effects of varying auditory input on schizophrenic hallucinations', *British Journal of Psychiatry* 139: 122–7.

Miles, C. P. (1977) 'Conditions predisposing to suicide', *Journal of Nervous and Mental Disease* 164: 231–46.

Mueser, K. T., Bellack, A. S., Douglas, M. S. and Wade, J. H. (1991) 'Prediction of social skill acquisition in schizophrenic and major affective disorder patients from memory and symptomatology', *Psychiatry Research* 37: 281–96.

Neale, J. M. and Oltmanns, T. F. (1980) *Schizophrenia*, New York: Wiley.

Overall, J. E. and Gorham, D. R. (1962) 'The Brief Psychometric Rating Scale', *Psychological Reports* 10: 799–812.

Paul, G. L. and Lentz, R. J. (1977) *Psychosocial Treatments of Chronic Mental Patients: Milieu Versus Social Learning Programs*, Cambridge, Mass.: Harvard University.

Paul, G. L., Redfield, J. P. and Lentz, R. J. (1976) 'The inpatient scale of minimal functioning: a revision of the social breakdown syndrome gradient index', *Journal of Consulting and Clinical Psychology* 44: 1021–2.

Power, C. T. (1974) 'The time sample behavioural checklist: observational assessment of patient functioning', *Journal of Behavioural Assessment* 1: 199–210.

Rattenburg, F. R., Harrow, M., Stoll, F. J. and Kettering, R. L. (1984) *'The Personal Ideation Inventory: on dimensions of delusional thinking*, New York: Microfiche Publictions.

Rosen, A. J., Turett, S. E., Davuner, J. H., Johnson, P. B., Lyons, J. S. and Davis, J. M. (1980) 'Pharmacotherapy of schizophrenia and affective disorders: behavioural correlates of diagnostic and demographic variables', *Journal of Abnormal Psychology* 89: 378–89.

Roy, A. (1982) 'Suicide in chronic schizophrenia', *British Journal of Psychiatry* 141: 171–7.

Rutter, M. and Brown, G. W. (1966) 'The reliability and validity of measures of family life and relationships in families containing a psychiatric patient', *Social Psychiatry* 1: 38–53.

Saccuzzo, D. P. and Braff, D. L. (1981) 'Early information processing deficit in schizophrenia', *Archives of General Psychiatry* 38: 175–179.

Shapiro, M. B. (1961) 'A method of measuring psychological changes specific to the individual psychiatric patient', *British Journal of Medical Psychology* 34: 151–5.

Slade, P. D. (1972) 'The effects of systematic desensitization on auditory hallucinations', *Behaviour Research and Therapy* 10: 85–91.

Spitzer, R. L. and Endicott, J. (1978) *Schedule for Affective Disorders and Schizophrenia – Lifetime version (SADS-L)*, New York: New York State Psychiatric Institute.

Spitzer, R. L. and Fleiss, J. L. (1974) 'A re-analysis of the reliability of psychotic diagnosis', *British Journal of Psychiatry* 125: 341–7.

Strauss, J. and Carpenter, W. (1972) 'The prediction of outcome in schizophrenia. I. Characteristics of outcome', *Archives of General Psychiatry* 27: 739–46.

Subotnik, K. L. and Nuechterlein, K. H. (1988) 'Prodromal signs and symptons of schizophrenic relapse', *Journal of Abnormal Psychology* 97: 405–12.

Tarrier, N. (1987) 'An investigation of residual psychotic symptoms in discharged schizophrenic patients', *British Journal of Clinical Psychology* 26: 141–3.

Vaughn, C. E. and Leff, J. P. (1976) 'The influence of family and social factors on the course of psychiatric illness: a comparison of schizophrenic and depressed neurotic patients', *British Journal of Psychiatry* 129: 125–37.

Westermeyer, J. F., Harrow, M. and Marengo, J. T. (1991) 'Risk for suicide in schizophrenia and other psychotic and non-psychotic disorders', *Journal of Nervous and Mental Disease* 179: 259–66.

Wing, J. K., Cooper, J. E. and Sartorious, N. (1974) *The Measurement and Classification of Psychiatric Symptoms*, Cambridge: Cambridge University Press.

Wykes, T. and Sturt, E. (1986) 'The measurement of social behaviour in psychiatric patients: an assessment of the reliability and validity of the SBS', *British Journal of Psychiatry* 148: 1–11.

Wykes, T., Sturt, E. and Katz, R. (1990) 'The prediction of rehabilitative success after three years', *British Journal of Psychiatry* 157: 865–70.

Wykes, T., Katz, R., Sturt, E. and Hemsley, D. R. (1992) 'Abnormalities of response processing in a chronic psychiatric group: a possible predictor of failure on rehabilitation programmes', *British Journal of Psychiatry* 160: 244–52.

Zahn, T. P. and Carpenter, W. T. (1978) 'Effects of short term outcome and clinical improvement on reaction time in acute schizophrenia', *Journal of Psychiatric Research* 14: 59–68.

Zubin, J. and Spring, B. (1977) 'Vulnerability – a new view of schizophrenia', *Journal of Abnormal Psychology* 86: 103–26.

Chapter 16

Schizophrenia

Treatment

David R. Hemsley

INTRODUCTION

There are a number of ways in which a discussion of the diverse psychological approaches to the treatment of schizophrenic symptoms might be organised. This review will begin by considering the growing literature on broadly cognitive-behavioural approaches to the positive symptoms of schizophrenia. Some interventions appear promising, although for the most part the research consists of case reports or case series rather than controlled studies. In this context will be raised the important issue of whether the emphasis in treatment should be on the training of effective coping strategies rather than the elimination of abnormal experiences.

Subsequent sections will deal with family intervention, group- and individual-based behavioural management programmes, and social-skills training. All have been investigated systematically. An interesting recent development has been the attempt to modify the cognitive impairment prominent in schizophrenia, although the results are at present inconclusive.

It has become increasingly apparent that in treating patients who have received the diagnosis of schizophrenia, it is crucial to deal with dimensions of psychopathology, such as depression and anxiety, which are not considered the 'core phenomena' of the disorder. Indeed, satisfactory outcome may be more dependent on the modification of such disturbances than the psychotic phenomena themselves. Techniques successfully employed with non-schizophrenic patients may well be useful, but one cannot assume that 'the same functional relationships would be treated by the same treatment techniques regardless of whether the person exhibited the problem in isolation or . . . in association with many other problem behaviours which might allow the classification of the person in a different nosological category' (Paul, 1974: 197–8).

DRUG TREATMENT

Psychological approaches to the treatment of the schizophrenic patient must be viewed in the context of the almost universal use of anti-psychotic medication, at least in the acute phase of the disorder. A large number of well controlled studies have demonstrated that such medication has a beneficial effect for many acute schizophrenics. However, some do not respond favourably, and among those who are discharged, serious social and occupational deficits often remain, indicating the clear need for additional therapeutic approaches. Further, neuroleptic drugs, in addition to their anti-psychotic properties produce a number of side effects, some of which, such as tardive dyskinesia, may prove irreversible. The use of medication over an extended period therefore requires careful consideration.

Gardos and Cole's (1976) review indicated that phenothiazines prevent serious relapses for about 40 per cent of out-patient schizophrenics, the remainder doing as well without maintenance medication. As yet, the identification of the latter group is dependent on patients being given a drug-free trial, any deterioration being treated by a resumption of medication. As was indicated in the preceding chapter, the environment to which the patient returns may interact with the effect of anti-psychotic drugs, these being of value in those returning to homes showing high levels of EE (Vaughn and Leff, 1976). A detailed discussion of such issues is provided by Hirsch (1986).

Anti-psychotic medication is therefore often employed in conjunction with a variety of psychological treatment approaches. In general, the latter interventions are instituted once optimal medication effects have been obtained and residual/additional problems assessed: neuroleptics may often increase patients' responsivity to procedures such as social-skills training. In part this may be attributable to the reduction in cognitive disorganisation following medication: Hersen *et al.* (1975) report a case in which a patient failed to respond to a token programme or skills-oriented group therapy throughout the first month of hospitalisation, but following medication was able to benefit from both.

As with drug treatment in other situations, there may be problems with compliance. Although these difficulties may be reduced by the use of long-acting injections of neuroleptics, psychological approaches may also be employed to increase drug-taking compliance.

COGNITIVE-BEHAVIOURAL APPROACHES TO POSITIVE SYMPTOMATOLOGY

Delusions

Watts *et al.* (1973) attempted to modify the delusional beliefs of three chronic paranoid schizophrenics. They concentrated on beliefs admitted to when the patient was questioned, rather than spontaneous talk about delusions. Confrontation was minimised and a hierarchy was made use of, whereby the least strongly held parts of the patient's delusion were tackled first. The patient was not required to abandon his own beliefs, just to consider the facts relating to, and arguments for them; as many lines of evidence as possible were raised against the beliefs. The patients were encouraged to voice the arguments against the delusions and such expressions were endorsed and expanded by the therapist. Following six sessions all three patients showed significant reductions in the strength of their delusional beliefs, although these were not completely abandoned.

Milton *et al.* examined the effects of two contrasting types of verbal intervention in a larger sample of persistently deluded patients. Belief modification, similar to that employed by Watts *et al.* (1973), was compared with confrontation. The latter began with the most strongly held beliefs and the therapist was to be 'firm and consistent, but polite, in rejecting the patients beliefs' (Milton *et al.*, 1978: 128). Both treatments produced a slight fall in the strength of delusion after five sessions. There was a further fall six weeks later in the belief-modification group, raising the possibility that this type of intervention may initiate changes which continue after its conclusion. None of this group showed an increase in overall disturbance, as assessed by the Brief Psychiatric Rating Scale (BPRS). In contrast, three of the seven patients in the confrontation groups had raised BPRS scores after the fifth session, and in two of them this persisted at six weeks. Alford (1986) also reported a single case study employing a cognitive intervention with significant effects on delusional beliefs which were maintained at three-month follow-up. A larger study by Chadwick and Lowe (1990) suggested that substantial reductions in delusional belief conviction could be achieved in a relatively small number of sessions. The components of treatment included a structured verbal challenge, employing a non-confrontational approach (cf. Milton *et al.*, 1978), and this was supplemented by a phase of reality testing in which the patient agreed to a test of his delusional beliefs. Of the six patients, two completely rejected their beliefs and three others significantly reduced their belief conviction. At six-month follow-up, there was evidence for maintenance of therapeutic effect. Interestingly, patients' initial response to a hypothetical contradiction of their belief appeared predictive of outcome (cf. Chapter 15).

While all of the above studies have focused on delusional beliefs, others have employed operant procedures to modify delusional speech. There is, however, an obvious danger in equating the presence or absence of a particular symptom with its verbal expression. An early case study (Richard *et al.* 1960), of a patient expressing delusional ideas, employed social approval for non-delusional speech in individual sessions. Although increases in rational conversation resulted, changes in stimulus conditions were followed by considerable deterioration. Nevertheless, a two-year follow-up under the original training conditions found that gains had been maintained. Subsequently, Ayllon and Houghton (1964) combined positive reinforcement and extinction to manipulate delusional speech. They first demonstrated that it was possible to increase the proportion of delusional speech by these methods, and then by reversing the contingencies, caused the patient's delusional speech to drop to a stable 15 per cent – initially it had been 50 per cent.

Wincze *et al.* (1972) examined the effects of tokens and feedback on the delusional speech of a group of chronic paranoid schizophrenics. Although both methods resulted in a decrease in delusional speech in experimental sessions for the majority of patients, there was no spontaneous generalisation of improvement to the ward setting; nor were independent psychiatrists able to detect any changes in the patients' delusions or mental status. However, generalisation training in the ward with a subgroup of patients resulted in half showing a significant improvement.

Liberman *et al.* (1973) treated four chronic paranoid patients with daily sessions which continued only as long as the patient spoke rationally. An evening 'chat' served as a reinforcer and its length was dependent on the amount of rational speech produced in daily sessions. After fifteen sessions dramatic improvements were demonstrated in daily sessions, with some generalisation to the evening 'chat'. However, during routine interactions on the ward, delusions continued to be expressed at a similar rate.

It is therefore apparent that, although operant procedures may result in a reduction in delusional speech within a treatment setting, this is rarely complete, and spontaneous generalisation is seldom found. There is no evidence of an alteration in patients' beliefs as a result of such interventions. In addition, the majority of studies have been carried out on patients showing coherent, systematised delusions rather than those which are constantly changing.

Hallucinations

Auditory hallucinations generally respond well to phenothiazine medication, although this is not always the case. Relatively few attempts have been made to modify such experiences by alternative methods. A major problem has been investigators' reliance, for the most part, on verbal report to indicate abnormal experiences. It is apparent that patients' reports might, with relative ease, be modified without any change in the underlying experience. Although some (e.g. Haynes and Geddy, 1973) have used as their dependent variable 'hallucinatory behaviour' – such as quiet talking and mumbling which does not appear as a response to any identifiable stimulus – the relationship of this to the frequency of abnormal experiences may be limited.

A study by Slade (1972) illustrates the use of a careful functional analysis to generate a treatment programme for persistent auditory hallucinations. The patient was required to record the occurrence of his voices and to rate a number of mood states and environmental conditions. It was found that he was more likely to record hallucinations when in a state of high internal arousal and in an environment of relatively low stimulation. On the basis of an enquiry into the situations giving rise to 'tension' a hierarchy was drawn up and systematic desensitisation carried out; this resulted in a decrease in frequency of reported hallucinatory experiences. A subsequent case report (Slade, 1973) substantially replicated these findings, although *in vivo* desensitisation was necessary. The successful use of systematic desensitisation was also reported by Alumbaugh

(1971), but Lambley (1973) cautions the need to be alert to the possible occurrence of new aberrant behaviours when such a single-symptom-based approach to treatment is used.

Operant procedures have been claimed as effective in the treatment of schizophrenic hallucinations. Thus Rutner and Bugle (1969) required a schizophrenic patient to record the frequency of auditory hallucinations for three days and then publicly displayed her frequency chart. Praise and attention were contingent on a reduction in reported hallucinations. Hallucinations had decreased dramatically before reinforcement contingencies were in force; they subsequently reduced to zero and no more were recorded at six-month follow-up. It was therefore difficult to know the reason for this patient's changed report.

Time out has also been employed in an attempt to suppress hallucinations (Haynes and Geddy, 1973). This involved removing the patient from her normal social environment and placing her in isolation in a small unfurnished room for ten minutes. As indicated above, the target was 'hallucinatory behaviour'. A considerable reduction in hallucinatory behaviour was achieved after thirty-five days but no follow-up was reported. A similar approach was employed in a single case study reported by Belcher. Undesirable behaviours associated with hallucinatory experiences resulted in 'a mild noxious consequence of contingent exercise' (Belcher, 1988: 70). A marked decrease in such behaviours was achieved, and maintained at one-year follow-up. Fonagy and Slade (1982) have observed that white noise presented concurrently with hallucinatory reports produced a reduction in their frequency, some generalisation of treatment effects being observed in all patients treated.

In one of the few controlled studies in this area Weingaertner (1971) employed three matched groups of patients, all known to experience hallucinations. Two groups were provided with shock boxes and asked to self-administer shock whenever they heard voices, and for one of these groups the current had been disconnected and hence no shock resulted. A third group received no treatment. The reports of hallucinations of all three groups decreased to an equivalent extent.

The implications of the above research are unclear. Controlled studies have produced negative results, but the case studies suggest that a number of procedures may diminish the report of hallucinations. Those employing non-operant procedures (e.g. Slade, 1972) may with greater justification be seen as possibly affecting the perceptual experience. Slade and Bentall (1988) suggest that three change processes may be operative in these various treatment strategies. First, focusing the concurrent self-monitoring of hallucinatory experiences; second, anxiety reduction; third, distraction.

The studies using operant procedures are less convincing and raise obvious ethical issues. On occasions a reduction in report of, and behaviour associated with, hallucinatory experiences may aid rehabilitation. As Al-Issa notes, it is possible that 'the occurrence [of reports] of hallucinations could thus be confined to socially acceptable situations' (Al-Issa, 1976: 158). Such interventions must, however, monitor closely any possible undesirable effects of the programme, particularly patient distress.

General cognitive-behavioural strategies

The moderately encouraging results from the mainly small-scale and uncontrolled trials considered above have led to the development of broad-based therapeutic packages incorporating many of these techniques. Examples include those of Kingdon and Turkington (1991a) and Fowler (1991), the latter a development of an earlier treatment approach (Fowler and Morley, 1989). The two therapy manuals share many important features, and Kingdon and Turkington (1991b) have reported promising findings in an uncontrolled study of sixty-four consecutively referred patients; the approach appeared acceptable both to them and to their relatives. Members of the group are being maintained on low levels of medication and have required minimal hospitalisation.

Both manuals emphasise the need for discussion and explanation of schizophrenic symptomatology, and the importance of identifying precursors of psychotic relapse. In addition to belief change approaches directed at the patients' delusions and hallucinations, there is an increasing emphasis on the development of effective coping strategies for abnormal experiences, rather than their elimination. It is clear that many patients spontaneously develop a range of coping responses (e.g. Breier and Strauss, 1983; Falloon and Talbot, 1981). The systematic application of those which prove effective would form part of the intervention. Allen and Bass (1992) provide a recent example of this approach.

It is also increasingly recognised that psychological approaches should target the anxiety and depression which are frequently prominent in those with a diagnosis of schizophrenia. There is no reason to think that the standard cognitive-behavioural strategies will be ineffective with this population. The disturbing incidence of suicide in such patients (see Westermeyer et al., 1991) and its link with cognitive features of depression (see Chapter 15) clearly indicate the importance of psychological assessment and intervention. Thus Fowler's manual emphasises the importance of distinguishing suicide/self-harm in the context of psychotic experiences, and that resulting from a 'rational' appraisal of life circumstances and extreme demoralisation.

MODIFICATION OF ABNORMALITIES IN THE FORM OF SPEECH

The expression of delusions – a disturbance in the content of speech – is usually distinguished from abnormalities in its form. There is the further feature in some schizophrenics of poverty of speech, which in its most extreme form presents as mutism.

Meichenbaum (1969) reinforced relevant and coherent responses to a question and ignored or fined incoherent, irrelevant or rambling replies. Two reinforcement groups were used, one receiving social reinforcement for correct responses and a negative social reaction for incorrect, the other being regulated by a system based on tokens. Both reinforcement groups improved more on the specifically trained behaviour than two control groups and showed greater changes in general measures of thinking.

Subsequently, Meichenbaum and Cameron (1973) developed a new technique, 'training schizophrenics to talk to themselves'. The patient is shown by the experimenter how to think aloud and how to employ this to solve a problem; he or she copies this procedure and is gradually taught to internalise the strategy. The therapists then attempt to make the patient sensitive to interpersonal cues indicating that his or her speech has been incoherent, and to use these as a signal to initiate self-instruction and change his or her behaviour. This programme resulted in a greater reduction in incoherent speech than was achieved in a control group receiving social reinforcement alone.

A similar procedure was employed in a subsequent case report by Meyers *et al.* (1976), self-instructions of the following type being presented to the patient cumulatively, one or two per session: 'I must pay attention', 'People think it's crazy to ramble on. I won't ramble on'. The therapist demonstrated aloud the use of self-instruction and an appropriate response to a question. After three such demonstrations the patient imitated until he could produce three consecutive appropriate performances. This pattern was repeated with whispered self-instruction and then replaced by covert self-instruction. A marked reduction in the frequency of inappropriate verbalisation in generalisation sessions and improved verbal behaviour were directly responsible for the decision to discharge the patient. Others have, however, failed to replicate these findings (e.g. Margolis and Steinberg 1976).

There have been several reports of attempts to reinstate speech in mute schizophrenics. Thus Sherman (1965) used reinforcement and imitative procedures with three psychotic patients, one of whom had a history of thirty-three years' complete mutism, the others near mute. Although some success was achieved in such tasks as naming objects and replying appropriately to therapists' questions, replies tended to consist of only one or two words. Both this and subsequent studies illustrate the problem of moving from the stage of single words to that of using complex language in communication. Indeed, some have seen poverty of speech as one method of adaptation to a severe disturbance of thinking, and hence, although verbalisation may be achieved, coherent speech may prove much more difficult. As Baker writes on the use of operant procedures to reinstate speech, 'for some patients speech was automaton-like, it was spoken quietly and mechanically and the content and form were predictable. Often nothing involving thought could be conditioned' (Baker, 1971: 333). Problems were also noted by Glickman *et al.* (1974), who found that operant procedures were effective in increasing gross verbal output but not the specific response class which was being reinforced.

Fraser *et al.* (1981) reported the more successful use of behaviour modification in the treatment of a schizophrenic with a 48-year history of mutism.

Intervention consisted of the application of shaping, prompting, modelling, fading, reinforcement and extinction procedures. After sixteen sessions incoherent words and phrases were mumbled by the patient. The first simple word was spoken in session 33, and in 69 the first complete sentences. After forty hours of treatment he was using sentences in response to questions. The study demonstrated that it is not sufficient to reinforce only single words and expect that sentence production will emerge spontaneously.

FAMILY INTERVENTION

A number of attempts at behavioural intervention in a family setting have been made, with mixed results. Some authors, such as Hudson (1975), have reported on the difficulties encountered. These included fear of a patient's responses if a programme of selective reinforcement were to be implemented, relatives being judged unable to cooperate, suggested goals not being agreed by the family, non-compliance by the patient, and family concern that relapse might occur if intensive rehabilitation procedures were employed. In part these reflect the general difficulties with operant procedures with schizophrenics, to be discussed below, in that they may fail to take into account the antecedents of behaviour, including anxiety, delusions and hallucinations, and their covert consequences, such as relief from anxiety.

Others (such as Cheek et al., 1971) have presented more favourable results. They aimed to assist parents better to observe the behaviour of the patient, their own behaviours in family interactions, and the relationship between them. They then taught parents how to maintain or modify behaviour by the systematic application of rewards and punishment. Methods included lectures, films, role-playing, group progress reports and discussions, and homework assignments. Although no control group was employed, a group of 'convalescent' schizophrenics showed improvements in a number of areas of functioning including household routines, a reduction in hostile behaviour, and increased social participation. According to the families, a major benefit was the opportunity to meet others with similar problems and share information about ways of handling them.

In view of the well-established relationship between the level of EE shown by relatives and the outcome of schizophrenic patients living with them (Chapter 15) several studies have used this as a basis for designing family intervention strategies. Leff et al. (1982) selected a group of schizophrenic patients in high contact with high EE relatives. The patients, who were all maintained on neuroleptic drugs, were randomly assigned to two groups, one receiving routine out-patient care, the other a package of social interventions. This consisted of (1) an education programme on schizophrenia, (2) a relatives' group (originally seen as a way of bringing together high EE and low EE relatives with the aim of altering the coping styles of the former; it was also hoped to counter the sense of isolation felt by many relatives of schizophrenics), and (3) family sessions, which had the aim of reducing EE and/or social contact by means of a variety of techniques. The relapse rate in the control group was 50 per cent, compared with 9 per cent in the experimental group. Either or both of EE and face-to-face contact were lowered in 73 per cent of treatment families. The evidence is thus suggestive of a causal role for EE in schizophrenic relapse. At two-year follow-up the results were slightly less impressive, 40 per cent in the treatment group having relapsed, compared with 68 per cent in the control group. However, there was minimal therapeutic contact between the team and the families following the first nine months, and it may be more appropriate to work on a continuing basis with families, as suggested by Tarrier *et al.* (1989).

Lam (1991) has reviewed the major family intervention studies in schizophrenia which have reported two-year outcomes (Leff *et al.*, 1982; 1985; 1988; 1990; Falloon *et al.*, 1982; 1985; 1987; Hogarty *et al.*, 1986; 1987; Tarrier *et al.*, 1988; 1989). Despite various methodological problems, the findings are for the most part encouraging. Somewhat less effective appeared to be an intervention which adopted a more psychodynamic approach. Lam suggests that the successful treatment packages share a number of common components:

(a) A positive approach and genuine working relationship, involving emphasis on the family's ability to change, and an avoidance of blame
(b) Providing structure and stability
(c) Focus on 'here and now'
(d) Use of family concepts
(e) Cognitive restructuring; the education programme aims to enable relatives to make sense of the patient's behaviour and experiences
(f) A behavioural approach which sets realistic goals and breaks these into small steps
(g) Improving communication

It appears clear that family therapy which employs a specific structured problem-solving approach and which also includes an educational component is useful in reducing family distress and schizophrenic relapse. The majority of families in the above studies involved parents providing care and support for their schizophrenic offspring. However, Bennun and Lucas (1990) have reported results suggesting that a similar approach may be beneficially employed in the treatment of couples where one partner has a long-standing diagnosis of schizophrenia. A series of case studies indicated a reduction in both positive and negative symptomatology following an intervention emphasising problem-solving, altering patterns of communication, and crisis management.

A number of important issues remain to be addressed. First, Tarrier (1991) has pointed out that many families either fail to become engaged, or withdraw from treatment at an early stage. A range of factors clearly influence treatment adherence, and Tarrier suggests that an awareness of those which are operating within a given family may suggest ways of maintaining the therapeutic interaction. Second, for the most part, studies have not directly assessed what are the crucial aspects of the multi-component treatment package. Third, the mechanisms of therapeutic change are far from clear, and the research lacks a clear theoretical framework. Tarrier (1989) has argued that successful outcome results from a reduction in environmental stress, to which schizophrenic patients are particularly vulnerable as a result of their well-documented dysfunctions in information-processing and arousal regulation. Hence a complex, vague or emotionally charged environment would lead to information overload and reappearance of positive symptoms. Consistent with this, MacCarthy *et al.* (1986) have reported a relationship between critical comments – a crucial component of EE – and relatives' more variable response to problem behaviours.

Behavioural approaches to chronic handicap

Ambitious attempts to modify the behaviour of institutionalised schizophrenic patients have involved the implementation of Token Economy Programmes (TEP). Tokens are provided following the occurrence of therapeutically desirable behaviours and are exchangeable for material rewards and privileges. The programmes require the clear specification of treatment goals and reinforcement contingencies. The majority of TEPs have focused on self-care behaviours, job performance and the control of grossly disruptive behaviour. Details of such procedures, and the difficulties which may be encountered, have been presented by Hall and Baker (1973). Although promising results have been obtained in a number of studies, Hall *et al.* (1977) indicate that much TEP research suffers from serious methodological deficits, and they suggest a number of requirements for research in this area. Their own study compared three groups: one acted as an own-ward control, the second received contingent tokens, social reinforcement and informational feedback as a consequence of appropriate behaviour, and the third group received contingent social reinforcement and feedback, together with a matched number of non-contingent tokens. At fifteen months both treatment groups had improved to a similar extent, which raises doubts about tokens as a causative factor in improvement. The authors stress the need to monitor psychiatric state as well as target behaviours. It is also apparent that explicit programmes have to be developed if sustained independent functioning in the community is to be achieved.

The most ambitious and methodologically adequate attempt to evaluate the effectiveness of learning-theory principles in the treatment of the schizophrenic patient is presented by Paul and Lentz (1977). The utility of these behavioural methods was compared with that of a milieu programme and standard hospital treatment. The patients' behaviour was regularly assessed by observers using measures whose reliabilities were carefully monitored. Patients in both treatment groups showed significant improvement over their initial levels of adjustment, particularly during the first six months. Areas assessed included instrumental role performance, self-care, and interpersonal skills. The behavioural programme resulted in larger gains than the milieu group and was clearly superior in terms of overall functioning. At the end of four years 10.7 per cent of the social-learning group had been discharged to independent functioning without read-mission, compared to 7.1 per cent in the milieu group and none of the controls. In addition the social-learning group was superior in terms of 'significant releases', that is, a minimum continuous community stay of ninety days.

However, as Hall (1989) points out, ward-wide token programmes have now largely been superseded by individual and group behavioural programmes within wards, hostels or group homes. As was noted previously, behavioural approaches also form part of many family intervention packages. Although there has been a marked reduction in the number of long-stay patients in psychiatric hospitals, there continue to be a number of settings in which group behaviour programmes are possible when patients have therapeutic targets in common. However, these require a consistency in staff practices which can usually only be achieved by a formal training. An example is provided by Milne (1986), who describes in detail the development of a ward-oriented training programme for nurses. In other situations, individualised behavioural interventions are most appro-priate (see Garety and Morris, 1984). In both group and individual treatment approaches there is increasing awareness of the importance of involving patients as much as is feasible in the determination of therapeutic objectives.

LIMITATIONS OF OPERANT PROCEDURES

Despite the frequent use of operant procedures in the modification of schizo-phrenics' behaviour, there remain a number of limitations to this approach; some may be understandable in terms of the well-established abnormalities of cognitive functioning in schizophrenia (Hemsley, 1978). Problems fall into three broad classes: lack of response, concurrent deterioration in non-target aspects of schizophrenic behaviour, and failures of generalisation.

With the non-responding patient it becomes necessary to decide whether intensified behavioural procedures should be implemented or whether the operant paradigm is inappropriate. It appears probable that one factor affecting the 'responsiveness' of a patient is the complexity of the response required of him or her. This has received little consideration although there are obvious differences between requiring shoes to be laced and asking patients to participate in a social situation or produce coherent speech.

Prior to the adoption of formal operant procedures it was noted that for some patients intensive rehabilitation procedures could result in a deterioration in certain aspects of schizophrenic behaviour. An example is provided by Pryce (1977). The possibility of similar problems occurring with operant procedures necessitates the concurrent monitoring of important aspects of patients' be-haviour not directly being modified. A problem in considering the changes produced as a result of operant procedures is the frequent presentation of aver-aged data: this may represent an improvement in some patients, a deterioration in others. A report by Kowalski et al. (1976) noted that nonparanoid schizophrenics showed a sharp decline in performance on introduction of a TEP. This was followed by a slow recovery to about the original level. In contrast, paranoid schizophrenics showed immediate improvement, which was continued if erratic. The author suggests that this may have been attributable to the paranoids' generally superior cognitive and behavioural integrity. There is also evidence (Hall *et al.*, 1977) that if too many behaviours are identified as targets, any improvement in certain areas may be accompanied by a deterioration in other behaviours. This may be attributable to some patients' inability to attend to more than a few targets at once.

Hudson (1975) encountered problems when attempting to employ behaviour-modification techniques with chronic schizophrenics in the community. Five cases where it was possible to institute a programme were reported. In one case attendance at a club was achieved but was short-lived and the patient's delusional talk increased. Another patient, who on discharge lay in bed all day, was rewarded for increased social interaction but eventually refused to allow hospital staff to enter and had to be readmitted to hospital on account of a recurrence of florid symptoms. These examples are deliberately selective, but do suggest that a minority of schizophrenics may show increased behavioural abnormalities when confronted with programmes requiring more complex decision-making than they have previously been accustomed to. In addition, there remains little to contradict the conclusion of a review of operant procedures (Keeley *et al.*, 1976) that evidence relating to long-term and/or generalised change is conspicuous by its absence, and the meagre evidence available raises serious doubts about our ability to go 'beyond management' (ibid: 292). Nevertheless, methods of improving generalisation have been put forward (Liberman, 1976: 188) and have received considerable attention in the literature on social-skills training in schizophrenia which is considered in the next section.

SOCIAL-SKILLS TRAINING

The importance of social functioning to successful adjustment has been stressed by several authors, and it clearly plays an important role with regard to both employment and hospitalisation. Hence the numerous studies attempting to improve the social skills of schizophrenic patients. A broad definition of social skills is provided by Trower *et al.*, who suggest that they comprise 'the ability to [understand] other people's use of elements of expression . . . to [convey] impressions through appropriate verbal and non-verbal behaviours . . . to affect behaviour and feelings of others in ways the person intends and which are socially acceptable . . . and to influence the environment sufficiently to attain basic personal goals' (Trower *et al.*, 1978: 2–5).

Social-skills training programmes usually involve three major techniques: modelling, practice and feedback. Video- or audiotaped modelling is often employed, practice usually involves role-playing, and feedback includes instruction in alternative responses and reinforcement of successful performance. These procedures, either alone or in combination, are usually more effective than no treatment, although much of the literature consists of individual case studies.

Wallace (1981) and his colleagues have developed an integrated assessment and treatment package, based on a role-playing format. However, rather than train patients in a sequence of discrete skills, they assess all variables after role-playing and apply various training techniques if deficiencies are indicated. Results of a controlled study have indicated less relapse and rehospitalisation among schizophrenic patients receiving this programme than among patients randomly assigned to equally intensive 'holistic health therapy'. It must be noted, however, that others have reported less successful social-skills programmes with schizophrenics (e.g. Lauterbach *et al.*, 1979). The residual cognitive impairment shown by many patients may be one reason for such negative findings, and Shepherd has suggested that 'a slow rate of presentation, and some kind of pure part or progressive part learning method, may reduce other information processing problems . . . . It is necessary to break down the task into small units each one of which must be thoroughly mastered before proceeding to the next and before attempting to chain the units into a complete response' (Shepherd, 1978a: 258). Matson and Stephens (1978) noted that an initial problem with their social-skills training package was developing responses, instructions and feedback simple and concise enough to be understood by regressed patients. With one subject all responses had to be four words or fewer before she could memorise and repeat them accurately.

The major problems with social-skills training with schizophrenics are those of generalisation and durability. Much research relies almost entirely on outcome measures tied closely to the treatment setting. Interventions must be shown to affect functioning outside the immediate treatment context. Shepherd (1977) developed a method of assessing patients' social functioning using independent observers in a setting completely different from the treatment groups, and was initially unable to find any evidence of the training having improved the interaction skills of patients in a day hospital.

Subsequently, a number of changes in procedure were implemented (Shepherd 1978b). These involved an increase in the duration and frequency of treatment sessions, a greater emphasis on setting targets, organising reinforcements and even conducting complete sessions in contexts other than the treatment group, and a greater attempt to take account of individual differences. Results suggested a clear improvement in social functioning for a treated group, this being observable by independent raters in a setting quite separate from that of treatment. Shepherd suggests that it may be more useful to think of such patients' social difficulties as chronic disabilities requiring effective systems of management rather than as symptoms requiring treatment. This view is supported by Matson and Stephens' observation that although social-skills training produced improvements which generalised to settings outside the treatment context, behaviour rapidly deteriorated following the cessation of the programme. They conclude that, in addition to a knowledge of skills, 'natural reinforcers in the environment may be necessary to sustain appropriate behaviour' (Matson and Stephens, 1978: 75).

It is therefore apparent that the emphasis should be on training those responses most relevant to everyday life, and which thus have the highest probability of natural reinforcement. The training of responses relevant to functioning outside the treatment setting will often require sessions in the natural environ- ment, such as shops and restaurants, and therapists will need to accompany patients to new situations. It may also prove essential to persuade significant people in a patient's environment, such as his or her family, to reinforce new, socially appropriate responses.

More recent large-scale clinical trials (Bellack *et al.*, 1984; Wallace and Liberman, 1985) have indicated that these approaches can enable patients to acquire and maintain new skills, and that such training can have a significant impact on relapse. There is continuing debate, however, on the role of conscious cognitive operations in interpersonal behaviour and in particular the role of problem-solving processes in social skills. Thus Liberman *et al.* (1986) have argued that training should focus primarily on enhancing such cognitive skills as generating multiple response alternatives and evaluating their respective utility before emitting a response. An example of this approach is provided by Hansen *et al.* (1985). However, the review by Bellack *et al.* concluded that 'further research on problem-solving training programmes is clearly warranted, but the validity of the problem-solving model and the utility of the training is uncertain' (Bellack *et al.*, 1989: 101).

MODIFICATION OF COGNITIVE IMPAIRMENT

As indicated in Chapter 15, there has been considerable research into schizo-phrenics' cognitive impairment. Occasionally this has suggested direct intervention procedures: thus Schwartz-Place and Gilmore, having demonstrated schizo-phrenics' failure to organise information at an early stage of processing, note that 'specific training in awareness of organization and segmentation may be useful in helping the schizophrenic organize his or her environment' (Schwartz-Place and Gilmore, 1980: 417). A more elaborate approach has been proposed by Magaro and his colleagues (e.g. Magaro *et al.*, 1986) and by Spaulding *et al.* (1986). A number of successful case studies have been reported (e.g. Adams *et al.*, 1981) but more systematic research is required. A controlled study by Olbrich and Mussgay also indicated that neuropsychological dysfunctions could be reduced by cognitive training. However, the effect was limited to more complex functions rather than elementary mechanisms. The authors speculate that their results might best be explained 'by assuming instigation of compen-satory mechanisms . . . . Training programmes may achieve success not by restoring a deficient repertoire but largely through the development of normal cognitive strategies. Thus a promising goal of future work in this area should be the identification of compensatory strategies and of training techniques to promote them' (Olbrich and Mussgay, 1990: 368). The parallels with approaches to the rehabilitation of patients with known brain damage are apparent. As Hemsley (1987) pointed out, research into cognitive impairment in schizophrenia has sought to specify the capacity restrictions of particular stages of processing. Cognitive psychologists are, however, increasingly interested in the strategies employed in the use of these stages to achieve particular goals. There is therefore the possibility that patients who remain cognitively impaired might be trained to utilise the most appropriate strategies to minimise the behavioural abnormalities shown in a given situation.

The self-instructional training employed by Meichenbaum and Cameron (1973) may be viewed as one such coping strategy. They claimed the successful modification of attention, thought, and language behaviour in schizophrenia. Less encouraging results employing this technique have, however, been reported by Bentall *et al.* (1987), who encountered difficulties in teaching self-instruction to the subjects and inadequate generalisation of treatment effects.

When considering training in coping strategies it is important to consider those which are employed spontaneously by patients in response to cognitive and perceptual abnormalities (Hemsley, 1977). These have been well documented (e.g. Falloon and Talbot 1981; Breier and Strauss 1983). However, for some patients in whom the cognitive disturbance has largely remitted or been success-fully treated, certain behavioural abnormalities resulting from previously adaptive strategies, such as narrowed scanning, slowed responding and social withdrawal, may no longer be serving a useful purpose. In such cases operant procedures may be employed to reverse these deficits. The preceding chapter noted the importance of assessing the level of residual cognitive impairment in the planning of rehabilitation programmes.

The direct modification of schizophrenics' cognitive dysfunctions plays a crucial role in the multi-faceted treatment programme described by Brenner *et al.* (1990). This attempts an integrated approach to cognitive, communicative and social skills. Several controlled studies have supported the utility of this approach, and treatment gains appear to be maintained at eighteen-month follow-up. There is continuing research on the precise role played by the remedi-ation of cognitive deficits. Brenner *et al.* acknowledge that, 'Although the overall results of the various studies point to the conclusion that the therapeutic effects are based on reducing cognitive deficits they could essentially also be due to a training in effective compensation strategies' (Brenner *et al.*, 1990: 186). They also accept the importance of considering 'compensatory dysfunctions', such as an attentional style which attempts to reduce information intake. In such cases (cf. Hemsley, 1977), 'direct therapeutic interventions intended to normalize cognitive disorders without simultaneous control of the quantity of information available or of psychophysiological arousal would be detrimental' (Brenner *et al.*, op. cit.: 187). Their wide-ranging approach to treatment merits continuing investigation to clarify the mechanisms of therapeutic change and the specifi-cation of those patients most likely to benefit.

REFERENCES

Adams, H. E., Malateska, V., Brantley, P. J. and Turkal, I. D. (1981) 'Modification of cognitive processes: a case study of schizophrenia', *Journal of Consulting and Clinical Psychology* 49: 460–4.

Alford, B. (1986) 'Behavioural treatment of schizophrenic delusion: a single case experimental analysis', *Behaviour Therapy* 17: 637–44.

Al-Issa, I. (1976) 'Behaviour therapy and hallucinations: a sociocultural approach', *Psychotherapy: Theory, Research and Practice* 13: 156–9.

Allen, H. and Bass, C. (1992) 'Coping tactics and the management of acutely distressed schizophrenic patients', *Behavioural Psychotherapy* 20: 61–72.

Alumbaugh, R. V. (1971) 'Use of behaviour modification techniques toward reduction of hallucinatory behaviour: a case study', *Psychological Record* 21: 415–17.

Ayllon, T. and Haughton, E. (1964) 'Modification of symptomatic verbal behaviour of mental patients', *Behaviour Research and Therapy* 2: 87–97.

Baker, R. (1971) 'The use of operant conditioning to reinstate speech in mute schizophrenics', *Behaviour Research and Therapy* 9: 329–36.

Belcher, T. L. (1988) 'Behavioural reduction of overt hallucinatory behaviour in a chronic schizophrenic', *Journal of Behaviour Therapy and Experimental Psychiatry* 19: 69–71.

Bellack, A. S., Turner, S. M., Hersen, M. and Luber, R. F. (1984) 'An examination of the efficacy of social skills training for chronic schizophrenic patients', *Hospital and Community Psychiatry* 35: 1023–8.

Bellack, A. S., Morrison, R. L. and Mueser, K. T. (1989) 'Social problem-solving in schizophrenia', *Schizophrenia Bulletin* 15: 101–16.

Bennun, I. and Lucas, R. (1990) 'Using the partner in the psychosocial treatment of schizophrenia: a multiple single case design', *British Journal of Clinical Psychology* 29: 185–92.

Bentall, R. P., Higson, P. J. and Lowe, C. F. (1987) 'Teaching self instructions to chronic schizophrenic patients: efficacy and generalization', *Behavioural Psychotherapy* 15: 58–76.

Breier, A. and Strauss, J. S. (1983) 'Self control in psychotic disorders', *Archives of General Psychiatry* 40: 1141–5.

Brenner, H. D., Kraemer, S., Hermanutz, M. and Hodel, B. (1990) 'Cognitive treatment in schizophrenia', in E. R. Straube and K. Hahlweg (eds) *Schizophrenia: Concepts, vulnerability and intervention*, New York: Springer (161–92).

Chadwick, P. D. J. and Lowe, C. F. (1990) 'The Measurement and modification of delusional beliefs', *Journal of Consulting and Clinical Psychology* 58: 225–32.

Cheek, F. E., Laucius, J., Mahncke, M. and Beck, R. (1971) 'A behaviour modification training program for parents of convalescent schizophrenics', in R. D. Rubin, H. Feusterheim, A. A., Lazarus and C. M. Franks (eds) *Advances in Behavior Therapy. Vol. 2*, New York: Academic Press.

Falloon, I. R. H. and Talbot, R. E. (1981) 'Persistent auditory hallucinations: coping mechanisms and implications for management', *Psychological Medicine* 11: 329–34.

Falloon, I. R. H., Boyd, J. L., McGill, G. W., Razani, J., Moss, H. B. and Gilderman, A. M. (1982) 'Family management in the prevention of exacerbations of schizophrenics: a controlled study', *New England Journal of Medicine* 306: 1437–46.

Falloon, I. R. H., Boyd, J. L., McGill, G. W., Williamson, M., Ranzani, J., Moss, H. B., Gilderman, A. M. and Simpson, G. M. (1985) 'Family management in the prevention of morbidity in schizophrenia: clinical outcome of a two year longitudinal study', *Archives of General Psychiatry* 42: 887–96.

Falloon, I. R. H., McGill, C. W., Boyd, J. L. and Pederson, J. (1987) 'Family management in the prevention of morbidity of schizophrenia: a social outcome of a two-year longitudinal study', *Psychological Medicine* 17: 59–66.

Fonagy, P. and Slade, P. (1982) 'Punishment vs negative reinforcement in the aversive conditioning of auditory hallucinations', *Behaviour Research and Therapy* 20: 483–92.

Fowler, D. (1991) 'Draft manual for the cognitive-behavioural management of the functional psychoses', unpublished manuscript, Fulbourn Hospital, Cambridge.

Fowler, D. and Morley, S. (1989) 'The cognitive-behavioural treatment of hallucinations and delusions: a preliminary study', *Behavioural Psychotherapy* 17: 267–82.

Fraser, D., Anderson, J. and Grime, J. (1981) 'An analysis of the progressive development of vocal responses in a mute schizophrenic patient', *Behavioural Psychotherapy* 9: 2–12.

Gardos, G. and Cole, J. D. (1976) 'Maintenance antipsychotic therapy: Is the cure worse than the disease?', *American Journal of Psychiatry* 133: 32–6.

Garety, P. A. and Morris, I. (1984) 'A new unit for long stay psychiatric patients: organization, attitude and quality of care', *Psychological Medicine* 14: 183–92.

Glickman, H. S., Di Scipio, W. J. and Hollander, M. A. (1974) 'Modeling and reinforcement techniques with hospitalized psychotics', in W. J. Di Scipio (ed.) *The Behavioural Treatment of Psychotic Illness*, New York: Behavioural Publications.

Hall, J. (1989) 'Chronic psychiatric handicaps', in K. Hawton, P. M. Salkovskis, J. Kirk and D. M. Clark (eds) *Cognitive Behaviour Therapy for Psychiatric Problems*, Oxford: Oxford University Press (315–38).

Hall, J. and Baker, R. (1973) 'Token economy systems: breakdown and control', *Behaviour Research and Therapy* 11: 253–63.

Hall, J. N., Baker, R. D. and Hutchison, K. (1977) 'A controlled evaluation of token economy procedures with chronic schizophrenic patients', *Behaviour Research and Therapy* 15: 261–84.

Hansen, D. J., St. Lawrence, J. S. and Christoff, K. A. (1985) 'Effects of interpersonal problem solving training with chronic aftercare patients on problem solving component skills and effectiveness of solutions', *Journal of Consulting and Clinical Psychology* 53: 167–74.

Haynes, S. N. and Geddy, P. (1973) 'Suppression of psychotic hallucinations through time out', *Behaviour Therapy* 4: 123–7.

Hemsley, D. R. (1977) 'What have cognitive deficits to do with schizophrenic symptoms?', *British Journal of Psychiatry* 130: 167–73.

Hemsley, D. R. (1978) 'Limitations of operant procedures in the modification of schizophrenic functioning: the possible relevance of studies of cognitive disturbance', *Behavioural Analysis and Modification* 3: 165–73.

Hemsley, D. R. (1987) 'An experimental psychological model for schizophrenia', in H. Hafner, W. F. Gattaz and W. Janzarik (eds) *Search for the causes of schizophrenia*. Vol. 1, New York: Springer.

Hersen, M., Turner, S. M., Edelstein, B. A. and Pinkstan, S. G. (1975) 'Effects of phenothiazines and social skills training in a withdrawn schizophrenic', *Journal of Clinical Psychology* 31: 588–94.

Hirsch, S. R. (1986) 'Clinical treatment of schizophrenia', in P. B. Bradley and S. R. Hirsch (eds) *The Psychopharmacology and Treatment of Schizophrenia*, Oxford: Oxford University Press.

Hogarty, G. E., Anderson, C. M., Reiss, D. J., Kornblith, S. J., Greatwald, D. P., Javana, C. D. and Madonia, M. J. (1986) 'Family psycho-education, social skills training and maintenance chemotherapy in the after care treatment of schizophrenia. I: one year affects of a controlled study on relapse and expressed emotion', *Archives of General Psychiatry* 43: 633–42.

Hogarty, G. E., Anderson, C. M. and Reiss, D. J. (1987) 'Family psychoeducation, social skill training and medication in schizophrenia: the long and short of it', *Psychopharmacology* Bulletin 23: 12–13.

Hudson, B. L. (1975) 'A behaviour modification project with chronic schizophrenics in the community', *Behaviour Research and Therapy* 13: 239–41.

Keeley, S. M., Sherberg, K. M. and Carbonell, J. (1976) 'Operant clinical intervention: behaviour management or beyond? Where are the data?' *Behavior Therapy* 7: 292–305.

Kingdon, D. G. and Turkington, D. (1991a) 'Cognitive behaviour therapy with a normalizing rationale in schizophrenia: a treatment manual', unpublished manuscript, Dept. of Psychiatry, Bassetlaw District General Hospital, Notts.

Kingdon, D. G. and Turkington, D. (1991b) 'The use of cognitive behaviour therapy with a normalizing rationale in schizophrenia', *Journal of Nervous and Mental Disease* 79: 207–11.

Kowalski, P. A., Daley, G. D. and Gripp, R. F. (1976) 'Token economy: Who responds how?' *Behaviour Research and Therapy* 14: 372–4.

Lam, D. H. (1991) 'Psychosocial family intervention in schizophrenia: a review of empirical studies', *Psychological Medicine* 21: 423–41.

Lambley, P. (1973) 'Behaviour modification techniques and the treatment of psychosis: a critique of Alumbaugh', *Psychological Record* 23: 93–7.

Lauterbach, W., Pelzer, U. and Awiszus, D. (1979) 'Is social skills training effective in European schizophrenics?' *Behavioural Analysis and Modification* 3: 21–31.

Leff, J., Kuipers, L., Berkowitz, R., Eberlein-Vries, R. and Sturgeon, D. (1982) 'A controlled trial of social intervention in the families of schizophrenics', *British Journal of Psychiatry* 141: 121–34.

Leff, J., Kuipers, L., Berkowitz, R. and Sturgeon, D. (1985) 'A controlled trial of social intervention in the families of schizophrenics: two year follow-up', *British Journal of Psychiatry* 146: 594–600.

Leff, J., Berkowitz, R., Shavit, N., Strachan, A., Glass, I. and Vaughn, C. (1988) 'A trial of family therapy v. a relatives group for schizophrenia', *British Journal of Psychiatry* 153: 58–66.

Leff, J., Berkowitz, R., Shavit, N., Strachan, A., Glass, I. and Vaughn, C. (1990) 'A trial of family therapy v. a relative control group for schizophrenia: two year follow-up', *British Journal of Psychiatry* 157: 571–7.

Liberman, R. P. (1976) 'Behaviour therapy for schizophrenia' in L. Jolyon D. West and and E. Flinn (eds) *Treatment of Schizophrenia: Progress and Prospects*, New York: Grune and Stratton.

Liberman, R. P., Teigan, J., Patterson, R. and Baker, V. (1973) 'Reducing delusional speech in chronic paranoid schizophrenics', *Journal of Applied Behaviour Analysis* 6: 57–64.

Liberman, R. P., Meusen, K. T., Wallace, C. J., Jacobs, H. E., Eckman, T. and Massel, H. K. (1986) 'Training skills in the psychiatrically disabled: learning coping and competence' *Schizophrenia Bulletin* 12: 631–47.

MacCarthy, B., Hemsley, D. R., Schrank-Fernandez, C., Kuipers, E. and Katz, R. (1986) 'Unpredicatability as a correlate of expressed emotion in the relatives of schizophrenics', *British Journal of Psychiatry* 48: 727–31.

Magaro, P. A., Johnson, M. and Boring, R. (1986) 'Information processing approaches to the treatment of schizophrenia', in R, Ingram (ed.) *Information Processing Approaches to Clinical Psychology*, London: Academic Press.

Margolis, R. B. and Steinberg, K. M. (1976) 'Cognitive self instruction in process and reactive schizophrenics: A failure to replicate', *Behaviour Therapy* 7: 668–71.

Matson, J. L. and Stephens, R. M. (1978) 'Increasing appropriate behaviour of explosive chronic psychiatric patients with a social skills training package', *Behaviour Modification* 2: 61–76.

Meichenbaum, D. H. (1969) 'The effects of instructions and reinforcement on thinking and language behaviour in schizophrenics', *Behaviour Research and Therapy* 8: 147–52.

Meichenbaum, D. H. and Cameron, R. (1973) 'Training schizophrenics to talk to themselves: a means of developing attentional controls', *Behaviour Therapy* 4: 515–34.

Meyers, A., Mercatoris, M. and Sireta, A. (1976) 'Use of covert self instruction for the elimination of psychotic speech', *Journal of Consulting and Clinical Psychology* 44: 480–2.

Milne, D. (1986) *Training Behaviour Therapists*, London: Croom Helm.

Milton, F., Patwa, V. K. and Hafner, R. J. (1978) 'Confrontation vs. belief modification in persistently deluded patients', *British Journal of Medical Psychology* 51: 127–30.

Olbrich, R. and Mussgay, L. (1990) 'Reduction of schizophrenia deficits by cognitive training: an evaluative study', *European Archives of Psychiatry and Neurological Science* 239: 366–9.

Paul, G. L. (1974) 'Experimental-behavioural approaches to "schizophrenia"', in R. Cancro, N. Fox, and L. Shapiro (eds) *Strategic Interaction in Schizophrenia*, New York,: Behavioral Publications (187–200).

Paul, G. L. and Lentz, I. (1977) *Psychosocial Treatments of Chronic Mental Patients: Milieu Versus Social Learning Programs*, Cambridge, Mass.: Harvard University Press.

Pryce, J. G. (1977) 'The effects of social changes in chronic schizophrenia: a study of forty patients transferred from hospital to a residential home', *Psychological Medicine* 7: 127–39.

Richard, H. C., Dignam, P. J. and Horner, R. F. (1960) 'Verbal manipulations in a psychotherapeutic relationship', in L. Krasner, and L. P. Vilman (eds) *Case Studies in Behavior Modification*, New York: Holt, Rinehart and Winston.

Rutner, I. T. and Bugle, C. (1969) 'An experimental procedure for the modification of psychotic behaviour', *Journal of Consulting and Clinical Psychology* 33: 651–3.

Schwartz-Place, E. J. and Gilmore, G. C. (1980) 'Perceptual organization in schizophrenia', *Journal of Abnormal Psychology* 89: 409–18.

Shepherd, G. W. (1977) 'Social skills training: the generalization problem', *Behavior Therapy* 8: 1008–9.

Shepherd, G. W. (1978a) 'Treatment in natural and special environments', in M. P. Feldman and J. Orford (eds) *The Social Psychology of Psychological Problems*, New York: John Wiley.

Shepherd, G. W. (1978b) 'Social skills training: the generalization problem: some further data', *Behaviour Research and Therapy* 16: 287–8.

Sherman, J. A. (1965) 'Use of reinforcement and imitation to reinstate verbal behaviour in mute psychotics', *Journal of Abnormal and Social Psychology* 70: 155–64.

Slade, P. D. (1972) 'The effects of systematic desensitization on auditory hallucinations', *Behaviour Research and Therapy* 10: 85–91.

Slade, P. D. (1973) 'The psychological investigation and treatment of auditory hallucinations', *Behaviour Research and Therapy* 46: 293–6.

Slade, P. D. and Bentall, R. P. (1988) *Sensory Deception: A Scientific Analysis of Hallucination*, London: Croom Helm.

Spaulding, W., Storm, L., Goodrich, V. and Sullivan, M. (1986) 'Applications of experimental psychopathology in psychiatric rehabilitation', *Schizophrenia Bulletin* 4: 560–77.

Tarrier, N. (1989) 'Effect of treating the family to reduce relapse in schizophrenia: a review', *Journal of the Royal Society of Medicine* 82: 423–4.

Tarrier, N. (1991) 'Some aspects of family interventions in schizophrenia. I: Adherence to intervention programmes', *British Journal of Psychiatry* 159: 475–80.

Tarrier, N., Barrowclough, C., Vaughn, C., Bamrah, J. S., Porceddu, K., Watts, S. and Freeman, H. (1988) 'The community management of schizophrenia: a controlled trial of a behavioural intervention with families to reduce relapse', *British Journal of Psychiatry* 153: 532–42.

Tarrier, N., Barrowclough, C., Vaughn, C., Bamrah, J. S. Porceddu, K., Watts, S. and Freeman, H. (1989) 'Community management of schizophrenia: a two year follow-up of a behavioural intervention with families', *British Journal of Psychiatry* 154: 625–8.

Trower, P., Bryant, B. and Argyle, M. (1978) *Social Skills and Mental Health*, Pittsburgh: University of Pittsburgh Press.

Vaughn, C. E. and Leff, J. P. (1976) 'The influence of family and social factors on the course of psychiatric illness', *British Journal of Psychiatry* 129: 125–37.

Wallace, C. J. (1981) 'The social skills training project of the Mental Health Clinical Research Center for the study of schizophrenia', in J. P. Curran and P. M. Martin (eds) *Social Skills Training: a Practical Handbook for Assessment and Treatment* , New York: Guilford.

Wallace, C. J. and Liberman, R. P. (1985) 'Social skills training for patients with schizophrenia: a controlled clinical trial', *Psychiatry Research* 14: 239–47.

Watts, F. N., Powell, G. E. and Austin, S. V. (1973) 'The modification of abnormal beliefs', *British Journal of Medical Psychology* 46: 359–63.

Weingaertner, A. H. (1971) 'Self administered aversive stimulation with hallucinating hospitalized schizophrenics', *Journal of Consulting and Clinical Psychology* 36: 422–9.

Westermeyer, J. F., Harrow, M. and Marengo, J. T. (1991) 'Risk for suicide in schizophrenia and other psychotic and non-psychotic disorders', *Journal of Nervous and Mental Disease* 179: 259–66.

Wincze, J. P., Leitenberg, H. and Agras, W. S. (1972) 'The effects of token reinforcement and feedback on the delusional verbal behaviour of chronic paranoid schizophrenics', *Journal of Applied Behaviour Analysis* 5: 247–62.

Chapter 17

Problems related to sexual variation
Investigation

A.J. Chalkley

In the 1940s and 1950s it was common to talk of the 'Sexual Perversions'. A well-known study in the 1960s was entitled *Sexual Deviation* (Storr, 1964). Since then new terms such as 'variation', 'anomaly' and 'atypicality' have been used with varying frequency.

These changes suggest a slow evolution towards a more liberal climate of opinion, but the sense of crisis in the field that has been around for twenty years or so persists. Of course not everybody is liberal and, even if they were, it is not always clear what standpoint a liberal person should take towards some of the problems certain sorts of sexual variation present. Clinical psychologists, particularly in the United States, have become increasingly involved with the problems of the sexual offender. This, though, presents a set of issues as much to do with offending as with sexual variation. It raises issues about the adequacy of present law in relation to sexual variation, but it leaves aside those sexual variations that are within the law.

The crisis is perhaps better reflected in the low levels of referral encountered in routine clinical practice, once forensic work has been excluded. Many clinicians are relieved to be spared an area of work that is so fraught with ethical difficulties. The possibility remains that there are circumstances when a person distressed about some aspect of a sexual variation may be well served by a clinician.

It is on that basis that assessment is approached in this chapter.

DEFINITION AND FOCUS

Conventional syndromes

The usual way of describing sexual variations has been by means of a typology based on the idea of co-occurring features. The more salient categories have sometimes been recognised medical diagnoses, but the system has been adopted by clinical psychologists as well as psychiatrists. The typology has been used to define patient populations in research and, besides that, provides the only generally accepted shorthand for communications among clinicians. The six most commonly identified categories in the UK and the USA are given below. Homosexuality would at one time have been included, but not now.

1 *Exhibitionism*, in which people freely expose their genitals in culturally inappropriate settings, such as public parks and playgrounds, probably becoming sexually aroused.
2 *Fetishism*, in which fantasy or overt behaviour is directed to an unususal degree towards clothing, parts of the body, hard or soft materials, or a wide variety of personal accessories, such as handkerchiefs or enemas.
3 *Paedophilia*, in which adults fantasise romantically or erotically about children and make contacts of various kinds with them, valuing children for qualities such as their innocence, good looks or smooth skin.
4 *Sadomasochism*, in which fantasies focus to an unusual extent on the themes of dominance and submission (usually both), and sexual activity involves coercion, restriction and in some measure pain.
5 *Transsexualism*, in which someone feels himself or herself to be a member of the opposite sex (although uncomfortably aware of his or her biological identity), and seeks to live as and be taken for a member of the opposite sex.
6 *Transvestism*, in which fantasies focus on clothes and the identity they convey, and relaxation and satisfaction are sought by periodic cross-dressing, in whole or part, in clothing of the opposite sex.

DSM III–R classifies the majority of these as 'paraphilias' and comments that 'these are practically never diagnosed in females' (American Psychiatric Association, 1987: 280). It respects a logical separation between sadism and masochism, includes frotteurism (almost never mentioned in the recent literature), and voyeurism. The term 'transvestic fetishism' replaces transvestism. Transsexualism is separately classified as a Gender Identity Disorder. 'Ego Dystonic Homosexuality' is treated as a sexual disorder in its own right. It has been argued by Gert (1992) that the definition of paraphilias does not meet the APA's definition of mental disorders in general which requires the experience of suffering or an increased risk of suffering. The APA's definition of paraphilia does not seem to imply a risk of suffering.

These are not the only terms available. Annon and Robinson (1980) listed about 110 'traditional labels for assumed or possible sexual disorders' ranging from Adamism to Zoophilia, of which at least half might still be claimed as variations. Even among the six categories there is the possibility of confusion. For example, it is difficult in practice sometimes to distinguish the paedophile from the exhibitionist (Mohr *et al.*, 1964), transsexuals were for long subsumed among transvestites, and transvestites before that among fetishists.

Another problem is the controversial presumption that there is always something abnormal about belonging to one or more of these groups. Any claim that membership is statistically unusual is hard to substantiate, given the social taboos on asking for this kind of information. Their numbers are not confined to people presenting themselves to clinicians. Gosselin and Wilson (1980) found only 15 per cent of a self-help group of sadomasochists wanted to be rid of their sexual preference. Prince and Bentler (1972), who received replies from 504 readers of the American magazine *Transvestia* found that 76 per cent of their sample had never consulted a psychiatrist.

The two groups most often represented in clinical settings are probably exhibitionists and paedophiles (114 and 56 cases respectively discharged from the Maudsley Hospital in the six years from 1970 to 1975, between 4 and 5 per cent of all adult psychiatric discharges for those years). These are often forensic cases and present a selected population. Otherwise, given the large non-clinical population, the question arises whether variant preferences *per se* should not be seen as normal. One experimental study suggests that self-exposing can in some settings arouse normal people as well as exhibitionists (Langevin *et al.*, 1979), while another indicates that normal adults will respond sexually to slides and videotapes of girls as young as 8 years old (Freund *et al.*, 1972).

To conclude, a number of conventional syndromes have been recognised and are referred to by clinicians. They have their uses, but at the same time sufficient shortcomings for it to be undesirable to base an assessment upon them.

Psychological concerns

In contrast to researchers, clinicians have been less interested in exhibitionism, fetishism, and so on in their own right than in the ways these may, in certain circumstances, lead people to express concerns in clinical settings. The few observations made here about concerns have been influenced by the general discussions by Shapiro (1975), Landfield (1975) and Fisch *et al.* (1982) on the nature of 'psychological dysfunctions', 'complaints' and 'problems' (respectively) in clinical psychology. A concern is not the same as a 'symptom'. The complainer need not be the patient. Parents and partners may also express concerns to psychologists, and in due course seek treatment in their own right. A concern is principally self-report. It can, of course, be investigated objectively and may have overt behavioural referents, but it is subjective in the sense that it implicates someone's perception of a state of affairs. Moreover, the concern is likely to convey a sense of distress. Distress may imply disablement. The disablement could be viewed as 'real' (incapacitating fear of supermarkets, dependence on a fetish for sexual arousal) or metaphorical (inability to change lifestyle or cope with problems, a sense of 'stuckness').

What constitutes a concern is normally treated as self-evident, rightly or wrongly. However, in dealing with a referral for a problem of sexual variation, the difficulties involved in defining a focus for treatment do seem to be more than usually large. An attempt is made in the following paragraphs to draw on some empirical evidence and identify common types of concern. Most of the categories are logically independent of one another, but a patient may very easily present concerns in more than one category.

1 *The patient perceives himself or herself to be too dependent on a rather narrow range of stimuli for sexual arousal.* The major source of sexual satisfaction may be hard to find. Some fetishes are inherently rare: for example, a certain shade of red hair, a person wearing a deaf aid, or someone with a calliper. A man may be unable to make love to his partner if she does not wear a certain item of clothing (Chalkley and Powell, 1983). Spengler (1977), who surveyed 245 sadomasochistic men in West Germany, reported that 15 per cent of them could not achieve orgasm without sadomasochistic activity. This applied particularly to those who took a more passive role or were exclusively sadist or masochist.

2 *The patient experiences a distressing block on normal forms of sexual expression.* A substantial number of the paedophiles investigated by Wilson and Cox (1983) believed that normal adult sexual relations were disgusting, fear-provoking, horrifying or pointless. To the extent that conventional forms of sexual expression are viewed as merely inappropriate rather than unacceptable, the matter is unlikely to be presented as of concern. Patients may report a period in the past when, incarcerated in some remote spot or in prison, they were severely limited in their sexual lives (McGuire *et al.*, 1965). They may feel that they have missed out and view their preferences as fixed. Alternatively, such blocks may be temporary, but recurring, tending to reflect difficulties with intimate relationships (Groth and Birnbaum, 1978).

3 *The patient has worries related to some aspect of a particular sexual preference.* Such anxieties may relate to the variation or to something else which the patient perceives as preventing the enjoyment of a particular sexual preference. A man may worry about what cross-dressing implies about his sexual identity or his adequacy as a husband, or he may be worried about the effects of frequent masturbation to particular fantasies. Someone wishing to discuss his or her homosexuality may be concerned about where it leaves existing heterosexual relations, whether to come out, where the law stands, how to cope with other people's prejudices about gays, what is now known about and what precautions should be taken against AIDS, and so on.

4 *A partner is concerned about a particular sexual preference.* Often important people know nothing, or next to nothing, about a patient's sexual variation. In Spengler's group, two-thirds of the sample claimed that their father, mother and siblings were ignorant of their sadomasochism. So were a large proportion of colleagues, friends and wives. Among transvestites the practice is again kept very private. The responses of partners who are told, or find out, vary considerably. Those who object, according to Brierley (1979), tend to do so because they feel that their husband is not 'all man', or because they feel not loved for themselves alone, or because they fear abandonment. Alex Comfort's view was that 'a transvestite with an informed and unscared wife usually finds that his compulsion, whatever its cause, doesn't spoil his sex life in the male

role' (Comfort, 1972: 212). With other sexual practices, a partner, however liberated, is more likely to raise objections if there is one ritual which seems a source of undue preoccupation, if it is long and complicated, if anxiety hinders sexual intercourse, or if it blatantly belies any feeling of human warmth or tenderness.

5 *The patient questions his or her sexual identity.* Both homosexuals and transvestites may question their sexual identity. Transsexuals experience this problem in more extreme form, expressing in many cases acute distress with their biological status as male or female. Often this may come with a request for sex-change surgery, presented as a matter of urgency, possibly with talk of suicide. Bancroft (1990) advises clinicians to make clear that decisions about surgery will involve other clinicians. This makes it easier for the patient to express ambivalence about undergoing the operation.

6 *The patient reports difficulty in controlling impulses.* Many sexual variations may be associated with, or actually be defined by, overt behaviour, and this may be perceived as difficult to control. Examples are peeping, publicly displaying the genitals, touching or rubbing oneself against strangers, following, pursuing, stealing, hoarding or hiding, dressing in rubber or leather, binding, gagging, or otherwise constricting oneself in polythene or rubber (sometimes to the point of asphyxiation), cross-dressing, dirtying or soiling.

These are not the only concerns that an interview with a sexually variant patient may elicit. Other concerns of a psychological nature, perhaps associated with a psychiatric diagnosis, will be taken into account. The matter of integrating concerns related to sexual variation with these others and deciding treatment priorities in the light of both is considered in Chapter 18.

Legal concerns

There are in the United Kingdom and in other countries numerous ways of committing sex-related offences. In the UK they include unlawful sexual intercourse (that is, where a person is under 16 or is for some other reason unable to give consent), incest, buggery (that is, anal intercourse), indecent assault (that is, bodily contact with overt sexual suggestion without consent), gross indecency with a child (which includes an invitation to a child to perform a sexual act), gross indecency between males, indecent exposure, and breach of the peace (a common law catch-all offence with which a person cross-dressing may be charged). Transvestites become vulnerable to a number of prostitution-related charges if, for example, they are found out at night alone with heavy rouge and lipstick. The law in the UK is particularly severe where children are involved. Since the 1990 Children Act came into force, it has become clear that clinicians are no longer protected by their duty of confidentiality to an (adult) patient where this risks conflicting with the interests of a child.

OTHER CRITERION VARIABLES

Criterion variables mean here those variables in which a clinician is interested. Up to now the issue has been the definition of the concerns at which treatment is to be directed. There are other factors which correlate with those concerns and which might be of value in explaining them, as well as factors standing in less close relationship to them that might contribute, none the less, to decisions about interventions or to predictions about outcome. Which of these other criterion variables a clinician chooses to investigate depends mainly on the theories the clinician explicitly or implicitly holds.

Theories

Analytic theory envisaged a similar disorder of personality underlying the psychopathology of all the sexual perversions. The earlier learning theory accounts of sexual variation were mostly theories of 'deviant arousal', and the questions asked ones about why some people are attracted to the 'wrong' things. With some problems it seems plausible to think in terms of deviant arousal, with others not. It appears more appropriate to fetishism and perhaps paedophilia than to exhibitionism or transsexualism. It depends if there is an identifiable stimulus to which the patient is attracted. The patient may expressly state an attraction; or an attraction may be inferred from the patient's response to an audiotaped description of a particular object or event; or it may be just suggested by something the patient does, such as hoarding or cross-dressing. In this last situation the clinician is in a position similar to that of an ethologist who hypothesises attraction from the animal's subsequent appetitive or consummatory behaviour (Beach, 1976).

With some types of behaviour, however, it is extremely difficult to find any sort of descriptive generalisation to make about effective stimuli, antecedent or consequent. Langevin et al. (1979) investigated exhibitionism. They concluded that it was easier to say what exhibitionists were not attracted to than to what they were. They were attracted to a woman's figure, but compared to a non-deviant control group they were not more attracted to young girls, men, women attending to men's genitals, or women experiencing either pleasure or shock.

Nowadays theories seem to be becoming more piecemeal as researchers identify several 'areas of concern' (Annon and Robinson, 1980), or 'components' of sexual behaviour (Barlow, 1977). Annon and Robinson broke down deviant arousal into problems related to object choice and to behaviour. They added a category called 'identity' (disturbances of gender identity, sex role and body image). Barlow retained 'deviant sexual arousal', but suggested that 'normal sexual arousal' should be investigated too, as well as 'heterosexual social skills' and 'gender role deviations'. These developments allow more phenomena to be considered. They have the further advantage of drawing out different explanations of logically distinct entities. There is no reason, for example, why the same factors should explain both why a man is attracted to ladies' underwear and why he steals it, let alone why any single intervention should be equally effective in treating both.

Theories have come to focus more on maintenance than acquisition. That is because the factors which cause problems to persist are no longer so likely to be perceived as the same as those which brought them on in the first place. Questions about early experience would, though, be important in a cognitive-behavioural framework if the clinician felt a patient held over-strong and perhaps inaccurate beliefs about the contribution of early experience to the current situation, beliefs which made the difficulties worse.

Maintaining factors

The issues that theories deal with have grown in number, but they still do not address themselves to all the psychological concerns covered earlier. They therefore do not cover areas which to a clinician would seem very important. Many in fact are directed at attempting to explain a variation and not why a variation has become a problem.

One set of hypotheses has sought to link neurological damage and one or another type of sexual variation. Reports have linked brain damage, particularly temporal lobe lesions, with fetishism (e.g. Mitchell *et al.*, 1954), transvestism (e.g. Davies and Morganstern, 1960), sadomasochism (e.g. Kolarsky *et al.*, 1967), exhibitionism (e.g. Hooshmand and Brawley, 1969), paedophilia (e.g. Lesniak *et al.*, 1972), and transsexualism (e.g. Hoenig and Kenna, 1979). For the most part these are reports of single cases, presenting a sexual anomaly, also found to be neurologically impaired. However, studies which have taken the presence of brain damage as their starting point and which have included relatively large numbers of patients have tended to report a low incidence of sexual variation (Kolarsky *et al.*, 1967; Shukla *et al.*, 1979).

Behind this sort of investigation is the idea that by having a lesion of some kind the patient may be predisposed to acquire 'odd' and highly specific types of sexual attraction; but the theory could also be an explanation of poor impulse control. Epstein (1960) brought together eleven cases of fetishism from the literature, summarily characterised by 'increased organismic excitability'. Among the features they shared were urges to perform certain motor acts, marked readiness of sexual arousal by the fetish and sexual arousal from what would be seen as non-erotic items like safety pins. Several of these patients had been confirmed as having, and others may have had, neurological disorders.

In contrast to Epstein's report of selected cases of 'marked readiness of sexual arousal by the fetish', are a number of cases where levels of sexual interest seem to have been rather low (e.g. Hoenig and Kenna, 1979; Buis, 1966). Crawford (1979), discussing sexual offenders, pointed out that many of them also had sexual dysfunctions, such as impotence or premature ejaculation.

Such problems may arise with people whose levels of confidence are already low. Eleven of Chalkley and Powell's forty-eight patients suffered either from fits or some other stigmatising condition, such as severe acne: one patient was seeking plastic surgery for a 'beaky' nose; another, who thought his nose was too long, covered it with his hand in conversation. Over a quarter of the sample, whose median age was 28, were judged by the psychiatrist to be socially anxious, and seventeen had never had sexual intercourse. Patients in other studies have been assessed as deficient in social skills (see, for example, Barlow *et al.*, 1977).

The perception the patient has of himself as abnormal may be heightened by the particular label that society attaches to him or which he attaches to himself. Wilson and Cox (1983) asked members of the Paedophile Information Exchange how they felt about their sexual preference. Among the seventy-seven replies were many emotionally charged ones: 'disturbed', 'guilty', 'ashamed ', 'sad', 'hopeless', 'depressed', 'bitter', 'angry'. Righton (1981) argued that the public's perception of the typical paedophile is reinforced by the language experts use to express their opinions. He cited the use of phrases such as 'morbid interest' and 'disease of the morals'. Perhaps the growth of minority interest groups over the last twenty years has done something to change the particular picture society has of some groups. It is less likely that it has done anything to reduce sexual stereotyping

Reasons why a partner might complain about a sexual variation have already been mentioned. The partner may anticipate that sex will end in failure, or in physical or psychological harm to one or both, or may find that a particular sexual practice fails to conform to a cherished idea of what is sexual, moral, decent or normal. Alternatively, the sexual variation and the concerns that are expressed about it may both be explained by other difficulties in the relationship. There may be sexual dysfunction. Anger and anxiety about rejection are thought likely to inhibit sexual arousal (Jehu, 1980). There is a small amount of experimental and clinical evidence that variant sexual behaviour may occur at the same time as negative mood states such as fear, depression and hostility (Weissman, 1957; Stoller, 1974; La Torre, 1980).

It seems likely that the persistence of some of these psychological concerns, particularly those related to over-dependence on a particular object or event, real or imagined, may involve consummatory sexual activity, either masturbation or intercourse accompanied by fantasies (McGuire *et al.*, 1965). Powerful reinforcers such as these are likely to strengthen and shape the images, events or actions to which the patient maintains an attraction. Those that are not associated with masturbation are likely in time to be perceived as less attractive than those that are.

STANDARDISED PROCEDURES

Ideally there would be standardised procedures for the assessment of all the variables covered so far. In this way the clinician could be reassured about the psychometric validity of the methods being used. It might also make assessment quicker. It would be particularly useful if at a first interview the clinician could turn to a readily available questionnaire or inventory and be sure of obtaining from it an adequately precise statement of the patient's concerns, one which would provide a dependable and useful starting point. However, as elsewhere in psychology, there is no evidence that all relevant aspects of patients' experience can be properly assessed by any pre-set procedure. Such a procedure would need to be able to cover an enormous amount of ground in very great detail. This finding is predicted by the theory that psychological variables are 'relatively specific' (Spearman, 1927; Shapiro, 1970).

Subjective report and observation

The main implication of relative specificity is for the initial assessment of psychological concerns, where the content of the problem is a priority. Procedures are required which are both flexible and accurate. This appears to throw the clinician back on the interview (Shapiro, 1979), whatever its shortcomings.

A key requirement of the interview is to ensure adequacy of coverage. A clinician will want a description which will permit both the inclusion of the types of concern outlined earlier and additional concerns, related or unrelated, which also form part of the overall picture. My own practice has been to use a form of Personal Interview (available from the writer) and go on from there to construct a Personal Questionnaire (Shapiro, 1961; see also Lindsay and Powell, Chapter 1), containing statements of the patient from the Personal Interview. Questions fall into nine categories which, while used with most patients, are specific enough to help elaborate concerns related to sexual variation: (1) crisis; (2) communication; (3) explanations; (4) others; (5) acceptability; (6) practical; (7) control; (8) desperation; (9) stuckness.

From such a general descriptive procedure, certain specific questions may be suggested and in some cases psychometric 'tests' exist to clarify these. (Conte (1983) contains a general review of paper-and-pencil tests of sexual functioning; see also de Silva, Chapter 9).

How does this patient's self-reported and observed behaviour compare with that of members of particular gender identity groups? In the light of what was written earlier about syndromes, it is probably fair to argue that diagnostic tests are of limited utility. There have, though, been a number of this kind of self-report measure over the years. Freund *et al.* (1977) published a 29-item gender-identity scale based on self-reported behaviour. Items were chosen on the basis of their ability to distinguish between various male groups. The authors' view was that the earlier part of the scale helped differentiate transvestites from transsexuals (on the assumption that transvestites are heterosexual and transsexuals are not), and the later part helped to differentiate transsexual homosexuals from non-transsexual homosexuals. Barlow *et al.* (1979) describes a checklist of sex-role behaviour.

How common, frequent or powerful are this patient's sexual fantasies? The potentially most useful questionnaire material probably relates to sexual fantasy. A number of studies present relevant data. Inevitably the information is not very precise and tends to deal with categories of fantasy rather than particular fantasies. All the studies survey a 'normal' population, but include items which a patient might regard as deviant. Sue (1979) surveyed the fantasies of American male and female college students during coitus. Crepault and Couture (1980) reported on 94 male francophone Canadians between 20 and 45 years old. In this group 14.9 per cent often fantasised about women wearing exciting clothing and accessories, where 8.5 per cent frequently imagined scenes where women were tied up and stimulated sexually. Wilson's (1978) book contained a Sex Fantasy Questionnaire and data about a group of men and women 'of relatively high occupational status' to whom the questionnaire had been administered. Although a patient's score on a particular item could not be compared with the sample, it was possible to compare scores on any of four factor-analytically derived scales drawn from these items and named 'exploratory', 'intimate', 'impersonal', and 'sado-masochistic'. Smith and Over (1991) and Meuwissen and Over (1991) present sex fantasy questionnaire data for men and women (respectively the MSFQ and FSFQ). They were interested both in mean degree of arousal and in mean frequency of use of the fantasies. The sample size and original item pool for the FSFQ was considerably larger than for the MSFQ. In both studies only the results for the twenty-five most highly arousing items were included, all with factor loadings greater than 0.40. The item pools contained fantasies about commonly experienced sexual activities rather than imaginary and make-believe material. These two questionnaires may help clinicians assess the strength and frequency of common fantasies among patients who may also experience uncommon ones.

Is this particular transsexual patient suitable for sex-change surgery? There would appear to be no test with predictive validity. A study by Walinder *et al.* (1978) found poor post-operative outcome associated with prior presence of unstable personality, inadequacy of self-support (for example, failure to obtain or hold down a job), inadequate support from family or close friends, inappropriate physique, and less than one occasion of full heterosexual coitus. There is evidence that a popular but previously unvalidated criterion (whether the patient has successfully negotiated an extended period of living and working in the desired gender role) also predicts post-operative adjustment (Meyer and Reter, 1979).

Physiological measures

According to Barlow (1977), who reviewed the subject at length, until Zuckerman's (1971) paper a number of different responses were considered suitable physiological measures of sexual arousal. However, Zuckerman argued that most of them, for example cardiac rate and pupil size, could be affected by many other psychological variables.

For the assessment of sexual arousal in men this meant more attention was given to penile erection, considered – perhaps unsurprisingly – by Zuckerman to be the best physiological measure. Clinicians have tended on the whole to prefer measures of penile circumference to the more sensitive but technically more complicated measure of penile volume devised by Freund *et al.* (1965). A comparison of the two types of measure showed them sometimes to change in opposite directions (McConaghy, 1974).

There are two main methods of measuring change in penile circumference. What is normally recorded with both is the maximum amplitude of response to a given stimulus expressed as a percentage of what circumference the patient's full erection gives. The first method was described by Bancroft *et al.* (1966) and in more detail by Bancroft (1974). It is a transducer (that is, it converts a physical change in the body into an electrical reading), consisting of a ring of 18 cm of silicone rubber filled with mercury and fitted with electrodes. As the penis becomes erect it lengthens the rubber tube and the mercury inside it. At the same time the diameter of the mercury is reduced and this increases the resistance of the circuit. The patient can himself place the ring, which is stabilised by a piece of perspex, over his penis. The other method was described by Barlow *et al.* (1970). It is a mechanical strain gauge set into an incomplete ring of surgical metal with a thin plastic coating. The incomplete ring is actually two half rings attached to each other at one end where the gauge 'platform' is. The material is pliant and as penile circumference increases, a strain is created at the gauge platform. This is converted into an electrical reading. Again, the patient can place the ring himself. The apparatus of Barlow *et al.* appears to be the harder to set up. Where repeated measures have been made, some reliability problems have been reported with it (Eccles *et al.*, 1988).

From the mid-1970s there began to appear physiological methods for the measurement of sexual arousal in women. The most researched is the vaginal photoplethysmograph (Sintchak and Geer, 1975). This records vasocongestion in the vagina either in terms of blood volume (DC coupling), or pulse amplitude (AC coupling). The patient inserts a clear acrylic probe about the size and shape of a tampon into her vagina. It contains a light source and a light detector. Blood changes affect the amount of light which gets back to the light detector and the output of the photoelectric transducer. Issues to do with the application and operation of this apparatus are reviewed by Hatch (1979).

For the most part, physiological measures do not present direct measurement of the criterion variables considered earlier, and this raises the issue of their criterion validity. Methodologically they seem to owe something to the taste prevalent especially in the early years of 'behavioural assessment', for 'hard', reliable measures. One could argue that for the average clinician, dealing mainly with a voluntary clientele, self-reports of anxiety, impulsivity, and of course sexual arousal are preferable. Where self-reported and physiological arousal fail to correlate – perhaps a quarter of cases (Abel *et al.*, 1981) – it is not a straightforward issue to decide which is the more appropriate measure. 'Non-admitters' may falsify their reports, but it also appears possible to suppress erectile response (Henson and Rubin, 1971). Further discussion of some of these issues is to be found in McConaghy (1989).

There does, though, appear to be a case for the clinical use of physiological measures in certain circumstances. A study by Abel *et al.* (1975) suggests that some patients may be unwittingly deceived about what excites them. The authors made successive audiotape recordings of a description of a fetish. The patient believed his fetish was white or brown sandals with open treads. When a description was replayed to him it evoked only 20 per cent of the patient's full erection on the penile plethysmograph. When the tape was remade to focus on the holding and caressing of the foot, and its smell and smooth touch, the figure went up to 75 per cent.

Physiological measures, like other standardised procedures, have a distinct but limited role in assessment. The clinician's principal strategy is to interview with the aim of eliciting clear statements of psychological concerns and then, in the light of the hypotheses that have suggested themselves, go on to verify or clarify his or her ideas about those concerns in terms of related criterion variables.

REFERENCES

Abel, G. G., Blanchard, E. B., Barlow, D. H. and Mavissakalian, M. (1975) 'Identifying specific erotic cues in sexual deviations by audiotaped descriptions', *Journal of Applied Behavioral Analysis* 8: 247–60.

Abel, G. G., Blanchard, E. B., Murphy, W. D., Becker, J. B. and Djenderedjian, A. (1981) 'Two methods of measuring penile response', *Behavior Therapy* 12: 320–8.

American Psychiatric Association (1987) *Diagnostic and Statistical Manual of Mental Disorders. 3rd edn Revised*, Washington, DC: American Psychiatric Association.

Annon, J. S. and Robinson, C. H. (1980) 'Sexual disorders', in A. E. Kazdin, A. S. Bellak and M. Hersen, (eds) *New Perspectives in Abnormal Psychology*, New York: Oxford University Press.

Bancroft, J. (1974) *Deviant Sexual Behaviour: Modification and Assessment*, Oxford: Clarendon Press.

Bancroft, J. (1990) *Human Sexuality and Its Problems. 2nd edn.*, Edinburgh: Churchill Livingstone.

Bancroft, J., Jones, H. and Pullan, B. (1966) 'A simple transducer for measuring penile erction with comments on its use in the treatment of sexual disorders', *Behaviour Research and Therapy* 4: 239–41.

Barlow, D. H. (1977) 'Assessment of sexual behavior', in A. R. Ciminero, K. S. Calhoun and H. S. Adams (eds) *Handbook of Behavioral Assessment*, Wiley: New York.

Barlow, D. H., Becker, R., Leitenberg, H. and Agras, W. S. (1970) 'A mechanical strain gauge for recording penile circumference change', *Journal of Applied Behavioral Analysis* 3: 73–6.

Barlow, D. H., Abel G. G., Blanchard, E. B., Bristow, A. R. and Young, L. D. (1977) 'A heterosocial skills behavior checklist for males', *Behavior Therapy* 8: 229–39.

Barlow, D. H., Hayes, S. C., Nelson, R. O., Steele, D. L., Meeler, M. E. and Mills, J. R. (1979) 'Sex role motor behavior: a checklist', *Behavioral Assessment* 1: 119–38.

Beach, F. A. (1976) 'Cross-species comparisons and the human heritage', *Archives of Sexual Behavior* 5: 469–81.

Brierley, H. (1979) *Transvestism*, Oxford: Pergamon Press.

Buis, C. (1966) 'A child's spectacles as fetish', *Psychiatria, Neurologia, Neurochirurgia* 69: 359–62.

Chalkley, A. J. and Powell, G. E. (1983) 'The clinical description of forty-eight cases of sexual fetishism', *British Journal of Psychiatry* 142: 292–5.

Comfort, A. (1972) *The Joy of Sex*, London: Quartet Books.

Conte, H. R. (1983) 'Development and use of self-report techniques for assessing sexual functioning: a review and a critique', *Archives of Sexual Behavior* 12: 555–76.

Crawford, D. A. (1979) 'Modification of deviant sexual behaviour: the need for a comprehensive approach', *British Journal of Medical Psychology* 52: 151–6.

Crepault, C. and Couture, M. (1980) 'Men's erotic fantasies', *Archives of Sexual Behavior* 9: 565–81.

Davies, D. M. and Morganstern, F. S. (1960) 'A case of cysticerosis, temporal lobe epilepsy and transvestism', *Journal of Neurology, Nerosurgery and Psychiatry* 23: 247–9.

Eccles, A., Marshall, W. L. and Barbaree, H. E. (1988) 'The vulnerability of erectile measures to repeated assessments', *Behaviour Research and Therapy* 26: 176–83.

Epstein, A. W. (1960) 'Fetishism: a study of its psychopathology with particular reference to a proposed disorder in brain mechanisms as an etiological factor', *Journal of Mental and Nervous Disorders* 133: 247–53.

Fisch, R., Weakland, J. H. and Segal, L. (1982) *The Tactics of Change. Doing Therapy Briefly*, San Francisco: Jossey-Bass.

Freund, K., Sedlacek, J. and Knob, K. (1965) 'A simple transducer for mechanical plethysmography of the male genitals', *Journal of the Experimental Analysis of Behavior* 8: 169–70.

Freund, K., McKnight, C. K., Langevin, R. and Cibiri., S. (1972) 'The female child as surrogate object', *Archives of Sexual Behavior* 2: 119–33.

Freund, K., Langevin, R., Satterburg, J. and Steiner, B. (1977) 'Extension of the gender identity scale for males', *Archives of Sexual Behavior* 6: 507–19.

Gert, B. (1992) 'A sex caused inconsistency in DSMIIIR', *The Journal of Medicine and Philosophy* 17: 155–71.

Gosselin, C., and Wilson, G. D. (1980) *Sexual Variation*, London: Faber & Faber.

Groth, A. N. and Birnbaum, H. J. (1978) 'Adult sexual orientation and attraction to underage persons', *Archives of Sexual Behavior* 7: 175–81.

Hatch, J. P. (1979) 'Vaginal photoplethysmography: methodological considerations', *Archives of Sexual Behavior* 8: 357–74.

Henson, D. E. and Rubin, H. B. (1971) 'Voluntary control of eroticism', *Journal of Applied Behavioral Analysis* 4: 37–41.

Hoenig, J. and Kenna, J. C. (1979) 'EEG abnormalities and transsexualism', *British Journal of Psychiatry* 134: 293–300.

Hooshmand, H. and Brawley, B. W. (1969) 'Temporal lobe seizures and exhibitionism', *Neurology* 19: 1119–24.

Jehu, D. (1980) *Sexual Dysfunction. A Behavioural Approach to Causation, Assessment and Treatment*, Chichester: Wiley.

Kolarsky, A., Freund, K., Machek, J. and Polak, D. (1967) 'Male sexual deviation: association with early temporal damage', *Archives of General Psychiatry* 17: 735–42.

Landfield, A. W. (1975) 'The complaint: a confrontation of personal urgency and professional construction', in D. Bannister (ed.) *Issues and Approaches in the Psychological Therapies*, London: Wiley.

Langevin, R., Paitich D., Ramsay, G., Anderson, C., Kamrad, J., Pope, S., Geller, G., Pearl, L., and Newman, S. (1979) 'Experimental studies of the etiology of genital exhibitionism', *Archives of Sexual Behavior* 8: 307–31.

La Torre, R. A. (1980) 'Devaluation of the human love object: heterosexual rejection as a possible antecedent to fetishism', *Journal of Abnormal Psychology* 89: 295–8.

Lesniak, R., Szmusik, A. and Chrzanowski, R. (1972) 'Case report: multidirectional disorders of sexual response in a case of brain tumour', *Forensic Science* 1: 333–8.

McConaghy, N. (1974) 'Measurements of change in penile dimensions', *Archives of Sexual Behavior* 3: 381–8.

McConaghy, N. (1989) 'Validity and ethics of penile circumference measures: a critical review', *Archives of Sexual Behavior* 18: 357–69.

McGuire, R. J., Carlisle, J. M. and Young, B. G. (1965) 'Sexual deviations as conditioned behaviour: a hypothesis', *Behaviour Research and Therapy* 2: 185–90.

Meuwissen, I. and Over, R. (1991) 'Multidimensionality of the content of Female Sexual Fantasy', *Behaviour Research and Therapy* 18: 179–89.

Meyer, J. K. and Reter, D. J. (1979) 'Sex re-assignment. Follow-up', *Archives of General Psychiatry* 36: 1010–15.

Mitchell, W., Falconer, W. A. and Hill, D. (1954) 'Epilepsy with fetishism relieved by temporal lobectomy', *Lancet* 2: 626–30.

Mohr, J. W., Turner, R. E. and Jerry, M. B. (1964) *Paedophilia and Exhibitionism: a Handbook*, Toronto: University of Toronto Press.

Prince, V. and Bentler, P. M. (1972) 'Survey of 504 cases of transvestism', *Psychological Reports* 31: 903–17.

Righton, P. (1981) 'The Adult', in B. Taylor (ed.) *Perspectives on Paedophilia*, London: Batsford.

Shapiro, M. B. (1961) 'A method of measuring psychological changes specific to the individual patient', *British Journal of Medical Psychology* 34: 151–5.

Shapiro, M. B. (1970) 'The intensive investigation of the single case', in P. Mittler (ed.) *The Psychological Assessment of Mental and Physical Handicaps*, London: Methuen.

Shapiro, M. B. (1975) 'The requirments and implications of a systematic science of psychopathology', *Bulletin of the British Psychological Society* 28: 149–55.

Shapiro, M. B. (1979) 'Assessment interviewing in clinical psychology', *British Journal of Social and Clinical Psychology* 18: 211–18.

Shukla, G. D., Srivastava, O. N. and Katiya, B. C. (1979) 'Sexual disturbances in temporal lobe epilepsy: a controlled study', *British Journal of Psychiatry* 134: 288–92.

Sintchak, G. and Geer, J. (1975) 'A vaginal photoplethysmograph system', *Psychophysiology* 12: 113–15.

Smith D. and Over R. (1991) 'Male sexual fantasy: multidimensionality in content', *Behaviour Research and Therapy* 18: 267–75.

Spearman, C. (1927) *The Abilities of Man*, New York: Macmillan.

Spengler, A. (1977) 'Manifest sadomasochism in males. Results of an empirical study', *Archives of Sexual Behavior* 6: 441–56.

Stoller, R. S. (1974) 'Hostility and mystery in perversion', *International Journal of Psychoanalysis* 55: 424–34.

Storr, A. (1964) *Sexual Deviation*, Harmondsworth, Middx.: Penguin.

Sue, D. (1979) 'Erotic fantasies of college students during coitus', *Journal of Sex Research* 15: 299–305.

Walinder, J., Lundstrom B. and Thuwe, I. (1978) 'Prognostic factors in the assessment of male transsexuals for sex re-assignment', *British Journal of Psychiatry* 132: 16–20.

Weissman, P. (1957) 'Some aspects of sexual activity in a fetishist', *Psychoanalytic Quarterly* 26: 494–507.

Wilson, G. D. (1978) *The Secrets of Sexual Fantasy*, London: Dent.

Wilson, G. D. and Cox, D. N. (1983) *The Child-Lovers*, London: Peter Owen.

Zuckerman, M. (1971) 'Physiological measures of sexual arousal in the human', *Psychological Bulletin* 75: 297–329.

Chapter 18

Problems related to sexual variation
Treatment

A.J. Chalkley

INTRODUCTION

Treatment is not the only response that problems related to sexual variation have elicited. Some interventions seem to have deterrent and incapacitating aspects (electric shock, hormone treatment and stereotactical surgery, for example), and with some types of sexual variation, treatment itself presents some potential interference with a person's right to get on with his or her own life. A reasonable case can be made for treatment only if attention is constantly paid to what clinician and patient are trying to achieve, and the focus of concern is kept constantly in mind. A man, on the whole, might be expected to be most unwilling to be rid of his homosexuality. On the other hand, he might be very worried about making an impulsive approach to a young man twenty years his junior, and thereby risking his career (McConaghy *et al.*, 1981). Most clinicians would probably be willing to work on this man's anxiety about his homosexuality and the difficulty he experienced in controlling impulses, if not his attraction to other men.

This distinction between sexual variation and the problems sometimes associated with it was made in the preceding chapter. It was suggested that, while there was a generally accepted typology of sexual variations, this typology was unsatisfactory in a number of ways. The chapter went on instead to approach assessment through six categories of 'concern' derived from clinical sources but not validated in any very systematic way. This approach is taken again here. In the second section, consideration is given to which treatments seem most suitable for each area of concern. Certain interventions require more detailed discussion, and these are covered in the third section. The first section deals with published outcome studies.

PUBLISHED OUTCOME STUDIES

By no means every type of concern regularly features as a dependent variable in the relevant outcome literature, and so it is often difficult to say with any degree of assurance what treatment works or does not work with each category, let alone to identify related prognostic and treatment variables. The question at this point is to what extent different types of treatment are successful on their own terms.

Modifying arousal patterns

Most of the procedures researched in the literature have been based on learning theory. Their original objective was to modify arousal patterns. On the whole these procedures date back some time, but there have been one or two recent developments, for example 'stimulus satiation' (Lo Piccolo, 1985). The two which are probably best known are 'orgasmic reconditioning' (Marquis, 1970), and 'covert sensitisation' (Cautela, 1967; Cautela and Wisocki, 1971). These are described later in the chapter. There are other phrases to describe these procedures or modifications of these procedures. Orgasmic reconditioning has been described as 'counter-conditioning' (Jackson, 1969), as 'arousal conditioning' (Keller and Goldstein, 1978), and as 'masturbation training'. Covert sensitisation has sometimes been seen as aversion therapy (Callahan and Leitenberg, 1973), but recently more often contrasted with it (McConaghy et al., 1981), leaving aversion therapy to cover electric shock, emetics and unpleasant smells.

Early reports of orgasmic reconditioning were favourable, but during the later 1970s concern began to be expressed on a number of grounds. Reports had been largely evaluations of single cases or multiple single cases. Furthermore, there was little evidence that the treatment worked when assessed on 'harder' behavioural and physiological measures (Conrad and Wincze, 1976). A number of explanations were offered as to why the approach appeared to be less effective than at first it promised. In his original version, Marquis asked the patient to masturbate to whatever fantasy he found most arousing (presumably the 'deviant' one), and then to switch to a more appropriate fantasy at the point he felt orgasm to be inevitable. Keller and Goldstein (1978) pointed out that this was backward conditioning because the unconditional stimulus (US) (masturbation) preceded the conditional stimulus (CS) (more appropriate fantasy). Arguing that a forward-conditioning paradigm was in theory more effective, they provided a clinical illustration using the alternative sequence.

Another problem with orgasmic reconditioning from the perspective of classical conditioning theory derived from Kamin's finding that if a conditional emotional response had been established using one CS and if an attempt was made to condition a second CS in the presence of the first (that is in the sequence CS1, CS2, US), when the second CS was presented on its own, it was found that no conditioning had taken place. There had been a 'blocking' effect (Kamin, 1969).

Kantorowitz (1978) highlighted other problems in the discussion section of an analogue study. Patients, he thought, might use deviant imagery to 'salvage' sexual arousal or sense that they achieved orgasm 'in spite of' the use of appropriate, but to their mind essentially rather unattractive, stimuli. Kremsdorf et al. (1980) reported a case study of a successful treatment of a 20-year-old paedophile by methods which sought to remove some of these difficulties. The study was unusual in reporting improvement on three physiological indices: percentage erectile strength to deviant and to non-deviant stimuli, and latency of ejaculation.

There are some parallels to be drawn with the literature on covert sensitisation. Here again there were reports that the treatment had been successful with single cases. The early papers tended to focus on procedure and only later was attention shifted to the outcome criteria. When this happened, it was found that there was little evidence that covert sensitisation or any other procedure designed primarily to suppress 'deviant arousal' could bring about long-term sexual reorientation. However, it was discovered that covert sensitisation was as good as, if not better than, electric shock on all measures assessed, and, since it was cheaper, led to fewer drop-outs, could be more easily self-administered and probably made more therapists less uncomfortable, it became the preferred treatment (Callahan and Leitenberg, 1973; McConaghy et al., 1981). This conclusion was drawn against a background increasingly sensitive to any attempt to interfere with a person's freedom to live in the sexual style he or she chose, subject to their not causing harm to or imposing on others (see, for example, Davison, 1977).

The survival of any 'suppressant' technique into the 1980s therefore required some clarification of what such treatments achieved and were expected to achieve. In their paper, McConaghy et al. (1981) argued that some people might want help in controlling unwanted sexual impulses. To refuse them treatment would itself raise ethical objections, and at present the most effective of the empirically tested procedures was covert sensitisation. Moreover, they added that if the procedures did not reorientate a person sexually but did affect his or her behaviour, a theory was required which accounted, not for the way treatment affected what a person was attracted to, but for how his or her overt behaviour towards it was determined. Geer and Fuhr (1976) considered the contribution of distraction and McConaghy et al. (1981) cited psychophysiological evidence to support an explanation in terms of 'behaviour completion' mechanisms. These are further examples of the trend away from 'deviant arousal theory'.

Overcoming social and relationship difficulties

'Adjunctive treatments' have been described in the literature for some time and modifying arousal patterns seen as insufficient. Clinicians have argued that it is necessary to increase appropriate forms of social and sexual interaction for major improvements to take place (Barlow, 1977). They have concentrated on a variety of issues including, on the one hand, reports of aversion to female genitalia or negative emotional feelings brought on by seeing naked members of the opposite sex and, on the other hand, descriptions of social interactions characterised by poor affect, poor voice production, and poor conversation.

A number of individual case studies contain reports of the successful use of systematic desensitisation and of skills training, and these appear in turn to have been fairly successful in increasing the sexual responses judged appropriate (see Barlow (1973) for an early review; later papers by Turner and Van Hasselt (1979), and Crawford and Allen (1979). These procedures still tend to be seen as 'adjunctive' (by implication less important), in much of the literature, although programmes have become broader in scope over the last dozen years or so (Brownell, 1980).

A case for giving priority to cognitive and relationship difficulties over sexual deviance has been argued recently by Marshall et al., (1991). They described two successive treatment studies of exhibitionists carried out by their group. Outcome was measured in terms of recidivism rates. Study One (N = 44, recidivism about 35 per cent over eight years) focused mainly on deviant arousal, but also included desensitisation or flooding to reduce anxiety, and modelling and role-play to enhance conversation skills. In Study Two (N = 17, recidivism about 24 per cent over four years), covert sensitisation was retained but electrical aversion therapy was dropped; the rationale for covert sensitisation was clearly presented as meant to help to develop control over thoughts rather than to serve as a punishment for deviant sexual feelings; and greater attention was given to developing skills for dealing with stress: assertiveness training, stress-management, cognitive restructuring and training in relationship skills.

Management of gender identity

The assessment of transsexuals for sex-change surgery was discussed in the preceding chapter. Not all patients ultimately opt for surgery and, among those that do, not all are selected. Conn (1979) found fifteen studies that had been published between 1966 and 1978 and established the percentage of successful or neutral outcome for each one: the figures turned out to be high with a median of 92 per cent. A more recent study of male-to-female transsexuals suggests that overall sexual adjustment is often unchanged by surgery; in one, only a third of those who had a vaginal construct had a functioning vagina and, again, only a third were rated as having a fair or good sexual adjustment after sex reassignment (Lindemalm et al., 1986). A study of forty female-to-male transsexuals reported an increase in polycystic ovarian disease (Futterweit et al., 1986).

Sex-change surgery is scarcely psychological treatment, but a psychologist could well be involved in its preparation. He or she might also be involved where attempts were made to re-socialise and sexually reorientate a patient in his or her biological role. There have been reports of success with this approach in papers published by Barlow et al. (1973) and Barlow et al. (1979). In the first study, a 17-year-old male, who had been seeking a sex-change but had been rejected – for the time-being at any rate – as too young, agreed to have his sexual identity treated. There is a description of how posture and vocal characteristics were changed and male sexual fantasies taught. The second study reports a favourable follow-up and a comparable success with another patient a few years older than the first. It also describes a third patient, who gave up feminine gender-identity while choosing to remain homosexual. It may be expected that many psychologists who are faced in due course with a referral of this kind will find themselves in something of a dilemma, since for the majority of patients the option is less than wholly attractive.

INTERVENTIONS WITH PARTICULAR CONCERNS

This section takes up the categories of concern proposed in the previous chapter and makes some suggestions about interventions that might be tried with each. Some of these are adaptations of procedures discussed fully elsewhere in the book. Others are described more fully in the section that follows on general and specific interventions. It is likely that concerns will fall into a number of different categories and, as a result, that a number of different interventions will be attempted. Furthermore, it would be expected in a clinical population that other target problems will be present, quite possibly related to sexual concerns, for example, affective disturbance, guilt and hopelessness.

Over-dependence on a narrow range of stimuli. This is a target area where orgasmic reconditioning could be used to advantage. The aim of treatment would be to expand the number of stimuli the patient finds attractive, not to substitute something else for them. The procedure initially involves an assessment of the attractive features of each stimulus (that is, an analysis of the 'effective stimuli' or 'attributes'), and then seeks a gradual increase in range by masturbation training to fantasies or in situations where some features are varied and others held constant. Alternatively, there may be room for some degree of normalising. After all, many people pursue unattainable ideals and compromise as circumstances require. A move to a larger population centre might improve a patient's chances of achieving his or her quest.

More normal sexual relationships seem blocked in the long or short term. The patient may complain of social and emotional obstacles to what he or she considers would be an appropriate sexual life. Where there is a partner, work with the couple might aim to: (1) facilitate understanding of the blocks, (2) help resolve them by commitments to specific changes and challenging beliefs cognitively, (3) aid the expression and communication of affect, and (4) identify negative patterns of interaction. These suggestions are taken from Bancroft (1990) and represent the 'psychotherapeutic component' of his approach to sexual problems. For clinical or practical reasons, individual work is often necessary. Other interventions include desensitisation of social anxieties and social-skills training.

Among paedophiles with stable erotic preferences for children, one review suggests that prominent themes will include the idealisation of childhood, overwhelming anxiety about adult heterosexuality, and a belief about their inability to exercise power and control in an adult relationship. Among people who molest from time to time, a corresponding theme identified is anger and resentfulness about perceived expectations within intimate relationships, with child mole-station occurring at such times (Lanyon, 1986). In respect of exhibitionists, Marshall *et al.* (1991) felt that their patients often had a sense of being taken advantage of by others, suffered from a lack of intimacy which created feelings of deprivation, and experienced resentment arising from a need to be perfect. Exhibitionism had become a way of dealing with negative emotions.

For many patients, social contacts may, at least in the short term, be im-practicable. Bernard Zilbergeld's book *Men and Sex*, is written for men whether or not they have partners (Zilbergeld, 1980). Particularly useful topics for men without partners are those on masturbation, touching, virginity and abstinence, and working out one's needs. These discussions seem likely to help a patient gain understanding and acceptance of himself sexually. If what is required is some-thing simple and factual (for men and women), then Ward (1988) is useful. Some organisations for the physically handicapped have begun to look at the sexual needs of their members and offer practical advice.

The patient has worries related to a particular sexual preference. Beliefs about a sexual preference likely to be elicited include the notions that it is inexplicable, inadmissible, unusual, odd or monstrous. Other worries relate more to the consequences of a sexual preference.

Most issues have been approached within a counselling framework. The main focus is on self-acceptance and not on changing sexual preferences. 'Counselling towards self-acceptance, greater inward and external openness, living with un-certainty but still developing and growing, are more fruitful avenues to go down' (Sketchley, 1989a: 249). Historically, the recurring issues were identified and addressed by the specialist organisations that grew up during the 1970s (and earlier) like the Legal Action Group, Brook Advisory Centre, Albany Trust, Beaumont Society, Campaign for Homosexual Equality, Gay Switchboard and Lesbian Line. Who should counsel gay people is considered by Rochlin (1985). Much may be at stake when a patient is considering approaching a specialist organisation of this kind, and a person may use a clinician to clarify what help is being sought and how the organisation is best approached. Clinicians need to have familiarity with the other counselling issues, because while they may not routinely be referred patients for counselling on these matters, they will en-counter them when they see members of sexual minority groups for other reasons. Treatment might therefore need to take account of issues associated with coming out (Beane, 1981), and also factors complicating the relationships of gay, lesbian and bisexual couples (Peplau, 1982; Wolf, 1985). There are couples where one partner has come out and the other has not. Some couples are troubled by the absence of traditional sets of rules for the relationship, the lack of external support, the absence of gender roles, and – having given so much more up to live together – expectations of perfection.

The psychotherapeutic needs of gay men have grown more complex as a result of the AIDS epidemic (Morin *et al.*, 1984). Many people in their thirties have had to come to terms with friends' deaths or faced death and the effects of debilitating illness themselves. Counselling people with AIDS needs to take account both of the uneven progression of the illness and the stage reached in a person's response both to being HIV positive and having AIDS itself: shock or deep shock; adjustment and discharging feelings verbally; acceptance and restoring a sense of being in control; taking stock of the implications, decisions and preparation for death. The stages do not necessarily progress in a logical fashion (Miller, 1986; 1987). These issues are summarised in Sketchley (1989b), who also considers ways of helping the 'unwilling client' whose response to AIDS is complicated by low self-esteem.

The partner is concerned about a particular sexual preference. Where a partner has concerns, there are tactical issues to consider. The clinician has to decide who (partner or patient) is the more concerned and the more amenable to change, who to see, and how far the difficulties should be formulated for the couple as a relationship rather than a personal problem. During the course of couple therapy, where issues about particular sexual preferences are likely to come up, the starting point may well be counselling (Annon, 1974). This involves: (1) a certain amount of information about the commonplaceness of sexual tastes and preferences; (2) help for the couple in trying to talk about them; (3) an atmosphere of permission and appropriate reassurance; (4) exploration of how to incorporate aspects of fantasy and behaviour into the couple's sexual life. The partner may need additional help in understanding why a particular sexual preference contains an unpleasant meaning. It may seem to a wife that the patient wants to end the relationship or heap humiliation upon her. It may relate to themes from the partner's past, or seem symbolic of wider and more pervasive (non-sexual) issues in the relationship, or have features (rages, compulsive urges) that encourage the partner to view the behaviour as 'sick'. A wife or husband may need help in saying no to those activities which remain fear-provoking or distasteful.

The clinician may or may not feel that the patient requires individual help. On occasion, though, it may be helpful not to see the couple together at first and to explore the couple's shared concerns with them later.

There are uncertainties and difficulties over sexual identity. A bisexual patient may come to a psychologist expressing uncertainty about his or her true sexual identity. Establishing that a person need not be wholly heterosexual or homosexual still leaves unresolved the issue of how the patient is to live as a bisexual, although it does allow a shift from one big issue to a number of smaller problems. And it raises questions such as what sort of relationships the patient currently wants to explore and how these relate to longer-term goals.

A transsexual or transvestite patient may come with a request for help in living as a member of his or her elected sex. This may be preparatory to sex-reassignment surgery. It is helpful if the clinician knows something about different aspects of gender management. These are considered by Kessler and

McKenna (1978). Yardley (1976) presents a case study in which a female therapist helped a male–female transsexual with various social skills over the course of twenty two-hour sessions. They covered body and head movement, facial expression, body tonus, posture, gesture, gaze, voice, courtship behaviour and social interaction in general. Brierley (1979), whose book included a discussion of the 'management' of the transsexual and the transvestite patient, emphasised the contribution of beauticians and speech therapists. A male patient who seeks to be taken for female has cosmetic and other difficulties to overcome before he is recognised as a woman. He needs to know what clothing and make-up should be worn by someone of his age and build. In Brierley's view, undertaking professional training to develop the upper register of the voice is likely to be more effective than hormone treatment. (He felt that too much store is set on oestrogen treatments by patients and potential hazards are disregarded.)

Bancroft (1990) has suggested that sometimes homosexuality or a transvestite 'double role' may be acceptable alternatives to complete transsexualism. In his experience, there is sometimes systematic variation in the strength of the transsexual identification. He also mentions that a person may particularly press for a sex-change if a partner finds the idea of a homosexual relationship unacceptable.

Difficulty in controlling impulses. Reasons for impulsive behaviour need to be explored. They can be idiosyncratic. For example, the writer saw one man who felt that to stop picking fights with small boys he was attracted to would be further proof of his cowardice, and that to experience cowardice would lead to mental illness and in due course to hospitalisation. This dictated the content of an intervention directed at coping with a feeling rather than controlling an impulse. None the less, its aim was to stop a behaviour (which it did, although without affecting its attractiveness). There are a number of general procedures that a clinical psychologist might offer to help a patient who wants to stop himself or herself from behaving in ways he or she sees as problematic: self-monitoring of situations and circumstances in which impulses become strong, self-control methods and covert sensitisation. A therapist might also consider using olfactory aversion, since it involves procedures over which the patient rather than the therapist has effective control and which the patient can apply as the situation demands. Maletzky and George (1973) described the use of valeric acid to assist covert sensitisation. They explained that it was normally used in perfumes, flavourings and pharmaceuticals, and listed its advantages as 'non-corrosive, inexpensive, readily obtainable' and 'colourless'. The valeric acid was soaked into balls of cotton wool and kept in a pill bottle, and the patient took a sniff when he felt the occasion demanded. Marshall (1974), adopting an idea suggested to him by S.J. Rachman, used smelling salts.

GENERAL AND SPECIFIC INTERVENTIONS

The previous edition of this chapter headed this section 'cognitive and behavioural techniques', while acknowledging that the best known techniques had encountered ethical and practical objections which had been incompletely addressed. To think in terms of techniques can have a punitive and distancing quality which does not commend itself, and the word has been dropped. The second two of the four interventions described here (the specific ones), if used, need to be set alongside other treatments. Used in isolation, they suggest an impoverished formulation.

Remedying 'the flawed intellectual framework'

Gagnon and Simon spoke of the 'flawed intellectual framework' in which sexual phenomena are viewed: 'The sexual actor in our culture lives in schizophrenic detachment from his nonsexual life. He feels his sex impulses are autonomous' (Gagnon and Simon 1973: 285). They went on to argue that sexual impulses tend to be seen as a natural 'drive', although this name is probably misleading. In any case the strength of this drive is, they also suggest, very often exaggerated.

Perhaps clinicians reared on ethology and comparative psychology are, if anything, more likely to see what is going on as a disturbance of a 'natural' function. The risk is that formulations will address the sexual problem in isolation and, in particular, pay insufficient attention to the patients' social world (Plummer, 1984). The risk is the greater because patients with sexual variation tend anyway to be viewed as isolated. The psychologist therefore needs to place a patient's sexual experience in the context of what has been happening in the patient's life as a whole. Rooth (1980) asked his sexually impulsive patients about other areas in which they had been slow to develop or had difficulty in coping. He also suggested that the patient be invited to explore links between sexual behaviour and changes in mood and environment.

At the outset of treatment a descriptive formulation based on the whole range of difficulties encountered during the assessment creates choices for patient and therapist within a broader framework. A man in his thirties had presented, by the end of the fifth session, the following set of concerns based on the interview categories outlined in the preceding chapter:

- fear of exposing my secrets
- sense of something dark and seedy within me
- worry about my sexual preferences
- difficulty coping with confrontations
- feeling of irritation with people
- uncomfortable feeling towards my mother
- upset about break-up of a recent relationship
- sense of frustrated energy within
- restlessness
- lethargy
- gnawing pain in my guts

- strong impulse to dress in rubber material
- urge to cut myself off from people

The patient was concerned not only that his therapist would label him a 'rubber fetishist', but also that treatment would be restricted to his fetishism. He was distressed by his uncomfortable feelings inside and by the sense of perpetual struggle to maintain contact with the outside world. With this man and with other people, the interrelationship of particular concerns as they fluctuate over time is used to clarify confusion over the nature of the difficulties. Sometimes it is the linking of sexual and non-sexual issues that is helpful, sometimes the express decision not to focus on the sexual concern to begin with that seems to be most appreciated.

Other ways of reducing guilt and fostering collaboration

Beck *et al.* (1979), writing about the cognitive therapy of depression, proposed that the patient's 'chief problem' became the most pressing of a number of 'target symptoms'. The framework here also allows that the patient may have a number of different concerns, instead of just one, albeit large, such as deviant arousal. Unlike the account of Beck *et al.*, though, the framework has not included specific reference to a psychiatric condition or much emphasis on underlying entities, such as exhibitionism and fetishism. None the less, this leaves open the issue of whether it may not be to the advantage of some sex-variant patients to be able to attribute how they feel to an 'illness' such as exhibitionism, rather than to themselves.

This could apply to some of those patients who come with problems of sexual identity which are understandable as transsexualism. Without this label they may have no very satisfactory way of interpreting their experience. Other types of patient may not find the diagnostic terminology very helpful, but may be grateful if the cliniciain conveys an understanding of how they feel their sexual tastes to have been limited in ways not of their own choosing. The assurance that someone understands may ease a sense of guilt and pre-empt their adopting the distressing position that they are inadequate or lack self-control.

At an early stage, the clinician will, none the less, probably want to lay emphasis on how what the patient thinks and does maintains the problem, and to hint at the possibility of changes following quite small variations of habit and routine. One way to establish this behavioural reframe is to focus on assessment. Three ways of doing this are: (a) further clarification of target problems in terms of antecedent and consequent events; (b) goal setting, with subgoals to allow for more successes along the way and to help the patient avoid seeing treatment as an all-or-nothing affair; and (c) self-monitoring with the possibility of short-term therapeutic gain through 'reactivity' and the implicit message to the patient that treatment is a collaborative venture.

Sometimes the clinician may want to help the patient normalise the sexual problem. One way of doing this is to relate statistically the patient's sexual preferences to those of other people, either the general population or a particular non-clinical population. There is actually very little known about the sexual preferences of the general population, but enough to suggest that even the least socially approved of the sexual variations, exhibitionism and paedophilia, are not unrelated to normal sexual tastes and practices. This matter was considered in the preceding chapter. While the patient may be a member of a minority group in whose eyes he or she is not abnormal, society's response to some has been extreme. Plummer (1981) described what can happen to an unpopular minority organisation such as the Paedophile Information Exchange.

Orgasmic reconditioning

There are a number of different procedures derived from classical conditioning theory. Possibly the best known is Marquis's version of orgasmic reconditioning (Marquis, 1970). The approach taken here has departed from Marquis's in a number of respects, to take account of the subsequent theoretical literature as well as likely treatment aims. It is based on the idea of pairing a succession of progressively more adaptive fantasies (CS2, CS3, CS4, and so on), with masturbation (US). It assumes there is one very unadaptive fantasy to which the patient already masturbates (CS1) and views as in some way problematic. In fact there is probably more than one such and a series of more adaptive fantasies may need to be created around each. In contrast to some other masturbation training procedures, the patient does not bring the unadaptive fantasy to mind while masturbating.

To begin with, the patient is told something about conditioning in general and how it will affect sexual response. (In this chapter masturbation training has been presented as a way of decreasing the patient's dependence on a rather narrow range of stimuli.) The patient may feel anxious or guilty about masturbation (being found out, thinking it is harmful or wrong, not being too sure how to do it). Cousins (1980) covers some of these points. Marquis (1970) suggests a relaxation technique can be helpful.

Therapist and patient discuss how the patient wants to increase the number of stimuli he or she finds attractive. Something like this might be said: 'With masturbation you have complete control over what you fantasise to. You can choose your favourite fantasy every time. You get a better and better idea of what you really like; and in the end, maybe, you always choose much the same thing. It's nice in a way, but it may feel limiting. Actually, what you like is special to you for a number of different reasons. But often one has forgotten what they are. What most attracts you is special for having so many attractive things about it'. The attractive things could be viewed as attributes of CS1. Attributes could be thought of as falling into three categories:

Sensory – physical properties of people or things, particularly visual and tactile properties, such as shape, colour and texture.

Instrumental – events that happen to people or things, actions that people, including the patient, initiate.

Symbolic – themes that characterise the fantasy as a whole and link with other areas of the patient's life: fun, adventure, risk, dominance, strength, protection, submission, relief, security, aesthetic satisfaction, physical pleasure.

When alternative fantasy material is discussed, the patient is invited to take existing fantasies as the starting point and to find others which have attributes in common, or similar attributes, and which build on or modify particular attributes. If it is decided to drop some, or play them down, others are included as compensation.

The patient is told when practising to fantasise around the chosen material. When it is reasonably well in mind, the patient is told to begin to masturbate. This should be repeated a number of times (perhaps three or four), before going on to an orgasm, if wished. There are theoretical reasons for supposing that the learning process will be undermined if the patient substitutes the CS1 for CS2 etc., during masturbation. An agreement not to do this is sometimes made part of a therapeutic contract. If there are difficulties achieving or maintaining arousal, the therapist may suggest a lubricating cream be applied to the genitals to make them more sensitive to the touch. A vibrator can be bought to help the patient get an erection (Roles, 1972). If the patient gets an erection to CS1, but not to CS2 etc., treatment is going too fast and needs to be broken down into smaller steps. Care should be taken to ensure an adequate frequency of masturbation: to masturbate less often reduces the number of pairings and slows down learning; to masturbate more often reduces the patient's arousal level when pairings take place.

Covert sensitisation

As with orgasmic reconditioning, it is important in covert sensitisation to be clear about the aim of the therapy. Rather than set out to accomplish complete sexual orientation, a more valid application of the intervention is to help with impulse control (McConaghy *et al.*, 1981). This is explained to the patient who is told something about conditioning and how this applies in the treatment about to be received. In the therapy, aversive situations are imagined to develop as the patient is on the point of performing the behaviour found arousing but which he or she wishes to restrain.

The procedure described here follows the instructions of Cautela and Wisocki (1971). The patient and therapist decide on what the situations are in which impulse control is sought. They also decide in what way these situations will become aversive and may for this purpose use a Life History Questionnaire or Fear Survey Schedule. Cautela and Wisocki include as examples verbal abuse from onlookers, being arrested and charged, and the reproaches of a respected teacher. Patient and therapist also discuss a second series of scenes where the patient experiences relief following the abandonment of the intended course of action. They may draw upon a reinforcement schedule for ideas about how these situations will be made satisfying and pleasant.

Descriptions of the aversion and aversion-relief scenes are written down, each one being something between 150 and 300 words long. The patient is asked to relax. The therapist reads out about ten of the aversion extracts (not necessarily ten different ones). Each time the patient tries to run over the scene. After this, patient and therapist work through ten aversion-relief scenes in the same way. Between sessions, held about twice a week, the patient practises the aversion – aversion-relief sequence. This should continue for three months. If a patient reports difficulty in imagining the scenes, Cautela and Wisocki suggest: (1) the scene may be described in more detail; (2) more sensory modalities may be invoked in the description; (3) the patient may be asked to pay closer attention to what properties of the situations are found aversive or attractive; (4) pictures may be used; or (5) tape recordings may be made during the session for use at home.

Clinicians who are reluctant to tackle impulse control by this method may prefer to concentrate on other target problems that the patient presents and take the view that, by dealing adequately with these, impulse control will no longer be a source of concern.

CONCLUSIONS

This chapter and the preceding one have been concerned with the investigation and treatment of concerns related to sexual variation. These concerns have been mainly limited to those of the patient, although mention has been made of partners whose own concerns may be amenable to treatment in their own right. Issues of management and control, as opposed to treatment, have not been considered.

Good methodology can help avoid ethical pitfalls. It has been argued that it is important to work from a sound descriptive base. The alternative imprisons the clinician in some stereotype of the 'sex variant patient', which, even were it a benign stereotype, does not do justice to the particular person. In any case, a benign stereotype which, for example, excludes the possibility that a person who cross-dresses may act out aggressively, and simply equates non-violence with feminity, may be as misleading as any other (Langevin, 1985). Sexual difficulties take their place alongside others.

The literature has moved a long way from postulating a single unifying disorder of character, and some way from over-narrow formulations in terms of drive theory ('deviant arousal'); and it has become more empirical and functional. It has been argued that some of the treatments associated with the heyday of behavioural approaches continue to be important where patients see themselves as over-dependent on certain sexual fantasies and where they wish for help in controlling sexual behaviour. The ability to counsel on particular topics is necessary. Also required is a wide variety of other cognitive and behavioural interventions; and there is a growing recognition of the need to understand patients' past and present relationships. There are now far more issues on which it is judged legitimate to focus. This makes more demands on the therapist, but increases therapeutic options.

REFERENCES

Annon, J. S. (1974) *The Behavioral Treatment of Sexual Problems. Vol. 1*, Honolulu: Enabling Systems.

Bancroft, J. (1990) *Human Sexuality and its Problems. 2nd edn*, Edinburgh: Churchill Livingstone.

Barlow, D. H. (1973) 'Increasing heterosexual arousal', *Behavior Therapy* 4: 657–71.

Barlow, D. H. (1977) 'Assessment of sexual behavior', in A. R. Ciminero, K. S. Calhoun and H. E. Adams (eds) *Handbook of Behavioral Assessment*, New York: Wiley.

Barlow, D. H., Reynolds, E. J. and Agras, W. S. (1973) 'Gender identity change in a transsexual', *Archives of General Psychiatry* 28: 569–76.

Barlow, D. H., Abel, G. G. and Blanchard, E. B. (1979) 'Gender identity change in transsexuals', *Archives of General Psychiatry* 36: 1001–17.

Beane, J. (1981) 'I'd rather be dead than gay: counselling gay men who are coming out', *Personnel and Guidance Journal* 60: 222–6.

Beck, A. T., Rush, A. J., Shaw, B. F. and Emery, G. (1979) *Cognitive Therapy of Depression*, Chichester: Wiley.

Brierley, H. (1979) *Transvestism*, Oxford: Pergamon Press.

Brownell, K. D. (1980) 'Multifaceted behavior therapy', in D. J. Cox and R. J. Daitzman (eds) *Exhibitionism: Description, Assessment, and Treatment*, New York: Garland STPM Press.

Callahan, E. J. and Leitenberg, H. (1973) 'Aversion therapy for sexual deviation: contingent shock and covert sensitization', *Journal of Abnormal Psychology* 81: 60–73.

Cautela, J. R. (1967) 'Covert sensitization', *Psychological Reports* 20: 459–68.

Cautela, J. R. and Wisocki, P. A. (1971) 'Covert sensitization for the treatment of sexual deviations', *The Psychological Record* 21: 37–48.

Conn, P. (1979) 'Studies in Gender Identity: exercises in the survey and assessment of a sex-change population', unpublished M. Phil. thesis, Institute of Psychiatry, London.

Conrad, S. R. and Wincze, J. P. (1976) 'Orgasmic reconditioning: a controlled study of its effects upon the sexual arousal and behavior of adult male homosexuals', *Behavior Therapy* 7: 155–66.

Cousins, J. (1980) *Make It Happy. What Sex is All About*, Harmondsworth, Middx.: Penguin.

Crawford, D. A. and Allen, D. V. (1979) 'A social skills training programme with sex offenders', in M. Cook and G. Wilson (eds) *Love and Attraction: Proceedings of an Annual Conference*, Oxford: Pergamon.

Davison, G. C. (1977) 'Homosexuality: the ethical challenge', *Journal of Homosexuality* 2: 79–81.

Futterweit, W., Weiss, R. A. and Fagerstrom, R. M. (1986) 'Endocrine evaluation of forty female-to-male transsexuals: increased frequency of Polycystic Ovarian Disease in female transsexualism', *Archives of Sexual Behavior* 15: 69–78.

Gagnon, J. H. and Simon, W. (1973) *Sexual Conduct. The Social Sources of Human Sexuality*, Chicago: Aldine.

Geer, J. H. and Fuhr, R. (1976) 'Cognitive factors in sexual arousal: the role of distraction', *Journal of Consulting and Clinical Psychology* 44: 238–44.

Jackson, B. T. (1969) 'A case of voyeurism treated by counterconditioning', *Behaviour Research and Therapy* 7: 133–4.

Kamin, L. J. (1969) 'Predictability, surprise, attention and conditioning', in R. Church and B. Campbell (eds) *Punishment and Aversive Behavior*, New York: Appleton-Century-Crofts.

Kantorowitz, D. A. (1978) 'An experimental investigation of pre-orgasmic reconditioning and post-orgasmic deconditioning', *Journal of Applied Behavioral Analysis* 11: 23–4.

Keller, D. J. and Goldstein, A. (1978) 'Orgasmic reconditioning reconsidered', *Behaviour Research and Therapy* 16: 299–300.

Kessler, S. J. and McKenna, W. (1978) *Gender: An Ethnomethodological Approach*, Chichester: Wiley.

Kremsdorf, R. B., Holmen, M. L. and Laws, D. R. (1980) 'Orgasmic reconditioning without deviant imagery: a case report with a paedophile', *Behaviour Research and Therapy* 18: 203–7.

Langevin R. (1985) *Erotic Preference, Gender Identity and Aggression in Men: New Research Studies*, Hillsdale N.J.: Lawrence Erlbaum Associates.

Lanyon, R. I. (1986) 'Theory and treatment in child molestation', *Journal of Counselling and Clinical Psychology* 54: 176–82.

Lindemalm G., Korlin D. and Uddenberg N. (1986) 'Long-term follow-up of "sex change" in thirteen male-to-female transsexuals', *Archives of Sexual Behavior* 15: 187–210.

Lo Piccolo, J. (1985) 'Guidelines for treatment of sex offenders', unpublished paper.

McConaghy, N., Armstrong, M. S. and Blaszczynski, A. (1981) 'Controlled comparison of aversive therapy and covert sensitization in compulsive homosexuality', *Behaviour Research and Therapy* 19: 425–34.

Maletzky, B. M. and George, F. S. (1973) 'The treatment of homosexuality by assisted covert sensitization', *Behaviour Research and Therapy* 11: 655–7.

Marquiss, J. N. (1970) 'Orgasmic reconditioning: changing sexual object choice through controlled masturbation fantasies', *Journal of Behavior Therapy and Experimental Psychiatry* 1: 263–71.

Marshall, W. L. (1974) 'A combined treatment approach to the reduction of multiple fetish-related behaviors', *Journal of Consulting and Clinical Psychology* 42: 613–16.

Marshall, W. L., Eccles A. and Barbaree, H. E. (1991) 'The treatment of exhibitionists: a focus on sexual deviance versus cognitive and relationship features', *Behaviour Research and Therapy* 18: 129–35.

Miller, D. (1986) 'How to counsel patients about HIV disease – those who have it and those who fear it', *Maternal and Child Health* 11: 322–30.

Miller, D. (1987) *Living with AIDS and HIV*, London: Macmillan.

Morin, S., Charles, K. and Malyon, A. K. (1984) 'The psychological impact of AIDS on gay men', *American Psychologist* 39: 1288–93.

Peplau, L. T. (1982) 'Research on homosexual couples: an overview', *Journal of Homosexuality* 8: 3–8.

Plummer, K. (1981) 'The paedophile's progress: a view from below', in B. Taylor (ed.) *Perspectives on Paedophilia*, London: Batsford.

Plummer, K. (1984) 'Sexual diversity: a sociologiocal perspective', in K. Howells (ed.) *The Psychology of Sexual Diversity*, Oxford: Blackwell.

Rochlin, M. (1985) 'Sexual orientation of the therapist and therapeutic effectiveness with gay clients', in J. C. Gonsoriek (ed.) *A Guide to Psychotherapy with Gay and Lesbian Clients*, New York: Harrington Park Press.

Roles, S. (1972) 'A serious look at sexual aids', *World Medicine*, October 4: 17–22.

Rooth, G. (1980) 'Exhibitionism: an eclectic approach to its management', *British Journal of Hospital Medicine* April: 366–70.

Sketchley, J. (1989a) 'Counselling and sexual orientation', in W. Dryden, D. Charles-Edwards and R. Woolfe (eds) *Handbook of Counselling in Britain*, London: Routledge.

Sketchley, J. (1989b) 'Counselling people affected by HIV and AIDS', in W. Dryden, D. Charles-Edwards and R. Woolfe (eds) *Handbook of Counselling in Britain*, London: Routledge.

Turner, S. M. and Van Hasselt, V. B. (1979) 'Multiple behavioral treatment in a sexually aggressive male', *Journal of Behavior Therapy and Experimental Psychiatry* 10: 343–8.

Ward, B. (1988) *Sex and Life, 2nd edn*, London: Macdonald.

Wolf, T. J. (1985) 'Marriage of bisexual men', *Journal of Homosexuality* 11: 135–48.

Yardley, K. M. (1976) 'Training in feminine skills in a male transsexual', *British Journal of Medical Psycholgy* 42: 329–39.

Zilbergeld, B. (1980) *Men and Sex: A Guide to Sexual Fulfilment*, Glasgow: Fontana.

Chapter 19

Drug and alcohol problems
Investigation

Michael Gossop

CONCEPTS

It is interesting to ask how particular issues come to be marked out as 'social problems'. Drug addiction and alcoholism are currently so well defined as such that it is worth reminding ourselves that they were not always seen so clearly in this way. The use of opium was completely unrestricted in England until 1868, and even after 1868 restrictions were minimal for many years. At this time the drug was sold and used on a considerable scale. It was used in many different preparations, but most commonly in the form of opium pills, or as a tincture of opium in alcohol (laudanum). Vendors often had their own special preparations to be used to quieten children. One of the most striking features of this state of affairs is the sense of complete normality which surrounded the open sale of opium (Berridge and Edwards, 1981).

For many years around the turn of the century cocaine too was used widely and with enthusiasm. Sigmund Freud tried the drug both orally and by injection and was impressed by the sense of well-being that it created. Soon he was giving it to his friends, to his fiancée, to his sisters and to his patients. He wrote articles in praise of it, describing 'the exhilaration and lasting euphoria which in no way differs from the normal euphoria of a healthy person'. In a letter to his fiancée he described one of his articles as 'a song of praise to this magical drug' (Gossop, 1993). Cocaine was sold in the form of cigarettes, in nose sprays, in chewing gum and in soft drinks (Coca-Cola, that symbol of the American way of life, contained cocaine until 1906). One hundred per cent pure cocaine could be freely bought over the counter of the local chemist. It was also commercially available in wine.

The enthusiasm for cocaine was as marked among the medical profession as among the general public, and Sir Clifford Albutt took it with him on a walking tour of the Alps to amaze his fellow climbers with the increased energy he hoped that it would give him. In his textbook of medicine, co-written with Humphrey Rolleston, he had this to say of another drug: 'The sufferer is tremulous and loses his self-command, he is subject to fits of agitation and depression. He loses colour and has a haggard appearance. As with other such agents, a renewed dose of the poison gives temporary relief, but at the cost of future misery'. This drug, which was so clearly identified as a problem, was coffee.

The manner in which drug problems[1] come to be defined and identified as such involves a tangle of social, moral and political factors. This is true both at the individual level and at the wider social level. The person who drinks a bottle of whisky every day, whose social world is collapsing and whose liver is burning up, is comparatively easy to recognise as having an alcohol problem. But there would be no such agreement about the person who becomes drunk on Friday and Saturday nights. With illicit drugs, the issues are further confused. The use of any illegal drug is almost automatically identified as a drug problem, even though the user may not be dependent upon the drug and may suffer from no medical or psychological complications as a result of his or her drug-taking. Society seems to be excessively eager to identify drug problems where illegal drugs, such as heroin or cocaine, are involved, and reluctant to recognise such problems when they involve legally available or medically sanctioned drugs, such as alcohol or tranquillisers.

Although this chapter (and the later one dealing with treatment) is primarily concerned with alcohol and illicit drugs, it is perhaps worth mentioning tobacco, and particularly cigarette smoking. Current research is this area regards smoking in terms of the self-administration of a powerful drug (nicotine), and Russell (1976) describes cigarette smoking as 'probably the most addictive and dependence-producing object-specific self-administered gratification known to man'. Nor is it an activity without its attendant hazards. Hundreds of thousands of deaths each year have been attributed to smoking.

Unlike heroin, however, cigarettes are legally available (indeed there are powerful industrial interests trying to promote their use); they are widely used and do not lead to the sort of immediate and dramatic forms of intoxication that follow the intravenous use of heroin. Nor do cigarettes produce the powerful and dramatic changes in behaviour and consciousness that follow heavy alcohol use. In many respects, smoking may be clearly regarded as an addiction. None the less, the use of different drugs raises different issues and not all can be easily incorporated within the framework of these chapters. It is with some regret, therefore, that smoking is largely omitted from the present discussion. Readers wishing to learn more of the reasons why so many people need to inhale the smoke from rolls of burning leaves are referred to the useful book by Ashton and Stepney (1982).

Drug and alcohol problems

One aspect of assessment that continues to bother clinicians is the apparently straightforward matter of determining the drug or alcohol usage of the patient. In part this is complicated by the belief of many clinicians who feel that alcoholics and addicts are unreliable informants. However, there is no clear evidence to support the idea that self-reported information provided by addicts and alcoholics is necessarily unreliable. Although there may well be occasions on which such groups may distort or conceal information, there are numerous research studies that have found that both alcoholics and drug addicts can be reliable informants, regardless of the type of information that is sought. Studies by Sobell and Sobell (1978), Hesselbrock *et al.* (1983) and Ball (1967) have shown this. Busto *et al.* (1983), for instance, looked at the use and abuse of benzodiazepines by alcoholics and found that alcoholics were accurate informants on this matter. In the Maudsley Relapse Study, the concordance between self-reported opiate use and the results of laboratory urine screening was found to be 93–99 per cent (Gossop *et al.*, 1989). There are some suggestions that, when response distortion occurs, it is often in the direction of over-reporting undesirable behaviour rather than denying or under-reporting (Sobell and Sobell, 1978; Gossop, 1978). In broad terms it seems that researchers are more likely to regard addicts and alcoholics as reliable informants and clinicians to distrust them. This may be due in part to the 'demand characteristics' of the different situations in which researchers and clinicians approach such people. However, the research evidence gives little support to the view that self-report data obtained from addicts or alcoholics is necessarily unreliable and untrustworthy.

None the less, when assessing either alcohol or drug problems it is good practice to use objective measures to determine the presence or absence of a variety of intoxicants that might be used by the individual, and also, wherever possible, to use procedures that provide a quantitative estimate of dose levels. This may not always be feasible. In the case of the illicit drugs, even the drug-taker is unlikely to know the contents or purity of the substances that he or she is using. Street 'heroin', for instance, may also contain barbiturates or methaqualone, and 'ecstasy' may contain amphetamines or LSD. The actual heroin content of street samples may vary from very high quality products to almost completely inert samples; in some United States' samples, heroin content as low as 0.5 per cent has been found (Gossop, 1993). Electronic breathalysers are sometimes used as a quick and easy method for the detection of blood-alcohol, and laboratory tests for some drugs can be conducted on blood samples.

For ordinary clinical purposes it is usually not necessary to obtain a fully detailed account of everything that has happened over a lifetime of drinking or drug-taking. Assessment should aim to chart major events (onset of daily drinking, first injection, appearance of withdrawal symptoms, etc.). Alcohol intake is commonly monitored in terms of 'units' (where one unit is equal to approximately half a pint of beer, cider or lager, to a single measure of spirits, or to a small glass of wine). Consumption of more than 50 units per week for a man, or more than 35 units for a woman, is likely to be harmful, and recommended levels are lower than that. Much problem drinking will involve episodic or 'binge' drinking, where very large quantities of alcohol are taken but not on a regular daily basis. Assessment of alcohol intake should be revised to take account of different drinking patterns.

There has been a continuing struggle to define and conceptualise the problems associated with the use of drugs and alcohol in objective terms. These attempts have not always been conspicuously successful. The concept of 'abuse' as applied to drugs or alcohol is among the least satisfactory notions, and it is tempting to agree with Szasz, who states:

> Drug addiction or drug abuse cannot be defined without specifying the proper and improper uses of certain pharmacologically active agents. The regular administration of morphine by a physician to a patient dying of cancer is the paradigm of the proper use of a narcotic; whereas even its occasional self-administration by a physically healthy person for the purpose of 'pharmacological pleasure' is the paradigm of drug abuse. I submit that these judgments have nothing whatever to do with medicine, pharmacology or psychiatry. They are moral judgments. Indeed, our present views on addiction are astonishingly similar to some of our former views on sex.
>
> (Szasz, 1972)

In their review, Edwards *et al.* (1981) pointed to some of the ideas that lurk beneath the notions of 'abuse' and 'misuse'. These include:

1 *Unsanctioned use* – the use of a drug that is not approved by a society or by a powerful group within that society. This has often been categorised as abuse.
2 *Hazardous use* – the use of a drug that will probably lead to harmful consequences for the user (either to psychological dysfunction or to physical damage). Edwards *et al.* (1981) illustrate this term with reference to a person who smokes twenty cigarettes a day: this practice may not cause him any actual harm but it is known to be hazardous.
3 *Dysfunctional use* – use of a drug that is leading to impaired psychological or social functioning (for example, loss of job or marital problems).
4 *Harmful use* – use of a drug by a person to whom it is known to have caused tissue damage or mental illness.

This analysis helps to clarify some of the implications of terms such as 'drug abuse', and it also helps to focus attention upon what sorts of problems we ought to be concerned about. Each of the four categories of drug problem described above may cause difficulties for the drug taker and each may require different sorts of intervention. The use of illegal drugs (unsanctioned use), particularly by very young people, may cause huge concern and it can lead to serious social sanctions, including being expelled from school, loss of job, or imprisonment, and it may cause enormous worry to the family and friends of the user. However, it need not in itself be associated with *clinical* problems. Equally, drug-taking may lead to many different types of problem. The acute intoxication that follows heavy drinking often leads to hazardous behaviours and not infrequently to actual harm. This sort of behaviour may or may not be a cause for intervention by the clinical psychologist.

DEPENDENCE AND ADDICTION

The term 'dependence' was formally introduced as an alternative to 'addiction' by the WHO in 1964. This reformulation carried with it an attempt to distinguish between the physical and psychological components of dependence. There undoubtedly can be circumstances in which physical dependence is seen in a relatively 'pure' form. For example, physical dependence upon morphine and methadone develops in the isolated segments of the spinal cord in spinal dogs and also in decorticated dogs (Vogel *et al.*, 1948). Another example that has been given is that of the surgical patient who receives opiates for pain relief and shows withdrawal symptoms when the drug is stopped but who shows no desire to continue taking the drug. However, the physical and psychological components tend to be inextricably linked in such a way that it is difficult to maintain a distinction between them.

Tolerance and withdrawal

For many years the concepts of tolerance and withdrawal provided the twin pillars that supported the concept of addiction. It can be readily demonstrated that repeated administration of certain drugs leads to progressive decreases in some of their effects. This occurs with the euphoric and analgesic effects of opiates such as heroin and methadone. It also occurs with alcohol. Early studies of addiction identified the development of tolerance with the tendency of addicts to increase the dose they were taking or to increase the frequency with which they took the drug. With the growth of tolerance, symptoms of withdrawal are often found when the drug is discontinued. In the case of the classic drugs of addiction (notably heroin and alcohol), there occurred a fairly predictable set of symptoms which was characterised as the 'withdrawal syndrome' of that drug.

The opiate withdrawal syndrome is often regarded as a paradigm of the withdrawal state, though the symptoms of withdrawal vary according to the particular drug of dependence. Opiate withdrawal is not the most physically hazardous of the responses to discontinuation of an addictive drug (withdrawal from alcohol, barbiturates or benzodiazepines can create more serious problems). Early opiate withdrawal symptoms (8 to 12 hours after the last use) of unmodified heroin withdrawal include watering eyes, runny nose, yawning and sweating. The peak intensity generally occurs between 36 and 72 hours after the last use, and symptoms include chills, hot and cold flushes, diarrhoea, stomach cramps and muscle spasms. Insomnia is a common symptom throughout withdrawal and is very distressing to many addicts. Thereafter, the severity of such symptoms declines over a period of one or two weeks though there may be residual symptoms for a much longer period, especially with respect to conditioned withdrawal symptoms which may be elicited by drug-related stimuli long after the unconditioned physiological response to withdrawal has passed.

The alcohol withdrawal syndrome, in its mild form, includes symptoms of irritability, sleeplessness and tremor, and, in its severe form, hallucinations, disorientation, memory impairment and seizures. Severe symptoms occur 48 to 60 hours after withdrawal. In the complete syndrome, delerium tremens may develop abruptly, frequently at night. Often it is preceded by increasing restlessness and feelings of apprehension and disorientation. Panic, disorientation and hallucinations increase as the syndrome develops. Delerium tremens usually subsides after about 2 to 3 days but it has a significant morbidity and mortality due to injuries which may be sustained during DTs or to dehydration and ciculatory collapse, hypothermia and pneumonia.

For many years these two features, tolerance and withdrawal, were universally accepted as the defining characteristics of physical dependence. It is increasingly clear, however, that tolerance occurs to drugs that are generally agreed to be not physically addictive, such as amphetamines and cannabis. Similarly, there are withdrawal-like responses to the discontinuation of these drugs after regular use (Gossop et al., 1982a). Whether or not one calls these responses 'withdrawal symptoms' is a semantic rather than a scientific problem. In addition, cocaine, which was once regarded as not truly 'addictive' because it did not lead to an opiate-type withdrawal syndrome has been found to create severe dependence problems in many users, especially when it is smoked (as freebase or 'crack').

Both tolerance and withdrawal have been observed in relation to habitual behaviours that do not involve the use of drugs at all. In the case of compulsive gambling, for instance, there is a marked tendency to 'escalate the dose', and, in a study involving members of Gamblers Anonymous, Wray and Dickerson (1981) found such symptoms of withdrawal as irritability, restlessness, anxiety, sleeplessness, depressed mood and poor concentration. The same sort of responses are frequently shown by compulsive eaters under dietary control.

In what has become a classic paper, the phenomena of tolerance and withdrawal were more precisely delineated and rechristened as neuroadaptation (Edwards et al., 1981). This paper suggested that the neurophysiological processes of neuroadaptation should be seen as just one of the cluster of factors that go together to create the dependence syndrome, and that the essence of dependence was the psychological desire for drugs. Although less theoretical weight is now attached to the processes of neuroadaptation, their clinical significance should not be underestimated. For the individual who is physically dependent upon a drug the prospect of withdrawal may provoke serious anxiety (Eiser and Gossop, 1979). Also, the discomfort of withdrawal symptoms may interefere with treatment interventions and may in some circumstances lead to the patient's opting out of treatment. For these reasons, it remains important to monitor and reduce the distress and discomfort caused to the patient by withdrawal symptoms.

Measures of withdrawal

A self-completion questionnaire for the assessment of the opiate withdrawal syndrome, the Short Opiate Withdrawal Scale (SOWS) is shown in Table 19.1. This scale has been found to be quick and easy to administer; most subjects can complete it in less than a minute. It provides clinically useful information which is relevant to the planning and delivery of individually based and group treatment programmes. The scale also offers a convenient and informative instrument for the study of detoxification procedures (Gossop, 1990).

The attempt to fit the addictive disorders into a traditional category-based psychiatric classification system has been conspicuously unsuccessful (Gossop, 1981). Such approaches have focused upon specific *substances* without sufficiently recognising the variation in drug-taking *behaviours* and *problems*. Many have also been based upon the concepts of tolerance and withdrawal as essential characteristics of drug dependence, such as *DSM III* which noted that 'the diagnosis requires the presence of physiological dependence' (Kuehnle and Spitzer, 1981). It is a mistake to confine the social and psychological complexities of the dependence disorders within such narrow physiological boundaries.

The change of terminology from addiction to dependence was introduced partly to encourage the move away from a categorical view of addiction as a state (is this person dependent/addicted?) to the notion of dependence as a dimension (how severely dependent/addicted is this person?).

Table 19.1 Short opiate withdrawal scale

Name: *Date:*

Please put a tick in the appropriate box if you have had any of the following *during the last 24 hours.*

	None	*Mild*	*Moderate*	*Severe*
Feeling sick				
Stomach cramps				
Muscle spasms/twitching				
Feelings of coldness				
Heart pounding				
Muscular tension				
Aches and pains				
Yawning				
Running eyes				
Insomnia/problems sleeping				

Source: Gossop (1990)

The essence of dependence is that the relationship between the user and their drug is altered. Initially, people may use drink or drugs for many reasons but the decision to use or not is one which is taken by the person as a voluntary choice. With the development of dependence the person becomes increasingly pre-occupied by the drug and feels some degree of compulsion to use it. The initial reasons for drinking or taking drugs may or may not still be present, but with the development of dependence, new factors are added which complicate the picture and increase the likelihood of drug-taking.

Various attempts have been made to define precisely what is meant by dependence. Edwards *et al.*, (1981) suggested that dependence should be re-garded as a syndrome in which the use of a particular drug, or even of a wide range of drugs, assumes a much higher priority than other behaviour that once had a higher value. Dependence occurs as part of a wider pattern of behaviour, in which not all the components of the dependence syndrome need be present, nor always at the same intensity. Among the various cognitive, behavioural and physiological effects that are said to make up the dependence syndrome are the following:

A feeling of compulsion to take drugs
A desire to stop taking drugs
A relatively stereotyped pattern of drug-taking
Signs of neuroadaptation (tolerance and withdrawal symptoms)
The salience of drug-taking behaviour relative to other priorities and the
    tendency to return to drug-taking soon after a period of abstinence.

According to this formulation, none of these items is in itself sufficient to define drug dependence, and the assessment of a dependence upon drugs or alcohol must rely upon multiple criteria. However, a strong case can be made for the centrality of the desire or compulsion to use drugs. Gossop (1989a) noted that, of these elements, 'the sense of compulsion would seem to be an essential ingredient. It contradicts our understanding of what we mean by an "addiction" that someone could be said to be addicted to something but not experience a strong need for it.' In this respect, dependence must ultimately be regarded as a psychological phenomenon.

The concept of dependence has attracted criticism. Some critics have com-plained that the notion of a dependence syndrome threatens to perpetuate some of the undesirable implications of the old-fashioned disease concept of addiction. Certainly, if the aim of treatment is to convince the alcoholic or the addict that they are not helpless victims of a disease process and that they can control their actions, then such disease implications are unhelpful and should be avoided.

Shaw (1979) complained that the dependence syndrome gives undue em-phasis to the elements of compulsion and 'loss of control', and that alcoholics and drug addicts should not be seen as passive victims of their dependence since they are able to demonstrate control over some aspects of their drug-taking (Mello and Mendelson, 1971; Gottheil *et al.*, 1972). It has also been suggested that the emphasis upon the loss-of-control component of dependence can serve to draw attention away from the more complex issues of why a person uses drugs and the circumstances in which drugs are used. Shaw illustrates his reservations about the clinical value of the dependence syndrome by reference to the hypothetical case of a women who drinks in response to various problems in her life:

She may begin to get drunk with increasing regularity. Simultaneously, the regularity and heaviness of the drinking will increase her tolerance to alcohol and she will gradually have to consume more and more alcohol to get drunk. Additionally, she may begin to suffer more severe withdrawal symptoms and the desire to ward off or relieve some of these symptoms may become further motivation for increased consumption. At this point, she might be classified as 'an alcoholic' or as 'severely dependent'. However neither term would be an explanation of how or why she had got herself into this position, and presuming her 'impaired control' of alcohol to be her 'leading symptom' might well confuse the issue. Of course, if she were not intellectually conscious of her real reasons for continually getting drunk, then the effect of her increasing tolerance and withdrawal would mean she had to consume more and more to become drunk or to ward off withdrawal, and she might indeed experience this as becoming unable to 'control' her intake. If she also felt a degree of guilt about her behaviour, then she might also feel she was under a 'compulsion' to drink (since one can only experience a 'compulsion' to do something if at the same time there is a feeling one ought not to do it). But to accept the statement at face value that she was 'compelled' to drink would be no *explanation* for her behaviour – the experience of feeling compelled and lacking self control was rather her surface interpretation of underlying conflicting motivations. On the other hand, to explain to the woman that she had an increased tolerance level, was experiencing increasing withdrawal effects, and that these alterations were developing interactively with the dynamics of the marital relationship and the place of drinking within it, would begin to make some scientific and therapeutic sense.

(Shaw, 1979: 343–4)

Much of Shaw's objection is directed towards the notion of dependence as an explanatory concept, and in his formulation, dependence is better seen as an attribution. It seems odd, therefore, that Shaw finds no place for the concept, since attributions may themselves be important factors in determining behaviour. Gutierres and Reich (1988) found that attributional style was related to outcome among illicit drug users in rehabilitation. Similarly, Bradley *et al.* (1992) found that addicts' beliefs about their ability to control episodes of drug-taking (a central aspect of the concept of dependence) were related to the probability of relapse.

Also, the value of the concept should perhaps be judged not merely by argument but in terms of its uses in clinical practice and in research. Although agreeing with some of Shaw's criticisms, Hodgson (1980) has been more enthusiastic about the concept of dependence and suggested that a dimensional (rather than a categorical) concept has direct clinical relevance. In the study of Orford *et al.* (1976), it was found that controlled drinking and abstinence were equally probable treatment outcomes, suggesting that clinicians should not be committed to total abstinence as the only goal; but when the data were re-analysed according to severity of dependence, it was found that the severely dependent tended to be either abstinent or uncontrolled and that only the moderately dependent were drinking in a controlled way. Armor (1980) also found that severity of dependence appeared to be related to abstinence or controlled drinking as treatment outcomes.

Measures of dependence

Hodgson (1980) suggests that severity of dependence is an important variable which should be assessed in process and treatment research, and a questionnaire (the Severity of Alcohol Dependence Questionnaire) has been devised that is said to offer a reliable measure of alcohol dependence (Stockwell *et al.*, 1979). A similar instrument (Severity of Opiate Dependence Questionnaire) has been devised for the measurement of opiate dependence (Sutherland *et al.*, 1986; Phillips *et al.*, 1987). More recently, a shorter Severity of Dependence Scale has been used for the measurement of dependence upon different types of illicit drug (Gossop *et al.*, 1992).

DIMENSIONS OF DEPENDENCE AND PROBLEMS

The behaviours contributing to and resulting from 'addiction' or 'dependence' have traditionally been the most frequent reasons for drug or alcohol users presenting to a treatment service. It is clear that many people who use drink and drugs find that they have very great difficulty in giving up the habit. However, a clear distinction should be made between dependence and the various types of problems that may be associated with the consumption of drugs or alcohol. Drug and alcohol problems may be of many different sorts. Some of the more obvious difficulties may arise in connection with physical health, mental health, social functioning and criminal behaviour.

From the perspectives of prevention and treatment, the targets involve both the avoidance and the reduction of harm. Intervention will seek to reduce the risks associated with drug-taking – the likelihood of harm. Strang (1992) has discussed the complex relationship between risk and harm. The notion of risk relates to the possibilities of an event occurring. Harm is related to the event itself. Some harms are readily quantifiable, but others may only become apparent with the passage of time. In the case of liver damage related to chronic heavy drinking, the degree of risk is related to the drinking behaviour and not to the occurrence of liver damage. In addition, some forms of harm are clearly categorical rather than dimensional in nature (one is either infected with HIV or not), whereas the behaviours that are associated with the harm are more readily incorporated within a dimensional framework. In general it may be more appropriate to see infection as a single event of harm. This might be distinguished from the notion of accumulated risk in which the overall probability of harm may be understood in terms of the sum total of probabilities surrounding many different actions, events and circumstances. A dimensional representation of drug and alcohol problems might therefore reflect behavioural risk as well as the accumulation of specific instances of actual harm incurred through events.

The problematic use of alcohol or drugs may relate to risk as well as to actual harm, and one obviously risky type of behaviour which might then be included within this dimension would be the repeated sharing of injecting equipment with other drug users (or, in the case of alcohol, regularly driving a motor vehicle after consuming large quantities of alcohol). It is clear that such activities put the individual at greatly increased risk of incurring harm through infection or accident. Treatment interventions might seek (for many reasons) to reduce needle-sharing in an HIV seropositive drug injector, and a reduction in sharing behaviour would be reflected in a lowered score on the problems dimension relating to risky and harmful health behaviours.

The dependence and problems dimensions should be regarded as conceptually separate.[2] It is clear that many people experience social, legal, psychological and health problems as a result of their drinking without being dependent. Examples might include the individual who is not a regular drinker but who on one occasion gets drunk and falls down the stairs, or who becomes involved in a motor vehicle accident because of his or her impaired driving performance. During the past decade, drug workers have been forced to respond to the threat of HIV infection and AIDS. The appearance of HIV and the recognition of drug injectors as a high-risk group has had profound significance for the development of services for drug-takers. In particular it has produced a re-examination of treatment goals, and it has reinforced awareness of the very serious harm that may follow from even a single episode of drug injection. With the attention to HIV risks there has also been a 'rediscovery' of other sorts of previously neglected and potentially fatal physical and medical problems, such as hepatitis B infection. Many of the drug-takers who become infected with hepatitis or HIV do so within the first few weeks of starting to inject drugs (and at a time when they are unlikely to be seriously dependent upon drugs). This is a consequence of the increased likelihood of sharing injecting equipment among inexperienced injectors.

There are drug takers who are dependent upon drugs but who experience little or no harm as a consequence. One notable example is Dr William Halstead, one of the greatest American surgeons, and a founder of the prestigious Johns Hopkins Medical School. For most of his life Halstead used amounts of 200 mg or more of morphine but was able to continue his successful medical career. Stimson (1973) also described a group of 'stable' heroin addicts. Like many of the heroin addicts in the UK prior to the development of youth drug cultures in

1960s, this group tended to be working, legitimately supported, with little involvement in crime and 'leading a relatively normal life'. On the twin dimensions of problems and dependence, they could be scored as high on dependence but low on problems. In Figure 19.1(b) they would probably be located in sector E (in contrast to the example of the non-dependent drinker described above whose accident might place him or her in sector D or G according to the severity of the accident).

The stereotypical 'junkie' or alcoholic would be more likely to occupy sector F in Figure 19.1(b). Such individuals tend to be characterised as being severely dependent as well as having many drug problems. The chronic heavy drinker who experiences impaired control of his or her alcohol consumption and who shows impaired brain function provides one such case. In his description of the more chaotic heroin users in his study, Stimson noted that 'The Junkies [v.s.] emerge as the opposite to the Stables in nearly every respect. Nearly all . . . support themselves by stealing . . . their drug use involves . . . the sharing of equipment with which to inject themselves . . . they report the highest incidence of physical complications . . . they eat poorly' (Stimson, 1973: 178–9).

In reality, it is improbable that these two dimensions will be fully independent of each other. In many instances, there are likely to be positive correlations between severity of dependence and problems. The likelihood of cases falling into the sectors A, B or F (in Figure 19.1(b)) could be expected to be greater than that of cases falling into sectors E or G. This is a question which is open to empirical investigation. In a recent investigation of heroin addicts (Gossop *et al.*, 1993a; b), it was found that severity of dependence was positively associated with a range of high-risk behaviours. The more severely dependent heroin users were more likley to be involved in prostitution in order to obtain either drugs or money for drugs; they were also more likely to inject drugs and to use injecting

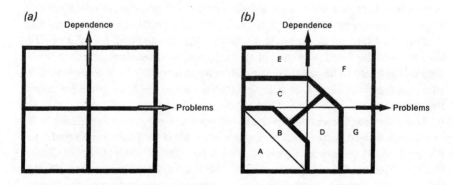

Figure 19.1 Dimensions of dependence and problems

equipment after it had been used by others. These risk behaviours are directly related to life-threatening conditions such as hepatitis and HIV infection.

In the case of alcohol, there is often a direct link between addiction and the development of certain health consequences. These may include damage to the central nervous system, the liver, the gastrointestinal system, and the pancreas and the heart.

THEORETICAL APPROACHES TO DRUG AND ALCOHOL PROBLEMS

Theories are not just systematic attempts to explain events, they also operate as ways of observing and interpreting the world. Theories and concepts contain within themselves types of bias or orientation as to what sort of empirical phenomena should be observed and what sort of procedures should be used to observe them. Moreover, we approach everything in the light of preconceived theory, and the manner in which we attempt to assess the problems of drug or alcohol dependence is influenced by theoretical preconceptions.

This creates many opportunities for misunderstanding as there are a variety of different models, theories and perspectives upon the addictive disorders. Nathan (1980) lists these different approaches under the following headings: biophysical and genetic, socio-cultural, psychoanalytic and behavioural. He reserves his main focus of attention for what he calls 'the social learning perspective'. Milby (1981) distinguishes between theories that are concerned with limited aspects of dependence (mainly with such phenomena as tolerance and withdrawal), and those that attempt a broader explanation of addictive behaviour. This is a distinction which is of some considerable importance. Milby divides the theories concerned to explain tolerance and withdrawal into four types: those that postulate metabolic changes, receptor-site theories, two-factor opponent-process theories and cellular-adaptation theories. He divides the more comprehensive theories into a further five types. These are psychoanalytic theories, the metabolic-disease theory, the artificially-induced-drive theory, learning-theory accounts and the opponent-process theory.

Whatever the scientific merit (or otherwise) of these different models, a clinical understanding of drug and alcohol problems needs to retain a more interactionist view of their aetiology. Drug and alcohol problems are produced and influenced by a wide range of different factors. Social, psychological and pharmacological factors may all be involved. But it is likely that they will be involved in different degrees for different individuals. As a result, a fixed theoretical stance will force a narrow attitude. A simple model of the manner in which psychological and social factors interact with pharmacological factors in the development of drug and alcohol problems is shown in Figure 19.2. Social, psychological and pharmacological factors may all lead to problems; and, in addition, all of these factors may also interact with the others to produce drug and alcohol problems.

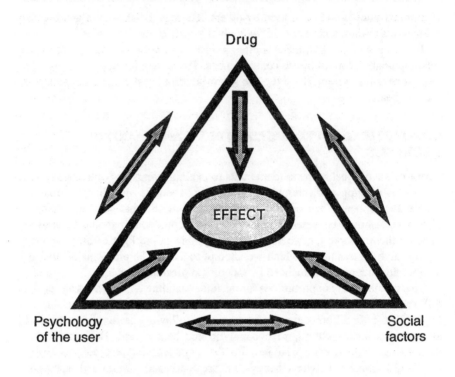

Figure 19.2 Interaction of drug, individual/psychological factors and social
factors in determining drug effects

Physiological approaches

For many years the treatment of drug addiction and alcoholism was dominated
by physicians whose medical background encouraged them to look for biochemical and physiological explanations of these problems. There has always
been a strong research interest in physiological changes that occur in response to
drugs, and many workers have held that there must be some physiological
mechanism underlying the addictive disorders.

There have also been suggestions that some people may have a biochemical
predisposition to alcoholism. No metabolic studies of alcoholism indicate a
difference in the rate at which alcoholics and non-alcoholics absorb alcohol,
though there have been suggestions that alcoholics differ from non-alcoholics in
terms of the route by which they metabolise alcohol. However, of the metabolic
differences so far demonstrated between alcoholics and non-alcoholics, most
should be seen as a consequence rather than a cause of the dependence (Dietrich,
1976). Also, although there is some data to suggest that genetic factors make a
contribution to alcoholism, it is not clear whether this effect is specific to

alcoholism *per se* or whether it is related to a general predisposition to psychiatric disorder (Murray, 1979).

One of the most influential research advances to occur during the 1970s was the discovery of opiate receptor sites and the identification of naturally occurring brain chemicals, the endorphins and enkephalins. Kosterlitz and Hughes (1977) suggested that opiates suppress the release of neuro-transmitters normally controlled by enkephalins, and that there is a compensatory enzymatic response to those, such that increasing amounts of opiates are needed to maintain the effect. When the opiates are withdrawn, the enkephalins are unable to stimulate the tolerant receptor complexes. If supported by research, this hypothesis would provide a sound physiological basis for the explanation of the mechanisms of tolerance and withdrawal.

More recently, there has been great interest in the possibility that the dopamine reward system may provide a neurochemical basis underlying the compulsive use of drugs. Much of the work on dopamine mechanisms has been done with cocaine, but the involvement of the dopamine system has also been implicated in connection with the use of several other drugs, including other stimulants, such as amphetamine and nicotine, as well as sedative drugs, such as alcohol. An excellent review of the neuropharmacological basis of reward is provided by Liebman and Cooper (1989). These authors offer a word of caution against the over-enthusiastic interpretation of findings in this field: 'Much of the interest in brain-stimulation reward is based upon the implicit assumption that an understanding of this phenomenon will provide new insights into the neuro-biology of motivation . . . . At this juncture, this goal is still a long way from being achieved' (Liebman and Cooper, ibid.: 93).

Some people with drug and alcohol problems may be brain-damaged, either as a result of their prolonged consumption of the substance (as with alcohol) or as a result of overdoses or accidents associated with their use of drink or drugs. The Wernicke-Korsakoff Syndrome is a consequence of thiamine (vitamin B_1) deficiency, which causes damage to the periventricular area of the brain and manifests itself primarily through impairments of memory. Alcoholic brain damage may also cause impaired balance and movement and blurring of vision. It is less clear whether, or to what extent, illicit drug use causes brain damage. Studies of long-term, high-dose opiate addicts have not shown any direct heroin-related damage (Strang and Gurling, 1989). Cocaine and other stimulant drugs may cause serious cardiovascular accidents in a minority of users (Gossop, 1987).

Conditioning approaches

Wikler (1948) first proposed that conditioning factors played an important role in drug addiction. Animals will increase their rate of operant responding when this is followed by intravenous opiates, CNS stimulants, such as amphetamines or cocaine, or sedatives, such as the barbiturates. In Wikler's view, drug-related behaviours and objects become secondary reinforcers as a result of their repeated pairings with the primary drug-related reinforcement. Similarly, stimuli regularly associated with withdrawal symptoms acquire conditioned aversive properties. There is ample experimental confirmation of these effects (e.g. Kumar and Stolerman, 1977), and it is consistent with the comments of several addicts who have described a craving for drugs when they visited places they associated with buying or using drugs. Wikler suggests that the high relapse rate among addicts may be due to incomplete extinction of both positive and negative secondary reinforcers.

Following the work of Wikler, another line of conditioning research has led to the opponent-process explanation of tolerance. This Pavlovian model suggests that conditioned responses to a variety of drugs (including opiates and alcohol) are opposite in direction to the unconditioned effects. Among the evidence for this is the fact that when the usual cues for administration of a drug are presented without the drug, there is an enhancement of the compensatory conditioned responses (Siegel, 1976). With the gradual increase in the strength of the conditioned responses, the unconditioned drug effect decreases (that is, tolerance occurs). The display of tolerance, therefore, is dependent upon prior experiences in the drug-administration environment as well as upon the drug. Tolerance shares many similarities with memory or learning processes. Both tolerance and learning are retained over long periods of time: both are disrupted by electroconvulsive shock, frontal cortical stimulation and metabolic inhibitors (Siegel, 1979).

There is an apparent contradiction between these conditioning accounts. In Wikler's theory the conditioned response is similar to the observed drug effect, whereas in Siegel's account, the conditioned response appears to oppose the drug effect. Unless it is possible to predict the nature and direction of the conditioned response, the value of any conditioning theory is seriously threatened. One attempt to resolve this matter was made by Eikelboom and Stewart (1982) who argued that the apparently contradictory predictions result from a misunderstanding about the nature of the unconditioned stimulus and the unconditioned response when drugs are used in conditioning studies. The drug-administration itself cannot necessarily be assumed to be the actual unconditioned stimulus nor the observed drug effect the unconditioned response. Eikelboom and Stewart suggested that a drug should be considered to be an unconditioned stimulus only when it acts on the afferent arm of the CNS and that only those drug effects which are CNS-mediated physiological reactions should qualify as unconditioned responses.

Personality theories

The personality disorder model has always had a profound influence upon psychiatric thinking about drug and alcohol dependence. Indeed, at one time, psychiatric nosologies tended to define drug addiction in terms of personality disorder (as in *DSM II*). This formulation derives from psychoanalytic thinking about character neurosis (cf. Gossop, 1981). People who become dependent upon a drug are said to be predisposed towards this because of their personality characteristics; the addiction itself is seen as symptomatic of this underlying problem.

A huge amount of personality research has been published, and the cynical reader may be tempted to view this in terms of the ease with which such publications can be generated. Cattell himself (1946) has described the excessive use of personality questionnaires as 'the nadir of scientific inventiveness and subtlety'. This vast sea of publications has done little to support the personality disorder view of the dependence disorders. Certainly it is clear that there is no single addictive personality. Addicts and alcoholics are impressively heterogeneous populations.

There is, however, good evidence that many addicts and alcoholics who seek treatment show signs of psychological difficulties or 'abnormal' personality profiles. Gossop and Eysenck (1980) compared a group of more than 200 addicts at three London treatment centres with normal controls. The addicts differed from the normal group on each of the four scales of the Eysenck Personality Questionnaire, but the most pronounced effect was the extremely high neuroticism scores of the addicts, who seemed to be troubled by affective difficulties, mainly by anxiety and depressive feelings. A review of the alcoholic personality literature also suggested that high levels of neuroticism were reported with some frequency (Barnes, 1979). Other studies have suggested that clinical samples of addicts and alcoholics score highly on measures of hostility, psychopathic deviation as measured by the MMPI, and tough-mindedness as measured by the P Scale of the Eysenck Personality Questionnaire (Gossop and Roy, 1976; Miller, 1976; Gossop and Eysenck, 1980). These findings are probably due, at least in part, to social selection processes by which the more psychologically disturbed individuals seek, or are directed towards, treatment agencies.

There is some data to suggest that the drug upon which a person becomes dependent may be chosen because of its self-medicating effects. Teasdale (1972) suggested that stimulant drugs were frequently used to reduce social anxieties (see Chapter 20). Similarly, Gossop and Roy (1976) suggested that opiate addicts might be using drugs to cope with the distress associated with hostile and aggressive feelings. As yet, these suggestions about the specific links between psychological problems and choice of drug have not been followed up by further research. However, drugs are powerful tools for altering the subjective state of the user, and it is clear that many people run into difficulties because of the way in which their drug reduces feelings of psychological discomfort. The distress associated with anxiety, anger and depression can be reduced by many commonly abused drugs. Where this sort of self-medication occurs, it may be appropriate to consider the possibilities of setting up a suitable programme directed towards treating the underlying problem.

Social perspectives

The social context affects drug-taking in many ways, from the broadest socio-cultural level to the specific circumstances in which a drug is used. One of the simplest determinants of drug-taking is availability. It is surprising how often this obvious factor has been ignored. It is not necessary to invoke complex pharmacological or psychological explanations to understand why the rate of alcoholism among barmen is so high. One might make a similar point about the abuse of drugs by medical personnel. And in the case of the illicit drugs, availability may also play a powerful role in leading to drug-taking.

As a result of the Iranian revolution, heroin producers moved into the northern areas of Pakistan (as well as other parts of Afghanistan and India) in the late 1970s, taking with them their technologies for manufacturing heroin from opium. This led to a massive heroin production and distribution industry. Because of the vast quantities of the drug, it soon became easily and cheaply available in most parts of Pakistan. In a country which had virtually no heroin addicts in the mid-1970s, the number of addicts had risen to more than half a million (one estimate put the figure at about 700,000) by the latter half of the 1980s (Gossop, 1989b).

Many investigators have pointed to the impact that cultural patterns have on rates of alcoholism. First-generation Italian Americans and Jewish Americans, both from cultures in which drug-taking occurs in a family or religious setting, are likely to drink but unlikely to become alcoholics (Calahan, 1978). Irish Americans, on the other hand, who are more likely to drink in pubs, have lower consumption rates but higher alcoholism rates. As these groups become less culturally distinct in later generations, their rates of alcoholism become more similar.

In the United States, Blacks and Puerto-Ricans are massively over-represented among American addicts. The early studies which looked for social correlates of drug addiction, pointed to social and economic disadvantage: low economic status, low educational attainment, disrupted family life and crowded housing conditions were strongly related to addiction (Chein et al., 1964). However, this observation is itself culturally limited. In Britain, this pattern was not evident for many years. With the changes that have occurred during the 1980s there is now more concordance between the British and American patterns, with increased concentrations of illicit drug users in some socially deprived inner city areas. In contrast to the American experience, it is somewhat surprising that the incidence of illicit drug problems (notably heroin addiction) among immigrant groups, such as West Indians and Asians, still seems to be lower than might be anticipated.

The immediate social influences upon drug-taking are perhaps important in terms of assessment and treatment. Social influence, for instance, is one of the factors that contributes to the development of drinking patterns among adolescents (Jessor and Jessor, 1975), and social factors often continue to play an important role in maintaining deviant patterns of drinking or drug-taking. An important part of assessment involves the elucidation of the social context in which drug-taking generally occurs. The bases of alcohol addiction in the solitary drinker may be quite different from those in the social pub drinker or in the expense-account businessperson.

The same applies to drug addiction. In his study of heroin addicts, Stimson (1973) distinguished between four types of users; these he called Junkies, Two-Worlders, Loners and Stable addicts. There were marked differences between these groups in terms of their drug-taking habits, physical health, contact with the junkie subculture, criminal involvement and employment. In a seven-year follow-up of this sample Oppenheimer et al. (1979) found that, among those people who had ceased to be dependent on opiates, there was a general improvement in social functioning, and Wille (1978) suggested that for those addicts who gave up drugs themselves, without formal treatment, this improvement may have preceded rather than followed their becoming abstinent.

There is a growing body of research which is concerned with self-change among drug abusers – that is, with changes in drug-taking patterns, including cessation, that occur without any formal treatment. In the case of cigarette smokers, for example, the majority of people give up smoking without any sort of formal treatment intervention (Schacter, 1982). Similarly, it is increasingly clear that many people with alcohol problems also give up without treatment (Saunders and Kershaw, 1979).

In an early study of self-change among heroin users, Schasre (1966) studied heroin users who had not yet progressed to a fixed pattern of dependent use. It is interesting, and contrary to some formulations of the natural history of drug addiction, that one reason for stopping was an awareness by the user of the onset of physical dependence. Indeed, awareness of the appearance of physical withdrawal symptoms was one of the more frequently cited reasons for stopping. This study also shows how various contingencies can markedly affect continued drug use. Half of the subjects stopped because they moved away from the neighbourhood, or their supply was otherwise interrupted. In this respect, Schasre's findings anticipate those of Robins et al.'s (1974) landmark studies of drug use among Vietnam veterans.

Biernacki (1986) investigated a group of heroin addicts who had deliberately chosen not to become involved in treatment as a way of giving up. The majority believed either that there was no need for formal treatment because they could take care of themselves or that treatment would not help. For Biernacki's subjects, breaking away from addiction was often accomplished by moving away (geographically) from the location in which the drug-taking patterns had been established. In other cases, the moving away was achieved by the person putting a 'social distance' between themselves and their previous drug using friends and environments. The manner in which drug users (including dependent users) give up drugs is an important issue which has only recently begun to be properly investigated.

A COGNITIVE PERSPECTIVE

Each of the theories that has been presented so briefly provides, at best, a partial explanation of different aspects of the addictive disorders. One aspect of drug and alcohol dependence that has been underrated is the meaning that the use of drugs has for the individual. People do not suddenly and inexplicably fall victim to drug addiction and alcoholism. They are actively involved in the use of drugs, and their attitudes, beliefs, intentions and expectations play an important role in this involvement with drugs.

There has, for instance, been some dispute about whether or not alcohol reduces anxiety and tension, and different empirical findings have been reported. It may be more pertinent to note that many alcoholics *expect* alcohol to reduce tension (Stockwell *et al.*, 1977), and this may be as influential in the decision to drink as any pharmacological effect. Marlatt *et al.* (1973) showed the importance of such expectations by demonstrating that the drinking of alcohol subjects was determined by the belief that they were drinking alcohol rather than by any pharmacological effects. Marlatt and Rohsenow (1980) have also pointed out how the beliefs and expectations of the user can induce craving and can lead to the 'loss of control' effect.

Despite this, some traditional theories imply that drug and alcohol dependence can be explained as if they were the result of forces acting upon the user over which he or she has no control. The implications of such views can lead to serious errors in assessment and treatment. An important part of assessment involves the clarification of the person's beliefs about drugs and alcohol. Both the clinician and the patient must explore and try to understand the social and psychological meaning of drug-taking. Too often those involved in treatment have attempted to deny or ignore the user's own perceptions of their drug use. Such failures to acknowledge the personal significance of drug-taking are likely to provoke resistance or hostility on the part of the user and may well interfere with their efforts to do without drugs.

Robinson (1972) indicated how the acceptance of a 'sick-role' view of alcoholism may interfere with treatment because of the assumption that sick people cannot cure themselves by their own efforts: once a disease is contracted, it can only be cured by outside (medical) intervention. The same assumption about sickness, control and responsibility applies to drug addiction. Eiser and Gossop (1979) looked at the ways in which a group of addicts at a London drug-dependence clinic interpreted their own drug-taking. One way was to see it as a form of sickness, or as symptomatic of some underlying disorder which needed to be treated by doctors. Another way of looking at addiction emphasised the addict's unwillingness or inability to do without drugs.

It is not altogether reassuring that some addicts see their addiction as a sickness, an interpretation that seems to account for their drug-taking and simultaneously to absolve them of responsibility for altering it. Studies have found that these views have been related to treatment. Gossop *et al.* (1982b) noted that fear of withdrawal appeared to be an important barrier to in-patient treatment. Those addicts who were most afraid of withdrawal tended not to seek in-patient treatment and were more likely to drop out of treatment prematurely. Bradley and Gossop (1983) also found differences between first-time attenders and regular drug-clinic patients in their view of drug-taking. New patients were more likely to emphasise the 'hooked' and 'sick' aspects of their drug use. It is not clear whether the attitudes of each individual change as they move through different phases of treatment or whether the results reflect some sort of selection process in which the addicts whose views fit in with staff attitudes remain in treatment and others drop out. Either way, the addicts' views of their own drug-taking are important and need to be taken into account.

Among the most basic issues which need to be explored are the following. Why has the person sought treatment, and why at this particular time? In what ways do they feel better or different when they take drugs/alcohol? (Many people have quite definite beliefs about how drugs and alcohol improve their ability to function.) How do they expect to feel when they have stopped using drugs? Do they have any confidence in their ability to regulate their drug use or do they believe in the 'one drink, one drunk' view? Do they want to give up drugs/alcohol entirely? (Many heroin addicts, for instance, do not see the use of either alcohol or cannabis as in any way related to their difficulties.) Other central questions that need to be asked concern the obstacles to maintaining change once the person has stopped using drugs. The factors that assist or impede the initial stages of change (getting off) may be quite different to those that assist or impede the maintenance of change (staying off).

CLINICAL IMPLICATIONS

The implicit and explicit theoretical perspective of the clinician is likely to have an important influence upon his or her treatment approach. However, it must be recognised that the factors that may lead to the development of drug and alcohol problems are diverse. The best guidelines for assessment and treatment in individual cases will be suggested by the circumstances surrounding that individual. As such, assessment of drug and alcohol problems is not merely an important and necessary precursor of treatment; it is a vital part of treatment. Without an appropriate and individually based assessment, the clinician will not know precisely how to target any treatment intervention. This failure of assessment is one of the commonest problems in the treatment of drug and alcohol problems and is often a factor associated with the application of inappropriate treatment methods or 'broad-spectrum' treatment packages.

NOTES

1   For the purposes of this chapter, unless otherwise specified, alcohol will be regarded as a 'drug', and drinking will be incorporated within the broader meaning of the term 'drug-taking'.

2   It should be obvious from this discussion that drug and alcohol problems cannot easily
    be conceptualised as a unidimensional construct. It is discussed as such here (as in
    Figure 19.1, p. 370) primarily because it is useful conceptually to distinguish problems
    from dependence. It was felt to be unnecessarily convoluted to refer both to the
    dimension of dependence as well as to the various dimensions of problems or harm
    that can follow from the use of drugs. In practice, however, it is probably unhelpful to
    attempt to confine the complexities of problematic drug use and harm within any
    single dimension, and for clinical or research purposes a multi-dimensional formu-
    lation is more likely to be used in which physical health, social functioning, and so on
    are considered separately.

REFERENCES

Armor, D. J. (1980) 'The Rand report and the analysis of relapse', in G. Edwards and
    M. Grant (eds) *Alcoholism Treatment in Transition*, London: Croom Helm.
Ashton, H. and Stepney, R. (1982) *Smoking*, London: Tavistock.
Ball, J. (1967) 'The rehability and validity of interview data obtained from 59 narcotic
    drug addicts', *American Journal of Sociology* 72: 350–4.
Barnes, G. E. (1979) 'The alcoholic personality: a re-analysis of the literature', *Journal
    for Studies on Alcoholism* 40: 571–634.
Berridge, V. and Edwards, G. (1981) *Opium and the People*, London: Allen Lane.
Biernacki, P. (1986) *Pathways from Heroin Addiction*, Philadelphia: Temple University
    Press.
Bradley, B. P. and Gossop, M. R. (1983) 'Differences in attitudes towards drug-taking
    among drug addicts: implications for treatment', *Drug and Alcohol Dependence* 10:
    361–6.
Bradley, B., Gossop, M., Brewin, B., Phillips, G. and Green, L. (1992) 'Attributions and
    relapse in opiate addicts', *Journal of Consulting and Clinical Psychology* 60: 470–2.
Busto, U., Simpkins, J., Sellers Edward, M., Sisson, B. and Segal, R. (1983) 'Objective
    determination of benzodiazepine use and abuse in alcoholics', *British Journal of
    Addiction* 78: 429–35.
Calahan, D. (1978) 'Implications of American drinking practices and attitudes for prevention
    and treatment of alcoholism', in G. A. Marlatt and P. E. Nathan (eds) *Behavioural
    Approaches to Alcoholism*, New Brunswick, NJ: Rutgers Center of Alcohol Studies.
Cattell, R. B. (1946) *Description and Measurement of Personality*, New York: World
    Books.
Chein, I., Gerard, D. L., Lee, R. S. and Rosenfeld, E. (1964) *Narcotics, Delinquency and
    Social Policy. The Road to H*, London: Tavistock.
Dietrich, R. A. (1976) 'Biochemical aspects of alcoholism', *Psychoneuroendocrinology*
    1: 325–46.
Dole, V. P. and Nyswander, M. E. (1967) 'Heroin addiction – a metabolic disease',
    Archives of Internal Medicine 120: 19–24.
Edwards, G. (1977) 'The alcohol dependence syndrome: usefulness of an idea', in
    G. Edwards and M. Grant (eds) *Alcoholism: New Knowledge and New Responses*,
    London: Croom Helm.
Edwards, G., Arif, A. and Hodgson, R. (1981) 'Nomenclature and classification of drug
    and alcohol related problems: a W.H.O. memorandum', *Bulletin World Health
    Organisation* 59: 225–42.
Eikelboon, R. and Stewart, J. (1982) 'Conditioning of drug-induced physiological
    responses', *Psychological Review* 89: 507–28.
Eiser, J. R. and Gossop, M. R. (1979) ' "Hooked" or "Sick": addicts' perceptions of their
    addiction', *Addictive Behaviours* 4: 185–91.

Gossop, M. (1978) 'A comparative study of oral and intravenous drug-dependent patients on three dimensions of personality', *International Journal of the Addictions* 13: 135–42.

Gossop, M. (1981) *Theories of Neurosis*, Berlin: Springer.

Gossop, M. (1987) 'Beware cocaine', *British Medical Journal* 295: 945.

Gossop, M. (1989a) *Relapse and Addictive Behaviour*, London: Routledge.

Gossop, M. (1989b) *Heroin Detoxification: Guidelines for Family Doctors and Primary Health Care Workers*, Islamabad: Pakistan Narcotics Control Board.

Gossop, M. (1990) The development of a Short Opiate Withdrawal Scale (SOWS), *Addictive Behaviors* 15: 487–90.

Gossop, M. (1993) *Living with Drugs, 3rd edn*, Aldershot: Ashgate.

Gossop, M. R. and Eysenck, S. B. G. (1980) 'A further investigation into the personality of drug addicts in treatment', *British Journal of Addictions* 75: 305–11.

Gossop, M. and Roy, A. (1976) 'Hostility in drug dependent individuals: its relation to specific drugs, and oral and intravenous use', *British Journal of Psychiatry* 128: 188–93.

Gossop, M., Bradley, B. and Brewis, R. (1982a) 'Amphetamine withdrawal and sleep disturbance', *Drug and Alcohol Dependence* 10: 177–83.

Gossop, M. R., Eiser, J. R. and Ward, E. (1982b) 'The addicts' perceptions of their own drug taking: implications for the treatment of drug dependence', *Addictive Behaviours* 7: 189–94.

Gossop, M., Green, L., Phillips, G. and Bradley, B. (1989) 'Lapse, relapse and survival among opiate addicts after treatment', *British Journal of Psychiatry* 154: 348–53.

Gossop, M., Griffiths, P., Powis, B. and Strang, J. (1992) 'Severity of dependence and route of administration of heroin, cocaine and amphetamine', *British Journal of Addiction* (forthcoming).

Gossop, M., Griffiths, P., Powis, B. and Strang, J. (1993a) 'Severity of heroin dependence and HIV risk. I. Sexual behaviour', *AIDS Care* 5: 149–57.

Gossop, M., Griffiths, P., Powis, B. and Strang, J. (1993b) 'Severity of heroin dependence and HIV risk. II. Sharing injecting equipment', *AIDS Care* 5: 159–68.

Gottheil, E., Murphy, B. F., Skoloda, T. E. and Corbett, L. O. (1972) 'Fixed interval drinking decisions', *Quarterly Journal Studies on Alcohol* 33: 325–40.

Gutierres, S. E. and Reich, J. W. (1988) 'Attributional analysis of drug abuse and gender', *Journal of Social and Clinical Psychology* 7: 176–91.

Hesselbrock, M., Babor, T. F., Hesselbrock, U., Meyer, R. E., and Workman, K. (1983) '"Never believe an alcoholic"? On the validity of self-report measures of alcohol dependence and related constructs', *International Journal of the Addictions* 18: 593–609.

Hodgson, R. (1980) 'The Alcohol Dependence Syndrome: a step in the wrong direction? A discussion of Stan Shaw's critique', *British Journal of Addiction* 75: 255–63.

Hodgson, R., Stockwell, T., Rankin, H. and Edwards, G. (1978) 'Alcohol dependence: the concept, its utility and measurement', *British Journal of Addiction* 73: 339–42.

Jessor, R. and Jessor, S. L. (1975) 'Adolescent development and the onset of drinking: a longitudinal study', *Journal of Studies on Alcohol* 36: 27–51.

Kosterlitz, H. W. and Hughes, J. (1977) 'Opiate receptors and endogenous opioid peptides in tolerance and dependence', in M. M. Gross (ed.) *Alcohol Intoxication and Withdrawal*, New York: Plenum.

Kuehnle, J. and Spitzer, R. (1981) '*DSM III* Classification of substance use disorders', in J. Lowinson and P. Ruiz (eds) *Substance Abuse: Clinical Problems and Perspectives*, Baltimore: Williams and Williams.

Kumar, R. and Stolerman, I. P. (1977) 'Experimental and clinical aspects of drug dependence', in L. I. Iverson and S. D. Iverson, (eds) *Handbook of Psychopharmacology*, New York: Plenum Press.

Liebman, J. and Cooper, S. (1989) *The Neuropharmacological Basis of Reward*, Oxford: Clarendon Press.

Marlatt, G. A. and Rohsenow, D. J. (1980) 'Cognitive processes in alcohol use: expectancy and the balanced placebo design', in N. K. Mello (ed.) *Advances in Substance Abuse*, Greenwich, Conn.: JAI Press.

Marlatt, G. A., Damming, B. and Reid, J. B. (1973) 'Loss of control drinking in alcoholics: an experimental analogue', *Journal of Abnormal Psychology* (8)1: 233-241.

Mello, N. K. and Mendelson, J. H. (1971) 'Drinking patterns during work contingent and non-contingent alcohol acquisition', in N. K. Mello and J. H. Mendelson (eds) *Recent Advances in Studies of Alcoholism*, Washington: NIMH.

Milby, J. B. (1981) *Addictive Behaviour and its Treatment*, New York: Springer.

Miller, W. R. (1976) 'Alcoholism scales and objective assessment methods: a review', *Psychological Bulletin* 83: 649-74.

Murray, R. (1979) 'Alcoholism', in P. Hill, R. Murray and A. Thorley (eds) *Essentials of Postgraduate Psychiatry*, London: Academic Press.

Nathan, P. E. (1980) 'Etiology and process in the addictive behaviours', in W. R. Miller (ed.) *The Addictive Behaviours*, New York: Pergamon.

Oppenheimer, E., Stimson, G. V. and Thorley, A. (1979) 'Seven-year follow-up of heroin addicts: abstinence and continued use compared', *British Medical Journal* 2: 627-30.

Orford, J., Oppenheimer, E. and Edwards, G. (1976) 'Abstinence or control: the outcome of excessive drinkers two years after consultation', *Behaviour Research and Therapy* 14: 409-18.

Phillips, G., Gossop, M., Edwards, G., Sutherland, G., Taylor, C. and Strang, J. (1987) 'The application of the SODQ to the measurement of the severity of opiate dependence in a British sample', *British Journal of Addiction* 82: 691-9.

Robins, L., Davis, D. and Goodwin, D. (1974) 'Drug use by US Army enlisted men in Vietnam: a follow-up on their return home', *American Journal of Epidemiology* 99: 235-49.

Robinson, D. (1972) 'The alcohologist's addiction: some implications of having lost control over the disease concept of alcoholism', *Quarterly Journal Studies on Alcohol* 33: 1028-42.

Russell, M. A. H. (1976) 'Tobacco smoking and nicotine dependence', in R. G. Gibbins *et al.* (eds) *Research Advances in Alcohol and Drug Problems. vol. 3*, New York: Wiley.

Saunders, W. and Kershaw, P. (1979) 'Spontaneous remission from alcoholism – a community study', *British Journal of Addiction* 74: 251-6.

Schacter, S. (1982) 'Recidivism and self-cure of smoking and obesity', *American Psychologist* 37: 436-44.

Schasre, R. (1966) 'Cessation patterns among neophyte heroin users', *International Journal of the Addictions*, 1: 23-32.

Shaw, S. (1979) 'A critique of the concept of the alcohol dependence syndrome', *British Journal of Addiction* 74: 339-48.

Siegel, S. (1976) 'Morphine analgesic tolerance: its situation specificity supports a Pavlovian conditioning model', *Science* 193: 323-5.

Siegel, S. (1979) 'The role of conditioning in drug tolerance and addiction' , in J. D. Keehn (ed.) *Psychopathology in Animals*, New York: Academic Press (143-68).

Sobell, L. C. and Sobell, M. B., (1978) 'Validity of self-reports in three populations of alcoholics', *Journal of Consulting and Clinical Psychology* 46: 901-7.

Stimson, G. (1973) *Heroin and Behaviour*, Shannon: Irish University Press.

Stockwell, T. R., Hodgson, R. J. and Rankin, H. J. (1977) 'An experimental look at the use of alcohol for tension-reduction by alcoholics', paper presented at International Conference on Experimental and Behavioural Approaches to Alcoholism, Bergen, Norway.

Stockwell, T., Hodgson, R., Edwards, G., Taylor, C. and Rankin, H. (1979) 'The development of a questionnaire to measure severity of alcohol dependence', *British Journal of Addiction* 74: 79–87.

Strang, J. (1992) 'Discussion document for consultation group on concepts and definitions of harm reduction', 3rd International Conference on the Reduction of Drug Related Harm, Melbourne, Australia.

Strang, J. and Gurling, H. (1989) 'Computerized tomography and neuropsychological assessment in long-term high-dose heroin addicts', *British Journal of Addiction* 84: 1011–19

Sutherland, G., Edwards, G., Taylor, C., Phillips, G., Gossop, M. and Brady, R. (1986) 'The measurement of opiate dependence', *British Journal of Addiction* 81: 485–94.

Szasz, T. (1972) 'The ethics of addiction', *Harpers Magazine*, April.

Teasdale, J. D. (1972) 'The perceived effect of heroin on the interpersonal behaviour of heroin-dependent patients, and a comparison with stimulant-dependent patients', *International Journal of Addictions* 7: 533–48.

Vogel, V. H., Isbell, H. and Chapman, K. W. (1948) 'Present status of narcotic addiction', *Journal of the American Medical Association* 138: 1019–26.

Wikler, A. (1948) 'Recent progress in research on the neurophysiologic basis of morphine addiction', *American Journal of Psychiatry*, 105: 329–38.

Wille, R. (1978) 'Cessation of opiate dependence: processes involved in achieving abstinence', *British Journal of Addiction* 73: 381–4.

Wray, I. and Dickerson, M. (1981) 'Cessation of high frequency gambling and "withdrawal" symptoms', *British Journal of Addiction* 76: 401–5.

Chapter 20

Drug and alcohol problems
Treatment

Michael Gossop

Although the dependence disorders are usually an important part of the drug and alcohol problems that lead to clinical intervention, it is important to keep in mind the broad range of problems and difficulties that can arise as a result of the use of drugs and alcohol. In many respects our concepts of the dependence disorders are more like earlier notions of 'mental illness'. Terms such as 'addiction' may appear to denote a specific disorder but they are better regarded as pointing to a vague and loosely defined collection of problems. As a result, it makes no more sense to ask how to treat addiction than it does to ask how to treat 'mental illness'. What is required is some more precise specification of the underlying dimensions or factors. The failure to acknowledge this has led to futile efforts to identify a single 'treatment of choice' which could be applied to all (or at least to most) cases of drug or alcohol dependence. During the past twenty or thirty years, every imaginable type of treatment intervention has been used in this area, and it is depressing to find that almost every one of them has been put forward as a sort of 'magic bullet' that will finally solve the problem of the addictive disorders.

As has been stated in the preceding chapter, drug and alcohol treatments should be tailored to the needs of the individual. This apparently simple and uncontentious statement turns out to have complex and far-reaching implications if seriously applied in clinical practice. The first implication is that there is not, nor can there be expected to be, any single best treatment for these problems. Both aetiology and outcome are influenced by a broad range of different factors. The treatment of drug and alcohol problems very seldom involves procedures that are any different from those which the clinical psychologist or other clinician will be familiar with as a result of his or her training and experience with other types of patient. Learning how best to treat drug and alcohol patients seldom requires the acquisition of new skills. It more often involves learning how to apply existing skills to these problems.

GOALS OF TREATMENT

Traditional descriptions of assessment procedures for behaviour modification programmes as offered by Kanfer and Phillips (1970) provide excellent guidance for those involved in the treatment of drug problems. Information is needed about the target behaviours, the reinforcement parameters maintaining them, opportunities in the patient's environment for maintaining other more desirable responses, and the patient's ability to observe and reinforce himself or herself. It is characteristic of such approaches that their data are often direct samples of behaviour in specific situations and not indirect and generalised signs of personality predispositions.

For all types of drug problems which require treatment, the intervention offered should be tailored to the needs of the particular individual. It is essential, for instance, that a thorough assessment should identify, *for each individual case*, the nature of the problem and appropriate and achievable goals for treatment. In addition, the treatment process should identify as early as possible those particular factors that are likely to assist or hamper the achievement of the treatment goal(s).

Examples of types of treatment goals might include the following:

1 Reduction of psychological, social or other problems not directly related to the drug problem
2 Reduction of psychological, social or other problems related to the drug problem
3 Reduction of harmful or hazardous behaviour associated with the use of drugs
4 Attainment of controlled, non-dependent, or non-problem drug use
5 Attainment of abstinence from problem drug
6 Attainment of abstinence from all drugs

These six examples are not, of course, mutually exclusive. It is possible, for instance, to set as treatment goals the attainment of abstinence *and* the improvement of psychosocial functioning in areas unrelated to drug-taking. It is, however, useful to distinguish between those treatments which are aimed directly at the drug problem and those that have an indirect or hypothetical relationship to the target problem.

One issue that has provoked controversy for many years concerns the possibilities of treatment goals other than abstinence – and in particular that of teaching alcoholics to regain control over their drinking. The first serious challenge to the idea that the only treatment goal for alcoholics was total abstinence was presented in a paper by Davies (1962). This showed that some alcoholics could return to normal drinking, and the publication of these results prompted a good deal of harsh criticism from the traditionalists. Fox asserted that: 'Among my own approximately 3,000 patients not one has been able to achieve [controlled drinking], although almost every one of them tried' (Fox, 1967).

In recent years there has been ample confirmation of Davies's original findings: it is clear that, for some alcoholics, moderate drinking is a realistic goal of treatment. None the less, there remains some doubt about the practical clinical significance of this. Glatt, for instance, has expressed this doubt in the following terms:

> In theory, therefore, there seems no reason why the great majority of alcoholics could not continue to drink in moderation, perhaps indefinitely. In practice, however, under conditions and stresses of ordinary day-to-day living . . . relatively few such drinkers can realistically hope to achieve moderate drinking for longer than relatively short periods.
>
> (Glatt, 1983)

Pattison, on the other hand, has argued that the emphasis upon abstinence as a criterion of successful treatment is unhelpful.

> First, abstinence is not the only goal of alcoholism rehabilitation. Other goals include improvement in emotional, inter-personal, vocational and physical health. Second, abstinence is not necessarily correlated with improvement in these other areas of life health. Abstinence may be associated with function deterioration in these other areas. Third, some alcoholics do not become abstinent yet demonstrate major improvements in all areas of life function.
>
> (Pattison, 1976)

The application of goals other than abstinence to the treatment of heroin and opiate addiction has often been linked to drug substitution treatments. The provision of maintenance drugs has generally been based upon an assumption that this might lead to improvement in other aspects of the addict's social and psychological functioning. In some cases, it has been asserted that the success of maintenance programmes should only be measured in such terms and that the dosage of the drug used should not be a criterion of treatment outcome (Newman, 1977). In America, this approach has been epitomised by the methadone-maintenance programmes. These have been effective in many cases, though the strength of the evidence supporting methadone maintenance has been much overrated (Gossop, 1978). There is, however, a sufficient core of data to support the suggestion that some addicts will show improvement in other areas of their life if given a controlled supply of maintenance drug. In a British study, Gossop et al., (1982b) found that some of the most difficult long-term opiate addicts attending a drug clinic showed improvements in social functioning after being prescribed an increased dose of opiates. The results of this study should be interpreted with caution, but they do at least serve as a reminder that there are other indicators of treatment success than abstinence. Abstinence from drugs continues to be regarded as the ultimate goal in the treatment of drug abuse, and this is also the most certain method of reducing harm through the prevention of HIV infection among drug abusers. However, the total elimination of drug-injecting is not an achievable goal. Nor is it sensible to expect any treatment intervention to be one hundred per cent effective. It is necessary to face up to the implications of the fact that some drug-takers will continue to abuse drugs and some will continue to take them by injection. Harm reduction programmes usually adopt a hierarchy of goals such as that shown in Figure 20.1.

Much of the controversy about abstinence as a treatment goal has centred around the problems concerning treatment matching. It is generally accepted that not all alcoholics will be able to regain control over their drinking, and there is some suggestion that those who are able to may be a comparatively small minority. Pattison (1976) suggests that the proportion of alcoholics who develop normal drinking patterns, either after treatment or after changes in their social circumstances may be between 10 and 15 per cent. As a result, many clinicians continue to support abstinence as a general treatment goal on the grounds that the attempt to predict which individuals will be successful in regaining control over their drinking remains little more than guesswork (Glatt, 1983). 'So long as no one knows what it takes to reactivate [alcoholism] in any individual who is

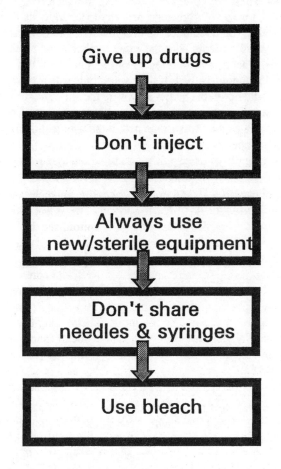

Figure 20.1 A hierarchy of treatment goals

addicted . . . the prudent alcoholic in remission should not put himself on trial' (Keller, 1972). Some studies have suggested that moderate drinking is more likely to be an appropriate goal for moderately dependent than for heavily dependent alcoholics (Orford *et al.*, 1976), and that the patient's attitude to controlled drinking, their age, employment and pre-treatment patterns of drinking may be important selective factors (Heather and Robertson, 1981), but beyond these rather general observations there is little empirical evidence or sound theory to which the clinician can turn for guidance.

The state of affairs is worse still in drug dependence where there are even fewer guidelines to help the clinician match the needs of the individual addict to the treatment programme. One unfortunate consequence of this is that clinical decisions are frequently taken on an idiosyncratic and somewhat arbitrary basis (Gossop and Connell, 1983). Another is that many treatment agencies shy away from the exasperating difficulties of attempting to match treatment to the needs of the individual. Instead of a greater sensitivity to the individual differences that clearly exist within the population of drug addicts, there has too often been a tendency to treat all patients with the same methods and to enforce the same treatment goals. The legend of Procrustes recounts how this robber waylaid travellers and tied them to a bed. If they were longer than the bed, he chopped off the parts that did not fit the bed; if they were too short, he stretched them until bed and traveller were of matching lengths. The treatment of dependence disorders often resembles the Procrustean bed in the way that the needs of patients are forced to accommodate the treatment being offered.

A valuable reminder of these points was provided by a recent US Institute of Medicine report of alcoholism treatments, though the point applies with equal force to the treatment of all types of drug problems. Drug and alcohol treatment agencies might profitably have it inscribed on the walls of their consulting rooms.

> Which kinds of individuals, with what kinds of . . . problems, are likely to respond to what kinds of treatments by achieving what kinds of goals when delivered by which kinds of practitioners?
>
> (US Institute of Medicine, 1990)

TREATMENT APPROACHES

Stages of changes

Prochaska and DiClemente (1982) found that smokers who were attempting to give up reported moving through certain stages of change. These stages of change, which have since been reported for all of the addictive disorders, were described as *Precontemplation, Contemplation, Action* and *Maintenance*.

Precontemplation is a stage in which people are not intending to change their behaviour. Many individuals in this stage are not aware, or are not sufficiently aware, that they have problems though others around them (family, friends, doctors) may be acutely aware of this. When precontemplators approach treatment services it is usually because they are under pressure from others. Contemplation is a stage in which individuals show an awareness of their problem. They begin to think about making changes but have not yet made serious commitments to take action. People may be stuck in the contemplation stage for long periods.

Action is the stage in which people modify their behaviour, experiences, and/or environment in order to overcome their problems. People, including professionals, often equate change with action and consequently overlook the important work that prepares individuals for action. The maintenance stage is the time in which people work to prevent relapse and consolidate their gains attained during action. Maintenance is itself an active stage.

Subsequently, a further stage of *Relapse* was added to this cycle of change (Prochaska and DiClemente 1986). Relapse is a frequent problem for people trying to give up addictive behaviours and many relapsers move back into the contemplation stage and make serious intentions to quit within a year. These stages of change are usually represented in some sort of 'revolving door' model. Change need not involve any orderly progression through the different stages and some people with addictive behaviour problems may become stuck in one of the stages.

One useful implication of this sort of model is that it draws attention to the different processes of change that may be appropriate to different stages of change (Prochaska and DiClemente, 1983). The matching of processes and stages of change can serve as an important guide to therapists. For example, patients in the precontemplation stage should be helped to recognise and develop an awareness of their problems rather than being guided directly towards behavioural change. Patients in the contemplation stage are most open to consciousness-raising interventions (such as self-monitoring procedures or educational methods) and may be resistant to the interventions of a directive action-oriented therapist. During the action stage patients are likely to require specific practical help with behaviour change procedures as well as encouragement and support. Just as preparation is required for action, so preparation is equally important for the maintenance stage, and specific relapse prevention methods may play a valuable role. It is interesting that therapists as well as patients can become stuck in a favoured stage of change.

Social-behavioural treatments

One of the most influential models of treatment to be described in recent years has been the Relapse Prevention model (Marlatt and Gordon, 1985). Marlatt suggested that Relapse Prevention be seen as a self-management programme designed to enhance the maintenance stage of the habit-change process (Marlatt, 1985). The goal of Relapse Prevention is to teach individuals who are trying to change their drug-taking behaviour how to anticipate and cope with the pressures and problems that may lead towards a relapse, and Relapse Prevention is presented as a cognitive-behavioural treatment approach based upon the principles of social learning theory. The foundations of this model are the notions of high-risk situations and the coping strategies available to the individual.

In a series of studies of alcoholics, Litman and her colleagues looked at the interaction between: (a) situations perceived to be dangerous for the individual in that they may precipitate relapse; (b) the coping strategies available within the individual's repertoire to deal with these situations; (c) the perceived effectiveness of these coping behaviours; and (d) the individual's self-perception and self-esteem and the degree of learned helplessness with which they view their situation (summarised in Litman, 1986). Relapsers were compared with survivors. Individuals with a multiplicity of coping styles were more likely to survive, and the factor of cognitive control was the strongest discriminator between relapsers and survivors. From this work, Litman proposed her 'conceptual framework for alcoholism survival' (Litman, 1980) which looked at the stages of survival rather than viewing it as an all-or-nothing phenomenon. In the early stages of survival, avoidance and positive thinking are both viewed as effective coping behaviours; although at later stages in survival, there will be greater use of positive thinking alone. Litman argued that this work provided further support for individually tailored treatment programmes which are designed according to the resources and vulnerabilities of each individual rather than their broad diagnostic category (Litman 1986).

The factors associated with relapse in former heroin addicts have also been studied (Gossop et al., 1987, 1989). A group of eighty opiate addicts who had recently completed in-patient detoxification were followed up during the six-month period very soon after discharge. A disturbingly high proportion of subjects used opiates again in the period immediately after leaving treatment. Eighty-one per cent used opiates at least once during the six-month period, and in most cases, the lapse occurred very soon after discharge; 11 used them within the first 24 hours, and a total of 32 subjects (42 per cent) had lapsed within one week (Gossop et al., 1989). The authors concluded that the time immediately after leaving treatment should be considered a critical period during which the treatment group is at extremely high risk. The results of this study also provided more grounds for optimism when looked at over a longer term, since many of the subjects were able to avoid a full relapse to addictive use of opiates. At six months, 45 per cent of the sample were abstinent from all opiates (as confirmed by urine screening) and living in the community. Of the eleven categories of relapse precipitants included in the study, the three factors that were found to be most often associated with the initial lapse were negative mood states, cognitive factors, and external situations (Bradley et al., 1989). Almost two-thirds of those who lapsed indicated that cognitive factors, usually some explicit decision or plan to return to opiate use were implicated in their initial lapse. More than half indicated that some negative mood state (sadness, boredom, tension or anxiety) preceded their lapse. These associated factors occasionally occurred as single relapse precipitants, but more often they occurred as either clusters (several simultaneous relapse factors) or as sequences (one or more factors leading on to others).

Relapse prevention

Over the last couple of decades, the emphasis in treatment programmes has shifted, and greater attention is now being paid to relapse as a process in its own right and to ways of preventing relapse. The explanatory hypotheses for these treatment approaches are very varied. In their review of relapse prevention approaches in the alcohol field, Donovan and Chaney (1985) list models ranging from the neurological to the behavioural. As Donovan and Chaney point out, the popularity of models changes over time and reflects the dominant mode of thought at a given time in history.

In Marlatt's model, attention is turned away from an alleged preoccupation with detoxification to a consideration of aftercare. It is suggested that there has been a mistaken emphasis on the problem of cessation of drug use, when what is required is more emphasis on the difficulties encountered in maintenance of the change once cessation has occurred. In a study of 311 patients addicted to a variety of drugs, Marlatt found that high-risk situations could be grouped into negative emotional states (accounting for 35 per cent of relapses), interpersonal conflict (16 per cent of relapses), or indirect or direct social pressure (20 per cent of relapses) (Marlatt and George, 1984). Craving and urges might be triggered by environmental and internal cues, and an important first task for the client is to develop a keen sense of awareness of the way in which these internal and external triggers may contribute towards the development of a high-risk situation. Clients are encouraged to keep regular diaries detailing use of drugs and the extent to which they have encountered possible precipitants of relapse, and a summary of their response. The therapist may assist in conducting a behavioural analysis of these situations and teaches the client how to conduct such a behavioural analysis themselves. Structured problem-solving techniques are employed alongside rehearsal/role-play. The client is warned of the dangers of the way in which covert planning may lead to relapse, and of Apparently Irrelevant Decisions (unfortunately, in view of subsequent developments, these were given the acronym 'AIDs'). Such decisions may 'by chance' lead the client to happen to find himself or herself outside his or her old drug dealer's house. The client must learn to spot early warning signals for these potential relapse situations.

On those occasions when people begin to experience craving, they must allow the feeling to wash over and beyond them by adopting a technique which Marlatt somewhat poetically refers to as 'urge-surfing'. This may be assisted by relaxation techniques, distraction, or other coping strategies. On occasions when there is a breakdown of resolution and drugs are taken, then the person must learn to reassume control, realising that drug use or abstinence is not an uncontrollable on/off behaviour.

Specific intervention strategies which might be considered would include possible muting of the conditioned-stimulus-response relationship, correcting of some identified physical or psychological handicap, or a relapse rehearsal so as to develop alternative coping strategies; and these should be supplemented by global self-control strategies, such as the learning of new 'positive addictions' and consideration of strategies for stimulus control and stimulus avoidance.

Where addiction problems are related to underlying anxiety disorders, treatment will involve the application of treatment techniques which are appropriate to anxiety management. Where deconditioning of craving is required, the clinician will be guided by the same principles and apply the same procedures that would be appropriate, for instance, to systematic desensitisation of phobic states. Where the acquisition of new behavioural coping skills is required the therapist will attempt to do this in the same way as with any other type of patient.

Enhancing self-efficacy

Annis (1986) has presented a relapse prevention model based on social learning approaches and, in particular, self-efficacy theory (Bandura, 1977; 1982; Wilson, 1978a; b). The self-efficacy model predicts that a successful treatment exerts its influence by enhancing the client's own efficacy expectations (defined as a judgement that one has the ability to execute a certain behaviour pattern (Annis, 1986)). Efficacy expectations will influence initiation, generalisation and maintenance of coping behaviours. The strength of the efficacy expectations will determine how long the coping behaviours will be maintained under stress. Thus, the disease model and a reliance on absolute abstinence are regarded as counter-productive in so far as they minimise the client's own self-efficacy expectations. In addition, an outcome expectation based on a 'one drink-one drunk' philosophy is likely to become self-fulfilling so that the event of lapse becomes more catastrophic. Annis recommends systematic teaching of self-regulatory and social skills so that the recovering alcoholic is better equipped to cope with 'slips'. Self-efficacy theory predicts that treatment is effective only in so far as it increases the client's own expectations of what they can themselves achieve and maintain. Emphasis is placed on the importance of enhancing the coping abilities of recovering alcoholics with sporadic drinking episodes which occur after periods of abstinence. Annis uses her own questionnaires for eliciting information from alcoholics (for example, the Situational Confidence Questionnaire and Inventory of Drinking Situations; see Annis, 1986), following which performance tasks can be ranked according to the particular patient's ratings of self-efficacy. Treatment is seen as comprising two phases – phase 1 is concerned with initiating changes in drinking behaviour, while phase 2 deals with consolidation of this progress associated with mastery experiences. Annis (1986) predicted that the extent of progress during phase 2 will be influenced by the four factors identified by Bandura (1977). These include: (1) a perceived high-risk situation; (2) achievement of success through only moderate effort; (3) primarily internal attribution of success; and (4) the success being part of a more general improvement.

Self-control training

Another social-behavioural approach to treatment that deserves mention is that developed by Miller and his colleagues (Miller, 1977; 1978). This includes the following components (for the treatment of alcohol dependence):

1 *Goal-setting* – the determination of specific, appropriate limits for drinking.
2 *Self-monitoring of alcohol consumption* – self-monitoring is increasingly recognised as an important component of treatment for the addictive behaviours. It not only provides valuable assessment data but can also produce a therapeutic or reactive effect. This has been noted in the treatment of alcohol problems, overeating and smoking (e.g. Sobell and Sobell, 1973).
3 *Rate-control training*, designed to alter the person's style of drinking.
4 *Self-reinforcement training* to encourage progress in treatment.
5 A *functional analysis* of drinking behaviour designed to teach the person the circumstances surrounding their craving for, and use of, alcohol, with training in stimulus-control procedures.

      (It is clear that there is a range of cues which increases the desire to drink (or to take drugs) after a period of abstinence. These vary from person to person but may include dysphoric mood states such as anxiety or depression, social settings such as parties, the presence of other drinkers, withdrawal symptoms, and so on. The similarities between compulsive disorders and the addictions are discussed by Hodgson (1982). To the extent that both the addict and the therapist can identify and understand the cues that are associated with an increase in craving and compulsions, measures can be taken to modify the potency of such cues or to avoid exposure to them.)
6 *Alternative-skills training* to teach coping skills to be used instead of drinking. (For example, where alcohol consumption increases in response to work or family stress, this may involve learning new skills or strengthening existing skills which respond directly to such issues and which help to lessen the problems occurring at work or within the family.)

Behavioural self-control training differs from some other treatments in its explicitly educational orientation. Several studies have looked at its effectiveness in the treatment of alcoholics. Most of these have compared it with other treatments and have found that each produced comparable and substantial amounts of improvement. Miller (1978), for instance, compared it with two treatments, electrical aversion therapy and another multi-model treatment package. All three programmes produced substantial improvement rates at one-year follow-up. The evaluative studies of behavioural self-control training have generally reported high rates of improvement (60 to 80 per cent) (e.g. Caddy and Lovibond, 1976) and if these rates continue to be supported in further studies, it may turn out to be a useful treatment option. Although most of the current research studies have been with alcoholics, there is no reason why the procedures of behavioural self-control training should not be adapted for use with drug addicts.

Motivational interviewing and motivational milieu therapy

The term 'motivation' has a somewhat dubious history in relation to the treatments of addictive behaviours. Einstein and Garitano pointed to the circularity in the way that this term has so often been misused:

> The general approach is that if the drug abuser patient gets better – translated that means he gives up his drugs of choice – he was a good and motivated patient and was able to profit from our professional expertise and skill. We cured him. If the patient continues his drug use, this is manifest evidence that he was not motivated, and a poor treatment risk who could not profit from our skill.
>
> (Einstein and Garitano, 1972: 235)

This circularity has been a major factor in leading to a dissatisfaction with the concept of motivation. It is because of this sort of problem that it has been suggested that the concept of motivation is useless and should be discarded. However, it may not be necessary to reject the term completely. It has been shown that when motivation is operationally defined (for example, in terms of the strength of the addict's desire for in-patient treatment), this is one of the principal determinants of how long addicts subsequently remain in an in-patient treatment programme (Gossop, 1978). The concept can therefore be rescued from circularity and it can be shown to relate to treatment response. However, it remains an inherently problematic concept, especially when used without clear definition. It is simplistic to regard motivation as an unchanging or as an entirely 'internal' factor. However, the extent to which it changes in response to external social and environmental factors requires further clarification.

In recent years, the term has re-emerged in relation to a form of treatment known as 'motivational interviewing'. This has been found to be a useful tool in many stages of treatment but it has been particularly useful in helping people who are at early stages of change (such as precontemplators).

Miller's original account of motivational interviewing describes its application with problem drinkers (Miller, 1983). Here, motivation is conceptualised as an interpersonal process, and the behaviour of the therapist is seen as having considerable influence on the subsequent attributions and behaviour of the client. Miller puts forward alternative views for mechanisms such as denial, which he does not regard simply as inherent in the alcoholic, but as a product of the way in which the counsellor has chosen to interact with the problem drinker. The aim of therapy is to increase levels of cognitive dissonance until a critical mass of motivation is achieved at which point the client is willing to consider change alternatives. Miller uses the model of process of change (Prochaska and DiClemente, 1983; 1986) in his discussion and explanation of his model to project movement from precontemplation and contemplation to determination and action. In the six-step sequence for implementing motivational interviewing, Miller emphasises how important it is that the therapist initially adopts an almost exclusively empathic stance using the techniques operationalised by Carl Rogers. However, this process is soon modified to be subtly selective in its reflection so as to reinforce statements of concern and elicit self-motivational statements. Clients then construct their own inventory of problems related to drinking to express their concern and identify possible changes which they might consider. The role of the therapist is to encourage the active involvement of the client in the identification of the problem and in the cost-benefit analysis of the various available options, as described by Janis and Mann (1977). The approach is intended to enhance the importance of personal responsibility and the internal attribution of choice and control, and the therapist must help the client to avoid treatment 'short circuits' from low self-esteem, low self-efficacy and denial, and the dangers of the 'alcoholic' label and of binary thinking (i.e. alcoholic vs. not alcoholic).

One of the interesting features of Miller's model is the way in which Rogerian reflective listening is used selectively. The therapist must be aware that he is not just being reflective but is subtly steering the client towards change. One of the main purposes behind the Rogerian stance is the active involvement of the client. The therapeutic style is not truly reflective, as the client's comments are fed back in a modified form and are selected so as to increase dissonance. This selection must be a clandestine operation and the therapist should include doubts expressed by the client so as to preserve the credibility of the procedure. The patient's own terminology should be used as far as possible. As Miller says, 'The counsellor should not put words in the client's mouth, because this will be easily detected as a ploy'. There is a real concern that not only would this particular treatment contact be fruitless, but there may be a boomerang effect in which the individual realises that he or she is being coerced and is then more likely to follow an exactly opposite course of action. The internal attribution of this moulded feedback generates dissonance, which must then be directed in an appropriate direction. The therapist should not discuss treatment options or alternatives until this critical mass of motivation is reached; and even then, the alternative intervention options should include no special intervention and also self-directed change strategies as well as traditional treatment options. The therapist assists the client in identification of appropriate goals and in the implementation of strategies to achieve these changes.

More recently, van Bilsen and his colleagues have used a similar approach with heroin addicts (van Bilsen and van Emst, 1986; van Bilsen, 1988). They describe their motivational milieu therapy (MMT) as a humanistic approach which should not be looked upon as a convincing process (i.e. convincing the client to do something about his or her drug use) but should be seen as the supervision of a process of decision-making in which the client makes the decisions. They describe an approach very similar to that of Miller (and indeed make appropriate credits), and summarise their approach as comprising three phases: the eliciting phase during which a non-judgemental style is adopted so as to obtain information on the attitudes and behavioural patterns of the subject; the information phase during which there is feedback from the therapist; and the negotiation phase during which therapist and client discuss the possible changes which the client may wish to implement. However, van Bilsen's description of the work of MMT seems closer to more traditional work in which the therapist assists the patient in decision-making (e.g. Janis and Mann, 1977), and lacks Miller's intriguing inclusion of deliberate manipulation of the patient's own language during the feedback by the therapist so as to generate dissonance. Van Bilsen's approach may be regarded as more honest, but the price for this honesty may be a more dilute treatment in which all responsibility is placed with the client. The therapist may feel more comfortable with such an approach, but it may be that Miller's more Machiavellian approach will be more likely to bring about change despite its requirement on the therapist to be more actively involved in the identification and planning of the behaviour change.

Conditioning treatments

Several attempts have been made to apply conditioning principles to the behavioural treatment of dependence disorders. Two basic approaches to altering the eliciting properties of drug-related stimuli include (1) attempts to reduce the power of drug-related conditioned stimuli through classical extinction (repeated presentation of the CS not followed by drug administration), also commonly referred to as cue exposure, and (2) counter-conditioning of other responses to the same drug-related CS.

Cue exposure methods have attracted a good deal of attention in recent years. It is possible to trace the origins of such methods back to the earliest studies of Pavlov in which it was shown that animals can acquire responses to contextual stimuli that have been previously associated with the onset of drug effects. The clinical implications of this were recognised by Wikler (1948) who noted that the self-administration of heroin (or other opiates) by drug-takers is associated in a unique and frequent manner with many environmental variables, such as the sight and smell of the drug itself, the rituals surrounding drug-taking, drug-using peers, dealers, specific locations, etc. These acquire the properties of discriminative stimuli in operant conditioning. The same variables tend also to be paired with the abstinence effects and become classically conditioned to these environmental stimuli (Wikler, 1980). Drug-seeking and drug-taking behaviours are powerfully reinforced thousands of times during the course of a person's drug-using career.

Similar procedures have established an important role in the treatment of phobic and obsessive-compulsive behaviour, and they are variously referred to as flooding, exposure, participant modelling and response prevention (Hodgson, 1982). Such forms of treatment rely upon the idea that a strong urge to carry out a compulsion will go away if the urge is resisted. When applied to alcoholism, a programme may be designed in which the therapist first identifies those events that act as signals or cues for drinking (such cues may be internal feelings, such as anxiety or depression, or external situations, such as particular bars or pubs): the alcoholic is then systematically exposed to these cues and is assisted to avoid drinking in response to them (Hodgson, ibid.). It is further assumed that conditioning processes play an important role in the establishment of cues. Examination of the role of classical conditioning in the experience of drug effects and subsequent dependence has produced apparently conflicting findings. On the one hand, conditioned euphoria may occur in the presence of drug-related cues (O'Brien et al., 1974). However, there is also convincing evidence that the abstinence syndrome can be conditioned as a response to specific environmental stimuli in both animals and man (Wikler et al., 1953; Wikler, 1965). Subsequent study has demonstrated the role of both unconditioned and conditioned drug effects as reinforcers (Stewart et al. 1984). Equally, it has been found that both conditioned agonist effects and conditioned withdrawal are extinguished following repeated exposure of the conditioned stimuli in the absence of the original (unconditioned) stimulus (Siegel, 1983).

In the clinical setting, the patient is exposed to cues (identified during assessment, and possibly including drug-related cues such as the sight of injecting equipment, social cues such as meeting other drug users, or internal cues such as anxiety or boredom) which would usually have triggered an episode of drinking or drug-taking. During this exposure session, the patient may be supervised, may be in a protected environment in which there is no access to drink or drugs, or may (in the case of alcohol) have previously taken an aversive drug such as disulfiram. The aim is to break down the stimulus-response relationship that has developed to alcohol itself and to various conditioned stimuli, by exposing the patient to the stimuli in sessions when these are not associated with the response of drinking. This approach may be used to achieve abstinence, but it has also been used as part of programmes aimed at controlled drinking (Heather and Robertson, 1986). O'Brien and his colleagues have used this same theoretical approach with opiate addicts, exposing them to drug-related cues, such as needles and syringes and the drugs themselves (Childress et al., 1984; 1988).

In their day to day life, addicts are likely to be confronted by various stimuli which have been conditioned to different aspects of their drug-taking behaviours. These conditioned stimuli will elicit conditioned responses which in turn are likely to lead to drug-seeking and drug-taking (Powell et al., 1990). Such effects may be experienced by the user as 'craving'. This term has been criticised as being poorly defined. However, it appears to be a useful concept for addicts, who seem to understand what they mean by it, often report experiencing it prior to using and during recovery, and have been able to rate its strength in clinical studies (O'Brien and Childress, 1991). Cue exposure treatments have often been used as a means of reducing craving.

In the treatment of a 43-year-old alcoholic, Hodgson and Rankin (1976) used an interesting *in vivo* desensitisation procedure which involved the subject's being given daily drinks of vodka under carefully controlled conditions. They reported a gradual reduction in craving and found significant improvement at six months.

O'Brien and his colleagues in Philadelphia have carried out a series of trials of cue exposure with different types of drug problems. In work with methadone-maintained opiate addicts, Childress *et al.* (1984; 1988) demonstrated habituation of subjective craving, and the clinical status of addicts who received cue exposure treatments was encouraging at follow-up. Other work done with people dependent upon cocaine Childress *et al.* (1988) showed significant responses to cocaine-related cues after twenty-eight days' cue exposure treatment. However, the clinical uses of cue exposure have not been fully established. In a recent clinical trial of cue exposure treatments for opiate addicts at the Maudsley Hospital in London, cue exposure was not found to produce any significant improvement when compared to standard treatment methods (unpublished data).

Other sorts of behaviour therapies for addiction problems have been based upon the principle of counter-conditioning, though such methods are less frequently used now than they once were. Such techniques have often involved techniques intended to pair incompatible or aversive consequences with specific stimuli associated with the use of drink or drugs.

Some of the earliest counter-conditioning studies, for instance, attempted to establish a conditioned aversion to alcohol or to whatever drug to which the person had become addicted. Both chemical and electrical forms of aversion therapy were being used to treat alcoholics as early as the 1930s. Voegtlin (1940) used chemically induced nausea in the treatment of alcoholics and claimed an abstinence rate of more than 60 per cent after one year. More recently, Wiens *et al.* (1976) reported a 63 per cent abstinence rate. In contrast, however, is the study of Wallerstein (1956) in which only 4 per cent of the alcoholics treated with chemical aversion therapy achieved abstinence.

The variability of successful outcome rates for electrically based procedures has been even greater. Miller (1978), for instance, found no difference between the effectiveness of behavioural treatment programmes with and without an electrical aversion component. Vogler *et al.* (1975), on the other hand, reported an 80 per cent reduction in alcohol consumption among alcoholics in a multi-model programme who received electrical aversion compared with 41 per cent in the condition without aversion therapy. There have been several small case studies of electrical aversion with opiate addicts (e.g. Teasdale, 1973). These have offered little confirmation of its value in drug, as opposed to alcohol, addiction; though even with alcoholics, Hodgson (1972) has commented that there must be considerable doubt as to the effectiveness of aversion therapies.

Covert sensitisation, a sort of aversion therapy which uses imagined scenes as aversive events, has also been used in treatment. Callner and Ross (1980) have expressed optimism about its value, describing it as 'particularly applicable' to the dependence disorders, though there seems to be little empirical support for their claim. Hedberg and Campbell (1974) compared covert sensitisation with several other treatments in a trial with alcoholic patients. They found that electrical aversion was the least effective of the treatments but covert sensitisation led to lower rates of improvement than either systematic desensitisation or behavioural family therapy.

Group therapies

Of all the procedures used in psychological medicine, 'group therapy' is both one of the most commonly used and one of the most poorly defined. Groups are variously run according to strict psychoanalytical principles, as psychodrama groups, problem-solving groups, experiential groups, support groups and, in some cases, according to no clear guidelines at all.

Not surprisingly, groups are one of the most difficult treatment options to evaluate, and, despite their widespread acceptance, most claims made on their behalf represent no more than subjective impressions of the authors. Improvement rates (defined in different ways) have been claimed which vary between 0 per cent and 82 per cent.

Alcoholics Anonymous and its lesser known cousin, Narcotics Anonymous, are forms of group therapy, albeit rather special forms. These treatments have had enormous success in many countries, notably in the United States, where they are often the dominant treatment modality. Essentially, they can be regarded as self-help or mutual-support groups. They are unusual, though by no means unique, in that they have explicitly religious aspects. AA has no interest in reasons for drinking and regards all such reasons merely as excuses. It believes that alcoholics drink because of a compulsion to do so and that they have lost control over their drinking whether or not they are aware of this.

Alcoholics Anonymous describes itself most fully in 'The Big Book' (Alcoholics Anonymous, 1955) in which it claims that 50 per cent of the alcoholics who attend AA attain abstinence immediately and permanently, and that a further 25 per cent subsequently achieve this – an eventual 75 per cent abstinence rate. No research evidence is offered to substantiate these claims. None the less, many workers are convinced of the effectiveness of AA. Zuska and Pursch (1980) state that 'there is no longer any doubt that Alcoholics Anonymous is responsible for the sobriety of more alcoholics than any other single treatment modality', and that doctors who wish to learn about alcoholism should attend occasional AA meetings; 'Not the least of what is learned will be that alcoholism is generally misdiagnosed and mismanaged by physicians.'

Several studies have attempted to evaluate AA. From a review of the available literature, Bebbington (1976) suggested that 26 per cent may represent a reasonable minimum success rate. Jindra and Forslund (1978) suggest that an upper limit to the effectiveness of AA may be about 50 per cent abstinence for about one year.

For such a widespread and significant treatment system, surprisingly little is known about AA. Even less is known about Narcotics Anonymous. However, research on the therapeutic community Synanon suggested that, as with AA, there is a high rate of individuals who fail to complete treatment but that among those who do remain, the outcome is often good (Scott and Goldberg 1973). Such forms of treatment can be effective for some people but should not be seen as a treatment model for everyone with a dependence disorder.

Psychotherapy

As with many other psychological treatments, there is general confusion about what actually happens during psychotherapy. The term itself is frequently used to refer to talking treatment based upon psychodynamic or psychoanalytic principles. Unfortunately, the influence exerted by psychoanalysis has not been matched by its clarity, and in any precise form both the doctrine itself and its procedures have managed to remain obscure (Gossop, 1981).

There is a widespread feeling among psychotherapists that the basic personality structure of alcoholics and drug addicts makes them poor candidates for psychotherapy (e.g. Selzer, 1967). In their extensive review of treatment options, Miller and Hester (1980) conclude that psychoanalytically oriented psychotherapy is not a treatment of choice for alcoholics, having an effectiveness lower than, or at best equivalent to, alternative treatment methods.

However, in an area which is conspicuously badly served by evaluative research, the study of Woody *et al.* (1981) is interesting. These authors compared a form of psychotherapy called supportive-expressive therapy with two other types of treatment, cognitive-behavioural therapy (as developed, and in this study supervised, by Beck), and drug-counselling. Supportive-expressive therapy is analytically based and aims to help the client identify and work through problematic relationship issues. It also pays special attention to the meaning that drug-taking has for the addict. Woody *et al.* found that opiate addicts receiving psychotherapy improved more than the counselling group in terms of their depressive difficulties and in their use of opiates and other psychoactive drugs. Addicts receiving cognitive-behavioural therapy also improved but there was no difference between this treatment and either of the others. The authors conclude that some opiate addicts can benefit from psychotherapy and that psychotherapy can add something to routine counselling services.

Medical treatments

It is not unusual for addicts and alcoholics to need medical attention. Many addicts, especially barbiturate and opiate users, take overdoses (Gossop *et al.*, 1975); and the behaviour of drug addicts, particularly the intravenous injection of drugs, makes them prone to such diseases as AIDS, hepatitis, septicaemia and bacterial endocarditis. Alcohol dependence is also associated with various health hazards, and chronic long-term use is known to cause damage to the liver, the pancreas and the brain.

The fact that chronic heavy use of alcohol leads to brain damage may have implications for psychological treatment. The cortical atrophy found among heavy drinkers is associated with confusion, disorientation, difficulties in concentration, and in its later stages produces a state indistinguishable from senility. Clearly in such advanced cases there are huge obstacles to conducting any therapeutic programme that requires complex and integrated psychological skills. However, it is not fully known to what extent the less severe states of neurological impairment may interfere with the patient's ability to understand, remember and carry out the requirements of therapy (Glass, 1991).

The most immediate medical feature of treatment is often the detoxification of the user. Many drugs, notably heroin and other opiates, produce physical dependence such that the addict suffers from withdrawal symptoms when he or she stops taking the drug. This is true of the barbiturates and the benzodiazepines (Valium, Mogadon, Librium, and so on), and alcohol too has a serious withdrawal syndrome. The psychological significance of the withdrawal phase is seen differently by different people. Some authors are inclined to see it as a relatively unimportant matter. Kleber (1981), for instance, described the opiate withdrawal syndrome as being like a dose of flu. However, it is clear that many addicts are very frightened of withdrawal (Gossop et al., 1982a), and for some this may be a reason or excuse for not attempting to give up drugs.

Although detoxification has, in the past, occasionally been regarded as a sufficient treatment for drug dependence, it is more usual to see the process of withdrawing the person from his or her drugs as the first stage of a wider treatment programme. Detoxification itself can be attempted either on an in-patient or an out-patient basis. In a national survey of over 16,000 American addicts, Joe and Simpson (1974) found that opiate addicts were twice as likely to be detoxified successfully as in-patients than they were as out-patients. This difference was even greater in a British study which found that 81 per cent of in-patients successfully completed detoxification from opiates compared to only 17 per cent of out-patients (Gossop et al., 1986). In the area of alcoholism, however, it has been suggested that only a minority of individuals need to be withdrawn from alcohol in an in-patient setting and that out-patient detoxification is a safe and effective alternative (Miller and Hester, 1980). Indeed, Edwards and Guthrie (1967) found no difference between the outcome rates at one year of alcoholics randomly assigned to either in-patient or out-patient treatment programmes. In-patient detoxification is usually achieved within a period of a few weeks by administering a gradually reducing dose of the drug of dependence (as in the case of the opiates) or of a substitute drug (as with alcohol dependence). Out-patient detoxification is more often attempted over a somewhat longer period.

One of the enduring myths of the addictions is that alcoholism and drug dependence are themselves diseases which can be treated by traditional medical procedures. The idea that the addictions are a form of illness emerged largely as a more humane alternative to the punitive approaches that were current, especially in America, earlier this century (Gossop, 1982). But well-intentioned though they were, such views have had a damaging effect upon the development of treatment options because of the way they have focused upon the search for a drug that will itself cure the addictions.

Although minor tranquillisers are often prescribed for alcoholics, there is little to suggest that this leads to any significant benefit. Mayer and Myerson (1971), for instance, found lower rates of improvement on drinking measures among patients treated with tranquillisers than among those receiving no medication. Kissin *et al.* (1970) found that a combination of tranquillisers and anti-depressants led to an abstinence rate of 16 per cent, compared with 22 per cent for either psychotherapy or 'standard hospital treatment'. Various other drugs have also been used, but the research literature offers little support for the effectiveness of psychoactive medication in the treatment of alcoholism (Pattison, 1977). The use of such drugs is particularly ill-advised with drug addicts, since most addicts rapidly acquire a taste for them, especially the benzodiazepines. The abuse of these drugs grew at a considerable rate during the 1970s and 1980s and although there has been increasing recognition of these problems among the medical profession, it continues to be a serious and under-rated drug problem (Gossop, 1982).

The use of disulfiram (Antabuse) represents a special form of drug treatment. Disulfiram is an alcohol-sensitising drug. When combined with alcohol, this drug inhibits the enzyme aldehyde dehydrogenase and produces a violent and unpleasant reaction with such symptoms as dizziness, sweating, nausea and vomiting. Anyone taking disulfiram cannot drink alcohol without risking this reaction, and the drug has been used to help ex-alcoholics to remain abstinent. Unfortunately attempts to evaluate the protective effects of disulfiram are be-devilled by the fact that patients who elect to take the drug are substantially different from those who refuse to take it: 'The effective use of disulfiram requires a cooperative individual who will comply with the treatment regimen, taking the drug consistently' (US Institute of Medicine, 1990). This introduces a powerful confounding effect into treatment evaluation studies. But, with the huge reservations that follow from this, the findings of Armor *et al.* (1978) can be noted that patients taking disulfiram do better than others who are not taking it. In a controlled, blinded, multi-centre study, Fuller *et al.* (1986) found that disulfiram as it is usually used in out-patient departments was no more effective than counselling alone in leading to continuous abstinence, though their results also indicated that the patients who responded best to disulfiram tended to be older, more socially stable men who had a history of relapses. There are further doubts about disulfiram treatments because of the unpredictability of serum disulfiram levels, and several recent studies have raised questions about the safety of disulfiram itself.

Similar attempts have been made to treat opiate addicts with antagonist drugs that block the euphoric effects of opiates. Naltrexone, for instance, is an orally administered, synthetic, long-acting competitive antagonist at opiate receptor sites. These drugs operate in a different manner from disulfiram since they block the euphoric effects of opiates without producing nausea or any physically aversive responses. Again, although a few addicts may benefit from treatment with antagonists, there has been some difficulty in persuading them to take these drugs. In an early American study, of the 735 addicts who agreed to take part in a trial of one of these drugs, 543 (74 per cent) dropped out before receiving even the first dose (O'Brien and Greenstein, 1981). Because of these difficulties in the induction period and because of the high drop-out rates during the first month of treatment, the usefulness of antagonists has tended to be limited to a small segment of the opiate-addicted population and this type of approach has tended to be best suited to those addicts who are strongly and consistently motivated to give up opiates. With such people, the antagonists can be a useful supportive measure. Studies of middle-class and professional opiate addicts, for instance, have shown good clinical outcomes with naltrexone (Ling and Wesson, 1984; Washton et al., 1984).

Methadone has been extensively used in the treatment of opiate addiction for many years and, since the advent of HIV and AIDS, maintenance treatments have had a considerable boost in popularity because of their link with 'harm-reduction' treatment goals. In January 1989 there were 667 methadone-maintenance programmes in the United States. These were treating approximately 80,000 addicts. Methadone treatments are used in many countries. However, there is enormous variation between programmes and in the manner in which this methadone is given. In a six-country survey, Gossop and Grant (1991) found differences in the number of patients treated, dispensing practices, the type of methadone administered, in dose levels and time limits for prescribing, entry criteria, attendance requirements, and in staffing. Any or all of these factors could be expected to have an important effect upon treatment effectiveness. Because of these very considerable differences in the way in which maintenance treatments are actually delivered, methadone maintenance should be regarded as a broad treatment approach rather than as a specific procedure or type of procedure.

The earliest and most vigorous advocates of this form of treatment were Dole and Nyswander (1965), who suggested that methadone maintenance blocked the addict's craving for heroin and led to a general improvement in social functioning. Several authors have asserted that the effectiveness of methadone maintenance is beyond question, and at least one textbook of psychiatry attaches to it the extravagant success rate of 70 to 90 per cent (Anderson and Solomon, 1971). However, the proponents of methadone maintenance may have done no favours for this form of treatment by overstating its merits.

One of the most detailed and convincing studies of methadone-maintenance treatments has recently been published by Ball and Ross (1991). This evaluation study looked at more than 400 patients in six different programmes. The results indicated that, as long as patients remain in methadone programmes, there are significant reductions in illicit drug-taking as well as in other target behaviours (for example, reductions in criminal behaviour). However, such treatment gains tend to be lost when patients leave the programme or when their maintenance drugs are stopped. In view of the claims made for methadone maintenance as a harm-reduction treatment, it is interesting that Ball and Ross found that, although methadone maintenance was associated with reductions in the *frequency* of needle-sharing, there were no significant reductions in the percentages of patients who shared injecting equipment.

TREATMENT IN PERSPECTIVE

In the treatment of the dependence disorders, any attempt to summarise the state of the art runs a serious risk of being swamped in a tedious litany of research findings and outcome figures. Sometimes it appears that the longer the recital, the less clear the position becomes. Treatments which are hailed as successes in one study appear in others as abject failures. At present it is must be acknowledged that it is difficult for the clinician to find clear and unequivocal indications about how to treat someone with a drink or drugs problem.

Traditional evaluative-research designs have not been especially helpful. These have generally been set up to answer questions such as, 'Are drug/alcohol-dependent patients more likely to improve when given treatment X or treatment Y?' In view of the individual variation within drug-dependent or alcoholic groups, this question is not appropriate. To return to the analogy of mental illness, it is not appropriate to set up research studies to answer the question, 'Are mentally ill patients more likely to improve after receiving treatment X or Y?' At the very least, the question requires that attention be drawn to the differential response of certain types of psychological problems to certain types of interventions.

In answer to the question, 'How good are treatments for alcoholism?', Clare reaches a number of pessimistic conclusions, notably that 'a small proportion of alcoholics achieve abstinence within six and twelve months of receiving treatment, whatever the nature, intensity and duration of the treatment concerned' (Clare, 1977). An earlier review of treatments for drug addiction reached a similar conclusion:

There is no relationship between time spent in treatment and the outcome of treatment. There is no relationship between the type of treatment and the outcome of treatment. Whoever the agent of therapy is, whether he be the aggressive social worker, the Rogerian counsellor, the pastoral counsellor, the psychoanalytically oriented psychotherapist, the clinician who uses methadone

maintenance, or the ex-addict giving mutual aid, the end result is not significantly different.

(Einstein, 1966)

Such pessimism is no longer warranted. There is now an impressive accumulation of evidence from recent research that shows that even people with severe
dependence upon drink and drugs can recover from their addictions (Biernacki,
1986; Gossop *et al.*, 1989). In many respects, it is atypical for addicts to remain
addicted throughout their lives. The majority will give up at some point. The
earlier pessimism about outcome now looks somewhat out of date.

To a large extent the negative expectations about the role of treatment in
producing change may be seen to have followed from confusions about the
unitary nature of addictive behaviours as well as about the application of inappropriate methodological procedures. For the moment, it would be helpful if
clinical practice and evaluative research were to focus less upon the application
of specific treatment interventions and to pay more attention to matching
treatments to the social and psychological characteristics of the person at whom
such treatment is directed. As in many other follow-up studies, Polich *et al.*'s
investigation of the course of alcoholism (Polich *et al.*, 1981) found that the

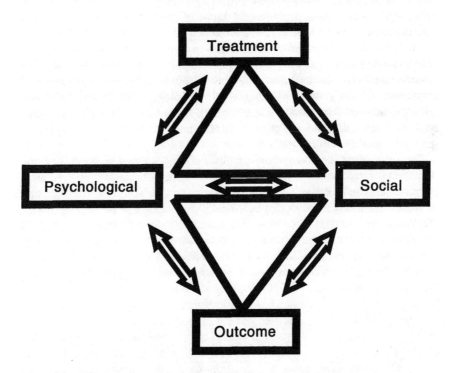

Figure 20.2 Effects of treatment, psychological and social factors upon
outcome

social and psychological characteristics of the subject sample at admission were a powerful determinant of their subsequent behaviour. Polich *et al.* comment that 'such subject factors as drinking history and social surroundings had more effect on outcomes than did any measured treatment factors'.

Raw has published a valuable review of treatments for smoking dependence in which he makes precisely this point.

> A major shortcoming of almost all treatment research in smoking is that it focuses interest on *treatment* to the exclusion of interest in subjects and subject variables . . . Thus a new 'treatment' is discovered and lauded but which actually accounts for relatively little variance in outcome and is seen subsequently to 'disappear' (be swamped) when compared more carefully with other treatments or with 'nonspecific' procedures.
>
> (Raw, 1978: 473)

The treatments that are provided for drug and alcohol problems provide only a relatively small input to the world of the drug-taker or drinker. As in the determination of drug problems, the psychology of the individual and the social setting in which the individual lives exert powerful influences upon outcome. For the therapist in the treatment setting it may be tempting to believe that treatment factors are more powerful than they really are. However, it can be misleading to underrate the potential input of factors outside the treatment context. Hubbard *et al.* note that, 'The role of treatment is to change behaviours and psychological states and to direct clients to community resources during and after treatment', and that 'Programmes have no direct control on behaviour after clients leave treatment. Rather, treatment should influence posttreatment behaviour indirectly through changes in psychological states and behaviour during treatment' (Hubbard *et al.*, 1989: 35). In this sort of model, treatments directed at the maintenance of change after treatment should be seen as operating indirectly, as shown in Figure 20.2.

The same point is made by Edwards, who offered a strong warning about the limitations of treatment and suggested that excessive enthusiasm about treatment effectiveness can be misguided; this enthusiasm can be 'constrained to the point of tunnel vision if it assumes that treatment influences are so paramount that all that has to be asked is 'Does treatment work?' with every other influence . . . discounted . . . . Treatment is more accurately conceived as being at best a timely nudge or whisper in a long life course' (Edwards, 1989).

Several excellent treatment outcome studies have been published recently. One is that of Moos *et al.*, (1990), looking at the context, process and outcome of treatments for alcoholism. These workers interviewed over 400 people with drinking problems, before, during, and 6 to 8 months after leaving 5 residential treatment programmes. The study is critical of previous 'black box' evaluations of alcoholism treatment and provides a wealth of detail about the experiences of the people during treatment as well as about their assessments of the quality of treatment environments. Moos *et al.* then followed up over 100 people who returned to their families, and 82 of these were followed up 10 years after treatment. In addition, those followed up to 2 and 10 years were compared to matched controls drawn from the community, and the spouses and children of the ex-patients were also followed up and compared to matched controls. The authors conclude that treatment led to substantial improvements in drinking behaviour. The study also looks carefully at how much of the outcome variance can be attributed to pre-treatment personal factors, intensity and quality of treatment, and the family and wider social context. The evidence about treatment impact is more encouraging than that reported in many studies, though individual and social factors also played an important role in determining outcome.

In the field of drug problems, a major study has recently been completed in the United States. The Treatment Outcome Prospective Study (TOPS) involved more than 11,000 people who entered treatment for drug problems at 41 treatment programmes (Hubbard *et al.*, 1989). Samples were interviewed at 3 months, 1 year, 2 years, and 3 to 5 years after leaving treatment. The study showed substantial decreases in the abuse of opiates and other drugs after treatment. Reductions in drug-taking continued to be found even up to the longer-term 3- to 5-year follow-up. Interestingly, in relation to the increased awareness of applying cost/benefit analysis to treatment, the TOPS study demonstrated the 'substantial crime-related and other costs . . . of drug abusers prior to treatment and the substantial reductions in these costs both during and following participation in treatment'.

REFERENCES

Alcoholics Anonymous (1955) *The Story of How Many Thousands of Men and Women Have Recovered from Alcoholism*, New York: AA Publishing.
Anderson, D. and Solomon, P. (1971) 'Drug dependence', in P. Solomon and V. D. Patch (eds) *Handbook of Psychiatry*, Los Altos, Calif.: Large Medical Publications.
Annis, H. (1986) 'A relapse prevention model for treatment of alcoholics', in W. Miller and N. Heather (eds) *Treating Addictive Behaviours*, New York: Plenum.
Armor, D. J., Polich, J. and Stanbul, H. (1978) *Alcoholism and Treatment*, New York: Wiley.
Ball, J. and Ross, A. (1991) *The Effectiveness of Methadone Maintenance Treatment*, New York: Springer.
Bandura, A. (1977) *Social Learning Theory*, Englewood Cliffs, NJ: Prentice-Hall.
Bandura, A. (1982) 'Self-efficacy mechanisms in human agency', *American Psychologist* 27: 122–47.
Bebbington, P. E. (1976) 'The efficacy of Alcoholics Anonymous: the elusiveness of hard data', *British Journal of Psychiatry* 128: 572–80.
Biernacki, P. (1986) *Pathways from Heroin Addiction*, Philadelphia: Temple University Press.
Bradley, B. P. and Gossop, M. R. (1983) 'Differences in attitudes towards drug-taking among drug addicts: implications for treatment', *Drug and Alcohol Dependence* 10: 361–6.
Bradley, B., Phillips, G., Green, L. and Phillips, G. (1989) 'Circumstances surrounding the initial lapse to opiate use after detoxification', *British Journal of Psychiatry* 154: 354–9.

Caddy, G. and Lovibond, S. (1976) 'Self-regulation and discriminated aversive conditioning in the modification of alcoholics' drinking behavior', *Behavior Therapy* 7: 223–30.

Callner, D. A. and Ross, S. M. (1980) 'Behavioral treatment approaches to drug abuse', in J. Ferguson and C. Taylor (eds) *The Comprehensive Handbook of Behavioral Medicine. Vol. 3*, New York: SP Medical and Scientific Books.

Childress, A. R., McLellan, A. and O'Brien, C. (1984) 'Measurement and extinction of conditioned withdrawal-like responses in opiate dependent patients', in L. Harris (ed.) *Problems of Drug Dependence*, Washington: NIDA Monogr, 49: 212–19.

Childress, A. R., McLellan, A., Ehrman, R. and O'Brien, C. (1988) 'Classically conditioned responses in opioid and cocaine dependence: a role in relapse?' in B. Ray (ed.) *Learning Factors in Substance Abuse*, Washington: NIDA Monogr, 84: 25–43.

Clare, A. W. (1977) 'How good is treatment', in G. Edwards and M. Grant (eds) *Alcoholism, New Knowledge and New Responses*, London: Croom Helm.

Davies, D. L. (1962) 'Normal drinking in recovered alcohol addicts', *Quarterly Journal of Studies on Alcohol* 23: 94–104.

Dole, V. P. and Nyswander, M. E. (1965) 'A medical treatment for diacetymorphine (heroin) addiction', *Journal of the American Medical Association* 193: 646–50.

Donovan, D. and Chaney, E. (1985) 'Alcoholic relapse prevention and intervention: models and methods', in A. Marlatt and J. Gordon (eds) *Relapse Prevention*, New York: Guilford.

Edwards, G. (1989) 'As the years go rolling by. Drinking problems in the time dimension', *British Journal of Psychiatry* 154: 18–26.

Edwards, G. and Guthrie, S. (1967) 'A controlled trial of in-patient and out-patient treatment of alcohol dependency', *Lancet* 1: 555–9.

Einstein, S. (1966) 'The narcotics dilemma: who is listening to what?' *International Journal of the Addictions* 1: 1–6.

Einstein, S. and Garitano, W. (1972) 'Treating the abuser: problems, factors and alterations', *International Journal of the Addictions* 7: 321–31.

Fox, R. (1967) 'A multidisciplinary approach to the treatment of alcoholism', *American Journal of Psychiatry* 123: 769–78.

Fremouw, W. J. and Brown, J. P. (1980) 'The reactivity of addictive behaviors to self-monitoring: a functional analysis', *Addictive Behaviors* 5: 209–17.

Fuller, R., Branchey, D., Brightwell, R., Derman, C., Emrick, F., Iber, K., James, R., Lacoursiere, K., Lowenstam, I., Maany, D., Neiderhiser, J. and Shaw, S. (1986) 'Disulfiram treatment of alcoholism: a Veterans Administration cooperative study', *Journal of the American Medical Association* 256: 1449–55.

Glass, I. (1991) 'Alcoholic brain damage: what does it mean to patients?' *British Journal of Addiction* 86: 819–21.

Glatt, M. M. (1983) 'Alcohol dependence: the "lack of control" over alcohol and its implications', in M. Glatt and J. Marks, *The Dependence Phenomenon*, Lancaster: MTP Press.

Gossop, M. R. (1978) 'A review of the evidence for methadone maintenance as a treatment for narcotic addiction', *Lancet* 1: 812–15,

Gossop, M. R. (1981) *Theories of Neurosis*, Berlin; Heidelberg; New York: Springer.

Gossop, M. R. (1982) *Living with Drugs*, London: Temple Smith.

Gossop, M. (1987) 'Beware cocaine', *British Medical Journal* 295: 945.

Gossop, M. R. and Connell, P. H. (1983) 'Drug dependence: who gets treated?' *International Journal of the Addictions* 18: 99–109.

Gossop, M. R. and Eysenck, S. B. G. (1980) 'A further investigation into the personality of drug addicts in treatment', *British Journal of Addiction* 75: 305–11.

Gossop, M. and Grant, M. (1991) 'A six-country survey of the content and structure of heroin treatment programmes using methadone', *British Journal of Addiction* 86: 1151–60.

Gossop, M. R., Cobb, J. P. and Connell, P. H. (1975) 'Self-destructive behaviour in oral and intravenous drug dependent groups', *British Journal of Psychiatry* 126: 266–9.

Gossop, M. R., Eiser, J. R. and Ward, E. (1982a) 'The addicts' perceptions of their own drug-taking: implications for the treatment of drug dependence', *Addictive Behaviors* 7: 189–94.

Gossop, M. R., Strang, J. and Connell, P. H. (1982b) 'The response of out-patient opiate addicts to the provision of a temporary increase in their prescribed drugs', *British Journal of Psychiatry* 141: 338–43.

Gossop, M., Johns, A. and Green, L. (1986) 'Opiate withdrawal: in-patient versus out-patient programmes and preferred versus random assignment to treatment', *British Medical Journal* 293: 103–4.

Gossop, M., Green, L., Phillips, G. and Bradley, B. (1987) 'What happens to opiate addicts immediately after treatment: a prospective follow-up study', *British Medical Journal* 294: 1377–80.

Gossop, M., Green, L., Phillips, G. and Bradley, B. (1989) 'Lapse, relapse and survival among opiate addicts after treatment', *British Journal of Psychiatry* 154: 348–53.

Heather, N. and Robertson, I. (1981) *Controlled Drinking*, London: Methuen.

Hedberg, A. and Campbell, L. (1974) 'A comparison of four behavioural treatment approaches to alcoholism', *Journal of Behaviour Therapy and Experimental Psychiatry* 5: 251–6.

Heather, N., Whitton, B. and Robertson, I. (1986) 'Evaluation of a self-help manual for media-recruited problem drinkers: six-month follow-up results, *British Journal of Clinical Psychology* 25: 19–34.

Hodgson, R. (1972) 'Behaviour Therapy', in G. Edwards and M. Grant (eds) *Alcoholism – New Knowledge and New Responses*, London: Croom Helm.

Hodgson, R. J. (1982) 'Behavioral psychotherapy for compulsions and addictions', in J. R. Elser (ed.) *Social Psychology and Behavioral Medicine*, New York: Wiley.

Hodgson, R. J. and Rankin, H. J. (1976) 'Modification of excessive drinking by cue exposure', *Behaviour Research and Therapy* 14: 305–7.

Hodgson, R., Stockwell, T. and Rankin, H. (1979) 'Can alcohol reduce tension?' *Behaviour Research and Therapy* 17: 459–66.

Hubbard, R., Marsden, M., Rachal, V., Harwood, H., Cavanaugh, E. and Ginzburg, H. (1989) *Drug Abuse Treatment: A National Study of Effectiveness*, Chapel Hill: University of North Carolina Press.

Janis, I. and Mann, L. (1977) *Decision Making: A Psychological Analysis of Conflict, Choice and Commitment*, London: Collier Macmillan.

Jindra, N. J. and Forslund, M. A. (1978) 'Alcoholics Anonymous in a western US city', *Journal of Studies on Alcoholism* 39: 110–20.

Joe, G. W. and Simpson D. D. (1974) 'Research on patient retention in treatment', cited in J. B. Milby (1981) *Addictive Behaviour and its Treatment*, New York: Springer.

Kanfer, F. and Phillips, J. (1970) *Learning Foundations of Behaviour Therapy*, New York: Wiley.

Keller, M. (1972) 'On the loss of control phenomenon in alcoholism', *British Journal of Addiction* 67: 153.

Kissen, B., Platz, A. and Su, W. H. (1970) 'Selective factors in treatment choice and outcome in alcoholics', in N. K. Mello and J. H. Mendelson (eds) *Recent Advances in Studies of Alcoholism*, Washington: US Government Printing Office.

Kleber, H. D. (1981) 'Detoxification from narcotics', in J. Lowinson and P. Ruiz (eds) *Substance Abuse*, Baltimore: Williams & Wilkins.

Kraft, T. (1969) 'Successful treatment of a case of chronic barbiturate addiction', *British Journal of Addiction* 64: 115–20.

Ling, W. and Wesson, D. (1984) 'Naltrexone treatment for addicted health-care professionals: a collaborative private practice experience', *Journal of Clinical Psychiatry* 45: 46–8.

Litman, G. (1980) 'Relapse in alcoholism', in G. Edwards and M. Grant (eds) *Alcoholism Treatment in Transition*, London: Croom Helm.

Litman, G. (1986) 'Alcoholism survival: the prevention of relapse', in W. Miller and N. Heather (eds) *Treating Addictive Behaviours*, New York: Plenum.

Marlatt, G. A. and George, W. (1984) 'Relapse prevention: introduction and overview of the model', *British Journal of Addiction* 79: 261–73.

Marlatt, G. A. and Gordon, J. R. (1985) *Relapse Prevention*, New York: Guilford.

Mayer, J. and Myerson, D. J. (1971) 'Out-patient treatment of alcoholics: effects of status, stability, and nature of treatment', *Quarterly Journal of Studies on Alcoholism* 32: 620–7.

Miller, W. R. (1977) 'Behavioural self-control training in the treatment of problem drinkers', in R. B. Stuart (ed.) *Behavioural Self-Management, Strategies, Techniques and Outcomes*, New York: Brunner/Mazel.

Miller, W. R. (1978) 'Behavioural treatment of problem drinkers: a comparative outcome study of three controlled drinking therapies', *Journal of Consulting and Clinical Psychology* 46: 74–86.

Miller, W. (1983) 'Motivational interviewing with problem drinkers', *Behavioural Psychotherapy* 11: 147–72.

Miller, W. R. and Hester, R. K. (1980) 'Treating the problem drinker: modern approaches', in W. R. Miller (ed.) *The Addictive Behaviours*, New York: Pergamon.

Moos, R., Finney, J. and Cronkite, R. (1990) *Alcoholism Treatment: Context, Process and Outcome*, New York: Oxford University Press.

Newman, R. G. (1977) *Methadone Treatment in Narcotic Addiction*, New York: Academic Press.

O'Brien, C. and Childress, A. R. (1991) 'Behaviour therapy of drug dependence', in, I. Glass (ed.) *Addiction Behaviour*, London: Routledge.

O'Brien, C. P. and Greenstein, R. A. (1981) 'Treatment approaches: opiate antagonists', in J. H. Lowinson and P. Ruiz (eds) *Substance Abuse: Clinical Problems and Perspectives*, Baltimore: Williams and Wilkins.

O'Brien, C., Chaddock, B., Woodey, G. and Greenstein, R. (1974) 'Systematic extinction of addiction-associated rituals using narcotic antagonists', *Psychosomatic Medicine*, 36: 458.

Orford, J. (1985) *Excessive Appetites*, New York: Wiley.

Orford, J., Oppenheimer, E. and Edwards, G. (1976) 'Abstinence or control: the outcome for excessive drinkers two years after consultation', *Behaviour Research and Therapy* 14: 409–18.

Pattison, E. M. (1976) 'Non-abstinent drinking goals in the treatment of alcoholism', *Archives of General Psychiatry* 33: 923–30.

Pattison, E. M. (1977) 'Ten years of change in alcoholism treatment and delivery', *American Journal of Psychiatry* 134: 261–6.

Polich, J. M., Armor, D. J. and Braiker, H. B. (1981) *The Course of Alcoholism*, New York: Wiley.

Powell, J., Gray, J., Bradley, B., Kasvikkis, Y., Strang, J., Barratt, L. and Marks, I. (1990) 'The effects of exposure to drug-related cues in detoxified opiate addicts: a theoretical review and some new data', *Addictive Behaviors* 15: 339–54.

Prochaska, J. and DiClemente, C. (1982) 'Transtheoretical therapy: toward a more integrative model of change', *Psychotherapy, Theory, Research and Practice* 19: 276–8.

Prochaska, J. and DiClemente, C. (1983) 'Stages and processes of self-change in smoking: towards an integrative model of change', *Journal of Consulting and Clinical Psychology* 5: 390–5.

Prochaska, J. and DiClemente, C. (1986) 'Toward a comprehensive model of change', in, W. Miller and N. Heather (eds) *Treating Addictive Behaviors*, New York: Plenum.

Raw, M. (1978) 'The treatment of cigarette dependence', in Y. Israel, F. Glaser, H. Kalant, R. Popham, W. Schmidt and R. Smart (eds) *Research Advances in Alcohol and Drug Problems. Vol. 4*, New York: Plenum.

Scott, D. and Goldberg, H. (1973) 'The phenomenon of self-perpetuation in Synanon-type drug treatment programmes', *Hospital and Community Psychiatry* 24: 231–3.

Selzer, M. L. (1967) 'The personality of the alcoholic as an impediment to psychotherapy', *Psychiatric Quarterly* 41: 38–45.

Siegel, S. (1983) 'Classical conditioning, drug tolerance, and drug dependence', in R. Smart, F. Glaser, Y. Israel, H. Kalant, R. Popham and W. Schmidt (eds) *Research Advances in Alcohol and Drug Problems*, New York: Plenum.

Sobell, L. C. and Sobell, M. B. (1973) 'A self feedback technique to monitor drinking behaviour in alcoholics', *Behaviour Research and Therapy* 11: 237–8.

Stewart, J., de Wit, H. and Eikelboom, R. (1984) 'Role of unconditioned and conditioned drug effects in the self-administration of opiates and stimulants', *Psychological Review* 91: 251–68.

Teasdale, J. (1972) 'The perceived effect of heroin on the interpersonal behaviour of heroin-dependent patients, and a comparison with stimulant-dependent patients', *International Journal of the Addictions* 7: 533–48.

Teasdale, J. (1973) 'Conditioned abstinence in narcotic addicts', *International Journal of the Addictions* 8: 273–92.

US institute of Medicine (1990) *Broadening the Base of Treatment for Alcohol Problems*, Washington: National Academy Press.

van Bilsen, H. (1988) 'Motivating drug users to change', in G. Bennett (ed.) *New Directions in the Treatment of Drug Abuse*, London: Routledge.

van Bilsen, H. and van Emst, A. (1986) 'Heroin addiction and motivational milieu therapy', *International Journal of the Addictions* 21: 707–13.

Voegtlin, W. L. (1940) 'The treatment of alcoholism by establishing a conditioned reflex', *American Journal of Medical Sciences* 199: 802–10.

Vogler, R. E., Compton, J. V. and Weissbach, T. A. (1975) 'Integrated behaviour change techniques for alcoholism', *Journal of Consulting and Clinical Psychology* 43: 233–43.

Wallerstein, R. S. (1956) 'Comparative study of treatment methods for chronic alcoholism', *American Journal of Psychiatry* 113: 228–33.

Washton, A., Pottash, A. and Gold, M. (1984) 'Naltrexone in addicted business executives and physicians', *Journal of Clinical Psychiatry* 45: 39–41.

Wiens, A. N., Montague, J. R., Manaugh, T. S. and English, C. J. (1976) 'Pharma cological aversive counter-conditioning to alcohol in a private hospital: one year follow-up', *Journal of Studies on Alcoholism* 37: 1320–4.

Wikler, A. (1948) 'Recent progress in research on the neurophysiologic basis of morphine addiction', *American Journal of Psychiatry* 105: 329–38.

Wilker, A. (1965) 'Conditioning factors in opiate addiction and relapse', in D. Wilner and G. Kassenbaum (eds) *Narcotics*, New York: McGraw Hill.

Wikler, A. (1980) *Opioid Dependence*, New York: Plenum.

Wikler, A., Fraser, H. and Isbell, H. (1953) 'N-Allylnormorphine: effects of single doses and precipitation of acute abstinence syndromes during addiction to morphine, methadone or larine in man (post-addicts)', *Journal of Pharmacology and Experimental Therapeutics* 109: 8–20.

Wille, R. (1980) 'Case studies I. Natural processes of recovery', in G. Edwards and A. Arif (eds) *Drug Dependence in a Socio-Cultural Context*, Geneva: WHO.

Wilson, G. T. (1978a) 'Booze, beliefs and behaviour: cognitive processes in alcohol use and abuse', in P. E. Nathan, G. A. Marlatt and T. Loeberg (eds) *Alcoholism: New Directions in Behavioural Research and Treatment*, New York Plenum.

Wilson, G. T. (1987b) 'The importance of being theoretical: a commentary on Bandura's "Self-efficacy: towards a unifying theory of behavioural change"', *Advances in Behaviour, Research and Therapy* 1: 217–30.

Woody, G. E., O'Brien, C. P., McLellan, A. T. and Mintz, J. (1981) 'Psychotherapy for opiate addiction: some preliminary results', *Annals of the New York Academy of Sciences*, 362: 91–100.

Zuska, J. and Pursch, J. (1980) 'Long-term management', in S. Gitlow and H. Peyser (eds) *Alcoholism: A Practical Treatment Guide*, New York: Grune and Stratton.

Chapter 21

Problems in the elderly
Investigation

R.T. Woods

INTRODUCTION

At present the number of *very* elderly people is increasing; more and more people are living beyond the age of 75 years. The previous rapid growth in the over 65-years age group has now stabilised. The increase in this older age group is especially important as they are much more likely to make extensive use of health and social services than the 65- to 74-year-olds. In some sections of society this is seen as a crisis. For clinical psychologists it represents a considerable challenge, to develop methods that will contribute to the psychological well-being of elderly people and of those who care for them.

Of some encouragement is the fact that most elderly people are not infirm, highly dependent or confused. For example, three-quarters of the over-75s do not have any degree of dementia. Indeed studies of adjustment in the elderly often identify a sizeable group of 'supernormal' elderly people – well-adjusted, mature and capable. Considerable untapped potential for self-help exists among the elderly, with the more able helping those needing support. Also encouraging is the huge variability in interests, abilities, opinions, experiences, health and lifestyle among elderly people; they have had longer to develop along different paths than younger people – 'elderly' often covers an age span of thirty years. Chronological age is an imperfect predictor of physical or mental health, so that generalisations about older people are likely to be misleading and in need of qualification. Old age is no more a disease than childhood – some would describe it rather as the penultimate stage of development. Not all elderly people require assessment or treatment; as with younger people, there must be a particular reason for psychological input.

Psychometric assessment was traditionally the major task of clinical psychologists with elderly patients. Now treatment and management of the problems of elderly people and those who care for them predominate. Assessment remains none the less important: any worthwhile treatment programme must be founded on a careful assessment and formulation. The questions and concerns to be addressed by the assessment and its content must, however, be re-evaluated. The book *Assessment of the Elderly*, edited by Beech and Harding (1990), provides

414 The Handbook of Clinical Adult Psychology

useful reviews of a number of the specific assessment measures commonly used with older people, as well as discussions of general themes.

WHY ASSESS THE ELDERLY?

A preoccupation of psychological assessment with older people has been differential diagnosis, particularly between depression and dementia. However, formal psychological assessments have been used for a number of other purposes:

- the measurement of the occurrence and extent of decline in cognitive functioning
- the early detection of Alzheimer's Disease and other dementias
- the characterisation and differentiation of the cognitive deficits in the various dementias
- monitoring change over time (e.g. describing the natural history of dementia)
- evaluating the response of the elderly person to a range of interventions (e.g. exercise, certain drugs, psychological interventions) and examining side effects (e.g. of anti-depressants on memory)
- identification of patients suitable for particular treatments
- selection of appropriate placements and services for the elderly person
- provision of feedback to elderly people and/or their carers, regarding the person's strengths and weaknesses (including neuropsychological deficits) and possible compensatory strategies

A basic distinction should be drawn between diagnostic assessment and descriptive assessment. The former has the primary aim of discriminating, and eventually assigning the patient to some category or other. The latter aims to delineate the patient's profile of psychological functioning, the pattern of abilities and deficits, thus providing information potentially useful for a number of the above purposes. The purpose of an assessment must always be carefully clarified, as different strategies and procedures will be indicated for different objectives.

Diagnostic assessment

Considerable energy has been expended over the years in developing tests which discriminate between groups of elderly patients diagnosed as having depression or dementia, and – most importantly for the assessment of the individual case – have low rates of error in category-allocation. Examples of these tests include various WAIS indices, learning and speed tests (such as the Kendrick Cognitive Tests for the Elderly), discussed in more detail in subsequent sections.

A major difficulty is that the tests are developed and standardised on clear-cut cases of depression and dementia. The very cases (i.e. the less clear-cut) where psychological assessment might be requested to aid diagnosis are excluded from the standardisation groups! Typically, where the diagnosis is doubtful, the psychological test results are equivocal. This is illustrated by the Kendrick Tests, which identified nearly perfectly clear-cut acute cases but misclassified almost half of a sample of long-stay psychiatric patients (Kendrick *et al.*, 1979; Gibson *et al.*, 1980).

Base-rates must also be considered. A diagnostic test's usefulness depends on the relative proportions of the diagnostic groups in those actually to be tested. A large preponderance of one group means an extremely high level of discrimination will be required of the test if it is to be more efficient than simply allocating all the patients to the extremely frequent diagnostic group. Cut-off points for different diagnoses need to be determined locally according to these base-rates.

Using clinical diagnosis to validate the tests inevitably introduces error, as diagnosis can never be a totally reliable procedure. On average, across eighteen studies, 10 per cent of cases initially diagnosed as organic dementia were later rediagnosed as depression (DesRosiers, 1992). Diagnostic tests validated only against a clinical diagnosis made at one point in time will be inadequate. In order to look at differences between the various forms of dementia it will probably be necessary to rely on post-mortem validation of clinical diagnoses for some time to come.

Using diagnostic tests is problematic but is it, nevertheless, worthwhile? The implications of the alternative diagnoses should be considered. At present a diagnosis of depression leads to some form of treatment, whilst one of dementia typically gives rise to predictions of a poor prognosis and deterioration. There is much to be said for not applying the label of dementia in doubtful cases, and for always treating depression when it is apparent, regardless of cognitive status. If dementia is also present (dementia and depression are by no means mutually exclusive) it will eventually become apparent, whilst in many cases after the successful treatment of the depression, doubts about cognitive deterioration will soon be resolved. The development of more effective pharmacological interventions for various dementias may in the next few years make such decisions more complex.

Refraining from using psychological tests simply as diagnostic tests is a good reminder that diagnosis consists of bringing together a variety of types of information about a person, of which cognitive test results are only one. In this differential diagnosis other features, such as mood, history of the disorder, and so on, are usually as relevant as cognitive status.

Descriptive assessment

Here, the emphasis is on describing aspects of the patient's psychological function and changes in them. This may still aid diagnosis. The difference here is that a poor score on, say, a learning test leads immediately to an evaluation of possible reasons for failure, not to a diagnostic statement that probably reflects only one of several explanations of poor test performance.

Descriptive assessment has its own problems. Perhaps as a result of the traditional emphasis on diagnostic testing, the range of psychological functions that can be readily assessed is fairly limited, the effects of repeated assessment have not been ascertained for many tests, and the relationship between test results and real-life behaviour is often uncertain.

If this type of assessment is pursued, however, it becomes possible to offer a distinctly psychological contribution to the care of the elderly patient. Assessment of change in function enables the effects of interventions (psychological or otherwise) to be evaluated, or the rate of change, say, in a person with dementia to be estimated. A detailed description of current levels and patterns of ability and dysfunction and of changes in these over time can be of assistance in counselling patients and/or their carers. This may assist in developing strategies for adapting to, or coping with, the deficits (Volans and Woods, 1983).

Descriptive assessment may be validated by its predictive power in certain instances, for example, where it is used to aid placement, or allocation of treatments or support services, or to measure rate of decline.

NORMAL AGEING

Making sense of a descriptive psychological assessment requires some knowledge of age-related changes in the normal elderly person. Good reviews are provided by Stuart-Hamilton (1991) and Kimmel (1990), and Birren and Schaie's comprehensive text (1990) contains detailed reviews; here the central issues will be discussed.

The misleading WAIS–R (Wechsler Adult Intelligence Scale–Revised)

The WAIS–R norms show IQ peaking at about 25, declining steadily to age 65 or so before decreasing more rapidly. These are *age differences*, obtained by the cross-sectional method of assessing groups of subjects of all ages at one point in time. The cohort of subjects born in, say, 1950 is compared with the cohort born in 1915. Subjects do not then differ simply in age but also in early medical care, nutrition, housing, education, occupational opportunities, and so on.

Longitudinal studies, following the same subjects over a number of years should give a better indication of *age changes*. Undertaking a lifespan longitudinal study restricts the findings to tests initially available and takes many researchers. Owens (1966) followed up subjects who had taken the Army Alpha Test at age 19. Thirty years later they had shown a general improvement, and by age 61 had shown little loss – a marked contrast to the Wechsler norms. Studies of older subjects over periods of seven to twenty years do show some decline, usually in performance scores, beginning in the sixties, with verbal scores also declining in older subjects. Longitudinal results can also be misleading because of practice effects, both in terms of familiarity with the particular test and the test situation. Selective drop-out is also a problem. Subjects available for retest have higher initial scores than those who drop out (Siegler and Botwinick, 1979). With every retest there is an increasingly selected sample.

Schaie (1990) and his colleagues, in a series of classic studies, have succeeded in combining the two methods. Subjects from all age groups were assessed initially and then re-assessed after seven, fourteen and twenty-one years. These four cross-sectional assessments were carried out both on the same subjects (longitudinal or repeated measures) and on fresh subjects (independent measures) in this 'cross-sequential' design. The longitudinal assessments showed least decline, the cross-sectional most, with independent measures intermediate. Decline appeared much later than the WAIS norms suggest, at age 50 on some functions, 60 or 70 on others.

The crucial point from this complex research, where it has in fact proved impossible to unravel all the variables involved, is that cohort differences can be as large as age changes over much of the lifespan. This emphasises the need for frequent up-dating of age norms.

Multi-dimensional changes

Whatever the methodology used to measure them, different functions appear to decline at different rates. Verbal, well-learned and consolidated – 'crystallised' – abilities decline more slowly than 'fluid' abilities, involving flexible reasoning in novel situations. Speed of processing seems particularly affected, at the level of central decision-making rather than simply of peripheral response. It is debatable whether this slowing is completely responsible for the early loss on performance abilities, where speed of performance is often emphasised, but it is widely regarded as a key factor.

It has been argued that current tests are based on those predicting educational and occupational attainment of children and adults. If abilities more relevant to cognitive demands on older people were assessed, an increase in ability might emerge, in knowledge of practical information (Demming and Pressey, 1957) or in wisdom and integrative abilities.

Individual differences

There is a great variability in rate of change of intellectual abilities among elderly people. A distinction between chronological age and functional age needs to be made – although functional ages would be more accurate, different aspects changing at different rates. Schaie (1990) demonstrates that the vast majority of older people show stability in at least some areas of cognitive function over a seven-year period, and that the pattern of change probably differs considerably between individuals. Holland and Rabbitt (1991) illustrate with data from a digit span test across different age groups that whilst mean scores decrease with age, there is a marked increase in variance with age – while some are declining, others are maintaining or improving function. There are, then, differences between individuals as well as within the individual's profile of performance. It is now recognised that an individual may retain or develop further ability in a particular cognitive domain – perhaps through interest, experience or opportunity – while other areas show decline. This process has been described as 'encapsulation' (Rybash et al., 1986). It finds parallels in the work of Baltes and Lindenberger (1988) on 'selective optimization', where the older person is viewed as maximising the use of reduced cognitive resources by focusing on areas and tasks which have meaning and value and utility for him- or herself. Performance can accordingly be improved by providing practice and appropriate motivation, with considerable scope for plasticity of function.

To talk in terms of a single ageing process is then misleading: a number of other factors must also be taken into account in making sense of lower group means of older people on cognitive tests. Situational factors include fatigue (Furry and Baltes, 1973), cautiousness (Birkhill and Schaie, 1975) and older people evaluating their own performance more negatively (Bellucci and Hoyer, 1975). It is important to examine older people's strategies and approach to the task and their perception of what is expected from them, not just the level or speed of their performance (Rabbitt, 1982).

Among longer term factors related to reduced cognitive performance, physical health is crucial. For example, Wilkie and Eisdorfer (1971) showed that subjects aged 60 to 69 with raised diastolic blood pressure declined more on the WAIS over a ten-year period than those with normal blood pressure. Holland and Rabbitt (1991) review the literature of the effects of a range of health problems – respiratory disease, diabetes, hypertension, etc. – on cognition in older people. The phenomenon of terminal drop – a decline in cognitive function in the years before death – is also relevant (and probably related), and has been observed up to ten years before death (see Stuart-Hamilton, 1991). The person's physical activity level and medication may also influence cognitive performance, and in turn have a relationship to physical health problems. Finally, the cognitive effects of psychiatric disorders, both organic and functional, are well established. A representative sample of elderly people could include up to 25 per cent with a psychiatric disorder (depending on the definition of depression). Considerable individual variability is understandable given the variety of factors leading to cognitive loss in the elderly. Age per se is not a causal variable – simply a crude index of other events and processes occurring in time.

THE ASSESSMENT OF COGNITIVE ABILITIES

Intellectual function

Two major measures of global intellectual function have been extensively used. Raven's Progressive Matrices (Standard and Coloured) and Mill Hill Vocabulary Scale (Raven et al., 1976) provide indications of performance and verbal intellectual levels respectively; they are fairly simple and quick to administer. Limited old-age norms are available (Orme, 1957). The Wechsler Adult Intelligence Scales (WAIS) are more time-consuming, requiring a highly trained tester, but tap a richer variety of skills and modalities. As they can only be used individually, the assessor is able to observe the patient's approach to the tasks and to consider alternative hypotheses for apparent deficits.

The revised version of the WAIS, the WAIS–R (Wechsler, 1981) was standardised in the USA on a representative sample of adults up to age 75. When assessing someone above this age, norms are now available for groups of 75- to 79-year olds and for those aged 80 and over (Ryan et al., 1990). The original WAIS (Wechsler, 1955) had norms for over-75s, which had some utility (Savage et al., 1973). However, in view of the cohort effects described above, it should only be used now for retesting a patient initially assessed on the WAIS.

The WAIS is a lengthy test for elderly people. A number of short forms have been evaluated by Crawford et al. (1992a) on a normal sample, which reflected the age distribution of over 16s in the UK, so that around a quarter were over 60. They provide regression equations and tables for calculating Full Scale, Verbal and Performance IQs from combinations of two, four, six and seven sub-tests. Generally, the more sub-tests administered, the better the prediction. For older people specifically, a four sub-test short form (Comprehension and Vocabulary, Block Design and Object Assembly) was developed by Britton and Savage (1966) for the WAIS; by consulting Crawford et al.'s equations it can confidently be used with the WAIS–R. Crawford et al. suggest substituting Similarities for Vocabulary, as the latter is now less likely to be used as an indicator of pre-morbid function (see below). The verbal and performance sub-tests included in both these short forms should give good estimates of the 'Verbal' and 'Perceptual Organisation' factors which emerge reliably in factor analytic studies of the WAIS–R (Crawford et al., 1989).

Much effort has been expended on developing methods of assessing whether or not the person's current level of intellectual function represents a decline from previous levels. In view of the previous discussion of the differing trajectories of distinct domains of cognitive function over the lifespan, this is perhaps a rather simplistic approach, but which does have clinical relevance in relation to disorders associated with global cognitive decline. A number of the available strategies have been reviewed by van den Broek and Bradshaw (1990).

Ideally, a comparison would be made with a measure of intellectual function administered during the person's middle years. Such an assessment is rarely, if ever, available. Alternatively, the current assessment is treated as a baseline, and then repeated after an appropriate time interval, to indicate whether any decline is ongoing. This latter approach will not detect a non-progressive change occurring before the first testing. In both instances some caution is required. Where possible, the same measure should be used on each occasion, as each test of intellectual function may produce slightly different IQ estimates. Practice effects and normal variability in cognitive function must be taken into account. These considerations may mean that quite a large change – of 15 IQ points, say – may have to be present for it to be considered clinically significant.

Some guide to pre-morbid function may be provided by demographic variables, such as occupation, level of education, and so on. Attempts have been made to draw up regression equations to make quantitative predictions using these variables, with rather limited success. Particularly with the current generation of older people, where educational opportunities were even less equitably available than today, these indices are likely to be unreliable in the individual case. They may be used in a positive sense, in that, for example, an older person who achieved well in higher education and/or in one of the professions might be safely assumed to be of above average intellectual level; however, no assumptions could be made regarding someone who left school at 14, and worked as, say, a labourer.

Another approach makes use of the apparent differential decline in various aspects of cognitive function. A number of formulae have been devised to compare WAIS sub-tests which are thought to 'hold' and 'not hold', producing various Deterioration Quotients. Or the Verbal and Performance IQ's have been compared to produce a Verbal–Performance Discrepancy Score. Essentially, these indices have proved to be of little value in discriminating older people with a dementia from those who are unimpaired (Savage *et al.*, 1973; van den Broek and Bradshaw, 1990). Partly this relates to the wide variability in patterns of cognitive function in the normal population; a person may have a fairly large difference between Verbal and Performance IQ's, greater than could be attributed to errors of measurement, without this being particularly unusual. Another factor is the variability in patterns of change, between individuals and within the same person at different stages of the disorder. Thus, at first, performance abilities may well show more decline, but verbal abilities may later decline more, reducing the discrepancy, with performance levels showing a 'floor' effect.

Vocabulary test scores have been evaluated as a possible indicator of pre-morbid intellectual levels and the comparison between the Mill Hill Vocabulary Scale and Raven's Progressive Matrices as an indication of decline was on this basis. Whilst vocabulary is still used in studies of normal ageing (e.g. Holland and Rabbitt, 1991) as a stable index of life-long levels, it has been shown to decline in dementia (O'Carroll *et al.*, 1987) and tests of word-reading ability are now thought to give a more accurate index of pre-morbid intellectual level (Nelson and McKenna, 1975). The National Adult Reading Test (NART; Nelson, 1982) consists of words unlikely to be read correctly unless the person is familiar with them. The Revised form (Nelson and Willison, 1991) has been standardised against the WAIS–R. Other data is available on the Schonell Reading Test in conjunction with both the WAIS and Raven's Matrices (Ruddle and Bradshaw, 1982). In each case a predicted intellectual level is derived from the reading test score and compared with the current assessed level. The Schonell is particularly useful for those patients who are able to read very few of the NART words, as it is more sensitive in the low average range. Conversely, it has a low 'ceiling', so that the NART must be used with those of above average ability. The NART has been criticised for being over-long, and Beardsall and Brayne (1990) have shown the first 25 of the 50 items to give a good estimate of overall performance. Other possible problems with the test have been described by Baddeley *et al.* (1993), who are developing the 'Spot the Word' test as an alternative. This lexical decision test requires the subject to choose which of two letter strings presented is actually a word.

Despite the usefulness of these tests in descriptive assessment of the older person, the use of the discrepancy between pre-morbid and current intellectual level as a diagnostic index should be treated with as much caution as any other attempt to arrive at a diagnostic formulation from only one type of evidence.

Memory and learning

Deficits in these areas are well-established in both dementia and depression. The person with dementia shows a relatively mild reduction in primary memory but has a marked secondary-memory problem (Morris and Kopelman, 1986). The memory deficit in depression is less severe and less universally found, but has led to the use of the term 'pseudodementia', and probably is the major factor in the mis-diagnosis of depression as dementia. Sahakian (1991) concludes that cognitive impairments in depression in older people do not disappear entirely when recovery from the depression occurs; there may well be at least a sub-group of elderly people with depression whose disorder is related to some degree of cerebral dysfunction, distinct from dementia. The pattern of memory impairment is in some ways similar to that found in early dementia; differences may lie in a greater tendency to random errors in dementia, and to automatic processing being less impaired in depression, with impairments tending to be in areas requiring effortful processes. People with dementia tend to have a wider range of impairments, aphasia, apraxia and agnosia, for example. However, in the early stages of dementia, when memory difficulties predominate, distinguishing the disorders on cognitive tests may not be feasible.

Primary memory is typically assessed using the digit-span test from the WAIS–R and the visual span from the Wechsler Memory Scale – Revised (Wechsler, 1987). A number of measures of secondary memory are available, reflecting different memory modalities, and, to an extent, different aspects of the memory process; unfortunately, the relationship of test paradigms to models of memory is not always clear. Among memory tests currently available are:

Kendrick Object Learning Test (OLT – Kendrick, 1985)

This test, involving free recall of a number of common objects presented pictorially, is acceptable to patients, but would benefit from a recognition or cued-recall format. It does have two parallel forms, and data on six-week retest aids its longitudinal use. The OLT Quotient should be calculated, giving a descriptive measure of the patient's performance in relation to his or her peer group; the diagnostic index is not recommended.

Recognition Memory Tests (Warrington, 1984)

This test uses a forced-choice recognition format, where the patient is required to indicate which of two stimuli he or she was shown previously. The test is in two parts, using single words and faces respectively, with 50 items in each. The test enables an interesting comparison to be made between verbal and non-verbal aspects of memory. Norms are available up to age 70; the recognition format tends to be more acceptable than free recall, but leads to a high chance level, with moderately impaired patients with dementia performing at chance levels.

The Rivermead Behavioural Memory Test (Wilson et al., 1985)

Designed to assess everyday memory quickly and simply, and to reflect real-life performance more than conventional tests, this battery contains a useful variety of memory tests, including – unusually – tests of prospective memory, that is, remembering to do something in the future, rather than some past event. The four parallel forms are especially useful for reassessment purposes, and there is a useful supplement to the test manual, giving norms for 119 older adults, aged 70 to 94 (Cockburn and Smith, 1989). Ironically some of the most useful sub-tests are very similar to conventional tests, for example, prose recall, face recognition and orientation; the behavioural aspects play a relatively minor role. The scoring system does not allow detailed interpretation of performance on particular sub-tests in comparison with the standardisation sample.

Wechsler Memory Scale – Revised (Wechsler, 1987)

The original scale was much criticised, but widely used as a brief test covering rapidly a variety of areas of memory function. The revised version takes many of the criticisms on board, but in so doing has become much more unwieldy and daunting for use with older people. Five indices may be derived from the full battery: general memory; attention/concentration; verbal memory; visual memory; and delayed recall. In contrast to the Rivermead, many of the items appear meaningless, and motivation may be an issue for some patients, for example, in attempting to learn pairings of words that have no apparent association, in the paired-associates sub-test. However, many of the sub-tests stand as tests in their own right (e.g. logical memory, digit span, paired associates) and sub-tests may be used selectively. Norms in the manual are up to age 74 only at present.

Fuld Object Memory Evaluation (Fuld, 1977)

This ambitious test begins with the patient identifying by touch (and sight, if necessary) ten objects hidden in a bag. The objects are removed and memory for them tested over five trials using a selective reminding paradigm (the subject is told on each occasion only those items he or she is unable to recall); delays are filled with verbal fluency tasks and a measure of recognition memory is also included. Even mood is assessed by contrasting the number of 'happy' and 'sad' words produced in a given time interval in two of the verbal fluency tasks. Norms are available for various populations, including some up to age 90, and there are two parallel forms. However, the test often feels over-demanding for older patients; perhaps a simpler version should be developed?

The Benton Visual Retention Test (Benton, 1974)

This is a commonly used test of immediate visual memory (Crookes and McDonald, 1972). A series of ten line drawings of shapes of increasing complexity are shown to the patient for ten seconds each; the patient draws them immediately each is removed. The copying version of the test (where the stimuli are not removed) provides a control for the effects of visuo-spatial, rather than memory difficulties. A detailed scoring system allows for analysis of the type of errors made.

Speed

The Digit Copying Test, one of the Kendrick Cognitive Tests for the Elderly, measures psycho-motor speed simply and acceptably. It is preferable to the WAIS Digit Symbol Test as it is less complex and relies less on memory and comprehension of instructions. The Digit Copying Quotient should be calculated to facilitate comparison with other aspects of the patient's abilities. Speed of performance may be impaired both in dementia and, to a lesser extent, in depression. In a number of research studies, reaction-time tests have been used, and these would be an obvious method of assessing speed of information processing. However, these have usually been associated with the various computerised test batteries that have been developed (see p. 431).

Language

Many aphasia batteries exist, but none specifically for older people. The Schuell Minnesota Aphasia test is wide-ranging, has a useful short form (Powell *et al.*, 1980), and has been standardised on normal elderly people (Walker, 1980). The Token Test (De Renzi and Vignolo, 1962; De Renzi and Faglioni, 1978) tests comprehension of instructions of increasing linguistic complexity, and is useful in delineating the extent of a receptive deficit.

Many batteries include a naming test; a specific test of nominal dysphasia – the Graded Naming Test – has been produced by McKenna and Warrington (1983), which comprises 30 line drawings of increasing difficulty. Norms are available up to age 70. Williams *et al.* (1989) present data on a similar test – the Boston Naming Test – for patients with dementia and normal controls, and suggest a 30-item version of the original 60-item test. In dementia the difficulty in naming is thought to also reflect difficulty in recognising the object, whereas the dysphasic may clearly recognise the object but still be unable to name it (Kirshner *et al.*, 1984).

Verbal fluency may be assessed by asking the patient to name as many words as possible beginning with a certain letter, in a particular time (Whitehead, 1973), or name members of a particular set (for example, country names; Isaacs and Akhtar, 1972). Hart *et al.* (1988) provide data on a small number of patients with Alzheimer-type dementia and normal elderly controls on both types of fluency tests. There is some evidence that verbal fluency scores are highly correlated with verbal intellectual level (Miller, 1984), and so the approach of Crawford *et al.* (1992b) in using NART scores to derive a predicted verbal fluency score for comparative purposes has much to commend it.

Stevens *et al.* (1992) report the use of verbal fluency tests and the Boston Naming Test in a memory clinic context, and provide some useful data on their usefulness in assessing early dementia.

The Anomalous Sentences Repetition Test (Weeks, 1988) involves the patient repeating a number of 'sentences', which, while syntactically correct, do not make sense. This is an area of function thought to be particularly sensitive to the effects of dementia, and the test has been designed very much with diagnosis in mind, rather than as an index of an aspect of language function. There are four parallel forms, the test is brief and reported to be acceptable to patients, with norms up to and beyond age 80. Data on its use in clinical settings will be of interest.

Neuropsychological batteries

These have been developed for use with younger patients and should be used cautiously unless old-age norms are available. For example, normal old people show poor performance on some parts of the Halstead-Reitan Battery (Klisz, 1978) and on other neuropsychological tests (Benton *et al.*, 1981). Generally, length and difficulty-level make such batteries unsuitable for elderly patients, although Blackburn and Tyrer (1985) report positively on the value of a shortened version of Luria's Neuropsychological Investigation in older patients. More straightforward clinical testing will be informative with many elderly patients. Examples of such a clinical approach are provided by Holden and Woods (1988), Holden (1988) and Church and Wattis (1988).

Brief cognitive assessment

By using brief cognitive tests clinicians can quantify clinical data in a structured and standardised form. Such tests should always have been given before patients are referred for detailed cognitive assessment, as simple tests of information and orientation have often proved at least as valid as more detailed cognitive tests (e.g. Pattie and Gilleard, 1979). Many such tests exist; the 12-item information/ orientation sub-test of the Clifton Assessment Procedures for the Elderly (CAPE) is widely available, and has been extensively researched (Pattie 1988). The CAPE also includes a concentration test and screening items for reading and writing as well as a behaviour rating scale (see p. 428). Other frequently used tests include Hodkinson's (1972) 10-item Abbreviated Mental Test (AMTS) and the rather longer Mini-Mental State Examination (MMSE; Folstein et al., 1975).

Which of the various tests is used in practice will depend on the setting, how brief the test has to be, and personal preference. The various measures have high inter-correlations (e.g. Orrell et al., 1992), and all are liable to be influenced by the patient's level of education; those with a below average education may score poorly on such tests, despite being unimpaired; those with a high level of education may maintain high scores despite actual cognitive decline. The MMSE has been shown to be particularly susceptible to this effect (e.g. Christensen and Jorm, 1992). The MMSE may also be criticised for combining a number of items tapping quite distinct areas of function (memory, concentration, praxis, etc.) into a single total score. Different patients may have identical scores but quite different patterns of performance on this test. Orrell et al. (1992) indicate that it is the memory and orientation items that discriminate best between groups of depressed and dementing patients.

Assessing other areas of function is important – for example, in describing the pattern of impairment, such as dementia with dysphasia, or dementia of frontal type. To achieve this, a profile is required rather than a single score. The Middlesex Elderly Assessment of Mental State (MEAMS; Golding, 1989) achieves just this, including twelve brief neuropsychological screening tests, including orientation, naming, drawing, arithmetic and perceptual tasks. It is brief, easy to administer and available in two parallel forms. Some clinical data is already available – as this grows, the usefulness of the test will be enhanced. The Cambridge examination for mental disorders of the elderly (CAMDEX; Roth et al., 1988) is a psychiatric diagnosis scale for older people that includes CAMCOG, a screening test again covering a range of neuropsychological functions, and incorporates the MMSE and AMTS. Each area of function has relatively few items, but it is reported to show sufficient differentiation at higher levels of function to be of value in the detection of mild dementia (Huppert, 1991).

Example of descriptive cognitive assessment

Referral Dr C., a 69-year-old retired general practitioner, presented at a Memory Clinic with complaints of mild memory impairment, worsening over the past year.

Assessment The aim was not primarily to show that Dr C. did or did not have dementia, but to describe her current cognitive function, provide feedback on this, perhaps to suggest ways of coping with any memory deficit, and perhaps to monitor any change over time. Dr C. was seen on two occasions, approximately six weeks apart.

Results

WAIS–R
Full-scale IQ 145
Verbal IQ 136
Performance IQ 142

Kendrick Cognitive Tests

Assessment I OLTQ 113 DCTQ 144
Assessment II OLTQ 123 DCTQ 136

Warrington Recognition Memory Test

Words: Raw score 47; Percentile 75+
Faces: Raw score 38; Percentile 25
Face Discrepancy Score: 9; Percentile 5–10

Comments Dr C.'s performance on the WAIS–R confirmed a high life-long and current level of function. The NART would be redundant at this level. The sub-tests showed a consistent pattern, with none falling significantly below the others. The initial administration of the Kendrick Tests showed excellent psychomotor speed, but a rather lower score on Object Learning. To explore this further, on the second assessment session the Kendrick Tests were re-administered, showing again excellent speed, and a slightly improved level of new learning. The Recognition Memory Tests showed a major discrepancy between verbal and non-verbal memory, with a poor score on the face recognition test. Dr C. was counselled regarding the specificity of the difficulty identified, in the context of high overall levels of function, and encouraged to use verbal memory strategies wherever possible.

Moral Increasingly, awareness of Alzheimer's disease will lead to older people having concerns regarding changes that they perceive in their cognitive function. This should result in a rediscovery of careful cognitive assessment as a means of working with the client through an understanding of the basis for his or her concerns.

ASSESSMENT OF ADJUSTMENT

Several self-report 'life-satisfaction' and 'morale' scales have been developed specifically for the elderly. Among those widely used have been the Philadelphia Geriatric Center Morale Scale (Lawton, 1975) and the Life Satisfaction Index, which is available in a number of forms (Twining, 1990), including the brief version described by Bigot (1974). This has eight items on two sub-scales, 'acceptance-contentment' and 'achievement-fulfilment'. Gilleard et al., (1981) provide useful normative clinical data and suggest that the latter sub-scale reflects a more stable attitudinal component of morale, based on past life achievements and experiences.

The PGC Morale Scale and the LSI show considerable overlap with depression scales, although demoralisation and depression in the elderly are not necessarily identical constructs (Gurland, 1980). Gilleard et al., (1981) used the LSI and Schwab Depression Scale to monitor depression in the elderly. Gallagher et al., (1982) report normative and reliability data on the Beck Depression Inventory with normal and depressed elderly people and conclude that it is an adequate clinical screening instrument. The Geriatric Depression Scale (Yesavage et al., 1983) has a simpler response format (Yes/No) than the Beck, and is now extensively used as a self-report measure for depression in older people. O'Neill et al. (1992) suggest that this scale is more effectively administered by a rater, rather than being given to the older person to complete. An alternative is the SELFCARE (D) scale, which has been developed as a 12-item self-report measure for use in primary care settings (Bird et al., 1987).

A number of observer-rated scales are available (see Montgomery, 1988), which may assist in overcoming some of the problems inherent in self-report measures with older people (such as visual acuity problems, inappropriateness of items, etc.). In assessing patients with cognitive impairment for mood disturbance – where self-report may be particularly unreliable – the observer-rated Depressive Signs Scale developed by Katona and Aldridge (1985) may prove useful.

Other aspects of adjustment have been explored even less. Teri and Lewinsohn (1982) have modified the Pleasant and Unpleasant Events Schedules for the elderly, though both are still rather lengthy. Lam et al. (1987) have used several scales relevant to cognitive therapy with groups of depressed and non-depressed older people, such as the Automatic Thoughts Questionnaire, Dysfunctional Attitudes Scale and the Hopelessness Scale. Lam and Power (1991) report the use of the Significant Others Scale as a measure of social support in an elderly primary care population. As psychological treatment of depression in the elderly develops, further assessment measures will be needed.

ASSESSMENT OF BEHAVIOUR

Often, particularly in dementia, a person's actual behaviour – level of function, excesses and deficits – is very important in finding a suitable placement or in monitoring change. Behaviour can be assessed in several ways.

Rating scales

Here, those familiar with an elderly person's day-to-day behaviour (usually nurses, care attendants, or relatives) complete the scales from their uncontrolled, unsystematic observations of the person, perhaps over a specified time period. Many different scales are in use, differing in behavioural areas covered, range and depth of content, length and format. The purpose of the assessment should guide the choice of scale. Long scales are only likely to be completed conscientiously by busy care staff if the results are immediately relevant to patient-management.

There are a number of scales indicating a deteriorated elderly patient's general functional ability and degree of care needed (Woods and Britton, 1985). These scales include aspects of behaviour such as toileting, feeding, mobility, and so on. Among the most frequently used are the Crichton Geriatric Rating Scale (Robinson, 1977); the Behaviour Rating Scale from the Clifton Assessment Procedures for the Elderly (CAPE; Pattie and Gilleard, 1979; Pattie, 1988); the Brighton Clinic Adaptive Behaviour Scale (BCABS; Ward *et al.*, 1991). They vary greatly in their depth of coverage and particularly in their coverage of 'problem' behaviour. Inter-rater reliabilities tend to be much lower for items such as aggression and social disturbance than for ratings of physical functioning, suggesting that they are more difficult to define and rate objectively. The Clifton is probably most useful for general screening. It gives four factor scores (physical disability, communication difficulties, apathy and social disturbance) and has extensive norms for a variety of elderly populations (Pattie, 1988). The BCABS has been designed to be particularly appropriate for rating patients with severe dementia, and has been used in comparisons of long-term care environments (Lindesay *et al.*, 1991).

These scales are not ideal for an elderly person being cared for at home by a relative. The emotional involvement and 24-hour commitment of a relative mean that different behaviours from those emphasised in an institutional setting will affect the ability to cope. Greene *et al.*'s Behavioural and Mood Disturbance Scale (Greene *et al.*, 1982) is intended for completion by relatives. It has three factors: apathy/withdrawal, active disturbance and mood change. Gilleard's Problem Check-list (Gilleard, 1984) has also been widely used in this context, and informant questionnaires, such as that developed by Jorm *et al.* (1989), are now frequently used to rate cognitive decline. Skills and activities relevant to less impaired elderly people are included in the Instrumental Activities of Daily Living Scale (Lawton and Brody, 1969) and the Functional Activities Questionnaire (Pfeffer *et al.*, 1982), covering food preparation, laundry, transport use, financial responsibility, and so on. Domestic, leisure, work and outdoor activities are assessed on Holbrook and Skilbeck's 15-item Activities Index (Holbrook and Skilbeck, 1983).

Structured observation

Here, in contrast, a person's performance is assessed in a structured situation. This method underlies the Performance Test of Activities of Daily Living (PADL) (Kuriansky and Gurland, 1976; Macdonald et al., 1982). It includes seventeen tasks which, with props, can be administered as a standardised structured interview. It may detect adaptive behaviour not prompted or encouraged in the ward environment: conventional rating scales are inevitably affected by the extent to which independence is reinforced and allowed by the care regime. However, underfunctioning on the PADL could occur if the patient is affected by the situation's unfamiliarity, has difficulty in understanding the instructions, or has test-anxiety or motivation difficulties.

Skurla et al. (1988) have developed the ADL Situational Task, which aims to focus more on memory and reasoning, and less on motor tasks than the PADL. It has four tasks, again with standardised equipment, materials and instructions, and specified prompts. The tasks include making a cup of coffee and using money to purchase two items. Mahurin et al. (1991) have devised a longer measure on similar lines, the Structured Assessment of Independent Living Skills (SAILS).

Direct observation

Behaviour in the natural environment is systematically observed, usually using some kind of sampling procedure to keep the quantity of data collected to manageable proportions: perhaps only particular behaviours will be observed, or observations will be made at set-time intervals, although Godlove et al., (1982) showed that this sampling is not always essential with elderly people. Direct observation requires considerable preparation, allowing time for adaptation to the observer's presence by both elderly people and staff, and careful definition of behaviours and the settings in which they are to be observed.

Some studies have looked at 'engagement' to assess the proportion of residents involved in some kind of activity, interacting with people or materials (Jenkins et al., 1977). The behavioural definitions can be extended to give a more detailed description of behaviour (McFadyen, 1984; Macdonald et al., 1985; Ward et al., 1992). Baltes et al. (1980) have used direct observation to assess the important sequential relationships in residents' and staff behaviour, and Lindesay et al. (1991) report its use in comparisons of long-term care settings for people with severe dementia.

ASSESSMENT OF THE ENVIRONMENT

Methods of assessing institutional environments can assist in identifying features needing change and in monitoring intervention attempts. A comprehensive and detailed measure is the Multi-phasic Environmental Assessment Procedure

(MEAP) (Moos and Lemke, 1980), designed for and standardised on settings for the elderly. Physical and architectural features, resident and staff characteristics, the social climate and aspects of the setting's policies and regime are all covered. An example of its use is in comparing different types of care philosophy (Benjamin and Spector, 1992).

The MEAP is rather long, and not specifically geared to environments for people with dementia. Some studies, such as Lindesay et al.'s (1991) evaluation of a new type of small, homely unit for people with severe dementia (the domus), have used selected scales from the MEAP. Others have selected and adapted items from across the various scales; thus Willcocks et al. (1987) report a national survey of residential homes on a number of environmental variables. Bowie et al. (1992) have developed six scales assessing aspects of the ward environment for use specifically in long-term care facilities for people with dementia, and report reliability and validity data. There is likely to be increasing interest in such measures, with more emphasis being placed on improving the quality of long-term care. Kitwood (1992) has developed a direct observational method, dementia care mapping, which focuses further on the quality dimension, evaluating the extent to which the environment and staff practices enhance, or detract from, the personhood of the dementia sufferer.

In community settings, it is of great importance to assess relatives' feelings of strain arising, for example, from looking after a person suffering from dementia. Some studies (e.g. Gilleard, 1984) have used non-specific measures of distress, such as the General Health Questionnaire (Goldberg, 1978) or the Beck Depression Inventory (see p. 427). Other scales have been developed that more specifically assess strain arising directly from the relative's care-giving (e.g. Greene et al., 1982; Gilleard, 1984).

PRACTICAL CONSIDERATIONS

Several practical points are important.

First, sensory deficits are more common in older people. Care must be taken that the patient can see and hear adequately, with glasses or hearing aid if necessary. If the sensory impairment is severe and uncorrectable, tests using only the unimpaired modalities will be needed. With deaf patients, written instructions can be useful for some tests.

Second, older patients may take longer to adjust to the testing situation and often more time needs to be spent putting the patient at ease, establishing an atmosphere of cooperation and trust, and explaining the purpose of the assessment and its benefits for the patient.

Third, the patient is likely to be helped by supportive encouragement during testing. This usually has to be of a general nature; often it is useful to explain that everybody fails on some items because of the test design. Patients often underestimate their performance level and realistic positive evaluations are often possible. Unrealistic praise where the patient's failure is blatantly evident is unhelpful.

The session should be paced gently – a rushed, pressured session will increase the apparent impairment level. Several short sessions are preferable to a lengthy one, to minimise the effects of fatigue. Ending each session on a note of success helps to maintain future cooperation. The difficulty level of the tests used should be carefully reviewed so that the patient experiences as little overt failure as possible, particularly early in the session.

It has been argued that using tests that appear to be relevant to the patient's everyday life will increase motivation (Kendrick, 1982), but this whole concept of 'ecological validity' needs further development (Volans and Woods, 1983). What is clear is that tests exposing the elderly patient to repeated overt failure are stressful, reduce cooperation and should be used with caution. Paradoxically, tests that appear too similar to real life may increase the stress on the patient, whereas tests that are more in the form of a game may be more acceptable.

FUTURE DIRECTIONS

Considerable scope for development exists. Currently, many severely impaired elderly patients are virtually untestable conventionally, partly because tests emphasise exposure of deficits rather than of remaining abilities. All patients may be assessed behaviourally. Future behaviour-rating scales need to be developed more rationally, using, for example, Guttman scaling to give the maximum information more efficiently. Detailed scales of particular areas – continence, feeding, and so on – with the skills broken down into their component parts, would be useful in designing the intervention programmes that are increasingly used. The widespread emphasis on the assessment of need that has accompanied the implementation of the Community Care legislation in the UK poses a challenge for psychologists to contribute to the development of strategies of assessment that lead to effective and appropriate packages of care for older people requiring assistance with living in the community.

It was hoped that automated testing would allow cognitive assessment of patients untestable conventionally (Miller, 1980). Despite the doubts of Kendrick (1982) regarding the acceptability of computerised tests for the current elderly generation, a number of reports of the development of such methods have appeared (e.g. Carr et al., 1986b; Sahakian, 1990; Simpson et al., 1991). The capabilities of microcomputers provide an excellent opportunity to devise a new generation of tests, emphasising success rather than failure, suitable for repeated use, and taking into account information-processing models currently used in experimental psychology, including consideration of the strategies the patient adopts. Using response speed measures allows differentiation between patients even in error-free performance. Computer graphics can be used to increase the attractiveness and interest of the materials, and the various studies have reported that such batteries are well received by elderly people, including those with dementia. There is some evidence that performance is enhanced through the use of a touch-sensitive screen rather than through response buttons (Carr et al.,

1986a). These batteries have yet to become widely used clinically; in part this may relate to the time required for test development; by the time the test is complete, the next generation of computer hardware has appeared! However, as they are used increasingly in research studies, it does seem likely that eventually computerised tests will become more commonplace.

REFERENCES

Baddeley, A., Emslie, H. and Nimmo-Smith, I. (1993) 'The Spot-the-Word test: a robust estimate of verbal intelligence based on lexical decision', *British Journal of Clinical Psychology* 32: 55–65.

Baltes, M. M., Burgess, R. L. and Stewart, R. B. (1980) 'Independence and dependence in self-care behaviours in nursing home residents: an operant observational study', *International Journal of Behavioural Development* 3: 489–500.

Baltes, P. B. and Lindenberger, U. (1988) 'On the range of cognitive plasticity in old age as a function of experience: 15 years of intervention research', *Behavior Therapy* 19: 283–300.

Beardsall, L. and Brayne, C. (1990) 'Estimation of verbal intelligence in an elderly community; a prediction analysis using a shortened NART', *British Journal of Clinical Psychology* 29: 83–90.

Beech, J. R. and Harding, L. (ed.) (1990) *Assessment of the Elderly*, Windsor: NFER-Nelson.

Bellucci, G. and Hoyer, W. J. (1975) 'Feedback effects on the performance and self-reinforcing behaviour of elderly and young adult women', *Journal of Gerontology* 30: 456–60.

Benjamin, L. C. and Spector, J. (1992) 'Geriatric care on a ward without nurses', *International Journal of Geriatric Psychiatry* 7: 743–50.

Benton, A. L. (1974) *The Revised Visual Retention Test*, New York: Psychological Corporation.

Benton, A. L., Eslinger, P. J. and Damasio, A. R. (1981) 'Normative observations on neuropsychological test performance in old age', *Journal of Clinical Neuropsychology* 3: 33–42.

Bigot, A. (1974) 'The relevance of American life satisfaction indices for research on British subjects before and after retirement', *Age and Ageing* 3: 113–21.

Bird, A. S., Macdonald, A. J. D., Mann, A. H. and Philpot, M. P. (1987) 'Preliminary experience with the SELFCARE (D): a self-rating depression questionnaire for use in elderly, non-institutionalized subjects', *International Journal of Geriatric Psychiatry* 2: 31–8.

Birkhill, W. R. and Schaie, K. W. (1975) 'The effect of differential reinforcement of cautiousness in intellectual performance among the elderly', *Journal of Gerontology* 30: 578–83.

Birren, J. E. and Schaie, K. W. (eds) (1990) *Handbook of the Psychology of Aging, 3rd edn*, San Diego: Academic Press.

Blackburn, I. M. and Tyrer, G. M. B. (1985) 'The value of Luria's neuropsychological investigation for the assessment of cognitive dysfunction in Alzheimer-type dementia', *British Journal of Clinical Psychology* 24: 171–9.

Bowie, P., Mountain, G. and Clayden, D. (1992) 'Assessing the environmental quality of long-stay wards for the confused elderly', *International Journal of Geriatric Psychiatry* 7: 95–104.

Britton, P. G. and Savage, R. D. (1966) 'A short form of WAIS for use with the aged', *British Journal of Psychiatry* 112: 417–18.

Broek, M. D. v. d. and Bradshaw, C. M. (1990) 'Intellectual decline and the assessment of premorbid intelligence', in J. R. Beech and L. Harding (eds) *Assessment of the elderly*, Windsor: NFER-Nelson (13–28).

Carr, A. C., Woods, R. T. and Moore, B. J. (1986a) 'Automated cognitive assessment of elderly patients: a comparison of two types of response device', *British Journal of Clinical Psychology* 25: 305–6.

Carr, A. C., Woods, R. T. and Moore, B. J. (1986b) 'Developing a microcomputer-based automated testing system for use with psychogeriatric patients', *Bulletin of the Royal College of Psychiatrists* 10: 309–12.

Christensen, H. and Jorm, A. F. (1992) 'Short report: effect of premorbid intelligence on the Mini-Mental State and IQCODE', *International Journal of Geriatric Psychiatry* 7: 159–60.

Church, M. and Wattis, J. P. (1988) 'Psychological approaches to the assessment and treatment of old people', in J. P. Wattis and I. Hindmarch (eds) *Psychological Assessment of the Elderly*, Edinburgh: Churchill Livingstone (151–79).

Cockburn, J. and Smith, P. T. (1989) *The Rivermead Behavioural Memory Test; Supplement 3: Elderly People*, Titchfield, Hampshire: Thames Valley Test Company.

Crawford, J. R., Allan, K. M., Stephen, D. W., Parker, D. M. and Besson, J. A. O. (1989) 'The Wechsler Adult Intelligence Scale – Revised (WAIS–R): factor structure in a UK sample', *Personality and Individual Differences* 10: 1209–12.

Crawford, J. R., Allan, K. M. and Jack, A. M. (1992a) 'Short-forms of the UK WAIS–R: regression equations and their predictive validity in a general population sample', *British Journal of Clinical Psychology* 31: 191–202.

Crawford, J. R., Moore, J. W. and Cameron, I. M. (1992b) 'Verbal fluency: a NART-based equation for the estimation of premorbid performance', *British Journal of Clinical Psychology* 31: 327–9.

Crookes, T. B. and McDonald, K. G. (1972) 'Benton's visual retention test in the differentiation of depression and early dementia', *British Journal of Social and Clinical Psychology* 11: 66–9.

Demming, J. A. and Pressey, S. L. (1957) 'Tests "indigenous" to the adult and older years', *Journal of Counselling Psychology* 4: 144–8.

De Renzi, E. and Faglioni, P. (1978) 'Normative data and screening power of a shortened version of the Token test', *Cortex* 14: 41–9.

De Renzi, E. and Vignolo, L. A. (1962) 'The token test: a sensitive test to detect receptive disturbances in aphasias', *Brain* 85: 665–78.

DesRosiers, G. (1992) 'Primary or depressive dementia: clinical features', *International Journal of Geriatric Psychiatry* 7: 629–38.

Folstein, M. F., Folstein, S. E. and McHugh, P. R. (1975) '"Mini Mental State": a practical method for grading the cognitive state of patients for the clinician', *Journal of Psychiatric Research* 12: 189–98.

Fuld, P. A. (1977) *Fuld Object Memory Evaluation*, Windsor: NFER-Nelson.

Furry, C. A. and Baltes, P. B. (1973) 'The effect of age differences in ability extraneous performance variables on the assessment of intelligence in children, adults and the elderly', *Journal of Gerontology* 28: 73–80.

Gallagher, D., Nies, G. and Thompson, L. W. (1982) 'Reliability of the Beck Depression Inventory with older adults', *Journal of Consulting and Clinical Psychology* 50: 152–3.

Gibson, A. J., Moyes, I. C. A. and Kendrick, D. (1980) 'Cognitive assessment of the elderly long-stay patient', *British Journal of Psychiatry* 137: 551–7.

Gilleard, C. J. (1984) *Living with Dementia*, Beckenham, Kent: Croom Helm.

Gilleard, C. J., Willmott, M. and Vaddadik, S. (1981) 'Self-report measures of mood and morale in elderly depressives', *British Journal of Psychiatry* 138: 230–5.

Godlove, C., Richard, L. and Rodwell, G. (1982) *Time for action: an observation study of elderly people in four different care environments*, Sheffield: Social Services Monographs.

Goldberg, D. (1978) *Manual of the General Health Questionnaire*, Windsor: NFER-Nelson.

Golding, E. (1989) *Middlesex Elderly Assessment of Mental State*, Titchfield, Hampshire: Thames Valley Test Company.

Greene, J. G., Smith, R., Gardiner, M. and Timbury, G. C. (1982) 'Measuring behavioural disturbance of elderly demented patients in the community and its effect on relatives: a factor analytic study', *Age and Ageing* 11: 121–6.

Gurland, B. J. (1980) 'The assessment of the mental health status of older adults', in J. E. Birren and R. B. Sloane (eds) *Handbook of Mental Health and Aging*, Englewood Cliffs, NJ: Prentice-Hall.

Hart, S., Smith, C. M. and Swash, M. (1988) 'Word fluency in patients with early dementia of Alzheimer type', *British Journal of Clinical Psychology* 27: 115–24.

Hodkinson, H. M. (1972) 'Evaluation of a mental test score for assessment of mental impairment in the elderly', *Age and Ageing* 1: 233–8.

Holbrook, M. and Skilbeck, C. E. (1983) 'An activities index for use with stroke patients', *Age and Ageing* 12: 166–70.

Holden, U. P. (1988) *Neuropsychology and Ageing: Definitions, Explanations and Practical Approaches*, London: Croom Helm.

Holden, U. P. and Woods, R. T. (1988) *Reality Orientation: Psychological Approaches to the 'Confused' Elderly, 2nd edn.*, Edinburgh: Churchill Livingstone.

Holland, C. A. and Rabbitt, P. (1991) 'The course and causes of cognitive change with advancing age', *Reviews in Clinical Gerontology* 1: 81–96.

Huppert, F. A. (1991) 'Neuropsychological assessment of dementia', *Reviews in Clinical Gerontology* 1: 159–69.

Isaacs, B. and Akhtar, A. J. (1972) 'The set test: a rapid test of mental function in old people', *Age and Ageing* 1: 222–6.

Jenkins, J., Felce, D., Lunt, B. and Powell, E. (1977) 'Increasing engagement in activity of residents in old people's homes by providing recreational materials', *Behaviour Research and Therapy* 15: 429–34.

Jorm, A. F., Scott, R. and Jacomb, P. (1989) 'Assessment of cognitive decline in dementia by informant questionnaire', *International Journal of Geriatric Psychiatry* 4: 35–9.

Katona, C. L. E. and Aldridge, C. R. (1985) 'The dexamethasone suppression test and depressive signs in dementia', *Journal of Affective Disorders* 8: 83–9.

Kendrick, D. C. (1982) 'Why assess the aged? A clinical psychologist's view', *British Journal of Clinical Psychology* 21: 47–54.

Kendrick, D. C. (1985) *Kendrick Cognitive Tests for the Elderly*, Windsor: NFER-Nelson.

Kendrick, D. C., Gibson, A. J. and Moyes, I. C. A. (1979) 'The revised Kendrick battery: clinical studies', *British Journal of Social and Clinical Psychology* 18: 329–40.

Kimmel, D. (1990) *Adulthood and Aging, 3rd edn*, New York: Wiley.

Kirshner, H. S., Webb, W. G. and Kelly, M. P. (1984) 'The naming disorder of dementia', *Neuropsychologia* 22: 23–30.

Kitwood, T. (1992) 'Quality assurance in dementia care', *Geriatric Medicine* September: 34–8.

Klisz, D. (1978) 'Neuropsychological evaluation in older persons, in M. Storandt, I. C. Siegler and M. F. Elias (eds) *The Clinical Psychology of Aging*, New York: Plenum Press (71–96).

Kuriansky, J. and Gurland, B. (1976) 'The performance test of activities of daily living', *International Journal of Aging and Human Development* 7: 343–52.

Lam, D. H., Brewin, C. R., Woods, R. T. and Bebbington, P. E. (1987) 'Cognition and social adversity in the depressed elderly', *Journal of Abnormal Psychology* 96: 23–6.

Lam, D. H. and Power, M. J. (1991) 'Social support in a general practice elderly sample', *International Journal of Geriatric Psychiatry* 6: 89–93.

Lawton, M. P. (1975) 'The Philadelphia Geriatric Center Morale scale: a revision', *Journal of Gerontology* 30: 85–9.

Lawton, M. P. and Brody, E. (1969) 'Assessment of older people: self-maintaining and instrumental activities of daily living', *Gerontologist* 9: 179–86.

Lindesay, J., Briggs, K., Lawes, M., Macdonald, A. and Herzberg, J. (1991) 'The domus philosophy: a comparative evaluation of a new approach to residential care for the demented elderly', *International Journal of Geriatric Psychiatry* 6: 727–36.

Macdonald, A. J. D., Mann, A. H., Jenkins, R., Richard, L., Godlove, C. and Rodwell, G. (1982) 'An attempt to determine the impact of four types of care upon the elderly in London by the study of matched groups', *Psychological Medicine* 12: 193–200.

Macdonald, A. J. D., Craig, T. K. J. and Warner, L. A. R. (1985) 'The development of a short observational method for the study of the activity and contacts of old people in residential settings', *Psychological Medicine* 15: 167–72.

McFadyen, M. (1984) 'The measurement of engagement in the institutionalised elderly', in I. Hanley and J. Hodge (eds) *Psychological Approaches to the Care of the Elderly*, London: Croom Helm.

McKenna, P. and Warrington, E. K. (1983) *The Graded Naming Test*, Windsor: NFER-Nelson.

Mahurin, R. K., DeBettignies, B. H. and Pirozzolo, F. J. (1991) 'Structured assessment of independent living skills: preliminary report of a performance measure of functional abilities in dementia', *Journal of Gerontology* 46: P58–66.

Miller, E. (1980) 'Cognitive assessment of the older adult', in J. E. Birren and R. B. Sloane (eds) *Handbook of Mental Health and Aging*, Englewood Cliffs, NJ: Prentice-Hall.

Miller, E. (1984) 'Verbal fluency as a function of a measure of verbal intelligence and in relation to different types of cerebral pathology', *British Journal of Clinical Psychology* 23: 53–7.

Montgomery, S. A. (1988) 'Measuring mood', in J. P. Wattis and I. Hindmarch (eds) *Psychological Assessment of the Elderly*, Edinburgh: Churchill Livingstone (138–50).

Moos, R. and Lemke, S. (1980) 'Assessing the physical and architectural features of sheltered care settings', *Journal of Gerontology* 35: 571–83.

Morris, R. G. and Kopelman, M. D. (1986) 'The memory deficits in Alzheimer-type dementia: a review', *Quarterly Journal of Experimental Psychology* 38A: 575–602.

Nelson, H. E. (1982) *The National Adult Reading Test*, Windsor: NFER-Nelson.

Nelson, H. E. and McKenna, P. (1975) 'The use of current reading ability in the assessment of dementia', *British Journal of Social and Clinical Psychology* 14: 259–67.

Nelson, H. E. and Willison, J. (1991) *National Adult Reading Test: Test Manual*, Windsor: NFER-Nelson.

O'Carroll, R. E., Baikie, E. M. and Whittick, J. E. (1987) 'Does the National adult reading test hold in dementia? *British Journal of Clinical Psychology* 26: 315–16.

O'Neill, D., Rice, I., Blake, P., Walsh, J. B. and Coakley, D. (1992) 'The geriatric depression scale: rater-administered or self-administered', *International Journal of Geriatric Psychiatry* 7: 511–15.

Orme, J. E. (1957) 'Non-verbal and verbal performance in normal old age, senile dementia and elderly depressives', *Journal of Gerontology* 12: 408–13.

Orrell, M., Howard, R., Payne, A., Bergmann, K., Woods, R., Everitt, B. S. and Levy, R. (1992) 'Differentiation between organic and functional psychiatric illness in the elderly: an evaluation of four cognitive tests', *International Journal of Geriatric Psychiatry* 7: 263–75.

Owens, W. (1966) 'Age and mental abilities: a second adult follow-up', *Journal of Educational Psychology* 51: 311–25.

Pattie, A. H. (1988) 'Measuring levels of disability – the Clifton Assessment Procedures for the Elderly', in J. P. Wattis and I. Hindmarch (eds) *Psychological Assessment of the Elderly*, Edinburgh: Churchill Livingstone (61–80).

Pattie, A. H. and Gilleard, C. J. (1979) *Manual for the Clifton Assessment Procedures for the Elderly (CAPE)*, Sevenoaks: Hodder & Stoughton Educational.

Pfeffer, R. I., Kurosaki, T. T., Harrah, C. H., Chance, J. M. and Filos, S. (1982) 'Measurement of functional activities in older adults in the community', *Journal of Gerontology* 37: 323–9.

Powell, G. E., Bailey, S. and Clark, E. (1980) 'A very short version of the Minnesota Aphasia test', *British Journal of Social and Clinical Psychology* 19: 189–94.

Rabbitt, P. (1982) 'How to assess the aged? An experimental psychologist's view: some comments on Dr Kendrick's paper', *British Journal of Clinical Psychology* 21: 55–9.

Raven, J. C., Court, J. H. and Raven, J. (1976) *Manual for Raven's Progressive Matrices and Vocabulary Scales*, London: H K Lewis.

Robinson, R. A. (1977) 'Differential diagnosis and assessment in brain failure', *Age and Ageing* 6 (Supplement): 42–9.

Roth, M., Huppert, F. A., Tym, E. and Mountjoy, C. Q. (1988) *CAMDEX – Cambridge Examination for Mental Disorders of the Elderly*, Cambridge: Cambridge University Press.

Ruddle, H. V. and Bradshaw, C. M. (1982) 'On the estimation of premorbid intellectual functioning: validation of Nelson and McKenna's and some new normative data', *British Journal of Clinical Psychology* 21: 159–65.

Ryan, J. J., Paolo, A. M. and Brungardt, T. M. (1990) 'Standardisation of the WAIS–R for persons 75 years and older', *Psychological Assessment: a Journal of Consulting and Clinical Psychology* 2: 404–11.

Rybash, J. M., Hoyer, W. J. and Roodin, P. A. (1986) *Adult Cognition and Aging: Developmental Changes in Processing, Knowing and Thinking*, New York: Pergamon.

Sahakian, B. J. (1990) 'Computerized assessment of neuropsychological function in Alzheimer's disease and Parkinson's disease', *International Journal of Geriatric Psychiatry* 5: 211–13.

Sahakian, B. J. (1991) 'Depressive pseudodementia in the elderly', *International Journal of Geriatric Psychiatry* 6: 453–8.

Savage, R. D., Britton, P. G., Bolton, N. and Hall, E. (1973) *Intellectual Functioning in the Aged*, London: Methuen.

Schaie, K. W. (1990) 'Intellectual development in adulthood', in J. E. Birren and K. W. Schaie (eds) *Handbook of the Psychology of Aging, 3rd edn*, San Diego: Academic Press (291–309).

Siegler, I. C. and Botwinick, J. (1979) 'A long-term longitudinal study of the intellectual ability of older adults – the matter of selective subject attrition', *Journal of Gerontology* 34: 242–8.

Simpson, P. M., Surmon, D. J., Wesnes, K. A. and Wilcock, G. K. (1991) 'The cognitive drug research computerized assessment system for demented patients: a validation study', *International Journal of Geriatric Psychiatry* 6: 95–102.

Skurla, E., Rogers, J. C. and Sunderland, T. (1988) 'Direct assessment of activities of daily living in Alzheimer's disease: a controlled study', *Journal of American Geriatrics Society* 36: 97–103.

Stevens, S. J., Pitt, B. M. N., Nicholl, C. G., Fletcher, A. E. and Palmer, A. J. (1992) 'Language assessment in a memory clinic', *International Journal of Geriatric Psychiatry* 7: 45–51.

Stuart-Hamilton, I. (1991) *The Psychology of Ageing: An Introduction*, London: Jessica Kingsley.

Teri, L. and Lewinsohn, P. (1982) 'Modification of the Pleasant and Unpleasant Events schedules for use with the elderly', *Journal of Consulting and Clinical Psychology* 50: 444–5.

Twining, C. (1990) 'Assessment of personal adjustment', in J. R. Beech and L. Harding (eds) *Assessment of the elderly*, Windsor: NFER-Nelson (87–99).

Volans, P. J. and Woods, R. T. (1983) 'Why do we assess the aged?' *British Journal of Clinical Psychology* 22: 213–14.

Walker, S. (1980) 'Application of a test for aphasia to normal old people', *Journal of Clinical and Experimental Gerontology* 2: 185–98.

Ward, T., Murphy, E. and Procter, A. (1991) 'Functional assessment in severely demented patients', *Age and Ageing* 20: 212–16.

Ward, T., Murphy, E., Procter, A. and Weinman, J. (1992) 'An observational study of two long-stay psychogeriatric wards', *International Journal of Geriatric Psychiatry* 7: 211–17.

Warrington, E. K. (1984) *Recognition Memory Test Manual*, Windsor: NFER-Nelson.

Wechsler, D. (1955) *Manual for the Wechsler Adult Intelligence Scale*, New York: Psychological Corporation.

Wechsler, D. (1981) *Manual for the Wechsler Adult Intelligence Scales – Revised*, New York: Psychological Corporation.

Wechsler, D. (1987) *Wechsler Memory Scale – Revised*, New York: Psychological Corporation.

Weeks, D. J. (1988) *The Anomalous Sentences Repetition Test*, Windsor: NFER-Nelson.

Whitehead, A. (1973) 'Verbal learning and memory in elderly depressives', *British Journal of Psychiatry* 123: 203–8.

Wilkie, F. and Eisdorfer, C. (1971) 'Intelligence and blood pressure in the aged', *Science* 172: 959–62.

Willcocks, D. M., Peace, S. M. and Kellaher, L. A. (1987) *Private Lives in Public Places*, London: Tavistock.

Williams, B. W., Mack, W. and Henderson, V. W. (1989) 'Boston naming test in Alzheimer's disease', *Neuropsychologia* 27: 1073–9.

Wilson, B. A., Cockburn, J. and Baddeley, A. D. (1985) *The Rivermead Behavioural Memory Test*, Titchfield, Hampshire: Thames Valley Test Company.

Woods, R. T. and Britton, P. G. (1985) *Clinical Psychology with the Elderly*, London: Croom Helm/Chapman and Hall.

Yesavage, J. A., Brink, T. L. and Rose, T. L. (1983) 'Development and validation of a geriatric depression scale: a preliminary report', *Journal of Psychiatric Research* 17: 37–49.

Chapter 22

Problems in the elderly
Treatment

R.T. Woods

INTRODUCTION

The two major mental health problems in old age are the dementias and depression. Around 5 per cent of over-65s suffer from a dementing condition; there is a sharp increase in prevalence in the over-80s, with perhaps 20 per cent of a representative sample having this diagnosis when examined by a psychiatrist. Depression that would be rated as severe would be identified in 4 per cent of over-65s; this would include those with psychotic features and those requiring in-patient hospital treatment. Thirteen per cent would have a milder form of depression, primarily with lowered mood, and around 3 per cent would have a generalised anxiety disorder, 10 per cent would have phobic disorders, mainly agoraphobia (Lindesay *et al.*, 1989). In this sample, 40 per cent of phobic patients were judged also to be depressed. Readers are referred to Jacoby and Oppenheimer (1991) for a comprehensive account of psychiatric disorders in late life or to Wattis and Church (1986) for a concise, practical approach.

PSYCHOLOGICAL TREATMENT OF THE DEMENTIAS – INTRODUCTION

The natural history of the dementias is usually considered to be of progressive deterioration in a range of cognitive abilities and self-care skills, often accompanied by disorders of behaviour. It is unlikely that a psychological treatment completely reversing its effects could be developed. The aim should be to improve the quality of life both of individuals with dementia and of their supporters. In recent years it has become widely acknowledged that these disorders have a great impact on the families of sufferers, often associated with high levels of strain and depression (Morris *et al.*, 1988). Interventions with the sufferer may entail attempts to change particular aspects of behaviour, and to maintain function as much as possible, rather than to reverse the whole process. 'Management' may be a more apt description than treatment (Miller, 1977). Generally, interventions have to become part of the person's environment if their effects are to continue.

Most approaches were developed in institutional settings, and there is generally even less evidence for their effectiveness with the majority of elderly people with dementia who live in the community, supported by relatives, friends, neighbours and formal support services; adaptations can be made for their use in day-care and domestic settings. Psychological approaches specifically geared to family care-givers will be discussed in a later section.

Sensory deprivation

Early attempts to 'treat' dementia psychologically aimed at stimulating patients in a variety of ways (see Holden and Woods, 1988). An analogy was drawn between the behaviour of the person with dementia and the cognitive and perceptual disturbances of young, healthy volunteers exposed to lengthy, extreme deprivation of sensory stimulation. The sensory deprivation of elderly people was attributed to a combination of loss of sensory acuity, the unstimulating environment of many old-age institutions, and the person's own withdrawal from their environment. Sensory deprivation, it was argued, would be especially damaging to patients with dementia as their impaired recent memory forces reliance on external stimulation to maintain appropriate environmental contact.

Whether or not the analogy holds – and the evidence in favour is at best circumstantial – these early studies set the pattern for many subsequent efforts. Attempts were made to change the physical environment and to introduce care regimes and group-work encouraging more independence, socialisation and activity. Recent studies which have attempted to evaluate the impact of offering particular forms of stimulation to patients with severe dementia include Norberg et al. (1986) (music, touch, and various objects), Gaebler and Hemsley (1991) (music) and Haughie et al. (1992) (pet dogs). What is particularly notable from these studies is both the responsivity of patients with severe dementia to aspects of their environment and the detailed, careful observation needed to identify this response. There is a real risk of patients being 'written off' as completely unresponsive because the response is not immediately apparent.

Physical environment

Even though existing buildings are difficult to change, some aspects are modifiable. The classic example is the arrangement of chairs in day-rooms and lounges. Several studies (see Holden and Woods, 1988) have demonstrated that placing chairs in smaller groups around coffee-tables increases the amount of social interaction between residents. This increase in interaction is by comparison with that occurring when chairs are in the traditional around-the-walls arrangement, which allows conversation only with immediate neighbours at each side – even this being uncomfortable! Other physical changes include the provision of clear signposting to help residents find their way around (Hanley, 1981) and the use in front of the exit door of either grid-patterns on the floor (Hussian and Brown, 1987) or a full-length mirror (Mayer and Darby, 1991), both of which reduced to an extent the frequency of patients wandering out of the wards involved.

These, and other physical factors, are being considered much more in the design of new buildings for people with dementia (Manser, 1991; Marshall, 1992; Netten, 1993). Current designs emphasise small living units, with a maximum of ten residents living in each, typically with individual bedrooms and domestic-scale communal areas, with the aim of achieving a 'homely' atmosphere and minimising as far as possible the person's deficits. Increasingly, the overall impact of these designs is being subject to evaluation in relation to its effect on residents and staff (for example, in the UK, the 'domus' schemes – Lindesay *et al.*, 1991; in France, the 'cantou' – Ritchie *et al.*, 1992), but the physical environment cannot in fact be separated from the regime of care provided. Most institutions cater for the physical needs of residents with dementia fairly well. Providing food, drink, shelter, help with self-care, and so on is relatively straightforward, although often demanding. A good institution also attempts to meet the person's much more complex psychological needs.

Ideal care

If residents' quality of life is to be maximised and an attempt made to meet psychological needs, the institutional environment must encourage these aspects:

1 Individualisation of care – for example, residents should be toileted according to their natural pattern of micturition, rather than at certain set times, en bloc; activities, games, music, and so on should be geared to individual tastes and preferences, and there should be individual care plans (Holden and Woods, 1988).
2 Residents' sense of control over their environment – in any communal living arrangements, some control is lost. Residents' committees may be inappropriate for those with severe cognitive impairment, but choices can still be made available, and should be presented so that the individual can respond. For example, Davies and Snaith (1980a) show how, in some settings, menu choices are either removed or presented in an over-complex manner.
3 Residents' independence – in the case of people with dementia, maintaining skills is easier than retraining. The environment should elicit and reinforce the residents' remaining abilities, and not differentially reinforce inappropriate or dependent behaviour, as so often happens (Baltes, 1988). This means that residents must be given sufficient time to feed or dress themselves, say, and not be fed or dressed for the sake of speed, or to avoid disruption of a rigid routine. Incontinence, screaming, wandering, and so on must not capture all the available staff attention – or the problems will become worse.
4 Treatment of the resident with dementia as a person – certainly he or she is disabled, often severely, but he or she still has the right to be respected and

not treated as an object, vegetable, doll, or child. He or she has experienced adulthood, and is attuned to the humiliation of public failure, being talked over, and the other indignities often seen in institutions. The resident's lack of insight or poor memory cannot be cited to imply that it does not matter. Apart from the humanitarian principle involved, it seems likely that people with dementia will function at their best in an environment which is structured so that individuals can experience some success and retain some independence, and not just know failure and indignity; where they can feel secure and not over-stressed; where others care about them and they can care about others. Kitwood, in a series of influential papers (e.g. Kitwood, 1990; Kitwood and Bredin, 1992) argues that what he describes as the 'malignant social psychology' around the dementia sufferer, which treats the person as less than a person, devaluing, invalidating and patronising, exacerbates and accelerates the neurological dysfunction. The essence of maintaining function then becomes person-centred care, which recognises and seeks out the personhood of the dementia sufferer.

Changing the environment

An important implication of our brief overview of the 'ideal' institution is that the success of the typical intervention study, focusing on one aspect of the environment, may well depend on other features of the environment. For example, introducing a weekly activity session may have a huge impact in a setting where no activities are routinely offered, but be less significant in a unit where individualised activities are part of daily life (an example of this is described by Head et al., 1990). Where residents are de-humanised the activity session may be drawn into the general atmosphere and become another experience of failure for the residents; in another setting, adopting a person-centred approach, activities may be more closely matched to each resident's abilities and interests, and be more beneficial. Generalisation of findings across settings assumes similarities in attitude and regime.

For example, large differences in meal-time atmosphere between two comparable geriatric wards were reported by Davies and Snaith (1980b). On one ward it was a social occasion, on the other little interaction occurred (mostly staff-initiated), patients were offered fewer choices, and there were many instances of patients' choices being denied by staff. The differences seemed to relate to the physical environment, social distance between staff and patients, and the ward sister's role. Changing one of these (the physical setting) by having patients sit around a table, successfully increased the amount of interaction, temporarily at least (Davies, 1982). It is worth noting that the person in charge of a unit may have a crucial effect on expectations, attitudes and style of care.

Similarly, Melin and Gotestam (1981) showed improved eating skills and social interaction in patients with dementia at meal-times by changing from a system with rigid time-limits, where slow patients were fed by staff, to one where unlimited time was given, and the social character of the occasion emphasised, allowing more choice and independence. In the same study, increases in social interaction and activity were noted when more choice and independence was allowed.

Brane *et al.* (1989) described their regime as 'integrity promoting care'. It involved individualised care, choices being encouraged, a more home-like atmosphere, personalised clothes and possessions, and the prompting of activities whilst allowing patients to proceed at their own pace. After three months a variety of improvements were noted in patients on this ward in comparison with a control group receiving traditional care. Mood, motor performance, confusion, anxiety and distractibility were areas where benefits were reported.

Behaviour modification

Despite considerable interest and speculation, there are still relatively few reports of the successful application of behaviour modification to patients clearly identifiable as having dementia (Patterson and Jackson, 1980; Holden and Woods, 1988; Woods and Britton, 1985).

Successful interventions have included reduced wandering and other inappropriate and stereotyped behaviour (Hussian, 1981), increasing orientation (see next section), increasing social interaction and participation (Carstensen and Erickson, 1986), inceasing mobility (Burgio *et al.*, 1986) and increasing participation in activities (Burton, 1980). Eliciting the desired behaviour through cueing or prompting, or providing a powerful discriminative stimulus for the behaviour, has often proved to be the key element of the programme, rather than the reinforcement schedule *per se*. For instance, progress in the Burgio *et al.* study aimed at increasing mobility was so rapid that the authors concluded that the opportunity to walk must have been an important component. Presumably environmental contingencies in this nursing home setting may have discouraged walking, with staff perhaps finding it more convenient to have residents in wheelchairs. This is a good example of the existence of 'excess disabilities', where the person functions at a worse level than that determined by their dementia, in response to the behaviour and attitudes of their care-givers; this also exemplifies Kitwood's concept of a 'malignant social psychology'.

The common, and difficult to manage, problem of incontinence has been the subject of mixed results when behavioural approaches have been applied. Schnelle *et al.* (1989) and Burgio *et al.* (1988) successfully used a prompted voiding procedure, where nursing home residents are simply asked on a regular schedule, say, hourly, whether they wish to use the toilet, and continence is systematically reinforced. The aim here is not independent toileting, and in fact self-initiated toileting became less frequent in the latter study. Rona *et al.* (1986) used a more complex procedure, aiming to increase independent toileting, with mixed results. Patients who had been incontinent less than once a day showed some improvements, while those who had been more frequently incontinent did not respond to the training programme.

Continence requires a number of different skills – finding the toilet, recognising it, adjusting clothing, and so on – and is affected in older people by a number of physical factors. Multi-modal approaches, tackling physical, psychological and environmental aspects, analysing the factors leading to incontinence in each case, and adapting toileting regimes to individual patterns of micturition, offer most help in this area (Hodge, 1984).

Reality orientation

Reality orientation (RO), as described by Holden and Woods (1988), seeks to orientate the person verbally and behaviourally. The aim is to help dementing patients to be more aware of what is happening around them and to be able to use this information in their daily lives. Confused or rambling talk is systematically not reinforced. Informal or 24-hour RO is carried out throughout the day, in every interaction between staff and patient. The patient is encouraged to make use of memory aids, signs and notice. RO sessions are intended to supplement informal RO. A small group of three to four patients meets, usually daily, for about half a hour. Through structured activities and discussions, individuals are helped to succeed by the use of cues, prompts and reinforcement of appropriate behaviour.

A number of controlled evaluations are reviewed by Holden and Woods (1988). In a variety of settings a small, but significant, effect of RO sessions on measures of verbal orientation has been reported. Twenty-four-hour RO has been the subject of fewer evaluations, although there have been several studies demonstrating the efficacy of specific training sessions in helping disorientated patients find their way around the ward or home, often using signposting (e.g. Lam and Woods, 1986). Reeve and Ivison (1985) showed improvements in spatial orientation following the implementation of a 24-hour RO programme. Similarly, Williams et al. (1987) showed significant cognitive and behavioural improvements associated with 24-hour RO. The use of past memories to foster contact has often been used in RO sessions, and has attracted interest as an approach in its own right. Reminiscence therapy has been used with individuals and in small groups (Norris, 1986; Thornton and Brotchie, 1987; Woods et al., 1991) with photographs, archive recordings and items from the past being used to stimulate a variety of personal memories. Evaluative studies with people with dementia are few, and no clear picture has yet emerged of its effects. Head et al. (1990) found an increase in interaction in one group, compared with an alternative activity, but a group in another day-centre failed to show a differential benefit from involvement in reminiscence activities. Baines et al. (1987) similarly report results from two groups, with only one one showing improvements in orientation and function outside the group. It is clearly an enjoyable activity for many older people with dementia, but as yet there is little evidence of its impact continuing after the group session, or of its being more effective within a group in increasing interaction than other activities.

Dissatisfaction with RO, which can be applied in a rather rigid, unfeeling fashion if too much emphasis is put on 'correcting' the person rather than seeking to understand their attempts at communication (Dietch et al., 1989), has led to increasing interest in Validation Therapy (Feil, 1989), where attempts are made to discern and respond to the emotional content of what the person says, rather than focusing on the factual content. Evaluative studies are beginning to appear (Morton and Bleathman, 1991; Bleathman and Morton, 1992), but to date the conclusion would have to be as for reminiscence; a useful addition to the repertoire of techniques for use in group and individual work with people with dementia, but with no clear evidence of persisting effects or of greater benefits generally than other approaches. Woods (1991) shows that the core techniques of validation therapy are not incompatible with the RO approach when it is used in a sensitive, individualised manner, and argues that to see alternative approaches as competitors may detract from the need to find the most effective strategy for working with a particular individual at a specific point in time.

Staff attitudes

Generally evaluations of these approaches have concentrated on changes in patients' behaviour, even though changing staff attitudes and behaviour may be equally important in institutions. For example, reminiscence may have a particular value in that it puts people with dementia for once in a position where they have something to give, by describing events and experiences to others, who have not shared these experiences. This enables staff to see the individual in the context of their whole life – work, relationships, interests, and so on – which could help greatly in the individualisation of care. Indeed in the Baines et al. study, staff knowledge of residents' personal information increased for residents participating in reminiscence (and RO) groups. Other approaches may also lead to attitudinal change; Ingstad and Gotestam (1987) report positive changes in staff attitudes on a ward for patients with severe dementia following the changes to the environment described by Melin and Gotestam (1981).

In any setting it is important to make a careful analysis of staff attitudes and expectations and the organisational framework, and to avoid rushing in with an 'off-the-shelf' treatment package. Usually careful, persistent, patient work is needed with key staff, at all levels, if the intervention is to have any chance of being satisfactorily implemented. For example, before RO is introduced, staff must seriously consider whether the environment is one to which it is worth being orientated. An individualised care-planning approach provides opportunities to focus on the individualisation of care, based on individual needs, assets and deficits, and for setting treatment goals in personalised care plans, identifying where the person is currently under-functioning. Barrowclough and Fleming (1986) show that staff in residential homes can be trained effectively to use this approach, which fits well with the integrative framework described by Holden and Woods (1988). This individualised approach also maps well onto care management as implemented by Challis *et al.* (1988) with elderly people with dementia and their carers in the community.

Care staff have a difficult task in coping with a disorder that has a natural history of progressive deterioration and which is physically and mentally demanding. Even reducing the rate of deterioration does not bring the reward of seeing the patient improve. Staff need help to identify the more subtle, but potentially important, changes in quality of life that may be possible; mutual support and encouragement is vital in this stressful and taxing work. These aspects need consideration by psychologists as much as – if not more than – the details of the treatment packages to be implemented.

Interventions with family care-givers

In recent years awareness has grown of the key role of family care-givers in supporting elderly people with dementia at home, and of the heavy price paid by many carers in terms of strain and depression. They find themselves having to cope with the effective loss of the person as he or she was, as well as coping day-by-day with an unpredictably changing pattern of decline in the person's cognitive and self-care abilities, often accompanied by behavioural disturbances that are difficult to manage in a domestic setting.

At least three strategies for psychological interventions involving family care-givers have been described. The first is to teach the care-giver to use behavioural techniques to modify the behaviour of the person with dementia. Pinkston *et al.* (1988) used this approach with 66 carers, targeting a range of areas, including self-care, aggression and walking; single-case designs were used to evaluate changes in target behaviours, with over 75 per cent showing improvement. In an interesting single-case study, Green *et al.* (1986) taught a carer to use social reinforcement to increase the amount, the spontaneity and appropriateness of her cognitively impaired husband's verbal behaviour. When this strategy is effective it can also serve to help the care-giver feel a greater sense of control and less powerlessness, and could potentially improve his or her own mood. In a small pilot study, Hinchliffe *et al.* (1992) showed that two carers who were taught successfully to use behavioural management techniques to reduce specific irritating behaviours reported dramatic reductions in strain. However, many relatives are first seen in a crisis, often when the strain is becoming unbearable. These techniques might be better taught earlier, whilst the strain is more manageable, or to supporters less emotionally involved. Other techniques, such as reminiscence, can be used to facilitate communication between the elderly person and their relatives (Davies, 1981); family members are well placed to use personal prompts – photograph albums, heirlooms, and the like.

The second strategy focuses specifically on the care-giver's feelings of stress, by teaching the use of stress-reduction approaches. Gendron *et al.* (1986) offered carers training sessions in relaxation and assertiveness, and report benefits in stress reduction, assertiveness and problem-solving skills compared with untreated control carers at six-month follow-up. Sutcliffe and Larner (1988) taught a small group of carers anxiety management and anger control methods; this intervention was associated with greater strain-reduction than the provision of information regarding dementia.

The third strategy is broadly educational, and in addition to elements of the first two approaches will also address cognitive aspects – the care-giver's perceptions of and attributions about the situation – and ways of maximising support from formal services and from family and friends. Lovett and Gallagher (1988) taught problem-solving skills in what they describe as a 'psycho-educational intervention' and found reductions in levels of depression; however, not all studies have found improvements in the key variables of depression and strain when a control group has been used (e.g. Zarit *et al.*, 1987). Brodaty (1992) provides a helpful review of this literature, and highlights the weaknesses of studies to date, which have often used training periods that are too brief and have not targeted sufficiently carers with high strain levels. Brodaty and Gresham (1989) brought both patient and carer into a special hospital unit, with carers receiving training in coping strategies whilst patients attended memory retraining sessions. Carers reported less strain at twelve-month follow-up compared with a control group of carers, whose relatives had been admitted for an equivalent period without them, so that they had received respite rather than training. The control patients tended to enter institutional care at an earlier stage than the relatives of carers who had received training. Debate continues regarding the advantages of individual counselling in relation to group approaches, and the use of peer-group counsellors (carefully trained and supervised), rather than professional therapists (Toseland *et al.*, 1989; Toseland and Smith, 1990). This is clearly an area where there is great potential, but a great deal more work needs to be done in developing individually tailored approaches before the strain and depression which weigh down many carers can be tackled with confidence.

TREATMENT OF AFFECTIVE DISORDERS

Introduction

Psychological treatment for depression seems to be offered less often to older people than to younger adults. Although effective pharmacological treatments are widely available, there are difficulties in their long-term use with some elderly patients with particular physical health problems. Relapse rates are relatively high (Murphy, 1982), a significant number of patients recover only partially, being left with disabling symptoms, and as many as a tenth do not improve at all. There is, then, certainly scope for psychological approaches to supplement physical treatments. In this section the focus will be on cognitive-behaviour therapy. Readers interested in psychotherapy with the elderly are referred to Knight (1986; 1992) and Smyer *et al.* (1990).

Generally there are probably more similarities than differences between the treatment of younger and older patients. A number of special points are none the less worth considering.

Physical health

Depression is closely linked to ill-health in older people (Pitt, 1991). Somatic symptoms are common in depressed elderly people and depression may present as a physical illness. Conversely, physical illnesses may present as, or precipitate, depression. Medication for various physical complaints may influence mood or interfere with treatment. A person's health may affect the range of achievable targets, or the energy he or she can devote to treatment. It is advisable to work closely with a medical colleague, so that treatment can be guided by the best available assessment of the patient's physical problems. Sensory impairments are also relevant. Loss of visual acuity may hamper the use of written materials in cognitive therapy, unless suitably modified. Hearing losses of even a mild degree may disrupt group work (see Rabbitt, 1988) and can render the giving of relaxation instructions a taxing task! Portable voice amplifiers, with headphones for the patient and microphone for the therapist, have proved helpful for some patients with hearing loss.

Cognitive decline

Some writers (e.g. Church, 1983; 1986) have drawn attention to cognitive changes in older people, particularly in abstract ability, and have suggested these may make it more difficult to apply therapies involving abstract ideas. Cognitive therapy might then need to be more practically and behaviourally based. It is not clear to what extent actual age-changes are occurring; generational differences are also likely to be operating. There are great individual differences between patients, and therapy needs to be carefully tailored to each patient's intellectual capabilities. Many elderly patients find recording automatic thoughts quite difficult, for example; some, however, will be able to do this.

Loss

Most elderly people have experienced a number of losses – work, health, sensory systems, family home, perhaps, as well as loved ones. In assessing the depressed patient it is important to consider the impact of the various losses the person has experienced, and the ways in which the person has attempted to cope with them. Parkes (1992), in a helpful review, suggests that anguish may be less extreme when an older person loses a spouse and that somatic symptoms are more pronounced. There may be a greater tendency towards withdrawal and for them, in contrast to younger people, anticipatory grief may do more harm than good: having an opportunity to prepare for the person's death may be outweighed by the strain of caring for a terminally ill person, with its consequent social isolation.

Each grief reaction is, of course, different: much depends on the nature of the relationship with the person who dies. The components of grief identified with younger people can also help describe grief in older people, but no definite sequence should be assumed. Shock and disbelief are often the initial reactions; protest and yearning, searching for the dead person, disorganisation and despair, including features of anger and guilt, may occur later. Detachment and reorganisation are usually seen as the endpoint of the grief process.

One implication of these multiple losses is that the person may be undergoing real-life hardships. Therapy needs to help the person distinguish depressive hopelessness and helplessness from a realistic appraisal of his or her limitations. Cognitive distortions are harder to identify when the person does have a number of physical or social limitations with which to contend.

Patients' expectations

Steuer and Hammen (1983) comment that older patients may be more likely to wait passively for help to be given to them by the 'expert', and more unwilling to try new patterns of behaviour, or to abandon old ones. This may be a particular difficulty where the patient has long-standing chronic problems. Emery (1981) refers to the need for 'treatment socialisation', to educate a person as to the nature of his or her condition and the treatment to be employed to correct misconceptions and false expectations. This is probably a generational consideration, rather than one related to age *per se*.

Therapists' expectations

Dysfunctional beliefs are not confined to patients! Therapists need to examine their own attitudes and beliefs about the elderly, to become aware of their own negative stereotypes. Frequent contact with healthy, coping old people is a valuable means of combating such attitudes (Emery, 1981). Therapists should be aware of local community resources and facilities, so that patients can be helped to make informed choices as they develop their problem-solving skills. Sometimes a little practical help can be immensely beneficial in relieving anxiety, but it is important to recognise that not all emotional problems have practical solutions; a patient may be just as unhappy in a new house as in the old one if the basic problem is one of making friendships, for example.

'Rambling' and 'poor memory'

Occasionally a patient has difficulty in focusing on the salient points and insists, for example, on recounting a particular story at great length. Emery (1981) suggests establishing an agenda for each session, with the clear understanding that the patient will be interrupted if he or she wanders from the topic. Depressed elderly people occasionally complain of poor memory – indeed some would argue that an elderly person complaining of poor memory is much more likely to be depressed than dementing (Feehan *et al.*, 1991). Cognitive assessment may be able to provide evidence of the adequacy of an individual's memory compared with that of his or her peers, and writing down homework tasks or targets can both reduce memory load and serve as an example of how to use memory aids to minimise memory failures.

APPLICATIONS OF COGNITIVE BEHAVIOUR THERAPY WITH THE ELDERLY

Anxiety disorders

A number of elderly people do report specific fears (Lindesay *et al.*, 1989) – most commonly regarding lack of confidence in going out. This may follow a specific trauma such as a fall or an attack in the street. Depression may follow if an individual is thus cut off from favoured sources of reinforcement. Graded exposure or systematic desensitisation can be successfully used. Woods (1982) describes two cases where the person was unable to go out. Thyer (1981) reports successful *in vivo* exposure therapy with an elderly woman suffering from a debilitating fear of dogs. Hussian (1981) used 'stress inoculation training' to help four elderly people overcome anxiety about travelling in a lift. This training included the practising of positive coping statements, and was initially carried out imaginally to reduce anxiety to a level where *in vivo* exposure was possible. Relaxation and other anxiety-management procedures can be taught to elderly people (Garrison, 1978). It is important to emphasise the 'relaxation' rather than the 'exercise' component; some elderly patients have been known to view the exercises as a means of muscle development, and have focused exclusively on the tension phase of the relaxation technique!

King and Barrowclough (1991) report the use of cognitive-behavioural interventions with ten out-patients (mean age 73) with anxiety disorders. In essence, the treatment involved assisting the person to re-interpret their anxiety symptoms. Rather than perceiving them as life-threatening or catastrophic, they were encouraged to view them as non-threatening, benign physical sensations. Techniques such as hyperventilation provocation tests and controlled breathing training – often now used with younger patients experiencing panic attacks (see Lindsay, Chapter 8) – were used to facilitate this process where appropriate. Nine of the ten patients showed a decrease in symptoms after treatment (an average of eight sessions) and this improvement was generally maintained at follow-up after three to six months. Holden (1988) provides a useful description of strategies for assisting elderly patients where hyperventilation is a major factor, and Ost (1992) reports a single-case study of a 68-year-old patient with a phobia of choking where cognitive restructuring of the patient's catastrophic thoughts proved to be the key to the intervention's success.

Cognitive therapies for depression

There is a significant literature on the use of cognitive therapy with depressed elderly people (see reviews by Morris and Morris, 1991; Woods, 1992). Steuer and Hammen (1983) report four cases treated in their cognitive therapy groups, using techniques for behavioural activation, problem-solving and cognitive restructuring. Emery (1981) also provides some illustrative case histories; patients were helped to become aware of their automatic thoughts and to evaluate cognitive distortions and misattributions. The most systematic outcome data have been provided by Gallagher and Thompson and their colleagues, with their clinical approach well described by Thompson et al. (1986). Thompson et al. (1987) report a comparative study where depressed out-patients were assigned to either cognitive or behavioural or insight-oriented psychotherapy for sixteen to twenty individual sessions over four months. The behavioural therapy involved encouraging patients to increase their participation in activities they found pleasant, following Lewinsohn's model of depression (Lewinsohn, 1975). All three therapies seemed equally effective in reducing depression by the end of treatment, in comparison with a waiting-list control group. Although in an earlier study (Gallagher and Thompson, 1982), patients treated with insight-oriented therapy tended to be more depressed and to relapse more often during the one-year follow-up period, in the later study no differences emerged between treatment approaches at one- or two-year follow-ups (Gallagher-Thompson et al., 1990). These and other studies provide evidence that cognitive therapy, suitably fitted to the individual's abilities and needs, is a viable and potentially effective treatment for depressed elderly people. However, there is as yet no indication that it is superior to other treatment modalities, and further work is clearly required to identify the most effective components of each.

Grief therapy

Few applications have been reported (see Fasey, 1990; Parkes, 1992). Parkes (1980) concludes that supportive counselling can reduce the risk of breakdown in a high-risk bereaved elderly person to that in a low-risk case. Risk factors include an unsupportive family (or no family), an ambivalent relationship with the deceased, a particularly traumatic loss, and another concurrent major life-crisis. Although it is difficult to establish exactly when a grief reaction becomes 'abnormal', behavioural analyses have identified at least two patterns (Gauthier and Marshall, 1977). The first is where the normal grief reaction is avoided. There may be a 'conspiracy of silence', with family and friends 'protecting' the bereaved person by not mentioning the loss, and perhaps advising them not to attend the funeral. The distressing emotional response is avoided, at the cost of never adjusting to the loss. The second pattern is where the grief reaction is extended, where family and friends continue to give attention to the person's grief, giving them special treatment because of it, at a point when the person could take up old activities again or follow new directions. In this case therapy aims to help family and friends encourage this more appropriate behaviour, and to help the patient gradually start living once more. Where grief is avoided, guided mourning may be helpful (Hodgkinson, 1982). Here the person is helped to go through the emotional reaction in a safe environment, using mementoes or images of the dead person to elicit the grief. Woods and Britton (1985) illustrate the use of these methods. More recently, Kavanagh (1990) has described a cognitive-behavioural approach to grief therapy. This incorporates the previously mentioned strategies of controlled exposure to bereavement cues and gradual increasing of activities and roles, with an additional emphasis on appraisal of excessively negative cognitions and increasing the availability of social support. It should be emphasised that not every elderly person who is bereaved requires treatment, and it is becoming clear that there are more individual differences in bereavement reactions than was acknowledged in the past (Wortman and Silver, 1989; Stroebe and Stroebe, 1991). A flexible, individualised approach is necessary.

Involving the family in treatment

Even where no relationship problems are immediately apparent, it is always worth, with the patient's permission, seeing family members or significant others. They may be able to assist in the treatment plan, or place the person's problems in a broader context. It may well be that the problem does have a relationship component that would not emerge if only the patient were seen. Treating such problems involves sessions with the patient and family together, encouraging open communication of feelings, experiences and needs, joint problem-solving, and mutual reinforcement. Where the relationship problem is long-standing, goals may have to be limited. For example, it may be possible to encourage a couple to spend more time apart, even if no improvement in the quality of interaction is attainable. Some marital problems seem to arise from couples having to spend more time together following, say, the husband's retirement: this may upset a precarious equilibrium that had enabled the couple to tolerate each other previously.

With so many difficulties occurring in a family context, increasingly family therapy is being applied where the older person is the identified patient, based on systems theory approaches, and this is likely to be a major area of development in older people's mental health services (Benbow et al., 1990).

Therapy for sexual problems

In this area, above all others, the influences of myths about normal ageing, the expectations of current generations of elderly people and therapists' negative stereotypes combine to produce a situation where no help is usually either available or requested. Our knowledge of the potential for sexual functioning to continue into advanced old age is increasing (e.g. Corby and Solnick, 1980; Comfort, 1980; Baikie, 1984). An interaction with physical problems is evident. Thus diabetes may lead to reduced sexual function in older men; heart problems probably do not directly affect sexual performance, but may result in such anxiety about the effects of exertion that intercourse is avoided. Sound medical advice is desirable in these cases; psychological treatment may involve giving 'permission' to continue sexual activity (Comfort, 1980) or advising on strategies for continued sexual enjoyment where disability or circumstances prevent a previous pattern being maintained. Little is yet known of the efficacy of standard sex-therapy procedures with the elderly.

Other disorders

Some success has been reported in the treatment of insomnia (Friedman *et al.*, 1991; Morgan, 1987) using relaxation and stimulus-control techniques.

A few case reports suggest that paranoid delusions can be modified by giving feedback on misinterpretations and training the patient to substitute the paranoid ideas with rational thoughts (Hussian, 1981: 175; Carstensen and Fremouw, 1981).

Problem drinking may be less common in old age (Mishara and Kastenbaum, 1980; Seymour and Wattis, 1992), but does occur. Some continue earlier patterns of heavy drinking, others drink heavily in reaction to a loss. No specific treatment guidelines are available, but careful behavioural analysis may indicate a place for family work, grief therapy, or work on increasing social contacts.

Benzodiazepines continue to be widely prescribed for elderly people (Sullivan *et al.*, 1988; Higgitt, 1992), and often for extended periods, despite considerable concern regarding the long-term effects, in terms of dependence, and the side effects on older people in particular. Jones (1990/1991) showed that the provision of training in relaxation procedures, together with support and counselling, was associated with a doubling in the number of elderly patients in a primary care setting stopping or reducing this medication compared with a control group. There are also indications that relaxation therapy may be helpful for elderly people with tension headaches (Arena *et al.*, 1988).

Group work

Many of the above approaches can be, and have been, applied in a group setting. For example, Yost *et al.* (1986) describe cognitive therapy groups for elderly depressed people. Groups need to be fairly small (say, six or so) to help overcome hearing and communication difficulties. The leader may actively have to encourage members to listen to one another, to prevent one member from monopolising the group and others from remaining quiet. Group cohesion has to be developed, and this is often facilitated by life-review, sharing details of background and past experiences. The performance of homework tasks can be greatly facilitated by the group setting, by encouragement and praise from the peer group. An educational model is often appropriate, including didactic instruction, modelling and behavioural rehearsal of skills, with group members providing each other with appropriate feedback.

Conclusions

There is tremendous scope for cognitive-behaviour therapy in the treatment of affective disorders in older people. Many questions remain but, in general, approaches used with younger clients are often applicable. The most important special consideration may prove to be that elderly people show great individual differences.

Treatment plans must, then, be carefully individually tailored; standard treatment 'packages' are of little general use given the diversity of people and problems encountered. This diversity leads to an attractive feature of work with the elderly. The psychologist working with older people can take on a great variety of roles: neuropsychological assessment, support of relatives, advising and training care staff in the management of patients with dementia and their problems, cognitive therapy, family therapy, grief therapy . . . . The possibilities for improving the quality of life of the elderly and their supporters are challenging, and waiting to be grasped!

REFERENCES

Arena, J. G., Hightower, N. E. and Chong, G. C. (1988) 'Relaxation therapy for tension headache in the elderly: a prospective study', *Psychology and Aging* 3: 96–8.

Baikie, E. (1984) 'Sexuality and the elderly', in I. Hanley and J. Hodge (eds) *Psychological Approaches to the Care of the Elderly*, Beckenham, Kent: Croom Helm.

Baines, S., Saxby, P. and Ehlert, K. (1987) 'Reality orientation and reminiscence therapy: a controlled cross-over study of elderly confused people', *British Journal of Psychiatry* 151: 222–31.

Baltes, M. M. (1988) 'The etiology and maintenance of dependence in the elderly: three phases of operant research', *Behavior Therapy* 19: 301–19.

Barrowclough, C. and Fleming, I. (1986) 'Training direct care staff in goal-planning with elderly people', *Behavioural Psychotherapy* 14: 192–209.

Benbow, S., Egan, D., Marriott, A., Tregay, K., Walsh, S., Wells, J. and Wood, J. (1990) 'Using the family life cycle with later life families', *Journal of Family Therapy* 12: 321–40.

Bleathman, C. and Morton, I. (1992) 'Validation therapy: extracts from 20 groups with dementia sufferers', *Journal of Advanced Nursing* 17: 658–66.

Brane, G., Karlsson, I., Kihlgren, M. and Norberg, A. (1989), 'Integrity-promoting care of demented nursing home patients: psychological and biochemical changes', *International Journal of Geriatric Psychiatry* 4: 165–72.

Brodaty, H. (1992) 'Carers: training informal carers', in T. Arie (ed.) *Recent advances in psychogeriatrics – 2*, Edinburgh: Churchill Livingstone (163–171).

Brodaty, H. and Gresham, M. (1989) 'Effect of a training programme to reduce stress in carers of patients with dementia', *British Medical Journal* 299: 1375–9.

Burgio, L. D., Burgio, K. L., Engel, B. T. and Tice, L. M. (1986) 'Increasing distance and independence of ambulation in elderly nursing home residents', *Journal of Applied Behavior Analysis* 19: 357–66.

Burgio, L., Engel, B. T., McCormick, K., Hawkins, A. and Scheve, A. (1988) 'Behavioral treatment for urinary incontinence in elderly in-patients: initial attempts to modify prompting and toileting procedures', *Behavior Therapy* 19: 345–57.

Burton, M. (1980) 'Evaluation and change in a psychogeriatric ward through direct observation and feedback', *British Journal of Psychiatry* 137: 566–71.

Carstensen, L. L. and Erickson, R. (1986) 'Enhancing the social environments of elderly nursing home residents: are high rates of interaction enough?', *Journal of Applied Behavior Analysis* 19: 349–55.

Carstensen, L. L. and Fremouw, W. J. (1981) 'The demonstration of a behavioural intervention for late-life paranoia', *Gerontologist* 21: 329–33.

Challis, D., Chessum, R., Chesterman, J., Luckett, R. and Woods, R. (1988) 'Community care for the frail elderly: an urban experiment', *British Journal of Social Work* 18 (Supplement): 13–42.

Church, M. (1983) 'Psychological therapy with elderly people', *Bulletin of the British Psychological Society* 36: 110–12.

Church, M. (1986) 'Issues in psychological therapy with elderly people', in I. G. Hanley and M. Gilhooly (eds) *Psychological Therapies for the Elderly*, London: Croom Helm.

Comfort, A. (1980) 'Sexuality in late-life', in J. E. Birren and R. B. Sloane (eds) *Handbook of mental health and aging*, Englewood Cliffs, NJ: Prentice-Hall.

Corby, N. and Solnick, R. L. (1980) 'Psychosocial and physiological influences on sexuality in the older adult', in J. E. Birren and R. B. Sloane (eds) *Handbook of Mental Health and Aging*, Englewood Cliffs, NJ: Prentice-Hall.

Davies, A. D. M. (1981) 'Neither wife nor widow: an intervention with the wife of a chronically handicapped man during hospital visits', *Behaviour Research and Therapy* 19: 449–51.

Davies, A. D. M. (1982) 'Research with elderly people in long-term care: some social and organisational factors affecting psychological interventions', *Ageing and Society* 2: 285–98.

Davies, A. D. M. and Snaith, P. (1980a) 'Meal-time problems in a continuing-care hospital for the elderly', *Age and Ageing* 9: 100–105.

Davies, A. D. M. and Snaith, P. (1980b) 'The social behaviour of geriatric patients at meal-times: an observational and an intervention study', *Age and Ageing* 9: 93–9.

Dietch, J. T., Hewett, L. J. and Jones, S. (1989) 'Adverse effects of reality orientation', *Journal of American Geriatrics Society* 37: 974–76.

Emery, G. (1981) 'Cognitive therapy with the elderly', in G. Emery, S. D. Hollon and R. C. Bedrosian (eds) *New directions in cognitive therapy*, New York: Guilford.

Fasey, C. N. (1990) 'Grief in old age: a review of the literature', *International Journal of Geriatric Psychiatry* 5: 67–75.

Feehan, M., Knight, R. G. and Partridge, F. M. (1991) 'Cognitive complaint and test performance in elderly patients suffering depression or dementia', *International Journal of Geriatric Psychiatry* 6: 287–93.

Feil, N. (1989) *Validation: the Feil method, 2nd edn*, Cleveland, Ohio: Edward Feil Productions; Bicester: Winslow Press.

Friedman, L., Bliwise, D. L., Yesavage, J. A. and Salom, S. R. (1991) 'A preliminary study comparing sleep restriction and relaxation treatments for insomnia in older adults', *Journal of Gerontology* 46: P1–8.

Gaebler, H. C. and Hemsley, D. R. (1991) 'The assessment and short-term manipulation of affect in the severely demented', *Behavioural Psychotherapy* 19: 145–56.

Gallagher, D. and Thompson, L. (1982) 'Treatment of major depressive disorder in older adult out-patients with brief psychotherapies', *Psychotherapy: Theory, Research and Practice* 19: 482–90.

Gallagher-Thompson, D., Hanley-Peterson, P. and Thompson, L. (1990) 'Maintenance of gains versus relapse following brief psychotherapy for depression', *Journal of Consulting and Clinical Psychology* 58: 371–4.

Garrison, J. E. (1978) 'Stress management training for the elderly: a psychoeducational approach', *Journal of American Geriatrics Society* 26: 397–403.

Gauthier, J. and Marshall, W. L. (1977) 'Grief: a cognitive-behavioural analysis', *Cognitive Therapy and Research* 1: 39–44.

Gendron, C. E., Poitras, L. R. and Engels, M. L. *et al.* (1986) 'Skills training with supporters of the demented', *Journal of American Geriatrics Society* 34: 875–80.

Green, G. R., Linsk, N. L. and Pinkston, E. M. (1986) 'Modification of verbal behavior of the mentally impaired elderly by their spouses', *Journal of Applied Behavior Analysis* 19: 329–36.

Hanley, I. G. (1981) 'The use of signposts and active training to modify ward disorientation in elderly patients', *Journal of Behaviour Therapy and Experimental Psychiatry* 12: 241–7.

Haughie, E., Milne, D. and Elliott, V. (1992) 'An evaluation of companion dogs with elderly psychiatric patients', *Behavioural Psychotherapy* 20: 367–72.

Head, D., Portnoy, S. and Woods, R. T. (1990) 'The impact of reminiscence groups in two different settings', *International Journal of Geriatric Psychiatry* 5: 295–302.

Higgitt, A. (1992) 'Dependency on prescribed drugs', *Reviews in Clinical Gerontology* 2: 151–5.

Hinchliffe, A. C., Hyman, I., Blizard, B. and Livingston, G. (1992) 'The impact on carers of behavioural difficulties in dementia: a pilot study on management', *International Journal of Geriatric Psychiatry* 7: 579–83.

Hodge, J. (1984) 'Towards a behavioural analysis of dementia', in I. Hanley and J. Hodge (eds) *Psychological Approaches to the Care of the Elderly*, London: Croom Helm.

Hodgkinson, P. E. (1982) 'Abnormal grief: the problem of therapy', *British Journal of Medical Psychology* 55: 29–34.

Holden, U. P. (1988) 'Hyperventilation', in U. P. Holden (ed.) *Neuropsychology and Ageing: Definitions, Explanations and Practical Approaches*, London: Croom Helm (177–92).

Holden, U. P. and Woods, R. T. (1988) *Reality Orientation: Psychological Approaches to the 'Confused' Elderly*, 2nd edn, Edinburgh: Churchill Livingstone.

Hussian, R. A. (1981) *Geriatric Psychology: A Behavioral Perspective*, New York: Van Nostrand Reinhold.

Hussian, R. A. and Brown, D. C. (1987) 'Use of two-dimensional grid patterns to limit hazardous ambulation in demented patients', *Journal of Gerontology* 42: 558–60.

Ingstad, P. J. and Gotestam, K. G. (1987) 'Staff attitude changes after environmental changes on a ward for psychogeriatric patients', *International Journal of Social Psychiatry* 33: 237–44.

Jacoby, R. and Oppenheimer, C. (eds) (1991) *Psychiatry in the Elderly*, Oxford: Oxford University Press.

Jones, D. (1990/1991) 'Weaning elderly patients off psychotropic drugs in general practice: a randomised controlled trial', *Health Trends* 22: 164–6.

Kavanagh, D. J. (1990) 'Towards a cognitive-behavioural intervention for adult grief reactions', *British Journal of Psychiatry* 157: 373–83.

King, P. and Barrowclough, C. (1991) 'A clinical pilot study of cognitive-behavioural therapy for anxiety disorders in the elderly', *Behavioural Psychotherapy* 19: 337–45.

Kitwood, T. (1990) 'The dialectics of dementia: with particular reference to Alzheimer's disease', *Ageing and Society* 10: 177–96.

Kitwood, T. and Bredin, K. (1992) 'Towards a theory of dementia care: personhood and well-being', *Ageing and Society* 12: 269–87.

Knight, B. (1986) *Psychotherapy with Older Adults*, Beverly Hills: Sage.

Knight, B. (1992) *Case-histories in Psychotherapy with Older Adults*, Beverly Hills: Sage.

Lam, D. H. and Woods, R. T. (1986) 'Ward orientation training in dementia: a single-case study', *International Journal of Geriatric Psychiatry* 1: 145–7.

Lewinsohn, P. M. (1975) 'The behavioural study and treatment of depression', in M. Hersen, R. Eisler and B. Miller (eds) *Progress in Behavior Modification – 1*, London: Academic Press.

Lindesay, J., Briggs, K. and Murphy, E. (1989) 'The Guys/Age Concern survey: prevalence rates of cognitive impairment, depression and anxiety in an urban elderly community', *British Journal of Psychiatry* 155: 317–29.

Lindesay, J., Briggs, K., Lawes, M., Macdonald, A. and Herzberg, J. (1991) 'The domus philosophy: a comparative evaluation of a new approach to residential care for the demented elderly', *International Journal of Geriatric Psychiatry* 6: 727–36.

Lovett, S. and Gallagher, D. (1988) 'Psychoeducational interventions for family caregivers: preliminary efficacy data', *Behavior Therapy* 19: 321–30.

Manser, M. (1991) 'Design of environments', in R. Jacoby and C. Oppenheimer (eds) *Psychiatry in the elderly*, Oxford: Oxford University Press (550–70).

Marshall, M. (1992) 'Designing for confused old people', in T. Arie (ed.) *Recent Advances in Psychogeriatrics – 2*, Edinburgh: Churchill Livingstone (201–16).

Mayer, R. and Darby, S. (1991) 'Does a mirror deter wandering in demented older people?', *International Journal of Geriatric Psychiatry* 6: 607–9.

Melin, L. and Gotestam, K. (1981) 'The effects of rearranging ward routines on communication and eating behaviours of psychogeriatric patients', *Journal of Applied Behavior Analysis* 14: 47–51.

Miller, E. (1977) 'The management of dementia: a review of some possibilities', *British Journal of Social and Clinical Psychology* 16: 77–83.

Mishara, B. L. and Kastenbaum, R. (1980) *Alcohol and Old Age*, New York: Grune & Stratton.

Morgan, K. (1987) *Sleep and Ageing*, London: Croom Helm.

Morris, R. G. and Morris, L. W. (1991) 'Cognitive and behavioural approaches with the depressed elderly', *International Journal of Geriatric Psychiatry* 6: 407–13.

Morris, R. G., Morris, L. W. and Britton, P. G. (1988) 'Factors affecting the emotional well-being of the caregivers of dementia sufferers', *British Journal of Psychiatry* 153: 147–56.

Morton, I. and Bleathman, C. (1991) 'The effectiveness of validation therapy in dementia: a pilot study', *International Journal of Geriatric Psychiatry* 6: 327–30.

Murphy, E. (1982) 'Social origins of depression in old age', *British Journal of Psychiatry* 141: 135–42.

Netten, A. (1993) *A Positive Environment? Physical and Social Influences on People with Senile Dementia in Residential Care*, Aldershot: Ashgate.

Norberg, A., Melin, E. and Asplund, K. (1986) 'Reactions to music, touch and object presentation in the final stage of dementia: an exploratory study', *International Journal of Nursing Studies* 23: 315–23.

Norris, A. (1986) *Reminiscence*, London: Winslow Press.

Ost, L. (1992) 'Cognitive therapy in a case of choking phobia', *Behavioural Psychotherapy* 20: 79–84.

Parkes, C. M. (1980) 'Bereavement counselling', *British Medical Journal* 281: 3–6.

Parkes, C. M. (1992) 'Bereavement and mental health in the elderly', *Reviews in Clinical Gerontology* 2: 45–51.

Patterson, R. L. and Jackson, G. M. (1980) 'Behavior modification with the elderly', *Progress in Behavior Modification* 9: 205–39.

Pinkston, E. M., Linsk, N. L. and Young, R. N. (1988) 'Home-based behavioral family treatment of the impaired elderly', *Behavior Therapy* 19: 331–44.

Pitt, B. (1991) 'Depression in the general hospital setting', *International Journal of Geriatric Psychiatry* 6: 363–70.

Rabbitt, P. (1988) 'Social psychology, neurosciences and cognitive psychology need each other; (and gerontology needs all three of them)', *Psychologist* 12: 500–6.

Reeve, W. and Ivison, D. (1985) 'Use of environmental manipulation and classroom and modified informal reality orientation with institutionalized, confused elderly patients', *Age and Ageing* 14: 119–21.

Ritchie, K., Colvez, A., Ankri, J., Ledesert, B., Gardent, H. and Fontaine, A. (1992) 'The evaluation of long-term care for the dementing elderly: a comparative study of hospital and collective non-medical care in France', *International Journal of Geriatric Psychiatry* 7: 549–57.

Rona, D., Wylie, B. and Bellwood, S. (1986) 'Behaviour treatment of day-time incontinence in elderly male and female patients', *Behavioural Psychotherapy* 14: 13–20.

Schnelle, J. F., Traughber, B., Sowell, V. A., Newman, D. R., Petrilli, C. O. and Ory, M. (1989) 'Prompted voiding treatment of urinary incontinence in nursing home patients: a behavior management approach for nursing home staff', *Journal of American Geriatrics Society* 37: 1051–7.

Seymour, J. and Wattis, J. P. (1992) 'Alcohol abuse in the elderly', *Reviews in Clinical Gerontology* 2: 141–50.

Smyer, M. A., Zarit, S. H. and Qualls, S. H. (1990) 'Psychological intervention with the aging individual', in J. E. Birren and K. W. Schaie (eds) *Handbook of the Psychology of Aging*, San Diego: Academic Press (375–403).

Steuer, J. L. and Hammen, C. L. (1983) 'Cognitive-behavioural group therapy for the depressed elderly; issues and adaptations', *Cognitive Therapy and Research* 7: 285–96.

Stroebe, M. and Stroebe, W. (1991) 'Does "grief-work" work?', *Journal of Consulting and Clinical Psychology* 59: 479–82.

Sullivan, C. F., Copeland, J. R. M. and Dewey, M. E., Davidson, I. A., McWilliam, C., Saunders, P., Sharma, V. K. and Voruganti, L. N. P. (1988) 'Benzodiazepine usage amongst the elderly: findings of the Liverpool community survey', *International Journal of Geriatric Psychiatry* 3: 289–92.

Sutcliffe, C. and Larner, S. (1988) 'Counselling carers of the elderly at home: a preliminary study', *British Journal of Clinical Psychology* 27: 177–8.

Thompson, L. W., Davies, R., Gallagher, D. and Krantz, S. E. (1986) 'Cognitive therapy with older adults', in T. L. Brink (ed.) *Clinical Gerontology: A Guide to Assessment and Intervention*, New York: Haworth: (245–79).

Thompson, L. W., Gallagher, D. and Breckenridge, J. S. (1987) 'Comparative effectiveness of psychotherapies for depressed elders', *Journal of Consulting and Clinical Psychology* 55: 385–90.

Thornton, S. and Brotchie, J. (1987) 'Reminiscence: a critical review of the empirical literature', *British Journal of Clinical Psychology* 26: 93–111.

Thyer, B. A. (1981) 'Prolonged *in-vivo* exposure therapy with a 70-year-old woman', *Journal of Behaviour Therapy and Experimental Psychiatry* 12: 69–71.

Toseland, R. W. and Smith, G. C. (1990) 'Effectiveness of individual counselling by professional and peer helpers for family caregivers of the elderly', *Psychology and Aging* 5: 256–63.

Toseland, R. W., Rossiter, C. M. and Labrecque, M. S. (1989) 'The effectiveness of peer-led and professionally led groups to support family caregivers', *Gerontologist* 29: 465–71.

Wattis, J. and Church, M. (1986) *Practical Psychiatry of Old Age*, London: Croom Helm.

Williams, R., Reeve, W., Ivison, D. and Kavanagh, D. (1987) 'Use of environmental manipulation and modified informal reality orientation with institutionalized confused elderly subjects: a replication', *Age and Ageing* 16: 315–18.

Woods, R. T. (1982) 'The psychology of ageing: assessment of defects and their management', in R. Levy and F. Post (eds) *The Psychiatry of Late Life*, Oxford: Blackwell (68–113).

Woods, R. T. (1991) 'What can be learned from studies on reality orientation?' in G. Jones and B. Miesen (eds) *Care-giving in Dementia*, London: Routledge (121–36).

Woods, R. T. (1992) 'Psychological therapies and their efficacy', *Reviews in Clinical Gerontology* 2: 171–83.

Woods, R. T. and Britton, P. G. (1985) *Clinical Psychology with the Elderly*, London: Croom Helm/Chapman and Hall.

Woods, R. T., Portnoy, S., Head, D. and Jones, G. (1991) 'Reminiscence and life-review with persons with dementia: which way forward?' in G. Jones and B. Miesen (eds) *Care-giving in Dementia*, London: Routledge (137–61).

Wortman, C. B. and Silver, R. B. (1989) 'The myths of coping with loss', *Journal of Consulting and Clinical Psychology* 57: 349–57.

Yost, E. B., Beutler, L. E., Corbishley, M. A. and Allender, J. R. (1986) *Group Cognitive Therapy: A Treatment Approach for Depressed Older Adults*, Oxford: Pergamon Press.

Zarit, S. H., Anthony, C. R. and Boutselis, M. (1987) 'Interventions with care-givers of dementia patients: comparison of two approaches', *Psychology and Aging* 2: 225–32.

Chapter 23

Rehabilitation
Investigation

A. Lavender and F.N. Watts

INTRODUCTION

Rehabilitation is so widely misunderstood that this chapter must begin with an attempt to clarify the concept. Many practitioners clearly have an unduly circumscribed notion of what constitutes rehabilitation, confining it to certain clinical conditions, activities or settings. Within psychiatric disorders, on which this chapter will concentrate, rehabilitation is often thought of as only for people diagnosed schizophrenic, whereas in fact clients with conduct disorders also need help in restoring their social adjustment as well as in treatment of their specific presenting problem (Watts and Bennett, 1991). In terms of activities, rehabilitation is often identified with low-level manual work of a kind for which there is decreasing call in an advanced economy. Rehabilitation for other kinds of paid employment and for other social roles, such as domestic and family roles, is often poorly developed. In terms of setting, rehabilitation is often seen as appropriate only to long-stay mental hospitals, sometimes to the point of regarding the aim of rehabilitation as nothing more than the discharge of patients from hospital.

These connections with the old psychiatric hospitals and with resettlement have led to rehabilitation being a less fashionable descriptor as services have become more community-based (Lavender and Holloway, 1988). In addition, for many of the clients, the term rehabilitation is something of a misnomer in that habilitation, that is, helping people to function for the first time would more accurately describe the work. Nevertheless, the term still provides a good description of the kind of work that is important for people with long-term and severe cognitive and emotional problems.

Rehabilitation is most appropriately considered as a conceptual framework concerned with objectives. In general terms, the objective of rehabilitation is to help clients to optimise their social performance in as socially valued a context as possible. A variety of treatment methods can contribute to this, and there is no sharp boundary between treatment practices and rehabilitation practices. However, rehabilitation is characteristically concerned with achieving positive objectives of good social and emotional adjustment, in contrast with much 'treatment', which is concerned with reducing distress, disturbance or deviance. It is also concerned with social-interactional rather than intra-individual objectives. Whereas much 'treatment', from medication to psychoanalysis, focusses mainly on the individual, rehabilitation is concerned to help the individual to make a good social adjustment. This requires attention to the social environment as well as to the individual, and to the interaction between them.

The aim of rehabilitation is essentially one of 'normalisation', which involves judgements about the viability of the interaction between the individual and a particular social environment. This usually means avoiding extremes of both over-protection and under-protection. Many clients require some degree of 'shelter' from potential stresses, and need support in coping with them. Expectations of clients that take no account of these needs for shelter and support can be counter-productive and lead to an inherently unstable social adjustment. On the other hand, providing an unnecessarily sheltered environment gives people no opportunity to make the best use of their abilities, and may indeed lead to atrophy of these abilities and to a patronising style of care that undermines autonomy and dignity.

This notion of a comprehensive assessment is vital to the development of sensible and coherent intervention programmes. Within case management systems (Intagliata, 1982; Beardshaw and Towell, 1990) or the care programme approach (Department of Health, 1990), which are increasingly being integrated into services for people with long-term mental health problems, comprehensive assessment is a crucial component. In both traditional rehabilitation teams and the more recently formed community teams which are attempting to implement case management/care programming, clinical psychologists are often in a position to take a lead role in helping such teams to formulate individual programmes based on a comprehensive assessment. The general skills in the analysis and use of objective information that a psychologist contributes to a clinical team are often at least as valuable as expertise in any specific therapeutic interventions.

ASSESSMENT OF THE CONTEXT OF REHABILITATION

Before considering the assessment of the individual, attention needs to be given to the context in which rehabilitation is to take place. The kind of environment in which clients live (or which they enter for day-time activities) can markedly hinder or facilitate rehabilitation. Three aspects will be considered: the physical environment, the management practices adopted, and external contacts (Lavender, 1985). Though it is in long-term residential environments, such as the remaining long-stay hospital wards, that environments unconducive to rehabilitation are most likely to be found, they do arise in other community-based contexts. Individuals can become as institutionalised in a small residential setting or a family home as in a psychiatric hospital.

Physical environment

The quality of the physical environment and the amenities provided can facilitate or impede progress towards rehabilitation (Holahan, 1976). The most careful approach to the assessment of the physical environment of wards so far developed is that of Morris (1969), which consisted of four measures. The first was a simple measure of overcrowding based on the number of beds per ward. The others were measures of the homeliness and comfort of the dormitories and the day areas, the amenities available in the dormitories and day areas, and the adequacy of washing and toilet facilities. Raynes *et al.* (1979) developed a related 'Index of the Physical Environment' and Lavender (1984), as part of the Model Standards Questionnaire, developed a similar scale to measure the quality of the physical environment. More recently Leiper *et al.* (1992a; b) have developed the QUARTZ system, which includes a schedule assessing the physical environment of residential and day-care settings and which draws on both the Model Standards Questionnaires and the writings on social role valorisation (Wolfensberger, 1982).

Management practices

A series of research studies has developed measures of the management practices which are an important part of the social environment in rehabilitation units. These include the study of three psychiatric hospitals by Wing and Brown (1970), the study of institutions for handicapped children by King *et al.* (1971), the study of institutions for mentally handicapped adults by Raynes *et al.* (1979), the study of psychiatric day-centres in the community by Shepherd and Richardson (1979), the study of sheltered care facilities by Segal and Moyles (1979), the study of a hospital-hostel by Wing (1982) and the study of long-stay psychiatric hospital wards by Lavender (1987). There is substantial overlap in the practices that have been assessed in these studies. These can be classified in terms of three dimensions (Lavender, 1985). First, autonomy–restrictiveness, that is, the extent to which clients are allowed to take decisions for themselves. Second, personalisation–depersonalisation, that is, the extent to which individuals have personal possessions and privacy. Finally, social integration–segregation, that is, the extent to which the staff's and clients' worlds are separated (for example, whether activities and facilities are shared and uniforms worn). Clifford and Wolfson (1989) have attempted to build on these ideas and produce a measure, FACE, which provides ratings across a variety of similar dimensions as a means of assessing the quality and appropriateness of care.

Outside contact

A third important factor in rehabilitation is the extent to which patients in the unit have outside contact. This is likely to be a problem mainly in residential settings, but not exclusively so. Patients living with their families in the community can be equally cut off from outside contact. Various measures of contact that residents have with the community have been developed including those of Morris (1969), Raynes *et al.* (1979), Lavender (1984) and Clifford *et al.* (1989). There are several forms of contact to be considered, including indirect contact by letter or telephone (both to and from the client), visits to the client/resident by relatives, friends or volunteers, and visits by the client/resident to places and people in the surrounding community. Constraints on contact should also be assessed, including restricted visiting hours, supervision of mail and cumbersome procedures for negotiating leave.

It is useful to be able to assess these various aspects of the quality of care offered in particular settings in a single comprehensive measure. Lavender (1984) developed such a measure, the Model Standards Questionnaire, for this purpose within psychiatric hospitals. Clifford *et al.* (1989) and Leiper *et al.* (1992a; b) extending this earlier work, have produced a more comprehensive measure as part of a quality assurance system designed to improve the quality of care within a larger range of mental health settings. It is important to remember that, for individuals, the quality of care offered is dependent on how well the total range of contexts provide adequate opportunities for role performance and social support that is covered rather than the quality of care offered by individual units.

ASSESSMENT OF SOCIAL FUNCTIONING

It is important to make a comprehensive assessment of clients' capacity for social functioning. As a preliminary to this it is prudent to assess physical and psychological health. Physical health is especially important in the most disabled clients who may have been neglected in long-term hospitals or, if living in the community, may not make proper use of the health services. Many of the more basic physical health functions, such as poor eyesight or hearing, dental problems, birth-control problems, menstrual problems and weight problems, can be screened for by any member of the rehabilitation team. The relevant experts become involved in the consequent action (for instance, an appointment with the optician for a patient who is seriously short-sighted but who has never had spectacles). Physical problems of this kind obviously need to be identified and remedied if any progress with rehabilitation is to be made.

There are many aspects of psychological health that are relevant to rehabilitation. Hall (1980) provided a convenient review of rating scales for the assessment of long-term patients, many of which concentrate primarily on psychological disturbance rather than social functioning. The assessment of anxiety, aggression and sexual behaviour do not need to be considered here, except to make the point that what matters as far as rehabilitation is concerned is how far problems in these areas affect people's capacity to function in social roles. It is striking how well some people can function despite serious psychological problems. The final part of the health assessment concerns a client's attitude to his or her physical and mental health. Clients' preoccupations with psychological or physical symptoms, convictions that 'illness' prevents their making any progress in rehabilitation, or excessive anxieties about relapse, all create obstacles to rehabilitation.

A number of well-developed scales now exist for systematically assessing social functioning. These include the REHAB scale (Baker and Hall, 1983), the Community Placement Questionnaire and Problems Questionnaire (Clifford, 1986; 1987) and the Functional Performance Record (Mulhall, 1990). Each of these assessment measures has a slightly different purpose, some are concerned with assessing needs for services, others with assessing needs for individual programmes, and some claim to do both. However, whether carrying out informal or formal assessments of individuals, it is important to include minimally the following functional capacities:

1 Personal memory and orientation (knowing names of parents and relatives, knowing birthdays, personal memory of childhood and adult life)
2 Literacy and numeracy (reading, writing, spelling, arithmetic, understanding money, knowing current prices)
3 Self-care (personal hygiene, washing, care of clothing, care of personal health, care of appearance, care and cutting of hair, use of toilet, basic first aid)
4 Home-management skills (cooking, shopping, cleaning, sewing, simple house repairs, budgeting, use of appliances, household laundry, use of gas, electricity and water services)
5 Use of community facilities (public transport, social security, shops, entertainment, financial services and health services)
6 Employment skills (job search, application and interview, occupational skills and abilities).

In addition, clients' capacities for social interaction and making effective social relationships need to be assessed. When any particular social role is under consideration (for example, as an employee, spouse or parent) the relevant role functions need to be assessed. A thorough social history is a valuable starting point, noting, for example, the variety of social roles that have been assumed over the years, what factors have led to these being successful, and whether the social history represents an orderly developmental sequence in which experience gained in one context has been utilised in another. Watts and Bennett (1977) have provided some illustrative information for employment on the predictive validity of summary indices derived from a social history. For example, it is more important in predicting stable resettlement in work to know how much stable employment a person has had than to know whether or not he or she has also had periods of doing casual jobs. Changes in type of work are more significant than changes of job, especially in those areas where job changing is commonplace.

The social history needs to be supplemented by careful observation of current social functioning. In interpreting observational data, it is important to keep the conceptual distinction between competence and performance clearly in mind. 'Competence' here means whether people have in their repertoire of skills those that are needed to function in a particular social role; 'performance', whether in practice people deploy these skills appropriately to attain a satisfactory level of functioning. To give an example, a client living alone may have it within his competence to change his clothes and bed-linen, which are relatively simple manual skills. However, when actually in a bed-sitter, he may not perform these skills adequately because he fails to remember, because he lacks discretion about how often they should be changed, or because he does not think it matters.

Performance thus involves skills, judgements and values that are not involved in basic competence in the component skills. It is usually necessary in a social role to have:

1 a capacity for taking the viewpoint of another person, 'decentering' in Piagetian terminology, so that it is possible to discern other people's expectations and to anticipate other people's reactions to alternative lines of conduct
2 an ability to relate immediate actions to long-term consequences and to take actions that will lead only to delayed 'gratification'
3 problem-solving skills for generating a variety of possible ways of reaching an objective, and choosing the most appropriate one.

There are also aspects of social performance that involve values, such as acceptance of the desirability of reciprocity in relationships (in other words, that there is 'trade-off' in a relationship between what people do for each other) and of the appropriateness of accepting obligations to other people and of regarding oneself as accountable for one's actions (Phillips, 1968).

Motivation for a social role also interacts with competence in determining performance. Structured interviews are probably the best way of assessing motivation, as Griffiths (1974) has shown for motivation for employment. In assessing motivation it is helpful to try to identify the potential sources of both satisfaction and dissatisfaction (Watts, 1983a). Motivation should not be regarded as a stable personality trait, but depends on perceptions of potential satisfactions and dissatisfactions and of personal and social resources. The enhanced social status and self-esteem with social roles, especially employment, is probably the most powerful source of motivation. This has to be balanced against the stresses they create for those who are emotionally vulnerable. Of course, emotional stresses can be reduced by the acquisition of confidence and coping skills (Pearlin and Schooler, 1978), thus changing the net balance of motivation.

Competence can be assessed in any setting where the facilities exist for the exercise of the skill being assessed. Thus competence in cooking can be assessed in any kitchen. However, people's exercise of their cooking skills in feeding themselves adequately can only be assessed in a setting where they are left to do this relatively autonomously, such as the client's home. Employment skills similarly need to be assessed in a realistic work setting (Pilling, 1991). In general, assessments of performance should be made in the setting where the client will be required to use the skill. The assessments need to be made by people who are aware of the standards of performance required. Many rating skills which yield useful data in the hands of experienced raters, such as Griffith's scale for work behaviour (Griffiths, 1973), are not well enough anchored for use by naive raters. However, even where assessments are made in a realistic setting, caution must still be exercised in generalising about performance from one setting to another. In the natural social environment, people are seldom required to exercise their competence completely autonomously. They usually have support in the form of advice or encouragement, or have people who will perform tasks for them from time to time. Exactly what support is available may make a crucial difference to the level of performance, and one of the objectives of the assessment should be to identify what minimal level of support is necessary for adequate performance. This will have important implications for the kind of setting in which the patient is resettled.

Acceptable performance in a normal social context also involves general capacities for social behaviour and role relationships that are at least as important as specific task competence. For example, Watts (1978) showed that relationships with co-workers in an occupational rehabilitation unit was the best predictor of subsequent re-employment. Response to supervision and enthusiasm showed some predictive power, especially in psychotic patients. Task performance failed to predict at all. The contribution of social behaviour to acceptable domestic performance is also important. Patients living in bed-sitters will make unacceptable tenants if their social interaction with the landlady is unacceptable, however good their household skills may be.

Finally, there are specific skills involved in the acquisition of roles that may be different from those required for their performance. For employment, inappropriate behaviour at interview (Searls et al., 1971) is closely related to failing to obtain employment. What employers look for is honesty and openness, information about job skills, personal adaptability, information about previous jobs, and an ability to respond to the interviewer's questions (Barbee and Kiel, 1973). It is also relevant to assess what connections with the world of employment the client has, because hearing about jobs through personal contacts is the most common precursor of getting a job (Jones and Azrin, 1973). In domestic roles, similar skills in self-presentation and relevant contacts will be equally important, but have been less well investigated (Parry, 1991).

SOCIAL INTEGRATION AND SUPPORT

Finally, an assessment needs to be made of the breadth of patients' social integration and support (MacCarthy, 1988). There is a wealth of evidence that patients with good social integration have a more favourable outcome following an episode of psychological disturbance; for example, people diagnosed as schizophrenic with a relatively good record of social adjustment have a better outcome in terms of early discharge from hospital and successful resettlement in the community (Watts, 1983b). Whilst it has been long recognised that people, in particular relatives, are sources of considerable social support which affect subsequent relapse (Vaughn and Leff, 1976), there is little research investigating families' needs in the long term (Atkinson, 1986; Shepherd, 1991).

Normally, social integration involves a considerable range of contacts which tend to fall into separate but partly interconnected clusters. Pattison *et al.* (1975) found that the number of primary social contacts in the normal population averages at between twenty and thirty. For neurotic patients it is ten to twenty but for psychotic patients, only four to five. Slightly different definitions of primary contacts have been used by different workers, but it is convenient to regard as such all the relatives, friends, neighbours and colleagues named by an individual as being people with whom he or she is in regular contact. The Interview Schedule for Social Interaction being developed by Henderson and his colleagues (e.g. Henderson and Duncan-Jones, 1982) covers the number of people currently available in the categories of: (1) those affectionately close, (2) friends, (3) work associates, and (4) casual contacts. Henderson's Interview Schedule is one of a variety of interview schedules available for the assessment of the community adjustment of psychiatric patients (Weissman, 1975). In addition to the number of contacts, it is helpful to look at the separate dimensions of the depth of relationships and the proportion of time spent in social contact (Phillips, 1968).

The functions served by different kinds of social contact are diverse. Weiss (1974) has suggested the following classification, which has been adopted in Henderson's Interview Schedule:

1 Attachment (giving a sense of security and place in society)
2 Social integration (people with whom concerns are shared and with whom services can be exchanged in the area for common interest)
3 Opportunities for nurturance of others
4 Reassurance of worth (role relationships with family or work colleagues that give a sense of being valued)
5 A sense of a reliable alliance (usually from kin)
6 Obtaining of guidance (access to a trusted mentor when under stress)

This classification, though useful, is only one of many that could be devised. For example, it does not explicitly include the concept of a 'confidant' as it has been used in Brown and Harris's work on vulnerability to depression (Brown and Harris, 1978).

Two general points need to be remembered in any assessment of how far such functions are met for individual clients. One is that there are considerable individual differences in the extent of these various needs. This means it is important to look not just at the objective extent of social support in these various categories, but at how satisfied individuals are with what is available to them. Henderson *et al.* (1978) have found that people diagnosed as neurotic often feel that their needs are unmet even where they have a substantial primary network. The second general point concerns the extent to which one aspect of social integration can substitute for another. There is evidence that different sources of support fulfil different functions (see Bennett and Morris, 1983, for a review). For example, neighbours are used for immediate help of a very limited kind, whereas kin are used for more substantial help, which may take longer to obtain but which is more prolonged (MacCarthy, 1988).

There is also a distinction, which is particularly important for rehabilitation, between social contacts providing opportunities for the exercise of role responsibilities (3 and 4 in Weiss's framework) and those providing opportunities of obtaining help. For some people, employment is important in providing an opportunity for the discharge of responsibilities. However, as the opportunities for open employment decline, other opportunities for role performance, through constructive voluntary activities, contributions to family or neighbourhood welfare, or sheltered employment, become increasingly important as alternatives (Holloway, 1988). There are, of course, many opportunities for role responsibilities in the home, and it is important to know who does what, how this particular pattern of responsibilities arose, what scope for change there is, and how disagreements in this area are resolved (Shepherd, 1983). Where the family expectations of the client are low, performance also tends to be low (e.g. Freeman and Simmons, 1963); though there may in some cases be quite pronounced limitations to what clients can do for themselves, and they may need to be 'sheltered' from expectations that they cannot meet. It is most important if clients are to maintain their independence and not become unnecessarily disabled that they should be encouraged to do as much as possible.

Interestingly, high expectations do not seem to increase the risk of a return of psychological disturbance so much as intense emotional involvement which has been described as a high level of expressed emotion (MacCarthy, 1988). The most influential single aspect of the latter is the number of critical comments made by relatives about the patient, the criteria being based partly on context and partly on vocal tone (Kuipers, 1979). Critical comments are related to the risk of relapse in both schizophrenic and depressed patients, though the mechanism of the effect is probably different in the two cases. In schizophrenia, it is also important to consider how much contact there is between the patient and the family, as this interacts with the level of criticism (Vaughn and Leff, 1976). Where the level of criticism is high, it is particularly important to make arrangements that will keep the amount of contact down to moderate levels.

In considering the suitability of an environment, the general criteria are whether it will meet the client's needs and aspirations, will lead to a stable adjustment that is not at risk of breaking down, and will provide no more than the minimum shelter and support beyond what would normally be available. If there are gaps in the naturally occurring support system, consideration needs to be given to how these can be remedied. Sometimes interventions with the family can result in its providing an increased level of support (MacCarthy, 1988). However, there will be many patients for whom there is no prospect of the family or social network providing the necessary support. In these cases it will be necessary to arrange for the rehabilitation services to provide supplementary or secondary support, though this clearly cannot wholly fulfil the functions of natural support systems (Shepherd, 1991). Both in the interests of efficient service-delivery and of maintaining the client's independence, supplementary support should be no more extensive than is necessary. Members of rehabilitation or community care teams need to know what supplementary facilities are available in the community and, when relevant, within the hospital. A network of facilities is essential to provide accommodation with the necessary level of supervision for those who cannot live independently (Garety, 1988), opportunities for sheltered employment or other day activities for those who cannot achieve open employment (Pilling, 1988), and secondary social support to supplement the primary social network (Shepherd, 1991).

MONITORING OF CHANGE

Finally, in rehabilitation, as in other areas, it is important to have ways of monitoring whether interventions designed to improve patients' social adjustment have the effect intended. Such consideration needs to be taken into account at the assessment stage in order that measures can be used which will make such evaluations possible. A range of assessment measures exist, including formal and standardised rating scales assessing clients' behaviour (e.g. Baker and Hall, 1983; Mulhall, 1990), measures assessing clients' quality of life (Rolleston, 1990), and more qualitative measures which remain underdeveloped in the area of rehabilitation (Watts, 1989). Usually, choosing an appropriate measure is dependent on the individual problems of the client and the unique circumstances that exist in the rehabilitation setting(s).

In the case of individual clients, Shepherd (1983) recommends the use of a simple but flexible goal-attainment scaling assessment procedure for this purpose. For example, five levels of outcome can be formulated in advance, ranging from the 'most unfavourable treatment outcome thought likely' to the 'best anticipated treatment success'. The various levels usually need to be developed separately for each individual and for each outcome variable. The degree of change achieved can then be related to the scale points agreed at the start of rehabilitation. The method has been used successfully by Pilling (1988) and provides an attractive standard approach to the quantification of change that can be applied to a heterogeneous group of patients.

CONCLUSION

Rehabilitation assessments need to be made of both the individual and the environment. The environmental assessments required range from assessments of rehabilitation units themselves to assessments of the natural community. The assessments of individuals that are needed range from basic capacities for relatively independent living to the higher-level capacities required for social roles. In neither case are there many satisfactory standard assessment techniques. The clinical psychologist needs rather to operate with a sufficient conceptual grasp both of rehabilitation, to know what needs to be assessed, and of the fundamentals of psychological assessment, to be able to generate satisfactory procedures that are applicable in local circumstances.

REFERENCES

Atkinson, J. M. (1986) *Schizophrenia at Home: A Guide to Helping the Family*, London: Croom Helm.

Baker, R. and Hall, J. N. (1983) *REHAB: Rehabilitation Evaluation. Hall and Baker*, Aberdeen: Vine Publishing.

Barbee, J. R. and Kiel, E. C. (1973) 'Experimental techniques of job interview training for the disadvantaged: videotape feedback, behaviour modification and microcounselling', *Journal of Applied Psychology* 58: 209–13.

Beardshaw, V. and Towell, D. (1990) *Assessment and Case Management: Implications for the Implementation of Caring for People*, Kings Fund Institute Briefing Paper No. 10, London: Kings Fund.

Bennett, D. H. and Morris, I. (1983) 'Support and rehabilitation', in F. N. Watts and D. H. Bennett (eds) *Theory and Practice of Psychiatric Rehabilitation*, Chichester: Wiley.

Brown, G. W. and Harris, T. (1978) *Social Origins of Depression: A Study of Psychiatric Disorder in Women*, London: Tavistock.

Clifford, P. (1986) *Community Placement Questionnaire*, London: National Unit for Psychiatric Research and Development.

Clifford, P. (1987) *Problems Questionnaire*, London: National Unit for Psychiatric Research and Development.

Clifford, P. and Wolfson, P. (1989) 'FACE: a functional assessment of care environments', unpublished paper and questionnaire, National Unit for Psychiatric Research and Development, London.

Clifford, P., Leiper, R., Lavender, A. and Pilling, S. (1989) *Assuring Quality in Mental Health Services: The QUARTZ System*, London: Free Association Press.

Department of Health (1990) *Health and Social Services Department. Caring for people, the Care Programme Approach for people with a mental illness referred to the specialist psychiatric services*, HC(90)23/LASSC(90)11, Lancashire: DOH.

Freeman, H. E. and Simmons, O. G. (1963) *The Mental Patient Comes Home*, New York: Wiley.

Garety, P. (1988) 'Housing', in A. Lavender and F. Holloway (eds) *Community Care in Practice*, Chichester: Wiley.

Griffiths, R. D. P. (1973) 'A standardised assessment of the work behaviour of psychiatric patients', *British Journal of Psychiatry* 123: 403–8.

Griffiths, R. D. P. (1974) 'Rehabilitation of chronic psychiatric patients: an assessment of their psychological handicap, an evaluation of the effectiveness of rehabilitation and observations of the factors which predict outcome', *Psychological Medicine* 4: 316–25.

Hall, J. N. (1980) 'Ward rating scales for long-stay patients: a review', *Psychological Medicine* 10: 277–88.

Henderson, S. and Duncan-Jones, P. (1982) *Neurosis and the Social Environment*, London: Academic Press.

Henderson, S., Duncan-Jones, P., McAuley, H. and Ritchie (1978) 'The patients' primary group', *British Journal of Psychiatry* 132: 74–86.

Holahan, C. J. (1976) 'Environmental change in a psychiatric setting; a social systems analysis', *Human Relations* 29: 153–66.

Holloway, F. (1988) 'Day care and community support', in A. Lavender and F. Holloway (eds) *Community Care in Practice: Services for the Continuing Care Client*, Chichester: Wiley.

Intagliata, J. (1982) 'Improving the Quality of Community Care for the Chronically Mentally Disabled: The Role of Case Management', *Schizophrenia Bulletin* 8: 655–74.

Jones, R. J. and Azrin, N. H. (1973) 'An experimental application of a social reinforcement approach to the problem of job-finding', *Journal of Applied Behaviour Analysis* 6: 345–53.

King, R. D., Raynes, N. V. and Tizard, J. (1971) *Patterns of Residential Care*, London: Routledge and Kegan Paul.

Kuipers, L. (1979) 'Expressed emotion: a review', *British Journal of Social and Clinical Psychology* 18: 237–43.

Lam, D. H. (1991) 'Psychosocial family intervention in shizophrenia: a review of empirical studies', *Psychological Medicine* 21: 423–41.

Lavender, A. (1984) *Evaluation in Settings for the Long Term Psychologically Handicapped*, London: Kings College Hospital Medical School, University of London.

Lavender, A. (1985) 'Quality of care and staff practices in long term settings', in F. N. Watts (ed.) *New Developments in Clinical Psychology*, Leicester: BPS/Wiley.

Lavender, A. (1987) 'Improving the quality of care on psychiatric hospital rehabilitation wards', *British Journal of Psychiatry* 150: 476–81.

Lavender, A. and Holloway, F. (1988) 'An Introduction', in A. Lavender and F. Holloway (eds) *Community Care in Practice: Services for the Continuing Care Client*, Chichester: Wiley.

Leiper, R., Lavender, A., Pilling, S. and Clifford, P. (1992a) *Structures for the Quality Review of Mental Health Settings: The QUARTZ Schedules*, Brighton: Pavilion.

Leiper, R., Pilling, S. and Lavender, A. (1992b) *Implementing a Quality Review System: The QUARTZ Manuals*, Brighton: Pavilion.

MacCarthy, B. (1988) 'The Role of Relatives', in A. Lavender and F. Holloway (eds) *Community Care in Practice: Services for the Continuing Care Client*, Chichester: Wiley.

Morris, P. (1969) *Put Away: A Sociological Study of Institutions for the Mentally Retarded*, London: Routledge & Kegan Paul.

Mullhall, D. (1990) *Functional Performance Record*, London: NFER.

Parry, G. (1991) 'Domestic roles', in F. N. Watts and D. H. Bennett (eds) *Theory and Practice of Psychiatric Rehabilitation, 2nd edn*, Chichester: Wiley.

Pattison, E. M., Defrancisco, D., Wood, P., Frazier, H. and Crowder, J. (1975) 'A psychosocial kinship model for family therapy', *American Journal of Psychiatry* 132: 1246–51.

Pearlin, L. I. and Schooler, C. (1978) 'The structure of coping', *Journal of Health and Social Behaviour* 19: 2–21.

Phillips, L. (1968) *Human Adaption and its Failures*, New York: Academic Press.

Pilling, S. (1988) 'Work and the continuing care client', in A. Lavender and F. Holloway (eds) *Community Care in Practice*, Chichester: Wiley.

Pilling, S. (1991) *Rehabilitation and Community Care*, London: Routledge.

Raynes, N. V., Pratt, M. W. and Roses, S. (1979) *Organisational Structure and the Care of the Mentally Retarded*, London: Croom Helm.

Rolleston, M. (1990) 'Controlled Study of Quality of Life – Long Term Patients Resettled in the Community', unpublished thesis submitted in partial fulfilment of the BPS Diploma in Clinical Psychology, Leicester.

Searls, D. J., Wilson, L. T. and Miskimins, R. W. (1971) 'Development of a measure of unemployability among restored psychiatric patients', *Journal of Applied Psychology* 55: 223–5.

Segal, S. P. and Moyles, E. W. (1979) 'Management style and institutional dependency in sheltered care', *Social Psychiatry* 14: 159–65.

Shepherd, G. W. (1983) 'Planning the rehabilitation of the individual', in F. N. Watts and D. H. Bennett (eds) *Theory and Practice of Psychiatric Rehabilitation*, Chichester: Wiley.

Shepherd, G. W. (1988) 'Evaluation and service planning', in A. Lavender and F. Holloway (eds) *Community Care in Practice: Services for the Continuing Care Client*, Chichester: Wiley.

Shepherd, G. W. (1991) 'Foreword: Psychiatric rehabilitation for the 1990s', in F. N. Watts and D. H. Bennett (eds) *Theory and Practice of Psychiatric Rehabilitation*, 2nd edn, Chichester: Wiley.

Shepherd, G., Holloway, F. and Richardson, A. (1979) 'Organisation and interaction in psychiatric day centres', *Psychological Medicine* 9: 573–9.

Vaughn, C. and Leff, J. P. (1976) 'The influence of family and social factors on the course of psychiatric illness', *British Journal of Psychiatry* 129: 125–37.

Watts, F. N. (1978) 'A study of work behaviour in a psychiatric rehabilitation unit', *British Journal of Social and Clinical Psychology* 17: 85–92.

Watts, F. N. (1983a) 'Employment', in F. N. Watts and D. H. Bennett (eds) *Theory and Practice of Psychiatric Rehabilitation*, Chichester: Wiley.

Watts, F. N. (1983b) 'Socialisation and social integration', in F. N. Watts and D. H. Bennett (eds) *Theory and Practice of Psychiatric Rehabilitation*, Chichester: Wiley.

Watts, F. N. (1989) 'Qualitative research', in F. N. Watts and G. Parry (eds) *Behavioural and Mental Health Research: A Handbook of Skills and Methods*, London: Erlbaum.

Watts, F. N. and Bennett, D. H. (1977) 'Previous occupational stability as a predictor of employment after psychiatric rehabilitation', *Psychological medicine* 7: 709–12.

Watts, F. N. and Bennett, D.H. (1991) 'Neurotic, affective an conduct disorders', in F. N. Watts and D. H. Bennett (eds) *Theory and Practice of Psychiatric Rehabilitation*, 2nd edn, Chichester: Wiley.

Weiss, R. S. (1974) 'The provision of social relations', in Z. Rubin (ed.) *Doing Unto Others*, Englewood Cliffs, NJ: Prentice-Hall.

Weissman, M. M. (1975) 'The assessment of social adjustment: a review of scales', *Archives of General Psychiatry* 32: 357–65.

Wing, J. K. (1982) 'Long-term community care; experience in a London borough', *Psychological Medicine*, Monograph Supplement 2.

Wing, J. K. and Brown, G. W. (1970) *Institutionalism and Schizophrenia: A Comparative Study of Three Mental Hospitals, 1960–1968*, Cambridge: Cambridge University Press.

Wolfensberger, W. (1982) *The Principle of Normalisation in Human Services*, Toronto: National Institute of Mental Retardation.

Chapter 24

Rehabilitation

Intervention

A. Lavender and F.N. Watts

INTRODUCTION

Psychological interventions in rehabilitation can be divided into those in which
the psychologist works directly with the individual, and those in which he or she
works with the network of people who are in more regular contact with the client
(whether the ward staff and rehabilitation team, or the client's family and social
network). Both are important. In Chapter 23 we proposed that the objective of
rehabilitation is to enable people to make the best use of their abilities in as
valued a social context as possible. This involves equipping clients to function at
their optimum level, either by intervening directly with individuals or by providing training and support for those who interact with them. It is also important
to consider whether the social environments in which a client is currently
operating are appropriate or whether alternatives need to be found.

The settings in which rehabilitation is carried out are extremely varied, in
terms of both location (hospital/community) and function (day activities/
residential). Some provide training in specific skills, others seek to achieve their
goals through the general way in which the unit is conducted and staff interact
with patients. In this brief chapter we consider first how units, usually residential
ones, can create the conditions in which the capacity for normal living can be
re-acquired or acquired for the first time. Next we turn to units designed to
provide training for some specific social role. We have deliberately not made a
sharp distinction here between occupational programmes and domestic or
socialisation programmes, as we want to bring out the common principles which
apply to both. Lastly we look at how the community needs to be involved in
rehabilitation.

THE SOCIAL ENVIRONMENT OF REHABILITATION

Crucial to any rehabilitation environment is the way in which clients are treated
by those around them. If they are provided with a merely custodial pattern of
care, with no encouragement of autonomy, independence and the exercise of
skills, no progress towards habilitation or rehabilitation can be expected. Though

custodial care is probably still most common in the long-stay wards of psychiatric hospitals, it can be found in other community settings, including hostels, day-centres and even in family homes (Lamb, 1982). This is an important point to understand at the present time when many of the psychiatric hospitals have closed or are in the process of closing and returning 'patients to the community'. Such a move is of little value if the same 'institutionalising' pattern of care is reproduced in a different setting. The practices adopted in a setting which hopes to have a rehabilitative function are as important as where it is situated.

There are two key issues in the modification of staff practices in rehabilitation settings. One relates to the kind of practices that are regarded as conducive to rehabilitation. The other issue, which cuts across it, relates to the methods by which staff practices can best be modified.

With regard to the first issue, the following examples illustrate the kind of staff practices that have been regarded as desirable for rehabilitation:

1 The use of operant programmes which provide patients with rewards for rehabilitation targets, such as self-care skills (e.g. washing and dressing), home-management skills or social interaction skills. Commonly, such operant programmes are run concurrently for all the clients on the ward, with tokens being used as the immediate reward. The extensive research evidence on token-economy (Kazdin, 1977) and social-learning programmes (Paul and Lentz, 1978) shows that useful improvements in target behaviours are often achieved, especially in self-care skills.

2 The introduction of 'therapeutic community' principles of democratic decision-making and personal accountability, in which regular general meetings of all staff and patients on the unit are the key element (Jones, 1968). Often this is also incidentally accompanied by a general increase in patient activities.

3 Modification of settings' practices to permit greater scope for autonomous, individual behaviour and greater extra-unit activities. Procedures for analysing unit practices were described in Chapter 23. These provide a framework within which staff can be given feedback on their current practices to help them to identify which are likely to be unconducive to rehabilitation. Specific targets for change in staff practices can thus be identified. Lavender (1987) has demonstrated the efficacy of such an approach.

It would be attractive to be able to formulate general conclusions about the relative effectiveness of these approaches, but for various reasons this is not possible. One problem is that it is difficult to find relatively pure exemplifications of them. The introduction of a token-economy programme is very often associated with more general changes in the style of ward management, and 'therapeutic community' programmes often involve the introduction of a variety of activity programmes as well as the basic elements of democratic decision-making and accountability. Many programmes, as Marks *et al.* (1968) point out, are 'hybrids' between reinforcement programmes and therapeutic communities.

Perhaps a more important reason why general answers cannot be given about the effectiveness of any of these programmes is the problem of what they should be compared with. Each kind of programme can be regarded as an explicit, focused way of remedying poor unit practices. Any of them is likely to represent an advance on the practices of an unenlightened setting. However, a good setting would already have incorporated many of the elements of all three types of programme as part of what Maxmen *et al.* (1974) call 'rational hospital psychiatry'. This leaves relatively little scope for improvement as a result of the introduction of specific new programmes. Even a comparison between the relative effectiveness of two kinds of specific programme would depend on how far their important elements had already been incorporated informally into unit practices. This tends to render all comparisons inconclusive, even the exceptionally thorough study of Paul and Lentz (1978), which obtained better results with a social-learning programme based on token-economy principles than for milieu therapy.

A particular issue that has to be considered carefully in connection with token-economy programmes is that, if rewards are to have a significant effect, then the environment has to be controlled so that whatever is being used as a reward is not freely available to the client in other ways. The possible advantages of the operant programme need to be balanced against the possibly counter-rehabilitation effects of control of the environment.

Shepherd (1980) has pointed out that settings programmes of apparently different kinds often have similar limitations. There is a danger that any approach if applied insensitively will prove over-stimulating and lead to the relapse of some people with schizophrenia (Hemsley, 1978). There are also serious problems in obtaining results that generalise from one setting to another and which persist for long periods of time. It is a general problem in rehabilitation that gains are often specific to the situation in which they are achieved and do not transfer (e.g. Hollingsworth and Foreyt, 1975). Indeed there is often little correlation between which clients function best in two different settings (e.g. Ellsworth *et al.*, 1968). It is difficult to avoid the conclusion that much of what passes for rehabilitation is no more than 'social influence' of a transitory kind (Watts, 1976).

The second key issue is how to introduce a new practice or programme into a setting in a way that will secure the cooperation of the staff. This is a question of prime importance, which has received much less attention than it deserves, though there has been some work on how to train staff to implement token-economy programmes (Kazdin, 1977), the results of which are salutory and probably apply equally to the introduction of other kinds of changes in staff practices. Formal didactic instruction may convey the principles on which the programme is based but does not seem to affect how well staff carry it out (Milne, 1985). Also, merely telling staff what behaviours to reinforce has little effect. Instruction needs to be followed up by supervised practice (Gardner, 1972). Several studies have shown that staff carry out programmes more effectively if they monitor their own performance or are given feedback on their performance by others (Kazdin, 1977: 143–5). Objective feedback is more effective if it is accompanied by social praise (Cossiart *et al.*, 1973); feedback alone is not sufficient. Daily telephone calls can be a useful way of providing feedback and encouragement (Stoffelmayr *et al.*, 1979).

Insufficient attention has been given to the many reasons why staff may be reluctant to change their practices in the desired direction. Lavender (1985) suggested that if some care is taken to identify these and an effort made to deal with them, fuller cooperation is likely to be achieved and changes in practices are likely to be more permanent. There is a dismal record of special programmes being introduced with initial enthusiasm, and collapsing as soon as the psychologist ceases to be heavily involved. Institutions are often adept at nullifying the efforts of the 'hero innovator' (Giorgiades and Phillimore, 1975). Sometimes, staff reluctance to modify setting/team practices may be used on practical problems. On other occasions, staff anxieties are the critical factor. For example, it was agreed that a particular nurse, helped by a student nurse, should take a long-stay client to the shops and help him to use them. A series of practical reasons for failing to carry out this assignment was produced. In the end, it transpired that the nurse was anxious about revealing her own incompetence in front of the student nurse. In settings where poor rehabilitation practices persist, they will often be the result of such anxieties about change. However, there will also often be key staff who are confident enough to be able to support constructive change, and it is important to identify and work through these 'healthy' elements in the system. Among the literature on this topic, Menzies (1959) has proposed a psychodynamic framework for understanding staff practices, and Bridger (1981) has set out a more general psychodynamic approach to understanding organisational behaviour.

The scope for changes in institutional practices is often limited by the constraints imposed by the wider institution in which the setting/team is located and by the differing professional loyalties and backgrounds of staff. It is important to identify the constraints on change that external professional hierarchies may bring to bear, and to seek to secure the active support of senior staff. However, a well-integrated team can often make changes in its own style of working if it has sufficient commitment to doing so. With this in mind, Watts and Bennett, (1983) have argued for the importance in rehabilitation of fostering an integrated staff team in which decisions are made collectively and all members of the staff are encouraged to take initiatives of their own in response to the changing needs of clients. However, besides the considerable difficulty in developing this style of teamwork, there are potential problems associated with it which need to be monitored (Pilling, 1991). It is likely to create a degree of role conflict and ambiguity that staff may find stressful (Braga, 1972). There is also a danger of staff cohesiveness producing both the intolerance of dissent and the suspicion of staff in related institutions who do not belong to the team. Such a team capable of facing and tackling these problems and operating a system for assessing, intervening and monitoring individualised programmes of care is an essential component of a high-quality rehabilitation service (Lavender and Holloway, 1992).

PREPARATION FOR SOCIAL ROLES

Most hospital-based rehabilitation services had, and some still have, training units designed to retrain clients in home-management skills as a preparation for independent living, and in occupational skills as a training for employment or other work roles. In the community-based services it is rare that replicas of such provision are established. There are good reasons for this, such as attempting to avoid providing facilities offering institutional styles of care and skills training not relevant to community settings. There are also problematic reasons for not providing such services, including thinly disguised money-saving devices and/or the failure of health and social services to agree about whether this is part of social (social services responsibility) or health (NHS responsibility) care, and/or simply lack of adequate service planning.

The client in any setting needs to be involved at the outset in decisions about which social roles are to be the target of rehabilitation. Trying to rehabilitate people for roles they are not interested in having is simply ineffective as well as being ethically dubious. The problem is that clients who are very anxious about their ability to cope with a job or with independent living may deal with their anxiety by deciding that they do not want to do it. As their confidence increases during rehabilitation they may take a different view. The rehabilitation worker needs to try to understand clients' reluctance, rather than just take it at face value as a reason for not proceeding with rehabilitation. Within each role area, it is important to have tasks that are relevant to the clients. Jones *et al.* (1956) illustrate this nicely in their description of how clients with character disorders showed no enthusiasm for industrial production work, but took rehabilitation much more seriously when instead they were asked to work on improving living conditions in the bomb-damaged building in which the unit was housed. Equally, clients in a domestic rehabilitation programme may, for example, all be given help with cooking, where the real problems for some of them may be with shopping or using appliances. Considerable resourcefulness and flexibility are required if a rehabilitation/community team is to adapt its programme to the real needs of clients.

There are however, common elements in the psychological skills needed for social roles. Work can be defined, following Jaques, as the exercise of discretion within prescribed limits to reach an agreed goal (Bennett, 1970). Work, in this sense, occurs in many other contexts apart from employment. Caring for young children is clearly work, though not employment. Work has 'manifest' functions, for example, monetary benefits, and 'latent' functions, such as the opportunities it provides for the exercise of general psychological skills such as structuring time and exercising discretion, for the structural social contact that it involves, and for the self-respect that it gives (Jahoda, 1979; Pilling, 1988; 1991). Though open employment, where available, may be a very good way of providing these benefits, they can also be obtained in other contexts.

Different kinds of settings are needed at different stages of rehabilitation. Initially clients' performance often falls short of what will eventually be required. The objective is to help them through skills training and encouragement gradually to improve their level of performance. The mistake often made at this stage is simply providing clients with a standard set of activities, with no analysis of their needs or monitoring of progress. At a late stage of rehabilitation, the setting should either be the clients' community-based setting or aim to provide conditions as close as possible to those that will be found in that setting. For employment skills, if the aim is for the person to move to open employment, the setting should offer normal working hours, style of supervision and commercial pressures. Unless such settings are available, no reasonable assessment can be made of whether clients can employ their skills appropriately or are ready to move to an open unsheltered environment. The expectations of 'normal' performance in such a unit can be a powerful way of achieving 'normal' performance. Such settings also give the client confidence about being able to make the transition between the rehabilitation unit and normal living or working conditions. The conditions and staff behaviour required at early and late stages of rehabilitation make it possible to do both in the same setting. It also needs to be recognised that some clients may not be able to gain open employment, because of shortage of opportunities or failure to develop sufficient levels of skill. In such cases it becomes important to develop within services a range of sheltered employment opportunities (Pilling, 1988).

Watts (1983a) has described the need to organise rehabilitation in a series of increasingly demanding settings in the context of general principles of socialisation. From research in a variety of both adult- and child-socialisation contexts, two dimensions have emerged that can be characterised roughly as making task demands and providing support. Manipulating these two in the most appropriate way is at the heart of successful rehabilitation. At early stages, clients are often only willing to respond to limited task demands in the context of high levels of support. Otherwise they may seek to withdraw from the rehabilitation programme and may show increased 'illness behaviour' (Shepherd, 1983: Chapter 6). The kind of support required varies from client to client. What matters is that they should feel supported. If the initial level of demands and support is successfully judged, gradually improving patient performance results. Increasing levels of demands can then produce increasing levels of performance. This in turn produces enhanced self-evaluation which can have pervasive positive effects on the prospects for successful rehabilitation.

As Lazarus (1966) has argued, reactions to task demands are influenced by a 'secondary appraisal' process based on a person's estimate of his or her own resources and of those available from others to meet the task demands. Increasing self-evaluation can be expected to increase people's ability both to respond to task demands constructively without avoidance and illness behaviour, and also to do this with less reliance on the support and resources of others. This, in turn, makes it possible to reduce the levels of support somewhat as reha- bilitation proceeds, though care needs to be taken to ascertain the minimum necessary 'maintenance level' of support. As increasing self-confidence is so important in rehabilitation there is a place for teaching new skills that may not be directly required in employment. For example, teaching arithmetic or yoga may, in different ways, increase a patient's sense of being able to cope with demands, even though these skills may not be directly required.

There is some literature on the use of behavioural methods to modify work-related behaviour in a variety of settings (Andrasik *et al.*, 1981; Watts, 1983b). The targets selected for skills training should be those that will make the most difference to whether people will succeed in open employment or, if this is not appropriate, in other sheltered community facilities. It is usually unrealistic to try to improve skills on all fronts. In rehabilitation, low productivity is the problem for which specific remedial programmes have most often been reported, though it is not the most critical determinant of employability. Giving graphic feedback on productivity, providing social stimulation and reward for good performance, and providing financial incentives on a piece-rate basis have all been shown to be useful. Walker (1979), in a representative study, found that the best results were obtained with a combination of these approaches. Desensitisation can be used to tackle excessive anxiety about mistakes, about criticism, or about learning new tasks. Probably the key factor is to ensure at the outset that the client sees his or her anxiety as a problem that needs to be overcome. Self-instruction methods are also a potentially useful means of anxiety management that focus specifically on the change in attitude that is often the key to success in rehabilitation.

The point was made in the preceding chapter that social behaviour is a critical determinant of employability and consequently social-skills training seems likely to be relevant. Liberman *et al.*'s broad-based definition of social-skills training seems most applicable to rehabilitation and focuses on verbal and non-verbal strengths and weaknesses, and interventions designed to improve functioning in these areas (Liberman *et al.*, 1986). The problem of generalisation (Shepherd, 1986) remains for any social-skills approaches, in that improvement in the therapeutic situation often does not transfer to the 'real' settings. A number of studies (Gillen and Heimberg, 1980; Liberman *et al.*, 1987) have shown how methods such as role-playing, videotape feedback and problem-solving techniques can produce significant improvements in skills and particularly in interviewing behaviour, and yet there appears to be little direct evidence that this improves the chances of actually obtaining employment.

Though training in employment skills is better developed and researched than training in domestic skills, the same principles apply. Specifically, there needs to be a careful selection of target variables, the provision of feedback and incen- tives for performance, and help in overcoming anxiety. Anthony (1980) has presented skills training as the central feature of rehabilitation, and argued that it is important to improve performance in a variety of social roles. An interesting attempt to improve the 'expressive' aspects of social interaction was a programme designed to improve the capacity of mothers to play effectively with their pre-school children (Lindsey *et al.*, 1978). The lack of skills in play shown by mothers, who were attending a rehabilitation-oriented day-hospital, was striking. The group used participant modelling to help the mothers enter into the children's world, exchange talk with them, and showed approval at their self-expression. Parry (1991) has provided a full discussion of the development of rehabilitation programmes for family roles. Training in skills of independent living that have been developing for the mentally handicapped could be applied in psychiatric rehabilitation. Of work in this area, reviewed by Lutzer *et al.* (1981), that of Cuvo was particularly impressive and includes operant programmes focusing on using coins, making emergency telephone calls and using public transport. The results have been encouraging, though the long-term benefit of the programmes on the level of functioning in the everyday environment have not been fully demonstrated.

The majority of clients using rehabilitation services suffer at some time in their lives from psychotic experiences. Psychological attempts to understand these experiences from a psychoanalytic tradition have a long history (Freud, 1911; Frosch, 1983), although from a cognitive perspective such developments are more recent (Bentall, 1990). Frosch (1983), in his impressive review, however, points out that whilst psychoanalysis has played a role in understanding the psychotic process, the extent to which this has been translated into meaningful therapy may be challenged. Interventions derived from cognitive models are being developed, including the use of techniques to alter the strength of beliefs in delusion (Chadwick and Lowe, 1990) and strategies to improve the client's ability to cope with psychotic experiences (O'Sullivan, 1991). Slade (1990) provides a useful review of these cognitive as well as behavioural approaches. Such interventions are likely to prove helpful for clients as they attempt to develop their social roles.

LINKS WITH THE COMMUNITY

Rehabilitation needs not only to prepare clients for roles in society, but to help them facilitate their entry into positions in society where they can exercise these roles. This is illustrated by the growing sophistication of programmes designed to help clients find jobs. One of the most impressive of these is the job-finding club that clients attended each day until they found a job (for example, see Azrin *et al.*, 1975; Jacobs *et al.*, 1984). The club provided a comprehensive structuring of the job-seeking process, which the clients were expected to regard as a full-time activity. They were encouraged to make full use of all sources of information about vacancies and to explore every reasonable lead. Training was given in how to arrange job interviews and how to behave at them. Clients in the club took a median of fourteen days to find a job compared to fifty-three for the control group, and also tended to obtain higher-level jobs. A good rehabilitation service also needs a range of facilities for helping clients who do not reach open employment to maintain their occupational skills. Indeed, as Shepherd (1991) and Pilling (1991) have pointed out, the opportunities to work, especially for the most disabled clients, have decreased considerably in recent years.

For these clients, sheltered workshops (Pilling, 1988) are particularly important. Usually such workshops tolerate a shortfall in some particular area from the expectation that would obtain in open employment whilst still providing remunerative employment. An alternative is the use of sheltered 'enclaves' within industry (Wansborough and Cooper, 1980). There will also be patients for whom voluntary work or other constructive leisure activities provide the most appropriate opportunities for them to use their work skills. Such settings include drop-in centres (Milroy, 1985) and related Clubhouse Schemes (Beard *et al.*, 1982). A rehabilitation/community team needs a wide range of community contacts to know what is available and to guide clients in their search.

Similar issues arise regarding re-entry into living accommodation in the community. If clients are being discharged home after a stay in hospital, the family and sometimes friends, need to be involved in the discharge process. Well before the final discharge the client should visit the home for trial periods to identify the skills that he or she will need in the home. The remaining period in hospital can then be used to help him or her to acquire them (O'Brien and Azrin, 1973). It is also important to explore how compatible are the expectations of the client and the family or residential staff (Jacobson and Klerman, 1966) and again to try to harmonise these before the final discharge, with the aim that the staff/families' expectations of the client should be as high as is realistic. It is especially helpful if opportunities can be found for the client to make a positive contribution to the home that will be genuinely welcomed by other members of the family and staff.

When the client is at home, it is important that the family or residential staff should have good access to advice and support. One economical way in which this can be done for families is through a self-help group of relatives (Priestley, 1979; Kuipers *et al.*, 1989) with some professional involvement. The functions of this kind of group are to disseminate information about such practical matters as accommodation and welfare benefits, and to provide an opportunity for relatives to learn to cope with any feelings of anger, self-blame, or shame about the client. The relatives can also encourage each other to lead their own lives and not to be totally absorbed with 'caring' for the mentally ill member of the family. There should also be access to professional help when crises develop. Langsley *et al.* (1969) and Hoult (1986) have demonstrated the effectiveness of a crisis-intervention service for families in preventing hospital admission.

Recently, prompted by the work of Brown *et al.* (1958; 1966) and Wynne and Singer (1963), much interest has focused on the concept of Expressed Emotion within the family. The level of Expressed Emotion is experimentally determined by the frequency of critical comments and positive remarks, and ratings of hostility, emotional over-involvement and warmth in an audiotaped interview with a relative of a client. High EE is demonstrated when the relative makes six or more critical comments, and/or scores a rank of one or more on hostility, and/or three or more on emotional over-involvement. Vaughn and Leff (1976) and Tarrier *et al.* (1988), amongst many others, have found a strong relationship between relapse and living with a high EE relative. Vaughn and Leff's study further indicated that, in a low EE family, medication did not significantly reduce the chances of relapse, whilst in high EE families, medication had a significant effect in reducing the chances of relapse. This work clearly has important implications for intervention in rehabilitation and it remains surprising that interventions based on these studies have not been more widely adopted (Lavender, 1992). This is particularly true given the success of interventions with families aimed at reducing the levels of expressed emotion (Leff *et al.*, 1982; Falloon *et al.*, 1982). Lam (1991) provides a useful review of the major components in such interventions.

Finally, attempts can be made to involve members of the social network in the client's rehabilitation to ensure that all clients have access to support in the community. The value of a close confidant has been established for those prone to depression (Brown and Harris, 1978). People diagnosed as suffering from schizophrenia also benefit from support (Goldstein and Caton, 1983) but may prefer relatively casual relationships. The needs of socially unengaged clients, who tend to have a very small primary-contact group, have no close confidant, and who do not engage in active contact with those around them but nevertheless do not report subjective loneliness, are particularly likely to be misunderstood. Such clients, while living independently in the community, often value being able to visit non-demanding facilities, where support can be gained from others without involving high levels of contact (Bender and Pilling, 1985). Volunteers can play an important part in rehabilitation, and can augment the support network (Holloway, 1988). The results of programmes which encourage volunteers to support clients and help them to develop the skills needed in the community are encouraging especially in rehabilitation (Anthony and Carkhuff, 1977) and to act as advocates for people living in hospitals and the community (Lavender and Holloway, 1992). However, here as in all aspects of rehabilitation, there is a danger of becoming over-attached to routine as well as replacing funded services with voluntary help in a way that is not sustainable in the long term. It was emphasised in Chapter 23 that different sources of support serve different functions and are not interchangeable. It is essential to consider for individual clients which aspects of support are most seriously deficient and how these can best be provided for as long as is necessary.

CONCLUSION

This chapter has focused on the general principles that should guide work in rehabilitation. The specific objectives of rehabilitation with different clients are so diverse and the techniques involved so numerous that they cannot be described in a single chapter. Also, many of the therapeutic methods used in rehabilitation are not specific to it, and have been described in other chapters of this book. The important thing to grasp about rehabilitation is its general approach to helping clients, concerned, for example, with positive objectives of good adjustment and with seeing the patients needs and capacities from a social-interactional perspective. Rehabilitation services usually founder because the people involved do not understand the general principles that should be guiding their work. Psychologists should be well equipped to contribute to rehabilitation or community teams if they have a strong grasp of these principles.

REFERENCES

Andrasik, F., Heimberg, J. S. and McNamara, J. R. (1981) 'Behavior modification of work and work related problems', in M. Hersen, R. M. Eisler and P. M. Miller (eds) *Progress in Behavior Modification. Vol II*, New York: Academic Press.

Anthony, W. A. (1980) *The Principles of Psychiatric Rehabilitation*, Baltimore: University Park Press,

Anthony, W. A. and Carkhuff, R. B. (1977) 'The functional professional therapeutic agent', in A. S. Gurman and A. M. Razin (eds) *Effective Psychotherapy: A Handbook of Research*, Oxford: Pergamon.

Azrin, N. H., Flores, T. and Kaplan, S. J. (1975) 'Job-finding club: a group assisted program for obtaining employment', *Behaviour Research and Therapy* 13: 17–27.

Beard, J., Probst, R. and Malamud, T. J. (1982) 'The Fountain House model of psychiatric rehabilitation', *Psychosocial Rehabilitation Journal* 5: 47–53.

Bender, M. D. and Pilling, S. (1985) 'A study of variables associated with under attendance at a psychiatric day hospital', *Psychological Medicine* 15: 395–402.

Bennett, D. H. (1970) 'The value of work in psychiatric rehabilitation', *Social Psychiatry* 5: 224–30.

Bentall, R. P. (ed.) (1990) *Reconstructing Schizophrenia*, London: Routledge.

Braga, J. L. (1972) 'Role therapy, cognitive dissonance theory and the interdisciplinary team', *Interchange* 3: 69–78.

Bridger, H. (1981) 'The contribution of organisational development at the level of the whole organisation', in K. Trebesch (ed.) *Organisation Development in Europe*, Berne: Paul Haupt.

Brown, G. W. and Harris, T. (1978) *Social Origins of Depression*, London: Tavistock.

Brown, G. W., Carstairs, G. and Topping, G. (1958) 'Post-hospital adjustment of chronic mental patients', *Lancet* (ii): 685–9.

Brown, G. W., Bone, M., Dalison, B. and Wing, J. K. (1966) *Schizophrenia and Social Care*, Oxford: Oxford University Press.

Chadwick, P. and Lowe, C. F. (1990) 'The measurement and modification of behavioural beliefs', *Journal of Consulting and Clinical Psychology* 58: 225–32.

Cossiart, A., Hall, R. V. and Hopkins, B. C. (1973) 'The effect of experimenters' instructions, feedback and praise on teacher praise and student attending behaviour', *Journal of Applied Behaviour Analysis* 89–100.

Ellsworth, R. B., Foster, L., Childers, B., Arthur, G. and Kroeker, D. (1968) 'Hospital and community adjustment as perceived by psychiatric patients, their families and staff', *Journal of Consulting and Clinical Psychology*, Monograph Supplement: 1–41.

Falloon, I. R. H., Boyd, J. L., McGill, G. W., Razani, J., Moss, H. B. and Gilderman, A. M.

(1982) 'Family management in the prevention of exacerbation of schizophrenia', *New England Journal of Medicine* 306: 1432–40.

Freud, S. (1911) 'Psychoanalytic notes on an autobiographical account of a case of paranoia (Dementia Paranoides)', *Standard Edition* (1958) London: Hogarth Press (12: 3–82)

Frosch, J. (1983) *The Psychotic Process*, New York: New York University Press.

Gardner, J. M. (1972) 'Teaching behaviour modification to non-professional', *Journal of Applied Behaviour Analysis* 5: 517–21.

Gillen, R. W. and Heimberg, R. G. (1980) 'Social skills training for the job interview: review and prospects', in M. Hersen, R. M. Eisler and P. M. Mill (eds) *Progress in Behaviour Modification. Vol. 10*, New York: Academic Press.

Giorgiades, N. J. and Phillimore, L. (1975) 'The myth of the hero innovator and alternative strategies for institutional change', in C. C. Keirman and F. Woodford (eds) *Behaviour Modification with the Severely Retarded*, Amsterdam: Associated Scientific Publishers.

Goldstein, J. and Caton, C. L. M. (1983) 'The effects of the community environment on chronic psychiatric patients', *Psychological Medicine* 13: 193–8.

Hemsley, D. H. (1978) 'Limitation of operant procedures in the modification of schizophrenia functioning: the possible relevance of studies of cognitive disturbance', *Behaviour analysis and Modification* 2: 165–73.

Hollingsworth. R. and Foreyt, J. P. (1975) 'Community adjustment of release token economy patients', *Journal of Behaviour Therapy and Experimental Psychiatry* 6: 271–4.

Holloway, F. (1988) 'Day care and community support', in A. Lavender and F. Holloway (eds) *Community Care in Practice: Services for the Continuing Care Client*, Chichester: Wiley.

Hoult, J. (1986) 'Community care of the acute mentally ill', *British Journal of Psychiatry* 149: 137–44.

Hudson, B. L. (1975) 'A behaviour modification project with chronic psychophrenics in the community', *Behaviour Research and Therapy* 13: 339–4.

Jacobs, H. E., Kardashian, S., Keel Keinberg, R., Ponder, R. and Simpson, A. R. (1984) 'A skills oriented model for facilitating employment among psychiatrically disabled persons', *Rehabilitation Counselling* December: 87–96.

Jacobson, N. S. and Klerman, G. L. (1966) 'Interpersonal dynamics hospitalized depressed patients' home visits', *Journal of Marriage and the Family* 28: 94–102.

Jahoda, M. (1979) 'The impact of unemployment in the 1930s and 1970s', *Bulletin of the British Psychological Society* 32: 309–14.

Jones, M. (1968) *Beyond the Therapeutic Community: Social Learning and Social Psychiatry*, New Haven, Conn.: Yale University Press.

Jones, M., Pomryn, B. A. and Skellern, E. (1956) 'Work therapy', *Lancet* 343–4.

Kazdin, A. E. (1977) *The Token Economy: A Review and Evaluation*, New York: Plenum.

Kuipers, L., McCarthy, B., Hurry, J. and Harper, R. (1989) 'Counselling the Relatives of the Mentally Ill, II. A low cost support model', *British Journal of Psychiatry* 154: 775–82.

Lam, D. H. (1991) 'Psychosocial family interventions in schizophrenia: A review of empirical studies', *Psychological Medicine* 21: 423–41.

Lamb, H. R. (1982) *Treating the Long-term Mentally Ill*, New York: Jossey Bass.

Langsley, D. G., Flomenhaft, K. and Machotka, P. (1969) 'Follow-up evaluation of family crisis therapy', *American Journal of Orthopsychiatry* 39: 753–6.

Lavender, A. (1985) 'Quality of care and staff practices in long term settings', in F. N. Watts (ed.) *New Developments in Clinical Psychology*, Chichester: BPS/Wiley.

Lavender, A. (1987) 'Improving the quality of care on psychiatric hospital rehabilitation wards', *British Journal of Psychiatry* 150: 476–81.

Lavender, A. (1992) 'Schizophrenia', in M. Power and L. Champion (eds) *Adult Psychological Problems: An introduction*, London: Falmer Press.

Lavender, A. and Holloway, F. (1988) 'Introduction', in A. Lavender and F. Holloway (eds) *Community Care in Practice: Services for the Continuing Care Client*, Chichester: Wiley.

Lavender, A. and Holloway, F. (1992) 'Models of Continuing Care', in M. Birchwood and N. Tarrier (eds) *Innovations in the Management of Schizophrenia*, Chichester: Wiley.

Lazarus, R. S. (1966) *Psychological Stress and the Coping Process*, New York: McGraw Hill.

Leff, J., Kuipers, L., Berkowitz, R., Eberllen-Fries, R. and Sturgeon, D. (1982) 'A controlled trial of social intervention in the families of schizophrenic patients', *British Journal of Psychiatry* 148: 727–31.

Liberman, R. P., Mueser, K. T., Wallace, C. J., Jacobs, H. E., Eckman, T. and Massel, H. K. (1986) 'Training skills in the psychiatrically disabled: learning coping and competence', *Schizophrenia Bulletin* 12: 631–47.

Liberman, R. P., Jacobs, H. E., Boone, S. E., Foy, D. W., Donahoe, C. P., Falloon, I. R. H., Blackwell, G. and Wallace, C. J. (1987) 'Skills training for the community adaptation of schizophrenia', in J. S. Strauss, W. Baker and H. D. Brenner (eds) *Psychosocial Treatment of Schizophrenia*, Toronto: Hans Huber.

Lindsey, C. R., Pound, A. and Radford, M. (1978) 'A co-operative playgroup in a psychiatric day hospital', *Group Analysis* 11: 289–96.

Lutzer, J. R., Martin, J. A. and Rice, J. M. (1981) 'Behavior therapy in rehabilitation', in M. Hersen, R. M. Eisler and P. M. Miler (eds) *Process Behavior Modification, Vol. 12*, New York: Academic Press.

Marks, J., Somoda, B. and Schalock, R. (1968) 'Reinforcement vs. relationship therapy for schizophrenics', *Journal of Abnormal Psychology* 73: 397–406.

Maxmen, J. S., Tucker, G. J. and Lebow, M. D. (1974) *Rational Hospital Psychiatry: The Reactive Environment*, New York: Brunner/Mazel.

Menzies, I. E. (1959) 'Case study in the functioning of social systems as a defence against anxiety', *Human Relations* 13: 95–121.

Milne, D. L. (1985) 'An observational evaluation of the effects of course training in behaviour therapy on unstructured ward activities and interaction', *British Journal of Clinical Psychology* 24: 149–58.

Milroy, A. (1985) 'Some reflections on the experience of the North Derbyshire Mental Health Service Project. Tontine Road, Derbyshire', in T. McAusland (ed.) *Planning and Monitoring Community Mental Health Centres*, London: Kings Fund Centre.

Mitchell, S. F. and Birley, J. L. T. (1983) 'The use of ward support by psychiatric patients in the community', *British Journal of Psychiatry* 142: 9–15.

O'Brien, F. and Azrin, N. H. (1973) 'Interaction-priming: a method of reinstating patient family relationships', *Behaviour Research and Therapy* 11: 133–6.

O'Sullivan, K. (1991) 'Dimensions of coping with auditory hallucinations', unpublished thesis submitted in partial fulfilment of the BPS Diploma in Clinical Psychology, Leicester.

Parry, G. (1991) 'Domestic roles', in F. N. Watts and D. H. Bennett (eds) *Theory and Practice of Psychiatric Rehabilitation, 2nd end*, Chichester: Wiley.

Paul, G. L. and Lentz, R. J. (1978) *Psychosocial Treatment of Chronic Mental Patients: Milieu versus Social-Learning Programmes*, Cambridge, Mass.: Harvard University Press.

Pilling, S. (1988) 'Work and the continuing care client', in A. Lavender and F. Holloway (eds) *Community Care in Practice: Services for the Continuing Care Client*, Chichester: Wiley.

Pilling, S. (1991) *Rehabilitation and Community Care*, London: Routledge.

Priestley, D. (1979) 'Helping a self-help group in schizophrenia and the family', in J. K. Wing and R. Olsen (eds) *Community Care of the Mentally Disabled*, Oxford: Oxford University Press.

Shepherd, G. W. (1980) 'The treatment of social difficulties in special environments', in P. Feldman and J. Oxford (eds) *Psychological Problems: the Social Context*, Chichester: Wiley.

Shepherd, G. W. (1983) *Institutional Care and Rehabilitation*, London: Longman.

Shepherd, G. W. (1986) 'Social skills training in schizophrenia', in C. R. Hollin and P. Trower (eds) *Handbook of Social Skills Training: Vol. 2*, Oxford: Pergamon Press.

Shepherd, G. W. (1991) 'Foreword: Psychiatric rehabilitation for the 1990s', in F. N. Watts and D. H. Bennett (eds) *Theory and Practice of Psychiatric Rehabilitation, 2nd edn*, Chichester: Wiley.

Slade, P. D. (1990) 'The behavioural and cognitive treatment of psychotic symptoms', in R. P. Bentall (ed.) *Reconstructing Schizophrenia*, London: Routledge.

Stoffelmayr, B. E., Lindsay, W. and Taylor, V. (1979) 'Maintenance of staff behaviour', *Behaviour Research and Therapy* 17: 271–3.

Tarrier, N., Barrowclough, C., Vaughn, C., Bamrah, J. S., Porcedon, K., Watts, S. and Freeman, H. L. (1988) 'The community management of schizophrenia. A controlled trial of family intervention to reduce relapse', *British Journal of Psychiatry* 153: 532–44.

Vaughn, C. E. and Leff, J. P. (1976) 'The influence of family and social factors on the course of psychiatric illness; a comparison of schizophrenic and depressed neurotic patients', *British Journal of Psychiatry* 129: 125–37.

Walker, L. G. (1979) 'The effect of some incentives on the work performance of psychiatric patients at a rehabilitation workshop', *British Journal of Psychiatry* 134: 427–35.

Wansborough, N. and Cooper, P. (1980) *Open Employment After Mental Illness*, London: Tavistock.

Watts, F. N. (1976) 'Social Treatments', in H. J. Eysenck and G. D Wilson (eds) *A Textbook of Human Psychology*, Lancaster: MTP.

Watts, F. N. (1983a) 'Socialisation and social integration', in F. N. Watts and D. H. Bennett (eds) *Theory and Practice of Psychiatric Rehabilitation*, Chichester: Wiley.

Watts, F. N. (1983b) 'Employment', in F. N. Watts and D. H. Bennett (eds) *Theory and Practice of Psychiatric Rehabilitation*, Chichester: Wiley.

Watts, F. N. and Bennett, D. H. (1983) 'Management of the staff team', in F. N. Watts and D. H. Bennett (eds) *Theory and Practice of Psychiatric Rehabilitation*, Chichester: Wiley.

Wynne, L. C. and Singer, M. T. (1963) 'Thought disorder and family relations', *Archives of General Psychiatry* 9: 199–206.

Chapter 25

An introduction to health psychology

Robert J. Edelmann

HEALTH PSYCHOLOGY DEFINED

Although the interplay between mind and body has long been recognised, in the past two decades the importance of psychological processes in the experience of health and illness has become increasingly acknowledged. This has been prompted by a number of factors. As acute infectious disease has been brought under control, the relative proportion of illness which involves chronic disease has steadily increased. The leading causes of death today include heart disease, cancer and stroke, all of which are influenced by lifestyle factors, such as diet, smoking and exercise. In addition, with chronic illnesses, such as asthma, diabetes and arthritis, where 'curing the disease' has less relevance, people live and cope with physical symptoms and associated emotional reactions for many years. In such instances, self-care and self-control methods are important aspects of health care. Allied to these issues, the last two decades have seen the development of effective behavioural techniques and allied research endeavours directed towards lifestyle modification, reducing distress associated with the experience of treatment and surgery and facilitating coping and adaptation to illness.

The interest of psychologists in these developments is attested to by the emergence of the term health psychology in the mid 1970s to describe the application of psychological theory and practice to physical health problems (Stone, 1991). (See, for example, the special issue, of the *Journal of Consulting and Clinical Psychology*, 1992: 60(4), which reviews developments over the past decade.) The most widely referred to definition of the field is that proposed by Joseph Matorazzo and adopted with minor revisions by the Division of Health Psychology of the American Psychological Association in 1980. This states that

> Health Psychology is the aggregate of the specific educational, scientific, and professional contributions of the discipline of psychology to the promotion and maintenance of health, the prevention and treatment of illness, and the identification of etiologic and diagnostic correlates of health, illness, and related dysfunction and analysis and improvement of the health care system and health policy formation.
>
> (Matorazzo, 1980: 815)

This definition thus reflects a broad continuum of concern ranging from factors which determine a person's health to those which influence one's ability to cope with illness. Issues pertaining to the former include health promotion and disease prevention, and the experience of becoming ill and receiving medical treatment; these issues are dealt with in the first part of the chapter. Coping with illness forms the basis of the second part of the chapter. Psychological contributions to health promotion and disease prevention focus on three broad issues: the identification of behavioural risk factors relating to chronic life-threatening illness; the investigation of factors which determine health-related behaviours; and the extent to which people can be prompted to modify their lifestyles by adopting healthy behaviour. Psychological contributions to understanding the experience of becoming ill and receiving medical treatment also focus on three broad issues: communication between doctor and patient; compliance with medical advice; and reactions to hospitalisation and surgery.

Although there may be many instances in physical health contexts when it may be appropriate for clinical psychologists to work with individual clients, there are also many instances when clinical psychologists might be asked to recommend practices to improve patient care or to promote health. This might involve ward-based interventions or more general strategies aimed at communicating information to patients or the general public via health information campaigns. The intention behind the material presented in this chapter is to provide an introduction to health psychology for clinical psychologists who are either involved in health-care research or who are working in general medical practice or receiving referrals from physicians in hospitals.

PSYCHOLOGY IN HEALTH AND ILLNESS

Determinants of health-related behaviour

Lifestyle and health

A number of authors have recognised that lifestyle plays a critical role in illness and, conversely, that lifestyle change is a major factor in health promotion and the prevention and treatment of disease (e.g. Jeffery, 1989). Known behavioural risk factors include smoking, use of illicit drugs, excessive consumption of alcohol, dietary habits and lack of sufficient exercise. In addition, many thousands of people are injured each year in car accidents or in accidents at home or work that could have been prevented.

It is difficult to assess the extent to which each lifestyle factor poses a threat to health, as lifestyle elements usually occur together as a constellation. Thus, someone who smokes and drinks is likely to engage in poor dietary habits and inadequate exercise. However, some risk factors clearly have more potential for damage to health than others. For example, unprotected sex is clearly a major risk factor for AIDS. In addition, it has been estimated that a quarter of all deaths from cancer could be avoided simply by modification of smoking habits, while coronary heart disease would be decreased by one-fifth if men aged 35 to 55 reduced their weight by 10 per cent (Kannel and Eaker, 1986). The case for exercise is less clear although 'evidence suggests that regular physical activity may reduce the incidence and severity of chronic disease and perhaps extend the life span by a few years' (Bouchard *et al.*, 1990). Others have argued more strongly that 'the evidence that a sedentary life-style lowers life expectancy for both men and women and contributes independently to the development of many prevalent chronic diseases is substanital and still increasing' (Dubbert, 1992: 616). The evidence for other risk factors, such as cholesterol, is rather more equivocal.

Although deficient diets are now quite rare in the western world, dietary imbalances or being extremely underweight or overweight have been linked to many acute and chronic illnesses. High-fat diets have been linked to cancers of the breast, colon, rectum and prostate, as well as being implicated in heart disease and stroke. In contrast, high-fibre diets may protect against cancers of the colon or rectum. It is well established that obesity is strongly linked to high blood pressure, raised plasma cholesterol and coronary heart disease (Johnston and Steptoe, 1989). Obesity is also related to other health-threatening conditions, including diabetes and gall bladder disease.

Excessive alcohol consumption can have direct effects, for example, through cirrhosis of the liver, or indirect effects, such as increasing the likelihood of car accidents; excessive alcohol consumption is also associated with hypertension. Smoking is a major risk factor for the development of emphysema and chronic bronchitis; cigarette smokers are almost twice as likely to die from heart disease as are non-smokers; smokers are also more likely to develop lung cancer, cancer of the mouth and cancer of the bladder. When combined with alcohol, cigarette smoking increases the likelihood of cancer of the larynx, oesophagus and oral cavity. Combined with other coronary risk factors, such as high cholesterol, cigarette smoking increases cardiovascular risk. Smoking during pregnancy has been linked to an increased risk of retarded foetal growth or spontaneous abortion. Involuntary or 'passive' smoking also increases the risk of disease and death (Garland *et al.*, 1985).

Those who live a sedentary lifestyle are more likely to develop and die from coronary heart disease than those who take regular exercise, although the former are also more likely to be at risk of coronary heart disease because they are overweight or smoke (Dishman *et al.*, 1985). Studies suggest that regular exercise decreases risk of a number of life-threatening illnesses, including coronary heart disease and cancer (Blair *et al.*, 1989), as well as helping in the management of diabetes, obesity and depression (Koplan *et al.*, 1989).

Accidents involving traffic and accidents at home or at work represent one of the major causes of preventable death, particularly amongst children, adolescents and young adults. Yet, until recently, relatively little psychological research has been devoted to understanding and reducing these risks. An interest in child safety behaviour is likely to be an important future area of health psychology research (e.g. Ampofo-Boateng and Thomson, 1989).

In each of the above instances, rather than having to treat physical disease or injury, the best way of dealing with the problem is by prevention or modification of the behaviour so that physical disease or injury do not occur. Whether someone will practise healthy behaviour is, however, influenced by social, emotional and cognitive factors. With regard to the latter, two theories of lifestyle change, Fishbein's theory of reasoned action (Ajzen and Madden, 1986; Fishbein and Ajzen, 1975) and the health belief model (Becker, 1974), have been particularly influential.

Theories of lifestyle change

Fishbein's theory of reasoned action

This theory holds that much of our behaviour is under voluntary control and is guided by intention (Fishbein and Ajzen, 1975). Intention is influenced both by our own attitude towards that behaviour and subjective norms about the appropriateness of it. Subjective norms derive from what we believe other people think it is appropriate to do (normative beliefs) and our motivation to comply with these norms. For example, if I intend to stop smoking to become healthier and I both believe that my behaviour change will have the desired outcome and that important others will approve of my action, I will have a strong intention to act. Although Fishbein's model has been used to predict a wide range of behaviours, its use has been limited with regard to health related behaviours. There has been some research showing the utility of the model in predicting exercise intention and behaviour (Wurtele and Maddux, 1987) and breast versus bottle feeding (Manstead *et al.*, 1983).

More recently, Ajzen and Madden have presented a revised version of the theory, referred to as the theory of planned behaviour (Ajzen and Madden, 1986). In addition to attitudes and subjective norms, they suggest it is important to recognise the individuals' perceived control over the target behaviour, a component similar to Bandura's self-efficacy concept (Bandura, 1977). The results of a recent study concerning the practice of testicular self-examination (TSE) for signs of testicular cancer provides support for the extended theory (Brubaker and Wickersham, 1990). Intention to perform TSE was significantly related to attitude toward performing TSE and subjective norm (the likelihood that significant others would want the person to perform TSE), while consideration of perceived self-efficacy (confidence in ability to perform TSE) and knowledge of TSE improved prediction of intention.

One problem with the theory, however, is that it does not account for irrational decisions people make about their health, such as failing to seek medical treatment when symptoms of illness exist. A further problem is that intentions and behaviour are not necessarily related. That is, the behaviour may not always follow the intention. Indeed, the relationship can be moderated by a range of factors including prior experience and past history of performing health related behaviours.

Health belief model

The health belief model was developed specifically to explain and predict health related behaviour (Becker, 1974). Initially developed to predict preventive health behaviours, the model has also been used to predict behaviour of both acutely and chronically ill patients. According to the model, the likelihood that an individual will take preventive action is dependent upon two factors: an assessment of the perceived threat of a health problem and an evaluation of the pros and cons of taking action. The perceived threat of illness is a function of the individual's perception of the seriousness of the health problem, his or her perceived susceptibility to it, and cues to action. The latter can take many forms such as mass media campaigns, a reminder letter from doctor or dentist, family illness, or the perception of one's own symptoms. Perceived threat of illness is influenced by demographic factors, such as age or gender, personality factors, and knowledge about or prior contact with the health problem.

In considering the pros and cons of taking preventive action people consider whether the perceived benefits, such as reducing their health risks, outweigh the perceived barriers or costs of taking such action. Such costs may well involve actual financial consideration, but may also involve less tangible concerns, such as time. Thus, people who feel threatened by an illness, and who feel that the benefits of having checks outweigh the costs, are more likely to take preventive action.

The model has generated a great deal of research, much of which has supported its predictions. With regard to health-promotion behaviours, research has been directed towards issues such as participation in screening programmes for cervical cancer and altering risk factors, such as giving up smoking and dietary change. In reviewing 24 such studies Janz and Becker (1984) conclude that intention to take-up of preventive behaviours is more likely by those who believe that they are susceptible to the condition in question, that the resulting illness will have serious effects and that the benefits of taking preventive action exceed the costs. Similar findings have been reported with regard to the extent that people follow treatment advice (Becker and Rosenstock, 1984). Furthermore, studies have shown that cues to action, such as reminders to perform breast self-examination (Craun and Deffenbacher, 1987), influence people's decisions to take preventive action.

In spite of the utility of the model and the research it has generated, it is not without its critics. For example, it does not account for health-related behaviours such as tooth-brushing that people perform habitually; secondly, there is no standard way of measuring components such as perceived susceptibility or seriousness. This no doubt accounts for varying results across studies and the fact that not all studies support the health belief model (e.g. Weisenberg *et al.*, 1980); thirdly, as with the theory of reasoned action, no account is taken of the fact that the costs and benefits of behaviour change may vary over time. In addition, both theories assume rational decision-making; that is, that people make careful appraisals of the medical risks involved in performing a particular behaviour and modify their behaviour accordingly. Yet, as a number of studies suggest, people's decision-making tends to deviate from rationality. A frequent research finding is that people are unrealistically optimistic about their health (Weinstein, 1982; 1987); having little experience of health threats, we may underestimate our vulnerability or find it difficult to imagine what a serious illness would be like. In reality, behaviour change frequently results from less well defined factors (Weinstein, 1988).

Health promotion and disease prevention

The aim of health promotion is to enable people to increase control over, and improve, their health. This refers to the practice of good health behaviours, such as a balanced diet, the practice of preventive health behaviours, such as breast self-examination, and the avoidance of health-compromising behaviours, such as excessive smoking or alcohol consumption. The aim of psychologists and other interested parties is thus to intervene with the healthy rather than the ill in order to maximise and enhance their health. Health education programmes are particularly important in this respect; these have three central aims:

1 To provide health-related information
2 To change health-related attitudes to those which are conducive to health
3 To change health-related behaviour in ways which are more likely to foster good health

Inevitably, providing information is a more straightforward matter than changing attitudes or behaviour (Kirscht, 1983), and public health campaigns are frequently ineffective. In both addressing this issue and in translating information about risk into effective intervention strategies, it is important to understand key concepts of risk behaviour. These are absolute, relative and population attributable risk. Absolute risk is the likelihood that someone will contract a disease over a certain period of time; thus, in the USA, the absolute risk that a 40-year-old man will die of lung cancer in one year is 11 in 100,000 (Mattson *et al.*, 1987). Relative risk is the ratio of the chance of disease in those exposed to a risk factor compared to those who are not; thus, the relative chance of lung cancer in a 40-year-old heavy smoker, compared with that of a non-smoker, is about 10 to 1 (Mattson *et al.*, 1987). Finally, population attributable risk is the number of cases which might not have occurred had the risk not been present; thus, in the USA, about 101,000 deaths per year are attributable to smoking (Jeffery, 1989). In thinking about public health campaigns, the population attributable risk provides important cues to action although such behaviours may have low or moderate absolute personal risk. Thus, although within a population of one million 35-year-old heavy smokers 10,000 will die unnecessarily from their habit before the age of 45 (Jeffery, 1989), the ten-year absolute risk of lung cancer for a 35-year-old man who is a heavy smoker is only about 0.3 per cent (Mattson *et al.*, 1987). Given the tendency for individuals to focus on their own relative risk rather than the population risk, it is perhaps not surprising that population-wide health campaigns often meet with limited success.

More success is often acheived by aiming information at high-risk populations, that is, those who are identified as being particularly vulnerable to a disease. Coronary prevention programmes, encouraging dietary, exercise and habit change in those at substantial risk of heart disease, are widely practised (e.g. Shekelle *et al.*, 1985). The safe-sex and anti-sun exposure campaigns are more recent examples.

Safe-sex

Although sexually transmitted diseases are widespread, most can be treated or managed with drugs; AIDS is a major exception. Estimates about the potential spread of the AIDS virus (HIV) make disturbing reading (Osborn, 1988). Changing people's behaviour is virtually the only way of reducing the risk of infection. The first such attempts concentrated very much on the use of fear-arousing warnings, although there is a large body of research suggesting that behaviour change is more likely if information is not presented in an overly fear-arousing manner. Rather, it is important to present people with concrete steps that they can take on their own behalf (Solomon and DeLong, 1986). Indeed, more recent campaigns have focused on providing information and advice. The former often involves challenging frequent misconceptions about the transmission of the HIV virus; for example, that hugging or touching an infected person can transmit the virus, or that only homosexuals or drug users can have AIDS (Batchelor, 1988).

The emphasis of advice, often through media campaigns or health education leaflets, has been to encourage:

1 Safe-sex practices by selecting sexual partners carefully, avoiding practices that may injure bodily tissues, and using condoms in all forms of sexual intercourse except within long-term monogamous relationships.
2 Avoiding sharing needles or syringes.

Others have pointed out that, for prevention efforts to be effective it is important to work with the issues of a given population so that interventions are tailored to their needs; for example, towards ethnic/cultural dynamics (e.g. Mays and Cochran, 1988) or the needs of adoloescents (e.g. Flora and Thoresen, 1988) as well as gay communities (e.g. Joseph *et al.*, 1987). Thus, for AIDS messages to be effective they must have personal relevance, be presented by individuals with whom the group concerned can identify and be delivered at a community level

(Mays and Cochran, op. cit.). As Becker and Joseph (1988) note, interventions targeted towards specific groups using 'tried and true' behavioural principles need to be implemented.

There is some evidence that people are becoming more knowledgeable about AIDS and that campaigns are having some impact on sexual practices, particularly in gay communities (e.g. Joseph *et al.*, 1987). Interestingly, Joseph *et al.* found that use of safer-sexual practices was unrelated to knowledge of AIDS, perceived risk or perceived efficacy of safer-sex behaviour, but was related to people's belief that their peers were changing their habits. This finding has relevance to Fishbein's theory of reasoned action, although this theory did not guide the study. At least within gay communities, there is evidence that AIDS education and prevention campaigns have resulted in the most profound modifications of personal health-related behaviour ever recorded (Stall *et al.*, 1988).

Anti-sun exposure

It is well established that excessive exposure to the sun's rays plays a significant causal role in the development of skin cancer and that the incidence of such cancers is increasing yearly. Yet, many cases could be prevented by using sun blocks, wearing protective clothing or simply staying out of the sun. Unfortunately, the rich and famous are often seen as relaxed and adventurous if they have dark tans; such people often serve as role models (Keesling and Friedman, 1987), and hence a potentially dangerous behaviour is reinforced. In spite of the fact that many cases of skin cancer could be prevented by attitude and behaviour change, little attention has been paid to this problem by health psychologists. With the ever-increasing incidence of such cancers, and spurred by the threat of atmospheric ozone depletion and harmful UV rays, anti-sun exposure campaigns are likely to increase in the future.

Illness and medical treatment

Seeking medical care

Although it might seem a relatively straightforward matter to consult a medical practitioner because of symptoms of illness, it is quite clear that many people have symptoms of potentially serious illness to which they fail to respond, while others seek medical care for seemingly trivial symptoms (Edelmann, 1992). Reactions to physical symptoms vary as a function of a range of factors. For example, women use medical services more than men even when medical care required by women during pregnancy and childbirth is excluded. Verbrugge (1985) suggests several possible explanations for this. For example, women may develop more illnesses than men (i.e. chronic conditions and non-fatal chronic diseases, such as arthritis or migraine, rather than fatal chronic disease).

However, as a result of sex-role stereotypes, men may be more reluctant to report experiencing symptoms.

Symptom interpretation and health-care seeking is also likely to be influenced by people's own explanations for their symptoms and their beliefs about the effectiveness of medical care. For example, consultation is more likely when a symptom becomes frightening or is perceived as threatening (Zola, 1973). Further, in line with the health belief model, the greater the person's belief in the effectiveness of medical care, the more likely he or she is to use health services (Crandall and Duncan, 1981). Social factors also act as triggers for people to seek medical help for symptoms. According to Zola (op cit.), people are more likely to seek medical care after experiencing a crisis in a relationship, when a symptom threatens to limit a person's social interactions, and when there is approval or encouragement from others for seeking help.

Delay in seeking medical care is not uncommon and can occur at three phases: appraisal delay (the time taken to interpret a symptom as a sign of illness), illness delay (the time from the patient's decision that he or she is ill to the decision to seek care), and utilisation delay (the time from deciding to seek care to actually obtaining medical help) (Safer et al., 1979). For a disease like cancer, delay can be life-threatening. At the other end of the spectrum are those patients who consult the doctor repeatedly when there is no need. The term hypochondriacal has been used to refer to those who are preoccupied with symptoms in the absence of identifiable organic pathology. Warwick and Salkovskis (1990) argue that hypochondriacal patients are more likely to misinterpret bumps and blemishes as signs of illness and as a result repeatedly check their symptoms and seek medical information and reassurance.

There are, then, a variety of reasons why people misuse, fail to use, or delay their use of health services. In addition to those factors mentioned above, health-care utilisation is also influenced by the patient's experience of medical consultations as discussed below.

Communication with patients

In summarising research, Ley commmments that 'in general, patients want information about their condition and their treatment but many feel that they are not told enough, many do not understand what they are told, and many do not remember what is said' (Ley, 1989: 74). Inevitably, patients differ in the amount of information they want and doctors differ in the amount of involvement they invite from patients. Clearly a mismatch between them will detrimentally affect their relationship. In a classic study analysing doctor–patient interactions, Byrne and Long (1976) identified styles of interaction ranging from doctor-centred to patient-centred. The former tended to involve closed questions, with the doctor focusing on the first problem presented by the patient, while ignoring attempts by the patient to raise other problems. The latter involved use of more open-ended questions, with the doctor encouraging the patient to provide more information and inviting participation from the patient in decision-making. Even though the doctors' styles differed, each individual doctor used a consistent style for all the patients that he or she treated. By failing to respond to each patient as an individual a mismatch in expectations is almost inevitable.

Studies have consistently demonstrated that patients prefer doctors who show sensitivity, warmth and concern to those who appear detached and unconcerned (DiMatteo, 1985). In addition, patients are more satisfied with consultations if they are given the opportunity to explain their problem(s) to someone who listens to them and gives them a clear explanation of their condition and the treatment offered (Feletti *et al.*, 1986). This is a particularly important issue given that research suggests there is a strong link between patients' satisfaction with the consultation and compliance with medical advice. Korsch *et al.* (1968), in an evaluation of mothers attending an out-patient paediatric clinic, found that those who were very satisfied with the doctor's warmth, concern and communication of information were three times more likely to comply with medical advice than those who were dissatisfied.

Non-compliance

Patient non-compliance with medical regimes, or indeed with psychological interventions, is thought to be widespread. DiMatteo and DiNicola (1982), who cite studies showing a wide variation in non-compliance rates, estimate that, on average, one-third of all patients do not cooperate with medical recommendations given to them for short-term treatment, and half or more do not cooperate with long-term treatments. Between 20 and 80 per cent of patients drop-out of smoking cessation or weight change treatment programmes (Dunbar and Agras, 1980). Non-cooperation can occur in many ways. For example, patients may fail to follow through recommendations relating to weight loss or smoking cessation designed to prevent illness; they may fail to adhere to interventions designed to lower blood pressure or they may fail to adhere to medical regimens designed to alleviate illness, by varying the amount of medication consumed or the number of days over which it is taken. At the very least, non-compliance results in the wastage of health resources. However, it may also result in the recurrence of symptoms or the onset of illness.

The wide variations in the estimates of compliance no doubt reflect assessment difficulties. Results are frequently based upon pill counts, doctor or therapist reports or patient self-reports. In published research, the latter is the most frequently used method of assessing compliance (Caron, 1985). Given that patients are likely to be reluctant to admit to non-compliance the true extent of non-compliance may exceed current estimates. Some of the more reliable assessments such as tests to check for signs of carbon dioxide or nicotine in the blood in relation to smoking cessation are not likely to be practicable in day-to-day clinical practice. Inevitably, non-compliance is often gauged on the basis of clinical judgement.

Factors influencing compliance

Three broad factors relating to compliance have been investigated: patient characteristics, aspects of the treatment and the doctor–patient relationship. The search for specific characteristics which will predict who will or who will not comply with treatment has not proved to be very productive. The health belief model, discussed on p. 490, has been applied rather more effectively. Patients who do not cooperate with their treatment are likely to believe that they are less susceptible to their illness, believe less in the efficacy of modern medicine and believe that the costs of treatment are too high.

Other variables influencing compliance include the extent to which patients understand what is being said to them during a consultation and the amount they are subsequently able to recall. In summarising a number of studies examining patients' understanding of the diagnosis of their medical condition and the medical regime prescribed, Ley (1988) notes that the number of patients judged by experts not to have understood their medication regime varied from 5 per cent to as many as 69 per cent. Many such patients will no doubt fail to comply with the correct medication dosage or timing.

Even if patients understand, they may fail to recall what they are told. In reviewing a number of studies of memory for medical information, Ley (1988) reports that the amount of medical information recalled by hospital patients ranged from 40 to 70 per cent.

The nature of the patient's illness and treatment prescribed will also influence compliance. For an acute illness with unpleasant symptoms, which are directly alleviated by medication, the probability of compliance is high. In contrast, for a chronic illness requiring treatment of long duration, compliance is likely to be poor (Sackett and Snow, 1979); compliance with treatment for diabetes is reviewed in the second part of this chapter. In addition, the more complex the treatment regimen the less likely it is that the treatment will be followed precisely (Haynes, 1976). If the treatment requires a major change in lifestyle, such as for a weight loss or smoking cessation programme, then adherence to the total programme is likely to be low (ibid.). Compliance is also likely to be poor if side effects occur. Indeed, some have argued that, in view of such effects, non-compliance can sometimes be adaptive. However, if the patient gauges that the benefits of treatment outweigh the side effects, the patient is likely to comply with the treatment.

The experience of treatment

'The prospect of undergoing an unpleasant medical procedure may be anxiety-provoking for a number of reasons: patients might be concerned with the pain and discomfort they expect to experience; they might be unfamiliar with the procedure and they might have concerns about the diagnoisis or prognosis' (Edelmann, 1992: 207). Patients who are more anxious prior to surgery are more likely to report post-operative pain, require more analgesic medication, stay in hospital longer and report more anxiety and depression during their recovery period (Anderson and Masur, 1983). This has led to a body of research investigating various strategies designed to reduce pre-operative anxiety and post-operative distress across a range of operative procedures including dental surgery. In the latter case, interventions have also been directed towards management of moderate fear and avoidance of dental treatment.

Psychological techniques designed to prepare patients for surgery include giving information, psychotherapy, modelling, behaviour management, cognitive-behaviour therapy and/or hypnotic procedures. There is evidence that all have some beneficial effects in reducing distress, although the mechanism by which this might operate is far from clear. In addition, the numerous reviews of this work which have appeared within the past decade (e.g. Ludwick-Rosenthal and Neufeld, 1988) have all referred to methodological difficulties which prevent any firm conclusion from being drawn. Problems include the frequent failure to include adequate control groups; a failure to ascertain whether the specific psychological intervention is actually being used by the patients concerned; the use of combinations of treatments, making it difficult to ascertain whether there is one particular effective ingredient; different outcome measures in different studies; and heterogeneous subject populations, both in terms of the operative procedure they are undergoing and in terms of their past history with these procedures.

The most effective intervention, in terms of both behavioural and self-report indices, seems to be modelling, particularly in the case of children, although the review by Saile *et al.* (1988) presents a more cautious assessment. Cognitive-behavioural interventions seem to offer promise, but there are few evaluative studies using this approach and those studies which have been conducted have tended to use a multi-component package (e.g. Wells *et al.*, 1986).

With regard to fear of dental treatment and dental avoidance, several case reports attest to the efficacy of desenitisation either used alone (e.g. Klepac, 1975) or in combination with modelling (e.g. Kleinknecht and Bernstein, 1978) both for reducing fear and promoting regular dental visits. Group comparison studies suggest that flooding, coping skills training, applied relaxation, self-instructional training and cognitive-behaviour therapy also meet with some degree of success on both anxiety and treatment measures (Gauthier *et al.*, 1985; Getka and Glass, 1992; Jerremalm *et al.*, 1986).

CONCLUSIONS AND RECOMMENDATIONS

Health psychology has a major role to play in terms of both health promotion and disease prevention and in furthering our understanding of the experience of becoming ill and receiving medical treatment. Gaining a clearer understanding of factors which prompt people to misuse, fail to use, or delay their use of health service provision, or which prompt them to practice healthy behaviour could have a profound effect upon behaviour change. The latter has implications for a range of life threatening illnesses, including, most recently, AIDS and skin cancer. Indeed, clinical psychologists have long been involved in efforts to influence various health-related behaviours, such as encouraging people to stop smoking or change their diet to reduce cardiovascular risk, although this has often been at the level of the individual or group. The role of clinical psychologists in planning and designing campaigns and advising on community-level interventions is likely to be important in the future, as evidenced by recent attemps to control the spread of the AIDS virus (Morin, 1988).

Psychology also has an important role to play both in facilitating self-management of illness and in reducing distress and anxiety associated with surgical intervention. Again, the role of clinical psychologists in advising and planning at ward or hospital level cannot be overestimated.

MANAGING CHRONIC ILLNESS

Chronic illness refers to any condition which involves some disability, caused by non-reversible pathological change and which requires training or motivation on the part of patients to care for themselves. Such conditions can range from the relatively minor, such as partial hearing loss, to the severe and life threatening, such as cancer, coronary heart disease and diabetes. Chronic illness is increasing for two main reasons: (1) improved treatment in the initial critical stages of acute illness or trauma (e.g. stroke, myocardial infarction) means that more people survive and hence have to live with the longer-term consequences of such illness; (2) within the western world the relative proportion of elderly people is increasing, and such a population is more prone to develop chronic illness. Chronic illness presents the individual with a range of challenges. In addition to the physical effects and pain associated with chronic illness, people are also likely to face emotional and social problems. Sexual dysfunction as a result of illness and/or treatment is also common; for example, it may be associated with hypertension, myocardial infarction and cancer (Anderson et al., 1989).

In addition, medical regimes for treating the symptoms of chronic illness may have unpleasant physical consequences (for example, chemotherapy) or may be difficult to follow (for example, in the treatment of diabetes). Psychological interventions can thus be directed towards pain management, cognitive-behavioural interventions designed to help people cope with the psychological effects of illness or reactions to treatment, maximising support or working with families, cognitive-behavioural interventions designed to enhance self-management of illness in addition to psychosexual counselling, or counselling to assist the process of adjustment to disfigurement or disability.

In order to discuss these issues in context, physical and emotional aspects of illness, in addition to the influence of the person's cognitive evaluations and social support resources as factors moderating the impact of chronic illness will be briefly reviewed.

The impact of chronic illness

Physical problems and chronic illness

Physical problems arising from chronic illness include both those associated with the illness itself and those which are allied to any associated treatment. Physical problems associated with illness include pain, such as chest pain experienced by cardiovascular patients, loss of breath associated with respiratory disorders, metabolic changes associated with cancer, or physical disability associated with multiple sclerosis or spinal cord injury. In addition, patients whose physical appearance is affected by illness, such as in the case of severe burns or mastectomy, may face a major crisis concerning their sense of self as a result of their altered appearance.

Unfortunately, the medical treatment for disease is often more debilitating than the disease itself. Cancer patients receiving chemotherapy often face nausea, vomiting, hair loss and skin discolouration (Burish et al., 1987). Cancer patients receiving radiation therapy have to cope with burning of the skin and gastro-intestinal problems (Nail et al., 1986).

Emotional reactions to chronic illness

Immediately after a chronic illness is diagnosed, patients are often in a state of crisis marked by physical, social and psychological disequilibrium (Moos, 1977). Anxiety, depression and denial are common reactions. While such reactions might be usual, and even beneficial at certain stages of adjustment to chronic illness, they may also impede recovery or treatment. It is thus important to identify adaptive and maladaptive reactions and to offer psychological treatment as appropriate.

Anxiety varies throughout the course of a disease. For example, serial measurements of anxiety in coronary patients admitted to hospital suggest that anxiety is highest on admission to the coronary care unit and immediately after transfer to the ward. It then falls rapidly over the following week, rising just prior to discharge and falling to the lowest level at four months post discharge, although returning to work is associated with a further increase in anxiety (Thompson et al., 1987). Subsequently, every episode of angina pectoris, which may occur for many months or even years post discharge, is likely to provoke further anxiety both for patients and their families (Langosch, 1984). Uncertainty associated with initial outcome and subsequent change in life almost inevitably prompts an increase in anxiety; similar increases in anxiety are associated with medical tests or treatment. While anxiety in such circumstances is not unusual, sustained high levels of anxiety can be problematic because they interfere with good adjustment. Research suggests that highly anxious patients cope poorly with radiotherapy for cancer (Graydon, 1988) and show poorer recovery from myocardial infarction, including a reduced subsequent return to work (Maeland and Havik, 1987).

Depression is also a common reaction to chronic illness, with as many as one-third of such in-patients reporting at least moderate symptoms of depression (Rodin and Voshart, 1986). Increased depression has been shown to be associated with illness severity in the case of Parkinson's disease (Dakof and Mendelsohn, 1986), the amount of pain and the extent of disability in relation to rheumatoid arthritis (Hawley and Wolfe, 1988; Fitzpatrick et al., 1988), degree of physical impairment in relation to diabetes (Littlefield et al., 1990), and with lack of social support or negative life events in cancer patients (Bukberg et al., 1984). Although depression can occur at any phase of the adjustment process, it is likely to occur somewhat later than anxiety, being associated with a realisation by patients of the implications of their condition. As with anxiety, depression similarly impedes rehabilitation and recovery. For example, depressed in comparison with non-depressed stroke patients are likely to remain in hospital for a longer period of time (Cushman, 1986). Myocardial infarction patients who are depressed are less likely to return to work one year later and are more likely to be hospitalised (Stern et al., 1977). Unfortunately, because many of the symptoms of depression, such as loss of appetite, weight loss and sleeplessness, are also symptoms of disease, depression is not always diagnosed and treated.

A final common reaction to diagnosis is denial or avoidance of the implications of illness. In the short term such a reaction can save the patient from having immediately to face the full range of problems posed by their illness, possibly providing them with time to mobilise other coping strategies. Hence it serves a protective function. For example, myocardial infarction patients with high levels of denial of impact of the condition while hospitalised show least short-term emotional upset. (Havik and Maeland, 1990). In the longer term, however, denial may impede the process of recovery, as patients may fail to monitor their condition or follow medication regimes, or fail to change their lifestyle in a way which would enhance their quality of life. Thus, in the longer term, denial or avoidance coping may be a risk factor for adverse response to illness (Felton et al., 1984). In one recent report, escape-avoidance coping was associated with more emotional distress for cancer patients, 72 per cent of whom had been diagnosed with initial cancers in the previous five years (Dunkel-Schetter et al., 1992). In contrast, patients who have a confrontative response, who seek advice or support, who focus on the positive and who believe they can personally control their illness tend to show less psychological distress (e.g. Affleck et al., 1987; Dunkel-Schetter et al., op. cit.). Effective management may thus depend upon identifying which strategies facilitate recovery at which stages of illness and for which particular patients. Such knowledge can subsequently be used to assist patients in the process of developing effective coping. In the longer term, patients' beliefs about their illness can play a major role in affecting adjustment.

Cognitive evaluation of chronic illness

Chronic illness is almost inevitably associated with life change. This may involve dietary control, vigilance for symptom recurrence, alteration in daily activities or a more generally restricted lifestyle. How people adapt to chronic health problems is influenced to a considerable degree by their evaluation, perception and reaction to their illness.

Self-blame has been shown to be related to poor adjustment in some studies (e.g. Kiecolt-Glaser and Williams, 1987, in relation to burn patients) and good adjustment in others (e.g. Bulman and Wortman, 1977, in relation to accident victims). In a review of illness attributions and adjustment, Turnquist *et al.*, (1988) comment that patients who report any implicit or explicit causal explanation for their illness seem to have more positive physical or emotional outcome than patients who fail to report a causal explanation. However, blaming someone else, such as family members or work colleagues has been shown to be more consistently maladaptive (e.g. Affleck *et al.*, 1987).

A further consistent finding is that patients who believe that they can control their illness show better psychological adjustment than patients without such beliefs. This is independent of whether or not the physical side of illness is controlled. Consistent findings have been obtained for patients with cancer (e.g. Taylor *et al.*, 1984), rheumatoid arthritis (Affleck *et al.*, 1987), stroke (Partridge and Johnston, 1989) and patients with spinal cord injuries (Schulz and Decker 1985).

It seems, however, that the role of health-related cognitions is constrained by the physical realities of disease. Dakof and Mendelsohn (1989) found that, for patients with mild to moderate impairment from Parkinson's disease, a sense of control, a belief that things could be worse and an ability to put negative thoughts out of their mind was related to positive psychological adjustment. Patients with severe impairment, however, reported elevated passivity or depression regardless of their beliefs. Similar findings have been reported by Rosenbaum and Palmon (1984) for patients with epilepsy. For patients with low to moderate seizure frequency, lower anxiety and depression was associated with a belief that their seizures could be controlled. Patients with high frequency of seizures reported negative affect irrespective of beliefs about controllability of seizures. In spite of these findings, however, psychological interventions aimed at encouraging more effective health-related cognitions could produce beneficial effects for many patients.

Social support

Adapting to chronic illness is also enhanced by having an effective system of social support (Wallston *et al.*, 1983). The relationship between good social relationships and positive adjustment to illness has been reported for cancer patients (e.g. Neuling and Winefield, 1988), rheumatoid arthritis patients

(Fitzpatrick *et al.*, 1988; Goodenow *et al.*, 1990), persons with diabetes (Littlefield *et al.*, 1990) and patients with spinal cord injuries (Schulz and Decker, 1985). In addition, studies have found that social support from family and friends reduces distress during recovery from coronary heart disease (e.g. Fontana *et al.*, 1989), a supportive marriage is associated with better diabetes control (e.g. Marteau *et al.*, 1987), and patients with AIDS who perceive themselves as having more available social support experience less depression and helplessness (Zich and Temoshok, 1987). One possibility is that the 'right kind' of support assists the individual's coping efforts. Thus, effective social support depends upon a match between what one needs and what one receives from those within one's social network. A recent study (Dakof and Taylor, 1990) suggests that different people within a social network are valued for providing different types of support. Emotional support is valued from those we are closer to at a personal level, while information and advice are valued from experts.

Yet, chronic illness can serve as a threat to social resources. Disruption in the life of one family member inevitably affects the lives of others. Chronic illness may lead to social withdrawal, while friends who normally provide social support may feel unable to deal with the ill person and hence withdraw this support (Wortman and Dunkel-Schetter, 1979). Psychological interventions for chronic illness could thus usefully address issues relating to social support. Increasing the effectiveness of existing support resources, facilitating support groups, involving families of the chronically ill in treatment, as well as helping the families themselves to cope, are all areas where psychology can contribute.

Psychological interventions

Given the physical and emotional aspects of chronic illness and its treatment, and the fact that adverse effects can to some extent be ameliorated by both cognitive appraisal and social resources, rehabilitation efforts can usefully be directed at each of these factors. At the physical level, cognitive-behavioural interventions for pain control are likely to have an increasingly important role to play, as is the psychological management of adverse emotional reactions to chronic illness. As noted above, strategies for modifying cognitive appraisal or influencing a person's social resources are also likely to promote more positive psychological adjustment. As illustration, three specific aspects of psychological intervention with chronic illness will be briefly reviewed in this final section: strategies for achieving pain reduction, strategies for modifying negative emotional reactions, and strategies for managing adverse reactions to treatment or difficulty adhering to treatment regimes.

Coping with pain

The control of pain remains a serious problem for many patients with chronic illness. For example, Dalton and Feuerstein (1988) estimate that 25 per cent of cancer patients do not find relief from pain. Although medication remains the primary method for treating cancer-related pain, behavioural methods are now also being used (Davis *et al.*, 1987).

Cognitive-behavioural interventions for pain have also been explored in relation to rheumatoid arthritis. For example, O'Leary *et al.* (1988) randomly assigned patients to either a cognitive-behavioural programme, where they were taught skills in managing stress, pain and symptoms of the disease, or an arthritis information group, who received a self-help book giving details of arthritis self-managment. Results indicated that those in the cognitive-behavioural group experienced reduced pain and joint inflammation and improved psychosocial functioning.

Although psychologists have contributed extensively to the study and management of chronic pain, this has generally been in relation to muscle or joint pain, especially low back pain, vascular pain, especially migraine headaches, and phantom limb pain. Less attention has been paid to pain associated with cancer or rheumatoid arthritis. Not only might psychological interventions help in pain control, they could also help to limit the consequences of pain, such as sleep disturbance, irritability and other behavioural difficulties.

Coping with emotions

A number of studies have investigated the utility of psychological interventions for helping patients to cope with anxiety and/or depression in both the acute phase of illness (for example, immediately post myocardial infarction or subsequent to the diagnosis of a potentially life-threatening disease) and during the course of chronic disease (for example, in relation to asthma).

In the former case, there is some evidence that psychological intervention during the acute coronary care phase can have a beneficial outcome on both psychological and medical parameters (e.g. Gruen, 1975; Thompson and Meddis, 1990). In one of the earliest studies, Gruen randomly assigned seventy myocardial infarction patients to either a control group receiving standard hospital care or a treatment group receiving support, reinforcement and reassurance. Those receiving the intervention fared better on a number of measures, including days hospitalised and anxiety both in hospital and at four-month follow-up (Gruen, op. cit.). In a more recent report, Thompson and Meddis randomly assigned sixty male myocardial infarction patients admitted to a coronary care unit with a first-time acute myocardial infarction to either a treatment group receiving in-hospital counselling in addition to routine care, or a control group which received routine care only. The counselled group reported significantly less anxiety and depression in comparison with the routine care group both in hospital and at six-month follow-up. Taken together with other findings, this led Thompson and Meddis to comment that 'such simple intervention in the acute phase is therapeutically beneficial, efficient and economic, and should be offered routinely to patients who have suffered a first MI' (Thompson and Meddis, 1990: 247).

In relation to newly diagnosed cancer patients, Worden and Weisman (1984) evaluated the efficacy of two different four-session psychotherapeutic interventions for lowering emotional distress and improving coping skills in relation to a no-treatment control group. In the first, patient-centred treatment, the therapist's role was to help patients identify and explore ways of solving problems they were experiencing. In the second, problem-focused intervention, patients were provided with a specific step-by-step approach to problem-solving. Both treatment groups had significantly lower emotional distress at each of a series of follow-up assessments and resolved problems more effectively in comparison with the control group. There were no differences between the two intervention groups.

With the course of any disease patients understandably experience varying emotional reactions. Determining the relationship of psychological factors to the course of a disease and developing effective intervention programmes is of particular importance. A number of studies have evaluated psychological interventions in coronary heart disease subsequent to hospital discharge. For example, Burgess *et al.*, (1987) randomly assigned 180 post MI patients to either a cardiac rehabilitation programme, consisting of cognitive-behavioural counselling, or standard cardiological aftercare. At three months the cardiac rehabilitation group reported less distress, anxiety and depression than the control group, although at thirteen-month follow-up none of the between-group differences was significant. However, in reviewing the evidence from a range of studies evaluating psychological interventions post MI, Bundy comments that 'most have been successful on some outcome measures' (Bundy, 1989: 170).

A range of interventions, including hypnosis, relaxation, systematic desensitisation and contingency management, have also been used as treatment for asthma (e.g. Yorkston *et al.*, 1974). Although the aim of such treatments has frequently been to improve lung function, there is little evidence of their efficacy in this regard. Such treatments are, however, meaningful when tension or anxiety are secondarily associated with asthma. Psychological interventions have also been used to help patients and their spouses cope with the psychological consequences of a range of other chronic illnesses, including cancer (e.g. Heinrich and Schag, 1985) and stroke (Krantz and Deckel, 1983). Such interventions have a clear role to play in improving the person's ability to cope with a disease once it has been diagnosed.

Problems associated with medical treatment

There are two main problems associated with medical treatment that have proved amenable to psychological intervention: adverse effects of medical treatment and problems adhering to the medical regime. The former includes nausea and vomiting associated with chemotherapy, or anxiety and panic associated with dialysis treatment of end-stage renal disease. The issues of adhering to a medical regime have been extensively investigated in relation to diabetes.

Although there are a number of unpleasant side effects of the drugs involved in chemotherapy these are often made worse by psychologically conditioned reactions to the treatment experience. Patients may experience anticipatory nausea and vomiting (ANV) without having had any chemical treatment at all. Factors associated with ANV include severity of post-treatment nausea and vomiting and anxiety; younger patients are also more likely to develop ANV (Morrow et al., 1991; Watson and Marvell, 1992). ANV seems to be particularly resistant to medication so that considerable attention has been focused upon psychological intervention (see Carey and Burish, 1988 and Morrow and Dobkin, 1988 for reviews). These include relaxation training (e.g. Burish and Lyles, 1981), systematic desensitisation (Morrow, 1986), relaxation training with guided imagery (e.g. Burish et al., 1987) and cognitive/attentional distraction (e.g. Redd et al., 1987). Thus, Burish and Lyles (1981) found that patients taught relaxation immediately prior to chemotherapy, allied with guided mastery used when relaxed and while drugs were administered, showed lower levels of both patient-and nurse-reported distress, nausea and anxiety than a no-relaxation control group. In a further report, Burish et al. (1987) taught one group of patients relaxation and guided mastery prior to their first cycle of chemotherapy. During the fourth and fifth cycles of chemotherapy, when ANV might be expected to occur, the incidence of ANV was significantly lower for the treated group than for the no-treatment control. In another study, Morrow (1986) found that systematic desensitisation was superior to relaxation, counselling or a no-treatment control in reducing ANV.

There are several posible explanations for how and why psychological interventions are effective (Carey and Burish, 1988; Morrow and Dobkin, 1988). One possibility is that these techniques distract patients sufficiently to divert attention from the chemotherapy treatments so that conditioning no longer occurs. Certainly this may be the case in those studies using relaxation, guided imagery or cognitive distraction where attention is diverted to either pleasant bodily sensations or pleasant images, but would seem less likely to apply in the case of systematic desensitisation which specifically focuses attention on aversive stimuli associated with the chemotherapy experience. A second possibility is that relaxation is the effective component. Certainly research suggests that relaxation as a treatment for ANV reduces physiological arousal (Burish et al., 1987) and may also reduce the subjective anxiety component that may serve as a conditioned stimuli for ANV. Relaxation may also decrease muscular contractions in the gastrointestinal tract, thus having a direct effect of reducing the likelihood of nausea and vomiting. Few studies exist comparing different interventions for ANV; such studies could perhaps clarify the mechanism by which psychological therapies operate.

Relaxation has also been shown to be effective in reducing anxiety and panic associated with dialysis as treatment for end-stage renal disease. In conjunction with systematic desensitisation and contingency management, relaxation has also been found to be effective in reducing frequency of vomiting behaviours accompanying dialysis (see Long, 1989).

In addition to alleviating distress associated with treatment, psychological interventions have been effectively used to improve adherence to treatment. The treatment goal for diabetes is to keep blood sugar at normal levels. This is accomplished through insulin injections, weight control, exercise, dietary control, such as reduced sugar and carbohydrate intake, and stress management. The regime is made more complex by the need to modify each of these factors over time depending upon the level of activity of the patients and their self-monitored blood glucose level. Inevitably, such a self-regulation programme involving voluntary restriction of diet, engaging in exercise, and the accurate monitoring of blood-glucose levels is no easy matter. Diet and exercise seem the most difficult aspects of diabetic treatment to manage and, although research is contradictory, poor social support and psychological stress seem to be associated with poor self-management (Goodall and Halford, 1991). In order to improve self-regulation of diabetes, a variety of interventions have been applied; these include information-giving, skills training and behaviourally based interventions.

The underlying assumption of many diabetes education programmes has been that people with diabetes do not manage their condition effectively because they lack the necessary knowledge. Although a range of such education studies report improvements in knowledge about diabetes, this does not translate into better long-term glycaemic control or to decreased hospitalisation (Goodall and Halford, 1991; Shillitoe, 1988). A small number of studies (e.g. McCulloch *et al.*, 1983) have provided skills training and feedback in addition to basic information. McCulloch *et al.* required patients to make choices from a menu, recognising and selecting appropriate quantities of permitted food from those available, receiving immediate appropriate feedback from a dietician. Seven days later, self-report food records showed improved dietary management for the feedback groups in comparison with two comparison groups provided with education or information alone.

A number of studies have evaluated behavioural interventions to improve diabetes management in children, adolescents and adults. Those involving adults have been aimed primarily at weight loss, although some have focused on helping patients engage in approriate self-injection or on effective monitoring of blood sugar levels. Results from such studies have not been encouraging, leading one group of researchers (Wing *et al.*, 1986) to suggest that the most effective self-regulation treatment programme might involve a multiple intervention package teaching patients to monitor blood sugar accurately and to use this information as a basis for making changes in behaviour through self-injection, reinforcing themselves for efforts to improve blood sugar control, managing stress, controlling diet and exercising.

Psychological interventions aimed at children and adolescents include systematic goal setting, self-monitoring, behavioural contracting, supervised exercise programmes and skills training. For example, Carney *et al.* (1983)

operated a token reinforcement programme where points were given for appropriately and accurately testing glucose levels. In addition, they made parental praise contingent upon the test being performed without prompting within ten minutes of the appropriate time. Although improved self-management and glycaemic control were acheived, the small sample (three children) and limited follow-up (four months) limit conclusions. Unfortunately these are common criticisms of many studies in this area.

A further issue of particular relevance to adolescents is the part played by peer pressure in causing deviation from management regimes. This has led some to evaluate social-skills training to promote assertive resistance to such pressure, although results have not necessarily been positive. For example, Gross *et al.*, (1983) found an improved level of social skills in the 9- to 12-year-old children who participated in their study, but no improvements in glycaemic control.

CONCLUSIONS AND RECOMMENDATIONS

Within the past few decades the relative proportion of illness which involves chronic disease has steadily increased. In such instances, coping with pain, physical, social and emotional problems has more relevance than 'curing the disease'. Psychological interventions can thus be directed towards pain management, helping patients and their families cope with the emotional and social effects of both the illness and its treatment, and enhancing self-management with regard to medical treatment. Although clinical psychologists have contributed extensively to the study and management of chronic pain, especially low back pain, less attention has been paid to psychological management of pain associated with cancer or rheumatoid arthritis. In contrast, a number of studies attest to the utility of psychological interventions for helping patients cope with anxiety and/or depression in the acute phase of illness (e.g. post myocardial infarction), immediately post diagnosis of a potentially life-threatening disease (e.g. cancer) and during the course of chronic disease (e.g. asthma). In addition, psychological interventions have proved to be particularly useful in helping patients cope with adverse effects of medical treatment (e.g. nausea and vomiting associated with chemotherapy and anxiety/panic associated with dialysis) and for improving self-management of illness (e.g. diabetes). A major goal for clinical health psychology in the future is likely to involve further development of effective interventions for helping people cope with the psychological consequences of chronic illness and its treatment. Implementation of such interventions is likely to be facilitated by active involvement of clinical psychologists at two levels: the operationalisation of psychological care at the point of delivery of medical care, and training other health professionals in psychological techniques for helping chronically ill patients and their families cope with illness and treatment.

REFERENCES

Affleck, G., Tennen, H., Pfeiffer, C. and Fifield, C. (1987) 'Appraisals of control and predictability in adapting to chronic disease', *Journal of Personality and Social Psychology* 53: 273–9.

Ajzen, I. and Madden, T. J. (1986) 'Prediction of goal-directed behavior: Attitudes, intentions, and perceived behavioral control', *Journal of Experimental Social Psychology* 22: 453–74.

Ampofo-Boateng, K. and Thomson, J. A. (1989) 'Child pedestrian accidents: A case for preventive medicine', *Health Education Research* 5: 265–74.

Anderson, B. L., Anderson, B. and deProsse, C. (1989) 'Controlled prospective longitudinal study of women with cancer: 1. Sexual functioning outcomes', *Journal of Consulting and Clinical Psychology* 57: 683–91.

Anderson, K. O. and Masur, F. T. (1983) 'Psychological preparation for invasive medical and surgical procedures', *Journal of Behavioral Medicine* 6: 1–40.

Bandura, A. (1977) Self-efficacy: 'Toward a unifying theory of behavioral change', *Psychological Review* 84: 191–15.

Batchelor, W. F. (1988) 'AIDS 1988: The science and the limits of science', *American Psychologist* 43: 853–8.

Becker, M. H. (ed.) (1974) 'The health belief model and personal health behavior', *Health Education Monograph* 2: 324–508.

Becker, M. H. and Joseph, J. G. (1988) 'AIDS and behavior change to reduce risks: A review', *American Journal of Public Health* 78: 394–410.

Becker, M. H. and Rosenstock, I. M. (1984) 'Compliance with medical advice', in A. Steptoe and A. Mathews (eds) *Health Care and Human Behaviour*, London: Academic Press.

Blair, S. N., Kohl, H. W., Paffenberger, R. S. Jr, Clark, D. G., Cooper, K. H. and Gibbons, L. W. (1989) 'Physical fitness and all-cause mortality: a prospective study of healthy men and women', *Journal of the American Medical Association* 262: 2395–401.

Bouchard, C., Shephard, R. J., Stephens, T., Sutton, J. R. and McPherson, B. D. (1990) 'Exercise, fitness, and health: the consensus statement', in C. Bouchard, R. J. Shephard, T. Stephens, J. R. Sutton and B. D. McPherson (eds) *Exercise, Fitness and Health*, Champaign, Ill.: Human Kinetics Press.

Brubaker, R. G. and Wickersham, D. (1990) 'Encouraging the practice of testicular self-examination: a field application of the theory of reasoned action', *Health Psychology* 9: 154–63.

Bukberg, J., Penman, D. and Holland, J. C. (1984) 'Depression in hospitalized cancer patients', *Psychosomatic Medicine* 46: 199–212.

Bulman, J. R. and Wortman, C. B. (1977) 'Attributions of blame and coping in the "real world": Severe accident victims react to their lot', *Journal of Personality and Social Psychology* 35: 351–63.

Bundy, C. (1989) 'Cardiac disorders', in A. Broome (ed.) *Health Psychology: Process and Applications*, London: Chapman and Hall.

Burgess, I. S., Lerner, D. J., D'Agostino, R. B., Vokanas, P. S., Hartman, C. R. and Gaccione, P. (1987) 'A randomised control trial of cardiac rehabilitation', *Social Science and Medicine* 24: 359–70.

Burish, T. G. and Lyles, J. N. (1981) 'Effectiveness of relaxation training in reducing aversive reactions to cancer chemotherapy', *Journal of Behavioral Medicine* 4: 65–78.

Burish, T. G., Carey, M. P., Krozely, M. G. and Greco, F. A. (1987) 'Conditioned side effects induced by cancer chemotherapy: prevention through behavioral treatment', *Journal of Consulting and Clinical Psychology* 55: 42–8.

Byrne, P. S. and Long, T. G. (1976) *Doctors Talking to Patients*, London: HMSO.

Carey, M. P. and Burish, T. G. (1988) 'Etiology and treatment of the psychological side effects associated with cancer chemotherapy: a critical review and discussion', *Psychological Bulletin* 104: 307–25.

Carney, R. M., Schechter, K. and Davis, T. (1983) 'Improving adherence to blood glucose testing in insulin-dependent diabetic children', *Behavior Therapy* 24: 247–54.

Caron, H. S. (1985) Compliance: 'The case for objective measurement', *Journal of Hypertension* 3 (Supplement 1): 11–17.

Crandall, L. A. and Duncan, R. P. (1981) 'Attitudinal and situational factors in the use of physician services by low income persons', *Journal of Health and Social Behavior* 22: 64–77.

Craun, A. M. and Deffenbacher, J. L. (1987) 'The effects of information, behavioral rehearsal, and prompting on breast self-exams', *Journal of Behavioral Medicine* 10: 351–65.

Cushman, L. A. (1986) 'Secondary neuropsychiatric complications in stroke: Implications for acute care', *Archives of Physical Medicine and Rehabilitation* 69: 877–9.

Dakof, G. A. and Mendelsohn, G. A. (1986) 'Parkinson's disease: the psychological aspects of a chronic illness', *Psychological Bulletin* 99: 375–87.

Dakof, G. A. and Mendelsohn, G. A. (1989) 'Patterns of adaption to Parkinson's disease', *Health Psychology* 8: 355–72.

Dakof, G. A. and Taylor, S. E. (1990) 'Victims' perceptions of social support: what is helpful to whom?' *Journal of Personality and Social Psychology* 58: 80–9.

Dalton, J. A. and Feverstein, M. (1988) 'Biobehavioral factors in cancer pain', *Pain* 32: 137–47.

Davis, M., Vasterling, J., Bransfield, D. and Burish, T. G. (1987) 'Behavioral interventions in coping with cancer-related pain', *British Journal of Guidance and Counselling* 15: 17–28.

DiMatteo, M. R. (1985) 'Physician–patient communication: promoting a positive health care setting', in J. C. Rosen and L. J. Solomon (eds) *Prevention in Health Psychology*, Hanover, NH.: University Press of New England.

DiMatteo, M. R. and DiNicola, D. D. (1982) *Achieving Patient Compliance*, New York: Pergamon.

Dishman, R. K., Sallis, J. F. and Orenstein, D. R. (1985) 'The determinants of physical activity and exercise', *Public Health Reports* 100: 158–71.

Dubbert, P. M. (1992) 'Exercise in behavioral medicine', *Journal of Consulting and Clinical Psychology* 60: 613–18.

Dunbar, J. M. and Agras, W. S. (1980) 'Compliance in medical instructions', in J. M. Ferguson and C. B. Taylor (eds) *Comprehensive Handbook of Behavioural Medicine, Vol. 3*, New York: Spectrum.

Dunkel-Schetter, C., Feinstein, L. G., Taylor, S. E. and Falke, R. L. (1992) 'Patterns of coping with cancer', *Health Psychology* 11: 79–87.

Edelmann, R. J. (1992) *Anxiety: Theory, Research and Intervention in Clinical and Health Psychology*, Chichester: John Wiley.

Feletti, G., Fireman, D. and Sanson-Fisher, R. (1986) 'Patient satisfaction with primary-care consultations', *Journal of Behavioral Medicine* 9: 389–400.

Felton, B. J., Revenson, T. A. and Hinrichsen, G. A. (1984) 'Stress and coping in the explanation of psychological adjustment among chronically ill adults', *Social Science and Medicine* 18: 889–98.

Fishbein, M. and Ajzen, I. (1975) *Belief, Attitude, Intention and Behavior: An Introduction to Theory and Research*, Massachusetts: Addison-Wesley.

Fitzpatrick, R., Newman, S., Lamb, R. and Shipley, M. (1988) 'Social relationships and psychological well-being in rheumatoid arthritis', *Social Science and Medicine* 27: 399–403.

Flora, J. A. and Thoresen, C. E. (1988) 'Reducing the risk of AIDS in adolescents', *American Psychologist* 43: 965–70.

Fontana, A. F., Kerns, R. D., Rosenberg, R. L. and Colonese, K. L. (1989) 'Support, stress, and recovery from coronary heart disease: A longitudinal causal model', *Health Psychology* 8: 175–93.

Garland, C., Barrett-Conner, E., Suaret, L., Criqui, W. H. and Wingard, D. L. (1985) 'Effects of passive smoking on ischemic heart disease mortality of nonsmokers', *American Journal of Epidemiology* 121: 645–50.

Gauthier, J., Savard, F., Halle, J. P. and Dufour, L. (1985) 'Flooding and coping skills training in the management of dental fear', *Scandinavian Journal of Behaviour Therapy* 14: 3–15.

Getka, E. J. and Glass, C. R. (1992) 'Behavioral and cognitive-behavioral approaches to the reduction of dental anxiety', *Behavior Therapy* 23: 443–8.

Goodall, T. A. and Halford, W. K. (1991) 'Self-management of diabetes mellitus: a critical review', *Health Psychology* 10: 1–8.

Goodenow, C., Reisine, S. T. and Grady, K. E. (1990) 'Quality of social support and associated social and psychological functioning in women with rheumatoid arthritis', *Health Psychology* 9: 266–84.

Graydon, J. E. (1988) 'Factors that predict patients functioning following treatment for cancer', *International Journal of Nursing Studies* 25: 117–24.

Gross, A. M., Heimann, L., Shapiro, R. and Schulz, R. M. (1983) 'Children with diabetes: Social skills training and hemoglobin Alc levels', *Behavior Modification* 7: 151–64.

Gruen, W. (1975) 'Effects of brief psychotherapy during the hospitalization period on the recovery process in heart attacks', *Journal of Consulting and Clinical Psychology* 43: 223–32.

Havik, O. E. and Maeland, J. G. (1990) 'Patterns of emotional reactions after myocardial infarction', *Journal of Psychosomatic Research* 34: 271–85.

Hawley, D. J. and Wolfe, F. (1988) 'Anxiety and depression in patients with reumatoid arthritis: a prospective study of 400 patients', *Journal of Rheumatology* 15: 932–41.

Haynes, R. E. (1976) 'A critical review of the "determinants" of patient compliance with therapeutic regimes', in D. L. Sackett and R. B. Haynes (eds) *Adherence, Compliance, and Generalization in Behavioral Medicine*, New York: Brunner/Mazel.

Heinrich, R. L. and Schag, C. C. (1985) 'Stress and activity management: group training for cancer patients and spouses', *Journal of Consulting and Clinical Psychology* 53: 439–46.

Janz, N. K. and Becker, M. H. (1984) 'The health belief model: a decade later', *Health Education Quarterly* 11: 1–47.

Jeffery, R. W. (1989) 'Risk behaviors and health: contrasting individual and population perspectives', *American Psychologist* 44: 1194–202.

Jerremalm, A., Jansson, L. and Ost, L.G. (1986) Individual response patterns and the effects of different behavioural methods in the treatment of dental phobia', *Behaviour Research and Therapy* 24: 587–96.

Johnston, D. and Steptoe, A. (1989) 'Hypertension', in S. Pearce and J. Wardle (eds) *The Practice of Behavioural Medicine*, Oxford: BPS Books/Oxford University Press.

Joseph, J. G., Montgomery, S. B., Emmons, C., Kessler, R. C., Ostrow, D. G., Wortman, C. B., O'Brien, K., Eller, M. and Eshleman, S. (1987) 'Magnitude and determinants of behavioral risk reduction: longitudinal analysis of a cohort at risk for AIDS', *Psychology and Health* 1: 73–96.

Kannel, W. B. and Eaker, E. D. (1986) 'Psychosocial and other features of coronary heart disease: Insights from the Framingham Study', *American Heart Journal* 112: 1066–73.

Keesling, B. and Friedman, H., S. (1987) 'Psychosocial factors in sunbathing and sunscreen use', *Health Psychology* 6: 477–93.

Kiecolt-Glaser, J. K. and Williams, D. A. (1987) 'Self-blame, compliance, and distress among burn patients', *Journal of Personality and Social Psychology* 53: 187–93.

Kirscht, J. P. (1983) 'Preventive health behavior: a review of research and issues', *Health Psychology* 2: 277–301.

Kleinknecht, R. A. and Bernstein, D. (1978) 'Assessment of dental fear', *Behaviour Research and Therapy* 9: 626–34.

Klepac, R. K. (1975) 'Successful treatment of avoidance of dental work by desensitization or increasing pain tolerance', *Journal of Behavior Therapy and Experimental Psychiatry* 6: 307–10.

Koplan, J. P., Caspersen, C. J. and Powell, K. E. (1989) 'Physical activity, physical fitness, and health: time to act', *Journal of the American Medical Association* 262: 2437.

Korsch, B. M., Gozzi, E. K. and Francis, V. (1968) 'Gaps in doctor–patient communication: 1. Doctor–patient interaction and patient satisfaction', *Journal of Pediatrics* 42: 855–71.

Krantz, D. S. and Deckel, A. W. (1983) 'Coping with coronary heart disease and stroke', in T. G. Burish and L. A. Bradley (eds) *Coping with Chronic Disease: Research and Applications*, New York: Academic press.

Langosch, W. (1984) 'Behavioural interventions in cardiac rehabilitation, in A. Steptoe and A. Mathews (eds) *Health Care and Human Behaviour*, London: Academic Press.

Ley, P. (1988) *Communicating with Patients: Improving Communication, Satisfaction and Compliance*, London: Croom Helm.

Ley, P. (1989) 'Improving patients' understanding, recall, satisfaction and compliance', in A. Broome (ed.) *Health Psychology: Process and Applications*, London: Chapman & Hall.

Littlefield, C. H., Rodin, G. M., Murray, M. A. and Craven, J. L. (1990) 'Influence of functional impairment and social support on depressive symptoms in persons with diabetes', *Health Psychology* 9: 737–49.

Long, C. L. (1989) 'Renal care', in A. Broome (ed.) *Health Psychology: Process and Applications*, London: Chapman & Hall.

Ludwick-Rosenthal, R. and Neufeld, R. W. J. (1988) 'Stress management during noxious medical procedures: An evaluative overview of outcome studies', *Psychological Bulletin* 104: 326–42.

McCulloch, D. K., Mitchell, R. D., Ambler, J. and Tattersall, R. B. (1983) 'Influence of imaginative teaching of diet on compliance and metabolic control in insulin dependent diabetes', *British Medical Journal* 28: 1858–61.

Maeland, J. G. and Havik, O. E. (1987) 'Psychological predictors for return to work after a myocardial infarction', *Journal of Psychosomatic Research* 31: 471–81.

Manstead, A. S. R., Proffitt, C. and Smart, J. L. (1983) 'Predicting and understanding mothers' infant-feeding intentions and behavior: testing the theory of reasoned action', *Journal of Personality and Social Psychology* 44: 657–71.

Marteau, T. M., Bloch, S. and Baum, J. D. (1987) 'Family life and diabetes control', *Journal of Child Psychology and Psychiatry* 28: 823–33.

Matorazzo, J. D. (1980) 'Behavioral health and behavioral medicine: frontiers for a new health psychology', *American Psychologist* 35: 807–17.

Mattson, M. E., Pollack, E. S. and Cullen, J. W. (1987) 'What are the odds that smoking will kill you?' *American Journal of Public Health* 77: 425–31.

Mays, V. M. and Cochran, S. D. (1988) 'Issues in the perception of AIDS risk and risk reduction activities by Black and Hispanic/Latino women', *American Psychologist* 43: 949–57.

Moos, R. H. (1977) *Coping with Physical Illness*, New York: Plenum.

Morin, S. F. (1988) 'AIDS: The challenge to psychology', *American Psychologist* 43: 838–45.

Morrow, G. R. (1986) 'Effect of the cognitive hierarchy in the systematic desensitisation of anticipatory nausea in cancer patients: a component comparison with relaxation only, counselling and no treatment', *Cognitive Therapy and Research* 10: 421–66.

Morrow, G. R. and Dobkin, P. L. (1988) 'Anticipatory nausea and vomiting in cancer patients undergoing chemotherapy treatment: prevalence, etiology, and behavioral interventions', *Clinical Psychology Review* 8: 517–56.

Morrow, G. R., Lindke, J. and Black, P. M. (1991) 'Anticipatory nausea in cancer patients: Replication and extension of a learning model', *British Journal of Psychology* 82: 61–72.

Nail, L. M., King, K. B. and Johnson, J. E. (1986) 'Coping with radiation treatment for gynecologic cancer: Mood and disruption in usual function', *Journal of Psychosomatic Obstetrics and Gynaecology* 5: 271–81.

Neuling, S. J. and Winefield, H. R. (1988) 'Social support and recovery from breast cancer: Frequency and correlates of supportive behavior by family, friends and surgeon', *Social Science and Medicine* 27: 385–92.

O'Leary, A., Shoor, S., Lorig, K. and Holman, H. R. (1988) 'A cognitive-behavioral treatment for rheumatoid arthritis', *Health Psychology* 7: 527–44.

Osborn, J. E. (1988) 'The AIDS epidemic: six years', in L. Breslow, J. E. Fielding and L. B. Lave (eds) *Annual Review of Public Health, Vol. 9*, Palo Alto, Calif. :Annual Reviews.

Partridge, C. J. and Johnston, M. (1989) 'Perceived control and recovery from stroke', *British Journal of Clinical Psychology* 28: 53–60.

Redd, W. H., Jacobson, P. B., Die-Trill, M., Dermatis, H., McEvoy, M. and Holland, J. (1987) 'Cognitive/attentional distraction in the control of conditioned nausea in paediatric cancer patients receiving chemotherapy', *Journal of Consulting and Clinical Psychology* 55: 391–5.

Rodin, G. and Voshart, K. (1986) 'Depression in the medically ill: an overview', *American Journal of Psychiatry* 143: 696–705.

Rosenbaum, M. and Palmon, N. (1984) 'Helplessness and resourcefulness in coping with epilepsy', *Journal of Consulting and Clinical Psychology* 52: 244–53.

Sackett, D. L. and Snow, J. C. (1979) 'The magnitude of compliance and non-compliance', in R. B. Haynes, D. W. Taylor and D. L. Sackett (eds) *Compliance in Health Care*, Baltimore: Johns Hopkins University Press.

Safer, M. A., Tharps, Q. J., Jackson, T. C. and Leventhal, H. (1979) 'Determinants of three stages of delay in seeking care at a medical clinic', *Medical Care* 17: 11–29.

Saile, H., Burgmeier, R. and Schmidt, L. R. (1988) 'A meta-analysis of studies of psychological preparation of children facing medical procedures', *Psychology and Health* 2: 107–32.

Schulz, R. and Decker, S. (1985) 'Long-term adjustment to physical disability: The role of social support, perceived control, and self-blame', *Journal of Personality and Social Psychology* 48: 1162–72.

Shekelle, R. B., Hulley, S. B., Neaton, J. D., Billings, J. H., Borhani, N. O., Gerace, T. A., Jacobs, D. R., Lasser, N. L., Mittlemark, M. B. and Stamler, J. (1985) 'The MRFIT behavior pattern study: II. Type A behavior and incidence of coronary heart disease', *American Journal of Epidemiology* 122: 559–70.

Shillitoe, R. W. (1988) *Psychology and Diabetes: Psychosocial Factors in Management and Control*, London: Chapman & Hall.

Solomon, M. Z. and DeLong, W. (1986) 'Recent sexually transmitted disease prevention efforts and their implication for AIDS health education', *Health Education Quarterly* 13: 301–16.

Stall, R. D., Coates, T. J. and Hoff, C. (1988) 'Behavioral risk reduction for HIV infection among gay and bisexual men', *American Psychologist* 43: 878–85.

Stern, M. J., Pascale, L. and Ackerman, A. (1977) 'Life adjustment post-myocardial infarction: determining predictive variables', *Archives of Internal Medicine* 137: 1680–85.

Stone, G. C. (1991) 'An international review of the emergence and development of health psychology', in M. Jansen and J. Weinman (eds) *The International Development of Health Psychology*, Reading, UK: Harwood Academic Publishers.

Taylor, S. E., Lichtman, R. R. and Wood, J. V. (1984) 'Attributions, beliefs about control, and adjustment to breast cancer', *Journal of Personality and Social Psychology* 46: 489–502.

Thompson, D. R. and Meddis, R. (1990) 'A prospective evaluation of in-hospital counselling for first time myocardial infarction men', *Journal of Psychosomatic Research* 34: 327–48.

Thompson, D. R., Webster, R. A., Cordle, C. J. and Sutton, T. W. (1987) 'Specific sources and patterns of anxiety in male patients with first time myocardial infarction', *British Journal of Medical Psychology* 60: 343–8.

Turnquist, D. C., Harvey, J. H. and Anderson, B. L. (1988) 'Attributions and adjustment to life-threatening illness', *British Journal of Clinical Psychology* 27: 55–65.

Verbrugge, L. M. (1985) 'Gender and health: an update on hypotheses and evidence', *Journal of Health and Social Behavior* 26: 156–82.

Wallston, B. S., Alagna, S. W., De Vellis, B. and De Vellis, R. F. (1983) 'Social support and physical health', *Health Psychology* 2: 367–91.

Warwick,. M. C. and Salkovskis, P. M. (1990) 'Hypochondriasis', *Behaviour Research and Therapy* 28: 105–17.

Watson, M. and Marvell, C. (1992) 'Anticipatory nausea and vomiting among cancer patients: a review', *Psychology and Health* 6: 97–106.

Weinstein, N. D. (1982) 'Unrealistic optimism about susceptibility of health problems', *Journal of Behavioral Medicine* 45: 441–60.

Weinstein, N. D. (1987) 'Unrealistic optimism about susceptibility to health problems: Conclusions from a community-wide sample', *Journal of Behavioral Medicine* 10: 481–500.

Weinstein, N. D. (1988) 'The precaution adoption approach', *Health Psychology* 7: 355–86.

Weisenberg, M., Kegeles, S. S. and Lund, A. K. (1980) 'Children's health beliefs and acceptance of dental preventive activity', *Journal of Health and Social Behavior* 21: 59–74.

Wells, J. K., Howard, G. S., Nowlin, W. F. and Vargas, M. J. (1986) 'Presurgical anxiety and postsurgical pain and adjustment: Effects of a stress inoculation procedure', *Journal of Consulting and Clinical Psychology* 54: 831–5.

Wing, R. R., Epstein, L. H ., Nowalk, M. P. and Lamparski, D. M. (1986) 'Behavioral self-regulation in the treatment of patients with diabetes mellitus', *Psychological Bulletin* 99: 78–89.

Worden, J. W. and Weisman, A. D. (1984) 'Preventive psychosocial intervention with newly diagnosed cancer patients', *General Hospital Psychiatry* 6: 243–9.

Wortman, C. B. and Dunkel-Schetter, C. (1979) 'Interpersonal relationships and cancer: A theoretical analysis', *Journal of Social Isues* 35: 120–55.

Wurtele, S. K. and Maddux, J. E. (1987) 'Relative contribution of protection motivation theory components in predicting exercise intentions and behavior', *Health Psychology* 6: 453–66.

Yorkston, N. J., McHugh, R. B., Brady, R., Serber, M. and Sergeant, H. G. S. (1974) 'Verbal desensitization in bronchial asthma', *Journal of Psychosomatic Research* 18: 371–6.

Zich, J. and Temoshok, L. (1987) 'Perceptions of social support in men with AIDS and ARC: Relationships with distress and hardiness', *Journal of Applied Social Psychology* 17: 193–215.

Zola, I. K. (1973) 'Pathways to the doctor – from person to patient', *Social Science and Medicine* 7: 677–89.

Chapter 26

Disorders of eating and weight
Investigation
Jane Wardle

INTRODUCTION

Weight is important in our culture, especially for women. Obese people and anorexics, although they lie at opposite ends of the weight spectrum, may both be victims of cultural expectations of thinness. The two weight disorders have now been joined by bulimia nervosa, which is characterised by an eating pattern of extreme dietary restriction alternating with voracious overeating. Obesity, anorexia and bulimia are all associated with a variety of physical health hazards and reduced psychological well-being.

Research into the psychological processes which underlie these disorders points to some communalities and some differences. A negative body image is found in all three groups, along with chronic, though not necessarily successful, dietary restraint. Eating and exercise patterns are often abnormal, and likewise hunger, appetite and satiety may be disturbed. All three problems are strikingly more common in women. Anorexic and bulimic patients are predominantly female, and many more women than men seek professional or commercial help with weight reduction. This sex difference is generally attributed to the fact that cultural pressures for thinness fall heavily on women, producing what has been described as 'the tyranny of slenderness' (Chernin, 1983). Few women escape these pressures, so a negative body image and attempts at weight control are common in the normal weight population (Dwyer *et al.*, 1970; Wardle and Marsland, 1990). Many women have a body size that is well above the fashionable ideal size, and possibly above the medically prescribed ideal weight. However, it is possible that attempted conformity to an ideal size may confer a greater risk for anorexia, bulimia or obesity (Wooley *et al.*, 1979; Garner, 1985; Wardle, 1988; Brownell, 1991).

Clinical assessment in the area of weight and eating, as in other areas, consists of an attempt to produce a systematic and objective description of the individual patient. Initially this may be part of a diagnostic process, but it also provides the baseline data from which a treatment plan may be evolved, and against which changes can be assessed. In clinical practice, verbal enquiry, in the form of an interview with the patient and other informants, is the basic method, and all other assessments essentially supplement this. Structured interviews or inventories, such as the Eating Disorder Examination (Cooper and Fairburn, 1987), the Interview for Diagnosis of Eating Disorders (Williamson, 1990) or the Stanford Eating Disorders Questionnaire (Agras, 1987), can be used to gather information systematically and are suitable for use by less experienced interviewers. Standardised tests, such as the Eating Disorders Inventory (Garner 1991) or the Anorexic Cognitions Questionnaire (Mizes and Klesges, 1990), have their place more obviously in research settings, but can usefully contribute to data gathering in a clinical setting. Finally, a medical examination is often necessary in conditions such as these, which have physical as well as psychological symptoms. These broader methods of enquiry will point to the specific areas which need detailed investigation with cognitive tests, rating scales and behavioural records.

INVESTIGATION OF OBESITY

Background

Excess weight is widely agreed to be one of the major health problems of the twentieth century in the western world. The definition of obesity is somewhat arbitrary because body fatness is a continuous variable. At or above 20 per cent overweight there is a reliable association with morbidity and mortality (Mayer, 1968; National Institute of Health, 1985; Jeffery, 1992). Body fat distribution, as well as total body fat, is now known to be related to disease risk. High levels of abdominal fat appear to confer greater risk than fat distributed on the limbs (Björntorp, 1988). This may go some way towards explaining the differences in the relationship between obesity and disease in men and women, since obese men are more likely to have central obesity and women to have peripheral obesity. The other aspects of weight which is attracting increasing attention is weight variability. Lissner et al. (1988) and Hamm et al. (1989) are among a number of workers who have shown that greater weight variability increases cardiovascular disease (CVD) risk. At present these finding must be evaluated cautiously, since they are cross-sectional rather than experimental. However, they must raise the concern that treatments which are effective in the short term but ineffective in the long term (and therefore promote weight cycling) could be harmful to health (Wing, 1992).

Assessment of family history is also important, since several studies strongly suggest that there is a genetic component to the variability in body weight (Stunkard et al., 1986). Finding a positive family history in an individual case cannot conclusively establish a genetic aetiology, nor does it have any implications for treatment. However, from the perspective of the patient, it is important to understand that a larger body size may be an inherited characteristic.

Epidemiological surveys in most western countries indicate that the prevalence of obesity is related to age, sex and social class (Osancová and Hejda, 1975; Sobal and Stunkard, 1989). Silverstone (1968) in a general practice sample in London found that 52 per cent of the men and 66 per cent of the women were at least 15 per cent above their ideal weight. There was a striking increase with age, especially in women, and the prevalence in the fifth decade was more than double that in the third decade. Similarly the prevalence of obesity in social classes 4 and 5 was more than double that in social classes 1, 2 and 3. The medical significance of obesity lies in its identification as a risk factor for a variety of medical problems; hypertension, hypercholesterolemia, gall bladder disease, osteoarthritis and diabetes are more common and more serious in obese people (Bray, 1976; National Institute of Health, 1985). Obesity may also confer an additional risk in smokers or people with a family history of CVD. The psychological significance of obesity appears to derive primarily from a cultural view that fatness is unattractive. Reduced popularity, occupational and medical discrimination, and a poor self-image have all been shown to characterise obese people (Allon, 1982).

Assessment of body fat

The term obesity refers to an excess of body fat, which in itself is not easily measurable. There are several different techniques available to estimate fatness, each of which has some drawbacks. The simplest is weight, which should be assessed on a lever- rather than a spring-type balance. Weight, however, is not a direct measure of fatness, as lean body mass is included, and some conversion must be performed. A comparison with a standard weight for height is also often used, with the most common standard being the Metropolitan Life Insurance Company's table for desirable weights, i.e. the weights associated with the lowest mortality (Metropolitan Life Insurance, 1983). For children, comparison with normative data for height and weight is the usual approach (Falkner, 1962). Many epidemiological surveys use the ratio of height and weight known as the 'Body Mass Index' (Florey, 1970). If height (H) is measured in metres and weight (W) in kilograms, the ratio W/H^2 offers a good estimate of body fatness, and the same values apply to adult men and women. Levels of BMI greater than 25 indicate overweight and greater than 30, obesity. All the methods which depend on weight assessment have the disadvantages that there is no easy way to take account of body build. Even the Metropolitan tables, which are organised by frame size, include only a crude criterion for making this judgement, based on elbow width.

A more direct assessment of fatness is obtained from measures of skinfold thickness, where the depth of subcutaneous fat is used as a guide to total body fat. There are a number of bodily sites where these measures may be taken, the most common being biceps, triceps, sub-scapular and supra-iliac. Specially designed callipers are available, which should be used according to careful procedural instructions (Grimes and Franzini, 1977). The measurements can then be compared with standardised tables such as those in Durnin and Womersley (1974). However, with fatter patients, reliable measurements are extremely difficult to achieve, and simple measurements of body circumference (waist, thighs, etc.) will be just as useful. In view of the observations that abdominal or central obesity may be particularly hazardous to health, measures of fat distribution are also useful. At present the ratio of waist to hip circumference is often used, with values greater than one indicating abdominal obesity.

Assessment of eating behaviour

Obesity results from an energy imbalance between energy input and output, but until recently theoretical and therapeutic efforts have been devoted largely to the input side. Obesity was believed to result from excessive food intake, itself the result of faulty eating habits and/or a faulty satiety mechanism. The obese were thought to eat too much, too often and too fast, and behavioural treatments have generally been predicated on this view (Mahoney, 1975). The main evidence for the so-called 'obese eating style' was obtained in a series of laboratory studies (Schachter and Rodin, 1974) performed on college students, from which the concept of 'externality' has been developed. Externality is essentially hypersensitivity to external appetitive cues, and combined with a supposed insensitivity to internal satiety cues, this was thought to account for obese overeating. However, naturalistic research on the eating style of obese eaters has almost entirely failed to confirm the laboratory findings. Food type, eating speed and eating frequency rarely differentiate obese from normal weight groups (Kissileff *et al.*, 1978). The existence of an eating style specific to obese people has therefore been seriously questioned, and its aetiological significance cannot be assumed. In terms of the quantity of food eaten, the conclusion from numerous food intake studies has been that the obese on average eat no more than their normal-weight counterparts (Garrow, 1974; Braitman *et al.*, 1985). Most investigators would now agree that overeating, in the sense of eating more than is normal for the social group, cannot be assumed to characterise all obese people. One possibility is that energy intake is high during the dynamic phase, but once weight has stabilised, energy intake falls to normal levels.

The nutrient composition of the diet of obese people is attracting increasing attention in view of the evidence that diet can affect cardiovascular risk. Several aspects of diet are implicated in disease risk, including fat intake, saturated/poly-unsaturated fat ratio, fibre intake, fruit and vegetable intake, and vitamin intake. In relation to weight, there is some evidence that a higher fat intake is conducive to weight gain (Schutz *et al.*, 1989). In view of this, it is important to assess diet more fully, using analysis of either dietary diaries or food frequency records. In either case, advice from a nutritionist is likely to be essential.

In a clinical setting, the assessment of energy input, along with eating style, becomes an issue of practical importance, rather than of diagnostic relevance, and a full assessment of food intake is necessary to ascertain if and where the changes can be made. Ideally, intake of food should be reported by external observers, but that is rarely possible, and the basic assessment tool has been the diary, usually formalised to give information on time, place, quantity and circumstance of eating. An example of such a diary is given in Table 26.1. A careful, weighed-food record is the ideal from the nutritionist's point of view, but few patients are prepared to undertake this. It is also likely to be highly reactive – that is, the measurement method will influence the parameter being measured. Using tables of calorific values, some estimate of daily caloric intakes can be made from the diary records if necessary.

The main criticism of self-monitoring as an assessment device is the opportunity for deception. It has been argued that the obese eat unconsciously and hence cannot report on their intake, and, of course, there is a strong element of social desirability involved. Self-monitoring of all kinds is also highly reactive. If at all possible, someone who lives or eats with the patient should be interviewed to get some confirmation of the record. Failing that, the success of the endeavour depends upon the establishment of a therapeutic alliance in which patient and therapist work together for change, and the advantages of a true record are clear to the patient.

The patterns of food intake should also be assessed; this includes when and where food is consumed and the circumstances (moods or settings) which promote food intake. This information may be obtained from the diary record, although some psychometric measures have been developed. Most obese people, along with many normal weight, attempt to regulate new food intake in accordance with cognitively derived rules about avoiding weight gain. This has been termed 'dietary restraint' (Herman and Mack, 1975) and has been implicated in some of the abnormalities of eating style which have been reported in obese people (Hibscher and Herman, 1977; Wardle 1988). It has been argued that externally or emotionally cued eating represent disinhibition of cognitive restraint, whereby powerful urges to eat are released by stress or temptation. In view of the possible role of restraint as a causal agent in overeating, it may be important to assess dietary restraint, and this can be done with the original Restraint Scale (Polivy et al., 1978), or with one of the questionnaires which

Table 26.1 Food intake record form

Date:

Time	Place/Company	Hunger rating	Food eaten	Satiety rating

include a scale for re-trained eating, such as the Three Factor Eating Questionnaire (TFEQ) (Stunkard and Messick, 1985) or the Dutch Eating Behaviour
Questionnaire (DEBQ) (Van Strien *et al.*, 1986; Wardle, 1987a). Externally and
emotionally cued eating have hitherto been assessed principally from diary
records, but both the DEBQ and the TFEQ include scales to assess these areas of
overeating in everyday life. This may be a more practical way of characterising
an individual's eating style.

Appetite

A commonly expressed view has been that obese people fail to recognise internal
cues of hunger and satiety, and thus their food intake is not governed by the
'normal' mechanisms (Schachter and Rodin, 1974). Early research provided
some confirmation of this view (Stunkard and Fox, 1971), but in a series of
elegant experiments Wooley and her colleagues have shown that few subjects of
any weight are sensitive to the caloric content of food they have eaten (see
Wooley and Wooley, 1975). Ratings of fullness after eating, hunger at various
times after eating, and amount eaten at the next meal failed to differentiate high
and low calorie intakes in obese or normal subjects. The exception was salivary
responses to palatable food, which remained high in obese subjects after the
normal weight subjects had satiated (Wooley *et al.*, 1975). These studies,
however, also failed to control for dietary restraint, and when that was taken into
account, the results showed that dieters of all weights had abnormal salivation
responses, suggesting that restraint can disturb appetite mechanisms (Klajner *et
al.*, 1981).

Craving for food, or for specific food, is often reported by people with
difficulties in controlling their eating. Chocolate cravings are probably the most
well-known and have sometimes been interpreted in the framework of addictive
behaviours. If food cravings are reported and are problematic, then they could be
recorded systematically on the diet record form. Therapeutic efforts could well
be directed towards the development of adaptive appetite responses, and so
assessment of some appetite variables is called for. The most convenient method
is to include ratings of hunger and fullness on the food intake record (see Table
26.1). Additionally, a more detailed evaluation of the patient's appreciation of
internal sensations of hunger might be obtained using an inventory of hunger
symptoms, such as that developed by Garfinkel (1974).

Energy expenditure

Unlike food intake, energy expenditure has received little attention in the therapeutic literature. By far the biggest proportion of energy intake is used for resting
metabolic processes such as thermoregulation, with muscular activity accounting for less than one-third in normal adults. Comparisons between obese and
normal subjects have in the past suggested that there may be a lowered metabolic

rate in the obese, especially in those who have been restricting their food intake (Bray, 1969). It has also been suggested that obese subjects may lack the normal metabolic means to burn off excess food intake, that is, a dietarily induced thermogenesis (Shetty *et al.*, 1981). A lower metabolic rate has been found to be associated with greater weight gain at follow-up (Ravussin *et al.*, 1988); however, in one of the few studies of energy expenditure over the longer term in free-living subjects, obese people were found to have higher not lower metabolic rates (Prentice *et al.*, 1986).

Assessment of physical activity levels, using pedometers, films, direct observation and self-report, have been used to compare energy expenditure levels. On balance, the research suggests that the obese (adults or children) are slightly less active than normal weight people (Johnson *et al.*, 1956; Stunkard, 1958; Stefanik *et al.*, 1959; Griffiths and Payne, 1976). However, inferences about causal processes are, of course, hard to draw from these studies, as the lowered activity need not be causal. It could be a consequence of weight gain, or of the dietary restriction so often practised by overweight subjects. The value of measures of activity come not from questions about the cause of obesity, but to set targets for intervention.

In principle, assessment should cover all aspects of energy balance, but this is rarely practicable. Metabolic assessments are not routinely performed, both because the assessment techniques are highly specialised and because metabolic activity is not yet an appropriate target of therapeutic intervention. Activity levels can usefully be assessed and may be included in therapeutic targets. A number of methods of assessing exercise levels have been developed (La Porte, 1989). In a clinical setting, self-report, backed up if at all possible by observer report, is the most relevant technique and again a diary form is usually used. Activities can be recorded in one column with duration and circumstances in others. The crudity of the measure precludes an accurate translation to calorific output, although a rough calculation may be made on the basis of available tables (Brownell and Stunkard, 1980). Pedometers can also be used to give a rough index of activity, and can prove valuable in providing regular feedback, thus motivating increases in activity level. Finally, a fitness assessment based on heart-rate responses to a standard physical work task could be carried out, although medical supervision may be advisable. Changes in fitness level can serve to reinforce exercise programmes.

Body image

Obesity is not only a medical problem but also a psychological and personal one. Western cultural ideals of beauty, especially for women, demand a minimum of body fat. The obese are therefore seen as physically unattractive, and furthermore as personally responsible for their unattractiveness. This leads to ridicule and lowered popularity as well as to active discrimination in educational and occupational spheres (Allon, 1982). Not surprisingly, therefore, overweight people have been shown to have a negative body image (Jourard and Secord, 1955) and low self-esteem (Monello and Mayer, 1963). There is also evidence that their body image is inaccurate and that they view themselves as larger than they are, as well as being very dissatisfied with their appearance (Pearlson *et al.*, 1981).

Self-esteem may be assessed on standardised scales (e.g. Rosenberg, 1965). Body image and body size perception have usually been assessed with idiographic techniques, although careful choice of technique may permit comparisons with published data. In the case of body image, simple ratings of the attractiveness of listed body parts is the simplest method of assessment of satisfaction. The Body Shape Questionnaire (Cooper *et al.*, 1987) was not developed for obese subjects but could also be used to give a quantitative evaluation of dissatisfaction. Techniques of body size estimation have proliferated and details are given in the section on anorexic assessment.

The salience of any of these attitudinal factors is again a matter for clinical judgement in the individual case. It would, however, be wise to bear in mind that behavioural techniques rarely achieve large weight losses, and consequently, improvement in body image and self-esteem may become an important component of therapeutic success.

INVESTIGATION OF ANOREXIA NERVOSA

Anorexia nervosa has an unequal sex distribution, and much more strikingly so than obesity, with fewer than 10 per cent of anorexic cases being male. Epidemiological studies put the incidence between 1 and 6 per 100,000 of the population (King 1989; Hoek, 1991). The prominent characteristic of anorexia nervosa is a weight abnormality, but whereas obesity refers to a specific biological parameter, anorexia nervosa is a diagnostic term implying a cluster of symptoms. The precise specification of symptoms varies but there is agreement on certain central physical and psychological characteristics. These are described by Russell as: (a) behaviour leading to marked weight loss, (b) amenorrhoea (or, in the case of men, loss of sexual interest) and (c) a morbid fear of fatness (Russell, 1970). The *DSM III–R* (American Psychiatric Association, 1987) definition includes: (a) refusal to maintain body weight, (b) fear of weight gain, (c) disturbance of body image, and (d) amenorrhoea. To complete the diagnosis there should be an absence of any other medical or psychiatric condition which might account for the symptoms, although concurrent psychological disturbances, especially depression, are not uncommon.

The identification of anorexia does not on the whole pose a diagnostic problem to mental health professionals, although it is undoubtedly sometimes missed at the primary care level. However, it is a complex disorder with considerable variability between patients, so careful description and quantification of the particular behavioural and attitudinal characteristics of each patient is crucial. In addition to those variables directly associated with weight and eating, such as a fear of weight gain, carbohydrate avoidance and body size over-estimation, there are a number of other features that have been said to have fundamental significance in the development of the disorder. These include fear of growing up (Crisp, 1970), a pervasive sense of ineffectiveness (Bruch, 1973), perfectionism (Halmi *et al.*, 1977; Slade, 1982), excessive achievement motivation (Dally and Gomez, 1979) and family problems (Minuchin *et al.*, 1978). Co-morbidity (see Halmi *et al.*, 1991) should be assessed, especially in relation to depression, obsessive-compulsive disorder and substance abuse.

It is now accepted that there is more than one sub-type of anorexia: 'restrictive anorexia' in which weight control is achieved exclusively by dietary restriction, and 'bulimic anorexia', in which large quantities of food are eaten but the fattening effects are avoided by inducing vomiting or taking large quantities of laxatives. Bulimic anorexia may be a sub-type of anorexia (Casper *et al.*, 1980), or it may reflect a different phase of the anorexic illness (Dally and Gomez, 1979). There is some evidence for differences in personality, psychopathology and outcome between restrictive and bulimic patients (Casper *et al.*, op. cit.; Garfinkel *et al.*, 1980), with restrictive patients generally being younger and less socially and sexually experienced, and having a better prognosis under current management regimes. From a diagnostic point of view, the distinction between bulimic anorexia and named bulimia nervosa is primarily one of weight, and most workers now recognise that an area of overlap exists between these two conditions (Fairburn, 1983; Fairburn and Garner, 1986).

There is abundant evidence that anorexic patients show disturbances in biological function with evidence for a range of neuro-endocrine and physiological alterations (Morley and Blundell, 1988; Fava *et al.*, 1989; Turner and Shapiro, 1992), some of which may develop soon after, or even before, significant weight loss, and others of which are probably a response to malnutrition and emaciation. These disturbances tend to be reversible and disappear on weight gain (Beumont *et al.*, 1976). There are also cardiovascular, biochemical, gastrointestinal and neurological complications which can result from the weight control methods or from the vigorous weight restoration procedures used in treatment. The effects of the disorder can be fatal, and mortality figures as high as 21 per cent have been reported (Steinhausen and Glanville, 1983). The assessment of anorexic patients is therefore an area which demands close cooperation between medical and behavioural experts.

Weight

Regular assessment of weight is essential in treatment but poses a number of practical problems. Patients may try to mislead the therapist by hiding heavy objects in their clothes to produce an apparent weight gain, and this should be guarded against. Weighing is also always an emotional matter for the patient, and time should be set aside to discuss it.

Eating behaviour

There is no doubt that the diets of anorexic patients are abnormal, being not only low in calories, but also specifically lacking carbohydrate or fat. Many anorexics prefer to eat alone and will avoid family meals, parties and other social occasions involving eating, although paradoxically some have a great interest in preparing food and serving it to others.

The choice of an appropriate assessment technique depends partly upon the treatment setting. An in-patient setting permits close and continuous observation of the patient's behaviour, therefore generating objective data but in an abnormal environment. In an out-patient setting, the monitoring of behaviour is usually dependent upon self-report of some kind, unless the patient is closely supervised by family members. There are a number of standard assessment devices which have been developed primarily in a research setting, but which can provide a starting point in the clinical investigations. Slade (1973) produced a scale to be used by ward staff to identify eating practices, food disposal techniques, and activity. Based on a present/absent distinction, this scale has so far been validated only with respect to diagnosis, but it might also be possible to use it to monitor change.

In an out-patient setting, there is a self-report measure of symptoms and behaviour, the Eating Attitudes Test (EAT), developed by Garner and Garfinkel (1979). This should help to locate problem areas for treatment as well as give a quantitative assessment of severity. A more detailed identification of the supposed underlying psychological dimensions is possible with the Eating Disorder Inventory (EDI) (Garner 1991). This comprises eight attitude subscales: drive for thinness, bulimia, perfectionism, body dissatisfaction, ineffectiveness, distress, interoceptive awareness and maturity fears. Standardisation data are available for restrictive and bulimic anorexics as well as male and female normal comparison groups.

The interviews and questionnaire assessments described above generate retrospective reports on intake and appetite, but in a clinical setting some continuous and ongoing record is usually required. The usual form of self-report is a diary in which time, place, quantity and kind of food eaten is recorded. A column on the record form in which to record self-induced vomiting or laxative abuse, behaviours which patients often regard as particularly shameful, may persuade them to reveal these. The validity of such a record is, of course, threatened by the ambivalence which many patients have about therapeutic cooperation, therefore continued stress on the importance of veracity is critical, along with external confirmation where possible.

Appetite

It was at one time assumed that the weight loss of anorexic patients reflected a loss of appetite, hence the name *anorexia* which means absence of appetite.

However, clinical research findings have indicated that appetite for food can be retained and the food restriction is an act of will (Garfinkel, 1974). Early work on anorexia in a laboratory setting suggested that anorexics were less sensitive than normal weight subjects to internal sensations of hunger (Coddington and Bruch, 1970). Both Wardle and Ogden (1989) and Halmi et al. (1989) have found lower hunger ratings. Abnormalities of satiety seem well established (Halmi et al., op. cit.) and clinical reports indicate that anorexics feel bloating, pain and weight gain after eating (Garfinkel, op. cit.). There is also some evidence of abnormality of satiety from the Cabanac and Duclaux (1979) sucrose aversion procedure. Normal subjects show a relative aversion to the taste of sucrose after the ingestion of sucrose, unlike obese and anorexic subjects (Garfinkel et al., 1978; Wooley et al., 1975). The communality between obese and anorexics in this response suggests that it may again be a consequence of dietary restriction.

Assessments of hunger, as well as of urges to eat and food cravings, should be part of the clinical investigation of each patient. If appropriate, rating scales for these appetitive characteristics can be included on the dietary record form.

Activity

Excessive exercising is another anorexic weight-loss device, and one which may be adopted by normal men and women (Yates, 1991). Social changes in attitudes to exercise may influence judgements on the abnormality of this behaviour, nevertheless information about time spent in vigorous exercise should be obtained. This will again be a matter for ward staff observation in the case of an in-patient, and for the diary record in the case of the out-patient.

Body image

The contrast between the emaciated appearance of anorexic patients and their statement that they are too fat is often striking. From her clinical observations, Bruch (1962) proposed that anorexic patients had a disturbance of body image, and in 1973, Slade and Russell reported a first systematic attempt to study this. Using the estimation of linear body width at four body parts, they showed that anorexic patients markedly overestimated body size, and subsequent studies, using a variety of different body size estimation techniques, have consistently confirmed this (Garner et al., 1976; Pierloot and Houben, 1978). However, whereas in the original study, control women were accurate in estimating their body size, this accuracy has not been confirmed in subsequent studies, and normal women have been found to overestimate their body size to much the same degree as anorexic patients (Button et al., 1977). The erosion of this difference between anorexic patients and normal women has therefore influenced the theoretical significance of body image distortion, but recent models of anorexia circumvent this problem by incorporating overestimation as one of many setting conditions for the development of anorexia nervosa (Garfinkel and Garner, 1982; Slade, 1982).

The current status of the body size overestimation in anorexia is best described as salient to but not specific to the condition. In a therapeutic setting it is usually important to assess the degree of overestimation, as patients themselves are often unaware of it. Many assessment techniques have been developed, including moving lights (Slade and Russell, 1973), distorting mirrors (Shipman and Sohlkhan, 1967), and distorting photographs (Garner et al., 1976). The reliability of any of these instruments is dependent upon consistency in the instruction given to the subject. Probably the commonest and easiest technique is Slade and Russell's method, which depends only upon obtaining two point light sources which may be moved closer or further away from one another. The body width is measured with callipers and can then be compared with perceived width to produce an index of overestimation (Slade and Russell, op. cit.).

Another approach to body image consists in establishing the patient's own view of her ideal weight and size, and comparing this with her healthy weight. An approximate guide to healthy weight is obtained from the pre-morbid weight if there was a time in her teens when she was fully grown but not dieting. Failing this, healthy weight should be established by using desirable weight for height norms, such as those of the Metropolitan Life Insurance Company (1983). The difference between the patient's notion of her ideal weight and her healthy weight gives some indication of the misperception of body size.

Finally, psychometric instruments, such as the Body Shape Questionnaire (Cooper et al., 1987) or the body dissatisfaction subscale of the Eating Disorder Inventory (Garner, 1991), can be included to quantify dissatisfaction.

INVESTIGATION OF BULIMIA NERVOSA

Bulimia nervosa is the only one of the three conditions discussed in this chapter which is essentially an eating rather than a weight disorder. It is characterised by episodes of bingeing which are generally followed by some means of getting rid of the food, such as self-induced vomiting or excessive laxative intake. Food intake between the binges is usually highly restrictive. This practice of over-eating and purging, reminiscent of the Roman orgy, is well established in a subgroup of anorexic patients (Beumont et al., 1976), but has only more recently been identified in normal weight women. A variety of labels have in the past been used for the condition including 'the dietary chaos syndrome' (Palmer, 1979) and 'compulsive eating', but Russell (1979) coined the term 'bulimia nervosa' when he described a series of thirty patients who were preoccupied with food, were fearful of fatness, and in whom bingeing and vomiting alternated with strict dieting. He saw the condition as 'an ominous variant of anorexia nervosa'. The majority of patients (24 out of 30), and of other case series (Pyle et al., 1981; Fairburn and Cooper, 1982), had a history of anorexia nervosa in its full strength, or in attenuated form. The link between dieting and bingeing is also found in normal women (Wardle, 1980), and it seems likely that dietary restriction plays an important role in the aetiology of bulimia nervosa (Wardle and Beinart, 1981). Available evidence suggests that bulimia is a common condition; Fairburn and Cooper (op. cit.) received over 1,000 replies to an advertised request for information from women who practised vomiting as a means of weight control, and screening studies of university students indicate an incidence of around 13 per cent (Halmi *et al.*, 1981). An estimate of the frequency in clinical settings is obtained from *DSM III* diagnoses in a university clinic where Stangler and Printz (1980) found that 15.1 per cent of the women patients had the diagnosis of bulimia. It is now agreed that *DSM III* may have used over-inclusive criteria, but nevertheless bulimia nervosa in its full form has been estimated at more than 8/100,000 (Hoek, 1991).

The overlap with anorexia nervosa is apparent in the many common features concerning attitudes to food and weight expressed by patients in these two groups. As far as differential diagnoses are concerned, *DSM III–R* has an explicitly hierarchical diagnostic system, that is, the use of the term bulimia depends upon the exclusion of anorexia nervosa, and the British literature suggests an implicitly hierarchical model. Essentially this means that a patient with a fear of fatness and an eating disorder would attract the diagnosis of 'anorexia nervosa (bulimic type)' if underweight, and 'bulimia nervosa' if normal weight. An overweight patient with this disorder would pose less of a diagnostic problem, as obesity is not a psychiatric diagnosis and hence there is no mutual exclusion. There is, however, a danger that bulimia could go undiagnosed in obese patients if the popular (but false) stereotype of obese people as compulsive eaters is believed.

Aetiological theories of bulimia stress the patient's attempt to conform to cultural ideas of thinness, which result in food intake and body weight well below biologically appropriate levels (Garner *et al.*, 1980; Wardle and Beinart, 1981; Slade, 1982). This is maintained for a while, but eventually the combined psychological and physiological pressures to eat provoke a breakdown of restriction. This is followed by guilt, renewed restraint, then more and larger binges. Clinical reports indicate that binges are more likely at times of boredom, anxiety, depression, loneliness and temptation (Johnson and Larson, 1982; Abraham and Beumont, 1982), and after intake of even small quantities of 'forbidden' food. These circumstances have many parallels with the failures of regulation shown by normal dieters in laboratory studies (Herman, 1980), suggesting that the mechanisms may be similar.

If vomiting and purging are present, they will almost always have developed after dieting has been established. Patients report that they 'learned' to vomit from the published work on anorexia and bulimia, from friends, or from therapists (Chiodo and Latimer, 1983). Vomiting and purging are commonly viewed by the patient as a temporary solution to be utilised until control is re-established. In fact the reverse occurs, with binges increasing in size and frequency after vomiting begins. The vomiting carries a number of health risks as well as being, for most patients, a source of shame and anxiety. The maintenance of the eating abnormality appears to follow from the interdependence of dieting, bingeing and vomiting, and all treatments have been based on explicit attempts to bring one or more of these components under control. Assessment of patients who present with this type of eating disorder is essentially similar to the assessment of anorexic patients: body image, weight, appetite and food intake all being imported areas. The main difference concerns the specific focus on the pattern, content and circumstances of eating, in order to identify and control the eating abnormality. Structured interviews for eating disorders offer a useful method of collecting information systematically. Combined with some psychometric measures, it probably offers the best assessment method. Cooper and Fairburn's Eating Disorder Examination is a 62-item inventory designed for bulimia nervosa (Cooper and Fairburn, 1987).

Food intake for the bulimic patient is usually clearly divided into two kinds: bingeing and controlled eating. Patients themselves can readily say whether a particular episode was a binge or not. Comparisons between binges and normal intakes reveal differences in circumstances, quantity and quality as well as timing. A binge is likely to consist of high-calorie food and drinks, in large quantity, consumed in private, and generally terminated by running out of supplies or severe physical discomfort. It is then often followed by vomiting or laxative use. Non-binge eating on the other hand consists of small quantities of low-calorie food and drink which may be eaten publicly. These features go some way to defining a binge, but an objective definition is elusive as patient reports indicate that the core characteristic of a binge is the frame of mind in which the eating takes place. Most researchers explicitly or implicitly are forced to accept the patient's own definition of a binge (Abraham and Beaumont, 1982; Johnson and Larson, 1982). A sense of abandonment of control is critical for a binge, whereas 'normal' eating is usually highly controlled. Heatherton and Baumeister (1992) have proposed that the escape from self-awareness which occurs with the binge plays an important role in the maintenance of binge eating.

Standardised instruments to assess attitudes and patterns of eating include those developed primarily for anorexia such as the Eating Attitudes Test (Garner and Garfinkel, 1979) and some of the subscales of the EDI (Garner 1991). The Anorexic Cognitions Questionnaire (Mizes and Klesges, 1990) covers similar ground. Emotionally cued eating is usually very common in bulimic patients and can be assessed with the emotional eating subscale of the DEBQ (Van Strien et al., 1986). There is also a scale for binge eating tendencies (the BULIT; Smith and Thelen, 1984) which has some standardisation data. Together with a measure of dietary restraint, these instruments can provide a quantitative index of the eating abnormality.

No psychometric device will substitute for detailed food records, which ideally would be kept by observers, but in practice are kept by the patient him- or herself. As the bingeing may vary considerably both within and between patients, long record-keeping is required with the inevitable compliance problems.

Fortunately many patients regard the dietary record as a useful aid, and hence are generally cooperative. A record form that has separate sections for binge and non-binge intakes simplifies the data processing. Basic frequency data can be obtained from these records along with more detailed information about the antecedents and consequences of eating.

CONCLUSION

Throughout this chapter, the emphasis has been on the assessment of variables closely related to eating and weight. The full range of clinical interviews, structured interviews, psychometric instruments, rating scales and diary records can be useful in defining and evaluating the eating problem. The results of full assessment offer not just a descriptive account of the problem but also a source of insight for the patient. The self-monitoring process can also serve to enhance self-control. It is important that the emphasis on eating and weight should not be taken to imply that eating problems can be understood in isolation. In the clinical setting the eating problem should always be placed in the context of a full psychological assessment.

REFERENCES

Abraham, S. F. and Beumont, P. J. V. (1982) 'How patients describe bulimia or binge eating', *Psychological Medicine* 12: 625–35.

Agras, W. S. (1987) *Eating Disorders: Management of Obesity, Bulimia, and Anorexia Nervosa*, New York: Pergamon.

Allon, M. (1982) 'The stigma of overweight in everyday life', in Wolman, B. B. (ed.) *Psychological Aspects of Obesity*, New York: Van Nostrand Reinhold.

American Psychiatric Association (1987) *Diagnostic and Statistical Manual of Mental Disorders, 3rd edn Revised*, Washington, DC: American Psychiatric Association.

Beumont, P. J. V., George, G. C. W. and Smart, D. E. (1976) '"Dieters" and "vomiters and purgers" in anorexia nervosa', *Psychological Medicine* 6: 617–32.

Björntorp, P. (1988) 'The associations between obesity, adipose tissue distribution and disease', *Acta Medica Scandinavia* (Supplement) 723: 121–34.

Braitman, L. E., Adlin, E. V. and Stanton, J. L. (1985) 'Obesity and caloric intake: the National Health and Nutrition Examination Survey of 1971–1975 (Hanes 1)', *Journal of Chronic Diseases* 38: 727–32.

Bray, G. A. (1969) 'Effect of caloric restriction on energy expenditure in obese patients', *Lancet* 2: 397.

Bray, G. A. (1976) *The Obese Patient*, Philadelphia: W.B. Saunders.

Brownell, K. D. (1991) 'Dieting and the search for the perfect body: where physiology and culture collide', *Behaviour Therapy* 22: 1–12.

Brownell, K. D. and Stunkard, A. J. (1980) 'Physical activity in the development and control of obesity', in A. J. Stunkard (ed.) *Obesity*, Philadelphia: W. B. Saunders.

Bruch, H. (1962) 'Perceptual and conceptual disturbances in anorexia nervosa', *Psychological Medicine* 24: 187–94.

Bruch, H. (1973) *Eating Disorders: Obesity, Anorexia and the Person Within*, New York: Basic Books.

Button, E. J., Fransella, F. and Slade, P. D. (1977) 'A reappraisal of body perception disturbance in anorexia nervosa', *Psychological Medicine* 7: 235–43.

Cabanac, M. and Duclaux, R. (1970) 'Obesity: Absence of satiety aversion to glucose', *Science* 168: 496–7.

Casper, R. C., Eckert, E. D., Halmi, K. A., Goldberg, S. C. and Davis, J. M. (1980) 'Bulimia. Its incidence and clinical importance in patients with anorexia nervosa', *Archives of General Psychiatry* 37: 1030–34.

Chernin, K. (1983) *Women Size. The Tyranny of Slenderness*, London: The Women's Press.

Chiodo, J. and Latimer, P. R. (1983) 'Vomiting as a learned weight-control technique in bulimia', *Journal of Behaviour Therapy and Experimental Psychiatry* 14: 131–5.

Coddington, R. C. and Bruch, J. (1970) 'Gastric perceptivity in normal, obese and schizophrenic subjects', *Psychosomatics* 11: 571–9.

Cooper, P., Taylor, M., Cooper, Z. and Fairburn, C. (1987) 'Development of the Body Shape Questionnaire', *International Journal of Eating Disorders* 6: 485–90.

Cooper, Z. and Fairburn, C. G. (1987) 'The eating disorder examination: a semi-structured interview for the assessment of the specific psychopathology of eating disorders', *International Journal of Eating Disorders* 6: 1–8.

Crisp, A. H. (1970) 'Premorbid factors in adult disorders of weight, with particular reference to primary anorexia nervosa', *Journal of Psychosomatic Research* 14: 1–22.

DaCosta, M. and Halmi, K. A. (1992) 'Classifications of anorexia nervosa: the question of subtypes', *International Journal of Eating Disorders* 11: 305–13.

Dally, P. and Gomez, J. (1979) *Anorexia Nervosa*, London: William Heinemann.

Durnin, J. V. and Womersley, J. (1974) 'Body fat assessed from total body density and its estimation from skinfold thickness', *British Journal of Nutrition* 21: 681–9.

Dwyer, J. (1992) 'Nutritional remedies: reasonable and questionable', *Annals of Behavioural Medicine* 14: 120–5.

Dwyer, J. T., Feldman, J. J. and Mayer, J. (1970) 'The social psychology of dieting', *Journal of Health and Social Behaviour* 11: 269–87.

Fairburn, C. G. (1983) 'Bulimia nervosa', *British Journal of Hospital Medicine* (June): 537–42.

Fairburn, C. G. and Cooper, P. J. (1982) 'Self-induced vomiting and bulimia nervosa; an undetected problem', *British Medical Journal* 284: 1153–55.

Fairburn, C. G. and Garner, D. M. (1986) 'The diagnosis of bulimia nervosa', *International Journal of Eating Disorders* 5: 403–19.

Falkner, F. (1962) 'Some physical growth standards for white North American children', *Pediatrics* 29: 467–74.

Fava, M., Copeland, P. M., Schweiger, U. and Herzog, D. B. (1989) 'Neurochemical abnormalities of anorexia nervosa and bulimia nervosa', *American Journal of Psychiatry* 146: 963–71.

Florey, C. D. V. (1970) 'The use and interpretation of ponderal index and other weight/height ratios in epidemiological studies', *Journal of Chronic Diseases* 23: 93–103.

Garfinkel, P. E. (1974) 'Perception of hunger and satiety in anorexia nervosa', *Psychological Medicine* 4: 309–15.

Garfinkel, P. E. and Garner, D.M. (1982) *Anorexia Nervosa: A Multidimensional Perspective*, New York: Brunner Mazel.

Garfinkel, P. E., Moldofsky, H., Garner, D. M., Stancer, H. C. and Coscina, D. V. (1978) 'Body awareness in anorexia nervosa: Disturbances in body image and satiety', *Psychosomatic Medicine* 40: 487–98.

Garfinkel, P. E., Moldofsky, H. and Garner, D. M. (1980) 'The heterogeneity of anorexia nervosa: Bulimia as a distinct subgroup', *Archives of General Psychology* 37: 1036–40.

Garner, D. M. (1985) 'Iatrogenesis in anorexia nervosa and bulimia nervosa', *International Journal of Eating Disorders* 4: 701–26.

Garner, D. M. (1991) *Eating Disorder Inventory 2*, Odessa, Fla.: Psychological Assessment Resources Inc.

Garner, D. M. and Garfinkel, P. E. (1979) 'The Eating Attitudes Test: an index of the symptoms of anorexia nervosa', *Psychological Medicine* 9: 273–9.

Garner, D. M., Garfinkel, P. E., Stancer, H. C. and Moldofsky, H. (1976) 'Body image disturbances in anorexia nervosa and obesity', *Psychosomatic Medicine* 38: 227–36.

Garner, D. M., Garfinkel, P. E., Schwartz, D. and Thompson, M. (1980) 'Cultural expectations of thinness in women', *Psychological Reports* 47: 483–91.

Garrow, J. S. (1974) *Energy Balance and Obesity in Man*, New York: Elsevier.

Goldberg, S. C., Halmi, K. A., Eckert, E. D., Casper, R. C., Davis, J. M. and Roper, M. (1980) 'Attitudinal dimensions in anorexia nervosa', *Journal of Psychosomatic Research* 15: 239–51.

Griffiths, M. and Payne, P. R. (1976) 'Energy expenditure in small children of obese and non-obese patients', *Nature* 260: 698–700.

Grimes, W. B. and Franzini, L. R. (1977) 'Skinfold measurement techniques for estimating percentage body fat', *Journal of Behaviour Therapy and Experimental Psychiatry* 8: 65–9.

Halmi, K. A., Goldberg, S. C., Eckert, E., Casper, R. and Davis, J. M. (1977) 'Pretreatment evaluation in anorexia nervosa', in R. A. Vigersky (ed.) *Anorexia Nervosa*, New York: Raven Press (43–54).

Halmi, K. A., Falk, J. R. and Schwarts, E. (1981) 'Binge eating and vomiting: A survey of a college population', *Psychological Medicine* 11: 697–706.

Halmi, K. A., Sunday, S., Puglisi, A. and Marchi, P. (1989) 'Hunger and satiety in anorexia and bulimia nervosa', *Annals of the New York Academy of Science* 575: 431–45.

Halmi, K. A., Eckert, E., Marchi, P., Sampugnaro, V., Apple, R. and Cohen, J. (1991) 'Comorbidity of psychiatric diagnoses in anorexia nervosa', *Archives of General Psychiatry* 48: 712–18.

Hamm, P., Shekelle, R. B., Stamler, J. (1989) 'Large fluctuations in body weight during young adulthood and twenty-five-year risk of coronary death in men', *American Journal of Epidemiology* 129: 312–18.

Hawkins, R. C. and Clement, P. F. (1980) 'Development and construct validation of a self-report measure of binge eating tendencies', *Addictive Behaviours* 5: 219–26.

Heatherton, T. F. and Baumeister, R. F., (1992) 'Binge-eating as escape from self-awareness', *Psychological Bulletin* 110: 86–108.

Herman, P. (1980) 'Restrained eating', in A. J. Stunkard (ed.) *Obesity*, Philadelphia: W. B. Saunders.

Herman, C. B. and Mack, D. (1975) 'Restrained and unrestrained eating', *Journal of Personality* 43: 547–60.

Hibscher, J. A. and Herman, C. P. (1977) 'Obesity, dieting and the expression of "obese" characteristics', *Journal of Comparative and Physiological Psychology* 97: 374–80.

Hoek, H. W. (1991) 'The incidence and prevalence of anorexia nervosa and bulimia nervosa in primary care', *Psychological Medicine* 21: 455–60.

Jeffery, R. W. (1992) 'Is obesity a risk factor for cardiovascular disease?' *Annals of Behavioural Medicine* 14: 109–12.

Johnson, C. B. and Larson, R. (1982) 'Bulimia: An analysis of moods and behaviour', *Psychological Medicine* 44: 341–51.

Johnson, M. L., Bucke, B. S. and Mayer, J. (1956) 'Relative importance of inactivity and overeating in the energy balance of obese high-school girls', *American Journal of Clinical Nutrition* 4: 37–44.

Jourard, S. M. and Secord, P. R. (1955) 'Body cathexis and the ideal female figure', *Journal of Abnormal and Social Psychology* 50: 243–6.

King, M. B. (1989) 'Eating disorders in a general practice population' in *Psychological Medicine*, Cambridge: Cambridge University Press 19: 1–34.

Kissileff, H., Jordan, H. and Levitz, L. (1978) 'Eating habits of obese and normal weight humans', in G. A. Bray (ed.) *Recent Advances in Obesity Research* 2, London: Newman.

Klajner, F., Herman, C. P., Polivy, J. and Chhabra, R. (1981) 'Human obesity, dieting and anticipatory salivation to food', *Physiology and Behaviour* 27: 195–8.

La Porte, R. E. (1989) 'Evaluating interrelationships among physical fitness and activity measurements', in T. F. Drury (ed.) *Assessing Physical Fitness and Physical Activity in Population Bases Surveys* 'DHHS-PHS Report 89-1253), Washington, DC.: US Government Printing Office.

Lissner, L., Bengtsson, C., Lapidus, L., Larsson, B., Bengtsson, B. and Brownell, K. (1988) 'Body weight variability and mortality in the Gothenburg prospective studies of men and women', in P. Björntorp and S. Rössner (eds) *Obesity in Europe 88*, London: John Libbey (55–60).

Mahoney, M. J. (1975) 'The obese eating style: bites, beliefs and behaviour modification', *Addictive Behaviors* 1: 47–53.

Mayer, J. (1968) *Overweight: Causes, Cost and Control*, Englewood Cliffs, NJ: Prentice-Hall.

Metropolitan Life Insurance Company (1983) '1983 Metropolitan Height and Weight Tables', *Statistical Bulletin* (Jan–June): 3–9.

Minuchin, S., Rosman, B. L. and Baker, L. (1978) *Psychosomatic Families: Anorexia Nervosa in Context*, Cambridge, Mass.: Harvard University Press.

Mizes, J. S. and Klesges, R. C. (1990) 'Validity, reliability, and factor structure of the Anorectic Cognitions Questionnaire', *Addictive Behaviors* 14: 589–94.

Monello, L. F. and Mayer, J. (1963) 'Obese adolescent girls. An unrecognised "minority", group?, *American Journal of Clinical Nutrition* 13: 35–9.

Morley, J. E. and Blundell, J. E. (1988) 'The neurobiological basis of eating disorders: some formulations', *Biological Psychiatry* 23: 53–78.

National Institute of Health (1985) 'Health implications of obesity', *Annals of Internal Medicine* 103: 1073–77.

Osancová, K. and Hejda, S. (1975) 'Epidemiology of obesity', in T. Silverstone (ed.) *Obesity Pathogenesis and Management*, Lancaster: Medical and Technical Publishing Company.

Palmer, R. L. (1979) 'The dietary chaos syndrome: A useful new term', *British Journal of Medical Psychology* 52: 187–90.

Pearlson, G. D., Flournoy, L. M., Simonson, M. and Slavney, P. R. (1981) 'Body image in obese adults', *Psychological Medicine* 11: 147–54.

Pierloot, R. A. and Houben, M. E. (1978) 'Estimation of body dimensions in anorexia nervosa', *Psychological Medicine* 8: 317–24.

Polivy, J., Herman, P. and Warsh, S. (1978) 'Internal and external components of emotionality in restrained and unrestrained eaters', *Journal of Abnormal Psychology* 87: 497–504.

Prentice, A. M., Black, A. E., Coward, W. A., Davies, H. L., Goldberg, G. R., Murgatroyd, P. R., Ashford, J., Sawyer, M. and Whitehead, R. G. (1986) 'High levels of energy expenditure in obese women', *British Medical Journal* 292: 983–7.

Pyle, R. L., Mitchell, J. E. and Eckert, E. D. (1981) 'Bulimia: A report of 34 cases', *Journal of Clinical Psychology* 42: 60–4.

Ravussin, E., Lillioja, S., Knowler, W. C., Christin, L., Freymond, D., Abbott, W. G. H., Boyce, V., Howard, B. V. and Bogardus, C. (1988) 'Reduced rate of energy expenditure as a risk factor for body-weight gain', *New England Journal of Medicine* 318: 462–72.

Rosenberg, (1965) *Society and Adolescent Self Image*, Princeton, NJ: Princeton University Press.

Russell, G. F. M. (1970) 'Anorexia nervosa: its identity as an illness and its treatment', in J. H. Price (ed.) *Modern Trends in Psychological Medicine 2*, London: Butterworth.

Russell, G. F. M. (1979) 'Bulimia nervosa: an ominous variant of anorexia nervosa', *Psychological Medicine* 9: 429–48.

Schachter, S. and Rodin, J. (1974) *Obese Humans and Rats*, Washington DC: Erlbaum-Halstead.

Schutz, Y., Flatt, J. P. and Jéquier, E. (1989) 'Failure of dietary fat intake to promote fat oxidation: a factor favoring the development of obesity', *American Journal of Clinical Nutrition* 50: 307–14.

Shetty, P. S., Jung, R. T., James, W. P. T., Barrand, M. A. and Callingham, B. A. (1981) 'Post prandial thermogenesis in obesity', *Clinical Science* 60: 519–25.

Shipman, W. and Sohlkhan, N. (1967) 'Body image distortion in obese women', *Psychosomatic Medicine* 29: 540.

Silverstone, J. T. (1968) 'Obesity', *Proceedings of Royal Society of Medicine* 61: 371–5.

Slade, P. (1973) 'A short anorexic behaviour scale', *British Journal of Psychiatry* 122: 83–5.

Slade, P. (1982) 'Towards a functional analysis of anorexia nervosa and bulimia nervosa', *British Journal of Clinical Psychology* 21: 167–81.

Slade, P. and Russell, G. F. M. (1973) 'Experimental investigations of bodily perceptions in anorexia nervosa and obesity', *Psychotherapy and Psychosomatics* 22: 259–363.

Smith, M. C. and Thelen, M. H. (1984) 'Development and validation of a test for bulimia', *Journal of Consulting and Clinical Psychology* 52: 863–72.

Sobal, J. and Stunkard, A. J. (1989) 'Socioeconomic status and obesity: a review of the literature', *Psychological Bulletin* 105: 260–75.

Stangler, R. S. and Printz, A. M. (1980) 'DSM III. Psychiatric diagnosis in a university population', *American Journal of Psychiatry* 137: 937–40.

Stefanik, P. A., Heald, F. P. and Mayer, J. (1959) 'Caloric intake in relation to energy output of obese and non-obese adolescent boys', *American Journal of Clinical Nutrition* 7: 55–62.

Steinhausen, H. C. and Glanville, K. (1983) 'Follow-up studies of anorexia nervosa: a review of research findings', *Psychological Medicine* 13: 239–49.

Stunkard, A. J. (1958) 'Physical activity, emotions and human obesity', *Psychosomatic Medicine* 20: 366–72.

Stunkard, A. J. and Fox, S. (1971) 'The relationship of gastric motility and hunger. A summary of the evidence', *Psychosomatic Medicine* 33: 123–34.

Stunkard, A. J. and Messick, S. (1985) 'The three factors eating questionnaire to measure dietary restraint, distribution and hunger', *Journal of Psychosomatic Research* 29: 71–84.

Stunkard, A. J. and Pestka, J. (1962) 'The physical activity of obese girls', *American Journal of Diseases of Childhood* 103: 812–17.

Stunkard, A. J., Sorensen, T. I. A., Hanis, C., Teasdale, T. W., Chakraborty, R., Schull, W. J. and Schulsinger, F. (1986) 'An adoption study of human obesity', *New England Journal of Medicine* 314: 193–8.

Turner, M. St. J. and Shapiro, C. M. (1992) 'The biochemistry of anorexia nervosa', *International Journal of Eating Disorders* 12: 179–93.

Van Strien, T., Frijters, J. E. R., Bergers, G. P. A. and Defares, P. B. (1986) 'The Dutch eating behaviour questionnaire for assessment of restrained, emotional and external eating behaviour', *International Journal of Eating Disorders* 5: 295–315.

Walsh, B. T., Kissileff, H. R. and Hadigan, C. M. (1989) 'Eating behaviour in bulimia', *Annals of the New York Academy of Sciences* 575: 446–55.

Wardle, J. (1980) 'Dietary restraint and binge eating', *Behaviour Analysis and Modification* 4: 201–9.

Wardle, J. (1987a) 'Eating style: a validation study of the Dutch Eating Behaviour Questionnaire in normal subjects and women with eating disorders', *Journal of Psychosomatic Research* 31: 161–9.

Wardle, J. (1987b) 'Compulsive eating and dietary restraint', *British Journal of Clinical Psychology* 26: 47–55.

Wardle, J. (1988) 'Cognitive control of eating', *Journal of Psychosomatic Research* 32: 607–12.

Wardle, J. and Beinart, H. (1981) 'Binge eating: a theoretical review', *British Journal of Clinical Psychology* 20: 97–109.

Wardle, J. and Ogden, J. (1989) 'Cognitive and physiological effects on hunger and food intake', *Annals of the New York Academy of Sciences* 575: 585–7.

Wardle, J. and Marsland, L. (1990) 'Adolescent concerns about weight and eating: A social developmental perspective', *Journal of Psychosomatic Research* 34: 377–91.

Williamson, D. A. (1990) *Assessment of Eating Disorders: Obesity, Anorexia, and Bulimia Nervosa*, New York: Pergamon.

Wing, R. R. (1992) 'Weight cycling in humans: a review of the literature', *Annals of Behavioral Medicine* 14: 113–19.

Wooley, O. W. and Wooley, S. C. (1975) 'The experimental psychology of obesity', in T. Silverstone (ed.) *Obesity Pathogenesis and Management*, Lancaster: Medical and Technical Publishing Company.

Wooley, O. W., Wooley, S. C. and Woods, W. A. (1975) 'Effect of calories on appetite for palatable food in obese and non-obese humans', *Journal of Comparative and Physiological Psychology* 89: 619–25.

Wooley, O. W., Wooley, S. C. and Dyrenforth, S. R. (1979) 'Obesity and Women II. A neglected feminist topic', *Women's Studies international Quarterley* 2: 81–92.

Yates, A. (1991) *Compulsive Exercise and the Eating Disorder: Towards an Integrated Theory of Activity*, New York: Brunner/Mazel.

Chapter 27

Disorders of eating and weight
Treatment

Jane Wardle

INTRODUCTION

Psychological treatments of the disorders of eating and weight have run a variable course. On the one hand, psychological approaches seem ideally suited to such abnormalities of behaviour as excessive eating, and some spectacular successes have been achieved with uncontrolled case series (Stuart, 1967; Garfinkel *et al.*, 1973). On the other hand, the disorders have not responded to treatment with the ease predicted by simple behavioural models. The prevailing view of the long-term impact of behavioural treatments on obesity (Wilson and Brownell, 1980; Garner and Wooley, 1991) or anorexia (Garfinkel and Garner, 1982) has lost its earlier optimism.

Initially behavioural treatments for eating disorders were based on an operant management procedure in which weight or eating targets were set and rewarded. The principles of classical conditioning have also been involved more recently, with suggestions that conditioned responses to food cues could be extinguished through cue exposure methods (Wardle, 1990; Schmidt and Marks, 1988; Jansen *et al.*, 1989). Greater emphasis has also been given to the cognitive elements of control of eating, and this has led to the emergence of a more optimistic note in the treatment literature. Combined cognitive and behavioural therapeutic packages are now routinely recommended (Fairburn, 1985; LeBow, 1989).

In common with the treatments for other habit disorders, however, the real challenge is not the initial behaviour change, but long-term maintenance. It is now widely acknowledged that behaviour change is often short-lived, and that new treatments must demonstrate a realistic acceptance of this.

TREATMENT OF OBESITY

Background

The 'problem' of obesity has attracted increasing attention in the western world over the past few decades for two reasons. First, the evidence that obesity is hazardous to health has accumulated (National Institute of Health, 1985; Jeffery, 1992) and while other risk factors such as hypertension can go unnoticed, obesity is a highly visible risk factor. Second, social attitudes to weight have increasingly emphasised a slim or androgynous body shape for women. Whereas fatness was once valued, and still is in some parts of the world, in the West it is now stigmatised (Sobal, 1991). The combination of health and aesthetic considerations has led to an unprecedented interest in weight loss. As many as 70 per cent of women have at some time tried to lose weight, only a few of whom are likely to have been at serious risk of disease because of their weight.

Treatments for obesity have consistently emphasised control of food intake, although the particular aspect of the diet which is targeted has varied. In the late nineteenth century, William Banting had a well-publicised success in losing weight with a low carbohydrate diet (Banting, 1863). Since that time an enormous literature, both popular and scientific, has detailed an innumerable variety of diets that are claimed to promote weight loss (see Dwyer, 1980; 1992). Expenditure on slimming products and services is at unprecedented levels, which probably owes as much to commercial interests as to the needs of the overweight population.

There is no doubt that if energy input is consistently less than energy output then weight loss occurs. The difficulty lies not simply in obtaining a negative energy balance but in maintaining it for long enough to achieve significant and sustained fat loss. Psychological, environmental and physiological factors will all tend towards the restoration of energy balance. In terms of weight loss, the results of dietary treatments for obesity have not been promising, and as Brownell and Wadden pointed out, 'recovery from cancer is more likely than recovery from obesity' (Brownell and Wadden, 1983). The assumption that body size can be altered at will is increasingly being challenged (Brownell and Wadden, 1992).

Behavioural treatments for obesity may be viewed as providing the framework within which the patient can comply with the essential nutritional recommendations concerning food intake and activity. Ferster et al. (1962) provided the first account of the development of a programme of weight control. It aimed to limit the frequency and speed of eating by teaching self-control procedures. These involved minimising exposure to the discriminating stimuli for eating, rewarding moderate and appropriate eating, and reducing the reinforcement value of eating. The first systematic application of these techniques was reported by Stuart (1967) who treated eight obese women with dramatically effective results, thus setting the stage for widespread development of the behavioural approach to obesity. Until very recently there has been little more than procedural variation on the theme of learning to control food intake.

One approach has been to apply behavioural strategies to increasing activity level. Pi-Sunyer (1987) has argued that obese people do not increase their food intake to match higher levels of energy expenditure, so a negative energy balance might be facilitated by increasing activity levels. However, the treatment outcome data suggests that activity levels are more relevant to maintenance of a new body weight than achieving significant weight loss (Perri *et al.*, 1986). In a second new development, the idea of modifying cognitions has been adopted as routine in current treatment programmes, although there is no consensus on what kind of cognitions are suitable targets for treatment. In some cases the cognitive approach is directed towards modifying the thoughts which might promote or prevent dietary lapses, as in Alan Marlatt's relapse prevention work (Marlatt, 1985; Sternberg, 1985). In other cases, negative thoughts about the self, for example about appearance, are targeted in their own right (Wardle, 1989). There has also been considerable interest in the possibility of achieving faster and greater initial weight loss through the use of very low calorie diets (VLCD) combined with behaviour therapy. Wadden and Stunkard (1986) achieved good results in the short term with a combined treatment, getting an average weight loss of 19.25 kg. However, at the three-year follow-up, many clients had regained a good deal of their lost weight and the total weight loss had declined to 6.53 kg with no significant advantage to the combined treatment group (Wadden *et al.*, 1988). Despite this poor outcome, there is still optimism that combining VLCD, behaviour therapy and better maintenance programmes could achieve sustained weight loss.

Notwithstanding the developments in the therapeutic repertoire, there has, however, been an important shift in attitude. The great confidence expressed in the early treatment reports has shifted to a more cautious view as psychologists and physiologists have realised that a significant and enduring reduction in fatness is not necessarily accessible to all overweight patients. Some reports (Wooley and Wooley, 1979; Wardle, 1989; Garner and Wooley, 1991) have emphasised the value of accepting that some patients may never achieve their target weight. Under these circumstances, assistance in the acquisition of improved physical and psychological well-being *despite* obesity is an important component of therapy. In this context, improving the quality of obese people's diet, increasing their exercise levels and helping them to adopt a more positive self-image have all been adopted as treatment targets. In this way it is possible to achieve reduction in cardiovascular risk factors (e.g. cholesterol, hypertension) and improve psychological well-being, even if the goal of weight loss cannot be met. Recent evidence suggests that even minimal weight loss can reduce risk factor levels significantly (Blackburn and Kanders, 1987).

Most of the cognitive-behavioural treatment programmes for obesity involve the following components: (a) self-monitoring of behaviour, (b) targeting of treatment goals, (c) identification and modification of discriminating stimuli, (d) alteration in eating style, (e) reduction in energy intake, (f) increase in activity level, and (g) identification of self-defeating cognitions. More detailed advice is included in the following books: Stuart (1967); Stuart and Davis (1972); Mahoney and Mahoney (1976); Stunkard and Mahoney (1976); Jeffery and Katz (1977); Agras (1987); and LeBow (1989). Each of the techniques will be described briefly in the following sections.

Self-monitoring

Record-keeping, using forms such as those shown in the many treatment manuals (e.g. Jeffery and Katz, 1977; Agras, 1987; LeBow, 1989), is the mainstay of the assessment procedure but may make a therapeutic contribution as well. The settings, timing and motivational states in which eating takes place can be identified, and will provide information on which to base the stimulus control procedures. Patients report that the self-monitoring procedures can themselves produce change (Ost and Gottestam, 1976), and some studies have suggested that they can produce a weight loss comparable to a more complex behavioural programme (Romanczyk *et al.*, 1973). The mechanism of the effect remains unclear, although it is assumed to lie in the increased opportunities for change which result from greater self-awareness. One implication of this is that the baseline information produced from self-monitoring is likely to under-represent the extent of any behavioural problems. Continued monitoring of weight or eating may also make a contribution to maintenance. If recommendations are given concerning the steps to be taken if weight regain exceeds a defined limit, then the continued monitoring should enhance longer-term weight control. The drawback of this approach is that continued and possibly obsessive attention to weight and eating could engender costs in quality of life which outweigh the benefits of weight loss. Certainly the obsession about weight expressed by western society has probably caused more problems than it has solved.

Target setting

The obvious target for obesity treatment is weight or fatness reduction, and usually some goal or a series of subgoals are set in this area. The choice of target weight will be based on a number of factors, including the desirable weight (Metropolitan Life Insurance Company, 1983), the weight history, health considerations, and the therapist's knowledge of the likely weight that patients lose in treatment. The typical weight loss has been around 10 lb for almost any behavioural treatment which has been evaluated (Jeffery *et al.*, 1978), although individual studies have produced better results in the short term (e.g. Wadden and Stunkard, 1986). Subgoals of weekly weight loss are generally set fairly low (1–2 lb per week), both in order to minimise the effects of starvation and because there is some evidence that realistic goal setting is associated with better results. It should be noted that target losses of 10–20 lb may be of more statistical than personal significance to someone who is grossly overweight. It is essential, therefore, that weight targets are discussed fully and realistically at the start of treatment.

If exercise is involved as part of the treatment procedure, then a change in fatness (for example, body circumference) rather than weight might represent a more appropriate goal, because it would give a better representation of changing bodily composition. The new approaches to obesity management, in which improvements in risk profile are targeted, demand a different set of goals. They may be behavioural (for example, dietary choice or activity levels) or physiological (for example, lipid levels, fitness).

Stimulus control – identification and modification of discriminative stimuli

The notion of stimulus control was put forward by Ferster *et al.* (1962). It was an instance of the general proposition that reinforcement principles could be self-applied as easily as they could be externally controlled. Ferster proposed that eating behaviour is part of a behavioural chain under control of environmental cues and consequences which, if manipulated appropriately, will result in the regulation of food intake without calling upon 'will power'. On the basis of interviews and dietary records, the antecedent conditions for eating can be identified and appropriate modification strategies applied.

Stuart and Davis (1972) and Brownell (1987) list a number of areas of antecedent stimuli which they have found useful to modify. These include the presence of desirable foods around the house, the situations in which eating takes place, and the activities which take place during eating. In other words, people tend to eat in response to the availability of desirable food, to eat while they talk or watch television, and to eat in several rooms of their home. Limitation of food purchasing and restriction of eating to a single particular setting may reduce total intake.

Eating is also assumed to have powerful and immediate positively reinforcing consequences, that is, it is pleasurable. The adverse consequences of a positive energy balance, such as fatness and reduced fitness, all lie in the future. Most behaviour therapy techniques are therefore set in the context of operant technologies, and self-reinforcement or external reinforcement paradigms appear in some form in order to bridge the time before weight loss occurs. In some programmes, clients deposit money or valued possessions to be returned or given away according to treatment results (Mann, 1972). Clients can also be trained in the principles of reinforcement and encouraged to alter their lifestyle so that pleasant events are contingent upon the performance of target behaviours or the achievement of goals. Examples of this approach might be to make some pleasurable activity contingent upon the avoidance of snacks, the performance of exercise plans, or the completion of a food shopping programme.

Studies which evaluate stimulus control procedures on their own tend to indicate that weight is reduced by the typical amount, usually around 1–2 lb per week, but while some studies have shown it to be better than other behavioural procedures (Beneke *et al.*, 1978), others have failed to show a specific effect. Clear identification of self-control as an effective therapy procedure requires the demonstration that it has produced the desired behaviour change, that this behaviour change is not produced without this specific training, and that the behaviour change is responsible for the weight loss. Many authors have commented that the relationship between self-control therapy, functional change and weight loss remains to be clarified (e.g. Brownell and Stunkard, 1978; Jeffery *et al.*, 1978).

Altering eating style

The 'obese eating style', as it was once known, has been characterised in terms of quicker eating and fewer chews per bite (Schachter, 1971; Stuart and Davis, 1972). The implications of this for aetiology and management of obesity have depended upon the theory that the food in the stomach provides, after a delay, some kind of satiety signal. Thus, slower eating supposedly gives time for the satiety signal to operate, but fast eating is completed before satiety mechanisms are activated. In fact, the evidence for fast eating in the obese is equivocal, and the contribution of fast eating to weight gain, or slowed eating to weight loss, remains to be demonstrated (Mahoney, 1975).

There may, however, be other reasons for reducing eating speed, such as increasing the time over which pleasurable eating takes place, reducing 'guilty stuffing', and affording the overweight person some direct evidence of control. On this basis, reduction in eating speed via pauses between mouthfuls can be part of the behavioural approach.

The aspect of eating style which is attracting increasing attention is 'emotional eating' (Ganley, 1988; Wardle *et al.*, 1992). Eating in response to negative emotional states is a common pattern, and in cases where the patient's goal is control of eating, it can prove especially difficult. If, for example, depression triggers a dietary violation, which in turn causes self-blame and further depression, the stage is set for a full-scale relapse. Mechanisms of this kind may promote and maintain binge-eating. If emotional eating is a regular feature of the patient's eating style, then it is vital to include it in the treatment targets. Helping the patient to develop and use alternative (and preferably incompatible) responses to negative moods would therefore be important.

Altering food intake

There is still little or no dissension from the view that obese people need to eat differently. It is assumed that they need to take in less energy and to alter their sources of energy towards complex carbohydrates and away from fats. Behavioural change does not obviate the need for caloric reduction, and most treatments are designed to make the dietary change easier. In other words, the behavioural treatment is the vehicle in which the dietary change is placed. Ideally the recommendations that the therapist makes will be nutritionally sound at the same time as taking account of the subject's dietary preferences. General nutritional education may help some subjects to make food choices which conform to the diet while being personally satisfying, so that the reduction of caloric intake is implemented in a way which will cause the least disruption in lifestyle. Some obese subjects are already well informed about food composition and energy content, but most will need to be supplied with this information. The stress on calorie counting in the diets of the 1960s and 1970s has given way to an emphasis on low-fat diets. There have been suggestions that diets which are low in fat will minimise fat storage and may make it easier to tolerate a degree of caloric restriction.

Outcome research on behavioural treatment has often compared a combined behavioural/nutritional treatment with a simple nutritional approach, and typically shows a marginal advantage when behavioural treatment is included (Penick *et al.*, 1971; Levitz and Stunkard, 1974; Wilson and Brownell, 1980). The growing evidence that diet and obesity may contribute independently to cardiovascular risk suggests that a shift to a 'healthy eating' diet would be advised for most obese patients. This will necessitate education and training in selecting a diet which is low in saturated fat and high in fibre and antioxidant vitamins. Learning to understand food labelling is a first step. There are also a number of cookery books available which specialise in low-fat and high-fibre recipes, which could be useful.

Increasing energy output

Early behaviour therapy work made only a token gesture towards increasing energy output. In part this was because it has been thought hard to establish increments in behaviour; indeed obese people themselves are often more willing to agree to a decrease in food than an increase in activity. Such a preference may be a good guide to the behaviour change which will be most easily acquired, but it does not necessarily predict maintenance. There is some evidence in normal subjects that exercise, once established, can function as its own reinforcer, because a reduction in activity level is aversive (Glasser, 1976). A second reason for ignoring exercise is that it has been thought to contribute little to weight loss. Most fat people ascribe to this view. However, there is now evidence that exercise contributes in several ways over and above its direct calorie cost. It appears to affect the process of energy balance in that subjects who exercise lose more weight than would be predicted by the direct caloric cost of the exercise (Bray, 1976). This could be due to appetite suppression, or to a more subtle metabolic change. Exercise-induced weight loss also seems to circumvent the reduction in basal metabolic rate which plagues dieters (Mayer, 1968). Finally, exercise is known to preserve lean tissue during weight loss. Subjects who lose weight by caloric restriction alone lose both fat and lean tissue, whereas regained weight is predominantly fat. Cycles of losing and regaining weight may therefore result in an increased proportion of bodily fat. Subjects who lose weight as a result of dietary restriction combined with exercise tend to preserve lean tissue, and this therefore prevents progressive replacement of fat for lean tissue in the total bodily composition (Parízková, 1977; Brownell and Stunkard, 1980; Thompson *et al.*, 1982).

One uncontrolled series showed that subjects who walked for an extra thirty minutes a day, lost 22 lb in one year (Gwinup, 1975). Stalonas *et al.* (1978) found exercise to be equal to dietary control during the treatment period, and more effective in the follow-up period. Likewise Dahlkoetter *et al.* (1979) and Perri *et al.* (1986) found that a diet/exercise combination group lost more weight during follow-up than a diet-only group. At present it seems unlikely that exercise programmes will offer substantially superior weight loss, but they may have an important part to play in prevention of relapse after treatment.

A quite different reason for including exercise in the treatment programme for obesity involves the reduction of physical risk factors. Almost all of the physical risk factors of obesity (high blood pressure, high lipid level, etc.) are also affected by exercise, which can therefore override the ill effects of obesity (Boyer and Kasch, 1970). Furthermore, accumulating evidence suggests that exercise has beneficial effects on body image, self-esteem and mood, all of which are of specific relevance to overweight people (Bouchard *et al.*, 1990).

The benefit of exercise depends upon the patient complying with the exercise programme, and compliance in this area is notoriously low. Cardiovascular fitness programmes with well-motivated subjects often have a compliance rate of less than 60 per cent; in a group of healthy volunteers only 35 per cent were fully compliant with a fitness programme (Ballantyne *et al.*, 1978). Results of exercise programmes for obese patients have produced similar results (Gwinup, 1975; Krotkiewski *et al.*, 1977), but more recently compliance has been improved by the adoption of the techniques of behaviour modification (Dahlkoetter *et al.*, 1979; Perri *et al.*, 1986). A paired support system for the participants, between sessions, and a monetary deposit which would be forfeited for non-attendance, are strategies which may be helpful.

Improving body image

The negative body image of obese people poses a unique problem in the field of eating disorders. Patients with anorexia or bulimia are usually at or below the socially prescribed ideal weights. Obese people, by definition, are over this weight, and the therapist is likely to share the cultural preference for a slim appearance. Management of a negative body image may therefore be more similar to management of other stigmatised physical conditions. Sobal (1991) has recommended a four-component strategy: (1) recognise the problem of stigma, (2) be ready for stigmatising situations, (3) react appropriately, (4) repair the problems that stigmatising may have caused. This could be a very useful framework for helping obese patients to tolerate their condition. At the same time, techniques to improve body image could be used. These would include cognitive strategies (for example, reducing negative self-statements) and behavioural methods (for example, using graded exposure to embarrassing situations such as swimming or dancing) (Butters and Cash, 1987; Dworkin and Kerr, 1987). Many obese patients have an extensive list of avoidances ranging from clothes shopping to sexual contact. Helping them overcome these fears could be an important part of their rehabilitation process.

Planning the exercise programme depends not just upon choosing the right level of activity, but also upon the context in which it is given. Behavioural principles, such as stimulus control, self-monitoring and reinforcement, are now being used to advantage to increase compliance. Stimulus control procedures suggest that exercise programmes incorporating marginal change in simple daily activities should be easier to follow (requiring less 'will power') than those demanding, for example, attendance after work at some distant gymnasium. Feedback of results via a self-monitored programme covering amount of activity, fitness, fatness, etc., is likely to add to the programme, as well as a system of rewards. These could be self-administered (for example, watching a favourite television programme only after completion of exercise, allocate money to be spent on self or on a favourite charity, according to weekly compliance), or externally administered, for example, by friends, partner or therapist (Wysocki *et al.*, 1979).

The choice of exercise depends in part on the anticipated benefits. If fitness is the primary concern, high-intensity activity incorporating sustained increase in heart rate is essential (Morehouse and Gross, 1975). In this case it is very important to ensure that medical advice is taken on the exercise programme. A regime involving strenuous exercise (e.g. swimming, cycling, jogging, dancing) sustained for 15–30 minutes and carried out at least three times a week over 10–12 weeks will result in increased cardiovascular fitness, reduced body fat, and increased lean tissue. This latter will be reflected primarily in reduction in skinfold thickness, and more slowly, if at all, in weight reduction.

If cardiovascular risk reduction and weight reduction rather than fitness are the main goals, the exercise need not be so strenuous. Walking, gardening, light exercise and other 'lifestyle activities' can be beneficial to health and may help energy balance. The main aim would be to increase the proportion of time spent in effortful activity. This can be achieved by specific prescription, for example, 30 minutes' walking each day; or by the substitution of more for less energy-consuming activities, for example, climbing stairs instead of using lifts, and walking instead of driving. Values for the caloric cost of activities are given in Brownell and Stunkard (1980).

Reducing negative thinking

Behaviour therapy in general is coming to include more references to cognitive processes, and the behavioural treatment of obesity is no exception (Leon, 1979). The earliest uses of cognitive manipulations in obesity treatment tended towards an aversive approach. Horan *et al.* (1975), and many since, have recommended the fat person to adopt a negative and critical style of self-talk. This was intended as a salient negative reinforcer which would motivate dieting. It is paired with positive images of a new and slim feature self which can be used to reward moderation. The disadvantage of this approach concerns the emphasis on negative cognitions in patients who are in any case known to have a poor self-image, low popularity, and to suffer abuse and discrimination because of their size. In the many cases where obesity cannot be significantly reduced, or where weight reduction leaves the self-esteem problem unchanged, a therapeutic package which has included training in low self-esteem cannot be recommended.

The opposite approach is closer to current thinking on the treatment of obese patients. Fostering a positive self-image and encouraging a growth in self-esteem, utilising the techniques of cognitive therapy, should be a routine part of treatment. Positive thinking is likely to contribute to a better mood and to higher expectations for change (Mahoney and Mahoney, 1976). Cognitive strategies for improving body image can be very helpful. In addition to the identification and modification of negative thoughts, it might be valuable to acquaint fat patients with current knowledge and obesity. This includes the fact that most obese people eat no more than thin people, that mild to moderate obesity carries no health risk for women, that obesity is largely biologically determined, that dieting reduces metabolic rate and enhances the tendency to store fat, and finally that there is, as yet, no effective treatment. In this context patients could be given more recent literature on obesity which summarises these points, such as papers by Wooley and her colleagues (Wooley and Wooley, 1979; Garner and Wooley, 1991) or the book by Marcia Millman (1980). At the same time, the benefits of healthy eating and an active lifestyle, both of which may have positive psychological and medical consequences, can be emphasised. Elements of Polivy and Herman's 'undieting' programme (Polivy and Herman, 1992) could also be helpful.

Conclusion

The proportion of the population who are overweight is rising while social pressures towards slenderness are persisting. Weight control probably represents one of the major concerns for women in the western world. Under these circumstances, the pressure to offer treatment is great but the risk of exploitation even greater. On present evidence, obese people have little chance of losing significant amounts of weight. It is incumbent upon psychologists not to promise too much or to contribute to the patient's sense of failure when the outcome is poor.

Wooley and Wooley's guidelines (1979) to those offering treatment for obesity are even more appropriate today and are summarised as follows:

1 Health care professionals should not impose their values on patients by criticising their weight or insisting on unwanted treatment.
2 Patients should be advised of the health risks associated with obesity in a form which will allow the most accurate appraisal of the risk to that individual.
3 Patients should be given whatever information is available on the short-term and long-term success rate of that treatment.

4 Patients should be helped to make an autonomous decision.
5 Patients who choose to remain heavy should be offered help in adjusting to the consequences of that decision.
6 Patients who fail to lose weight should be offered help.
7 Therapists should help to relieve undue pressures on the overweight to conform to social norms.

(Wooley and Wooley, 1979: 77)

The situation is not, however, entirely without hope. Weight control is sought for two reasons, one concerned with health-risk modification and the second with the negative body image of fatter people. The balance of these two motives can vary across patients. Even if weight control is not a realistic possibility, reducing health risks and improving body image may be attainable. Cardiovascular risk is reduced both by adoption of a healthy (but not necessarily calorically restricted) diet and by increasing activity levels. Body image may be susceptible to a combination of cognitive and behavioural strategies.

THE TREATMENT OF ANOREXIA

Background

Anorexic patients often have a good pre-morbid personality and relatively acute problems. Their difficulties have attracted the therapeutic efforts of many different schools of therapy, but they have proved surprisingly resistant to change.

The principal psychological characteristics of anorexia involve abnormalities of food intake resulting in low weight, and an abhorrence of weight gain. In addition to these difficulties, many patients express conflicts over issues of control, sexuality, achievement and maturation, all of which may have aetiological significance. The classic picture of anorexia nervosa is of an emaciated young woman who refuses to eat more than small amounts of low-calorie food. However, it has been clear for some time that a proportion of anorexic patients, probably around 50 per cent, binge and either vomit or abuse laxatives. Several authors have suggested that the differences between the restrictor and bulimic subtypes imply that they should be separate diagnoses (DaCosta and Halmi, 1992). Unlike obesity, which is usually readily identified by the patients themselves, anorexia nervosa is not characterised by insight. Most anorexic patients have distortions of body image and a fear of fatness which makes them very reluctant to accept any treatment which involves weight gain. Initially, therefore, it may be necessary to devote considerable effort to persuading the patient to participate in treatment, or in cases where the weight loss reaches life-threatening levels, to institute compulsory treatment procedures. The medical consequences of anorexia can be very serious, and death from the complications of long-term starvation, vomiting or laxative abuse is frighteningly common. A careful assessment of the patient's physical state is vital in order to evaluate the metabolic symptoms, renal function, liver function and nutritional status (Turner and Shapiro, 1992).

Treatment procedures for anorexia have tended towards a two-pronged approach. Nursing and medical efforts are directed at immediate weight restoration and metabolic regulation, often in an in-patient setting. Then, after some weight change is achieved, psychological treatments are directed at the attitudes and beliefs that supposedly underlie the weight problem. Unfortunately success has been correspondingly divided: weight restoration, in the short term, seems possible for most patients, but a more permanent change has proved much harder. Longer-term follow-ups of anorexia treatment reveal the continuation of abnormalities in eating patterns and attitudes, as well as a high relapse rate (Hsu et al., 1979; Garfinkel and Garner, 1982; Kreipe et al., 1989).

Management of weight

Severe weight loss often demands in-patient treatment, and this has been the setting of most reports of management techniques, although it is recognised that some patients can be treated entirely on an out-patient basis (Barcai, 1971; Agras and Werne, 1981; Yates, 1990; Herzog et al., 1992).

Behavioural treatment approaches to anorexia were first reported in 1965 (Hallsten, 1965; Bachrach et al., 1965), and alone, or in combination with pharmacological or psychotherapeutic treatment, they have become the main-stay of current management practices. The essence of the behavioural approach is feedback and reinforcement of weight gain. The first reports used removal of 'privileges' (visitors, clothes, television, phone calls), which were reinstated systematically according to achievement of weight gain (Bachrach et al., 1965; Leitenberg et al., 1968). Blinder et al., (1970) extended this to include access to exercise, which in view of the anorexic patient's known preference for high levels of activity, provided a particularly suitable source of reinforcement. The implementation of reinforcement procedures generally begins with collection of baseline information on eating and weight over the course of a week or so. A target weight is established at the beginning of treatment, which is based on past healthy weight, or on some approximation (90 per cent, for example) of matched population ideal weight (Metropolitan Life Insurance Company, 1983). A more or less formal contract is then drawn up, defining the intermediate weight increase targets and the reinforcement schedules. Current ethical guidelines would probably rule out many of the reinforcers which have been used – 'the use of reinforcement techniques in therapeutic programmes should involve exclus-ively the provision of goods or privileges which improve on this basic standard' (Royal College of Psychiatrists et al., 1980: Chapter 4, para. 49) – so access to baths, telephone, etc. could not be limited but no restriction is placed on the provision of extra privileges, such as staff attention, special outings, magazines, etc., which can be used to reward weight gain.

Weight gain is usually achieved by consumption of high-calorie meals, and a daily caloric allowance of 3,000 to 5,000 is recommended, with a lower allowance being used initially (Halmi *et al.*, 1975). Nursing management procedures involve encouraging and persuading the patient to consume these extra-large meals (e.g. Morgan and Russell, 1975), but in the operant-based programmes food intake is left to the patient, and only weight is monitored. This may have some advantage as it avoids conflict about food. Nutritional education is also necessary, as the patients have often lost sight of what constitutes normal or healthy eating.

The average weight gain for treatments of all types is 3–4 lb per week (Van Buskirk, 1977), and so weight gain targets of around a half a pound a day would be appropriate. Higher rates of weight gain are widely believed to be too disturbing for patients to tolerate, as well as having unpleasant physical side effects.

Most patients can and do comply successfully with this regime, but at some personal cost, for weight gain is the one thing that they have been avoiding assiduously, and they understandably experience some distress when it is imposed. Comments from staff and family referring to the patient's improved appearance can also be construed negatively, as many patients will have been actively pursuing a frail and unhealthy appearance.

Operant techniques gained popularity when they demonstrated the possibilities of achieving weight gain without drugs or coercive procedures. A series of individual case studies had shown that weight gain was related to the reinforcement procedure (Blinder *et al.*, 1970; Garfinkel *et al.*, 1973; Bhanji and Thompson, 1974). However, controlled studies have not shown the expected clear-cut average; Eckert *et al.*, (1979), in a randomised control trial, found that 'milieu therapy' produced the same immediate gain as reinforcement procedures, and Garfinkel *et al.* (1977), in a retrospective study, found no differences between behavioural and psychotherapeutic techniques at follow-up. Good effects have also been reported for a combination of family therapy and behaviour modification (Rosman *et al.*, 1975), and for a more strictly psychotherapeutic approach (Crisp, 1965; Hall and Crisp, 1987; Crisp *et al.*, 1991), though this latter would certainly include an informal system of encouragement and support for weight gain. In one of the few controlled trials, Crisp *et al.* (1991) compared specialist in-patient treatment, or specialist out-patient treatment (group or individual), with referral back to primary care physician or local psychiatric service. The three specialist services achieved similar weight increases, all of which were higher than the controls. On other measures, the differences between treated and control cases failed to reach significance.

Present evidence, therefore, would suggest that treatment approaches based on any one of several different theoretical positions will give good results in terms of short-term weight gain. The implication of this is that the power of the treatments may lie in the features common to the different programmes, such as the patient's acceptance of the need for treatment, the patient's removal from the home environment, or staff approval of eating and weight gain, rather than in the specific components. Guidelines are given by Halmi (1985) or Agras (1987).

Management of 'anorexic attitudes'

After weight gain is under way, most patients are offered further therapy, often on an out-patient basis. This is variously conceptualised as treating the underlying problems which had resulted in the weight loss (Bruch, 1973), encouraging generalisation of operant treatment effects (Halmi *et al.*, 1975), dealing with conflicts aroused by weight gain and physical maturation (Crisp, 1980), or tackling the abnormal attitudes to weight and food (Garfinkel and Garner, 1982). Many different approaches have been used but no controlled studies exist to demonstrate unequivocally the efficacy of any long-term treatment. In some cases treatment involves the application of a particular therapeutic approach, such as classical psychoanalysis (Silverman, 1974), family therapy (Minuchin *et al.*, 1978) or behaviour modification (Halmi *et al.*, 1975). More commonly, however, experienced clinicians have developed their own approaches, which are derived from several theoretical backgrounds and are aimed at the specific difficulties which the anorexic patients are believed to experience Bruch (1973), Selvini-Palazolli (1974), Crisp (1980), Garfinkel and Garner (1982) and Garner and Bemis (1985) have all given detailed and sensitive accounts of their clinical work, but there are as yet no outcome data from which to make an informed choice between these approaches.

All clinicians, however, agree on certain features of the anorexic patient's psychological background which require therapeutic attention, and some of the common components of therapy are discussed in the following sections.

Relationship with the therapist

A supportive relationship with a therapist is an important part of treatment for anorexic patients. This is not always easy to achieve because anorexic patients are ambivalent about treatment, especially when it involves weight gain. A sensitive understanding of the meaning to the patient of weight and fatness are crucial, along with a straightforward and fairly directive therapeutic style. At times many patients will understandably attempt to mislead the therapist, in an effort to avoid feared consequences of treatment, and this must be dealt with without damaging the relationship. Garner (1985) has emphasised the powerful negative emotional reactions which anorexic patients elicit in some of those treating them, and recommends a number of steps which may be taken to reduce these. Among the most important is the provision of an experienced therapist as a role model, who understands the interdependence between the physical, psychological and social factors in the disorder, and has a genuine fondness for these kinds of patients.

Modification of body image

Many patients describe themselves as fat and some have a grossly exaggerated image of their body size. Careful measurements of body image and feedback of the results could provide the possibility of change. Even more impact might be produced with videotapes of the patient alongside other women whose body size she can assess without distortion. In addition to confronting the patient with information about the true size of her body, she should be supplied with some strategies for reinterpreting her distorted perceptions. These should include generating counter arguments, or learning to give less attention to perceptual information (Garner and Bemis, 1985). Cognitive-behavioural approaches to body image modification are being developed (Butters and Cash, 1987).

Familial/social interactions

For patients still in close contact with the family, the many complex and enmeshed patterns of interaction, communication and reinforcement may curtail positive change (Strober and Humphrey, 1987). Even without full-blown family therapy, any therapist should investigate the family situation, and evaluate and modify those areas which are opposing improvement. This may range from exploring the need for the family to have a 'sick' member, to assessing the possibility that family and friends of anorexic patients actually admire an anorexic appearance (Branch and Eurman, 1980). In this context the therapist should remember that dieting is endemic in women, and that female members of the patient's family may be motivated by similar pressures but be less 'successful', so a degree of envy could be involved. Many clinicians have also commented on the difficulty that anorexic patients have in organising separate and autonomous lives, and in so far as this is outside the boundaries of normal adolescent difficulties, support and guidance may be helpful.

All descriptive research on anorexic patients, especially those who are restrictive rather than bulimic, confirms that they are introverted and socially anxious (Beumont et al., 1976; Casper et al., 1980). This is enhanced by secondary social avoidance caused by fears of encountering situations in which eating is expected. Exploration of the patient's fears and difficulties in social situations may reveal several problem areas which can then be dealt with, allowing the patient to resume a more normal social life. Difficulties are also often reported in the area of psychosexual functioning, and it is commonly believed that the illness is intricately bound up with avoidance of sexual maturity (Crisp, 1980). However, when anorexic patients are interviewed in detail about their sexual knowledge, attitudes and experience before the onset of illness, there is little evidence that they differ from normal young women. Once the anorexic pattern is established, however, most, but not all, patients report a reduction in libido (Beumont et al., 1981; Burvat-Herbaut et al., 1983).

Challenging anorexic attitudes and beliefs

One of the characteristics of anorexia which is widely viewed as the major barrier to long-term improvement is the patient's unswerving belief in the essential wrongness of fatness and eating, and the rightness of thinness and restraint. The first stage of modification involves enabling the patient to identify these beliefs, and to understand the subtle line between the social pressures for thinness which result in fashion models with anorexic proportions, and the pathological drive for thinness that is destroying the patient's own life. Likewise, cultural pressures for dieting, which involve labelling certain foods as 'bad' and 'fattening', must be understood as the background for the over-enthusiasm with which anorexic patients take up dietary restriction.

Anorexic patients are likely to be unaware of the physiological and psychological effects of starvation which are amply documented by Keys *et al.* (1950). Discussion of this may provide valuable insights, and may increase the patient's motivation for change. This can then be followed up with adequate nutritional education. These insights should pave the way for relinquishing the anorexic position, and can then be followed with a cognitively based treatment approach. Garner and Bemis (1985) and Garfinkel and Garner (1982) have elaborated some of the distortions of thinking which anorexic patients commonly report, and other suggestions for intervention are given by Wardle (1989).

Conclusion

The longer-term follow-up studies of anorexia nervosa, whatever the method of treatment, do not give encouraging results (Steinhausen and Glanville, 1983). Many patients lose weight again after discharge, and of those who do not lose weight significant numbers become overweight (Seidensticker and Tzagournis, 1968). Even at normal weight, many patients continue to have eating abnormalities and some begin to binge and vomit, while others show finickiness and restrictiveness. In Crisp's series of 19 patients who had gained weight to matched population levels, followed by out-patient psychotherapy, only 9 were said to be 'better' (Crisp, 1965), and in the 1979 series (Hsu *et al.*, 1979), only 48 out of 100 came in the 'good' outcome category. Likewise, Morgan and Russell (1975) had to readmit more than half of their patients in the four years following the first admission, and Morgan *et al.* (1983), reporting on their series of patients treated largely in an out-patient setting, found that 42 per cent of their patients had failed to recovery completely. Higgs *et al.* (1989) report a similarly poor outcome and Kreipe *et al.* (1989) describe the emergence of bulimia nervosa in almost 50 per cent of cases.

At present the factors predictive of a good prognosis all tend to be general rather than specific to the psychopathology of anorexia or the mode of treatment, and include early onset, short duration of illness before referral, good pre-morbid personality and good family relationships. Nevertheless, it is the specific symptoms, such as fear of fatness, which cannot be shifted. Future research effort needs to be directed towards these difficult problems and towards the process of change, so that the outcome of treatment can begin to be understood in terms of the therapeutic process.

TREATMENT OF BULIMIA

Background

Bulimia nervosa is a more recently identified, but increasingly common, disorder experienced primarily by young women. The main feature is bouts of massive overeating (binges), which take place against the background of severe self-imposed dietary restriction. The eating binges are often (but not always) followed by self-induced vomiting or excessive laxative intake. The psychological characteristics of the patients have much in common with anorexia nervosa, in that abhorrence of fatness is the main drive. Many patients have a history of anorexia nervosa, or of a period of dietary restriction and weight loss, after which the binges began (Russell, 1979; Fairburn and Cooper, 1984; Pyle *et al.*, 1981). Conversely, a significant proportion of anorexic patients have, or develop, a bulimic eating pattern, emphasising the close links between these disorders (Garfinkel *et al.*, 1980; Dally and Gomez, 1979; Hsu *et al.*, 1979; Kreipe *et al.*, 1989). Fear of weight gain and disturbance of body image are also central to the disorder.

The crucial diagnostic difference between anorexia nervosa and bulimia nervosa is weight: a diagnosis of anorexia nervosa demands low body weight, whereas most patients who ask for help with bulimia are of low normal body weight or, more rarely, overweight. However, Garner *et al.* (1985a) have questioned the validity of the distinction between bulimia with and without anorexia nervosa, and find evidence that bulimic anorexics more closely resemble normal weight bulimics than restrictive anorexics. A second difference concerns the perception of illness: bulimic patients are usually aware of the abnormality of their behaviour, and are disturbed both by their preoccupation with food and their bingeing. Consequently they are more likely to seek help than anorexic patients for whom denial of illness is a hallmark.

The treatment literature for bulimia consists both of case series, and more recently of some controlled trials (Freeman *et al.*, 1988; Fairburn *et al.*, 1991). There has been a tremendous growth of interest in this area, and in recent years treatment reports for bulimia have much outnumbered treatment reports for anorexia nervosa. Certain consistent themes run through this treatment literature, including normalising eating habits and reducing the over-valuation of slimness. The behavioural and cognitive treatment programmes can be in individual or group settings, and are usually on an out-patient rather than an in-patient basis. It seems very likely that the group setting can provide support and advice for the individual members in an effective fashion, but in some cases the need for careful development of an individual treatment programme might override the advantages of group support. For the most part the published literature tends towards a cognitive and behavioural orientation, although feminist therapists have emphasised what they see as the fundamental conflicts in the psychology of women as the root causes of eating problems (Orbach, 1984). Accordingly they recommend psychoanalytically based treatment approaches. However, there is no substantial evidence for a fundamental disturbance of personality in women with bulimia, and consequently the more straightforward behavioural and cognitive approaches appear to offer the best form of treatment. There has also been some interest in pharmacological or combined pharmacological/behavioural treatments. In one study, combined treatment appeared to be better than antidepressants alone and possibly better than behaviour therapy alone, at least in the short term (Agras *et al.*, 1992).

In some cases, the vomiting has been targeted, on the understanding that vomiting reinforces the binge eating (Welch, 1979; Rosen and Leitenberg, 1982). In other cases, the emphasis has been on the control of the binge eating *per se* (Fairburn, 1981; Smith and Medlik, 1983; Lacey, 1983), while others put more emphasis on the resumption of unrestrictive eating patterns (Garner *et al.*, 1985b). Johnson *et al.* describe what they call a 'symptom management' approach, which incorporates a range of cognitive and behavioural strategies (Johnson *et al.*, 1987). As for the treatment of anorexia, the quality of the relationship with the therapist is considered very important. The components of treatment are described briefly in the following sections.

Self-monitoring of food intake, vomiting and preoccupation with food

Initially this is used as an assessment device, but for most patients it becomes a valued part of their system of control, and allows an objective evaluation of intake at times where anxiety prevents proper recall. Some patients have requested diaries to help them get through a difficult time (e.g. Christmas), after the end of formal treatment, and it could well be recommended as a maintenance procedure.

Modification of food intake

Many patients cannot even remember when they last ate normally, and considerable coaching is required. Almost all therapies involve encouraging the patient to relinquish restraint and return to normal eating. A daily food intake of approximately 2,000 calories, in the form of three meals with two to three snacks, seems to be suitable for most patients, but in many cases detailed instructions are necessary in order to avoid doubt and conflict. Great stress is placed on continuation of normal eating even if a binge has occurred. At first it is wise to avoid 'dangerous' foods, but these can be introduced gradually. Some patients have found it very helpful to have copies of diary sheets from normal eaters (or better still, treated patients) for comparison.

Like anorexic patients, bulimic patients seem surprised to discover that food preoccupation, craving, failures of satiety and bingeing are likely to be caused by food deprivation. It is often helpful to describe the studies of eating abnormalities in dieting subjects (Herman and Polivy, 1980; Wardle, 1987) and the effects of starvation (Keys *et al.*, 1950). An excellent 'psychoeducational' programme is outlined by Garner *et al.* (1985b).

Hunger and satiety also prove problematic and many patients have trouble in identifying these states. In some programmes patients are urged to try to be more responsive to their body needs; to monitor their feelings and eat only when they are 'really' hungry. However, the literature on food intake regulation suggests that this may be a difficult course of action. Patterns of hunger and satiety may develop in response to times and amounts of eating. The patient's long-standing habits of eating and vomiting will almost certainly have disrupted the links between internal state and subjective experience. The most helpful model seems to be a learning model, that is, that hunger and satiety require both a regular meal pattern (Booth, 1980) and retention of food eaten. Food records bear this out, and most patients gradually acquire hunger and satiety around their regular mealtimes.

Exposure to 'forbidden' food

Bulimic patients divide food into two kinds, one is called 'bad', 'banned', 'forbidden' or 'dangerous', and is consumed only in a binge. The other is 'good'. The former is invariably food of a high calorie density, while the latter is 'diet food', such as fruit, vegetables, cottage cheese, etc. In response to the sight, thought or taste of dangerous food, they become very anxious and conflicted and are at risk of a binge.

In normalising eating, most therapists accept the need for a balance between stimulus control and exposure. In order to reduce binge frequency at first, exposure to binge situations should be limited and the patient helped to recruit support to avoid a binge. Gradually the feared food can be re-introduced and feared situations re-entered. Exposure seems to be useful, and the introduction of 'bad' food eaten first with the therapist, and then alone, can erode the list of 'bad' foods. Some clinicians describe this in terms of exposure and response prevention, though opinions vary as to whether the 'response' in question is eating (Schmidt and Marks, 1988; Jansen *et al.*, 1989) or vomiting (Rosen and Leitenberg, 1982). However, there is now some doubt over whether response prevention of vomiting is a valuable therapeutic component (Agras *et al.*, 1989).

Reduction of vomiting and laxative abuse

Essentially this is approached initially by stressing the dangers of electrolyte disturbance (Mitchell *et al.*, 1983; Johnson *et al.*, 1987), and the role that vomiting plays in maintaining bingeing (calibrating the satiety system to massive intakes, and avoiding the consequences of bingeing). At this point patients can usually be asked to stop, or a series of reducing frequency targets can be set. Surprisingly, elimination of vomiting and laxative abuse does not always prove difficult. In other cases, active exposure and response prevention can be included with a programme in which the patient eats until she has the urge to vomit and then resists. However, in a controlled study, the exposure group showed little more improvement than the no-exposure group (Leitenberg *et al.*, 1988).

Coping with the urge to eat

The most common approach is to identify the environmental/cognitive cues, and to counsel avoidance of, or distraction from, these cues until normal intake is established. The most common triggers are being alone and unoccupied, and being in the presence of 'bad' food. Monitoring of the craving may convince the patient that a delay will allow the urge to decay, but this does not always occur. At such times, giving in to the urge in a 'civilised' fashion (cook the food, eat it slowly at a table) will have the best chance of averting a whole series of binges.

Managing preoccupation with weight

Concern with weight, and feeling fat is usually distressingly intense (Robinson *et al.*, 1983), and most patients weigh themselves frequently. The intensity of the feeling, however, is unrelated to actual weight, being prompted by eating, the feeling of tight clothes, or sometimes by negative moods. Many patients also report avoidance of certain social and sexual situations, where they feel that 'fatness' will be noticed.

Identification of the disturbing thoughts should be followed by obtaining the patient's cooperation in dealing with them as negative thoughts (Beck, 1976). At that point a combined cognitive and behavioural approach, as described by Fairburn (1981) or Garner and Bemis (1985) should be used. Wooley and Kearney-Cooke (1985) have described an approach to body image disturbance which emphasises the cultural meaning of thinness. It is often also helpful to encourage the patient to take up some form of vigorous exercise (running, aerobics, swimming), which can often be associated with an improvement in body image.

Conclusion

When the condition of bulimia nervosa was first described it was thought to carry a poor prognosis (Russell, 1979), because bulimic patients did badly under a nursing management regime, and bulimic anorexics were known to do less well in treatment than those who are purely restrictive (Casper *et al.*, 1980). However this pessimism may have been premature, as subsequent case reports have generally reported positive results after out-patient treatment on a weekly basis over three to four months (Fairburn, 1988). Studies which have utilised comparison of a multi-component package with a no-treatment control group, have confirmed that treatment is effective (Lacey, 1983, Freeman *et al.*, 1988). Further controlled studies have indicated that full cognitive-behavioural treatment is more effective than a brief intervention (Ordman and Kirschenbaum, 1985), non-directive group therapy (Kirkley *et al.*, 1985), or interpersonal psychotherapy (Fairburn *et al.*, 1991). However, most studies find that many of the patients are not dramatically improved by the treatment, and there is always a serious problem of relapse. Abstinence from symptoms is also comparatively rare (Garner, 1987). For that reason, it is necessary to continue to explore treatment approaches to this distressing problem.

REFERENCES

Agras, W. S. (1987) *Eating Disorders: Management of Obesity, Bulimia and Anorexia Nervosa*, New York: Pergamon.

Agras, W. S. and Werne, J. (1981) 'Disorders of eating', in Turner *et al.* (eds) *Handbook of Clinical Behaviour Therapy*, New York: Wiley.

Agras, W. S., Schneider, J. A., Arnow, B., Raeburn, S. D., and Telch, C. F. (1989) 'Cognitive-behavioral and response-prevention treatments for bulimia nervosa', *Journal of Consulting and Clinical Psychology* 57: 215–21.

Agras, W. S., Rossiter, E. M., Arnow, B., Schneider, J. A., Telch, C. F., Raeburn, S. D., Bruce, B., Perl, M. and Koran, L. M. (1992) 'Pharmacologic and cognitive-behavioural treatment for bulimia nervosa: a controlled comparison', *American Journal of Psychiatry* 149: 82–7.

Bachrach, A. J., Erwin, W. J. and Mohr, J. P. (1965) 'The control of eating behaviour in an anorexic by operant conditioning techniques', in L. P. Ullman and J. Krasner (eds) *Case Studies in Behavior Modification*, New York: Holt, Rinehart and Winston.

Ballantyne, D., Clark, A., Dyker, G. S., Gillis, C. R., Hawthorne, V. M., Henry, D. A., Hole, D. S., Murdoch, R. M., Semple, T. and Stewart, G. M. (1978) 'Prescribing exercise for the healthy: Assessment of compliance and effects on plasma lipids and lipoproteins', *Health Bulletin* (July): 169–79.

Banting, W. (1863) *Letter on Corpulence Addressed to the Public*, London: Harrison.

Barcai, A. (1971) 'Family therapy in the treatment of anorexia nervosa', *American Journal of Psychiatry* 128: 286–90.

Beck, A. T. (1976) *Cognitive Therapy and the Emotional Disorders*, New York: International University Press.

Beneke, W. M., Paulson, B. and McReynolds, W. T. (1978) 'Long-term results of two behavior modification weight loss programmes using nutritionists as therapists', *Behavior Therapy* 9: 501–7.

Beumont, P. J. V., George, G. C. W. and Smart, D. E. (1976) '"Dieters" and "vomiters and purgers" in anorexia nervosa', *Psychological Medicine* 6: 617–32.

Beumont, P. J. V., Abraham, S. F. and Samson, K. G. (1981) 'The psychosexual histories of adolescent girls and young women with anorexia nervosa', *Psychological Medicine* 11: 131–40.

Bhanji, S. and Thompson, J. (1974) 'Operant conditioning in the treatment of anorexia nervosa', *British Journal of Psychiatry* 124: 166–72.

Blackburn, G. L. and Kanders, B. S. (1987) 'Medical evaluation and treatment of the obese patient with cardiovascular disease', *American Journal of Cardiology* 60: 55g–58g.

Blinder, B. J., Freeman, D. and Stunkard, A. J. (1970) 'Behaviour therapy of anorexia nervosa: affectiveness of activity as a reinforcer of weight gain', *American Journal of Psychiatry* 126: 1093–8.

Booth, D. A. (1980) 'Acquired behaviour controlling energy intake and output', in A. J. Stunkard (ed.) *Obesity*, Philadelphia: W. B. Saunders.

Bouchard, C., Shephard, R. J., Stephens, T., Sutton, R. J. and McPherson, B. D. (eds) (1990) *Exercise, Fitness, and Health: A Consensus of Current Knowledge*, Champaign, Ill.: Human Kinetics Publishers.

Boyer, J. L. and Kasch, F. W. (1970) 'Exercise therapy in hypertensive men', *Journal of the American Medical Association* 211: 1668–71.

Branch, C. H. H. and Eurman, L. H. J. (1980) 'Social attitudes toward patients with anorexia nervosa', *American Journal of Psychiatry* 137: 631–2.

Bray, G. A. (1976) *The Obese Patient*, Philadelphia: W. B. Saunders.

Brownell, K. D. (1987) *The learn program for weight control*, Philadelphia, PA: University of Pennsylvania School of Medicine.

Brownell, K. D. and Jeffery, R. W. (1987) 'Improving long-term weight-loss: pushing the limits of treatment', *Behavior Therapy* 18: 353–74.

Brownell, K. D. and Stunkard, A. J. (1978) 'Behaviour therapy and behaviour change: uncertainties in programs for weight control', *Behaviour Research and Therapy* 16: 301.

Brownell, K. D. and Stunkard, A. J. (1980) 'Physical activity in the development and control of obesity', in A. J. Stunkard (ed.) *Obesity*, Philadelphia: W. B. Saunders.

Brownell, K. D. and Wadden, T. A. (1983) 'Behavioral and self-help treatments', in M. R. C. Greenwood (ed.) *Obesity*, New York: Churchill Livingstone.

Brownell, K. D. and Wadden, T. A. (1992) 'Etiology and treatment of obesity: understanding a serious, prevalent and refractory disorder', *Journal of Consulting and Clinical Psychology* 60: 505–17.

Bruch, H. (1973) *Eating Disorders, Obesity, Anorexia and the Person Within*, New York: Basic Books.

Burvat-Herbaut, M., Hebbinckuys, P., Lemaire, A. and Burvat, J. (1983) 'Attitudes towards weight, body image, eating, menstruation, pregnancy, and sexuality in 81 cases of anorexia, compared with 288 normal control schoolgirls', *International Journal of Eating Disorders* 2: 45–59.

Butters, J. W. and Cash, T. F. (1987) 'Cognitive-behavioral treatment of women's body-image dissatisfaction', *Journal of Consulting and Clinical Psychology* 55: 889–97.

Casper, R. C., Eckert, E. D., Halmi, K. A., Goldberg, S. C. and Davis, J. M. (1980 'Bulimia. Its incidence and clinical importance in patients with anorexia nervosa', *Archives of General Psychiatry* 37: 1030–4.

Channon, S. and Wardle, J. (1989) 'Cognitive-behavioural treatment of eating disorders', in J. Scott, M. Williams and A. Beck (eds) *Cognitive Therapy in Clinical Practice*, London: Routledge.

Crisp, A. H. (1965) 'A treatment regime for anorexia nervosa', *British Journal of Psychiatry* 112: 505–12.

Crisp, A. H. (1980) *Anorexia Nervosa: Let Me Be*, London: Academic Press.

Crisp, A. H., Norton, K., Gowers, S., Halek, C., Bowyer, C., Yeldman, D., Levett, G. and Bhat, A. (1991) 'A controlled study of the effect of therapies aimed at adolescent and family psychopathology in anorexia nervosa', *British Journal of Psychiatry* 159: 325–33.

DaCosta, M. and Halmi, K. A. (1992) 'Classifications of anorexia nervosa: the question of subtypes', *International Journal of Eating Disorders* 11: 305–13.

Dahlkoetter, J., Callahan, E. G. and Linton, J. (1979) 'Obesity and the unbalanced energy equation: exercise vs eating habit change', *Journal of Consulting and Clinical Psychology* 47: 898–905.

Dally, P. and Gomez, J. (1979) *Anorexia Nervosa*, London: William Heinemann.

Dishman, R. K. (1991) 'Increasing and maintaining exercise and physical activity', *Behavior Therapy* 22: 345–78.

Dworkin, S. H. and Kerr, B. A. (1987) 'Comparison of interventions for women experiencing body image problems', *Journal of Counseling Psychology* 34: 136–40.

Dwyer, J. (1980) 'Sixteen popular diets', in A. J. Stunkard, (ed) *Obesity*, Philadelphia: W. B. Saunders.

Dwyer, J. (1992) 'Nutritional remedies: reasonable and questionable', *Annals of Behavioral Medicine* 14: 120–5.

Eckert, E. D., Goldberg, S. C. and Halmi, K. A., Caspar, R. C. and Davis, J. M. (1979) 'Behaviour Therapy in Anorexia Nervosa', *British Journal of Psychiatry* 134: 55–9.

Fairburn, C. G. (1981) 'A cognitive-behavioural approach to the management of bulimia', *Psychological Medicine* 11: 697–706.

Fairburn, C. G. (1985) 'Cognitive-behavioral treatment for bulimia', in D. M. Garner and P. E. Garfinkel (eds) *Handbook of Psychotherapy for Anorexia Nervosa and Bulimia*, New York: Guilford Press.

Fairburn, C. G. (1988) 'The current status of the psychological treatments for bulimia nervosa', *Journal of Psychosomatic Research* 32: 635–45.

Fairburn, C. G. and Cooper, P. J. (1984) 'The clinical features of bulimia nervosa', *British Journal of Psychiatry* 144: 238–46.

Fairburn, C. G. and Garner, D. M. (1989) 'The diagnosis of bulimia nervosa', *International Journal of Eating Disorders* 5: 403–19.

Fairburn, C. G., Jones, R., Peveler, R. C., Carr, S. J., Solomon, R. A., O'Connor, M. E., Burton, J. and Hope, R. A. (1991) 'Three psychological treatments for bulimia nervosa', *Archives of General Psychiatry* 48: 463–9.

Ferguson, J. M. (1975) *Learning to Eat: Behaviour Modification for Weight Control*, Palo Alto, Calif.: Bull.

Ferster, C. B., Nurnberger, J. I. and Levitt, E. B. (1962) 'The control of eating', *Journal of Mathematics* 1: 87–109.

Freeman, C. P. L., Barry, F., Dunkeld-Turnbull, J. and Henderson, A. (1988) 'Controlled trial of psychotherapy for bulimia nervosa', *British Medical Journal* 296: 521–5.

Ganley, R. M. (1988) 'Emotional eating and how it relates to dietary restraint, disinhibition, and perceived hunger', *International Journal of Eating Disorders* 7: 635–47.

Garfinkel, P. E. and Garner, D. M. (1982) *Anorexia Nervosa: A Multidimensional Perspective*, New York: Brunner Mazel.

Garfinkel, P. E., Kline, S. A. and Stancer, H. C. (1973) 'Treatment of anorexia nervosa using operant conditioning techniques', *Journal of Nervous and Mental Disease* 157: 428–33.

Garfinkel, P. E., Moldofsky, H. and Garner, D. M. (1977) 'The role of behaviour modification in the treatment of anorexia nervosa', *Journal of Paediatric Psychology* 2: 113–21.

Garfinkel, P. E., Moldofsky, H. and Garner, D. M. (1980) 'The heterogeneity of anorexia nervosa: bulimia as a distinct subgroup', *Archives of General Psychology* 37: 1036–40.

Garner, D. M. (1985) 'Iatrogenesis in anorexia nervosa and bulimia nervosa', *International Journal of Eating Disorders* 4: 701–26.

Garner, D. M. (1987) 'Psychotherapy outcome research with bulimia nervosa', *Psychotherapy and Psychosomatic* 48: 129–40.

Garner, D. M. and Bemis, K. M. (1985) 'Cognitive Therapy for anorexia nervosa', in D. M. Garner and P. E. Garfinkel (eds) *Handbook of Psychotherapy for Anorexia Nervosa and Bulimia*, New York: Guilford Press.

Garner, D. M., Fairburn, C. G. and Davis, R. (1987) 'Cognitive-behavioral treatment for bulimia nervosa: a critical appraisal', *Behavior Modification* 11: 398–431.

Garner, D. M. and Garfinkel, P. E. (1980) 'Socio-cultural factors in the development of anorexia nervosa', *Psychological Medicine* 10: 647–56.

Garner, D. M., Garfinkel, P. E. and O'Shaughnessy, M. (1985a) 'The validity of the distinction between bulimia with and without anorexia nervosa', *American Journal of Psychiatry* 142: 581–7.

Garner, D. M., Rockert, W., Olmsted, M. P., Johnson, C. and Coscina, D. V. (1985b)

'Psychoeducational principles in the treatment of bulimia and anorexia', in D. M. Garner and P. E. Garfinkel (eds) *Handbook of Psychotherapy for Anorexia Nervosa and Bulimia*, New York: Guilford Press.

Garner, D. M. and Wooley, S. C. (1991) 'Confronting the failure of behavioral and dietary treatments for obesity', *Clinical Psychology Review* 11: 729–80.

Glasser, W. (1976) *Positive Addiction*, New York: Harper and Row.

Gwinup, G. (1975) 'Effect of exercise alone on the weight of obese women', *Archives of International Medicine* 135: 676–80.

Hall, A. and Crisp, A. H. (1987) 'Brief psychotherapy in the treatment of anorexia nervosa: outcome at one year', *British Journal of Psychiatry* 151: 185–91.

Hallsten, E. A. (1965) 'Adolescent anorexia nervosa treated by desensitisation', *Behaviour Research and Therapy* 3: 87–91.

Halmi, K. A. (1985) 'Behavioral management for anorexia nervosa', in D. M. Garner and P. E. Garfinkel (eds) *Handbook of Psychotherapy for Anorexia Nervosa and Bulimia*, New York: Guilford Press.

Halmi, K. A., Powers, D. and Cunningham, S. (1975) 'Treatment of anorexia nervosa with behaviour therapy', *Archives of General Psychiatry* 32: 93–7.

Heatherton, T. F. and Baumeister, R. F. (1992) 'Binge-eating as escape from self-awareness', *Psychological Bulletin* 110: 86–108.

Herman, P. E. and Polivy, I, J. (1980) 'Restrained eating', in A. J. Stunkard (ed.) *Obesity*, Philadelphia: W. B. Saunders.

Herzog, D. B., Keller, M. B., Strober, M., Yeh, C. and Pai, S-Y. (1992) 'The current status of treatment for anorexia nervosa and bulimia nervosa', *International Journal of Eating Disorders* 12: 215–20.

Higgs, J. F., Goodyer, I. M. and Birch, J. (1989) 'Anorexia nervosa and food avoidance emotional disorder', *Archives of Diseases of Childhood* 64: 346–51.

Hoberman, H. M. and Kroll-Mensing, D. (1991) 'Eating disorders in adolescents', *Current Opinion in Psychiatry* 4: 542–8.

Horan, J. J., Baker, S. B., Hoffman, A. M. and Shute, R. E. (1975) 'Weight loss through variations in the covenant control paradigm', *Journal of Consulting and Clinical Psychology* 43: 68–72.

Hsu, L., Crisp, A. H. and Harding, B. (1979) 'Outcome of anorexia nervosa', *Lancet* 1: 61–5.

Jansen, A., Van den Hout, M. A., De Loof, C., Zandbergen, J. and Griez, E. (1989) 'A case of bulimia successfully treated by cue exposure', *Journal of Behavior Therapy and Experimental Psychiatry* 20: 327–32.

Jeffery, R. W. (1992) 'Is obesity a risk factor for cardiovascular disease?', *Annals of Behavioral Medicine* 14: 109–12.

Jeffery, R. W., Wing, R. R. and Stunkard, A. J. (1978) 'Behavioral treatment of obesity: the state of the art 1976', *Behavior Therapy* 9: 189–99.

Jeffrey, D. B. and Katz, R. G. (1977) *Take It Off and Keep It Off*, Englewood Cliffs, NJ: Prentice-Hall.

Johnson, C., Connors, M. E. and Tobin, D. L. (1987) 'Symptom management of bulimia', *Journal of Consulting and Clinical Psychology* 55: 668–76.

Jordan, H. A., Levitz, L. S. and Kimbrell, G. M. (1977) *Eating is Okay: A Radical Approach to Weight Loss, The Behavioral Control Diet*, New York: Rawson.

Keys, A., Brozek, J., Henschel, A., Mickelson, O. and Taylor, H. L. (1950) *The Biology of Human Starvation*, Minneapolis: University of Minnesota Press.

Kirkley, B. G., Schneider, J. A., Agras, W. S. and Bachman, J. A. (1985) 'Comparison of two group treatments for bulimia', *Journal of Consulting and Clinical Psychology* 53: 43–8.

Kreipe, R. E., Churchill, B. H. and Strauss, J. (1989) 'Long term outcome in adolescents with anorexia nervosa', *American Journal of Diseases of Children* 143: 1322–7.

Krotkiewski, M., Sjostrom, L. and Sullivan, L. (1977) 'Effects of long term training on adipose tissue cellularity and body composition in hypertrophic and hyperplastic obesity', *International Journal of Obesity* 2: 395.

Lacey, J. H. (1983) 'Bulimia nervosa, binge eating, and psychogenic vomiting: a controlled treatment study and long term outcome', *British Medical Journal* 286 (21 May 1983): 1609.

LeBow, M. D. (1981) *Weight Control: The Behavioral Strategies*, New York: John Wiley.

LeBow, M. D. (1989) *Adult Obesity Therapy*, New York: Pergamon.

Leitenberg, H., Agras, W. S. and Thomson, L. E. (1968) 'A sequential analysis of the effect of selective positive reinforcement in modifying anorexia nervosa', *Behaviour Research and Therapy* 6: 211–18.

Leitenberg, H., Rosen, J. C., Gross, J., Nudelman, S. and Vara, L. S. (1988) 'Exposure plus response-prevention treatment of bulimia nervosa', *Journal of Consulting and Clinical Psychology* 56: 535–41.

Leon, G. R. (1979) 'Cognitive-behavior therapy for eating disturbances', in P. C. Kendall and S. D. Hollon (eds) *Cognitive-Behavioral Interventions*, New York: Academic Press.

Levitz, L. S. and Stunkard, A. J. (1974) 'A therapeutic coalition for obesity: Behavior modification and patient self help', *American Journal of Psychiatry* 131: 423–7.

Lichtman, S. and Poser, E. (1983) 'The effects of exercise on mood and cognitive functioning', *Journal of Psychosomatic Research* 27: 43–52.

Linden, W. (1980) 'Multi-component behavior therapy in a case of compulsive binge eating followed by vomiting', *Journal of Behavior Therapy and Experimental Psychiatry* 11: 297–300.

Long, C. G. and Cordle, C. J. (1982) 'Psychological treatment of binge eating and vomiting', *British Journal of Medical Psychology* 55: 139–45.

Mahoney, M. J. (1975) 'The obese eating style: bites, beliefs and behaviour modification', *Addictive Behaviors* 1: 47–53.

Mahoney, M. J. and Mahoney, K. (1976) *Permanent Weight Control: A Total Solution to the Dieter's Dilemma*, New York: Norton.

Mann, R. A. (1972) 'The behaviour-therapeutic use of contingency contracting to control an adult behaviour problem: weight control', *Journal of Applied Behaviour Analysis* 5: 99–109.

Marlatt, G. A. (1982) 'Relapse prevention: a self-control programme for the treatment of addictive behaviour', in R. B. Stuart (ed.) *Adherence, Compliance and Generalisation in Behavioural Medicine*, New York: Brunner/Mazel.

Marlatt, G. A. (1985) 'Situational determinants of relapse and skill-training interventions', in G. A. Marlatt and J. R. Gordon (eds) *Relapse Prevention*, New York: Guilford.

Mayer, J. (1968) *Overweight: Causes, Cost and Control*, Englewood Cliffs, NJ: Prentice-Hall.

Metropolitan Life Insurance Company (1983) '1983 Metropolitan Height and Weight Tables', *Statistical Bulletin* (Jan–June): 3–9.

Millman, M. (1980) *Such a Pretty Face: Being Fat in America*, New York: Norton.

Minuchin, S., Rosman, B. L. and Baker, L. (1978) *Psychosomatic Families: Anorexia Nervosa in Context*, Cambridge, Mass.: Harvard University Press.

Mitchell, J. E., Pyle, R. L., Eckert, E. D., Hatsukami, D. and Lentz, R. (1983) 'Electrolyte and other physiological abnormalities in patients with bulimia', *Psychological Medicine* 13: 273–8.

Mitchell, J. E., Davis, L., Goff, G. and Pyle, R. (1986) 'A follow-up study of patients with bulimia', *International Journal of Eating Disorders* 5: 441–50.

Morehouse, L. E. and Gross, L. (1975) *Total Fitness*, New York: Simon & Schuster.

Morgan, H. G. and Russell, G. F. M. (1975) 'Value of family background and clinical features as predictors of LT outcome in anorexia nervosa: 4 year follow-up of 41 patients', *Psychological Medicine* 5: 355–71.

Morgan, H. G., Purgold, J. and Welbourne, J. (1983) 'Management and outcome in anorexia nervosa. A standardised prognostic study', *British Journal of Psychiatry* 143: 282–7.

National Institute of Health (1985) 'Health implications of obesity', *Annals of Internal Medicine* 103: 1073–7.

Orbach, S. (1984) 'The construction of femininity: some critical issues in the psychology of women', paper presented at the Third Annual Conference Center for the study of Anorexia and Bulimia (November 1984), New York.

Ordman, A. M. and Kirschenbaum, D. S. (1985) 'Cognitive-behavioral therapy for bulimia: an initial outcome study', *Journal of Consulting and Clinical Psychology* 53: 305–13.

Ost, L. G. and Gotestam, K. G. (1976) 'Behavioural and pharmacological treatments for obesity: an experimental comparison', *Addictive Behaviors* 1: 331–8.

Parízková, J. (1977) *Body Fat and Physical Fitness*, Netherlands: Martinus Nijhoff.

Penick, S., Filon, R., Fox, S. and Stunkard, A. J. (1971) 'Behavior modification in the treatment of obesity', *Psychosomatic Medicine* 33: 49–55.

Perri, M. G., Lauer, J. B., McAdoo, W. G., McAlister, D. A. and Yancey, D. Z. (1986) 'Enhancing the efficacy of behavior therapy for obesity: effects and aerobic exercise and a multicomponent maintenance program', *Journal of Consulting and Clinical Psychology* 52: 404–13.

Pi-Sunyer, F. X. (1987) 'Exercise effects on calorie intake', *Annals of the New York Academy of Sciences* 449: 94–103.

Polivy, J. and Herman, C. P. (1992) 'Undieting: a program to help people stop dieting', *International Journal of Eating Disorders* 11: 261–8.

Pyle, R. L., Mitchell, J. E. and Eckert, E. D. (1981) 'Bulimia: A report of 34 cases', *Journal of Clinical Psychology* 42: 60–4.

Robinson, R. G., Tortosa, M., Sullivan, J., Buchanan, E., Andersen, A. E. and Folstein, M. F. (1983) 'Quantitive assessment of psychologic state of patients with anorexia nervosa or bulimia: response to caloric stimulus', *Psychosomatic Medicine* 45: 283–92.

Romanczyk, R. G., Tracey, D. A., Wilson, F. T. and Thorpe, G. L. (1973) 'Behavioral techniques in the treatment of obesity: A comparative analysis', *Behaviour Research and Therapy* 11: 629–40.

Rosen, J. C. and Leitenberg, H. (1982) 'Bulimia nervosa: Treatment with exposure and response prevention', *Behavior Therapy* 13: 117–24.

Rosen, J. C. and Leitenberg, H. (1985) 'Exposure plus response prevention treatment of bulimia', in D. M. Garner and P. E. Garfinkel (eds) *Handbook of Psychotherapy for Anorexia Nervosa and Bulimia*, New York: Guilford Press.

Rosen, J. C., Minuchin, S., Leibman, R. and Baker, L. (1975) 'Input and output of family therapy in anorexia nervosa', in J. L. Claghorn (ed.) *Successful Psychotherapy*, New York: Brunner/Mazel.

Rosman, B. L., Minuchin, S., Leibman, R. and Baker, L. (1975) 'Input and outcome of family therapy in anorexia nervosa', in J. L. Claghorn (ed.) *Successful Psychotherapy*, New York: Brunner/Mazel.

Royal College of Psychiatrists, Royal College of Nursing and British Psychological Society (1980) *Behaviour Modification: Report of a Joint Working Party*, London: HMSO.

Russell, G. F. M. (1979) 'Bulimia nervosa: an ominous variant of anorexia nervosa', *Psychological Medicine* 9: 429–48.

Schachter, S. (1971) 'Some extraordinary facts about obese humans and rats', *American Psychology* 26: 129–44.

Schachter, S. and Rodin, J. (1974) *Obese Humans and Rats*, Washington DC: Erlbaum-Halstead.

Schmidt, U. and Marks, J. (1988) 'Cue exposure to food plus response prevention of binges for bulimia: a pilot study', *International Journal of Eating Disorders* 7: 663–72.

Seidensticker, J. F. and Tzagournis, M. (1968) 'Anorexia nervosa – clinical features and long term follow-up', *Journal of Chronic Diseases* 21: 361–7.

Selvini-Palazolli, M. (1974) *Anorexia Nervosa*, London: Chaucer Publishing Company.

Silverman, J. A. (1974) 'Anorexia nervosa: Clinical observations in a successful treatment plan', *Journal of Paediatrics* 84: 68–73.

Smith, G. R. and Medlik, L. (1983) 'Modification of binge eating in anorexia nervosa: A single case report', *Behavioural Psychotherapy* 11: 249–56.

Sobal, J. (1991) 'Obesity and nutritional sociology: a model for coping with the stigma of obesity', *Clinical Sociology Review* 9: 125–41.

Sobal, J. and Stunkard, A. J. (1989) 'Socioeconomic status and obesity: a review of the literature', *Psychological Bulletin* 105: 260–75.

Stalonas, P. M., Johnson, W. G. and Grist, M. (1978) 'Behaviour modification for obesity: the evaluation of exercise, contingency management and program adherence', *Journal of Consulting and Clinical Psychology* 46: 463–9.

Steinhausen, H. C. and Glanville, K. (1983) 'Follow-up studies of anorexia nervosa: a review of research findings', *Psychological Medicine* 13: 239–49.

Stern, J. S. (1983) 'Diet and exercise', in M. R. C. Greenwood (ed.) *Obesity*, New York: Churchill Livingstone.

Sternberg, B. (1985) 'Relapses in weight control: definitions, processes, and prevention strategies', in G. A. Marlatt, and J. R. Gordon (eds) *Relapse Prevention*, New York: Guilford.

Strober, M. and Humphrey, L. L. (1987) 'Familial contributions to the etiology and course of anorexia nervosa and bulimia', *Journal of Consulting and Clinical Psychology* 55: 654–9.

Stuart, R. B. (1967) 'Behavioural control of overeating', *Behaviour Research and Therapy*, 5: 357–65.

Stuart, R. B. and Davis, B. (1972) *Slim Chance in a Fat World: Behavioral Control of Obesity*, Champaign, Il.: Research Press.

Stunkard, A. J. and Mahoney, M. J. (1976) 'Behavioural treatment of the eating disorders', in H. Leitenberg (ed.) *Handbook of Behavior Modification and Behavior Therapy*, Englewood Cliffs, NJ: Prentice-Hall.

Stunkard, A. J., Foch, T. T. and Hrubec, Z. (1986) 'A twin study of human obesity', *Journal of the American Medical Association* 256: 51–4.

Thompson, J. K., Jarvie, G. J., Lahey, B. B. and Cureton, K. J. (1982) 'Exercise and obesity: Etiology, physiology and intervention', *Psychological Bulletin* 91: 55–79.

Turner, M. St. J. and Shapiro, C. M. (1992) 'The biochemistry of anorexia nervosa', *International Journal of Eating Disorders* 12: 179–93.

Van Buskirk, S. W. (1977) 'A two-phase perspective on the treatment of anorexia nervosa', *Psychological Bulletin* 84: 529–38.

Wadden, T. A. and Stunkard, A. J. (1986) 'Controlled trial of very low-calorie diet, behavior therapy, and their combination in the treatment of obesity', *Journal of Consulting and Clinical Psychology* 54: 482–8.

Wadden, T. A., Stunkard, A. J. and Liebschutz, J. (1988) 'Three-year follow-up of the treatment of obesity by very low-calorie diet, behavior therapy, and their combination', *Journal of Consulting and Clinical Psychology* 56: 925–8.

Wardle, J. (1987) 'Compulsive eating and dieting restraint', *British Journal of Clinical Psychology* 26: 47–55.

Wardle, J. (1989) 'The management of obesity', in S. Pearce and J. Wardle (eds) *The Practice of Behavioural Medicine*, Oxford: Oxford University Press.

Wardle, J. (1990) 'Conditioning processes and cue exposure in the modification of excessive eating', *Addictive Behaviors* 15: 387–93.

Wardle, J. and Beinart, H. (1981) 'Binge eating: a theoretical review', *British Journal of Clinical Psychology* 20: 97–109.

Wardle, J., Marsland, L., Sheikh, Y., Quinn, M., Fedoroff, I. and Ogden, J. (1992) 'Eating style and eating behaviour in adolescents', *Appetite* 18: 167–83.

Welch, G. J. (1979) 'The treatment of compulsive vomiting and obsessive thoughts through graduated response delay, response prevention and cognitive correction, *Journal of Behaviour Therapy Experimental Psychiatry* 10: 77–82.

Wilson, G. T. and Brownell, K. D. (1980) 'Behaviour therapy for obesity: An evaluation of treatment outcome', *Archives of Behavior Research Therapy* 3: 49–86.

Wooley, O. W., Wooley, S. C. and Dyrenforth, S. R. (1979) 'Obesity and women II. A neglected feminist topic', *Women's Studies International Quarterly* 2: 81–92.

Wooley, S. C. and Kearney-Cooke, A. (1985) 'Intensive treatment of bulimia and body-image disturbance', in K. D. Brownell and J. P. Foreyt (eds) *Handbook of Eating Disorders*, New York: Basic Books.

Wooley, S. C. and Wooley, O. W. (1979) 'Obesity and women I. A closer look at the facts', *Women's Studies International Quarterly* 2: 69–79.

Wooley, S. C., Wooley, O. W. and Dyrenforth, S. R. (1979) 'Theoretical, practical and social issues in behavioural treatments of obesity', *Journal of Applied Behavioural Analysis* 12: 3–25.

Wysocki, T., Hall, G., Iwata, B. and Riordan, M. (1979) 'Behavioural management of exercise: contracting for aerobic points', *Journal of Applied Behaviour Analysis* 12: 55–64.

Yates, A. (1990) 'A current perspective on the eating disorders II. Treatment, outcome, and research directions', *Journal of the American Academy of Child and Adolescent Psychiatry* 29: 1–9.

Chapter 28

Cardiovascular and respiratory disease
Investigation

C. Bundy

CORONARY HEART DISEASE/ISCHAEMIC HEART DISEASE

Coronary heart disease (CHD) is a chronic progressive disease primarily affecting the coronary arteries. It is an acquired disease and has been associated with a more affluent lifestyle enjoyed by the western world. The pathological process is a gradual build-up of metabolic by-products within the artery walls which narrows and hardens the vessels. This process is known as atherosclerosis. There are a number of clinical manifestations of CHD including angina pectoris (AP), hypertension, myocardial infarction (MI), or sudden death (SD). Each of these conditions may present as a medical emergency. CHD causes one-third of all deaths in men under 65 and a quarter of all deaths (Davies, 1987), and it is therefore the biggest single cause of death in British men.

Although AP may be the least life-threatening clinical manifestation of CHD it is not benign: stable AP may become uncontrolled or unstable and may precipitate an MI. Spasm of the coronary arteries may dislodge an atheromatous plaque which may further lodge in a small vessel.

Epidemiological research has implicated a number of factors which contribute to CHD. These include: smoking, a positive family history, age, sex, hypertension, hyperlipidaemia, obesity, lifestyle, the Type A Behaviour pattern (TABP) and stress (e.g. Shaper *et al.*, 1981; Keys *et al.*, 1980). Smoking is the single most important of the known risk factors for heart disease. Any or all of these factors may be involved at any stage of the disease process, but a combination of one or more factors confers a degree of risk which is more than simply additive.

Angina pectoris (AP)

Approximately one million middle-aged British men are affected by AP (Fox, 1988). AP is painful ischaemia of the myocardium due to the transient interruption of the blood supply. The disrupted supply may be due to progressing disease or to coronary artery spasm.

Psychologists involved with this client group have traditionally viewed the

CHD population as homogeneous, even though AP patients tend to be slightly older and have different psychological characteristics from post-MI patients. Current researchers are beginning to identify these differences and more attention is being given to AP patients as a separate group.

Psychological assessment of AP patients can contribute to the understanding of AP in three main ways: by (a) mapping the psychosocial factors associated with AP, (b) assessing the extent of corroboration of pain and disability reports with the documented severity of the disease, and (c) determining the psychosocial triggers of AP attacks. This assessment will form part of the overall assessment of AP.

The main psychosocial factors known to be associated with AP are neuroticism, anger and hostility, and TABP. Neuroticism as measured by the Eysenck Personality Inventory (EPI) has consistently been associated with AP; however, there is no causal relationship implied. Neuroticism and related factors, such as hypochondriasis and anxiety, have also been shown to be related to general health and pain complaints, which was initially confusing. Only with the recent possibility of witnessing the presence of coronary disease through angiography has the confusion lessened. Prior to angiography the diagnosis of AP relied heavily on patients' reports of symptoms; recent angiographic studies have shown that high levels of neuroticism were inversely related to documented CHD but very closely related to self-reports of chest pain. Therefore, neuroticism seems to be correlated with illness behaviour and not actual severity of illness. As a result, neuroticism has been shown to be more closely associated with AP than with other forms of CHD (Jenkins *et al.*, 1978) and people with high levels of neuroticism who complain of chest pain are more likely to be diagnosed as having AP than those who are not high in neuroticism despite there being no differences in the incidence of arteriosclerosis shown on angiography (Costa and McCrae, 1987). In view of these findings, researchers in this area recommend the use of psychometric tests to detect high levels of neuroticism as part of the overall management of this client group (see, for example, Elias and Robbins, 1987).

The TABP is associated with AP, although less so than with MI, and more recent research on the sub-components of the TABP complex has implicated anger and hostility as the main pathogenic factors. The detection of hostility usually relies on the Cook–Medley 50-item subscale of the MMPI (Cook and Medley, 1954) and the Spielberger State-Trait Anger Scale for the detection of anger (Spielberger *et al.*, 1983). The Cook–Medley scale appears to be tapping a generally negative attitudinal set and basic mistrust of others, which has been labelled cynicism. This factor correlates strongly with the potential for hostility found in the videotaped structured interview, the 'gold standard' measure of TABP.

Hostility is strongly associated with the incidence of CHD events such as MI (Barefoot *et al.*, 1983), and prospectively with risk of death from CHD, malignancies, and all other causes (Williams and Anderson, 1987).

Investigation of the route by which anger/hostility and TABP affect CHD has focused on the neuroendocrine pathway. A psychosocial event which is cognitively appraised as challenging or threatening results in the fight–flight response. Heart rate and blood pressure increase along with increased secretion of epinephrine, norepinephrine, cortisol and prolactin but, interestingly, not testosterone. When a similar challenge arises via a physical task, such as a reaction time task, the pattern of response is somewhat different; this time significant increases in norepinepherine and testosterone are seen, but no subsequent rise in epinepherine, cortisol or prolactin occurs. With this background knowledge, the results of mentally challenging tasks can be investigated using hormonal detection, ECG and arteriographic equipment, all of which may ultimately help to clarify the relationship between cognitive activity and psychological responses.

Hypertension

Hypertension is a risk factor for MI and sudden cardiac death as well as cerebrovascular accidents (CVA) or strokes. It may be a primary disease or secondary to renal or other organ disease. Essential hypertension mainly affects middle-aged men who are overweight and smoke, but it is not exclusive to that group of people.

Blood pressure is measured by occluding (usually) the brachial artery with an inflatable cuff and slowly releasing the obstruction. The initial surge of bloodflow back into the artery is audible through a stethoscope: this is the systolic pressure; the second audible sound of the pressure reaching background pressure is the diastolic. The readings are expressed as systolic (the higher value) over diastolic (the lower value) in millimetres of mercury (mmHg). There is some controversy regarding desirable levels of blood pressure and what is considered hypertensive varies (Carroll, 1992). However, most people involved in this area of work would agree that a persistent diastolic pressure between 110 and 120 mmHg is hypertensive.

Hypertension is not a 'visible' disease. That is, in its early history, the patient experiences no symptoms. Therefore its detection relies on the patient's presenting for either routine health screening or as a result of some other medical problem. In its traumatic form it presents because persistent high pressure damages the medial lining in the vessel walls, resulting in an aneurysm that ruptures, causing death of surrounding tissue wherever it occurs.

Accurate measures of blood pressure are difficult because a host of physiological and psychological factors can influence it (Carroll, 1992). Normal blood pressure varies with even routine activity and high blood pressure may vary even more. Patients should be made aware of this when they are taught self-monitoring of their blood pressure. Frequent random checks can provide an accurate pressure profile and activity sampling simultaneously can yield a very useful picture. There are a number of simple manual and automatic blood pressure monitors, and although ambulatory monitoring equipment is available, it is too unreliable at present to be considered appropriate for use with all patients with hypertension. As patients become more able to monitor their blood pressure, they can begin to identify the accompanying physical symptoms and the thoughts and feelings that coincide with episodes of elevated blood pressure. This self-monitoring may form the basis of psychological treatment programmes for these patients.

Recent research has concentrated on the effects of prolonged hypertension on cognitive functioning. Typical studies have examined three broad areas: neuropsychological functioning, general functioning, such as IQ and memory, and reaction time. It has been hypothesised that persistent hypertension causes cognitive damage through cerebral lesions or increased/decreased blood supply. However, there is very little evidence to support this hypothesis. There is no doubt that hypertensive patients differ from normotensive patients on a number of indices of intellectual performance, but recent thinking suggests these differences may be more likely to be associated with the increased trait and state anxiety in some hypertensives than due to brain pathology (Elias *et al.*, 1987). However, this area is fraught with difficulties, as most subjects involved will be receiving anti-hypertensive medication, which itself can cause adverse cognitive effects. Other areas of psychological investigation have included the effects of anger and hostility on blood pressure and the correlation between mood and hypertensive episodes, all of which are useful when designing psychological interventions aimed at helping people to understand the interplay between mental and physiological activity.

Excessive lability of blood pressure and excessive sympathetic arousal are potential causal mechanisms in hypertension (Steptoe *et al.*, 1984) and may also accelerate atherosclerosis, induce coronary spasm and exacerbate cardiac arrythmias (see, for example, Krantz and Manuck, 1984). TABP has been shown to be associated with similar physiological changes. Assessment of these changes involves presenting a stressful stimuli, either passive in the form of upsetting films or active in the form of coping tasks, such as problem-solving or mental arithmetic tasks, and measuring changes before and after in physiological measures, such as blood pressure, heart rate, breathing patterns, muscle tension via EMG and skin resistance via GSR (see, for example, Carroll, 1984). Some time must be taken to allow the patient to acclimatise to this form of assessment, as some find the procedure itself stressful, which may present misleading findings. Although this procedure is mainly used for assessment purposes, it can also be used as a form of bio-feedback to highlight the importance of the interplay between psychological and physiological functioning.

Myocardial infarction (MI)

The main early work investigating psychological factors and CHD concentrated on the search for the 'coronary-prone' personality. This was later shown to be an over-simplification, and it is now widely accepted that a collection of factors or behavioural styles are associated with MI rather than a single coronary-prone personality. Psychological and behavioural factors also play a role in recovery and rehabilitation after MI, and the factors influencing the three stages of pre-morbidity, post-MI and rehabilitation may be different or overlap.

Pre-morbidity

The most consistent and yet controversial psychological risk factor of CHD is surely the TABP. This pattern is characterised by a sense of time urgency, a driving need for achievement and excessive ambition, impatience, over-involvement with work, and high anger and hostility. The TABP can be measured by a videotaped structured interview (SI) or by self-report questionnaires. The SI is a reliable, well validated measure of TABP. This interview consists of twenty-five questions which aim to measure impatience, competitiveness and hostility. The questions are asked in a provocative way, and the style of response is measured along with the words used (Carroll, 1992). Although it is generally accepted to be the most reliable measure of TABP, there are difficulties associated with its use as users have to be trained by approved trainers and it can be time-consuming to conduct. The questionnaire method of assessment has shown some association with CHD but the strength of association can differ with the use of different instruments. The 'gold standard' assessment is the SI, and this has been shown to be predictive of CHD and coronary events, such as MI and AP in at least three studies (Rosenman et al., 1975; Haynes, et al., 1980; Kornitzer et al., 1981). However, the association between TABP and CHD is not a universal finding: the Multiple Risk Factor Intervention Trial, a large-scale American study, showed no connection between SI-assessed TABP and the development of CHD (see MRFIT, 1982). Further analyses of the global TABP complex have highlighted hostility as the main pathogenic factor, the other components showing weaker associations with CHD (Dembroski et al., 1985).

A number of other psychosocial factors have been linked to CHD to greater or lesser extent, and these include smoking, low socio-economic status (Shaper and Pocock, 1987), low physical activity (Menotti and Seccareccia, 1985), work stress in the form of low work status, poor sense of job control and high perceived responsibility (Tyroler et al., 1987), and, finally, life events (Siegrist et al., 1982). It is more likely that these factors are linked with the risk of major illness including MI rather than specifically with CHD.

Post-MI

The most prominent factors to emerge at this stage of the disease are anxiety and depression, both of which can influence immediate recovery from MI and return to normal life (Nagle et al., 1971). It has been estimated that up to 30 per cent of all post-MI patients will experience clinical levels of anxiety, depression, or both (see, for example, Cassem *et al.*, 1968). Although the majority of post-MI studies on anxiety have used questionnaire measures, such as the Hospital Anxiety/ Depression Scale (Zigmond and Snaith, 1983) or the State-Trait Anxiety Inventory (Spielberger, 1972), some have used psycho-physiological assessments also (see, for example, Fielding, 1980; Langosch *et al.*, 1982). Acute anxiety, if left unresolved, can lead to a chronic sense of lack of control over one's life, and this may have a major impact on the patient's rehabilitation and return to normal life.

Rehabilitation

Depression is the most commonly experienced problem in this phase of recovery; in some instances it has been shown to persist for up to three years post-MI (Verwoerdt and Dovenmuhle, 1964). Excessive illness behaviour and neuroticism account for a great deal of continuing 'disability' and even chronic invalidism. To what extent these factors influence daily living is poorly researched, but it is thought that they are better predictors of chronicity than the extent of the original event (Smith, *et al.*, 1984). It follows, then, that assessment of anxiety and depression is necessary in the post-MI and rehabilitation phases, as they can severely impair recovery and adjustment to everyday living.

Cardiac arrhythmias

Acute emotional distress can influence the electrical activity of the heart via higher nervous system functioning (Lown *et al.* 1980). In an already damaged heart (from previous MI), this is potentially lethal. Psychological factors, such as self-reported high levels of stress and feelings of social isolation, have been shown to be predictive of sudden death in men who had just experienced MI (Ruberman *et al.*, 1984). Reports of serious life stress immediately preceding an MI has also been shown to be a predictive characteristic of patients who experienced recurrent coronary events (Byrne, 1981). There are also reports of recent loss of a loved one (Cottington *et al.*, 1980) and recent psychiatric illness (Talbot *et al.*, 1977) being associated with increased risk of sudden cardiac death.

In a piece of cardiological research on post-MI patients, experimental psychological stress in the form of mental arithmetic has also been shown to have electro-physiological effects (measured by ECG, echocardiography and programmed ventricular stimulation), most notably reduced ventricular refractory periods, transient ventricular tachycardia and ventricular fibrillation (Tavazzi *et al.*, 1986).

Two potential pathways by which mental activity influences electro-physiology have been suggested; these are response to challenge via the sympathetic-adrenal medullary activation or response to vigilance via the pituitary-adrenal cortical system (Eliot and Buell, 1985). Both of these characteristic responses are able to induce cardiac arrhythmias.

There is clearly a role for psychological assessment of those considered most at risk of developing potentially lethal arrhythmias, assessment which may take the form of a psychological interview, standardised psychological testing for anxiety, and evaluation of psycho-physiological responsiveness to emotional trauma.

ASTHMA

Asthma is generally considered a young person's disease and over 60 per cent of all asthmatics are under 16 years. The form of asthma suffered by the young is usually a response to common allergies such as those to pollen or dust mites. The other form of asthma, with no known cause, more often affects older people. An asthmatic attack is usually characterised by inflammation and oedema of the bronchioles, accompanied by broncho-constriction and excessive production of mucus (see, for example, Creer, 1982). This tends to result in a wheezing cough, rapid inspiration, and a feeling of congestion and panic. Patients who experience this are often admitted to hospital as emergency cases and are extremely agitated and frightened.

Despite earlier assertions to the contrary, psychological factors probably do not play a causal role in asthma. However, psychological factors can trigger an asthmatic attack, and they undoubtedly exacerbate symptoms during an attack (see, for example, Horton et al., 1978). Wheezing can be elicited by emotionally charged situations (ibid. 1978), and family dynamics can influence the severity of asthma (Purcell et al., 1969). It is also likely that psychological factors influence the course of the illness and adaption to life with asthma. The assessment of the psychological triggers and influencing factors in asthma will provide very useful information on which to base the comprehensive treatment of this condition and, of course, will provide the basis for any psychological treatment programme.

CHRONIC BRONCHITIS (CB)

Chronic bronchitis, as its name implies, is a long-term progressive inflammation of lung tissue, which produces wheezing, breathlessness, coughing, excessive sputum production, pain or discomfort in the chest, and fatigue (see, for example, Foxman et al., 1986). It is often accompanied by emphysema, the thickening and hardening of the alveoli that results in poor oxygen/carbon dioxide exchange in the lungs. Both CB and emphysema can give rise to right-sided heart failure. The commonest cause of CB is smoking.

CB is a relatively common disease in the UK, affecting mainly older people, 60 years plus, and it is claimed that CB accounts for more lost working days than any other disease (Morgan, 1987).

Psychological factors are prominent in CB. Worry, anxiety (Foxman et al., 1986) and depression (Rutter, 1977) are common. High levels of neuroticism have been witnessed in CB patients (Peach and Pathy, 1981), and elevated hostility levels in this group have been shown to predict undue disability (i.e. disability in excess of that warranted by their physical condition) (Morgan *et al.*, 1983). Furthermore, attitudes to treatment and beliefs about the efficacy of exercise are thought to be better predictors of functional disability than the physiological markers of the severity of the disease (Morgan *et al.*, op. cit.). It is worth mentioning a word of caution on this point. In this age group there is often more than one illness present, so assessing the contribution that CB alone makes to the overall level of disability is often extremely difficult. However, a clear psychological profile of the influencing factors in CB will enable clinicians to provide an assessment of the extent of damage and limitations that may be due to physical factors.

HYPERVENTILATION

The hyperventilation syndrome (HVS) is thought to be a psychological disorder, which produces symptoms of panic and somatic symptoms that can be mistaken for CHD or respiratory disorders, such as asthma. The predominant symptom is chest pain but other symptoms commonly experienced include epigastric pain, palpitations, tachycardia, shortness of breath and sighing, and tingling in the fingers (see, for example, Freeman and Nixon, 1985). Investigation will often reveal ECG changes that are indistinguishable from those produced by CHD (see, for example, Bass *et al.*, 1983).

The symptoms of HVS are thought to be due to rapid shallow breathing which over-inflates the lungs and causes mechanical compression of the stomach. This rapid overbreathing increases tension in the chest wall muscles also. The depletion of carbon dioxide resulting from overbreathing is thought to cause neurochemical changes, which result in increased tone in the heart muscle and blood vessels, causing them to contract spasmodically, and the ECG changes are most probably due to coronary spasm (Freeman and Nixon, 1985). These changes can occur in healthy patients (BASS *et al.*, 1983), but the situation is more complicated when HVS occurs in patients who also have coronary disease.

To differentiate between a diagnosis of HVS and CHD, many patients will undergo skilled and costly investigations usually culminating in a coronary angiogram, which may reveal no evidence of coronary disease. If HVS is suspected, the clinician will attempt to induce symptoms by getting the patient to hyperventilate (using the hyperventilation provocation tests, HVPT) whilst having ECG and lung function investigations. If this can induce characteristic symptoms that disappear when the patient's breathing returns to normal, a positive diagnosis can be made. Considerable doubt has been thrown on the validity of the HVPT (see Lindsay, Chapter 7). Production of the symptoms alone is by no means conclusive, and possible organic causes should be excluded before the diagnosis of HVS is made.

REFERENCES

Barefoot, J. C., Dahlstrom, W. G. and Williams, R. B. (1983) 'Hostility, CHD incidence and total mortality: a twenty-five year follow-up study of 225 physicians', *Psychosomatic Medicine* 245: 59–63.

Bass, S. C., Wade, C. and Gardener, N. N. *et al*, (1983) 'Unexplained breathlessness and psychiatric morbidity in patients with normal and abnormal coronary arteries', *Lancet* I: 605–9.

Byrne, D. G. (1981) 'Type A behavior: Live events and MI: independent or related risk factors?' *British Journal of Medical Psychology* 54: 371–7.

Carroll, D. (1984) *Biofeedback in Practice*, London: Longman.

Carroll, D. (1992) *Health Psychology. Stress Behavior and Disease*, London: The Falmer Press.

Cassem, N. R., Hackett, T. P. and Wishnie, H. A. (1968) 'The coronary care unit – an appraisal of the psychological hazards', *New England Journal of Medicine* 279(25): 1365–70.

Cook, W. W. and Medley, D. (1954) 'Proposed hostility and pharisaic-virtue scale for the MMPI', *Journal of Applied Psychology* 38(6): 414–18).

Costa, P. T. and McCrae, R. R. (1987) 'Neuroticism, somatic complaints and disease: Is the bark worse than the bite? *Journal of Personality* 55: 2.

Cottington, E. M., Kuller, L. H., Matthews, K. A. and Talbot, T. T. E. (1980) 'Environmental events preceding sudden death in women', *Psychosomatic Medicine* 42: 567–74.

Creer, T. L. (1982) 'Asthma', *Journal of Consulting and Clinical Psychology* 50(6): 912–21.

Davies, P. (1987) 'Confronting coronary heart disease', *The Health Service Journal* 23 (April).

Dembroski, T. M., MacDougall, J. M., Williams, R. B. *et al*., (1985) 'Components of Type A, hostility and anger in relationship to angiographic findings', *Psychosomatic Medicine* 247: 219–33.

Elias, M.F. and Robbins, M. A. (1987) 'Use of cinearteriography in behavioural studies of patients with chest pain in the absence of clinically significant coronary artery disease', in J. W. Elias and P. H. Marshall (eds) *Cardiovascular Disease and Behaviour*, London: Hemisphere.

Elias, M. F. and Robbins, M. A. and Schultz, N. (1987) 'Influence of essential hypertension on intellectual performance; causation or speculation?' in J. W. Elias and P. H. Marshall (eds) *Cardiovascular Disease and Behavior*, London: Hemisphere.

Eliot, R. S. and Buell, J. C. (1985) 'Role of emotions and stress in the genesis of sudden death', *Journal of American College of Cardiologists* 5: 95b–98b.

Fielding, R. (1980) 'A note on behavioral treatment in the rehabilitation of myocardial infarction patients', *British Journal of Social and Clinical Psychology* 19: 157–61.

Fox, R. M. (1988) 'Silent ischaemia: clinical implications in 1988', *British Heart Journal* 60: 363–6.

Foxman, B., Sloss, R. M., Lohr, N. K. and Brook, R. H. (1986) 'Chronic bronchitis: prevalence, smoking habits impact and anti-smoking advice', *Preventative Medicine* 15: 624–31.

Freeman, L. J. and Nixon, P. G. F. (1985) 'Chest pain and the hyperventilation syndrome – some etiological consideration', *Postgraduate Medical Journal* 61: 957–61.

Haynes, S. G., Feinleib, M. and Kannel, W. B. (1980) 'The relationship of psychosocial factors to coronary heart disease in the Framingham study: III. Eight year incidence of coronary heart disease', *American Journal of Epidemiology* III: 37–58.

Horton, D. J., Suda, W. L. and Kinsman, R. A. (1978) 'Bronchoconstrictive suggestion in asthma: a role for airways' hyperreactivity and emotions', *American Review of Respiratory Disease* 117: 1029–38.

Jenkins, C. D., Rosenman, R. H. and Zyzanski, S. J. (1978) 'Coronary prone behavior: one pattern or several?', *Psychosomatic Medicine* 40: 25–43.

Keys, A. (1980) *Seven Counties: A Multivariate Analysis of Death and Coronary Heart Disease*, Cambridge, Mass.: Harvard University Press.

Kornitzer, H., DeBacker, G. and Kittel, F. *et al.*, (1981) 'The Belgian Heart Disease Prevention Project: Type A behavior pattern and the prevalence of coronary heart disease', *Psychosomatic Medicine* 43: 133–45.

Krantz, D. S. and Manuck, S. D. (1984) 'Psychophysiologic reactivity and risk of CHD: a review and methodological critique', *Psychological Bulletin* 94(3): 435–64.

Langosch, W., Brodner, G. and Seer, T. *et al.*, (1982) 'Behavior therapy with CHD patients: results of a comparative study', *Journal of Psychosomatic Research* 26: 475–84.

Lown, B., De Silva, R. A., Murawski, B. J. and Reich, P. (1980) 'Psychophysiological factors in sudden cardiac death', *American Journal of Psychiatry* 137: 1325–35.

Menotti, A. and Seccareccia, S. (1985) 'Physical activity at work and job responsibility as a risk factor for fatal coronary heart disease and other causes of death', *Journal of Epidemiology and Community Health* 39: 325–9.

Morgan, A. D. (1987) 'Chronic bronchitis, disability and the attitudes and beliefs of patients', *Midwife and Health Visitor-Community Nurse* 23(3): 104–8.

Morgan, A. D., Buchanan, D. and Peck, D. S. *et al.*, (1983) 'Psychological factors contributing to disproportionate disability in chronic bronchitis', *Journal of Psychosomatic Research* 27(4): 259–63.

MRFIT (1982) 'Risk factor changes and mortality results', *Journal of the American Medical Association* 248: 1465–7.

Nagle, R., Gangola, R. and Picton-Robinson, I. (1971) 'Factors influencing return to work after myocardial infarction', *Lancet*, II: 454–6.

Peach, H. and Pathy, H. S. (1981) 'Follow-up study of disability among elderly patients discharged from hospital with exacerbations of chronic bronchitis', *Thorax* 36: 585–9.

Purcell, K., Brady, K. and Chai, H. *et al.*, (1969) 'The effect of asthma in children of experimental separation from the family', *Psychosomatic Medicine* 31: 144–64.

Rosenman, R. H., Brand, R. J. and Jenkins, C. D. *et al.* (1975) 'Coronary heart disease in the WCGS. Final follow-up experience of eight years', *Journal of the American Medical Association* 233: 872.

Ruberman, W., Chaudhary, B. S., Goldberg, J. D. and Weinblatt, E. (1984) 'Social influences on mortality after myocardial infarction', *New England Journal of Medicine* 311: 552–9.

Rutter, B. (1977) 'Some psychological concomitants of chronic bronchitis', *Psychological Medicine* 7: 45964.

Shaper, A. G. and Pocock, S. J. (1987) 'Risk factors for ischaemic heart disease in British men', *British Heart of Journal* 57: 11–16.

Shaper, A. G., Pocock, S. J. and Walker, M. (1981) 'British regional heart study: cardiovascular risk factors in middle-aged men in 24 towns', *British Medical Journal* 283: 179–86.

Siegrist, J., Dittman, K., Rittner, K. and Webber, I. (1982) 'The social context of active distress within patients with early myocardial infarction', *Social Science and Medicine* 16: 443–53.

Smith, T. W., Follick, N. J. and Korr, K. S. (1984) 'Anger, neuroticism, Type A behavior and the experience of angina', *British Journal of Medical Psychology* 57: 249–252.

Spielberger, C. D. (1972) *Anxiety: Current Trends in Theory and Research*, New York: Academic Press.

Spielberger, C. D., Jacobs, G. Russell, S. (1983) 'Assessment of anger: the State-Trait

Anger Scale' in J. N. Butcher and C. D. Speilberger (eds) *Advances in Personality Assessment, Vol. 2*, Hillsdale, NJ: LEA.

Steptoe, A., Melville, D. and Ross, A. (1984) 'Essential hypertension and psychological functioning: a study of factory workers', *British Journal of Clinical Psychology* 21: 303–11.

Talbot, T. T. E., Detre, K., Kuller, L. H. and Perper, J. (1977) 'Biologic and psychosocial risk factors of sudden death from coronary disease in white women', *American Journal of Cardiology* 39: 858–64.

Tavazzi, L., Zotti, A. M. and Rondanelli, R. (1986) 'Role of psychologic stress in the genesis of lethal arrhythmias in patients with coronary artery disease', *European Heart Journal* 7 (Supplement A): 99–106.

Tyroler, H. A., Cobb, L. A. and Haynes, S. G. *et al* (1987) 'Task Force One: Environmental risk factors in coronary artery disease', *Circulation* 76 (I Part 2): 139–44.

Verwoerdt, A. and Dovenmuhle, R. H. (1964) 'Heart disease and depression', *Geriatrics* 19: 856–63.

Williams, R. B. Jr and Anderson, N. B. (1987) 'Hostility and coronary heart disease', in J. W. Elias and P. H. Marshall (eds) *Cardiovascular Disease and Behaviour*, London: Hemisphere.

Zigmond, A. S. and Snaith, R. P. (1983) 'The hospital anxiety and depression scale', *Acta Psychiatrica Scandinavica* 67: 361–70.

Chapter 29

Cardiovascular and respiratory disease
Treatment

C. Bundy

INTERVENTION IN CORONARY HEART DISEASE/ISCHAEMIC HEART DISEASE

Psychological intervention may be applied to most stages of the CHD process: either to primary prevention of CHD (before the disease is manifest), during the acute stage most commonly following MI, or at the rehabilitation or post-rehabilitation (secondary prevention) phase. The type of intervention that can be used ranges from psychotherapy through cognitive-behavioural techniques to behavioural strategies. Therapeutic intervention prior to the 1970s consisted mainly of psychotherapy or behavioural modification of high-risk behaviours. However, with the development of interactive models of stress came the introduction of more comprehensive packages of treatment which employed more than one technique.

Prevention

The basic approach to primary prevention is through health education, which is based on the assumption that communication of the risk factors in the aetiology of CHD will result in the people targeted altering their lifestyle and behaviours accordingly. It has been used on a small scale with individuals and small groups and on a large scale involving whole communities. Two notable studies involving communities are the Stanford Three Communities Project in the USA and the North Karelia project in Finland (see, for example, Kottke *et al.*, 1984; Puska *et al.*, 1983). Both of these studies used mass media saturation with advice and information on heart disease risk and healthy eating and behaviour. The North Karelia project showed significant reductions in smoking, serum cholesterol and systolic blood pressure.

The Stanford project compared (1) no structured intervention with (2) the use of education alone with (3) education plus behavioural tuition on self-control of blood pressure and of weight and smoking, combined with specific advice on nutrition. The results for the education plus instruction group were excellent: a 30 per cent reduction in coronary risk was demonstrated, compared with a 10 per cent reduction for the education alone group. The 30 per cent coronary risk reduction was also accompanied by a reduction in risk for other related diseases, such as strokes and respiratory disorders. On an individual level, behavioural skill training plus extended individual counselling, as compared with a one-off physician contact, has been shown to result in significant improvements in weight, diet, cholesterol and triglyceride levels, and smoking (Meyer and Henderson, 1974).

Much of the work on primary prevention has concentrated on TABP modification and will therefore be discussed more fully in that section of this chapter.

One of the few studies to compare a psychological intervention (education, cognitive-behavioural rehearsal) with a physical intervention (aerobic conditioning) is reported by Long (1984). Anxiety and tension, perceived self-efficacy and exercise capacity were measured in 61 self-selected 'stressed' people. Large changes in tension and anxiety were reported in both groups but neither group proved superior, rather they were thought to be complementary. Despite the positive changes in CHD risk behaviour reported as a result of health education alone and combined with cognitive behavioural strategies, the question remains whether this translates into decreases in CHD incidence. It is likely that there will be a delay while the changes in lifestyle materialise into real CHD reductions, and psychologists can play a key role in assisting this transition.

Acute phase

The most common form of intervention used at this stage of the CHD process is described as individual or small group psychotherapy, but in reality it includes counselling and anxiety management training. Lenzer and Aronson (1972) report individual psychotherapy with patients who were being transferred from coronary care units to the main wards. Those given preparation showed less emotional distress, lower catecholamine levels and lower cardiac complications than those who acted as control patients. The most systematic study with patients in this phase was conducted by Gruen (1975), who randomised seventy patients to supportive psychotherapy or no treatment while they were being medically treated on a coronary care unit (CCU). The active treatment group were rated as less anxious and depressed, they experienced fewer cardiac problems, and stayed for fewer days on the coronary care unit and in the hospital after the coronary care unit. This form of psychological input appears to be beneficial to the patients and furthermore is reported to be relatively cost-effective to administer.

Rehabilitation and secondary prevention

Many forms of psychological intervention, ranging from behavioural techniques through to psychotherapy, have been used with varying degrees of success at this phase of the CHD process. The current treatment of choice is a package of education, supportive psychotherapy and cognitive-behavioural skills training.

The education component usually involves information about MI, diet, resumption of work and a healthy lifestyle, and in some instances involves recognition of physiological arousal and the accompanying thoughts, feelings and behaviour. The skills training most often centres around modification of TABP but can extend to include the use of bio-feedback and relaxation, assertiveness training and anger management.

There are many notable studies of psychological intervention at this stage; most programmes are based on relaxation training and some also include other treatments, such as exercise training (for a good review, see Langosch, 1984). One of the most comprehensive treatment packages is described by Ornish *et al.* (1983; 1990) and is the only programme to concentrate on AP. A combination of dietary changes, stress management training and lifestyle alterations, including graded exercise training, was used on CHD patients. The results from these studies not only show marked reductions in angina with increased exercise tolerance but also claim to reverse the atherosclerosis, and the evidence shown on angiography is very convincing. The authors make no claim regarding which component of the treatment package affected this reversal, and this is clearly an area of future involvement for psychologists with this otherwise overlooked client group.

Conclusions and recommendations

Psychological intervention can be conducted at any time phase of the illness, prior to diagnosis, during the acute stage and during rehabilitation. Psychological interventions based on a cognitive-behavioural approach, especially those which are skills-based, are broadly effective, but supportive psychotherapy can also be useful for a subgroup of people. Interventions that include more than one type of treatment appear to be generally more effective than single treatments alone, and these effects are seen on physiological and psychological measures.

Case history

Mr D. was a 53-year-old manager of a small restoration business. He lived with his wife. They had two sons who were in their thirties, with their own families. Although the family described themselves as 'comfortably off', they also described their lifestyle as a legacy from their respective poor backgrounds. Both were smokers and consumed the upper limit of the recommended alcohol intake for their weight. They ate at restaurants frequently and entertained friends at home regularly. They were both overweight and admitted to eating 'all the wrong foods'. Mr D. played golf once a week and Mrs D. enjoyed an occasional swim. Both sons were regular exercisers but had a similar lifestyle to their parents.

Mr D. suffered his first episode of chest pain while playing golf and, thinking it was indigestion, played on. Some episodes occurred later, mainly while he was taxing himself mentally and physically. He was seen by a cardiologist, who conducted an exercise tolerance test and ECG, and then explained that Mr D. probably had angina. Mr D. was placed on the waiting-list for an angiogram to confirm the diagnosis and was told to stop smoking. He made no concessions in his lifestyle, either dietary or behavioural. Two weeks before he was due to have the angiogram, he suffered an MI and was admitted as an emergency to the CCU. Although Mr D. recovered from the MI, his angina had become much worse and was severely inhibiting his lifestyle. After being discharged home he experienced a panic attack for which he was re-admitted to the CCU with a suspected MI. When this was not confirmed he was referred to the psychology service.

A lifestyle assessment together with a psychological profile of his behavioural style and characteristic traits was conducted, along with a thorough assessment of his physical abilities and cardiological status. Mr D. was shown to have recovered well from his MI; he had a mild degree of coronary occlusion and his exercise tolerance limit was reasonable for his age. He was, however, highly anxious, as measured by HADS, highly hostile, as measured by the Cook and Medley Hostility Scale, and scored extremely high on neuroticism, as measured by EPI (N). He did not display TABP, as measured by the Jenkins Activity Survey.

A mixed programme of rehabilitation was prescribed for Mr D. He joined an exercise group at the hospital, which included other post-MI patients and which he attended four mornings a week for twelve weeks. He also joined an SMT group, which was complementary to the exercise programme and which included post-MI and AP patients. The SMT group included five types of relaxation training, ranging from progressive muscular relaxation to self-hypnosis. It was based on a cognitive-behavioural therapy, which had been adapted by the clinical psychologists involved to the special needs of the MI/AP population. It included anger management, pain control (after Meichenbaum, 1985), education about lifestyle and what an MI was, the connection between thoughts, feelings and behaviour, and potential psychological triggers of AP. The group of eight to ten people met twice a week for one and a half hours for seven weeks. During this time Mr D. was expected to practise relaxation at home and complete homework assignments which included making changes in lifestyle and behavioural style.

At the end of the rehabilitation Mr D. was experiencing infrequent attacks of AP only, as recorded by an angina diary and a 24-hour ECG tape. He no longer required regular, prescribed anti-anginal medications, his exercise tolerance had improved significantly on a progressive exercise bicycle test, and he now went swimming and cycling twice a week. He claimed to have stopped smoking and his anxiety and hostility scores were significantly lower than before the programme. Mr D.'s wife and sons had changed their lifestyle accordingly. Mrs D. no longer smoked and both sons were giving up cigarettes also; their diet had changed to include a lower fat intake by their dietary report and they were beginning to lose weight. Both sons had requested a cholesterol check, which registered on the high normal ranges, and this, they said, was a further incentive to change their food intake.

At one-year follow-up Mr D. continued his progress and now described himself as fitter than he had ever been. He had not experienced any further panic attacks or problems as a result of the MI but still experienced the occasional AP episode, which he described as his 'stressometer'. Perhaps the most notable success in this case history is the continued improvements made by the rest of the family, none of whom now smoked, all of whom had lost weight and described their lifestyle as 'significantly healthier than before'. The sons reported a decrease in their cholesterol level and had maintained their fitness. Somewhat ironically, Mr and Mrs D. described Mr D.'s MI as 'the best thing' that had happened to their family.

TYPE A BEHAVIOUR PATTERN (TABP)

It is not possible to talk about the psychological treatment of CHD without including TABP modification. Attempts to alter this behavioural risk factor have enjoyed much attention in the literature over the last twenty years, and the results from early studies are anything but consistent, with some authors reporting major reductions in TABP scores and some reporting no change or short-lived changes (for an excellent review of TABP modification, see Johnston, 1982). There are many difficulties associated with these early studies, the most notable of which centre around a confusion of interventions and a mis-match of outcome measures, some choosing to use self-rated TABP in all its various forms and some using the videotaped structured interview method. Some studies have compared healthy TABP men, with post-MI TABP men but it is now more generally accepted that they do not constitute a homogeneous group.

Despite the controversy surrounding attempts to alter TABP, it is generally agreed that, with an appropriate intervention, reductions in TABP scores are likely. There are a number of well-conducted studies demonstrating this (see, for example, Friedman et al., 1986; Thurman, 1985; Gill et al., 1985), but by far the largest TABP modification programme to date is the Recurrent Coronary Prevention Project (Friedman et al., op. cit.). This study is particularly noteworthy because it was conducted on post-MI patients rather than a healthy population; in it over 800 patients were allocated to a group receiving cardiac counselling alone or cardiac counselling plus TABP modification (these techniques are described in detail by Thoresen et al., 1982). Assessments of the outcome measures were taken annually for the first three years and finally at four and a half years. Both of the treatment groups reduced their TABP scores, but the combined counselling and TABP modification group reduced their scores significantly more than the counselling alone group. Similarly, MI re-infarction rates were almost halved in the combined treatment group (12.9 per cent) when compared with the counselling alone group (21.2 per cent). The most encouraging finding, however, was that subjects who had reduced their TABP at the end of one year, irrespective of which treatment they had received, had fewer re-infarctions over the research period than those who did not change their TABP. This appears to present strong support for the assertion that specific interventions aimed at modifying TABP not only reduce the target behaviour but also reduce the associated CHD endpoint, MI.

Case history

Dr H. was a 43-year-old academic, who was referred to the psychological service following medical counselling after his recent MI. He was married, with three children in their teens, and his wife was the owner of a small catering business. Dr H. was the head of the mathematics department at the local university and spoke often of his ambition to have the largest department in a British university. He was already the youngest appointed professor. During the initial interview. Mrs H. spoke of her husband's insatiable appetite for competition; he was a very keen squash player and cyclist and 'even competed with himself'. She described how, when the children were young, he would beat them at children's games and never allow them to win. This he described as 'character building'. During the interview Dr H. constantly checked his watch and seemed irritable and impatient. He described himself as energetic, enthusiastic and very intolerant of slow people.

As part of a detailed assessment Dr H. completed a videotaped interview for TABP, and questionnaire measures of hostility, anger, anxiety and neuroticism. His medical treatment had been completed and, as he had made an unremarkable recovery from the MI two months previously, he was not receiving any medical treatment at the time. During the interview, Dr H. displayed characteristic signs of hostility, potential for aggression, impatience and competitiveness. His questionnaire results indicated a very high hostility score, high state and trait anger, above normal levels of neuroticism and scores indicating clinical anxiety.

Dr H. was counselled regarding these findings and, after some discussion, agreed to enrol in a TABP management course the following week. He attended ten small-group meetings, lasting one and a half hours, of TABP modification, which included:

1 Education on the nature of TABP and the potential pathway between it and CHD, and the nature of the relaxation response;
2 Self-appraisal of cognitions and cognitive restructuring;
3 Anxiety management;
4 Anger control (including assertiveness training);
5 A variety of relaxation techniques, ranging from simple meditative techniques through progressive muscular relaxation to self-hypnosis.

Each session allowed patients to provide real-life examples of the subject being discussed and pooling of coping styles and resources, and ended with a twenty-minute period of relaxation. Between sessions, behavioural assignments were set, and a diary of responses was kept, providing examples for the forthcoming session. Measures of TABP, hostility, anger, anxiety and neuroticism, as used during initial assessment, were taken before and after treatment and at the half-way stage.

Significant reductions in TABP, as rated by the Jenkins Activity Survey, along with significant reductions in state anxiety and anger were seen at both time phases. Hostility scores reduced, but not significantly, and there was no change in either neuroticism or trait-anger scores. Dr H. described himself as significantly more relaxed and less intense, and had begun to notice improvements in his relationships with his family and staff, which he ascribed to the assertiveness training/ anger control. He claimed that the sessions on time management had enabled him to work more productively. At one-year follow-up, the reductions in TABP were maintained, trait-anger and anxiety were non-significantly lower than the final assessment, and Dr H. maintained that the ten sessions had given him an alternative way of dealing with frustrations and with the pressure that he recognised he had placed himself under. His enthusiasm for his treatment, marginally short of evangelism, had encouraged him to send all of his staff to a private TABP modification course, which he claimed had cost his department £10,000 over the past year but had earned the department much more in terms of revenue from grant-giving bodies by making his team the most 'productive' in the university.

Hypertension

Hypertension is very often associated with TABP and because both are independent risk factors of CHD (Review Panel, 1981), a number of studies have attempted to alter them separately (e.g. Irvine et al., 1986) or together (e.g. Bennett et al., 1991). The modification of TABP outlined above can easily be adapted to the hypertensive population but may need to be expanded to include other forms of behavioural management relevant to the hypertensive population, such as diet, weight control and improvement of compliance.

The simplest intervention with this client group is education and self-monitoring. The medical management of hypertension frequently fails to include impressing the importance of regular and sustained medication-taking; patients often stop taking the tablets if they feel better or following some arbitrary time limit. When given a brief, simple explanation of how their medication, works in their condition many patients increase their adherence to their regime. Similarly, when patients are told about potential side effects and the reason why some side effects occur, they are more likely to adhere to a medical regime (Haynes et al., 1976). Keeping a diary of medication use and noting side effects is also useful to promote as part of a self-monitoring package, the rationale being that greater involvement in the treatment would result in a more accurate reporting of progress and less likelihood of patients abandoning their treatment. Other general methods of treatment focus on changing further CHD risk factors which interact with hypertension either to exacerbate the hypertension itself or increase the risk of other cardiac events (such as MI or angina), or a combination (Kannel, 1977). The focus in Kannel's behavioural treatment is on smoking, weight control, salt intake control, alcohol and caffeine reduction where they are excessive. There is some, albeit patchy, support that reducing salt intake (Beard et al., 1982) and weight (Basler et al., 1982) can help control episodes of hypertension in mild and obese hypertensive patients. There is evidence that daily self-monitoring of blood pressure alone can gradually reduce the pressure at least as much as other psychological interventions, such as relaxation training. However, there is some discrepancy between the reductions that occur in measurements taken in the patient's home and at the clinic, and whether these reductions are due to feedback alone or whether they represent long-term habituation to monitoring is unclear (Chesney et al., 1987).

Formal relaxation training, even when used alone, can have a lowering effect on blood pressure. These findings have been consistently reported from 1976, but the early studies contained many methodological weaknesses, such as high drop-out rates, confusion of treatments and the use of non-homogeneous groups. Meditation techniques have been shown to reduce blood pressure significantly when compared with no treatment (Seer and Raeburn, 1980), as has progressive muscular relaxation (Southam et al., 1982), but the most convincing studies have compared treatments that are comparable.

In a study which combined progressive muscular relaxation with meditative techniques and compared them with an information-only intervention, significant reductions in BP occurred in the combined intervention group. Furthermore, these reductions were maintained or increased at three-month follow-up and at four-year follow-up (Patel et al., 1985). Similar significant findings were found when relaxation/meditative techniques were compared with either an attention control procedure (Patel and Marmot, 1988) or no active treatment (Jorgensen et al., 1981). When relaxation training was compared with medical treatment alone or in conjunction with supportive psychotherapy, relaxation proved to be the superior treatment (Taylor et al., 1977).

The most comprehensive comparison of psychological treatments in mildly hypertensive patients is described by Chesney *et al.* (1987). One hundred and fifty-eight subjects were randomly allocated to one of five groups: relaxation training alone; relaxation training plus cognitive restructuring; relaxation plus bio-feedback; relaxation plus behaviour modification (salt, smoking and caffeine reduction); or a combination of relaxation, bio-feedback and cognitive restructuring. These groups were compared with a control group receiving measurement of blood pressure only. When the clinic blood pressure readings were compared, there were no differences between the groups, who all showed significant reductions. However, only the intervention groups showed reductions in work-site measurements, with the relaxation plus cognitive treatment showing the greatest reductions in both systolic and diastolic blood pressure.

Conclusions

The overall conclusion from the work on psychological therapy for hypertensive patients is that most treatments can be effective: from simple monitoring of blood pressure to elaborate cognitive therapy. No one method has proved conclusively superior. However, where a combination of education plus skills training plus bio-feedback and cognitive therapy has been used, the results are very encouraging and this multi-level approach might be the most effective treatment of choice.

Case history

Mr W. was a 58-year-old self-employed builder. He lived with his wife, who was a 54-year-old housewife. The Ws had three children, who were grown up and had their own families but lived close to their parents. Mr W. was identified as being mildly hypertensive (a diastolic pressure between 90 and 105 mmHg) by his GP following a Well-Person check at the surgery. He was offered the opportunity to take part in stress management training with a group of nine other people twice a week for ten weeks. Measures of TABP were taken, using the Jenkins Activity Survey, and anger was assessed using the Spielberger Anger Expression Scale. The Derogatis Stress Profile was used to measure self-reported stress. Blood pressure recordings were made before and after each session of stress management training and were used to provide feedback to each session.

Stress management training consisted of a combination of education about blood pressure and the role of stress, relaxation training, and cognitive restructuring, TABP modification, especially changing time urgency and the anger response. Homework consisted of regular self-monitoring of blood pressure and keeping a diary recording stressful events.

During the sessions it became clear that Mr W. was experiencing difficulties with his marriage, and the problem was traced at least in part to his unassertiveness. Whenever he was required to be assertive, he became defensive and aggressive, and this resulted in feelings of guilt and depression. He subsequently withdrew from the relationship and this caused further tension. Mr W. identified this as his main source of stress, and from the information he kept in his stress/BP diary he was able to see the direct effects on his blood pressure. As a result of participation in the group, he was able to enlist the help of the other members in identifying his responses, in helping to change his accompanying thoughts and in providing himself with an opportunity to practise a more assertive, less aggressive response to certain problems.

At the end of the programme Mr W.'s blood pressure measured significantly lower consistently. He also appeared to be calmer and reported feeling more in control. His stress profile scores had reduced, but not significantly, and his TABP scores were unchanged from the initial borderline level. However, the anger expression scores had changed significantly. He now reported feeling less angry and also expressing less anger. At six-month follow-up the same pattern of response prevailed, and Mr W. continued to report increased feelings of well-being and control. He also claimed that improvements in his relationship with his wife were helping to maintain his blood pressure improvements. At this stage his blood pressure fell into the 80 and 90 mmHg diastolic range, and he was no longer considered at risk for further CHD.

ASTHMA

Much of the research on psychological aspects of respiratory disease has included mixed groups of people: with asthma, bronchitis and other lung disorders. Typical areas of work include: the relationship between alexithymia (a general disturbance of mood and thinking characterised by somatic expression of some intra-pyschic conflict) and hospitalisation (e.g. Dirks et al., 1981); panic/fear reactions in respiratory illness (e.g. Dirks et al., 1977); personality traits and pulmonary functioning (e.g. Biro and Sebej, 1977); and behavioural management of lung disease (Parker, 1985). Where patients with only asthma have been studied, two broad psychological techniques have been applied, psychotherapy and behavioural methods. Where psychotherapy has been used, it has been based on psychoanalytic theories of over-dependence and attachment to the mother, and the asthmatic attack is viewed as an inhibited, repressed cry. However, from the available literature, there is little evidence for unusual relationships between mother and asthmatic child, rather there is some evidence that asthmatics patients tend to be well-adjusted people (see, for example, Gauthier et al., 1977). There is also no evidence supporting the repressed cry theory. There is equally no evidence that psychotherapy alone alleviates asthma; any improvements that are reported are likely to be coincidental (Creer, 1982).

Behavioural strategies have proved to be somewhat more successful. A controlled treatment of systematic desensitisation to fear-provoking cues in twenty-six children showed a small improvement in forced expiratory volume (FEV1) when compared with no active treatment (Miklich *et al.*, 1977). One of the problems associated with this study is that some patients made large improvements, but these were obscured when averaged with the data from other subjects who did not improve much. This has led to a call for asthmatic patients to act as their own comparison controls, to minimise comparisons between subjects. Other related techniques include teaching symptom discrimination (teaching patients to assess when asthmatic attacks are imminent) and using physical markers of attacks such as lung function tests to provide the patient with physiological feedback. Teaching hospital staff how not to reinforce illness behaviour, by removing television, books and the opportunity to interact with other children when the asthma patient was admitted, has proved useful in reducing length of stay, as has teaching the patient self-management strategies (see, for example, Weiss, 1981).

More recent approaches to the psychological management of asthmatic patients have included using decision flow-charts in which decisions and response to possibilities during an asthma attack can allow patients to take early preventive action (Pal-Hegedus, 1988); a combination of behavioural coping strategies, bio-feedback and the use of hypnosis (Brown and Fromm, 1988), all of which report some degree of success in minimising symptoms. The importance of providing basic education regarding asthma to patients should not be overlooked, particularly in relation to the correct use of medication. Many asthmatics rely on self-administered medication, and active participation in treatment is considered essential to good management.

Case history

Ms M. was a 30-year-old teacher in a further education college. She had been suffering from asthma since she was 18. She was very well informed about her condition and took a great deal of responsibility for her own management. Her physician was very happy for her to take responsibility and he referred her to the psychology service for basic relaxation training.

After many weeks of observing Ms M. prior to, during and following asthmatic attacks (some experimentally induced by the medical team), it became apparent that her rapid shallow breathing in the early pre-asthmatic stage exacerbated attacks. Her psychological profile was normal except for a high score on the panic/fear scale (MMPI).

A programme of seven sessions was agreed on, during which deep breathing techniques were taught. These included diaphragmatic breathing of slow deep breaths with exhalation being of the same duration as inhalation (Soskis, 1986). Parallel sessions on progressive muscular relaxation and self-hypnosis were also conducted. The sessions were conducted on an individual basis in the patient's home. The three-month assessment at the chest clinic of the local hospital revealed a 30 per cent decrease in the number of asthmatic attacks experienced. This was accompanied by a 100 per cent decrease in attacks that required hospitalisation. This pattern of improvements continued for the one-year follow-up with a 75 per cent decrease in hospital admissions. Ms M. used relaxation and self-hypnosis on average once weekly and reported no adverse side effects of using these techniques. She reported a general improvement in well-being and control but this was not systematically measured. She now teaches these techniques, with the physician's permission, to patients who attend the chest clinic.

CHRONIC BRONCHITIS

Psychological aspects of chronic bronchitis and emphysema have been sadly neglected both from a research and an intervention perspective. Much of the treatment which a psychologist can offer will be crisis intervention and sympton control. However, as the single biggest cause of chronic bronchitis and emphysema is smoking, smoking cessation programmes may also be offered. As previously mentioned, psychological factors are major determinants of functional disability for a number of people. It is important, therefore, to examine critically the actual level of functional ability. This can only be done in participation with the health care team so as not to undermine the input from the other professionals involved.

Psychological intervention with this client group has usually occurred in the context of a general rehabilitation programme (see, for example, Agle *et al.*, 1973) and may amount to no more than simple relaxation training. There are few reports of specific psychological interventions with these patients. One such study (Rosser *et al.*, 1983) compared a group of patients receiving analytic psychotherapy with another group given supportive psychotherapy and a nurse-led group that concentrated on practical issues of bronchitis. All groups were compared with a non-active treatment group, who received weekly laboratory tests only. All the groups were followed up six months later. The results suggested that both psychotherapy groups 'underwent psychodynamic change' but the analytical psychotherapy group showed no positive benefits over and above that. The supportive psychotherapy group reduced their psychiatric symptoms, as assessed by the General Health Questionnaire, and increased their exercise tolerance. The nurse-led discussion group improved their breathlessness but at the same time increased their depression scores. The results from this study must be viewed with caution, as some of the treatment groups contained as few as five patients and these results have not been replicated.

Case history

Ms Z. was a 62-year-old ex-psychiatric nurse. She had been diagnosed as having chronic bronchitis and emphysema seven years previously. Until now she had received only medical treatment, usually during acute attacks, and the medical team felt Ms Z. would benefit from general physical rehabilitation including some relaxation and breathing training. Prior to starting treatment an exercise-tolerance test was performed to determine the target level of training; this was estimated to be 20 per cent below the potential maximum for her age group. Following a detailed psychological assessment, which included state anxiety and depression, Ms Z. began a twelve-week course of aerobic training designed to her specific requirements. This was conducted with a group of eleven other people with a similar diagnosis, who began at the same time, and was carried out twice a week for one and a half hours at a time. A third session, conducted by a nurse and a clinical psychologist with the same people, was designed to support and educate people who had recurrent bouts of bronchitis. Members were encouraged to reveal their feelings and any problems they wished to share and to discuss specific problems associated with their diagnosis. This ran for twelve sessions. Autogenic relaxation training and breathing exercises (after Jacobson, 1978) were taught during the physical rehabilitation sessions by a physiotherapist with an interest in chest medicine.

At the end of the twelve weeks, a repeat exercise-tolerance test and anxiety/depression scales were given. Ms Z. had shown a marked improvement in her level of tolerated exercise and was able to perform significantly better (heart and respiratory rate were used as indicators) at her entry exercise tolerance level. She had noticed an improvement in her ability to perform everyday tasks. Her initial anxiety scores had not been abnormally high but her depression scores were high, placing her in the clinically depressed band. The second measures showed her depression scores were reduced below clinical levels.

Ms Z.'s physician and the physiotherapist involved with her treatment felt there was a marked improvement in both her physical and psychological condition but the reports were not measured systematically.

Follow-up of Ms Z. one year later showed a small fall-off of physical fitness but levels remained above the level at entry to the programme. The depression scores were the same as those post-treatment and anxiety scores were also unchanged.

HYPERVENTILATION

Breathing training has also been used with some success for the group of people who are labelled hyperventilators. This is a form of bio-feedback and sometimes involves instruments which measure the rate and quality of inspiration and expiration (Grossman *et al.* 1985). The simplest technique is to get patients to re-breathe their expired air by breathing into a brown paper bag. This technique works during a hyperventilation attack when the aim is to restore carbon dioxide to normal levels in the blood (see Lindsay, Chapter 8). Strategies which aim to prevent attacks can range from relaxation training to comprehensive programmes of cognitive-behavioural stress management training.

Hyperventilation has more usually been viewed as the physical manifestation of some underlying psychological/psychiatric disorder, such as chronic anxiety or panic disorder, and as such is treated indirectly by behavioural, cognitive-behavioural or psychodynamic methods. Where this is thought to be the case, the reader is referred to the relevant literature on treatment of anxiety/panic disorders (see Lindsay, Chapter 8). Where hyperventilation is thought to be a precursor of asthma or coronary artery spasm, the treatment, although essentially the same as that for panic disorder generally, would tend to be more focused on the hyperventilation. Here, simple behavioural strategies, such as relaxation training including breathing control training and bio-feedback, are probably the most successful.

Unfortunately hyperventilation can exacerbate angina in patients with cardio-vascular disease (Freeman and Nixon, 1985), and so treatment of such patients should be done in collaboration with physicians.

Case history

Mr C. was a 58-year-old man with chronic stable angina pectoris. Mr C. had attended the cardiology out-patients department for the previous three years following the diagnosis of his condition. He complained often that his angina would get worse when 'he was uptight'. He was referred for assessment to determine the suitability of joining a stress management training programme. After initial assessment, it was revealed that he was highly anxious and hostile and was extremely 'Type A', therefore he was suitable for treatment. However, Mr C. refused to take part in the project and declined any involvement with a psychologist. It was felt that he would benefit from being taught breathing control, as his hyperventilation frequently exacerbated angina attacks and myocardial ischaemia, as seen on cardiac testing. The psychologist discussed the treatment with a physiotherapist who had a particular interest in cardiac disorders, and she agreed to teach relaxation and breathing control to Mr C. which involved deep, slow diaphragmtic breathing with controlled inspiration and expiration times.

After ten sessions of training Mr C. performed an exercise test. Hyperventilation was induced during this test, but he very successfully controlled his breathing and stopped the hyperventilation at will. During this time he also exhibited some control over the ischaemia, measured by ST-segment depression, a characteristic deviation from the normal pattern displayed on an ECG monitor from the patients heart tracing. Mr C.'s cardiologist felt that Mr C. had benefited from the training and invited him to join the current stress management training group. Mr C. agreed to participate and completed the twelve-week course, having participated fully in each session.

REFERENCES

Agle, D. P. *et al.* (1973) 'Multidisciplinary treatment of chronic pulmonary insufficient: I Psychologic aspects of rehabilitation', *Psychosomatic Medicine* 35: 41–9.

Basler, H. D. *et al.* (1982) 'Psychological group treatment of essential hypertension in clinical practice', in A. Mathews and A. Steptoe (eds) *Behavioral Medicine*, Leicester: British Psychological Society (57–64).

Beard, C. *et al.* (1982) 'Randomised controlled trial of a no added sodium diet for mild hypertension', *Lancet* II: 455–8.

Bennett, P. *et al.* (1991) 'Treating type A behaviors and mild hypertension in middle aged men', *Journal of Psychosomatic Research* 35(2/3): 209–23.

Biro, V and Sebej, F. (1977) 'Personality traits and respiration changes sensorimotor load in asthmatics', *Studia Psycholgia* 19(4): 314–17.

Brown, D. P. and Fromm, E. (1988) 'Hypnotic treatment of asthma', *Advances* 5: 15–27.

Chesney, M. A. *et al.* (1987) 'Relaxation training at the worksite: I The untreated mild hypertensive', *Psychosomatic Medicine* 49: 250–73.

Creer, T. L. (1970) 'The use of a time out from positive reinforcement procedure with asthmatic children', *Journal of Psychosomatic Research* 14: 117–20.

Creer, T. L. (1982) 'Asthma', *Journal of Consulting and Clinical Psychology* 50(6): 912–21.

Derogatis, L. R. (1986) 'The Derogntis Stress Profile (DSP): quantification of psychological stress', *Advancess in Psychosomatic Medicine* 003: 1.

Dirks, J. F. *et al.* (1977) 'Panic/fear: a personality dimension related to length of hospitalisation in respiratory illness', *Journal of Asthma Research* 14(2): 61–71.

Dirks, J. F. *et al.* (1981) 'Alexithymia and the psychomaintenance of bronchial asthma', *Psychotherapy and Psychosomatics* 36(1): 63–71.

Freeman, L. J. and Nixon, P. G. F. (1985) 'Chest pain and the hyperventilation syndrome – some aetiological considerations', *Postgraduate Medical Journal* 61: 957–61.

Friedman, M. *et al.* (1986) 'Alteration of Type A behavior and reduction in cardiac recurrences in post-myocardial infarction patients. Summary results of the RCCP', *American Heart Journal* 112(4) 653–65.

Gautheir, Y. *et al.* (1977) 'The mother–child relationship and the development of autonomy and self-assertion in young (14–30 months) asthmatic children', *Journal of the American Academy of Child Psychiatry* 16: 109–31.

Gill, J. J. *et al.* (1985) 'Reduction of Type A behavior in healthy middle-aged American military officers', *American Heart Journal* 110: 503–14.

Grossman, D., DeSwart, J. C. G. and DeFares, P. B. (1985) 'A controlled study of breathing therapy for treatment of hyperventilation syndrome', *Journal of Psychosomatic Research* 29: 49–58.

Gruen, W. (1975) 'Effects of brief psychotherapy during the hospitalisation period on the recovery process in heart attack', *Journal of Consulting and Clinical Psychology* 43: 223–32.

Haynes, R. B., Sackett, D. L. and Gibson, E. S. *et al.* (1976) 'Improvement of medication compliance in uncontrolled hypertension', *Lancet* I: 1265–8.

Irvine, M. J. *et al.* (1986) 'Relaxation and stress management in the treatment of essential hypertension', *Journal of Psychosomatic Research* 30: 437–50.

Jacobson, E. (1978) *You Must Relax*, New York: McGraw-Hill.

Jenkins, C. D. (1979) *Form C: Jenkins Activity Survey*, New York: Psychological Corporation.

Johnston, D. W. (1982) 'Behavioral treatment in the reduction of coronary risk factors: Type A behavior and blood pressure', in A. Mathews and A. Steptoe (eds) *Behavioral Medicine*, Leicester: British Psychological Society (43–56).

Jorgensen, R. S. *et al.* (1981) 'Anxiety management training in the treatment of essential hypertension', *Behaviour Research and Therapy* 19: 467–74.

Kannel, W. E. (1977) 'Importance of hypertension as a major risk factor in cardiovascular disease', in Genet, Koiw and Kuchel (eds) *Hypertension, Pathology and Treatment*, New York: McGraw-Hill.

Kottke, T. E., Puska, P., Salonen, J. T. *et al.* (1984) 'Changes in perceived heart disease risk and health during a community based heart disease prevention programme: the North Karelia Project', *Public Health Briefs* 74: 12.

Langosch, W. (1984) 'Behavioural interventions in cardiac rehabilitation', in A. Steptoe and A. Mathews (eds) *Health Care and Human Behaviour*, London: Academic Press (301–24).

Lenzer, A., and Aronson, A. (1972) 'Psychiatric vignettes from a CCU', *Psychosomatics* 13: 179–84.

Long, B. D. (1984) 'Aerobic conditioning and stress inoculation: A comparison of stress management interventions', *Cognitive Therapy and Research* 8(5): 517–42.

Meichenbaum, D. (1985) *Stress Inoculation Training*, Oxford: Pergamon Press.

Meyer, A. J. and Henderson, J. B. (1974) 'Multiple risk factor reductions in the prevention of cardiovascular disease', *Preventative Medicine* 3: 225.

Miklich, D. R. *et al.* (1977) 'The clinical utility of behavior therapy as an adjunctive treatment for asthma', *The Journal of Allergy and Clinical Immunology* 60: 285–94.

Ornish, D. *et al.* (1983) 'Effects of stress management training and dietary changes in treating ischaemic heart disease', *Journal of the American Medical Association* 249: 1.

Ornish, D., Brown, S. E., Scherwitz, L. W. *et al.* (1990) 'Can lifestyle changes reverse coronary heart disease?' *Lancet* 336: 129–33.

Pal-Hegedus, C. (1988) 'Behavioral treatment in childhood asthma. Special issue: health psychology', *Revista-Latinoamericana de Psicologia* 20(1): 71–80.

Parker, S. R. (1985) 'Future directions in behavioral research related to lung disease', *Annals of Behavioral Medicine* 7(4): 21–5.

Patel, C. F. and Marmot, M. (1988) 'Can general practitioners use training in relaxation and management of stress to reduce mild hypertension?', *British Medical Journal* 296: 21–4.

Patel, C. *et al.* (1985) 'Trial of relaxation in reducing coronary risk: Four year follow-up', *British Medical Journal* 290: 1103–6.

Puska, P. *et al.* (1983) 'Changes in risk factors for CHD during 10 years of a community intervention programme: the North Karelia Project', *British Medical Journal* (17 December 1983): 287.

Review Panel on Coronary-prone Behavior and Coronary Heart Disease (1981) 'Coronary prone behavior and coronary heart disease: a critical review', *Circulation* 63: 1199–215.

Rosser, R., Denford, J. and Heslop, W. *et al.* (1983) 'Breathlessness and psychiatric morbidity in chronic bronchitis and emphysema: a study of psychotherapeutic management', *Psychological Medicine* 13: 93–110.

Seer, P. and Raeburn, J. M. (1980) 'Meditation training and essential hypertension: a methodological study', *Journal of Behavioral Medicine* 3: 59–71.

Soskis, D. A. (1986) *Teaching Self Hypnosis: An Introductory Guide for Clinicians*, New York: W. W Norton.

Southam, M. A. *et al.* (1982) 'Relaxation training: blood pressure lowering during the working day', *Archives of General Psychiatry* 39: 715–17.

Taylor, C. *et al.* (1977) 'Relaxation therapy and high blood pressure', *Archives of General Psychiatry* 34: 339–42.

Thoresen, C. E. *et al.* (1982) 'The RCCP. Some preliminary findings', *Acta Medica Scandinavica* (Supplement) 660: 172–92.

Thurman, C. W (1985) 'Effectiveness of cognitive-behavioral treatments in reducing Type A behavior among university faculty – one year later', *Journal of Counselling Psychology* 32: 445–8.

Weiss, J. B. (1981) 'Superstuff', in *Self-Management Educational Programs for Childhood Asthma, Vol 2: Manuscripts*, Bethesda, Md.: National Institute of Allergic And Infectious Diseases.

Chapter 30

Disorders of sleep

Investigation

S.J.E. Lindsay and M. Jahanshahi

INTRODUCTION

Sleep, far from being an unchanging state of low arousal, is characterised by continuously varying activity of body movement, dreaming, and physiological and biochemical systems (Kleitman, 1963). One variable, the electrical activity of the brain recorded in electroencephalography (EEG), however, has been used more than any other to identify changes in sleep.

Accordingly, sleep has been described as consisting of four stages, which are undergone repeatedly throughout the night (Empson, 1989; Williams *et al.*, 1974).

Body movement and muscular activity, indicated typically by changing electrical potentials in chin and forehead muscles, decrease from stages 1 to 3. However, in stage 4 there is an increase in muscular activity. Sleep-walking and night terrors occur most often then (*British Medical Journal*, 1980; Carlson *et al.*, 1982). Nevertheless, that is the stage of deepest sleep, when the subject is least easily wakened (Webb and Cartwright, 1978). Subjects usually find it impossible to recall events occurring in stage 4. As sleep progresses, the subject usually spends less time in stage 4.

During Rapid Eye Movement (REM) sleep, which occurs mostly following a lightening of stage 2 sleep, dreams are most frequent (Empson, 1989). In REM sleep, the subject's musculature (apart from the respiratory muscles) is in a state of 'flaccid paralysis' (Empson, 1989).

These characteristics of sleep change with age, elderly subjects spending less of the night in stage 4 than do younger subjects. Infants spend a large proportion of their sleep in REM sleep (Empson, 1989).

Many environmental variables also influence the course and characteristics of sleep (Webb and Cartwright, 1978), and may have special significance for the clinical investigation of sleep problems (see Table 30.1). Unusually high room temperature (Schmidt-Kessen and Kendel, 1973), noise, meaningful signals, such as the sound of a familiar name (Webb and Cartwright, op. cit.), and strenuous or unaccustomed exercise close to the time of sleep (Horne and Porter, 1976) may all retard the onset or interrupt the course of sleep. Chronic cardiac illness (Johns, 1970), toothache (Sheiham and Croog, 1981) and depression (Williams and Karacan, 1973) can have similar effects. The intake of some beverages (e.g. Horlicks) can favour sleep (Southwell *et al.*, 1972). Others, especially those containing caffeine (coffee and tea), can impair sleep. Even the quality of beds themselves has been studied, but the effects of hard and soft mattresses are inconsistent (Kleitman, 1963).

Environmental variables may also affect the structure of sleep. For example, Bunnell *et al.* (1983) found that exhaustive exercise increased the amount of stage 4 sleep. Sleep deprivation also increases the amount of stage 4 and REM sleep compared with baseline on the first night of return to normal sleep (Berger and Oswald, 1962). Changes in sleep-activity cycles, as in shift work, do not appear to change the stages of sleep significantly but do curtail the duration of sleep (Tepas, 1982).

The significance of many variables is debatable because often they affect characteristics of sleep whose own importance is not clear (Hartmann, 1973). For example, alcohol intake reduces the amount of REM sleep (Williams and Salamy, 1972) but innumerable investigations of REM sleep and dreaming have given few clues about the significance of REM and dreaming (Empson, 1989). Major questions about sleep itself remain unanswered. What restorative functions does it serve? How much sleep is necessary (Empson, 1989; Hartmann, 1973; Webb and Cartwright, 1978)?

There are many abnormalities of sleep (American Psychiatric Association, 1987). The following do not appear to affect its quantity or quality: bedwetting and soiling, night terrors, sleep-walking, sleep-talking, and head- and body-rocking. More disruptive are hypersomnia, nightmares and insomnia (Bixler *et al.*, 1979), and sometimes snoring.

Snoring, when it interrupts the client's airflow (a condition known as obstructive sleep apnoea), can impair the quality and quantity of sleep. At least thirty such episodes of ten seconds each are said to define this condition (Jennett, 1984). Investigation thus requires careful observation by an independent party. People who habitually snore during sleep may be exposed to increased risk from cardiovascular disease (D'Allesandra and Magelli, 1990), although the causal relationship between these problems is not clear.

INSOMNIA

Insomnia is probably the most common disorder of sleep (Bixler *et al.*, 1979). It may affect as many as 35 per cent of adults at any one time, and as many as 50 per cent may have suffered from the problem (ibid.). Elderly people and women are more liable to suffer from insomnia (ibid.), but estimates of the incidence vary considerably. Of particular interest to clinical psychologists is the increased likelihood of insomnia in depressed clients (Williams and Karacan, 1973). Insomnia has been linked with poor physical health, abuse of drugs and alcohol, and impaired efficiency at work and in social relationships (Lacks and Morin, 1992).

Insomnia can be experienced as frequent occurrence of the following: delay in falling asleep (sleep-onset insomnia), which is probably the most common form of insomnia (Roth *et al.*, 1976), insufficient duration of sleep, frequent awakenings (sleep maintenance insomnia), early final awakening (terminal insomnia), lack of enjoyment in sleeping, feeling tired after sleeping, falling asleep readily during the day and experiencing poor performance in diurnal activities following unsatisfactory sleep (Monroe, 1967; Coates *et al.*, 1982; Thoresen *et al.*, 1981). Insomniacs may report only one or many of these complaints.

It would appear that it is the subject's dissatisfaction with sleep which has been the outstanding criterion for identifying insomnia, certainly in all the studies reported here and in the succeeding chapter, because there have been notable instances of subjects who have apparently been none the worse for habitually sleeping for only three hours per night (Jones and Oswald, 1968).

Moreover, most of the studies of insomnia available for this review have examined subjects who have been recruited by some form of advertisement. They may therefore differ in a number of critical but indeterminate ways from people who experience difficulties in sleeping but who do not volunteer for research. In addition, such sampling would not include subjects who have trouble in falling and remaining asleep according to EEG criteria but, like the two cases reported by Jones and Oswald (1968), do not experience corresponding difficulties. Hence it is probable that cases of insomnia will come to the attention of clinical psychologists, because the clients believe that they have difficulties in sleeping.

Many adults who complain of insomnia overestimate the time it takes them to fall asleep and underestimate the total duration of their sleep (Frankel *et al.*, 1976; Carskadon *et al.*, 1976; Franklin, 1981) in comparison with EEG, other objective criteria and the reports of observers. Borkovec *et al.* (1981) have reported that many insomniac subjects wakened from stage 2 sleep report that they have not been asleep.

Trinder (1988) has reviewed the evidence which had suggested (Borkovec, 1979) that it may be appropriate to identify two classes of insomniacs: pseudo (experiential) insomniacs, who complain of sleeping difficulties but who have little or no corresponding objective evidence of this; and idiopathic (objective) insomniacs who, by EEG and other criteria, do have difficulties in falling and staying asleep. Borkovec *et al.* (1979) identified pseudo insomniacs as those subjects who reported time to the onset of sleep that was consistently at least one and a half times as long as the time to the onset of their stage 1 EEG. Objective insomniacs were those whose corresponding ratios were less than one and a half.

THEORIES OF INSOMNIA

There are several theories which have attempted to explain the occurrence of insomnia (Borkovec, 1979; Espie, 1991). Some concentrate on hypotheses about the EEG characteristics of sleep in insomniacs (Gillard, 1976) but only those which have influenced the development of behavioural treatments will be described here briefly. This will be done mainly by describing differences between insomniacs and non-insomniacs.

A number of authors have sought to distinguish between primary insomnia and secondary insomnia that results from psychiatric disturbances such as depression and psychosis (Williams and Karacan, 1979). Bixler *et al.*, (1979) found that 35 per cent of adults who complained of difficulty in falling asleep had required some help for an emotional problem in the previous year. Insomnia may be secondary to physical illness also. Bixler *et al.*, (op. cit.) found that 60 per cent of insomniacs had a recurring general health problem, 22 per cent having had to go to hospital for this in the previous year.

Unfortunately, in many cases it may be difficult to distinguish cause and effect in variables which are correlated with insomnia and which distinguish insomniacs from others. For example, a number of studies have suggested that insomniacs are frequently affected by troublesome thoughts in the delay before sleep (Lichstein and Rosenthal, 1980; Van Egeren *et al.*, 1983). This may be the consequence of lying awake and worrying about not being able to sleep and/or it may be the cause, as most subjects believe, of difficulty in falling asleep.

Freedman and Sattler (1982) asked insomniacs and non-insomniac subjects to describe their thinking on five occasions during a fifteen-minute period before sleeping. They had to say whether their thinking was real or unreal, in or out of control, repetitive or otherwise, pleasant or unpleasant, and how anxiety-provoking. A five-point rating of consciousness was also completed. It must be difficult to give such information when about to fall asleep, and none of these measures had any proven validity or reliability. Moreover, the reactive effects of these procedures, which might include delaying the onset of sleep, are not clear. There were, in any case no differences in these cognitive variables between the groups.

Van Egeren *et al.* (1983) found that subjects' beliefs about the reasons for their difficulties in falling asleep (their attributions recorded in an interview before the study) predicted their estimates of habitual delays in falling asleep. The content of subjects' reported thoughts (thoughts favouring sleep, such as thinking about feeling drowsy; neutral thoughts or anti-sleep thoughts) predicted the time to fall asleep reported by subjects in the laboratory. No variable of thought-content or attribution of sleep difficulties was significantly associated with objective measures of time to sleep onset.

There have been several studies of the personalities of insomniacs suggesting that more of them can be described as highly neurotic or chronically anxious than normative controls (Coursey *et al.*, 1975; Haynes *et al.*, 1974; Frankel *et al.*, 1973) but other studies have not found this (e.g. Gering and Mahrer, 1972). Some studies have indicated that insomniacs show greater physiological activity in some variables than controls up to the point of falling asleep (Monroe, 1967; Freedman and Sattler, 1982) especially in EMG (electromyogram) records. However, Good (1975) found no significant correlations between measures of

EMG and time to sleep onset. The variance in the latter, however, might not have been sufficient in that study to obtain a significant correlation in any case. With all these studies, cause and effect relationships between insomnia and other variables are unclear.

A frequent and ironic contribution to the occurrence of insomnia results from hypnotic medication prescribed to promote sleep onset and reduce the frequency of awakening. Withdrawal of barbiturates and even the benzodiazepines such as Mogadon (nitrazepam) and Temazepam (temazepam), which are now most frequently prescribed, can make it much more difficult for subjects to fall asleep than before being prescribed the medication (c.f. Kales *et al.*, 1978). In addition, the hypnotic effect of such medication can be lost within two weeks of its continuous use and may be associated with even greater difficulties in falling asleep (ibid.). This may result in demands from the client for increased dosages. This leads to further tolerance, and so on (Williams, 1980).

INFLUENCES ON INSOMNIA: CONCLUSIONS AND RECOMMENDATIONS

The numerous factors which may retard the onset and reduce the quantity and quality of sleep are summarised in Table 30.1. Because the preceding discussion has been unable to make many reliable generalisations about the variables which contribute to insomnia, single-case experimentation (see Morley, Chapter 37) will be necessary to evaluate the contribution of certain variables for each client. A Sleep Disturbance Questionnaire (Espie *et al.*, 1989) has been developed to distinguish different types of insomnia determined by certain client variables: the experience of high physical tension, continuous worry before sleep, and pre-sleep activity incompatible with sleep. No test-retest reliability has been reported for this measure (Espie, 1991), and so the assumption that insomniacs do consistently describe their difficulties in these ways remains to be tested.

SUBJECTIVE MEASURES OF INSOMNIA

Most behavioural studies have relied on self-report of insomnia variables which have shown acceptable test-retest reliability equivalent to that of EEG variables (Coates *et al.*, 1982).

When, as in most cases, the complaint of insomnia is expressed by the client, it is important for him or her to keep a sleep diary in which daily accounts of the variables shown in Table 30.2. are entered. A baseline period of at least two weeks will probably be necessary.

The client's partner or room-mate can keep a similar record of the first two variables. After collecting baseline data, it will be desirable to ask the client to discontinue taking hypnotic medication and to try and reduce day-time naps.

Independent variables (Table 30.1) should also be recorded on a chart marked with half-hourly intervals. Other useful self-report measures already available

Table 30.1 Variables which can influence sleep

Excessive caffeine intake (e.g. coffee, tea)

Hypnotic medication: tolerance from prolonged use (2 weeks +); withdrawal of

Incompatible bedtime activities (e.g. reading in bed, eating in bed, busy
     preparation for the next day)

Heavy meals shortly before bedtime

Vigorous physical exercise shortly before bedtime

Worry (e.g. about not being able to sleep; about effect of sleep loss on
     day-time work; about events in sleep such as myoclonic spasm)

Chronic anxiety evident also in day-time

Unpredictable sensory stimulation (noise, light, etc.)

Significant signals (e.g. child crying; sounds of morning awakening in others in
     the household)

Disturbance of activity–rest cycles (e.g. changes from day to night shift)

Established night-shift working/day-time sleeping

Intense sensory stimulation (e.g. high temperature/humidity)

Oversleeping during day-time

Chronic physical health problems (e.g. producing chronic pain such as
     toothache or backache)

Frequent need for urination (e.g. as side effect of medication, or from physical
     problems, such as enlargement of the prostate gland)

Side effects of medication for chronic health problems

Psychiatric problems, especially depression

Respiratory difficulties (e.g. obstructive sleep apnoea)

Day-time stress

Nocturnal panics

include the Leeds Sleep Evaluation questionnaire (Parrott and Hindmarch, 1980) and the Stanford Sleepiness Scale (Hoddes *et al.*, 1973).

OBJECTIVE MEASURES OF INSOMNIA

Unfortunately, EEG recording equipment is rarely available to clinicians for recording data corresponding to the variables noted in the preceding section. Adequate EEG sleep-recording (Williams *et al.* 1974; Rosekind *et al.*, 1978) is probably too expensive as yet for such purposes. Hence other devices have been devised for the objective recording of insomnia. For all such devices the clinician should be aware of possible reactive effects, especially in their delaying sleep when they are first used (e.g. Schmidt and Kaelbling, 1971; Coates *et al.*, 1979). Recording of EEG is, nevertheless, still desirable for research purposes and for detecting certain disorders, such as obstructive sleep apnoea, a form of

Table 30.2 Variables to be recorded in a daily sleep diary

On rising from each night's sleep with the aid of a bedside clock, the client records
1 The time when the lights were put out
2 The time when he or she believes that he or she fell asleep
3 An estimate of the total duration of sleep
4 An estimate of the total number of awakenings
5 The time of final awakening
6 Satisfaction with the night's sleep (a rating scale of up to 11 points, 'no satisfaction' to 'maximum possible satisfaction'). Alternatively the client can provide a rating of how rested he or she felt on waking (cf. Chapter 1)
Recorded during the day:
7 The occurrence and duration of day-time naps

respiratory interruption during sleep, and nocturnal myoclonus (involuntary muscle spasm).

Franklin (1981) has described a device with a switch which the client has to keep pressed in order to keep a clock running. The automatic release of the switch when the client falls asleep stops the clock to record sleep onset latency. Records with this device have corresponded to observer's estimates of the subject's time to fall asleep (ibid.). An improved version allows for the client's accidental release of the switch before sleep onset (Viens *et al.*, 1988).

Kelley and Lichstein (1980) have described a Sleep Assessment Device (SAD) where a repeated 'soft' auditory signal at ten-minute intervals from a tape recording requires the client to give a reply which is itself recorded. This monitors time to fall asleep, number of subsequent awakenings and duration of each awakening. Subjects have reported that the SAD did not disturb their sleep (Lichstein *et al.*, 1982). The number of awakenings immediately following the tone was similar to the number which preceded it.

The most commonly used procedure in clinical practice, however, has been estimates by observers of subjects' time to fall asleep. The observers may call the client's name at intervals until the client no longer responds. Unfortunately, this procedure is unreliable for clients who take a long time to fall asleep: the observer falls asleep before the client (Coates *et al.*, 1982).

There appear to be no reliable guidelines or normative data to suggest when the complaint of insomnia is severe enough to justify behaviourial intervention. Indeed, because of the many variables which influence sleep and because of the uncertainty about the function of sleep and its many characteristics, normative data would be difficult to obtain (Webb and Cartwright, 1978).

In adults up to the age of 40, if the client is concerned about delay in sleep onset of forty minutes or more, or less than six and a half hours sleep on more than two nights per week, treatment would probably be desirable.

OTHER ABNORMALITIES OF SLEEP

Detailed analysis of investigative procedures for less frequent disorders, such as nocturnal bruxism (see Glaros and Rao, 1977), abnormal body and head movement (Lindsay *et al.*, 1982), sleep-walking (*British Medical Journal*, 1980) and night terrors (Carlson *et al.*, 1982), is beyond the scope of this chapter, largely because there are few tested psychological treatment interventions. However, a number of reviews (op. cit.) deal with aetiological issues both biological and behavioural, environmental influences and monitoring procedures.

All these problems are often especially disturbing to the client's partners and family who might therefore be the primary sources of data. The influence of independent variables (Table 30.1) on these problems could be investigated by single-case experimentation.

Excessive time spent in sleep is a common complaint amongst young people (Bixler *et al.*, 1979). Investigators should ensure that excessive sleepiness during the day is not the result of night-time insomnia. However, in two conditions, subjects can find it almost impossible to stay awake even after a night's sleep: narcolepsy (Empson, 1989) and in some cases of post-viral debility (Guilleminault and Mondin, 1986). Again there are probably no satisfactory psychological treatments for either problem. Psychologists may have a role in helping clients to adjust to these afflictions.

Obstructive sleep apnoea, for which there are some psychological interventions (see Chapter 31), can be a cause of insomnia (Empson, 1989).

Finally, Fenwick (1986) has drawn attention to the need to distinguish between activities occurring during dreaming (REM sleep) and during night terrors (deep sleep). He comments on a case in which a man, who had murdered his wife, put forward the defence that he had committed the act during a dream which he described in detail. This explanation is at odds with the muscular paralysis (Empson, 1989) during REM sleep and with the common inability to recall the content of dreaming during night terrors when complex body movement is possible.

REFERENCES

American Psychiatric Association (1987) *Diagnostic and Statistical Manual of Mental Disorders, 3rd edn Rev.*, Washington, DC: American Psychiatric Association.

Berger, R. J. and Oswald, I. (1962) 'Effects of sleep deprivation on behaviour, subsequent sleep and dreaming', *Journal of Mental Science* 108: 457–65.

Bixler, E. O., Kales, A., Soldatos, C. R., Kales, J. D. and Healey, S. (1979) 'Prevalence of sleep disorders in the Los Angeles Metropolitan area', *American Journal of Psychiatry* 136: 1257–62.

Borkovec, T. D. (1979) 'Pseudo (experiential) insomnia and idiopathic (objective) insomnia: theoretical and therapeutic issues', *Advances in Behaviour Research and Therapy* 136: 1257–62.

Borkovec, T. D., Grayson, J. B., O'Brien, G. T. and Weerts, T. C. (1979) 'Relaxation treatment of pseudo insomnia and idiopathic insomnia: an electroencephalographic evaluation', *Journal of Applied Behaviour Analysis* 12: 37–54.

Borkovec, T. D., Lane, T. W. and van Oot, P. H. (1981) 'Phenomenology of sleep among insomniacs and good sleepers: wakefulness experience when cortically asleep', *Journal of Abnormal Psychology* 90: 607–9.

British Medical Journal (1980) 'Unquiet sleep', *British Medical Journal* 281: 1660–1.

Bunnell, D. E., Bevier, W. and Horvath, S. M. (1983) 'Effects of exhaustive exercise on the sleep of men and women', *Psychophysiology* 20: 50–8.

Carlson, C. R., White, D. K. and Turkat, I. D. (1982) 'Night terrors: a clinical and empirical review', *Clinical Psychology Review* 2: 455–68.

Carskadon, M. A., Dement, W. C., Mittler, M. M., Guilleminault, C., Zarcone, V. P. and Spiegel, R. (1976) 'Self-reports v. sleep laboratory findings in 122 drug-free subjects with complaints of chronic insomnia', *American Journal of Psychiatry* 133: 1382–7.

Coates, T. J., Rosekind, M. R., Strossen, R. J., Thoreson, C. E. and Kirmil-Gray, K. (1979) 'Sleep recordings in the laboratory and home: a comparative analysis', *Psychophysiology* 16: 339–46.

Coates, T. J., Killen, J. D., George, J., Marchini, E., Silverman, S., Thoreson, C. (1982) 'Estimating sleep parameters: a multi trait–multimethod analysis', *Journal of Consulting and Clinical Psychology* 50: 345–52.

Coursey, R. D., Bucksbaum, M. and Frankel, B. L. (1975) 'Personality measures and evoked responses in chronic insomniacs', *Journal of Abnormal Psychology* 84: 239–49.

D'Allesandra, R. and Magelli, C. (1990) 'Snoring every night as risk of myocardial infarction: a case-control study', *British Medical Journal* 300: 1557–8.

Empson, J. (1989) *Sleep and Dreaming*, London: Faber and Faber.

✕ Espie, C. A. (1991) *The Psychological Treatment of Insomnia*, Chichester: Wiley.

Espie, C. A., Brooks, D. N. and Lindsay, W. R. (1989) 'An evaluation of tailored psychological treatment for insomnia', *Journal of Behavior Therapy and Experimental Psychiatry* 20: 143–53.

Fenwick, P. (1986) 'Murdering while asleep', *British Medical Journal* 293: 574–5.

Frankel, B. L., Buchbinder, R., Coursey, R. D. and Snyder, F. (1973) 'Sleep patterns and psychological test characteristics of chronic primary insomniacs', *Sleep Research* 2: 149.

Frankel, B. L., Coursey, R. D., Buchbinder, R. and Snyder, F. (1976) 'Recorded and reported sleep in chronic primary insomnia', *Archives of General psychiatry* 33: 615–20.

Franklin, J. (1981) 'The measurement of sleep onset latency in insomnia', *Behaviour Research and Therapy* 19: 541–8.

Freedman, R. R. and Sattler, H. L. (1982) 'Physiological and psychological factors in sleep-onset insomnia', *Journal of Abnormal psychology* 91: 380–9.

Gering, R. C. and Mahrer, A. R. (1972) 'Difficulty in falling asleep', *Psychological Reports* 30: 523–8.

Gillard, J. M. (1976) 'Is insomnia a disease of slow wave sleep?', *European Neurology* 14: 473–84.

Glaros, A. G. and Rao, S. M. (1977) 'Bruxism: a critical review', *Psychological Bulletin* 84: 767–81.

Good, R. (1975) 'Frontalis muscle tension and sleep latency', *Psychophysiology* 12: 465–67.

Guilleminault, C. and Mondin, S. (1986) 'Mononucleosis and chronic day-time sleepiness', *Archives of Internal Medicine* 146: 1333–5.

Hartmann, E. L. (1973) *The Functions of Sleep*, New Haven, Conn.: Yale University Press.

Haynes, S. N., Follingstad, D. and McGowan, W. (1974) 'Insomnia: sleep patterns and anxiety level', *Journal of Psychosomatic Research* 10: 431–6.

✕ Hoddes, E., Zarcone, V., Smythe, V., Phillips, R. and Dement, W. C. (1973) 'Quantification of sleepiness: A new approach', *Psychophysiology* 10: 431–6.

Horne, J. A. and Porter, J. M. (1976) 'Time of day effects with standardised exercise upon subsequent sleep', *Electroencephalography and Clinical Neurophysiology* 40: 178–84.

Jennett, S. (1984) 'Snoring and its treatment', *British Medical Journal* 289: 335–6.

Johns, M. W. (1970) 'Sleep habits and symptoms in male medical and surgical patients', *British Medical Journal* 2: 509–12.

Johnson, L. I. (1982) 'Sleep deprivation and performance', in W. Webb (ed.) *Biological Rhythms, Sleep and Performance*, New York: John Wiley.

Jones, H. S. and Oswald, I. (1968) 'Two cases of healthy insomnia', *Electroencephalography and Clinical Neurophysiology* 24: 378.

Kales, A., Scharf, M. and Kales, J. (1978) 'Rebound insomnia: a new clinical syndrome', *Science* 201: 1039–41.

Kelley, J. E. and Lichstein, K. L. (1980) 'A sleep assessment device', *Behavioural Assessment* 2: 135–46.

Kleitman, N. (1963) *Sleep and Wakefulness*, Chicago: University of Chicago Press.

Lacks, P. and Morin, C. M. (1992) 'Recent advances in the assessment and treatment of insomnia', *Journal of Consulting and Clinical Psychology* 60: 586–94.

Lichstein, K. L. and Rosenthal, T. L. (1980) 'Insomniacs' perceptions of cognitive vs. somatic determinants of sleep disturbance', *Journal of Abnormal Psychology* 89: 105–7.

Lichstein, K. L., Nickel, R., Hoelscher, T. J. and Kelley, J. E. (1982) 'Clinical validation of a sleep assessment device', *Behaviour Research and Therapy* 20: 292–8.

Lindsay, S. J. E., Salkovskis, P. M. and Stoll, K. (1982) 'Rhythmical body movement in sleep: a brief review and treatment study', *Behaviour Research and Therapy* 20: 523–6.

Marks, I. M. (1981) *The Care and Cure of Neurosis*, New York: John Wiley.

Monroe, L. J. (1967) 'Psychological and physiological differences between good and poor sleepers', *Journal of Abnormal Psychology* 72: 255–64.

Parrott, A. C. and Hindmarch, I. (1980) 'The Leeds Sleep Evaluation Questionnaire in psychopharmacological investigations: a review', *Psychopharmacology* 71: 173–9.

Rosekind, M. R. *et al.* (1978) 'Telephone transmission of polysomnographic data from subjects' homes', *Journal of Nervous and Mental Disease* 166: 448–51.

Roth, T., Kramer, M. and Lutz, T. (1976) 'The nature of insomnia. A descriptive summary of a sleep clinic population', *Comprehensive Psychiatry* 17: 217–20.

Schmidt, H. S. and Kaelbling, R. (1971) 'The differential laboratory adaptation of sleep parameters', *Biological Psychiatry* 3: 33.

Schmidt-Kessen, W. and Kendel, W. (1973) 'Influence of room temperature on night sleep in man', *Research in Experimental Medicine* 160: 220–33.

Sheiham, A. and Croog, S. H. (1981) 'The psychosocial impact of dental diseases on individuals and communities', *Journal of Behavioural Medicine* 4: 257–72.

Southwell, P. R., Evans, C. R. and Hunt, J. N. (1972) 'Effect of a hot milk drink on movement during sleep', *British Medical Journal* 2: 429–31.

Tepas, D. I. (1982) 'Work/Sleep time schedules and performance', in W. B. Webb (ed.) *Biological Rhythms, Sleep and Performance*, New York: John Wiley.

Thoresen, C. E., Coates, T. J., Kirnil-Grey, H. and Rosekind, M. R. (1981) 'Behavioural self-management in treating sleep maintenance insomnia', *Journal of Behavioural Medicine* 4: 41.

Trinder, J. (1988) 'Subjective insomnia without object findings: a pseudo-diagnostic classification?' *Psychological Bulletin* 103: 87–94.

Van Egeren, L., Hagner, S. N, Franzen, M. and Hamilton, J. (1983) 'Presleep cognitions and attributions in sleep onset insomnia', *Journal of Medicine* 6: 217–32.

Viens, M., De Koninck, J., Van den Bergen, R., Audet, R. and Christ, G. (1988) 'A refined switch-activated time monitor for the measurement of sleep-onset latency', *Behaviour Research and Therapy* 26: 271–4.

Webb, W. B. and Cartwright, R. D. (1978) 'Sleep and dreams', *Annual Review of Psychology* 29: 223–52.

Williams, R. L. (1980) 'Sleeping-pill insomnia', *Journal of Clinical Psychiatry* 41: 153–4.

Williams, R. L. and Karacan, I. (1973) 'Clinical disorders of sleep', in G. Usden (ed.) *Sleep Research and Clinical Practice*, New York: Brunner/Mazel.

Williams, R. L. and Karacan, I. (eds) (1979) *Sleep Disorders: Diagnosis and Treatment*, New York: John Wiley.

Williams, R. L., Karacan, I. and Hursch, C. J. (1974) *EEG of Human Sleep: Clinical Applications*, New York: John Wiley.

Williams, R. L. and Salamy, A. (1972) 'Alcohol and sleep', in B. Kissin and H. Begleiter (eds) *The Biology of Alcoholism 2*, New York: Plenum Press.

Chapter 31

Disorders of sleep
Treatment

S.J.E. Lindsay

INTRODUCTION

As insomnia is one of the most prevalent (Bixler *et al.*, 1979) and troublesome of sleep disorders, this chapter will concentrate on interventions for that problem. This is appropriate also because the treatment of insomnia has been investigated probably more comprehensively than the treatment of any other sleep disorder.

INSOMNIA

Pharmacological treatments

Undoubtedly, the ubiquitous treatment of insomnia is hypnotic medication and especially by benzodiazepines, such as triazolam, flunitrazepam, temazepam and flurazepam. The last of these has been recommended because it can retain its effectiveness throughout one month of continuous use (Kales *et al.*, 1975). It is also exceptional in that it usually does not, when withdrawn, produce 'rebound insomnia', a greater difficulty in sleeping than before the onset of treatment (Lader and Lawson, 1987; Kales *et al.*, 1983). Nevertheless, flurazepam, like other hypnotics, disrupts REM sleep, dreaming and the time spent in deep sleep (Kales *et al.*, 1975).

The hypnotic effect of benzodiazepines is lost within weeks of their first being taken: the development of tolerance. There is a widespread risk of over-dosing especially in anxious and depressed clients, who may be the most likely to be referred with insomnia to psychologists. Such clients may have become dependent on hypnotic medication. Some benzodiazepines, such as flurazepam, are eliminated only slowly from the body and so make subjects drowsy, impairing performance of tasks such as driving throughout the day (Cormack *et al.*, 1989; Kales and Kales, 1987). On the other hand, short-acting benzodiazepines may not allow subjects to sustain a full night's sleep. Withdrawal effects are numerous and distressing: anxiety during the day, great difficulty in sleeping, nightmares, depression, tremulousness, nausea, perceptual disturbances, such as hypersensitivity to stimuli, muscular aches, numbness, profuse sweating and headaches (Cormack *et al.*, op. cit.). For all these reasons, therefore, safe, effective alternatives to pharmacological treatment are highly desirable.

The need to withdraw patients from hypnotic medication

Withdrawal symptoms can persist for several weeks after the discontinuation of hypnotic medication. These symptoms often convince patients that they need the medication in order to sleep. Worse still, if patients undergo withdrawal during psychological treatment, they may attribute their distress to the psychological treatment itself or, at best, believe that psychological treatment is ineffective. Therefore, withdrawal should be complete before psychological treatment is attempted.

Most patients probably prefer to have their medication withdrawn gradually (Cormack *et al.*, 1989). Support in groups of clients withdrawing from hypnotics may be helpful (ibid.). Information about the effect of hypnotics on sleep (see preceding section) and their withdrawal effects has been recommended (Espie, 1991) under the headings: 'What sleeping pills do to your sleep'; 'What happens when you stop'; and 'Will you make it without them?' (this includes information about psychological treatment).

Psychological treatment of insomnia: further preliminaries

Investigation (see preceding chapter) may reveal that certain environmental influences have been impairing a client's sleep. For example, one client reported that her bed was next to a wall, which was adjacent to the main staircase in her block of flats. Not only was her sleep disturbed by latecomers, but it was also interrupted early in the morning by people going to work. A move to a quiet room was appropriate. Once all similar impediments to sleep have been removed, the following widely recommended practices should be followed, regardless of the psychological treatment proposed:

1 A set routine at a set time should be established in the hour or more before going to bed.
2 This routine should avoid, wherever possible, rousing activities; thus preparation for the next day, such as making sandwiches, should be done before this winding-down phase.
3 Naps should be avoided outside the main period of sleep.

Relaxation training as a treatment for sleep-onset insomnia

Given that the onset of sleep is characterised as a reduction in physical and cognitive activity, it would not be surprising if those procedures which have a similar effect in waking subjects were suitable for the treatment of insomnia.

Indeed, progressive muscular relaxation training (Espie *et al.*, 1989a), desensitisation (Steinmark and Borkovec, 1974), bio-feedback-assisted relaxation (Nicassio *et al.*, 1982), meditation (Woolfolk *et al.*, 1976) and autogenic training (Nicassio and Bootzin, 1974) have all been shown to have some favourable effects.

A number of studies reviewed in the previous edition of this chapter (Lindsay, 1987) have suggested that relaxation training has optimum effects on the experience of tension and its physiological correlates if the following are observed:

1 It is conducted over more than one session, the recommended number varying considerably from about four to ten (Bernstein and Borkovec, 1973), and many more (Lehrer, 1982).
2 It is at least supervised by the clinician (tape-recordings providing the instruction) or, better, conducted entirely by the therapist (Lehrer, 1982).
3 Tension exercises are included in training (see below).
4 There is a more than minimal (but indeterminate) level of prevailing tension or physical activity.
5 The relaxation is practised at home (Hillenberg and Collins, 1983) with the aid of audiotapes.
6 The subject has some control over training.

The coupling of EMG feedback, perhaps the most radical innovation in relaxation training conducted by the therapist, produces little further benefit (Beiman *et al.*, 1978). Focusing attention on physical sensations probably also produces no additional advantage.

The following is an example of relaxation instructions recommended by Morris (1985) and similar to procedures described by Bernstein and Borkovec (1973):

> 'Now hold your arms out and make a tight fist. Really tight. Feel the tension in your hands. I am going to count to three and when I say "three" I want you to drop your hands . . .
>
> 'Now put your tongue at the roof of your mouth. Press hard. (Pause) Relax and allow your tongue to come to a comfortable position in your mouth . . .'
>
> This tension-release cycle is repeated for many muscle groups throughout the body until finally the client is asked to 'make sure every muscle is relaxed – first your toes, your feet, your legs . . . shoulders, neck . . . forehead'. The clinician should make sure that the client continues to breathe in and out slowly.

With a few subjects who may find such tension-release exercises unpleasant (Heide and Borkovec, 1984), it may be advisable to concentrate on other techniques of relaxing, such as those focusing on pleasant imagery or meditation or autogenic instructions.

Borkovec and his colleagues have produced a series of studies supporting the efficacy of such tension-release relaxation in the treatment of insomnia (Borkovec *et al.*, 1975; Steinmark and Borkovec, 1974; Borkovec and Weerts, 1976; Borkovec *et al.*, 1979). The most consistent effects are in the improvement in the time which subjects take to fall asleep, this being apparent in both the reports from the clients themselves (Steinmark and Borkovec, 1974; Borkovec *et al.*, 1975) and in time to stage 1 of EEG sleep records (Borkovec and Weerts, 1976).

These effects are evident in counter-demand phases, where subjects are warned not to expect improvement, as well as in positive demand phases of treatment. Follow-up of subjects indicates that these effects are maintained up to five months after treatment (Steinmark and Borkovec, 1974; Borkovec *et al.*, 1975).

Borkovec's studies have been conducted mostly in young university volunteers with only moderate trouble in sleeping. Hence it is encouraging that Carr-Kaffashan and Woolfolk (1979) found that insomniacs, average age 40 years, recruited by advertisement from the community, fell asleep more quickly by an average of 46 per cent of baseline with relaxation-meditation training. This improvement was significantly greater than in a placebo treatment during a counter-demand phase. These insomniacs had had severe sleeping difficulties, having required 90 minutes or more to fall asleep on most nights according to their reports.

The study by Espie *et al.* (1989a) is less encouraging in that relaxation training was not effective in reducing time to fall asleep reported by patients referred by their doctors for treatment of chronic insomnia. Progressive relaxation did have a significant benefit on feelings of rest following sleep.

Carr-Kaffashan and Woolfolk (1979) claim also that there was no difference between severe and moderate insomniacs in the extent of improvement with relaxation-meditation. This is surprising since the severe insomniacs who were treated in this way improved by 50 per cent of baseline. Having taken just under 160 minutes on average to fall asleep, they were taking less than 80 minutes at the end of the counter-demand period.

The moderate insomniacs treated by relaxation-meditation changed for the better by approximately 30 per cent of baseline from about 60 minutes' to 40 minutes' delay in falling asleep. In absolute terms there may have been a much greater improvement for the severe insomniacs. However, it would appear that the sampling error in the data and the small number of subjects (only eight severe and eight moderate insomniacs) made it impossible to support that effect statistically. Relaxation training can substantially improve time to fall asleep in severe insomniacs even when they are led to expect no improvement (the counter-demand). However, recent studies have shown less impressive effects, possibly because more resistant subjects are being studied (Lacks and Morin, 1992).

Where relaxation is effective in reducing the time to fall asleeep, the mechanism of the effect has not been established (Borkovec, 1979; Coates and Thoresen, 1981). There has been no evident relationship between the extent of change in EMG activity and improvement in time to fall asleep, as Nicassio *et al.* (1982) have shown in a study of EMG bio-feedback and relaxation training. Hence there is no consistent support for the requirement that muscular activity should be reduced in order that insomniacs will report less difficulty in falling asleep.

There is also evidence that a wide range of conditions, including 'placebo' treatments, not amounting to progressive relaxation, are as effective as that treatment (Carr-Kafashan and Woolfolk, 1979; Nicassio et al., 1982), at least by subjects' reports.

Most of the studies quoted here have required the subjects to practise relaxation and similar activities in bed. The monotonous activity which this entails would also foster the onset of sleep (Bohlin, 1973). A doctoral project (Nau, 1977) has demonstrated that this effect is more pronounced where the subject is instructed to focus attention on such stimuli.

Similar mechanisms may also explain the moderate efficacy of insomniacs focusing their attention on visual imagery (Woolfolk and McNulty, 1983). Alternatively, relaxation and other treatment may work because they disrupt the worry which insomniacs believe impedes their sleep (see Chapter 30).

Conclusions

Training and practice in progressive muscular relaxation according to recommendations outlined in the preceding section can produce significant benefits for insomniacs in reducing the time to fall asleep and also in feelings of rest after sleep. However, it is not at all clear how this works. It may not be necessary to be especially competent in reducing tension and muscular activity to achieve this effect. In addition, the effects may not be large, and severe insomniacs may still take much longer than control subjects to fall asleep.

Stimulus control for sleep-onset insomnia

Hypotheses about stimulus control assume that, for insomniacs, bed and its surroundings have become a signal for being unable to fall asleep: for the worry and irritation with which that is associated. Attention is also drawn to other activities which at bedtime could be incompatible with sleep. Treatment therefore should produce, for the activity of going to bed, sleep as reinforcement. The characteristics of a stimulus-control programme are summarised in Table 31.1.

Turner and Ascher (1979) have reported a series of six subjects who fell asleep more quickly with a stimulus-control programme than in a baseline period according to their own reports. The stimulus-control procedure was also more effective than a quasi-desensitisation treatment. Espie et al. (1989a) showed that stimulus control, unlike relaxation, did reduce the time to fall asleep in a small sample of chronic insomniacs referred by their doctors.

Puder et al. (1983) describe the effects of stimulus control in elderly insomniacs, average age 67 years. The clients were required not to take naps during the day and to rise at a regular pre-determined time each morning. The subjects reported in sleep diaries that time to fall asleep decreased from over 60

Table 31.1 The characteristics of a stimulus-control programme for insomnia

1　Activities, incompatible with sleep, such as listening to the radio or eating, should be avoided in bed.

2　The bedroom should be used only for sleep.

3　The subject is advised not to go to bed until feeling sleepy. Care should be taken to ensure that the act of going to bed does not include activities, such as running upstairs or changing in a very cold room, which might rouse the subject at this time.

4　If the subject is then unable to fall asleep within ten minutes, he or she should get out of bed, move to another room and only return to bed when ready to fall asleep. (It is important to ensure that this room is not at a noticeably different temperature from that of the bedroom.)

5　Stage 4 should be repeated if sleep does not then occur.

6　The subject should wake with an alarm and rise at the same time each day.

7　He or she should not take naps.

minutes on average to about 30 minutes, an effect maintained at six-week follow-up. The study is especially notable because it has paid attention to the insomnia in elderly subjects for whom improvement has been regarded as less promising with behavioural treatment (Nicassio and Bootzin, 1974; Alperson and Biglan, 1979).

In conclusion, several studies, all using small samples, have shown that stimulus control can be a useful treatment for sleep-onset insomnia, and it may be especially worth considering for elderly subjects. However, as with relaxation training, the mechanisms of the beneficial effects are not understood. It is possible that stimulus-control programmes are effective because they deprive clients of sleep, which increases the likelihood of their falling asleep on returning to bed. Alternatively, or in addition, cognitive activity incompatible with sleep is curtailed by leaving the bedroom.

Other treatments for sleep-onset insomnia

Several other treatments have limited evidence to support their efficacy: counter-conditioning, attribution training (Davison *et al.*, 1973), and paradoxical intention (Espie *et al.*, 1989a) in which the subject tries to stay awake as long as possible. This has been used following the failure of relaxation training (Ascher and Turner, 1979; Ascher and Efran, 1978).

Combining treatments

It is discouraging to learn from the report of Turner *et al.* (1983) that stimulus control plus relaxation may make it more difficult for subjects to fall asleep. However, Lacks and Morin (1992) note a number of studies which have used multiple treatments. This requires further study, because there is little evidence that this approach is consistently more effective than treatments applied singly.

Self-help treatment

Morawetz (1989) describes the use of an instructional audiotape for insomnia (sleep-onset and sleep-maintenance). The tape detailed the requirements of a programme for stimulus control (for sleep-onset insomnia), relaxation (for nocturnal waking) and the scheduling of sleep (for early final waking). It was recommended that subjects purchase their own relaxation tapes. They were provided with written relaxation instructions.

It is not clear how well the clients followed the instructions. However, there were modestly significant improvements in sleep onset and in early waking in comparison with subjects who remained untreated on a waiting-list. The way in which the data are presented makes it difficult to assess the magnitude of the effects. However, in consideration of the ease and economy with which relaxation and other instructions can be given on tape, this is an approach which should receive further consideration.

Tailoring treatments to clients' needs

Because subjects differ in the factors which they say impede their sleep, it would be appropriate to choose (as in the preceding section) for each client treatments which correspond to those influences. However, there is as yet (Lacks and Morin, 1992) little encouragement for the efficacy of this approach. Espie *et al.* (1989b) found that treatments selected to match subjects had no greater effect than treatments allocated to clients at random.

Treatment of sleep-maintenance insomnia

In one of the few studies of difficulties in maintaining sleep, Lacks *et al.* (1983), in a sample of only fifteen subjects, found that both stimulus control and a quasi-desensitisation programme, a placebo treatment, appeared to influence a number of variables which defined sleep maintenance, including number of awakenings and total time awake after sleep onset. However, there was no evidence to indicate the superiority of stimulus control over the quasi-desensitisation which has been shown elsewhere to be almost as effective as relaxation training.

Morin and Azrin (1987), in a sample of seven subjects, found that stimulus control reduced the duration of awakenings, reported by the subjects, more than imagery control given to another group. There was no significant effect on frequency of awakenings, possibly because these were too few to permit a significant change. However, there is no clear reason why stimulus control should prevent awakenings and thus reduce their frequency. In a similar study of elderly subjects (Morin and Azrin, 1988), stimulus control improved duration of time asleep.

The evidence from these studies is that stimulus control is probably the most versatile treatment for insomnia capable of hastening the onset and reducing the time awake after the onset of sleep.

The use of hypnotic drugs in psychological treatments

Several of the treatment studies quoted in the foregoing have asked subjects to stop taking hypnotic medication before the start of behavioural programmes, but insufficient data are available to say what effect on treatment was produced by such withdrawal. It is always advisable to complete withdrawal before starting psychological treatment as noted on p. 602.

Hypnotics have been used in a behavioural programme where the subjects, given a therapeutic dosage, were told instead that they were receiving an ineffective concentration (Davison *et al.*, 1973). Thus it was intended that subjects would attribute improvement in sleep patterns to their own devices and therefore maintain that improvement after the withdrawal of the medication. It is not clear if that would be effective where the client has already been taking hypnotics for insomnia.

OTHER DISORDERS OF SLEEP

The management and treatment of nocturnal enuresis have been described by Doleys (1977) and Sacks and DeLeon (1983). Sacks and DeLeon (op. cit.) have emphasised the value of follow-up and retraining where bell-and-pad techniques are used.

A similar method, using an alarm to wake the client, has been described by Lindsay *et al.* (1982) for the treatment of head- and body-rocking.

For the treatment of recurrent nightmares, there have been few studies (Blanes *et al.*, 1993), but relaxation and desensitisation have shown some success (Miller and DiPilato, 1983). The nature of the latter procedure in that study is not clear but probably involves desensitisation to the content of recurrent dreams. Blanes *et al.* (op. cit.) draw attention to suggestions that encouraging the client to see a different, that is, happy, ending to the nightmare would be a cognitive procedure worth considering.

Finally, where snoring appears to interrupt sleep, continuous positive airway pressure may be an appropriate treatment (Jennett, 1984). This requires a device which delivers air to the client at increased atmospheric pressure via a facial mask. A less invasive procedure using a tongue-retaining device has also been used to improve respiration (Cartwright *et al.*, 1988).

REFERENCES

Alperson, J. and Biglan, A. (1979) 'Self-administered treatment of sleep onset insomnia and the importance of age', *Behavior Therapy* 10: 347–56.

⤙ Ascher, L. M. and Efran, J. S. (1978) 'Use of paradoxical intention in a behavioural program for sleep onset insomnia', *Journal of Consulting and Clinical Psychology* 46: 547–50.

↖ Ascher, L. M. and Turner, R. M. (1979) 'Paradoxical intention and insomnia: an experimental investigation', *Behaviour Research and Therapy* 17: 408–11.

Beiman, I., Israel, E. and Johnson, S. A. (1978) 'During training and post-training effects of live and taped extended progressive relaxation, self-relaxation and electromyogram biofeedback', *Journal of Consulting and Clinical Psychology* 46: 314–21.

Bernstein, D. A. and Borkovec, T. D. (1973) *Progressive Relaxation Training*, Champaign, Ill.: Research Press.

Bixler, E. O., Kales, A., Soldatos, C. R., Kales, J. D. and Healey, S. (1979) 'Prevalence of sleep disorders in the Los Angeles metropolitan area', *American Journal of Psychiatry* 136: 1257–62.

⟜ Blanes, T., Burgess, M., Marks, I. M. and Gill, M. (1993) 'Dream anxiety disorders (nightmares): a review', *Behavioural Psychotherapy* 21: 37–44.

Bohlin, G. (1973) 'Interaction of arousal and habituation in the development of sleep during monotonous stimulation', *Biological Psychology* 1: 99–114.

x Bootzin, R. R. and Nicassio, P. M. (1978) 'Behavioural treatments for insomnia', in M. Hersen *et al.*, (eds) *Progress in Behaviour Modification, vol. 6*, New York: Academic Press.

Borkovec, T. D. (1979) 'Pseudo (experiential) insomnia and idiopathic (objective) insomnia: theoretical and therapeutic issues', *Advances in Behaviour Research and Therapy* 2: 27–55.

Borkovec, T. D. and Weerts, T. C. (1976) 'Effects of progressive relaxation on sleep disturbance: an electroencephalographic evaluation', *Psychosomatic Medicine* 38: 173–80.

⟜ Borkovec, T. D., Kaloupek, D. G. and Slama, K. M. (1975) 'The facilitative effect of muscle tension-release in the relaxation treatment of sleep disturbance', *Behavior Therapy* 6: 301–9.

Borkovec, T. D., Grayson, J. B., O'Brien, G. T. and Weerts, T. C. (1979) 'Relaxation treatment of pseudo insomnia and idiopathic insomnia: an electroencephalographic evaluation', *Journal of Applied Behaviour Analysis* 12: 37–54.

⟜ Carr-Kaffashan, L. and Woolfolk, R. L. (1979) 'Active and placebo effects in treatment of moderate and severe insomnia', *Journal of Consulting and Clinical Psychology* 47: 1072–80.

Cartwright, R., Stefoski, D., Caldarelli, D., Kravitz, H., Knight, S., Lloyd, S. and Samuelson, C. (1988) 'Toward a treatment logic for sleep apnoea: the place of the Tongue Retaining Device', *Behaviour Research and Therapy* 26: 121–6.

⟜Coates, T. J. and Thoresen, C. E. (1981) 'Treating sleep disorders: few answers, some suggestions and many questions', in S. M. Turner, K. S. Calhoun and H. E. Adams, (eds) *Handbook of Clinical Behavior Therapy*, New York: John Wiley.

⟜Cormack, M., Owens, R. G. and Dewey, M. E. (1989) *Reducing Benzodiazepine Consumption*, New York: Springer-Verlag.

⟜ Davison, G. C., Tsujimoto, R. N. and Glaros, A. G. (1973) 'Attribution and the maintenance of behaviour change in falling asleep', *Journal of Abnormal Psychology* 82: 124–33.

Doleys, D. M. (1977) 'Behavioural treatments for nocturnal enuresis in children. A review of recent literature', *Psychological Bulletin* 84: 30–54.

Espie, C. A. (1991) *The Psychological Treatment of Insomnia*, Chichester: Wiley.

⟜Espie, C. A., Lindsay, W. R., Brooks, D. N., Hood, E. M. and Turvey, T. (1989a) 'A controlled comparative investigation of psychological treatments for chronic sleep-onset insomnia', *Behaviour Research and Therapy* 27: 79–88.

⟜Espie, C. A., Brooks, D. N. and Lindsay, W. R. (1989b) 'An evaluation of tailored psychological treatment of insomnia', *Journal of Behavior Therapy and Experimental Psychiatry* 20: 143–53.

Heide, F. J. and Borkovec, T. D. (1984) 'Relaxation-induced anxiety: mechanisms and theoretical implications', *Behaviour Research and Therapy* 22: 1–12.

Hillenberg, J. B. and Collins, F. L. (1983) 'The importance of home practice for progressive relaxation training', *Behaviour Research and Therapy* 21: 633–42.

Jennett, S. (1984) 'Snoring and its treatment', *British Medical Journal* 289: 335–6.

Kales, J. D. and Kales, A. (1987) 'Clinical selection of benzodiazepine hypnotics', *Psychiatric Medicine* 4: 229–41.

Kales, A., Kales, J. D., Bixler, E. O. and Scharf, M. M. (1975) 'Effectiveness of hypnotic drugs with prolonged use: flurazepam and pentobarbital', *Clinical Pharmacology and Therapeutics* 18: 356–63.

Kales, A., Soldatos, C. R., Bixler, E. O. and Kales, J. D. (1983) 'Rebound insomnia and rebound anxiety: a review', *Journal of Pharmacology* 26: 121–37.

Lacks, P. and Morin, C. M. (1992) 'Recent advances in the assessment and treatment of insomnia', *Journal of Consulting and Clinical Psychology* 60: 586–94.

Lacks, P., Bertelson, A. D., Sugerman, J. and Kunkel, J. (1983) 'The treatment of sleep-maintenance insomnia with stimulus control techniques', *Behaviour Research and Therapy* 21: 291–5.

Lader, M. and Lawson, C. (1987) 'Sleep studies and rebound insomnia: methodological problems, laboratory findings and clinical implications', *Clinical Neuropharmacology* 10: 291–312.

Lehrer, P. M. (1982) 'How to relax and how not to relax: a re-evaluation of the work of Edmund Jacobson – I', *Behaviour Research and Therapy* 20: 417–28.

Lindsay, S. J. E. (1987) 'Disorders of sleep: treatment', in S. Lindsay and G. Powell (eds) *A Handbook of Clinical Adult Psychology*, Aldershot: Gower.

Lindsay, S. J. E., Salkovskis, P. M. and Stoll, K. (1982) 'Rhythmical body movement in sleep: a brief review and treatment study', *Behaviour Research and Therapy* 20: 523–6.

Miller, W. R. and DiPilato, M. (1983) 'Treatment of nightmares via relaxation and desensitisation: a controlled evaluation', *Journal of Consulting and Clinical Psychology* 51: 870–7.

Morawetz, D. (1989) 'Behavioral self-help treatment for insomnia: a controlled evaluation', *Behavior Therapy* 20: 365–79.

Morin, C. M. and Azrin, N. H. (1987) 'Stimulus control and imagery training in treating sleep-maintenance insomnia', *Journal of Consulting and Clinical Psychology* 55: 260–2.

Morin, C. M. and Azrin, N. H. (1988) 'Behavioral and cognitive treatments of geriatric insomnia', *Journal of Consulting and Clinical Psychology* 56: 748–53.

Morris, R. J. (1985) 'Fear reduction methods', in F. H. Kanfer and A. P. Goldstein (eds) *Helping People Change, 3rd edn*, New York: Pergamon.

Nau, S. (1977) 'The soporific effect of monotonous stimulation as a function of instructional set and stimulus intensity', unpublished doctoral dissertation (quoted by Borkovec, 1979, q.v.).

Nicassio, P. and Bootzin, R. (1974) 'A comparison of progressive relaxation and autogenic training as treatments for insomnia', *Journal of Abnormal Psychology* 83: 253–60.

Nicassio, P. M., Boylan, M. B. and McCabe, T. G. (1982) 'Progressive relaxation, EMG biofeedback and biofeedback placebo in the treatment of sleep-onset insomnia', *British Journal of Medical Psychology* 55: 169–96.

Puder, R., Lacks, P., Bertelson, A. D. and Storandt, M. (1983) 'Short-term stimulus control treatment of insomnia in older adults', *Behavior Therapy* 14: 424–9.

Sacks, S. and DeLeon, G. (1983) 'Conditioning functional enuresis: follow-up after retraining', *Behaviour Research and Therapy* 21: 693–4.

Steinmark, S. W. and Borkovec, T. D. (1974) 'Active and placebo treatment effects on moderate insomnia under counter-demand and positive demand instructions', *Journal of Abnormal Psychology* 83: 157–63.

Turner, R. M. and Ascher, L. M. (1979) 'A within-subject analysis of stimulus-control therapy with severe sleep-onset insomnia', *Behaviour Research and Therapy* 17: 113–18.

Turner, R. M., Di Tomasso, R. and Giles, T. (1983) 'Failures in the treatment of insomnia: a plea for differential diagnosis', in E. B. Foa and P. M. G. Emmelkamp (eds) *Failures in Behavior Therapy*, New York: John Wiley.

Woolfolk, R. L. and McNulty, T. F. (1983) 'Relaxation treatment for insomnia: a component analysis', *Journal of Consulting and Clinical Psychology* 51: 495–503.

Woolfolk, R. L., Carr-Kaffashan, L., McNulty, T. F. and Lehrer, P. M. (1976) 'Meditation training as a treatment for insomnia', *Behavior Therapy* 7: 359–65.

Chapter 32

Chronic pain
Assessment

Shirley Pearce and Joyce Mays

INTRODUCTION

Chronic pain poses a major economic as well as medical problem. In the United Kingdom low back pain alone causes the loss of several million working days each year. Additionally, multiple medical and surgical interventions, medication expenses and attendant economic and family problems contribute to the hidden costs of chronic pain (Sternbach, 1986). Unfortunately, traditional medical and surgical approaches to the investigation and management of chronic pain have often been found to be of limited value. In some cases, the patient has no obvious physical pathology; in others, the treatment methods themselves have created further problems. These include addiction to analgesic medication and the development of painful scar tissue following surgery. In recent years increasing attention has been turned to the role of psychological factors in chronic pain problems and the development of models of pain which take account of the way in which the experience of pain is mediated by psychological factors (Melzack and Wall, 1988).

It is now accepted that, in pain of all kinds, physiological and behavioural processes are likely to interact. Psychological factors, including attention, mood, anxiety, cognition and memory, contribute directly to the perception of pain and the way it is experienced.

This and the following chapter will be concerned with psychological contributions to the assessment and management of chronic pain. Before these areas are reviewed, theories of pain will be introduced, and the distinction between chronic and acute pain will be outlined.

THEORIES OF PAIN

Early accounts of pain include the specificity theory (see Mountcastle, 1974) and the pattern theory (Crue and Carregal, 1975). Both of these have been found inadequate to account for a variety of physiological and psychological findings. In 1965 Melzack and Wall proposed the *gate control theory* of pain. This essentially provided an anatomical basis for the view that sensory input could be modulated by certain physiological and psychological processes. Input from the peripheral nociceptors was thought to pass through a neural 'gate' in the spinal cord before being transmitted to the brain. This gate may be opened or closed according to the relative activity in small and large afferent fibres, for example touch receptors, as well as the activity in fibres descending from the brain. The gate is also controlled by descending pathways from central cortical areas.

This model of pain therefore provides a mechanism by which psychological factors, such as attention, distraction, mood, expectations and personality, can exert an influence over pain perception. The theory is described at length in a number of places (Melzack, 1973; Wall, 1976; Melzack and Wall, 1988) and will not be discussed in detail here. However, there is evidence that the activation of descending fibres can trigger prolonged changes of receptive field and modality which differ from the fast neural inhibitions and excitations which have been the subject of earlier studies (McMahon and Wall, 1988). Such evidence may provide a basis for the existence of some of the proposed mechanisms.

The basic concept of input modulation is now widely accepted and the gate control theory is viewed as one of the most important theoretical advances in recent pain research, arguing for the importance of a multi-dimensional model of pain and distinguishing between the sensory and affective components of the subjective experience of pain.

Fordyce (1978) also suggests that activity in the physiological system is perceived at a subjective level both as a sensation (e.g. burning, pricking) and as an unpleasant affect (e.g. distress, discomfort). He further suggests that this negative affect motivates pain behaviours (wincing, taking pills), which are aimed at communicating the pain experience to those around and at reducing the intensity of the pain experience.

The further away from the level of nociception, the more other factors besides the level of physiological activity are likely to become implicated in the pain experience. For example, social and cultural variables are likely to influence pain behaviours perhaps as much as activity in the nociceptive fibres. Hence the concordance between these three systems, physiological, subjective and behavioural, may vary. Karoly (1985) has extended the 'three systems model' to include two additional factors: (a) 'lifestyle impact' (for example, marital distress or vocational change); and (b) 'information processing or central control' (for example, coping styles, problem-solving skills and health beliefs).

Philips (1987) outlines a model which deals with the relationship between two of Karoly's response levels. It describes the influence of cognitions on pain behaviour. Emphasis is placed on the expectations patients have about the effects of their actions and their beliefs about their capacity to control pain episodes. If self-efficacy is low, patients avoid activities that might provoke an increase in pain. Pain behaviours are viewed as avoidance behaviours which have the effect of maintaining the pain problem.

A model which has greater predictive power is that of Leventhal (1984), which uses very different concepts drawn from an information-processing view of emotion. In common with all more recent models, however, it proposes that the notion of a linear relationship between noxious stimulation and pain intensity must be discarded. Rather, a parallel-processing view is outlined. He proposes that central processing occurs at three hierarchically organised levels. The first involves the activation of an innate set of expressive motor reactions to environmental stimuli; for example, Izard and Dougherty (1982) identify changes in facial expressions in young children discriminating between different experiences such as pain, fear and anger with high inter-rater reliability. The second is the automatic encoding in memory of the emotional experience. This leads to the gradual development of a schematic system providing a record of the stimulus factors and their associated affective and expressive motor responses. At a higher level still, a set of abstract rules about emotional episodes and associated voluntary responses arises over time as a consequence of self-observation.

CHRONIC VS. ACUTE PAIN

Chronic pain has been distinguished from acute pain on the basis of two main variables: function and duration. Definitions based on function highlight the role of acute pain as a warning signal. The value of chronic pain is less clear, although it may serve to promote the inactivity which is sometimes necessary for successful recovery from serious injury (Bonica, 1977b; Wall, 1979). There is little empirical support for a functional distinction between acute and chronic pain, and researchers and clinicians have usually based their working definitions of chronicity on the duration of pain. Pain is often considered chronic if it persists for longer than six months (Sternbach, 1974).

Anatomic and neurophysiological differences between acute and chronic pain conditions have not been clearly established, although some surgical lesions have been shown to reduce the distress caused by persistent pain and yet leave the capacity to feel brief painful stimulation (pinpricks) unaffected (Sweet, 1980). However, recent research using positron emission tomography suggests that there may be differences in patterns of brain activation to painful stimuli between chronic pain patients and non-pain patients (Jones et al., 1991).

'PSYCHOGENIC' VS. 'ORGANIC' PAIN

Pain for which no clear physical cause can be identified is often labelled 'psychogenic' in origin. It is assumed that patients have some emotional, motivational or personality problem as the primary cause of their pain behaviours (Fordyce, 1978). For example, Engel (1959) identified a subgroup of patients without detectable lesions characterised by excessive guilt feelings, intolerance of personal success, and family histories featuring pain and aggression. However, this is not necessarily evidence that these factors play a causal role and indeed there is good evidence to suggest that psychological disturbance may be the result, rather than the cause, of chronic pain. For example, although pain patients show higher scores on the hysteria, depression and hypochondriasis scales of the MMPI, these scores decrease significantly after successful treatment of the pain (Sternbach, 1974; Sternbach and Timmermans, 1975).

The distinction between organic and psychogenic pain is therefore of little value, since psychological factors play a significant part in all cases of chronic pain. Nevertheless, this deeply entrenched concept does offer medical science a convenient label for those patients with identified pathology whose pain remains intractable despite the best efforts of practitioners to cure it. Equally, the label may provide an umbrella for organic conditions which may remain undetected or unidentified. Either way, the term does little to serve the interests of patients or practitioners, and for the purposes of this chapter no further distinction is made, since the methods described are of equal relevance to the assessment of pain whether or not organic pathology is suspected.

AIMS OF ASSESSMENT

Methods used for the assessment of physiological, subjective and behavioural components of pain will now be discussed in turn. However it is important to bear in mind the aims of the assessment. Broadly the three main aims in practice are:

1 To determine the suitability of a patient for treatment
2 To determine the individual patient's strengths and weaknesses so as to match or tailor a treatment programme effectively
3 To evaluate change during treatment and at follow-up periods.

THE ASSESSMENT OF PAIN BEHAVIOURS

The term 'pain behaviour' has been applied to a wide range of different activities. These include demands for medication and indices of its use, verbal complaints of pain, non-verbal responses, such as gasping or grimacing, pain-relieving activities (for example, rubbing or heating an affected location), and gross 'negative' behaviours, such as not getting out of bed and avoiding activities which may exacerbate pain. The measures described in the following sections are aimed at measuring these specific pain behaviours, but it must be remembered that the term pain behaviours in the broadest sense includes Karoly's concept of lifestyle impact, which may require more complex assessment. Marital distress, social interactions, recreational activities, employment status and domestic arrangements would be included in this category. Many aspects of such lifestyle impact are incorporated in the widely used Sickness Impact Profile (Bergner et al., 1976), adapted for use with chronic back pain patients (Follick et al., 1985).

Direct observation

Observer recordings of pain behaviour may be performed in clinical settings as well as in more natural environments. Ward assessments raise the question of the generalisability of the measurements obtained. Aspects of the ward may exacerbate the demonstration of pain, either by means of social influences, such as other patients manifesting pain behaviours, or by nursing staff providing reinforcement of pain behaviours. Hence caution must be applied in generalising one's findings to other settings. As a method to evaluate progress during an in-patient programme, however, direct observation on the ward may be very useful. Certain very specific pain behaviours are easily recorded by ward staff. For example, where nurses are the only source of drugs, medication intake can be easily recorded, as can requests for medication.

'Well behaviours', such as the number of sit-ups achieved in physiotherapy, can also be simply recorded. These are important measures of improvement and should be included among measures of outcome. Another important outcome measure, which is increasingly valued as a criterion for evaluating the efficacy of treatment programmes, is a 'back-to-work' measure. 'Field' assessment of the home and workplace is also currently being developed, not just as an aid to assessment but in conjunction with field management as part of treatment programmes aimed to complement institutional management (Cott *et al.*, 1990).

Finer aspects of pain behaviour, such as non verbal complaints of pain, may be helpful in the identification of environmental factors that may be maintaining pain. These may be assessed by a variety of direct observation techniques which are most readily applied in in-patient settings.

Pain behaviours have been recorded by frequency counts during specified intervals. For example, Rybstein-Blinchik (1979) reports frequency counts of both verbal and non verbal pain behaviours during thirty-second observation periods of discussion initiated by the therapist. Inter-rater reliability was high, but the generalisability of the count was reduced by the therapist's presence. In addition, the period of time sampled was very short. This may have limited the value of the measure in terms of evaluating outcome. Repeated time-sampling over longer time periods is likely to provide more relevant information.

Other approaches to direct observation of pain behaviours have involved the use of rating scales. For example, ratings by nurses of the frequency of three different types of pain behaviour observed during each shift. An example of more detailed ratings of pain behaviour is provided by Scott Richards, who describes the development of a pain behaviour scale. Nursing staff were asked to rate the frequency on three-point scales (none, occasional, frequent) of ten verbal and non verbal pain behaviours. The time to be sampled was a daily ward round, where the patient interacted with the therapy team in a semi-structured interview lasting approximately five minutes. He reports high inter-rater reliability for this measure, and moderate correlations with other measures such as level of physical activity and behavioural improvement during the in-patient programme (Richards *et al.*, 1982). Again, the time period sampled limits the external validity of the measure. In addition, whilst the use of a three-point rating scale may make the instrument easy to apply, it is also likely to reduce its sensitivity to change.

Attempts at obtaining measures of pain behaviours in natural settings include asking spouses or peers of patients to record pain behaviour (Fordyce, 1976). Unfortunately, a spouse may not be an entirely objective observer. A review of the problem of reactivity in observational measurement suggests that participant observers cannot be assumed to provide reliable data (Harris and Lahey, 1982).

Electromechanical devices

The move towards objectivity in the assessment of pain behaviour has led to the development of a number of rather bizarre electromechanical devices. The methods favoured in early studies are not much used today. Cairns *et al.* (1976) used an 'uptime' clock placed above the patient's bed, which recorded the amount of time the patient spent lying down. Although they report this to be a useful measure of 'uptime', it is dependent on the patient's not being able to lie down anywhere else in the ward. Accuracy of recording also requires that patients can be trusted not to 'play the system' by lying on their fellow ward mates' beds!

A slightly less problematic measure has been developed by Saunders. This is called a pedometer and consists of a recording device worn on the patient's wrist, which is activated by a microswitch on the leg. It therefore assesses gross movements and gives estimates of walking distance (Saunders *et al.*, 1978).

Self-observation

Self-observation has the advantage of providing measurements obtained from the patient's natural environment. Furthermore, it gives responsibility for the evaluation of progress directly to the patient.

Care should be taken to design self-recording schedules which will maximise patient compliance (Collins and Thompson, 1979). Simple targets for self-recording, such as the number of specific exercises achieved and medication intake, may provide more reliable information than very detailed measures (Melzack and Wall, 1989). It has been suggested that self-recordings should be used in conjunction with more objective behavioural measures, since discrepancies between the two types of measure may occur. Comparison of observer recordings of the activity of patients with self-monitoring data obtained from the patients themselves show considerable discrepancies. Similar discrepancies have been noted between self-monitoring data and uptime clock recordings (Sanders, 1983).

Such discrepancies may reflect some of the complex functional ramifications of pain and its meaning for the patient in a wider social context. For example, many patients, particularly at the start of treatment, may deny awareness of fluctuations in pain intensity in relation to environmental changes. Often the admission that social or interpersonal factors may exacerbate pain is seen as a statement that the pain is not real. The evaluation of a variety of treatment programmes is often particularly difficult in relation to pain intensity ratings. Outcome studies that show a decrease in pain ratings from admission to follow-up may not be statistically attributable to treatment. Deardoff *et al.* (1991) argue that patients may have had a tendency to inflate pain ratings when being evaluated for treatment. On follow-up, when either treatment was complete or obtaining treatment was no longer an issue, patients may have given more accurate pain level ratings.

MEASUREMENT OF THE SUBJECTIVE COMPONENT OF PAIN

Given current multi-dimensional models of pain which attempt to integrate both sensory and affective elements, it follows that assessment of pain experience must include a variety of measures to tap into both dimensions.

Measuring the quality and intensity of pain

Rating scales

Rating scales are the most commonly used measure in clinical pain research. They vary according to the number and nature of the anchor points supplied: numbers, words or presentation of visual analogue lines. The distribution of responses on verbal rating scales (VRS) and visual analogue scales (VAS) has been examined extensively. In general, VAS yield more uniform distributions. However, an initial assumption that this reflected their superior sensitivity (Scott and Huskisson, 1976) has been challenged by Gracely (1980), who argues that psychophysical literature suggests a tendency for responses to be spread over a constrained response range, regardless of intensity, spacing or frequency of the underlying stimulus continuum.

A fundamental objection to reliance on unidimensional rating scales concerns their failure to reflect the complexity of the pain experience. Attempts have been made to overcome this problem in two ways.

The first is by using combinations of rating scales. Price *et al.* (1987) used separate VAS ratings of the sensory and affective dimensions of pain. Previous research showed that VAS ratings approximated the properties of ratio scales (Price *et al.*, 1983) and were internally consistent (Price and Harkins 1987). In a comparison of different patient groups, Price *et al.* (1987) found score profiles consistent with expectations, in that chronic pain patients produced higher affective ratings than women in labour and volunteers exposed to experimental pain.

The second approach has involved using methods of cross-modality matching to validate the distinction between the two scales. Gracely (1980) describes the use of cross modality matching techniques to develop separate ratio scales for the sensory (intensity) and the affective (distress) aspects. Pharmacological interventions were shown to have differential effects on the two scales. Although these findings concern acute experimentally induced pain rather than chronic pain, they nevertheless demonstrate that reliance on single scales may distort conclusions concerning changes in the subjective component of pain.

Questionnaires

The McGill Pain Questionnaire (MPQ) (Melzack, 1975) is one of the most widely used pain descriptor questionnaires. It consists of seventy-eight pain adjectives arranged into twenty groups, each reflecting slightly different qualities of pain. Some groups describe sensory experiences (e.g. prickling, boiling, hot, scalding), others describe affective qualities (e.g. sickening, fearful, punishing, cruel), and yet others describe evaluative aspects of pain (e.g. annoying, miserable, trouble-some). Subjects are asked to indicate which words describe their pain, and the questionnaire may be scored to derive either an index reflecting the intensity of the words checked or more simply the number of words checked in each of the three categories. Modified card-sort versions of the MPQ are discussed by Reading (1983). The reliability of the adjective groupings has been assessed by Prieto et al. (1980), Byrne et al. (1982) and Reading et al. (1982). Turk et al. (1985) studied the internal structure of the questionnaire by using confirmatory factor analysis. Melzack and Katz (1992) and Torgerson (1986) discuss these findings in depth, together with the rationale for using factor analytic methods to delineate the dimensions of the MPQ. In summary, the MPQ may be considered a useful measure of the qualitative aspects of pain but caution should be attached to its use as a quantitative measure.

Assessment of mood, anxiety and depression

In accordance with a multi-dimensional model of pain, assessment of depression (for example, by the Beck Depression Inventory) and anxiety (for example, by the Spielberger State-Trait Anxiety Inventory) is obviously important to the evaluation of the chronic pain patient. Assessment of mood can, however, be problematic with the chronic pain patient, as some variables, such as fatigue, insomnia and changes in appetite, may be symptoms frequently associated with the physical aspects of the condition itself. The development of the Hospital Anxiety and Depression Scale (HADS) by Zigmund and Snaith (1983) over-comes some of these difficulties, and it is important in the light of the stated aims of assessment to obtain as accurate a measure of mood as possible. As it is now accepted that the experience of pain encompasses sensory and affective ele-ments, one would expect treatment outcomes to show improvements in mood.

Pain diaries

A major problem in the evaluation of chronic pain is that of spontaneous fluctuations over time. Measures of the efficacy of a therapeutic intervention must therefore be based on an adequate sample of the problem. Fluctuations in pain intensity in the patient's natural environment may provide important clues about situations likely to exacerbate or ameliorate pain and hence help determine the level and nature of treatment intervention. Relying on patients' memories of pain fluctuations even in the week or so prior to consultation is likely to produce unreliable data. Andrasik and Holroyd (1980) found discrepancies between diary records of headache frequency and intensity and recollections made at interview. The latter tended to underestimate the problem when compared with diary records. It is therefore reasonable that diary records should play a prominent role in the assessment of pain. Every effort should be made, however, to ensure that patients complete their ratings regularly, so that the unreliability of retrospective recordings may be avoided. Ideally, diary records should be compared to independent ratings or direct observation. Whilst Follick et al. (1984) found high associations between self-report and spouse observations, Fordyce et al. (1984) found little relationship between pain reports and pain behaviour. Despite a positive correlation between pain reports and resulting limitation, there was little relationship between health-care utilisation, behaviour and pain reports. It is likely that a range of factors influence the closeness of association between self and others' ratings, and this in itself may be an interesting source of information for the overall clinical assessment.

The use of experimental pain measures

Early attempts to estimate the intensity of clinical pain by using comparisons with experimentally induced pain sensations centred upon the research of Hardy et al. (1952). In practice the qualitative differences between experimental pain and most clinical pain conditions made the scale very hard to operate. The scale has therefore fallen into disuse. Pain induced by the Tourniquet Pain Method has been used more widely. This is a method described by Sternbach (1974) in which the tourniquet is used to induce pain to a level comparable to the clinical pain. A 'Tourniquet Pain Ratio' can be computed. Although this technique has been shown to be reliable, questions surround its validity. Sternbach et al. (1977) showed that the Tourniquet Pain Ratio was insensitive to the changes induced by various doses of analgesic medication.

The assessment of pain-related cognitions

Although the meaning that patients ascribe to their pain experience has long been considered important to their adjustment, it is only recently that researchers have begun to explore the role of patient beliefs in adjustment to chronic pain. Several types of cognitions have been examined, including thoughts about the controllability of pain, attributions about one's own ability to use specific pain-coping strategies, and expectations about the possible outcomes of various coping efforts. The results of this research are well reviewed by Jenson et al. (1991).

Beliefs

Beliefs or cognitions which patients have regarding their pain problem, the consequences of an event and their ability to cope with the event have been hypothesised to have an impact on functioning in two ways. First, beliefs about the implications of events may have a direct influence on mood. Negative thoughts that emphasise catastrophic consequences and/or one's perceived inability to control these consequences may contribute or lead to depression. Second, beliefs may influence adjustment indirectly through their impact on coping efforts. For example, pain patients who believe that they are capable of exercising regularly may be more likely to initiate and persist in a regular exercise programme.

Beliefs about pain are commonly accessed via questionnaires, such as the Beliefs about Pain Control Questionnaire (Skevington, 1990), which is derived from the Multidimensional Health Locus of Control Questionnaire (MHLC; Wallston and Wallston, 1978). This questionnaire assesses the extent to which people believe that they have personal control over their pain (Internal Scale), or that fate, doctors or other influential people control their pain (Chance and Powerful Other Scales).

Coping

Coping has been defined as purposeful efforts to manage or vitiate the negative impact of stress. Coping efforts or activities have been categorised along several dimensions. Lazarus (1984) and Coyne and Holroyd (forthcoming) have, for example, divided coping strategies into two major types: those that serve to manage the negative emotions associated with stress (emotion-focused coping); and those that are directed at solving or relieving the problem (problem-focused coping). In the field of chronic pain, some researchers categorise coping efforts into active and passive dimensions (Brown and Nicassio, 1987). Active strategies are defined as responses requiring a person to initiate some action to manage pain (such as exercise). Passive strategies, on the other hand, involve withdrawal or giving up control to an external force or agent (for example, resting or using medication).

Perceived control over pain

Rudy et al. (1988) investigated the relationship of perceived control and perceived interference of pain in life activities to depression. Higher levels of perceived control and lower levels of perceived interference with activities were both associated with lower levels of depression. Furthermore, both predictor variables made independent contributions to the prediction of depression, suggesting that each may be important in determining psychological adaptation to chronic pain. Findings also showed support for the hypothesis that perceived control and perceived interference mediate the relationship between pain severity and depression. A study by Strong *et al.* (1990) found that the more chronic low back pain patients endorsed a sense of control over pain, the less likely they were to report that pain interfered with their daily functioning. Jenson *et al.* (1987) found that the perceived controllability of pain predicted self-reported use of relaxation to cope with pain, and greater exercise immediately following treatment in a multidisciplinary pain programme.

Perceived helplessness

A dimension closely related to that of perceived control over pain is perceived helplessness. Using a learned helplessness model of depression as a theoretical framework, Nicassio *et al.* (1985) developed the Arthritis Helplessness Index. In a variety of studies, patients with scores indicating perceived helplessness on this scale showed a passive pain coping style and a greater degree of psychological and physical disability. The scale has also shown a negative relationship to active coping efforts. On a similar measure developed by Flor and Turk (1988) for chronic pain patients, those with scores suggesting greater perceived helplessness reported greater pain severity, interference with activities and greater health-care utilisation.

THE ASSESSMENT OF THE PHYSIOLOGICAL COMPONENT OF PAIN

Physiological assessments of chronic pain can be broadly divided into two groups. The first consists of attempts to isolate physiological changes which may play a causal role in the development of pain and which may occur in the absence of obvious tissue pathology. An example of this would be the investigation of the electromyographic changes thought to underlie tension headache or of the vascular changes believed to cause migraine. In the second category there are investigations of physiological changes thought to occur as a response to the subjective experience of pain. In fact, this distinction may have little validity in chronic pain conditions, where the relationship between cause and effect is generally unclear.

Holmes and Wolff (1952) found back pain patients showed generalised muscular hyperactivity under conditions of physical activity and emotional stress. They believed that this represented voluntary guarding. That is, the patients voluntarily tensed those muscles to protect themselves against further pain and hence probably exacerbated their original pain.

Keefe and Block (1982) report a number of unpublished studies by Wolff *et al.* which support the view that back pain patients show abnormalities of muscular activity when compared with non-pain subjects. While normal subjects show low symmetrical levels of EMG activity from recordings on both sides of the lumbar spine, back pain patients show asymmetry of lumbar muscle activity either during static activity or during movements such as bending or twisting.

Wolf *et al.* (1982) showed that training patients to produce more regular EMG patterns was associated with a reduction in subjective reports of pain and with increased levels of activity. It seems likely that, whatever the initial cause of pain, the awkward movements patients make to avoid stressing the painful area may provoke physiological changes which exacerbate or maintain the original problem. Appropriate assessment of physiological variables potentially associated with the pain may therefore be important in identifying possible levels of therapeutic intervention.

Although some studies do support the view that tension headache patients have higher resting levels of muscle tension (e.g. Philips, 1977), there is now a large body of evidence which suggests that raised levels of muscle tension may not be a sufficient condition for the development of tension headache. A number of studies have failed to find differences between tension headache patients and other headache subjects or normal controls (Martin and Mathews, 1978; Pearce and Morley, 1981). This does not necessarily mean that changes in muscle tension are not involved in the experience of headache. It does suggest, however, that there is not a one-to-one relationship between EMG and subjective experience of pain. This is what would be expected from a theory of pain as an experience comprising activity in three potentially discordant systems. The important conclusion from these observations is that measurement of the physiological variables, even for conditions where they have traditionally been thought to play a causal role in development, may not be particularly useful for diagnostic purposes. Certainly the measurement of *resting* levels will be of limited value in diagnosis, although physiological responses to stress may be more valuable (Cohen *et al.*, 1978). As a way of monitoring the therapeutic processes associated with particular outcomes, information about changes in related physiological systems may be of some interest.

REFERENCES

Andrasik, F. and Holroyd, K. A. (1980) 'Reliability and Concurrent Validity of Headache Questionnaire Data', *Headache* 20: 44–6.

Bergner, M., Bobbitt, R. A. and Pollard, W. E. (1976) 'The Sickness Impact Profile: validation of the health status measure', *Medical Care* 14: 56–67.

Bonica, J. J. (1977a) *Advances in Neurology: International Symposium on Pain*, New York: Raven Press.

Bonica, J. J. (1977b) 'Neurophysiologic and pathologic aspects of acute and chronic pain', *Archives of Surgery* 112: 750–61.

Brown, G. K., and Nicassio, P. M. (1987) 'The development of a questionnaire for the assessment of active and passive coping strategies in chronic pain patients', *Pain* 31: 53–65.

Byrne, M., Troy, A., Bradley, L. A., Marchisello, P. J., Geisinger, K. F., Van der Heide, L. and Prieto, E. J. (1982) 'Cross validation of the factor structure of the McGill Pain Questionnaire', *Pain* 13: 193–201.

Cairns, D., Thomas, L., Mooney, V. and Pace, J. B. (1976) 'A comprehensive treatment approach to chronic low back pain', *Pain* 2: 301–8.

Cohen, M. J., Riddes, W. H. and McArthur, O. L. (1978) 'Evidence for physiological response stereotopy in migraine headache', *Psychosomatic Medicine* 40: 344–9.

Collins, F. L. and Thompson, J. K. (1979) 'Reliability and standardisation in the assessment of self-reported headache pain', *Journal of Behavioural Assessment* 1: 73–86.

Cott, A., Anchel, H., Goldberg, W. M., Fabich, M. and Parkinson, W. (1990) 'Non-institutional treatment of chronic pain by field management: an outcome study with comparison group', *Pain* 40: 183–94.

Coyne, J. C. and Holroyd, K. (forthcoming) 'Stress, coping and illness: a transactional perspective', in T. Millon, C. Green and R. Meagher (eds) *Handbook of Health Care Clinical Psychology*, New York: Plenum Press.

Crue, B. L. and Carregal, E. J. A. (1975) 'Pain begins in the dorsal horn – with a proposed classification of the primary senses', in B. L. Crue (ed.) *Pain: Research and Treatment*, New York: Academic Press.

Deardoff, W. W., Rubin, H. S., and Scott, D. W., (1991) 'Comprehensive multi-disciplinary treatment of chronic pain: a follow-up study of treated and non-treated groups', *Pain* 45: 35–43.

Dubuisson, D. and Melzack, R. (1976) 'Classification of clinical pain descriptors by multiple group discriminant analysis', *Experimental Neurology* 51: 480–7.

Edwards. L. (1992) 'An Investigation of Cognitive Processes in Chronic Pain', unpublished Ph.D. thesis, University of London.

Engel, G. L., (1959) 'Psychogenic pain and the pain prone patient', *American Journal of Medicine* 26: 899–918.

Flor, H. and Turk, D. C. (1988) 'Chronic back pain and rheumatoid arthritis: predicting pain and disability from cognitive variables', *Journal of Behavioral Medicine* 11: 251–65.

Follick, M. M., Ahearn, D. and Laser-Wolston, N. (1984) 'Evaluation of a daily diary for chronic pain patients', *Pain* 19: 377–82.

Follick, M. J., Smith, T. W. and Ahern, D. K. (1985) 'The Sickness Impact Profile: a global measure of disability in chronic low back pain', *Pain* 21: 67–76.

Fordyce, W. E. (1976) *Behavioural Methods for Chronic Pain and Illness*, St Louis: C.V. Mosby.

Fordyce, W. E. (1978) 'Learning processes in pain', in Sternbach R A (ed.) *The Psychology of Pain*, Raven Press, New York.

Fordyce, W. E., Brena, S. F., Holcomb, R. J., DeLateur, B. J. and Loeser, J. D. (1978) 'Relationship of patient semantic pain descriptions to physician diagnostic judgements, activity level measurements and MMPI', *Pain* 5: 293–303.

Fordyce, W. E., Lansky, D., Calsyn, D. A., Shelton, J. L., Stolov, W. C. and Rock, O. L., (1984) 'Pain measurement and pain behaviour', *Pain* 10: 53–69.

Gracely, R. J. (1979) 'Psychophysical assessment of human pain', *Advances in Pain Research and Therapy* 3: 805–24.

Gracely, R. J. (1980) 'Psychological assessment of human pain', in J. J. Bonica and D. Albe-Fessard (eds) *Advances in Pain Research and Therapy*, New York: Raven Press.

Gracely, R. H., McGrath, P. and Dubner, R. (1978) 'Ratio scales of sensory and affective verbal pain descriptors', *Pain* 5: 5–18.

Hanvik, L. J. (1951) 'MMPI profiles in patients with low back pain', *Journal of Consulting Psychology* 15: 350–3.

Hardy, J. D., Wolff, H. G., and Goodell, H. (1952) 'Pain sensations and reactions', New York: Hafner Publishing.

Harris, F. C. and Lahey, B. B. (1982) 'Recording system bias in direct observational methodology: a review and critical analysis of factors causing inaccurate coding behaviour', *Clinical Psychology Review* 2: 539–57.

Holmes, T. H. and Wolff, H. G. (1952) 'Life situations, emotions and backache', *Psychosomatic Medicine* 14: 18–33.

Izard, C. E. and Dougherty, A. (1982) 'Two complementary systems in measuring facial expressions in infants and children', in C. E. Izard (ed.) *Measuring Emotions in Infants and Children*, Cambridge: Cambridge University Press (56–73).

Jenson, M. P., Karoly, P. and Huger, R. (1987) 'The development and preliminary validation of an instrument to assess patients' attitude toward pain', *Journal of Psychomatic Research* 31: 393–400.

Jenson, M. P., Turner, J. A., Romano, J. M. and Karoly, P. (1991) 'Coping with chronic pain: a review of the literature', *Pain* 47(3): 249–83.

Jones, A. K. P., Friston, K. J., Qi, L. Y., Harris, M., Cunningham, V. J., Jones, T., Feinman, C. and Frackowiak, R. S. J. (1991) 'The sites of action on the human brain studied with positron emission tomography', *Lancet* 338: 825.

Joyce, C. B., Zutshi, D. W., Hrubes, V. and Mason, R. M. (1975) 'Comparison of Fixed Interval and Visual Analog Scales for rating chronic pain', *European Journal of Clinical Pharmacology* 8: 415–20.

Karoly, P. (1982) 'Cognitive Assessment in Behavioural Medicine', *Clinical Psychology Review* 2: 421–34.

Karoly, P. (ed.) (1985) *The Assessment of Pain: Concepts and Procedures in Management Strategies in Health Psychology*, New York: Wiley.

Keefe, F. J. and Block. A. R. (1982) 'Development of an observation method for assessing pain behaviour in chronic low back pain patients', *Clinical Psychology Revue* 9: 549–68.

Keefe, F. J., Brown, C., Scott, D. S. and Ziesat, H. (1962) 'Behavioural assessment of chronic pain', in F. J. Keefe and J. A. Blumenthal (eds) *Assessment Strategies in Behavioural Medicine*, New York: Grune and Stratton (Ch. 11).

Kremer, E. F., Atkinson, J. H. and Ignetzi, R. J. (1982) 'Pain measurement: the Affective Dimensional Measure of the McGill Pain Questionnaire with a cancer pain population', *Pain* 12: 153–64.

Lazarus, R. A. and Folkman, S. (1984) *Stress, Appraisal and Coping*, New York: Springer.

Leventhal, H. (1984) 'A perceptual-motor theory of emotion', *Advances in Experimental Social Psychology* 17: 117–83.

McMahon, S. B. and Wall, P. D. (1988) 'Descending inhibition and excitation of spinal cord lamina I projection neurones', *Journal of Neurophysiology* 59: 1204–19.

Martin, P. and Mathews, A. M. (1978) 'Tension Headaches: a psychophysiological investigation and treatment', *Journal of Psychosomatic Research* 22: 389–99.

Melzack, R. (1973) *The Puzzle of Pain*, New York: Basic Books.

Melzack, R. (1975) 'The McGill Pain Questionnaire: major properties and scoring methods', *Pain* 1: 275–99.

Melzack, R. and Katz, M. (1992) 'The McGill Pain Questionnaire: appraisal and current status', in D. C. Turk and R. Melzack (eds) *The Handbook of Pain Assessment*, New York: Guildford Publications.

Melzack, R. and Wall, P. D. (1965) 'Pain mechanisms: a new theory', *Science*, 150: 971–9.

Melzack, R. and Wall, P. D. (1988) *The Challenge of Pain*, 2nd edn, London: Penguin Books.

Melzack, R. and Wall, P. D. (1989) *Textbook of Pain*, London: Churchill Livingstone.

Mountcastle, V. B. (1974) 'Pain and Temperature Sensibilities', in V. B. Mountcastle (ed.) *Medical Physiology*, St Louis: C. V. Mosby.

Nicassio, P. M., Wallston, K. A., Callahan, L. F., Herbert, M. and Pincus, T. (1985) 'The measurement of helplessness in rheumatoid arthritis', *Journal of Rheumatology* 12: 462–7.

Pearce, S. and Erskine, E. (1989) 'Chronic pain' in S. Pearce and J. Wardle (eds) *The Practice of Behavioural Medicine*, Oxford: BPS Books/Oxford University Press.

Pearce, S. and Morley, S. (1981) 'An experimental investigation of pain production in headache patients', *British Journal of Clinical Psychology* 20: 275–81.

Philips, C. (1977) 'The modification of tension headache using EMG feedback', *Behavioural Research Therapy* 15: 119–29.

Philips, H. C. (1987) 'Avoidance behaviour and its role in sustaining chronic pain', *Behaviour Research and Therapy* 25: 273–9.

Pollard, W. E., Bobbitt, R. A., Bergner, M., Marsh, D. P. and Gilson, B. S. (1976) 'The Sickness Impact Profile: reliability of a health status measure', *Medical Care* 14: 146–55.

Price, D. D. and Harkins, S. W. (1987) 'The combined use of visual analogue scales and experimental pain in providing standardized assessment of clinical pain', *Clinical Journal of Pain* 3: 1–8.

Price, D. D., McGrath, P. N., Raffi, A. and Buckingham, B. (1983) 'Validation of visual analogue scales as ratio scales measures for chronic and experimental pain, *Pain* 17: 45–56.

Price, D. D., Harkins, S. W. and Baker, C. (1987) 'Sensory affective relationship among different types of clinical and experimental pain', *Pain* 28: 297–307.

Prieto, E. J., Hopson, L., Bradley, L. A., Byrne, M., Geisinger, K. F., Midax, D. and Marchisello, P. J. (1980) 'The language of low back pain: factor structure of the McGill Pain Questionnaire', *Pain* 8: 11–19.

Reading, A. E. (1982) 'A comparison of the McGill Pain Questionnaire in chronic and acute pain', *Pain* 13: 185–92.

Reading, A. E. (1983) 'Testing pain mechanisms in persons in pain', in P. D. Wall and R. Melzack (eds) (1989) *Textbook of Pain*, London: Churchill Livingstone.

Reading, A. E., Evertt, B. S. and Sledmere, C. M. (1982) 'The McGill Pain Questionnaire: a replication of its construction', *British Journal of Clinical Psychology* 21: 339.

Richards, J. S., Nepomuceno, C., Riles, M. and Suer, Z. (1982) 'Assessing pain behaviour: the UAB pain behaviour scale', *Pain* 14: 393–8.

Rudy, T. E., Kerns, R. D. and Turk, D. C. (1988) 'Chronic pain and depression: toward a cognitive-behavioural mediation model', *Pain* 35: 129–40.

Rybstein-Blinchik, E. (1979) 'Effects of different cognitive strategies on chronic pain experience', *Journal of Behavioral Medicine* 2: 93–101.

Sanders, S. H. (1983) 'Automated versus self-monitoring of the "Up-Time" in chronic low back pain patients: a comparative study', *Pain* 15: 399–407.

Saunders, K. J., Goldstein, M. K. and Stein, G. H. (1978) 'Automated measurement of patient activity on a hospital rehabilitation ward', *Archives of Physical Medicine and Rehabilitation* 59: 255–7.

Scott, J. and Huskisson, E. C. (1976) 'Graphic representation of pain', *Pain* 2: 175–84.

Skevington, S. M. (1990) 'A standardised scale to measure beliefs about controlling pain (BPCQ): a preliminary study', *Psychology and Health* 4: 221–32.

Spielberger, C. D., Gorush, R. L. and Lushene, R. (1970) *Manual for the State-Trait Anxiety Inventory*, Palo Alto, Calif.: Consulting Psychologist's Press.

Sternbach, R. A. (1974) *Pain Patients: Traits and Treatments*, New York: Academic Press.

Sternbach, R. A. (1978) 'Clinical aspects of pain', in R. A. Sternbach (ed.) *The Psychology of Pain*, New York: Raven Press.

Sternbach, R. A. (1986) 'Pain and daily "Hassles" in the USA: findings of the Nuprin Pain Report', *Pain* 27: 69–80.

Sternbach, R. A. and Timmermans, G. (1975) 'Personality changes associated with reduction of Pain', *Pain* 1: 177–81.

Sternbach, R. A., Wolf, S. R., Murphy, R. W. and Akeson, W. H. (1973) 'Traits of pain patients: the low back "Loser"', *Psychosomatics* 14: 226–9.

Sternbach, R. A., Deems, L. M., Timmermans, G. and Huey, L. Y. (1977) 'On the sensitivity of the Tourniquet Pain Test', *Pain* 3: 105–10.

Strong, J., Ashton, R., Cramond, T. and Chant, D. (1990) 'Pain intensity, attitude and function in low back pain patients', *Australian Journal of Occupational Therapy* 37: 179–83.

Swanson, D. W., Maruta, T. and Swenson, W. M. (1979) 'Results of behaviour modification in the treatment of chronic pain', *Psychosomatic Medicine* 41: 55–61.

Sweet, W. H. (1980) 'Central mechanisms of chronic pain (neuralgias and certain other neurogenic pain)', in J. Bonica (ed.) *Pain: Association for Research in Nervous and Mental Diseases, Vol. 58*, New York: Raven Press.

Torgerson, W. S. (1986) *Critical Issues in Verbal Pain Assessment: Multidimensional and Multivariate Issues*, Washington DC: American Pain Society.

Turk, D. L., Rudy, T. E. and Saveloy, P. (1985) 'The McGill Pain Questionnaire reconsidered: confirming the factor structure and examining appropriate uses', *Pain* 21: 385–97.

Turner, J. A. (1982) 'Comparison of group progressive – relaxation training and cognitive-behavioural group therapy for chronic low back pain', *Journal Consulting and Clinical Psychology* 50: 757–65.

Wall, P. D. (1976) 'Modulation of pain by non-painful events', in J. J. Bonica and D. Albe-Fessard (eds) *Advances in Pain Research and Therapy, Vol. 1*, New York: Raven Press.

Wall, P. W. (1979) 'On the relation of injury to pain', *Pain* 6: 253–60.

Wallston, K. A. and Wallston, B. S. (1978) 'Development of the Multidimensional Health Locus of Control (MHLC) Scale', *Health Education Monographs* 6: 160–70.

Wolf, S. L. and Basmajian, J. V. (1978) 'Assessment of paraspinal electromyographic activity in normal subjects and in chronic back pain patients using muscle biofeedback devoice', in E. Asmussen and K. Jorgenson (eds) *Biomechanics VI. Proceedings of the Sixth International Congress of Biomechanics*, Baltimore: University Park Press.

Wolf, S. L., Nacht, M. and Kelly, J. L. (1982) 'EMG feedback training during dynamic movement for low back pain patients', *Behavior Therapy* 123: 395–496.

Wolff, B. B. (1978) 'Behavioural measurement of human pain', in R. A. Sternbach (ed.) *The Psychology of Pain*, New York: Raven Press.

Zarkowska, E. A. (1981) 'The relationship between subjective and behavioural aspects of pain in people suffering from low back pain', unpublished M. Phil dissertation, University of London.

Zigmund, A. S. and Snaith, R. P. (1983) 'The Hospital Anxiety and Depression Scale', *Acta Psychiatrica Scandinavia* 67: 361–70.

Chapter 33

Chronic pain
Psychological approaches to management

Shirley Pearce and Joyce Mays

INTRODUCTION

The management of chronic pain is one of the most widespread and difficult challenges facing health-care professionals. Whilst many acute pain episodes respond to traditional medical intervention and are successfully resolved, for a significant number of patients pain becomes chronic and unresponsive to any single modality of treatment. As the pain condition persists, patients typically become more desperate for a cure, greatly increasing the risk of iatrogenic complications. The cost of chronic pain can be counted not only in terms of patient suffering but also in terms of socio-economic factors, including decreased work functioning, attendant family problems and increased health-care expenditure (Sternbach, 1986).

It is now well accepted that pain is a multi-dimensional phenomenon involving sensory, affective, motivational, environmental and cognitive components. It is likely that as pain persists, nociceptive input becomes less important in influencing suffering and pain behaviours, while other areas become more predominant. The management of chronic pain has evolved considerably in relation to the growing awareness that chronic pain does not respond to uni-dimensional treatments and that it is maintained by multiple factors. In response to this awareness, a variety of different treatment approaches have been established, which will be described in this chapter, together with a summary of the current state of outcome research in this area. An exhaustive review of the outcome literature will not be attempted, since several reviews are already available (Jenson *et al.*, 1991; Latimer, 1982; Linton, 1982; Pearce, 1983; Turner and Chapman, 1982a; b). Techniques such as relaxation and bio-feedback, which are widely used in other areas and which have been covered in other sections of this volume, will not be described in detail. Greater attention will be paid to describing approaches, such as contingency management and cognitive intervention, whose application to chronic pain presents rather different problems from those in other areas of clinical psychology. Psychological methods will be categorised into those concerned primarily with the behavioural, cognitive and physiological components of pain respectively. Finally, some of the methodological problems limiting the conclusions regarding the strength and nature of the association between coping strategies and adjustment in chronic pain patients will be outlined.

THE MODIFICATION OF PAIN BEHAVIOURS

Contingency management

The development of contingency management approaches for the treatment of chronic pain derives from Fordyce's view of chronic pain as primarily a behavioural problem. Fordyce considered that, in some cases, pain behaviours can be maintained largely by their reinforcing consequences, rather than by underlying physiological processes. The term pain behaviours is now commonly used to refer to both the learned and unlearned respondent and operant responses which contribute to and comprise chronic illness behaviours. Among the relevant and often discussed environmental variables that may strengthen illness are (1) reinforcement of pain behaviours by significant others; (2) avoidance behaviours in the form of restrictions in work, exercise, and even the most routine of daily activities; (3) litigation and income protection plans (that is, income contingent on disability); and (4) unemployment or the failure to return to work following treatment or recovery. Pain behaviours may be either positively reinforced, for example by social factors, such as attention and concern from family members, or negatively reinforced, for example by avoidance of unwanted responsibilities. The aim of operant programmes is to increase the frequency of well behaviours and decrease that of pain behaviours. Reduction in pain intensity is not specified as an aim. Indeed, in clinical practice it is generally explained to the patient that the programme is not aiming to remove their pain but rather to help them cope better with it and resume normal activities despite it. There is an underlying assumption that, once the patient is active again and engaged in more distracting activities, attention to the pain sensations will be reduced and hence pain intensity will diminish. The methods used to achieve these aims are described in detail by Fordyce (1976). Briefly, patients are admitted to specialised programmes for periods of between two and six weeks. During this time staff give no attention to pain behaviours or requests for analgesics but provide considerable social reinforcement for targeted well behaviours. Physical therapy programmes are developed to increase patient activity levels. Daily exercise quotas are determined on the basis of patients' initial tolerance levels. Each day the quota is increased so that the patient becomes able to manage significantly more than the initial level. Progress is charted graphically and staff attention, or some other desirable event, is made contingent on successful daily completion of the quota.

There is some support for the view that pain behaviours and activity levels in chronic pain patients can be controlled by altering reinforcement contingencies in this way. McArthur et al. (1987) review some of the literature dealing with the effect on activity levels of contingent social reinforcement. Typically, groups of patients are admitted to behavioural pain management programmes, usually conducted in in-patient facilities and of short duration (for example, four to six weeks). Such programmes can produce dramatic results, but have frequently failed to produce adequate maintenance on follow-up (Keefe and Gil, 1985). This may suggest that, although activity levels may be altered by environmental manipulation, any therapeutic approach based solely on this method is likely to have considerable problems in generalising beyond the treatment environment.

Reducing levels of medication is also an important aim of the operant programmes. This is done by establishing initial drug requirements by putting the patient on a free operant schedule for a few days immediately after admission. The amount of medication required is then provided in a strong-tasting masking vehicle called the 'pain cocktail'. The patient is unable to tell from its appearance or taste how strong the concoction is. This pain cocktail is provided on a time contingent rather than pain contingent or PRN basis; the patient has to take it every four hours whether in pain or not. If it is refused, the patient must wait until the next time interval is up before medication is available again. In this way the association between pain and medication should be broken. The active ingredients of the pain cocktail are gradually reduced so that by discharge the patient should be consuming only the inert substance.

Multi-method

Since these early studies which investigated operant methods, in-patient programmes have become widespread in the USA and have expanded beyond dependence on contingency management and increased exercise to include a range of psychological therapies, for example, group therapy, bio-feedback, body mechanics, relaxation training and education.

The evaluation of such programmes is frequently confounded by the inclusion of a mixture of therapeutic ingredients within the operant programme. An example of such multi-method outcome studies is provided by Seres and Newman (1976). They describe the progress of 100 patients in a treatment programme incorporating operant conditioning along with physical therapy, body mechanics, bio-feedback, relaxation training and education. Despite their positive results, an uncontrolled study of this kind offers little information about the relative efficacy of any one of its ingredients. More recent studies although based on programmes with controlled follow-up and improved assessment methodology, still reflect similar problems inherent in a *multi-method* programme. For example, McArthur *et al.* (1987) review a large sample of chronic low back pain patients from admission to a multidisciplinary programme through to initial and long-term follow-up over a period of six months to five years following treatment. Favourable outcomes were achieved by many of the respondents, and in several of the measures a good degree of stability was observed. The therapeutic techniques used on the programme included bio-feedback, attribution-based psychotherapy, patient-controlled medication reduction, physical reconditioning, vocational counselling, educational presentations, pool and recreational therapy, and assertiveness training.

Experimental design issues

Isolating effective variables

With so many therapeutic techniques, it is evidently a challenge to researchers to tease apart those variables which may be most effective. One such attempt by Sanders (1983) used component analysis of an operant treatment programme and a multiple-baseline single-case study design to compare relaxation, an operant activity programme, assertiveness and a functional analysis of pain. Measures of uptime, pain report and medication consumption were used to evaluate change. Findings showed that relaxation contributed most to overall improvement, followed by the operant activity programme. Jensen *et al.* (1991), in a comprehensive critical review, suggest that the paucity of true experimental designs may be partially addressed with greater utilisation of such single-subject designs which could provide data uniquely suited to understanding an individual's coping process over time. Other studies attempting to evaluate operant methods have been reviewed by Turner and Chapman (1982b), Linton (1982), Kerns and Turk (1983) and Latimer (1982).

Control groups

In addition to the problem of multiple ingredients, few studies have employed 'no-treatment' control groups. An early study to use a comparison group of any kind was that of Roberts and Reinhardt (1980). They compared the progress of three groups of patients: first, those accepted onto the operant programme; second, treatment refusers; and third, those who were rejected from the trial. Clearly these are not comparable groups, and it is not surprising to find that the treated group did better than the other two groups on measures of adjustment and occupational status follow-up. They also showed greater reductions in self-reported medication intake and ratings of pain-related interference with daily activities.

More recently, Guck *et al.* (1985) used a no-treatment comparison group to investigate an in-patient pain programme. In this study comparison group members had been accepted for treatment in the programme but lacked the financial ability or insurance coverage to begin treatment. Of the treated group, 60 per cent were considered a success using the criteria of Roberts and Reinhardt. Alternatively, none of the comparison group met these criteria. While the comparison group in Guck's study represents an improvement over rejected patients, there may still be important socio-economic and age differences between the treatment and no-treatment groups which it could be argued may confound results. Recently,

Deardoff *et al.* (1991) similarly compared a group of chronic pain patients treated in a comprehensive multidisciplinary pain programme with a group of patients who were accepted but not treated due to lack of insurance authorisation. Comparisons were made at evaluation and at a follow-up period averaging eleven months later. From evaluation to long-term follow-up, both the treated and non-treated groups showed significant decreases in self-report pain ratings and interference with activities ratings. However, only the treated group showed a decrease in addictive medication use and increase in work functioning. The return to work rate for the treated group was 48 per cent, with an additional 28 per cent of the patients being returned to vocational rehabilitation. None of the non-treated group returned to work or vocational rehabilitation.

Alternative comparison groups

Whilst the trend in the USA has traditionally been for in-patient treatment settings, the development of pain management programmes in the UK has reflected fundamental differences in health-care provision. Limited resources and facilities available to psychologists in the UK have contributed to difficulties in developing a consistent management approach. In some cases this has led to patients being treated on an out-patient basis. Skinner *et al.* (1990) report on the evaluation of a cognitive-behavioural treatment in out-patients with chronic pain. The programme, which took place for one afternoon a week for eight weeks, was conducted by a multidisciplinary team aiming to increase patients' skills for coping with chronic pain and its social, emotional and physical consequences. Results paralleled the findings of US studies with patients showing increase in activity, improvement in mood, increased coping skills, and decreased medication use and physical disability from assessment to one-month follow-up. A long-term follow-up to this study, the COPE programme, is currently additionally comparing a group-based treatment programme with an individual out-patient programme in an attempt to isolate variables which may contribute to the success of such programmes.

The use of out-patient settings may in fact have some advantages compared to the in-patient programmes favoured until recently in the USA in that they may partially overcome some of the problems of generalisability. Whilst in-patient programmes may produce impressive results in the short term, improvements have often not always been maintained when the patient returns to a more everyday environment, where family and social reinforcement may remain largely unaltered.

Out-patient programmes, on the other hand, mean that patients must handle day-to-day difficulties in their normal environment whilst on the programme. Support during such a programme may help patients initiate and maintain changes in family and social dynamics as well as day-to-day activities which may help break up patterns of positive and negative reinforcement of pain behaviours.

This idea has recently been extended to look at home-based programmes, and in the USA the advantages of home-based compared to out-patient programmes are currently being evaluated. Cott *et al.* (1990) compared patients who completed an interdisciplinary out-patient programme with a group who additionally received 'field management'. Field management through the use of specially trained field consultants is a mechanism by which interdisciplinary interventions can be implemented in non-institutional settings. Field consultants are drawn from a variety of applied backgrounds, such as psychology, education, nursing and physical education, and trained by behavioural psychologists in the principles of objective behavioural analysis, standard behavioural and cognitive-behavioural rehabilitative concepts, and the disease-illness distinction model.

In the study reported by Cott *et al.* (1990), field visits to patients' homes consisted of activities aimed at assessing and modifying functional capacity, general fitness and illness behaviours. Observations were also made of the patient's response to pain and the responses of family/significant others to illness behaviours. These behavioural observations made in the home and/or workplace were valuable in establishing (a) actual levels of functioning, (b) the degree to which the home environment was structured to promote invalidism (for example, who does the housework), and (c) the degree to which limitations on activity were a function of the environment, as indicated by discrepancies between the range or nature of activities performed at home versus those observed at the clinic or workplace. In this way a tailored treatment programme was designed, employing learning-based strategies aimed at identifying and modifying the relevant environmental contingencies and maladaptive cognitions that maintained the patient's pain behaviours.

Results showed that, in the group of field-managed patients, 84 per cent had a successful outcome as defined by (a) return to work and (b) reduced limitations on work, exercise, and daily living activities, compared with a successful outcome for 61 per cent of those completing the out-patient programme. Corey *et al.* (1987) showed similar results using home-based management, with 69.4 per cent of patients maintaining improved functional status at an average thirteen-month follow-up.

COGNITIVE METHODS

The use of cognitive coping strategies to influence the experience of pain has a long history. The term cognitive implies that these are techniques that influence pain through the medium of one's thoughts, as distinguished from behavioural techniques that modify overt behaviour, or physical intervention. The cognitive events altered may include an individual's attentional processes, images and/or self-statements.

Fernandez and Turk (1989), in a comprehensive study, found terminological inconsistency a major difficulty in reviewing the literature, in that several authors have employed different terms for what are apparently the same strategies. They argue that, while the several intuitive taxonomies which have been developed to enable the classification of cognitive coping strategies may serve as interesting points of departure, they are too idiosyncratic and open to disagreement to be generally useful.

Fernandez and Turk favour the development of categories first developed by Wack and Turk (1984) using the statistical approach of multi-dimensional scaling to develop an empirically derived taxonomy of cognitive strategies. Subsequently cluster analysis was employed to identify eight categories of coping strategies which were labelled:

1 Pleasant imaginings
2 Rhythmic cognitive activity
3 External focus of attention
4 Pain acknowledging
5 Dramatised coping
6 Neutral imaginings
7 Breathing activity
8 Behavioural activity.

In a subsequent study, Wack and Turk (1984) replicated these findings with a new sample of subjects. The first six of these categories were used to group cognitive strategies, as the last two categories relate to non-cognitive techniques.

Strategies involving a redirection of attention away from the site of stimulation, for example, viewing slides of landscapes or watching TV, were classified as external focus of attention. Those strategies involving imagery of neither a pleasant nor unpleasant quality, for example, imagined attendance of a lecture, were classified as neutral imagery. Strategies involving a dramatised reconstruction of the context in which nociception occurs, for example, imagining the pain as arising from an injury sustained during a football game, were classed as dramatised coping. Those involving cognitive activity of a repetitive or systemised nature, for example, counting backwards from 100 by threes, were classed as rhythmic cognitive activity. Strategies involving a reappraisal of the nociceptive stimulation in terms of objective sensation, for example, concentration on the sensation of dullness associated with nociception induced by cold water, were classed as pain acknowledging. The final category of pleasant imagery comprised those strategies involving imagining some pleasant scene or event, such as sitting in comfort and listening to music.

In evaluating the efficacy of such cognitive coping strategies, Fernandez and Turk report that meta-analysis of fifty-one relevant research studies reveals that 85 per cent of the investigations showed that cognitive strategies had a positive effect in enhancing pain tolerance/threshold or attenuating pain ratings as compared to no-treatment controls. They also point out that, in many of these studies, control groups were not prevented from the spontaneous use of such strategies. They further found that cognitive strategies provided a significant advantage over expectancy (placebo) controls. As for the relative efficacy, each individual class of strategy attenuated pain significantly, with imagery strategies tending to be most effective, whereas strategies involving repetitive cognitions or acknowledgement of sensations associated with pain were among the least effective.

It should be pointed out that the majority of the studies on which these findings were based pertain largely to acute pain induced in laboratory conditions. Whilst this does not diminish the usefulness of the classification categories nor the utility of the strategies in a clinical setting with chronic pain patients, care should be taken in extrapolating these results directly.

It has been suggested that the usefulness of cognitive strategies in ameliorating the effect of pain can be explained theoretically in terms of attentional models of processing. Limited-capacity models of attention, for example, as proposed by Broadbent (1958), Shiffrin and Schneider (1977) and Triesman (1964), provide one plausible explanation of the results. These models propose that attention is finite in capacity, and that given competing stimuli, attention becomes selective by filtering out or excluding part of the incoming information.

In clinical practice, explanations to patients based on models of attention are readily accepted and provide a rationale for the need to learn cognitive strategies, as cognitive coping strategies can be seen as impinging on the amount of attention available for nociception; that is, distraction displaces the processing of nociceptive information, thereby attenuating perceived pain. The differential efficacy of types of strategies as outlined by Fernandez and Turk may also possibly be explained in terms of attention. For example, imagery strategies were generally found to be superior to pain acknowledgment possibly because they produce greater distraction from pain. Similarly rhythmic cognitive activity might not have been sufficiently effective possibly because of its repetitive and monotonous quality, which is not ideal for capturing attention.

These attentional processes may also be accompanied by unique patterns of physiological activity. Melzack and Wall (1982) suggest that attention exerts its modulating effect on pain by way of descending cortical influences on a 'gate' in the dorsal horns of the spinal cord. Achterberg (1984) points out that higher brain centres are active during imaging, and Fernandez and Turk argue that these, in turn, may exert inhibitory effects on the gate when such strategies are employed during pain.

Cognitive stress management methods

Historically, stress has been viewed either as an event requiring adaptation, such as a significant life event, or a response within the individual, such as increased heart rate or blood pressure. More recently, Lazarus and Folkman (1984) have conceptualised stress as involving a relationship or transaction between environmental events and individual responses. This more broadly based view of stress has been widely adopted, possibly because it incorporates the multiple factors now thought to influence stress processes.

Stress is associated with chronic pain in a number of ways. First, research has demonstrated significant relationships between the experience of stress and both the incidence and severity of painful conditions. For example, in one study of a sample of community volunteers with chronic low back pain (Turner *et al.*, 1987), pain was identified by 35 per cent as the most stressful aspect of their lives. Equally, some of the more common consequences of chronic pain, such as loss of income or marital difficulties, may themselves be viewed as significant stressors.

A growing number of investigators have used models of stress and coping to help explain the differences in adjustment found among chronic pain patients. Although preliminary, some consistent findings are beginning to emerge. For example, patients who believe they can control their pain, who avoid catastrophising about their condition, and who believe they are not severely disabled appear to function better than those who do not (Jenson *et al.*, 1991).

Stress management techniques involve teaching the patient to identify and monitor cognitive responses to stressful situations and then develop alternative more constructive responses. In a group outcome study with tension headache sufferers, Holroyd *et al.* (1977) compared cognitive stress management with EMG bio-feedback and a waiting-list control condition. Cognitive stress management was found to be more effective than bio-feedback in reducing headache frequency and duration. Since bio-feedback is generally accepted as an effective method for tension headache, this might be considered powerful support for the effectiveness of cognitive stress management. However, Holroyd and Andrasik (1978) found no difference among groups receiving (a) cognitive stress management alone, (b) cognitive stress management and relaxation training, or (c) a control headache discussion group. All showed significant reductions in headache activity whilst a symptom-monitoring group showed no such reduction. Holroyd and Andrasik explain the improvement in the headache discussion group by suggesting that similar cognitive changes occurred despite the lack of active cognitive training.

Unfortunately, this conclusion can neither be confirmed nor disproved, since cognitive responses to stressful events were not assessed. An alternative interpretation might be that all three groups were responding to a common non-specific component of the three therapies – for example, the arousal of expectations of improvement. An attempt to look more closely at the active ingredients of cognitive stress management training for chronic pain is provided by Mitchell and White (1977), who used a dismantling design with successive stages of treatment being available to a reduced proportion of the initial sample of migraine patients. Their results support the view that the main reduction in headache frequency occurred as a result of active treatment, namely relaxation and cognitive stress management rather than from placebo components of the programme.

METHODS AIMED AT PHYSIOLOGICAL CHANGE

Relaxation and bio-feedback

Relaxation training has been widely used in the treatment of chronic pain, and there are a number of reasons why relaxation may be effective in lowering pain. First, relaxation training may have a general effect on levels of muscle tension throughout the body. Second, relaxation may be associated with anxiety reduction, in which case pain might be perceived as less intense (Woodforde and Merskey, 1972). Third, the relaxation procedure itself may serve a distracting function in that attention to the exercises and relaxing mental imagery may reduce attention paid to unpleasant sensory input. Fourth, it may act to increase patients perceived control over their physiological activity and their pain. Since the belief that one has control over a painful event has been shown to increase pain tolerance (Thompson, 1981), relaxation training may have an indirect effect by altering the level of perceived control.

Studies investigating the value of relaxation training in the treatment of tension headache generally report encouraging results (e.g. Fichtler and Zimmerman, 1973; Tasto and Hinkle, 1973; Warner and Lance, 1975). Most reports, however, have described uncontrolled outcome studies or are largely anecdotal. A number of studies have compared relaxation training with EMG bio-feedback (Chesney and Shelton, 1976; Haynes and Griffin, 1975; Cox et al., 1975) and have shown both to be more effective than a no-treatment control. It is therefore reasonable to conclude that relaxation training may be an effective treatment for tension headache.

A similar picture emerges for the role of relaxation in the treatment of migraine (e.g. Andreychuk and Skriver, 1977; Blanchard et al., 1978). In other chronic pain conditions there have been relatively few investigations of its value. Gessel and Alderman (1971) describe case studies of relaxation training for patients with myofascial pain dysfunction. Although they report encouraging results, the study is methodologically weak. Therapists' judgements of progress were used to evaluate outcome, no control groups were included, and follow-up data were not obtained.

Relaxation has also been used within a desensitisation framework in the treatment of dysmenorrhoea (Tasto and Chesney, 1974; Chesney and Tasto, 1975). Both these studies reported reductions in menstrual symptoms following the desensitisation procedure and the later report suggests that desensitisation may be more effective for patients with spasmodic rather than congestive dysmenorrhoea.

Bio-feedback has also been shown to be effective for some groups, although again its mode of action is unclear. Four main types of bio-feedback have been applied to the problem of chronic pain (Turner and Chapman, 1982a). The first of these, EEG bio-feedback, aims to induce a state similar to relaxation by training patients to increase alpha wave activity. Studies investigating its value for headaches have produced conflicting results. Melzack and Perry (1975) have reported on a study that has used EEG feedback for conditions other than headache. With mixed chronic pain patients, they found that hypnosis in combination with alpha feedback was more effective than either alone. These mixed results are perhaps not altogether surprising in view of the uncertain status of the psychological state associated with increased alpha activity.

EMG bio-feedback has also been most extensively used for tension headache, on the assumption that pain arises from raised levels of muscle tension in the frontalis and other muscles of the head and neck. Although a range of studies (see Turner and Chapman, 1982a) show that EMG bio-feedback is effective for tension headache only one study has suggested that it may be more effective than relaxation training alone (Hutchings and Reinking, 1976). EMG and thermal bio-feedback for chronic headaches are well reviewed by Chapman (1986).

Studies investigating the value of EMG bio-feedback for non-headache states (mainly back pain, phantom limb and arthritis) are reviewed by Linton (1982). He concludes that these generally show reductions in pain ratings and tension in the target muscles, although the studies are largely uncontrolled and the clinical significance of the pain reductions is not possible to assess.

Skin temperature feedback has been used almost exclusively for migraine on the assumption that increases in peripheral blood-flow (which occur with increases in skin temperature) are associated with decreases in cranial sympathetic activity. Since migraine is thought to be due to excessive vascular responsivity, this reduction in cranial sympathetic activity should lower the frequency of migraine headache. This basic assumption, like that of the role of muscle tension levels in the development of tension headache, remains unproven. Although a number of studies have suggested that skin temperature feedback may be effective (Turin and Johnson, 1976), others have shown that false feedback can also produce reductions in headache frequency (Mullinix et al., 1978). This suggests that the treatment may be having powerful non-specific effects.

Blood volume pulse feedback is another approach that has been used exclusively for migraine headache. The assumption has been that teaching patients to decrease cranial pulse amplitude via volume feedback will reduce extracranial vascular dilatation and hence reduce headache frequency. Although preliminary studies are encouraging, further investigations are required before the value of this kind of feedback can be adequately assessed.

It should be concluded that the quality of investigations for the efficacy of relaxation training and various forms of bio-feedback in the treatment of chronic pain has been rather poor. The standard has been highest for headache, and here the evidence suggests that relaxation training may be just as effective as the more complicated and expensive bio-feedback procedures. This conclusion is also supported by the meta-analytic review of outcome studies by Blanchard et al. (1980). For a review, see Andrasik and Blanchard (1983). How these methods produce their effects unfortunately remains unclear. The majority of studies have still not incorporated placebo control procedures whose credibility has been demonstrated to be equal to that of the 'true' treatments. In the absence of such controls, we cannot conclude that relaxation and bio-feedback have been shown to have specific effects. The need for a careful evaluation of non-specific factors is particularly evident where bio-feedback is concerned. The inherent credibility of this ostensibly scientific procedure with its costly and impressive equipment has led Stroebel and Glueck (1973) to describe it as the 'ultimate placebo'.

GENERAL ISSUES IN THE APPLICATION OF PSYCHOLOGICAL TREATMENT METHODS TO CHRONIC PAIN PATIENTS

Treatment credibility

Unlike patients with anxiety or depression, pain patients typically do not formulate their difficulties in psychological terms. Most chronic pain patients, with the possible exception of those with headache, believe that there is an organic cause for their distress. They may therefore be unwilling to accept a psychological approach to treatment and may construe the referral to a psychologist as a sign that the doctors are not taking their pain seriously or that they are thought to have imaginary pain. In several areas of psychotherapy research it has been shown that the credibility of therapy rationales and the appropriateness of patient expectations may be important determinants of the effectiveness of particular techniques (Frank *et al.*, 1978; Shapiro, 1981). These factors are likely to have special significance in the management of chronic pain patients. In the clinical setting there are a number of variables which, although not yet empirically tested, seem likely to affect the initial credibility of therapeutic methods designed for use with this group. These will be briefly discussed.

Method of referral

The most unpromising start is likely to occur when the patient is referred to a psychologist based in a psychiatric unit where little collaboration is possible with the referring medical source and where the patient has not been given further follow-up appointments with the medical staff. This may perpetuate the notion that there are two kinds of pain, real and imaginary, and that the patient is thought to be suffering from the latter variety.

A better arrangement is likely to be for the psychologist to work alongside the medical staff. Involvement in the patient's initial medical assessment, either as an observer or perhaps in the pain assessment itself, may result in the psychologist's being more readily accepted as a part of the pain investigation and treatment programme. Psychological treatment will not, therefore, be seen as a last ditch resort for only the most unpromising patients. It may also reinforce the view that psychological variables play an important part in all pain experience. At the very least, psychologists receiving pain patient referrals from medical staff should attempt to see the patient in the pain clinic or medical out-patient

clinic and should consult closely with other staff, such as doctors, physiotherapists and occupational therapists. In American pain clinics, psychologists
are now a recognised and regular part of the personnel and in Britain clinics are
beginning to employ psychologists.

Explanation of pain and treatment rationale

Leventhal *et al.* (1980) suggest that it is essential for patients to attempt to
understand and regulate any treatment in order to maximise compliance. They
suggest that it is incorrect to view patients as passive objects who need to be
pushed to action by means of education and motivational devices. They argue
that patients are active agents taking in and interpreting information. In their
opinion, the view of the patient as an object is a heritage of medical and
behaviourist models, which regard patients as passive uninformed targets and
practitioners as active prescribing experts. In their 'common sense theory of
illness', they suggest that three basic sources of information are likely to shape
and change patients' theory of illness. These are (1) bodily experience, (2)
information from the external social environment, for example, health-care
providers, family, media, and (3) information based on past experience of illness.

A study by Johnson and Leventhal (1974) illustrates this theory. They argued
that if fear interfered with coping, the reduction of fear could facilitate patients'
ability to cope with objective situational demands. In a study of patients about to
undergo endoscopic examination, patients were given information preparing
them for the sensory experiences entailed, for example, numbness of the throat
caused by anaesthesia, the gagging sensation caused by the optic fibre tube, the
fullness of the stomach when inflated with air. By preparing patients to observe
and objectify these specific sensory experiences, they suggest that these sensations were converted into cues for coping rather than cues of threat. Results
showed that prepared patients showed less heart rate acceleration, much less
gagging, and exerted control over the rate at which they swallowed the optic
fibre tube.

In view of the potential discrepancy between patients' views of their painful
condition and the psychologists' understanding of pain, it will be important in
the initial stages of contact to provide a framework for patients to understand
how psychological and physical variables can interact to affect the intensity of
their pain and the distress it engenders. If the patient can come to understand a
model of pain in which desynchrony may occur between its different dimensions, then the credibility of psychological intervention is likely to be increased.

GENERAL CONCLUSIONS

There is growing evidence to suggest that psychologists can make a contribution
to the management of chronic pain conditions using methods directed at the
behavioural, cognitive and physiological components of pain. The overall quality of

research on these methods has been poor, however, and few conclusions may yet be drawn concerning the role of specific procedural variables. In view of the multi-dimensional nature of pain, it seems important that the approach adopted should be tailored to the pattern of pain responses exhibited by the individual patient. Pain management approaches have developed away from early uni-dimensional therapeutic approaches based solely on contingency management towards more broadly based cognitive-behavioural interventions. Holzman *et al.*, (1986) point out that the general goal of most cognitive-behavioural programmes is to develop on the part of the patient a reconceptualisation of his or her pain. It is possible that as research into process factors is extended, these changes in beliefs may emerge as the most important predictors of outcome.

Kanfer and Karoly (1982) suggest that for self-management to operate, there must be a shift in the patient from well-established, habitual, automatic but ineffective responses towards systematic problem-solving, long-term control of affect, and behavioural persistence. Techniques are employed to teach the patient to recognise and alter the association between thoughts, feelings, behaviours and environmental stimuli, and pain. Therapeutic gain is enhanced when the patient is actively involved and accepts responsibility for change.

REFERENCES

Achterberg, J. (1984) 'Imagery and medicine: pschophysiological speculations', *Journal of Mental Imagery* 8: 1–14.

Andrasik, F. and Blanchard, E. B. (1983) 'Application of biofeedback to therapy', in C. E. Waken (ed.) *Handbook of Clinical Psychology: Therapy Research and Practice*: Homewood, Ill.: Dorsey (1123–64).

Andreychuk, T. and Skriver, C. (1977) 'Hypnosis and biofeedback in the treatment of migraine headache', *International Journal of Clinical and Experimental Hypnosis* 23: 172–83.

Blanchard, E. B., Andrasik, F., Ahles, T. A., Teders, S. J. and O'Keefe, D. (1980) 'Migraine and tension headache: a meta-analytic review', *Behavior Therapy* 11: 613–31.

Blanchard, E. B., Theobald, D., Williamson, D., Silver, B. and Brown, D. (1978) 'Temperature biofeedback in the treatment of migraine headaches', *Archives of General Psychiatry* 35: 581–8.

Broadbent, D. E. (1958) *Perception and Communication*, London: Pergamon Press.

Chapman, S. L. (1986) 'A review and clinical perspective on the use of EMG and thermal biofeedback for chronic heachaches', *Pain* 27: 1–43.

Chesney, M. A. and Shelton, J. L. (1976) 'A comparison of muscle relaxation and electromyogram biofeedback treatments for muscle contraction headache', *Journal of Behaviour Therapy and Experimental Psychiatry* 7: 115–21.

Chesney, M. and Tasto, D. (1975) 'The effectiveness of behaviour modification with spasmodic and congestive dysmenorrhoea', *Behaviour Research and Therapy* 13: 245–54.

Corey, D. T., Etlin, D. and Miller, P. C. (1987) 'A home-based pain management and rehabilitation programme: an evaluation', *Pain* 29(2): 219–30.

Cott, A., Anchel, H., Goldberg, W. M., Fabich, M. and Parkinson, W. (1990) 'Non-institutional treatment of chronic pain by field management: an outcome study with comparison group', *Pain* 40: 183–94.

Cox, D. J., Freundlich, A. and Meyer, R. G. (1975) 'Differential effectiveness of electro-myographic feedback, verbal relaxation instructions and medication placebo with tension headaches', *Journal of Consulting and Clinical Psychology* 43: 892–8.

Deardoff, W. W., Rubin, H. S. and Scott, D. W. (1991) 'Comprehensive multidisciplinary treatment of chronic pain: a follow-up study of treated and non-treated groups', *Pain* 45: 35–43.

Fernandez, E. and Turk, D. C. (1989) 'The utility of cognitive coping strategies for altering pain perception: a meta-analysis', *Pain* 38(2): 123–36.

Fichtler, H. and Zimmerman, R. R. (1973) 'Changes in reported pain from tension headaches', *Perceptual and Motor Skills* 36: 712.

Fordyce, W. E. (1976) *Behavioural Methods for Chronic Pain and Illness*, St. Louis: C.V. Mosby.

Fordyce, W. E., Fowler, R. and Lehmann, J. (1968) 'Some implications of learning in problems of chronic pain', *Journal of Chronic Disorders* 21: 179–90.

Fordyce, W. E., Fowler, R. S., Lehmann, J. F., Delateur, B. J., Sand, P. L. and Treischmann, R. B. (1973) 'Operant conditioning in the treatment of chronic pain', *Archives of Physical Medicine and Rehabilitation* 54: 399–408.

Frank, J., Huehn-Saric, R., Imber, S. and Liberman, B. (1978) *Effective Ingredients of Successful Psychotherapy*, New York: Brunner/Mazel.

Gessel, A. H. and Alderman, M. (1971) 'Management of myofascial pain dysfunction syndrome of the temperomandibula joint by tension control training', *Pychosomatics* 12: 302–9.

Guck, T. P., Skultety, F. M., Meilman, P. W. and Dowdy, E. T. (1985) 'Multidisciplinary follow-up study: evaluation with a no-treatment control group', *Pain* 21: 295–306.

Haynes, S. and Griffin, P. (1975) 'Electromyographic biofeedback and relaxation instructions in the treatment of muscle contraction headaches', *Behavior Therapy* 6: 672–8.

Holroyd, K. A. and Andrasik, F. (1978) 'Coping and the self-control of chronic tension headache', *Journal of Consulting and Clinical Psychology* 46: 1036–45.

Holroyd, K. A., Andrasik, F. and Westbrook, T. (1977) 'Cognitive control of tension headache', *Cognitive Therapy and Research* 1: 121–33.

Holzman, A. D., Turk, D. C. and Kerns, R. D. (1986) 'The cognitive-behavioural approach to the management of chronic pain', in A. D. Holzman and D. C. Turk (eds) *Pain Management: A Handbook of Psychological Approaches*, New York: Pergamon.

Hutchings, D. F. and Reinking, R. H. (1976) 'Tension headaches: what form of therapy is most effective?' *Biofeedback and Self-Regulation* 1: 190–93.

Jenson, M. P., Turner, J. A., Romano, J. M. and Karoly, P. (1991) 'Coping with chronic pain: a review of the literature', *Pain* 47(3): 249–83.

Johnson, J. E. and Leventhal, H. (1974) 'Effects of accurate expectations and behavioural instructions on reactions during a noxious medical examination', *Journal of Personality and Social Psychology* 29: 710–18.

Kanfer, F. H. and Karoly, P. (1982) 'The psychology of self-management: abiding issues and tentative directions', in P. Karoly and F. H. Kanfer (eds) *Self-management and behaviour change*, Elmsford, New York: Pergamon.

Keefe, F. J. and Gil, K. M. (1985) 'Recent advances in the behavioural assessment and treatment of chronic pain', *Annals of Behavioural Medicine* 7: 11–16.

Kerns, R. D. and Turk, D. C. (1983) 'Psychological treatment for chronic pain: a selective review', *Clinical Psychology Review* 3: 15–26.

Latimer, P. R. (1982) 'External contingency management for chronic pain: a critical review of the evidence', *American Journal of Psychiatry* 139(10) 1308–12.

Lazarus, R. A. and Folkman, S. (1984) *Stress, Appraisal, and Coping*, New York: Springer.

Leventhal, H., Meyer, D. and Nerenz, D. (1980) 'The common-sense representation of illness danger', in S. Rachman (ed.) *Contributions to Medical Psychology, Vol. 2,* Oxford: Pergamon.

Linton, S. J. (1982) 'A critical review of behavioural treatments for chronic benign pain other than headache', *British Journal of Clinical Psychology* 21: 321–37.

McArthur, D. L., Cohen, M. J., Gottlieb, H. J., Naliboff, B. D. and Schandler, S. L. (1987) 'Treating chronic low back pain. I Admission to initial follow-up. II Long-term follow-up', *Pain* 29: 1–22; 23–38.

Melzack, R. and Perry, C. (1975) 'Self-regulation of pain. The use of alpha-feedback and hypnotic training for the control of chronic pain', *Experimental Neurology* 46: 452–69.

Melzack, R. and Wall, P. D. (1982) *The Challenge of Pain,* New York: Basic Books.

Mitchell, K. R. and White, R. G. (1977) 'Behavioural self-management: an application to the problem of migraine headaches', *Behavior Therapy* 8: 213–22.

Mullinix, J. M., Norton, B. J., Hack, S. and Fishman, M. A. (1978) 'Skin temperature biofeedback and migraine', *Headache* 17: 242–4.

Pearce, S. (1983) 'A review of cognitive-behavioural methods for the treatment of chronic pain', *Journal of Psychosomatic Research* 27: 431–40.

Roberts, A. H. and Reinhardt, L. (1980) 'The behavioural management of chronic pain: long-term follow-up with comparison groups', *Pain* 8: 151–62.

Rosenstiel, A. K. and Keefe, F. J. (1983) 'The use of coping strategies in chronic low-back pain patients: relationship to patients' characteristics and current adjustment', *Pain* 17: 38–44.

Rybstein-Blinchik, E. (1979) 'Effects of different cognitive strategies on chronic pain experience', *Journal of Behavioural Medicine* 2: 93–101.

Sanders, S. H. (1983) 'Component analysis of a behavioural treatment programme for chronic low-back pain', *Behavioural Therapy* 14: 697–705.

Seres, J. L. and Newman, R. (1976) 'Results of treatment of chronic low back pain at the Portland Pain Centre', *Journal of Neurosurgery* 45: 32–6.

Shapiro, D. (1981) 'Comparative credibility of treatment rationales. Three tests of expectancy theory', *British Journal of Clinical Psychology* 20: 111–22.

Shiffrin, R. M. and Schneider, W. (1977) 'Controlled and automatic human information processing. II Perceptual learning, automatic attending, and a general theory', *Psychological Review* 84: 127–90.

Skinner, J. B., Erskine, A., Pearce, S., Rubenstein, M., Taylor, M. and Fosters, C. (1990) 'Evaluation of a cognitive behavioural treatment programme in out-patients with chronic pain', *Journal of Psychosomatic Research* 14: 13–19.

Sternbach, R. A. (1986) 'Pain and daily "Hassles" in the USA: findings of the Nuprin Pain Report, *Pain* 27: 69–80.

Stroebel, C. F. and Glueck, B. C. (1973) 'Biofeedback treatment in medicine and psychiatry: an ultimate placebo?' *Seminars in Psychiatry* 5(4): 379–93.

Tasto, D. L. and Chesney, M. A. (1974) 'Muscle relaxation therapy for primary dysmenorrhoea', *Behavioural Research and Therapy* 5: 668–672.

Tasto, D. L. and Hinkle, J. E. (1973) 'Muscle relaxation treatment for tension headaches', *Behaviour Research and Therapy* 11: 347–9.

Thompson, S. C. (1981) 'Will it hurt less if I can control it? A complex answer to a simple question', *Psychological Bulletin* 90: 89–101.

Triesman, A. M. (1964) 'Monitoring and storage of irrelevant messages in selective attention', *Journal of Verbal Learning and Behaviour* 3: 449–59.

Turin, A. and Johnson, W. G. (1976) 'Biofeedback therapy for migraine headaches', *Archives of General Psychiatry* 33: 517–19.

Turner, J. A. (1982) 'Comparison of group progressive-relaxation training and cognitive-behavioural group therapy for chronic low back pain', *Journal of Consulting and Clinical Psychology* 50: 757–65.

Turner, J. A. and Chapman, C. R. (1982a) 'Psychological intervention for chronic pain: a critical review. 1. Relaxation and training and biofeedback', *Pain* 12: 1–21.

Turner, J. A. and Chapman, C. R. (1982b) 'Psychological interventions for chronic pain: a critical review. 11. Operant conditioning, hypnosis and cognitive-behavioural therapy', *Pain* 12: 23–46.

Turner, J. A. and Clancy, S. (1986) 'Strategies for coping with chronic low-back pain: relationship to pain and disability', *Pain* 24: 355–64.

Turner, J. A., Clancy, S. and Vitaliano, P. P. (1987) 'Relationships of stress, appraisal and coping to chronic low-back pain, *Behaviour Research and Therapy* 25: 281–8.

Wack, J. T. and Turk, D. C. (1984) 'Latent structure in strategies for coping with pain, *Health Psychology* 3: 27–43.

Warner, G. and Lance, J. (1975) 'Relaxation therapy in migraine and chronic tension headache', *Medical Journal of Australia* 1: 298–301.

Woodforde, J. M. and Merskey, H. (1972) 'Personality traits of patients with chronic pain', *Journal of Psychosomatic Research* 16: 167–72.

Chapter 34

Introduction to neuropsychology and neuropsychological assessment

Graham E. Powell and Barbara A. Wilson

The purpose of this chapter is to introduce the topics of neuropsychology, neuropsychological assessment and assessment for neuropsychological rehabilitation. We will introduce the language of neurology and neuropsychology, describe the physical brain and its main components, outline the structure and function of the lobes, indicate what tasks and tests might be used to detect dysfunctions of important regions, give classifications of the main neuropsychological disorders, and finally, deal with the process of interviewing, assessment and report writing.

TERMINOLOGY

The student new to neuropsychology can find the terminology of the brain a real obstacle to interest and understanding, and it certainly puts many people off the whole area. Therefore, we begin with a glossary of useful high frequency words.

Spatial orientation terminology

mid-line   the line or plane dividing left and right hemispheres
medial   at or on the mid-line
mesial   towards the mid-line
lateral   on the side; away from the mid-line
superior   above
inferior   below
anterior   in front; towards the face
posterior   behind; towards the back of the head
central   on the plane dividing anterior from posterior
caudal   towards the spinal cord
rostral   away from the spinal cord
ventral   towards the chest and abdominal surface; towards the top of the brain in humans
dorsal   towards the back surface; towards the bottom of the brain in humans
ipsilateral   on the same side of the body

contralateral   on the other side of the body
proximal   near
distal   far

Anatomical terminology

neuron   a nerve cell capable of transmitting an impulse
gyrus   a bump or elevation on the surface of the brain
sulcus   the groove or fissure between two gyri
grey matter   concentration of nerve cell bodies
white matter   concentration of nerve cell projections (axons)
cortex   the grey matter covering the outside surface of the brain and tucked into
the sulci
lobe   an area of brain usually, but not always, marked off from the rest of the
brain by prominent sulci
lobule   a major feature within a lobe; one or two prominent gyri, say.
ventricle   space in the brain through which cerebro-spinal fluid (CSF) runs
pia mater, arachnoid, dura mater   the three tough layers or membranes
between brain and skull
meninges   the above three layers taken together

Lesion terminology

lesion   any damage whatsoever to the brain
sclerosis   death of any brain tissue
-oma   suffix indicating abnormal growth as in neuroma (tumour of the neurons);
glioma (tumour of the glial cells that act as supportive structures of the brain);
and meningioma (tumour of the meninges)
neoplasm   any new growth of tissue (i.e. tumour)
angioma or arteriovenous malformation (AVM)   knot or tangle or growth of
distended blood vessels
stroke   general term for the behavioural and cognitive effects of a cerebro-
vascular accident
cerebro-vascular accident (CVA)   damage done by a spontaneous disruption of
blood supply, usually attributable to degeneration of the arteries, as in old age,
arteriosclerosis or certain diseases
haemorrhage   bleeding
haematoma   a collection of blood in one site
infarct   localised area of damage due to an interrupted blood supply
ischaemia   inadequate flow of blood
embolism   the obstruction of blood flow, e.g. by a blood clot or air bubble
aneurysm   abnormal swelling of a blood vessel
infectious diseases   those that affect the brain include bacterial meningitis,
tuberculous infection, brain abscess, neurosyphilis, leptospirosis (e.g.

encephalitis and myelitis), and viral infections (e.g. meningitis, encephalitis, rabies, Creutzfeldt-Jakob disease)

demyelinating diseases affecting the myelin sheaths of axons; includes multiple sclerosis

diseases affecting the basal ganglia includes Parkinsonism and Huntingdon's chorea

dementia a general term for any disease causing progressive deterioration of the CNS, including many of the above but especially Alzheimer's disease (pre-senile dementia) and Pick's disease (senile dementia), or, inclusively, senile dementia Alzheimer's type (SDAT)

head injury an imprecise term implying either a blow to the head or rapid acceleration/deceleration of it; or penetration by a foreign body or skull fragments

brain injury a slightly less imprecise term to screen out cases of only superficial damage to the face or head (e.g screens out facial cuts and broken jaws); includes only those cases with damage to the CNS.

Functional terminology

afferent fibre neuron conveying information into a given area; from the sense organ, for example

efferent fibre pathway conveying information to a given area; to the muscles, for example

neuro-transmitter the chemicals by which neurons communicate with each other at their synapses, especially acetylcholine, dopamine, norepinephrine, serotonin and gamma aminobutyric acid

function the specific job, or information-processing capacity, of a given area

functional system the linkage of several areas of brain (i.e. several functions) to subserve a complex task (e.g. walking, reading)

primary or nuclear zone a 'projection' area of brain receiving or sending impulses to the periphery

secondary zone brain surrounding primary zones where information is decoded or encoded into a complex cognition

tertiary zone areas where secondary zones overlap, responsible for the most complex mental activity including cross-modal processing

association cortex any cortex outside the primary zones

localisation of function the attempt to map a function on to one area of cortex, or to map a functional system on to several connected areas

plasticity of function the extent to which intact areas of brain can come to subserve a new function

lateralisation of function the extent to which a given function is localised in one or other of the hemispheres

dominance as for localization but with special reference to language functions *concussion*   temporary disturbance of cognitive processing including confusion and minor memory upset after mild head injury

unconsciousness   the state in which the person exhibits a degree of reduced responsiveness to the environment after head injury; the eyes are closed

coma   unconsciousness, usually for a prolonged period, of varying depth

persistent vegetative state   the person appears to be awake but does not respond to the environment in any meaningful way and requires total physical care, such as feeding and toileting

Terminology and investigations

X-rays   simple X-rays are still used in order to detect fractures of the skull; they are poor at visualising the soft tissues of the brain

Electroencephalogram (EEG)   the changing electrical activity over different areas of the brain, usually recorded as a paper trace

evoked potentials (EPs)   reaction of the EEG recording to sensory stimuli such as sounds, lights or tactile sensation, usually obtained by averaging over many trials

computerised transaxial tomography (CT)   computer-enhanced picture of the brain based on repeated low intensity X-rays taken from different angles

positron emission tomography (PET)   typically, radioactively labelled glucose or oxygen is taken up by the brain and the radioactivity that is detected is converted into a picture; often used to measure blood flow.

single-photon emission computed tomography (SPECT)   similar to PET but uses single photons rather than X-rays

magnetic resonance imaging (MRI)   computer generated picture of the brain based upon radio waves given off by brain tissue as it relaxes after being in a strong magnetic field

OVERALL FEATURES OF THE BRAIN

Gross divisions of the brain

The cortex (or neocortex because of its recency in evolutionary terms) is grouped together with the most immediate subcortical structures (i.e. basal ganglia, limbic system, olfactory bulb, lateral ventricles and thalamus) to constitute the *fore brain*. The remaining structures (epithalamus, hypothalamus, third ventricle, tegmentum, cerebral aqueduct, cerebellum, pons, fourth ventricle and medulla oblongata) are less involved in complex sensory integration and more concerned with basic, primitive physiological functioning, such as the control of level of arousal; these structures are collectively known as the *brain stem*. Beneath the brain stem comes the *spinal cord*. The gross divisions of the brain are well presented by magnetic resonance images in Kolb and Whishaw (1990: 854–60).

The gyri and lobes of the cortex

The cortex divides, to some extent arbitrarily, into four lobes, frontal, parietal, occipital and temporal, often divided at their boundaries by prominent gyri and sulci (see Figures 34.1 and 34.2). The lobes refer simply to broad regions of brain and do not imply functional unity.

Cytoarchitectonic areas

The cortex can also be divided into areas with a similar structure of nerve cells. The cortex is 50–100 cells thick, arranged in six layers. In various areas different layers will predominate, hence giving rise to Brodman's well-known map of cortical structure published in 1909, depicted in a simplified fashion in Figure 34.3. Some areas have histologically distinct boundaries; other areas merge into each other.

Subcortical structures

These will be detailed in the section on pp. 667–70, but for the moment the medial view of the brain in Figure 34.4 will orientate the reader to the location of some of the major structures.

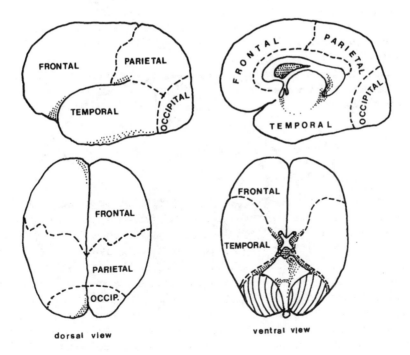

Figure 34.1 The lobes of the brain

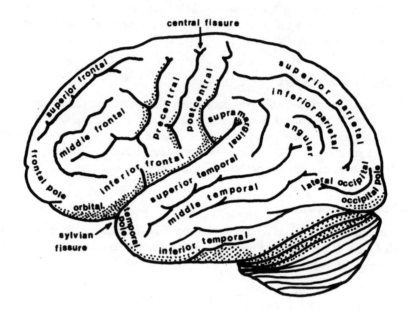

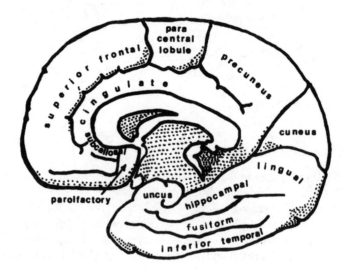

Figure 34.2 The main gyri of the brain

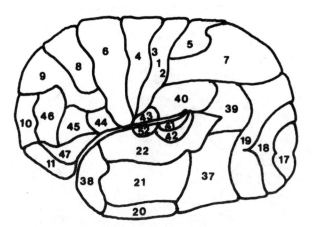

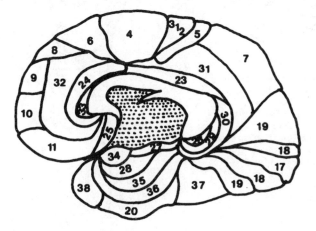

Figure 34.3 Simplified version of Brodman's map

The ventricles of the brain

The CSF-filled spaces in the brain used to be visualised by air encephalogram (AEG) but now this technique has been overtaken by CT images. A knowledge of their structure, given in Figure 34.5, is important because (1) their damage can lead to a blockage of CSF flow, which can give rise to an increase in cranial pressure, crushing cortex against the skull or causing the head to swell if the skull is still malleable as in childhood hydrocephalus, and (2) distortions in their shape and size are a clue to the site and nature of space-occupying lesions. There are four ventricles. The first and second are the lateral ventricles, with anterior, posterior and inferior horns extending into the frontal, occipital and temporal

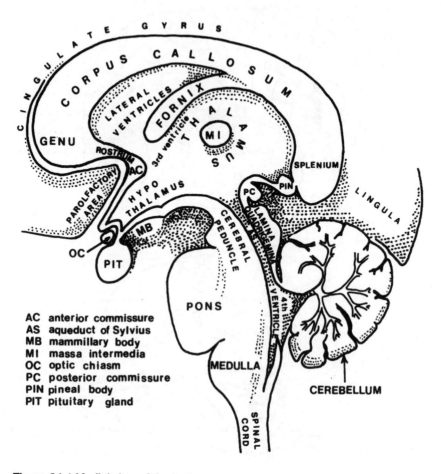

Figure 34.4 Medial view of the brain

lobes respectively. The third ventricle is on the mid-line; one should note the 'hole' in the third ventricle, which is where the left thalamus joins the right thalamus (called the intermediate mass of the thalamus). The new student should firmly grasp this landmark as it accurately locates the thalamus and thence all remaining lower structures in relation to the cortex. The flow of CSF continues down a fine tube (cerebral aqueduct, aqueduct of Sylvius) to the fourth ventricle).

The blood supply

Arteries take oxygenated blood to the brain and veins drain it away. Because damage and abnormalities of the blood supply (e.g. aneurysm, embolism,

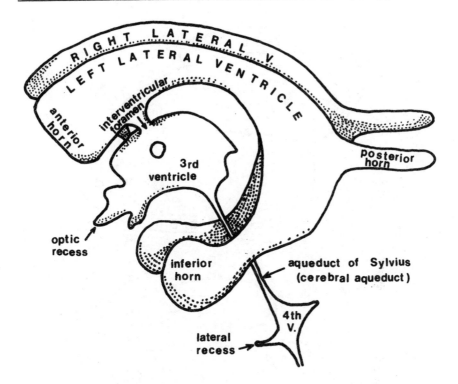

Figure 34.5 The ventricles of the brain

ischaemia) can impair cortical activity, it is necessary to know the three main cerebral arteries and the regions of cortex they fuel, as outlined in Figure 34.6.

The nerve supply

The brain is supplied with its sensory data and outputs motor commands via twelve cranial nerves entering at various points at the base. The nerves are: I olfactory (smells); II optic (vision); III oculomotor (reactions to light, lateral movement of eyes, eyelid movement); IV Trochlear (vertical eye movement); V Trigeminal (masticatory movements); VI Abducens (lateral eye movement); VII Facial (facial movements); VIII Auditory vesibular (hearing); IX Glossopharangeal (tongue and pharynx); XI Spinal accessory (neck muscles and viscera); XII hypoglossal (tongue muscles).

The projection zones of the cortex

The sense data arrive at the cortex, via the cranial nerves above, at a few

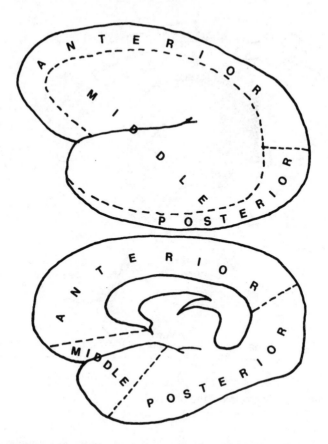

Figure 34.6 The areas of the cortex supplied by the anterior, middle and posterior cerebal arteries

well-defined points known as the 'nuclear' or 'primary' zones (Luria, 1966; 1973). The four primary zones (three sensory and one motor) are located as in Figure 34.7. A knowledge of these primary zones is the first step towards a functional topography of the cortex. The location of secondary and tertiary zones is also indicated, but it must be remembered that although primary and secondary zones are well demarcated, the boundaries between secondary and tertiary areas are somewhat hazy.

The primary, secondary and tertiary areas can be superimposed on Brodman's cytoarchitectoaic map as indicated in Table 34.1 (Kolb and Whishaw, 1980).

Main connections between regions of the cortex

There is naturally a flow of information between all the regions of the cortex.

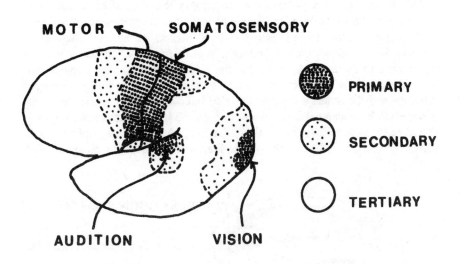

Figure 34.7 The functional zones of the cortex

Table 34.1 Functional areas of the cortex mapped on to Brodman's system

Functional area	Brodman's area
(a) Vision	
primary	17
secondary	18, 19, 20, 21, 37
(b) Audition	
primary	41
secondary	22, 42
(c) Body senses	
primary	1, 2, 3
secondary	5, 7
(d) Sensory, tertiary	7, 22, 37, 39, 40
(e) Motor	
primary	4
secondary	6
eye movement	8
speech	44
(f) Motor, tertiary	9, 10, 11, 45, 46, 47

Source: Kolb and Whishaw (1980, revised 1990)

The flow from primary to secondary to tertiary has already been mentioned implicitly, and is part of a more general pattern of each neuron being connected to its neighbours, but there is also a flow of information between more distal regions. Such a flow tends to occur along a few main pathways that are represented in Figure 34.8. Note that the information exchange between one hemisphere and the other occurs through two main bundles of fibres, the corpus callosum and the anterior commisure, also indicated in Figure 34.8, and also through the hippocampal commisure, in Figure 34.11. Naturally the cortex is also linked to subcortical sites, via the projection pathways, for example. The subcortical connections of the cortex will be dealt with in the section on pp. 667–70.

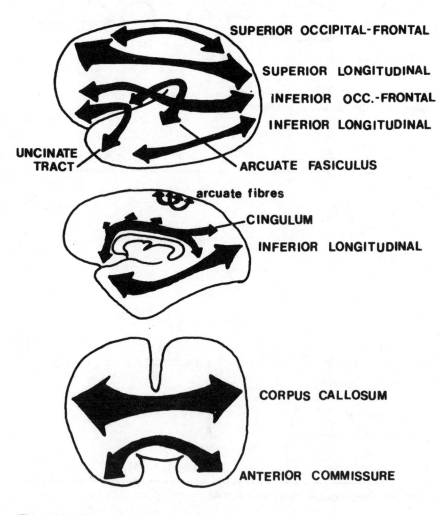

Figure 34.8 The main cortical pathways

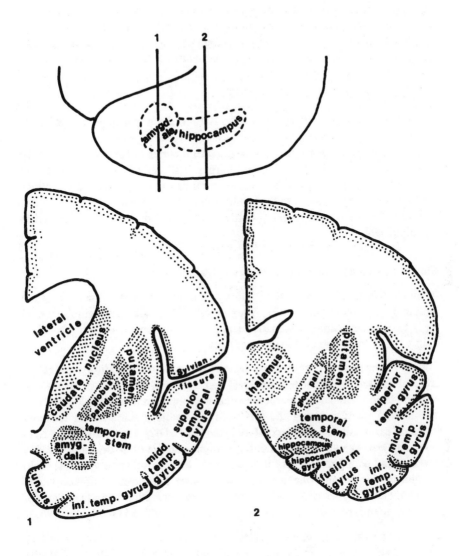

Figure 34.9 Cross-sections through the temporal lobe

TEMPORAL LOBES

Summary of structure

The lateral surface comprises the superior, middle and inferior temporal gyri. The insular cortex, hidden from view within the Sylvian fissure, comprises three more gyri – the uncus, fusiform gyrus and parahippocampal gyrus – and are phylogenetically older and sometimes termed the archicortex. The archicortex also includes two subcortical or limbic structures, namely the amygdala and the hippocampus. The two cross-sections through the temporal lobe shown in Figure 34.9 make clear the external and internal structures of the temporal lobe.

Summary of connections

The sensory input to the temporal lobe is from the auditory pathways to the superior temporal gyrus at area 41, known as Herschl's gyrus.

As for cortico-cortical connections, the lateral cortex of the left temporal lobe is connected to that of the right via the corpus callosum, whilst the left and right archicortex is connected via the anterior commissure. Other distal connections are as given in Figure 34.8, to the frontal and occipital lobes.

Internally, the lateral temporal cortex is closely connected to the amygdala and hippocampus.

Functions and dysfunctions of the temporal lobes

It follows from the foregoing description of the structure and connections of the temporal lobe that its functioning is not unitary. There are four main functional areas to consider: auditory sensation and perception, language comprehension, long-term memory and personality or affect.

Auditory sensation is disturbed by lesions to the primary auditory projection areas of the left and right hemispheres, that is, Herschl's gyrus, or area 41. A bilateral lesion here could produce cortical deafness, but a unilateral lesion will not, instead merely raising the threshold for auditory sensation in the contralateral ear. Lesions to the secondary areas (22 and 42), especially on the right side, may lead to auditory agnosia; for example, amusia (tone deafness, melody deafness and poor perception of rhythm, tempo and prosody of music or speech) or agnosia for sounds (the inability to interpret the meaning of non-verbal sounds). Other higher order deficits of auditory perception include deficits of selective attention on dichotic listening tasks (Schulhoff and Goodglass, 1969).

Language comprehension, too, is affected by unilateral lesions to the secondary zones (especially area 22) but this time on the left side in particular. Clinically this is known as Wernicke's aphasia, but also termed sensory aphasia, acousticognostic aphasia, acoustico-mnestic aphasia or receptive aphasia. The precise symptoms vary according to how close the lesion is to the primary zone. Closer lesions will create disorders of the more elementary processes involved in decoding speech, whereas lesions more distant from the primary zone will create higher level semantic or symbolic processing problems. At the lowest level there can be problems in perceiving and identifying phonemic characteristics; such patients might, for example, fail to discriminate between similar phonemes such as 'da – ta'. Further into the secondary area, the meanings of words might become obscure for patients, shown in the way they might fail to follow instructions adequately; there will be difficulties in naming objects (nominal aphasia); and recall of appropriate words can become difficult, patients often complaining of the tip-of-the-tongue phenomenon. There is naturally an effect on speech, which may become incoherent if words are used which fail to obey the rules of normal semantic relationships. There may be a more generalised deficit in the ability to organise material into meaningful classes or categories, which is related to some extent to a memory problem (Wilkins and Moscovitch, 1978).

Lesions to the posterior, tertiary portions of the temporal lobe around the agular gyrus cause special problems since the area overlaps with the tertiary zones of the occipital and parietal lobes. The understanding of single words may be perfect but there is a problem synthesising all the elements of a sentence, especially if it demands placing these elements into a logical or spatial schema (e.g. if Sam is taller than Bill and Tom is shorter than Sam, then who is the tallest?) Lesions here can also affect reading by disrupting cross-modal processing from the visual to auditory form (e.g. Luria, 1973, in his discussion of semantic aphasia).

Long-term memory is most profoundly affected when both temporal lobes are damaged in their medial or hippocampal aspects, as in bilateral temporal lobectomy for the relief of focal epilepsy (Falconer *et al.*, 1955). The hippocampus or bi-temporal syndrome is one of severe anterograde amnesia; that is, an almost complete inability to learn and retain new material. Unilateral damage to the anterior, medial or hippocampal aspects of the temporal lobe causes deficits dependent upon the site of damage. Left temporal lobectomies create a mild verbal learning and memory defect (Blakemore and Falconer, 1967; Rausch, 1981), which varies in severity in part according to the amount of hippocampus removed (Jones-Gotman and Milner, 1978). Patients are poor, for example, at remembering a prose passage across a delay of an hour or so, and are slow to learn lists of paired associates. Right temporal lobectomies, on the other hand, cause mild non-verbal or spatial memory defects, again varying in intensity according to the extent of hippocampal excision (Corkin, 1965; Milner, 1965). There may be difficulties in remembering faces, for example, or complex drawings or in learning routes or mazes.

Personality problems have long been associated with temporal lobe epilepsy and temporal lobe lesions. They include aggression (Falconer *et al.*, 1955); alterations in sexual habits and desires, religiosity and paranoia (see Bear and Fedio, 1977, for a review); breakdown of a psychotic or thought disordered nature with a left site (Flor-Henry, 1969); and disturbances of emotion or emotional control with right sites (Lishman, 1968).

A general point should be made at this juncture which applies to the analysis and description of all the lobes and their functions. It is easy to talk in terms of syndromes (e.g. bi-temporal syndrome) or groups of symptoms (e.g. 'amnesia' or memory problems), and neurology and neuropsychology have made great progress by doing this. However, there is usually considerable controversy about whether syndromes exist or not and, if they do, what they comprise and what the underlying functional deficit is. An alternative to broad labels and group experiments is to analyse each case in fine detail and gradually to build a model of cognitive processes underlying observed deficits (Ellis and Young, 1988).

Tests of temporal lobe functioning

Clinical observations in the foregoing areas may all suggest the need for further neuropsychological (and psychiatric) assessment.

Dealing with memory testing: first some tests should be verbal in nature to detect left temporal involvement, such as:

1 Delayed recall of the Logical Memory passages of the Wechsler Memory Scale (Powell, 1979; Rausch, 1981; Delaney *et al.*, 1980; Milner, 1967; 1975)
2 Performance on the verbal form of Meyer's paired associate learning test (Meyer, 1957; 1959; Meyer and Yates, 1955; Blakemore and Falconer, 1967)
3 Performance on the paired associate learning sub-test of the Wechsler Memory Scale (Rausch, 1977)

Conversely, some tests should be spatial or non-verbal in nature to detect right temporal impairment, such as:

1 Delayed recall of the Rey figure (Rey, 1959; Powell, 1979; Taylor, 1969)
2 The Benton visual retention test (Benton, 1955)
3 Immediate and delayed recall condition of the visual reproduction subtest of the Wechsler Memory Scale (Delaney *et al.*, 1980; Rausch, 1981)
4 Visual or tactile maze learning (Corkin, 1965; Milner, 1965)
5 Recognising recurring nonsense figures (Kimura, 1963)

Language tests which might be usefully employed are:

1 The token test in which subjects have to follow increasingly complex instructions (De Renzi and Vignolo, 1962; McNeil and Prescott, 1978)
2 The naming and receptive tests in the Minnesota test of the differential diagnosis of aphasia (Schuell and Sefer, 1973; Powell *et al.* 1980), or the Boston diagnostic aphasia test (Goodglass and Kaplan, 1972), or the neurosensory centre comprehensive examination for aphasia (Spreen and Benton, 1969).

THE PARIETAL LOBES

Summary of structure

From the lateral perspective, immediately behind the central fissure is the post-central gyrus (areas 1, 2, 3) followed by the superior parietal lobule (5, 7), the inferior parietal lobule (43, 40) and the angular gyrus. From a medial view, the parietal lobe comprises the posterior part of the paracentral lobule (1, 2, 3, 5) and the precuneus (7, 31).

Summary of connections

The anterior portion of the parietal lobe (area 1, 2, 3, or the post-central gyrus) is the projection site for somatosensory information; a primary zone feeding information into the remaining parietal areas. The secondary and tertiary zones, having analysed and integrated this basic sensory data, project to the frontal and temporal cortex. Descending projections are to the basal ganglia and spinal cord.

Functions and dysfunctions of the parietal lobe

From the preceding description, it follows that the main functions of the parietal lobe are (1) to receive and discriminate basic somatosenory data, (2) to analyse and 'perceive' such data, (3) to relate these data to auditory and visual information available from the temporal and occipital cortex, and (4) to help control bodily movements.

Somatosensory discrimination includes touch, sense of body position (kinaesthesis), pain, temperature and vibration. Increases in the threshold for these data occur only with lesions to the rolandic area in the post central gyrus (Semmes *et al.*, 1960; Corkin, 1964; Corkin *et al.*, 1970), detectable on such tests as two-point discrimination, pressure sensitivity and point localisation.

Outside this primary zone, lesions produce a transient sensory loss, but disorders of *tactile perception* become common. The patient may display astereognosis, being the inability to identify the object manipulated in the hands whilst blindfolded (Hecaen and Albert, 1978; Brown, 1972).

With lesions to the tertiary zones the patient can be deficient on *cross-modal matching* tasks (tactual-visual, visual-tactual, auditory-visual), as found by Butters and Brody (1968), who confirmed that the ability to match auditory and visual signals is a prerequisite for reading. Finally, as for *motor functions*, the parietal lobe in areas 7 and 40 contributes to gross (not fine) limb movement. Therefore the apraxia (motor disorder) seen after parietal lobe lesioning tends to be confined to whole body or whole limb movements, not involving, say, fine finger or facial movements (Geschwind, 1975; Kimura, 1980).

This four-way division of function, based on structure, does not quite do justice to the complexity of the parietal lobes, since lesions here can create a 'bewildering array' of symptoms. The common feature to this array tends to be that the task requires some kind of spatial analysis. This includes poor visual object recognition and a reduced ability to recognise objects from usual views (Warrington and Taylor, 1973). It is found rather more frequently in left than right cases (Warrington and Rabin, 1970). Other left-sided symptoms include disorders of reading or alexia; disorders of mental arithmetic, especially when problems require some spatial representation, as in the use of columns to add and subtract (Luria, 1973); and left-right orientation (Benton, 1959). Disturbances of spatial analysis also include problems of reaching and eye movement, as found in Balint's syndrome. Other signs of parietal lobe damage tend to indicate a right-sided focus, including contralateral neglect in which the patient behaves and talks as if the left side of the body and of visual space does not exist (Battersby *et al.*, 1956), and anosognosia (the failure to perceive illness or dysfunction). There may also be a general disturbance of body language.

Still other symptoms can be found with either left or right lesions, including the inability to draw or make up three-dimensional constructions out of sticks or cubes, termed constructional apraxia (Piercy *et al.*, 1960). However, constructional apraxia may not be a single entity, and left and right lesion cases may fail the same constructional task but for rather different reasons (Benton, 1967): left cases because verbal analysis and motor control is deficient; right analysis because a 'spatial analysis' centre is deficient. Therefore one can conceive of an executive deficit versus a perceptual one.

Finally, the parietal lobes have a specific role to play in short-term memory, around the angular gyrus (areas 39 and 40) (Warrington and Weiskrantz, 1973).

Tests of parietal lobe function

Somatosensory function is assessed by the clinical tests, such as two-point discrimination, already mentioned (Corkin *et al.*, 1970), whilst at the higher level the Seguin–Goddard formboard (Teuber and Weinstein, 1954) can be used to assess tactile form recognition. Visual recognition tests include Gollin's incomplete figures (Warrington and Rabin, 1970) or the Mooney Closure test.

The ability to deal with spatial relationships can be assessed on a wide variety of tests including Block Design and Object Assembly of the WAIS; copying the Rey figure; the copy version of the Benton visual retention test (Benton, 1962); and Semmes locomotor map (Semmes *et al.*, 1963).

Tests of mathematical functions are included in Luria's test battery (Christensen, 1975) under the quasi-spatial synthesis section and in the standardised version of the tests, known as the Luria Nebraska Neuropsychological Battery (Golden, 1981).

Other characteristics of parietal lobe damage, such as apraxia, unilateral neglect and cross-modal matching, are more frequently detected through clinical observation and ad hoc tests than by any standardised tests.

THE OCCIPITAL LOBES

Summary of the structure

On the lateral surface, the occipital lobe comprises the lateral occipital gyrus and the occipital pole, merging indistinctly into the parietal and temporal lobes. On the medial surface are the cuneus and lingual gyrus, separated from the parietal lobe by the parieto-occipital fissure. The occipital lobe comprises areas 17, 18 and 19, arranged in an idiosyncratic concentric fashion (19 surrounding 18 in turn surrounding 17).

Summary of connections

Area 17 receives afferents direct from the retina along a route including the optic nerve, optic chiasm, optic tract and the lateral geniculate nucleus, and then genisculostriate radiations to the cortex. But it should be noted that visual information also reaches the tertiary visual cortex via a second pathway called the tectopulvinar system: optic nerve, superior colliculus, lateral posterior thalamus, pulvinar, areas 20 and 21. Connections radiate from the primary nucleus to the secondary area (18, or the parastriate region) and thence to the tertiary areas (19, or peristriate region). Distal connections are with the temporal lobes (inferior longitudinal tract) and frontal lobes (e.g. superior and inferior occipito-frontal tracts).

Functions of the occipital lobes

The geniculostriate system is mainly involved in the perception of form, colour and pattern, and the tectopulivinar system in locating a visual stimulus in space. Hence, the latter tends to locate objects to be analysed in detail by the former.

Lesions of any part of the geniculostriate system up to and including the primary cortical zones will produce visual field defects, such as hemianopia (blindness in the left or right visual fields) or scotomas (blind spots), which are sometimes coped with by constant tiny eye movements referred to as nystagmus.

Lesions in the secondary or tertiary areas cause higher level defects of which the visual agnosias are the most relevant here:

1 Visual object agnosia, a deficit in naming, using or recognising objects presented visually in the absence of such a deficit when the same objects are presented tactually, most common after left lesions
2 Simultanagnosia, when only one aspect of a stimulus can be perceived at any one time
3 Prosopagnosia, the inability to recognize faces, mainly found after right lesions
4 Colour agnosia and colour anomia, perhaps most related to left lesions
5 Colour imperception or achromatopsia, being the inability to distinguish hues, especially after right-sided damage
6 Pure word blindness or agnosic alexia or alexia without agraphia, the inability to read words but with a retained ability to write them – a disconnection syndrome of the left hemisphere.

Tests of occipital lobe functioning

Visual field defects can be accurately mapped by a visual field analyser presenting points of light to different locations. The agnosias are usually detected by *ad hoc* tests.

THE FRONTAL LOBES

Summary of structure

The frontal lobes make up one third of the mass of the cerebrum and are the newest part of the brain. The frontal lobe is divided from the parietal by the central fissure, and from the temporal lobe by the Sylvian fissure. On the lateral surface we have superior, middle and inferior frontal gyri, which lie between the frontal pole anteriorly and the precentral gyrus posteriorly. On the medial surface there is the cingulate gyrus which follows the arched curve of the corpus callosum, and the parolfactory area surrounding the olfactory bulb. The cortex itself is often divided up into *granular* and *agranular* types, depending upon whether cell layers II and IV are prominent or absent. Areas 4 and 6 and part of 8 and 44 are agranular and lie immediately anterior to the central fissure. The remaining areas are termed frontal granular cortex or pre-frontal cortex.

Summary of connections

The frontal lobes have no area receiving primary sense data, but the pre-frontal region does receive afferents from the visual, auditory and somatosensory areas, usually by way of the parietal lobe. The pre-frontal region also receives rich projections from subcortical structures, most especially the dorsomedial nucleus of the thalamus. Also importantly, the cingulate area receives afferents from the thalamus, specifically its anterior nucleus. On the efferent side, area 4 is a primary zone projecting ultimately to all muscular systems, and is hence known as the motor cortex. The pre-frontal region sends projections to parietal, temporal and cingulate cortex and to many subcortical structures, notably the basal ganglia, dorsomedial nucleus of the thalamus, amygdala, hippocampus and hypothalamus.

Functions of the frontal lobe

The broad functional divisions of the frontal lobes are shown in Figure 34.10, from the lateral perspective.

The motor strip controls movement, including, in the face area, all movements of the speech apparatus, such as the lips, tongue and pharynx, that is, a primary zone in Luria's terminology. The premotor zone, a secondary area, organises individual movement into ordered sequences (Kolb and Milner, 1981).

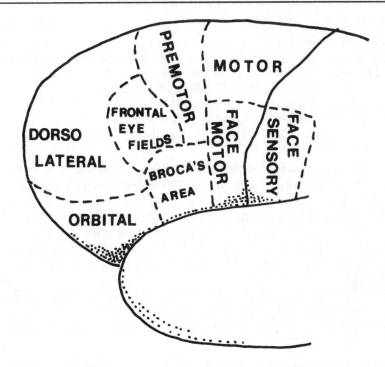

Figure 34.10 The broad functional divisions of the frontal lobes

Lesions in and around the face area can, for example, cause dysarthria – the inability to speak rapidly and accurately or, on the reception side, to discriminate phonemes properly (Taylor, 1979). In a conceptually related manner, lesions to the frontal eye fields disrupt voluntary gaze, causing difficulties in the systematic searching of an array of shapes, for example (Teuber, 1964; Tyler, 1969, Guitton *et al.*, 1982), or a disruption of the patient's scanning of a complex picture when trying to abstract the most important features (Luria, 1973). There can also be a general loss of fine movement (Kuypers, 1981) or strength (Leonard *et al.*, 1988).

The remaining areas are tertiary, and lesion effects broadly (very broadly) fall into three categories: Broca's aphasia (44 on the left); changes in the highest of intellectual and cognitive functions (dorsolateral); and changes in personality (orbital and cingulate). In *Broca's aphasia* it is the expressive side of language that is most disrupted: patients can understand most words and sentences (unless they are extremely complex grammatically) but their speech is hesitant, dysfluent and ungrammatical; their writing follows suit. Repetition and reading aloud is also impaired, and in common with other aphasias, naming can be poor.

A variety of *high level intellectual and cognitive skills* can be disrupted after dorsolateral frontal lesions, including:

1 Loss of abstract thinking or a tendency to think in a concrete fashion (Goldstein, 1944)
2 Deficits in planning or problem-solving, in which patients approach tasks in a haphazard trial-and-error manner (Crown, 1952) and show deficits in forming strategies (Shallice, 1982; Shallice and Evans, 1978)
3 Rule-breaking (Miller, 1985; Walsh, 1978)
4 Poor visuo-constructional skills, related to poor planning, in which patients cannot spatially organise all the elements of the pattern to be reproduced (Luria and Tsvetkova, 1964)
5 Poor error evaluation, as already suggested by poor rule-following, caused by a lack of self-monitoring or a failure of verbalisation to control action (Konow and Pribram, 1970)
6 Inflexibility or rigidity, so that the patient cannot shift easily from one 'set' to another (Milner, 1964), and generally reduced spontaneity
7 Loss of verbal fluency (left-sided), where speech lacks spontaneity and is impoverished in content (adynamia or dynamic aphasia, but not a true aphasia)
8 Loss of design fluency (right-sided), in which the drawing of nonsense shapes or 'doodles' is inhibited (Jones-Gotman and Milner, 1977)
9 Disturbances to temporal memory (Smith and Milner, 1984; Freedman and Oscar-Berman, 1986).

Finally, as for lesions to the orbital and cingulate cortex, their effects on *personality* are fairly well established through studies of orbital (modified) leucotomy and cingulotomy (O'Callaghan and Carroll, 1982, provide a thorough summary; also Walsh, 1976). There is a significant reduction in the patient's appreciation of aversive emotional states, with reduced anxiety, depression and neuroticism. This can be understood by viewing the cingulate cortex as the primary cortical projection area for the 'emotional' circuits and processes of the limbic system. Naturally, if both orbital and dorsolateral cortex is destroyed, then more major personality changes occur – extreme inertia coupled with disinhibition or impulsivity is common, and this is why 'standard' leucotomy or lobotomy is no longer performed.

Tests of frontal lobe functioning

Clinical observation can usually reveal deficits in motor control, and interviews, backed up by standardized questionnaires, usually pinpoint personality change, such as disinhibition and reduced initiative.

Expressive language deficits can be assessed formally on the appropriate sections of standard batteries, such as the Minnesota test (Schuell and Sefer, 1973) or the aphasic screening battery (Russell *et al.*, 1970).

The abstract thinking deficit and inability to shift categories can be observed with the Colour-Form Sorting Test (Goldstein and Sheerer, 1941), the Halstead

Cateogory Test (Halstead, 1947) or the Wisconsin Card Sorting Test (Grant and Berg, 1948; Milner, 1964; Nelson, 1976). Fluency in the verbal sphere can be assessed on Thurstone's (or the 'Chicago') written word fluency test (Milner, 1964; Pendleton et al., 1982), and in the spatial sphere by design fluency (Jones-Gotman and Milner, 1977). Examples of both are given by Kolb and Whishaw (1990). An oral verbal fluency test can also be used (Benson, 1986; Bornstein, 1986). Planning programmes of action can be assessed on the Porteus Maze Test (Porteus, 1965), the Trail Making Test (Reitan, 1966) or by copying complex figures such as the Rey. Planning and the verbal regulation of behaviour is further assessed in Luria's tests (Christensen, 1975; Golden, 1981).

SUBCORTICAL STRUCTURES

So much for the functions of the cortex – now what lurks beneath? We will deal with four main systems: the limbic system, the basal ganglia, the thalamus and the hypothalamus.

The limbic system

The limbic system (limbic lobe or reptilian brain) is a collection of structures with a variety of functions. One of its main identifying features is the fornix, which arches underneath the corpus callosum and sweeps posteriorly round and underneath the thalamus (Figure 34.11). Papez's circuit (hippocampus to the mammillary bodies to the thalamus to the cingulate gyrus and back to the hippocampus) is well known to be implicated in emotion, and the mammillary bodies and hippocampus have become involved in theories of memory, inhibition and learning.

The basal ganglia

Clarity of definition is lacking somewhat here. The basal ganglia can be taken to include the corpus striatum (i.e. caudate nucleus, putamen, globus pallidus and claustrum), the subthalamic nuclei, the substantia nigra and the amygdaloid nucleus (although this last is most often thought of in the context of the limbic system). Figure 34.12 shows how the basal ganglia lie beneath the cortex, its approximate shape, and its lateral relationship to the thalamus.

Historically, the principal functions of the basal ganglia have been thought of as motor, there being a dominant projection from the motor cortex to the caudate nucleus and putamen. Hence, damage to the basal ganglia (as in Parkinsonism) produces changes in muscle tone and fine motor control. More recent research (Hassler, 1978) also relates these structures to sensory motor integration and motivation.

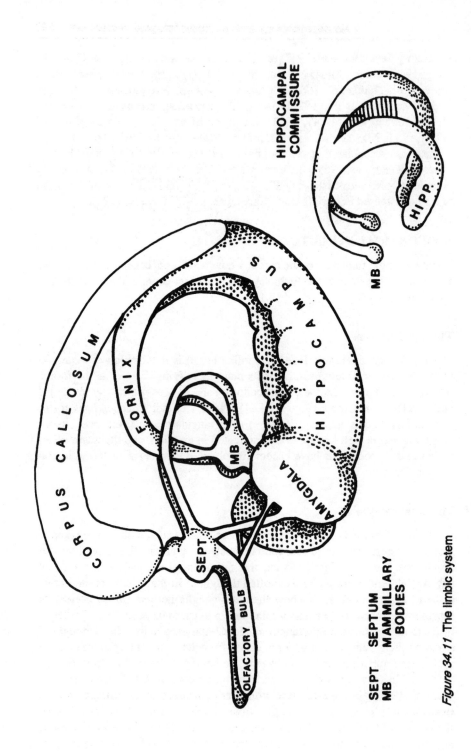

SEPT   SEPTUM
MB   MAMMILLARY
        BODIES

Figure 34.11 The limbic system

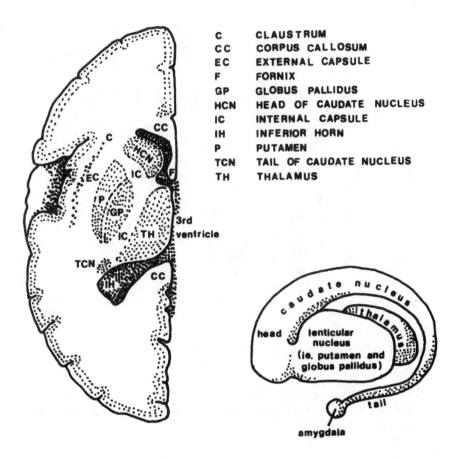

C	CLAUSTRUM
CC	CORPUS CALLOSUM
EC	EXTERNAL CAPSULE
F	FORNIX
GP	GLOBUS PALLIDUS
HCN	HEAD OF CAUDATE NUCLEUS
IC	INTERNAL CAPSULE
IH	INFERIOR HORN
P	PUTAMEN
TCN	TAIL OF CAUDATE NUCLEUS
TH	THALAMUS

Figure 34.12 The basal ganglia

Thalamus

The thalamus, situated under the arch of the corpus callosum and fornix, lies on the medial surface of the hemispheres, its left and right portions joined by the intermediate mass. It is a massive relay station for sensory information radiating projections to all parts of the cortex as indicated in Figure 34.13.

Hypothalamus

The hypothalamus is a collection of nuclei at the base of the brain below the thalamus. It is intimately connected with the limbic system and, via the pituitary, the release of hormones. Thus it is the most important link between the neural and endocrine systems. It is divided into at least nine nuclei (pre-optic, para

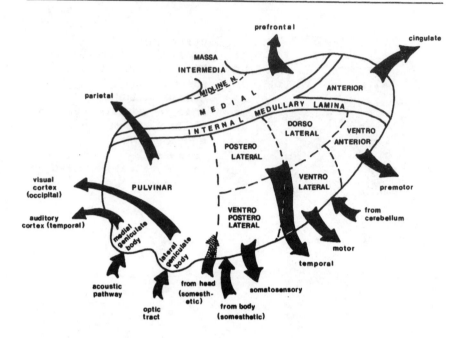

Figure 34.13 The main projections of the thalamus

ventricular, anterior, supraoptic, lateral, dorsal, dorsomedial, ventromedial and posterior). Some of these nuclei and their position in the brain are indicated in Figure 34.14.

THE CLASSIFICATION OF DISORDERS

Many disorders have already been mentioned as the functions of the cortex have been described. The following subsections will complete the breakdown of functions into disorders, and terms that have not yet been introduced will be briefly described. These disorders may arise from a wide variety of aetiologies including vascular problems (ischaemia, haemorrhage, aneurysms), head injury (closed, penetration, crushing injuries), epileptic foci, tumours (gliomas, meningioma, metastatic), infections such as meningitis and degenerative disorders such as multiple sclerosis, Parkinsonism and Alzheimer's disease. The aetiology will not affect the nature of the disorder *per se*, but will relate to rate of onset, pattern of other associated symptoms and prognosis.

Disorders of movement

The general term for higher order disorders of movement is *apraxia*: the inability

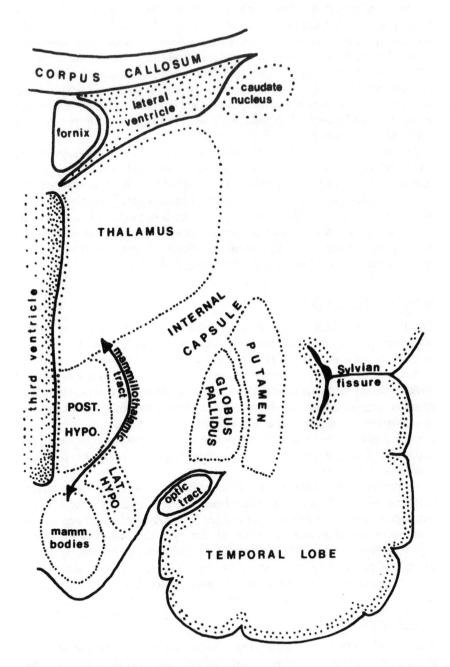

Figure 34.14 The position of the hypothalamus

to carry out purposeful movements on command in the absence of primary sensory or motor impairment. The apraxias include *ideomotor apraxia*, when the sequencing of a complex gesture is intact but each constituent element is performed badly; *ideational apraxia* when individual simple movements are intact but the sequence of a complex gesture is disordered; *constructional apraxia*; and *drawing apraxia*. Less common apraxias include *melokinetic apraxia* when involuntary movements of facial expression are intact but voluntary movement is impaired; *unilateral limb apraxia*; and *frontal apraxia*, the disorder involving a difficulty in initiating movements.

Lower level movement disorders include *ataxia*, the failure of coordination or an irregularity of the flow of muscle action, often found after damage to the cerebellum; *hemiplegia*, the paralysis to one side of the body; *paraplegia*, the paralysis of the lower half of the body as after spinal cord injury; *paralysis*, the loss of movement or sensation in one part of the body; and *paresis*, slight and incomplete paralysis. Abnormal movements are sometimes seen, including slow writhing movements (athetosis), involuntary jerks (chorea) and spasticity (increase in muscle tone) and intention tremor (e.g. Parkinsonism).

Disorders of language

The five basic syndromes are *Broca's aphasia* (alternatively named motor, efferent motor, non-fluent, expressive or encoding aphasia); *Wernicke's aphasia* (sensory, acoustic-amnestic, decoding); *conduction aphasia*, in which it is hypothesised that the pathway between Wernicke's and Broca's area is severed to create a failure in the ability to repeat; *transcortical aphasia* (isolation syndrome) being the isolation of the speech circuit from remaining cortex, leading to a preserved ability to repeat but a low level of spontaneous speech; and *angular gyrus syndrome* in which a lesion in the parieto-occipito temporal area impairs reading and causes prominent anomic aphasic symptoms (although anomia is common in all syndromes).

Some other terms that may be encountered are probably not true aphasias, such as dynamic aphasia (lack of spontaneous speech after pre-frontal lesions and really one aspect of a general behavioural inertia) and afferent motor aphasia (disturbed articulatory abilities caused by disrupted feedback from the speech apparatus due to a lesion in the postcentral gyrus). Language problems stemming from right or non-dominant lesions are gradually becoming recognised, including deficits of prosody and gesture (Benson, 1986).

The agnosias

These are disorders of higher cognitive understanding and integration in the absence of sensory loss. In the visual modality they include *object agnosia*; *agnosia for drawings*; *prosopagnosia*; *colour agnosia*; *colour anomia*; *achromatopsia*; *visual-spatial agnosia*; and *simultagnosia*. In the auditory modality there is *amusia* and *agnosia for sounds*. In the somatosensory mode is *astereognosis*; *anosognosia*; *anosodiaphosia*; *autopognosia* (failure to localize and name body parts); *asymbolia for pain*; *finger agnosia*; *right–left disorientation*; and *unilateral neglect*.

Memory disorders

These are usually defined by aetiology or type or locus of damage. We have the *bilateral hippocampal syndrome* with profound anterograde amnesia across all modalities, although motor learning is rather better preserved; *unilateral hippocampal (temporal) syndrome*, as found after unilateral temporal lobectomy; *Korsakoff syndrome* resulting from severe vitamin B_1 deficiency, as found in chronic alcoholism, and consisting of an inability to lay down new memories, loss of some old memories, confabulation to 'make good' gaps in memory, meagre content in conversation, and lack of insight and empathy; *electroconvulsive shock syndrome* when, for the treatment of severe depression, a 70–120 volts AC current is passed through the temporal lobes for about one half a second, producing amnesia for the treatment and retrograde amnesia for events prior to the shock, and two to three weeks of anterograde amnesia, all of which can be reduced if the shock is administered unilaterally; *transient global amnesia*, which is temporary complete retro- and anterograde amnesia due, say, to a transient ischaemic attack; *traumatic amnesia*, consisting of a shrinking retrograde amnesia and a diminishing anterograde amnesia (post-traumatic amnesia or PTA); *frontal amnesia*, the failure of the intention to recall; *dementing amnesia*, the anterograde amnesia found in old age especially; and *disassociative* or *hysterical amnesia*, which is a motivated, temporary amnesia created by the secondary gain it accrues. Theories of memory and amnesia are covered by Baddeley (1990).

Disorders of intellect and related processing

Widespread diffuse lesions and lesions to the frontal lobe may well produce deficits that affect performance on tests of intelligence in fairly general or non-specific ways. Such deficits include slowed information processing (Gronwall, 1977) and problems with attention (Gentilini *et al.*, 1989). Other deficits which may be observed in the process of assessing intelligence, and which have already been mentioned in preceding sections, are disturbances to the ability to make abstractions, to organise responses, to plan solutions, to monitor one's own performance, to comprehend complex instructions and to retain appropriate amounts of material in mind whilst solving problems.

Disorders of emotional and related processing

It has been known for a long time that brain injury can cause changes to emotions, social behaviour, and personality, in both animals and humans, but these changes have not been conveniently organised into 'syndromes' as has been achieved with language or memory disorders. As has already been mentioned, a pattern of inertia coupled with disinhibition and impulsivity is often linked with frontal injury, and a relationship between anger or aggression and temporal lesions and temporal lobe epilepsy is well known (Bear and Fedio, 1977). However, there are many more subtle emotional and related changes that are still poorly understood, including the perception of emotion in others (Tompkins and Mateer, 1985), the use of facial expression and gesture, the perception of social cues, the interpretation of social behaviour, and changes in humour (Birhle *et al.*, 1986). In addition, the links between brain injury and frank psychiatric disorder, either of a schizophrenic/psychotic or affective/depressive nature, are still unclear though fascinating (Silberman and Weingartner, 1986).

LOSS AND RECOVERY OF FUNCTION: THE EXAMPLE OF HEAD INJURY

Loss of function

Loss of function is due to several factors, including the *lesion trauma* itself, which halts the passage of the nerve impulse; *retrograde degeneration* of the axon between cell body and trauma; *anterograde degeneration* of the distal portion of the axon beyond the trauma site; *transneuronal degeneration*, being the degeneration of neurons to which the dying neuron is connected; the *alteration of neurochemical pools*, being an upset to nervous transmission over the whole brain; *vascular disruption*, such as haemorrhage; *diaschisis*, or the functional shock to a group of cells when they lose their afferents; *oedema*, or swelling which can crush the brain against the skull; and finally *raised CSF pressure* which can compress the brain.

Recovery of function

Mechanisms of recovery of function fall into three categories as shown in Table 34.2. An outstanding discussion of recovery is to be found in Finger *et al.* (1988).

Head injury

Head injury requires a special mention; first, because it is the commonest reason for loss of brain function in children and younger adults that the neuropsychologist will encounter; second, because it demonstrates very well the whole process of loss and recovery of function; and third, because it well illustrates the diversity of consequence arising from an injury to the brain.

The frequency of head injury varies considerably between countries, and in the USA has been estimated at 300–450 per 100,000 per year (Kolb and Whishaw,

Table 34.2 Mechanisms of recovery of function

Physiological mechanisms

Recovery from diaschisis	A diminution of the functional shock caused by deafferentation
Regeneration	Regrowth of previous connections, not seen in humans apart from random regenerative sprouting
Collateral sprouting	Neighbouring axons take over vacated synaptic sites
Re-routing	Axons seek new targets when previous ones are destroyed
Relatively ineffective/silent synapses	Pre-existing or dormant connections are innervated
Denervation supersensitivity	De-afferented tissue becomes hyper responsive to residual connections
Nerve growth factor	Protein encouraging growth in damaged neurons and reinneration

Structural mechanisms

Redundancy	The same message is carried by more than one fibre
Equipotentiality	The idea that (some) brain tissue is non-specific in its functions
Levels of representation	If higher level analysis is destroyed then lower level information still exists to be utilised
Substitution	The concept of a structural safety net comprising previously unused tissue
Vicaration	Substitution by adjacent area
Multiple control	Some functions are undertaken by more than one centre
Sparing	Those processes surviving damage in a specific area

Process mechanisms

Simple functional substitution or behavioural compensation	Tasks are solved by an entirely different functional system
Re-routing	Reorganising the flow of processing to avoid a damaged area
Plasticity	An area of brain learns to perform a new task

1990). Of these, 200–300 will be admitted to hospital (Gronwall *et al.*, 1990; Jennett and Frankowski, 1990). The rate is about twice as high for men than for women (Kraus and Nourjah, 1989), and it peaks at more than 600 per 100,000 for young men, who are more likely to be involved in motor accidents, assaults and sporting injuries. The rate is, in general, elevated in childhood and again during old age, when falls are most likely. Forty-two per cent are due to road traffic accidents, 23 per cent to falls, 14 per cent to assault, and bicycle (not involving cars), sports and recreation activities account for 6 per cent each. Other causes account for 8 per cent (Kraus and Nourjah, op. cit.; see also Jennett and Frankowski, op. cit.). Aetiology varies from centre to centre, depending upon the availability of firearms, the socio-demographic characteristics of the community, the extent of alcohol abuse, and so forth.

The mechanisms of head injury are well described by Stalhammar (1990) and Pang (1989). The primary injuries occur at the time of impact. In blunt injuries, there is an epidural haematoma at the site of impact, a brain contusion at the site of impact as the skull bends in and as the brain is accelerated, and brain contusions at the opposite side of the skull as the brain, having accelerated, hits and decelerates against the inside opposite surface. There are contusions as the brain is pulled over the bony protuberances and ridges on the base of the skull, causing particular damage to the poles of the frontal and temporal lobes. There are shearing and tensile strains within the white matter, as the brain rotates in relation to the head and as counter-rotational forces are set up between the two hemispheres, all causing the axons to snap (diffuse axonal injuries). Blood vessels also shear and bleed. There is a similar pathology in acceleration/deceleration injuries (whiplash) but without haematoma and contusion at an impact site. In penetration injuries (Roy and Cooper, 1990), one has to distinguish between high-velocity military weapons, and civilian small-calibre, low-muzzle-velocity bullets, the former being 'incompatible with survival'. There is laceration and tearing along the track of both brain tissue and blood vessels and an instant rise in intracranial pressure as shock waves spread out, again causing contusion and haemorrhage at distal sites. The secondary effects of the brain injury can be due to lack of oxygen to the brain (hypoxic and ischaemic or hypotensive ischaemia) caused by damage to other organs; inadequate blood supply to the brain as blood pressure drops; raised intracranial pressure; brain swelling; the development of space-occupying lesions by way of haematomas; and the results of infection, especially in penetrating injuries. There are tertiary changes to metabolism and degenerative changes in the white matter.

The severity of the brain injury is often measured by the length of post-trauma amnesia (10 min. = very mild; 10–60 min. = mild; 1–24 hrs = moderate; 1–7 days = severe; > 7 days = very severe). The depth of unconsciousness is often measured on the Glasgow Coma Scale (Teasdale and Jennett, 1974). The best eye opening is rated 1–4, the best motor response 1–6, and the best verbal response 1–5, thus yielding scores ranging from 3 to 15. In terms of severity, 3–5 is very severe, 6–8 severe, 9–12 moderate, and 13–15 is mild (this is the worst GCS score on the first day).

Outcome, which is correlated negatively with initial severity, is often grossly measured by the Glasgow Outcome Scale (GOS; Jennett and Bond, 1975) in which 1 = death, 2 = persistent vegetative state, 3 = severe disability, relying on help at least once every 24 hrs, 4 = moderate disability and 5 = good recovery and ability to return to work. As an example of outcome, after severe injury, 40 per cent die, 5 per cent are left in vegetative state, 10 per cent have severe disability, 20 per cent moderate disability and 25 per cent make a good recovery (Levin *et al.* 1990). After moderate injury, 38 per cent make a good recovery and 49 per cent have a moderate disability. After mild injury, 78 per cent make a good recovery and 22 per cent have a moderate disability.

Many of the details of recovery and residual effects are given in Lezak (1989). There are many subtle effects and repercussions even when an apparently good recovery has been made. For example, Brooks *et al.* (1986) found, in a five-year follow-up, that 74 per cent of patients who had had severe injury complain of some personality change, and 50 per cent of mood change, irritability and temper, and the reports of memory problems and fatigability are nearly as high. Even mild head injury has a pronounced effect. At one month after mild injury Dikmen *et al.* (1986) report that nearly 40 per cent of patients are not yet working properly, over 50 per cent have headaches, over 60 per cent are fatigued, over 70 per cent are irritable and over 50 per cent have memory and anxiety problems.

THE PROCESS OF NEUROPSYCHOLOGICAL TESTING

Purpose

Neuropsychological testing is undertaken for a variety of reasons and the exact nature of the tests given will be dictated by the precise purpose. Such purposes include:

1 To detect organic impairment
2 To localise the site of organic lesioning
3 To aid diagnosis
4 To assess the current level of functioning so as to detect deterioration and to give a descriptive basis for rehabilitation
5 To yield research data on the mechanisms of a dysfunction
6 To give a baseline against which degree of recovery can be judged
7 To make a prediction as to whether a particular surgical intervention, such as a temporal lobectomy, should take place.

Testing without a reasonable purpose is pointless, and it is up to the clinical neuropsychologist to decide what is reasonable. The principles and practice of neuropsychological assessment are well described in Spreen and Strauss (1991) and Lezak (1983).

The basic procedure

Neuropsychological testing begins with a clear statement of purpose. Next come the screening observations, which include:

1 Reading the notes (Table 34.3)
2 Observing the patient (Table 34.4)
3 Interviewing the patient (Table 34.5)
4 Giving various standardised tests, as have been described throughout this
   chapter.

On the basis of these results a second phase assessment will frequently be
required, often with a much greater emphasis upon the ingenuity and experience

Table 34.3 Checklist of background information on the patient to be collected
                prior to testing

1 Purpose of the investigation
2 Demographic variables
      age
      sex
      handedness
      education
      profession
      previous brain injuries
      brief medical history
3 Results of previous investigations
      neurological examination
      previous psychology tests
      EEG and EPs
      AEG
      CAT
      MRI
      angiogram
      X-rays
      biochemical tests
      previous diagnosis
4 History of the lesion
      site of trauma
      age at which damage occurred
      time since lesion occurred
      history of seizures
      history of anoxia
      length of unconsciousness
      history of retrograde amnesia
      nature of lesion
      reports from any operations
      history of any cognitive defects
      history of any emotional and social changes
5 Factors affecting testing
      drug levels
      recent seizure activity
      mood and motivation
      relevant deficits, such as visual or motor problems, that might interfere
         with other tests

Table 34.4 Checklist of observations to make on the patient during general interaction and testing

1	Motor behaviour	Tics and mannerisms Limb weaknesses Awkward gaits and limps Tremor Awkwardness of movement (clumsiness, jerkiness, slowness) Writing ability Handedness
2	Language	Amount of speech Volume and prosody of speech Understanding of verbal instructions Unusual structure of speech (e.g. telegraphese and agrammatism) Unusual content of speech (word-finding difficulties, neologisms, paraphrasia) Difficulties of pronunciation (oral apraxias, dysarthrias)
3	Memory	Orientation in time and place (e.g. age, date, hospital) Recall of instructions Recall of therapist's name Recall of what had occurred in the session Recall of recent history
4	Style of performance	Self-talk, self-instruction Haphazardness vs. systematisation of performance Persistence Concentration Error checking Speed Concreteness in abstract tasks Perseveration
5	Spatial and visual awareness	Neglect of one side of body or environment Confusions of left or right orientation Attendance to only one side of tasks Whether glasses are used Viewing material from odd angles Holding material close to the eyes Failure to recognise objects
6	Personality	Activity level (lethargic or fatigued to overactive) Anxiety level Extraversion (withdrawn vs. friendly) Inappropriateness (e.g. over-familiarity) Overt psychiatric symptoms Impulsiveness Insight into deficits

Table 34.5 Questions to ask the patient (and a close informant if possible).
These are examples only

1 General questions to get the patient talking
   How has the injury affected your life?
   How has it changed you?
   What problems have cropped up?
2 Work
   How has it affected your employment?
   Do you find work more difficult?
      become tired easily?
      find it hard learning new things?
      feel under pressure?
3 Social
   What do you do in your spare time with friends?
   Do you have many friends?
      meet new people?
      find you have lost friends?
      have any worries about people?
      get anxious in company? about what?
4 Personality
   Do you enjoy some things?
      get really low sometimes?
      lack energy? etc.
   What sort of person are you?
   How do others see you?
5 Motor
   Do you have any problems   walking?
                                   moving?
                                   co-ordinating?
                                   with clumsiness?
6 Language
   Do you have to ask people to repeat things?
      get stuck in conversations for something to say?
      find words just won't come out?
      stumble over pronouncing words?
7 Memory
   What sort of things do you forget?
   How are you at learning things?
   Do you remember facts?
8 Spatial
   Do you bump into things you didn't notice?
      get confused looking at pictures?
      get left and right mixed up?
      get lost when going somewhere?
9 Targets
   Over the last month, what problems have you had to worry about?
   In the coming week or so, is there anything to do that you are worrying about?
   What are the most important things that you cannot do?
   Where shall we start?

of the tester. It may well be necessary, for example, to make up *ad hoc* tests to examine some specific skill, or to design a single-case experiment to examine a model of the dysfunction, or to observe the patient in real-life settings so as to clarify rehabilitation goals. To carry out this second stage properly requires a good working knowledge of the neuropsychological literature above and beyond the manuals of the standard tests.

Assessment for rehabilitation purposes

For rehabilitation purposes the assessment as given in Table 34.6 must make a clear statement of the strengths and weaknesses of the patient; not just what he or she cannot do, but what he or she can do. For example, there is little point in embarking upon an image-mediated memory therapy programme if the patient's ability to form visual images is minimal; and there is little point in setting up a visual symbol system for an aphasic patient if he or she also has spatial agnosia problems. The examination, then, of cognitive strengths and weaknesses will determine the gross strategy of the treatment.

Next, the assessment should pinpoint specific targets for treatment; that is, translate the observed cognitive defect (for example, 'a spatial memory problem') into real-life goals (for example, the ability to remember the route to the toilets). This must of necessity involve forward planning; what type of environment will

Table 34.6 Factors to be taken into account in regard to rehabilitation

1 Areas of brain damaged

2 Functions disrupted

3 Probability of spontaneous recovery of these functions

4 Areas of brain intact

5 Functions intact

6 Factors that might affect progress on a rehabilitation programme
   - e.g. insight
           motivation
           social and interpersonal behaviour
           neurotic and psychiatric disorder

7 Physical factors influencing the design of a rehabilitation programme
   - e.g. ambulatory skills

8 Environmental factors influencing the outcome of a rehabilitation programme
   - e.g. attitude of spouse
           attitude of previous employer
           local state of unemployment and jobs available
           financial restrictions

the patient be moving to and what will be the most important requirements? Such forward planning must also take into account 'environmental' problems, such as shortages of suitable placements or restrictions of financial resources.

The identification of rehabilitation goals is not necessarily an easy matter. Consider memory disorders. Laboratory measures of memory do not correlate highly with self-reports of memory problems (Bennett-Levy et al., 1980; Sunderland et al., 1983), and therefore cannot be considered a sufficiently useful measure; but the accuracy of the self-report measures themselves must in some cases be doubted, since the filling-in of the questionnaire itself requires the exercise of memory. For example, our own experience of Korsakoff patients who have filled in the Subjective Memory Questionnaire (Bennett-Levy and Powell, 1980) is that they score above the normal mean, rating themselves as having a better than average memory in spite of their profound amnesia. Clearly, there is no substitute for the direct observation of patients in the actual settings in which they are required.

Finally, the assessment must describe the patient as a person: his or her aims, aspirations, personal difficulties, priorities, motivation and fears. It is the person being rehabilitated, not a collection of neuropsychological terms.

The report

Neuropsychological reports usually contain: a section on usual demographic variables; statement of purpose and for whom the report is prepared; educational record; occupational record; sources of information (e.g. interview and test of the patient, interview with relative, other reports available); description of the accident/ injury; history of effects and treatment; summary of previous tests; test-taking behaviour; present cognitive test results; personality; psychological state (for example, presence of associated or concurrent depression or post-traumatic stress disorder); comments and conclusions; prognosis or implications for treatment or management.

REFERENCES

Baddeley, A. (1990) Human Memory: Theory and Practice, Hove: Lawrence Erlbaum Associates.

Battersby, W. S., Ender, M. B., Pollack, M. and Kahn, R. L. (1956) 'Unilateral "spatial agnosia" ("inattention") in patients with cerebral lesions', Brain 79: 68–93.

Bear, D. M. and Fedio, P. (1977) 'Quantitative analysis of interictal behaviour in temporal lobe epilepsy', Archives Neurology 34: 454–67.

Bennett-Levy, J. and Powell, G. E. (1980) 'The Subjective Memory Questionnaire (SMQ): an investigation into the self-reporting of "real-life" memory skills', British Journal of Social Clinical Psychology 19: 117–88.

Bennett-Levy, J., Polkey, C. E. and Powell, G. E. (1980) 'Self-report of memory skills after temporal lobectomy – the effect of clinical variables', Cortex 16: 543–57.

Benson, D. F. (1986) 'Aphasia and lateralization of language', Cortex 22: 71–86.

Benton, A. L. (1955) The Visual Retention Test, New York: Psychological Corporation.

Benton, A. L. (1959) *Right-left Discrimination and Finger Localization*, New York: Hoeber Medical, Harper Row.

Benton, A. L. (1962) 'The visual retention test as a constructional praxis task', *Confinia Neurologica* 22: 141–55.

Benton, A. L. (1967) 'Constructional apraxia and the minor hemisphere', *Confina Neurologia* 29: 1–16.

Benton, A. L. (1968) 'Differential behavioural effects in frontal lobe disease', *Neuropsychologia* 6: 53–60.

Birhle, A., Brownell, H. H., Powellson J. A. and Gardner H. (1986) 'Comprehension of humorous and non-humorous materials by left and right brain-damaged patients', *Brain and Cognition* 5: 185–203.

Blakemore, C. B. and Falconer, M. A. (1967) 'Long-term effects of anterior temporal lobectomy on certain cognitive functions', *Journal of Neurology, Neurosurgery and Psychiatry* 30: 364–7.

Bornstein, R. A. (1986) 'Contributions of various neuropsychological measures to detection of frontal lobe impairment', *International Journal of Clinical Neuropsychology* 8: 18–22.

Brooks, N., Campsie, L., Symington, C., Beattie, A. and McKinlay, W. (1986) 'The five-year outcome of severe blunt head injury: a relative's view', *Journal of Neurology, Neurosurgery and Psychiatry* 49: 764–70.

Brown, J. (1972) *Aphasia, Apraxia and Agnosia*, Springfield, Ill. : Charles C. Thomas.

Butters, N. and Brody, B. A. (1968) 'The role of the left parietal lobe in the mediation of intra-and cross-modal associations', *Cortex* 4: 328–43.

Christensen, A. L. (1975) *Luria's Neuropsychological Investigation*, Copenhagen: Muskgaard.

Corkin, S. H. (1964) 'Somesthetic function after cerebral damage in man', unpublished doctoral thesis, McGill University.

Corkin, S. (1965) 'Tactually-guided maze learning in man: effects of unilateral and bilateral hippocampal lesions', *Neuropsychologia* 3: 339–51.

Corkin, S. B., Milner, B. and Rasmussen, T. (1970) 'Somatosensory thresholds', *Archives of Neurology* 23: 41–58.

Crown, S. (1952) 'An experimental study of psychological changes following prefrontal lobotomy', *Journal of General Psychology* 47: 3–41.

Delaney, R. C., Rosen, A. J., Mattson, R. H. and Novelly, R. A. (1980) 'Memory function in focal epilepsy: a comparison of non-surgical, unilateral temporal lobe and frontal lobe samples', *Cortex* 16: 103–17.

De Renzi, E. and Vignolo, L. A. (1962) 'The token test: a sensitive test to detect receptive disturbances in aphasics', *Brain* 85: 665–78.

Dikmen, S., McLean, A. and Temkin, N. (1986) 'Neuropsychologies and psychological consequences of minor head injury', *Journal of Neurology, Neurosurgery and Psychiatry* 49: 1227–32.

Ellis, A. W. and Young, A. W. (1988) *Human Cognitive Neuropsychology*, London: Lawrence Erlbaum Associates.

Falconer, M. A., Hill, D., Meyer, A., Mitchell, W. and Pond, D. A. (1955) 'Treatment of temporal-lobe epilepsy by temporal lobectomy: a survey of findings and results', *Lancet* 1: 827–37.

Finger, S., LeVere, T. E., Almli, C. R. and Stein. D. G. (eds) (1988) *Brain Injury and Recovery: Theoretical and Controversial Issues*, New York: Plenum Press.

Flor-Henry, P. (1969) 'Psychosis and temporal lobe epilepsy: a controlled investigation', *Epilepsia* 10: 363–88.

Freedman, M. and Oscar-Berman, M. (1986) 'Bilateral frontal lobe disease and selective delayed response deficits in humans', *Behavioural Neuroscience* 100: 337–42.

Gentilini, M., Nichelli, P. and Schoenhuber, R. (1989) 'Assessment of attention in mild

684 The Handbook of Clinical Adult Psychology

head injury', in H. S. Levin, H. M. Eisenberg and A. L. Benton (eds) *Mild Head Injury*, New York: Oxford University Press.

Geschwind, N. (1975) 'The apraxias: neural mechanisms of disorders of learned movement', *American Scientist* 63: 188–95.

Golden, C. J. (1981) 'A standardized version of Luria's neuropsychological tests', in S. Silskov and T. J. Bull (eds) *Handbook of Clinical Neuropsychology*, New York: Wiley-Interscience.

Goldstein, K. (1944) 'Mental changes due to frontal lobe damage', *Journal of Psychology* 17: 187–208.

Goldstein, K. and Scheerer, M. (1941) 'Abstract and concrete behaviour: an experimental study with special tests', *Psychological Monographs* 43: 1–151.

Goodglass, H. and Kaplan, E. (1972) *The Assessment of Aphasia and Related Disorders*, Philadelphia: Lea and Febiger.

Grant, A. D. and Berg, E. A. (1948) 'A behavioural analysis of degree of reinforcement and ease of shifting to new responses in a Weigl-type card sorting', *Journal of Experimental Psychology* 38: 404–11

Gronwall, D. (1977) 'Paced auditory serial addition task: a measure of recovery from concussion', *Perceptual and Motor Skills* 44: 367–73.

Gronwall, D., Wrighton, P. and Waddell, P. (1990) *Head Injury: The Facts*, Oxford: Oxford University Press.

Guitton, D., Buchtal, H. A. and Douglas, R. M. (1982) 'Disturbances of voluntary saccadic eye-movement mechanisms following discrete unilateral frontal-lobe re-movals', in G. Lennerstrand, D. S. Lee and E. L. Keller (eds) *Functional Basis of Ocular Motility Disorders*, Oxford: Pergamon Press.

Halstead, W. C. (1947) *Brain and Intelligence*, Chicago: University of Chicago Press.

Hassler, R. (1978) 'Striatal control of locomotion, intentional actions and of integrating and perceptive activity', *Journal of Neurological Science* 36: 187–224.

Hecaen, H. and Albert, M. L. (1978) *Human Neuropsychology*. New York: John Wiley and Sons.

Jennett, B. and Bond, M. (1975) 'Assessment of outcome after severe brain damage', *Lancet* 480–4.

Jennett, B. and Frankowski, R. F. (1990) 'The epidemiology of head injury', in R. Braakman (ed.) *Handbook of Clinical Neurology, Vol. 13(57): Head Injury*, Amsterdam: Elsevier Science Publishers.

Jones-Gotman, M. and Milner, B. (1977) 'Design fluency: the invention of nonsense drawings after focal cortical lesions', *Neuropsychologia* 15: 653–74.

Jones-Gotman, M. and Milner, B. (1978) 'Right temporal lobe contribution to image mediated verbal learning', *Neuropsychologia* 16: 61–71.

Kimura, D. (1963) 'Right temporal lobe damage: perception of unfamiliar stimuli after damage', *Archives of Neurology* 8: 264–71.

Kimura, D. (1980) 'Neuromotor mechanisms in the evolution of human communication', in H. D. Steklis and M. J. Raleigh (eds) *Neurobiology of Social Communication in Primates: An Evolutionary Perspective*, New York: Academic Press.

Kolb, B. and Milner, B. (1981) 'Performance of complex arm and facial movements after focal brain lesions', *Neuropsychologia* 19: 505–14.

Kolb, B. and Whishaw, I. Q. (1980) *Fundamentasl of Human Neuropsychology*, San Francisco: W. H. Freeman.

Kolb, B. and Whishaw, I. Q. (1990) *Fundamentals of Human Neuropsychology, 3rd edn*, New York: Freeman and Company.

Konow, A. and Pribram, K. H. (1970) 'Error recognition and utilization produced by injury to the frontal cortex in man', *Neuropsychologia* 8: 489–91.

Kraus, J. F. and Norjah, A. P. (1989) 'The epidemiology of mild head injury', in

H. S. Levin, H. M. Eisenberg and A. L. Benton (eds) *Mild Head Injury*, New York: Oxford University Press.

Kuypers, H. G. J. M. (1981) 'Anatomy of the descending pathways', in V. B. Brooks (ed.) *The Nervous System, Handbook of Physiology, Vol. 2*, Baltimore: Williams and Wilkins.

Leonard, G., Jones, L. and Milner, B. (1988) 'Residual impairment in handgrip strength after unilateral frontal-lobe lesions', *Neurospychologia* 26: 555–64.

Levin, H. S., Hamilton, W. J. and Grossman, R. G. (1990) 'Outcome after head injury', in R. Braakman (ed.) *Handbook of Clinical Neurology, Vol. 13(57): Head Injury*, Amsterdam: Elsevier Science Publishers.

Lezak, M. D. (1983) *Neuropsychological Assessment, 2nd edn*, New York: Oxford University Press.

Lezak, M. (ed.) (1989) *Assessment of the Behavioural Consequences of Head Trauma*, New York: Alan R. Liss Inc.

Lishman, W. A. (1968) 'Brain damage in relation to psychiatric disability after head injury', *British Journal Psychiatry* 114: 373–410.

Luria, A. R. (1966) *Higher Cortical Function in Man*, New York: Basic Books.

Luria, A. R. (1973) *The Working Brain*, London: Penguin.

Luria, A. R. and Tsvetkova, L. D. (1964) 'The programming of constructive activity in local brain injuries', *Neuropsychologia* 2: 95–108.

McNeil, M. R. and Prescott, T. E. (1978) *Revised Token Test*. Baltimore: University Park Press.

Meyer, V. (1957) 'Cognitive changes following temporal lobectomy for the relief of focal temporal lobe epilepsy', unpublished Ph. D. thesis, University of London.

Meyer, V. (1959) 'Cognitive changes following temporal lobe lobectomy for relief of temporal lobe epilepsy', *Archives of Neurology Psychiatry* 81: 299–09.

Meyer, V. and Yates, A. S. (1955) 'Intellectual changes following temporal lobectomy for psychomotor epilepsy', *Journal of Neurolology Neurosurgery and Psychiatry* 18: 44–52.

Miller, L. (1985) 'Cognition risk taking after frontal or temporal lobectomy I. The synthesis of fragmented visual information', *Neuropsychologia* 23: 359–69.

Milner, B. (1964) 'Some effects of frontal lobectomy in man', in J. M. Warren and K. Akert (eds) *The Frontal Granular Cortex and Behaviour*. New York: McGraw-Hill.

Milner, B. (1965) 'Visually-guided maze learning in man: effects of bi-lateral hippocampal, bilateral frontal, and unilateral cerebral lesion', *Neuropsychologia*, 3: 317–38.

Milner, B. (1967) 'Brain mechanisms suggested by studies of temporal lobes', in F. L. Darley (ed.) *Brain Mechanisms Underlying Speech and Language*. New York: Grune and Stratton.

Milner, B. (1968) 'Effects of different brain lesions on card sorting', *Archives of Neurology* 9: 90–100.

Milner, B. (1975) 'Psychological aspects of focal epilepsy and its neurosurgical management', in D. P. Purpura, J. K. Penry and R. D. Walter (eds) *Advances in Neurology, Vol. 8*. New York: Raven Press.

Nelson, H. E. (1976) 'A modified card sorting test sensitive to frontal lobe defects', *Cortex* 12: 313–24.

O'Callaghan, M. A. J. and Carroll, D. (1982) *Psychosurgery: A Scientific Analysis*. Lancaster: MTP Press.

Pang, D. (1989) 'Physics and Pathophysiology of closed head injury', in M. Lezak (ed.) *Assessment of the Behavioral Consequences of Head Trauma*, New York: Alan R. Liss, Inc.

Pendleton, M. G., Heaton, R. K., Lehman, R. A. W. and Hulihan, D. (1982) 'Diagnostic utility of the Thurstone Word Fluency Test in neuropsychological evaluations', *Journal of Clinical Neuropsychology* 4: 307–17.

Piercy, M., Hecaen, H. and Ajuriaguerra, J. de (1960) 'Constructional apraxia associated with unilateral cerebral lesions – left and right sided cases compared', *Brain* 83: 225–42.

Porteus, S. D. (1965) *Porteus Maze Test: Fifty Years' Application*, Palo Alto, Calif.: Pacific.

Powell, G. E. (1979) 'The relationship between intelligence and verbal and spatial memory', *Journal of Clinical Psychology* 35: 335–340.

Powell, G. E., Bailey, S. and Clark, E. (1980) 'A very short version of the Minnesota Aphasia test', *British Journal of Social and Clinical Psychology* 19: 189–94.

Rausch, R. (1977) Cognitive strategies in patients with unilateral temporal lobe excisions, *Neuropsychologia*, 15: 385–95.

Rausch, R. (1981) 'Lateralization of temporal lobe dysfunction and verbal encoding', *Brain and Language* 12: 92–100.

Reitan, R. M. (1966) 'A research programme on the psychological effects of brain lesions in human beings', in N. R. Ellis (ed.) *International Review of Research in Mental Retardation, Vol. 1*, New York: Academic Press.

Rey, A. (1959) *Le Teste de copie de figure complexe*, Paris: Edition Centre de Psychologie Appliquée.

Roy, R. and Cooper, P. R. (1990) 'Penetrating injuries of the skull and brain', in R. Braakman (ed.) *Handbook of Clinical Neurology, Vol. 13(57): Head Injury*, Amsterdam: Elsevier Science Publishers.

Russell, E. W., Neuringer, C. and Goldstein, G. (1970) *Assessment of Brain Damage: A Neuropsychological Key Approach*, New York: Wiley.

Schuell, H. and Sefer, H. (1973) *Differential Diagnosis of Aphasia: Revised*, Minneapolis: University of Minnesota Press.

Schulhoff, C. and Goodglass, H. (1969) 'Dichotic listening: side of brain injury and cerebral dominance', *Neuropsychologia* 7: 149–60.

Semmes, J. S., Weinstein, S. and Teuber, H.-L. (1960) *Somatosensory Changes after Penetrating Brain Wounds in Man*, Cambridge, Mass. : Harvard University Press.

Semmes, J., Weinstein, S., Ghent, L. and Teuber, H.-L. (1963) 'Correlates of impaired orientation in personal and extra-personal space', *Brain* 86: 747–72.

Shallice, T. (1982) 'Specific impairments of planning', *Philosophical Transactions of the Royal Society London*, B298: 199–209.

Shallice, T. and Evans, M. E. (1978) 'The involvement of the frontal lobes in cognitive estimation', *Cortex* 14: 294–303.

Silberman, E. K. and Weingartner, H. (1986) 'Hemispheric lateralization of functions related to elusion', *Brain and Cognition* 5: 322–53.

Smith, M. L. and Milner, B. (1984) 'Differential effects of frontal-lobe lesions on cognitive estimation and spatial memory', *Neuropsychologia* 22: 697–705.

Spreen, O. and Benton, A. L. (1969) *Neurosensory Center Comprehensive Examination for Aphasia*, Victoria, Canada: University of Victoria.

Spreen, O. and Strauss, E. (1991) *A Compendium of Neuropsychological Texts: Administration, Norms and Commentary*, New York: Oxford University Press.

Stalhammer, D. A. (1990) 'The mechanisms of brain injury', in R. Braakman (ed.) *Handbook of Clinical Neurology, Vol. 13(57): Head Injury*, Amsterdam: Elsevier Science Publishers.

Sunderland, A., Harris, J. E. and Baddeley, A. D. (1983) 'Do laboratory tests predict everyday memory?', *Journal of Verbal Learning and Verbal Behaviour* 22, 341–57.

Taylor, L. B. (1969) 'Localization of cerebral lesions by psychological testing', *Clinical Neurosurgery* 16: 269–87.

Taylor, L. (1979) 'Psychological assessment of neurosurgical patients', in T. Rasmussen and R. Marino (eds) *Functional Neurosurgery*, New York: Raven Press.

Teasdale, A. and Jennett, B. (1974) 'The Glasgow Coma Scale', *Lancet* 2: 81–4.

Teuber, H.-L. (1964) 'The riddle of frontal lobe function in man', in J. M. Warren and K. Akert (eds) *The Frontal Granuar Cortex and Behaviour*, New York: McGraw-Hill.

Teuber, H.-L. and Weinstein, S. (1954) 'Performance on a formboard task after penetrating brain injury', *Journal of Psychology* 38: 177–90.

Tompkins, C. A. and Mateer, C. A. (1985) 'Right hemisphere appreciation of intonational and linguistic indications of affect', *Brain and Language* 24: 185–203.

Tyler, H. R. (1969) 'Disorders of scanning with frontal lobe lesions', in S. Locke (ed.) *Modern Neurology*, London: Churchill.

Walsh, K. W. (1976) 'Neuropsychological aspects of modified leucotomy', in W. H. Sweet (ed.) *Neurosurgical Treatment in Psychiatry, Pain and Epilepsy*, Baltimore: Unversity Park Press.

Walsh, K. W. (1978) *Neuropsychology: A Clinical Approach*, Edinburgh: Churchill Livingstone.

Warrington, E. K. and Rabin, P. (1970) 'Perceptual matching in patients with cerebral lesions', *Neuropsychologia* 8: 475–87.

Warrington, E. K. and Taylor, A. M. (1973) 'The contribution of the right parietal lobe to object recognition', *Cortex* 9: 152–64.

Warrington, E. K. and Weiskrantz, L. (1973) 'An analysis of short-term and long-term memory defects in man', in J. A. Deutsch (ed.) *The Physiological Basis of Memory*, New York: Academic Press.

Wilkins, A. and Moscovitch, M. (1978) 'Selective impairment of semantic memory after temporal lobectomy', *Neuropsychologia* 16: 73–9.

Chapter 35

Neurological problems
Treatment and rehabilitation

Barbara A. Wilson and Graham E. Powell

THE POTENTIAL ROLE AND CONTRIBUTION OF CLINICAL PSYCHOLOGY

Most treatments available to brain-injured patients are currently provided by doctors, nurses, physiotherapists, occupational therapists and speech therapists. Recently, however, it has become apparent that clinical psychology also has much to offer.

First, clinical psychologists can contribute to the nature of the treatment itself, using their knowledge of specific training techniques. The appropriate techniques have been described by Powell (1981; 1983) and Wilson (1991a) and are outlined in Table 35.1 as they pertain to the various neuropsychological dysfunctions.

Second, the clinical psychologist's expertise in matters of assessment can help define treatment goals and aid in an improved monitoring of patient progress. Indeed, under some circumstances, such monitoring can itself have a therapeutic impact; it can reinforce patient and staff motivation and can foster an atmosphere of mutual cooperation.

Third, the clinical psychologist has a knowledge of research design, research methodology and statistics. This is important in the investigation of patient dysfunction (thereby refining treatment targets) and in the evaluation of treatment efficacy – a sadly neglected topic in many of the helping professions.

The problems confronting the clinical psychologist working with brain-injured people derive from a variety of sources – including the effects of strokes, traumatic head injury, brain tumours, brain surgery, degenerative diseases, metabolic and endocrine disorders, intracerebral infections, nutritional deficits, birth traumas and toxic disorders. The problems themselves may usefully be broken down into three overlapping categories. First, there are the deficits that stem directly from the lesioning of neural tissue, including aphasia, apraxia, disinhibition, memory deficits, unilateral neglect, and so forth. Second, there are the problems that have been learned after brain damage, like yelling for attention, fear of physiotherapy, talking too much to avoid doing a particular activity, or limping for no reason other than secondary gain. Third, there are those problems which predate or coexist with the neurological damage. These are problems

Table 35.1 Some of the treatment techniques used to alleviate neurological
problems

A *Language disorders*
  1 Approaches that treat language as comprising behaviours that can be
     shaped:
     e.g. operant shaping using positive reinforcement
           operant shaping using negative reinforcement for inappropriate
              utterances
           token economy programmes
           modelling of desired 'behaviours'
           feedback of performance
           programmed learning
  2 Approaches that attempt to engage the non-dominant hemisphere:
     e.g. melodic intonation therapy
           lateralised input (visual auditory or tactile) to the right hemisphere only
           recoding of words into visual forms
  3 Approaches that build up an entirely new vehicle for the expression of
     thoughts and cognition:
     e.g. sign language
           pictorial vocabulary books to be pointed to (e.g. BLISS)
           artificial languages (e.g. Visual Communication System)
B *Memory dysfunction*
  1 External, artificial memory storage:
     e.g. notebooks
           diaries
           lists
  2 Internal, cognitive strategies of organising information to be recalled:
     e.g. first letter mnemonics
           the loci method
           the peg method
  3 The increase of the depth of processing of material to be recalled:
     e.g. reading for meaning or for implications
           reading with a view to answering pre-defined questions
  4 The recoding of information into patterns that can be stored and retrieved:
     e.g. verbal to visual recoding
           verbal to motor recoding
           face–name imaginal associations
  5 The use of both the verbal and the non-verbal memory systems (dual
     encoding):
     e.g. pictorial remediation of word pairs
           pictorial illustrations of prose passages
C *Seizure disorders*
  1 Behavioural manipulations of the environment:
           Removal of immediate and delayed secondary gains
           Addition of immediate negative reinforcement
           Interruption of pre-seizure behavioural chains
  2 Changing the emotional impact of certain environmental stimuli:
           Desensitisation to feared epileptogenic circumstances
           General reduction of anxiety
           Increased ability to relax
           Insight into the reasons for emotional stress

Table 35.1 Continued

    3 Habituation to epileptogenic sensory stimuli:
          Graded exposure
    4 Bio-feedback:
          of the sensori-motor rhythm (SMR)
          of fast activity in general
          of alpha rhythm
D *Motor disorders*
    1 Feedback paradigms:
      e.g. EMG feedback of muscle activity in paralysis and spasticity
            motor movement feedback in cases of voluntary motor disorder
              (e.g. torticollis and tremor)
            performance feedback (on distance walked, height of leg lifted, etc.)
    2 Reinforcement approaches:
      e.g. rewards for goals attained
            time out for inappropriate voluntary behaviours
    3 Sundry techniques:
      e.g. massed practice
            pacing of motor skills
            mental practice of skills
            verbal direction of voluntary movements

which are not caused by the tissue loss but adversely affect rehabilitation or prognosis and must be dealt with or accommodated to. These include aggressive tendencies, marital difficulties, arthritis, obesity, and a whole range of others. Table 35.2 shows how patients' problems can be divided in this manner.

The rest of this chapter provides some illustrations of these problems and the methods used to treat them. The most common impediments found in brain-damaged adults after head injury (Brooks, 1984), strokes (Nicols, 1979) and sundry neurological problems (Lishman, 1978) are likely to be:

1 Motor difficulties, such as hemiplegia, apraxia and ataxia. These are often accompanied by spasticity and loss of muscle tone. Physiotherapists will probably be involved in the treatment of these.
2 Cognitive deficits, such as memory, language and perceptual impairments. Speech therapists and occupational therapists are most likely to be treating these, if indeed they are being treated at all.
3 Behaviour problems, such as shouting, swearing, and disinhibition, and
4 Emotional problems such as anxiety, anger, fear and depression. If these are being treated then a psychologist may be asked to advise on management. However, it is frequently the case that no psychologist is available, so all other staff may be trying to manage as best they can with varying degrees of success. In most cases, families of patients will find that eventually they have to struggle with no support.

Table 35.2 Examples of some problems commonly found in neurological patients

Problem	Resulting directly from brain damage	Learned after brain damage	Pre-dating or co-existing with brain damage
Behaviour problems	Disinhibition and impulsivity after frontal lobe damage	Yelling for attention	Aggression
Fears/ Anxieties	An increase in these is more likely after temporal subcortical damage	Fear of physiotherapy	Fear of spouse leaving and of the future in general
Social skills	Language disorders clearly affect social interaction	Talking too much to avoid task	Psychopathic personality. Social phobic
Depression	Sometimes correlated with left hemisphere damage, but has also been related to right damage	Resulting from role change	Manic/depressive personality
Motor	Hemiplegia, apraxia, and Parkinsonism may all result from different sites of damage	Attention-seeking limp	Arthritis, congenital abnormalities
Memory problems	Poor learning and poor retention over time are the frequent con-comitants of temporal damage	May learn to exaggerate memory deficit. Compensation neurosis	Function/hysterical amnesia
Speech, language and reading	Dysarthria, dysphasia, and acquired dyslexia may all be evident after left lesions	Elective mutism	Developmental dyslexia, stammering, elective mutism
Unilateral neglect	Right parietal damage	(Unlikely to be learned)	(Unlikely to be learned)
Obesity	Chronic overeating can result from hypothalamic damage	Resulting from less exercise	Always overweight

5   Handicaps resulting from frontal lobe damage, such as perseveration, apathy, mutism and difficulty with organising and planning behaviour. Again, these are largely untreated, although all paramedical staff may become involved, depending on the circumstances.

The major question we need to ask is how can clinical psychologists help in situations like these? Let us look at each subsection in turn.

MOTOR PROBLEMS

Behaviour principles can sometimes be used to alleviate motor difficulties or even restore lost function. Usually it is desirable to combine forces with a physiotherapist or perhaps a neurologist. In certain situations patients may refuse to cooperate, arguing that it is too difficult for them to learn to walk or push their wheelchairs. On other occasions patients may be unwilling to participate in therapy, owing to the erroneous belief that they merely have to wait passively for their arm or leg to return to normal. Clinical psychologists may be able to circumvent this unwillingness to cooperate by the use of appropriate reinforcement. For example, many patients find that by complaining and refusing to cooperate they will escape from the unpleasant or difficult task in hand. If they refuse to propel the wheelchair, somebody else will eventually push them; if they complain sufficiently about their exercises, they will be allowed to rest for a while or the physiotherapist will give them extra attention. Rest and attention are frequently very powerful reinforcers in a rehabilitation setting (Series and Lincoln, 1978). The solution here may be found simply by providing the rest and attention following success or achievement rather than following complaints or failure. Thus, if a particular patient finds an exercise or activity fatiguing he or she should certainly be allowed to rest but after, say, spending three or four minutes on the exercise or after completing the exercise a given number of times. The guiding rule is to begin with a target the patient will achieve very easily. It is better to make the goals too easy, as it is always possible to move ahead. If the goals are too hard to achieve, then everyone may become despondent. Feedback is another powerful reinforcer for neurological patients and one that is often overlooked. Simply informing people how well they are doing and providing charts or graphs to confirm this may lead to dramatic results. One 34-year-old spinal patient, reported by Carr and Wilson (1983), developed pressure sores through failing to push his buttocks up from his wheelchair at regular intervals. Physiotherapists, nurses and doctors tried to convince him of the importance of skin care and the necessity to lift himself for four seconds every ten minutes. The man ignored their advice, cajoling and subsequent anger. However, when the psychologists fitted a device to his wheelchair which recorded the number of lifts made every hour, the rate of lifting increased and the pressure sores healed. It is possible that feedback may also benefit other motor disorders, such as limb apraxia. For example, a simple device which emits a signal wherever a certain angle is obtained might improve the apraxic patient's positioning of a faulty arm or leg. The biggest difficulty is in designing a piece of equipment easily fitted to a knee or hip or elbow which is both sensitive to angle of movement and comfortable to wear. Bio-feedback is effective in the laboratory, but something is needed for everyday wear in natural situations. Such a device has been made for the physiotherapy department at Rivermead Rehabilitation Centre in Oxford by Maynard Projects of Oxford. The device – a mercury tilt switch – is a phial with two contacts and a bubble of mercury. When the device is horizontal the mercury bridges the gap between the contacts and an auditory signal is emitted. Although this has not yet been used for apraxic patients, it has been used for a stroke patient who continually drooped her head forward. The device was attached to a woolly hat and in order to avoid the signal's beep she had to keep her head upright.

A recent paper by Robertson and Cashman (1991) describes the treatment of a 29-year-old woman with unilateral neglect and frontal lobe difficulties. These resulted from multiple cerebral infarcts following cardiac surgery. The woman presented problems in physiotherapy because she walked with her left heel held up and in a highly unstable position. After she had failed to learn to lower her heel when walking, a pressure-sensitive switch, attached to a buzzer on her belt, was inserted under her left heel. A training programme followed, which included setting goals and charting progress. Her walking improved and generalised to non-therapy situations.

An alternative form of feedback is bio-feedback, that is, a procedure in which some aspect of an individual's functioning is systematically monitored and fed back to the individual in the form of an auditory or visual signal. Psatta (1983) described the use of bio-feedback with epileptic patients and showed a gradual normalisation of their EEG recordings. Imes (1984) found bio-feedback showed more clear-cut results than group psychotherapy in the treatment of stroke patients, and Thompson (1987), also working with stroke patients, found significant improvement in control of innervated leg muscles. This was particularly likely between weeks 5 to 16 of training.

COGNITIVE PROBLEMS

In the first edition of this book we said that this was possibly the most neglected area in neurological rehabilitation or treatment. Since then there has been a considerable increase in cognitive rehabilitation, with two journals (*Cognitive Rehabilitation*, published by Neuroscience Publishers, Indianapolis, and *Neuropsychological Rehabilitation*, published by Lawrence Erlbaum Associates, Hove) devoted largely to this topic. Numerous articles have appeared in the past five years (see, for example, Sturm and Willmes, 1991, and Kerkoff *et al.*, 1992). Despite this growth of interest it is still true that some doctors fail to recognise the enormous implications of changed intellectual functioning following a stroke, head injury or other central nervous system damage. Of those who do recognise the handicap caused by cognitive impairments, many will fail to appreciate that some amelioration or re-education is possible. Many cognitive deficits, such as unilateral neglect, amnesia or agnosia, will be totally misunderstood by the patients themselves, by their relatives and by staff working with them. People with memory deficits, for example, often think they are going crazy. People with unilateral neglect often deny there is anything the matter. People with acquired dyslexia may think they need new glasses. People with aphasia may be shouted at or treated like children by relatives or some professionals – or conversely they may be treated as if they understood everything said to them because their non-verbal skills are still intact. Diller said, 'Remediating cognitive deficit remains the greatest challenge to those concerned with rehabilitation of the brain-injured' (Diller, 1976: 13). Some techniques and new approaches already exist and others are currently being developed. There are, however, well-established principles and strategies that can be incorporated into our treatment programmes: for example, positive reinforcement, extinction, shaping, errorless learning, modelling and prompting. We can also borrow and adapt techniques from other fields within psychology: for example, we can use teaching techniques developed for use with mentally handicapped people, reality orientation from geriatrics, and behaviour therapy from adult and child psychiatry. Wilson (1989; 1991a) provides clinical examples of these.

One of the commonest cognitive impairments following brain damage is memory disorder, and this is certainly one of the problems frequently noted by relatives. The range of difficulties included under the heading of memory impairment is wide but almost always includes problems with new learning and retaining certain kinds of new information. For the majority of memory-impaired people, it is unrealistic to expect any treatment to restore their memory to its pre-morbid level (Wilson, 1991b). The exceptions are those still in the recovery phase, when the memory problems are transient (even here, it is the recovery process rather than training which is probably responsible for improvement). On the other hand, there are several approaches clinical psychologists can use in an attempt to ameliorate the memory problems, and the field of memory therapy is expanding (see, for example, Wilson and Moffatt, 1992). Two guiding principles would be: (1) do not set your sights too high; if the goals are small they are more easily obtainable. It is always simpler to extend the goals or aims following success than it is to backtrack after failure, when patients, relatives and staff may become disillusioned with the whole process. (2) Rather than ask the question, 'How can I improve this person's memory?' it is usually more profitable to ask, 'What is the best way for this person to retain new information?' Inherent in the first question is the implication that generalisation will occur, that is, that any method taught will be used in other settings. In practice such generalisation rarely occurs. Thus it is possible to teach new names, new skills or new routes by a particular method, but patients, by and large, do not subsequently use the methods spontaneously to improve their learning of names or skills or routes. Instead, it is the therapist or relative who has to impose the strategy whenever it is necessary for the patient to learn further information. Nevertheless, finding the most effective learning method for an individual can still be a valuable aid in reducing the effects of the deficit.

The approaches which may be considered for amelioration of memory problems are: (a) Re-arranging the environment to make life easier for a memory impaired person. For example, in one geriatric unit in the United States all the lavatory doors were painted a different colour from all the other doors. The result was that more patients 'remembered' where to go and the rate of incontinence decreased (described in Harris, 1980). Labelling doors and painting lines from one room to another may achieve the same end; (b) a second approach is to teach or encourage people to bypass their poor memory by using external aids, such as diaries, notebooks, noticeboards or tape recorders. Sohlberg and Mateer (1989) provide a description of a treatment programme to teach the use of compensatory memory books.

One man who has had a left temporal lobe tumour removed (Wilson, 1981b) keeps a paper and pencil in every room in his house, writes down immediately anything he wants to remember and, if he has to go upstairs to fetch something, writes down what it is before he goes. He manages to get round his memory problems remarkably well. Timers can also serve a useful purpose – alarm clocks, digital alarm watches, kitchen timers and calculators that have an alarm system (see Harris, 1980, and Wilson and Moffat, 1992) for a more detailed description of these). Sometimes timers are sufficient on their own to remind the person to do something. Sometimes it may be necessary to use a timer in conjunction with a notebook or diary (Fowler et al., 1972), and sometimes a timer can be used to shape behaviour by gradually increasing the interval over which new information has to be retained (Wilson, 1987a). A third approach is to teach various internal strategies or mnemonics, such as visual imagery (Jones, 1974; Wilson, 1987b), elaborate coding (Crovitz, 1979), special rehearsal techniques (Glasgow et al., 1977; Wilson, 1987b) or a combination of these methods (Wilson, 1987b). A recent study demonstrating the effects of specific strategy training for memory-impaired patients is reported by Berg et al., (1991).

Another frequently encountered group of cognitive deficits resulting from brain damage acquired in adulthood is that of perceptual disorders. Included under this heading are difficulties with visual recognition, spatial relationships, depth perception, constructional tasks and, perhaps the most common, unilateral spatial neglect or left inattention. The majority of perceptual disorders result from posterior and right hemisphere damage and may be very handicapping for normal everyday functioning. Right hemisphere stroke patients, for example, usually take longer to rehabilitate than left hemisphere stroke patients (Denes et al., 1982). Unfortunately, such problems are often not recognised or understood by patients and relatives. Even professionals frequently fail to realise how disruptive such problems may be. Left inattention, for example, can impair reading ability, as the patient may not 'see' the beginning of the line. One of our patients said his favourite item on the menu was 'late' pudding. He never saw the 'choco' at the beginning. These patients often bump into doorways or catch their hands in the wheelchair spokes if staff are not very careful. They may also miss cutlery, pills or clothes if these are placed on their left-hand side. Even when the grosser deficits subside, more subtle and less obvious ones may remain (Halligan et al., 1991). These can severely impair the patient's driving ability and performance in other complex tasks where divided attention is necessary. Left inattention is often accompanied by a hemianopia but can exist independently. The hemianopia itself cannot explain the inattention, as hemianopia is equally likely after a left hemisphere stroke. Inattention (of the right side), however, is far less likely after left hemisphere strokes.

There is a current surge of interest in both the theoretical and clinical implications of neglect (e.g. Robertson, 1989; Halligan et al., 1991; Zoccolotti and Judica, 1991 and Robertson (forthcoming)). One of the earliest reported treatments for the reduction of neglect was the visual scanning training by Diller and his colleagues (Diller and Weinberg, 1977; Weinberg et al., 1979; Diller, 1980). A more recent treatment is that of Joanette and Brouchon (1984) involving contralesional limb activation. Robertson et al., (1992) describe three single-case studies in which they attempt to replicate the findings of Joanette and Brouchon and to determine whether the improvement is due to perceptual cueing or to ipsilesional hemsiphere activation. Robertson et al. found an improvement in all three patients and suggested that the effects relied more on contralesional limb activation than on perceptual anchoring.

Many right-brain-damaged patients have problems with recognition of pictures taken from certain angles (Warrington and Taylor, 1973). When shown a picture of a bucket as seen from above, for example, they may think it is a fried egg or a headlamp. They usually have no problem, however, identifying a bucket seen from the side. The difficulty, therefore, cannot be explained by poor visual acuity or by dysphasia. Examples of real-life manifestations of this problem are sometimes offered by patients. One woman who had a right hemisphere stroke saw a black cardigan lying on her hospital bed. She thought it was a cat and spoke to it. When she saw the cardigan from another angle, she realised it was not a cat. She was then overcome with embarrassment, because she thought the other people in the ward would think she was crazy to talk to a cardigan. Sometimes people with this kind of perceptual difficulty become suspicious and think people are deliberately playing tricks on them. One woman who was copying a mosaic pattern said that every time she looked back to check the original design, she thought someone had played a trick on her and had changed it, as the original looked different each time she saw it. Treatment for such difficulties can include (a) explanation, (b) practice in seeing things from different angles in attempts to re-educate, (c) feedback on progress or success rate, and (d) compensatory strategies, such as checking objects from several angles, making sure the patient draws close to objects before trying to identify them, taking care that the lighting is good and encouraging verbal descriptions whenever possible. This problem of recognition from certain angles is not the same as visual object agnosia which is a more severe recognition disorder. However, there is some commonality in that neither can be explained by sensory or language deficits. Visual object agnosia is very rare, but three patients have been treated by one of the present authors, and some improvement in recognition of objects and pictures is possible (see Wilson, 1990).

The final group of cognitive problems to be discussed here are those associated with language disorder. Most aphasic or dysphasic patients receive treatment from a speech therapist, but there are at least three ways in which a clinical psychologist may also contribute. First, by working with speech therapists to devise and implement a treatment programme. One patient, for example, was a young man who had previously had a large left fronto-parietal tumour removed, resulting in a severe global dysphasia. His speech therapist asked the clinical psychologist to collaborate on a language comprehension programme, and an approach similar to that used in comprehension programmes for mentally handicapped children was devised (see Howlin, 1980). A prompting and fading procedure was used to teach discrimination between two dissimilar items, with other items added singly as the earlier ones were mastered.

A more recent example of a psychologist and a speech therapist working together to reduce word-finding deficits of dysphasic patients is that of Davis and Pring (1991). They compared semantic and phonological approaches to treatment, finding both helpful. Furthermore, they found that generalisation to non-target items occurred and that the therapeutic effects lasted up to six months.

Second, a psychologist may provide language therapy after the speech therapist has decided not to continue. Such discontinuation on the part of a speech therapist may arise because of shortage of time and/or because the patient no longer appears to be benefiting from speech therapy. Psychological intervention in such a case will normally be primarily concerned with alternative communication systems rather than working towards restoration of normal language functioning. Of course, many speech therapists will also be involved in alternative communication programmes, but their intervention is almost always time-limited and psychologists may be in a position to continue treatment for a few patients for a longer period. One globally aphasic man, for example, was first seen by his psychologist five years post stroke – long after speech therapy has ceased. He was taught to use symbols adapted from the work of Gardner *et al.* (1976). It took three 45-minute sessions a week for nine months before the man used the symbols for expressive communication. The symbols helped his comprehension from a much earlier stage.

Third, a psychologist may work alongside a speech therapist on aspects of disordered communication not stressed in detail during the speech therapy sessions. Acquired dyslexia could be such a case. Some kinds of dyslexia, for example, deep dyslexia and surface dyslexia, are found in association with expressive and receptive language disorders. A psychologist could perfectly well attempt to improve certain aspects of these reading disorders. Other acquired dyslexias, such as letter-by-letter reading and agnosia alexia, are usually associated with perceptual disorders, such as visual object agnosia or Balint's Syndrome (see Rubens, 1979, for a more detailed description). In the perceptually based dyslexics, speech therapists (at least in the UK) are less likely to be involved, and here psychologists may be the only people interested in remediation. Some success has been demonstrated in such cases (Wilson and Baddeley, 1986 and Wilson, 1987b).

BEHAVIOUR PROBLEMS

In one sense, all the problems or difficulties described so far can be called behaviour problems if we define behaviour as meaning anything a person says or does which can be observed or inferred. Usually, however, behaviour problems refer to those phenomena which disrupt or are detrimental to a person's lifestyle or treatment. Frequently encountered after head injury, these disruptive behaviours may take the form of yelling, tantrums, aggression, refusing to get up or go to a particular therapy, and talking all the time. All these are examples of behavioural excesses, but behavioural deficits are also encountered and may be equally disruptive to treatment regimes or to independent living. These deficits may take the form of withdrawal, apathy, fearfulness and mutism. In general, the best approach is to follow the steps one would usually follow in designing a behavioural assessment/treatment programme: specify the target behaviour, select the goals or aims of treatment, obtain baselines, select the method of treatment, begin treatment, monitor progress, modify treatment if necessary and evaluate the course of treatment (Powell, 1981). It is, of course, essential to bear in mind the nature of the neurological and neuropsychological impairments. Thus, if someone with behaviour problems has a severe memory deficit, there is no point expecting him or her to remember that the reward for not yelling for two days is a trip into town next week. The programme may need to be written down for the patient, feedback charts may be necessary, and daily or hourly reminders from a particular therapist may also be desirable. Any of the techniques used in behaviour therapy and behaviour modification are potentially useful with brain-damaged and other neurologically impaired patients, provided the neurological and neuropsychological status is taken into account.

Some examples may show the range of such behavioural approaches. The first is of a 58-year-old stroke patient referred for fear of the hydrotherapy pool. This woman had always been terrified of water. A straightforward desensitisation programme was used very successfully, but care had to be taken over the preliminary relaxation exercises. Because of her hemiplegia, the tense-and-release exercises normally used by a clinical psychologist were inappropriate as these could lead to an increase in spasticity of her hemiplegic arm and leg. After discussion with her physiotherapist, an alternative relaxation method was used, whereby the patient only relaxed her good side and imagined the hemiplegia side relaxed. The programme began with imaginal desensitisation but rapidly changed to *in vivo* because of inability to feel any anxiety in the imaginary situations.

The second example is of a 22-year-old head-injured girl who was frightened of physiotherapy. This fear had obviously developed after her head injury. In her particular case, she was physically very disabled, the exercises were difficult for her, and before coming to the rehabilitation centre, she appeared to have received some harsh treatment in another department. All these factors seemed to have contributed to her fear of physiotherapy. In her case, baselines were taken of the

amount of time spent in each of five exercises. One exercise, 'head balancin
she actually enjoyed doing – no doubt because it was easy for her. Of the others,
three were particularly disliked and she spent less than two minutes on each of
these before complaining. A multiple baseline procedure was used in which one
of the three most disliked exercises was treated each week. The first week after
baselines the patient was (a) asked to try and increase the amount of time spent
on that exercise, (b) given verbal feedback on her performance, (c) given visual
feedback by means of a graph, and (d) allowed to spend several minutes on the
head-balancing exercises if she reached her target (the Premack Principle). For
the remaining disliked exercises, baselines were still taken but no encouragement given. The following week, another disliked exercise was included in the
treatment, and in the third week, the final exercise was added (see Figure 35.1).
Thus it can be seen that improvement only occurred after treatment was initiated.
It cannot be explained by natural recovery or improvement over time.

The final example in this section is of a young man who had received a head
injury some twelve months before the programme began. He constantly called
out to anyone in sight during his physiotherapy and occupational therapy sessions,

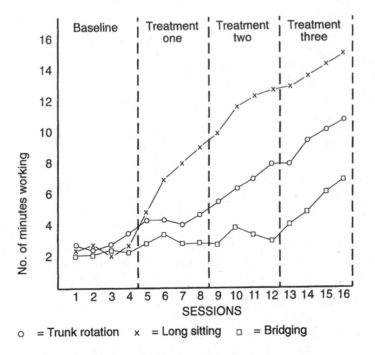

Figure 35.1 A multiple baseline procedure for physiotherapy exercises

own treatment and that of the other patients. His physio-
al therapist and psychologist collected baselines on the
alled out during a session, following which he was informed
ure. A contract was made that if he could manage not to call
cutive days, he could go to the pub for lunch with the three
einforcement proved to be very powerful and, with some false
out decreased satisfactorily. The pub lunches gradually became
mor   o obtain, that is, he had to increase the number of days when he
did not ca   ut, but over a period of several weeks the problem abated. This
particular young man had a good verbal memory, so it was not difficult for him
to remember the contract. He had considerable motor problems, however, so
going to the pub was indirectly therapeutic in encouraging him to manage
without his wheelchair (he used his wheelchair as far as the pub door but insisted
on walking into the pub with the help of sticks). Further discussion of this topic
is to be found in Wood (1987) and an imaginative case study is described by
Alderman and Ward (1991).

EMOTIONAL PROBLEMS

Emotional problems are common after brain injury and are partly dependent on
the site of the brain injury. A brain stem stroke, for example, may result in
marked and rapid changes in emotional behaviour whereby the person might
range from tears to laughter in the space of a few minutes. Panic, fear, grief and
other emotional difficulties, can, of course, result from non-organic causes, such
as failure to understand the cognitive changes, uncertainty about the future, role
change and loss of motor function.

Depression, stress, anxiety and anger are emotions which are commonly seen
in non-brain-injured people but which can interact in abnormal ways following
brain injury due to the influence of impaired cognition.

As we saw earlier in the examples about fear, it is not always easy to
distinguish between emotional, cognitive and behaviour problems, and
interactions between these may occur. The woman who was frightened of
physiotherapy, for example, felt the emotion fear because of the cognitive
difficulties and this caused her to exhibit behaviour problems in her therapy
sessions.

An interesting strategy used with head-injured patients with temper tantrums
resulting from poor self-control is described by McKinlay and Hickox (1988).
The acronym used for the strategy is ANGER, which stands for

A = Anticipate the trigger situations
N = Notice the signs of rising anger
G = Go through your temper regime
E = Extricate yourself from the situation if all else fails
R = Record how you coped; lessons for the future

Problems resulting from frontal lobe damage (the dysexecutive syndrome)

Because over a third of the human brain is comprised of frontal lobes, there is a bewildering variety of frontal lobe deficits many of which may cause particularly severe management or treatment problems (see Chapter 34). Because it is inadequate and potentially misleading to specify a syndrome in terms of its localisation, Baddeley and Wilson (1988) suggested the term dysexecutive syndrome (DES) to describe the functional deficits shown by these patients. One of the biggest handicaps of frontally damaged patients is their inability to organise and plan their behaviour. This makes it almost impossible for them to get to grips with their difficulties and find solutions to them. The patients who constantly fight to remedy their deficits are, almost always, those with posterior damage. The actual physical and cognitive handicaps of this latter group may, in fact, be far more serious than those of the frontal patients, who may be completely intact physically with few language, perceptual or memory disorders. Unfortunately they usually lack the insight, determination and motivation to help themselves. To some extent such patients can be helped by providing a structure for them: Luria and Tsvetkova (1964), for example, show how frontal patients can be helped to accomplish certain tasks if the tester or experimenter imposes an overall structure. Thus, in a block design task, placing a transparent sheet with a 3×3 grid marked on it over the stimulus card can enable frontal patients to complete a nine-block design successfully. It is sometimes possible to provide such a structure for DES patients in everyday situations. One man, for example, who had sustained a depressed fracture of the frontal bone, became very passive and lacking in initiative. He lay in bed in the mornings until told to get up: once up, he sat on the bed until told to go to the lavatory; he then stayed there until told to get washed and shaved, and so forth. A card was given to this man with the morning's activities listed on it: (1) get up, (2) go to the lavatory, (3) wash, (4) shave, (5) get dressed, (6) go to breakfast. A nurse gave him the card first thing in the morning and told him to follow the instructions. He did this and the steps were gradually faded out. The first one was omitted a week later, the second step a few days after that, and so forth. The man continued to do all the steps required with occasional verbal prompting. Timers can also help in some cases. A kitchen timer or alarm, or calculator with a built-in timer can act as a cue for frontal patients to commence the next step or activity.

A simple reward system has been used on at least two occasions with two of our frontal patients who do not initiate conversation. Both had received severe head injuries. They were not dysphasic and could answer direct questions. However, they rarely spoke when not being questioned. At first tokens and praise were given for any speech. Later, rewards were given only for unsolicited speech. So successful was one of these programmes that one patient began talking too much, and another programme was necessary to reduce over-talkativeness!

Two very different and successful treatment programmes for DES patients have recently been published. One is a group study (von Cramon et al., 1991) in which patients with problem-solving deficits are given specific problem-solving training. These patients show significantly greater improvement on a number of frontal lobe or executive tests in comparison with a control group who received memory training. The second is a single-case study in which a DES patient showed severe behaviour problems. Treatment involved two behavioural techniques, known as 'response cost' and 'cognitive overlearning'. Following successful treatment, generalisation to a ward setting was seen to occur.

It is possible that other problems, such as perseveration, may be amenable to behavioural approaches. Feedback, for example, on the number of times a phrase or movement or activity has been repeated may help in reducing the frequency. An auditory signal, such as a buzzer or a word, might be the most appropriate way to provide such feedback. Investigations of possible treatment methods for these and other problems are urgently required. We also need to know to what extent training patients with the DES in tasks they typically find difficult (for example, fluency, visual search and category sorting) generalises to problems encountered in everyday life. Shallice (1982), for example, describes the 'Tower of London' puzzle, which requires planning ahead and which frontal patients may be unable to solve. Would training on this activity help planning generally? What is the best way to teach such skills? Is chaining, or prompting, or modelling most effective? This is a field ripe for investigation by clinical psychologists.

REFERENCES

Alderman, N. and Ward, A. (1991) 'Behavioural treatment of the dysexecutive syndrome: reduction of repetitive speech using response cost and cognitive overlearning', *Neuropsychological Rehabilitation* 1: 65–80.
Baddeley, A. D. and Wilson, B. A. (1988) 'Frontal amnesia and the dysexecutive syndrome', *Brain and Cognition* 7: 212–30.
Berg, I., Koning-Haanstra, M. and Deelman, B. (1991) 'Long-term effects of meaning rehabilitation: a controlled study', *Neuropsychological Rehabilitation* 1: 97–111.
Brooks, D. N. (1984) *Closed Head Injury*, Oxford: Oxford University Press.
Carr, S. and Wilson, B. (1983) 'Promotion of pressure relief exercising in a spinal injury patient: a multiple baseline across settings design', *Behavioural Psychotherapy* 11: 329–36.
Cramon, D. Y. von, Mathes-von Cramon, G. and Mai, N. (1991) 'Problem-solving deficits in brain-injured patients: a therapy approach', *Neuropsychological Rehabilitation* 1: 45–64.
Crovitz, H. (1979) 'Memory retraining in brain damaged patients: the airplane list', *Cortex* 15: 131–4.
Davis, A. and Pring, T. (1991) 'Therapy for word-finding deficits: more on the effects of semantic and phonological approaches to treatment with dysphasic patients', *Neuropsychological Rehabilitation* 1: 135–45.
Denes, G., Semenza, C., Stoppa, E. and Lis, A. (1982) 'Unilateral spatial neglect and recovery from hemiplegia', *Brain* 105: 543–52.
Diller, L. (1976) 'A model for cognitive retraining in rehabilitation', *Clinical Psychologist* 19: 13–15.
Diller, L. (1980) 'The development of a perceptual-remediation program in hemiplegia', in L. Ince (ed.) *Behavioral Psychology in Rehabilitation Medicine: Clinical Applications*, Baltimore: Williams and Wilkins.

Diller, L. and Weinberg, J. (1977) 'Hemi-inattention in rehabilitation: the evolution of a rational remediation program', in E. A. Weinstein and R. P. Friedland (eds) *Advances in Neurology, Vol. 18*, New York: Raven Press.

Fowler, R., Hart, J. and Sheehan, M. (1972) 'A prosthetic memory: an application of the prosthetic environment concept', *Rehabilitation Counselling Bulletin*, 15: 80–5.

Gardner, H., Zurif, E. B., Berry, T. and Baker, E. (1976) 'Visual communication in aphasia', *Neuropsychologia* 14: 275–92.

Glasgow, R., Zeiss, R., Barrera, M. and Lewinsohn, P. (1977) 'Case studies on remediating memory deficits in brain damaged individuals', *Journal of Clinical Psychology* 33: 1049–54.

Halligan, P. W., Cockburn, J. and Wilson, B. A. (1991) 'The behavioural assessment of unilateral neglect', *Neuropsychological Rehabilitation* 1: 5–32.

Harris, J. E. (1980) 'We have ways of helping you remember', *Concord, The Journal of the British Association for Service to the Elderly* 17: 21–7.

Howlin, P. (1980) 'Language training', in W. Yule and J. Carr (eds) *Behaviour Modification for the Mentally Handicapped*, London: Croom Helm.

Imes, C. (1984) 'Interventions with stroke patients: EMG biofeedback, group activities, cognitive retraining', *Cognitive Rehabilitation* 2: 4–17.

Joanette, Y. and Brouchon, M. (1984) 'Visual allesthesia in manual pointing: some evidence for a sensori-motor cerebral organization', *Brain and Cognition* 3: 152–65.

Jones, M. (1974) 'Imagery as a mnemonic aid after left temporal lobectomy: contrast between material specific and generalized memory disorders', *Neuropsychologia* 12: 21–30.

Kerkoff, G., Munbinger, U., Eberte-Straus, A. and Stogerer, E. (1992) 'Rehabilitation of hemianopic alexia in patients with postgeniculate visual field disorders', *Neuropsychological Rehabilitation* 2: 21–42.

Kolb, B. and Wishaw, I. Q. (1980) *Fundamentals of Human Neuropsychology, 3rd edn*, San Francisco: W. H. Freeman.

Lishman, W. A. (1978) *Organic Psychiatry*, Oxford: Blackwell Scientific Publications.

Luria, A. R. and Tsvetkova, L. D. (1964) 'The programming of constructive ability in local brain injuries', *Neuropsychologia* 2: 95–108.

McKinlay, W. W. and Hickox, A. (1988) 'How can families help in the rehabilitation of the head injured?' *Journal of Head Trauma Rehabilitation* 3: 64–72.

Nicols, P. J. R. (1979) *Rehabilitation Medicine: The Management of Physical Disabilities*, London: Butterworths.

Oldfield, R. C. and Wingfield, A. (1965) 'Response latencies in naming objects', *Quarterly Journal of Experimental Psychology* 17: 273–81.

Powell, G. E. (1981) *Brain Function Therapy*, Aldershot: Gower.

Powell, G. E. (1983) 'Psychological assessment and treatment strategies in the rehabilitation of brain damaged patients', in S. Rachman (ed.) *Contributions to Medical Psychology, Vol. 3*, Oxford: Pergamon Press.

Psatta, D. M. (1983) 'EEG and clinical survey during biofeedback treatment of epileptics', *Neurologie et Psychiatrie* 21: 63–75.

Robertson, I. (1989) 'Anomalies in the lateralisation omissions in unilateral left neglect: implications for an attentional theory of neglect', *Neuropsychologia* 27: 157–65.

Robertson, I. (forthcoming) 'The rehabilitation of attentional and hemi-inattentional disorders', in G. Humphreys and J. Riddoch (eds) *Cognitive Neuropsychology and Cognitive Rehabilitation*, Hove: Lawrence Erlbaum Associates.

Robertson, I. and Cashman, E. (1991) 'Auditory feedback for walking. Difficulties in a case of unilateral neglect: a pilot study', *Neuropsychological Rehabilitation* 1: 175–83.

Robertson, I., North, N. and Geggie, C. (1992) 'Spatio-motor cueing in unilateral left neglect: three case studies of its therapeutic effects', *Journal of Neurology, Neurosurgery and Psychiatrry* 55: 799–805.

Rubens, A. B. (1979) 'Agnosia', in K. M. Heilman and E. Valenstein (eds) *Clinical Neuropsychology*, New York: Oxford University Press.

Series, C. and Lincoln, N. (1978) 'Behaviour Modification in physical rehabilitation', *Occupational Therapy*, July: 222–4.

Shallice, T. (1982) 'Specific impairments of planning', *Philosophical Transactions of the Royal Society of London* B298, 199–209.

Sohlberg, M. M. and Mateer, C. (1989) 'Training use of compensatory memory books: a three-stage behavioural approach', *Journal of Clinical and Experimental Neuropsychology* 11: 871–91.

Sturm, W. and Willmes, K. (1991) 'Efficacy of a reaction training on various attentional and cognitive functions in stroke patients', *Neuropsychological Rehabilitation* 1: 259–80.

Thompson, S. B. (1987) 'A micro-computer-feedback system for improving control of completely innervated leg muscle in adult cerebrovascular accident patients', *British Journal of Occupational Therapy* 50: 161–6.

Warrington, E. K. and Taylor, A. (1973) 'The contribution of the right parietal lobe to object recognition', *Cortex* 9: 152–64.

Weinberg, J., Diller, L., Gordon, W., Gerstman, L., Lieberman, A., Lakin, P., Hodges, G. and Ezrachi, O. (1979) 'Training sensory awareness and spatial organization in people with right brain damage', *Archives of Physical and Medical Rehabilitation* 60: 491–6.

Wilson, B. A. (1981a) 'A survey of behavioural treatments carried out at a rehabilitation centre for stroke and head injuries', in G. Powell (ed.) *Brain Function Therapy*, Aldershot: Gower.

Wilson, B. A. (1981b) 'Teaching a man to remember names after removal of a left temporal lobe tumour', *Behavioural Psychotherapy* 9: 338–44.

Wilson, B. A. (1982) 'Success and failure in memory training following a cerebral vascular accident', *Cortex* 18: 581–94.

Wilson, B. A. (1987a) 'Single case experimental designs in neuropsychological rehabilitation', *Journal of Clinical and Experimental Neuropsychology* 9: 527–44.

Wilson, B. A. (1987b) *Rehabilitation of Memory*, New York: Guilford Press.

Wilson, B. A. (1989) 'Management of problems resulting from damage to the Central Nervous System', in S. Pearce and J. Wardle (eds) *The Practice of Behavioural Medicine*, Oxford: Oxford University Press (51–81).

Wilson, B. A. (1990) 'Cognitive rehabilitation for brain-injured adults', in B. G. Deelman, R. J. Saan and A. H. Van Zomeren (eds) *Traumatic Brain Injuring: Clinical, Social and Rehabilitational Aspects*, Lisse, Netherlands: Swets and Zeitlinger (121–43).

Wilson, B. A. (1991a) 'Behaviour therapy in the treatment of neurologically impaired adults', in P. R. Martin (ed.) *Handbook of Behavior Therapy and Psychological Science: An Integrative Approach*, New York: Pergamon (227–52).

Wilson, B. A. (1991b) 'Long term prognosis of patients with severe memory disorders', *Neuropsychological Rehabilitation* 1: 117–34.

Wilson, B. A. and Baddeley, A. D. (1986) 'Single case methodology and the remediation of acquired dyslexia', in G. Pavlides and D. Fisher (eds) *Dyslexia: Neuropsychology and Treatment*, Hillsdale NJ: Lawrence Erlbaum Associates.

Wilson, B. A. and Moffat, N. (1992) *Clinical Management of Memory Problems, 2nd edn*, London: Chapman and Hall.

Wilson, B. A., White, S. and McGill, P. (1983) 'Remediation of acquired alexia following a gunshot wound', paper presented at the Second World Congress on Dyslexia, Greece.

Wood, R. L. (1987) *Brain Injury Rehabilitation: A Neurobehavioural Approach*, London: Croom Helm.

Zoccolotti, P. and Judica, A. (1991) 'Functional evaluation of hemineglect by means of a semi-structured scale: personal extrapersonal differentiation', *Neuropsychological Rehabilitation* 1: 33–44.

Chapter 36

Psychological evidence in court

Gisli H. Gudjonsson

INTRODUCTION

The word 'forensic' is derived from the Latin *forensis*, which specifically refers to the Roman Forum. Therefore, the use of the term forensic is most appropriately restricted to evidence pertaining to the court. In line with this correct use of the term, Haward defines forensic psychology as 'that branch of applied psychology which is concerned with the collection, examination and presentation of evidence for judicial purposes' (Haward, 1981: 21).

The term forensic psychology is used more broadly by some American writers (e.g. Weiner and Hess, 1987), who view this speciality as any 'professional practice' and 'research endeavour' where psychology and the law interact. The term criminological psychology would be more appropriate to use in that context.

The present chapter deals specifically with psychological evidence in court; therefore Haward's definition of forensic psychology is ideal, because it focuses on the two main features of forensic psychology. These are (1) the collection and examination of evidence (for example, by assessing suspects, victims and witnesses, and by studying documents); and (2) the presentation of evidence, written or oral, in judicial proceedings.

This chapter highlights some of the unique contributions that psychologists can make and the types of problem that may arise when they prepare court reports and present evidence in court.

The contributions that psychologists can make to judicial proceedings are influenced, to a large extent, by the legal framework within which they have to work. Individual legal systems have their own 'law of evidence' or 'rules of evidence' which govern the admissibility and presentation of evidence before the court (Gudjonsson, 1992a; b). Therefore, any discussion about psychological evidence in court must address the legal constraints within which such evidence is going to be allowed. I shall accordingly discuss briefly the English legal system and the significant changes that have taken place in recent years with regard to the admissibility of psychological evidence.

It is now about a century since psychologists began to provide the courts with psychological evidence (Gudjonsson, 1991). In that time the scope of forensic psychology has grown immensely. This has resulted in increased demand for psychological services, with psychologists functioning more independently than ever before in judicial proceedings (Gudjonsson, 1984a; b; 1985; 1987a). The growth in the demand for court reports has occurred in both civil and criminal proceedings.

THE LEGAL FRAMEWORK

Each country has its own legal system. Broadly speaking, two main types of legal system exist, which are typically referred to as 'inquisitorial' and 'adversarial', respectively. The former system, which is favoured in other European countries, is based on the foundation that justice is best served by the court itself searching for the facts in the case by listening to witnesses and examining all the available material surrounding the case. Further police investigations may be ordered if the judge considers it necessary. Under this system, it would be the responsibility of the court to commission psychological and psychiatric reports, and all reports would be made available to the judge.

The 'adversarial' system, on the other hand, which is used in English law, is based on the assumption that justice is best derived from direct confrontation by the defence and prosecution sides rather than from an inquiry.

The main advantage for psychologists working within an inquisitorial system is that expert witnesses have access to all the salient documents and far more background information about the case than when instructed within an adversarial system (Gudjonsson, 1984a). Furthermore, their findings are not suppressed when deemed to be unfavourable to one side, which is often the case in England (Gudjonsson, 1992a). The main disadvantage for psychologists of working within an inquisitorial system is that the role of psychologists tends to be rather limited, with psychiatric evaluations dominating (Gudjonsson and Petursson, 1984).

The main reason for this seems to be that the inquisitorial approach to legal issues is less inclined to stimulate the development of new ideas than the adversarial approach. However, it is worth remembering that until the 1970s the role of British psychologists in forensic evaluations was very limited indeed, with most referrals coming from psychiatrists (Gudjonsson, 1985).

From the point of view of an expert witness, there are some distinct advantages with the adversarial system. First, psychologists are more likely to be instructed to address specific issues rather than being required to give a general psychological profile of the defendant (i.e. the instructions tend to be more focused). Second, psychologists working within an adversarial system are more likely to be required to give oral evidence in court, which means that their testimony is potentially open to rigorous cross-examination. This has the advantage of making expert witnesses more careful in their examination of defendants and overcomes some of the dangers of unsubstantiated opinions being uncritically accepted by the court. Indeed, I would argue that the adversarial system makes psychologists more aware of the strengths and limitations of their evidence and encourages them to look for improved methods and techniques (Gudjonsson, 1985), thereby stimulating empirical research (Gudjonsson, 1992a).

Within the English and Scottish legal systems, cases can be divided into civil and criminal proceedings. Criminal cases are generally brought against defendants by the Crown Prosecution Service in England and Wales or the Procurator Fiscal in Scotland, who are acting on behalf of the State. A civil proceeding involves all those cases brought before the court which are not criminal. Action is typically brought against another individual or company with the intention of seeking financial compensation for such matters as a breach of contract or personal injury. Civil cases may also involve family issues (e.g. child-care proceedings, divorce) and property disputes.

Clark (1987) points out that there are important differences between English and Scottish law which influence the ways in which psychological and psychiatric evidence is treated by the court. In Scotland the Procurator Fiscal is responsible for considering and evaluating all evidence against the accused before the case goes to court. Where necessary and appropriate, the Procurator Fiscal may ask the experts questions about their evidence prior to the court hearing in order to clarify their evidence and limit its over-inclusiveness. The Crown Prosecution Service in England and Wales has no such clarification function. Another important difference between English and Scottish law that affects expert evidence is that juvenile justice in Scotland is administered through Children's Hearings, where the emphasis is on determining what steps can be taken to ensure an outcome that is in the best interests of the child rather than deciding on guilt or innocence.

Most civil litigation is dealt with by the County Court. However, the Magistrates' Courts, which deal with up to 98 per cent of all criminal cases, also process some civil cases, such as domestic disputes and child-care proceedings. The Crown Court deals with the most serious criminal cases and provides defendants with a trial by jury in contested cases. The Crown Court also deals with cases committed for sentence from the Magistrates' Court. When defendants wish to appeal against the decision of magistrates, this is heard in the Crown Court. Further appeals are heard in the Court of Appeal, which is divided into civil and criminal divisions. Final appeals, which are generally on points of law and of general public importance, are heard in the House of Lords.

Clinical psychologists sometimes give evidence in the Magistrates' Court, particularly in juvenile and domestic cases (Lane, 1987; Parker, 1987). In the Crown Court they tend to be instructed in the most serious cases, such as those involving sexual offences and violence, including murder. The role of clinical psychologists in such cases is very varied (Cooke, 1980; Haward, 1981; Blau, 1984; Weiner and Hess, 1987; Lloyd-Bostock, 1988).

THE ROLES OF THE FORENSIC PSYCHOLOGIST

The different roles of psychologists in judicial proceedings have been described in detail by Haward (1981; 1990). He identifies four main roles and describes the types of court where psychologists may find themselves giving evidence. These roles are referred to by Haward as 'experimental', 'clinical', 'actuarial' and 'advisory'.

In the *experimental role*, psychologists perform a unique function which is generally outside the expertise of forensic psychiatrists. Because in this role human behaviour is studied by experimentation rather than by a clinical interview, it requires the ability and knowledge to apply psychological principles and techniques to unique forensic problems. On occasions it involves devising ingenious experiments, both in civil and criminal cases (Haward, 1981; 1990).

For example, Gudjonsson and Sartory (1983) used an experimental procedure involving a polygraph as an aid to the diagnosis of blood-injury phobia, which resulted in the overturning on appeal of a defendant's conviction for failing to provide a specimen of blood in a suspected drunken driving case. The case involved a young man who had been stopped by the police for suspected drunken driving. The man was breathalysed by the police. After failing two breathalyser tests, he was asked to provide a specimen of blood for analysis, which he refused to do on the basis that he was mentally unable to do so. The man was subsequently convicted in the Magistrates' Court for failing to give a specimen. He appealed against his conviction on the basis that he was a genuine blood phobic and therefore had a reasonable excuse for failing to provide a specimen of blood. The man was referred to the present author for an assessment of the genuineness of his alleged blood-injury phobia. At the time it was known in the clinical psychology literature (Sartory *et al.*, 1977) that genuine blood-injury phobia was associated with unique cardiac reactions (lowering of heart rate and blood pressure), which could be monitored physiologically by a polygraph (Gudjonsson, 1992a). A polygraph examination of the man's heart rate to blood-related and neutral items clearly indicated that he exhibited cardiac reactions typical of blood-injury phobia (Gudjonsson and Sartory, 1983). This evidence was presented by the present author at the man's appeal and his conviction was overturned by the judges.

In another case, an experimental procedure was applied to a case of alleged rape of a person with severe learning disability in order to differentiate between areas of the victim's reliable and unreliable testimony (Gudjonsson and Gunn, 1982). The victim's testimony was the main prosecution evidence against six defendants. In view of the victim's learning disability, the prosecution was concerned about the likely reliability of her evidence against the defendants and how she would be able to cope with cross-examination in court. A detailed psychological examination indicated that she was able to distinguish between facts and fantasy when the facts were clear to her, but when she was unsure of the facts she became readily suggestible to questioning. Most importantly, those of her statements that had no objective basis could be easily altered under pressure, whereas those answers that were correct could not be altered. The psychological findings were presented to the jury at the Old Bailey in order to provide them with guidelines by which they could discriminate between the reliable and unreliable evidence as pertaining to the case being tried. Five of the six defendants were convicted. This case, which subsequently stimulated the development of the Gudjonsson Suggestibility Scales (Gudjonsson, 1992a), demonstrated how a highly suggestible person with learning disability was capable of giving reliable testimony pertaining to basic facts she clearly remembered.

Haward (1981) highlights the forensic importance of experiments into perception and memory. This kind of evidence falls into two distinct categories. First is general evidence about scientific findings concerning the limitations of human memory and its fallibility, particularly in relation to eyewitness identification evidence (Loftus, 1979). This kind of expert evidence, which is commonly presented in the courts in the United States of America, is not admissible in Britain (Davies, 1983). This relates to the fact that British courts are reluctant to admit evidence of a general nature, which does not directly focus on abnormality in the personality or mental state of the defendant.

The second type of scientific evidence, which is admissible in the British courts, relates to experiments directly relevant to the individual case. For example, in one case described by Haward (1981), four motorcyclists had been involved in a collision with a sports car. Three of them were charged with dangerous driving on the basis that a police officer claimed to have seem them earlier in the day travelling at a dangerously high speed. The basis of the police officer's identification of the motorcyclists was that he had been able to memorise their registration numbers when he had seen them earlier in the day. Haward carried out an experiment on a sample of 100 normal subjects and demonstrated that the police officer would have been extremely unlikely to have been able to record the registration numbers as he had claimed (that is, the findings indicated that none of the 100 subjects had been able to replicate the police officer's claimed perceptual efficiency under experimental conditions).

The *clinical role* is most appropriately fulfilled by chartered clinical psychologists. This is the most common role among psychologists who have been instructed to prepare a court report (Gudjonsson, 1984a; b; 1985) and overlaps with the role fulfilled by forensic psychiatrists. Here the psychologist interviews a client and carries out the required assessment, which may include extensive psychometric testing (for example, the administration of tests of intelligence, neuropsychological functioning, personality and mental state) and behavioural data (Gudjonsson, 1985). The nature of the assessment will, of course, depend upon the instruction of the referral agent and the type of problem being assessed. Clients may need to be assessed on more than one occasion. In addition, whenever possible and appropriate, informants should be consulted for providing corroboration and further information. Previous reports, including school reports and psychological and psychiatric assessments, should be obtained whenever they are likely to be relevant to the present assessment.

The *actuarial role* refers to the application of statistical probabilities to events and behaviour. This role is not confined to psychologists and is commonly used by statisticians and other scientists when interpreting observational and behavioural data. The type of probabilities and observational data analysed by psychologists may include estimating the probability that a person with a given psychological deficit could earn a living or live independently in the community (Haward, 1981).

The *advisory role* generally consists of psychologists advising counsel about what questions to ask when cross-examining psychologists who are testifying for the other side. For example, the prosecuting counsel may request that a psychologist sits behind him in court and advises him how to cross-examine the defence psychologist. Reports by psychologists are increasingly being subjected to peer review by an expert for the other side. That expert may have carefully studied the psychological report and, in addition, may have carried out an assessment of the defendant.

Having another psychologist in court evaluating one's testimony has been reported to increase the stress experienced when psychologists testify (Gudjonsson, 1985). Sometimes there is considerable disagreement between the opinions of psychology experts and this may result in lengthy and stressful cross-examination (Tunstall *et al.*, 1982). When preparing a court report psychologists should always assume that their report will be subjected to a careful peer review by the other side. Even if it is not, lawyers are becoming increasingly familiar with psychological testimony and are able to ask some very searching questions. The psychologist must be thoroughly familiar with the development and validation of the instruments and tests used.

PSYCHOLOGISTS' CONTRIBUTIONS TO CRIMINAL PROCEEDINGS

In criminal proceedings, most legal systems involve three distinct stages: Pre-trial, trial and sentencing. The nature and contribution of the psychological assessment will be influenced by the relevant legal issues. It is therefore essential that psychologists who are preparing court reports are familiar with the relevant legal concepts at each stage of the criminal proceedings, as well as being fully briefed about the legal issues in the case they are assessing.

Pre-trial issues

At the pre-trial stage, the defendant's fitness to plead and fitness to stand trial may be questioned by the defence (Chiswick, 1990). This happens when the defendant's physical or mental state at the time of the trial is such that proceeding with the case is thought to interfere with due process of the law (that is, the defendant may not have a fair trial if the case proceeds). The ability of the defendant to give adequate instructions to his or her lawyers, to understand the charge against him or her, to distinguish between a plea of guilty and not guilty, and to follow the proceedings in court are the main legal issues to be decided upon at the pre-trial stage. In England, fitness to plead and stand trial issues are generally raised only in serious cases because of their legal and clinical significance (ibid.).

The main problem for the forensic psychiatrist and psychologist, which applies equally to British and American expert witnesses, is that the legal constructs of fitness criteria are defined and described too inadequately in case law to enable the expert to evaluate satisfactorily the defendant's psychiatric and psychological vulnerabilities within the context of the legal criteria. This often means that the psychiatric evaluation is only going to be peripherally related to the legal criteria.

In the United States clinical psychologists are actively involved in this area of the criminal proceedings, where their role overlaps considerably with that of psychiatrists (Blau, 1984; Cooke, 1980; Weiner and Hess, 1987). Special psychological instruments, commonly referred to as 'Competency Tests', have been developed by American psychologists in order to assess objectively the psychological deficits that are relevant to the legal issues (Blau, 1984). Recent factor analytic studies into Competency Tests have raised concern about the lack of stable factor structure across different subject samples (Bagby et al., 1992). Bagby et al. recommend that what is needed is a further development of empirical measures that better match the legal construct of competency to stand trial.

In the United Kingdom, psychiatrists are mainly involved at this stage of the proceedings, and psychologists only occasionally become involved. In recent years, however, psychologists in England are being increasingly requested by defence lawyers to carry out a psychological assessment on these cases, because it provides the court with an objective and standardised assessment of the defendant's strengths and weaknesses. This may involve an assessment of the defendant's intellectual and neuropsychological status, as well as an assessment of problems related to anxiety and depression.

For example, in one case referred to the present author, a middle-aged man was charged with very serious criminal offences connected with the laundering of millions of pounds in proceeds from a robbery. He had been assessed by a number of psychiatrists, who were concerned about the defendant's fitness to stand trial because of a depressive illness which appeared to impair his ability to brief counsel and follow the proceedings in court. The case involved complicated international financial dealings where the defendant had to be able to cope with a lengthy trial and taxing cross-examination. The present author was asked to conduct a psychological investigation on the defendant, with a view to establishing whether or not he was fit to stand trial. The psychological assessment indicated that the defendant was severely depressed, which was accompanied by impaired intellectual functioning. In particular, he had serious attentional problems and slowness in cognitive processing which would have made it impossible for him to follow adequately the court proceedings, considering the complexity of the case. For example, he found it very difficult to concentrate on questions and tasks during the psychological assessment and it took him a long time to grasp intructions and complete simple tasks. This resulted in his failing to earn points on many of the timed subtests of the WAIS–R.

All the experts testified in court about the defendant's mental condition. The defendant was found unfit to stand trial and was provided with psychiatric treatment for his depression. Two years later he was considered by psychiatrists to be fit to stand trial and was convicted and given a substantial prison sentence.

Trial issues

In English law, a criminal offence consists of a number of different elements. These fall into two main categories and are referred to as *actus reus* and *mens rea* (see Leng, 1990, for a detailed review). The former comprises elements relevant to the criminal act itself, whereas the latter generally, but not exclusively, focuses on the mental state of the defendant. During the *actus reus* stage, the prosecution has to prove (a) that a criminal offence was committed, and (b) that the defendant committed it. Issues related to *mens rea* focus on the state of mind of the accused at the time of the alleged offence and its blameworthiness (for example, whether the offence was committed either intentionally or recklessly).

The criteria for establishing *mens rea* depend on the nature of the offence. The reason for this is that each offence is defined separately in law and there are no standard criteria for defining *mens rea* across different offences, even among related offences. Some offences do not require an element of *mens rea* for the defendant to be convicted (that is, they are offences of 'strict liability' and the prosecution only has to prove *actus reus*). However, in such cases, a mental condition relevant to *mens rea* can be used as mitigation at the sentencing stage.

Psychologists in England are commonly asked to prepare court reports which are relevant to both *actus reus* and *mens rea* issues and their involvement in such cases is expanding rapidly (Gudjonsson, 1986; 1992a; Fitzgerald, 1987).

The contribution of clinical psychologists to *mens rea* issues complements that of their psychiatrist colleagues (Gudjonsson, 1984b, 1986). This may include dealing with issues relevant to 'abnormality of mind' and diminished responsibility in cases of homicide and the question of intent in cases of alleged shoplifting.

Sentencing issues

Sentencing is the final stage in the criminal proceedings and takes place after the defendant has been found guilty of the charged offence. If the defendant is acquitted by the jury or magistrates, then he or she is free to go. Where the defendant pleads guilty or is convicted, the judge or the magistrates have to pass a sentence. Various sentencing options are available, depending on the nature of the offence and the circumstances of the case (Eysenck and Gudjonsson, 1989). These include a prison sentence, a financial penalty, probation, and community service orders. In the case of minor offences, a fine is the most common sentence. In more serious cases, depending on the nature of any aggravating features (for example, domestic burglaries carried out at night with the occupants in the house asleep), the defendant may be sentenced to prison or given up to 240 hours of community service (that is, given some tasks to do in the local community under close supervision).

Psychologists are less involved at the sentencing stage than their psychiatrist colleagues, but increasingly they are providing court reports about factors which are relevant to mitigation and sentencing (Gudjonsson, 1986). This includes offering an opinion about treatment options and likely prognosis. The advice given may involve offering treatment to persons convicted of sexual offences, compulsive shoplifting (Gudjonsson, 1987b), or car theft (Brown, 1985).

PSYCHOLOGICAL TESTING

There is very little information available about the extent to which psychological tests are used in forensic assessment. Forensic psychiatrists almost invariably base their assessment on a clinical interview and they do not, on the whole, have the necessary training or expertise for administering psychological tests. Clinical psychologists, on the other hand, have the advantage of being able to use standardised psychological tests for measuring functional skills and deficits, personality and mental status (Blau, 1984; Grisso, 1986; Heilbrun, 1992). This means that their evidence is generally more factually based than the evidence of psychiatrists, who rely almost exclusively on an opinion.

Gudjonsson (1985), in his survey of members of the British Psychological Society, found that 96 per cent of the psychologists studied said they generally used psychological tests when carrying out a forensic assessment. The most common tests used were those that focused on functional strengths and deficits, such as the WAIS and various neuropsychological tests. A small minority (9 per cent) said that they most commonly used personality tests, including the MMPI and the EPQ. In spite of the large proportion of psychologists who generally used psychological tests in their forensic assessment, most also relied on behavioural assessment and interview data. Therefore, although psychological tests are commonly applied when conducting a forensic assessment, they typically form a part of the overall assessment.

The extent to which psychological tests are used in a forensic assessment will depend on the practice and orientation of the individual psychologist concerned. However, it also depends on the instruction received from the referral agent and the nature of the problem to be assessed. For example, subjects referred specifically for assessment of intellectual functioning or neuropsychological status would invariably need to be tested, whereas in child custody cases the psychological assessment is typically heavily dependent on information obtained by interviews and observations (Keilin and Bloom, 1986). Where the instruction given by the referral agent is not clear, the psychologist will need to clarify the purpose of the assessment verbally or in writing. It is often useful to know the legal issues involved in a given case, so that the psychological assessment can be planned accordingly.

Heilbrun (1992) provides useful guidelines for the use of psychological testing in forensic assessment. These include:

1   The test used should be adequately documented and reviewed in the scientific literature and needs to contain a manual describing the test's development, psychometric properties, and procedure.
2   The reliability of the test chosen should be considered carefully (see Lindsay and Powell, Chapter 1).
3   The test chosen must be relevant to (i.e. valid for) the legal issue addressed, or the psychological construct underlying the legal issue (see Lindsay and Powell, Chapter 1). Preferably, relevance should be supported by published validation research, although on occasions justification for using a particular test may be made on theoretical grounds.
4   The standard administration recommended in the test's manual should be used, which normally requires a quiet and distraction-free testing environment.
5   The findings from a particular test should not be applied towards a purpose for which the test was not developed (e.g., making inferences about psychopathology, suggestibility or confabulation from the results of IQ tests). Interpretation of the results should be guided by population and situation specificity; that is, the closer the individual 'fits' the population and situation of those described in the validation studies, the greater the confidence one can express in the applicability of the results. Many tests used in forensic practice were standardised on non-forensic populations, which may make generalisability of the results difficult.
6   There is considerable controversy in the literature about clinical versus statistical predictions (e.g., Meehl, 1954; Sawyer, 1966). Using a combination of results from objective tests and actuarial data is preferable. Of course, very much depends on the type of assessment that is being carried out, and the circumstances under which the test is administered. For example, many clinical judgements of intellectual skills and suggestibility traits are often grossly wrong (Gudjonsson, 1992a), and objective measurements would give more reliable information than clinical judgements. Conversely, a clinical interview is often essential for assessing the person's current or past mental state, and this may be supplemented by objective tests, such as the General Health Questionnaire and the Beck Depression Inventory.
7   When interpreting the results from tests it is important that the 'forensic'

psychologist is sensitive to behaviours ('response style') that have a bearing on the validity of the results (e.g. defensiveness, evasiveness, denial and malingering).

One of the most important points that Heilbrun makes is that psychological testing should be viewed as a part of hypothesis testing. Thus, 'Psychological testing can serve as one source of information that can both formulate and confirm or disconfirm hypotheses about psychological constructs relevant to legal issues, but there are others as well: history, medical testing, interview data, and third-party observations of behaviour can all be used for these purposes' (Heilbrun, 1992: 268). Once the hypotheses have been formulated they need to be tested out by objective means.

ASSESSMENT IN CASES OF RETRACTED CONFESSION

Prior to the early 1980s most cases involving retracted or disputed confession were referred to psychiatrists, who were typically ill-equipped to assess the relevant psychological issues (Gudjonsson, 1992a). Following the present author's research activities in the area of suggestibility (Gudjonsson, 1983; 1984c) and false confession (Gudjonsson and MacKeith, 1988), and his involvement in a number of notable cases (Gudjonsson, 1992a; b), clinical psychologists are increasingly being referred cases where confession evidence is disputed. Legal precedents have been created in several recent cases in the Court of Appeal, where the criteria for admissibility of expert psychological evidence have been broadened. The English criminal courts have now become more accepting of psychological evidence. This has resulted in solicitors referring many more cases to psychologists for evaluation concerning psychological constructs relevant to the assessment of the reliability of confession evidence. The specific legal issues addressed in the assessment of these cases and the type of psychological examination that needs to be conducted are discussed in detail by Gudjonsson (1992a; b).

For a comprehensive assessment, Gudjonsson (1992a) recommends four groups of factors to be assessed:

1 Characteristics of the defendant (e.g. age, knowledge of legal rights, intelligence, memory capacity, personality)
2 The circumstances of the arrest and custody
3 The defendant's physical and mental state during custody and interrogation
4 Interrogative factors (e.g. the length and type of interrogation).

Most commonly, solicitors ask for an assessment of intellectual functioning and suggestibility. The type of suggestibility directly relevant to the assessment is 'interrogative suggestibility', which refers to the tendency of the individual to yield to leading questions and to give in to interrogative pressure (Gudjonsson and Clark, 1986; Gudjonsson, 1992a). This type of suggestibility, which differs in many ways from other types of suggestibility (for example, hypnotic suggestibility), can be objectively measured (Gudjonsson, 1984c, 1987c). The findings from the psychological testing may need to be interpreted within the context of the overall case, especially if the psychologist testifies in court. It is therefore important that the psychologist has access to all the relevant documents in the case before interviewing the defendant, including the tape-record interviews and a copy of the custody record.

THE DETECTION OF DECEPTION

The term 'deception' covers any attempt by an individual to distort or misrepresent his or her answers or performance. Deception can take a variety of forms and it is particularly rife in the context of a forensic assessment, where the responses of the individual are typically self-serving (Gudjonsson, 1992a).

A distinction must be drawn between cases where the individual 'fakes good' (that is, attempts to create a favourable impression by lying or cheating), and those where he or she is motivated to 'fake bad' (that is, pretend to be psychologically disordered, amnesic, or suffering from a cognitive deficit). Both types of deception can seriously threaten the validity of psychological tests and clinical assessment.

Deception is often classified into two groups, referred to as self- and other-deception, respectively (Gudjonsson, 1990). This distinction has both theoretical and clinical importance.

Self-deception, or lying to oneself, can distort the individual's responses during a clinical assessment. This can occur in two different ways. First, self-deception, unlike other-deception, acts like a mood regulator and is associated with denial of symptoms of psychopathology (Sackeim and Gur, 1979; Sackeim, 1983). Self-deception is a part of everyday behaviour and helps people to cope with stress and disappointments in life and protect their self-esteem. However, when extreme, it can seriously distort the clinical picture one may obtain during forensic assessment. When high levels of self-deception are suspected, the questionnaire developed by Sackeim and Gur (1979) can prove useful for objective monitoring.

The second type of self-deception that is commonly reported relates to cognitive distortions; these are particularly important when assessing sex offenders, who often have a strong tendency to justify, minimise and rationalise their criminal behaviour. Various scales have been developed to assess these kinds of distortion (Salter, 1988).

Other-deception means that people intentionally lie, or fake their answers on psychological tests, in order either to conceal or falsify information. It can range from 'impression management', (where the individual attempts to present himself or herself in a socially favourable light) to deliberate lying or malingering as a way of escaping punishment (e.g. avoiding the possibility of a criminal conviction or imprisonment) or to seek rewards (e.g. financial compensation in cases of head injury or post-traumatic stress disorder).

When assessing cases for court reports, psychologists should always be aware of the possibility that subjects, whether suspects, victims or witnesses, may be engaged in deception. Deliberate lying is undoubtedly the most common form of deception one encounters in forensic assessment. 'Faking bad' on psychological tests is much rarer, but it does occur on occasions and is not always easy to detect. If faking or malingering is suspected, then the psychologist should test this as far possible. Various methods for detecting malingering have been devised (Lezak, 1983; Gudjonsson and Shackleton, 1986; Rogers, 1988). These techniques are largely based on the assumptions that malingerers (a) do not know when to start faking to make it convincing; (b) tend to fail simple items whilst passing others of greater complexity; (c) find it difficult to gear their level of failure to the severity of their complaint; (d) make different types of errors on tests than persons with genuine impairment; and (e) are insuffiently familiar with the types of symptoms typically associated with a particular condition (e.g. psychosis, post-traumatic stress disorder).

Unfortunately, the techniques devised for detecting faking or malingering are, by and large, not objective or scientific. They may give certain indications about possible faking, but fail to provide clinicians with any indication of the false positive and false negative error rates which can be used to evaluate the likelihood of faking. The exception is the formula devised by Gudjonsson and Shackleton (1986), using Raven's Standard Progressive Matrices. The formula objectively works out the pattern of the person's performance across the five sets of items on the Matrices and gives a clear indication of the likelihood of faking according to established false positive and false negative error rates.

PRESENTING PSYCHOLOGICAL EVIDENCE

Most of the time psychologists will not be required to give evidence in person in court, often because the opposing side accepts the psychological report and does not require to cross-examine the psychologist on it. In the event of the findings being unfavourable, the defence would normally not forward a copy of the report to the prosecution and the psychologist would not be required to give evidence. If the psychologist has been instructed by the prosecution, then the report will invariably be forwarded to the defence, irrespective of whether or not the findings are favourable to the prosecution. Normally, if the defence decides to rely on the psychological report, then the report has to be served on the prosecution well in advance of the trial, and they may instruct their own expert to evaluate the report.

A psychological report sometimes contains both favourable and unfavourable findings. For example, a defendant may prove to possess poor intellectual abilities, but score low on tests of suggestibility, which by implication means that he or she may be able to cope reasonably well with interrogation in spite of limited cognitive abilities. Similarly, the psychologist may recommend treatment as an alternative to a custodial sentence, but he or she may also express reservations about the defendant's motivation or about the prognosis. When this happens, solicitors may request the psychologist to delete the unfavourable findings from the report or to alter the report in such a way as to make it look more favourable to the court. No psychologist should ever be tempted to comply with the solicitors' wishes to alter the report in such a way that it could mislead the court. The only time psychologists should consider altering the report is when the findings or terms used need to be clarified, or when a mistake has been made that needs to be corrected.

The way psychological findings are presented in a report is often of major importance to the court's understanding and appraisal of the report. The psychologist's findings must be presented clearly and succinctly. The conclusions and opinions drawn should be substantiated and made relevant to the issues addressed. When the findings are presented clearly, and are relevant to the legal issues, the report may be accepted by the respective legal advocates without the psychologist's having to give oral evidence. This commonly happens. In some instances the prosecution may withdraw the charges after considering the psychological findings, particularly in cases of learning disability and mental illness. In only about one fifth of retracted confession cases does the psychologist have to give oral evidence in court, sometimes both during the *voire dire* and the trial proper (Gudjonsson, 1992a). The great majority of civil cases involving compensation are settled out of court, so psychologists very infrequently have to testify in person.

Haward (1981), Carson (1990), Cooke (1990) and Lloyd-Bostock (1988) provide psychologists with useful information about how to present themselves and their findings when testifying in court. This includes knowing the difference between 'expert' and other witnesses The former can, with the permission of the legal advocates, sit in court and listen to other witnesses giving evidence before testifying themselves. This is often useful, because it provides the psychologist with a certain familiarity with the court's layout and the approach and strategy of the legal advocates. Another difference between expert witnesses and other witnesses is that the former are allowed to give opinions as well as factual (real) evidence. Ordinary witnesses are only allowed to give factual evidence. However, expert witnesses are well advised to concentrate on factual evidence and limit their opinions to evidence which can be substantiated by empirical testing (Carson, 1990).

Psychologists must be aware that courts are formal settings where certain rituals and conventions must be followed. For example, the expert witness should be formally dressed and speak slowly, clearly and confidently, and even when asked questions by different legal advocates, the psychologist should address his or her answers to the judge. The psychologist first provides evidence in Chief and he or she will then be cross-examined about the evidence, after which there may be re-examination of various matters raised during the cross-examination. When giving evidence, the psychologist can be asked probing and challenging questions by the legal advocates and the judge. The psychologist should always be fully prepared by knowing the basic facts of the case, being intimately familiar with the tests used in the assessment, and any relevant documents or tapes. Notes of the interviews with the client and the findings of any psychological test that they bring into court may be closely inspected. Psychologists should think carefully before answering questions. If they consider the question asked as being unreasonable or impossible to answer, which is often the case with hypothetical questions (Tunstall *et al.*, 1982), they should not hesitate to say so.

Giving evidence in court is a stressful experience for most expert witnesses. Attending court and listening to court proceedings before giving evidence is often helpful. The stress will be reduced as the psychologist becomes more experienced at giving evidence.

In addition to satisfactory training and experience, the most important factors for the 'forensic psychologist' are integrity, open-mindedness, a thorough assessment, good preparation, and clear presentation of the evidence.

CONCLUSIONS

Clinical psychologists are becoming independent of psychiatrists and they now typically receive instruction directly from solicitors rather than depending on referrals from their medical colleagues. Indeed, psychologists should always insist on being instructed directly by solicitors. The demand for the services and expertise of psychologists is growing rapidly. The recent Court of Appeal judgment in the case of *R. v. Raghip* demonstrates the increased acceptability of psychological evidence among legal advocates (Gudjonsson, 1992b). The case, which is publicly known as that of the 'Tottenham Three', is described in detail by Gudjonsson (1992a; b), who testified in the Court of Appeal in relation to Engin Raghip.

REFERENCES

Bagby, R. M., Nicholson, R. A., Rogers, R. and Nussbaum, D. (1992) 'Domains of competency to stand trial. A factor analytic study', *Law and Human Behavior* 16: 491–507.

Bartol, C. R. and Bartol, A. M. (1987) 'History of forensic Psychology', in I. B. Weiner and A. K. Hess (eds) *Handbook of Forensic Psychology*, New York: John Wiley and Sons.

Blau, T. H. (1984) *The Psychologist as an Expert Witness*, New York: John Wiley and Sons.

Brown, B. (1985) 'The involvement of psychologists in sentencing', *Bulletin of the British Psychological Society* 38: 180–2.

Carson, D. (1990) *Professionals and the Courts. A Handbook for Expert Witnesses*, Birmingham: Venture Press.

Chiswick, D. (1990) 'Fitness to stand trial and plead, mutism and deafness', in R. Bluglass and P. Bowden (eds) *Principles and Practice of Forensic Psychiatry*, London: Churchill Livingstone (171–8).

Clark, D. F. (1987) 'Psychological evidence in court', in G. Gudjonsson and J. Drinkwater (eds) *Psychological Evidence in Court*, Issues in Criminological and Legal Psychology 11, Leicester: British Psychological Society (58–64).

Cooke, D. (1990) 'Being an "expert" in court', *The Psychologist* 3: 216–21

Cooke, G. (ed.) (1980) *The Role of the Forensic Psychologist*, Springfield: Charles C. Thomas.

Davies, G. M. (1983) 'The legal importance of psychological research in eyewitness testimony. British and American experiences', *Journal of the Forensic Science Society* 24: 165–75.

Eastman, N. L. G. (1987) 'Clinical confidentiality: a contractual basis', in G. Gudjonsson and J. Drinkwater (eds) *Psychological Evidence in Court*, Issues in Criminological and Legal Psychology 11, Leicester: British Psychological Society (49–57).

Eysenck, H. J. and Gudjonsson, G. H. (1989) *The Causes and Cures of Criminality*, New York: Plenum Press.

Finch, J. D. (1984) *Aspects of Law Affecting the Paramedical Profession*, London: Faber.

Fitzgerald, E. (1987) 'Psychologists and the law of evidence: admissibility and confidentiality', in G. Gudjonsson and J. Drinkwater (eds) *Psychological Evidence in Court*, Issues in Criminological and Legal Psychology 11, Leicester: British Psychological Society (39–48).

Grisso, T. (1986) *Evaluating Competencies. Forensic Assessments and Instruments*, New York: Plenum Press.

Gudjonsson, G. H. (1983) 'Suggestibility, intelligence, memory recall and personality: an experimental study, *British Journal of Psychiatry* 142: 35–7.

Gudjonsson, G. H. (1984a) 'The role of the "forensic psychologist" in England and Iceland', *Nordisk Psykologi* 36: 256–63.

Gudjonsson, G. H. (1984b) 'The current status of the psychologist as an expert witness in criminal trials', *Bulletin of the British Psychological Society* 37: 80–2.

Gudjonsson, G. H. (1984c) 'A new scale of interrogative suggestibility', *Personality and Individual Differences* 5: 303–14.

Gudjonsson, G. H. (1985) 'Psychological evidence in court: results from the BPS survey', *Bulletin of the British Psychological Society* 38: 327–30.

Gudjonsson, G. H. (1986) 'Criminal court proceedings in England: the contribution of the psychologist as expert witness', *Medicine and Law* 5: 395–404.

Gudjonsson, G. H. (1987a) 'The BPS survey and its implications', in G. Gudjonsson and J. Drinkwater (eds) *Psychological Evidence in Court*, Issues in Criminological and Legal Psychology 11, Leicester: British Psychological Society (6–11).

Gudjonsson, G. H. (1987b) 'The significance of depression in the mechanism of compulsive shoplifting', *Medicine, Science and the Law* 27: (171–6).

Gudjonsson, G. H. (1987c) 'A parallel form of the Gudjonsson Suggestibility Scale', *British Journal of Clinical Psychology* 26: 215–21.

Gudjonsson, G. H. (1990) 'Self-deception and other-deception in forensic assessment', *Personality and Individual Differences* 11: 219–25.

Gudjonsson, G. H. (1991) 'Forensic psychology: the first century', *Journal of Forensic Psychiatry* 2: 129–31.

Gudjonsson, G. H. (1992a) *The Psychology of Interrogation, Confessions and Testimony*, Chichester: John Wiley & Sons.

Gudjonsson, G. H. (1992b) 'The admissibility of expert psychological and psychiatric evidence in England and Wales', *Criminal Behaviour and Mental Health* 2: 245–52.

Gudjonsson, G. H. and Clark, N. K. (1986) 'Suggestibility in police interrogation: a social psychological model', *Social Behaviour* 1: 83–104.

Gudjonsson, G. H. and Gunn, J. (1982) 'The competence and reliability of a witness in a criminal court', *British Journal of Psychiatry* 141: 624–7.

Gudjonsson, G. H. and MacKeith, J. A. C. (1988) 'Retracted confessions: legal, psychological and psychiatric aspects, *Medicine, Science and the Law* 28: 187–94.

Gudjonsson, G. H. and Petursson, H. (1984) 'Psychiatric court reports in Iceland 1970–1982', *Acta Psyciatrica Scandinavica* 70: 44–9.

Gudjonsson, G. H. and Sartory, G. (1983) 'Blood-injury phobia: a "reasonable excuse" for failing to give a specimen in a case of suspected drunken driving', *Journal of the Forensic Science Society* 23: 197–201.

Gudjonsson, G. H. and Shackleton, H. (1986) 'The pattern of scores on Raven's Matrices during "faking bad" and "non-faking" performance', *British Journal of Clinical Psychology* 25: 35–41.

Haward, L. R. C. (1981) *Forensic Psychology*, London: Batsford.

Haward, L. R. C. (1990) *A Dictionary of Forensic Psychology*, Chichester: MediLaw/ Barry Rose.

Heilbrun, K. (1992) 'The role of psychological testing in forensic assessment', *Law and Human Behaviour* 16: 257–72.

Keilin, W. G. and Bloom, L. J. (1986) 'Child custody evaluation practices: A survey of experienced professionals', *Professional Psychology: Research and Practice* 17: 338–46.

Lane, D. A. (1987) 'Psychological evidence in the juvenile court', in G. Gudjonsson and J. Drinkwater (eds) *Psychological Evidence in Court*, Issues in Criminological and Legal Psychology 11, Leicester: British Psychological Society (20–8).

Leng, R. (1990) '*Mens rea* and the defences to a criminal charge', in R. Bluglass and P. Bowden (eds) *Principles and Practice of Forensic Psychiatry*, London: Churchill Livingstone (237–50).

Lezak, M. D. (1983) *Neuropsychological Assessment, 2nd edn*, Oxford: Oxford University Press.

Lloyd-Bostock, S. M. A. (1988) *Law in practice. Applications of psychology to legal decision making and legal skills*, Leicester: British Psychological Society.

Loftus, E. (1979) *Eyewitness Testimony*, London: Harvard University Press.

Meehl, P. E. (1954) *Clinical versus Statistical Predictions*, Minneapolis: University of Minnesota Press.

Mitchell, S. and Richardson, P. J. (1985) *Archbold. Pleading, Evidence and Practice in Criminal Cases, 42 edn*, London: Sweet & Maxwell.

Parker, H. (1987) 'The use of expert reports in juvenile and magistrates' courts', in G. Gudjonsson and J. Drinkwater (eds) *Psychological Evidence in Court*, Issues in Criminological and Legal Psychology 11, Leicester: British Psychological Society (15–19).

Rogers, R. (ed.) (1988) *Clinical Assessment of Malingering and Deception*, New York: Guilford Press.

Sackeim, H. A. (1983) 'Self-deception, self-esteem, and depression: An adaptive value of lying to oneself', in J. Masling (ed.) *Empirical Studies of Psychoanalytic Theories, Vol. 1*, London: Lawrence Erlbaum Associates 101–57.

Sackeim, H. A. and Gur, R. C. (1979) 'Self-deception, other-deception, and reported psychopathology', *Journal of Consulting and Clinical Psychology* 47: 213–15.

Sartory, G., Rachman, S. and Grey, S. J. (1977) 'An investigation of the relation between reported fear and heart rate', *Behaviour Research and Therapy* 15: 435–8.

Salter, A. (1988) *Treating Child Sex Offenders and Victims. A Practical Guide*, London: Sage.

Sawyer, J. (1966) 'Measurement and prediction, clinical and statistical', *Psychological Bulletin* 66: 178–200.

Tunstall, O., Gudjonsson, G., Eysenck, H. and Haward, L. (1982) 'Professional issues arising from psychological evidence presented in court', *Bulletin of the British Psychological Society* 35: 329–31.

Weiner, I. B. and Hess, A. K. (1987) *Handbook of Forensic Psychology*, New York: John Wiley and Sons.

Chapter 37

Single-case methodology in psychological therapy

Stephen Morley

INTRODUCTION

Single-case methods are now well established in clinical psychology. Indeed, one measure of their establishment is a growing interest in their history (e.g. Miller, 1990). They were highly influential in the development of behaviour therapy in the 1950's (Eysenck, 1964), and Shapiro (1963) advocated the use of single-subject research methodology as the procedure of choice for investigating clinical phenomena. While Shapiro and his colleagues conducted many single-case investigations (Shapiro, 1963; 1966), it was the development of applied behaviour analysis in North America which led to a set of formal experimental designs. These were documented in a seminal paper by Baer *et al.* (1968). Since then single-case methods have been elaborated and refined: experimental designs have been extended, a range of statistical analyses for the data have been considered, and the methods have been extended to medicine with some success (Johannessen, 1991). There are now several excellent texts which cover the field in detail and anybody who considers using single-case methods extensively should consult one of them (Barlow and Hersen, 1984; Kazdin, 1982; Kratochwill, 1978; Kratochwill and Levin, 1992; Johnson and Pennypacker, 1980). The purpose of this chapter is to outline the rationale of single-case methods and to provide an overview of their use in investigating psychological therapies. Many examples are drawn from behavioural psychotherapy but the methods can be used to investigate other therapies (Parry *et al.*, 1986; Fonagy and Moran, 1990).

VALIDITY OF EXPERIMENTS

Experimental methods have been developed to eliminate plausible rival hypotheses which might explain a series of observations and to enable the investigator to make valid inferences about the available data. Campbell and his colleagues (Campbell and Stanley, 1966; Cook and Campbell, 1979) have provided an anatomy of experimental and quasi-experimental design. Although their discussion is focused on traditional comparisons between groups, the fundamental elements of their anatomy can be extended to experiments with single-cases. Campbell separates threats to valid interpretation into four groups:

- *Internal validity* describes factors concerned with the design and execution of a particular study, which may provide a plausible alternative account for the pattern of the results. They prevent one from concluding that the intervention was responsible for the change. Countering threats to internal validity is a prime task for the single-case-oriented clinician and researcher. The major threats will be discussed in this chapter.
- *External validity* is concerned with how far the results obtained in the particular study may be extended to other subjects, therapists and settings.
- *Statistical conclusion validity* is determined by whether the design and sampling characteristics of the study are appropriate for the aims of the study.
- *Construct validity* concerns the theoretical interpretations which may be placed on the data. In many group-based studies researchers are interested in the relationship between two constructs, for example, health status and exercise. These cannot usually be indexed by a single measure. It is usual to take multiple measures and examine the relationship between the various components of putative cause and effect. In the majority of single-case studies clinicians and researchers are interested in criterion variables, such as the number of panic attacks, frequency of self-mutilation, and the 'causal' variables are directly manipulated and measured. Issues of construct validity are not often discussed, but careful conceptual analysis of the measures and intervention should always be made (see Youell and McCullough (1974) for an example).

To these threats to the validity of interpretations we might add two other considerations:

- *Standard contextual alternatives* In any field of study there are well-known types of alternative hypotheses which can be put forward to explain data. In the case of psychological treatments, two such alternatives are 'expectation of therapeutic gain' and the general placebo effect. As a result of considerable research, there are now recognised procedures for designing outcome studies to take these explanations into account.
- *Non-standard alternatives* These are the alternative explanations in which the researcher is ultimately interested. They involve comparison between two competing theories.

FEATURES OF SINGLE-CASE EXPERIMENTS

Single-case methods attempt to overcome these threats to validity to enable the investigator to make valid interpretations of the data by the systematic investigation of single cases. There are, however, several features of these methods, which, although not confined to them, are most prominently displayed by them.

First, the original development of single-case experimental methods was inspired by a different approach to investigation from that of the traditional between-subjects design (Johnson and Pennypacker, 1980; Sidman, 1960). The most notable feature of this from a clinician's perspective is that single-case experiments can be data-driven. The design of the experiment may be constructed in response to the data as it is collected and analysed. There are, of course, penalties to be paid for such an approach, for example, the potential loss of experimental control, and one has to pay careful attention to reasons for implementing changes at each point (Morley, 1987; 1989). The flexibility inherent in single-case designs in investigating a phenomenon has great appeal for clinicians who wish to enhance the accountability of their work.

The second feature of single-case methods is that they are closely tied to ipsitive measures. Group-based studies frequently use assessments based on the shared variance of a measure (Shapiro, 1975). For example, questionnaire measures are developed through factor analyses which eliminate variance specific to the individual. In contrast, single-case methods allow the investigator to use measures which are of particular relevance to the individual subject. These may include personal questionnaire assessments of subjective state (Philips, 1986; Shapiro, 1961), frequency counts of particular behaviours or a variety of other measures (Cone, 1988). The exact choice of measure depends on the purpose of the investigation, the psychometric and scaling characteristics of available measures and on the practical constraints of implementing the measure. For example, many well-known psychometrically validated measures, such as the Beck Depression Inventory (Beck *et al.*, 1961), were not designed to be repeatedly administered over short periods of time. Their length and psychometric characteristics make them quite unsuitable for this purpose. They can, however, be used to track the resolution of a problem over longer periods of time. Other measures, such as personal questionnaires and short adjective checklists, are more suitable for frequent repeated applications. Morley (1989) has outlined an assessment-evaluation funnel as a strategy for measurement with single cases (see Figure 37.1).

The third feature of single-case method is the acknowledgement of variability in behaviour (including subjective state) within an individual. Group-based methods often obscure this and 'wash out' fluctuations in individual behaviour by pooling the data. Single-case methods offer a way of investigating fluctuations in behaviour over time, and the effects of treatments must be judged against these fluctuations. This focus on variability is problematic in some aspects. In the clinical context one often needs variability in behaviour to provide clues about the events which control and moderate the problem. Clinical problems which appear static and immune from influence are often difficult to formulate and understand. As Johnson and Pennypacker note, variability is the 'window through which to observe the workings of basic controlling relationships' (Johnson and Pennypacker, 1980: 70). On the other hand, single-case data is much more easily evaluated when there is little variability within different

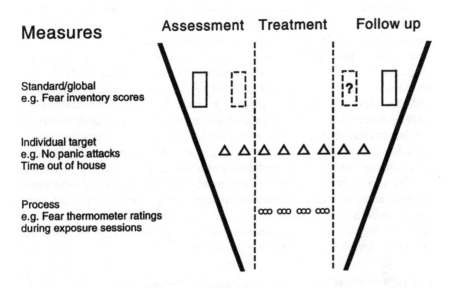

Figure 37.1 An assessment-evaluation funnel

The figure illustrates a general strategy for selecting measures for single-case studies and experiments. *Standard/global* measures are those which have been developed on known populations and for which there are appropriate psychometric data. These include assessments such as the Beck Depression Inventory and the SCL–90R. Ideally there should be norms for different clinical groups. In general, these measures should only be given two or three times: during the assessment phase, at the end of treatment and at follow-up. *Individual target* measures are those measures which index the client's complaint. They are normally ipsitive and developed for a particular client. Typical examples are frequency counts of target behaviour, and personal questionnaire measures and ratings of subjective states. These measures should be taken frequently during baseline and treatment conditions. Psychometric characteristics are usually those concerned with the inter-rater reliability and internal consistency of the measures. *Process* measures are taken more frequently than individual target measures. They may be used by investigators to track changes within a single session. For example, a therapist may track the intensity of pain while a client is engaged in imagery exercises. It is quite usual for process measures to be 'quick and dirty'.

Source: Reproduced with permission from Morley (1989)

experimental phases of the study. In laboratory conditions, and in artificially contrived field settings, investigators take considerable pains to ensure that the environment remains as constant as possible, and that there are no uncontrolled extraneous influences. In many clinical settings this is not possible and investigators must consider analysing variability through graphical or statistical means (Morley and Adams, 1989; 1991).

Single-case designs can be used for a number of purposes. Some writers have expressed the hope that clinicians will adopt them as part of routine practice (Salkovskis, 1984). This is an unobtainable goal for the busy clinician. Developing data collection protocols and conducting single-case experiments is undoubtedly time-consuming. It is, however, possible to incorporate aspects of single-case designs into daily clinical work, for example, assessment of a client on standardised measures at critical junctures (pre- and post-treatment). When clinicians have access to a population of clients with a common problem it is possible to develop a set of suitable measures and deploy a standard procedure for data collection. In such instances, simple experimental designs can be used to build up informative case series (Owens *et al.*, 1989). Within clinical practice the most appropriate use of single-case methods is perhaps to investigate unusual problems or monitor the development of new treatments. Finally, single-case methods may be used as the chosen research strategy for particular problems. These methods offer an extremely efficient way of investigating new treatments and can be combined with elements of traditional group designs to elucidate clinical problems (e.g. McKnight *et al.*, 1984).

SIX QUESTIONS FOR THE PRACTISING CLINICIAN

Questions about case formulation

Therapeutic intervention should always be preceded by a clinical formulation of the case. How clinicians make formulations is still unclear. Most schools of psychotherapy require that the individual should be understood in terms of their developmental history and the influence of the current social environment on their behaviour. Much of the relevant data is obtained through interviews with the client and others (family or care staff), examination of existing records and through direct observation. Clinicians may make judgements about causal influences by assessing how similar a particular client is to others they have seen with the same type of problem. They will try to identify the relationship between the occurrence of the problem and likely significant life events. They may use prospective, passive observational techniques to determine the covariation between current events and aspects of the problem behaviour. Although passive observation is not an experimental method, aspects of experimental method can be used to clarify the relationship between variables of interest. The most appropriate 'design' is one which makes explicit the covariation between antecedents, consequences and the target problem. In general, people, including clinicians, are rather poor at detecting covariation. One reason for this is that they do not appreciate the assessment of covariation, even in a simple 2×2 contingency table (Nisbett and Ross, 1980). This table is a valuable tool because it forces one to consider negative instances. Table 37.1 shows how using a contingency table can help in the formulation of a client's problem. This data was collected by an agoraphobic (Mrs C.), who ascribed her fears to being outside. Mrs C was instructed to keep a diary of when the panics occurred and the concurrent events. Panel (a) of Table 37.1 shows that there was only a weak association between being outside and panic. A content analysis of Mrs C.'s detailed diary and its subsequent tabulation showed that the important trigger event seemed to be certain types of assertive social interaction (see panel (b)). It was also clear from the diary that assertive responses were as likely to be demanded at home and were not just associated with being outside (see panel (c)). Shapiro (1966) reviews a variety of clinical descriptions applied to single cases in this manner (e.g. Metcalfe, 1956).

Mace and Lalli (1991) provide an elegant example of how a descriptive analysis based on passive observation of a problem may be enhanced by a subsequent experimental analysis. Experimental analyses have two important features. First, the order of the treatments is planned so that they are balanced across such features as the time of day, and the number of times in which they precede and succeed each other. Second, they are applied independently of the individual's behaviour, unless there are ethical reasons why certain treatments should not be applied in certain situations. Mace and Lalli's client, Mitch, was a 46-year-old man with moderate learning difficulties living in a community

Table 37.1 Assessing covariation between panic attacks and other events (see text for further details)

Panel (a) shows the association (lack of) between location and the occurrence of panic attacks

(a)

	At home	Outside
Panic attack	8	14
No panic attack	29	29

Panel (b) shows the association between charcteristics of the social situation and the occurrence of panic

(b)

	Assertion required	No assertion required
Panic	19	3
No Panic	0	58

Panel (c) shows that assertion was independent of location

(c)

	Assertion required	No assertion required
At home	8	0
Outside	11	3

facility. Mitch was observed to make frequent bizarre statements. Mace and Lalli initially observed Mitch as he moved around the house. They recorded the events preceding Mitch's talk and the consequences. This initial analysis suggested two hypotheses: (1) that Mitch's talk was positively reinforced by the staff paying attention to him, or (2) that the bizarre talk was negatively reinforced by the staff discontinuing instructing Mitch in independent living skills, or by Mitch withdrawing from the currently assigned task. Mace and Lalli tested these hypotheses by arranging four conditions which varied the task demands and consequences of social interaction. These were systematically varied in a controlled manner and Mitch's behaviour recorded. The outcome of this experiment can be seen in Figure 37.2.

The analysis of these data led to the development of two interventions, one in which Mitch was scheduled to receive attention on a variable-time schedule irrespective of his behaviour, and a second one in which Mitch was trained to initiate and maintain conversation which sustained social interaction with others. These successfully reduced Mitch's bizarre speech and increased the frequency with which he initiated conversations.

Simple questions about the outcome of treatment. 'Has the client improved?'

The most important question for client and clinician alike is whether the client recovers or improves. Leaving aside the question of whether any change in a measure is actually due to treatment, the minimal design requirements for

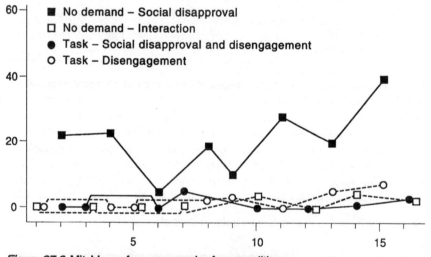

Figure 37.2 Mitch's performance under four conditions

It is clear from the figure that the condition in which Mitch received social disapproval for his bizarre talk was associated with increased levels of talk.

Source: Reproduced with permission from Mace and Lalli (1991)

determining improvement are 'pre-' and 'post-' intervention measures, but any change might be due to the unreliability of measurement. This concerns the issue of the internal validity of the study.

Testing is the general name given to effects which can occur when subjects are measured repeatedly. Each measure is likely to show different specific effects of testing. IQ scores and memory tests are likely to show practice effects, whereas people may learn to 'fake good' or 'bad' on personality tests and symptom checklists. Measurements may also be *reactive* so that the very act of measurement provokes a significant change in the subject's behaviour. Reactivity usually declines in time (see Rosenberg and Upper (1983) for a contrary example), so that changes between two occasions may not be due to a 'true' change but merely to a decrease in reactivity. Reactivity is a significant feature in behavioural observation but it can usually be removed by taking repeated measures, which are expected to stabilise after some time, or by using unobtrusive recording measures.

Changes in measures may also be due to *instrumentation*. This refers to a change in the calibration of the instrument itself. An example of this is 'observer drift', found when observers change their criteria for detecting or recording particular behaviours during the study (Kent and Foster, 1977): in this case the observers are the instrument. Consistent scoring can be maintained by repeated checking of the observers by independent judges. Self-report measures of symptom intensity are also subject to instrumentation effects, especially if no attempt is made to ensure that the scales have equally spaced intervals. The differential sensitivity across the scale may lead to problems, including 'ceiling' or 'floor' effects.

A final problem due to repeated measurement is *statistical regression*. If an investigator uses a test of less than perfect reliability, any score will only be an estimate of the true score. On repeating the test the person's score will change. If they initially scored at one extreme of the scale, the second score will tend toward the middle of the scale for purely statistical reasons. When standardised questionnaires are used in pre/post-designs the effect of repeated measurement can be estimated if a test-retest reliability coefficient is part of the standardisation. Investigators must first ascertain that the standardisation occurred in the population from which their client was drawn, that no treatment occurred between test and retest in the standard population, and that the test-retest period is similar to that used in the single case. If these conditions are met, it is possible to use the test-retest coefficient in a regression equation to predict where the individual's post-treatment score would fall if there had been no treatment.

The analysis of pre-/post-treatment changes

Jacobson and his colleagues (Jacobson and Revenstorf, 1988; Jacobson and Truax, 1991) have suggested criteria for the evaluation of clinically significant changes in psychotherapy. If individuals complete standardised measures in which normative data is available for a non-dysfunctional population and/or a dysfunctional group, Jacobson suggests that there are three criteria by which clincal significance may be operationalised:

(a) The level of functioning after therapy should fall outside the range of the dysfunctional population (more than two standard deviations, in the direction of the normal reference group).
(b) The level of functioning should fall within the range of the non-dysfunctional group.
(c) The level of functioning should place the client closer to the mean of the functional group than the mean of the dysfunctional group.

A graphic representation of these is shown in Figure 37.3.

Statistical approaches to analysing changes in an individual were discussed by Payne and Jones in 1957. Jacobson has applied this analysis to psychotherapy change scores. Jacobson's Reliable Change Index (RCI) (Jacobson and Revenstorf, 1988; Jacobson and Truax, 1991) is a statistical measure of whether the client has improved. The RCI determines whether the observed change is greater than the change which would be expected on the basis of the error in the measure. It is essentially a z score from a normal distribution. Computation of the RCI is very easy and is shown in Table 37.2.

The RCI does not take into account possible effects of regression to the mean. This can be analysed by using the standard error of prediction, if the mean and standard deviation of the normative sample is known. Hsu (1989) provides a clear explanation of this and a table which enables investigators to look up significant changes for a range of changes scores for tests with different test-retest reliabilities. A worked example of this approach is shown in Table 37.2. Hsu also notes that the same approach can be used to estimate whether a deterioration in a client's state is also reliable (ibid.). While it is probably reasonable to assume that regression to the mean occurs in many measures, there are occasions when it does not. Under these conditions, application of a correction formula may produce a Type II error, that is, concluding that a client's scores are unchanged when they have improved (Speer, 1992).

The use of these statistical criteria is dependent on the availability of appropriate normative data. For some client groups it is questionnable whether norms derived from fully functional samples can be meaningfully applied, for example, it may be inappropriate to apply such norms to people with schizophrenia. Furthermore, there are many measures applied to clinical groups for which no normative data are available. The application of Jacobson's clinical criteria and the statistical assessment of such changes must always proceed with due consideration on the part of the investigator.

Is the treatment effective?

The simple pre-/post-test design does not enable us to infer that the change

Overlapping distributions

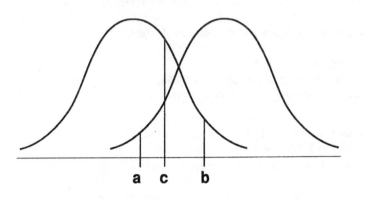

Non-overlapping distributions

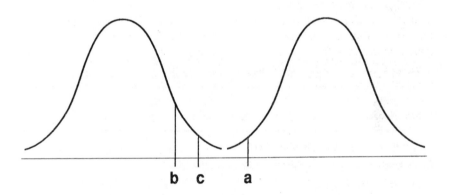

Figure 37.3 Diagrammatic representation of Jacobson's three definitions of significant clinical change

a = score falling outside the range of the dysfunctional group; b = score falling within the range of the functional group; c = score closer to the mean of the functional group. Jacobson suggests that when norms are available, criteria b and c are preferable. If the groups overlap, then c is preferable. When they do not overlap, b should be adopted. If norms for a functional group are not available, then a is the only criterion available. The figure shows the effect of adopting different criteria for overlapping and non-overlapping distributions.

Table 37.2 Calculating the Reliable Change Index (RCI)

(a) RCI using Jacobson's method

Standard error of measurement of a score $(SE_M) = SD \sqrt{(1 - r_{xx})}$

where:

SD = standard deviation of the population in the test

and

r_{xx} = the reliability of the test

Standard error of a difference score $(SE_{DIFF}) = 2(SE_M)^2$

Reliable Change Index (RCI) = $(x_1 - x_2) / (SE_{DIFF})$

where:

x_1 = pre-treatment score

x_2 = post-treatment score

The critical value for the RCI to be statistically significant = 1. 96

An example

Bill has a pre-treatment score of 70 on a standardised test of social anxiety, with a mean = 50, SD = 10 and test-retest reliability = 0. 8. After eight sessions of therapy his score (post-treatment) = 55. Is this change statistically reliable, or is it due to measurement error?

$(SE_M) = 10 \sqrt{(1 - 0. 8)} = 4. 47$

$(SE_{DIFF}) = 2(4. 47)^2 = 6. 32$

$RCI = \dfrac{70 - 55}{6.32} = 2. 37$

As this value exceeds 1. 96 we can be reasonably confident that Bill's improved status is not just due to the inherent unreliability of the test.

(b) RCI in which regression to the mean is considered (Hsu, 1989)

X = mean of the standardisation sample

SD = standard deviation of the population in the test

X_1 = pre-treatment score

and

$x_1 = X - X_1$ is the difference between the mean and pre-treatment score

X_2 = post-treatment score

and

$x_2 = X - X_2$ is the difference between the mean and post-treatment score

r_{xx} = the reliability of the test, this should be the test-retest coefficient

For a significant (reliable) change to occur, which is not due to regression to the mean, the value on the left-hand side of the inequality (>) must be greater than the value on the right-hand side.

Table 37.2 Continued

$$(x_1 - x_2) > (1 - r_{xx}) x_1 + \sqrt{1.96}(SD) \sqrt{1 - \{r_{xx}\}^2}$$

An example
Using the data for Bill we can ask if his improvement is due to regression to the mean.

$$(20 - 5) > (1 - 0.8)20 + 1.96(10) \sqrt{1 - 0.8^2} ?$$

$$15 > 4 + 19.6 \sqrt{1 - 0.64} ?$$

$$15 \not> 15.76$$

The observed change is not greater than that which could be accounted for by regression to the mean (but only just). We should be cautious in interpreting Bill's progress. Astute observers will note that in this case Bill's score is well within 1 SD of the mean of the normal population. The alternative interpretation is that Bill's initial score was overestimated by the unreliability of the test.

produced is due to therapy. Even if the testing, reactivity, instrumentation and regression threats have been eliminated, it could be hypothesised that the observed change is due to the effects of maturation or history. *Maturation* refers to changes occurring within the individual over a given period, which produce changes in the target variable, irrespective of treatment. Studies which involve children's acquisition of skills are obviously prone to this effect. *History* denotes the occurrence of an extra-treatment event producing a therapeutic effect on the target variable(s). For example, a student's anxiety about studying may be markedly relieved if he or she is told that the exams will contribute very little to the final assessment. This change might be erroneously taken as a treatment effect. A number of experimental designs have been suggested to control for these alternative hypotheses.

AB design or simple time series

A and B represent series of repeated observations under two conditions: baseline (A) and treatment (B). By taking repeated measurements, it is argued, testing, reactivity, regression and maturation may be assessed and controlled. Each of these threats would be expected to produce a systematic trend in the sequence of baseline data points. The effectiveness of the treatment is judged by the extent to which the data points shift when the intervention is introduced, and by whether this change is sustained throughout the intervention. Issues in evaluating this type of data are discussed at a later point.

To some extent this design can provide a control for the effects of history. If the client's behaviour is reasonably stable during baseline and treatment phases, despite the documented presence of various extraneous events, it is not unreasonable to infer that any major change occurring at the time of introducing treatment is due to the treatment.

Strictly speaking, the AB design is not a true experiment, as it is generally impossible to rule out all the threats to its internal validity. Nevertheless, the systematic collection of data throughout baseline (pre-treatment) and treatment conditions is a considerable advance on single observations obtained pre-and post-treatment. In general, repeated measurement can facilitate case management by providing the clinician with accurate feedback about formulation and treatment. Despite the advantages gained with repeated measures, two further issues must be considered.

First, as in all single-case work, one must be explicit about the factors determining the decision to change from baseline to treatment phases. Morley (1989) has outlined three criteria which are used.

1 Clinicians may decide to introduce a treatment as soon as possible in order to reassure the client. This is not good experimental practice, as it invariably means that the baseline is too short to enable the study to be evaluated. It may, of course, be possible to obtain a retrospective assessment of the baseline if there is suitable clinical documentation. While a rapid intervention is sometimes possible, it is often not desirable on clinical grounds, because a testable clinical formulation has not been developed.

2 Treatments may be applied as soon as the therapist is convinced that an adequate formulation of the case has been achieved. While this is a good clinical criterion, it is possible that a less than adequate number of baseline points will have been obtained.

3 Clinicians must be aware of the problems of a *reactive intervention*. Glass *et al.*, (1975) noted that it is possible for clinicians and experimenters to introduce a treatment in response to a deterioration in the baseline, perhaps brought about by a crisis. Although this is ethically understandable it is quite usual for crises to dissipate quickly, and if treatment had been with held, the client's score would have returned to a less extreme level. Extreme scores are also likely to be associated with significant personal or environmental events. These may provide important information about the factors controlling the target problem. Introducing an intervention in reaction to a marked change precludes the opportunity to investigate the source of the variability. An example of a reactive intervention and an investigation into it is given by Morley (1989, case study 2).

The second issue to consider concerns the problem of detecting a change in the client's behaviour due to treatment when there is variability in the data. Repeated measurements often reveal considerable variability. Under these conditions it is possible to attribute changes to treatment when they are more appropriately ascribed to natural variation. To some extent this problem can be ameliorated if longer baseline and treatment phases are used. It is then possible to estimate the extent of the variability (see the section on evaluation on p. 739) and take this into account when evaluating the effect of treatment interventions. Nevertheless, the presence of large variability in the baseline should lead the clinican to explore its sources. For example, careful plotting of the data may reveal systematic cycles (Morley and Adams, 1991; Cox and Klinge, 1976), which may relate to regular biological or environmental events. In general, an attempt should be made to correlate environmental changes with change in the target variable. This will often lead to a refined formulation. Johnson and Pennypacker (1980) provide an excellent analysis of variability from a behavioural perspective.

Despite the problems associates with the AB design it is widely used in clinical practice and in more systematic research. Its overriding advantage is that it fits in naturally with the requirements of investigators and clients alike. A combination of sufficient data points, careful documentation of treatment and extra-treatment events, and systematic and cautious analyses of variability and change justifies its continued use.

ABAB or the reversal design

Increased control over the threat of history is achieved if the treatment is withdrawn and the client's behaviour reverses to the original baseline. By increasing the number of treatment-baseline reversals this design strengthens the case against history as a plausible rival hypothesis. It would be stretching credulity to suggest that both the introduction and cessation of treatment coincided with appropriate extra-treatment changes.

There may be clinical and ethical reasons against using any design which entails a degree of reversal. Clinicians are understandably reluctant to reverse treatments which are seen to be effective, especially if the target problem is one which causes distress or danger to the client. It may also be clinically impossible to reverse certain behaviour. This can be partly circumvented by using brief probes which return the patient to baseline conditions. The hidden assumption in reversal designs is that the behaviour under investigation is maintained by environmental contingencies. Once learned, many classes of behaviour, for example speech and fear/avoidance reduction, do not require continuous external reinforcement to maintain them. Moreover, many cognitive-behavioural treatments and psychotherapeutic approaches aim to change the client's ability for self-control of the problem.

Changing criterion design (Hartmann and Hall, 1976)

This design circumvents some of the problems raised by the ABAB design. Baseline observations are made on a single target variable. This is followed by a series of treatment phases, each of which uses the same treatment applied to successively prescribed changes (criteria) in the target behaviour. For example, a smoker who regularly smoked 80–100 cigarettes per day was initially asked to reduce the number to 70 per day (Belles and Bradlyn, 1987). He agreed to fine himself $25.00 if he exceeded this criterion. Once this criterion was met it was reduced in sucessive steps to his agreed goal of five cigarettes per day. Each treatment phase thus acts as a baseline for its successor. Hartmann and Hall (1976) note that successive baselines should be long enough to rule out history, maturation and measurement threats to internal validity. Phases should also be of unequal length to ensure that the step-like changes in the criterion are not in synchrony with any natural changes in the target behaviour. This design can also be extended to probe performance under criteria which have not yet been instituted (Horner and Baer, 1978). A form of the changing criterion design has been used for many years in behaviour therapy; Wolpe (1958) described it as progression up a fear hierarchy.

Multiple baseline designs

The fundamental idea behind multiple baseline designs is the introduction of control variables. Treatment is introduced to one variable at a time. The assumption is that if only this variable changes, then the effects of a coincidental event (history) may be eliminated. The further assumption is that if an extra-treatment event causes the change in the target variable, then it will also influence control variables. There is an inconsistency in this argument (Kazdin and Kopel, 1975). It is assumed that treatments will have specific effects but that extra-treatment factors will have general effects. In practice this means that the interpretation of the design is dependent on the outcome. If specific changes occur with the treatment of each variable, then one might reasonably rule out history and maturation effects, but if untreated variables change with the introduction of a specific treatment it is unclear whether this is due to a generalised treatment effect, history or maturation. Nevertheless, this design does force clinicians to take note of more than one variable, a feature to be recommended in any clinical or experimental investigation. The design is, however, much weaker than a reversal or operant design in ruling out the threat of history.

There are a number of variants of the multiple baseline. The multiple baseline can refer to different target variables within the same subject (Bilsbury and Morley, 1979), the same behaviour in one subject observed in different environmental settings (Singh *et al.*, 1980), or to similar behaviour in several individuals in one setting. In the latter case it could be argued that the design is really a series of replications of the AB design. This is particularly so if clients are not investigated at the same time (Harris and Jensen, 1985; Hayes, 1985).

Why did the patient improve and what part of the treatment was responsible for the change?

The previous discussion of experimental design has focused on common threats to validity, but even apparently simple manipulations have alternative 'non-standard' interpretations which require special investigation to account for the mechanism of change. Consider the delivery of tokens in a token economy. Is their effectiveness due to the contingent delivery of the reinforcer, or to the coincidental increase in social contact between patient and therapist (Hall *et al.*, 1977)? Single-case methods enable clinicians to explore these issues. They are particularly useful for investigating rare disorders which are not easily amenable to controlled between-group (large n) studies.

Any experimental investigation of why a treatment works (a process question) involves a comparison between two or more conditions. It is clear that the same designs can be used to compare the relative effectiveness of two dissimilar treatments. Three designs are particularly suitable for this type of investigation. The multiple baseline design can be used if individuals have multiple symptoms. Each symptom (variable) can be treated by different methods and simple between-methods comparisons made. Rachman (1974) described a condition of primary obsessional slowness, characterised by excessively slow and meticulous self-care, in the absence of common obsessional symptoms, such as ruminations or anxiety reduction following the behaviour. Bilsbury and Morley (1979) and Bennun (1980) replicated Rachman's treatment methods: a package of participant modelling and prompting, shaping and pacing. They demonstrated specific independent improvements in each target symptom as it was treated. Clark *et al.*, (1982) used a multiple baseline method in an attempt to separate the effective components in the package.

It is also possible to investigate the impact of different treatments, or treatment components, on single target problems. There are a number of designs described in the literature and their nomenclature may be misleading. The common term for this type of design is an *alternating treatments design* (Barlow and Hersen, 1984). Early developments of this approach were drawn directly from infra-human operant work. In a multiple schedule design a single target behaviour is exposed to two or more different treatments (historically these were reinforcement schedules), and each treatment is associated with a discriminative stimulus. The main point of interest is whether stimulus control of the behaviour can be established. More recently, designs have been described in which two or more treatments are applied to a single target behaviour.

Ollendick *et al.*, (1981) reported three single-cases which illustrate the features of this approach. They compared the relative effectiveness of positive practice and physical restraint in reducing stereotypic behaviour in children with learning difficulties. Baseline observations were obtained for three sessions per day and each of these sessions was allocated in a balanced way to a treatment condition, although no treatment was given in this phase. During the treatment phase proper, the treatments were delivered so that they were balanced across the time of the day, and arranged so that each type of treatment followed and preceded the others in a systematic fashion. It was therefore possible to assess the relative effectiveness of each treatment independently of any extraneous and potentially confounding variables.

There are a number of constraints in using this design. It is necessary to use interventions which have a rapid and powerful effect within each session, so that there is a minimum 'warm-up' necessary. Generally speaking, there should be little carry-over effect, that is, the effect of one treatment does not continue into the next session. One must also choose target behaviour which is not too close to the floor or ceiling of the observation range. Problems with a very low probability of occurring during treatment sessions will mean that there are few opportunities for treatments to be applied. One feature of the alternating treatments design is that it is possible to designate one of the treatments as a no-treatment control. Ollendick *et al.* (1981) did this and were able to demonstrate that the target behaviour changed only when treatments were applied. This procedure helps to rule out the threats of history and maturation.

The third approach to investigating differential treatment effects in single cases is to extend the AB design by adding on successive phases in which treatment conditions are systematically related. Mace and Lalli (1991) provide an example of this approach in their treatment of Mitch. This approach can be used when the impact of the treatment is expected to be gradual, and when prolonged periods of observation and data collection are possible. Thus an experiment for investigating two treatments B and C and their interaction may be schematically represented as A–B–A–C–BC–B–A–C.

Will this treatment be of any use to other clients and clinicians?

This question concerns the external validity or generalisation of findings from an experiment, so it can only be answered empirically. Campbell and Stanley (1966), Cook and Campbell (1979) and Kratochwill (1978) provide excellent discussions of the issues contained in the concept of external validity. It is useful to consider three domains to which one might wish to generalise the findings of a case study.

1 Population validity: to which members of which populations is this procedure useful or applicable?
2 Ecological validity: how far can these findings be replicated with different experimenters, settings and measurement procedures?
3 Manipulation or construct validity (Cook and Campbell, 1979): will a conceptually similar intervention have the same effect? For example, it is tacitly assumed that a wide class of events are punishers, yet these events may not be interchangeable. An example of this is the differential effectiveness of shock and time out in their capacity to suppress self-mutilation in the Lesch-Nyhan syndrome (Anderson *et al.*, 1978). These investigators conducted a series of single-case studies demonstrating that shock was not an effective punisher, whereas time out from social reinforcement suppressed self-mutilation.

Questions pertaining to theory testing

We have already encountered the idea of theory testing in Question 1, where the theories were hypotheses about particular patients. It is possible to use single cases in testing well-articulated general theories about therapeutic processes, and this enables the clinician to contribute to research without recourse to generally expensive between-group studies (Biglan and Craker, 1982; Watts, 1979).

EVALUATING SINGLE-CASE DATA

Single-case data can be evaluated on clinical and experimental criteria. The overriding clinical criterion is whether the patient has achieved an acceptable level of improvement. Experimental criteria concern the confidence which one may have in the belief that the intervention produced the effect. These criteria are not synonymous. A client may improve considerably by the end of the intervention phase, yet it may not be possible to attribute this change to the effect of treatment.

The evaluation of single-case data has been a source of lively debate for a number of years. When formal designs were introduced through applied behaviour analysis (Baer et al., 1968), the application of statistical techniques was eschewed (Baer, 1977). This was because researchers trained in the philosophy of the analysis of behaviour conducted studies which paralleled laboratory ones. In particular they paid attention to two features. First they endeavoured to establish baseline conditions in which the individual could be considered to be in a steady state, that is, the mean level of the target behaviour was constant over time, and there was little variablity during the course of the baseline. The second feature was that they employed interventions which had relatively rapid, large-magnitude effects, producing changes in the target variable within the first few sessions (often within the first session). Under these conditions the data can be easily evaluated by plotting the data points against time. Figure 37.4 shows the effect that variations in several features of data have on the ability to evaluate the data by visual inspection.

As single-case methods became more widely known and used by non-operant psychologists the data became less easily amenable to analysis by visual inspection. A number of statistical approaches to analysing the data have been advocated. One solution has been to apply conventional parametric t and F tests to data. For example, a t test could be conducted to determine the difference between the means of the A and B phases of a study. A significant objection to using these tests is that they assume that each data point is independent and that the error components are uncorrelated. If this assumption is violated, then the inference based on the test is likely to be invalid. Furthermore, t and F tests are only sensitive to the changes in mean (repeated measures analyses of variance can assess trend), and would not be able to detect a change in the trend of the data. In general these tests are not recommended.

A second approach to the statistical analysis of single-case data has been to use time series analysis. Time series analysis has received considerable attention (Gottman, 1981; Gottman and Glass, 1978; Jones et al., 1977; McCain and McCleary, 1979). The method involves making a statistical model of the baseline

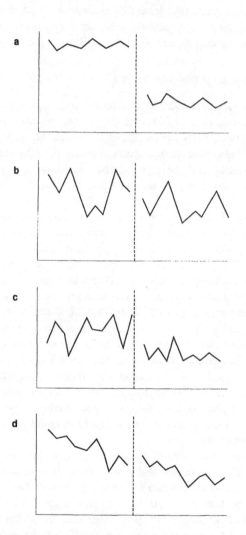

Figure 37.4 The effect of data feature variations on data evaluation by visual analysis

In panel (a) the baseline and treatment phases are stable with little variance. In addition the introduction of the treatment is associated with a large-magnitude shift in the series. This pattern of data is strongly suggestive of a treatment effect. Panel (b) shows the reverse of panel (a); here the data are very variable and there is little evidence of a shift in the series as the treatment is introduced. This series will require further analysis to enable a conclusion to be reached about the effectiveness of the treatment. Panel (c) shows a pattern of marked variability in the baseline but reasonable stability in the treatment phase. Although the data in the two phases overlap we may be quite confident that treatment has been effective. Panel (d) is difficult to interpret because of the apparent trend in the baseline and treatment phases.

phase and testing whether data from the intervention phase fit this model. Time series analyses possess several advantages; they can handle the problem of non-independence of errors, and they are capable of assessing changes in several features of the data (mean, trend, change in level at the point of intervention). They provide an elegant and powerful solution to the problems raised by conventional tests. Unfortunately, there are two practical problems in applying these tests to the bulk of single-case data obtained in a clinical setting. First, they require a considerable number of data points (at least fifty in each phase) in order to identify the statistical model of the data with any reliability. Second, they require a degree of statistical 'know-how' which is often beyond that which clinicians are willing to obtain. On balance they are not recommended for use.

One other approach to the statistical analysis of intervention effects merits attention, because it can be used with relatively small sample sizes (twenty or so data points), and because the analysis does not require the investigator to make assumptions about the distribution of the data. Randomisation tests use only the available data. The basic strategy of the test is to determine the exact probability with which the observed data, or a more extreme pattern of data, would occur. The major requirement of the test is that the scheduling of the intervention(s) shall be decided at random before the beginning of the study. Randomisation tests are relatively easy to conduct and can be adapted to test a range of hypotheses about the means, and trend in single-case data. Edgington (1980), Kazdin (1984), Levin et al., (1978), and Hand (1982) all provide introductions to this approach. Further examples can be found in Clements and Hand (1985).

All the above methods have centred on the application of statistics to determine the significance of the intervention. Statistics can also be used to help describe the data and to carry out analyses of whether segments of the data contain trends or other features. Morley and Adams (1989) have summarised a set of easily computable, non-parametric tests which can be used to explore the characteristics of single-case data, either as a prelude to further analysis, or to supplement visual inspection.

Despite the availability of a range of statistical methods, it is probable that most clinicians will rely on graphs and 'visual analysis' to draw conclusions. Indeed, even if statistical analyses are to be used, the data should be inspected and manipulated to highlight a variety of features. Parsonson and Baer (1978) have outlined the basics of preparing visual displays for single-case data. Morley and Adams (1991) have compiled a set of methods which enable an investigator to explore the data in some depth. Visual analysis has also been subjected to investigation in its own right (De Prospero and Cohen, 1979; Furlong and Wampold, 1982; Matyas and Greenwood, 1990; Wampold and Furlong, 1981), and it is clear that visual displays can be misinterpreted, especially when the data contain trends and variability.

CONCLUSIONS

Single-case methods have a long history in psychology and have been applied to clinical problems in a systematic manner for forty years. There is a range of formal designs which have been developed to circumvent threats to the valid interpretation of the data. Variations on the designs appear with regularity as inventive clinicians and researchers face new problems (e.g. Wacker *et al.*, 1990). Issues of interpretation and design continue to be debated (e.g. Higgins Hains and Baer, 1989) and new approaches to the analysis of data are being considered (e.g. White *et al.*, 1989). Single-case methods look set to continue evolving and expanding the range of problems to which they are applied.

NOTE

This chapter is dedicated with thanks and affection to Monte Shapiro: a superb teacher and compassionate clinician.

REFERENCES

Anderson, L., Dancis, J. and Alpert, M. (1978) 'Behavioural contingencies and self mutilation in Lesch-Nyhan disease, *Journal of Consulting and Clinical Psychology* 46: 529–36.

Baer, D. M. (1977) 'Perhaps it would be better not to know everything', *Journal of Applied Behavior Analysis* 10: 167–72.

Baer, D. M., Wolf, M. M. and Risley, T. R. (1968) 'Some current dimensions of applied behavior analysis', *Journal of Applied Behavior Analysis* 1: 91–7.

Barlow, D. H. and Hersen, M. (1984) *Single-Case Experimental Designs: Strategies for Studying Behavior Change, 2nd edn*, New York: Pergamon.

Beck, A. T., Ward, C. H., Mendelsohn, M., Mock, J. and Erbaugh, J. (1961) 'An inventory for measuring depression', *Archives of General Psychiatry* 4: 561–71.

Belles, D. and Bradlyn, A. S. (1987) 'The use of the changing criterion design in achieving controlled smoking in a heavy smoker: a controlled case study', *Journal of Behaviour Therapy and Experimental Psychiatry* 18: 1–6.

Bennun, I. (1980) 'Obsessional slowness: A replication and extension', *Behaviour Research and Therapy* 18: 595–8.

Biglan, A. and Craker, D. (1982) 'Effects of pleasant activities manipulation on depression', *Journal of Consulting and Clinical Psychology* 50: 436–8.

Bilsbury, C. D. and Morley, S. (1979) 'Obsessional slowness: a meticulous replication', *Behaviour Research and Therapy* 17: 405–8.

Campbell, D. T. and Stanley, J. C. (1966) *Experimental and Quasi-Experimental Designs for Research*, Chicago: Rand McNally.

Clark, D. A., Sugrim, I. and Bolton, D. (1982) 'Primary obsessional slowness: a nursing treatment programme with a 13-year-old male adolescent', *Behaviour Research and Therapy* 20: 289–92.

Clements, J. C. and Hand, D. J. (1985) 'Permutation statistics in single-case design', *Behavioural Psychotherapy* 13: 288–99.

Cone, J. D. (1988) 'Psychometric considerations and the multiple models of behavioral assessment', in A. S. Bellack and M. Hersen (eds) *Behavioral Assessment, 3rd edn*, New York: Pergamon.

Cook, T. D. and Campbell, D. T. (1979) *Quasi-Experimentation: Design and Analysis Issues for Field Settings*, Chicago: Rand McNally.

Cox, M. D. and Klinge, V. (1976) 'Treatment and management of a case of self burning', *Behaviour Research and Therapy* 14: 382–5.

De Prospero, A. and Cohen, S. (1979) 'Inconsistent visual analysis of intra-subject data', *Journal of Applied Behaviour Analysis* 12: 573–9.

Edgington, E. S. (1980) *Randomization Tests*, New York: Marcel Dekker.

Eysenck, H. J. (ed.) (1964) *Experiments in Behaviour Therapy*, Oxford: Pergamon.

Fonagy, P. and Moran, G. S. (1990) 'Studies on the efficacy of child psychoanalysis', *Journal of Consulting and Clinical Psychology* 58: 684–95.

Furlong, M. J. and Wampold, B. E. (1982) 'Intervention effects and relative variation as dimensions in experts' use of visual inference', *Journal of Applied Behavioural Analysis* 14: 415–21.

Glass, G. V., Willson, V. L. and Gottman, J. M. (1975) *Design and Analysis of Time Series Experiments*, Boulder, Colo.: Colorado Associated University Press.

Gottman, J. M. (1981) *Time-series analysis: A Comprehensive Introduction for Social Scientists*, Cambridge: Cambridge University Press.

Gottman, J. M. and Glass, G. V. (1978) 'Analysis of interrupted time series experiments', in T. R. Kratochwill (ed.) *Single Subject Research: Strategies for Evaluating Change*, New York: Academic Press.

Hall, J. N., Baker, R. D. and Hutchinson, K. (1977) 'A controlled evaluation of token economy procedures with chronic schizophrenic patients', *Behaviour Research and Therapy* 15: 261–83.

Hand, D. J. (1982) 'Statistical tests in experimental psychiatric research', *Psychological Medicine* 12: 415–21.

Harris, F. N. and Jensen, W. R. (1985) 'Comparisons of multiple-baseline across persons designs and AB designs with replication: issues and confusions', *Behavioral Assessment* 7: 121–7.

Hartmann, D. P. and Hall, R. V. (1976) 'The changing criterion design', *Journal of Applied Behaviour Analysis* 9: 527–32.

Hayes, S. C. (1985) 'Natural multiple baselines across persons: a reply to Harris and Jensen', *Behavioral Assessment* 7: 129–32.

Higgins Hains, A. and Baer, D. M. (1989) 'Interaction effects in multielement designs: inevitable, desirable and ignorable', *Journal of Applied Behavior Analysis* 22: 57–69.

Horner, R. D. and Baer, D. M. (1978) 'Multiple-probe technique: A variation of the multiple baseline', *Journal of Applied Behaviour Analysis* 11: 189–96.

Hsu, L. M. (1989) 'Reliable changes in psychotherapy: taking into account regression toward the mean', *Behavioral Assessment* 11: 459–67.

Jacobson, N. S. and Revenstorf, D. (1988) 'Statistics for assessing the clinical significance of psychotherapy techniques; issues, problems and new developments', *Behavioral Assessment* 10: 133–45.

Jacobson, N. S. and Truax, P. (1991) 'Clinical significance: a statistical approach to defining meaningful change in psychotherapy research', *Journal of Abnormal Psychology* 59: 12–19.

Johannessen, T. (1991) 'Controlled trials in single subjects', *British Medical Journal* 303: 173–4.

Johnson, J. M. and Pennypacker, H. S. (1980) *Strategies and Tactics of Human Behavioral Research*, Hillsdale, NJ.: Lawrence Erlbaum Associates.

Jones, B. R., Vaught, R. S. and Weinrott, M. (1977) 'Time-series analysis in operant research', *Journal of Applied Behaviour Analysis* 10: 151–66.

Kazdin, A. E. (1982) *Single Case Research Designs: Methods for Clinical and Applied Settings*, New York: Oxford University Press.

Kazdin, A. E. (1984) 'Statistical analyses for single-case experimental designs', in D. H. Barlow and M. Hersen (eds) *Single-Case Experimental Designs: Strategies for Studying Behaviour Change*, New York: Pergamon Press.

Kazdin, A. E. and Kopel, S. A. (1975) 'On resolving ambiguities in the multiple-baseline design: problems and recommendations', *Behavior Therapy* 6: 601–8.

Kent, R. N. and Foster, S. L. (1977) 'Direct observational procedures: Methodological issues in naturalistic settings', in, A. R. Ciminero, K. S. Calhoun and H. E. Adams (eds) *Handbook of Behavioural Assessment*, New York: Wiley.

Kratochwill, T. R. (ed.) (1978) *Single-Subject Research: Strategies for Evaluating Change*, New York: Academic Press.

Kratochwill, J. R. and Levin, J. R. (eds) (1992) *Single-Case Research Designs and Analysis*, Hove: Lawrence Erlbaum Associates.

Levin, J., Marascuilo, L. A. and Hubert, L. J. (1978) 'N = 1 Nonparametric randomization tests', in T. R. Kratochwill (ed.) *Single-Subject Research: Strategies for Evaluating Change*, New York: Academic Press.

Mace, F. C. and Lalli, J. S. (1991) 'Linking descriptive and experimental analyses in the treatment of bizarre speech', *Journal of Applied Behavioral Analysis* 24: 533–62.

McCain, L. J. and McCleary, R. (1979) 'The statistical analysis of the simple interrupted time-series quasi-experiment', in, T. D. Cook and D. T. Campbell *Quasi-Experimentation: Design and Analysis Issues for Field Settings*, Chicago: Rand McNally.

McKnight, D. L., Nelson, R. O., Hayes, S. C. and Jarrett, R. B. (1984) 'Importance of treating individually assessed response classes in the amelioration of depression', *Behavior Therapy* 15: 315–35,

Matyas, T. A. and Greenwood, K. M. (1990) 'Visual analysis of single case time series: effects of variability, serial dependence, and magnitude of intervention effects', *Journal of Applied Behavioral Analysis* 23: 341–51.

Metcalfe, M. (1956) 'Demonstration of a psychosomatic relationship', *British Journal of Medical Psychology* 29: 63–6.

Miller, E. (1990) 'Single-case experimentation: a seventeenth century example', *British Journal of Clinical Psychology* 29: 433–4.

Morley, S. (1987) 'Modification of auditory hallucinations: experimental studies of headphones and earplugs', *Behavioral Psychotherapy* 15: 240–51.

Morley, S. (1989) 'Single case research', in G. Parry and F. N. Watts (eds) *Behavioural and Mental Health Research: A Handbook of Skills and Methods*, Hove: Lawrence Erlbaum Associates.

Morley, S. and Adams, M. (1989) 'Some simple statistical tests for exploring single-case time series data', *British Journal of Clinical Psychology* 28: 1–18.

Morley, S. and Adams, M. (1991) 'Graphical analysis of single-case time series data', *British Journal of Clinical Psychology* 30: 97–115.

Nisbett, R. and Ross, L. (1980) *Human Inference: Strategies and Shortcomings in Social Judgement*, Englewood Cliffs, NJ: Prentice-Hall.

Ollendick, T. H., Shapiro, E. S. and Barrett, R. P. (1981) 'Reducing stereotypic behaviours: An analysis of treatment procedures utilizing an alternating treatments design', *Behavior Therapy* 12: 570–7.

Owens, R. G., Slade, P. D. and Fielding, D. M. (1989) 'Patient series and quasi-experimental design', in G. Parry and F. N. Watts (eds) *Behavioural and Mental Health Research: A Handbook of Skills and Methods*, Hove: Lawrence Erlbaum Associates.

Parry, G., Shapiro, D. A. and Firth, J. (1986) 'The case of the anxious executive: a study from the research clinic', *British Journal of Medical Psychology* 59: 221–33.

Parsonson, B. S. and Baer, D. M. (1978) 'The analysis and presentation of graphic data', Kratochwill, T. R. (ed.) *Single-Subject Research: Strategies for Evaluating Change*, New York: Academic Press.

Payne, R. W. and Jones, H. G. (1957) 'Statistics for the investigation of individual cases', *Journal of Clinical Psychology* 13: 115–21.

Philips, J. P. N. (1986) 'Shapiro personal questionnaire and generalised personal questionnaire techniques: a repeated measures individualised outcome measurement', in L. S. Greenberg and W. M. Pinsof (eds) *The Psychotherapeutic Process: A Research Handbook*, New York: Guilford Press.

Rachman, S. (1974) 'Primary obsessional slowness', *Behaviour Research and Therapy* 12: 9–18.

Rosenberg, H. and Upper, D. (1983) 'Problems with stimulus/response equivalence and reactivity in the assessment and treatment of obsessive-compulsive neurosis', *Behaviour Research and Therapy* 21: 177–80.

Salkovskis, P. M. (1984) 'Psychological research by NHS clinical psychologists: an analysis and some suggestions', *Bulletin of the British Psychological Society* 37: 375–7.

Shapiro, M. B. (1961) 'A method of measuring psychological changes specific to the individual psychiatric patient', *British Journal of Medical Psychology* 34: 151–5.

Shapiro, M. B. (1963) 'A clinical approach to fundamental research with special reference to the study of the single patient', in P. Sainsbury and N. Kreitman (eds) *Basic Research Techniques in Psychiatry*, London: Oxford University Press.

Shapiro, M. B. (1966) 'The single-case in clinical psychological research', *Journal of General Psychology* 74: 3–23.

Shapiro, M. B. (1975) 'The single variable approach to assessing the intensity of feelings of depression', *European Journal of Behavior Analysis and Modification* 1: 62–70.

Sidman, M. (1960) *Tactics of Scientific Research*, New York: Basic Books.

Singh, N. H. Dawson, M. J. and Gregory, P. R. (1980) 'Suppression of chronic hyperventilation using response-contingent aromatic ammonia', *Behavior Therapy* 13: 561–566.

Speer, D. C. (1992) 'Clinical significant change: Jacobson and Truax (1991) revisited', *Journal of Consulting and Clinical Psychology* 60: 402–8.

Wacker, D., McMahon, C., Steege, M., Berg, W., Sasso, G. and Melloy, K. (1990) 'Applications of a sequential alternating treatments design', *Journal of Applied Behavior Analysis* 23: 333–9.

Wampold, B. E. and Furlong, M. J. (1981) 'The heuristics of visual inference', *Behavioral Assessment* 3: 79–92.

Watts, F. (1979) 'The habituation model of systematic desensitization', *Psychological Bulletin* 86: 627–37.

White, D. M., Rusch, F. R., Kazdin, A. E. and Hartmann, D. P. (1989) 'Applications of meta-analysis in individual subject research, *Behavioral Assessment* 11: 281–96.

Wolpe J. (1958) *Psychotherapy by Reciprocal Inhibition*, Stanford: Stanford University Press.

Youell, K. J. and McCullough, J. P. (1974) 'Behavioral treatment of mucous colitis', *Journal of Consulting and Clincal Psychology* 43: 740–5.

Chapter 38

Experimental research designs

B.S. Everitt

INTRODUCTION

Much of the research undertaken in clinical psychology is concerned with the evaluation of treatment procedures. Fundamental to such research is the study in which groups of subjects are allocated in some way to a particular treatment condition and then measurements are taken on some dependent variable(s) of interest. In an investigation into the effect of a particular drug on reaction time, for example, an investigator may assign a number of subjects to receive the drug and a number to receive a placebo. The reaction time of each subject to some task will then be measured. This is the simplest example of a group design in which the effect of manipulating a single *independent* variable, treatment condition, on a single *dependent* variable, reaction time, is assessed. Other more complex examples will involve more than a single independent variable and the measurement of several dependent variables.

The analysis of such designs generally involves a statistical technique known as the *analysis of variance*, introduced by the statistician R. A. Fisher in the 1920s. Use of this method allows the investigator to separate the variability of a set of observations into component parts representing the variation due to the independent variables and that due to chance effects and measurement error. The latter might be considered 'background noise' against which it is hoped to detect some effect of interest. The simple two-group design, for example, attempts to uncover a difference between groups amongst the inherent variability of the individual observations.

EXPERIMENTAL AND OBSERVATIONAL STUDIES

Research studies can be divided roughly into those which are *observational* and those which are *experimental*. Both generally involve the comparison of two (or more) groups of subjects, one group which has received the new treatment or been exposed to a particular risk factor or whatever, and one group which has received only the normal treatment or a placebo, or has not been exposed to the risk factor etc. (Studies in which, for example, all patients are given a new treatment are generally either scientifically or ethically unacceptable.) The basic difference between the two types of study is the amount of control which the investigator has over the way in which groups of subjects to be compared are constructed. In an observational study there is usually essentially *no* control and in an experimental study generally *complete* control, although there are types of investigations which fall somewhere between these two extremes (see later).

Returning for the moment to the simple experimental study considered in the introduction, where a drug is to be compared with a placebo, subjects have to be allocated in some way to the two conditions. This is an extremely important aspect of any experimental study. If subjects are assigned by casual methods to one group or the other, there may well be factors associated with the assignment which are related to the dependent variable being measured, and these may cause a biased assessment of the group difference. If, for example, subjects who are first to volunteer are all placed in one group, then the two groups may differ in level of motivation and so subsequently in performance. The appropriate procedure for overcoming such a problem is, of course, the *random allocation* of subjects to groups. Whether a subject is to receive the drug or the placebo is decided, for example, by the toss of a coin. The primary benefit of randomisation lies in the *chance* (and therefore impartial) assignment of extraneous influences amongst the group to be compared, and it offers this control over such influences whether or not they are known by the experimenter to exist. Note that randomisation does not pretend to render the two samples equal with regard to such factors. But if the same procedure was applied in repeated samples, equality would be achieved in the long run. Thus randomisation ensures a lack of bias, whereas other methods of allocation may not. In an experiment which uses this method of forming the groups to be compared, the interpretation of a 'significant' group difference is largely unambiguous – its cause is the different treatments or conditions received by the groups.

In contrast to experiments are studies in which the independent variables come to the researcher, as it were, 'ready made'. In an investigation into the relationship between smoking and systolic blood pressure, for example, it would not be possible for the investigator to allocate subjects randomly to the two conditions, 'smoking' and 'non-smoking'. Instead the systolic blood pressure of naturally occurring groups of individuals who smoke and those who do not must be compared. Such observational studies may be analysed by essentially the same statistical methods as are used for experiments. Problems arise, however, in the interpretation of any group differences detected. A difference in the blood pressure of smokers and non-smokers, for example, would have three possible explanations:

1 Smoking causes a change in systolic blood pressure.
2 Level of blood pressure has a tendency to encourage or discourage smoking.
3 Some unidentified factors play a part in determining both the level of blood pressure and whether or not the subject smokes.

Somewhere between the observational study and the laboratory experiment come studies which attempt to alter the state of affairs in a non-laboratory environment. An example might be an educational programme designed to prevent smoking, introduced into one school but not another. After some suitable time period, the program might be assessed by comparing the two schools on, say, an outcome measure derived from pupils' responses to a questionnaire that asks them about smoking. This is not a rigorous experiment since it leaves many conditions uncontrolled, for example, possible differences between the backgrounds of the children who attend the two schools. Nevertheless, because such investigations are designed to come as close as possible to the ideal of a laboratory experiment, they are generally termed *quasi-experimental*.

Two possible alternatives to achieving control through random allocation should be mentioned, namely *matching* and *analysis of covariance*. Matching is the process by which the investigator attempts to 'equalise' the groups on a number of variables that are thought to affect the dependent variable. In the smoking and blood pressure investigation, for example, it might be considered sensible to obtain groups of smokers and non-smokers who have the same average age, or smokers and non-smokers might be matched 'one-to-one' for sex. Although matching is very popular amongst psychologists it does have a number of disadvantages. Foremost is that matching only controls for those extraneous variables actually identified by the investigator. There remains the possibility that other variables which may affect the response are uncontrolled.

Statistical control by means of analysis of covariance is discussed in the section beginning on p. 761.

THE ROLE OF MODELS IN THE ANALYSIS OF DATA

Models imitate the properties of 'real' objects in a simpler or more convenient form. A road map, for example, models part of the earth's surface, attempting to reproduce the relative positions of towns, roads and other features. Chemists use models of molecules to mimic their theoretical properties, which, in turn, can be used to predict the behaviour of real objects. A good model follows as accurately as possible the relevant properties of the real object, while being convenient to use.

Statistical models allow inferences to be made about an object, or activity, or process, by modelling some associated observable data. Suppose, for example, a child has scored 20 on a test of verbal ability, and after studying a dictionary for some time, scores 24 on a similar test. If it is believed that studying the dictionary has caused an improvement then a possible model of what is happening is:

20 = {person's initial score}

24 = {person's initial score} + {improvement}

The improvement can be found by simply subtracting the first score from the second.

Such a model is, of course, very naive, since it assumes that verbal ability can be measured exactly. A more realistic representation of the two scores, which allows for possible measurement error is:

$$x_1 = \gamma + \varepsilon_1$$
$$x_2 = \gamma + \delta + \varepsilon_2 \tag{1}$$

where x_1 and x_2 represent the two verbal ability scores, γ represents the 'true' initial measure of verbal ability and δ the improvement score. The terms ε_1 and ε_2 represent measurement error. Here the improvement score can be *estimated* as $x_2 - x_1$.

Such a model gives a precise description of what the investigator assumes is occurring in a particular situation – in this case it says that the improvement δ is considered to be independent of γ and is simply added to it. (An important point that needs to be noted here is that if you do not believe in a model, you should not perform operations and analyses on the data which assume it is true!)

Suppose now that it is believed that studying the dictionary does more good if the child already has a fair degree of verbal ability and that the various random influences which affect the test scores are also dependent on the true scores. Then an appropriate model would be:

$$x_1 = \gamma \varepsilon_1$$
$$x_2 = \gamma \delta \varepsilon_2 \tag{2}$$

Now the parameters are multiplied to give the observed scores, x_1 and x_2. Here δ might be estimated by dividing x_2 by x_1.

A further possibility is that there is a limit, λ, to improvement, and studying the dictionary improves performance on the verbal ability test by some proportion of the child's possible improvement, $\lambda-\gamma$. A suitable model would be:

$$x_1 = \gamma + \varepsilon_1$$
$$x_2 = \gamma + (\lambda - \gamma)\delta + \varepsilon_2 \tag{3}$$

With this model there is no way to estimate δ from the data unless a value of λ is given.

The decision about an appropriate model should be largely based on the investigator's prior knowledge of an area. In many situations, however, additive, linear models, such as that given in equation (1) are invoked by default, since such models allow many powerful and informative statistical techniques to be applied to the data. Analysis of variance techniques, for example, use such models, and in recent years *generalised linear models* have evolved which allow analogous models to be applied to a variety of data types, including those which involve categorical and ordinal dependent variables (see McCullagh and Nelder, 1989 for details).

THE ONE-WAY DESIGN

In the simplest type of research design used by psychologists, one independent variable is manipulated and the effect of this manipulation on a single dependent variable is assessed. This is the so-called *one-way design* or, if the groups are formed by random allocation, the *randomised groups design*. The question of major interest is whether the dependent variable can be considered to have the same mean value in the populations represented by each level of the independent variable. When this has only two levels, this question is addressed by way of the usual *t*-test, the relevant null hypothesis being:

$H_0: \mu_1 = \mu_2$

where μ_1 and μ_2 are the population means of the two groups. The *alternative hypothesis* might be *one-tailed*, for example,

$H_1: \mu_1 > \mu_2, H_1: \mu_1 < \mu_2$

or *two-tailed*,

$H_1: \mu_1 \neq \mu_2$

and the *t*-test might be *independent groups* or *paired*, dependent on how the subjects in each of the two groups were selected. Details of all the terms in italic and of how to perform a *t*-test are available in any elementary statistical textbook, for example, Altman (1991).

When the independent variable has more than two levels, say k, the appropriate null hypothesis is:

$H_o: \mu_1 = \mu_2 = \ldots = \mu_k$

with the alternative hypothesis generally being that not all the means are equal.

It is tempting to think that such a hypothesis might be tested by a series of *t*-tests on each pair of means. Such a procedure is however, not appropriate because of the following:

Suppose each *t*-test is performed at significance level α, so for any of the tests

Pr (rejecting the equality of the two means when hypothesis is true) = α

and, consequently

Pr (accepting the equality of the two means when hypothesis is true) = $1 - \alpha$

The total number of *t*-tests for all pairs of means amongst the k groups is

$N = k(k - 1)/2$ and so

Pr (accepting the equality of the two means for *all* *t*-tests performed when hypothesis is true) = $(1 - \alpha)^N$

and so, finally

Pr (rejecting the equality of the two means for *at least one* of the *t*-tests performed when hypothesis is true) $= 1 - (1 - \alpha)^N$

For particular values of k and $\alpha = 0.05$ this leads to:

k	N	Probability
2	1	$1 - (0.95)^1 = 0.05$
3	3	$1 - (0.95)^3 = 0.14$
4	6	$1 - (0.95)^6 = 0.26$
10	45	$1 - (0.95)^{45} = 0.90$

The probability of falsely rejecting the null hypothesis quickly increases above the chosen significance level, and it is clear that such an approach could give rise to misleading conclusions.

The appropriate procedure for testing the equality of k means is the analysis of variance, assuming, in general, the following linear model for the observations

$$x_{ij} = \mu + \alpha_i + \varepsilon_{ij} \tag{4}$$

where x_{ij} is the j-th observation in the i-th group, μ is the overall mean, α_i is the effect on an observation of being a member of the j-th group, and ε_{ij} is a random error term, assumed to be normally distributed with zero mean and variance σ^2. Assuming such a model the hypothesis of the equality of group means can be rewritten in terms of the αs as

$$H_0: \alpha_1 = \alpha_2 = \ldots = \alpha_k \tag{5}$$

The total variation in the observations is partitioned into that due to differences in the group means and that due to differences amongst observations within groups. Under the hypothesis of the equality of group means, both the between-group and within-group variances are estimates of σ^2. An F test of the equality of these two variances provides, consequently, a test of the hypothesis specified in equation (5).

To illustrate the analysis of the simple one-way design, an investigation described by Kapor (1981) will be used. Here the effect of knee-joint angle on the efficiency of cycling was studied. Efficiency was measured in terms of the distance pedalled on an ergocycle until exhaustion. The experimenter selected three knee-joint angles, 50°, 70° and 90°. Thirty subjects were available for the experiment and ten subjects were randomly allocated to each angle. The drag of the ergocycle was kept constant at 1.5 kp and subjects were instructed to pedal at a constant speed of 20 km/hour until exhaustion. The data are shown in Table 38.1.

Although the F tests used in the analysis of variance are known to be robust against even moderate departures from the assumptions of normality and homogeneity (that is, the population corresponding to each group has the same variance), it is good practice to make some effort to check for any obvious departures from either assumption. Here this is made a little difficult because of the relatively small number of observations in each group. In general, however,

Table 38.1 The effect of knee-joint angle on the efficiency of cycling

| | | Knee joint angle | |
	50°	*70°*	*90°*
Total	8.4	10.6	3.2
distance	7.0	7.5	4.2
covered	3.0	5.1	3.1
in kms	8.0	5.6	6.9
	7.8	10.2	7.2
	3.3	11.0	3.5
	4.3	6.8	3.1
	3.6	9.4	4.5
	8.0	10.4	3.8
	6.8	8.8	3.6

graphical techniques, such as *stem-and-leaf plots* and *probability plots* are likely to be most useful (see Altman, 1991). Formal tests of both normality and homogeneity are available but are not necessary in most circumstances. A simple graphical display of the knee-joint data is given in Figure 38.1. The 90° observations appear to contain two outliers, and the observations in the 50° condition appear to split into two groups. Here, however, these slight oddities of the data will be ignored.

The one-way analysis of variance table for the data is shown in Table 38.2. The size of the F ratio and its associated p value indicate clearly that the means of distance covered are not the same on the three conditions.

With two groups the interpretation of a significant difference is reasonably straightforward, but with three or more groups, further analysis may be required to find out how the means differ; whether they all differ, for example, or whether one group differs from the others, etc. In general there is no completely satisfactory answer to what should be done and a variety of so-called *multiple comparison techniques* have been developed which can often be helpful (see Klockars and Sax, 1986, for details). In the knee-joint example, however, a more straightforward approach can be adopted, since the groups have a clear ordering. In such cases, the variation between groups can be split into one degree of freedom components, representing variation due to *linear trend, quadratic trend* etc. If such an operation is carried out here, the results shown in Table 38.3 are obtained. Clearly the major difference between the groups is in terms of the quadratic component, reflecting the structure seen in Figure 38.1, with the mean distance covered rising from the 50° to 70° conditions and falling for the 90° condition.

When the dependent variable is considered to be on an *ordinal* rather than an interval scale, an equivalent procedure to the analysis of variance outlined in the foregoing is available, which uses only the *ranks* of the observations. It is known as the *Kruskal–Wallis test* (Altman, 1991, Chapter 9).

Ergocycle experiment – plot of data

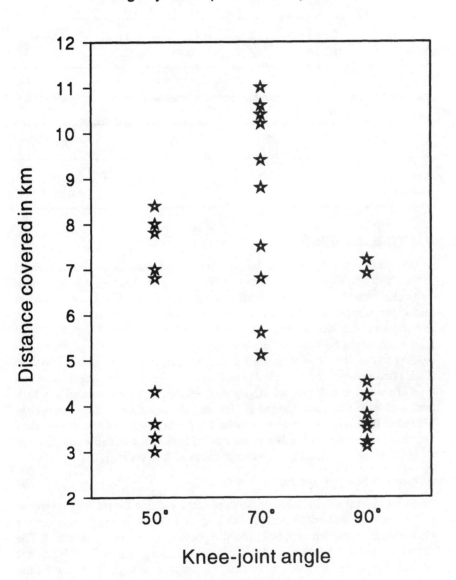

Figure 38.1 Graphical display of knee-joint data in *Table 38.1*

Table 38.2 Analysis of variance for knee-joint data

Source	SS	df	MS	F	p
Betn. angl	90.56	2	45.28	11.52	0.0002
Error	106.16	27	3.93		

Table 38.3 Linear and quadratic components of between-group variation for knee-joint data

Component	F	df	p
Linear	3.72	(1,27)	0.0644
Quadratic	19.27	(1,27)	0.0002

FACTORIAL DESIGNS

In the type of study discussed in the previous section, interest centred on looking at the effect of a single independent variable. It is often the case, however, that a particular variable may have one effect on people's behaviour in one situation and quite another effect in other circumstances. Consider, for example, an investigation into two schemes for teaching children to read. With backward readers, it might be that reading scheme A is more successful at improving reading scores, whilst with more advanced readers, reading scheme B is better. Such a finding would be described as an *interaction* between reading scheme and type of reader. In order to investigate such effects, a study is needed in which both variables can be examined at one and the same time. The appropriate procedure is usually known as a *factorial design*. In the case of two independent variables, where different subjects are studied under each possible combination of levels of the two variables, the model assumed for the data is

$$x_{ijk} = \mu + \alpha_i + \beta_j + \gamma_{ij} + \varepsilon_{ijk} \tag{6}$$

where x_{ijk} represents the value of the dependent variable for the k-th subject in the j-th level of one variable and the i-th level of the other, α_i and β_j represent the main effects of the two variables, and γ_{ij} represents their interaction effect. The three hypothesis of interest are (1) no difference in the means of the independent variable for the various levels of the first independent variable, (2) similar for the second independent variable, (3) no interaction effect between the two variables. In terms of the parameter in the model, these may be written as

$$H_0(1): \alpha_1 = \alpha_2 \ldots = \alpha_r = 0$$

$$H_0(2): \beta_1 = \beta_2 \ldots = \beta_c = 0 \tag{7}$$

$H_0(3)$: $\gamma_{ij} = 0$ $i = 1, 2 \ldots r, j = 1, 2 \ldots c$

where r and c are the number of levels of the two independent variables. Partitioning the total variance in the observations into parts representing variation between the levels of each of the independent variables and variation due to their interaction leads to F tests for each hypothesis (for details, see Winer, 1971; Chapter 5). The data shown in Table 38.4 will be used to illustrate this design. These data arise from an investigation into types of slimming regime. In this case the two independent variables are 'treatment', which relates to whether women attending a slimming clinic were advised to use a slimming manual or not as an addition to the regular package offered by the clinic, and 'status', that is, whether a woman was regarded as an 'experienced' or 'naive' slimmer. The dependent variable was a measure of weight change after three months. (For more details of this study, see Hand and Taylor, 1987).

The analysis of variance table for these data is shown in Table 38.5. Here each of the F tests is highly significant, including that corresponding to the hypothesis of no interaction. The presence of a significant interaction means that care is

Table 38.4 Slimming data

(a) Raw data

	Status	
	Novice	Experienced
No manual	− 5.85	− 2.42
	− 1.98	0.00
	− 2.12	− 2.74
	0.0	− 0.84
Manual	− 4.44	0.00
	− 8.11	− 1.64
	− 9.40	− 6.40
	− 1.50	− 6.15

(b) Table of means and standard deviations

	Status	
	Novice	Experienced
No manual		
Mean	− 2.49	− 1.50
SD	2.44	1.30
Manual		
Mean	− 7.51	− 1.89
SD	1.53	1.85

Table 38.5 Analysis of variance for slimming data

Source	SS	df	MS	F	p
Condition	29.40	1	29.40	8.76	0.012
Status	43.66	1	43.66	13.01	0.004
CS	21.46	1	21.46	6.40	0.026
Error	40.26	12	3.35		

required in arriving at a sensible interpretation of the results. First, a plot of the mean values in each of the four cells assists in explaining the interaction. A suitable plot is shown in Figure 38.2. Clearly the difference produced by giving novice slimmers access to the slimming manual is far greater than for experienced slimmers, where the effect is negligible. The significant main effects could be interpreted as indicating differences in the average weight change for novice and experienced slimmers, and for slimmers having access to the manual compared with those who do not, but here it is essentially the interaction effect which is of most interest.

The analysis of variance of even a simple factorial design with two factors becomes considerably more complicated if there are unequal numbers of observations in the four cells (see, for example, Hand and Taylor, 1987).

As the number of factors increases, a complete factorial design may require a large number of subjects. In a three-factor design, for example, where the factors have say p, r and q levels, the number of subjects required will be $p \times q \times r \times n$. So a $3 \times 3 \times 3$ design with ten subjects per cell will require 270 subjects. For this reason, complete factorial experiments with four factors or more are rarely performed. Alternatives are designs such as *latin squares*, which economise on subjects by assuming that certain interaction terms are absent. For more details about incomplete designs, see Winer (1971).

REPEATED-MEASURE DESIGNS

In the previous discussion of the difference between experimental and non-experimental studies, the advantages of random allocation were described. Foremost amongst these was the balance achieved in the groups on differences between subjects existing prior to the investigation. From the point of view of eliminating individual differences, there is, however, an alternative to random allocation, and that is to use the same subjects for all conditions. The primary purpose of such an arrangement is to provide a control on differences between subjects, and by using a same-subjects design, any individual peculiarities are equalised out over all conditions. Such studies, in which the same subjects are observed under all k levels of the independent variable, are usually referred to as *repeated measure* designs. The analysis of such designs poses more problems

Slimming data means and standard deviation bars

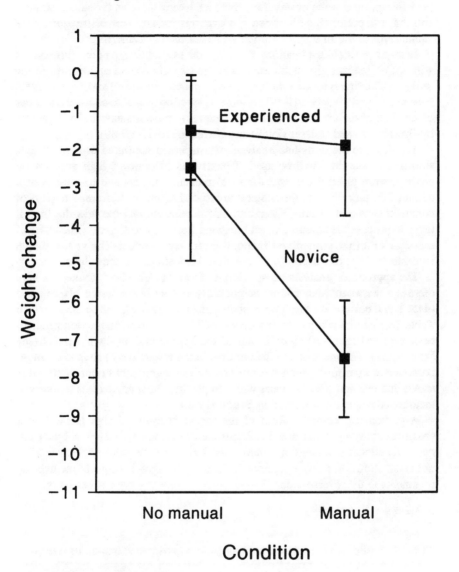

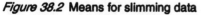

Figure 38.2 Means for slimming data

than for the designs considered earlier, since, to the extent that characteristics of individual subjects remain constant under different levels, pairs of observations will tend to be correlated rather than independent. Different assumptions about the pattern of these correlations lead to alternative F tests for assessing the effect(s) of the independent variable(s). In the simplest of such designs, for example, where a number of subjects each receive all of a number of treatments, the assumption that the observations for each treatment have the same variance, and that the correlations between observations for any pair of treatments are equal, leads to the straightforward analysis outlined in Table 38.6.

In many practical applications, however, the assumption of equal correlations will not be realistic. In such cases there are two alternative approaches to the analysis. The first is to use a *multivariate* procedure (see Hand and Taylor, 1987, for details), and the second is to use some 'correction factor' to adjust the degrees of freedom of the usual F tests. Possible correction factors have been suggested by Greenhouse and Geisser (1959) and Huynh and Feldt (1980).

To illustrate the complete analysis of a repeated measures design the data shown in Table 38.7 will be used. Two groups of subjects, high and low on anxiety, were given a perceptual task to process uni-, bi- and tri-dimensional stimuli. The task required the subjects to respond 'same' or 'different' to pairs of stimuli that varied in dimensionality. The dependent variable was the time it takes to process the stimuli pair and respond 'same' or 'different'. The order of presentation of the stimuli was randomised for each subject. The values shown in Table 38.7 are the mean 'same' reaction times of each of the subjects.

The appropriate analysis of variance is shown in Table 38.8. (Note that here there is a 'between' and 'within' subjects component in the design.) Here a test of the equal correlation assumption shows that it is justified, and so the F tests in Table 38.8 can be taken at their face value. The significant interaction needs to be interpreted first, and again a plot of the appropriate means is helpful (see Figure 38.3). The increase in reaction time in the low-anxiety group is far more pronounced than in the high-anxiety group. The significant effect of stimulus shows that reaction time increases with complexity. Other approaches to repeated measures designs are described in Everitt (1994).

A particularly common form of the repeat measures design is the 2×2 crossover study in which two treatments are to be compared. Here subjects are generally allocated at random to one of two groups; in one group subjects receive treatment A followed by treatment B, in the other group subjects receive the treatments in the reverse order. A possible model for this type of design is

$$x_{ijk} = \mu + \tau_{ij} + \alpha_k + \beta_u + \gamma_{uk} + \varepsilon_{ijk} \tag{8}$$

Table 38.6 Analysis of variance for a single-group repeated measures design

Source	SS	df	MS	F
Between subjects	SS	$n-1$	1 SS/$(n-1)$	
Between treatments	ST	$k-1$	2 ST/$(k-1)$	2/3
Subjects × treatments	SST	$(n-1)(k-1)$	3 SST/$(n-1)(k-1)$	

Table 38.7 Two-factor design with repeated measures on one factor

	Subject	uni	bi	tri
High Anxiety	1	502	580	640
	2	574	610	600
	3	480	520	580
	4	496	530	611
	5	520	600	620
	6	511	630	620
	7	493	586	601
	8	521	652	670
	9	440	593	485
Low Anxiety	10	451	670	707
	11	480	587	650
	12	513	650	680
	13	402	522	621
	14	472	690	680
	15	480	595	653
	16	395	552	651
	17	470	597	715
	18	576	789	835

Source: Broota (1989)

Table 38.8 Analysis of variance for data in *Table 38.7*

Source	SS	df	MS	F	p
Between subjects					
Anxiety	12421.5	1	12421.5	1.63	0.220
Error	122096.0	16	7631.0		
Within subjects					
Stimuli	24588.0	2	122922.0	123.69	<0.0001
Anxiety × Stimuli	31836.0	2	15918.0	16.02	<0.0001
Error	31802.00	32	993.81		

where τ_{ij} is the effect of the j-th subject in the i-th group, α_k is the effect of the κ-th period, β_u is the effect of the u-th treatment and γ_{uk} is the treatment × period

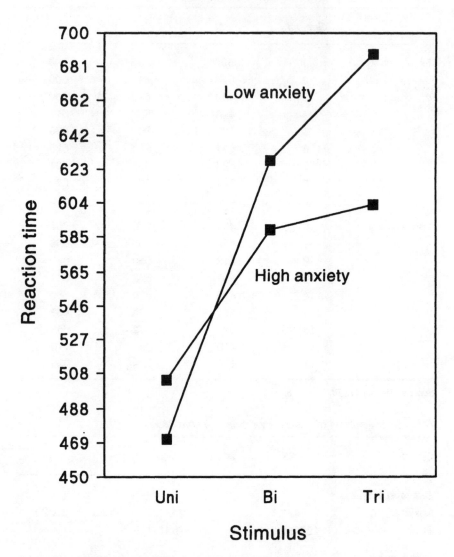

Figure 38.3 Means for anxiety data

interaction effect, more usually referred to as the *carryover* effect. There are several difficult issues involved with this type of design and these are discussed in, for example, Brown (1980), Zimmermann and Rahlfs (1980), Armitage and Hills (1982), and Jones and Kenward (1989). The most difficult issue concerns possible carryover effects, and it is generally recommended that a crossover design should not be used unless such effects can be discounted a priori.

ANALYSIS OF COVARIANCE

In the section on experimental and observational studies it was mentioned that researchers often attempt to overcome the disadvantages of studies where randomisation is not possible, either by matching subjects on variables thought to affect the dependent variable or by a method of statistical control known as the *analysis of covariance*. This method consists of measuring one or more concomitant variables in addition to the dependent variable of primary interest, and using these measurements to adjust, in some way, the dependent variable so that groups become more comparable. Only then are tests applied to assess group differences on the dependent variables. The data in Table 38.9, for example, are anxiety scores for patients having one of three different methods for extracting wisdom teeth. Scores were recorded before the operation and on discharge, using the Spielberger Anxiety Inventory. Here the investigator is primarily interested in group differences in anxiety on discharge, but wishes to *control* for initial level of anxiety. This may be done by using the analysis of covariance model:

$$y_{ij} = \mu + \alpha_i + \beta (x_{ij} - \bar{x}) + \varepsilon_{ij} \tag{9}$$

where x_{ij} is the anxiety score on discharge for the j-th subject in the i-th group and x_{ij} is the corresponding initial anxiety score. The other terms in the model are μ = overall mean, α_i = effect of the i-th treatment group, β = regression slope, ε_{ij} = residual or error term. The model assumes that (1) a linear relationship holds between the dependent variable and covariate, and (2) that the slope of this regression line is the same in each group.

Table 38.10 shows the results of a simple one-way analysis of variance for anxiety on discharge, and the results of an analysis of covariance using initial anxiety as a covariate. The simple analysis indicates no difference between methods of extraction, but the analysis of covariance suggests that after allowing for initial anxiety values, there is a difference between methods. The means for anxiety on discharge *adjusted* for initial anxiety shown in Table 38.10, indicate that it is higher for extraction method three than for the other two methods. (Adjusted estimates such as these must, of course, be interpreted with caution, since their values depend heavily on the assumptions of linearity and equal shape.)

The analysis of covariance was first introduced into statistics by R.A. Fisher (1932) as a means of reducing error variation and increasing the sensitivity of an experimental analysis to mean differences. The method depends upon identifying one or more measured covariates which are related to the response variable but not to the experimental treatment condition. (This is most often assured by measuring the covariate prior to the administration of the treatment.) By including concomitant measures in the analysis, residual variation can be reduced to the extent that it is attributable to the covariates, that is, to the extent that the criteria and covariates are linearly related.

As originally devised, the technique was used in combination with random

Table 38.9 Anxiety scores for patients undergoing wisdom tooth extraction by one of three methods

Method	Patient	Initial Anxiety	Anxiety on Discharge
One	1	30.2	32.0
	2	35.3	34.8
	3	32.4	36.0
	4	31.9	34.2
	5	28.4	30.3
	6	30.5	33.2
	7	34.8	35.0
	8	32.5	34.0
	9	33.0	34.2
	10	29.9	31.1
Two	11	32.6	31.5
	12	33.0	32.9
	13	31.7	34.3
	14	34.0	32.8
	15	29.9	32.5
	16	32.2	32.9
	17	31.0	33.1
	18	32.0	30.4
	19	33.0	32.6
	20	31.1	32.8
Three	21	29.9	34.1
	22	30.0	34.1
	23	29.0	33.2
	24	30.0	33.0
	25	30.0	34.1
	26	29.6	31.0
	27	32.0	34.0
	28	31.0	34.0
	29	30.1	35.0
	30	31.0	36.0

allocation to groups to increase the precision of the experiment. In psychology, however, analysis of covariance is often thought to be of no great use in a randomised design, but instead is often considered to be essential where subjects cannot be randomly allocated, as a means of removing potential sources of bias due to extraneous variables. For example, an investigator may be interested in determining whether normal subjects have different reaction times from schizophrenics or from depressed patients. A variable which clearly affects reaction

Table 38.10 Analysis of variance and covariance for anxiety scores in Table 38.9

(a) One way analysis of variance

Source	df	MS	F	p
Between Methods	2	4.32	2.13	0.14
Error	27	2.02		

(b) Analysis of covariance

Source	df	MS	F	p
Initial anxiety	1	18.44	13.23	0.001
Between Methods	2	10.12	7.26	0.003
Error	26	1.39		

(c) Adjusted means

Method 1—33.21
Method 2—32.22
Method 3—34.48

time is age, and so it may be decided to use the analysis of covariance to adjust the comparisons of reaction time of the three groups for age.

Without questioning the specific assumptions of the method, namely, that reaction time is linearly related to age with the same regression slope in each group, there are still fundamental difficulties about such an analysis. First, as with the process of matching, there may be variables other than the measured covariate, age, that affect reaction time. Unless age acts as a surrogate for all of these, the comparison between groups could still be misleading. Second, after performing the analysis of covariance, the investigator will have an answer to the question, 'Conditional on having the same age, does the reaction time of normals, schizophrenics and depressives differ?' However, this may not be a sensible question, since schizophrenics may always be younger than depressed patients.

Such difficulties are discussed in more detail by Fleiss and Tanur (1972), and researchers contemplating the use of analysis of covariance should ensure that they are familiar with its possible problems.

SUMMARY

Group designs and the analysis of variance are essential tools in all branches of psychology. Research workers need to be familiar with at least the basics of such methods so that they can design sensible studies and analyse them appropriately. Nowadays, of course, they need not be familiar with the arithmetic of analysis of variance, since computers can find the mean squares and F values for even the most complex designs in a few seconds. However, this is not without its dangers, and it is not uncommon to find that much of the output from a complex program, such as SPSS's Manova or BMDP's 4V, is misunderstood by many of its users. It is important to remember that the availability of statistical packages (user-friendly or otherwise) does not mean that a visit to a statistician will not be beneficial. In general, it is essential!

REFERENCES

Altman, D. G. (1991) *Practical Statistics for Medical Research*, London: Chapman and Hall.

Armitage, P. and Hills, M. (1982) 'The two period cross-over trial', *The Statistician* 31: 119–31.

Broota, K. D. (1989) *Experimental Design in Behavioural Research*, New Dehli: Wiley Eastern.

Brown, B. W. (1980) 'The cross-over experiment for clinical trials', *Biometrics* 36: 69–79.

Everitt, B. S. (1994) *Statistical Methods for Medical Investigations*, 2nd edn, London: Edward Arnold.

Fisher, R. A. (1932) *Statistical Methods for Research Workers*, Edinburgh: Oliver and Boyd.

Fleiss, J. L. and Tanur, J. M. (1972) 'The analysis of covariance in psychopathology', in M. Hammer, K. Salzinger and S. Sutton (eds) *Psychopathology*, New York: Wiley.

Greenhouse, S. W. and Geisser, S. (1959) 'On methods in the analysis of profile data', *Psychometrika* 24: 95–112.

Hand, D. J. and Taylor, C. C. (1987) *Multivariate Analysis of Variance and Repeated Measures: A Practical Approach for Behavioural Scientists*, London: Chapman and Hall.

Huynh, H. and Feldt, L. S. (1980) 'Performance of traditional F test in repeated measures designs under covariance heterogeneity', *Communications in Statistics – Theory and Methods* A9: 61–74.

Jones, B. and Kenward, M. G. (1989) *Design and Analysis of Cross-Over Trials*, London: Chapman and Hall.

Kapor, M. (1981) 'Efficiency on ergocycle in relation to knee-joint angle and drag', unpublished Master's dissertation, University of Delhi.

Klockars, A. J. and Sax, G. (1986) *Multiple Comparisons*, Sage University Paper 61, Beverly Hills, Calif.: Sage Publications.

McCullagh, P. and Nelder, J. A. (1989) *Generalized Linear Models*, 2nd edn, London: Chapman and Hall.

Winer, B. J. (1971) *Statistical Principles in Experimental Design*, Tokyo: McGraw-Hill.

Zimmermann, H. and Rahlfs, V. (1980) 'Model building and testing for change over designs', *Biometric Journal* 22: 197–210.

Chapter 39

Single-case methodology in clinical neuropsychology

A.G.M. Canavan

INTRODUCTION

The aim of this chapter is to provide an outline of the kind of investigation that could be carried out subsequent to a standard clinical neuropsychological examination such as that described by Powell and Wilson in Chapter 34. Such investigations are indicated whenever a patient displays deficits that are not easy to interpret. It is assumed that these deficits (i.e. poor test performances) are due to some underlying dysfunction (i.e. disturbance of ability), and thus a clinical assessment will not be complete if the final report simply lists deficits. The nature of the underlying dysfunction needs to be determined, and this can only be achieved by the application of experimental methodology. For instance, it is one thing to report that a patient performs poorly on the Block Design sub-test of the Wechsler scales, but it is quite another thing to determine why the patient performs so poorly. This chapter is intended as an introduction to the latter kind of investigation.

It is not suggested that single-case studies should replace group studies as the proper method of investigation in neuropsychology, since it is clear that generalising from a single instance is a very risky undertaking. Indeed, Kolb and Whishaw go as far as to argue that '. . . studies of single-cases are not a legitimate basis for neuropsychological theory' (Kolb and Whishaw, 1980: 321). Equally though, the study of groups should not exclude detailed consideration of the individual: the two approaches are in fact complementary. Nevertheless, single-case studies are fraught with problems, and so a large part of this chapter will be devoted to a discussion of the difficulties inherent in such studies.

Another reason for the utilisation of single-case studies is that certain syndromes are so rare that there may never be a chance to employ a group design. A case in point is the patient H.M. (see p. 777), who suffered from such a serious amnesia as the consequence of a surgical procedure that the operation is unlikely to be repeated.

Single-case investigation may be useful in at least four other ways. First, there is the principle of 'fractionation of syndromes' to consider (Shallice, 1979). He states, 'If a patient is observed with less than the defining number of deficits for a syndrome, then the syndrome as a functional entity fractionates into more specific syndromes' (ibid.: 200). Second, conclusions drawn from single-case studies may provide hypotheses for further examination with a group study. Third, while single-cases may well form an insecure basis upon which to develop theories, it is often true that a single instance is all that is necessary in order to reject a hypothesis. Fourth, a thorough single-case investigation will always be of benefit to the patient in helping the neuropsychologist to design an optimal, individualised treatment plan.

Finally, as implied above, it should be emphasised that the kind of single-case study to be described in this chapter relies heavily on experimental methodology, and should be contrasted with the more casual observational studies made popular by Luria (e.g. Luria, 1968) and more recently by Sacks (1985). These authors have produced delightfully written, memorable accounts of patients with striking or unusual deficits, occasionally carrying out subtle environmental or behavioural manipulations aimed at throwing more light on the deficits, and have offered fascinating speculations as to the likely underlying dysfunctions. However, in the absence of painstaking experimental work, such studies remain at the level of clinical description, and will not be considered further here.

PERFORMING A CASE STUDY

Background data

It is obviously essential that background testing be exhaustive (see Powell and Wilson, Chapter 34), since the delineation of a specific deficit (or syndrome) may be achieved only by ruling out all other possible deficits. Thus a description of a 'specific' verbal memory deficit which lacked in background data regarding language functions in general would be unconvincing, as would the description of a 'specific' impairment in drawing skills in the absence of background data regarding other constructional abilities.

Realistically, this means that no single-case study can be carried out in a matter of a few hours. Given that most brain-damaged patients tire easily, and thus that individual testing sessions must be kept short in order to avoid fatigue effects, then in practical terms a thorough single-case study is going to cost both the patient and the examiner a number of weeks, or even months. As will be seen, in the case of H.M., the study might even run into years.

The background data should include the results of all physical investigations, and to this end the clinical neuropsychologist is being forced to become more and more familiar with the latest recording and imaging techniques and how to interpret their findings. It is beyond the scope of the present chapter to discuss these techniques here, but for overviews of EEG (electroencephalogram) and SCP (slow cortical potential) work, the reader is referred to Rockstroh *et al.* (1989) and Birbaumer *et al.* (1990), and for descriptions of PET (positron emission tomography), MRI (magnetic resonance imaging) and other brain imaging techniques, the reader is referred to Pfurtscheller and Lopes da Silva (1988) and Ottosson and Rostene (1989).

It is also true that the clinical neuropsychologist plays an essential role in certain semi-invasive investigations, such as the sodium amytal test, in which each hemisphere is in turn anaesthetised to allow the assessment of the other hemisphere's functions in isolation (e.g. Powell *et al.*, 1987), and it is likely that this role will continue to expand in the realm of PET and MRI scanning. Indeed, with a combination of the last two techniques it is now possible to localise, to a very fine degree, function (and dysfunction) within the living brain, and this will become a major aspect of single-case studies in the future. A recent example of how such imaging techniques can lead to important findings even when the sample size is n=1 is the study of Akshoomoff *et al.* (1992). The anatomical detail produced by MRI scanning allowed these authors to conclude that the neuropsychological deficits seen in their patient C.Z. were definitely due to cerebellar damage, thus confirming that the cerebellum contributes to cognitive ability (Bracke-Tolkmitt *et al.*, 1989) and not just motor skills.

While it cannot be emphasised too highly that the background data should include the results of all physical investigations, as well as details of surgical procedures and neuropathological findings where appropriate, it is, however, just as essential to present a clear report of the patient's educational and occupational background, special interests and disinterests, current motivational level and so forth, again as outlined by Powell and Wilson in Chapter 34. An example described previously (Canavan, 1987) should suffice to underline this point. The young female patient J.R. presented with extremely poor spelling and almost complete alexia following a closed-head injury. She was, however, able to read certain single words when the lettering was large enough, including 'little', 'tree', 'horse', 'saddle' and 'stirrup'. Her drawing abilities were also extremely impaired, except for retention of the ability to draw horses. These islands of ability would remain a mystery to any investigator who failed to take note of the patient's long-standing fascination for horses.

Ad hoc testing

Once all of the background tests have been performed, specification of the syndrome can proceed to the *ad hoc* testing phase. The background data may have revealed a single deficit on, for example, the Block Design sub-test of the Wechsler scales, or a pattern of deficits, but will not necessarily have thrown light upon the nature of the dysfunction(s) underlying such deficits. From this point on, the single-case study adopts an experimental methodology, involving the formation of hypotheses and the devising of critical tests to choose between them. The next sections are intended to help the investigator in going about this task.

Hypotheses derived from the test material itself

A consideration of the properties of the particular psychometric test that first elicited the deficit is a good starting point for a single-case study. To take the Wechsler Block Design sub-test again as an example, this involves arranging within a set time either four or nine red and white blocks into patterns according to a model presented either in the form of similar blocks (with the examiner demonstrating the solution) or in the form of a two-dimensional picture on a card (with no demonstration).

All of these variables (number of blocks, nature of model, time limit, presence or absence of demonstration) may be systematically explored using items additional to those present in the original test. Such parametric variation will determine the circumstances under which the patient succeeds or fails; a patient who is simply slow, for instance, or particularly sensitive to time demands, may well go on to complete the block designs given unlimited time, whereas a patient with a serious perceptual or visuo-constructive deficit will not benefit from being allowed extra time. Indeed, such patients often produce erroneous solutions quite quickly.

Again, exploring the factor as to whether or not the correct solution is first modelled by the examiner could lead to hypotheses concerning planning ability on the part of the patient. If the patient always succeeds when the solution is first modelled but otherwise fails, then further experiments could be devised to assess the patient's ability to formulate strategies and carry them out. Determining exactly how much help the patient needs, and which kind of help best facilitates performance, will obviously also represent the first steps in devising a suitable rehabilitation programme.

Psychometric variation of test properties, then, is in itself a beginning to the process of hypothesis testing that forms the basis of the neuropsychological single-case study.

Hypotheses derived from a consideration of functions underlying test performance

It is implicit in administering neuropsychological tests that they assess some underlying neuropsychological function. Unfortunately, it is not for the most part explicit what this underlying function might actually be. For instance, with the Block Design test described in the preceding section most researchers would agree that it assesses some kind of visuospatial constructive ability, with elements of planning and perceptual matching. But this is hardly an operational definition, open to experimental investigation. In fact, most tests available to the neuropsychologist measure some mixture of poorly defined 'primary' abilities, since most have not been constructed according to any particular theory of brain function.

Nevertheless, this shortcoming can prove a lively source of hypotheses for the single-case study. Consider verbal paired associate learning, for instance, usually taken as reflecting a verbal memory task (on the functional level) and left temporal lobe function (on the anatomical level). Verbal paired associate tests usually contain 'easy' pairs, such as *baby – cries* and *north – south*, and 'difficult' pairs, such as *obey – inch* and *crush – dark*. The former pairs tend to be learned quite well even by patients who have undergone left temporal lobectomy (Meyer and Yates, 1955; Goldstein *et al.*, 1988), who score at about 70 per cent of the level of healthy subjects (which is in fact a statistically significant impairment, but hardly a case of complete loss of function). The difficult pairs, on the other hand, pose a severe problem to such patients, who may learn to a level of only 7 per cent on average, or not at all in individual cases.

Data such as these, even from a single case, would be a convincing pointer to the anatomical location of the ability to form difficult verbal associations. They also provide a clue as to why total loss of either verbal or visuospatial memory functions is rarely seen after unilateral temporal lesions. At least three possibilities are raised, all of which may be regarded as hypotheses that could be tested in case studies.

The first possibility is that clinical neuropsychology lacks 'pure' tests of verbal and spatial abilities. That is to say, that tests considered to be purely verbal are in fact contaminated with visuospatial properties, while tests considered to be visuospatial in nature can in fact be verbalised. In the case of verbal paired associates, for instance, it might be argued that the easy pairs cited above could in fact be visualised, utilising the functions of the right hemisphere, while the difficult pairs would not lend themselves to such imagery. If this were so, the effect of left temporal lobectomy would be to abolish performance on the difficult pairs but not on the easy pairs – which is the result described above.

A second possibilty is that the easy pairs are extremely common and therefore overlearned pairs, while the difficult pairs are only rarely encountered, and unlikely to have been learned pre-operatively (or pre-injury). There is some evidence from animal learning studies (e.g. Chow and Survis, 1958; Orbach and Fantz, 1958) that overtraining can protect behaviours from the disruptive effects of lesions in cases where the same behaviours would be abolished completely by the same lesions had they been learned only to some minimal criterion.

A third possibility is also related to how commonly the associations occur in everyday life. In a paired associates test, recall is prompted by presentation of the first word in a pair; for instance, by saying either *baby?* or *obey?* in the example given above. If it is assumed that each of these words will generate a list of 'free' or 'natural' associations, it is likely that the list generated by *baby?* will include *cries!* whereas the list generated by the prompt *obey?* is unlikely to include *inch!* Thus, while the 'difficult' pairs constitute a genuine recall task, the 'easy' pairs may in contrast represent a recognition task. The data cited above could therefore be interpreted as evidence that left temporal lobectomy results in a dysfunction of verbal recall but not of verbal recognition.

A single-case study would present an ideal opportunity for investigating these three possibilities. For instance, if recognition memory were intact, other recognition memory tasks should be performed equally well, which would not be expected on the basis of the overtraining or visualisability hypotheses. Again, combinations such as *baby – jumps, baby – skips* or *baby – drives* could presumably be visualised, but should certainly be neither overlearned nor 'natural' associations. Finally, paired associates derived from a knowledge of the patient's lifelong occupations or hobbies, but non-visualisable and not usually associated outside that occupation or hobby, could form items for a third test in this case study. As noted in the section on control subjects (p. 776), appropriate control subjects would be necessary for all conditions.

Thus a consideration of the possible functions underlying task performance can in itself lead to the development of testable hypotheses in a case study.

Hypotheses derived from a consideration of the effects of the lesion

Locus, extent and type of lesion, as well as age at injury and time since it occurred, all play a role in interpreting the test performance of the individual patient and in carrying out the single-case study.

Lesions restricted to very small areas of cortex or to particular subcortical nuclei are somewhat rare, but obviously provide the best opportunity to define the function of a given anatomical structure. Patients with such lesions tend to have very specific deficits that are not always detectable with standardised test batteries, and which may not be particularly disruptive in daily life. It is certainly true, however, that no brain lesion, no matter how small, will ever be completely without effect, and so it is worth checking for subtle deficits even in patients with apparently normal test profiles.

The choice of which tests to use when investigating such patients will depend on the location of the lesion and knowledge as to which functions are typically disturbed by larger lesions in that region. Large lesions of occipital cortex, for instance, produce extensive anopia (loss of vision), and thus it is to be expected that small lesions or epileptic foci in this area will produce scotomas (small blind spots in the visual field) that may not be subjectively noticeable, but may be of clinical importance.

As another example, further testing of patients with lesions of left temporal or frontal cortex who do not display any gross dysphasia, dyslexia or dysgraphia may nevertheless reveal subtle language deficits, for instance, an inability to name specific classes of words, such as colour-names (a symptom known as colour anomia). This process of uncovering ever more specific deficits is what Shallice (1979) terms 'fractionation', and in the realm of language disorders this kind of study has seen something of a boom in recent years (see, for example, De Bleser, 1987; Shallice, 1988; Scott and Byng, 1989).

It must be admitted, however, that most patients seen in the clinic will have rather diffuse lesions which do not respect any particular anatomical boundaries, and in these cases very little can be said at the end of the study about localisation of function. Shallice urges further investigation of such patients despite this, with the aim of 'providing information relevant to theories of functional organisation of the systems underlying human cognition' (Shallice, 1979: 183). This 'functional approach' based upon single-case studies has led to the situation in which even conservative classification systems estimate as many as nine (Goodglass and Kaplan, 1972) or eleven (Mazzochi and Vignolo, 1979) different syndromes of language disturbance, virtually none of which can be traced back to particular anatomical pathology.

In contrast, the 'localisation approach', in which investigators attempt to specify exactly the structures involved in specific functions, has been meeting with more and more difficulties in recent years. For instance, although there is little doubt that expressive (Broca's) dysphasia is seen primarily following left frontal lobe lesions, whereas receptive (Wernicke's) dysphasia is commonly the result of more posterior left-sided lesions, there is growing documentation of cases of expressive dysphasia in which Broca's area remains intact, and of receptive dysphasia in which Wernicke's area is undamaged (e.g. Mazzochi and Vignolo, 1979). Furthermore, lesions of Broca's area alone do not lead to permanent dysphasic disturbance (Mohr, 1976). At present, in fact, it would seem that most dysphasic patients tend to have a mixture of expressive and receptive difficulties, in that those cases in the literature described as 'pure' Broca's or Wernicke's dysphasics are as a rule the least extensively investigated, whereas those cases who have been thoroughly diagnosed show only relative asymmetries between expressive and receptive dysphasia (see also Niebergall et al., 1976).

Nevertheless, these doubts concerning localisation of function and fractionation of syndromes call for many further, more precise, single-case studies, rather than argue against the value of studies already carried out. The extra precision required in the future is already available in the form of better imaging techniques on the one hand, and on the other the more refined experimental procedures increasingly being drawn from cognitive psychology.

It should also be noted, however, that one development within the 'localisation approach' is the growing acceptance that functions tend to be organised in systems rather than as separate entities, and that a large number of systems exist which display fairly non-specific functions. Implications of the former conclusion include acknowledging that even small lesions at any level in a serially organised system can have quite devastating effects on the system as a whole, and that many different lesions can have seemingly similar effects, albeit for different reasons. The recognition of non-specific systems has also become of increasing importance, particularly with regard to the neurotransmitter systems originating in the basal brain and brain stem. The dopaminergic system arising in the substantia nigra, for instance, may be regarded as non-specific in terms of cognitive function in that the neurons comprising this system do not directly process information themselves. Rather, the dopamine which they produce has a more general dampening function on other neurons in target structures, modulating their spontaneous activity and thereby increasing their signal to noise ratios (e.g. Rolls *et al.*, 1979; 1984). Given that the substantia nigra supplies the neostriatum (caudate nucleus and putamen), the tegmentum and the whole of the frontal cortex with dopamine, however, the consequent disruption of multiple functions following damage confined to this relatively tiny structure should not be too surprising. This is in fact the case in Parkinson's disease, and the similarities and differences between the Parkinsonian syndrome and the 'frontal lobe syndrome' have been the subject of much intensive investigation in recent years (e.g. Lees and Smith 1983; Canavan *et al.*, 1989a; b; 1990; Linden *et al.*, 1990).

It is in exactly this area that detailed investigations of individuals have been proposed as a preferred alternative to group studies. Shallice (1982), for instance, remarked upon the difficulty he had experienced in attempting to replicate many of the earlier findings regarding the effects of frontal lobe damage, and Canavan *et al.* (1985) questioned the usefulness of the concept of the 'frontal lobe syndrome' *per se*. The problem here is that there are at least five to seven functionally independent areas in the primate frontal lobe (Rosenkilde, 1979; Kolb and Whishaw, 1980), and thus Shallice (1982) argued that single-case studies will be more illuminating than group studies because of the great heterogeneity seen in patients classified as having frontal lobe lesions. This point is acknowledged nowadays even in group studies (e.g. Canavan *et al.*, 1989a; b; 1990), where data for individual patients are displayed additionally in graphs, rather than simply plotting group means, and such investigations may in a sense be considered 'multiple' single-case studies.

Returning now to the more general theme of interpreting the effects of brain damage, and developing hypotheses to be tested in single-case studies, it should not be forgotten that different types of lesion can have quite different effects on brain function. For instance, meningiomas may exert pressure on widespread parts of the brain, whereas gliomas are more likely to affect only the regions which they infiltrate. Again, slow-growing tumours may not be as devastating in their effects as fast-growing tumours, for the same reasons that serial surgical lesions are more sparing of function than single-stage removals of the same amount of tissue (Butters *et al.*, 1972). Closed-head injuries are likely to have widespread effects, but in particular, *contrecoup* effects – damage to areas exactly opposite to the site of external injury. Vascular lesions are also likely to have widespread effects, with anoxia affecting all regions supplied by the vessel in question. In particular, subcortical structures may be adversely affected by such lesions. Thus, for instance, a lesion of the anterior communicating or cerebral arteries, apart from affecting orbital and medial frontal cortex, may also affect limbic functioning (these arteries supply the cingulate gyrus and the anterior columns of the fornix), as well as the functioning of the neostriatum. Lesions such as these may have profound effects not only upon cognitive abilities but also upon motivational and motor mechanisms. A case study devoted to a description of the former, then, must take into account performance deficits possibly resulting from disruption of the latter.

Surgical resections are the easiest lesions to localise, and are certainly the most precise and circumscribed lesions to be found in the clinic, but it must be remembered that surgery is never carried out on a healthy brain, and thus interpretation of the post-operative syndrome is not always easy. In particular, the nature of the pathology requiring surgical intervention must be taken into account. For instance, removal of a meningioma may be carried out with minimal damage to underlying tissue, yet the pre-operative widespread effects of pressure from this space-occupying lesion may still be observed immediately post-operatively. Case studies could profitably illuminate the different courses of recovery in patients with differing clinical pictures in this respect. As another example, the lesioned area of a temporal lobe in an epileptic patient after temporal lobectomy may well extend beyond the area of surgical resection. Not only may there be retrograde degeneration in more posterior parts of the temporal lobe and projection areas of the thalamus, but also it is not uncommon to find at pathology that the hippocampus within the resected lobe is sclerotic, or in some other way damaged (see, for example, Goldstein et al., 1988; 1989). The suspicion must therefore be that hippocampal tissue in the spared regions of the temporal lobe is also affected. In short, the study of surgical removals in human beings is confounded by the fact that such interventions are carried out only on abnormal brains, and thus data gathered from such cases are more likely to reflect the underlying pathology than the intervention itself. It is quite possible, then, that studies of patients who have suffered missile wounds (see, for example, Newcombe, 1969), where there can be relatively little suspicion of previous pathology, are among the most valuable of the studies to be performed in the clinic.

It is also important to note that the presence of damaged tissue may be more devastating in its consequences for the patient than the complete removal of such tissue. Thus the presence of a small cortical scar may result in all of the deficits and symptoms associated with psychomotor epilepsy, while the removal of the scarred tissue may relieve the condition. Indeed, temporal lobe dysfunction (as opposed to temporal lobe resection), for example, has been implicated in many disorders of cognition, mood and motivation. Bear (1979), for instance, studying the behaviours of patients with temporal lobe epilepsy in their inter-ictal periods, characterised right temporal lobe epileptics as displaying obsessions, helplessness, sadness, moralistic fervour, emotional arousability and indulging in unusual sexual behaviour. On the other hand, left temporal lobe epileptics were described as being more angry, paranoid and dependent than the normal population. Again, Flor-Henry (1969; 1972) has suggested that right hemisphere epileptic foci are associated with manic depression and that left hemisphere foci are associated with paranoid schizophrenia. As early as 1981 Newlin et al. also concluded that schizophrenia is associated with left hemispheric abnormality, and there are now a host of PET-scan studies to support this position (e.g. Weinberger et al., 1986; 1988; Friston et al., 1992). Thus it is possible that certain types of lesion (for example, epileptic foci) are more likely to lead to disorganisation of function, whereas other types of lesion (for example, lesions involving loss of tissue) are more likely to lead to loss of function. This possibility is one which may be fruitfully explored with single-case studies, especially given the current availability of techniques for imaging brain activity in individual patients under defined circumstances.

Age at injury and time since it occurred are two final factors that have to be taken into account when performing a single-case study, and they are also both sources of hypotheses that could be tested with such studies. It has long been thought, for instance, that lesions occurring in early childhood are less disruptive of function than lesions that occur in adulthood. Woods and Teuber (1973), for example, demonstrated that language survives early damage to the left hemisphere, and Teuber (1975) demonstrated that recovery of various motor, somatosensory, visual and language functions is better in the 17–20 age group than in the 21–25 age group, which is better than in patients above the age of 26. These findings, especially as regards language recovery, have not gone completely without challenge (for a review, see Heywood and Canavan, 1987), but the fact remains that the pattern of deficits observed in any one patient following a specific lesion may differ from the pattern of deficits observed in another with the same lesion depending on the patients' ages at the time of injury and at the time of testing. This situation calls for detailed single-case studies and argues against group studies in which patients of varying ages and stages of recovery are mixed together. It also draws attention to a severe limitation on the generalisability of single-case studies, namely, that no one case can fully describe the pattern of deficits to be expected from any particular lesion.

Late deterioration in function is also a factor which single-case studies need to take into account. For instance, Hamlin (1970) was able to demonstrate deficits in patients fourteen years after frontal lobectomy which had not been present immediately after surgery. Geschwind (1974) has pointed out that the brains of such patients show marked and continuous shrinkage from the time of surgery onwards, and this is probably the neurological explanation underlying Hamlin's findings. As another example, this time from comparative research, but with important implications for human studies, the ability of the normal infant monkey to perform delayed response tasks depends on the integrity of the caudate nucleus (Goldman, 1974). During development the maturing prefrontal cortex begins to subserve a dominant role in such tasks. If dorsolateral prefrontal cortex is removed in monkeys after birth, the ability to perform delayed response tasks is unimpaired in infancy (Goldman, 1971). However, as the operated monkey matures, a deficit on delayed response tasks appears (Goldman, 1974; 1976). Thus the possibility of growing up into an impairment that was not obvious in infancy should be paid careful consideration.

Finally, short-term changes need also to be taken into account in single-case studies. For instance, the performance of patients may deteriorate drastically immediately after surgery because of the appearance of oedema, which usually reaches its peak by about the third post-operative day to disappear about three weeks later (Geschwind, 1974). Test results observed at this time will be unreliable, since areas of brain far removed from the surgical resection site may be affected, and since 'recovery' will take place rapidly. Clearly, little can be said about localisation of function in such cases, although it is often at this time that some of the most intriguing neurological symptoms occur, for instance, unilateral neglect. The difficulty in defining unstable syndromes does, of course, pose a major problem in single-case studies, but it also probably precludes the possibility of meaningful group studies.

In conclusion, merely considering the likely effects of type and time of lesion can lead to hypotheses worth exploring with single-case designs, and there is clearly a wealth of information to be won through such studies.

Hypotheses derived from the literature

The vast literature of experimental and comparative psychology is probably the most important source of hypotheses that can be profitably tested in the clinic. The study of patient D.B. (Weiskrantz et al., 1974) is a particularly good example of this kind of hypothesis testing. Damage to the geniculo-striate system, the primary pathway and processing area for visual perception, leads to clinical blindness, in which the patient is subjectively unaware of any form of visual stimulus. However, from their consideration of the comparative literature regarding residual visual function in monkeys following striatal ablation, Weiskrantz and colleagues decided to test the ability of the patient D.B. to point to objects in his hemianopic field. For D.B. this task must have been rather puzzling, in that he was being asked to point to things which he could not see. To his great surprise, he proved quite capable of achieving not only this but also of identifying whether lines presented in his blind field were horizontal or vertical, and could 'guess' a number of other basic features of stimuli too. The literature on this phenomenon, which has become known as 'blindsight', has burgeoned, mainly through the publication of single-case studies or at most small groups of patients (see Weiskrantz, 1986, or Cowey and Stoerig, 1991, for reviews), and it serves as a lesson that the pattern of deficits and residual function to be found in neurological patients comes often only through careful experimentation. In the case of blindsight, this involved testing patients for capabilities of which they themselves were unaware, and which had long been overlooked by examining physicians and psychologists.

Another example of a single-case investigation driven by consideration of the comparative literature is the study of patient C.B. reported by Heywood et al., (1987). C.B. suffered from cortical achromatopsia (colour blindness), a not unusual result of damage to the ventromedial occipitotemporal region. The area known as V4 in the monkey is located in this region, and it is known that the monkey's V4 is responsible for both colour vision and pattern recognition (e.g. Desimone et al., 1985; Heywood and Cowey 1987), and thus Heywood et al. decided to test C.B.'s visual functions in detail, to see if his deficit was indeed restricted to colour perception. The results they obtained were not entirely unambiguous, in that although they concluded that C.B.'s pattern discrimination was intact, he in fact had difficulties in reading small print and recognising faces (see Canavan and Sartory, 1990, for a detailed criticism). Nevertheless the study is a good demonstration of how hypotheses derived from the literature can be tested in practice in the single-case design.

Hypotheses derived from extrapolation and casual observation

As a final example of how a single-case investigation can come about, the study of patient T.M. reported by Halligan and Marshall (1991) is illuminating, not least because it aroused something of a controversy (see Mattingley and Bradshaw, 1991; Marshall and Halligan, 1991). The starting point of the investigation was a consideration of the possibility that, among the many visual areas of the human brain, there might be one set of spatial maps specialised for 'near space' and another for 'far space', corresponding to a reaching-field and a pointing- or throwing-field respectively. Halligan and Marshall reasoned that this should be demonstrable in patients suffering from hemi-neglect, in that cases must exist where near space is neglected but not far space. The opportunity to test this hypothesis arose when the patient T.M., a keen darts player, arrived in the clinic. He displayed a classic left visuospatial neglect within near space, transecting lines drawn on paper systematically to the right of midpoint in a line bisection task. However, when requested to bisect much longer lines located in far space by throwing darts at the midpoint, his performance was much better. Thus a mixture of extrapolation from the literature and observation of an individual's hobbies can lead to experimental investigations of the single case that throw light on the organisation and dissociation of functions in the human brain.

Control subjects

As in all experiments in which new tests are developed, the single-case design requires the assessment of a control group. The size of this comparison group need not be very large, particularly if the variance in the performance of the controls is very small or even zero, which will be the case when the test in question is performed at ceiling level by healthy subjects. In other cases, however, such as in the use of reaction-time tests, where variance in performance can be very large, it may be necessary to test ten or more controls in order to define the normal range of performance on the test.

The optimal composition of the control group is, in contrast, a matter of some debate. There is fairly good agreement that the control group should match the patient in age, gender and scores on all tests other than the particular test in question. There is less agreement as to how this matching should be achieved. Shallice (1979), for instance, recommends that matching be carried out with respect to premorbid intellect, while the present author has suggested that this could lead to some very dubious 'matches' (Canavan, 1987), particularly when a patient has undergone gross changes in intellect due to lesioning, or when pre-morbid intellect is unassessed. Consider, for example, the situation in which the patient's pre-morbid scaled scores on each of the performance tests of the WAIS–R are known to have been 15, while after injury these scores fell to 2 on the Block Design test and 10 on all others, with variations of Block Design being considered in the single-case study. The high correlations between these sub-tests in the normal population suggest they hold a lot in common, and if this communality is to be controlled for, then the correct comparison is a control group matched with the patient's current scores on the tests other than Block Design, rather than with pre-morbid scores.

Another problem with respect to finding appropriate controls, and one which is very difficult to overcome, is the question of motivation. For the patient performing the tests, motivation may be either very high, when expectations regarding the usefulness of the procedures in terms of treatment and recovery are high, or very low, when failure experiences and insight regarding the breadth of impairment are increasing. For the controls it is, of course, a completely different matter, particularly if they are performing at ceiling level and becoming rather bored. These differences will especially influence timed tests, and must certainly be taken into account.

Perhaps the best solution of all with regard to the above problems is to try to recruit the spouse and other members of the patient's family and circle of friends as control subjects, since these will be 'naturally' matched and can be persuaded that the testing is of some importance.

EXAMPLES OF SINGLE-CASE STUDIES FROM THE LITERATURE

H.M.

H.M. is probably the best-known and most intensively investigated single case in the literature (e.g. Scoville, 1954; Scoville and Milner, 1957; Corkin, 1965; 1968; Milner, 1965, 1966; Sidman et al., 1968; Milner et al., 1968), and thus only a brief overview of the main findings will be given here. The original publications cited above are recommended for further reading as a prototypical case study.

H.M. suffered a minor head injury accompanied by loss of consciousness at the age of 7. Three years later he developed *petit mal* seizures, and then *grand mal* seizures began at the age of 16. At the age of 27 he underwent bilateral mesial temporal-lobe excision for the relief of his intractable epilepsy: the prepyriform gyrus, uncus, amygdala, hippocampus and hippocampal gyrus were resected bilaterally. The operation resulted in a reduction in seizure frequency and profound anterograde amnesia.

Shortly after the surgery, H.M. had an IQ of 112, but was disoriented, being unable to give either the date or his age. His immediate reproduction of stories and drawings was below average, and it soon became apparent that his memory performance for new material was in fact limited to whatever items he was at that particular moment rehearsing, that is, to the contents of his short-term memory store. In contrast, he could remember the earlier years of his life with some clarity.

H.M. has been so thoroughly tested that it is possible to conclude that the anterograde amnesia was a quite specific deficit. He had no difficulties in sensation, perception, language function or motor ability, although it is true that he had a few fairly basic motivational deficits. For instance, he rarely complained of hunger or thirst, but would eat and drink when the appropriate things were offered to him. He also did not find electric shocks painful, and exhibited almost no electrodermal activity.

Six months after beginning a new job, he was unable to describe his daily duties or the place in which he worked, or how to get there. He also continued to fail to recognise his examiners, although they had been testing him over many years. Some things did, however, appear to register slowly in his long-term memory. In 1968, for instance, he was able to draw a plan of the place in which he had been living for more than eight years. He also seemed to be aware that his father had recently died. It is also of some theoretical importance that he retained the ability to learn new motor skills over a period of days, such as mirror drawing and performance on the pursuit rotor test, even though he would daily deny ever having seen the apparatus before.

Probably the most important aspect of the study of H.M., and the reason why his case is so often cited in the literature, is the combination of a total and specific functional loss with a circumscribed and documented lesion. Such cases are only rarely encountered in the clinic, the rule being that functions are usually lost only to some degree and in an overlapping fashion (e.g. Canavan and Sartory, 1990), and 'naturally occurring' lesions tend not to respect anatomical boundaries and are often difficult to define. This last problem, at least, should be alleviated in the future with the more common use of, for instance, magnetic resonance imaging techniques. Such new technology will probably herald an increase in the application and importance of single-case studies.

K.F.

This patient is often cited as the best example of a double dissociation to H.M., in that it is claimed that he has a specific impairment in auditory verbal short-term memory, with long-term memory intact. That this is actually not the case has been argued before (Allport, 1984; Canavan, 1987) and will be shown again in the following, but the studies performed on K.F. provide an excellent lesson in the application of experimental methodology to the neuropsychological investigation of the single subject that deserves to be treated in detail here.

K.F. suffered a parieto-occipital fracture in a motorcycle accident at the age of 17 years. Warrington and Shallice (1969) first studied him at the age of 28, when an AEG revealed prominent localised dilatation of the left trigone and occipital horn, with some dilatation of the left temporal horn. Upon standard neuropsychological examination, the authors were particularly impressed by the 'disproportionate' impairment of K.F.'s ability to repeat verbal stimuli, as evinced by his score on the Digit Span sub-test of the WAIS. Working on the basis that K.F. displayed a deficit on only the Digit Span task, Warrington and Shallice went on to explore systematically its multiple components, in the following fashion:

1 First, holding constant the WAIS presentation rate of one item per second, they determined K.F's ability to repeat digit-, letter- and word-strings of increasing length. By presenting many different strings of one to four items they were able to show that strings of one item were repeated near perfectly, while strings of four items were hardly ever repeated accurately, with strings of intermediate length showing a gradual decline in performance. Thus, they confirmed by experiment the original observation of impairment on the WAIS Digit Span sub-test, and extended it also to letter span and word span.

2 Next they held the number of items in the strings constant, but varied presentation rate from one item per half second to one item every two seconds, and were able to show that performance improved with slower presentation rates, which allowed greater time for rehearsal and the use of long-term memory.

3 They then examined 'continuous memory span', which simply required that K.F. identify the last item in strings differing in length. He was completely accurate on this task.

4 They then tested K.F.'s ability to match (rather than recall) digit-, letter- and word-strings of length one to four items, at a presentation rate of one item per second. His performance on this task was extremely good, compared to his ability to recall strings of similar length. For instance, he was able to match correctly 17 of the 20 four-item digit-strings. Curiously, Warrington and Shallice concluded: 'Any interpretation of his better performance in matching than in recall must be treated with some caution. A same-difference judgement is easier than an identification judgement and some correction for guessing is necessary' (Warrington and Shallice, 1969: 889). They did not, however, offer a 'guessing correction', and in end effect simply ignored this result, a point which will be returned to below.

5 Warrington and Shallice next demonstrated that K.F. was able to identify individual numbers and letters if he simply had to tap when a key item occurred in a string.

6 Identification of words in a forty-word list by category (e.g. colours, countries or animals) was also found to be near perfect.

7 Performance of the Digit Span test by pointing to numbers on a card was found to be no better than oral recall. It was therefore concluded that his impairment was not due to an expressive dysphasia.

8   Next, K.F. was required to report either the first or the second item in a two-item string, although he was not told which until after the string had been presented. He was poor at this task, but order of item had no effect.

9   A further test involved presenting either three or four items individually, which had to be repeated individually. After the final item K.F. was required to repeat all items in their order of presentation. This manipulation also facilitated his performance, in that he was correct on 13 of the 20 four-item strings of digits.

10 Visual presentation of digits and letters also led to improved performance.

11 Performance with tachistoscopic visual presentation also showed improvement, and thus the facilitation seen in (10) was not due simply to increased presentation time.

12 Long-term learning and memory was shown to be intact on tests of paired associates, incomplete words and pictures, and ten-word lists.

    This systematic variation of the multiple components of the Digit Span test, and expanded use of materials, provides a thorough lesson in how to go about *ad hoc* testing. However, the single-case study would not be complete at this point. Further tests of the experimental hypothesis (that auditory verbal short-term memory is specifically impaired) are now required. Shallice and Warrington (1970) therefore presented five further experiments, these being derived from a consideration of the literature on short-term memory rather than from a consideration of the components of the Digit Span task.

13 First, they determined K.F.'s Serial Position Curve for strings of ten high-frequency words. They found that the recency effect was reduced to one serial position instead of the normal value of about five or six. The recency effect is thought to be subserved by short-term memory, and so the prediction of a reduction in the effect was borne out.

14 In contrast, a modified version of the Peterson–Peterson procedure produced equivocal results. In this task, three three-letter words are spoken at a rate of one per second, and then a delay of from zero to fifteen seconds is imposed, during which a distracter task (counting) is performed. At the end of this period free recall is required. Normal subjects achieve about 95 per cent correct at zero delay, falling to about 25 per cent at the longest delay. K.F. achieved about 50 per cent correct throughout. The results, then, neither supported nor rejected the hypothesis that K.F. should be impaired with increasing delays.

15 The next experiment examined the effect of proactive interference on K.F.'s ability to recall pairs of letters. Ten series, each containing ten pairs of letters, were spoken aloud at a rate of one item per second. The result was that performance declined over the ten serial positions of each series, suggesting that 'in digit span situations, a considerable proportion of K.F.'s retrieval is from LTM' (Shallice and Warrington, 1970: 266), unlike retrieval of normal subjects, whose performances typically show a practice effect by improving over series.

16   A probe task then confirmed that K.F.'s recency effect was limited to one or two items, and also demonstrated that he was able to rehearse these items for up to twenty seconds.

17   A final test involved the 'missing scan' procedure, in which K.F. simply had to report which digit was missing from a limited series. Although he showed a 10–30 per cent superiority for missing scan over recall, this superiority was said not to reach the level shown by normal subjects (25–45 per cent). Shallice and Warrington thus concluded that his defect was not limited to one retrieval method.

This is an outstanding example of a thorough single-case study, but it must be documented here that it was carried out in vain, and that the conclusion drawn by its authors, namely, to have demonstrated a specific deficit in auditory verbal short-term memory, is not warranted. Indeed, a great strength of the studies described above is that they contain enough detail to allow other conclusions. First, the deficit was not consistent. It was more apparent on tests of free recall than on tests of recognition. Performance also improved when items were presented individually for immediate repetition and later serial recall, with visual presentation and with slower verbal presentation. Missing scan performance also showed improvement over standard testing, to this author's mind to within the reported control range, and the probe task showed that K.F. could hold two items in STM for up to twenty seconds. Furthermore, the Peterson–Peterson procedure showed that, under certain circumstances, K.F.'s performance was actually better than that of the controls. All in all, the results suggest that K.F.'s poor performance on the Digit Span test owes more to its language components than to its memory components.

   In fact, the first clue that this might be the case was already present in the very first experiment described above. It was noted there that 'strings of one item were repeated near perfectly'. In other words, K.F. was occasionally unable to repeat even single items. Now, in order to fail to repeat a string of items, it is sufficient simply to fail on one of them. Thus, for K.F., the probability of failing to reproduce a sequence was dependent upon the probability of failing to reproduce the individual items, and this probability increased with every additional item in the list. It is clear that it would not take very many items before K.F. would be completely unable to reproduce the string.

   The exact type of dysphasia from which K.F. suffered remains to date unknown, but Allport (1984) has attributed the Digit Span deficit in such patients to an impairment of phoneme (and word-form) discrimination. Indeed, Warrington and Shallice (1969) themselves should have considered the possibility of a dysphasic impairment, since they noted that K.F. had a performance IQ of 113, but a verbal IQ of only 79. This verbal–performance discrepancy is significant ($p < 0.001$) and occurs in less than 0.1 per cent of the population. Furthermore, K.F.'s Digit Span scaled score was not significantly different from his other verbal scaled scores (Canavan, 1987), indicating that he had severe verbal problems, but not a specific deficit. Added to this, his reading age on Schonell's Graded Word Reading Test fell just below the 9-year level, and in oral and written spelling he attained only the 6-year level. Warrington and Shallice further reported that 'His ability to express himself was halting, and some word-finding difficulty and circumlocutions were noted' (Warrington and Shallice, 1969: 886). They also observed some paraphasic errors, nominal dysphasia and difficulties in carrying out instructions which involved more than a single step. In short, he displayed many language difficulties over and above the impairment in repeating digits, and thus to have regarded this as a specific impairment worthy of special investigation was an extremely poor start to a case study. Nevertheless, the experiments described above remain a model example of single-case methodology in clinical neuropsychology.

L.M.

As a final example of an intensively investigated single case, the study of patient L.M., who suffered a specific loss of visual motion perception due to extrastriate cortical damage (Zihl et al., 1983), is to date the only detailed case of isolated cerebral akinetopsia that has been published, but despite this the findings were immediately accepted by the neurological world (see Zeki, 1991). Apart from the original report, L.M. has been further described by Hess et al. (1989), Baker et al. (1991) and Zihl et al. (1991), and together these studies provide a classical lesson in how a specific deficit may be painstakingly defined in order to reveal the underlying dysfunction.

The first study employed a battery of neuropsychological tests to document L.M.'s poor performance on motion-related visual tasks, and normal performance on other perceptual tasks not involving motion, such as Snellen and vernier acuity, temporal resolution, stereopsis, colour discrimination and saccadic localisation. Later studies used forced-choice discrimination psychophysics and sine-wave grating or random dot stimuli to confirm the specificity of the akinetopsia, but also to show that the dysfunction lay in the judgement of stimulus motion attributes, rather than in reduced sensitivity to moving stimuli. Such studies eventually led to the conclusion that extrastriate cortex (the area damaged bilaterally in patient L.M.) might be particularly involved in the processing of stimuli that suffer from an impoverished signal-to-noise ratio; a further intriguing speculation was that the akinetopsia might have arisen simply from a reduction in the number of neurons carrying directional information, rather than from an all-or-none loss of a discrete brain area or brain function.

In summary, this particular case study followed a course in which an already seemingly specific deficit in motion vision was ever more narrowly defined, with residual function being carefully documented, to the point where the nature of the underlying dysfunction could be clearly formulated. The result therefore not surprisingly took an important place in the neuroscience literature, even though it was based upon only a single case.

CONCLUSION

It is not suggested that single-case studies should replace group studies as the proper method of investigation in clinical neuropsychology. It is suggested, however, that more attention should be given to individual performances, and that even in group studies such data should not be sacrificed in statistical averaging.

Hypotheses worth testing in such studies can be drawn from a number of sources, varying from a consideration of the properties of the test material itself, through speculation about likely effects of the lesion, to simple, even casual observation.

Hopefully, it has been shown in this chapter that a wealth of information may be gleaned from careful single-case studies in clinical neuropsychology, and that the way forward involves little more than the application of experimental methodology and techniques in answering specific questions concerning individual patients.

REFERENCES

Akshoomoff, N. A., Courchesne, E., Press, G. A. and Iragui, V. (1992) 'Contribution of the cerebellum to neuropsychological functioning: Evidence from a case of cerebellar degenerative disorder', *Neuropsychologia* 30: 315–28.
Allport, D. A. (1984) 'Auditory-verbal short-term memory and conduction aphasia', *Attention and Performance* 10: 313–25.
Baker, C. L., Hess, R. F. and Zihl, J. (1991) 'Residual motion perception in a "motion-blind" patient, assessed with limited-lifetime random dot stimuli', *Journal of Neuroscience* 11: 454–61.
Bear, D. M. (1979) 'The temporal lobes: an approach to the study of organic behavioural changes', in M. S. Gazzaniga (ed.) *Handbook of Behavioural Neurobiology, Vol. 2, Neuropsychology*, New York: Plenum Press.
Birbaumer, N., Elbert, T., Canavan, A. G. M. and Rockstroh, B. (1990) 'Slow potentials of the cerebral cortex and behaviour', *Physiological Reviews* 70: 1–41.
Bracke-Tolkmitt, R., Linden, A., Canavan, A. G. M., Rockstroh, B., Scholz, E., Wessel, K. and Diener, H.-C. (1989) 'The cerebellum contributes to mental skills', *Behavioural Neuroscience* 103: 442–6.
Butters, N., Pandya, D., Stein, D. and Rosen, J. (1972) 'A search for the spatial engram within the frontal lobes of monkeys', *Acta Neurobiologia Experimentalis* 32: 305–30.
Canavan, A. G. M. (1987) 'Single-case methodology in neuropsychology', in S. J. E. Lindsay and G. E. Powell (eds) *A Handbook of Clinical Adult Psychology*, Aldershot: Gower.
Canavan, A. G. M. and Sartory, G. (1990) *Klinische Neuropsychologie – Ein Lehrbuch*, Stuttgart: Ferdinand Enke.
Canavan, A. G. M., Janota, I. and Schurr, P. H. (1985) 'Luria's frontal lobe syndrome: Psychological and anatomical considerations', *Journal of Neurology, Neurosurgery and Psychiatry* 48: 1049–53.
Canavan, A. G. M., Passingham, R. E., Marsden, C. D., Quinn, N., Wyke, M. and Polkey, C. E. (1989a) 'The performance on learning tasks of patients in the early stages of Parkinson's disease', *Neuropsychologia* 27: 141–56.
Canavan, A. G. M., Passingham, R. E., Marsden, C. D., Quinn, N., Wyke, M. and Polkey, C. E. (1989b) 'Sequencing ability in Parkinsonians, patients with frontal lobe lesions

and patients who have undergone unilateral temporal lobectomies', *Neuropsychologia* 27: 787–98.

Canavan, A. G. M., Passingham, R. E., Marsden, C. D., Quinn, N., Wyke, M. and Polkey, C. E. (1990) 'Prism adaptation and other tasks involving spatial abilities in patients with Parkinson's disease, patients with frontal lobe lesions and patients with unilateral temporal lobectomies', *Neuropsychologia* 28: 969–84.

Chow, K. L. and Survis, J. (1958) 'Retention of overlearned visual habit after temporal cortical ablation in the monkey', *Archives of Neurology and Psychiatry* 79: 640–6.

Corkin, S. (1965) 'Tactually-guided maze learning in man: Effects of unilateral excisions and bilateral hippocampal lesions', *Neuropsychologia* 3: 338–51.

Corkin, S. (1968) 'Acquisition of a motor skill after bilateral medial temporal-lobe excision', *Neuropsychologia* 6: 255–65.

Cowey, A. and Stoerig, P. (1991) 'Neurobiology of blindsight', *Trends in the Neurosciences* 14: 140–5.

De Bleser, R. (1987) 'From agrammatism to paragrammatism. German aphasiological traditions and grammatical disturbances', *Cognitive Neuropsychology* 4: 187–256.

Desimone, R., Schein, S. J., Moran, J. and Ungerleider, L. G. (1985) 'Contour, colour and shape analysis beyond the striate cortex', *Vision Research* 25: 441–52.

Flor-Henry, P. (1969) 'Psychosis and temporal lobe epilepsy: a controlled investigation', *Epilepsia* 10: 363–95.

Flor-Henry, P. (1972) 'Ictal and interictal psychiatric manifestations in epilepsy: specific or non-specific?' *Epilepsia* 13: 773–83.

Friston, K. J., Liddle, P. F., Frith, C. D., Hirsch, S. R. and Frackowiak, R. S. J. (1992) 'The left medial temporal region and schizophrenia. A PET study', *Brain* 115: 367–82.

Geschwind, N. (1974) 'Late changes in the nervous system: an overview', in D. G. Stein, J. J. Rosen and N. Butters (eds) *Plasticity and Recovery of Function in the Central Nervous System*, New York: Academic Press.

Goldman, P. S. (1971) 'Functional development of the prefrontal cortex in early life and the problem of neuronal plasticity', *Experimental Neurology* 32: 366–87.

Goldman, P. S. (1974) 'An alternative to developmental plasticity: Heterology of CNS structures in infants and adults', in D. G. Stein, J. J. Rosen and N. Butters (eds) *Plasticity and Recovery of Function in the Central Nervous System*, New York: Academic Press.

Goldman, P. S. (1976) 'Maturation of the mammalian nervous system and the ontogeny of behaviour', in J. S. Rosenblatt, R. A. Hinde, E. Shaw and C. Beer (eds) *Advances in the Study of Behaviour, Vol. 7*, New York: Academic Press.

Goldstein, L. H., Canavan, A. G. M. and Polkey, C. E. (1988) 'Verbal and abstract designs paired associate learning after unilateral temporal lobectomy', *Cortex* 24: 41–52.

Goldstein, L. H., Canavan, A. G. M. and Polkey, C. E. (1989) 'Cognitive mapping after unilateral temporal lobectomy', *Neuropsychologia* 27: 167–77.

Goodglass, H. and Kaplan, D. (1972) *The Assessment of Aphasia and Related Disorders*, Philadelphia: Lea and Febiger.

Halligan, P. W. and Marshall, J. C. (1991) 'Left neglect for near but not far space in man', *Nature* 350: 498–500.

Hamlin, R. M. (1970) 'Intellectual functions fourteen years after frontal lobe surgery', *Cortex* 6: 299–307.

Hess, R. F., Baker, C. L. and Zihl (1989) 'The "motion blind" patient: Low-level spatial and temporal filters', *Journal of Neuroscience* 9: 1628–40.

Heywood, C. A. and Canavan, A. G. M. (1987) 'Developmental neuropsychological correlates of language', in W. Yule and M. Rutter (eds) *Language Development and Disorders*, Oxford: Blackwell.

Heywood, C. A. and Cowey, A. (1987) 'On the role of cortical area V4 in the discrimination of hue and pattern in macaque monkeys', *Journal of Neuroscience* 7: 2601–17.

Heywood, C. A., Wilson, B. and Cowey, A. (1987) 'A case study of cortical colour 'blindness' with relatively intact achromatic discrimination', *Journal of Neurology, Neurosurgery and Psychiatry* 50: 22–9.

Kolb, B. and Whishaw, I. Q (1980) *Fundamentals of Human Neuropsychology*, San Francisco: Freeman.

Lees, A. J. and Smith, E. (1983) 'Cognitive deficits in the early stages of Parkinson's disease', *Brain* 106: 257–70.

Linden, A., Bracke-Tolkmitt, R., Lutzenberger, W., Canavan, A. G. M., Scholz, E., Diener, H. C. and Birbaumer, N. (1990) 'Slow cortical potentials in Parkinsonian patients during the course of an associative learning test', *Journal of Psychophysiology* 4: 145–62.

Luria, A. R. (1968) *Mind of a Mnemonist*, New York: Basic Books.

Marshall, J. C. and Halligan, P. W. (1991) 'Reply', *Nature* 352: 673–4.

Mattingley, J. B. and Bradshaw, J. L. (1991) 'Spatial maps', *Nature* 352: 673.

Mazzochi, F. and Vignolo, L. A. (1979) 'Localisation of lesions in aphasia: clinical-CT scan correlations in stroke patients', *Cortex* 15: 627–54.

Meyer, V. and Yates, A. J. (1955) 'Intellectual changes following temporal lobectomy for psychomotor epilepsy', *Journal of Neurology, Neurosurgery and Psychiatry* 18: 44–52.

Milner, B. (1965) 'Visually-guided maze learning in man: Effects of bilateral hippo-campal, bilateral frontal and unilateral cerebral lesions', *Neuropsychologia* 3: 317–38.

Milner, B. (1966) 'Amnesia following operation on the temporal lobes', in C. W. M. Whitty and O. L. Zangwill (eds) *Amnesia*, London: Butterworths.

Milner, B., Corkin, S. and Teuber, H. L. (1968) 'Further analysis of the hippocampal amnesic syndrome: 14-year follow-up study of H.M.', *Neuropsychologia* 6: 215–34.

Mohr, J. P. (1976) 'Rapid amelioration of motor aphasia', *Archives of Neurology* 28: 77–82.

Newcombe, F. (1969) *Missile Wounds of the Brain. A Study of Psychological Deficits*, Oxford: Oxford University Press.

Newlin, D. B., Carpenter, B. and Golden, C. J. (1981) 'Hemispheric asymmetries in schizophrenia', *Biological Psychiatry* 16: 561–82.

Niebergall, G., Remschmidt, H. and Lingelbach, B. (1976) 'Neuropsychologische Untersuchungen zur Rückbildung traumatisch verursachter Aphasie bei Kindern und Jugendlichen', *Zeitschrift für Klinische Psychologie* 5: 194–209.

Orbach, J. and Fantz, R. L. (1958) 'Differential effects of temporal neo-cortical resections on overtrained and non-overtrained visual habits in monkeys', *Journal of Comparative and Physiological Psychology* 51: 126–9.

Ottosson, D. and Rostene, W. (1989) *Visualisation of Brain Function*, New York: Stockton Press.

Pfurtscheller, G. and Lopes da Silva, F. H. (1988) *Functional Brain Imaging*, Bern: Huber.

Powell, G. E., Polkey, C. E. and Canavan, A. G. M. (1987) 'Lateralisation of memory functions in epileptic patients by use of the sodium amytal (Wada) technique', *Journal of Neurology, Neurosurgery and Psychiatry* 50: 665–72.

Rockstroh, B., Elbert, T., Canavan, A. G. M., Lutzenberger, W. and Birbaumer, N. (1989) *Slow Cortical Potentials and Behaviour, 2nd edn*, Munich: Urban and Schwarzenberg.

Rolls, E. T., Thorpe, S. J., Maddison, S., Roper-Hall, A., Puerto, A. and Perrett, D. (1979) 'Activity of neurons in the neostriatum and related structures in the alert animal', in I. Divac and R. G. E. Oberg (eds) *The Neostriatum*, Oxford: Pergamon Press.

Rolls, E. T., Thorpe, S. J., Boytim, M., Szabo, I. and Perrett, D. (1984) 'Responses of striatal neurons in the behaving monkey. 3. Effects of iontophoretically applied dopamine on normal rsponsiveness', *Neuroscience* 12: 1201–12.

Rosenkilde, C. E. (1979) 'Functional heterogeneity of the prefrontal cortex in the monkey: a review', *Behavioural and Neural Biology* 25: 301–45.

Sacks, O. (1985) *The Man Who Mistook His Wife for a Hat*, London: Duckworth.

Scott, C. and Byng, S. (1989) 'Computer-assisted remediation of a homophone comprehension disorder in surface dyslexia', *Aphasiology* 3: 301–20.

Scoville, W. B. (1954) 'The limbic lobe in man', *Journal of Neurosurgery* 11: 64–6.

Scoville, W. B. and Milner, B. (1957) 'Loss of recent memory after bilateral hippocampal lesions', *Journal of Neurology, Neurosurgery and Psychiatry* 20: 301–45.

Shallice, T. (1979) 'Case study approach in neuropsychological research', *Journal of Clinical Neuropsychology* 1: 183–211.

Shallice, T. (1982) 'Specific impairments of planning', *Philosophical Transactions of the Royal Society, London* B 298: 199–209.

Shallice, T. (1988) *From Neuropsychology to Mental Structure*, Cambridge: Cambridge University Press.

Shallice, T. and Warrington, E. K. (1970) 'Independent functioning of verbal memory stores: a neuropsychological study', *Quarterly Journal of Experimental Psychology* 22: 261–73.

Sidman, M., Stoddard, L. T. and Mohr, J. P. (1968) 'Some additional quantitative observations of immediate memory in a patient with bilateral hippocampal lesions', *Neuropsychologia* 6: 245–54.

Teuber, H. L. (1975) 'Recovery of function after brain injury in man', in *Ciba Foundation Symposium 34*, Amsterdam: Elsevier.

Warrington, E. K. and Shallice, T. (1969) 'The selective impairment of auditory verbal short-term memory', *Brain* 92: 885–96.

Weinberger, D. R., Berman, K. F. and Zee, R. F. (1986) 'Physiologic dysfunction of dorsolateral prefrontal cortex in schizophrenia', *Archives of General Psychiatry* 43: 114–24.

Weinberger, D. R., Berman, K. F. and Illowsky, B. P. (1988) 'Physiological dysfunction of dorsolateral prefrontal cortex in schizophrenia', *Archives of General Psychiatry* 45: 609–15.

Weiskrantz, L. (1986) *Blindsight. A Case Study and Implications*, Oxford: Oxford University Press.

Weiskrantz, L., Warrington, E. K., Sanders, M. D. and Marshall, J. (1974) 'Visual capacity in the hemianopic field following a restricted occipital ablation', *Brain* 97: 709–28.

Woods, B. T. and Teuber, H. L. (1973) 'Early onset of complementary specialisation of cerebral hemispheres in man', *Transactions of the American Neurological Association* 198: 113–17.

Zeki, S. (1991) 'Cerebral akinetopsia (visual motion blindness) A review', *Brain* 114: 811–24.

Zihl, J., von Cramon, D. and Mai, N. (1983) 'Selective disturbance of movement vision after bilateral brain damage', *Brain* 106: 313–40.

Zihl, J., von Cramon, D., Mai, N. and Schmid, C. (1991) Disturbance of movement vision after bilateral posterior brain damage. Further evidence and follow-up observations', *Brain* 114: 2235–52.

Chapter 40

Professional issues in the 1990s and beyond

New demands, new skills

Catherine Dooley

INTRODUCTION: WHAT ARE PROFESSIONAL ISSUES?

What is meant by professional issues? What does the term encompass as subject matter? This needs to be clarified before those issues which relate to adult clinical psychology can be adequately explored.

The definition of a 'profession'

In the present day the word 'professional' is used very broadly, tending to refer to anyone who is reliable and trustworthy. However there are clear distinctions in terms of expertise, authority, social importance, autonomy and self-regulation, commitment and reward (Windt *et al.* 1991) which identify the 'true' professional.

There is general agreement that the recognition of professions came originally from the three paradigm professions of medicine, law and the clergy. The later professions have followed a similar process of specialisation through the development of technical skills and expertise; however, to be granted professional status requires significant additional steps – the expertise must be unique to the profession; there must be formal training; and there must be clear standards of conduct by which the public are protected.

To quote from Dyer:

> To simplify, we may say that a profession may be defined by:
> (a) its knowledge, techniques and expertise;
> or
> (b) its ethics and values.
>
> (Dyer, 1991: 69)

Dyer considered that training was the means by which expertise and standards were developed and maintained rather than a separate factor; this assumption will be followed throughout this chapter.

The remit of professional issues

The work done on revising the examinations for the Diploma in Clinical Psychology of the British Psychological Society (Powell *et al.* 1993) entailed reviewing and categorising the curriculum that related to professional issues. Three main areas were identified to categorise the particular items which would be included in the curriculum:

- The profession and its context
- Personal and professional practise
- Ethical issues

In contrast to the earlier definition of a profession, when considering what 'professional issues' in the 1990s and beyond encompass, it was evident that the organisational context within which clinical psychologists work could not be excluded. A competent psychologist would need to understand the role and function of the National Health Service, social services, private and voluntary agencies, the legal domain, etc.

Professional issues for clinical psychology

It is important to consider why the definition of a profession essentially concentrates on the internal working of the profession, yet the field of professional issues incorporates the external world in which the professional operates and to which he or she relates. The answer is that all the original professionals and many of the later ones were self-employed and thus were not required, in quite the same way, to take into account society's perspective. In fact, one opinion is that a true profession cannot be salaried as it dilutes the main allegiance to the client (Toren, 1972).

It is proposed that it is exactly this shift in the position of professions which accounts for those professional issues with which clinical psychologists are at present wrestling; that – in common with many other professions within and outside the health services – clinical psychology is in transition from being an essentially self-defined and internally monitored profession to one which is required to market its skills in relation to the demand and requirements of outsiders and account publicly for the work that is done.

The rest of the chapter will develop this theme in relation to both the current preoccupations of the profession and the changing environment to which it relates. Some core themes will be identified and possible directions for action suggested.

CONTEMPORARY ISSUES IN CLINICAL PSYCHOLOGY

Internal dilemmas for the profession

New areas of work

The first and most striking feature within the field of adult psychology work is the increased demand for psychology services in many new areas of work. In recent years new disorders have appeared, such as AIDS/HIV; problems have been identified as requiring specialist intervention – for instance, to remedy the effects in adulthood of child sexual abuse (Cahill *et al.* 1991). In addition, new areas of application have developed, as, for instance, in primary health care and health psychology.

Options for psychology work are vast; resources are extremely limited. The MPAG report commissioned by the Department of Health to review clinical psychology services in the UK (Manpower Planning and Advisory Group, 1990) looked at the number of clinical psychologists (in all specialities); 25 per cent of districts had four or fewer staff; 50 per cent had seven or fewer; 75 per cent had eleven or fewer. This showed that the notion of the range of specialities first outlined in 1977 (Trethowan, 1977) and refined and extended by the Management Advisory Services Report (1989) is impractical in any but a small minority of district departments as presently constituted.

Waiting-lists

The result can be long waiting-lists, with many clients waiting months: 44.2 per cent of referrals are to departments where it may take over six months, and 15 per cent where it may take over a year, to be seen (Division News, 1993). A number of imaginative proposals for dealing with this problem have been suggested. These include group therapy, pre-therapy screening for individuals and groups, quota systems for referrals, the use of models of brief therapy and a *laissez-faire* policy to stimulate additional resources (summarised in Seager and Jacobson, 1993). White (1992) describes the use of local presentations and public lectures to promote psychological health.

The 'two-plus-one' model has been best developed and claims to be derived from research on those aspects of the therapeutic process which enhance the potency of brief therapy (Barkham and Shapiro, 1989). It has been criticised (Seager and Jacobson, 1993) as being a model of service delivery with the rationale of saving resources, rather than a model of therapy with the aim of enhancing benefit. However, it has to be recognised that better management of waiting-lists is at best a palliative for an underlying problem and a more long-term solution is required.

Recruitment difficulties

In addition, the recruitment problems which previously were specific to services such as substance abuse, forensic services and services to older people, where vacancy rates of 20–30 per cent (Manpower Planning and Advisory Group, 1990) were not uncommon, are now beginning to extend to the general adult speciality. The MPAG figures give a 17 per cent vacancy rate for adult mental health based on 1989 data (ibid. 49, Table 3), and more recent local surveys indicate that this is now rising. Psychologists in the less popular specialities, where psychology resources have always been limited, have dealt with chronic manpower problems and instability in staffing levels by providing clinical psychology expertise and services in indirect ways: through consultancy, staff training and service development work (Kat, 1991).

Psychologists who work with adult clients may now need to consider a shift in their way of working if they wish to maintain their involvement in a wide range of clinical specialities without being swamped by client referrals. There is a feeling that there is resistance to such a major shift in work which will be discussed later. However, the obvious answer to these difficulties is to increase the numbers of new entrants to the profession in the UK by increasing training places.

Limitations on training

Whilst the MPAG report identified the need to do so, its publication unfortunately was overtaken by events in relation to the 1991 NHS reforms. The interpretation of Working Paper 10 (Department of Health, 1989) removed any mechanism for central planning to increase training places; training is now explicitly a regional commitment and linked directly to projected manpower requirements (Richardson, 1992).

Thus, direct and indirect employers of clinical psychologists are the people who will determine the numbers entering the profession for the immediate future, and so they need to be able to make a clear and unequivocal case for employing clinical psychologists.

Community work and teams

There has also been a shift away from the traditional methods of delivery of psychology services in out-patient clinics or central psychology departments, where the client comes to see the psychologist with a defined need and receives direct and individual treatment for a finite period. The community care initiatives of the 1980s have moved more psychologists into community settings, often as part of community mental health teams. This has implications for the model of working and the means by which psychological health can be enhanced (Bender, 1976), most of which would be fully compatible with the aims and principles of clinical psychologists.

However, there is considerable concern about the method of delivery, specifically about the efficacy and efficiency of team work. Trepka and Marsh (1990) identify concerns for clinical psychologists which relate to role security – legitimacy, differentiation and status for the expertise of clinical psychologists. Pilgrim and Treacher (1992) saw this occurring partly because in community settings role-blurring and genericism rather than specialism has begun to characterise practice; they felt that psychologists were vulnerable given their lack of any statutory powers in comparison with other professionsals, such as doctors, nurses and social workers.

Competition

At a time when there is increased evidence for the value of clinical psychology expertise and therapeutic interventions, as described specifically in the research literature and addressed generally in Watts (1990), the profession of clinical psychology might feel that it can begin to relax in the confidence of its efficacy. Yet, at the same time, one finds a burgeoning of other therapists, any of whom claim similar levels of expertise. Psychiatric nurses may offer what appears superficially to be very much the same range of therapies as a psychology department; counselling psychology may or may not subsume the range of work of clinical psychologists, depending on which viewpoint one accepts; accordingly, a separate profession of health psychologists is proposed (Bennet and Wright, 1992).

The core function of the profession

These various elements do not make the profession confident about its expertise and role. This is not new, as Pilgrim and Treacher (1992) illustrate in their review of the history of the profession. In the MAS report (1989), Mowbray recommended that the profession worked on clarifying its core expertise; in response, the BPS's Division of Clinical Psychology has recently produced a statement *Core Purpose and Philosophy of the Profession,* (BPS/DCP, 1992) and the current analysis by the National Council for Vocational Qualifications in conjunction with the BPS may also clarify this.

The changing context to the work of clinical psychology

The NHS has never been in a settled state since its inception, but on the whole the regular changes within the health services have been largely aimed at the way that services were organised or the way that services were delivered. The 1991 reforms, however, were aimed at the very structure of the NHS itself, introducing features from the workings of the private sector into a public service. The full effects of this restructuring are not yet clear, and are unlikely to be so in the immediate future.

One thing is, however, evident: the way that psychology services are organised internally and in relation to their districts will become increasingly varied; the types of clinical psychology services will become much more individualised depending on the local situation.

Because of these two factors – the reforms not being fully implemented and psychology services probably becoming much more varied – it seems more appropriate to draw out the political and philosophical themes that underlie these changes and to illustrate the impact that they will have on psychology services. It should be clear from what follows that, on the whole, the major changes are likely to be permanent, as they appear to reflect a redefinition of both the purpose of the NHS and the means by which resources will be allocated.

The purchaser/provider split

The first, and obviously the most fundamental, change is that at the core of the 1991 reforms – the purchaser/provider split within the Health Service, so that DHAs now purchase health provision from provider units. This has resulted in a number of options for the organisation of psychology departments (within trusts; within directly managed units; as clinical directorates independent of, or combined with, other professions; as trading agencies). It opens up opportunities for clinical psychologists to sell services outside their main employers – to social services, to private health users, or even to industry.

Decentralisation

Initially the main purchaser was the District Health Authority, who would determine the health needs within a district and subsequently contract with hospital trusts and directly managed units for the provision of such services. However, the introduction of fundholding general practices, originally piloted in very limited ways, has now accelerated (Department of Health, 1992b), with the underlying implication that the government wishes to shift decisions about the use of resources away from districts down to the primary health level. Increasingly, therefore, departments are contracting to provide psychology services specifically for general practitioners who directly purchase such services and have very precise and clear demands.

There are both difficulties and opportunities from this aspect of the reforms; however, the immediate consequences are that departments now have more formal contracts with purchasers of service, closer monitoring of the provision of service, and are open to competition potentially from other psychology departments and certainly from other therapists who can offer a similar clinical service.

Marketing

A helpful way of considering the implications for therapy services is to consider the notion of 'marketing'. This approach does not imply that services should be planned and delivered solely on the basis of cost to the detriment of quality, or the commercialisation of services through slick, glossy images.

Technically, marketing requires research – looking for the appropriate 'market segments', finding out what are the priorities and wants of potential customers, and considering means and methods of responding to them. It entails communication and negotiation as the potential provider helps the purchaser to recognise options and approaches which will meet their needs. Above all, it requires that the 'customers' are taken seriously, whether or not one agrees with their priorities – a considerable shift for all professionals.

The implications are that if general practitioners wish for locally based services with high patient activity and turnover, clinical psychologists need to address this in the services they offer. If mental health services managers wish psychologists to work with long-stay patients on the acute admissions wards, the departments need to be able to respond. The different requirements of these two different purchasers would be reflected in very different contracts – one likely to be based more on direct client contact and volume of work, the latter likely to focus more on indirect contacts, staff supervision and training, and team work.

This change does not rule out professional standards and advice on the most appropriate services: obviously departments can decline to tender for work that they feel is misdirected. However, the customer has the option of looking elsewhere.

One can see from the examples given in the preceding paragraph how much more diversified psychology services are becoming. Psychologists will be required to work in different contexts in different ways depending on the local contract.

Accountability

It follows from this that all NHS work is more accountable, accessible to external scrutiny and thus open to criticism in a way that was never previously encountered.

The origins of this stem from the need to monitor the use of resources within the NHS. The NHS as a whole is one of the biggest bureaucracies within Europe and one of the largest employers in the world; the history of the NHS is largely the history of attempts to control and manage its vast resources in a way that makes best provision for the health care of the nation.

Thus originated the requirements that are now familiar to all psychologists: Körner returns to describe and quantify the work that psychologists perform; quality strategies, which require a clarification of the purpose, structure and delivery of clinical psychology services; clinical audit – a mechanism to allow review and analysis of the processes in the delivery of client services . . . Do they make a difference? Are they worth the effort? Is the information meaningful and relevant?

The development of service specifications within the formal contracts now required also formalise the amount of work (e.g. sessions per week), the type of work undertaken (direct and indirect client work etc.), and outcome measures, such as number of new referrals, volume of treatment sessions, etc. Although in many respects this is to be welcomed, as it will result in the provision of a clearer and more efficient service, there is also considerable concern that the loss of professional autonomy may reduce the efficacy of work if purchasers insist on a style of provision which is inappropriate. However, at least this is now being formally addressed for all professions in a systematic and comprehensive way which allows dialogue about assumptions, priorities and methods to take place; recent developments within the profession in this area will be described later.

The purpose of health care

There is a more fundamental shift, however, which is to do with the assumptions and purpose of health service provision, both in the UK and within the western world.

In the 1970s disillusion grew with the present form of services (Klein, 1983); namely, disillusion with the capacity of (medical) science to deliver technical solutions to prevent illness or cure disease. There is now increased interest, not only in preventative work, but in approaching health services in a more strategic way. This is epitomised with the recent publication of *The Health of the Nation* (Department of Health, 1992c), which sets out clear goals to reduce the incidence and prevalence of a wide range of physical disorders and – in a rather disappointing way (BPS, 1992) – certain mental health problems.

The revolt against professionalism

This has substantial implications for the status and practice of professional skills. Klein (1983) tracks the political shifts within the NHS and identifies two relevant trends since the 1970s – the revolt against the values of expertise and the increased interest in participatory democracy. Pilgrim and Treacher (1992) also refer to these trends which are primarily orientated at medical and nursing professions but which also sweep along the many other professions in their wake. The effects of such a change, which is manifest in such legislation as the Access to Information Act (1991), are that professions cannot claim the mystical power of technical (and esoteric) skill as the basis of their status but need to present their expertise in a way which is clearly relevant and meaningful to the consumers and users. They must be prepared to be called to account in the public arena for their professional decisions and actions.

Models of service provision

The changing demands on professionals will be discussed in further detail below, but first it seems useful to explore the shift in assumptions about health- care services that underlie the strategy. This has been conceptualised by Stacey (1977) as described in Ham (1993) as follows:

The model of service provision can be seen to be based on three opposing perspectives:

– Orientated towards the individual vs. collective health

- Focusing on functional fitness vs. welfare
- Curative in intent vs. preventative

Ham's contention is that the NHS was established and run with a curative purpose, focusing on the functional fitness of individuals, and that it is now shifting to an orientation which looks at maintaining and developing the collective well-being of the whole population, with an increased emphasis on prevention.

While the writing tends to use medical terminology, one can see that a similar shift is applicable within mental health services – and thus relates to adult clinical psychology.

One of the most important issues which comes out of this shift of emphasis is the current priority placed on equality of access to health services across all social groups and ethnic and cultural minorities. Mental health services have been criticised, particularly for their poor provision for women (*Clinical Psychology Forum*, 1989) and ethnic minorities (Littlewood, 1990; Rack, 1991), a criticism which is not just based on referral patterns and uptake of services but runs to the way that diagnosis reflects cultural and sexual stereotypes. This has been examined within clinical psychology services, where a survey of district departments (Goodwin and Power, 1986) reported a number of reasons for the difficulties in providing a service for clients from minority ethnic groups, such as language difficulties. Alladin (1986) felt that there were more fundamental issues, citing *inter alia* the models of clinical practice used and the relationship of ethnicity to psychological health needs.

WHERE DOES CLINICAL PSYCHOLOGY GO FROM HERE?

Although at one level clinical psychologists might feel quite comfortable with recent developments, since the profession would welcome such shifts in philosophy, it seems that they may still need to examine the values and assumptions underlying their work at a fundamental level to effect a structural change to the delivery of psychology services.

In order to emphasise this, a quotation – at length – will be given from David Hawks's introductory chapter to McPherson and Sutton's book *Reconstructing Psychological Practice* (1981).

Conclusions

It has been argued in this chapter that the relative scarcity of clinical psychologists is only a problem when clinical psychological practice is construed as providing a one-to-one therapeutic relationship. If it is accepted that clinical psychologists can never provide such a service, and it is questionable as to whether they should even attempt it, and instead of demanding more and more clinical psychologists, consideration is given to redefining the clinical task, radical implications for the individual and corporate practice of clinical psychology emerge.

Individual patients, if seen, should be seen in order that diagnostic and therapeutic skills can be developed with a view to giving them away and in order to reveal the working of more general principles of psychopathology. To continue to see individual patients exclusively, however, is not only to perpetuate a discriminatory activity, it is clearly impracticable given the prevalence of psychological disorder.

Nor is it only individual clinical psychological practice which warrants examination in the light of these premises. Much corporate clinical psychological practice appears not to reflect any consideration of priorities, whether of needs or of competence, but rather reflects the expectations of other professions and the idiosyncratic preferences of clinical psychologists . . . What would seem called for is much more corporate consideration of objectives, more concentration of scarce resources, offering the prospect of at least modest success.

(Hawks, 1981: 21)

Written in 1981, this predates most of the major changes within the NHS that have been catalogued, and yet it is probably as true today as ten years ago, particularly in the field of adult clinical psychology.

That is not to say that changes have not happened, nor that there are not many examples of good practice which demonstrate innovative and beneficial ways of providing effective services. However, it does seem that the profession has not fully integrated the changes into its core models of working and its practice skills; the contention of the remainder of this chapter is that there are integral blocks to this reconstitution, which, until resolved, will frustrate attempts to make radical amendments to the function of adult clinical psychology. In order to examine this, it is necessary to return to the two criteria for a profession.

Core expertise – a need to broaden and deepen

Hawks (1981), quoted above, referred to the way in which clinical psychology practice is construed as based on the provision of the one-to-one therapeutic relationship. This has always been much more the tradition within adult mental health work than in other fields, such as learning difficulties or even child work, where for various reasons psychologists have worked indirectly with carers. In a recent survey of all DCP members (presumably across all specialities), Norcross et al. (1992) found that only 6 per cent of psychologists had an overtly non-individual orientation (family/systems); in addition, using the figures they present, it appears that while psychologists do undertake group, couples and family therapy, this combined figure represents 26 per cent of time in comparison to the 74 per cent given to individual therapy.

There are a number of roots of such an emphasis. First, it represents the application of the model described above in relation to western medicine as a whole until recent years. In common with other professions in health services, clinical psychology has adopted the individually orientated curative approach by means of helping the client alter his or her dysfunctional beliefs and behaviours.

Second, there is considerable evidence to demonstrate that psychological therapy relates to and reflects the cultural assumptions of a particular society. Models of therapy that are commonly in use in western cultures all tend to focus on the individual's need to self-actualise and his or her right to utilise experiences in his or her own way and to discover his or her own meaning through this. Ho (1985) argued that there are ideological biases which underlie clinical psychology in the West which can be traced at least partly to the cult of individualism. The western perspective might be contrasted with individual therapy in Japan, where the aim is very different: the minimisation of self and the maximisation of others is the primary focus; effective functioning is not through self-development but through the maintenance of harmonious relationships based on the acceptance of obligation to others (Noon and Lewis, 1992).

Third, one other strand comes from the historical roots within psychology. Pilgrim and Treacher chart the development of clinical psychology and identify the dominance of empiricism, which prioritises methodology over theory and led to an aversion to theoretical systems building (Pilgrim and Treacher, 1992: 32–3). Later in the book they also highlight the way that experimental psychology has profoundly influenced the development of the profession rather than areas such as social psychology, which would have produced a very different type of clinical psychologist (ibid.: 130).

The truth of the matter is that the majority of trainees enter – and leave – clinical psychology training motivated to work with individual patients and gaining their reinforcement as clinicians in doing such work. However, the dilemma is that, once established in clinical practice, it is evident that it is impossible to reach the number of clients who might benefit from individual therapy. As Hawks (1981) saw it, the individual practitioners respond by either denial, over-simplification, or escape from the profession.

The very supremacy of the model of individual work means that other forms of therapy can seem to be inevitably second best; if one cannot 'cure' the patient, then one 'manages' their symptoms or behaviour, or improves their 'quality of life'. John Hall, in the introduction to his article 'Towards a psychology of caring' (Hall, 1990), examines reasons why psychologists should develop a psychological perspective on caring. He identifies a number of factors – for example, that positive treatment or intervention may not work, that a preoccupation with treatment may not be appropriate – suggesting an alternative 'ameliorative' or 'rehabilitative' model which concentrates on reducing the impact of symptoms rather than trying to tackle the symptoms direct (Miller et al., 1987).

However, integrative models which can combine the intra-psychic phenomena of the individual within their social system are still in their infancy; in particular, their applicability for the adult client tends to be either when all else fails, or in a compartmentalised fashion. This is particularly true if one considers the way in which family therapy/systemic work is seen: in child services, it is a core intervention; in work with older adults and in rehabilitation, it has a clear role. In normal adult psychology work, it is generally unusual and tends to be used for clients for whom individual work seems unlikely to be effective or for whom it has already failed.

It seems unlikely that the conflicts and dilemmas identified earlier will be resolved unless the supremacy of individual client work is challenged, not just at the practitioner level – which is fully recognised as inevitable – but also at a theoretical level, so that psychologists working within the adult sphere have a satisfying alternative which assists them in making rational judgements about the most appropriate method of delivering services.

In considering the ideas presented in different contexts, it can be seen that there are common themes. Parry (1990), cited by Pilgrim and Treacher, writes:

> Our strength, which we have got to get across, is that we are special because we combine knowledge of a wider client group, with knowledge about clinical skills with knowledge about psychological theories. Other professions may be skilled in one of these three areas, but only clinical psychologists can combine all three.

> (Pilgrim and Treacher, 1992: 159)

The BPS/DCP publication *Core Purpose and Philosophy of the Profession* stated that the profession:

> draws on a broad range of theories and approaches which reflect the multi-dimensional nature of personal experience and the influences upon it. For example, these may include psychological knowledge of the way biological factors, relationships, groups, organisations and society can interact and cause distress or enhance personal fulfilment.

> (BPS/DCP, 1992)

Their description of the range of work seems to indicate that there might be a limited group of clients who require detailed and intensive intervention by a clinical psychologist, whilst others require a psychologist to plan and support others in the use of psychological approaches.

To summarise, it seems that to function effectively and efficiently in the health services in the 1990s and – really more importantly – to have a sense of pride and satisfaction in the meaning and value of their work, psychologists working in the adult speciality need to reverse their priorities. Instead of maintaining their core identity as clinicians working with the individual client and then moving away from this model in the face of workplace realities, they need to start with the MAS model – that their core skill and identity is through their breadth of knowledge of theory and application of psychology; on the basis of this model, they must then identify those particular client groups that specifically need the individual attention of a clinical psychologist to alleviate their distress or disability.

Such a shift in approach has implications for training, both at a clinical skills level and in terms of the academic curriculum required to support such work; it can be questioned – as the MAS report does – whether one can train psychologists direct for Level 3 work or whether it comes through progression from more direct clinical roles; nevertheless, training would be geared towards increased emphasis on first principles and theory underlying clinical practice and there would need to be a greater focus on the methodology or application of such principles. Clinical development would focus less on the one-to-one client skills but balance this against training in group, family and systemic work; teaching and training skills would have greater importance.

In many respects what has been described is merely a shift in perspective and might seem straightforward to implement; however, the next section will examine potential barriers to such a shift and consider what methods are available to assist in the choice of priorities.

Ethics and values – the need to revise and extend

Ethical codes

One of the core dimensions of a profession is that it sets and monitors its own standards of conduct; for most professions this is epitomised by an ethical code, or code of conduct. This can be used in order to deal with unprofessional conduct or incompetent practice, either directly or in conjunction with the employing body. The BPS incorporated a code of conduct for clinical psychologists as part of the Royal Charter and uses this in relation to disciplinary procedures.

The code of conduct for clinical psychologists, in common with the majority of similar codes or guidelines, focuses essentially on the clinician's relationship and conduct with the individual client – dealing with issues of confidentiality, consent, and so on.

The basis of such codes comes from the tradition – as noted in the introduction – for earlier professions to be self-employed, so that the professional had a direct relationship with the client; the client – as a free agent – could decide which professional to use; the codes were designed to protect clients, once they had engaged professional services, from exploitation or mismanagement of their affairs. Such codes of conduct are to be welcomed and obviously still underlie all client work. They lay down the parameters within which the professionals can use their clinical judgement in order to plan the right treatment for the individual client. The basis of client work is the allegiance to the client, and ethical guidelines encode this. Psychologists have a duty to give the best service possible to the client (the duty of beneficence; Hare, 1991).

However, one needs to ask: who is 'the client?' Is it only those people actually seen and taken on for therapy; is it also those people who might or might not be referred, depending on the decision of, say, a psychiatrist? Or is it wider still, encompassing those people within the population who might benefit in some way directly or indirectly from the work of a clinical psychologist? In essence, what is being said is that psychologists – in common with many other professionals – need to recognise that they continually make covert decisions about resource allocation throughout their daily lives; however, this is often implicit and intuitively based, and so may not be fully identified as such.

Newman and Howard (1986) state that 'the most pervasive myth within the clinical community is that costs are the business of business and not a clinical concern'. Ham (1993) saw this as a feature of many professions within the health service, although focusing mainly on the medical profession, given its key role in the use of resources within the health service. In the 1980s and 1990s, doctors have been under increasing pressure to become involved in formal resource allocation through taking on posts such as clinical directors; some have adopted their new role with enthusiasm, others feel it is a fundamental betrayal of the clinical role and their right to advocate for their clients' best interests unhindered by reference to resource availability.

Richard Hare, in a useful summary of the philosophical basis of ethics (in relation to psychiatry) (Hare, 1991), proposes that there is no fundamental incompatibility between the two approaches. He differentiates between the 'absolutist' and the 'utilitarian' view. The absolutist perspective tends to see matters in absolute terms – focusing on rights and duties, which are seen to be inalienable and uncompromising. The utilitarian position is one where decisions would be made on the basis of the best interest of all those people affected.

A patient in treatment might seem, then, to be owed particular consideration by virtue of the commitment entered into, and a good clinician might well find it hard to refuse or limit effective treatment which the client really needs and would benefit from. A utilitarian approach would consider the best interests of both that client and potential clients who might also benefit from treatment, and weigh them up to make a final decision.

The absolutist, intuitive level, with its prima-facie duties and principles, is the main focus of everyday moral decisions for the clinician, and this has great utility in easing the work that has to be done; the utilitarian approach is required when there is conflict (for instance, in deciding how to deal with a waiting list) or when the intuitive judgements themselves are being appraised (for instance, during the clinical audit procedure to examine the most effective and efficacious treatment method).

To incorporate such issues into psychological practice requires additional work and additional skills. Some of this work is being achieved through the quality initiatives which are being developed throughout the country. The clarification of referral criteria, development of quality standards and establishment of effective information systems, all lay the basis of effective clinical audit. All such work entails the articulation of the underlying values and standards of psychology work, and explicit statements about the priorities of the service and the range of services being offered; procedures are laid open for internal and external monitoring to take place.

For clinical psychologists it is particularly important that their services should be well defined, efficient and effective, and appropriately costed; this is partly, as mentioned earlier, because there has been ambiguity and overlap between the skills of a clinical psychologist and others carrying out similar therapeutic procedures. There is perhaps greater urgency since, as services are costed more carefully, clinical psychologists can appear extremely expensive in comparison with other groups. It is important for the profession to demonstrate that they are not so much an expensive profession as a high-quality/'value-for-money' service.

Considerable work is being carried out on information systems, costing and clinical audit for clinical psychologists – the three aspects being interwoven to a certain extent; information is being gathered to allow identification of costs and to facilitate the effective audit of quality aspects of the service, one part of which will be 'value for money'.

Information systems

The Körner statistics still form the basis of much of the information gathered about the work of clinical psychologists, occasionally being supplemented by local surveys. It originally had two purposes: to gather information about costs and to allow the development of Performance Indicators (Pilling, 1991). The Körner System for clinical psychologists has two aspects: the routine collection of data concerning direct client contact with registered patients and a yearly activity survey, the Survey of Professional Activity. These measures have been criticised as inaccurate and crude, but it seems likely that they will remain as the basis of information gathered for the short-term future at least, albeit with more flexibility at local level.

It is unfortunate that the measures used are subjected to very crude analysis at regional level – the daily Körner forms measure new referrals and direct client contacts, which psychologists recognise as only one aspect of their client work, let alone their full range of professional services. Regions may divide the total cost of the whole service (taking no account of the other activities) by the number of new cases per year (taking no account of the mix of long- and short-term work etc.), which simplistic calculation presents clinical psychology services as expensive (Kat, 1993).

Pilling *et al.* (1990) describe an information system for workload measurement which is based on the Körner Minimum Data set; this was originally developed to allow accurate costing of services but also allows comparison of activity across and within departments, for example, between the specialities. The main features of the system are, first, that it covers the whole range of activities that psychologists engage in, including indirect client work, service planning and management, teaching and supervision, and research and development. Second, measures of 'overhead' activities have been established. Third, considerable effort was made to develop reliable and valid definitions for all these measures so that the system is robust enough to work in a range of settings.

This system, as mentioned above, was primarily developed to generate a method to identify unit costs for psychology. Kat (1993) describes an example of the use of the system to provide accurate costing in establishing contracts with purchasers. This identifies five types of services: 'direct' client work; clinical consultancy and project work with staff and carers; teaching, training and supervision of non-psychologists; 'organisational' consultancy; and research.

Other activities would be counted as 'supporting activities' or overheads – for instance, travel, CPD, training of psychologists, etc. – and apportioned to the five categories in proportion to the amount of time spent in each of them. This allows the generation of two types of unit costs – a cost per patient for direct client work and a cost per unit of time (either per hour or per session) for the other four categories. One can immediately perceive the value in this approach in enabling purchasers to choose between a service orientated primarily to direct client work and one which covers a wider range of more 'indirect' activities.

Clinical audit

This quite clearly relates closely to the above analysis. Auditing is part of the Quality Assurance process which is now entrenched within the NHS in the UK as a means to enhance client services. Clinical audit is concerned with the quality of the services provided by clinicians; it covers two areas: the efficiency and economy of the service and the 'value-for-money' component of services. It also attempts to address the far more complex aspect of efficacy: whether the service does in fact do what it claims to do, that is, whether a therapy service is effective in reducing distress and enhancing well-being for its clients.

The framework for the audit proposed by the Department of Health for four therapy professions, including clinical psychology, proposes four sections, each containing sub-sections (Berger, 1991).

The sections comprise

- *Audit of direct interventions*, which covers such issues as standards for assessment, professional standards for interventions, monitoring of outcomes and analysis of failures
- *Staffing*, dealing with adequate job descriptions, performance review and appropriate deployment of staff
- *Management and service*, which covers the adequacy of facilities and equipment, information about the service, equity of access, standards for referrals, waiting time and record-keeping. This section also includes the need to monitor unmet needs of the total client population
- *Audit of indirect interventions*, which includes setting professional standards and competence and the monitoring of outcomes

However, there also appear to be more formal methods that might be developed, which bear directly on the need to establish the circumstances in which clinical psychology's particular expertise is especially appropriate and to allow both psychologists and purchasers of the service to choose between options, using rational criteria and objective information.

Three approaches, which seem from their different perspectives to offer some assistance in such a task, are available. Although there is some clear overlap, they will be addressed separately. Each approach appears to be in its relative infancy in this country, particularly for mental health services.

1 There has been a general increase in interest in evaluation methods which relate research directly to improvements in mental health care, as epitomised in recent publications such as Milne (1987) and Parry and Watts (1989). Parry (1992) presents a particular methodology of linking psychotherapy research to audit procedures which appears both relevant and widely applicable.

   Parry takes the six dimensions on which a service's efficacy may be judged (Maxwell, 1984): relevance/appropriateness, equity, accessibility, acceptability, effectiveness and efficiency. For each of these areas she reviews relevant literature. The exercise both elaborates and supports the sort of decisions that clinicians make intuitively in planning the course of therapy – for instance, in determining which type of client suits which therapeutic intervention – and starts to clarify the circumstances in which more specialist therapy may be cost-effective – for instance, that for more severe problems psychoanalytical plans appear to be less costly than other orientations (and the opposite for less severe).

   Inevitably the article raises a number of questions and gives a number of indications for future investigation; however, it is likely that the methodology of tying clinical research to the requirements of audit would be applicable in many other areas.

2 Second, there is the work from health economics, where the focus is on comparing the costs of treatments to other factors – efficiency and effectiveness and benefits to the client (Drummond, 1986; McGuire et al. 1988; Department of Health, 1992a). There are a number of problems in applying the techniques in any situation, partly to do with the measures used; for instance, methods of assessing life change – such as Quality Adjusted Life Years – are questionable in their assumptions about what is an actual benefit and how it can be measured (Moore, 1990). However, although the measurement and methodology can be questioned, in many ways the use of the procedures themselves is valuable in laying bare the implicit assumptions and values by which people work; once made explicit they can then be reviewed.

   A useful application of this approach in relation to clinical psychology services was demonstrated by Robson et al. (1984), who found that the psychotropic drug bill in a general practice could be significantly decreased by having a psychologist work on site. Liberman et al. (1987) also showed that family therapy was a more cost-efficient intervention than individual treatment for people with schizophrenia.

   One can clearly see the utility of this approach, as it does allow the particular dilemma of the psychologist in adult mental health work to be addressed, of how to demonstrate, and in which particular client situation, that the expensive and specialised expertise of the psychologist is more effective than that of other therapists.

3 The third approach comes from the work on the psychology of problem-solving, decision-making and reasoning that has been applied to clinical reasoning (Elstein and Bordage, 1991, Chase, 1993). This work has been applied primarily within the medical context but has obvious relevance to the mental health field. The use of information-processing models allows the reasoning process to be described by analysing the thoughts and steps taken in addressing clinical problems; this relates the process to psychological elements and principles. The understanding of these methods can assist clinicians in identifying errors that they make in their reasoning, by virtue of such features as bounded rationality, misinterpretation of cues, bias shown by early hypotheses, over-emphasis on positive findings, and so on.

While this might appear esoteric and irrelevant to daily clinical practice, one can see its value as an exercise to identify errors and assist in more objective thought processes. To take a specific example, it would be fascinating to track the errors in reasoning that a clinician might make when dealing with a client from an ethnic minority, to identify the specific way that discrimination occurs within the clinical process.

This section aimed to present briefly some methodological developments which open up opportunities for clinical psychologists to analyse in greater depth and with greater specificity the processes that they use within their clinical practice. These should be helpful in assisting the identification of the particular expertise that psychologists bring to health services, thus enabling them to clarify the particular components of their work and so make rational choices in the delivery of service, based on more objective criteria which relate to the population as a whole.

CONCLUSION

This chapter started with the definition of any profession; it ends with, not so much a definition, but a shift in emphasis from introspection and internal monitoring to clinical psychology in an organisational context which places increasing demands on it. It has presented an outline of some of the areas that may require to be explored at a conceptual level, and the skills and methods that the profession may need to adopt in order to face the 1990s and beyond with confidence and a clear sense of its identity – both internally and in its present-ation to the external world.

REFERENCES

Alladin, W. (1986) 'Ethnic minorities and clinical psychology: an inside view of clinical psychology', *Clinical Psychology Forum* 5: 28–31.

Barkham, M. and Shapiro, M. (1989) 'Towards resolving the problem of waiting-lists: psychotherapy in two-plus-one sessions', *Clinical Psychology Forum* 23: 15–18

Bender, M. (1976) *Community Psychology*, London: Methuen.

Bennet, P. and Wright, S. (1992) 'Health psychology: discipline or profession?' *Clinical Psychology Forum* 40: 39–40

Berger, M. (1991) 'A framework for audit in clinical psychology', *Clinical Psychology Forum* 35: 42–4.

BPS (1992) *Response to 'The Health of the Nation'*, Leicester: BPS.

BPS/DCP (1992) *Core Purpose and Philosophy of the Profession*, Leicester: BPS/DCP.

Cahill, C., Llewelyn, S. P. and Pearson, C. (1991) 'Treatment of sexual abuse which occurred in childhood: a review', *British Journal of Clinical Psychology* 30: 1–12

Chase, J. (1993) 'Clinical decision making', in Powell *et al.* (1993) *Curriculum in Clinical Psychology*, Leicester: BPS/DCP.

Clinical Psychology Forum 22 (1989).

Department of Health (1989) *Education and Training: Working Paper 10, Cmnd 555*, London: Department of Health.

Department of Health (1990) *Manpower Planning Advisory Group: Clinical Psychology Project. Full Report*, London: Department of Health.

Department of Health (1992a) *Assessing the Effects of Health Technologies. Principles, Practice, Proposals'*, London: Department of Health.

Department of Health (1992b) 'The extension of the hospital and community health services elements of the GP fundholding scheme from 1 April 1993 – Supplementary guidance', *HSG* (92): 53, London: Department of Health.

Department of Health (1992c) *The Health of the Nation*, London: Department of Health.

Division News (1993) 'Report on D.C.P. survey of waiting list times in N.H.S clinical psychology services: 1992', *Clinical Psychology Forum* 53: 39–42.

Drummond, M. F. (1986) *Principles of Economic Appraisal in Healthcare*, New York: Oxford University Press.

Dyer, A. (1991) 'Psychiatry as a profession', in S. Bloch and P. Chodoff (eds) *Psychiatric Ethics, 2nd edn*, New York: Oxford University Press.

Elstein, A. S. and Bordage, G. (1991) 'Psychology of clinical reasoning', in J. Dowie and A. Elstein (eds) *Professional Judgement: A Reader in Clinical Decision Making*, Cambridge: Cambridge University Press.

Goodwin, A. and Power, R. (1986) 'Clinical psychology services for minority ethnic groups', *Clinical Psychology Forum* 5: 24–8

Hall, J. (1990) 'Towards a psychology of caring', *British Journal of Clinical Psychology* 29: 129–44.

Ham, C. (1993) *Health Policy in Britain: The Politics and Organisation of the N.H.S., 2nd edn*, Hong Kong: Macmillan.

Hare, R. (1991) 'The philosophical basis of psychiatric ethics', in S. Block and P. Chodoff (eds) *Psychiatric Ethics, 2nd edn*, New York: Oxford University Press.

Hawks, D. (1981) 'The dilemma of clinical practice – surviving as a clinical psychologist', in I. McPherson and A. Sutton (eds) *Reconstructing Psychological Practice* London: Croom Hall.

Ho, D. Y. F. (1985) 'Cultural values and professional issues in clinical psychology', *American Psychologist* 40: 1212–18.

Kat, B. (1991) *Models of Service in Clinical Psychology*, Leicester: BPS.

Kat, B. (1993) *GP Fundholding: News, and the Next Steps*, Leicester: BPS/DCP.

Klein, R. (1983) *The Politics of the National Health Service*, New York: Longman.

Liberman, R. P., Cardin, V., McGill, C. W., Falloon, I. and Evans C. D. (1987) 'Behavioural family management of schizophrenia: clinical outcome and costs', *Psychiatric Annals* 17: 610–19.

Littlewood, R. (1990) 'From categories to contexts: a decade of the "new cross-culture psychiatry"', *British Journal of Psychiatry* 156: 308–27.

McGuire, A., Henderson, J. and Mooney, G. (1988) *The Economics of Health Care – An Introductory Text*, New York: Routledge & Kegan Paul.

McPherson, I. and Sutton, A. (1981) *Reconstructing Psychological Practice*, London: Croom Helm.

Management Advisory Services (1989) *National Review of Clinical Psychology Services*, Cheltenham: M.A.S.

Manpower Planning and Advisory Group (1990) *Clinical Psychology Report*, London: Department of Health.

Maxwell, R. J. (1984) 'Quality assessment in health', *British Medical Journal* 288: 1470–2.

Miller, D. and Brown, B. (1988) 'Developing the role of clinical psychology in the context of AIDS', *The Psychologist* 2: 63–5.

Miller, E., Morley, S. and Shepherd, G. (1987) 'The trouble with treatment', *British Journal of Clinical Psychology* 26: 241–2.

Milne, D. (ed.) (1987) *Evaluating Mental Health Practice: Methods and Applications*, London: Croom Helm.

Moore, D. (1990) 'The limits of health care', in D. Evans (ed.) *Why Should We Care. Professional Studies in Health Care Ethics*, Hong Kong: Macmillan.

Newman, F. and Howard, K. (1986) 'Therapeutic effort, treatment outcome and national health policy', *American Psychologist* 41: 181–7.

Noon, J. M. and Lewis, J. R. (1992) 'Therapeutic strategies and outcomes: perspectives from different cultures', *British Journal of Medical Psychology* 65: 107–18.

Norcross, J., Brust, A. and Dryden, W. (1992) 'British clinical psychologists: I. A national survey of the BPS Clinical Division', *Clinical Psychology Forum* 40: 19–24

Parry, G. (1992) 'Improving psychotherapy services: applications of research, audit and evaluation', *British Journal of Clinical Psychology* 31: 3–20.

Parry, G. and Watts, F. (1989) *Behavioural and Mental Health Research: A Handbook of Skills and Methods*, Hove and London: Laurence Erlbaum Associates.

Pilgrim, D. and Treacher, A. (1992) *Clinical Psychology Observed*, London: Routledge.

Pilling, S. (1991) 'Monitoring clinical activity: the workload measurement system', in M. Berger (ed.) *Aspects of Audit: Collecting and Using Clinical Information*, *Association for Child Psychology and Psychiatry: Occasional Papers* 4: 10–15.

Pilling, S., Spencer, C. and Oddy, M. (1990) 'Workload measurement systems for clinical psychology', Paper prepared for the Service Development Sub-Committee of the British Psychological Society.

Powell, G., Young, R. and Frosch, S. (1993) *Curriculum in Clinical Psychology*, Leicester: BPS/DCP.

Rack, P. (1991) *Race, Culture and Mental Disorder*, London: Routledge.

Richardson, A. (1992) 'Training courses and working paper 10', *Clinical Psychology Forum* 41: 32–36.

Robson, M. H., France, R. and Bland, M. (1984) 'Clinical psychologists in primary care: controlled clinical and economic evaluation', *British Medical Journal* 288 1805–8.

Seager, M. and Jacobson, R. (1993) 'Two-Plus-One: Misunderstood or Incomprehensible? A Reply to Davis *et al.*', *Clinical Psychology Forum* 52: 16–22.

Toren, N. (1972) *Social Work. The Case of a Semi-Profession*, London: Sage.

Trepka, C. and Marsh, C. (1990) 'Community health teams and the role security of clinical psychologists', *Clinical Psychology Forum* 26: 20–2.

Trethowan, W. H. (1977) *The Role of Psychologists in the Health Services*, London: Department of Health.

Watts, F. N. (1990) *The Efficacy of Clinical Applications of Psychology*, Cardiff: Shadowfax Publishing.

White, J. (1992) 'How to get round the waiting list? Using the local press and public lectures to publicise stress', *Clinical Psychology Forum* 42: 6–9.

Windt, P. Y., Appleby, P. C., Battin, M. P., Francis, L. P. and Landesman, B. M. (1991) *Ethical Issues in the Professions*, Englewood Cliffs, NJ: Prentice-Hall.

Index

treatment evaluation 404–7; treatment
goals 384–8; Treatment Outcome
Prospective Study 407; withdrawal
363–8, 401
drugs *see* pharmacological treatment
Dutch Eating Behaviour Questionnaire
519, 527
Dyadic Adjustment Scale 209, 279
dysarthria 665
dysexecutive syndrome 701–2
Dysfunctional Attitudes Scale 93, 102,
127, 427
dyslexia, acquired 697
dysmenorrhoea 637
dyspareunia: female 202; male 201
dysphasia: rehabilitation 697; *see also*
aphasia
dysthymic disorder 131

early maladaptive schemas 132–4
Eating Attitudes Test 523, 527
eating behaviour: anorexia nervosa 523;
obesity 517–19, 539
Eating Disorder Examination 515, 527
Eating Disorder Inventory 515, 523, 525,
527
eating disorders: investigation 514–28;
treatment 534–54; *see also* anorexia
nervosa; bulimia nervosa
ejaculation: problems 200–1; treatment
218–19
elderly people: adjustment assessment
427; alcoholism 452; assessment
413–32; benzodiazepines 452;
cognitive abilities 416–26;
cognitive-behavioural therapy 449–53;
cognitive decline 447; dementia *see*
dementia; depression, assessment 427,
430; depression, cognitive therapies
450; depression, diagnosis 414–15;
depression, memory/learning deficits
421; depression, treatment 446–53;
environment, assessment 429–30;
family therapy 451; group therapy
452–3; hyperventilation 449–50;
intellectual function 418–21; learning
421–3; loss 447–8; marital problems
451; memory 421–3, 448–9;
neuropsychological batteries 424;
normal ageing 416–18; patients'
expectations 448; physical health 418,
447; sensory impairment 430, 447;

sexual problems 451–2; speed testing
423; treatment 438–53
electroconvulsive shock syndrome 673
electroconvulsive therapy 111
emotional problems, rehabilitation 700–2
endorphins 373
enkephalins 373
enuresis, nocturnal (bed-wetting) 608
environmental variables 15
epilepsy, temporal lobe 659, 773
ethical codes 799–801
ethnic minorities 795; drug/alcohol
dependence 376–7
exercise: anorexia nervosa 524; and
health 488; obesity 540–1
exhibitionism 330
expectations, realistic 39–40
exposure: flooding 175–9; imagined *see*
desensitisation, systematic; *in vivo*
175–9; obsessive-compulsive disorder
73, 75, 77–8
expressed emotion 303–4, 316–18, 480–1
Eysenck Personality Inventory 563
Eysenck Personality Questionnaire 375

family history 7
family therapy 451
Fear of Negative Evaluation Scale 163,
244–5
fears *see* phobias
feedback: interpersonal problems 256;
loops 12–13; motor disorders 692–3;
social skills training 256; treatment
technique 40–1; video 41; *see also*
bio-feedback
Feeling Good (Burns, 1980) 116
fetishism 330
finger agnosia 673
Fishbein's theory of reasoned action 489–90
flooding 175–9
flurazepam 601
follow-up 46
forensic psychology 705–19; deception,
detection of 716–17; presenting
psychological evidence 717–19;
psychological testing 713–15; retracted
confession 715–16; role of
psychologist 708–10
frontal lobe lesions: amnesia 673;
dysexecutive syndrome 701–2;
personality 666; single-case
methodology 772

marital conflict: attributions 274–5;
behavioural observation 277–8;
behavioural therapy 284–90; cognitive
model 284–6; elderly 451;
investigation 271–80; presenting
problems 273–4; questionnaires
275–80; social cognition 274
Marital Conflict Form 279
marital history 7
Marital Interaction Coding System 277–8
Marital Pre-Counselling Inventory 278–9
Marital Status Inventory 279
marital therapy 283–93; agencies 284;
behavioural 284–90; cognitive-
behavioural therapy 124; couple therapy
290–3; structural/strategic 287–9;
systems theory approach 286–7;
unilateral 289–90
marriage: affect, assessing 275–7; life cycle
272–3; satisfaction, assessing 277, 278–9
Marriage Inventory 279
Maudsley Obsessional-Compulsive
Inventory 62, 66–7
Means–End Problem-Solving Test 246
medical phobia 161–2, 497
medical screening see physical condition
medical treatment: adherence to treatment
506–7; adverse effects 504–5;
alcoholism 400–4; anxiety 496–7;
chronic illness 499; communication
with patients 494–5; compliance
495–6; drug addiction 400–4;
experience of treatment 496–7; seeking
493–4; see also physical condition
melokinetic apraxia 672
memory disorders 673; amnesia 659, 673;
court testimony 709; elderly patients
421–3, 448–9; long-term 659;
rehabilitation 694–5; rehabilitation
goals 682
memory testing 15–16, 660
meningiomas 772
mental handicap: court testimony 708–9;
social-problem-solving skills training
260; social skills training 260, 263–4
methadone maintenance 386, 403–4
Meyer's Paired Associate Learning Test
660
Middlesex Elderly Assessment of Mental
State 425
migraine: bio-feedback 638; relaxation
training 637

Mill Hill Vocabulary Scale 16, 418–19,
420
Mini-Mental State Examination 425
Minnesota Multiphasic Personality
Inventory 20, 563, 615, 666
Model Standards Questionnaire 461, 462
modelling 41–2; interpersonal problems
255; obsessive-compulsive disorder 73;
phobias 184
Montgomery–Asberg Scale 100
Mooney Closure Test 662
motor functions 661; disordered (apraxia)
661, 670–2; rehabilitation 692–3
Multidimensional Health Locus of
Control Questionnaire 621
Multiphasic Environmental Assessment
Procedure 429–30
Multiple Affect Adjective Check-List 164
Multiple Risk Factor Intervention Trial
566
mutism 315–16
myocardial infarction 565–7

naltrexone 403
narcolepsy 597
Narcotics Anonymous 399–400
National Adult Reading Test 16, 420–1
negative automatic thoughts 117–21
neuroleptic (antipsychotic) drugs 310
neurological problems see brain damage
neuropsychological testing 677–82;
elderly patients 424
neuropsychology 645–82; single-case
methodology 765–83; terminology
645–8; see also brain damage
neuroticism 562
night terrors 597
nightmares 608
North Karelia Project 573
numeracy, assessment 17–18
Nurses' Observation Scale for In-patient
Evaluation 302
nystagmus 663

obesity: appetite 519; behavioural
treatment 535–6; body fat assessment
516–17; body image 520–1, 541–2;
diet 517, 539–40; dieting 535; eating
behaviour 517–19, 539; energy
expenditure 519–20, 540–1;
epidemiology 515–16; exercise 540–1;
exercise programmes 542; food intake,

visual hallucinations 6
visual object agnosia 663–4, 696
visual-spatial agnosia 672
vocational guidance 18
vomiting 525–7, 552–3

waiting-lists 789
Wakefield Self-Assessment Depression
   Inventory 93
Wechsler Adult Intelligence
   Scale–Revised 9, 18; Block Design
   Sub-test 662, 768, 777; elderly patients
   416–17, 419–20
Wechsler Memory Scale–Revised 422,
   660
Weissman's Interpersonal Psychotherapy
   111

Wernicke's aphasia 658, 672, 771
Wernicke–Korsakoff syndrome 373
Wessman–Ricks Scale 93–4
Wisconsin Card Sorting Test 667
Wolpe–Lazarus Assertiveness
   Questionnaire 244
women: agoraphobia 160; eating
   disorders 514; sexual dysfunction
   201–2
word blindness (agnosic alexia) 663

Yale–Brown Obsessive-Compulsive
   Scale 62
Young's cognitive therapy 132, 133–4

Zung Self-Rating Depression Scale
   99–100